Poetry
Criticism

Guide to Gale Literary Criticism Series

For criticism on	Consult these Gale series
Authors now living or who died after December 31, 1999	*CONTEMPORARY LITERARY CRITICISM (CLC)*
Authors who died between 1900 and 1999	*TWENTIETH-CENTURY LITERARY CRITICISM (TCLC)*
Authors who died between 1800 and 1899	*NINETEENTH-CENTURY LITERATURE CRITICISM (NCLC)*
Authors who died between 1400 and 1799	*LITERATURE CRITICISM FROM 1400 TO 1800 (LC)* *SHAKESPEAREAN CRITICISM (SC)*
Authors who died before 1400	*CLASSICAL AND MEDIEVAL LITERATURE CRITICISM (CMLC)*
Authors of books for children and young adults	*CHILDREN'S LITERATURE REVIEW (CLR)*
Dramatists	*DRAMA CRITICISM (DC)*
Poets	*POETRY CRITICISM (PC)*
Short story writers	*SHORT STORY CRITICISM (SSC)*
Literary topics and movements	*HARLEM RENAISSANCE: A GALE CRITICAL COMPANION (HR)* *THE BEAT GENERATION: A GALE CRITICAL COMPANION (BG)*
Asian American writers of the last two hundred years	*ASIAN AMERICAN LITERATURE (AAL)*
Black writers of the past two hundred years	*BLACK LITERATURE CRITICISM (BLC)* *BLACK LITERATURE CRITICISM SUPPLEMENT (BLCS)*
Hispanic writers of the late nineteenth and twentieth centuries	*HISPANIC LITERATURE CRITICISM (HLC)* *HISPANIC LITERATURE CRITICISM SUPPLEMENT (HLCS)*
Native North American writers and orators of the eighteenth, nineteenth, and twentieth centuries	*NATIVE NORTH AMERICAN LITERATURE (NNAL)*
Major authors from the Renaissance to the present	*WORLD LITERATURE CRITICISM, 1500 TO THE PRESENT (WLC)* *WORLD LITERATURE CRITICISM SUPPLEMENT (WLCS)*

ISSN 1052-4851

Poetry Criticism

Excerpts from Criticism of the Works of the Most Significant and Widely Studied Poets of World Literature

Volume 64

Michelle Lee
Project Editor

THOMSON

GALE

Detroit • New York • San Francisco • San Diego • New Haven, Conn. • Waterville, Maine • London • Munich

Poetry Criticism, Vol. 64

Project Editor
Michelle Lee

Editorial
Jessica Bomarito, Kathy D. Darrow, Jeffrey Hunter, Jelena O. Krstović, Thomas J. Schoenberg, Lawrence J. Trudeau, Russel Whitaker

Data Capture
Francis Monroe, Gwen Tucker

Indexing Services
Synapse, the Knowledge Link Corporation

Rights and Acquisitions
Lori Hines, Sue Rudolph, Shalice Shah-Caldwell

Imaging and Multimedia
Dean Dauphinais, Leitha Etheridge-Sims, Lezlie Light, Mike Logusz, Dan Newell, Christine O'Bryan, Kelly A. Quin, Denay Wilding, Robyn Young

Composition and Electronic Capture
Kathy Sauer

Manufacturing
Rhonda Dover

Associate Product Manager
Marc Cormier

LIBRARY OF CONGRESS CATALOG CARD NUMBER 91-118494
ISBN 0-7876-8698-0
ISSN 1052-4851

Printed in the United States of America
10 9 8 7 6 5 4 3 2 1

Contents

Preface vii

Acknowledgments ix

Literary Criticism Series Advisory Board xiii

Preface

*P*oetry Criticism (*PC*) presents significant criticism of the world's greatest poets and provides supplementary biographical and bibliographical material to guide the interested reader to a greater understanding of the genre and its creators. Although major poets and literary movements are covered in such Gale Literary Criticism series as *Contemporary Literary Criticism* (*CLC*), *Twentieth-Century Literary Criticism* (*TCLC*), *Nineteenth-Century Literature Criticism* (*NCLC*), *Literature Criticism from 1400 to 1800* (*LC*), and *Classical and Medieval Literature Criticism* (*CMLC*), *PC* offers more focused attention on poetry than is possible in the broader, survey-oriented entries on writers in these Thomson Gale series. Students, teachers, librarians, and researchers will find that the generous excerpts and supplementary material provided by *PC* supply them with the vital information needed to write a term paper on poetic technique, to examine a poet's most prominent themes, or to lead a poetry discussion group.

Scope of the Series

PC is designed to serve as an introduction to major poets of all eras and nationalities. Since these authors have inspired a great deal of relevant critical material, *PC* is necessarily selective, and the editors have chosen the most important published criticism to aid readers and students in their research. Each author entry presents a historical survey of the critical response to that author's work. The length of an entry is intended to reflect the amount of critical attention the author has received from critics writing in English and from foreign critics in translation. Every attempt has been made to identify and include the most significant essays on each author's work. In order to provide these important critical pieces, the editors sometimes reprint essays that have appeared elsewhere in Thomson Gale's Literary Criticism Series. Such duplication, however, never exceeds twenty percent of a *PC* volume.

Organization of the Book

Each *PC* entry consists of the following elements:

- The **Author Heading** cites the name under which the author most commonly wrote, followed by birth and death dates. Also located here are any name variations under which an author wrote, including transliterated forms for authors whose native languages use nonroman alphabets. If the author wrote consistently under a pseudonym, the pseudonym will be listed in the author heading and the author's actual name given in parenthesis on the first line of the biographical and critical introduction. Uncertain birth or death dates are indicated by question marks. Single-work entries are preceded by the title of the work and its date of publication.

- The **Introduction** contains background information that introduces the reader to the author and the critical debates surrounding his or her work.

- A **Portrait of the Author** is included when available.

- The list of **Principal Works** is ordered chronologically by date of first publication and lists the most important works by the author. The first section comprises poetry collections and book-length poems. The second section gives information on other major works by the author. For foreign authors, the editors have provided original foreign-language publication information and have selected what are considered the best and most complete English-language editions of their works.

- Reprinted **Criticism** is arranged chronologically in each entry to provide a useful perspective on changes in critical evaluation over time. All individual titles of poems and poetry collections by the author featured in the entry are printed in boldface type. The critic's name and the date of composition or publication of the critical work are given at the beginning of each piece of criticism. Unsigned criticism is preceded by the title of the source in which it appeared. Footnotes are reprinted at the end of each essay or excerpt. In the case of excerpted criticism, only those footnotes that pertain to the excerpted texts are included.

- Critical essays are prefaced by brief **Annotations** explicating each piece.

- A complete **Bibliographical Citation** of the original essay or book precedes each piece of criticism.

- An annotated bibliography of **Further Reading** appears at the end of each entry and suggests resources for additional study. In some cases, significant essays for which the editors could not obtain reprint rights are included here. Boxed material following the further reading list provides references to other biographical and critical sources on the author in series published by Thomson Gale.

Cumulative Indexes

A **Cumulative Author Index** lists all of the authors that appear in a wide variety of reference sources published by Thomson Gale, including *PC*. A complete list of these sources is found facing the first page of the Author Index. The index also includes birth and death dates and cross references between pseudonyms and actual names.

A **Cumulative Nationality Index** lists all authors featured in *PC* by nationality, followed by the number of the *PC* volume in which their entry appears.

A **Cumulative Title Index** lists in alphabetical order all individual poems, book-length poems, and collection titles contained in the *PC* series. Titles of poetry collections and separately published poems are printed in italics, while titles of individual poems are printed in roman type with quotation marks. Each title is followed by the author's last name and corresponding volume and page numbers where commentary on the work is located. English-language translations of original foreign-language titles are cross-referenced to the foreign titles so that all references to discussion of a work are combined in one listing.

Citing *Poetry Criticism*

When writing papers, students who quote directly from any volume in the Literary Criticism Series may use the following general format to footnote reprinted criticism. The first example pertains to material drawn from periodicals, the second to material reprinted from books.

Sylvia Kasey Marks, "A Brief Glance at George Eliot's *The Spanish Gypsy*," *Victorian Poetry* 20, no. 2 (Summer 1983), 184-90; reprinted in *Poetry Criticism*, vol. 20, ed. Ellen McGeagh (Detroit: The Gale Group), 128-31.

Linden Peach, "Man, Nature and Wordsworth: American Versions," *British Influence on the Birth of American Literature*, (Macmillan Press Ltd., 1982), 29-57; reprinted in *Poetry Criticism*, vol. 20, ed. Ellen McGeagh (Detroit: The Gale Group), 37-40.

Suggestions are Welcome

Readers who wish to suggest new features, topics, or authors to appear in future volumes, or who have other suggestions or comments are cordially invited to call, write, or fax the Associate Product Manager:

Associate Product Manager, Literary Criticism Series
Thomson Gale
27500 Drake Road
Farmington Hills, MI 48331-3535
1-800-347-4253 (GALE)
Fax: 248-699-8054

Acknowledgments

The editors wish to thank the copyright holders of the criticism included in this volume and the permissions managers of many book and magazine publishing companies for assisting us in securing reproduction rights. We are also grateful to the staffs of the Detroit Public Library, the Library of Congress, the University of Detroit Mercy Library, Wayne State University Purdy/Kresge Library Complex, and the University of Michigan Libraries for making their resources available to us. Following is a list of the copyright holders who have granted us permission to reproduce material in this volume of *PC*. Every effort has been made to trace copyright, but if omissions have been made, please let us know.

COPYRIGHTED MATERIAL IN *PC*, VOLUME 64, WAS REPRODUCED FROM THE FOLLOWING PERIODICALS:

Brick: A Literary Journal, v. 57, fall, 1997 for "A Talk with Anne Carson" by John D'Agata. Copyright © 1997 by *Brick: A Literary Journal*. All rights reserved. Reproduced by permission of the author.—*Canadian Literature*, spring, 2003; spring, 2004. Copyright © 2003, 2004 by the University of British Columbia. All rights reserved. Both reproduced by permission.—*Chicago Review*, v. 27, autumn, 1975; v. 45, 1999. Copyright © 1975, 1999 by *Chicago Review*. All rights reserved. Both reproduced by permission.—*Concerning Poetry*, v. 18, 1985. Copyright © 1985 by Western Washington University. All rights reserved. Reproduced by permission.—*Critical Quarterly*, v. 29, spring, 1987. Copyright © 1987 by *Critical Quarterly*. All rights reserved. Reproduced by permission of Blackwell Publishers.—*Denver Quarterly*, v. 32, summer/fall, 1997 for "The Cold Hectic Dawn and I" by Jeff Hamilton. Copyright © 1997 by *Denver Quarterly*. All rights reserved. Reproduced by permission of the author.—*English*, v. 40, spring, 1991. Copyright © 1991 by the English Association. All rights reserved. Reproduced by permission.—*Iowa Review*, v. 27, 1997 for "A_____ with Anne Carson" by John D'Agata. Copyright © 1997 by the University of Iowa. All rights reserved. Reproduced by permission of the author.—*Journal of Modern Literature*, v. 23, summer, 2000. Copyright © 2001 by Indiana University Press. All rights reserved. Reproduced by permission.—*Journal of Narrative Technique*, v. 3, January, 1973. Copyright © 1973 by the *Journal of Narrative Technique*. Reproduced by permission.—*Language and Style*, v. 18, winter, 1985 for "'Honey Dusk Do Sprawl': Does Black Minstrel Dialect Obscure *The Dream Songs*?" by Kathe Davis. Copyright © 1985 E. L. Epstein. Reproduced by permission of the author.—*Missouri Review*, v. 4, fall, 1980. Copyright © 1980 by the Curators of the University of Missouri. All rights reserved. Reproduced by permission.—*Modern Language Studies*, v. 18, fall, 1988 for "The Freedom of John Berryman" by Kathe Davis. Copyright, Northeast Modern Language Association 1988. Reproduced by permission of the publisher and author.—*New England Review and Bread Loaf Quarterly*, v. 7, winter, 1984 for "Flaubert in Florida" by Michael Ryan. Copyright © 1984 by Kenyon Hill Publishers. All rights reserved. Reproduced by permission of the author.—*Ohio Review*, v. 16, spring, 1975. Copyright © 1975 by the Editors of the *Ohio Review*. All rights reserved. Reproduced by permission.—*Parnassus*, v. 26, 2002 for "Truth, Beauty, and the Remote Control" by Mark Scroggins. Copyright © 2002 Poetry in Review Foundation, NY. Reproduced by permission of the author.—*Pequod*, n. 16-17, 1984. Copyright © 1984 by *Pequod*. All rights reserved. Reproduced by permission.—*Poetry*, v. 112, June, 1968 for "I Come to Speak for Your Dead Mouths" by James Wright. Copyright © 1968 by the Modern Poetry Association. Reproduced by permission of the Editor of Poetry and the Literary Estate of James Wright.—*Prairie Schooner*, v. 47, winter, 1973-74. Copyright © 1973-74 by University of Nebraska Press. Reproduced from *Prairie Schooner* by permission of the University of Nebraska Press.—*Raritan*, v. 16, fall, 1996. Copyright © 1996 by *Raritan: A Quarterly Review*. All rights reserved. Reproduced by permission.—*Revista Interamericana de Bibliografía/Inter-American Review of Bibliography*, v. 38, 1988. Reproduced by permission.—*Romance Notes*, v. 18, winter, 1977. Reproduced by permission.—*Southern Review*, v. 38, summer, 2002 for "Homage: Donald Justice" by Andrew Hudgins. Copyright © 2002, by the author. Reproduced by permission of the author.—*Symbiosis*, v. 3, April, 1999. Copyright © 1999 by The College of St Mark & St John. All rights reserved. Reproduced by permission.—*Symposium*, v. 28, summer, 1974. Copyright © 1974 by Helen Dwight Reid Educational Foundation. Reproduced with permission of the Helen Dwight Reid Educational Foundation, published by Heldref Publications, 1319 18th Street, NW, Washington, DC 20036-1802.—*Tennessee Folklore Society Bulletin*, v. 41, September, 1975. Copyright © by the Tennessee Folklore Society, 1975. All rights reserved. Reproduced by permission.—*Wallace Stevens Journal*, v. 17, fall, 1993. Copyright © 1993 by the Wallace Stevens Society, Inc. All rights reserved. Reproduced by permission.—*West Virginia History*, v. 24, January, 1963. Copyright © 1963 by the Department of Archives and History of West Virginia. Renewed 1991 by State of West Virginia Division of Culture and History, Archives & History. Reproduced by permission.

COPYRIGHTED MATERIAL IN *PC*, VOLUME 64, WAS REPRODUCED FROM THE FOLLOWING BOOKS:

Neruda, Regents of the University of California. Reproduced by permission of the University of California Press.—Santí, Enrico Mario. From **Pablo Neruda: The Poetics of Prophecy**. Cornell University Press, 1982. Copyright © 1982 by Cornell University Press. All rights reserved. Reproduced by permission of the author.—Schweitzer, Ivy. From "Puritan Legacies of Masculinity: John Berryman's Homage to Mistress Bradstreet," in **The Calvinist Roots of the Modern Era**. Edited by Aliki Barnston, Michael Tomasek Manson and Carol J. Singley. University Press of New England, 1997. Copyright © University Press of New England, Hanover, NH. All rights reserved. Reproduced by permission.—Stitt, Peter. From "The Art of Poetry: An Interview with John Berryman," in **Berryman's Understanding: Reflections on the Poetry of John Berryman**. Edited by Harry Thomas. Northeastern University Press, 1988. Copyright © 1988 by Harry Thomas. All rights reserved. Reproduced by permission.—Stroud, Parry. From **Stephen Vincent Benét**. Twayne Publishers, Inc. Copyright © 1982 by Twayne Publishers, Inc. Reproduced by permission of the Gale Group.

PHOTOGRAPHS AND ILLUSTRATIONS APPEARING IN *PC*, VOLUME 64, WERE RECEIVED FROM THE FOLLOWING SOURCES:

Benét, Stephen Vincent, photograph by Pirie MacDonald. The Library of Congress.—Berryman, John, photograph. AP/Wide World Photos.—Carson, Anne, photograph. AP/Wide World Photos.—Justice, Donald R., photograph by Miriam Berkley. Copyright © Miriam Berkley.—Neruda, Pablo, photograph by Jerry Bauer. Copyright © Jerry Bauer.

Thomson Gale Literature Product Advisory Board

The members of the Thomson Gale Literature Product Advisory Board—reference librarians from public and academic library systems—represent a cross-section of our customer base and offer a variety of informed perspectives on both the presentation and content of our literature products. Advisory board members assess and define such quality issues as the relevance, currency, and usefulness of the author coverage, critical content, and literary topics included in our series; evaluate the layout, presentation, and general quality of our printed volumes; provide feedback on the criteria used for selecting authors and topics covered in our series; provide suggestions for potential enhancements to our series; identify any gaps in our coverage of authors or literary topics, recommending authors or topics for inclusion; analyze the appropriateness of our content and presentation for various user audiences, such as high school students, undergraduates, graduate students, librarians, and educators; and offer feedback on any proposed changes/enhancements to our series. We wish to thank the following advisors for their advice throughout the year.

Stephen Vincent Benét
1898-1943

American poet, novelist, essayist, playwright, and short story writer.

INTRODUCTION

Benét is recognized as a noteworthy twentieth-century American poet. His best-known works adapt American myths, imagery, and themes to epic poetic form and exhibit a strong interest in history and legend. His poetic masterpiece, *John Brown's Body,* is a nationalistic epic poem that recounts the history of the Civil War. Although his verse has declined in popularity through the years, critics acknowledge his important contribution to American letters.

BIOGRAPHICAL INFORMATION

Benét was born on July 22, 1898, in Bethlehem, Pennsylvania. He was born into a military family: his father was a career military officer, and his grandfather was a general in the U.S. Army. Benét's older brother was the poet William Rose Benét. The boys were raised in California and Georgia, where his father was stationed in the military. Benét became interested in literature as a boy, and his early writings received awards from *St. Nicholas* magazine. In 1915 he entered Yale University and published his first book, *Five Men and Pompey.* He quickly became involved in the literary life at Yale, developing friendships with such figures as Thornton Wilder and Archibald MacLeish. While at Yale he published another book of verse, *The Drug Shop, or Endymion in Edmonstoun* (1917). In his senior year at Yale, he served as chairman for the *Yale Literary Magazine.* After his graduation in 1919, he worked briefly in advertising but returned to Yale for graduate studies. In 1920 he accepted a fellowship to study at the Sorbonne in Paris. While in Paris he published his first novel, *The Beginning of Wisdom,* and met his wife, Rosemary Carr. They returned to the United States and married in 1921. That same year he was awarded the Poetry Society of America Prize and a few years later won the *Nation* poetry prize.

After he was awarded a Guggenheim fellowship in 1926, he moved with his family to Paris, where he remained for the next few years. It was there that he wrote his best-known poetic work, *John Brown's Body* (1928), which earned him a Pulitzer Prize. He then

returned to the United States and began to write short stories in addition to his poetry, essays, and novels. He also wrote plays, radio plays, and adaptations of myth and folklore. In 1929 he moved to Los Angeles to try his hand at writing scripts for Hollywood films. However, he did not enjoy scriptwriting and returned to New York. In 1933 he accepted the editorship of the Yale Younger Poet Series and engaged in literary journalism. In 1939 he suffered from a nervous breakdown, which was complicated by the onset of severe arthritis. Politically, Benét became a strong and active voice for liberal causes; he wrote several propaganda essays warning readers of the growing fascist threat in Europe. He died from a heart attack on March 13, 1943. A year later, he won a Pulitzer Prize for his incomplete posthumous poem *Western Star.*

MAJOR WORKS

Benét wrote dramatic monologues, ballads, lyrics, and epic poems that focus on popular historical characters and subjects and concern moral and social values. His first major work, *The Ballad of William Sycamore* (1923), draws from American legends such as Davy Crockett, Daniel Boone, and Kit Carson to celebrate the rugged individualism and adventurous spirit of the pioneer scout William Sycamore. He also included other numerous stereotypical images of the American West in the poem and cited Sycamore's death as a metaphor for the passing of an entire era. In 1923 *King David* was also published. This two-hundred line poem adapts the story of David and Bathsheba from the Bible. The poem did attract some controversy for telling such an iconic story in a modern way, and reviewers criticized Benét's handling of David's adultery and his casual repentance. Considered Benét's poetic masterpiece, *John Brown's Body* is a history of the Civil War. Starting right before Brown's raid on Harper's Ferry, each section of the long poem is told from a different character's perspective and relates their experiences in various military campaigns. Benét utilized not only historical information to tell the story of the Civil War, but also used soldiers' letters and biographical material. Reviewers note the evenhandedness of his approach and argue that he treated his characters with respect and tolerance. In this way, critics view *John Brown's Body* as a nationalistic epic poem that stands out from Benét's other work. His final poem, *Western Star,* was published posthumously in 1944. Initially projected as a nine-volume epic poem on the American pioneer spirit and the settlement of the West, Benét only completed five thousand lines before his death in 1943. The finished portion of the poem chronicles the first English settlement in the New World.

CRITICAL RECEPTION

Benét's reputation has declined throughout the years. His penchant for archetypal American characters and themes, as well as his optimism and patriotism, is denigrated by reviewers who value more experimental and esoteric forms of verse. Such critics dismiss his poems as too conventional and hackneyed. However, others commentators assert that his poetry utilizes familiar characters and stories in appealing ways that are in concert with mainstream American culture. *John Brown's Body* remains his best-known and most highly regarded poetic work. Critics commend the importance of the subject matter and the epic scope of the poem, as well as Benét's careful craftsmanship. In theme and style he is often compared to Henry Wadsworth Longfellow, Carl Sandburg, and Edgar Lee Masters. Despite his decline in popularity, critics recognize Benét as an important figure in the American poetic tradition and praise his ability to create compelling and entertaining verse from American history and folklore.

PRINCIPAL WORKS

Poetry

Five Men and Pompey: A Series of Dramatic Portraits 1915
The Drug Shop, or Endymion in Edmonstoun 1917
Young Adventure: A Book of Poems 1918
Heavens and Earth: A Book of Poems 1920
The Ballad of William Sycamore, 1790-1880 1923
King David 1923
Tiger Joy: A Book of Poems 1925
John Brown's Body 1928
Ballads and Poems, 1915-1930 1931
A Book of Americans [with Rosemary Carr Benét] 1933
Burning City: New Poems 1936
The Ballad of the Duke's Mercy 1939
Nightmare at Noon 1940
Listen to the People 1941
Selected Works of Stephen Vincent Benét. 2 vols. (novels, short stories, poems, essays, and radio plays) 1942
Western Star 1943
The Last Circle: Stories and Poems (poems and short stories) 1946
Selected Poetry and Prose (poems and essays) 1960

Other Major Works

The Beginning of Wisdom (novel) 1921
Young People's Pride: A Novel (novel) 1922
Jean Huguenot (novel) 1923
Nerves [with John Chipman] (play) 1924
That Awful Mrs. Eaton [with John Chipman] (play) 1924
Spanish Bayonet (novel) 1926
The Barefoot Saint (short stories) 1929
The Litter of the Rose Leaves (short stories) 1930
James Shore's Daughter (novel) 1934
The Magic of Poetry and the Poet's Art (essays) 1936
The Devil and Daniel Webster (short stories) 1937
The Headless Horseman: An Operetta in One Act [with Douglas Moore] (play) 1937
The Devil and Daniel Webster: A Play in One Act (play) 1939
We Stand United: A Declaration (nonfiction) 1940
A Child is Born: A Modern Drama of the Nativity (play) 1942
They Burned the Books (play) 1942
O'Halloran's Luck, and Other Short Stories (short stories) 1944
We Stand United, and Other Radio Scripts (radio plays) 1945
Selected Letters (letters) 1960

CRITICISM

Harriet Monroe (review date October-March 1928-1929)

SOURCE: Monroe, Harriet. "A Cinema Epic." *Poetry* 33, no. 2 (October-March 1928-1929): 91-6.

[*In the following review, Monroe praises* John Brown's Body *as a singular achievement and calls the poem "a kind of cinema epic."*]

Here is a real book, a man-size book, a rousing American verse-tale, a kind of familiar super-journalistic epic, done by a young poet away from home, an impecunious young poet lingering for two years in France on a Guggenheim "Travelling Fellowship." Hats off to Stephen Vincent Benét! I have read his earlier poems—stories of King David, William Sycamore, and other adventurers, mere practice work in narrative—and I herewith joyously confess I should never have dreamed that **John Brown's Body** was in him. Mr. Benét was the first poet honored by the Guggenheim committee, and for their first two or three years the only one. A book like this, probably the most distinguished piece of work which any Guggenheim "fellow" has turned out, should encourage them to appoint more poets.

Epic is too heroic a word, no doubt, to stand alone as descriptive of this poem; a word associated too loftily with Homer and Virgil, with Dante and Milton; suggestive of masterpieces of the past, whose royal rhythms carry mythical gods and heroes through magical exploits. Mr. Benét's poem is a kind of cinema epic, brilliantly flashing an hundred different aspects of American character and history on the silver screen of an unobtrusively fluent and responsive style. The scene-shiftings are sometimes jerky, not always adroit; occasionally the scenario is faulty or the camera-work slipshod, conceding a too "happy ending," for example, in at least one detail of the enormous scheme; and one is forced to admit that the poem, like most epics, falls off somewhat toward the end—*Books VII* and *VIII* do not quite keep up the gallant stride with which the poem began.

But these are minor blemishes, to be admitted but not dwelt upon when there is so much to praise. Mr. Benét has held his reins well in hand, and kept to the straight road of his subject, riding lightly and gracefully a Pegasus which has more paces than a gaited horse. Most of the narrative passages run in a loosely-syllabled variously rhymed three-time pentameter; but one never has a chance to tire of this measure, for suddenly, with a change of mood or subject in the story, the lines will trot into tetrameters, or scuffle into free verse, or, as at the opening of *Book VII,* march solemnly into four-time hexameters. And the lyrics, which happily interrupt the narrative at intervals, are beautifully set to different song-measures, from the hymn-tune of *John Brown's Prayer* to the sapphics of Sally Dupré's lament for her wounded lover. In short, the technique shows admirable variety, with fewer lapses into dullness or prosiness than one would expect in so long a poem; it is carried without strain, is usually adequate, and often brilliantly skilful.

I have said there is much to praise, and perhaps one should praise first and longest the poet's whole-hearted abandonment to his

> American muse, whose strong and diverse heart
> So many men have tried to understand,
> But only made it smaller with their art
> Because you are as various as your land.
> . . . . .

> You are the buffalo-ghost, the broncho-ghost
> With dollar-silver in your saddle-horn,
> The cowboys riding in from Painted Post,
> The Indian arrow in the Indian corn.
> . . . . .

> The prairie-schooners crawling toward the ore,
> And the cheap car parked by the station door.

> Where the skyscrapers lift their shaggy plumes
> Of stranded smoke out of a stony mouth,
> You are that high stone and its arrogant fumes,
> And you are ruined gardens in the South,

> And bleak New England farms—

And so forth. Only a few lines may be quoted from that haughty and high-spirited *Invocation,* much as one would like to quote the whole; for there is nothing finer in the book than this key-note.

Then, after the *Prelude* in the slave-ship, and a few pages with minor characters—youth north and south—we have the bronze clangor of John Brown's magnificent prayer:

> I hear the rolling of the wheels,
> The chariots of war.
> I hear the breaking of the seals
> And the opening of the door.
> . . . . .

> Get, up, get up, my hardy sons;
> From this time forth we are
> No longer men, but pikes and guns
> In God's advancing war.

> And if we live, we free the slave,
> And if we die, we die;
> But God has digged His saints a grave
> Beyond the western sky.

Oh, fairer than the bugle-call
Its walls of jasper shine!
And Joshua's sword is on the wall,
With space beside for mine.

And should the Philistine defend
His strength against our blows,
The God who doth not spare His friend
Will not forget His foes.

It is strange how the tough, rough figure of this pioneer crusader has taken on the glamorous proportions of a heroic myth. Executed as a traitor, his tomb is now a state-guarded shrine, and there all the poets are heaping up their tributes. Lindsay, Masters, Sandburg have laid their imperishable wreaths, and now this younger poet dedicates a whole book to his memory, making his name the pivot on which his nation swung its mighty war.

We cannot follow here the various episodes, historic and fictional, which carry the poem on to the death of Lincoln and the end of the conflict. There is nothing finer than the John Brown chapter, but some of the battle-thunders, rolling at Shiloh or Antietam or Gettysburg, strike out as heroic a tune. Throughout, the poet stands as a twentieth-century observer of all the impassioned goings to and fro; seeing the astonishing events as parts of a patterned whole, the characters as heroes or supes of a vast drama which few of them understand. He sees the whimsical, the grotesque as well as the heroic—there is icy satire, for example, in his description of the congressmen who "came out to see Bull Run"—

The congressmen who like free shows and spectacles,
They brought their wives and carriages along;
They brought their speeches and their picnic-
   lunch. . . .
Some even brought a little whiskey, too—
(A little whiskey is a comforting thing
For congressmen in the sun, in the heat of the sun.)

The characterization is often marvellously vivid. Three leading actors in the drama, especially, stand out in full stature and color—Grant, Lee and Davis are like to be remembered as this poet paints them: thus they were, and are till the crack of doom. Lincoln's portrait is pretty well done, but less authoritative—for who can put into print or paint that strange and sombre figure, piteous, humorous and confoundingly wise! Some of the minor generals—Hooker, Meade, Beauregard—are vividly sketched in, and McClellan gets his dusty tag. And a few women are very much alive, mostly southern women: Mary Lou Wingate, who hated the North, and held the plantation and the South together through those tragic years—

                    as slightly made
And as hard to break as a rapier blade.

And her mammy and servant:

   Fat Aunt Bess is older than Time . . .
   The family despot, and the slave.

We have a whole panorama moving hardly before us on the luminous screen—soldiers, officers, civilians; aristocrats, slaves, sweethearts, lovers, killers; great and small, heroes and nobodies, they are all in the picture that moves along to the rumble of drums.

And as the picture moves, as the cinema epic swings along, the ghostly figure of John Brown reappears like a refrain:

                        That is my song.
   It is made of water and wind. It marches on.

A big book. A book which reaches out over this broad America, and looks not only backward but forward.

Alfred Kreymborg (essay date 1929)

SOURCE: Kreymborg, Alfred. "Youth Moves on Toward Maturity." In *Our Singing Strength: An Outline of American Poetry (1620-1930),* pp. 607-11. New York: Coward-McCann, Inc., 1929.

[*In the following excerpt, Kreymborg views Benét as a minor poet "attempting a major theme" in* John Brown's Body *and asserts that the poem is too ambitious in scope.*]

If Hart Crane has not yet found a theme large enough for his powers, it may be said that Stephen Benét, in **John Brown's Body,** attempted too large a canvas. But any failure on a grand scale is always admirable. It has been observed that recent American poets, in an effort to produce perfection, have become obsessed with polishing some microscopic image, or, haunted by cosmologies, have reduced the universe to polysyllabic abstractions in which human beings are beheld as atoms. If one now wearies of Imagism, one has also begun to weary of a poetic world in which the race is reduced to microbes underneath a lens fastened in the knowing eye of some poet who has read quite a few books on science and psychology, and holds an omniscient altitude by virtue of other men's discoveries. Benét and other young poets are returning to an older view of man—man, the heroic puppet—a view by no means romantic. The renewed interest in epic forms is based on this view, and the poet passionate enough to attempt nothing less than a major theme is the poet of to-morrow. America is old enough and rich enough in racial experience to offer major material. The modern movement in history and biography is an earnest of a larger, more expert examination of our past with reference to our present and future. A man need no longer import his writing material from abroad. Longfellow's day is long since past. So is Ezra Pound's. Obviously, but never obviously enough for certain esthetes, any race is a member of the human race. One need not be a chauvinist to detect the major tendencies of the American experiment. The theme as a whole is tremendous; and its myriad ramifications have minor details of a major character. It is time for the native poet to be writing poems on a universal scale; to show how large the little is, no matter how little. He no longer has to invent his themes; the less he invents the better. He may find them in the American tradition. The tradition may not be completely grounded, broadened, mellowed. Most things, in a continental experiment, may still lie ahead. The old experiment may be a failure, and the new fail even more tragically. But human beings were concerned in the tragedy. Their effort and failure, and their relation to one another along the way, reveal an endless succession of heroic themes. Major poets are the rarest of human beings. We have not had an epic poet since Whitman. But we have had many minor poets attempting a major theme. Benét is the most recent of these.

Though he is still a young man, he has been writing ballads and narratives for a number of years. His first book, *Five Men And Pompey,* was issued by The Yale University Press in 1915, when the poet was seventeen. Three other volumes of verse and four or five rather popular novels, not to mention a play or two, have followed rapidly. One does not object to the popular appeal behind Benét's work. In choosing the Civil War as the theme for *John Brown's Body,* he obeyed the tradition of epic writers from Homer down: they used material common to their own race and known to the average household for years and centuries. Possibly, we are still too close to the Civil War. We are only beginning to see it en masse, and to understand its motives, motives for the most part dark to its protagonists, darker still to its people, and darkest of all to the gray and blue men in the field. But certain facts are now apparent: we perceive their approximate order and realize that the greatest issue of the war was not the Negro question, not the saving of the Union or the defense of States' rights, but the economic issue. From John Brown's attack on Harpers Ferry to Lincoln's assassination, this issue is the undercurrent of Benét's saga. Benét, though still a young man, was so thoroughly saturated with the war, from infancy on, thanks to his father's memories, and has made so persistent a study of histories, biographies, newspapers, facts, hearsay, legends and lies, as to be the poet best fitted at present to compose a Civil War epic. His poem is a fascinating document, deriving part of its fascination from the familiarity of the theme and of the characters and issues involved. But it is a document rather than a major poem: a book

composed of glorious fragments of poetry, thrilling battlescenes, portraits of the leaders and portraits of minor characters.

No history has given us a more intimate feeling of the war: one feels everything and everybody: the Southern soil, the Northern soil, the border states, the European vultures, England and France—John Brown, Davis, Lincoln, Lee, Jackson, Beauregard, Longstreet, Pickett, MacClellan, Meade, Hooker, Grant—and the fictitious characters: the Wingates of Georgia, the Wingate home, the Southern aristocracy, Southern ladies, the gypsy-like Sally Dupré, the ladylike Lucy Weatherby, the marvelous Negroes, Cudjo, faithful to his masters, and Spade, the runaway slave who finds less freedom in the North—and the Northern protagonist, Jack Ellyat of Connecticut, and the dryad he falls in love with, Melora Vilas, and deserts after their first night—a beautiful lyric episode. And the soldiers themselves—the most vivid characters in the book—their vernacular—the Southern, the Yankee, the Mid-Western, each an accurate transcription. And the hell of it all, the inordinate suffering, the blind obstinacy, hatred of the war, love of commanders; and the laughter, the spoofing, vaingloriousness, heroism, cowardice, chicanery, humanity. The poem has a cinematographic scheme. It is the right scheme for so vast and swift a canvas. But the poet has failed in important particulars. Many of the shots are entirely unnecessary. Others come in at the wrong time. Often, a battlescene is interrupted for the sake of imposing a sardonic moral, a moral in the manner of Sandburg. Often, the poet stops a scene to tell you that historians have fabricated sentimental lies at this point. Then again, lyrics are introduced by way of underscoring the mood of a character or situation. These are written out of the poet's nature. Too often, he writes out of his own person. Such passages are fine in themselves, but obscure the dramatis personæ or retard the dramatic progression.

The order of the material follows the historic order— from Harpers Ferry, Fort Sumter, Bull Run, through Gettysburg, the Wilderness, Appomattox, the surrender, the death of Lincoln, the dirge of the South, and the birth of Northern industrialism out of John Brown's remains.

> Out of John Brown's strong sinews the tall skyscrap-
>   ers grow,
> Out of his heart the chanting buildings rise,
> Rivet and girder, motor and dynamo,
> Pillar of smoke by day and fire by night,
> The steel-faced cities reaching at the skies,
> The whole enormous and rotating cage
> Hung with hard jewels of electric light,
> Smoky with sorrow, black with splendor, dyed
> Whiter than damask for a crystal bride
> With metal suns, the engine-handed Age,

The genie we have raised to rule the earth,
Obsequious to our will
But servant-master still,
The tireless serf already half a god . . .

Finally, the poet urges the reader not to join shuddering
or adoring prophets:

Say neither, in their way,
"It is a deadly magic and accursed,"
Nor "It is blest," but only "It is here."

It seems to me that the poet should not have attempted
to recreate the war in its entirety. Born not far from
Gettysburg (Book Seven is a superb reproduction of the
battle), Benét might have produced a greater poem by
confining himself to the one high incident, reflecting
the whole war, and the heights and depths of the
Southern cause to which, by temperament, he throws
his larger sympathies. He could have employed the
same cast of characters, actual and fictitious, and given
us a more closely integrated drama. *John Brown's Body*
does not fail as history: as a revelation of America or of
the human race anywhere. Nor does it fail as poetry in
disparate fragments. But it does fail as drama. Raving
critics who called the book the greatest since the *Iliad*
and *Odyssey* were most unjust to Benét. One need only
go back to Goethe's *Faust* or to Whitman's *Leaves* to
see how unsparing such praise is. Goethe and Whitman
each spent a lifetime on works unfinished at their death.
Possibly, Benét has not yet finished *John Brown's Body.*
Perhaps he will revise and enlarge it down to his final
breath. What he has done with the theme has enough
grandeur for the grandeur to be carried on. I am heartily
glad the book is popular. But I trust, even more heartily,
the poet will not let his public give him the impression
that his work is done. The economic issues of any war
are also issues in the lives of poets. The success of his
book has freed Benét from the terrible bugaboo. He
may now invite his soul to loaf, and make his book a
companion of the Leaves. Walt, at the heart of hospital
camps, was certain no poet could encompass the Civil
War. It is time for some stripling to show the old
prophet where he was wrong. Stephen Benét has made
a fine start in that direction.

Morton Dauwen Zabel (review date August 1936)

SOURCE: Zabel, Morton Dauwen. "The American
Grain." *Poetry* 48, no. 5 (August 1936): 276-82.

[*In the following mixed review, Zabel delineates the
range of styles and themes in Benét's* Burning City.]

For twenty years Mr. Benét has been praised as a
prodigy, a patriot, an entertainer, and a prize-winner; it
has not been so easy to take him seriously as a poet.

But one becomes conscious of a wish to resist this difficulty and summon up a reasonable interest in a writer
so devoted to the American tradition that he has won, at
whatever sacrifice of critical respect or comparison with
the more formidable talents of his period, one of the
largest popular followings of the past two decades. His
verse is a survival of an abundant native line; it has
become a virtual guide-book of native myth and
folklore, their place-names, heroes, humors, and rever-
ences. He followed the mid-western poets of the pre-
War revival in this affection; one poem in *Burning
City,* a tribute to Vachel Lindsay which precedes another
to Walt Whitman, reminds us of this continuity. At a
moment when even special students of poetry are
expressing exasperation with the more rarefied pureties
of esthetic belief, when political contempt is directed
against intellectual verse and symbolist influences, when
a new order of lyric realism is being demanded of
Americans and the author of *John Brown's Body* is
held up at the Writers' Congress as a model of popular
eloquence to revolutionaries, Mr. Benét's day for sober
honors seems at last to have arrived. *Burning City*
claims attention on these grounds and one hopes to see
a practiced hand demonstrate to floundering proletarian
talents the right ways of using popular language and
subjects, of translating common human tastes and necessities into a verse that will surmount the futility of
convincing only those believers who require no conversion to the ways of light. The fact that Mr. Benét has
sensed this situation and turned to social and political
subject compels such curiosity. His new book opens
with a set of poems on political themes (**"Litany for
Dictatorships," "Ode to the Austrian Socialists,"**
etc.), and closes with a group of **"Nightmares"** of the
coming years—a *Blick ins Chaos* where angels in cellophane, synthetic rubber, and chromium sow the seeds
of a final confusion, and the termites of Manhattan
develop a taste for steel.

These are formidable subjects, but we find them approached with no fear or trembling. Mr. Benét follows
in a poetic line that is never so relaxed or self-confident
as in the presence of prophetic enormities that might
paralyze another order of poets to the point of speech-
lessness. This confidence is important; it indicates his
type—the romantic fabulist. It explains both the ease
with which he has spun past legends out of any stuff
that fell to hand—Biblical, historical, or fantastic—and
the temerity that produced in *John Brown's Body* a
whole text-book of dramatic and metrical varieties.
Ease of this kind is as enviable as it is convenient in a
poet who wants to work in the large dimensions of
popular myth. There can be no undue worry about refin-
ing allegory or imagery to the point of exact meaning,
no severe economy in a poem's structure, and no
privacy in its references. Such verse strives to be as
indulgent to the reader's attention as possible, and no
generosity is greater than that exhibited by Mr. Benét's

facile yarn-spinning imagination. His poem on Lindsay amounts to much more than a reproachful tribute to an ignored and neglected singer of the tribe: it shows how Mr. Benét derived, through Lindsay, from the bardic romantics who held sway in American poetry for over a century. Kipling, Masefield, Morris, and Rossetti might be studied as English revivalists of ballad and epic heroics, but not necessarily, for in America this tradition, in its homeliest form, was the living authority of text-books and family anthologies all the way from Neihardt, Riley, and Markham, back through Hay, Harte, and Miller, to the bearded dynasties of Longfellow and Bryant—a succession hostile to eccentric talent or refined taste, scornful of modernity or exotic influence, once the pride of the burgeoning Republic, and now chiefly a source of cheerful embarrassment to teachers and blushing incredulity to their students. Mr. Benét has aspired from his school-days to a place in this old American line. He has preferred, to the tests and risks of a loftier poetic hardihood, the homespun satisfactions recently expressed by Robert Frost:

> At least don't use your mind too hard,
> But trust my instinct—I'm a bard.

Toward such bardship he has mastered a profuse stock of native lore and made himself, next to Lindsay, the most proficient balladist on native themes in the century. If the sentiment of local traditions survives for future poets, it may be largely due to his efforts. One admits a strong pull on even the most guarded of patriotic feelings, as well as on human impulses over which vigilance may now be more safely relaxed.

Why then, with all these seductions, does one find the sympathy as rigid and skeptical as ever in reading ***Burning City***? It is chiefly because the book illustrates so flatly the distinction between bard and poet. To the fluent mill of such a talent, all is grist, not merely in subject-matter, but in language as well. Mr. Benét talks about social and moral degeneration, but there is little in imagery or phrasing to suggest that its meaning has penetrated his sensibilities or intelligence. He has roughly seized upon the moment's issues and causes, run them through the familiar meters and phrases of his instincts, and produced a passable verse journalism. It would be hoping too much to expect from this journeyman attitude anything very decisive in moral judgment or memorable as poetic meaning.

The most ambitious poem in the volume is the **"Ode to Walt Whitman."** Here is a full opportunity for displaying a love of American memories against a heroic theme, and the opening section is in fact a passage in Mr. Benét's most charming manner—pictures of provincial innocence moving loosely through a free verse that catches the spirit of Whitman very successfully, particularly in the image of footsteps and the approach of "Magnificent Death." The second part begins to dissipate this impressive effect by repetition and direct exposition; it betrays the absence of a central conception of Whitman as the dialogue between the poet and his interrogator descends to the most obvious contrasts between Whitman's dream of democracy and its present frustration ending with a suspended cliché:

> "Now they say we must have one tyranny or another
> And a dark bell rings in our hearts."

> "Was the blood spilt for nothing, then?"

There follows a hymn-like interlude which suggests an answer to this question by hinting that heroic visions are not successful in terms of small profits and quick returns: "He grows through the earth and is part of it like the roots of new grass." The form of this passage—brief unrhymed lines of two beats—is appealing, and some of the images are delicate, but they multiply and entangle themselves to disadvantage, and as a lyric interruption it hardly strengthens the formal unity of the poem as a whole. In Part 4 the ode's resolution is completely stultified by characteristic faults: it begins with some slovenly sarcasm on the cheap way the world has with its poets, and advances into a catalogue of "the glory of America" as glimpsed by Whitman, a broad flood of visions and splendors advancing toward "the restless-hearted always, forever, Mississippi, the god." This exhibits Mr. Benét's customary deftness in producing the tones and colors of native life, but never gets beyond suggesting a check-list of his familiar references, and ends with the desultory effect of having all been heard, too many times, before. In fact, it repeats—shorn of originality or concentration—the idea of Crane's *The River,* and invites a perilous contrast with what the theme becomes in the hand of a genuine poet.

It is this willingness to work in the loose run-of-mill material of the commonplace that besets all the more serious projects here. When one poem is entitled **"Litany for Dictatorships,"** it reveals its technique only too obviously: it turns out to be a long indiscriminate itemization of newspaper reports, atrocities, and horrors that finally arrives at a perfectly true and quite insignificant conclusion: "We thought we were done with these things, but we were wrong," upon which any daily editorial writer might improve. The same effect is produced in the poem on the Austrian socialists, and as for the *Nightmares,* whatever sense they convey of the impending catastrophe is cheapened as much by the juvenility of their spectres as by the reckless vulgarity of their style. These chromium-plated angels and swampy miasmas belong to thrillers by Wells or Conan Doyle, and their language should be reserved to *The New Yorker* or Paul Engle. Mr. Benét's success in echoing this last-named disciple is not the least of the discouragements his new book offers. In fact, since

Burning City presents quite a range of styles, it may be said that the nearer it gets to suggesting a notable model, the better its items are: at the lowest level it offers such trash as **"For City Spring"**; its reminders of the elegiac MacLeish are more moving; several poems of personal accent are charming—the poem on Lindsay, **"Girl Child,"** and **"The Lost Wife"**; a brief lyric that conveys a hint of Yeats—**"Memory"**—is probably the finest page in the volume.

The lessons offered to humanitarians by **Burning City** take the form of three emphatic negatives: (1) avoid hortatory sentences: they usually induce nothing but a false sense of power; (2) stop writing declarations, summons-to-arms, and "addresses to contemporaries": they are safer in the hands of editorial-writers and platform orators; and (3) beware of prophecy: it may be the surest way of deluding a valid ambition to poetry. If these cautions are properly admitted, Mr. Benét's instructions in wholesome sentiment and urgent indignation will offer a good deal more profit than otherwise.

F. O. Matthiessen (essay date 1948)

SOURCE: Matthiessen, F. O. "Poetry." In *Literary History of the United States,* Vol. II, edited by Robert E. Spiller, Willard Thorp, Thomas H. Johnson, and Henry Seidel Canby, pp. 1349-351. New York: Macmillan, 1948.

[*In the following excerpt, Matthiessen regards the poetry of Benét and Edna St. Vincent Millay as representative of the popular tastes of the 1920s.*]

In the years just at the end of the First World War when college undergraduates were more excited about contemporary American poetry than they had ever been before, such sinister thoughts were farthest from their minds. The popular taste of the twenties can be best caught in Edna St. Vincent Millay and Stephen Vincent Benét. Miss Millay's "Renascence" (1912) heralded her arrival at Vassar from Maine, and already contained the essence of what was to make her popular: an innocent freshness toward nature, which is none the less compounded out of the attitudes of the English romantic poets. She was soon to add the gamin boldness of the Greenwich Village Bohemian, and her quatrain about the candle burning at both its ends was hailed by the young anti-Victorians as their "Psalm of Life."

Her audience was increased by *Second April* (1921) and *The Harp-Weaver* (1923), and she was praised particularly by those who disliked the new intellectual poetry. The critical division over her work may be observed in the reception accorded *Fatal Interview* (1931). Some

did not hesitate to liken this sonnet sequence to Shakespeare's. Others, upon more exacting scrutiny, insisted that even the most striking of these sonnets, such as "O sleep forever in the Latmian cave," did not wholly escape incoherence of feeling and blurred syntax. The fairest comparison for Miss Millay's qualities and limitations would be with the posthumous sonnet sequence by Elinor Wylie in *Angels and Earthly Creatures* (1929). Turning seriously to poetry only during the last decade of her life, Mrs. Wylie demonstrated how a romantic sensibility could be strengthened and purified by a taste for the metaphysicals, whereas, despite the phrase from Donne that forms her title, Miss Millay's sonnets remain enthusiastically but loosely Keatsian. Mrs. Wylie was the more mature craftsman, even though her personal distinction may have caused her friends to exaggerate her original force. As Morton Zabel said in reviewing her work: "In literature, as in life, there is room only for a few important experiences, but for many amenities." Her rewarding amenity is her deft and delicate control of her traditional medium, in contrast with most of Edna Millay's work. Miss Millay is at her best when freest from any emulation of other writers, in a poem like "The Return" (1934), the simplest kind of personal lyric. When she tried to go beyond lyrics, she showed little skill—though she produced, to be sure, in *The King's Henchman* (1926), a workmanlike libretto for an opera. She shared generously in the protest against the execution of Sacco and Vanzetti, but the poems she wrote on that occasion are hardly memorable. When she sought, under the growing pressures of the late thirties, to stir up an awareness of international problems, she fell into thin sentiment and hackneyed phrases.

Stephen Benét, as the son of an army officer, was brought up in various parts of the United States, and absorbed an interest in the American scene and its historical background. His precocious first poems gave evidence of another absorption, in the literary ballad as handled by William Morris and other late nineteenth century poets. He was to fuse these two interests in some of his best work, ballads using the material of American folklore and humor, of which **"William Sycamore"** (1923) is probably the most notable. Like Edna Millay he was also to participate in the gay revolt against the Victorians, particularly in the ebullience of **"For All Blasphemers."**

In *John Brown's Body* (1928) he solidified his gifts and produced the most widely read long poem of the period. In the view of some readers this work established Benét as the first national poet of the dimensions called for by Whitman; but Harriet Monroe characterized it as "a cinema epic." Composed within a couple of years, this full-length novel in a variety of verse forms testifies to its author's technical facility, as well as to his gusto for the personalities of the Civil War. But there are many slack pages, his fictional plots are rather expected, and most of his characters are two-dimensional. Such a work raises the problem of popular art in modern society. Benét's talents have not been considered as of anything like the first order by many other poets; and *John Brown's Body* has kept its largest following among readers under twenty. But such an audience is not to be scorned in a democracy, and Benét's share in reviving the bright colors of our heroic legends puts him squarely in the succession from Longfellow and Lindsay. The most striking defect of this poem is in its passages of reflection, which skip over grave problems with a delusive jauntiness. Benét had grown to understand more of our history when he wrote his **"Ode to Walt Whitman"** against the background of the depression; and in **"Litany for Dictatorships"** (1936) and **"Nightmare at Noon"** (1940), he looked ahead, much more affectingly than Miss Millay, to the menace of the war. In *Western Star,* the first section of a long poem on which he had been working for some years at his death, he still manifested the same warm feeling for the American land, if little advance in technique beyond his first attempted epic.

Archibald MacLeish, who was at Yale just ahead of Benét, performed another serviceable function by being a kind of middleman of taste between the experimenters and the general public. Reading his work from *The Pot of Earth* (1925) down to *America Was Promises* (1939) is to be presented with a chronicle of the dominant new influences in that period. He began writing verse as an undergraduate, but he dated his own poetic career from 1923, when he gave up the practice of law and went to live in France. At that time he reflected Eliot's interest in *The Golden Bough,* particularly in the theme of cyclical death and rebirth. He also utilized Eliot's technique of sudden contrasts to convey the broken rhythm of contemporary existence. A few years later, in "Land's End," he was bringing to American readers the wide-space imagery of Perse's *Anabase.* He demonstrated how much he had learned from Pound's versification in *Conquistador* (1932), and in its most successful portion, "Bernál Diaz' Preface to His Book," he extended the world-weary attitude of Gerontion. But he had returned to America by the end of the twenties, and was soon responding to the new mood of social protest. His *Frescoes for Mr. Rockefeller's City* (1933) was dedicated to Sandburg, and in *Public Speech* and his radio play, *The Fall of the City,* he caught up some of the tones and accents of the younger poets, particularly Auden. MacLeish was characterized throughout these years by generous enthusiasms, as well as by a sensitive ear, but he was too suggestible to possess a style quite his own. The conspicuous exception was in some of his short lyrics, like "The Too Late Born," or "You, Andrew Marvell," authentic expressions of his own elegiac emotion.

Charles A. Fenton (essay date 1958)

SOURCE: Fenton, Charles A. "Angry Poet." In *Stephen Vincent Benét: The Life and Times of an American Man of Letters, 1898-1943,* pp. 274-96. New Haven, Conn.: Yale University Press, 1958.

[*In the following essay, Fenton considers Benét's personal and creative development during the 1930s.*]

> Taxi strike going on but don't see any of it in this neighborhood. . . .

The middle years of the 1930's, and of his own thirties, thus became for Benét a period of personal and professional crisis. The artistic duress of writing *James Shore's Daughter,* and the plain reality that he simply could not afford that kind of labor financially, nor perhaps temperamentally, invited him to slip permanently into the role of proficient hack. It was a tempting fate.

The luster of *John Brown's Body* would always give him a vocational edge over his competitors. It would be easy to rationalize his compromise from year to year, on the basis of domestic responsibility and momentary expediency. There would be the fragmentary notes for the long poem on the settlement of the West as occasional consolation; he could tinker with the poem for a few weeks every year or so. There could be Hollywood sorties in the winter and a writers' conference or two in the summer as a purge. That kind of an American literary career was being practiced by many of his contemporaries; from Washington Irving to Ben Hecht there was ample precedent for the self-limitation of one's talent.

Benét walked the very center of this particular professional road from time to time, and he was never completely removed from its environs, but from 1935 until his death he also traveled another route. He came to this alternative path as a result of various conditions. The insistence of his creative instincts was an important factor. So was his boredom with formula fiction, and his deep feeling about America; so, too, were such elements as his friendship with Archibald MacLeish, his profound admiration for Franklin Roosevelt, his appalled horror at totalitarianism, and his devotion to the concept of freedom. It was not an easy road, and none of these factors could ever have been much more than temporary irritants without his own determination to chart such a route.

"It is one of the hardest things in the world," he said later, "for the popular writer who has made a success at one sort of thing to branch out into another field. The bread-and-butter pressure is all the other way. 'Give us some more of your delightful stories about Southern mountaineers—or New York policemen—or Andaman islanders.'"[1]

Benét had learned this truth each working day from 1925 until this present moment. His stories about the American past had been resisted by every editor save those at *Country Gentleman* and the *Elks' Magazine*. He was encouraged and rewarded to remain faithful to the light contemporary material of his initial magazine successes. As a poet he was identified with the loose, folk verse of **John Brown's Body** or the rollicking wit of **"King David."** Editors urged him to maintain the familiar forms and tone; even the circulation magazines solicited verse from him for national holidays and tributes to Washington and Lincoln and, once, to Colonel Lindbergh. "Sorry," he wrote Brandt in 1931, when *Country Gentleman* had offered him a large price for such a poem. "I have tried to make Mr. Washington come down off his monument but with no success."

Benét was an acute and pitiless analyst of his own situation; he had begun to keep a diary for that very reason, as its candor and self-examination showed. "There comes a time in the life of every writer," he said once, "when he has said the first things he had to say and cannot say them over again in just the same way—and yet he must go on writing."[2] For him that time came in the mid 1930's.

* * *

Ever since 1915 his primary preoccupations had been the twin and frequently conflicting ones of a poetry that was largely subjective and the private relationships of his family and friends. His concern with politics had reached its peak during adolescence, when he created a temporary socialism from which to challenge the Colonel's benign conservatism. Like most of his generation he then became indifferent to politics as an undergraduate and later as a young man. He was thoroughly uninterested in the presidential campaign of 1920, Tom Chubb remembered, and such occasional political rallying-points of the 1920's as the Sacco-Vanzetti case got only the mildest response from him.

As late as 1932 he washed his hands of both major political parties and made the negative gesture of voting for Norman Thomas. Chubb felt that it was the rise of Hitler which aroused Benét to a public literary role. In reality, however, he could not insulate himself in 1933 and 1934 against the grim depression winters in New York. Long before he was fully aroused by totalitarian savagery he was stricken by the sight of white-collar workers wielding relief shovels in their shabby overcoats. "They were not used to digging," Benét wrote McClure. "You could tell by their shoulders."

MacLeish, far better informed about the national scene than most American writers of the period, was living in New York now. The two couples were congenial and saw a good deal of each other socially. MacLeish's own

poetry was shifting from the personal concerns of his early verse; now he was formulating his concept of public speech as the role of the poet in time of national emergency. In the fall of 1933 Benét spent a long dinner and evening with MacLeish, Farrar, and Hervey Allen. "Talk about really doing something about what we believe in," Benét noted in his diary, "both as regards literature and democracy."

At the same time his friendships with young writers were acquainting him with a literary generation which was obsessed with politics as his own at that age had been engrossed by aesthetics and individual self-fulfillment. They brought for his inspection and verdict not only their manuscripts but also their plans for new magazines and their manifestoes of protest. Benét was impressed by their conviction and touched by their confidence in him, which he characteristically regarded as misplaced. He was also skeptical of their optimism.

"Have lunch with ——— and his earnest wife at Automat," he wrote in his diary in 1934. "They are eager idealists &, like most e.i.'s, somewhat disingenuous as to the means they take to bring about the Kingdom of God."

He knew more about American history than any other major contemporary novelist or poet save Dos Passos. His creed as a liberal was grounded in his confidence in the American heritage and the good sense of the American people. "No," he told Paul Engle, when the latter inquired about his politics, "I am not a revolutionary." From the beginning he was thoroughly hostile not only to fascism but also to Marxism. His convictions about liberal American government were as strengthened by the hostility of native communists to F. D. R. as by the similar hatred of the President by the American rich. "At the moment," he said with satisfaction in 1936, "every element I dislike most in the country is allied against Roosevelt." Much of his political thinking began in this pragmatic, intuitive way.

"Govt. starts selling gold abroad," he wrote in his diary in 1933. "All stuffed shirt Wall St. people against it—so feel rather for it, while knowing nothing."

He was diffident about his own ignorance of geopolitics, which was by no means as complete as he imagined or pretended it to be. He regretted, however, the grim self-assurance and monomania of the new literary generation. "The life of a young radical," he noted in 1935, speaking of a young poet, "strikes me as dreary, or rather ———'s life does. He is too busy thinking about economics to laugh." Benét was doubtful of all panaceas and wary of doctrinal infallibility.

The 1930's were a time of pundits and wise men. Benét instead thought of himself as a rather confused liberal. He suspected that most Americans, when their self-interest was not too much involved, were very much like himself in their confused liberalism. He shared with his friend Robert Nathan a kind of urbane good-will, though soon his own liberalism became increasingly militant. In a letter to Nathan, congratulating him on the canine hero of his current fantasy, Benét summed up in an epitaph of light verse his doubts concerning the various loud certainties of the period.

> He was no Lippmann, I can see,
> Nor Heywood Broun, nor Dotty T.
> But he seems rather more like me.
>
> For he was liberally inclined
> But lacked their comprehensive mind.
> They know who's who. They know what's what.
> But he and I, I fear, do not,
> Who sniff the legs of grief and mirth
> And run bewildered on the earth.
>
> For he was liberally inclined
> But lacked the trained-dogmatic mind.
> And yet liked living, wet or dry.
> And so do I, and so do I.

As his political and social involvement became more and more broad Benét came to regard liberalism as a specific and definable creed, difficult to practice but essential to American principles. "If you're a liberal," he told a friend who was regretting its necessary ambiguities, "that means you're always out on a limb. It isn't very comfortable, on the limb, but then God never intended liberals to be comfortable. If he had, he'd have made them conservatives. Or radicals." Out of an historical perspective more extensive than the typical liberal's he found strength and verification. When Philip Barry despaired of America because of the vituperation of Roosevelt, Benét reassured him with tales of the invective which continually surrounded Lincoln. "His wide reading," said Barry's widow many years later, "made him much more knowledgeable about politics than Phil or the rest of our friends."[3]

Benét seemed to his friend Christopher LaFarge, the poet and short story writer, to be almost the ideal representative of a demanding political position. "He had a truly liberal mind," said LaFarge in 1954, "which liked to entertain and examine other people's ideas." LaFarge remembered that Benét would not argue; he would only discuss. There was nevertheless a realistic quality in his thinking which made his liberalism a permanent creed. "Roosevelt has made his purpose plain," Benét rejoiced in his diary in 1934, "and united all the pigs and Bourbons against him, which is fine." It was this same realism as much as his knowledge of history which made him so mistrustful of the native communists.

"I'm not very sold on Marxism as a doctrine," he wrote Paul Engle in 1935. "They have built it into too cast-iron a theory, and life seems to take pleasure in fooling cast-iron theories. Also, the leading professors over here are a little too witch-burning to suit me."

He was invited out to the University of Iowa again, in the spring of 1935. The long train ride across half the continent was a tonic and confirmation. "As always, traveling these miles," he told Engle, "I was impressed once more. My God, the cows, the chickens, the fruit-trees, the ploughlands, the abundance, depression or no depression! It is just so completely different from any European scene—the enormous backlog of energy possibility, in spite of any number of mistakes and lots of crooks."

In the meantime, however, he saw in New York and at Peace Dale the less attractive side of the American scene. He met people, he said, who regarded even Paul McNutt as a red; he was equally angered by the distorted coverage of the Washington news by the New York press. His and Rosemary's active social life took them into homes where the most obscene innuendoes about Roosevelt were regarded as documented fact. His sense of what was valuable in America was deeply offended. "It is curious," he noted in his diary after a summer in Rhode Island, "how many Eastern people really behave, once they've had money for 2 generations, with a sort of would-be Divine Right." There was a violence now in his reactions which replaced the earlier placidity.

"At Westbury," he wrote in his diary in 1933. "Go to overstuffed, stupid ———'s for lunch. Where are you going for the summer? Oh, what a party we had. We missed you at Palm Beach, etc. Enormous estate. [They] have made the supreme sacrifice by opening the golf course for charity. Goyas, etc.—but God, what human beings."

His sense of justice caused him to make a kind of footnote to this outburst. "Much better rich than ———," he noted a few days later of another host, but even here his acceptance was qualified. "If one has to have [the] rich, which may not be necessary." All but a handful of his friends were rabidly hostile to the New Deal. Only at the Century Club, and not always there, was he likely to find himself belonging to the majority. His objection to the anti-Roosevelt group was, as LaFarge pointed out, that they would not discuss; they would only argue. Benét joyously won their money when they challenged him to bet against Landon in 1936, but often there were bitter quarrels. "The election is in full swing here," he wrote McClure in 1936, "but New York, thank goodness, is a fairly impersonal place and I don't get into as many fights as I would have in Rhode Island."

Ethel Andrews—married now to John Harlan, corporation lawyer and future Supreme Court justice—was startled to see a Benét who was aroused in an entirely new way. When she was the hostess she tried to keep the conversation off politics. Benét's identification of the opposition was harsh and bitter. "It is horrible," he wrote Paul Engle, who was still in England, "to see the nervous violence of the comfortable ones once they get the idea that one cent of their precious money is being touched. It makes you feel degraded. The patriots and lovers of America who put their money in Newfoundland holding companies—the descendents of signers who talk about people on relief as if they were an inferior breed of dog. What a sorry class of rich we have here—their only redeeming feature is their stupidity."

The state of the nation became more and more his primary concern. "Try to write after dinner," he noted in his diary, "but waste time in idle thought about political situation instead." What he hoped for, and this was the appeal for him of the New Deal, was simply an America of more genuine opportunity. "If we could have fifteen years of decent government, Federal aid and Robert Moses," he told Engle, "this would be a good city to live in. They might even build new schools."

The letters he wrote to Engle were an important release for him. He took special pains with them, filling two and three single-spaced pages with detailed descriptions of national events and acute characterizations of contemporary motives. Always he ducked the mantle of sage and pundit. "All this is subject to change without notice," he told the young poet after making some tentative predictions, "and I never pretended to be a prophet anyway." Now, too, his short stories had additional comment on the current political and social scene. For the first time he began to give to his stories of the American past a sustained contemporary relevance.

He wrote, in "A Man from Fort Necessity," a good story about the young Washington. It was published in the *Saturday Evening Post*.[4] The parallel between the hatred of Roosevelt and Washington was apparent. "You can say that he wants to make himself a king or a dictator, if you like," says the innkeeper who had served with Washington in the French and Indian Wars. "Every man to his own brand of politics. But you'll have to say it outside; not in my house. He's a man that likes his way; yes, I'll grant you that. I don't give a shinplaster for a man that don't, myself; other people may be otherwise minded. But as for that New York newsletter and what it says about him, you can put that right back in your pocket while you're drinking my liquor."

In the spring of 1935, his mind preoccupied with the native fascism of Huey Long, Benét wrote an even more detailed parable for the times. In "Silver Jemmy" he drew the parallel between Jefferson and Aaron Burr on the one hand and Roosevelt and Long on the other. The

contemporary implications were harsh and telling. "He talked to me for some time," says the New Orleans aristocrat after an audience with Jefferson, "of his belief in 'the common man' and 'democracy'—beliefs which we know to be both subversive and impossible of realization . . . his influence is rapidly waning and his doctrine of 'the common man' has roused much resentment among the better educated. It seems likely that he will be the last President of this present confederation—and that the nation will then either fall apart of its own weight or give rise to some dictator."[5]

These were the months, after all, in which the Liberty League was born; these were months in which some of the hostility toward Roosevelt, and particularly among the class of whom Benét saw so much socially, became pathological. Many Americans in 1935 were questioning the utility of a democracy, weighing various alternatives. One of his friends announced emphatically that she would move to England—she didn't—if Roosevelt won in 1936. Benét listened to the tirades at Manhattan dinners and on Rhode Island beaches. Now, in "Silver Jemmy," he translated them into an historical perspective.

"It is the first time *you* have known them," the old creole tells his son, "the cries and the wild voices, the prophets of calamity. And yet they come not once in the life of a nation but many times. Your sons in their turn will know them, and their sons also."

Cosmopolitan, which eventually bought the story and finally published it in May 1936, was fearful of its theme and tone. They argued first that it needed more romance and a lighter touch. Benét made cheerful concessions to their anxiety about the love interest, but he refused to tamper with its basic statement. When a *Cosmopolitan* editor protested to Brandt that the story was too intellectual, Benét became thoroughly exasperated.

"If patriotism is intellectual," Benét wrote his agent, "so is the banking system—and Father Coughlin can fill Madison Square Garden by talking about the banking system, not about cuties. In other words, this happens to be a time when people are interested in things which might have been considered intellectual in '28. And any editor with brains can tie this story into the present with a ten word blurb. Doesn't the Cosmo think that a few men might like to read the magazine once in a while? This is a man's story, as I see it—but I'm damned if I think that's a defect, in principle."

The editorial timidity was chronic; it was not confined to *Cosmopolitan.* The *Saturday Evening Post* bought his notable antitotalitarian story, "The Blood of the Martyrs," but Benét was irritated by their attempts to soften its indictment. "Illustrator has done his best," he noted, "to portray all possible European types & thus avoid damages." Wesley Stout, successor to George Lorimer as editor of the *Post,* aroused Benét in memorable fashion when he objected to the opening paragraphs of "Schooner Fairchild's Class."[6] Stout's prose, as he denounced Benét's characterization of the story's central character in a letter to Brandt, was more oratorical than editorial.

Benét, Stout told Brandt, had created in Lane Parrington "not an individual but a stuffed shirt, an effigy of the conservative cause. It is a tract worthy of the immaculately conceived Harry Hopkins. I care not how ridiculous he may make his Parrington, as long as he does not offer him as a symbol of the blasphemy of opposing those selfless, consecrated knights of the Holy Grail." Stout thereupon suggested that the *Post,* which was then paying Benét $1250 a story, would nevertheless buy "Schooner Fairchild's Class" if the characterization of Lane Parrington was altered. Benét would have no part of it.

"I can't make any revisions," he wrote Brandt. "I wouldn't know where to begin if I wanted to. . . . The whole thing is pretty surprising to me—and pretty disappointing. Because if the *Post* is going to want the opinions of its editorial page stuck willy-nilly into its fiction—if you have to class-angle a story for the *Post* as you'd have to for the *New Masses,* only in reverse—there's no point in my trying to write for them. I can't work that way. Any magazine can make its own rules—but that seems to me a stupid policy for a general magazine. Where does Stout think he gets his three million circulation? From the Union League Club?"

Some of this kind of editorial pressure was removed when Ben Hibbs became fiction editor of *Country Gentleman* in 1934. Now Benét's Oldest Inhabitant stories were again welcomed there; his price rose gradually during the rest of the decade to $1500, and in 1934 and 1935 *Country Gentleman* bought and published four of his American tales.[7] The most interesting characteristic of these new stories was the confirmation they gave that Benét could not be labeled a merely regional or period writer. Beyond their common quality of a recurrent narrator they resembled each other only in their imaginative evocation of the American past. They might deal with the antebellum South or post-Appomattox bitterness, with the flatboat legends of the Mississippi or the covered-wagon caravans pressing across the mountains. He would write a clipper-ship story and a hunting story, a trotting story, a steamboat story, and a story about Yankee peddlers. Benét was roaming unrestricted through a hundred years of American history, the first genuinely national American story-teller since Washington Irving, more richly talented than the latter and thoroughly free of Irving's uneasy sense of American inadequacies.

Benét varied the historical fiction, as always, with a coating of trivialities, most of them published in *Redbook* and the *Delineator.*[8] "This is the Xmas story to Mr. Vetluguin's specifications for *Redbook,*" he wrote Brandt in August 1935. "If he likes it, stick him for it." Here too, however, as with the more substantial material of the American past, there was editorial perversity. *Redbook* also craved revisions and simplification.

"I think that is a little whimsical on Mr. Balmer's part," Benét told Brandt, when the agent sent him the *Redbook* suggestions, "[but] Vetluguin is a good egg, I'd like to please him, and if you consider it absolutely necessary, I'll make the revision. But I would like to point out to him or to Mr. Balmer that I have to have a little fun writing a story of this sort or it isn't going to be any good. I'm perfectly willing to work to any sort of specifications, but I think I ought to be allowed to put in my own doors and windows. If you revise and revise, and put in this and take out that, it gets to be like the movies and the thing goes dead and flat."

Neither in the historical material nor in the contemporary situations could he be entirely free of the taboos and restrictions. This long period of concentration on short stories, extending almost without interruption from April 1934, when *James Shore's Daughter* was published, until the late spring of 1935, had given him a legitimate sense of financial security. "I've made some money," he wrote his brother, "paid up the back bills and hope to be a little flusher this winter than I was last." His ideas about contemporary issues frustrated and truncated by the circulation magazines, but enjoying a reprieve from old debts, he began his most productive season of continuous poetry since **John Brown's Body** eight years before.

* * *

The poems Benét wrote in 1935 and 1936, of which the most permanently distinguished was **"Litany for Dictatorships"** and the most immediately famous the Nightmare series in the *New Yorker,* had their origins in Benét's various anxieties. His major anxiety was the perilous condition of human liberty in the twentieth century. He examined a number of different kinds of beleaguered freedom: political freedom in the **"Litany"**; artistic freedom in the stanzas to Vachel Lindsay called **"Do You Remember, Springfield?"**: technological freedom in the "New York" poems, and personal freedom in all of them.

The result was a group of poems, most of them written between the spring of 1935 and the late winter of 1936, which he could collect with satisfaction in **Burning City** in June 1936. They gave new status to his role as a national writer. In 1948 F. O. Matthiessen would cite **"Ode to Walt Whitman"** as evidence of Benét's grasp of the American heritage; in the **"Litany,"** Matthiessen felt, Benét recorded the issues "more affectingly" than any of his contemporaries. The *Nation* reported, quite rightly, that although the book lacked the high peaks of *John Brown's Body,* his growth was impressive. He was, said his fellow poet Donald Culross Peattie, "as nearly the national poet as any one has been since Whitman."[9]

Broad as his topics were, their original source was always the deeply subjective one which had been Benét's chief poetic strength since 1915. It was the quality which separated both him and these poems from the characteristic literature of protest of the 1930's. "She does not make the mistake of many young revolutionary poets," Benét had said approvingly of Muriel Rukeyser, "in thinking that a political statement is a poem because it is a political statement."[10] Nor did he himself make that error; he could not, since the poetic tradition in which he wrote was a personal one. Always, despite the grandeur of his subjects—Walt Whitman, the decay of a civilization, the preservation of democratic values—always these poems were superior to the conventional verse of a dialectic because of the intimate, nonportentous, unoratorical quality. Always there was the same relief from rhetoric which he gave to so brief a poem as **"Sparrow."**

> Lord, in your mercy let me be a sparrow!
> His rapid heart's so hot.
> And some can sing—song-sparrows, so they say—
> And, one thing, Lord—the times are iron, now.
> Perhaps you have forgot.
> They shoot the wise and brave on every bough.
> But sparrows are the last things that get shot.

Thus the poems of 1935 and 1936 were not only statements on the great questions but also intimate lyrics which examined his own situation as his thirties came to an end. Each group contained fragments of the other; this too gave the best of them a permanence that was rare in the social art of the 1930's. A basic theme, rising above the social declarations, was the recurrent celebration of the practice of poetry. He presented this statement in the large outlines of Whitman and Lindsay, and in the slighter verse of **"Thanks"** and **"Reply,"** where the celebration was private and immediate, and deeply moving in its candor.

> It is a long time, long.
> And so much wasted, yes.
> And other men, oh, yes,
> All the clever, better-placed men.
> And so much bad work for bread,
> The work that crawls in the hand
> And that I would do again.
>
> A long time, very long, yes.
> And the lateness beginning, yes.
> And everything that you say

> And the door shut with a weight.
> O lightning, o forked bough,
> Raining from the great sky,
> The fire burns in the hand
> Even this late.

This, too, was part of the origins of *Burning City.* Benét was feeling in his late thirties, under the stress both of conditions peculiar to his own situation and of others common to all men in this decade of tension, a compulsion to restate the moments of his life. He looked back to one war in **"Short Ode,"** ahead to another in **"1936."** There was a poem to his daughter and there were lyrics in which the presence of his love for his wife was dominant and tender. He celebrated the retention of his poetic gift—"The fire burns in the hand / Even this late"—as if in gratitude that it should still exist despite the uses to which he had sometimes put it. When an interviewer asked him why he had written **"Litany for Dictatorships,"** Benét replied that he wrote it because he had to. The beginnings of the New York series, as he noted in his diary, had been the repeated nightmares of his own sleep. He described the poems as angry poems.

"Feel much like writing these days," he noted in August 1935. He wrote steadily all that summer and fall, the **"Litany"** in mid-July, **"Girl Child"** and **"For Those Who Are as Right as Any"** at the end of the month, **"Sparrow"** and **"Old Man Hoppergrass"** in August, and **"Do You Remember, Springfield?"** and **"Memory"** in October. All through the last weeks of November and before and after the Christmas holidays he worked on **"Notes to Be Left in a Cornerstone."** He finished it toward the end of January. The *New Yorker* bought it immediately, enclosing their check for four hundred and eighteen dollars. "Highest price ever got for a poem," Benét wrote in his diary. "Quite stunned."

The *New Yorker's* response was characteristic of the impact which these poems were having and continued to have. He mailed **"Litany for Dictatorships"** to the *Atlantic Monthly* in mid-July; two days later Edward Weeks telephoned to say that he would pay a hundred and fifty dollars for it and planned to break open the September issue to make room for it. Benét began to think in terms of a collection of the poems. Farrar and Rinehart, to whom he had shifted completely when Dan Longwell moved from Doubleday to the Luce organization, were immediately anxious to get the book on their spring list. By the middle of December 1935 the jacket had been designed by Charlie Child.

Now, with the book a visualized reality in both his own and his publishers' minds, Benét was pressed again; his bank account grew thinner and he wrote once more for a deadline. The *New Yorker* check for **"Notes to Be Left in a Cornerstone"** went immediately on the back rent, fuel, and phone bills. The winter brought ominous warnings about his health. "Try to work afternoon & evening but with no success. The cold seems to freeze up the vital juices. Also have a continual pain in the back." By February the easy, buoyant mood and circumstances of 1935 had vanished. "I must finish this infernal book—get so I dream about it—but I will not do it sloppily."

He completed **"Ode to the Austrian Socialists"** at the end of February, however, and in March **"Short Ode"** and **"Complaint of Body, the Ass, against His Rider, the Soul."** By the end of March the grotesque race between time and money reached a climax. "Must finish book—must also make some money." On April 11, the day he finished typing the manuscript and making final revisions, his bank balance was down to two dollars.

"Hand to mouth for last 3½ years," he wrote in his diary, "& still going on. Should be used to it but am not—takes my courage now. You lose, in time, the first flair, when it is exciting to be broke, work days at a stretch, and redeem finances by some coup."

In April he got a check from Doubleday for four hundred and fifty dollars of current royalties on *John Brown's Body.* It was not even a respite; he paid the New York State income tax with it the same day. In early May, when he was proofreading the galleys of *Burning City,* his resources had again almost vanished; this time his account had shrunk to three dollars. The children's tuition had to be paid by June. He was encouraged by the publication of the book—"seems solid," he conceded—and by the high praise of most of the reviewers. What should have been a triumphant professional moment, however, was made wretched by poverty and self-reproach. "This degrading, humiliating and constant need of money is something that stupefies the mind and saps the vitality. Will I ever get free of it & be able to do my work in peace?"

Burning City sold well, yet he was still so broke in July that they had to remain in New York; the children spent a couple of weeks with Rosemary's relatives in Richmond. He borrowed two hundred and fifty dollars from Brandt. "Try to work on story in evening but no go. Owe lots of money. Am so tired of things being like that." He finished the new story on July 9 and sent it downtown to Brandt. "Will you give me a buzz on this?" he asked the agent. "I'm afraid it's a little long but I tried to get a lot of things in." Brandt read the manuscript and telephoned Benét immediately. "It's a honey," Brandt told him. He would send it to the *Post* right away.[11]

Benét had gone back in this story to the American nineteenth century, his imagination aroused by passages in Van Wyck Brooks' *The Flowering of New England.*

As he did so often, he also found a portion of his situation in a timeless legend that was as much universal as American. The particular legend he chose was a poignant clue to his frame of mind in June and July of 1936. During those weeks he, too, would have entertained a proposition from Satan. The hero of "The Devil and Daniel Webster" was the New England statesman, but the author's kinship was with Jabez Stone, the bedeviled farmer who worked a rocky strip of New Hampshire land.

"The Devil and Daniel Webster" consolidated the national role which had been slowly materializing for Benét ever since the publication of the ballads of 1922 and 1923. Though he wrote the story in ten days, it was in a very real sense the product of ten years of labor. Its realistic fantasy and extraordinary plausibility came from a decade's drafts and revisions of those fifteen Oldest Inhabitant stories which preceded it. In Daniel Webster he had found an ideal folk-hero. Webster was ambiguous enough for productive characterization, less remotely sacred and frozen than Lincoln, majestic in his strengths and weaknesses, national in his values. Just as Longfellow rehabilitated Paul Revere, so too had Benét revitalized another tarnished hero.

Americans responded to the story in a way that astonished the *Post,* who published it in the issue of October 24. Soon the magazine wooed Benét and Brandt with an attractive contract that pledged four stories a year for $1750 for each story. When Benét stopped off at Brandt's office he found himself, he said, "quite the white-headed boy. *Post* depending on me, etc." His publishers brought out the story in hard covers; it went through eleven editions during the next twenty years and was still in print in 1957. There were deluxe editions from fancy presses, with elaborate illustrations. It was precisely the kind of permanent classic which Benét had once denied "The Barefoot Saint" to be, "a story you can read in an hour but which you keep remembering for a long time."

When it was given the O. Henry Memorial Award as the best American short story of the year, Harry Hansen, the editor of the series, reported that it was one of the rare occasions when all the judges were unanimously of the same opinion. "Second and third readings," said one of them, "convince me of its fine chance for as near an approach to immortality as a short story can attain."[12] It was as widely anthologized as any single American tale by an American writer. It reached continuous and additional audiences as operetta, one-act play, and full-length movie.

Benét had begun with no more than a title, taken from the work sheet on which he listed phrases that seemed to have the promise of a good story in them. Not until several months later did he read Irving's "The Devil and Tom Walker," which was often supposed to have been his inspiration. All he had was a title, "The Devil in New England." His initial conception, harassed by bills as he was, after the publication of **Burning City,** and anxious for a quick sale, was to have the Devil come to a modern small town. "Then I tried shifting it back into the past," Benét explained later. "It seemed a good idea but I didn't know what I'd have him do when he got there."[13] It was at this point that he first visualized Webster as the Devil's antagonist.

"I had always thought of him," Benét said in 1941, "as an orator with one hand stuck in the bosom of his frock coat, till I read of him in Van Wyck Brooks' *The Flowering of New England.* Then he began to come alive and I read more about him."[14]

He did a good deal of research on Webster in late June of 1936, as was indicated not only by this story but also by its successors in the *Post,* "Daniel Webster and the Sea Serpent" and "Daniel Webster and the Ides of March."[15] Once he had fixed on Webster, the rest, he said, was easy. "Webster's strong point was oratory," he explained, "so naturally he'd have to meet the Devil in an oratorical contest and win."[16] The enormous success of the story required Benét to discuss it publicly in a way that he rarely did with his work.

"It's always seemed to me," he said later, "that legends and yarns and folk-tales are as much a part of the real history of a country as proclamations and provisos and constitutional amendments. . . . 'The Devil and Daniel Webster' is an attempt at telling such a legend . . . I couldn't help trying to show him in terms of American legend; I couldn't help wondering what would happen if a man like that ever came to grips with the Devil— and not an imported Devil, either, but a genuine, homegrown product, Mr. Scratch."[17]

After the publication of "The Devil and Daniel Webster" Benét became a story-teller to the nation. He could now write for the largest magazine in the United States stories about leprechauns and sea serpents, and about Nazi tyranny and American responsibilities. He wrote for the biggest audience that any American writer of his stature had ever possessed. For many of his readers his political and moral values were their only encounter with this particular set of national convictions.

His personal as well as his professional status was consolidated by "The Devil and Daniel Webster." The early summer of 1936 was the last period of truly desperate financial pressure which he had to endure. It ended dramatically in August, when, Jabez Stone-like, he found temporary prosperity: two more stories were sold to the *Post;* one of the studios unexpectedly bought the movie rights to a story called "Everybody Was Very

Nice" for twenty-five hundred dollars; and Rosemary inherited a thousand dollars from an aunt whom she scarcely knew. "Thus ends," Benét wrote in his diary, "one of the strangest weeks in our lives." Thereafter his income rose rapidly on the strength of the Daniel Webster success; it leveled off at between twelve and fifteen thousand dollars a year for the rest of his life.

There were still the nightmarish intervals when insurance and rent and tuition came suddenly due at a time when he was caught between stories. And, as his income grew, he assumed new responsibilities. Now he gave his mother additional funds; when he was flush he sent her checks for two or three thousand dollars. He increased his contributions to charity; he gave generously to most of the antifascist organizations. He never knew complete freedom from financial tension, but "The Devil and Daniel Webster" gave him an earning power which now at least was more realistically in balance with his responsibilities.

He had discovered and disciplined his fiction talent in the big slicks, though he'd had to escape the prison first. "[Writing]," Benét told the short story writer Pauli Murray in 1939, "is a job to be done, like any job—it's a profession to be learned, like any profession. It isn't learned in a month or a year—it takes time. But it can be learned." For evidence—though he was without that kind of vanity—Benét could have referred Miss Murray to back issues of *Country Gentleman* and the *Elks' Magazine* and *Cosmopolitan.* More particularly, however, the story was public verification that now he was what could not have been anticipated on the basis of his earlier work for *Metropolitan* and *Redbook* and *Liberty.* He had become an important and revered American man of letters.

Notes

1. SVB [Stephen Vincent Benét] and Rosemary Benét, "Mary Roberts Rinehart's Bread and Butter," *New York Herald Tribune Books,* 9 (October 19, 1941), 7.

2. SVB and Rosemary Benét, "Ernest Hemingway: Byron of Our Day," *New York Herald Tribune Books,* 9 (November 3, 1940), 7.

3. SVB to Robert MacAlarney, March 26, 1940; Ellen Barry to CAF (int.), August 28, 1954.

4. SVB, "A Man from Fort Necessity," *SEP, 212* (July 1, 1939), 18.

5. SVB, "Silver Jemmy," *Cosmopolitan, 100* (February 1936), 59.

6. SVB, "Schooner's Class," *Collier's, 101* (June 18, 1938), 14. Reprinted as "Schooner Fairchild's Class" in *Tales before Midnight.*

7. SVB, "Young Lovyer," *Country Gentleman, 104* (February 1934), 8; "The Natural-Born Fool," *Country Gentleman, 104* (August 1934), 10; "The Loves of the Roses," *Country Gentleman, 104* (November 1934), 16; "The Redheaded Woodpecker," *Country Gentleman, 105* (August 1935), 8.

8. SVB, "Witch's Spell," *Delineator, 124* (February 1934), 8; "Dec. 5, 1933," *Redbook, 62* (April 1934), 34; "Lisa and the Far Horizons," *Liberty, 11* (April 7, 1934), 11; "Marrying Town," *Delineator, 125* (September 1934), 8; "Early Morning," *Delineator, 126* (February 1935), 7; "Over the Bumps," *SEP, 207* (March 30, 1935), 10; "The Professor's Punch," *Delineator, 126* (April 1935), 42; "A Story by Angela Poe," *Harper's Bazaar* (July 1935), 38; "We'll Never Be Rich," *Redbook, 65* (July 1935), 38; "The Curfew Tolls," *SEP, 208* (October 5, 1935), 16; "Mystery Train," *Liberty, 12* (October 12, 1935), 14. "The Curfew Tolls" and "A Story by Angela Poe," both of them far superior to the rest of this group, were reprinted in *Thirteen O'Clock.*

9. Philip Blair Rice, "Chronicles in Verse," *Nation, 143* (July 18, 1936), 81; Donald C. Peattie, "A Singing Poet in the Tradition of the Bards," *New York Herald Tribune Books, 7* (June 14, 1936), [1].

10. SVB, ["Muriel Rukeyser"], *Trial Balances,* ed. Ann Winslow (New York, 1935), p. 201.

11. SVB, "The Devil and Daniel Webster," *SEP, 209* (October 24, 1936), 8. Brandt's comments are written in his hand on the note which Benét enclosed with the typescript.

12. Harry Hansen, "Introduction," *O. Henry Memorial Award Prize Stories of 1937* (New York, 1937), p. x.

13. Robert Van Gelder, "Mr. Benét's Work in Progress," *New York Times Book Review, 6* (April 21, 1940), 20.

14. SVB, "The Author Is Pleased," New York *Times* (September 28, 1941), p. 4.

15. SVB, "Daniel Webster and the Sea Serpent," *SEP, 209* (May 22, 1937), 18; "Daniel Webster and the Ides of March," *SEP, 212* (October 28, 1939), 18. The first of these stories was reprinted in *Thirteen O'Clock,* the second in *Tales before Midnight.*

16. Van Gelder.

17. SVB, "The Author Is Pleased."

Parry Stroud (essay date 1962)

SOURCE: Stroud, Parry. "The Minor Poetry: History, Love, Laughter, and Prophecy." In *Stephen Vincent Benét*, pp. 23-45. New York: Twayne Publishers, Inc., 1962.

[*In the following essay, Stroud provides a thematic and stylistic overview of Benét's minor poetry.*]

Stephen Vincent Benét was first a poet, and he remained essentially a poet throughout his career, although he disciplined himself into becoming a skilled writer of short stories, novels, and radio scripts.[1] His poetry has five major modes: the dramatic monologue; the ballad; the lyric; the prophetic; and the epic. Something of a national poet in the tradition of Whitman and Sandburg, Benét was, like Whitman, fundamentally a romantic poet, but in different ways and to considerably less consequence. Lacking Whitman's transcendental faith and philosophy, Benét was unable to give his poetry an overall unity, and his romanticism was refracted and fragmented. *John Brown's Body*[2] aside, Benét was a minor poet, though his unfinished *Western Star* (1943) must be reckoned with in gauging his potential stature. The nature and quality of Benét's poetic achievement have not yet been fully analyzed, despite a number of vigorous and perceptive reviews.

No discussion of Benét's poetry can go very far without entering the vexed and murky domains of the controversy over modern poetry. The placing of him in the romantic tradition of course takes him out of the neo-metaphysical tradition which is central in modern poetry. Irony sharpens a good many of Benét's poems, and he often deals with the modern world; but his is not a difficult poetry of wit or of startling juxtapositions all compact of symbolism. Benét's tastes were catholic, but he followed his own genius, and its roots were in the nineteenth century rather than in the seventeenth. Yet at his best he was a modern poet of his own sort.

Basil Davenport has pointed to the major components of Benét's romanticism: his fascination with the remote in time and place, his sense of the macabre, his sensitive awareness of landscape.[3] To these qualities should be added Benét's concern with emotion, with states of mind, rather than with ideas. His poetry is also vivid in its imagery, richly colored like that of many romantics. In this respect he resembles the nineteenth-century English poet, designer, and craftsman whose work most shaped Benét's poetry: William Morris.[4] Benét used the ballad form after the manner of Morris, and the octosyllabic couplets that Morris employed in some of his long narrative poems reappear in some of Benét's poems. Morris' technique of weaving song into narrative was paralleled by Benét in his two epics.

I *Five Men and Pompey*

Benét's first published book of poems, however, owed more to Robert Browning than to Morris. *Five Men and Pompey* (Boston, 1915) is a series of dramatic monologues spoken by Roman leaders on the eve of Caesar's accession to imperial power. Although the basic form derives from Browning, Benét gave his half-dozen portraits a collective significance of his own in that they trace the fall of the Roman Republic. In this way they herald Benét's *John Brown's Body,* some eleven years later, except that the American historical poem deals with the sundering and then the forging of a republic.

Benét himself regarded *Five Men and Pompey* as significant not only as the beginning of his poetic career, but as germinating the form of *John Brown's Body.*[5] Quite justifiably, he also saw it as superior to much of his work done in the early 1920's. The merit of *Five Men and Pompey* rests upon skillful characterization through the difficult form of the dramatic monologue, upon the successful introduction of dramatic action, and upon appropriate metrical variation of clear and vivid language. Although sometimes bombastic and melodramatic, the work reveals an auspicious talent far in advance of its author's seventeen years.

Sertorius is the actor in **"The Last Banquet"** as he wearily struggles to uphold the Republic while foreseeing the eventual victory of Pompey. Two former comrades of Sertorius attempt to assassinate him in a dramatic action that goes beyond anything Browning attempted—perhaps, indeed, too far for the form. But Sertorius comes alive out of history as he brokenheartedly calls for his love Nydia, all that remains for him. In the second monologue Lucullus dines with Cicero and Pompey and wavers between a longing for the old heady sense of conquest with his legions and nostalgia for a girl he had found during the sacking of a city. Subsequent portraits reveal Crassus preparing to leave his tent to face the encircling Parthian cavalry, Cicero groaning under the burden of adjudication, and Caesar in Gaul deciding to march on Ariminium to begin the civil war. Pompey comes last, after the decisive battle of Pharsalia. The day is Caesar's, and the Republic is gone; but Pompey dreams that "'somewhere, beyond all, there still endures / That pure Republic: its white walls shine'" (47). A similar concern with the fate of the American republic and with its ideal form was to appear in much of Benét's later poetry and prose.

This first published poem by Benét also reveals his technical versatility and forceful style. The rather irregular blank verse which predominates moves with proper emphasis according to the speaker, shifting from the leisurely movement of Lucullus' lines to the brisk directness of Caesar's speech. When Cicero broods on the treacheries of life, the meter changes to rhymed couplets in dactylic heptameters, somewhat in the manner of Swinburne. Crassus in his last moments reflects that "'To praise is hard, easy to damn. / I failed in this. Some other will succeed'" (24). Then his mood changes and he recalls the Republic's greatness:

> "Ere the first sword was sharpened and the first trumpet blown
> Rome looked upon the new-made lands and marked them for her own!
> Ere the first ship was timbered and the first rudder hung
> Rome held the oceans in her hands, splendid and stern and young!"

(26)

The metrical and syntactical balance and contrast in these lines make evident Benét's technical skill and his preference for pronounced rhythmical effects. His liking for vivid imagery drawn from the more familiar realms of life is demonstrated in Lucullus' lines comparing life to a platter of coins over which we exclaim. For him only one coin remains, an old Greek one sent him by Demetrius and reminiscent of the face of Lucullus' lost love. The passage borrows Byron's epithet "burning" for Greek beauty, perhaps intentionally, and the coin image lacks high originality, but it is appropriate and adds another dimension to the portrait of Lucullus because it shows his ability to conceive of his love in direct ways and to associate the coin of friendship with the remembered coin of love and beauty. The metaphor is striking and functions in two ways but does not possess the multiple meanings of much modern poetry.

Five Men and Pompey also differs from much modern poetry in that it has one of the great themes: the fate of a civilization. The poem's overall effect lies somewhere between melodrama and tragedy, and it hardly achieves greatness; but overall competence it does attain, despite youthful exuberances of meter and diction and drama. All in all, it is an astonishing achievement for a seventeen-year-old.

II "The Hemp" and Other Ballads

The two poems which followed the Roman portraits are inferior to them, particularly *The Drug-Shop; or, Endymion in Edmonstown.*[6] Although it won its author a poetry prize at Yale,[7] its chief importance is biographical. It reveals Benét's love and admiration for Keats and exemplifies again Benét's tendency to juxtapose romanticism and modern realism. In this instance he does so by placing Keats's mythological hero among the products of a twentieth-century American drugstore.

"The Hemp,"[8] written a year earlier than *The Drug-Shop,* retells in ballad form an incident drawn from early Virginia history: the story of the pirate Captain

Hawk, his rape of Sir Henry's daughter, and his eventual death at the hands of the vengeful father. This lurid tale Benét transformed into appropriately stirring metrics, with beats as emphatic as a marching drum's. Full of melodramatic imagery—for example, "His name bestrode the seas like Death"—the ballad compels attention by its controlled violence of sound and incident. It deflects critical esteem through its violent but superficial extremes of characterization and by its costume clichés of plot and setting. Yet Benét almost brings it off; he almost contrives a first-rate literary ballad.

Benét comes so close to this achievement because of his sure control of rhythm, which is unfalteringly adjusted to the story's development; because of the power of his descriptions; and because of a certain philosophical element. This increment of meaning is expressed partly through symbolism and partly through a refrain which becomes progressively more ominous. The hemp which Hawk swears will never hang him is finally grown by Sir Henry, is spun and twisted, made into rope, and finally placed around the pirate's neck. In the terminal refrain, *"the hemp clings fast to a dead man's throat, / And blind fate gathers back its seeds."* However, the symbolism of fate and seeds was not to have fruitful poetic issue until *John Brown's Body.* An extended ballad, **"The Hemp"** loses by its failure to employ either the compression of the finer folk ballads or the understatement and subtle metrical effects of William Morris' superb "The Haystack in the Floods."

Benét returned to the ballad, ultimately with better results, in subsequent volumes of poetry: *Young Adventure* (New York, 1918); *Heavens and Earth* (New York, 1920); and *Tiger Joy* (New York, 1925). **"Three Days Ride"**[9] is notable for a fine refrain with steadily darkening import, but this tale of aristocratic English lovers fleeing a villainous brother and his evil band is too familiar and too reliant upon the small change of a chase to merit serious consideration. **"Habberton's Plow,"**[10] a ballad with an American setting, is a grim story of a father who murders his daughter's lover, just returned from the Civil War, in order to keep the soldier from obtaining a New England farm. Thirty years later the daughter, while plowing, turns up her lover's skeleton and then kills her father with the plow blade. But Benét did not think as a New Englander in writing this poem, and the story could as well have taken place on the other side of the Atlantic. Stale romantic images like "aching June" are another source of the poem's disjunction of setting and style.

In a group of ballads collected in *Tiger Joy* (the title comes from Shelley's poetic drama *Prometheus Unbound*), Benét found styles perfectly suited to very different themes: thumping rhythms and Georgia hill dialect for **"The Mountain Whippoorwill"**;[11] swift,

flailing couplets for **"King David"**;[12] and clear, sweet pioneer music for **"The Ballad of William Sycamore (1790-1880)."**[13]

The first of these three poems—subtitled "A Georgia Romance"—drew on Benét's boyhood memories of that state and of North Carolina.[14] Benét said that in this poem he attempted to adapt the traditional ballad form to a contemporary American theme, to vary it as he chose, and to use colloquial speech—"get the note of the boxwood fiddle into it, if it could be done. I had heard the mountain fiddlers in the North Carolinas, and their tunes stuck in my head."[15] The result was more than a minor *tour de force* since Benét not only managed to suggest through the imagery and movement of his verse the swift country bowing, but the quality of life in the hills of Georgia and Carolina. The poem is lighted with touches of pioneer tall-tale humor and old-time religion. The narrator, winner of the Essex County Fiddlers' Show at a fair, is individualized as an imaginative orphan who conceives of his parents as a fiddle and a whippoorwill; and his initial bravado, followed by his genuine appreciation for his rivals' skill and his feeling that he has lost the contest, adds drama to his victory.

Benét's ability to suggest the range, movement, and quality of the fiddling does most to make the poem. Overwhelmed by Old Dan Wheeling's playing, who "fiddled the wind by the lonesome moon / . . . fiddled a most almighty tune," the storyteller calls on his identity with the mountains where he was born as his unique resource:

> Whippoorwill, singin' thu' the mountain hush,
> Whippoorwill, shoutin' from the burnin' bush,
> Whippoorwill, cryin' in the stable-door,
> Sing tonight as yuh never sang before!

Thus inspired, he wins. The sometimes coarse and violent language of this ballad is justified on the grounds of realism; also, it is modified by the genuine folk poetry which colors the poem. Repeated references to the whippoorwill—first as the mother of the narrator, then as a nature symbol whose singing represents both the fiddler and the fiddler's genius—provide another unifying device. **"The Mountain Whippoorwill"** was Benét's first ballad shaped wholly from native materials by his full resources for giving them life.

Benét's **"Ballad of William Sycamore,"** often chosen by editors of anthologies to represent his lyrical Americanism, deserves the widespread admiration accorded it by common readers and by at least some professional ones. The latter include the redoubtable F. O. Matthiessen, who was for the most part unfavorably disposed toward Benét's work but regarded this poem as notable.[16] The clarity and precision with which Benét sums up the life of a representative though idealized frontiersman are here precisely the qualities to be conveyed by the ballad meter, with its exact rhymes and beat as exciting as the frontier's "Money Musk," on which the pioneer is reared. Benét adroitly alternates iambics and dactyls and introduces just enough metrical variations in the short line to suggest a rippling song.

The clean, fresh life of the frontier is set forth in the succession of American images which move through the poem: the green fir that serves as the mother's doctor; the silver-handled ewer and bayberry candles that are boyhood memories; the snuff-brown frontiersmen with their long squirrel-rifles; the girl like a Salem clipper; and the sons sowed like apple-seed on the wagon trails. Like this last one, several of the images evoke birth or death, and the peaceful immortality of William Sycamore at the end moves the poem into the larger realm of myth. Sycamore's name, an image played upon in the image of the pine that attended his birth, suggests, of course, the evergreen symbol of immortality. His life-in-death continues in the wilderness earth from which he sprang and which he symbolizes; he is one of the innumerable sons of Natty Bumppo who fled westward from the encroaching towns. The poem which bears Sycamore's name has as intimate a relationship to the legends of the frontier which the American mind remembers. So long as the national mind does so, it will find this ballad rooted deep and strong in the country's history, and perhaps even deeper in the universal urge to be at one with nature in her wild, free beauty.

Benét's equally famed **"American Names,"**[17] written while he was living in Paris during the late 1920's and working on *John Brown's Body,* is an offshoot of the epic.[18] This ballad is a direct expression of Benét's love for his distant homeland, an emotion nourished rather than diminished by his temporary exile. The poem does not summon up as much history and legend as **"William Sycamore,"** but it draws some names, crisp and tangy as Winesaps, from American history in order to press from them the flavor of our native juices. Benét's line "I am tired of loving a foreign muse" echoes Emerson's historic utterance in his "American Scholar" address of 1821: "We have listened too long to the courtly muses of Europe."

Benét descends into no chauvinism in this statement: he concedes the unique beauties of Old World names and the cultures they symbolize and merely asserts his preference for the culture of his native land. Indeed, judged by traditional aesthetic criteria, Europe's names are more beautiful. Seine and Piave, the poet calls "silver spoons," and the names of some English counties are like "hunting tunes." Rue des Martyrs and Bleeding-Heart-Yard guard "a magic ghost." Yet the poet longs for American places, Yankee ships and Yankee dates, even for the preposterously comic Skunk-

town Plain; he yearns for a newer ghost. Henry and John—presumably Longfellow and Whittier—were not thus, but the poet wonders if they never watched for Nantucket light "after the tea and the laurels had stood all night." Here Benét associates the nineteenth-century New England poets with the borrowed English and classical culture which they represented.

"American Names" demonstrates the same sensitive control of meter that characterizes **"William Sycamore,"** as well as the same command of imagery, although much of the poem's effect comes from the connotations of proper names strategically placed.[19] The fourth stanza uses the objectionable term "blue-gum nigger," but Benét identifies him honorably as the singer of blues, the American music. A Salem tree (a majestic chestnut), a Santa Cruz rawhide quirt, and a bottle of Boston sea complete this list of American symbols. Each is recognizably American but not banal as an image: a lesser poet might have longed for Coney Island or a five-gallon Stetson. The poem's movement and meaning gather rising emphasis in the final stanza, with its succession of short, simple sentences and its assertion of a love returning home triumphant over the body's alien burial. Benét's final prayer that his heart be buried at Wounded Knee gives the poem deeper significance than it has hitherto possessed, since this South Dakota town was the scene of a tragic Indian massacre by the Seventh Cavalry in the final clash between Indians and government troops.[20] The poet thus identifies himself inextricably with the mixture of good and bad that is his country, and his choice of burial place implies a desire for national atonement and peace.

"King David" proved Benét's ability to employ the ballad for a non-American and more sophisticated purpose, although the poem undoubtedly has American religious implications. A scathingly satiric retelling of the biblical story of David, Uriah, and Bathsheba, it points up David's smug egotism and facile repentance of his sins. Benét's edged phrasing underscores criticism of the Old Testament concept of a God who is a jealous God, a crafty God, and a too-forgiving God; and he embellishes the story as told in II Samuel so as to emphasize David's lustfulness, deviousness, and pride. The broad ironies of the story emerge through Benét's trenchant characterizations and through stinging heroic couplets with their snapping terminal iambics. The sly insertions of the refrain—"The Lord God is a jealous God"—and its variations emphasize the mocking attitude of the poet in his guise as a devout contemporary chronicler. Benét masterfully combines striking, sensuous Hebrew metaphor—Bathsheba's body glimmers like the flesh of aloes in candlelight—with his own ironic imagery and vivid phrasing, to make **"King David"** a poem that fastens on the memory.

The six parts and two-hundred-odd lines of **"King David"** culminate with a triumphantly sardonic description of David's seven nights of repentance which end with the death of his and Bathsheba's child and with David's solacing of her out of his great contentment. She, being woman merely, grieves for a while, permits herself to be soothed, and conceives again. The name of this second child is Solomon (Benét puts the name in boldface), who is God's staff until the end of his days. Solomon's wisdom Benét slyly does not mention, but the reader may recall it as a criterion for the follies of David and, even more fundamentally, the absurdity of those who believe in a deity so debased by human characteristics as to smite hard the heathen and exalt such a ready sinner and successful supplicator as David.

The distinctions of this irreverent ballad won for it the coveted poetry award of *The Nation* for 1922, but it brought the editors of that eminent liberal journal a heavy influx of indignant letters objecting to Benét's supposed immorality and blasphemy. But although **"King David"** can be associated with the juvenile pseudo-diabolism of Benét's novel *The Beginning of Wisdom* (1921), with the skepticism reflected in *Jean Huguenot* (1923), another novel, and with his notable short poem **"For All Blasphemers,"**[21] it should not be taken as a full statement of his religious position. In his letters Benét refers to himself as an agnostic,[22] and his poem **"Hands"**[23] is deeply reverent. While **"King David"** offended many conventional or orthodox believers, it can be defended as moral in the sense that it challenges an uncritical acceptance of an Old Testament story. A religious ethic which praises a Deity harsh toward unbelievers while indulgent toward devout sinners, no matter how deliberately sinful and shallowly repentant, is a less consistently lofty system than its advocates prefer to believe. But whatever the reaction to the religious content of the poem, there is no denying its superb style and structure.

III OF YOUTH AND OF LOVE

The large majority of Benét's early poems are undistinguished by any exacting standard, ideological or aesthetic, and they particularly contrast with his handful of fine ballads. The title of *Young Adventure* indicates a group of poems dealing with some aspect of the American youth that continued to be one of Benét's major concerns, both as subject and audience. Portraits of a baby, of a boy, and of young love[24] succeed in plausibly presenting infantile, boyish, and youthful psychology, but in the romantically strained accents of Benét's least attractive style. **"Young Blood"**[25] is stuffed with clichés and is garishly dependent on the shock of revelation—in this instance, as sustained by a victim of a bachelor party on the eve of his wedding who finds himself in bed the next morning with a sleazy prostitute. **"The General Public"**[26] takes its epigraph from Browning's fine poem on Shelley and then proceeds to shatter the reader's memory of the Victorian's well-

sustained tone of wonder and understated climax with an overwrought, melodramatic picture of a persecuted Shelley with flame-like eyes. These and similar poems of Benét's can safely be consigned to their respective realms of the commonplace and the sensational.

Among the mass of Benét's minor poems gleam occasional diamond-like lyrics and some excellent light verse, including humorous poems and some fancies and bouquets for his lady. The **"Hands"** in the previously mentioned poem of this title belong to his wife, his brother, and to Benét himself. The delicate hands of his wife and the cultivated hands of his brother are contrasted with Benét's "children of affront, / Base mechanics at the most / That have sometimes touched a ghost." The poet asks a blessing upon the first four hands but for his own hands prays for an iron stake for them to attempt to break. The powerful first lines of the last stanza invoke the blessings of "God the Son and God the Sire / And God the triple-handed fire" in a magnificent metaphorical linking of the Trinity with the human objects of the poet's invocation. Benét asks finally only a blessing for "four hands of courtesy," and his humility is the proper attitude to precede the "Amen." The short hymn-like lines, liturgically emphatic rhythm, and rich though compact imagery of this lyric combine to give it a power out of proportion to its length.

Compression also characterizes Benét's next best short lyric, **"Memory,"**[27] though its intensity is uneven, heightening through the second of the two eight-line stanzas, after the more open statement of the first. Its poignancy comes from its seizing of the essences of life—love, birth, age, wisdom, death—and contrasting them in terse, unrhymed lines built with monosyllables, six to eight per line. His love was the best part of his life, the poet says; death does not matter, for life is a ghost in the flesh that comes and goes. With an almost choking ellipsis, the poet acknowledges that though the moon burns lamp-bright it will not have *that* brightness. . . . He said her name sleeping and waking. The underlying emotion—tragic awareness of the inevitable loss of life's dearest possession—surges through the silence of what is unsaid.

A delightful cluster of gay and fanciful tributes to his sweetheart (*Selected Works,* I, 353-62), whom he later married, tributes airy and delicate as a handful of silver milkweed spores on summer wind, includes the lovely **"To Rosemary"** (353-54). In it, her essence is as old music boxes, young tawny kittens, wild-strawberry seed, and something indefinable, fire in crystal. **"Nomenclature"** (354) is still finer, with its impressionistic descriptions of the qualities of names (some people have names "full of sizzling esses like a family quarrel of snakes") and its subtle appreciations of the lady's qualities, culminating in an ecstatic rush of words and images.

Charming enough to turn any lady's head, although they are styled for Benét's lady, are **"Difference"** (355), contrasting the wilderness map of his mind with her lovely and delicate psyche; **"To Rosemary, on the Methods by Which She Might Become an Angel"** (357), playfully prophesying the impudent nature of her immortality; and **"Dulce Ridentem"** (361), lightly celebrating his youth and her "moth-wing soul." **"Nonsense Song"** (356) weaves in a deft tribute to Rosemary, along with the fooling. **"In a Glass of Water Before Retiring"** (358-59) is as drowsily sweet music as a lady could wish, while the companion poem **"Evening and Morning"** (357-58) imaginatively traces the course of her sleep until break of day.

Several poems lying somewhere between the pathos of **"Memory"** and the playful gallantries of the fanciful poems complete the limited emotional spectrum of Benét's love poetry. The limitations arose simply from the sustained happiness of his courtship of a fine and charming woman and their marriage of more than twenty years, which was terminated only by Benét's death.[28] Throughout their long relationship Benét wrote poems to her, all of them testifying to the steadfastness of his affection. **"All Night Long"**[29] tells of the poet's vigil over the serene sleep of his beloved and of her awaking into the beautiful day. Their passion is indirectly suggested by an image of the rising morning; Benét is no anatomist of love. **"With a Gift of Silver Candlesticks"**[30] symbolically bestows one lovely gift for his wife's body, one for her spirit. The giving is a gesture gravely worshipful. Benét's love for his wife as expressed in his poems to her was deep and sensitive, wholly admirable; it was based on keen admiration for her loyalty, gaiety, wit, imagination, and highly individual beauty.

IV *A BOOK OF AMERICANS*

United also by mutual love of their native land, the Benéts collaborated in writing a clever series of verse biographies, *A Book of Americans* (1933). Benét conceived of the project in 1933 after seeing an exhibition of children's books,[31] and his and his wife's dedication of the book to their three children—"our other works in collaboration"—indicates the audience they wrote it for. Benét's lifelong interest in American youth found expression in verse portraits which sprang from the same creative impulse that, fusing humor and history, produced the Daniel Webster tales.

A Book of Americans consists of fifty-odd short poems about famous and infamous figures in American history; they range from Christopher Columbus to Woodrow Wilson and include such national villains as Aaron Burr. Mrs. Benét contributed the portraits of the five women—Pocahontas, Abigail Adams, Dolly Madison, Nancy Hanks, and Clara Barton—while her husband sketched the men, and described clipper ships, Negro spirituals, and some other unique products of the American imagination. A few collective portraits—notably of the Puritans and Pilgrims—are also provided. The result of the collaboration is a winning little book with the twin appeals of humor and insight, both historical and biographical, for adults not too stodgy to enjoy occasional quiet fun at the expense of some national heroes. (Wilson, Benét observes, eschewed his boyhood name of Tommy for his resounding public name.)

That vast and mysterious audience called "juvenile" doubtless includes many who would enjoy the nursery-rhyme meter, the clear, short rhymes, and the general freshness spiced with diverting surprises that the Benéts tucked into *A Book of Americans*. Ulysses S. Grant, the youthful reader will learn, was a great soldier and gentleman but a poor president, though an honest one. The poet, pondering the contradictions of human nature, reaches into his lexicon for a Scottish dialect word and concludes that men are "kittle cattle." But, he asks, "How many rhymers, children dear, / Have ever won a battle?" The point is made so sweetly that it should go down easily, though *kittle* and a few other grown-up words may bring calls for grown-up help.

Judicious praise and blame for the men and women portrayed are what the book's **"Apology"** asks of the reader, whether young or old; and the Benéts themselves observe the dictates of justice. Sometimes, however, there is nothing to laud, as with Daniel Drew, the nineteenth-century financial wizard, a "sanctimonious old sneak" whose death the poet terms fortunate, since it prevented Drew from further stealing. If the reader wonders why the poet dug up this tarnished scamp from history's refuse, the answer is that there were more men like Daniel Drew, and there still are. Obviously no one will question the presence of Crawford Long and William Morton, the little-known doctor and dentist who, working separately, discovered the anesthetic properties of ether and thus made possible painless surgery. Earnest patriots, however, may object to such generosity of spirit as Benét shows in reminding the reader that, although the triumph of Oliver De Lancey, the Tory—or Loyalist—general would have meant no Stars and Stripes, there are two sides to every question. Idolators of the Puritans and Pilgrims will resent Benét's observation that every time we think we are better than someone else and that he must do as we say or we'll whack him, the Puritan is still in our backyard. Fanatical anti-Puritans will criticize Benét's concluding emphasis on the Puritans' resolute courage, their never asking to fight with less than giants. *A Book of Americans* is marked by a largeness of vision and a tolerance characteristic of American liberalism at its best; it recognizes that our nation was built by many individuals and groups with varying mixtures of good and bad traits.

V Gothic Themes

That broad romantic hope of Benét's which was stirred by the American Dream contrasts strikingly with the midnight aspect of his romanticism. Sometimes, indeed, his sense of the macabre explored some frailty or sickness in the national soul, but it also had a more personal aspect. Several lyrics of medium emotional weight reveal the darker reaches of his mind, his rebelliousness, or his intermittent preoccupation with such Gothic themes as death or insanity.

"Architects"[32] follows the pattern of "Hands" in that it sets up distinctions between several persons close to the poet by means of a symbolic extension of identifying traits, but it expresses only the bleakest kind of faith. Benét contrasts his son's fortress of pride, his daughter's shield of wit, his wife's coffin of lead wrought from "counterfeit tears of mourners" in which she rests with the blessed calm of a long-dead saint, and the poet's own arid, craftily dug grave. It will not last till Judgment Day, he concedes, but it will not cripple him either; and though some may think it confining, when he enters it he can keep the "nakedness of an arrow." This somewhat obscure poem seems to restate Benét's stoic view of death, a conception relieved only by a wreath of poetry. "Architects" is Benét's closest approach to a modernist metaphysical poem: its five conventional quatrains enclose an involved structure packed with mortal ironies.

Irony wrenched into the grotesque is the pattern of "Ghosts of a Lunatic Asylum,"[33] which attempts to heighten the terrors of insanity by describing an abandoned institution haunted by the shades of the former inmates. Benét treats the theme superficially, however, and the effect lessens rather than accentuates the horror. Considerably more powerful is "Minor Litany,"[34] which makes use of a traditional Christian liturgical form to achieve a mordant irony. In a time of confusion, "with few clear stars," either public or private, the poet supplicates on behalf of those he calls the lost, the half-lost, and the desperate—in current terminology, the mentally ill. The cumulative effect of Benét's precisely stated—or understated—dictionary of types in need of, or already under the care of, psychiatrists is almost unbearably depressing. The poet calls first upon Christ for mercy, then upon Freud, then upon Life; and a later invocation near the end of the poem implores only the mercy of drugs. The final stanzas drive home the widespread and relentless incidence of psychic traumas and climax the rising note of hopelessness—the poor in mental health ye have always with ye, so to speak—inherent in a litany without God. The ending carelessly dissipates something of the carefully built-up mood by its half-facetious phrasing, and the total meaning is circumscribed by its descriptive and unanalytical approach; yet the poem is disturbing.

VI *Burning City*

The cream of Benét's poems thus far examined consists of his four fine ballads, three of them American flavored, of two exquisite lyrics, of a cluster of love poems, and of *A Book of Americans.* The ballads have an arresting originality of style and content; the love poems have a charming music Benét's own, and, in a sense, his wife's. *A Book of Americans* teaches and delights with an effectiveness out of proportion to its slightness. Yet in their totality these poems can lay claim to no more than a modest place in twentieth-century American poetry, nor did Benét claim more for them. In several ways—his general preference for traditional form, his unabashed love of his country, his somewhat ambiguous religious skepticism, his avoidance of complex symbolism and of distillations of themes remote from the commonalty of American experience—his poetry was vulnerable to attack on the critical battlegrounds of the 1920's and 1930's. The American themes were anathema to both Marxists and expatriates. The Metaphysical critics could find no elaborate interweavings of "wit"; and the whole center of this movement around T. S. Eliot was rooted in an implicit cultural, social, political, and religious anti-Americanism. Back of Eliot lay a significant tradition of cultural alienation stretching back to Nathaniel Hawthorne and crowned by Henry James. This tradition had, and has, numerous and well-entrenched supporters, particularly in the academic world.

A detailed examination of these points of view as they bear upon Benét's poetry is neither feasible nor necessary in this study. In a broad sense, America's growing political maturity and cultural resources, particularly in literature, have provided the answers to those who have held that an American literature in any way affirmative and rich was impossible of achievement. Marxist criticism offers for liberal critics a single viable insight: that class conflicts exist in life and may be reflected in literature. Metaphysical criticism has provided innumerable insights into individual works of literature and has been instrumental in shattering nineteenth-century literary traditions, a valuable accomplishment, on the whole. Narrowness and dogmatism have often attended this school, however. At any rate, its point of view is, I believe, adequately represented by the critic whose scrutiny of a volume of Benét's poetry I shall consider in detail.

Some criticism of Benét's poetry which may not be easily disposed of came from an avant-garde position during the 1930's. A later academic spokesman for this group was the distinguished F. O. Matthiessen, author of *American Renaissance* (1941), one of the finest scholarly and critical works of the twentieth century. Matthiessen, in his essay on modern American poetry in the definitive *Literary History of the United States*

(II, 1350-51), commented that "Benét's talents have not been considered as of anything like the first order by many other poets. . . ." The page which Matthiessen devoted to Benét in his survey left no room for critical analysis, though it is reasonable to suppose that many graduate students and professors have accepted the short essay as highly authoritative.

Earlier, another influential critic, in an extended attack from advanced positions held by the aesthetic (though not political) left, made clear in trenchant detail his reasons for disliking Benét. Morton Dauwen Zabel, editor of *Poetry* and a fine critic, in a review of Benét's **Burning City** (New York, 1936) in that important magazine, charged that Benét was the latest representative in a long line of American poets, going back to Long-fellow and Bryant, whom Zabel labels the "bardic romantics."[35] The whole tradition, according to Zabel, has been "hostile to eccentric talent or refined taste, scornful of modernity or exotic influence. . . ."

Zabel seizes on **Burning City** because it enables him to illustrate the distinction he wishes to make between a bard and a poet. The former, as exemplified by Benét, is, among other things, indiscriminating in both subject matter and style. Zabel asserts that although Benét discusses social and moral degeneration, he does not grasp their significance with either his sensibilities or his intelligence. Zabel concludes his general indictment with what amounts to critical banishment: Benét writes "passable verse journalism." Along with Benét, Zabel consigns to oblivion *The New Yorker,* which was publishing some of Benét's poetry, including **"Notes To Be Left in a Cornerstone,"** one of the longer poems in **Burning City.** Also damned are Paul Engle, the poet-professor whom Zabel regards as Benét's model, and H. G. Wells and Conan Doyle, the supposed progenitors of Benét's poems about the future. Zabel, spokesman for high art and the devoted seekers and practitioners of it and editor of the single most important American outlet for the new poetry, is intent on attacking not only the lower levels of popular literature but the more sophisticated upper strata of it occupied by *The New Yorker* and by certain academic circles.

Zabel carries on his attack against Benét through a scrutiny of **"Ode to Walt Whitman"** as the most ambitious poem in **Burning City.** After a severe though not injudicious analysis, Zabel concludes that the poem, despite some merits, is essentially derivative, uninspired, and obvious in meaning and technique. Since the basic issue raised by Zabel—the conflict between popular and élite art in a democracy—is a perennial one, and since his criticism of Benét as bard offers a fruitful means of appraising Benét's minor poetry, a point-by-point consideration of Zabel's analysis of the **"Ode"** is warranted.

Zabel begins by conceding that the first section of the ode is written in Benét's "most charming manner," a relative degree of praise that would be evasive were it not followed by the assertion that Benét's free verse catches Whitman's spirit very successfully, notably in the image of giant, approaching footsteps. The spatial limitations of Zabel's essay prevent him from spelling out the details of Benét's achievement here. Partly they reside in the fact that the footsteps symbolize not only the death that walks through *Leaves of Grass* but also suggest Walt himself in his marches across America as seer and prophet. They further suggest the personal identification with death that marks some of Whitman's poems, such as "When Lilacs Last in the Dooryard Bloom'd." Technically Benét's line in this section resembles Whitman's without duplicating it (in so far as Whitman's diversified free metrics could be paralleled). In its general movement, however, through the accumulation of reiterated facts and participial phrases, Benét's verse is finely evocative of Whitman's.

Notable also in this first section are Benét's imagery and phrasing. Drawn from the same native sources as Whitman's, they are similarly clear and concrete, or symbolically ambiguous. A picture of Death as "half-seen through the wet, sweet sea-fog of youth" awakens the surging echoes of Whitman's "Out of the Cradle Endlessly Rocking," his entangled childhood reminiscence of some crucial experience of death on Long Island. The lines which Benét gives Whitman to speak appropriately set off the calamus—generative symbol of a group of poems in *Leaves of Grass*—against nightbane, symbol of death and also of the night of "Out of the Cradle," in which the boy gains his knowledge of the universality of death and life. This sort of skillful alluding to Whitman's poetry is akin to borrowing, in respect to originality; but Benét also provides a fresh and noble American image which is characteristic of Whitman but does not occur in *Leaves of Grass.* This is a simile which likens Whitman to one of the great old herd-leaders among the buffalo, innocent, curly-browed, with "kingly eyes," who die on the plains and have their tongues cut out by hunters. The image is physically and symbolically apt, descriptive of Whitman in body, character, and final end. Not all of the imagery is so fine, but on the whole Zabel somewhat underrates the value of this section of the **"Ode,"** though he finally calls it "impressive."

In the second section of the poem Zabel notes a falling-off from the initial excellence because of repetition and direct exposition. He also declares that this part "betrays the absence of a central conception of Whitman as the dialogue between the poet and his interrogator descends to the most obvious contrasts between Whitman's dream of democracy and its present frustration. . . ." Zabel is correct in perceiving a general poetic decline in this section, although in only one or two instances is the imagery banal, as in "women with dry breasts." Some of it is on nearly as high a level as that in the first section; there is, for example, "bridges arched like the necks of beautiful horses," a simile which establishes a beautiful parallel between the modern industrial world and the animal world which Whitman loved. Again, to suggest the active principle of evil at work in the Depression, Benét fashions the powerfully repellent image of tentworms shrouding the trees of America. On the other hand, some of the exposition is flat and sacrifices the concentration and multiple suggestiveness of the tentworm metaphor. Lines such as "'We have made many, fine new toys'" and "'There is a rust on the land'" lie somewhere between the banal and the merely uninspired, and they partially bear out Zabel's charge.

Zabel's complaint that Benét engages in repetition is, however, unsupported, unless he means that there is some dilution of the theme of a land blighted by waste, injustice, and folly. Certainly the main elements causing the Depression require description, and this Benét provides, though not from the best of his imaginative resources. Zabel's assertion that Benét lacks a central conception of Whitman is equally unexplained; indeed, it is puzzling since in this section Benét sets forth his ideas about the causes and nature of the Depression, in answer to Whitman's questions as the latter rests on a hillside in his life-in-death. Benét's description reveals the compassion for the ill-clothed, ill-housed, and ill-fed and the anger over economic and social injustice that liberals felt during the Depression. This section is admittedly inferior to the first one, but its basic structure is surely inevitable. The alternative—to have Whitman make pronouncements about the Depression, to make him the principal spokesman in the section—would demand a conception of him as omnipresent and omniscient. Benét's method—to have him ask questions concerning his native land after having been wakened by his modern lovers—permits the tragedy of Whitman's final query: Was the blood of the Civil War spilt for nothing?

In the short third section, with its two- and three-beat lines and quiet intensity, Benét provides metrical and emotional relief from the extended gravities of the preceding section. A lone man, presumably a poet, who comes to seek the arbutus, a symbol of renewal connected with both the grass and the calamus symbols of Whitman, signifies reaffirmation of the American spirit and identification with the soil. Love and courage motivate the symbolic action. Zabel approves of the style of this passage and of the delicacy of some of its images, but he says of the latter that they are strung out and involved to poor effect. The section as a whole, Zabel believes, does not strengthen the formal unity of the poem. Unquestionably, however, the human and natural symbols in the section establish vital connections with Whitman. They also forecast the rising note of national affirmation which dominates the fourth and final section. Zabel's objection to the unharmonious structural role of this section is not valid. Moreover, Benét limits his images to an uncomplicated handful, though they are not taken from his freshest stock of native metaphor.

With Zabel's strictures on the opening passage of the fourth part of the ode, one may readily agree: Benét does lapse into "slovenly sarcasm" on the world's way with poets. His tone descends to the colloquial and the exasperated, and it is hardly saved by a succession of one-line descriptions of the terrible demises of poets other than Whitman. The remaining three-fourths of the section consist of a panoramic vision of America in the Whitman manner, slightly modified by Benét's quickness of perception, and finally centering on the Mississippi as the nation's great artery. Zabel acknowledges Benét's usual skill in catching here the texture of American life, but he damns this portion as a familiar checklist of Benét's usual references and says that it invites a dangerous comparison with the handling of the same theme by a true poet, Hart Crane. Zabel's vehemence is unwarranted, and his feeling that he has heard all this before remains unsubstantiated. Benét's conclusion for his ode nevertheless remains disappointing because of its obvious technique; superficially complimentary to Whitman, Benét neglects Whitman's preference for originality rather than convention.

My critical analysis of the **"Ode to Walt Whitman"** is thus in general agreement with Zabel's, although it parts company at several points concerning imagery, structure, and conception. Moreover, Zabel's initial insistence on Benét's lifelong ambition to become a bard in the genteel tradition is unfounded and illogical; it is difficult to reconcile Benét's admiration for Whitman—anathema to conservatives—with Zabel's charge.

Zabel consigns not only the tribute to Whitman but all the other more important poems in *Burning City* to the same critical trash heap of the commonplace. He singles out **"Litany for Dictatorships"** (12-16) and **"Ode to the Austrian Socialists"** (17-21) as examples of tedious cataloguing and banal thinking. The three nightmares—**"Metropolitan Nightmare"** (69-72), **"Nightmare, with Angels"** (73-75), and **"Nightmare Number Three"** (76-79)—Zabel castigates as juvenile in conception and vulgar in style, although he implies that they convey some sense of impending catastrophe. **"Metropolitan Nightmare"** and **"Nightmare Number Three"** merit some attention since they have been included in several anthologies and exemplify Benét in his role as prophet. These poems were followed in 1940 by a group which includes **"Nightmare for Future Reference"**[36] and **"Nightmare at Noon"**.[37] To these should be added **"Notes To Be Left in a Cornerstone"** (3-9), the best of the longer poems in *Burning City,* although Zabel does not mention it.

All of these poems are warnings of doom for America as represented by New York City. The forms of the catastrophe envisioned include destruction by natural causes, annihilation through war or through universal sterility brought on by war, and ruin of an unspecified sort brought on by collective madness for money or some other general folly or failure. The time is the present, the near future, or World War III; and the speaker or narrator is the poet or, in **"Nightmare Number Three,"** an average man. The style is prevailingly conversational, with only an occasional rise to a more lyrical line; and since the symbolism is easily grasped, these poems for the most part communicate their meaning with little effort on the part of the reader. The group is full of vivid descriptive detail organized for maximum effect. In two of the poems full revelation of the fateful circumstances comes in the last line. In **"Metropolitan Nightmare"** a termite found carrying in its jaw a bright crumb of steel brings realization of the terrible adaptation of the insects to a city of skyscrapers which they have invaded as a result of a change in the Gulf Stream. In **"Nightmare for Future Reference"**—an ironic title—an account of World War III and its sudden cessation when women revolt withholds until the last line the fact that the race can no longer reproduce itself.

The situation in these poems is unfolded with Benét's usual facility, and now and then an increment of meaning is furnished by indirection. **"Metropolitan Nightmare"** gains through the unstressed import of the indifference of New Yorkers to the silent peril come upon them, an attitude suggestive of a casualness about real though unstated dangers. Mostly, however, Benét makes his meaning explicit, sometimes to the point of overstatement; and in general these poems are superficial and contrived to produce sensational effects. **"Nightmare at Noon"** is more thoughtful than the others and is within the realm of reality, but its style never achieves any more distinction than a conversational irony or unechoing plainness.

"Nightmare Number Three," the best of the group except for **"Notes To Be Left in a Cornerstone,"** is a nondramatic monologue in which the speaker describes himself and his situation without attaining any insight into either. In his account of a revolt of the machines against their modern American masters, the hopelessly trapped fellow consoles himself with the thought of the gratitude his Plymouth must have for the swell French horn he gave it. Foolish senators, Wall Street brokers, and petty uses for the power of machines are manifestations of the enslavement of man by his creations. Now the machines have learned to think, while their creators have stopped thinking. Imaginative details such as the

octopus-tendrils of a telephone switchboard waving over the head of a strangled business executive make the poem arresting, though its ultimate quality is garish melodrama.

The mood and style of **"Notes To Be Left in a Cornerstone"** are quiet; yet they come close to creating an overwhelming sense of the tragedy in the fall of a great city. The cause of the disaster is hinted at only; Benét is unconcerned with the means of destruction. What absorbs him is the quality of life in New York, its variety and contradictions, its seasonal extremes, its ugliness and beauty. Benét conveys precisely and vividly the terrible heat of summer, the long cold of winter and its hushes broken only by the scritch-scratch of shovels, the sharp stimuli of fall, the short loveliness of spring, with the new moon over the gray water at the end of streets. Since all this has passed away, the poem is movingly elegiac. A dignified line, often pacing several feet beyond the limits of blank verse, bears securely the elegiac mood. Some lines are notable, as when the poet laments that maps and models can never represent the city as it was:

> They cannot restore that beauty, rapid and harsh,
> That loneliness, that passion or that name.

The next to last section of the poem falters a bit as Benét, in the manner of T. S. Eliot, introduces quasi-humorous names to indicate those New Yorkers who have gone with the city; but the final section rises again to poignancy and tragic resignation.

In this poem Benét demonstrates a sensibility, a range of perception and feeling, and a sensitive and powerful style that go beyond the best of his ballads, dramatic monologues, and lyrics. Although these combined powers are not reflected elsewhere in **Burning City,** they are in this poem the manifestation of the much greater talent that had earlier produced **John Brown's Body.** Any critical estimate of Benét as a poet must be based primarily on this epic.

Notes

1. Charles A. Fenton, *Stephen Vincent Benét: The Life and Times of an American Man of Letters, 1898-1943* (New Haven, Conn., 1958), pp. 36, 41, 96, and *passim.* Hereafter in these footnotes this work will be referred to as *Benét.*

2. *John Brown's Body* (Garden City, N.Y., 1928). This work has gone through a number of editions. The twenty-first, edited by Mabel A. Bessey (New York, 1941) is the one cited in the present study.

3. Introduction to *Stephen Vincent Benét: Selected Poetry and Prose* (New York, 1960).

4. Benét, letter to Paul Engle, Oct. 4, 1935, *Selected Letters of Stephen Vincent Benét,* ed. Charles A. Fenton (New Haven, Conn., 1960), p. 279. Hereafter this collection will be referred to as *Letters.*

5. Fenton, *Benét,* p. 41.

6. Privately printed by the Brick Row Book Shop, New Haven, Conn., 1917; reprinted in Benét's later collection of poetry, *Young Adventure* (Yale University Press, 1918).

7. Fenton, *Benét,* p. 56.

8. "The Hemp" appeared originally in *Century Magazine,* XCI (January, 1916), 342. Reprinted in *Selected Works of Stephen Vincent Benét,* 2 vols., ed. unidentified (New York, 1942), I, 371-75.

9. "Three Days' Ride," according to Fenton (*Benét,* n. 383), appeared originally in the *Yale Literary Magazine,* LXXXI (1915-16), 13. Reprinted in *Selected Works,* I, 389-92.

10. *Heavens and Earth,* pp. 30-37.

11. "The Mountain Whippoorwill" appeared first in *Century Magazine,* XXCVII (March, 1925), 635-39. Reprinted in *Tiger Joy, Ballads and Poems,* and *Selected Works,* I, 376-80.

12. "King David" was first published in the *Nation,* CXVI (Feb. 14, 1923), 117-79. Also published separately under the same title by Henry Holt & Co. in 1923; was included in *Tiger Joy, Ballads and Poems,* and *Selected Works,* I, 368-70.

13. "The Ballad of William Sycamore, 1790-1880" first appeared in the *New Republic,* XXXII (Nov. 8, 1922), 279. It was republished by the *Literary Digest,* LXXV (Nov. 25, 1922), 36, and by the Brick Row Book Shop, New York, 1923, as *The Ballad of William Sycamore.* Reprinted, *Tiger Joy, Ballads and Poems,* and *Selected Works,* I, 368-70. Benét changed the *New Republic* subtitle to "1790-1871" in subsequent printings. See Fenton, *Benét,* n. 9, p. 390.

14. Fenton, *Benét,* p. 148.

15. *Ibid.*

16. In *The Literary History of the United States,* 3 vols., eds. Spiller, Thorp, Johnson, and Canby (New York, 1946), II, 1350-51. See Fenton, *Benét,* pp. 126-29 for an analysis of the critical reception of the poem.

17. "American Names," *Yale Review,* XVII (Oct., 1927), 63-64. Reprinted, *Ballads and Poems,* pp. 3-4, and *Selected Works,* I, 367-68.

18. Fenton, *Benét,* p. 190.

19. See *Life,* XVI, 5 (Jan. 1931), 48-56, for a photographic essay on the American place-names in the poem.

20. "Wounded Knee," *Dictionary of American History* (New York, 1940), ed. James Truslow Adams.

21. *Selected Works,* I, 408.

22. Letter to Rosemary Carr, April 21, 1921, in *Letters,* p. 55.

23. *Selected Works,* I, 363-64.

24. Reprinted in *Selected Works,* I, 339-41.

25. *Ibid.,* pp. 343-44.

26. *Ibid.,* pp. 342-43.

27. *Burning City,* (New York, 1936) p. 53; *Selected Works,* I, 364.

28. See Fenton, *Benét, passim.*

29. *Selected Works,* I, 362.

30. *The Last Circle* (New York, 1946), pp. 303-4.

31. Fenton, *Benét,* pp. 255-56.

32. *Selected Works,* I, 409.

33. *Ibid.,* pp. 411-12.

34. *New Yorker,* XIV (Apr. 12, 1938), 21; *Selected Works,* I, 461-63.

35. "The American Grain," *Poetry,* XLVIII (August, 1936), 276-82.

36. *New Yorker,* XIV (Apr. 12, 1938). Reprinted in *Selected Works,* I, 457-61.

37. *Selected Works,* I, 464-68. "Nightmare at Noon" originally appeared in the *New York Times.*

Mary Lynn Richardson (essay date January 1963)

SOURCE: Richardson, Mary Lynn. "The Historical Authenticity of John Brown's Raid in Stephen Vincent Benét's *John Brown's Body*." *West Virginia History* 24, no. 2 (January 1963): 168-75.

[*In the following essay, Richardson investigates the historical authenticity of* John Brown's Body.]

INTRODUCTION

In the "Note" prefacing Stephen Vincent Benét's *John Brown's Body,* he says:

> In dealing with known events I have tried to cleave to historical fact where such fact was ascertainable. On the other hand, for certain thoughts and feelings attributed to historical characters, and for the interpretation of those characters in the poem, I alone must be held responsible.[1]

John Brown's raid at Harpers Ferry is covered by Benét in nine pages of poetry. The scene at the courthouse is covered in two pages. John Brown's last speech is then given, although several parts of it are omitted.[2]

In this paper I am comparing the historical accuracy of John Brown's raid at Harpers Ferry as told by Benét with that of other historical accounts available. Historians themselves differ in giving accounts of this, but even with their differences, they are important because the characters become less confused and more understandable when reading Benét's narrative. It is almost necessary to read Benét's account along with the material covered in this paper.

THE HISTORICAL AUTHENTICITY OF JOHN
BROWN'S RAID IN STEPHEN VINCENT BENÉT'S
JOHN BROWN'S BODY

In Benét's narrative no background information about John Brown's arrival in Harpers Ferry is given. Brown had rented the Kennedy Farm near the village of Sharpsburg and told people he was a mining prospector. He called himself "Isaac Smith".[3] "One day two large boxes arrived at the Kennedy Farm. Mining machinery, he told people. They believed him. Why not? The boxes actually contained 200 new rifles, 200 revolvers and—a thousand spearheads and tomahawks. And not an Indian within a thousand miles."[4]

Another account says that when wagon loads of heavy boxes arrived, a neighbor asked about them. John Brown said it was household goods and were not to be opened until "Mrs. Smith" arrived.[5]

Brown had no "well-defined purpose in attacking Harpers Ferry, save to begin his revolution in a spectacular way, capturing a few slaveholders and release some slaves."[6]

Benét's story begins with John Brown's descent into Harpers Ferry. "On the night of October 16, 1859 [Sunday], with eighteen men, five of whom were Negroes, he made the attack"[7] at 8:00.[8] Benét names six of the men: Kagi, Stevens, Dauphin Thompson, Oliver Brown, Dangerfield Newby, and Watson Brown.[9] The others of the total of twenty-two men were: Owen Brown, Barclay and Edwin Coppoc, John Edwin Cook, William Thompson, Francis J. Merriam, William Henry Leeman, Steward Taylor, Osborne Perry Anderson, John A. Copeland, Lewis Sherrard Leary, Shields Green, Albert Hazlett, Jerry Anderson and Charles Plummer Tidd.[10]

Benét describes the six men he mentioned fairly accurately. He calls Kagi "the self-taught scholar, quiet and cool."[11] John Kagi went to the district school and later attended an academy in Virginia.[12] He had also been called a "philosopher and scholar."[13]

Aaron D. Stevens is described by Benét as "the cashiered soldier, quiet and cool, a singing giant, gunpowder-tempered and rash."[14] "Stevens was hard to discipline and could seldom restrain his disposition to resist the daily tyrannies."[15] He also had a "beautiful baritone voice". "He did not affect the faith of a Christian. He was a devoted spiritualist, however, and died believing absolutely in the immortality of life."[16]

Dauphin Thompson is described by Benét as "the pippin-cheeked country-boy, more like a girl than a warrior."[17] Dauphin Thompson had just turned twenty-two and was the brother of William. Both were eventually slain.[18]

Benét says that Oliver Brown was "married last year when he was barely nineteen."[19] Hinton calls him the "boy-husband" who was just recently married and still very young.[20]

Benét calls Dangerfield Newby the "colored and born a slave, freeman now, but married to one not free who, with their seven children waited him South, the youngest baby just beginning to crawl."[21] Hinton says he was "thirty years old, mulatto, who was married to one not free and had seven children."[22]

Watson Brown was another of John Brown's sons. Benét inserts a portion of a letter from Watson Brown to his wife[23] which was not located in the sources used in this paper. He then gives his own opinion of Oliver Brown, whom he says had a face that has a "masculine beauty somewhat like the face of Keats."[24]

John Brown had assigned Owen Brown, Merriam, and Barclay Coppoc to watch the house at the Kennedy Farm, Tidd and Cook to cut the telegraph wires, Watson Brown and Taylor to hold the bridge over the Potomac, Kagi and Stevens to detain the bridge guard, Oliver Brown and William Thompson to hold the bridge over the Shenandoah, Jerry Anderson and Dauphin Thompson to occupy the engine house in the arsenal, Hazlett and Edwin Coppoc to hold the armory and during the night Kagi and Copeland were to seize and guard the rifle factory.[25]

Benét first tells of the capture of the rifleworks. "They tied up the watchmen and took the rifleworks."[26] DuBois says that Brown's men ordered the gate to be opened. The watchmen refused. They then ordered them to get the key, but the men refused. Brown's men got a crowbar and large hammer from a wagon and opened the door. They captured the two watchmen and left them in the custody of Jerry Anderson and Dauphin Thompson. Albert Hazlett and Edwin Coppoc held the armory for the time being.[27]

The excitement began and they took several prisoners. The raiding party, headed by Stevens and Cook, then went to Colonel Lewis Washingtgon's farm.[28]

"It is remarkable," said Governor Wise, speaking of the event, "that the only thing of material value which they took, besides his slaves, was the sword of Frederick the Great, which was sent to General Washington [great-uncle of Colonel Lewis Washington]. This was taken by Stevens to Brown, and the latter commanded his men with that sword in this fight against the peace and safety of Washington's native State!"[29]

Another account says that Cook had taken Lafayette's pistols and Frederick's sword which Colonel Washington had once shown them in courtesy.[30]

In reference to the slaves:

John Brown could not see the liberated slaves when they laid down the pikes or guns, which they had so uncomprehendingly and obediently carried about all day, and slunk off homeward through the trees.[31]

Benét covers this episode quite accurately, adding a description of the slaves who were acting as guards.[32]

Benét then tells of Patrick Higgins, the night watchman of the Maryland bridge being shot, leaving a bullet-crease in his scalp.[33]

Robert Penn Warren gives this account:[34]

The watchman who came to relieve Bill Williams met the guard on the bridge, struck Captain Owen Brown, and tore himself away from the men who seized him. "I didn't know what 'Halt' mint [sic] then any more than a hog knows about a holiday," once explained Patrick Higginson. . . .

Warren got the names confused, because the man's name was Patrick Higgins according to Villard[35] and duBois[36] and it also was Oliver Brown whom Higgins struck.

It was about this time that the B&O train was due in Harpers Ferry. Higgins got away and warned the train.[37] The train arrived at the station known as the Wager House[38] and Brown's men shot the colored porter.[39]

Heyward Sheppard, [sic, Shepherd] colored porter, came up from the rear of the train. The men remonstrated with Cromwell. There was the bark of a rifle from somewhere in the crowd and the porter fell with a mortal wound.[40]

This was, indeed an ill omen for the army of liberation. The first man to fall at their hands was neither a slaveowner nor a defender of slavery, nor one who suffered by it, but a highly respected man in full possession of his liberty and favored with the respect of the white community. He had not even offered to resist.[41]

The passengers in the train went to the Wager House and remained there.[42] At sunrise the train proceeded.[43] Benét tells of this in great detail. He interprets Shepherd's thoughts while dying as a man who had found his place in society.[44]

Benét then switches the scene back to the town. He mentions that a townsman named Boerley was killed. He does not tell anything about Boerley.[45]

Thomas Boerley, a local grocer, was the first white man killed by the raiders.[46] "He had walked out into the invading riflemen, still so sure of success, asked no questions about any man's errand; a man showed himself a fair target and that was enough."[47]

Benét tells of the attitude of the people in Harpers Ferry. They thought it was Nat Turner who had returned.[48]

What the South had been dreading ever since the Nat Turner insurrection of 1831 had come to pass: there was another servile uprising in the land. For years patrols had ridden the roads and men had watched of night lest the negroes turn upon their masters. It was an ever-present fear; that the Abolitionists wished the slaves to rise and kill their masters in their beds was a belief widely held in the South and often publicly expressed, and no happening that could be imagined contained a greater possibility of horror and bloodshed.[49]

"At daylight, every person who appeared in the street was taken prisoner, until they numbered between forty and fifty men."[50]

Benét next tells of the arrival of the militia. He says that the Jefferson Guards had no uniforms. Their weapons consisted of old squirrel rifles and shot guns loaded with spikes and scraps of iron.[51] DuBois verifies this. He says that Captain Rowan, who headed the volunteer company, "found one or two squirrel rifles and a few shot guns."[52]

Benét then rejoins the raiders in his account. He speaks of Kagi, who was holding the rifle-works, sending Brown messages to retreat. He says that Brown "neither replied nor heeded."[53]

John H. Kagi, who had been in possession of the Hall gun factory up the Shenandoah and who was the chief advisor of John Brown, had urged the leader several times during the morning to retreat, but Brown refused to turn about.[54]

The scene again changes back to the militia. Benét says, "Just about noon the Jefferson Guards took the Potomac Bridge and drove away the men Brown posted there."[55]

The militia began to arrive and the movements to cut off Brown's men began. The Jefferson Guards crossed the Potomac, came down to the Maryland side and seized the Potomac bridge. The local company was sent to take the Shenandoah bridge, leave a guard and march to the rear of the arsenal, while another local company was to seize the houses in front of the arsenal.[56]

Benét continues saying the other bridge, meaning the Shenandoah, was soon recaptured.[57] Redpath, in his *Echoes of Harper's Ferry,* published the year after John

Brown's raid said "the first attack was made by the Charlestown Guards at the Shenandoah Bridge. William Thompson was taken prisoner, unwounded. . . ."[58]

The first of the raiders were killed. Benét describes Dangerfield Newby again. He gives his thoughts on what Newby and Shepherd would say to each other.[59]

There are several accounts of Stevens and Watson Brown asking for a truce. Villard, duBois, and Redpath all verify Benét's account. Redpath's account is as follows:

> At the request of Mr. Kitzmiller, one of John Brown's hostages, Stevens went out of the Arsenal with him in order to enable him, if he could do so, to "accommodate matters" for the benefit of the prisoners. Stevens carried a flag of truce; but yet he was shot down and seized by the ruffianly militia.[60]

Benét then tells of Mr. Brua trying to calm the citizens. He then gives his own opinion of Brua as a man and a citizen.[61]

Other accounts say that "a brave prisoner named Joseph A. Brua went backward and forward"[62] "despite the desultory fire from the citizens"[63] "begging the citizens not to shoot, as they endangered the lives of Colonel Washington and the other prisoners."[64]

Benét then tells of other killings. He tells of Leeman, "a boy of eighteen and the youngest raider, trying to flee . . . from the engine-house . . . and killed on an islet in the Potomac."[65] DuBois says Leeman, who was taking a second message to Brown, was killed.[66]

The next person Benét mentions was Fontaine Beckham, mayor of the town. He tells how Beckham went to look at Heyward's body. Benét tells Beckham's thoughts while going to see Heyward and of his being killed, although he does not tell how he was killed.[67]

Warren gives this account:

> The kindly old Fontaine Beckham, agent for the railroad and mayor of the town was the next victim. The poor fellow, greatly disturbed by the death of his man, Sheppard, crept up on the trestlework near the station to watch the outlaws who were causing all this violence in the streets of his town. Crouching in the protection of the engine-house building, Edwin Coppoc saw a man peering around the corner of the water tank, some thirty yard. "If he keeps on peeking, I'm going to shoot." Coppoc fired, but missed. The prisoners recognized Beckham and shouted in protest, but Coppoc's rifle was raised again. Beckham crumpled up with his head twisted against the timbers of the trestle.[68]

Benét next mentions the killing of William Thompson, which has already been noted in this paper.[69] He mentions that Kagi and Oliver Brown were killed. DuBois

tells of the death of Kagi and Oliver Brown. Kagi fell and died in the water while trying to reach a large flat rock near the middle of the river.[70] Oliver Brown was shot and died without speaking a word.[71] Benét tells of Oliver Brown crying in agony and John Brown telling him to die like a man.[72]

Benét devotes the next several paragraphs to Brown's thoughts. He then begins to tell about the marines.[73] He tells of Lee's arrival. Lee offered the "honor of the attack" to the colonel of the militia, who declined, saying that Lee's men were paid for this kind of work, while theirs had wives and children.[74]

> Robert E. Lee, with one hundred marines, arrived just before midnight on Monday. . . .[75]

> Colonel Lee offered the privilege of the attack to Colonel Shriver of the Maryland militia, who declined for a sound reason. "These men of mine have wives and children at home. I will not expose them to such risks. You are paid for doing this kind of work.[76]

Benét then tells of Stuart taking a letter to Brown.[77] "J. E. B. Stuart was the first to recognize Brown as Osawatomie Brown of Kansas, whom he had once had as a prisoner."[78] When Brown would not surrender, Stuart gave the signal for the marines to attack.[79]

Benét then tells of John Brown watching the marines come and what the rifle-shots sounded like.[80] He does not mention Lieutenant Green by name. He refers to him as "the shadow."[81]

Warren, duBois, and Redpath all tell of Lieutenant Green's entrance into the engine house.[82] Green had a flimsy dress sword in hand and rushed to the rear of the building and jumped on top of the engine. "This is Osawatomie," Washington said, pointing to Brown. Green sprang about twelve feet at Brown, giving him an upward thrust with the sword,[83] then brought the hilt down several times on Brown's head until he laid still.

Benét says that two marines were down. He says that one of Brown's men was pinned to the wall with bayonets, another to the floor.[84]

Warren says "the first two Marines to follow Green fell the breach, and then their comrades were in with the bayonets. They caught one fellow, skulking beneath the engine, and pinned another clean to the wall with a single thrust."[85]

> Green shouted the order to hold, and the fight was over. It had lasted only some two or three minutes from the time the door gave under the impact of the ladder."[86] For nearly three hours the firing went on before he Brown saw the futility of further resistance."[87]

Benét says it had been a quarter of an hour since Stuart gave the signal for the storm.[88]

*"And now it was over.
　All but the long dying."*

Notes

1. Stephen Vincent Benét, *John Brown's Body* (Murray Hill, New York, 1928), p. vii.

2. Compare with "Testimonies of Capt. John Brown at Harper's Ferry with his address to the court". (New York, 1860), p. 15.

3. Frank Ball, "Harper's Ferry Episode." *West Virginia Review,* October, 1939.

4. Charles Carpenter, "John Brown in Harper's Ferry", *National Republic,* August, 1931.

5. Ball, *op.cit.*

6. Oswald, Garrison Villard, *John Brown 1800-1859.* (Boston, 1911), p. 427.

7. *Encyclopedia Britannicae.* (Chicago, 1960), vol. 4, p. 266.

8. B. Burghardt duBois, *John Brown* (Philadelphia, 1909), p. 308.

9. Benét, *op.cit.* p. 25.

10. Richard J. Hinton, *John Brown and His Men.* (New York, 1894).

11. Benét, *op.cit.*

12. Hinton, *op.cit.,* pp. 455-6.

13. *Ibid.,* p. 449.

14. Benét, *op.cit.*

15. Hinton, *op. cit.,* p. 493.

16. *Ibid.,* p. 499.

17. Benét, *op.cit.*

18. Hinton, *op.cit.,* p. 528.

19. Benét, *op.cit.*

20. Hinton, *op.cit.,* p. 332.

21. Benét, *op.cit.*

22. Hinton, *op.cit.* p. 505.

23. Benét, *op.cit.,* p. 26.

24. *Ibid.*

25. duBois, *op.cit.,* pp. 308-9.

26. Benét, *op.cit.*

27. duBois, *op.cit.* pp. 310-311.

28. *Ibid.,* p. 311.

29. James Redpath, *The Public Life of Capt. John Brown.* (Boston, 1860), p. 248.

30. Robert Penn Warren, *John Brown, the Making of a Martyr.* (New York, 1929), p. 354.

31. *Ibid.,* p. 372.

32. Benét, *op.cit.*

33. *Ibid.,* p. 27.

34. Warren, *op.cit.,* p. 356.

35. Villard, *op.cit.,* p. 432.

36. duBois, *op.cit.,* p. 309.

37. Villard, *op.cit.*

38. Ball, *op.cit.*

39. duBois, *op.cit.*

40. Ball, *op.cit.*

41. Villard, *op.cit.,* p. 433.

42. Redpath, *op.cit.*

43. duBois, *op.cit.,* 311.

44. Benét, *op.cit.,* pp. 27-8.

45. *Ibid.*

46. Benjamin Bradlee, "Harper's Ferry; 1959", *Newsweek.*

47. Warren, *op.cit.,* p. 358.

48. Benét, *op.cit.*

49. Villard, *op.cit.,* 436.

50. Redpath, *op.cit.,* p. 248.

51. Benét, *op.cit.,* p. 29.

52. duBois, *op.cit.,* p. 320.

53. Benét, *op.cit.*

54. Carpenter, *op.cit.*

55. Benét, *op.cit.*

56. duBois, *op.cit.,* p. 321.

57. Benét, *op.cit.*

58. Redpath, *op.cit.,* 252.

59. Benét, *op.cit.,* p. 30.

60. Redpath, *op.cit.,* p. 254.

61. Benét, *op.cit.,* p. 30-1.

62. Villard, *op.cit.,* p. 438.

63. Warren, *op.cit.,* p. 364.

64. Villard, *op.cit.*

65. Benét, *op.cit.,* p. 31.

66. duBois, *op.cit.,* p. 325.

67. Benét, *op.cit.,* pp. 31-2.

68. Warren, *op.cit.,* pp. 367-8.

69. See page 169.

70. duBois, *op.cit.*

71. *Ibid.*

72. Benét, *op.cit.,* p. 33.

73. *Ibid.*

74. *Ibid.,* p. 34.

75. duBois, *op.cit.,* p. 332.

76. Warren, *op.cit.,* 377.

77. Benét, *op.cit.,* 34.

78. duBois, *op.cit.*

79. *Ibid.*

80. Benét, *op.cit.,* p. 34-5.

81. *Ibid.,* p. 35.

82. Warren, *op.cit.,* p. 380; duBois, *op.cit.,* p. 333-4; Redpath, *op.cit.,* p. 262.

83. "It seems that Green's sword, in making the thrust, struck Brown's belt and did not penetrate the body. The sword was bent double. The reason that Brown was not killed when struck on the head was that Green was holding his sword in the middle, striking with the hilt and making only scalp wounds." duBois, *op.cit.*

84. Benét, *op.cit.*

85. Warren, *op.cit.*

86. *Ibid.*

87. Ball, *op.cit.*

88. Benét, *op.cit.*

John Griffith (essay date January 1973)

SOURCE: Griffith, John. "Narrative Technique and the Meaning of History in Benét and MacLeish." *Journal of Narrative Technique* 3, no. 1 (January 1973): 3-19.

[*In the following essay, Griffith compares the narrative techniques utilized in Benét's* John Brown's Body *and Archibald MacLeish's* Conquistador *and assesses the significance of these historical epics in the tradition of American verse.*]

When American historians at the end of the last century and the beginning of this one became involved in sharp controversy over the nature of historical truth and the historian's discipline, the lines their arguments took formed a paradigm of fundamental disagreements about the nature of truth in modern thought of the most various kinds—religious, artistic, literary, philosophical and scientific.

On one side of this historians' debate was the "scientific history" of the American Historical Association. Following the lead of Herbert Baxter Adams, who in the 1880s brought to American universities the German graduate seminar with its ideals of objectivity and scientific detachment, scientific historians (and between 1884, when Adams founded the AHA, and 1910 or 1912, virtually all professional American historians thought of themselves in those terms) took as their motto von Ranke's dictum that historiography should simply tell the past *wie es eigentlich gewesen.* With little epistemological self-examination, the scientific historians assumed that the facts of history were solid, fixed and finite, existing outside the mind of the historian; that these facts could be directly rendered in written history, objectively and without distortion; and that they were intrinsically coherent—that their causal relationships formed rationally understandable patterns, which would inevitably appear if the historian simply told the truth.[1] Thus the working historian could best spend his days collecting and establishing real facts, not in interpreting them. "For such a process we have the fortunate analogy of the physical sciences," wrote one of them, Albert Bushnell Hart. "Did not Darwin spend twenty years in accumulating data, and in selecting typical phenomena, before he so much as ventured a generalization? . . . In history, too, scattered and apparently unrelated data fall together into harmonious wholes; the mind is led to the discovery of laws; and the explorer into scientific truth is at last able to formulate some of those unsuspected generalizations which explain the whole framework of the universe."[2]

The other side of the controversy was a comparatively small and unsystematic but persuasive body of historical comment which contended that historical truth, just like any other kind of truth, is relative to the point of view of the truth-seeker. Frederick Jackson Turner, James Harvey Robinson, Carl Becker and Charles A. Beard were perhaps the most articulate of these relativist historians. Each in his own way attacked his "scientific" colleagues' faith in the absolute truth of history. Turner questioned the absolutists' belief that a *fact* is a fixed quantity. "Those who insist that history is simply the effort to tell the thing exactly as it was, to state the facts, are confronted with the difficulty that the fact which they would represent is not planted on the solid ground of fixed conditions; it is in the midst and is itself part of the changing currents, the complex and interacting influences of the time, deriving its significance as a fact from its relations to the deeper-seated movements of the age."[3] Robinson argued that every age distorts the past according to its own biases, inevitably; his advice was that historians should recognize this principle and distort wisely, in a good cause; they should "exploit [the past] in the interest of advance."[4] The urbane Becker satirized the naiveté of the very concept of a "discrete fact." Historical facts, he contended, were only images in someone's mind, each fact being compounded of smaller "facts" which could be atomized endlessly.[5] Beard rejected the scientists' faith that the totality of history could some day be recorded and its meaning known—this, wrote Beard, is the dream of omniscience, an epistemological absurdity.[6]

It was at the height of this controversy that Stephen Vincent Benét's *John Brown's Body* (1927) and Archibald MacLeish's *Conquistador* (1932) appeared. Both are long narrative poems on historical subjects. Both aroused considerable enthusiasm—moderate in the academies but remarkably great in the general reading public; it has been said they started a minor fad of historical poetry.[7] But despite their casual similarities, they are fundamentally and intensely different kinds of narrative verse. Benét proceeds on the epistemological assumptions of the scientific historian, even though he takes conscious and freely-declared liberties with scientific practice; MacLeish, like the relativists, writes with the defensive attitude of a historian who sees himself surrounded by scientists and is highly suspicious of their positivistic way of thinking. To compare the narrative techniques embodying these attitudes is to discover again the interdependence of form and meaning in literature, and at the same time to illuminate an aspect of our century's pervasive relativist-positivist controversy.

II

Allen Tate, puzzling over the lack of aesthetic unity in *John Brown's Body,* once asked: "Is it possible that Mr. Benét supposed the poem to be about the Civil War, rather than about his own mind?"[8] Actually, wrote Benét in a foreword which seems (but only seems) to answer Tate's question, "I do not think of the poem as being primarily a poem about war itself. What I was trying to do was to show certain realities, legends, ideas, landscapes, ways of living, faces of men that were ours."[9] The point of Tate's question and Benét's answer is the same: *John Brown's Body* makes the scientific historian's assumption that the truth—reality, the past—exists, independent of any human projection, waiting to be caught. Benét's Invocation describes his poem as an effort to reconstruct that past—

> To build again that blue, American roof
> Over a half-forgotten battle tune
> And call unsurely, from a haunted ground,
> Armies of shadows, and the shadow ground.
>
> (7)[10]

He often proclaimed the distinction between himself and the true historian. "Naturally," he writes of his poem, "it does not follow history in a strict sense—that is to say I have not described and do not mean to describe every battle, every fluctuation of fortune, every event . . . That is to say—it is a poem, an attempt at an interpretation, not a history or recital of events."[11] But the more he protests his freedom from the historian's formal responsibilities, the more clearly he reveals his controlling awareness of them. "As this is a poem, not a history," he writes in another note, "it has seemed unnecessary to me to encumber it with notes, bibliography, and other historical apparatus." Then he goes on to list his dozen major historical sources. "I have tried to cleave to historical facts where such fact was ascertainable."[12] Douglas Southall Freeman has said, "He could have fortified even his casual adverbs with footnotes."[13]

His attention is always outward, toward the past he is seeking to capture, rather than inward, toward what Tate seeks in the poem but fails to find, "some striking personal vision of life" which might give internal meaning to the poem's events and people. "It was a remarkable time—one of the great and crucial periods of our history," Benét declares. "And such things are worth writing about so they can be remembered."[14]

A few critical attempts have been made to establish an imaginative unity in the poem.[15] But no one has gotten around the patent fact that its strongest unifying feature is its conventional chronology of the war's battles and campaigns. As Benét said, "Except for the prologue and epilogue, the action of the poem is a continuous action, beginning shortly before the John Brown raid and ending shortly after the surrender at Appomatox."[16] Each of the eight books treats prominently one or more military events: Book I, Harper's Ferry; Book II, the firing on Fort Sumter and the Battle of Bull Run; Book III, Shiloh; Book IV, the campaigns of the East and the West, Fair Oaks, Fredericksburg, and other battles; Book V, Antietam and the hard winter of 1862; Book VI the Wilderness Campaign, Grant and Sherman at Vicksburg; Book VII Gettysburg; Book VIII, Sherman's march to the sea and the surrender at Appomatox. Included in this chronology are numerous other public events—the hanging of John Brown, the election of Lincoln, the formation of the Confederate cabinet, the appointment and dismissal of various generals, the death of Jackson, the death of Lincoln.

Metaphorically one might picture the poem as a kind of insulated cable At its core, advancing along a chronological line, is the war itself, the essential historical Civil War. The cable's outer surface is the ideal discipline of historiography, cultivated with the best modern scholarly tools—detachment, sobriety, open-mindedness, exhaustive research. It is only between this core and this outer surface that the poet exercises his license; his fancy is never allowed to drift too far from the "ascertainable facts" of his source books. "I want to be as accurate as possible wherever I can," he tells his editor.[17]

The fabric which encases the military chronology consists of a number of roughly graduated viewpoints from which the war is seen. Closest to the center are Benét's anonymous or near-anonymous historical figures, who see war only as personal experience, immediate and without much abstract meaning. Benét gleans from their letters and diaries:

> It is cold. It is wet. We marched till we couldn't stand
>   up.
> It is muddy here. I wish you could see us here.
> I wish everybody at home could see us here.
> They would know what war is like.
>
> (185)

Benét's fictitious figures, presented at their most unreflective and immediate in a kind of *style indirect libre,* produce more highly-wrought rhetoric but no broader sense of understanding. An example is Ellyat's impressions of the battle at Shiloh:

> A huge horse rose above the wall of the tent
> And hung there a second like a bad prodigy,
> A frozen scream full of hoofs.
>   He struck at its head
> And tried to get out from under as it lunged down
> But he wasn't quite quick enough.
>
> (128)

One remove from this are characters, fictional and historical, who try to formulate some larger meaning for the war—some, at least, personal moral lesson. Benét's Lincoln thinks:

> We can fail and fail,
> But, deep against the failure, something wars,
> Something goes forward, something lights a match,
> Something gets up from Sangamon County ground
> Armed with a bitten and blunted axe
> And after twenty thousand wasted strokes
> Brings the tall hemlock crashing to the ground.
>
> (222)

One more step away from the experiential core is the poet, writing in a summary way of the actors' attitudes and feelings, as in this passage from his description of the Army of Northern Virginia:

> Praying army,
> Full of revivals, as full of salty jests,
> Who debated on God and Darwin and Victor Hugo,
> Decided that evolution might do for Yankees
> But that Lee never came from anything with a tail,
> And called yourselves "Lee's miserables faintin'"
> When the book came out that tickled your sense of
>   romance.
>
> (189)

And then, at the outer layer of this texture of viewpoints, is the poet-historian in his study with his maps and battle-plans and his surveys of social history that give the large, disinterested perspective of the twentieth century.

> And so the game is played,
> The intricate game of the watchers overseas,
> The shadow that falls like the shadow of a hawk's
>   wing
> Over the double-chessboard until the end—
> The shadow of Europe, the shadows of England and
>   France,
> The war of cotton against the iron and wheat.
>
> (181)

My elaborate image of the poem as a core of historical events layered about with individual impressions at various distances implies, I think, something of the poem's essentially unplanned quality, even in the presence of such care and meticulous research. Benét depends on a rough historical calculus, assuming that if he assembles all the standard themes and viewpoints surrounding the war itself, then a significant configuration will inevitably form—the shape of "the golden prey" he sets after in his Invocation. It is a calculus which, Benét assumes, operates independent of his own imagination—the shape of history will automatically appear if the right facts and opinions and first-hand impressions are brought in.

Principles of selection are, of course, necessary, lest the poem reach to infinity. Like most of the historians who were his contemporaries, Benét doesn't seem to have done much conscious thinking about how one selects facts on which to focus. Generally his view of the Civil War accords with that which Thomas B. Pressly calls "the nationalist school," which he says "was characterized primarily by its spirit of nationalism and sectional reconciliation."[18] In this view, the Civil War had no major villain; Lincoln and Lee were both to be admired. "This so-called 'cult of Lincoln and Lee,'" says Pressly, "reflected the widespread agreement among historians that supporters of the Union, typified in Lincoln, and supporters of the Confederacy, typified in Lee, had acted in the main from honorable and justifiable motives." What caused the war, in this view, was not some*one* but some*thing*—as Pressly says, "inanimate forces were the primary cause of the conflict between North and South rather than the actions of evil individuals." Benét agrees:

> Sometimes there comes a crack in time itself.
> Sometimes the earth is torn by something blind.
> Sometimes an image that has stood so long
> It seems implanted as the polar star
> Is moved against an unfathomed force
> That suddenly will not have it any more.
> Call it the *mores,* call it God or Fate,

Call it Mansoul or economic law,
That force exists and moves.

(56)

As far as one can judge by its effect on his narrative technique, the most pervasive implicit thesis in Benét's interpretation is that the war resulted from what Pressly calls "deep-seated, fundamental, irreconcilable differences" between the country's sections. Following, whether consciously or not, Frederick Jackson Turner's image of the United States as a group of culturally discrete sections dynamically juxtaposed, Benét pictures the Civil War as primarily a conflict between the bourgeois Puritan temper of New England and the romantic-aristocratic Southern temper, embodied in the characters and customs surrounding Wingate Hall—

The full-rigged vessel, the sailing dream,
The brick and stone that were somehow quick
With a ghost not native to stone and brick,
The name held high and the gift passed on
From Wingate father to Wingate son

(165)

With the Wingate plantation—granted by England's Charles II to "our well-beloved John Wingate"—as the symbolic center, Benét presents an integrated series of Southern characters—Clay Wingate, the scion; Mary Lou Wingate, his mother, who "gathered the reins of the whole plantation" (161); Cudjo and Aunt Bess, the loyal slaves, and Spade, the runaway; the coquette Lucy and the slightly wild, barely respectable Sally Dupré; and all the young gallants who attend the soirées at Wingate Hall and ride in the Wingates' Black Horse Troop.

The Puritan coloration shows in a number of characters. The slave-trading skipper in the Prelude is a New Englander:

"I get my sailing orders from the Lord."
He touched the Bible. "And it's down there, Mister,
Down there in black and white—the sons of Ham—
Bondservants—sweat of their brows." His voice
   trailed off
Into texts.

(15)

The same Biblical fervor invests John Brown of Connecticut, and the lady abolitionists of the North:

Women praying,
Praying at night, in every house in the North,
Praying for old John Brown until their knees
Ached with stiff cold.
      Innumerable prayers
Inexorably rising, till the dark
Vault of the midnight was so thronged and packed
The wild geese could not arrow through the storm
Of terrible, ascendant, women's prayers

(53)

Young Jack Ellyat, the poem's Yankee hero, whose mother is one of those praying women, lacks their manifest piety, but his cultural background is plainly theirs. His moral earnestness and social innocence are key notes in his affair with Melora Villas, the western girl:

He told himself, "I'm all right,
I'm not like Bailey. I wouldn't sleep with a girl
Who never slept with anybody before
And then just go off and leave her."
      But it was Melora.
It wasn't seducing a girl. It was all mixed up.
All real where it ought to be something told in a
   sermon.

(149)

As for the other geographical sections, their representatives are more lightly sketched. But they, no less than Wingate and Ellyat, are clearly products of what Morton Zabel has called Benét's love of "the large dimensions of popular myth."[19] They are quintessentially conventional, drawn according to social and geographical types, depending on the most standard themes and images. John Vilas is a romantic individualist, set to hunting "the wilderness stone" as he avoids being caught up in the war. Benét said that he was meant to represent "the Border States and the growing West."[20] Luke Breckinridge of the Tennessee mountains is ignorant, superstitious, a hard-eyed feuder and a keen shot with his long rifle. Jake Diefer of Pennsylvania is a sturdy German peasant who goes to war and loses an arm and stolidly comes back to his plow again. Sophy is the lower-class Southern white, "scared chambermaid in Pollet's hotel," who would "like to smell sweet . . . like a lady" (266); Shippy, "the little man with sharp rat-eyes," is her counterpart from the North, a base-spirited peddler who carries spy-reports in his boots and dies whining. Bailey is Ellyat's fiercely provincial, ignorant, tough-talking Midwestern compatriot from Illinois.

There is a sense in which Benét's very epistemological assumptions require him to use such stereotypes. If, as his Invocation implies, the essential American past is to be found in an amalgamation or juxtaposition of a finite number of recognizable viewpoints—the "hundred visions" from which he proposes to make one—then those viewpoints must exist, and in finite number. The farther Benét might move toward imagining his characters as individuals, each with his own peculiarities, the more he fragments his quest for the historical truth—the more he strays away from those "harmonious wholes" which he and A. B. Hart and the other scientific historians believed in. To picture Clay Wingate as a Southern aristocrat who reads Byron and gambles and polishes his boots and his honor is a way of pointing the reader's attention outward, toward the historical "reality." Typical or stereotyped regional representatives are, perhaps, one kind of comprehensive historic fact to be discerned in the welter of particular instances.

This conception of significant truth as something to be caught rather than created has a crucial effect on the poem's schematic structure, or lack of it. Benét has made little apparent effort to establish a total meaning or pattern within the poem itself—a significant relationship between images, say, or between themes or even characters. Henry Seidel Canby has claimed to have found a moral unity in the poem, based on the fundamental theme of "the struggle of individuals caught in Karma."[21] But this is surely the laxest kind of pattern. Consider the particular "karmas" of the central figures: for Ellyat, a going away from home, a meeting with a lovely gypsy girl, a separation and a miraculous reunion; for Wingate, the bitter-sweet loss of the prettily romantic world of which Lucy Weatherby is queen, and the gaining of the more real, mysterious and sensuous love of Sally Dupré. For Diefer, dogged duty, resulting in the loss of an arm. For Spade, the break for freedom, the disillusionment by Northern cruelty, and the final subdued triumph of finding a job on Diefer's farm. For Lucy, a chivalric lark that goes sour. For Cudjo and Mary Lou Wingate the tragic destruction of the old aristocracy. For Lincoln, the running down of the quarry, God's intention; for Grant, professional success after a career of failure; for Lee, a Stoic lesson in defeat; for John Brown, martyrdom. To find the significance of these fates we look not to structural bonds and contrasts between them, but outward, to the historical reality they refer to.

The same centrifugal motion is visible in the poem's prominent rhetorical devices. They owe their impact, characteristically, to a tension between the poem and something outside it, rather than between parts of the poem itself. Benét relies, that is to say, on his audience's general familiarity with the central issues of the war, its leading heroes and the names of its great battlefields. His poetic trademark is the mild ironic spark he strikes between that general myth of the Civil War and his own wry, rather tight-lipped understatements about it. Lincoln, Lee, Grant, the ante-bellum South, Puritanical New England, the great American war—all have a popular romantic aura which Benét evokes in hundreds of allusions, most of them pointedly clipped and restrained.

> It is wrong to talk of Lincoln and a star together—that old rubbed image is a scrap of tinsel, a scrap of dead poetry—it dries up and blows away when it touches a man. And yet Lincoln had a star, if you will have it so—and was haunted by a prairie star.
>
> Down in the South another man, most unlike him but as steadfast, is haunted by another star that has little to do with tinsel, and the man they called "Evacuation" Lee begins to grow taller and to cast a longer shadow.

(112)

Just to name the famous battlefields can set the reverberations going.

> Follow the Indian names in the Indian West,
> Chickamauga and Chattanooga and all the words
> That are sewn on flags or cut in an armory wall.

(321)

Paul Engle has said of Benét's historical verse that "always there is the conviction that the act of history means little unless it ends in a human image, and the act of expressing poetry means little unless it works through mortal object, through used, known, touched, feared, accustomed detail."[22] The converse of this is also true, perhaps truer: that for Benét the human image, the mortal object has little meaning—an uncertain place in the mind's universe—unless it is rather solidly attached to standard historical landmarks. *John Brown's Body*'s most prestigious defenders have been historians, for most of its governing assumptions are rooted in historiography: strict regard for documented fact, chronological structure emphasizing great public events, attention to the geographical sections of the country, and so on. Benét's whole narrative technique is, in its own way, intended to be transparent, so historical reality can shine through. His manner is easy, relaxed, discursive, structurally uncomplicated, bearing little relation to the new poetics of Pound and Eliot and Williams or even Whitman. Above all, it is confident and unself-conscious, and it does what it was intended to do: convey with considerable reportorial felicity the solid, respectable history in which the poem's meaning is grounded.

III

Benét's linked conceptions of poetry and history were constant throughout his career. The narrative technique of *Western Star,* the historical epic he left unfinished at his death, is no different from that of *John Brown's Body*; it shows no change in its author's belief in the conventions of narrative historiography.

MacLeish has been much more concerned with the avant-garde in poetry, and more self-conscious about the way he and other writers look at the world and write about it; his poetry shows a consistency of steady change. Broadly, the path of his thinking follows that of Becker and Beard: at first (in prose and poetry written in the 1920s and early 1930s) he chafes under the strictures of absolute positivism, finding them naive and unsatisfying but very deeply entrenched in modern dogma and apparently inescapable; then, in the 1930s and 1940s, he proposes to supplant them by an effort of will—to choose his way of perceiving consciously and purposefully, and to project intentionally the kinds of meaning by which society can best be served; and finally (from about 1950 on), somewhat mellowly, he acquiesces in the unsystematic, unrigorous, fluid adjustment to scientific positivism which sophisticated modern humanists are always making.

It seems to have taken MacLeish some time to accept the idea that truth-telling of all kinds—whether in poetry, history, or science—is not a simple passive surrender to objective stimulus, but a purposeful act performed by the truth-teller. By the middle of the 1930s, though, he had become convinced of that principle. He saw that the dispassionate objectivity of science was really only one of a number of possible viewpoints, and one which might even be called morally reprehensible. In his most famous essay, *The Irresponsibles* (1940), he castigated artists and scholars of the twenties for their failure to go beyond science's image of man as an empty cipher, and to provide a human image which might better sustain the spirit. He came to argue that "poetry's one debt" to humanity was "an image of mankind in which men can believe again," a "great alternative to that knowledge by abstraction which science has imposed."[23]

But when he began writing verse during the First World War as a conscientious member of the Lost Generation, MacLeish announced that imagination had been overwhelmed in an age of science; the essence of art and the newly prevailing mood of scientism were fatally at odds. "Poetry," he wrote, "like any other art, can only reach its highest level in a universe of which man is the center. In a human world. And the world centered about man was destroyed by the impulses which produced the world explicable by science."[24] The scientific position seemed impregnable; that powerful advocate *proof*—concrete, objective proof—was on its side. Science was ugly but it was real, and it was here, a regrettable but unavoidable fact of life. It was a time for humanists to sit down by the waters of Babylon.

> Nature, the spayed bitch. We have been into her too deep and too sharp. The magic is out of her and the meaning. The voices that used to speak with authority from brooks and trees, the Voice that with even more authority from a mountain, the gestures of fleeting goat-form and fleeter thighs signifying at least direction, the half-horse, half-man speaking credibly to man the numb and incredible fact of horse, or half-tree, half-girl performing inwardly the miraculous metabolism of tree into talk, the goddess herself offering between corn-heavy breasts the actual communication with earth— are simply Not. Leaving young men alone with the awkward incommunicativeness of say a hill or an acorn.[25]

The very concept of *truth* as something spiritually nourishing, said MacLeish, was old-fashioned, a passing illusion in human history. "The truth lies backward. The truth has been known to Plato—to Georg Wilhelm Friedrich Hegel—to Professor Pollard reading the notes in the margin of his Jowett. The truth is something-that-has-been-known."[26] The only meaning which man could still legitimately proclaim is the mute, tentative, unintellectual testimony of the senses:

> I will tell you all we have learned,
>   I will tell you everything:
> The earth is round,
>   there are springs under the orchards,
>   The loam cuts with a blunt knife, beware of
> Elms in thunder,
>   the lights in the sky are stars—
> We think they do not see,
>   we think also
> The trees do not know nor the leaves of the grasses
>   hear us.
>
> ("Epistle to be Left in the Earth," 71)[27]

Over and over, in half a dozen volumes of verse published during the 1920s, MacLeish laments the loss of spiritual meaning. His poetry shows great reluctance to ask too much meaning of experience, an attitude shared by many intellectuals of the day, professional historians among them. Material things, historical facts are assumed to be real; beliefs, concepts, abstractions less so. "Every declaration about human affairs," wrote Charles Beard, "consists of two parts (perhaps hopelessly confused): a statement of fact or facts (real or alleged) and an expression of opinions. Only the facts can be authenticated with more or less precision."[28] But, says Beard, *facts,* for all their solidity, are dead, uninvigorating things. "There is nothing in any fact or set of facts that commands anybody to cherish them or do anything about them. In other words, there is nothing 'constructive' in historiography as such. The facts of chemical compounds do not tell the chemist what to do about them."[29]

It is just here, on the painful edge between the intellectual acceptance of mere phenomenalism and the emotional rebellion against it, that MacLeish tells the story of *Conquistador*—fills it with things, nouns, physical details, and virtually no interpretive comment other than an atmosphere of lingering despair. Its subject is the beleaguered human memory making its way through a welter of untranslatable physical experience, attempting to engage the past. The action of the poem occurs in the mind of its narrator, Bernal Diaz, one of Cortez' soldiers who has survived and become a neglected old man, and who is now intent on telling the story of the conquest authoritatively, from the standpoint of an intimate participant. But as he tells his story, his authority proves frail, adulterated with nostalgia and a numbing sense of loss.

The poem has some formal characteristics of an epic, but more crucially it is an expansive dramatic monologue. Except for a brief introduction, we hear in it only the voice of Diaz, a narrator who is emphatically not the poet himself. Meaning here is only the projection of a fictive mind, a self-defining, self-limiting complex of impressions. Larger contexts are neither affirmed nor denied. In MacLeish's Prologue (by contrast to Benét's Invocation) there is no talk of capturing essences or rebuilding pasts; here the past is a dream-world, inaccessible to the living.

> Time done is dark as are sleep's thickets:
> Dark is the past: none waking walk there:
> Neither may live men of those waters drink.

Here it is as Becker says: "The reality of history has forever disappeared, and the 'facts' of history, whatever they once were, are only mental images which the historian makes in order to comprehend it."[30] To Diaz, MacLeish's narrator, his memories are fixed and clear and precious—

> Like a cock's jewels of gravel and worn thin
> With the sleepless caul of the heart and hard and clean
>
> (324)

But to the poet and his reader they are mere "wind-blown words," impressions of shadows or a dream:

> before the staring
> Eyes go shadows of that ancient time:
> So does a man speak from the dream that bears his
> Sleeping body with it and the cry
> Comes from a great way off as over water
>
> (262)

Conquistador has a plot of sorts. Although MacLeish admittedly tampers with historical chronology, he does give a generally sequential account of Cortez' invasion, with some indication of the struggles he had with Montezuma, with his political enemies back in Cuba and in Spain, and with his own mutinous soldiers. But MacLeish's narrative technique is consistently designed to obscure that plot. Diaz' story comes piecemeal, jerkily, one detail at a time—

> And we ate nothing or ill: we ate roots: and our
> Bellies were bitter for bread among those mountains:
> So did we follow the waters: and we stood
>
> The third day clear of the unequal ground:
> Rocks over: snow hard in the crevices:
> And the hawks were under us turning and far down
>
> (306)

Diaz' vision moves across the Mexican panorama near-sightedly; particular physical details come clear, but the larger perspectives which in more orthodox histories provide geographical, social and historical bearings are methodically blurred or destroyed. Little attention is paid to such matters as when the action occurs, exactly where, how many men are involved, what their long-range purposes are; such concerns are either ignored or merely hinted at. Diaz' language is calculatedly alien—

odd, stiff, artificial, often broken by ellipses which remind us that the voice comes to us raggedly "from a great way off, as over water." The language is Biblical in some ways, with its strictly simplified conjunctions; Anglo-Saxon in its alliteration ("And late light in the loft air," 339; "Sea ruffled with squalls: ships scattering," 288); laced with archaisms ("the fat brach that he was," 336; "a glibbed boar in a bucket," 336; "they were well wealed," 315). Grammatical constructions are conspicuously unidiomatic, with nouns and modifiers grouped or inverted in peculiar ways:

> And the house was smooth and of clean walls and so
> spacious
> And well made and with lime and the stone set there
> was
> Place for us all and the guns and our goods and our
> Indians
>
> (325)

Much of the poem is about fighting, or the memory of fighting, and Diaz hardly distinguishes one battle from another. The enemy is always just "they," the soldiers' greatest aim is just to stay alive, and the lingering memory is of how physically wearisome it all was, and what dogged endurance it called for.

MacLeish had two primary sources for the details of his narrative: the *Historia Verdadera de la Conquista de la Nueva España* by the soldier Bernal Diaz del Castillo, and a foot-and-mule-back trip MacLeish himself took along the trail of the conquistadores in 1929. The second is fully as crucial to the poem as the first. Even a perfunctory comparison between the *Historia Verdadera* and MacLeish's version makes clear the extent to which MacLeish has broken down psychic reality until any abstracting would have to be done by the reader himself. His Diaz emphasizes elemental sense impressions in a way almost totally foreign to the historical Diaz. Where the historical Diaz explains, for instance, "I remember that whenever we fired our guns, the Indians gave great shouts and whistles, and threw up straw and earth so that we could not see what harm we had done them,"[31] his observation becomes for MacLeish's Diaz one cryptic item in a rush of impressions:

> And they near in the sun; and they took it shouting:
> And they threw dust in the air: when the smoke lifted
> The dead were vanished from the bloody ground.
>
> (313)

The one interpretive thesis which MacLeish adds to the *Historia Verdadera* is one that might at first seem rather inappropriately romantic in this grim poem: the notion that the Spanish conquests were a manifestation of man's westering instinct. MacLeish takes for his epigraph Odysseus' speech from the *Inferno*:

> "O frati," disi, "che per cento milia
> Perigli siete giunti all' occidente"—

"'O brothers,' I said, 'who through a hundred thousand perils have reached the west . . .'" Several times the poem's Diaz speaks of feeling the mysterious pull of the west:

> But as for us that returned from that westward country—
> We could not lie in our towns for the sound of the sea:
> We could not rest at all in our thoughts: we were young then:
>
> We looked to the west
>
>   (270)

The one other figure in the poem with enough substance to be called a character, Cortez himself, also explains the conquest in terms of a romantic desire to reach the west. He claims his soldiers go westward driven not by greed nor religious fanaticism but by the lure of adventure. Unwilling to live peacefully in Old World houses "limed with the dottle of dead bones," they turned bravely to "the new world toward us in the west." (296)

Such a romantic conception seems anomalous in a tough-minded modern poem unless one recognizes its source: two men with manifest axes to grind, emotional and political—a captain trying to rouse enthusiasm for a faltering crusade, and an old man trying to recapture the grandeur of his youth:

> We were the first that found that famous country:
> We marched by a king's name: we crossed the sierras:
> Unknown hardships we suffered: hunger
>
> Death by the stone knife: thirst: we fared by the
> Bitter streams: we came at last to that water:
> Towers were steep upon the fluttering air:
>
> We were the lords of it all
>
>   (267)

The westering motif is thus an aspect of the poem's mood of mildly boastful elegy; it is to be understood not historically but dramatically, as the rhetoric of an anxious captain and a nostalgic old soldier.

Conquistador is history told in the only way MacLeish could tell it in 1930. He believed that the poet's was essentially a social function, not a private one. The poet, he says, is the myth-maker—the artisan who casts into durable form stories which embody his people's spiritual truths. In other ages, these truths might consist of fairly elaborate moral, religious and aesthetic propositions that generate strong narrative form—the sequence of prohibition, temptation, transgression and damnation in the story of Adam and Eve, say, or the sequence of the mysterious birth, ministry, death and resurrection of Christ. But in the twentieth century, MacLeish believed, the sweep of science had reduced these fundamental spiritual truths—"the common inner life of man," as he put it—to nothing more than "the simplest emotion." "And since it is the common spiritual experiences of men with which poetry must concern itself," he wrote, "poetry [has] suffered."[32] The only myth possible in such an age is one dealing with those simple emotions, in the most fundamental of sensuous terms.[33] Hence the poetic hero becomes someone like the simple, earthy Diaz, whose mind acts out the "common spiritual experiences of men with which poetry must concern itself"—little else than blank submission to emotion and sensation. Later in his career—from about 1950 onward—MacLeish's poetry becomes mythic in a more traditional sense: he adopts the story of Job in the drama *J. B.*, Greek legend in the plays *The Trojan Horse* and *Herakles,* the pastoralism of Eden in *Songs for Eve,* and, most recently, a bit of modern American folklore in *Scratch,* a dramatization of Benét's "The Devil and Daniel Webster." In such works, removing himself from the time-bound world, he effectively resigns his place in the debate over the meaning of history. But in the early 1930s, *Conquistador* was his heroic effort to find meaning in the uncertain past; to abide by the large strictures of positivism and yet at the same time to fulfill the social function of myth by creating an artistic center in which readers could shed individual identity in a shared inner experience.

Notes

1. For a convenient summary of the principles of scientific history, see W. Stull Holt, "Historical Scholarship," in *American Scholarship in the Twentieth Century,* ed. Merle Curti (Cambridge: Harvard Univ. Press, 1953), pp. 83-110.

2. Quoted by W. Stull Holt, *Historical Scholarship in the United States, and Other Essays* (Seattle: Univ. of Washington Press, 1967), p. 24.

3. *The Early Writings of Frederick Jackson Turner,* ed. Everett E. Edwards and Fulmer Mood (Madison, Wisc.: University of Wisconsin Press, 1938), p. 52.

4. *The New History* (New York: MacMillan, 1912), p. 24.

5. *Detachment and the Writing of History,* ed. Phil L. Snyder (Ithaca, N.Y.: Cornell Univ. Press, 1958), pp. 43-47.

6. "Written History as an Act of Faith," *American Historical Review,* 39 (1934), 222-24.

7. Arthur Murray Kay, "The Epic Intent and the American Dream: The Westering Theme in Modern American Narrative Poetry," Diss. Columbia 1959.

8. "The Irrepressible Conflict," *Nation,* 127 (Sept. 19, 1928), 274.

9. Preface to the 1941 edition of *John Brown's Body,* ed. Mabel A. Bessey (New York: Farrar and Rinehart, 1941), p. xxxiii.

10. Page references are to the 1929 edition of *John Brown's Body* (Garden City, N.Y.: Doubleday, Doran and Co., 1929), the most popular of the poem's many editions.

11. *Selected Poetry and Prose,* ed. Basil Davenport (New York: Rinehart, 1960), p. 333.

12. Preface to the 1929 edition, p. vi.

13. Quoted by Charles Fenton, *Stephen Vincent Benét, The Life and Times of an American Man of Letters (1898-1943)* New Haven: Yale Univ. Press, 1958), p. 182.

14. Preface to Bessey edition, p. xxxiii.

15. See, for example, Parry Stroud, *Stephen Vincent Benét,* Twayne's United States Authors Series (New York: Twayne, 1962), pp. 57-72; and Paul L. Wiley, "The Phaeton Symbol in *John Brown's Body,*" *American Literature,* 17 (November 1945), 231-42.

16. *Selected Poetry and Prose,* p. 333.

17. Quoted by Fenton, p. 184.

18. *Americans Interpret Their Civil War* (Princeton, N. J.: Princeton Univ. Press, 1954), pp. 187-88.

19. "The American Grain," *Poetry,* 48 (August 1936), 277.

20. Preface to Bessey edition, p. xxxiv.

21. Introduction to the 1929 edition, p. x.

22. "American Search," *Poetry,* 63 (December 1943), 161.

23. *A Continuing Journey* (Boston: Houghton Mifflin, 1968), p. 226.

24. *A Time to Speak* (Boston: Houghton Mifflin, 1940), p. 152.

25. *Time to Speak,* p. 155.

26. *Time to Speak,* p. 154.

27. Page references for MacLeish's verse are to *The Collected Poems* (Boston: Houghton Mifflin, 1962).

28. *The Discussion of Human Affairs* (New York: MacMillan, 1936), p. 122.

29. *Discussion of Human Affairs,* p. 120.

30. *Detachment and the Writing of History,* p. 11.

31. *The Bernal Diaz Chronicles,* ed. and trans. Albert Idell (Garden City, N.Y.: Doubleday and Co., 1956), pp. 75-76.

32. *Time to Speak,* p. 153.

33. A related kind of poetry is that written *about* myth, or the failure of myth. Like Eliot, Joyce, Pound and others, MacLeish attempted this, in the highly Eliotic *The Pot of Earth,* 1925.

Eugene Wiggins (essay date September 1975)

SOURCE: Wiggins, Eugene. "Benét's 'Mountain Whippoorwill': Folklore atop Folklore." *Tennessee Folklore Society Bulletin* 41, no. 3 (September 1975): 99-114.

[*In the following essay, Wiggins examines "The Mountain Whippoorwill" within the context of American mountain fiddling and fiddler's contests.*]

I have been an admirer of Fiddlin' John Carson for over half a century. At the age of three I ran ecstatically up and down a bank behind my home when his early records were being played. (His "early" records were made when he was an old man, but people were just beginning to record such old men.) A few years later the spring on the phonograph had broken, and I was forced to stay put and turn the records with my finger. By then I had read Stephen Vincent Benét's poem subtitled **"How Hill-Billy Jim Won the Great Fiddlers' Prize."** Parts of it seemed so much in keeping with the general flavor of Fiddlin' John's music and lyrics that I wondered if some lines hadn't been stolen from songs of John I hadn't yet heard. Since then I have accumulated tapes of nearly all of John's recordings and now have no such suspicions.

By now, my estimate of both John and Benét has changed. In the case of John, my admiration for the music has been greatly diluted. Moments of amusement come oftener than moments of exhilaration, though those still come, too. My love for the *person* has grown. He was really a *hell* of an old fellow.

In the case of Benét the admiration is less, too. I see that he did not always follow Wordsworth's admonition about keeping the eye on the object. But the poem mentioned still attracts some attention, and I think it may be worthwhile to demonstrate that it shows a surprising knowledge of the folklore of mountain fiddling and of the nature of the lyrics which accompany fiddle tunes—a knowledge which shows itself fully only to one who has absorbed Fiddlin' John and his kind.

It also turns out that the poem probably has a direct connection with John, even though Benét did not, as I suspected as a child, steal from him. The poem seems to have been suggested by an account of John's defeat in a fiddlers' contest by Lowe Stokes.[1] [News stories are shown on pp. 113-14.]

This paper, then, will examine the poem in the context of fiddling and fiddlers' contests, with special reference to that contest which Benét probably read about in the *Literary Digest* before he wrote the poem. I shall bring in some things Benét probably did not know because I think they illustrate standard components of the sort of myth he was re-creating in the poem. I shall mention some things he almost certainly did not know, because I think there is some insight to be gained about the general workings of literature when we compare an author's guesses with the documents. I say "the documents" and not "the reality" because the reality about a fiddlers' contest a half century past is almost as elusive as Plato's true bed. Benét's poem might be considered a top stratum of what he calls "romance," suggesting that he did not see it as bed-rock realism and that he associated it with other "romantic" literature, probably literature in the "local-color" area. The account in the *Literary Digest* is a lower stratum of conventional folk belief mixed with gravels that must be fact. In the *Atlanta Journal* pieces about fiddlers' contests and their participants there is a stratum with more gravel of fact, but there is folklore there too, mainly recognizable as such by way of "good story" contradictions between various pieces. There is another stratum still in what I have been able to glean from those who remember Carson and Stokes.[2] I suppose it has more gravel of fact in it than the *Atlanta Journal* stratum, though a greater *in*accuracy about one sort of thing is combined with greater accuracy about another. I fear that I am sounding as if fact is better than folklore. For the Benét student it is not. We can believe far more easily that Benét knew material analogous to the folklore than that he knew many facts about the contest concerned or the persons in it.

There are five reasons to think Benét had read about the Stokes-Carson contest in the *New York Times* or (more likely) in the *Literary Digest*. The *Digest* article[3] is little more than a reprint of the *Times* editorial.

1. The *Times* and *Digest* stress the surprising victory of a notably rustic and notably young fiddler over old fiddlers and especially over one outstanding old fiddler. This is Benét's story.

2. They mention that both Stokes and Carson played "Hell Broke Loose in Georgia." Any evidence which can be had suggests that this was not a well-known tune title, which increases the probability that Benét, who makes this title a commanding motif in the poem, got the title from the printed source. Recordings in the 1920s under this title are few, and only two that I know of are performances of the same melody.[4] It is true that collectors find different melodies for rather widely known titles, but the tendency is what one would expect it to be. The records that Carson and Stokes (as a member of Gid Tanner's Skillet Lickers) made under this title do not contain the same melody. Carson's melody fits rather poorly the words of Benét's poem presumably supposed to be words to "Hell Broke Loose in Georgia" and Stokes' melody does not fit them at all. My conjecture is that the Carson-"Hawkins" melody of Benét's poem is the older and that the title goes back to the days of the gold rush in Georgia in the 1830s.[5] Should this be true, the title is old enough to have been well known, but I do not think it was.

3. Benét implied in a comment on the poem that his most vivid memories of mountain fiddlers were of fiddlers in North Carolina.[6] Why did he not use a North Carolina setting? Possibly because he had heard some fiddling while he lived in Augusta, possibly because he had lived in Georgia when the same age as his protagonist (whose age is not given but who is a child), but very likely because he recently had been informed or reminded that the big contest was in Georgia.

4. The *Times—Digest* account seems to have the misconception (though the wording does not leave one sure) that Stokes played an exceedingly long time as part of the contest.

> Endurance may have been a factor in winning the fiddler's crown for Stokes. He was twenty-two and Fiddlin' John was sixty-seven. After Stokes had played all day and long after midnight he announced that, "We play till milking time in Cartersville and the cows leave home." He started all over again with his Blue Ridge repertoire that had set the mountain folks dancing and his crowd stayed with him, "patting," "spanking," and cheering to the last. Youth for once won. Stokes is the youngest man to hold the championship.[7]

Fiddlers played only a few minutes each during the contest part of a convention, though there was a lot of fiddling before and after. One would prefer to think the author of this passage knew this, for he is wrong on enough counts at best. John was not sixty-seven but fifty-six. Cartersville was not any mountain hamlet; and while Stokes may be correctly quoted, if so, he was playing rube deliberately. The mistake about John's age is surely clerical, but it is in accord with the folk belief manifested throughout the piece that normally only very old fiddlers are good. That Stokes played all night is likely enough. The probability is that a good many people at the convention did so, though not without pause, and definitely not as part of the contest. Benét's Jim plays all night as part of the contest, which is the least realistic thing in the poem, but it seems right there. We do not leave reality as completely in this poem as in most tall tales about folk heroes, but we get something of the same effect. Benét surely doubted the truth of the *Digest* story on this point, or doubted that it really meant to say what it appears to, but he well may have found the idea for one of his best effects in someone else's ignorance or verbal fuzziness.

5. The lapse of time between the *Digest* article (December, 1924) and the publication of the poem (March, 1925) is a reasonable one for the belief that Benét got his idea from the article.

Let us postpone a direct examination of the poem long enough to look at what sources closer to Stokes and Carson say about them. We do not find much about Stokes in the *Atlanta Journal,* but a more urbane person is suggested there than is suggested in the *Digest.* We find that Stokes had played on WSB, Atlanta, on a number of occasions with a band called the Hometown Boys, in which "Mr. W. C. McMichen" was "leader and first violinist" and Stokes was "violinist."[8] The personnel shifted constantly (there was no pay). McMichen came and went and so did Stokes. At one time in 1923 the following was reported of Stokes, Riley Puckett, and Ted Hawkins.

> The three combine modern jazz with oldtime tunes in a way that makes them one of the most desirable entertainment outfits in the field.[9]

One who knew only what he got from early notices in the *Journal* would not suspect that this band eventually would flaunt its rusticity with the name Skillet Lickers, or even that it would be considered mainly a *country* band.

Lowe Stokes, then, is Benét's Hill-billy Jim only to the extent that he was young enough that some could think he was surprisingly young, and to the extent that he was a winning fiddler. What of Carson? The pickings are very different there. Nearly everything in Benét's poem concerning both winner and loser is paralleled by those facts or myths about Carson that were emphasized by Carson's admirers. It is doubtful that Benét knew anything more about Carson than what he probably read in the *Digest,* but the way he has restated what John's admirers liked to think about John is remarkable. Of course, John's admirers, especially by way of selection and emphasis, were thrusting John into folk hero molds known to them and known (much more consciously) by Benét. For instance, *The Little Shepherd of Kingdom Come* by John Fox, Jr., has parallels to the Hill-billy Jim story and the Carson story as revealed in pieces in the *Atlanta Journal.* This novel was so widely known that it almost certainly would have been known to Benét, to Carson's "press," and even to some of Carson's admirers. In all three cases there is a young mountain boy separated from any family who is a marvelous natural performer on an instrument (a banjo in Fox). In all three cases the Marvelous Child enters an alien environment and amazes people there. We wonder about Benét's line "Listen to my fiddle— Kingdom Come—Kingdom Come!" Is it onomatopoeia for fiddling as "Jug o' rum" is for frogs in the next line? Is it supposed to suggest exaltation? Is he putting in a fiddle tune title as he does elsewhere?[10] Was Fox's title somewhere in his mind?

John Carson was born in the mountains of Georgia in 1868, a generation after Fox's imaginary child prodigy. Fannin County then would have been little less isolated than a slightly earlier Kingdom Come, Kentucky. According to one story, John began to fiddle at five and turned professional at six, when he was given a dime and a stick of candy to play to a posse of revenuers long enough for the neighbors to hide their still.[11] According to another he was given his grandfather's fiddle on his tenth birthday and learned to play on the way home.[12] John's descent from the mountains is not clearly dated in one of the articles about him, but the implication is that it was not long after he was ten. The article continues,

> One day this barefoot boy was standing on a corner of a Tennessee town, playing his heart away, thinking of his far-away home and translating his thoughts into music. A big man, looking like one of those old southern planters, stood awhile listening.
>
> "What's your name?" the man asked.
>
> "John Carson," answered the boy.
>
> "It's Fiddlin' John from now on," said the man. . . .[13]

The man turns out to be Fiddlin' Bob Taylor, later governor of Tennessee. The use of the "barefoot boy" and "southern planter" stereotypes within this brief scope suggests that the writer wanted readers to see John in terms of things they had read before. The "far-away home" is another situation cliché—many popular songs of this period were about wanting to go 'way back to somewhere. Another source[14] says that the Tennessee town was Copperhill, which is about twenty miles from where John lived, but it is always good to get your sad protagonist farther away than that. In some versions of the encounter-with-Taylor story, Fiddlin' Bob buys the freshly-dubbed Fiddlin' John "his first suit of store-bought clothes."[15] Then, presumably, John could say with Benét's Jim,

> . . . I'm Hell broke loose in a new store shirt
> To fiddle all Georgia crazy.

John is quoted as saying he won the contest in Atlanta for the first time in 1899. His confession is,

> I was in Atlanta, in a little trouble over some whisky, when they had the contest. The sheriff got me out of jail to play, and when I won the first prize, he gave me some time off.[16]

We get two different accounts of the contest between Fiddlin' John and Governor Taylor. Each is more like Benét's story in some ways than is the other. According to the *Atlanta Journal,*

> It was in an old-timers' fiddling contest in Memphis. John and Bob both were there. Both played for the prize. The judges gave it to Bob, who was then the governor of the state.

Stepping to the front of the platform, Fiddlin' Bob, in a touching speech, told the audience that he believed the judges had given him the prize only because he was the governor. He said he could never hope to play like Fiddlin' John, and he resigned the prize in the latter's favor.[17]

According to the *Radio Digest,*

"Fiddlin' Bob," as he was popularly known, was recognized for his skill with the fiddle, and few had ever been found who were near enough his equal to make a competition interesting.

But on this momentous occasion, a new adversary was discovered. A hardy mountaineer was entered in the contest, who was the pride and hope of his friends who had come along with him to lend any moral support they could. The contest went on and it was a thrilling battle between the two favorites—Gov. Bob Taylor, and the unknown mountaineer. Then the finish and young Carson was declared winner and thereafter became known as Fiddlin' John, while Governor Taylor was so delighted with the young fellow's playing that right there on the spot, he bestowed his fiddle on the proud victor.[18]

Compare with this the close of Benét's story:

. . . I went to congratulate old man Dan,
—But he put his fiddle into my han'. . . .

Note also that John's youth is implicitly exaggerated here as his age was flatly exaggerated in the piece in the *Literary Digest* about his defeat by Stokes. Surely, as far as fiddling enthusiasts were concerned, the above story exaggerates his obscurity. "How Young Obscure Defeated Old Famous" is a popular story in which John eventually played both parts. Items in the *Atlanta Journal* cast him in different and contradictory roles during the rather brief period of his radio and recording popularity. In one he is just out of Fannin County and in another he has traveled widely; in one he plays only ancient songs and in another writes them all himself. The Cinderella motif appears: John hardly knows what to do with his wealth. Ed Kincaid, who played in his band, remembers no such problem. He remembers, instead, how the band came to a toll bridge and had to stop and play up the twenty cents toll. There was a sort of transformation in John's life, no doubt, and one journalist found a pair of pictures that transcend the usual pap as well as perhaps topping Charles Perrault and Horatio Alger and Stephen Vincent Benét. One shows a middle-aged man with a fiddle walking his way from Blue Ridge to the contest in Atlanta, over roads so muddy that he is carrying his shoes in his pocket. The other shows him fifteen years later, after the recordings, riding to the contest—nervous and much less happy—in an airplane.[19]

With this much indication of what things were like and what people wished to think they were like, let us take a closer look at Benét's poem. After some ten couplets in which the protagonist-narrator, Jim, describes himself and the mountains, he says,

Essex County has a mighty pretty fair,
All the smarty fiddlers from the South come there.

Despite the fact that there is no Essex county in Georgia, Benét has done just what he might have done with the very fullest knowledge of his background. He wanted a big victory for Jim, and yet he did not want to picture an auditorium in Atlanta. He wanted us to imagine (though it is true he does not describe it) the more bucolic, open-air setting that smaller fiddlers' contests had. It is true that the county seat of Essex County (whatever it may be) "wears man's smudge." There is tobacco spitting and fiddle tuning and even inept fiddlers. Things do not have the perfection and Blakean grandeur of the mountains. Still it isn't an auditorium in Atlanta. But we must have a big victory and a big prize for Jim. It is interesting to note that in a poem which has as its second title **"How Hill-billy Jim Won the Great Fiddlers' Prize"** we never learn what the prize was. The usual prize in the big one was a hundred dollar fiddle contributed by the Cable Piano Company. This would hardly do. A hundred dollars might, if it were a gold piece, but we don't really like it. Prizes for the smaller contests were cash prizes that would have seemed insignificant to Benét's readers or were things some merchant was willing to contribute, things that might be *too* picturesque. For instance, in a Copperhill contest one John Goolsby won a cash prize (amount not stated) for fiddling, "a bucket of lard for the largest family, and a lantern on his looks."[20] I suspect Benét dodges the prize for the same reasons he fictionalizes the setting—he wanted a big victory in a more idyllic setting than he thought the facts would give him.

The main "man to beat" for Jim is

Old Dan Wheeling, with his whiskers in his ears,
King-pin fiddler for nearly twenty years

If Benét was working from the story in the *Literary Digest,* this is his guess at the appearance of John Carson, whose appearance is not described there. In fact John is the little clean-shaven man one sees among the goatish figures in pictures taken at old fiddlers' conventions. But Benét is correct on the tendency toward hairiness. He may be a little lazy in characterizing the other two main contenders, Big Tom Sargent and Little Jimmy Weezer. The names show a facile contrast. If it were only names we wanted, we would turn to the *Atlanta Journal,* which gives us Laughing Gid Tanner, Red Neck Jim Lawson, Three-fingered Pop Tucker, and Wild Bill Thompson the Bee Man,

All sittin' roun' spittin high an' struttin' proud,
(Listen, little whippoorwill, yuh better bug yore eyes!)

Tun-atun-a-tunin' while the jedges told the crowd
Them that got the mostest claps 'd win the bestest
  prize.
Everybody waitin' for the first tweedle-dee,
When in comes a-stumblin-—hill-billy me!

There is no way to prove it, but I suspect that "hill-billy" was exactly the right word back in 1925. It was less common then than later. It was derogatory to a mild yet ill-defined extent. It was just about to become a generic term for a type of music, but this had not yet happened.

  Jim plunks down his dollar entry fee with

                    "There's my callin' card!
  An' anyone that licks me—well, he's got to fiddle
    hard!"

This is interesting. A certain shyness and modesty would not seem a poorer guess to many people. Folk music collectors find many people declaring they cannot play at all and then playing well. But there is evidence that the public liked a boastfulness in contest fiddlers, and fiddlers' contests were almost as much popularity contests as they were what they claimed to be. (This is one reason old men *did* tend to win—they had had time to make a lot of friends.) The main memory one informant has of a contest Carson won is of his loud and multiple-negative introduction of himself—"This is old John Carson from Fannin County, and nobody never taught old John nothin'!"[21] One of John's recordings[22] has him competing against another fiddler and each making a boasting speech before playing. John's speech—"I'm the best fiddler ever jerked the hairs of a hoss' tail across the belly of a cat"—probably is not meant to have the seriousness of Beowulf or Achilles or even that of the "ring-tailed roarers" of folklore. Still, whether he got the idea from hero literature or from some knowledge of fiddlers' contests, Benét is on solid ground in having his Jim boast.

Big Tom plays and the acclaim is great, but Jim does not seem to be worried by him. Little Jimmy plays, also winning great applause, and again Jim does not seem to be worried.

  Then came the ruck of the bob-tailed fiddlers,
  The let's-go-easies, the fair-to-middlers.

  They got their claps an' they lost their bicker,
  And settled back for some more corn-licker.

The vinous nature of fiddlers is a tradition well known and never denied by Georgia fiddlers of the 1920s, who picture themselves as moonshiners, bootleggers and sots in practically *all* the dramatic skits they recorded. The first pay accorded American folk music on radio, according to Ed Kincaid, was that the performers got to "slip back in the control room and drink them radio

fellers' whiskey." John and his frequently changing retinue were usually listed on the printed program in the *Atlanta Journal* as "Fiddlin' John Carson and his Cronies." This probably was regarded as a jocular listing by some people, but the men in the control room must have marvelled at its accuracy. So must have some people on Decatur Street, the street of the bootleggers, who would swap a pint or even a quart for a few tunes. "We never bought no whiskey," Kincaid remembers, "but we got our part."

Old Dan Wheeling begins to fiddle, and Jim sees that this one will be hard to beat.

  He fiddled high and he fiddled low
  (Listen, little whippoorwill: yuh got to spread yore
    wings!)
  He fiddled with a cherrywood bow.
  (Old Dan Wheeling's got bee-honey in his strings.)

The first impression may be that the "cherrywood bow" is poor. Whether or not he is aware that good bows are not made of cherry, the reader may ask, "Why is the kind of wood important?" Benét's intent probably is for a sort of synesthesia associating the music with the beauty of the cherry tree and the sweetness of the cherry fruit, possibly even making the cherry a symbol of lips and love as in some folksongs and in the "Cherry Ripe" songs of the Renaissance. The next line employs the same technique but may be better, in that one sees immediately what is being done.

Somewhat the same technique was being used, I think, in Benét's comment on the poem: "I was trying to . . . get the note of the boxwood fiddle into it."[23] A boxwood fiddle would be even less feasible than a cherrywood bow. Along with the same sort of synesthesia, I believe Benét was thinking about a poem by William Ernest Henley which is short enough to quote in full and which may throw some light on the total intent of the poem.

  The nightingale has a lyre of gold,
    The lark's in a clarion call;
  And the blackbird plays on a boxwood flute,
    But I love him the best of all.

  For his song is all of the joy of life,
    And we in the mad spring weather,
  We two have listened till he sang
    our hearts and lips together.[24]

Henley is aware that the song of the blackbird has been praised less frequently than has the song of the nightingale or the song of the lark, as Benét is aware that mountain fiddling has been praised less frequently than have many other types of music. But the blackbird and the fiddler have their own charm, and it is a charm furthered by *association*. When Old Dan Wheeling has finished, and the applause has been so great that there is no attempt to describe it except by saying "the crowd cut loose," Jim is momentarily distressed about his chances, but putting his fiddle to his shoulder and imagining himself back in the mountains helps a great deal. Then, before he begins to fiddle, he thinks about this associational evocative quality I am talking about.

> They've fiddled the rose an' they've fiddled the thorn,
> But they haven't fiddled the mountain-corn.
>
> They've fiddled sinful an' fiddled moral,
> But they haven't fiddled the breshwood laurel.
>
> They've fiddled loud and they've fiddled still,
> But they haven't fiddled the whippoorwill.

I do not see Old Dan's giving his fiddle to Jim at the end mainly as a way of trying to say, "Your rhythm, intonation, timbre, etc., are better than mine." I see him as trying to say, "I too know about the mountain corn and the breshwood laurel and the whippoorwill, and you will be able to evoke these things when I am gone." Then when the noise of the crowd begins, I see that, too, as a paeon to the mountain *experience*. I see the whole poem mainly as paeon to that experience.

When Benét has Jim actually start playing, the tone is markedly less elevated. It is as if Benét were aware that for many people mountain fiddling is just "dump-diddle dump" and does not evoke those things Jim has said he means to evoke.

> I started off with a dump-diddle dump
> (Oh, Hell's broke loose in Georgia!)
> Skunk-cabbage growin' by the bee-gum stump
> (Whippoorwill, yo're singin' now!)
>
> Oh, Georgia booze is mighty fine booze,
> The best yuh ever poured yuh,
> But it eats the soles right offen yore shoes,
> For Hell's broke loose in Georgia.

Even if we think of this as Essex County booze, and not as Decatur Street booze, the tone is rather low. I believe Benét, in the last four lines quoted, has aimed at what Walter Scott tried with ballads—a *passable* imitation. I think he has succeeded. Had he never written these lines and had I heard them for the first time on a Carson recording, I should not have thought them at all atypical. That they do not fit very well any melody I know called "Hell Broke Loose in Georgia" means little. They might fit one I don't know.

It is the latter part of the passage representing Jim's playing that gives most evidence of specific knowledge of folk material. It has less logical connection than the rest of the poem has, being pretty much a potpourri of disjointed phrases and sentence fragments. Such actually is the nature of many fiddle tune lyrics and of the fill-in phrases in square dance calling which come between the phrases that tell the dancers to do something.

Certain linguistic structures are common in the real thing, and Benét knew them. The smallest of these structures is the fiddle tune title pattern that goes noun—*in* or *on*—*the*—noun. Some of the better known tune titles that follow this pattern are "Turkey in the Straw," "Sugar in the Gourd," "Fire in [or *on*] the Mountain [or *Mountains,* as in the poem]," "Billy in the Lowground," "Paddy on the Turnpike," "Jenny on the Railroad," and "Rabbit in the Pea-patch." Sometimes prepositions other than *in* or *on* occur, as in "Hell among the Yearlings." "Natchez under the Hill" perhaps should not be included as the whole title can be thought of as a place name; but the recording which gave it as "Rat Cheese under the Hill"[25] gives us a lot *more* to think about. Benét gives "Turkey in the Straw" as the tune played by Tom Sargent. "Rabbit in the pea-patch" and "fire on the mountains" are phrases in the phrase potpourri, along with phrases such as "snakes in the grass" and "possum in the pot" which sound like tune titles and may be, but not to my knowledge. Obviously Benét would have preferred to create similar phrases for the most part, no matter how many actual titles he may have known.

A slight enlargement of this linguistic structure used in the titles gives us a sort of sentence fragment common in fiddle tune lyrics. We add adjectives and perhaps a verbal, but no predicate. Content-wise we usually are talking about the goodies of life, and sense a predicate in the understood phrase "consider the delights of." For instance Fiddlin' John:

> Whiskey by the gallon,
> Sugar by the pound,
> A great big bowl to put it in,
> And a spoon to stir it around.[26]

A song by Uncle Dave Macon has some predicates in the song as a whole but none in the stanzas below:

> Cattle in the pasture, hogs in the pen,
> Sheep on the ranch and wheat in the bin.
>
> Corn in the crib and poultry in the yard,
> Meat in the smokehouse and a big can of lard.
>
> Fruit in the cellar and cheese on the board,
> A big sack of coffee and sugar in the gourd.
>
> Hosses in the stable and money in the pocket,
> A baby in the cradle and a pretty woman to rock it.[27]

We have this sort of thing most purely in Benét, if we consider the grammar and the level of elevation both, in such lines as "Flapjacks flippin' on a red-hot griddle" part of Jim's playing. However, there is a tendency to substitute verbals for verbs throughout the poem. It begins in the opening couplets.

> Up in the mountains, it's lonesome all the time,
> (Sof' win' a slewin' thu' the sweet-potato vine).

Up in the mountains, it's lonesome for a child.
(Whippoorwills a-callin' when the sap runs wild).

If I were to digress from my main purpose it would be to offer the first of the above couplets as an example of what I meant early in this paper about Benét's not always keeping the eye on the object. Sweet potato vines hug the ground, and it is hard for me to believe that the wind slewing through them could be impressive, except to a potato bug. There seems to be too many apostrophes, too, and who *does* pronounce the *gh* in *through*?

To return to my purpose, let me say that one of the couplets used to represent Jim's playing uses a folk formula that has no name, as far as I know. It could be called the "sudden sittin' calamity formula." Benét's couplet goes,

Jonah sittin on a hickory bough,
Up jumps a whale—an' where's yore prophet now?

Whatever we call the formula, obviously this is like a verse in a folksong collected by Burl Ives.

Jaybird sittin' on a hickory limb,
Singing out his soul,
Along there came a big black snake
And swallowed that poor boy whole.[28]

And it is like a verse done by Lowe Stokes' partner Clayton McMichen.

Grasshopper sittin' on a sweet-potato vine (three times)
Along came a chicken and said, "He's mine!"[29]

There was a song of considerable popularity at the time Benét wrote his poem, "It Ain't Gonna Rain No More," which tended to accumulate such sudden sitting calamities. It was copyrighted in 1923 by Wendell Hall, The Red-Headed Music Maker, but it is an older song. One of Hall's verses:

Bullfrog sittin' on a lily pad,
Lookin' at the skies;
The lily pad broke and the frog fell in,
Got water in his eyes.[30]

My own childhood memories furnish another verse of this song which went,

A peanut sittin' on the railroad track;
His heart was all a-flutter;
Along came a train—choo, choo, choo—
Bam! Bam! peanut butter.

The couplet about Jonah is Benét's loudest echo of actual folk *words*. Knowing the likely structures, the likely tone, and the likely subject matter, he was easily able to furnish the words himself. One might wonder,

however, if the *whippoorwill* and the *hillbilly* of his titles owe anything to Uncle Dave Macon. Six months before the appearance of the *Digest* article about Stokes and Carson, Uncle Dave had recorded a "Hill Billie Blues." (The spelling reminds us that the word was not yet common.) The opening lines were,

I am a billie and I live in the hills;
I can whistle and sing like a whippoorwill.[31]

In evaluating the possibility of such influence, we should remember that Benét was not required to write on hillbilly music. He chose his subject over all others and chose to treat it with a realism which suggests that he knew the real thing and liked it.

There is a final comment which may be of interest to any whose partisanship has been aroused by the Carson-Stokes background. John did not, like Dan in the poem, give the victor his fiddle. Ed Kincaid remembers that "John got so mad he like to busted."

I'm still a little angry myself. Lowe was a far more polished fiddler, but it is John who reminds me of the mountain corn, and the brushwood laurel, and the whippoorwill.

Notes

1. That Benét was influenced by a brief report of this contest has been suggested by two fiddling enthusiasts in places known to other fiddling enthusiasts (a record jacket and a fiddlers' magazine) but not likely to be seen by many students of poetry. There has been no consideration of what Benét knew about fiddling beyond what he may have gotten from this brief and inaccurate report, or of the way he used that knowledge. The record jacket statement (County 526) is itself inaccurate as to the date of the contest, and the magazine note (*The Devil's Box,* September, 1969) leaves uncorrected the report's exaggeration of Carson's age, an exaggeration that is in accord with the sort of mythologizing I intend to consider. Within the scope of its few lines and its limited intent—mainly to show notice of fiddlers by a poet—the magazine note is good, however.

2. A major informat is Ed Kincaid of Morganton, Georgia, who played with Carson. I was directed to him by Kathie Thompson of Epworth, Georgia, who also directed me to other informants such as Dan Westmoreland and Lawrence Stanley, both of Ellijay, Georgia. Throughout my research, I have been more concerned with the Carson myth than with *facts* about him.

3. "The Fiddlin' Champion Receives His Crown," *Literary Digest,* LXXXIII (December 6, 1924), 70-71.

4. "Uncle Jim Hawkins" recorded the same melody that Carson recorded on Challenge 101. This record was vended by Sears, Roebuck, which probably caused the title to be better known than ever before, but not until after Benét's poem. According to Harlan Daniel, "Who Was Who? An Index of Hill Country Recording Pseudonyms," in *The American Folk Music Occasional* (New York: Oak, 1970), p. 66, Uncle Jim Hawkins would be William B. Houchens. However, he sounds more like Doc Roberts.

5. The very tenuous evidence for this conjecture (but nothing more than a conjecture is likely ever to appear—or any less tenuous evidence) is as follows. A Carson record entitled "Hell Bound for Alabama" (Okeh 45159, reissued on County 525) has the same melody as his "Hell Broke Loose in Georgia" (Okeh 45018). The later recording is wordless, but the former begins with the words

>Ain't no hell in Georgia
>Hell broke loose in Georgia

This flat contradiction occurs also in a song called "Hell Broke Loose in Georgia" (different melody) collected from Bascom Lamar Lunsford and printed in *The Frank C. Brown Collection of North Carolina Folklore.* Luke Highnight recorded a wordless melody (different from any mentioned) under the title "There's No Hell in Georgia" (Vocalion 5325). Such argument over Georgia's climate (or morality, or suffering, or whatever) is diffuse and thus probably old. On the record of "Hell Bound for Alabama" John seems to sing, "Never seen mutton in the old tin pan. . . ." It seems to make more sense as a gold-panner complaint, "Never seen *nothin'*. . . ." Admittedly *mutton* makes more sense, and the logic of the rest of the song is not really Aquinian. Some people cannot understand John at all. His teeth seem to have been poor, he seems to have preferred not to record cold sober, he rolled a large ball of candy around in his mouth as he sang, and he was from Fannin County. I think he says *mutton* but suspect the original was *nothin'.*

Another reason for thinking the title may date to gold rush times in Georgia is the "little Indian goes Georgie" in the Lunsford version (*The Frank C. Brown Collection of North Carolina Folklore,* V, 497). I can make no sense of it at all except by taking the *goes* to mean *exclaims,* a guess in itself, and by relating it to the desire of the Cherokees to stay on the gold land and the desire of the whites to get them off. Any theory dating this title, of course, is weakened by the multiplicity of times in Georgia's past when hell might have been said to break loose there.

6. Charles Fenton, *Stephen Vincent Benét* (New Haven: Yale University Press, 1960), p. 148.

7. "The Fiddlin' Champion Receives His Crown," 71.

8. *Atlanta Journal,* October 8, 1922, p. 11.

9. Ibid., June 17, 1923, p. 10.

10. The melody to Henry Clay Works' Civil War satire "Kingdom Coming" ("Year of Jubilo") makes a fair fiddle tune and probably has been played as such under that title. I have heard it fiddled under other titles.

11. *Atlanta Journal,* September 2, 1924, p. 7.

12. Rebecca Franklin, "Fiddlin' John's Been At It for 71 Years," *Atlanta Journal,* June 5, 1949. Reprinted in *Old Time Music* (Summer, 1971), p. 20.

13. Bert Collier, "Fiddlin' John on Broadway," *Atlanta Journal Magazine* (February 10, 1924), p. 1.

14. A song folio "Dixie's Champion of Champions," inside cover, P. C. Brockman published a good deal of John's material and a good deal of material under his name that he probably never performed, certainly not in arrangements such as were presented on paper.

15. *Atlanta Journal,* October 21, 1923, section B, p. 8. The clothes are also in the song folio mentioned just above.

16. Bert Collier, p. 1.

17. Ibid.

18. *Radio Digest,* November 7, 1925. Reprinted in Mark Wilson's pamphlet of liner notes for "The Old Hen Cackled and Rooster's Going to Crow," Rounder Records 1003.

19. Elinor Hillyer, "Fiddlin John Flies Home," *Atlanta Journal Magazine* (October 13, 1929).

20. George Gordon Ward, *The Annals of Upper Georgia Centered in Gilmer County,* 1965, p. 661. The "looks" probably were supposed to be unusually poor rather than unusually good, at least nominally. "Ugliest man" contests, really a sort of popularity contest, once were common in this section. The Atlanta fiddlers' convention with which we are concerned sometimes had a fifty-dollar fiddle for the "ugliest fiddler."

21. Mr. Lawrence Stanley.

22. "Who's the Best Fiddler?" Okeh 45448.

23. Quoted in Fenton, p. 148.

24. "To A.D.," in many anthologies.

25. Brunswick 458.

26. "Gonna Swing on the Golden Gate," Rounder 1003.

27. "Grey Cat on the Tennessee Farm," County 521.

28. "Saturday Night," Decca Album A-407.

29. "Soldier's Joy," County 506.

30. Victor 19171-A.

31. Vocalion B 14904, dated in Ralph Rinzler and Norm Cohen, *Uncle Dave Macon: A Bio-Discography,* JEMF Special Series No. 3.

Jared Lobdell (essay date 2003)

SOURCE: Lobdell, Jared. "123 College Street: Stephen Vincent Benét and the Development of an Historical Poetry for America." In *Stephen Vincent Benét: Essays on His Life and Work,* edited by David Garrett Izzo and Lincoln Konkle, pp. 107-27. Jefferson, N.C.: McFarland & Company, Inc., 2003.

[*In the following essay, Lobdell discusses the influence of Benét's Yale years on his development as a poet.*]

In those days, the address of the Elizabethan Club was 123 College Street, in a house built in 1804 on a block off the New Haven Green. The house is still there, still in the same place on College Street, but the number is now 459.

Back in 1894-95, Yale Professor William Lyon Phelps taught his first undergraduate course on Elizabethan drama. Among his students in that class was an apparently unremarkable junior named Alexander Smith Cochran, of the Yale Class of 1896, whose family owned a woolen mill in Yonkers. In 1906, Cochran wrote Billy Phelps from England, "saying that the course in Elizabethan Drama had awakened in him an acute interest in the literature of the period; that he had amused himself with collecting some rare books; and that in a few days he would send me his manuscript catalogue" (Phelps 292). Professor Phelps was "quite unprepared" for what followed, which was a catalogue of books worth (even in 1906) several hundred thousand dollars: "Shakespeare quartos, a copy of the first edition of the *Sonnets,* of Bacon's *Essays,* and so on."

The next year, Cochran wrote Phelps that he had a plan, that he was coming back to the United States, and that he wanted to discuss his plan with Phelps. Billy Phelps takes up the story:

> His plan was a good one. He wished to found at Yale an Elizabethan Club, because the one thing he had most missed at Yale was good conversation; that if

there were an undergraduate club, with a remarkable library as a nucleus, he thought students who loved literature and the arts would be glad to meet there, and talk informally and naturally about literature, both with their contemporaries and with congenial members of the Faculty. He would donate the club building, the library, and the endowment

[293]

He did, and not only that. By the time the Club opened in 1911, he had added more books to the collection, and at the great Huth sale in that year he bought all four Shakespeare folios, including (of course) the first—along with quite a number of other items. The club took off with "club nights" with distinguished guests, many of them English, in the years 1911-1914. Then it continued mostly bereft of its contacts with England through the war years, until 1919, when the English visitors streamed in once more—to meet an undergraduate population, some of whom had fought with the AEF in France, and some of whom were experimenting (at least in their minds) with the question of the American identity—no longer the Anglo-American identity, as with Henry James, or indeed with Alexander Smith Cochran.

To this club in the World War I years came a young undergraduate, Stephen Vincent Benét, born July 22, 1898, in Bethlehem, Pennsylvania, son of General (James) Walker Benét (b. 1857) and grandson of General Stephen Vincent Benét, sometime chief of ordnance, U.S. Army. (He was also brother of William Rose Benét, b. 1886, and nephew of Laurence Benét, 1863-1948, Yale 1884, and at this time commandant, American Ambulance and Hospital Service in France.) When Phelps wrote his autobiography, he remembered three undergraduates in particular from 1917-1918: "Three of my undergraduate students, who were in college at the same time, and intimate friends, have now [1939] become famous through creative literary work. The playwright, Philip Barry, 1918; the poet, Stephen Vincent Benét, 1919; the novelist Thornton Wilder, 1920" (661). But Barry graduated before the war was over, and there were others in the postwar group, Amos Niven Wilder (Thornton's older brother), Alfred Bellinger, and John Chipman Farrar (all three of them being among the first poets published in the Yale Series of Younger Poets)—and a nonpoet named Robert Coates, to whom we will return later. It is worthwhile to look at these other figures in this group, that we might call the Yale Renascence and that met at 123 College Street, and worthwhile to acknowledge poems written by those three of its less well-known figures, Bellinger (1893-1978), Farrar (1896-1974), and Amos Niven Wilder (1895-1993).

Alfred Bellinger taught classics and numismatics and history at Yale. He taught me the history of the later Roman Empire in graduate school in 1961-62, the year of his retirement. Chip Farrar founded the publishing house that still bears his name. My father was once his investment advisor, and he was by way of being a family acquaintance, though not a family friend. Amos Niven Wilder (son of Amos Parker Wilder) was a distinguished churchman whom I knew as the father of my friend at both Yale and Wisconsin, Amos Tappan Wilder, Yale 1962. The reason I mention the "nonliterary" ways I came to know these men is to suggest that in these years after World War I they were amateur writers, occasional writers, or scholarly writers, so that their eventual careers were in different (though related) areas: they wrote their poetry as part of the intellectual ferment of a sunshine age.

Bellinger's poem is a song from his collection *Spires and Poplars* (1920): "Bright as a single poppy in a field," is about the youthful joy of collegial bliss. Farrar's is another joyful song in classical meter from his *Forgotten Shrines* (1919): "Come to me, Pan, with your wind-wild laughter." (Compare Benét's dochmaics and other classical meters in his **"The First Vision of Helen"** noted in Basil Davenport, "Stephen Vincent Benét" in *Selected Works of Stephen Vincent Benét*, Vol. I, x).

I spoke of Amos Niven Wilder as a churchman: he was indeed a graduate of the Yale Divinity School (1924), a Congregationalist minister, editor of the *Journal of Religion,* president of the Society of Biblical Literature, and secretary to Albert Schweitzer. Perhaps "churchman" is an inadequate word. He was also the author of a long poem deriving from his experience in the First World War, *Battle-Retrospect* (1923), and a memoir of that experience, *Armageddon Revisited* (published after his death in 1993)—and a number of other books, some of them on the relationship of religion and poetry. Incidentally, he played tennis in the All-England Tournament of Wimbledon in 1922. In *Battle-Retrospect,* an initial bliss and joy give way to a terrible reality of a war in trenches. "That fluctuating roar, its rise and fall." There follows an extended Classical simile of a second-rate eighteenth-century variety: I, but probably no one else, am reminded of Akenside. But the point here is Wilder's translation of the experience of wartime France into the neo-Classical mode.

"And I have seen, or thought I saw, the gods." Once again, this is neo-Classical, and it may escape us that the imagery is that of the Angels of Mons or of Chesterton's "Ballad of St. Barbara." Now that is not to say that Wilder's poem is better than Chesterton's or better than Arthur Machen's story, but it is to say that Wilder has made a poet's attempt to recollect in tranquillity and form the recollection in a Classical mode: in that sense this is more a poem, more a made thing, and Wilder more a *makar,* more a conscious poet, than Chesterton or Machen. This is similar to what Bellinger did

with his poppy (already a World War I image), or Farrar did in general in his *Forgotten Shrines.*

Here is what the historian of the Yale Younger Poets series, George Bradley, says about these poets in his introduction to *The Yale Younger Poets Anthology.* He begins by quoting a comment by C. M. Lewis, the Classicist who was the editor of the Yale Series of Younger Poets from 1918 to 1923: the comment is from Lewis's introduction to *A Book of Verse of the Great War* (New Haven, 1917), and we will see its importance to our consideration of Benét and his historical poetry for America. "A critical curse lies upon the poetry of patriotism and war. The passion of patriotism is common to all right-minded men, and Criticism wants the uncommon. . . . The poet whose sole aim is to rekindle . . . old ardors will be fortunate if he escape the ninety-nine ways of banality; and even the hundredth way, unless he is a consummate artist, will hardly lead him to the very peaks of Parnassus" (xxvi). Bradley then goes on to say that "No survey of the Yale series [of Younger Poets] can avoid the assessment that its early volumes were banal, even if Lewis's ninety-nine ways to banality rather overestimates their variety. Put simply, these authors tried to say too much and thereby said too little. The first Yale Younger Poets knew that they were witnesses to history, and they believed they had been touched with fire as surely as Oliver Wendell Homes, Jr., and his Civil War companions before them" (xxvii).

They could not communicate their wartime experiences, however, because in any art, skill at the art must precede meaning, and "unexceptional imitation" of Classical verse is not sufficient skill for the meaning they wanted their poems to bear. William Rose Benét put it well in his review of volumes 5-8 of the series, in the *Yale Review* of October 1921, when he hoped of the poets "that they'll all learn thoroughly to put what they think in the way they actually think it and not in the way they think precedent demands that it should be put" (qtd. in Bradley xxx). Admittedly, it was the older and not the younger Benét brother saying this, but their attitudes were much the same. Though it is going outside the bounds of 123 College to look at this, the choices Stephen Vincent Benét made when he was editor of the series, from 1933 to 1942, show clearly how he welcomed poets who said what they thought in the ways they thought it, including James Agee, Muriel Rukeyser, Joy Davidman, Margaret Walker, and Reuel Denney. Not that Benét never wrote imitative verse, or even imitative poetry: **"The General Public"** is an example to the contrary. But it was done with impish humor—so much so that, in his Yale days, much of his purest imitative (and impish) verse found its way into the *Yale Record* (the humor magazine) and not the *Yale Lit.*

In other words, the poetry of this sunshine age right after World War I was largely derivative and even the sunshine was arguably that of an Indian summer. But the ferment was unmistakable, and the principal location was 123 College Street. Cochran was right, and there's more. If I hold the first printing of *Othello* in my hands, or Ben Jonson's own copy of his *Works,* or Izaak Walton's copy of the first edition of Milton's *Lycidas,* there bubble up in my mind not only thoughts for conversation with my like-minded friends but—more slowly and from deeper levels—thoughts of greater moment, about history and the nature of language and the peoples of this Earth. If I hold *Othello* and look at the Reynolds portrait of David Garrick in the front room of the club, I can be transported back in my imagination to Johnson's eighteenth century and history becomes a palpable thing. I can fancy Dr. Johnson there, dribbling snuff. So could—and did—Benét and his friends.

That's not American history, of course. Yet I believe the experience with *Othello* and Garrick carries over into experience with other histories, other rooms. Moreover, I believe that Benét had a similar experience in those rooms at the Elizabethan Club, with those books and those pictures and the visitors from England. One piece of evidence comes from a passage in *John Brown's Body,* Book Four, the passage on Wingate Hall: "So Wingate found it, riding at ease / The cloud edge lifting over the trees / A white-sail glimmer beyond the rise . . . Mounting, mounting, the shining spectre / . . . / The cloud expanding, the topsails swelling" (*Selected Works* 142). Now this is a description of Wingate Hall, but one can hear Alfred Noyes in "The Highwayman," and see Steve Benét sitting there in the front room at 123 College, listening to Noyes read his poem (which he did there during his visit to this country in 1919): "The moon was a ghostly galleon, tossed upon cloudy seas. . . ." Phelps said Noyes was the best public reader of his own poems of any poet he had ever heard (304).

Even if this gives us a source for the imagery, however, it might be asked why bring it up in this context. The answer lies in the fact that Noyes himself was historian as well as poet and he wrote historical poetry—"The Highwayman" is an example—speaking to what I have elsewhere called the Edwardian interest in "the past alive in the present" (18-19, 23). This is not only an Edwardian characteristic—it informs Rupert Brooke's "If I should die . . ."—and it is not only an English characteristic. The Americans who went to France during the "Great War" were immensely conscious of French history—recall the cry "LaFayette, we are here!"—as indeed Amos Niven Wilder, in particular, makes clear.

When they came back, they brought that consciousness with them. It had been in the poetry they grew up on— Noyes or Newbolt. It was in the poetry they read or heard at Yale. It was in the approach Phelps took to Shakespeare (and to the Age of Johnson). It had been

borne in on the returning servicemen by their service in the war, fighting in and across the immemorial countryside of France. Now it was brought home and nurtured in a United States of America suddenly excited and conscious of a new literary destiny of its own.

One can remember Benét's lines in the Invocation to *John Brown's Body,* describing both his characters and the genesis of the poem: "This flesh was seeded from no foreign soil / But Pennsylvania and Kentucky wheat" (*Selected Works,* I, 7). That is true, but the method of the seeding was formed by conversation and reading at 123 College. Yes, Benét had published a volume of verse at seventeen, before he came to Yale: the volume was *Five Men and Pompey.* But it was at Yale that he fell under the sway of Yale's sense of history, and especially of the sway of a sense of the past alive in the present. *Whose* sense of the past alive in the present? Along that line of inquiry, one can look at possible poetic connections with William Morris and the Pre-Raphaelite Brotherhood. But for the moment let us imagine a scene at 123, before the United States entered the war in the Spring of 1917.

The door to the club opens into a hall, with the stairs going up on the left and the entry to the front room on the right. There is a duty table in the hall, and the hall leads to the tea room. To the right of the tea room and behind the front room is the vault room: it is in the vault that the rare books are kept (including, as of 1998, first editions of Benét's books). Steve Benét is sitting, owlish or perhaps chipmunklike behind his round glasses, round-faced and round-cheeked, legs twisted schoolboy-fashion around the legs of the chair, cigarette at the ready, in the corner just inside the door to the front room.

The chair is one of a pair flanking the table where current issues of *Punch* are kept. (The bound volumes are upstairs on the shelves in the writing room.) Under the front windows of the room is a couch, with a coffee table in front, flanked by two armchairs. A couple of straight-backed chairs are against the walls. Today Chip Farrar and Amos Niven Wilder are on the couch, Bellinger in the chair on Farrar's side, Thornton Wilder (I think he may be visiting his brother) in the chair on his brother's side, Bob Coates in the other chair flanking the *Punch* table. Benét is reading. He begins by quoting Browning's line, "And did you once see Shelley plain?" in his squeaky, oddly inflected voice, smiling at the emphasis his inflections give.

"Shelley? Oh, yes, I saw him often then," / The old man said. A dry smile creased his face / With many wrinkles, "That's a great poem, now! / That one of Browning's! Shelley? Shelley plain? / The time that I remember best is this—. . . Round about / Struggled a howling crowd of boys, pellmell, / Pushing and jostling like a stormy sea, / With shouting faces . . . They all had clods, / Or slimy balls of mud. A few gripped stones. / And there, his back against a battered door, / His pile of books scattered about his feet, / Stood Shelley while two others held him fast, / And the clods beat upon him . . . all his face / Was white, a whiteness like no human color, / But white and dreadful as consuming fire. / His hands shook now and then, like slender cords / Which bear too heavy weights. He did not speak. / So I saw Shelley plain." "And you?" I said. / "I? I threw straighter than the most of them, / And had firm clods. I hit him—well, at least / Thrice in the face. He made good sport that night" (***Selected Works,*** I, 342-343).

The poem, **"The General Public,"** was written when Benét was a freshman, but he was as prone to read old poems as new, sitting there in the front room, and **"The General Public"** is a good example of what differentiated Benét from his peers. It is of course derivative, but it is derivative in a way that we might now link with the idea of intertextuality: he is using Browning's style in picking up from Browning's line and twisting it rather like a Moebius strip or Escher print. Not at all the same thing as youthfully imitating Housman's classicism (or even that of Gilbert Murray, or that less-tutored classicism of Rupert Brooke), which is what Bellinger and Farrar and even Amos Niven Wilder were all doing in some degree. It doesn't very much matter if it is intertextuality or Benét's "impish humor"—or both.

Impish or not, Benét had a passion for patriotism. What distinguished him from Bellinger and Farrar and Amos Niven Wilder, and half a dozen other poets of the time (and the Yale Younger Poets series), was that he was the poet who found a new way to sing his passion, eventually with consummate artistry. How did this happen. There may be a clue in the fact that the late Ian Ballantine (1916-1995), Benét's editor for his 1943 Pocket Books collection of short stories, included in the brief biography of Benét on the cover, the simple statement that Benét was a patriot. I asked Ballantine about this some years ago (at a science-fiction convention in Tarrytown, New York), and was given to understand that it had to do not with any doubts of Benét's patriotism (in light of his sometimes leftward politics), but with finding a single word to describe Benét's literary motivation. At the time I was surprised at the answer, but I am convinced he spoke truthfully.

In short, Benét was very much of his generation, the same generation as Bellinger and Farrar and Amos Niven Wilder. But he was not an occasional poet whose career was elsewhere, and he had that impish humor. Yet in the end, what influenced him as much as anything else to take the path so much different from the paths his peers took was his status as an "army brat" who spent his summers in Carlisle, Pennsylvania, and, more important and more germane to this essay, his apprecia-

tion of history, nurtured by the Elizabethan Club and by two others among his friends there. These are Thornton Niven Wilder (1897-1975), Amos's younger brother, and Robert Coates. Coates, like Alfred Bellinger, became an historian (but what a different kind of historian!), while Wilder's first books were historical novels, one Roman, and one based in the Americas—albeit in South America. Bob Coates's *magnum opus* was *The Outlaw Years: The History of the Land Pirates of the Natchez Trace* (1930, reprinted Bison Books 1986). Alfred Bellinger's *magna opera* included *Troy: The Coins* (Princeton 1961, reprinted 1979) and *Essays on the Coinage of Alexander the Great* (likewise reprinted 1979): the same year Bob Coates published *The Outlaw Years,* Bellinger was publishing a modest item in the American Numismatic Society's *Notes* (No. 42), "Two Hordes of Attic Bronze Coins." As I say, it was a very different kind of history, but history nonetheless, and Bellinger was devoted to it over a sixty-year career.

Wilder's South American novel was the one for which he won his first Pulitzer prize, *The Bridge of San Luis Rey* (1927), which plays off the "real history" of the memoirist who died in the collapse of the bridge against our knowledge of her two hundred years later. The Roman novel was *The Cabala* (1926), which plays off contemporary Rome against Virgil and the eternal city, and which Farrar in his review (*The Bookman,* 1926) called "brilliant, bitter, imaginative"—of which the second word is the one that should give us pause. It may be worthwhile here to quote what Wilder's mother wrote to Phelps after *The Cabala* and *The Bridge* were published—noting that Wilder dedicated *The Bridge* to his mother: "As for Thornton, I always knew him for a gifted and altogether a choice spirit. But I confess to you that I feared that his very fastidiousness might separate him from the common lot. I mean make him superior and highbrow. Now I know the humanity in him is strong enough to balance the other. So I am not so much 'proud' as thankful and content" (qtd. in Harrison 106). Wilder immersed himself in history—more in *The Bridge* than in *The Cabala*—and the reward was a loss of bitterness and a gain in humanity. (Nor was Phelps's contributions to this gain in humanity negligible.) In Benét, as later (almost) in Wilder with *The Skin of Our Teeth,* the bitterness dissolved in impish laughter, in intertextual humor, and (possible, given the time) in the use of history as objective correlative.

Wilder accepted the interidentification of times and places as the keynote or cornerstone of his vision—as in *Our Town* or *The Skin of Our Teeth* or even *The Merchant of Yonkers* (*Hello Dolly!*). That is almost the exact opposite of Benét's historical consciousness, one might say the mirror image of Benét's historical consciousness (on this interidentification, see my essay "Thornton Wilder and the Science-Fiction Anti-

Paradigm" in *Patterns of the Fantastic II,* Mercer Island WA 1985, 29-38). But it comes from the same root, the same concern over the relationship of past and present. One could argue that Wilder's father's move from the shores of Lake Mendota, Wisconsin, to China, in 1906 (when Thornton was eight) opened Thornton Wilder to almost a Spenglerian view of culture and history, while Benét's youthful summer visits to the area around Carlisle, including Gettysburg, and his "army brat" status, opened him to a sense of history inherent in the countryside. But in the 1920s the line of demarcation was not so clear: *The Cabala* and *The Bridge of San Luis Rey* both celebrate the past alive in the present, in almost the same way as Benét's freshman poem **"The General Public."**

I mentioned that Benét wrote much of his strictly imitative (and "impish") verse for the *Yale Record.* There was his **"The Game and the Poets"** in which Horace, Robert Burns, and John Masefield consider the Yale-Princeton game: I quote from the Masefield *pastiche* ("John Masefield Extends the Everlasting Mercy to the Tiger"): "By then I'd used up all my tricks, / 'I'm bloody in a bloody fix!' / I said—and searched the lawbooks through / To find some final crime to do, / The one huge, unforgiven sin / That bloody rots the heart within! / The sin that like a steel-tight jersey / Removes you from eternal mercy! I bloody shrank a bit at first / To crown my horrors with a worst! / But soon I yielded. Vileness filled me, / I went to Princeton—and it killed me!" (*The Yale Record Book of Verse* 17). There were half a dozen others in the 1922 collection of *Yale Record* verse: he has more poems in that collection than any other poet. Finally, my favorite when I first read it in 1951, his "Wander Song (From any of the popular magazines.)": "Give me the curlews calling on the gypsy patteran, / The pine-smoke whirling, falling, and the battered, open van! / Give me the fires of spring, lass, your warm red mouth to kiss! / (But, for Gawd's sake, gimme the twenty bucks I get for writing this!)"—I quote only the first of the three stanzas (*The Yale Record Book of Verse* 24).

What happened with Benét had something to do with his coming to Yale, and to 123 College Street, without an intermediary stop. The Wilder brothers went to Oberlin before they came to Yale, and Amos Niven Wilder was an ambulance driver in France, under Benét's uncle Laurence. For Amos, perhaps, the experience in France brought him to see that France existed as a kind of Blakean entity: I'm thinking of that passage in *The Marriage of Heaven and Hell* (Plate 11) where Blake writes that "The ancient poets animated all sensible objects with Gods or Geniuses, calling them by the names and adorning them with the properties of woods, rivers, mountains, lakes, cities, nations, and whatever their enlarged and numerous senses could perceive. And particularly they studied the genius of each city &

country. . . ." Thornton Wilder found an odd Spanish colonial *genius* in his creation of the Marquesa de Montemayor and Father Juniper and the collapse of a bridge on July 20, 1714. But Benét carried that realization into the creation of an historical poetry for the United States of America, seeking the American *genius,* the American spirit. (Yes, I know "Art has no nations—but the mortal sky / Lingers like gold in immortality" [**John Brown's Body, Selected Works,** I, 121-122]. So should we say *Ars longa, natio longior*?)

Not all at once did Benét begin this creation. If we read his poetry from his time at Yale we find an historical sense applied derivatively or intertextually in **"Three Days' Ride"** (*Selected Works,* I, 389-392), where the text is Browning's "How They Brought The Good New From Aix to Ghent"—and I believe, with Basil Davenport, that this is one of Benét's best early poems, with the increasing stress accompanying each variation within the refrain, up to "From Belton Castle to Solway side, / Though great hearts break, is three days' ride!" We find the same sense in **"The Retort Discourteous (Italy—sixteenth century)"** (*Selected Works,* I, 387-389). Listen to the last three quatrains: "Roll your hands in the honey of life, / Kneel to your white-necked strumpets! / You came to your crowns with a squealing fife / But I shall go out with trumpets! // Poison the steel of the plunging dart, / Holloa your hounds to their station! / I march to my ruin with such a heart / As a king to his coronation. // Your poets roar of your golden feats—/ I have herded the stars like cattle. / And you may die in the perfumed sheets, / But I shall die in battle."

It is worthwhile pausing over this because the technique is similar to that of Benét's humorous verse, as well as of **"The General Public"** and, indeed, of the later short stories. We might call it the technique of pointed contrast, and it is not much different from the classic *Punch*-line in the jokes in those copies of *Punch* on the table there in the front room of the Elizabethan Club. "Advice to persons about to marry—'Don't!'" Fife and trumpets, ruin and coronation, die in bed or die in battle, seeing Shelley plain to hit him, "Though great hearts break, is three days' ride"—all these have a twist at the end, a point, almost a *Punch*-line, to draw the pointed contrast. Also, there is the progressive increase in stress in the opening beats of the second line of the **"Three Days' Ride"** refrain, beginning "From Belton Castle to Solway side, / Hard by the bridge, is three days' ride" and going on to "Strive as you may, is three days' ride," then "Ride how you will, is three days' ride," then the dragged beat of "Though great hearts break, is three days' ride" (*Selected Works,* I, 387). (This is the progress noted by Basil Davenport in his Introduction to *Selected Works of Stephen Vincent Benét,* I, ix-x). The point is that Benét uses what one might call the tricks of poetry (or the tricks of verse) as part of his technique of pointed contrast. Moreover, he had this technique at hand in his undergraduate days, as indeed he had the techniques of classical meter shared by the rest of the young poets at 123 College Street—and some of them (whether in the *Lit* or the *Record*) could work the tricks of verse to the same end.

Benét, however, had something else, something shared more by young Coates than by his fellow poets. He had his interest in American history, and particularly in the history of the area of the first push westward. Doubtless some of this came from his father's Army career, his status as an Army brat, his summers in Carlisle. Doubtless also, there is a friend of Phelps, a colleague of his in the English department at Yale, a colleague in the Elizabethan Club, to whom we ought to devote brief attention here. His name was Henry Augstin Beers (1847-1926), and he was a short-story writer (stories collected in *A Suburban Pastoral,* 1894), historian of American letters (*Nathaniel Parker Willis,* 1885, and *The Connecticut Wits,* 1920), an historian of Yale (*The Ways of Yale in the Consulship of Plancus,* 1895), and an historian of American thought (*Four Americans: Roosevelt, Hawthorne, Emerson, Whitman,* 1919). What is particularly important for our endeavor is that in the years Benét was an undergraduate at Yale, the retired Professor Beers, a regular at the club, was thinking, and writing, about the interrelationship of the push westward and the American character. This not only in his consideration of Teddy Roosevelt (who, after all, wrote *The Winning of the West*), but also because of his friendship with the Harvard philosopher Josiah Royce. It is Royce's book on California in the American Commonwealths Series (1889) that is, I believe, the *textus receptus* for the interrelation of American West and American character, not least for its philosophical portrait of John Charles Frémont.

We may see some of the influence of this concern if we look briefly at a few of Benét's poems from a little after the Yale days, around the same time as *John Brown's Body* (to which we will come shortly). In particular, let us look at **"American Names"** (*Selected Works,* I, 398-402) on Jefferson, Audubon, and Daniel Boone. From **"American Names"** let us look particularly at ll. 10-15, ll. 23-25, and (simply because they are the best-known lines and put the rest in context), ll. 31-36: ". . . I will remember where I was born. / I will remember Carquinez Straits, / Little French Lick and Lundy's Lane, / The Yankee ships and the Yankee dates / And the bullettowns of Calamity Jane. / And I will remember Skunktown Plain. / . . . It is a magic ghost you guard / But I am sick for a newer ghost, / Harrisburg, Spartanburg, Painted Post. / . . . / I shall not rest quiet in Montparnasse. / I shall not lie easy in Winchelsea. / You may bury my body in Sussex grass, /

You may bury my tongue in Champmedy. / I shall not be there, I shall rise and pass. / Bury my heart at Wounded Knee."

Here are a few quatrains from *A Book of Americans* (note the title): "Thomas Jefferson, / What do you say / Under the gravestone / Hidden away? / . . . / I liked queer gadgets / And secret shelves, / And helping nations / To rule themselves / Jealous of others? / Not always candid? / But huge of vision / And open-handed / . . . / I got no riches. / I died a debtor. / I died free-hearted / And that was better . . ." (*Selected Works,* I, 398). Or on Audubon, "Some men live for warlike deeds, / Some for women's words. / John James Audubon / Lived to look at birds / . . . / Drew them all the way they lived / In their habitats. / (Lucy Bakewell Audubon / Sometimes wondered 'Cats?') . . ." (*Selected Works,* I, 400). In addition, there is the single quatrain on Daniel Boone, going—with a kind of reverse twist—from the almost comic lines on Audubon and the imitation schoolboy mnemonics of the lines on Jefferson (admittedly both of these show something of Rosemary Benét's hand) to the haunting "When Daniel Boone goes by, at night, / The phantom deer arise / And all lost, wild America / Is burning in their eyes" (*Selected Works* I, 402). I think it is not accidental that these are all three men of the push westward, even (though Audubon is late) of the first great push westward. Then there are Benét's lines on **"French Pioneers 1534-1759"**: "They came here, they toiled here, / They broke their hearts afar, / Normandy and Brittany, / Paris and Navarre / . . . / Marquette and Joliet, / Cartier, LaSalle, / Priest, corsair, gentleman, / Gallants one and all. / France was in their quick words, / France was in their veins. . . ." (*Selected Works,* I, 397-398).

Now let us look at Robert Myron Coates (1897-1973). After he graduated from Yale, Coates, like his friend Thornton Wilder, was a part of the circle that gathered in Paris around Gertrude Stein. His first published book (Paris 1926) is *The Eater of Darkness,* and in the Yale Library is a presentation copy of his *Yesterday's Burdens* (1933), inscribed to Gertrude Stein. He was a Leftist expatriate much of his life, a friend of Nathaniel West, and among his other books are *All the Year Round* (1943), *The Hour After Westerly and Other Stories* (1957), *Beyond the Alps* (1961), *The Man Just Ahead of You* (1964), and *The Farther Shore* (1966). But his important book for our purposes, as we noted, is his single sustained work of history, *The Outlaw Years: The History of the Land Pirates of the Natchez Trace* (1930). The major piece in the book is on Murrell and his conspiracy in the 1830s, but Sam Mason and the Harpes and other earlier figures appear in the earlier part of the book. These are Pennsylvanians (or northwest Virginians) turned Kentuckians, a part of the trans-Appalachian frontier in the years 1775-1820. It happens that I have worked a good bit in the manuscript sources for this period, and I have wished there was something on the northwest part of that frontier comparable to Coates's book on the Southwest part. (The distinction is between the Territory Northwest of the River Ohio in the Northwest Ordinance of 1787 and the Territory Southwest of the River Ohio at the same time.)

The Pennsylvania Rifle of 1775 became the Kentucky Rifle of 1800. Frontiersman Sam Mason left Youghoughania for "Caintuck" (one step ahead of a law particularly hard on horse thieves), and "This flesh was seeded from no foreign soil / But Pennsylvania and Kentucky wheat." The sources for *The Outlaw Years* are all in the Yale University Library, and so far as I have been able to tell, were there in 1920. **"American Names"** is, in a way, Benét's answer, from Yale and from his sense of American history, not only to the Great War French experience of Bellinger and Farrar and Amos Niven Wilder (and Uncle Laurence), but to the postwar French experience of Bob Coates and Thornton Wilder.

It is in a sense also an answer to the achievement of another Elizabethan Club member of an earlier generation (closer to William Rose Benét), a frequent visitor in Steve Benét's years, Brian Hooker: the name may not be familiar now, but a few years ahead of the Great War Hooker was the brilliant translator of Rostand's heroic comedy *Cyrano de Bergerac* for the 1924 production starring Walter Hampden (a production Benét saw with his brother and also, I believe, at the Keith-Orpheum in Washington with his uncle Laurence Benét: my parents were there). See how Hooker (or Rostand in the original) uses the French names: "We are the Cadets of Gascoyne, the defenders / Of Carbon de Castel-Jaloux. / Free fighters, free lovers, free spenders, / The Cadets of Gascoyne, the defenders / Of old homes, old names, and old splendors, / A proud and pestilent crew, / The Cadets of Gascoyne, the defenders, / Of Carbon de Castel-Jaloux." And the wonderful scene where Roxane is introduced to the Gascon Cadets (195): "Baron de Peyrescous de Colignac! . . . Baron de Casterac de Cahuzac—Vicomte de Malgouyre Estressac Lesbas d'Escarabiot—Chevalier d'Antignac-Juizet—Baron Hillot de Blagnac-Salechan de Castel-Crabioules—" (which should be enough names to set a thousand scenes—but note Benét's use of names in **"French Pioneers"**).

Then there is here, from Act IV of *Cyrano,* when the piper begins to play a Provençal melody, "Listen, you Gascons! Now it is no more / The shrill fife—It is the flute, through woodland far / Away, calling—no longer the hot battle-cry, / But the cool quiet pipe our goatherds play! / Listen—the forest glens . . . the hills . . . the downs . . . / The green sweetness of night on the Dordogne . . . / Listen, you Gascons! It is all Gascoyne!" (178). It is worth remembering that 1998 was

not only Benét's centennial but the centennial of *Cyrano,* which opened in Paris with Constant Coquelin in the title role on December 23, 1897, and in New York with Richard Mansfield in the title role on October 3, 1898 (both in French). Its translation by Brian Hooker seventy-five years ago was part of the Francophile days after World War I, along with James Branch Cabell's creation of Poictesme and Dunsany's stories of Carcassonne. Now, with all this in mind, let us listen again to the last stanza of **"American Names."** (Cabell was a favorite of Benét.)

"I shall not rest quiet in Montparnasse. / I shall not lie easy in Winchelsea. / You may bury my body in Sussex grass, / You may bury my tongue in Champmedy. / I shall not be there, I shall rise and pass. / Bury my heart at Wounded Knee." The last line, of course, has taken on a different meaning since Dee Brown used it as the title of his book on the tragic history of native Americans: its point for Benét is the contrast between the European graves, and especially the British and the French, of the war and the war poets, and the scenes of war in the United States. He picks up from the second stanza: "Seine and Piave are silver spoons, / But the spoonbowl-metal is thin and worn, / There are English counties like hunting-tunes / Played on the keys of a postboy's horn, / But I will remember where I was born." As it happens, I have visited (or even lived in) a number of the places Benét names in the poem—"Harrisburg, Spartanburg, Painted Post" among them—and I know something of the historical significance they had for him. The references may seem general or even generic, but for him they were specific, as specific as the reference in the next-to-last stanza, "Henry and John were never so / And Henry and John were always right? / Granted, but when it was time to go / And the tea and the laurels had stood all night, / Did they never watch for Nantucket Light?"

Henry and John, so far as I know, are Henry James, the American expatriate novelist, and John Singer Sargent, the American expatriate painter. James visited Phelps in New Haven in 1911 (*Autobiography* 551), but that was before Benét's time: he died in early 1916 in his flat in Chelsea. Sargent lived until 1925, but I have no idea whether Benét met him. In both cases, I suspect the references came through Phelps (or, to style him as he styled himself in his signature, "Wm Lyon Phelps"). Indeed Phelps plays a significant role in Benét's development of an historical poetry for America. Shortly after he first taught his course in Shakespeare at Yale, Professor Phelps (in 1897-98) taught a course in Chaucer and Browning. When he retired from teaching at Yale in 1933, Professor Chauncy Brewster Tinker, who had been an undergraduate member of that class, presented him with the autographed copy of Walter Savage Landor's 1845 sonnet on Browning, "with its fine reference to Chaucer" (*Autobiography* 909).

Moreover, at his retirement dinner at the New Haven Lawn Club that year, he was presented with a collection of unpublished Browning letters. For all his connection with Shakespeare in Alexander Smith Cochran's mind (and it was a true connection), Phelps was pre-eminently—in the Yale mind—a devotee of Robert Browning.

There is a tradition in English letters that runs from Chaucer to Dryden to Browning, and another that runs from Langland to Bunyan to Robert Smith Surtees, and then to Tolkien, who was of Benét's generation. The traditions sometimes intermingle in a given author—Kipling and William Morris are examples—and one may recall Morris's approach to history as a possible influence on Benét. My attention was called to this point by Basil Davenport (in his Introduction to **Selected Works,** I, ix), where he notes that the influence of Morris was at the point "where he is least dangerous as an influence, in the mood of mediaevalism combined with the brutal realism of 'Shameful Death' or 'The Haystack in the Floods'—and, making allowance for some youthful romanticism, the mood, here, of **'Three Days' Ride.'**" In other words, what Benét took from Morris is the application of imaginative detail in the re-creation of history, which is not unlike what he took from Browning. Benét himself recognized the influence, in his first novel, *The Beginning of Wisdom* (Davenport ix).

The evidence in Benét's undergraduate poetry (as, for example, **"The General Public"**) is that Browning had a significant effect on his writing, perhaps the most significant effect, in his developing a poetry out of history. He is part of that tradition from Chaucer to Dryden to Browning. But there was another of Phelps's poets who had nearly as much effect, and who helped make Benét's an historical poetry *for America*: that was (Nicholas) Vachel Lindsay, a guest at the Elizabethan Club in 1916, and indeed on at least two subsequent visits to New Haven (Phelps 629-632). Professor Phelps called Lindsay's best poems—"General William Booth Enters Heaven," "The Congo," and "The Santa Fe Trail"—"truly great, both in their soaring imagination and in their felicity of diction" (629). It is not hard to hear them behind Benét's historical poetry, and particularly his use of meter in the Wingate sections of **John Brown's Body.** The point here is that both Browning and Vachel Lindsay came to Benét in his under-graduate days through Phelps and (certainly in Lindsay's case, arguably in Browning's) 123 College Street. There was a quirk in Benét, linked to his manner and voice and intonation, possibly emphasized by Browning's humor and Lindsay's meter, and even by the issues of *Punch* there in the front room and upstairs on the shelves, a quirk which led to a curious result in his writing. A quirk, also, that links him with Chaucer and Dryden and Browning.

When we read **John Brown's Body,** we, like Basil Davenport (in his Introduction to **Selected Works,** I, x-xi), find that the long, loose, five- or six-beat line that carries the bulk of **John Brown's Body** at times comes perilously near prose, though "it can carry casual conversations without incongruity, or at need can deepen without any sense of abrupt transition for the nobility of Lincoln or Lee" (xi). Benét, like Brian Hooker in his translation of *Cyrano,* was striving to solve what Davenport calls "one of the primary problems of verse in our day, the finding of a form which may bear the same relation to our easygoing talk that, presumably, blank verse did to the more formal speech of an earlier generation" (x). But look how Hooker handled the problem. Here is the last passage of *Cyrano,* where he brilliantly uses "my white plume" to render *mon panache*: "What's that you say? Hopeless?—Why, very well!—/ But a man does not fight merely to win! / No—no—better to know one fights in vain! . . . / You there—who are you? A hundred against one—/ I know them now, my ancient enemies—/ Falsehood! . . . There! There! Prejudice—Compromise—/ Cowardice—What's that? No! Surrender? No! / Never!—never! . . . Ah, you too, Vanity! / I knew you would overthrow me in the end—/ No! I fight on! I fight on! I fight on! / Yes, all my laurels you have riven away / And all my roses; yet in spite of you, / There is one crown I bear away with me, / And tonight, when I enter before God, / My salute shall sweep all the stars away / From the blue threshold! One thing without stain, / Unspotted from the world, in spite of doom / Mine own!—And that is—that is—my white plume!" (255-256).

I was younger when I saw José Ferrer in the title role in *Cyrano* on Broadway than Benét when he saw Walter Hampden, but I know from conversations with some of Benét's friends and acquaintances that he came from the theatre quoting Hooker's text as I did (and as they did). But what is curious—what is part of this quirk I mentioned—is that Benét did not use his loose line to achieve the romantic heights that Hooker climbed. Instead, it is in his ruminative prose in the 1930s, which we will only touch on here, that he climbs those heights—as in "The Devil and Daniel Webster" or "Jacob and the Indians"—or plumbs the romantic depths. In **John Brown's Body,** which is his pre-eminent historical poetry for America, he asserts the American character in his long loose lines (or in his experiments in meter), not in the manner of Rostand's romantic look at France, or that of his own confreres, or even Browning's detached or quizzical look at times longer past. Davenport (xi, xiii) especially notes two of Benét's lines from **John Brown's Body**: first, as an example of Benét's individual meter, "It is over now, but they will not let it be over" and second, as a translation of a Roman epitaph "*Saltavit. Placuit. Mortuus est,*" "He danced with me. He could dance rather well. He is dead." It is good to pick out memorable lines, and there are many: I would add, "They came on to fish-hook Gettysburg in this way, after this fashion // Over hot pikes heavy with pollen, past fields where the wheat was high . . ." (*Selected Works,* I, 247). Fish-hook Gettysburg and fish-shaped Paumanok, and Walt Whitman is not only a character but an influence in *John Brown's Body*—yet Whitman was a lyric poet, and *John Brown's Body* is by way of being an epic (at least an epic ode), though there are lyrics in it. It is from lyrics or elegies one picks out the memorable lines.

Here's Browning loose-lined lyric in the epic, Benét quizzical, remembering his own youth, on a visit to Gettysburg: "You took a carriage to that battlefield. / Now, I suppose, you take a motor-bus, / But then, it was a carriage—and you ate / Fried chicken out of wrappings of waxed paper, / While the slow guide buzzed on about the war / And the enormous, curdled summer clouds / Piled up like giant cream puffs in the blue / . . . / And it was hot. You could stand and look / All the way down from Cemetery Ridge, / Much as it was, so clam and hot, / So tidy and great-skied. No men had fought / There but enormous, monumental men / Who bled neat streams of uncorrupting bronze . . ." (*Selected Works,* I, 260). I too have stood, with cold fried chicken, wrapped in wax paper, under the great-skied enormous summer clouds, looking down on Cemetery Ridge, looking at the monuments, in the deserted heat of a summer day before the centennial changed Gettysburg. I nod and say, yes, indeed, that is the way it is: I do not weep as I weep at the end of *Cyrano.* Here is one reason why. Here is the end of the ode that ends *John Brown's Body* (and listen! You may hear Tennyson's "Ode on the Death of the Duke of Wellington" and you may hear a little of William Butler Yeats—two more Phelps favorites, though Yeats visited the club before Benét's student days).

"So when the crowd gives tongue / And prophets, old or young / Bawl out their strange despair / Or fall in worship there, / Let them applaud the image or condemn / But keep your distance and your soul from them. / And if the heart within your breast must burst / Like a cracked crucible and pour its steel / White hot before the white heat of the wheel, / Strive to recast once more / That attar of the ore / In the strong mold of pain / Till it is whole again, / And while the prophets shudder or adore / Before the flame, hoping it will give ear, / If you at last must have a word to say, / Say neither, in their way, / 'It is a deadly magic and accursed,' / Nor 'It is blest,' but only 'It is here.'" Say not America is blest, or curst, but we are here. So ends the epic that began with the invocation, "American muse, whose strong and diverse heart / So many men have tried to understand / But only made it smaller with their art, / Because you are as various as your land. . . ." (One

may recall how, in that invocation, Benét turns away from Rupert Brooke, as he has turned away from France, "They planted England with a stubborn trust. / But the cleft dust was never English dust." The implicit reference is to "There shall be / In that rich earth a richer dust concealed, / A dust whom England bore, shaped, made aware, / Gave once her flowers to know, her fields to roam . . ." from Brooke's most famous sonnet.)

I mentioned Tennyson and his "Ode on the Death of the Duke of Wellington": here is an earlier part of the ode that ends *John Brown's Body* ("this man" in the first line is John Brown). "Bury the South together with this man, / Bury the bygone South. / Bury the minstrel with the honey-mouth, / Bury the broadsword virtues of the clan, / Bury the unmachined, the planters' pride, / The courtesy and the bitter arrogance, / The pistol-hearted horsemen who could ride / Like jolly centaurs under the hot stars. / Bury the whip, bury the branding-bars, / Bury the unjust thing / That some tamed into mercy. . . ." And then, eventually, "Bury this destiny manifest, / This system broken underneath the test, / Beside John Brown and though he knows his enemy is there / He is too full of sleep at last to care." Tying Benét to Tennyson through Phelps is a slightly dicey business, I admit: although reading Tennyson's *Maud* was the greatest poetic experience of Phelps's young life (*Autobiography* 144), he said later that "Tennyson was a great poet, but he did not have an interesting mind" (205). Still, Phelps did particularly direct attention to Tennyson's elegies—see his comparison of Tennyson with Milton in *Autobiography* 204-205—and it is important to remember that Phelps was an enthusiastic teacher and Benét an enthusiastic learner in matters of technical form and meter, odes, elegies, sonnets, anapests, dochmaics, and so on. Benét was not only a conscious but a conscientious formal experimenter in verse. The quirk was that his search for the pointed contrast or the ironic twist or the *Punch*-line meant that even the long loose lines of *John Brown's Body* could not be used as Hooker used his similar lines in *Cyrano.*

Now let us set against the tone of *John Brown's Body* these two scenes from the short stories of the 1930s. First is the trial scene in "The Devil and Daniel Webster," and the second is a double scene, Jacob's sojourn in the wilderness and his times at the house of Raphael Sanchez in "Jacob and the Indians." In "The Devil and Daniel Webster," Dan'l looks at the hell-bound judge and jury, and sees their eyes glittering like hounds before they get the fox, and he sweats like a man who has just missed falling into a pit in the dark. He speaks of common things, and how the jury are all men, and American men at that, and about the things that make a country a country and a man a man, about the freshness of a fine morning when you're young, and about the taste of food when you're hungry, and how these things sicken without freedom. He speaks of the wrongs that have been done, and how, out of the wrong and the right, the suffering and the starvations, something new has come, and even the traitors played a part in it. And as he speaks, he feels, all down his back and through his chest, the strength of being a man, and the voice speaking through him is like the forest and its secrecy, like the sea and its storms, like the cry of the lost nation, like the scenes of childhood (**Selected Works,** II, 32-45). There, in prose—and in a semihumorous cautionary tale at that—, is Benét's closest approach to unabashed Romanticism.

Or in "Jacob and the Indians," where he calls up a vision of the paths in eighteenth-century America, dark with the shadow of the forest and green with its green and through the green ran trails and paths that were not yet roads and highways, without the dust and scent of the cities of men, but with another look. There were pleasant streams and wide glades, untenanted but by the deer, and pressing in, huge and vast, the promise of a continent, a great and open landscape, life in it and death, the landscape Raphael Sanchez has described to young Jacob Weiss (**Selected Works,** II, 9-16). "They think this is a mine to be worked, as the Spaniards worked Potosi, but it is not a mine. It is something beginning to live, and it is faceless and nameless yet. But it is our lot to be part of it—remember that in the wilderness, my young scholar of the law" (**Selected Works,** II, 9).

All of which leaves us—where? Briefly summarizing, Benét came to Yale as a freshman in fall 1915, already a published poet. He shortly fell in with a group of students gathering at the Elizabethan Club at 123 (now 459) College Street, and under the influence of William Lyon Phelps, "America's favorite professor" and the literary doyen of the club (though the painter John Ferguson Weir, brought up at West Point before the Civil War, may have been the senior member). While his confreres looked to their experience in France in World War I for inspiration and history, and while the club itself focused (obviously) on English history, Benét and—on occasion—some of his friends (particularly Bob Coates in *The Outlaw Years*) looked toward American history for inspiration, and particularly the history of Pennsylvania and Pennsylvanians in the first push westward. Billy Phelps brought Browning and (among others) Vachel Lindsay to the table. Benét took them from the table, took them from the shelves, took them from Billy Phelps, and made them part of his great work.

I believe, as I said earlier, that books in the Yale Library (such as Augustine Walton's *A History of the Detection and Trial of John A. Murel,* 1835, or Charles Seals-field's *Frontier Life,* 1860) played a role in the interest in the push westward. That helps explain (in part) some

of the subject matter for Benét as for Coates. More to our point on form and technique, the circle in which Benét moved at Yale was a circle of conscious *makars,* creators of poems and *made* things. Because of Phelps's influence (and that of *Punch* and writing for the *Record*), and, through Billy Phelps, Browning's influence, Benét neither sought nor achieved the immediacy in his historical poetry that he achieved in his prose fiction. He remained in some ways the Classicist who translated "*Saltavit. Placuit. Mortuus est.*" This was not a weakness: it helped make possible the highly formal structure of **John Brown's Body** that I believe will help it to endure. I had the great good fortune in my teen years to hear Judith Anderson, Tyrone Power, and Raymond Massey in Charles Laughton's production of **John Brown's Body.** Its structure made that dramatic reading possible. There is more.

There is always, in America, the question of our part in the European tradition—European history or European literature. One may recall that George Washington believed a formal structure for the Continental Army necessary for us to take our place in the concert of nations. In somewhat the same way, Benét constructed a formal (if loose-lined) historical poetry for America, so we might take our place in the concert of history, and playing an equal part with England (but revealing our own *genius*) in a concert of letters.

Works Cited

Bellinger, Alfred R. *Spires and Poplars.* New Haven: Yale UP, 1920.

Benét, Stephen Vincent. *The Selected Works of Stephen Vincent Benét, Poetry and Prose.* 2 vols. New York: Farrar & Rinehart, 1942.

Bradley, George. "Introduction." *The Yale Younger Poets Anthology.* New Haven, 1998, xxvi-xxxii.

Bronson, Francis W., et al (eds.) *The Yale Record Book of Verse 1872-1922.* New Haven: Yale UP, 1922.

Davenport, Basil. "Stephen Vincent Benét." *The Selected Works of Stephen Vincent Benét, Poetry and Prose.* New York: Rinehart and Co., 1942, vii-xii.

Farrar, John Chipman. *Forgotten Shrines.* New Haven: Yale UP, 1919.

Harned, Joseph, and Neil Goodwin (eds.). *Art and the Craftsman: The Best of the Yale Literary Magazine 1836-1961.* New Haven: Yale UP, 1961.

Harrison, Gilbert. *The Enthusiast: A Life of Thornton Wilder.* New York: Ticknor & Fields, 1983.

Lobdell, Jared. *England and Always: Tolkien's World of the Rings.* Grand Rapids, Mich.: W. B. Eerdmans Publishing Co., 1981.

Phelps, William Lyon. *Autobiography, with Letters.* London: Oxford UP, 1939.

Rostand, Edmond. *Cyrano de Bergerac. an heroic comedy in five acts. A new version in English verse.* trans. Brian Hooker. New York: H. Holt & Co., 1924.

Wilder, Amos Niven. *Battle-Retrospect.* New Haven: Yale UP, 1923.

———. *Armageddon Revisited: A World War I Journal.* New Haven: Yale UP, 1994.

Gary Grieve-Carlson (essay date 2003)

SOURCE: Grieve-Carlson, Gary. "*John Brown's Body* and the Meaning of the Civil War." In *Stephen Vincent Benét: Essays on His Life and Work,* edited by David Garrett Izzo and Lincoln Konkle, pp. 128-41. Jefferson, N.C.: McFarland & Company, Inc., 2003.

[*In the following essay, Grieve-Carlson contends that* John Brown's Body *embodies Benét's belief that "the Civil War reflects the values of liberal democracy" and regards the poem as a "signal achievement in American poetry."*]

When Henry James asked William Butler Yeats to contribute a poem for a collection intended to raise money for the Allied cause in World War I, Yeats replied, "I think it better that in times like these / A poet's mouth be silent, for in truth / We have no gift to set a statesman right. . . ." Yeats plays to the common assumption that poetry is not the place where politics or history may be understood. But of course Yeats never believed that, or he never could have written "Easter 1916," "Nineteen Hundred and Nineteen," or many of his most powerful poems that deal with political and historical themes of Ireland and its quest for independence from England. Poetry's capacity to tell the truth about history, however, remains controversial. Stephen Vincent Benét's *John Brown's Body* (1928) appears after Ezra Pound's "Near Perigord" (1915) and the early *Cantos,* and after T. S. Eliot's *The Waste Land* (1922), poems which radically challenged our conventional thinking about history, not only in ideological but also in epistemological terms. The iconoclastic examples of Pound and Eliot are followed by Hart Crane (*The Bridge,* 1930), William Carlos Williams (*Paterson,* 1946-58), Robert Penn Warren (*Brother to Dragons,* 1953), and Charles Olson (*The Maximus Poems,* 1953-75). Benét's poem belongs in this modernist tradition because of certain stylistic elements, such as its multiple and fragmented narrative lines, but in many ways *John Brown's Body* is closer in spirit to the great narrative poems of the past, such as Longfellow's "Evangeline" or "The Midnight Ride of Paul Revere." Benét is also

closer to Longfellow than to the twentieth-century poets mentioned above in his refusal of historical iconoclasm. Epistemologically, he believes the past has a stable meaning, and that we can know it, and ideologically, he believes that the Civil War reflects the values of liberal democracy. Essentially he sees the meaning of the War as Lincoln saw it: the war results in "a new birth of freedom," a redeemed nation, a re-unified people. From our perspective in the twenty-first century, it is easy to forget how important and healing such an attitude toward the war was, even in 1928. The divisiveness spawned by the war was bitter, recriminatory, and enduring, and one of Benét's poem's great strengths is its honoring of both sides in the conflict and its affirmation of the restored union that emerged from the conflict. In order to achieve this, he emphasizes certain romantic, even sentimental, elements and evades certain troubling questions, and these aspects of the poem, along with its refusal to conform fully to the modernist aesthetic, have resulted in its precipitous fall from popularity. Although his poem has remained in print, it is rarely assigned in high school or college classes, and Benét is difficult to find in either American literature anthologies or the MLA bibliography. Nevertheless, *John Brown's Body* remains a signal achievement in American poetry.

In 1926 Benét (1898-1943), a Yale graduate who had also studied at the Sorbonne, won a Guggenheim grant—the first ever awarded for poetry—to research and write a long poem on the American Civil War. He moved to Paris, where the cost of living was more manageable, and wrote *John Brown's Body,* a poem of over three hundred pages and almost 15,000 lines, in less than two years. Benét was unsure of its quality; after 135 manuscript pages, he wrote to his brother, ". . . sometimes I think it will be the most colossal flop since Barlow's *Columbiad*" (Fenton 192). But the book's first readers felt otherwise. The Book of the Month Club selection for August 1928, *John Brown's Body* proved incredibly popular. It was Doubleday's biggest moneymaker between 1924 and 1934, selling over 130,000 copies in its first two years, and well over 200,000 copies to date (Fenton 219). In 1929 the book was awarded the Pulitzer Prize for Poetry, and at that time Benét was probably the most widely read poet in the United States. Sinclair Lewis mentioned *John Brown's Body* in his 1930 Nobel Prize acceptance speech as evidence of an American literary renaissance, and Allen Tate called it "the most ambitious poem ever undertaken by an American on an American theme." As late as 1962 Parry Stroud called the poem "decisively the closest approach to Homer and Vergil that an American poet had ever made" (46). To his credit, Benét was more modest than some of his critics. "A poet of greater faculties," he wrote to his publisher, John Farrar, "would have avoided my failures in it and my superficialities—and there are many of both" (Fenton 199). Later: "If the poem is to stand eventually, in any sort of way, it will do so because of a few passages in each Book and the mass-effect of the whole. The faults are many and glaring. But I could do no better, given such brains as I had" (Fenton 209). Benét's judgment has proven more accurate than Parry Stroud's.

However, despite its waning popularity, *John Brown's Body* has genuine strengths, particularly in its cataloguing of vivid emotional images: Ulysses Grant seeing that the Confederates have lit bonfires to celebrate the birth of George Pickett's son, and ordering his Union troops to do the same, then sending the baby a silver service several days before attacking the Confederate position; the secessionist Edmund Ruffin, who fired the first gun against Fort Sumter, walking in his garden after hearing the news of Lee's surrender, cloaking a Confederate flag around his shoulders, and shooting himself in the heart; Lincoln visiting Pickett's widow in Richmond, just before the surrender at Appomattox. In early reviews both Allen Tate, who refers to *John Brown's Body*'s "motion picture flashes," and Harriet Monroe, who calls the poem "a kind of cinema epic" (91), praise Benét's powerful and effective juxtaposition of images.

Benét is also a good storyteller, especially in terms of his ability to tell the tale of a complicated war in a coherent and engaging manner—the major battles, the broad political issues involved, character sketches of the chief figures on both sides (similar to John Dos Passos's short biographies in the *U.S.A.* trilogy). Unlike, say, *The Cantos* or *Paterson*, *John Brown's Body* is absorbing reading, almost novel-like in its ability to pull the reader along. Benét read voluminously as he worked on the poem—regimental histories, diaries, memoirs, autobiographies—and complained that he wanted still more to read. Both Samuel Eliot Morison, who wrote to Benét for permission to quote from *John Brown's Body* in his *The Growth of the American Republic,* and Lee's biographer Douglas Southall Freeman praised the poem for its historical accuracy (Fenton 182). Bruce Catton has called it the single best book, in some respects, ever written on the Civil War (Griffith 14), a judgment shared by Henry Steele Commager (Jackson 73).

Benét, however, insists he is not a historian; in his note prefaced to the book, he writes, "this is a poem, not a history," explaining the absence of notes and bibliography. However, he protests too much, for he then goes on to cite his chief sources and to explain his approach to history: "In dealing with known events I have tried to cleave to historical fact where such fact was ascertainable. On the other hand, for certain thoughts and feelings attributed to historical characters, and for the interpretation of those characters in the poem, I alone must be held responsible" (vii). Thus for Benét history is essentially a matter of fact, not interpretation. He complains in a *Saturday Review* essay of 1932:

> A good many of our recent biographies—or biografictions—whatever you choose to call them, have [been] rather like Mark Twain's reconstruction of the dinosaur, "three bones and a dozen barrels of plaster." The author might not always take the trouble to find out just what his subject did and when he did it—for that often requires a tiresome amount of research. But, as regards what the subject thought and felt, there the author was not merely all-wise but all-seeing . . .
>
> [Fenton 184-85]

The sharp distinction between "what his subject did and when he did it" and "what his subject thought and felt," and Benét's preference for the former, suggests that history ought to be comprised primarily of ascertainable fact, and that interpretation ought to be minimal. At another point Benét writes, only half in jest, "I wish prominent historians wouldn't contradict each other as much as they do. How's a poor poet to know which is right" (Fenton 348). If they'd take the time to do the "tiresome research" and resist the speculative interpretation, Benét implies, the contradictions would disappear.

Benét imagines history as essentially a stable, linear narrative whose meaning is accessible. Historical meaning is a function of accuracy, massive detail—what Ezra Pound called "the method of multitudinous detail," in contrast to his own "method of luminous detail"— and a variety of points of view subsumed within a coherent master narrative. Benét works hard to tell a story that both North and South can agree is true; to be objective, for Benét, is to be nonpartisan, and he treats both Northern and Southern historical characters with respect, depicting heroic behavior motivated by genuine, if somewhat obscure, ideals on both sides of the conflict. His fictional storylines are sentimental and sometimes simply unbelievable, and we might wonder why Benét, with his insistence on the supremacy of the fact, would include them. The answer lies in his inability to get the historical facts by themselves to generate the kind of meaning he wants to impart to the war. The fictional storylines tell accessible, romantic tales that end happily, tales in which suffering and destruction become redemptive and purposeful. In other words, Benét can make the war meaningful in his fictional storylines in a way that he cannot in the historiographic parts of the poem. As Aristotle says in the *Poetics,* poetry can tell universal truths, while history is confined to particular truths. Benét's scrupulous adherence to the particular truths of the Civil War prevents him from twisting history to suit his thematic goals, and so he relies on fictional narratives. But the war itself, in all its complications and refusal to conform to neat or simple meanings, keeps getting in his way.

Benét's difficulty with the war's meaning becomes clear early in the book when he considers the question of the war's cause. He points to the usual factors, especially the slavery question—the poem's preface describes a

Bible-quoting New England sea captain carrying a cargo of slaves from Africa to North America, and Book One describes John Brown's raid on Harper's Ferry. But rather than represent the war as the result of political, economic, and moral decisions made by particular human beings, Benét depicts the war as the inevitable product of large forces beyond human comprehension, thereby mystifying the war's causes. Early in the poem both Jack Ellyat, the main Northern fictional character, and Clay Wingate, the main Southern fictional character, experience supernatural premonitions of an imminent upheaval, so the war is presented as something like an act of God, the product of fate or destiny rather than human decisions.

Benét's representation of the war as the inevitable shedding of blood necessary for redeeming the nation from the sin of slavery is similar not only to the rhetoric of John Brown, but also to Lincoln's language in the Second Inaugural: ". . . if God wills that it [the war] continue, until all the wealth piled by the bond-man's two hundred and fifty years of unrequited toil shall be sunk, and until every drop of blood drawn with the lash, shall be paid by another drawn with the sword, as was said three thousand years ago, so still it must be said 'the judgments of the Lord, are true and righteous altogether'" (Hollinger 477). For Lincoln the war is mandated by God as punishment for America's sin: ". . . American slavery is one of those offences which, . . . having continued through His appointed time, He now wills to remove, and . . . He gives to both North and South, this terrible war, as the woe due to those by whom the offence came . . ." (Hollinger 476-77). Such rhetoric, though it places responsibility for the sin on both North and South and is thus nonpartisan, also serves to remove the war's justification and its consequences from human responsibility. Lincoln had no choice, he claims, but to go to war and to continue the war—God has given this war to the United States as a just punishment for its sins, and God determines its duration and the suffering it causes. Benét picks up on Lincoln's mystification because it furthers his thematic goal (similar to Lincoln's political goal) of a nonpartisan depiction of the war's causes and a redemptive depiction of its results.

It is clear, however, that Lincoln did not go to war against the Confederacy in order to abolish slavery, but rather to preserve the Union, and the Emancipation Proclamation, as Garry Wills persuasively argues in *Lincoln at Gettysburg,* is a military rather than a political or moral document; i.e., abolition in the rebelling states is necessary and justifiable only in order to put down the insurrection and preserve the Union. For Benét, too, the preservation of the Union takes priority over the abolition of slavery as the ultimate purpose for which the war is fought. But why is the preservation of the Union so important? The poem offers no explicit

answer, and elsewhere Benét offers only a vague notion of manifest destiny: "My sense of the union," writes Benét, "is of two majestic and continuing phases, the preservation of the Union and the continual restless movement of its people" (Fenton 344). The Civil War is essential to the fulfillment of that second phase, westward expansion, which is the subject of Benét's unfinished second epic, *Western Star,* the first volume of which won him a posthumous Pulitzer Prize in 1944. But Benét never explains why the preservation of the union and its overspreading the continent is necessary, or good, or worth 600,000 deaths. For most of his readers this may be a claim that needs no justification, a claim to be accepted without question; however, it is this kind of unexamined acceptance of conventional history that puts Benét at odds with the more iconoclastic poet-historians of his time.

If Benét is unclear on the war's causes, or more importantly its justification, he is able with his fictional storylines to tell coherent, meaningful tales associated with the war. His fictional characters, however, tend to be flat, and in some of them his Unionist bias seeps out. The Georgian Clay Wingate, for example, loves Sally Dupré, but the rigid class structure of the South drives him instead into the arms of the beautiful but vain and shallow Lucy Weatherby, a stereotypical Southern belle. The war is thus a good thing because it destroys the class system of the Old South, enabling the love of Clay and Sally to flower. Like the un-American Tories after the Revolutionary War, Lucy goes off to Canada, suggesting that the antebellum South was un-American in its Anglophilic, aristocratic pretensions. Jack Ellyat of Connecticut, who participates, somewhat unrealistically, in every major battle of the war, from Bull Run to Shiloh to Gettysburg, and is even incarcerated in the notorious Andersonville POW camp, falls in love with and impregnates Melora Vilas in Tennessee. After the war's end Melora, like Longfellow's Evangeline, travels the country in search of Ellyat, whom she finally finds and marries. Luke Breckinridge is a Southern Appalachian backwoodsman so stereotypically ignorant that he believes—literally, not figuratively—that the Yankees are the Redcoats, and the Civil War a reprise of the Revolutionary War. Cudjo, the slave who remains loyal to the Wingates even after Wingate Hall is burned by Sherman's troops, is counterbalanced by Spade, the runaway slave who makes the difficult journey north and eventually crosses the Potomac. He encounters racist taunts and exploitation even in the North, but eventually is hired by the Pennsylvanian Jake Diefer, who has lost an arm in the war and can no longer manage his farm by himself. With that image of racial harmony, Benét ignores the very painful history of black Americans between 1865 and the poem's publication in 1928, and evades the question of the depth of the nation's redemption from the sin of race-based slavery. The fictional happy endings—Melora reunited with Ellyat,

Sally Dupré winning Wingate from Lucy, Spade work-ing with Jake Diefer in an idyll of interracial harmony, Luke Breckinridge going home with the chambermaid Sophy—do for Benét what history alone can not: they justify the suffering wrought by the war, and turn the war into a Romantic tale of redemption. When Benét turns to history itself for such justification, however, he cannot find it because, to his credit, he is scrupulously faithful to the historical record, in all its tangled complexity.

Benét is in control of his material and its meanings, either fictional or historical, when he presents vignettes or images calculated to evoke a particular emotional response. Indeed, his historical vignettes are especially powerful because they are not reduced to the often sentimental meanings of the fictional storylines. When Benét moves away from romance and emotion, however, he sometimes loses control of his material and its mean-ings. This is most clear in his treatment of the abolition-ist John Brown, whose presence hovers over the entire poem. Readers have disagreed over the significance of Brown in the poem. John McWilliams claims that Abra-ham Lincoln, and not "the murderous John Brown," is the hero of the poem (61), while Henry Seidel Canby asserts that Brown, not Lincoln, is the poem's protago-nist (Benét, xii). Parry Stroud writes, "The gigantic myth of the corporeal death and spiritual rebirth of Brown . . . becomes an American version of the ancient Egyptian myth of Osiris and the Greek myth of Di-onysus" (70), the kind of exaggerated claim we might expect from a critic careless enough to identify Spade as a Wingate slave (54) when he is not. But if Brown is not Osiris or Dionysus, the terms "protagonist" and "hero" are also misleading. Of all the poem's critics, Allen Tate is the most perceptive on John Brown: "The symbol of John Brown becomes an incentive to some misty writing, and instead of sustaining the poem it evaporates in mixed rhetoric. Mr. Benét sees that the meaning of the War is related to the meaning of Brown; yet what is the meaning of Brown?" Because Benét never clearly answers that question, argues Tate, the war itself "has no meaning" in the poem.

Benét treats Brown ironically rather than romantically, but his irony is inconsistent. In the Prelude, the words of a Negro spiritual ask for a prophet or angel to free the slaves (12-13), and Brown sees himself as an instru-ment of God: he calls himself "Jehovah's rod" (23) and refers to himself and his followers as "pikes and guns / In God's advancing war" (25). Recalling his slaughter of five unarmed proslavery settlers in Kansas, Brown states, "Lord, God, it was a work of Thine, / And how might I refrain?" (24). Although this language is quite similar to Lincoln's in the Second Inaugural, Benét is uncomfortable with Brown's fanaticism, and he notes the irony that the first man killed by Brown's Harper's Ferry raiders was the black baggagemaster, Shepherd

Heyward. He notes also Brown's curious refusal, after seizing the armory's weapons, to retreat before the Virginia militia and federal troops could seize the Poto-mac Bridge and then surround him. Benét can be harsh in his depiction of Brown:

> He was a stone,
> A stone eroded to a cutting edge
> By obstinacy, failure and cold prayers.
> Discredited farmer, dubiously involved
> In lawsuit after lawsuit, Shubel Morgan [an alias
>   Brown used]
> Fantastic bandit of the Kansas border,
> Red-handed murderer at Pottawattomie,
> Cloudy apostle, whooped along to death
> By those who do no violence themselves
> But only buy the guns to have it done,
> Sincere of course, as all fanatics are,
> And with a certain minor-prophet air,
> That fooled the world to thinking him half-great
> When all he did consistently was fail
>
> [47]

Then Benét's speaker corrects himself, returning to the image of John Brown as a "stone eroded to a cutting edge," and asserting that despite his unreasoning and destructive temperament, Brown was also "Heroic and devoted" (48) in a stonelike manner, and that he was a passive instrument of a large historical force beyond his comprehension: "Call it the *mores,* call it God or Fate, / Call it Mansoul or economic law, / That force exists and moves. And when it moves / It will employ a hard and actual stone" (48). These lines echo the supernatural premonitions that Wingate and Ellyat experience early in the book, as well as Lincoln's Second Inaugural, in their suggestion that the war is the product of something like fate or destiny rather than human decisions. However, they also seem to suggest that what we call "That force" is unimportant, which suggestion is argu-able. If we call it "God," then history unfolds as Lincoln suggests in the Second Inaugural, or as Augustine sug-gests in *City of God*; if we call it "economic law," then history unfolds as Marx suggests it does. The difference is hardly insignificant, particularly with regard to the meaning of the Civil War. Yet Benét evades the ques-tion, largely, I think, because such a mystification of John Brown and the war's origins makes it easier to be nonpartisan (neither side is finally responsible for the war; destiny is responsible) and to effect the redemptive reconciliation between North and South that is, for Benét, the war's signal achievement.

In his failure and execution, John Brown becomes the catalyst that ignites the war, a "swift fire whose sparks fell like live coals / On every State in the Union" (48). Benét's dominant tone toward Brown, however, remains ironic, as in this description of contemporary accounts of the days before his execution:

> The North that had already now begun
> To mold his body into crucified Christ's,

Hung fables about those hours—saw him move
Symbolically, to kiss a negro child,
Do this and that, say things he never said,
To swell the sparse, hard outlines of the event
With sentimental omen.

                                        It was not so

                                                              [51]

Was Brown successful? No, according to the poem's narrator at this point: "The slaves have forgotten his eyes. / . . . / Cotton will grow next year, in spite of the skull. / Slaves will be slaves next year, in spite of the bones. / Nothing is changed, John Brown, nothing is changed" (52). But Brown's ghost replies, "There is a song in my bones" (52), "And God blows through them with a hollow sound" (53), and the poem's narrator admits, "I hear it" (53). That song, of course, faint as it is at first, will become "John Brown's Body," the tune of which will later be used for "The Battle Hymn of the Republic." Early in Book Two, which opens with the fall of Fort Sumter, Benét recalls Brown: "The stone falls in the pool, the ripples spread" (55).

At this point in the poem John Brown disappears, and the war takes center stage. He re-appears in 1862, at the end of Book Four, nearly three years after his execution, with the war in stalemate. The poem's narrator reports that certain Union soldiers claim to have seen him walking "in front of the armies" (183).

> A dead man saw him striding at Seven Pines,
> The bullets whistling through him like a torn flag,
> A madman saw him whetting a sword on a Bible,
> A cloud above Malvern Hill
>
>   [183]

"But these are all lies" (183), insists the narrator. Brown is dead, his goals unrealized. "The South goes ever forward, the slave is not free, / The great stone gate of the Union crumbles and totters, / The cotton-blossoms are pushing the blocks apart" (184). Nonetheless, the narrator affirms for Brown a crucial role in the war, invigorating Union morale and providing a sanctifying purpose for the war effort: "His song is alive and throbs in the tramp of the columns" (183).

Yet Benét's discomfort with Brown persists. He is at pains to distinguish the man from the symbol. "But his song and he are two" (183), Benét insists, and addressing the man, he says, "You did not fight for the union or wish it well, / You fought for the single dream of a man unchained" (184). Benét aligns Brown with those radical abolitionists who would sooner dissolve the union than countenance slavery, whereas for Benét, the preservation of the union is the primary justification of the war. For Benét abolition, which has led to the South's secession, becomes at the nadir of Union morale the means to the end of the Union's preservation. Addressing Brown directly, Benét says, "You fought for a

people you did not comprehend, / For a symbol chained by a symbol in your own mind, / But, unless you arise, that people will not be free" (184). So the man—failure, murderer, and fanatic—is transformed into and invoked as a symbol:

> Your song goes on, but the slave is still a slave,
> And all Egypt's land rides Northward while you moul-
>   der in the grave!
> Rise up, John Brown,
> (A-mouldering in the grave.)
> Go down, John Brown,
> (Against all Egypt's land)
> Go down, John Brown,
> Go down, John Brown,
> Go down, John Brown, and set that people free!
>
>   [185]

However, casting black slaves in the role of the captive Israelites, the American South as Egypt, and John Brown as the people's great deliverer, Moses, is an analogy that breaks down in several key respects. Moses was an Israelite, and their acknowledged leader, whereas Brown was not black; and far from being their acknowledged leader, his followers in the raid on Harper's Ferry included seventeen whites and only five blacks; Frederick Douglass, among others, had refused to join him. Finally, the Israelites eventually reached the Promised Land; whether American blacks have done the same, despite Benét's sunny depiction of Spade on Diefer's farm, is a far from settled question. Benét's attempt to separate, via irony, the man from the symbol remains problematic; Brown's moral intensity cannot be separated from his violence and fanaticism.

Brown indirectly accomplishes his goal—the Thirteenth Amendment abolishes slavery. But the means to that end—the Civil War—bring about much more than abolition and the preservation of the Union. Does the war effect the "new birth of freedom" that Lincoln prophesies at Gettysburg? Does it establish a nation committed to the moral ideals articulated by Jefferson in the Declaration of Independence? Having purged the nation of its sin (slavery), does it re-establish a covenantal relationship with God? Benét makes no such claims. In fact, on the consequences of the War he is remarkably close to Edmund Wilson, who describes

> the whole turbid blatant period that followed the Civil War—with its miseries of an industrial life that was reducing white factory workers to the slavery which George Fitzhugh had predicted, with its millionaires as arrogant and brutal as any Carolina planters, with the violent clashes between them as bloody as Nat Turner's rebellion or John Brown's raid upon Kansas, with its wars in Cuba and Europe that were our next uncontrollable moves after the war by which we had wrested California from the Mexicans and the war by which we had compelled the South to submit to the Washington government
>
>   [794]

Similarly, Robert Penn Warren writes that the War's consequences include "not only the Union sanctified by blood, but also Gould and Cook and Brady and the Crédit Mobilier and the Homestead blood and the Haymarket riot . . . the uncoiling powers of technology and finance capitalism, the new world of Big Organization" (153). At the end of his poem Benét makes remarkably similar points about what the war destroys, in addition to the institution of slavery and the agrarian values of the Old South, and what it brings about. Focusing on the irony inherent in the kind of nation the Civil War produced, Benét reminds us that Brown had been a shepherd and a farmer, not at home in towns or cities, and was a man more interested in the things of the spirit than in material prosperity. Yet ironically,

> Out of his body grows revolving steel,
> Out of his body grows the spinning wheel
> Made up of wheels, the new, mechanic birth,
> No longer bound by toil
> To the unsparing soil
> Or the old furrow-line,
> The great, metallic beast
> Expanding West and East,
> His heart a spinning coil,
> His juices burning oil,
> His body serpentine.
> Out of John Brown's strong sinews the tall skyscrapers grow,
> Out of his heart the chanting buildings rise,
> Rivet and girder, motor and dynamo,
> Pillar of smoke by day and fire by night,
> The steel-faced cities reaching at the skies,
> The whole enormous and rotating cage
> Hung with hard jewels of electric light,
> Smoky with sorrow, black with splendor, dyed
> Whiter than damask for a crystal bride
> With metal suns, the engine-handed Age,
> The genie we have raised to rule the earth,
> Obsequious to our will
> But servant-master still,
> The tireless serf already half a god—
>
>   [335]

Benét sees the kind of society, the kind of nation, the Civil War gave birth to, but he refuses, finally, to judge or to evaluate those consequences. In "Ars poetica," Archibald MacLeish writes, "A poem should not mean / But be," summarizing what the New Critics called "the heresy of paraphrase," according to which a poem's meaning depends on its particular combination of formal literary elements. Any attempt to paraphrase the poem's meaning involves an inevitable reduction of that combination of elements, which only exists as the complete poem itself. Benét treats history as the New Critics treat poetry, and the "heresy of paraphrase" becomes for him the heresy of historical interpretation or judgment. In the poem's final lines, he warns his readers about "prophets," or overtly biased, partisan historians, who look at what America has become and either "Bawl out their strange despair / Or fall in wor-

ship there" (336). Cautioning his reader against either approach, he continues, in the poem's final four lines:

> If you at last must have a word to say,
> Say neither, in their [the prophets who either "bawl"
>   or "worship"] way,
> "It is a deadly magic and accursed,"
> Nor "It is blest," but only "It is here"
>
>   [336]

For Benét, in interpreting the history of the Civil War and its consequences, our choices are limited to (1) the extreme reductivism of curse or blessing, or (2) silent acceptance. He chooses the latter, and he advises his reader to do so as well. One might argue that the choice is a version of the either-or fallacy, and is thus a false choice: after all, we can imagine interpretations of the Civil War that are neither curse, blessing, nor laconic acceptance. However, Benét is caught between his thematic goal—to depict the war as a tragic yet redemptive reconciliation of North and South that enables the reborn nation to fulfill its destiny—and his admirable adherence to the historical record. He cannot deny what Wilson and Warren observe about the war's effects, and he is honest enough to include such observations in his poem, yet he cannot bring himself to the dangerous conclusion that such observations, at least implicitly, undermine his theme. In other words, the Civil War and its intractable, hugely complicated history, its tangled mass of causes and effects, cannot be reduced to the thematic meaning that Benét, like Lincoln, wants to give it, and Benét is honest enough as a historian to concede implicitly this point. That this point cannot be easily or neatly synthesized with the poem's theme may be considered a weakness, but it also provides the kind of unresolved tension that gives the poem much of its power and interest. Unlike such historian-poets as Pound, Eliot, and Olson, Benét is neither a revisionist nor a skeptic. He is in the political mainstream; he is of the party of Lincoln, and *John Brown's Body* very effectively dramatizes Lincoln's conception of the war. And Lincoln's conception, after all, has become the nation's conception. It is certainly possible to take issue with Lincoln's conception of the war, as Warren and Wilson have done, but to criticize Benét for failing to do so is to criticize him for not having written a different poem, which is hardly fair.

Benét assumes the posture of the moderate antiextremist, the non-partisan who simply and objectively recounts what happened, making the war's significance clearer and more accessible in the themes of his fictional storylines, and in so doing he presents a meaningful tale of suffering, sacrifice, heroism, redemption, and reconciliation. Some of the hard, intractable questions about the war are omitted, and these aporia, along with the romantic emplotment of much of the narrative, are in part responsible for the poem's having fallen into critical disfavor. **John Brown's Body** rewards repeated reading, however, and along with such too often neglected poems on history as Archibald MacLeish's *Conquistador* and Robert Penn Warren's *Brother to Dragons,* Benét's poem stands as a major work within the genre of American narrative poetry that takes history as its subject.

Works Cited

Benét, Stephen Vincent. *The Selected Works of Stephen Vincent Benét Poetry and Prose.* New York: Farrar & Rinehart, Inc., 1942.

Fenton, Charles A. *Stephen Vincent Benét: The Life and Times of an American Man of Letters.* New Haven: Yale UP, 1958.

Griffith, John. "Stephen Vincent Benét," in *Dictionary of Literary Biography,* ed. Peter Quartermain, vol. 48, Detroit: Gale Research, 1985.

Hollinger, David A., and Charles Capper, eds. *The American Intellectual Tradition,* volume I. New York: Oxford UP, 1997.

Jackson, Frederick H. "Stephen Vincent Benét and American History." *The Historian* 17 (Autumn 1954): 67-75.

McWilliams, John. "The Epic in the Nineteenth Century." *The Columbia History of American Poetry.* New York: Columbia UP, 1993.

Monroe, Harriet. "A Cinema Epic." *Poetry* 33 (November 1928): 91-96.

Stroud, Parry. *Stephen Vincent Benét.* New York: Twayne, 1962.

Tate, Allen. "The Irrepressible Conflict." *The Nation* 127 (19 September 1928): 274.

Warren, Robert Penn. "Edmund Wilson's Civil War." *Commentary* 34 (August 1962): 151-58.

Wills, Garry. *Lincoln at Gettysburg: The Words That Remade America.* New York: Simon & Schuster, 1992.

Wilson, Edmund. *Patriotic Gore: Studies in the Literature of the American Civil War.* New York: Oxford UP, 1962.

FURTHER READING

Criticism

Bradley, George. Introduction to *The Yale Younger Poets Anthology,* edited by George Bradley, pp. xliii-liii. New Haven, Conn.: Yale University Press, 1998.

> Provides an overview of Benét's tenure as editor of the Yale Series of Younger Poets.

Jackson, Frederick H. "Stephen Vincent Benét and American History." *Historian* 17, no. 1 (autumn 1954): 67-75.

> Examines the role of American history in Benét's verse, focusing on his epic poem *John Brown's Body.*

Kretzoi, Charlotte. "Puzzled Americans: Attempts at an American National Epic Poem." In *The Origins and Originality of American Culture,* edited by Tibor Frank, pp. 139-48. Budapest, Hungary: Akadémiai Kiadó, 1984.

> Analyzes the attempts at an American epic by Borlow, Longfellow, and Benét.

John Berryman
1914-1972

(Born John Allyn Smith, Jr.) American poet, biographer, novelist, essayist, and critic.

INTRODUCTION

Berryman is regarded as a boldly innovative twentieth-century American poet. Critics associate him with a group of poets known as the "Middle Generation," which includes Delmore Schwartz, Randall Jarrell, Robert Lowell, and Theodore Roethke. Berryman's verse is often classified as confessional poetry, but some critics argue that this categorization is simplistic and belittling in that it does not take into consideration the craft and imagination imbued in his poems.

BIOGRAPHICAL INFORMATION

Berryman was born on October 25, 1914, in McAlester, Oklahoma. His father, a banker, moved the family to Florida when Berryman was a child and started a land speculation business. When the business failed, he committed suicide. Berryman's mother quickly remarried. These traumatic events profoundly influenced Berryman's life and work. In 1926 the family moved to New York, and two years later Berryman enrolled at the South Kent School in Connecticut. With its emphasis on athletics and competition, Berryman felt isolated and fell into depression, which resulted in a suicide attempt in 1931. After graduating early, he entered Columbia College (now known as Columbia University) in New York City. He was profoundly influenced by his professor Mark van Doren, a poet and scholar, and with his encouragement Berryman began to concentrate on poetry. His verse began appearing in periodicals such as *The Nation* and the *Columbia Review*. Berryman was named a Kellet Fellow, which allowed him to study in England at Cambridge University for two years. At Cambridge he met such prestigious writers as W. B. Yeats, T. S. Eliot, Dylan Thomas, and W. H. Auden. During this time, he was awarded the Oldham Shakespeare Scholarship. In 1939 he returned to New York City, working as a part-time editor for *The Nation,* and then as an instructor in English at Wayne State University in Detroit.

In 1940 Berryman became an instructor at Harvard University, where he taught for three years. That same year, several of his poems were published in *Five Young*

American Poets, a collection of verse written by Berryman, Mary Barnard, Randall Jarrell, W. R. Moses, and George Marion O'Donnell. He accepted a position at Princeton University in 1943, and remained there for the next ten years. He was awarded the American Academy Award for poetry in 1950, the same year he accepted a teaching position at the University of Washington, and then the University of Cincinnati. Known as a charismatic teacher, Berryman was affected by alcoholism and other personal problems, which emerge in his verse. These problems also caused his resignation from the Writer's Workshop at the University of Iowa, where he accepted a position in 1954. In 1955, the poet Allan Tate invited him to teach at the University of Minnesota, where Berryman remained for the rest of his life. In 1958 he was hospitalized for exhaustion and nerves, a pattern which would continue throughout the years. In 1965 he was awarded a Pulitzer Prize for *77 Dream Songs* (1964). After years of heavy drinking, he checked himself into a rehabilitation program in 1969. His struggle to quit drinking was the subject of his novel *Recovery* (1973). On January 7, 1972, he committed suicide by jumping off of the Washington Avenue Bridge in Minneapolis.

MAJOR WORKS

Berryman's first major book of poetry, *The Dispossessed* (1948), reflected the poet's chaotic personal life and growing sense of despair by utilizing the Holocaust as a metaphor for his own struggles. Reviewers recognized his artistic potential, but derided the volume as bitter and lacking deep feeling. His next volume, *Berryman's Sonnets,* which was not published until 1967, is a collection of sonnets in the Petrarchan form that describe his feelings of guilt, exhilaration, and hope resulting from an extramarital affair during his time at Princeton. These sonnets were published posthumously in *Collected Poems, 1937-1971* (1988), as *Sonnets to Chris.* Initially published in the *Partisan Review* in 1953, *Homage to Mistress Bradstreet* (1956) is one of Berryman's best-known works and is regarded as the breakthrough in his career. A fifty-seven stanza poem based on the life of the seventeenth-century American poet Anne Bradstreet, the piece was well received by critics for its poetic maturity.

It was the publication of *The Dream Songs* (1969) that catapulted Berryman to the forefront of American poetry. Comprised of two previously published collections—*77 Dream Songs* and *His Toy, His Dream, His Rest* (1968)—*The Dream Songs* is made up of 358 poems, or songs, composed of three, six-line stanzas. Deemed by most reviewers as obscure and abstruse, the songs revolve around the middle-age character of Henry, who is haunted by loss and acts out in often self-destructive ways. Critics have discussed parallels between Henry and Berryman, who claimed Henry was not his alter-ego. The collection garnered much critical attention, most of it mixed, but critics recognized the volume's contribution to American poetry and the poet won both the National Book Award and the Bollingen Prize for the collection. His last major work, *Love and Fame* (1970), is a collection of lyrics, most of which are confessional in nature. Reviewers regard the poems in this collection as his most revelatory and the most self-indulgent of his career. Berryman ended the volume with "The Eleven Addresses to the Lord," a series of poems that explores his religious faith.

CRITICAL RECEPTION

The critical reaction to Berryman's poetry centers on the confessional nature of his work, as commentators assess the extent to which his poems reflect his chaotic and self-destructive personal life. In this sense, he has

been compared to other confessional poets such as Sylvia Plath and Robert Lowell. Critics have traced the development of his verse, from technically proficient but unemotional poems that are dominated by the influences of other poets to audaciously original poems that adroitly explore his recurring obsessions: religious apostasy, spiritual desolation, adultery, professional and personal discipline, loss, guilt, retribution, and remorse. Commentators have identified a number of profound influences on his early work, particularly that of W. B. Yeats, W. H. Auden, Walt Whitman, Ezra Pound, and Delmore Schwartz. Viewing him as a brashly original and essential poet, critics have favorably assessed Berryman's contribution to twentieth-century American poetry.

PRINCIPAL WORKS

Poetry

Poems 1942
The Dispossessed 1948
Homage to Mistress Bradstreet 1956
His Thoughts Made Pockets and the Plane Buckt 1958
77 Dream Songs 1964
Berryman's Sonnets 1967
Short Poems 1967
His Toy, His Dream, His Rest 1968
†*The Dream Songs* 1969
Love and Fame 1970
Delusions, Etc. of John Berryman 1972
Selected Poems, 1938-1968 1972
Henry's Fate and Other Poems, 1967-1972 1977
‡*Collected Poems, 1937-1971* 1988
Selected Poems 2004

Other Major Works

Stephen Crane (biography) 1950
Recovery (novel) 1973
The Freedom of the Poet (essays) 1976
Stephen Crane: The Red Badge of Courage (criticism) 1981
We Dream of Honor: John Berryman's Letters to His Mother (letters) 1988
Berryman's Shakespeare (criticism) 1999

*This work includes *The Dispossessed* and *His Thoughts Made Pockets and the Plane Buckt.*

†This work includes *77 Dream Songs* and *His Toy, His Dream, His Rest.*

‡This work includes *Sonnets to Chris.*

CRITICISM

John Berryman and Peter Stitt (interview date 1972)

SOURCE: Berryman, John, and Peter Stitt. "The Art of Poetry: An Interview with John Berryman." In *Berryman's Understanding: Reflections on the Poetry of John Berryman,* edited by Harry Thomas, pp. 18-44. Boston: Northeastern University Press, 1988.

[*In the following interview, originally published in 1972, Berryman discusses the impact of fame on his life, his reaction to being classified as a confessional poet, and the influence of W. B. Yeats, W. H. Auden, and T. S. Eliot on his work.*]

On a Sunday afternoon in late July 1970, John Berryman gave a reading of his poems in a small "people's park" in Minneapolis near the west bank campus of the University of Minnesota. Following the reading, I introduced myself—we hadn't seen each other since I was his student, eight years earlier—and we spent the afternoon in conversation at his house. He had had a very bad winter, he explained, and had spent much of the spring in the extended-care ward at St. Mary's Hospital. I asked him about doing an interview. He agreed, and we set up an appointment for late October.

Berryman spent a week in Mexico at the end of the summer—and had "a marvelous time." A trip to upstate New York for a reading followed, and by early October he was back at St. Mary's. It was there that the interview was conducted, during visiting hours on the 27th and 29th of October.

He looked much better than he had during the summer, was heavier and more steady on his feet. He again smoked, and drank coffee almost continually. The room was spacious and Berryman was quite at home in it. In addition to the single bed, it contained a tray-table that extended over the bed, a chair, and two nightstands, one of which held a large AM-FM radio and the usual hospital accountrements. Books and papers covered the other nightstand, the table, and the broad window sill.

Berryman was usually slow to get going on an answer, as he made false starts looking for just the right words. Once he started talking, he would continue until he had exhausted the subject—thus some of his answers are very long. This method left unasked questions, and the most important of these were mailed to him later for written answers. In contrast to the taped answers, the written answers turned out to be brief, flat, and even dull. (These have been discarded.) By way of apology, he explained that he was again devoting his energies almost entirely to writing poetry.

An edited typescript of the interview was sent him in January 1971. He returned it in March, having made very few changes. He did supply some annotations, and these have been left as he put them.

[*Stitt*]: *Mr. Berryman, recognition came to you late, in comparison with writers like Robert Lowell and Delmore Schwartz. What effect do you think fame has on a poet? Can this sort of success ruin a writer?*

[Berryman]: I don't think there are any generalizations at all. If a writer gets hot early, then his work ought to become known early. If it doesn't, he is in danger of feeling neglected. We take it that all young writers overestimate their work. It's impossible not to—I mean if you recognized what shit you were writing, you wouldn't write it. You have to believe in your stuff—every day has to be the new day on which the new poem may be *it.* Well, fame supports that feeling. It gives self-confidence, it gives a sense of an actual, contemporary audience, and so on. On the other hand, unless it is sustained, it can cause trouble—and it is very seldom sustained. If your first book is a smash, your second book gets kicked in the face, and your third book, and lots of people, like Delmore, can't survive that disappointment. From that point of view, early fame is very dangerous indeed, and my situation, which was so painful to me for many years, was really in a way beneficial.

I overestimated myself, as it turned out, and felt bitter, bitterly neglected; but I had certain admirers, certain high judges on my side from the beginning, so that I had a certain amount of support. Moreover, I had a kind of indifference on my side—much as Joseph Conrad did. A reporter asked him once about reviews, and he said, "I don't read my reviews. I measure them." Now, until I was about thirty-five years old, I not only didn't read my reviews, I didn't measure them, I never even looked at them. That is so peculiar that close friends of mine wouldn't believe me when I told them. I thought that was indifference, but now I'm convinced that it was just that I had no skin on—you know, I was afraid of being killed by some remark. Oversensitivity. But there was an *element* of indifference in it, and so the public indifference to my work was countered with a certain amount of genuine indifference on my part, which has been very helpful since I became a celebrity. Auden once said that the best situation for a poet is to be taken up early and held for a considerable time and then dropped after he has reached the level of indifference.

Something else is in my head; a remark of Father Hopkins to Bridges. Two completely unknown poets in their thirties—fully mature—Hopkins one of the great poets of the century, and Bridges awfully good. Hopkins with no audience and Bridges with thirty readers. He says,

"Fame in itself is nothing. The only thing that matters is virtue. Jesus Christ is the only true literary critic. But," he said, "from any lesser level or standard than that, we must recognize that fame is the true and appointed setting of men of genius." That seems to me appropriate. This business about geniuses in neglected garrets is for the birds. The idea that a man is somehow no good just because he becomes very popular, like Frost, is nonsense also. There are exceptions, Chatterton, Hopkins of course, Rimbaud, you can think of various cases, but on the whole, men of genius were judged by their contemporaries very much as posterity judges them. So if I were talking to a young writer, I would recommend the cultivation of extreme indifference to both praise and blame, because praise will lead you to vanity and blame will lead you to self-pity, and both are bad for writers.

What is your reaction to such comments as: "If Berryman is not America's finest living poet, then he is surely running a close second to Lowell"?

Well, I don't know. I don't get any *frisson* of excitement back here, and my bank account remains the same, and my view of my work remains the same, and in general I can say that everything is much the same after that is over.

It seems that you, along with Frost and several other American writers, were appreciated earlier in England than in America.

That's true. More in Frost's case. Stephen Crane is another.

Why do you think this is true?

I wonder. The literary cultures are still very different. Right this minute, for example, the two best reviewers of poetry in English, and perhaps the only two to whom I have paid the slightest attention, are both Englishmen—Kermode and Alvarez. Of course, that's just a special case—ten years ago it was different, but our people have died or stopped practicing criticism. We couldn't put out a thing like the *Times Literary Supplement*. We just don't have it. Education at the elite level is better in England, humanistic education—never mind technical education, where we are superior or at least equal—but Cambridge, Oxford, London, and now the redbrick universities provide a much higher percentage of intelligent readers in the population—the kind of people who listen to the Third Programme and read the *Times Literary Supplement*. They are rather compact and form a body of opinion from which the reviewers both good and mediocre don't have to stand out very far. In our culture, we also, of course, have good readers, but not as high a percentage—and they are incredibly dispersed geographically. It makes a big difference.

You, along with Lowell, Sylvia Plath, and several others, have been called a confessional poet. How do you react to that label?

With rage and contempt! Next question.

Are the sonnets "confessional"?

Well, they're about her and me. I don't know. The word doesn't mean anything. I understand the confessional to be a place where you go and talk with a priest. I personally haven't been to confession since I was twelve years old.

You once said: "I masquerade as a writer. Actually I am a scholar." At another time you pointed out that your passport gives your occupation as "Author" and not "Teacher." How do your roles as teacher and scholar affect your role as poet?

Very, very hard question. Housman is one of my heroes and always has been. He was a detestable and miserable man. Arrogant, unspeakably lonely, cruel, and so on, but an absolutely marvelous minor poet, I think, and a great scholar. And I'm about *equally* interested in those two activities. In him they are perfectly distinct. You are dealing with an absolute schizophrenic. In me they seem closer together, but I just don't know. Schwartz once asked me why it was that all my Shakespearian study had never showed up anywhere in my poetry, and I couldn't answer the question. It was a piercing question because his early poems are really very much influenced by Shakespeare's early plays. I seem to have been sort of untouched by Shakespeare, although I have had him in my mind since I was twenty years old.

*I don't agree with that. One of **The Dream Songs,** one of those written to the memory of Delmore Schwartz—let me see if I can find it. Here, number 147. These lines:*

> Henry's mind grew blacker the more he thought.
> He looked onto the world like the act of an aged
>   whore.
> Delmore Delmore.
> He flung to pieces and they hit the floor.

That sounds very Shakespearian to me.

That sounds like *Troilus and Cressida,* doesn't it? One of my very favorite plays. I would call that Shakespearian. Not to praise it, though, only in description. I was half-hysterical writing that song. It just burst onto the page. It took only as long to compose as it takes to write it down.

Well, that covers scholarship. How about teaching? Does teaching only get in the way of your work as a poet?

It depends on the kind of teaching you do. If you teach creative writing, you get absolutely nothing out of it. Or English—what are you teaching? People you read twenty years ago. Maybe you pick up a little if you keep on preparing, but very few people keep on preparing. Everybody is lazy, and poets, in addition to being lazy, have another activity which is very demanding, so they tend to slight their teaching. But I give courses in the history of civilization, and when I first began teaching here I nearly went crazy. I was teaching Christian origins and the Middle Ages, and I had certain weak spots. I was okay with the *Divine Comedy* and certain other things, but I had an awful time of it. I worked it out once, and it took me nine hours to prepare a fifty-minute lecture. I have learned much more from giving these lecture courses than I ever learned at Columbia or Cambridge. It has forced me out into areas where I wouldn't otherwise have been, and, since I am a scholar, these things are connected. I make myself acquainted with the scholarship. Suppose I'm lecturing on Augustine. My Latin is very rusty, but I'll pay a certain amount of attention to the Latin text in the Loeb edition, with the English across the page. Then I'll visit the library and consult five or six old and recent works on St. Augustine, who is a particular interest of mine anyway. Now all that becomes part of your equipment for poetry, even for lyric poetry. The Bradstreet poem is a very learned poem. There is a lot of theology in it, there is a lot of theology in **The Dream Songs.** Anything is useful to a poet. Take observation of nature, of which I have absolutely none. It makes possible a world of moral observation for Frost, or Hopkins. So scholarship and teaching are directly useful to my activity as a writer.

But not the teaching of creative writing. You don't think there is any value in that for you as a poet.

I enjoy it. Sometimes your kids prove awfully good. Snodgrass is well known now, and Bill Merwin—my students—and others, and it's delightful to be of service to somebody. But most of them have very little talent, and you can't over-encourage them; that's impossible. Many of my friends teach creative writing. I'm not putting it down, and it certainly is an honest way of earning a living, but I wouldn't recommend it to a poet. It is better to teach history or classics or philosophy or the kind of work I do here in humanities.

You have given Yeats and Auden as early influences on your poetry. What did you learn from them?

Practically everything I could then manipulate. On the other hand, they didn't take me very far, because by the time I was writing really well, in 1948—that's the beginning of the Bradstreet poem and the last poems in the collection called **The Dispossessed**—there was no Yeats around and no Auden. Some influence from Rilke,

some influence from a poet whom I now consider very bad, Louis Aragon, in a book called *Crèvecoeur*—he conned me. He took all his best stuff from Apollinaire, whom I hadn't then read, and swept me off my feet. I wrote a poem called **"Narcissus Moving,"** which is as much like Aragon as possible, and maybe it's just as bad. I don't know. Then the Bradstreet poem—it is not easy to see the literary ancestry of that poem. Who has been named? Hopkins. I don't see that. Of course there are certain verbal practices, but on the whole, not. The stanza has been supposed to be derived from the stanza of "The Wreck of the Deutschland." I don't see that. I have never read "The Wreck of the Deutschland," to tell you the truth, except the first stanza. Wonderful first stanza. But I really just couldn't get onto it. It's a set piece, and I don't like set pieces. I'll bet it's no good—well, you know, not comparable with the great short poems. Then Lowell has been named. I see the influence of *Lord Weary's Castle* in some of the later poems in **The Dispossessed.** There's no doubt about it. In the Bradstreet poem, as I seized inspiration from *Augie March*, I sort of seized inspiration, I think, from Lowell, rather than imitated him. I can't think, offhand—I haven't read it in many years—of a single passage in the Bradstreet poem which distinctly sounds like Lowell. However, I may be quite wrong about this, since people have named him. Other people? I don't think so.

How about Eliot? You must have had to reckon with Eliot in one way or another, positively or negatively.

My relationship with Eliot was highly ambiguous. In the first place, I refused to meet him on three occasions in England, and I think I mentioned this in one of the poems I wrote last spring. I had to fight shy of Eliot. There was a certain amount of hostility in it, too. I only began to appreciate Eliot much later, after I was secure in my own style. I now rate him very high. I think he is one of the greatest poets who ever lived. Only sporadically good. What he would do—he would collect himself and write a masterpiece, then relax for several years writing prose, earning a living, and so forth; then he'd collect himself and write another masterpiece, very different from the first, and so on. He did this about five times, and after the *Four Quartets* he lived on for twenty years. Wrote absolutely nothing. It's a very strange career. Very—a pure system of spasms. My career is like that. It is horribly like that. But I feel deep sympathy, admiration, and even love for Eliot over all the recent decades.

You knew Dylan Thomas pretty well, didn't you?

Pretty well, pretty well. We weren't close friends.

Any influence there?

No. And that's surprising, very surprising, because we used to knock around in Cambridge and London. We didn't discuss our poetry much. He was far ahead of me. Occasionally he'd show me a poem or I'd show him a poem. He was very fond of making suggestions. He didn't like a line in a poem of mine, later published by Robert Penn Warren in the *Southern Review,* called **"Night and the City"**—a very bad poem modeled on a poem by John Peale Bishop called "The Return." Well, Dylan didn't like one line, and so he proposed this line: "A bare octagonal ballet for penance." Now, my poem was rather incoherent, but couldn't contain—you know, in the military sense—it couldn't contain that! I was very fond of him. I loved him, and I thought he was a master. I was wrong about that. He was not a master; he became a master only much later on. What he was then is a great rhetorician. Terrific. But the really great poems only came towards the end of World War II, I think. There was no influence.

Do you think he had an impulse towards self-destruction?

Oh, absolutely. He was doomed already when I first knew him. Everybody warned him for many years.

Can one generalize on that? So many of the poets of your generation have encountered at least personal tragedy—flirting with suicide, and so on.

I don't know. The record is very bad. Vachel Lindsay killed himself. Hart Crane killed himself, more important. Sara Teasdale—quite a good poet at the end, killed herself. Then Miss Plath recently. Randall—it's not admitted, but apparently he did kill himself—and Roethke and Delmore might just as well have died of alcoholism. They died of heart attacks, but that's one of the main ways to die from alcoholism. And Dylan died in an alcoholic coma. Well, the actual cause of death was bronchitis. But he went into shock in the Chelsea, where I was staying also, and they got him to the hospital in an ambulance, where he was wrongly treated. They gave him morphine, which is contraindicated in cases of alcoholic shock. He wouldn't have lived anyway, but they killed him. He lay in a coma for five days.

You were there, weren't you?

I was in the corridor, ten feet away.

What was it like to take high tea with William Butler Yeats?

All I can say is that my mouth was dry and my heart was in my mouth. Thomas had very nearly succeeded in getting me drunk earlier in the day. He was full of scorn for Yeats, as he was for Eliot, Pound, Auden. He thought my admiration for Yeats was the funniest thing in that part of London. It wasn't until about three o'clock that I realized that he and I were drinking more

than usual. I didn't drink much at that time; Thomas drank much more than I did. I had the sense to leave. I went back to my chambers, Cartwright Gardens, took a cold bath, and just made it for the appointment. I remember the taxi ride over. The taxi was left over from the First World War, and when we arrived in Pall Mall—we could see the Atheneum—the driver said he didn't feel he could get in. Finally I decided to abandon ship and take off on my own. So I went in and asked for Mr. Yeats. Very much like asking, "Is Mr. Ben Jonson here?" And he came down. He was much taller than I expected, and haggard. Big though, big head, rather wonderful looking in a sort of a blunt, patrician kind of way, but there was something shrunken also. He told me he was just recovering from an illness. He was very courteous, and we went in to tea. At a certain point, I had a cigarette, and I asked him if he would like one. To my great surprise he said yes. So I gave him a Craven-A and then lit it for him, and I thought, "Immortality is mine! From now on it's just a question of reaping the fruits of my effort." He did most of the talking. I asked him a few questions. He did not ask me any questions about myself, although he was extremely courteous and very kind. At one point he said, "I have reached the age when my daughter can beat me at croquet," and I thought, "Hurrah, he's human!" I made notes on the interview afterwards, which I have probably lost. One comment in particular I remember. He said, "I never revise now"—you know how much he revised his stuff—"but in the interests of a more passionate syntax." Now that struck me as a very good remark. I have no idea what it meant, and still don't know, but the longer I think about it, the better I like it. He recommended various books to me, by his friend, the liar, Gogarty, and I forget who else. The main thing was just the presence and existence of my hero.

William Faulkner once ventured to rate himself among contemporary novelists. He rated Thomas Wolfe first, himself second, Dos Passos third, Hemingway fourth, and Steinbeck fifth.

Oh, no! Really? That's deluded! The list is abominable. I think what must have happened is this. There are two ways to rank writers: in terms of gift and in terms of achievement. He was ranking Wolfe in terms of gift. Wolfe had a colossal gift. His achievement, though—to rank him first and Hemingway fourth is openly grotesque.

Would you be interested in doing this, in ranking yourself among contemporary American poets?

I don't think I could do it. I'll tell you why. First, most of these characters are personal friends of mine, and you just don't sit around ranking your friends. After I published *The Dispossessed* in '48, I quit reviewing poetry. By that time I knew most of the people writing verse, and how can you deliver a fair judgment of the man you had dinner with the night before? Preposterous! It's supposed to be easy, but actually it's impossible. My love of such poets as Schwartz, *In Dreams Begin Responsibilities,* Roethke, and Lowell, *Lord Weary's Castle,* is very great. I would love to be in their company, and I feel convinced that I am, but I don't want to do any ranking. It's just not a sweat.

In **The Dream Songs** *there is a passage about assistant professors becoming associate professors by working on your poems. How do you feel about being cannon fodder for aspiring young critics and graduate students?*

As for the graduate students, some of the work they do is damned interesting. A woman somewhere in the South did an eighty-page thesis investigating the three little epigraphs to the *77 Dream Songs* and their bearing on the first three books of the poem. I must say that her study was exhaustive—very little left to be found out on that subject! But it's good, careful work. I take a pleased interest in these things, though there is ineptness and naïveté, and they get all kinds of things wrong and impute to me amazing motives. Another woman thought I was influenced by Hebrew elegiac meter. Now, my Hebrew is primitive, and I don't even know what Hebrew elegiac meter is—and, moreover, neither does she. It's a harmless industry. It gets people degrees. I don't feel against it and I don't feel for it. I sympathize with the students.

The professional critics, those who know what the literary, historical, philosophical, and theological score is, have not really gone to work yet, and may not do so for a long time yet. I did have a letter once from a guy who said: "Dear Mr. Berryman, Frankly I hope to be promoted from assistant professor to associate professor by writing a book about you. Are you willing to join me in this unworthy endeavor?" So I joined him. I answered all his questions. I practically flew out to pour out his drinks while he typed.

I would like to change the subject now and talk about your work. Let's start with **The Dream Songs.** *As you know, there is some controversy over the structure of the work—why it was first published in two volumes, why it consists of seven sections of varying lengths, and so on. What structural notion did you have in mind in writing it?*

Several people have written books about **The Dream Songs,** not published, and one of them, a woman, sees it as a series of three odysseys, psychological and moral, on the part of Henry, corresponding vaguely to Freud's differentiation of the personality into superego or conscience, ego or façade or self, and id or unconscious. Each has a starting point and a terminus and so forth. I don't know whether she is right or not, but if so, I did not begin with that full-fledged conception when I wrote the first dream song.

I don't know what I had in mind. In **Homage to Mistress Bradstreet** my model was *The Waste Land,* and **Homage to Mistress Bradstreet** is as unlike *The Waste Land* as it is possible for me to be. I think the model in **The Dream Songs** was the other greatest American poem—I am very ambitious—"Song of Myself"—a very long poem, about sixty pages. It also has a hero, a personality, himself. Henry is accused of being me and I am accused of being Henry and I deny it and nobody believes me. Various other things entered into it, but that is where I started.

The narrative such as it is developed as I went along, partly out of my gropings into and around Henry and his environment and associates, partly out of my readings in theology and that sort of thing, taking place during thirteen years—awful long time—and third, out of certain partly preconceived and partly developing as I went along, sometimes rigid and sometimes plastic, structural notions. That is why the work is divided into seven books, each book of which is rather well unified, as a matter of fact. Finally, I left the poem open to the circumstances of my personal life. For example, obviously if I hadn't got a Guggenheim and decided to spend it in Dublin, most of book VII wouldn't exist. I have a personality and a plan, a metrical plan—which is original, as in **Homage to Mistress Bradstreet.** I don't use other people as metrical models. I don't put down people who do—I just don't feel satisfied with them.

I had a personality and a plan and all kinds of philosophical and theological notions. This woman thinks the basic philosophical notion is Hegelian, and it's true that at one time I was deeply interested in Hegel. She also thinks, and so do some other people, that the work is influenced by the later work of Freud, especially *Civilization and Its Discontents,* and that is very likely. For years I lectured on the book every year here at Minnesota, so I am very, very familiar with it—almost know it word by word. But at the same time I was what you might call open-ended. That is to say, Henry to some extent was in the situation that we are all in in actual life—namely, he didn't know and I didn't know what the bloody fucking hell was going to happen next. Whatever it was he had to confront it and get through. For example, he dies in book IV and is dead throughout the book, but at the end of the poem he is still alive, and in fairly good condition, after having died himself *again.*

The poem does not go as far as "Song of Myself." What I mean by that is this: Whitman denies that "Song of Myself" is a long poem. He has a passage saying that he had long thought that there was no such thing as a long poem and that when he read Poe he found that Poe summed up the problem for him. But here it is, sixty pages. What's the notion? He doesn't regard it as a literary work at all, in my opinion—he doesn't quite say so. It proposes a new religion—it is what is called in Old Testament criticism a wisdom work, a work on the meaning of life and how to conduct it. Now, I don't go that far—*The Dream Songs* is a literary composition, it's a long poem—but I buy a little of it. I think Whitman is right with regard to "Song of Myself." I'm prepared to submit to his opinion. He was crazy, and I don't contradict madmen. When William Blake says something, I say thank you, even though he has uttered the most hopeless fallacy that you can imagine. I'm willing to be their loving audience. I'm just hoping to hear something marvelous from time to time, marvelous and true. Of course *The Dream Songs* does not propose a new system; that is not the point. In that way it is unlike "Song of Myself." It remains a literary work.

Christopher Ricks has called **The Dream Songs** *a theodicy. Did you have any such intention in writing the poem?*

It is a tough question. The idea of a theodicy has been in my mind at least since 1938. There is a passage in Delmore's first book, *In Dreams Begin Responsibilities,* which goes: "The theodicy I wrote in my high school days / Restored all life from infancy." Beautiful! He is the most underrated poet of the twentieth century. His later work is *absolutely* no good, but his first book is a masterpiece. It will come back—no problem. So that notion's always been with me. I can't answer the question. I simply don't know. I put my stuff, in as good condition as I can make it, on the table, and if people want to form opinions, good, I'm interested in the opinions. I don't set up as a critic of my own work. And I'm not kidding about that.

You once said that, among other things, a long poem demands "the construction of a world rather than the reliance upon one already existent." Does the world of **The Dream Songs** *differ from the existent world?*

This is connected with your previous question. I said that **The Dream Songs** in my opinion—only in my opinion—does not propose a new system, like Whitman. But as to the creation of a world: it's a hard question to answer. Suppose I take this business of the relation of Henry to me, which has interested so many people, and which is categorically denied by me in one of the forewords. Henry both is and is not me, obviously. We touch at certain points. But I am an actual human being; he is nothing but a series of conceptions—my conceptions. I brush my teeth; unless I say so somewhere in the poem—I forget whether I do or not—he doesn't brush his teeth. He only does what I make him do. If I have succeeded in making him believable, he performs all kinds of other actions besides those named in the poem, but the reader has to make them up. That's the world. But it's not a religious or philosophical system.

Where did you get the name "Henry"?

Ah, big sweat about that too. Did I get it from *The Red Badge of Courage* or *A Farewell to Arms* or what? O.K., I'll tell you where it came from. My second wife, Ann, and I were walking down Hennepin Avenue one momentous night. Everything seemed quite as usual, but it was going to puzzle literary critics on two continents many years later. Anyway, we were joking on our way to a bar to have a beer, and I decided that I hated the name Mabel more than any other female name, though I could mention half a dozen others that I didn't like either. We had passed from names we liked to names we disliked, and she decided that Henry was the name that she found completely unbearable. So from then on, for a long time, in the most cozy and affectionate lover kind of talk—we hadn't been married very long at this time—she was Mabel and I was Henry in our scene. So I started the poem. The poem began with a song that I killed. I've never printed it. It set the prosodic pattern, but for various reasons I killed it. It had not only a hero but a heroine. It was mostly about Henry, but it also had Mabel in it. It began:

> The jolly old man is a silly old dumb
> with a mean face, humped, who kills dead.
> There is a tall who loves only him.
> She has sworn "Blue to you forever,
> grey to the little rat, go to bed."
> I fink it's bads all over.

It winds up:

> Henry and Mabel ought to but can't.
> Childness let's have us honey—

Then, for reasons which I don't remember, I wiped Mabel out and never printed that song. For a long time after that, every now and then Ann would complain that Mabel didn't seem to be taking any part in the poem, but I couldn't find myself able to put her back in the poem, so it has no heroine. There are groups of heroines, but no individual heroine. By the way, that first song sounds quite good. Maybe I ought to pull it out.

You once said in speaking of **Homage to Mistress Bradstreet** *that you started out thinking you would write a fifty-line poem and ended up with fifty-seven stanzas. When you started* **The Dream Songs,** *did you know how long it was going to be or how far you were going to go?*

No, I didn't. But I was aware that I was embarked on an epic. In the case of the Bradstreet poem, I didn't know. The situation with that poem was this. I invented the stanza in '48 and wrote the first stanza and the first three lines of the second stanza, and then I stuck. I had in mind a poem roughly the same length as another of mine, "**The Statue**"—about seven or eight stanzas of eight lines each. Then I stuck. I read and read and read and thought and collected notes and sketched for five years, until, although I was still in the second stanza, I had a mountain of notes and draftings—no whole stanzas, but passages as long as five lines. The whole poem was written in about two months, after which I was a ruin for two years. When I finally got going, I had this incredible mass of stuff and a very good idea of the shape of the poem, with the exception of one crucial point, which was this. I'll tell you in a minute why and how I got going. The great exception was this; it did not occur to me to have a dialogue between them—to insert bodily Henry into the poem . . . *Me,* to insert me, in my own person, John Berryman, *I,* into the poem . . .

Was that a Freudian slip?

I don't know. Probably. Nothing is accidental, except physics. Modern physics is entirely accidental. I did not have the idea of putting him in as a demon lover. How he emerged was this. The idea was not to take Anne Bradstreet as a poetess—I was not interested in that. I was interested in her as a pioneer heroine, a sort of mother to the artists and intellectuals who would follow her and play a large role in the development of the nation. People like Jefferson, Poe, and me.[1] Well, her life was very hard in many, many ways. The idea was to make it even harder than it had been in history. There is a lot of history in the poem. It is a historical poem, but a lot of it is invented too. I decided to tempt her. She was unbelievably devoted to her husband. Her few really touching passages, both in verse and in prose, are about her love for her husband, who was indeed a remarkable man—and she was a remarkable woman, and she loved him, with a passion that can hardly be described, through their whole life together, from the age of sixteen on. I decided to tempt her. I could only do this in a fantasy; the problem was to make the fantasy believable, and some people think I have completely failed with that. It is not for me to judge. I am deeply satisfied. I only do the best I can—I think I succeeded and some other people do too.

So, with the exception of the dialogue in the middle— that's the middle third of the poem—all the rest was one whole plan, but it took a series of shocks to get it going. What happened? My wife and I were living in Princeton, had been for a year. She was in the hospital in New York for an operation, what they call a woman's operation, a kind of parody of childbirth. Both she and I were feeling very bitter about this since we very much wanted a child and had not had one. So I had very, very strong emotions and solitude. Second, at this point Saul Bellow had almost finished *Augie March,* his first important novel and one of the great American novels, I think. His later novels are far more important still, but

Augie March is a landmark. He had almost finished that and wanted me to see it. We didn't know each other very well—since then he has become perhaps my best friend—but he was living just a few blocks away. I remember sitting in my chair, drinking as usual, reading the typescript. It was very long, about 900 pages. I was amazed. The word "breakthrough" has become kind of a cliché. Every two minutes somebody in *Life, Time,* or *Fortune* has a breakthrough. But the term does describe something that actually happens. A renaissance. Suddenly, where there was pure stasis, the place is exploding. For example, the twelfth century—suddenly Europe was blazing with intelligence and power and insight, fresh authority, all the things that had been missing for centuries. I recognized in *Augie March* a breakthrough— namely, the wiping out of the negative personality that had created and inhabited his earlier work. Some critics like those novels, but in my opinion they're shit. They're well written, and if you look closely you can see a genius coming, but the genius is absolutely not there—he is in a straightjacket. In *Augie* he's there.

My plans for the Bradstreet poem had got very ambitious by that time. I no longer had any idea of a fifty-line poem. That was five years before. My idea was now very ambitious. The Bradstreet poem is just as ambitious as **The Dream Songs.** Saul once said to me that it is the equivalent of a 500-page psychological novel. That is exactly my opinion, also—in spite of the fact that it is short, the poem is highly concentrated. So I was exhilarated. One of my pals had made a major attempt. You know, these things don't happen very often. Most even very fine artists don't try to put up the Parthenon, you know, and most of those who do turn out to be imposters. Merely grandiose, like Benjamin Haydon, Keats's friend. A very good, very minor painter who thought he was Michelangelo, then killed himself. It's hard to take the risk of joining that terrible, frightful company. Contemptible, pathetic, they move your heart but they draw you to scorn. Saul had decided to make a big attempt, so my idea of my poem improved.

And the third thing was that I had recently reread, for the first time in many years, *Anna Karenina,* which I think is the best portrait of a woman in world literature. You just can't mention any other attempt at a woman, except perhaps *Madame Bovary.* I recently reread it for a seminar I am giving, and I have a very high regard for it. It's a beauty. It deserves its reputation, which is saying a lot. But *Anna Karenina* is even greater. The only woman in American literature is Hester Prynne, and she is very good. I have great respect for her and the book, but **Mistress Bradstreet** is much more ambitious. It is very unlikely that it is better, but it attempts more.[2] So again my notion of my poem expanded. The fourth thing that got me going was this. I had been in group therapy. The analyst who had been treating me individually for several years set up a group. There were two lawyers, a chemist, an alcoholic housewife, a psychiatric social worker, and me. I tried to run the group, of course, and they all killed me. I would leave, and come back, and so on, but it was a shattering business—I mean emotionally shattering—much more so than individual therapy had been. That had been kind of cozy. Well, I got fed up and left the group forever, and this left me blazing with hostility and feelings of gigantism, defeated gigantism. So these four things— the deep wound of Eileen's tragic operation, Saul's wonderful daring, Tolstoy's commanding achievement, and the emotional shock of my experience with the group—swung me into action, and suddenly I was on fire every second.

What was your method of composition on that poem? You must have worked very hard to finish it in two months.

I started out writing three stanzas a day, but that was too much, so I developed a more orderly method. I got one of those things that have a piece of glassine over a piece of paper, and you can put something in between and see it but not touch it. I would draft my stanza and put it in there. Then I would sit and study it. I would make notes, but I wouldn't touch the manuscript until I thought I was in business—usually not for hours. Then I'd take it out, make the corrections, put it back in, and study it some more. When I was finally satisfied, I'd take it out and type it. At that point I was done—I never touched any stanza afterward. I limited myself to one a day. If I finished at eleven in the morning, I still did not look at the next stanza until the next morning. I had a terrible time filling the hours—whiskey was helpful, but it was hard.

Do you consider your latest book, **Love & Fame,** *a long poem?*

Love & Fame is very shapely and thematically unified, and in that it resembles a long poem. But it is absolutely and utterly not a long poem at all; it's a collection of lyrics. The last eleven all happen to be prayers, but even there each poem is on its own. This is even more true in the earlier sections. It is unified through style and because most of the poems are autobiographical, based on the historical personality of the poet. By historical I mean existing in time and space, occupying quanta.

How does the composition of **Love & Fame** *compare with that of your earlier work? Did you write these poems more quickly than the long poems?*

The composition was like that of the Bradstreet poem, and to some extent like that of **The Dream Songs,** many of which were also written in volcanic bursts. Not all. I worked daily over a period of years, but sometimes I would write fifty in a burst and then not write any for months. The Bradstreet poem, as I say, took two months. **Love & Fame** took about three months.

What made you turn back to the short form after having written two long poems?

When I finished **The Dream Songs,** two years ago, I was very tired. I didn't know whether I would ever write any more poems. As I told you, it took me two years to get over the Bradstreet poem before I started **The Dream Songs.** Your idea of yourself and your relation to your art has a great deal to do with what actually happens. What happened in this case was something that contradicted my ideas, as follows. I saw myself only as an epic poet. The idea of writing any more short poems hadn't been in my mind for many years. The question after **The Dream Songs** was whether I would ever again attempt a long poem, and I thought it improbable, so I didn't expect to write any more verse.

But suddenly one day last winter I wrote down a line: "I fell in love with a girl." I looked at it, and I couldn't find anything wrong with it. I thought, "God damn it, that is a *fact.*" I felt, as a friend of mine says: "I feel comfortable with that." And I looked at it until I thought of a second line, and then a third line, and then a fourth line, and that was a stanza. Unrhymed. And the more I looked at it, the better I liked it, so I wrote a second stanza. And then I wrote some more stanzas, and you know what? I had a lyric poem, and a very good one. I didn't know I had it in me! Well, the next day I knocked out a stanza, changed various lines, this and that, but pretty soon it looked classical. As classical as one of the *Rubáiyát* poems—without the necessities of rhyme and meter, but with its own necessities. I thought it was as good as any of my early poems, and some of them are quite good; most of them are not, but some are. Moreover, it didn't resemble any verse I had ever written in my entire life, and moreover the subject was entirely new, solely and simply myself. Nothing else. A subject on which I am an expert. Nobody can contradict me.[3] I believe strongly in the authority of learning. The reason Milton is the greatest English poet except for Shakespeare is because of the authority of his learning. I am a scholar in certain fields, but the subject on which I am a real authority is me, so I wiped out all the disguises and went to work. In about five or six weeks I had what was obviously a book called **Love & Fame.**

I had forty-two poems and was ready to print them, but they were so weird, so unlike all my previous work, that I was a little worried. I had encouragement from one or two friends, but still I didn't know what to do. I had previously sent the first poem to Arthur Crook at the *Times Literary Supplement.* He was delighted with it and sent me proof. I in turn was delighted that he liked the poem, so I corrected the proof and sent him five more—I didn't want the poem to appear alone. So he printed the six, which made up a whole page—very nice typographically—and this was further encouragement. But I still wasn't sure. Meanwhile, I was in hospital. I was a nervous wreck. I had lost nineteen pounds in five weeks and had been drinking heavily—a quart a day. So I had my publisher in New York, Giroux, Xerox a dozen copies, which I sent out to friends of mine around the country for opinions. It is a weird thing to do—I've never heard of anybody else doing it—but I did it, looking for reassurance, confirmation, wanting criticism and so on, and I got some very good criticism. Dick Wilbur took **"Shirley & Auden,"** one of the most important lyrics in Part I—some of the poems are quite slight and others are very ambitious—and gave it hell. And I agreed—I adopted almost every suggestion.

I also got some confirmation and reassurance, but there were other opinions as well. Edmund Wilson, for whose opinion I have a high regard, found the book hopeless. He said there were some fine lines and striking passages. How do you like that? It is like saying to a beautiful woman, "I like your left small toenail; that's very nice indeed," while she's standing there stark naked looking like Venus. I was deeply hurt by that letter. And then other responses were very strange. Mark Van Doren, my teacher, an old, old friend and a wonderful judge of poetry, also wrote. I forget exactly what he said, but he was very heavy on it. He said things like "original," and "will be influential," and "will be popular," and so on, but "will also be feared and hated." What a surprising letter! It took me days to get used to it, and it took me days even to see what he meant. But now I see what he means. Some of the poems are threatening, very threatening to some readers, no doubt about it. Just as some people find me threatening—to be in a room with me drives them crazy. And then there is a good deal of obscenity in the poems, too. And there is a grave piety in the last poems, which is going to trouble a lot of people. You know, the country is full of atheists, and they really are going to find themselves threatened by those poems. The *Saturday Review* printed five of them, and I had a lot of mail about them—again expressing a wide variety of opinion. Some people were just purely grateful for my having told them how to put what they'd felt for years. Then there are others who detest them—they don't call them insincere, but they just can't believe it.

There has always been a religious element in your poems, but why did you turn so directly to religious subject matter in these poems?

They are the result of a religious conversion which took place on my second Tuesday in treatment here last spring. I lost my faith several years ago, but I came back—by force, by necessity, because of a rescue ac-

tion—into the notion of a God who, at certain moments, definitely and personally intervenes in individual lives, one of which is mine. The poems grow out of that sense, which not all Christians share.

Could you say something more about this rescue action? Just what happened?

Yes. This happened during the strike which hit campus last May, after the Cambodian invasion and the events at Kent State. I was teaching a large class—seventy-five students—Tuesday and Thursday afternoons, commuting from the hospital, and I was supposed to lecture on the Fourth Gospel. My kids were in a state of crisis—only twenty-five had shown up the previous Thursday, campus was in chaos, there were no guidelines from the administration—and besides lecturing, I felt I had to calm them, tell them what to do. The whole thing would have taken no more than two hours—taxi over, lecture, taxi back. I had been given permission to go by my psychiatrist. But at the beginning of group therapy that morning at ten, my counselor, who is an Episcopalian priest, told me that he had talked with my psychiatrist, and that the permission to leave had been rescinded. Well, I was shocked and defiant.

I said, "You and Dr. So and So have no authority over me. I will call a cab and go over and teach my class. My students need me."

He made various remarks, such as "You're shaking."

I replied, "I don't shake when I lecture."

He said, "Well, you can't walk and we are afraid you will fall down."

I said, "I can walk," and I could. You see I had had physical permission from my physician the day before.

Then the whole group hit me, including a high official of the university, who was also in treatment here. I appealed to him, and even he advised me to submit. Well, it went on for almost two hours, and at last I submitted—at around eleven-thirty. Then I was in real despair. I couldn't just ring up the secretary and have her dismiss my class—it would be grotesque. Here it was, eleven-thirty, and class met at one-fifteen. I didn't even know if I could get my chairman on the phone to find somebody to meet them. And even if I could, who could he have found that would have been qualified? We have no divinity school here. Well, all kinds of consolations and suggestions came from the group, and suddenly my counselor said, "Well, I'm trained in divinity. I'll give your lecture for you."

And I said, "You're kidding!" He and I had had some very sharp exchanges. I had called him sarcastic, arrogant, tyrannical, incompetent, theatrical, judgmental, and so on.

He said, "Yes, I'll teach it if I have to teach it in Greek!"

I said, "I can't believe it. Are you serious?"

He said, "Yes, I'm serious."

And I said, "I could kiss you."

He said, "Do." There was only one man between us, so I leaned over and we embraced. Then I briefed him and gave him my notes, and he went over and gave the lecture. Well, when I thought it over in the afternoon, I suddenly recalled what has been for many years one of my favorite conceptions. I got it from Augustine and Pascal. It's found in many other people too, but especially in those heroes of mine. Namely, the idea of a God of rescue. He saves men from their situations, off and on during life's pilgrimage, and in the end. I completely bought it, and that's been my position since.

What about the role of religion in your earlier works? I remember that when the Sonnets came out, one critic, writing in the New York Review of Books, *spoke of "the absence of thematic substance" in your poems generally. Another critic, writing in the* Minnesota Review, *picked this up and disagreed with it, pointing out what he felt was a firm religious basis in the sonnets— the question of guilt and atonement, etc. What would you say about the role of religion generally in your poetry?*

It's awfully hard for me to judge. I had a strict Catholic training. I went to a Catholic school and I adored my priest, Father Boniface. I began serving Mass under him at the age of five, and I used to serve six days a week. Often there would be nobody in the church except him and me. Then all that went to pieces at my father's death, when I was twelve. Later, I went to a High Church Episcopalian school in Connecticut, called South Kent, and I was very fond of the Chaplain there. His name was Father Kemmis, and, although I didn't feel about him as I had about Father Boniface as a child, I still felt very keen, and was a rapt Episcopalian for several years. Then, when I went to Columbia, all that sort of dropped out. I never lost the sense of God in the two roles of creator and sustainer—of the mind of man and all its operations, as a source of inspiration to great scientists, great artists, saints, great statesmen. But my experience last spring gave me a third sense, a sense of a God of rescue, and I've been operating with that since. Now the point is, I have been interested not only in religion but in theology all my life. I don't know how much these personal beliefs, together with the interest in theology and the history of the church, enter into particular works up to those addresses to the Lord in *Love & Fame.* I really think it is up to others— critics, scholars—to answer your question.

By the way, those addresses to the Lord are not Christian poems. I am deeply interested in Christ, but I never pray to him.[4] I don't know whether he was in any special sense the son of God, and I think it is quite impossible to know.[5] He certainly was the most remarkable *man* who ever lived. But I don't consider myself a Christian. I do consider myself a Catholic, but I'd just as soon go to an Episcopalian church as a Catholic church. I do go to Mass every Sunday.

Let's turn to new directions. What has happened to the poem about heaven set in China, titled **"Scholars at the Orchid Pavilion,"** *which you were working on a couple of years ago? Are you still working on that?*

I intended that to be rather a long poem. As with the Bradstreet poem, I invented the stanza—it's a very beautiful, sort of hovering, seven-line stanza, un-rhymed—and wrote the first stanza and stuck. I then accumulated notes on Chinese art history in most of the major forms. Chinese art is much more complicated than ours—they have many forms. I have a whole library on Chinese art and early Chinese philosophy, Chinese history, Chinese folk tales, ghost stories, all kinds of Chinese stuff. I even tried to learn classical Chinese one time, but I decided after a few days that it was not for me.

Anyway, I finally decided that I was nowhere, that all this accumulation of knowledge was fascinating and valuable to me, but that I was personally not destined to write a Chinese epic. So at that point I felt fine, and I wrote a second stanza, and a third stanza, and a fourth stanza. They're not as good as the first stanza, but they are all pretty good. And then I put some asterisks and that's what I'll publish sooner or later. I may say, **"Scholars at the Orchid Pavilion: A Fragment."**

Where do you go from here?

I have written another book of poetry, called **Delusions.** It won't be out for some time yet, however. We're doing a volume of my prose, probably spring or fall of '72. After that—I am very much interested in the question, or will be when I get my breath back from the composition of the last nine months. I've written over a hundred poems in the last six months. I'm a complete wreck. I'm hopelessly underweight, and the despair of about four competent doctors. When I get my breath back—it may be next spring—maybe I'll begin to think. I don't know whether I'll ever write any more verse at all. The main question is whether I will ever again undertake a long poem, and I just can form no idea.

There are certain subjects that have interested me for a long time, but nothing commanding and obsessive, as both the Bradstreet poem and **Dream Songs** were. What is involved in the composition of a long poem, at least by my experience, is five to ten years. I don't know how long I'll live. Probably I wouldn't be able to begin it for—well it took me two years to get over the Bradstreet poem. I finished **The Dream Songs** only two years ago, and I've written two more books since, besides a lot of other literary work. I've been working on a play, an anthology, and revising the volume of my criticism. I probably wouldn't get to it for at least three to five years. That makes me getting on to sixty. Taking on a new long poem at the age of sixty is really something. I have no idea whether I would still have the vigor and ambition, need, that sort of thing, to do it.

I have a tiny little secret hope that, after a decent period of silence and prose, I will find myself in some almost impossible life situation and will respond to this with outcries of rage, rage and love, such as the world has never heard before. Like Yeats's great outburst at the end of his life. This comes out of a feeling that endowment is a very small part of achievement. I would rate it about fifteen or twenty percent. Then you have historical luck, personal luck, health, things like that, then you have hard work, sweat. And you have ambition. The incredible difference between the achievement of A and the achievement of B is that B *wanted* it, so he made all kinds of sacrifices. A could have had it, but he didn't give a damn. The idea that everybody wants to be president of the United States or have a million dollars is simply not the case. Most people want to go down to the corner and have a glass of beer. They're very happy. In *Henderson the Rain King,* the hero keeps on saying, "I want. I want." Well, I'm that kind of character. I don't know whether that is exhausted in me or not, I can't tell.

But what I was going on to say is that I do strongly feel that among the greatest pieces of luck for high achievement is ordeal. Certain great artists can make out without it, Titian and others, but mostly you need ordeal. My idea is this: the artist is extremely lucky who is presented with the worst possible ordeal which will not actually kill him. At that point, he's in business. Beethoven's deafness, Goya's deafness, Milton's blindness, that kind of thing. And I think that what happens in my poetic work in the future will probably largely depend not on my sitting calmly on my ass as I think," "Hmm, hmm, a long poem again? Hmm," but on being knocked in the face, and thrown flat, and given cancer, and all kinds of other things short of senile dementia. At that point, I'm out, but short of that, I don't know. I hope to be nearly crucified.

You're not knocking on wood.

I'm scared, but I'm willing. I'm sure this is a preposterous attitude, but I'm not ashamed of it.[6]

Notes

1. Get the delusion (J. B., March 1971).
2. Delusion (J. B., March 1971).
3. Delusion (J. B., March 1971).
4. Situation altered; see "Ecce Homo," poem to be published in the *New Yorker* (J. B., March 1971).
5. Delusion (J. B., March 1971).
6. Delusion (J. B., March 1971).

Michael Berryhill (essay date 1972)

SOURCE: Berryhill, Michael. "Introduction: The Epistemology of Loss." In *John Berryman: A Checklist,* edited by Richard J. Kelly, pp. xxi-xxxi. Metuchen, N.J.: The Scarecrow Press, 1972.

[*In the following essay, Berryhill considers the sense of loss in Berryman's verse and examines the major allusions, idioms, and themes in his poetry.*]

Our dead frisk us, & later they get better at it,
our wits are stung astray
till all that we can do is groan, bereft:
tears fail: and then we reckon what is left,
not what was lost.

("Dream Song #325")

As Richard Kelly mentions in his preface, this checklist was in preparation some months before John Berryman's suicide on January 7, 1972. What was intended to bring us up to date must now serve us to "reckon what is left," though I suspect that for some time we will grieve like Henry, against all his good advice, for what is lost. It will be particularly difficult because so much of Berryman's personality was in his poetry. Every line about suicide reverberates with his act, every anguished lament for the loss of his friends is intensified and possibly distorted by our loss of Berryman, a loss which we now feel to be lurking, ominous and certain throughout the poems. The poems convert Berryman's grief at his loss into our grief at our loss.

The New Critics coined a phrase for this: "the affective fallacy." Because the poem moves us, we think it good. But did the texture and meaning of the language move us, or was the feeling provoked by some event or action external to the poem? There are obvious limitations to this approach—all language is embedded in experience external to the poem itself—but it is a useful admonition.

If we are to "reckon what is left," we already have available the poems which John Berryman, in his lifetime, cared to publish, and on which his reputation is certain to rest: **The Dispossessed, Berryman's Sonnets, Homage to Mistress Bradstreet, The Dream Songs, Love and Fame,** and **Delusions, Etc.** which was in proof before he died. Other things are sure to follow—an uncompleted autobiographical novel on which he was working the autumn before his death, uncollected and unpublished poems, possibly some stories written but never published.

1. ALLUSIONS

In an interview for *The Paris Review* Berryman maintained that he was "equally interested" in scholarship and writing, but unlike Housman, for whom the two activities were "perfectly distinct," in him they were "closer together." Anyone who has read a few of the **Dream Songs** knows that they are studded with references to painting, music, literature, philosophy, biography and movies which will drive the best-read to the reference room. These flashes of learning must seem, to some critics, pretentious. Yet they are as essential to the poetry as to the man. Berryman was a brilliant and thorough student at Columbia, who took his learning seriously. He failed a course of his friend and mentor, Mark Van Doren, for admitting to having read only seventeen of forty-two books on the syllabus, despite having made an "A" on the final. Upon graduation from Columbia, Berryman was awarded a fellowship to Cambridge, England, where he studied Shakespeare and wrote poems for two years. After teaching at Harvard and Princeton, Berryman settled down at the University of Minnesota in 1955 as a professor in the Humanities Program, where he taught courses in the history of civilization until his death in 1972. His classes at Minnesota were always filled, and his reputation as a lecturer was high, though he was sometimes acid towards students who asked what he considered to be stupid questions.

For a man for whom books were a way of life, and for a man who wrote about his life, the mention of books was inescapable. Occasionally a poem which seems quite clear will be punctuated with some indigestible phrase from a foreign language, or some abstruse reference which requires assistance. Generally, I sense that these difficulties do not exist out of perversity or a desire to be obscure, but out of a genuine love for a wide range of studies. When Berryman taught the Gospels in his Humanities class, his studies were not merely for lecture's sake, but also for his own religious and poetic quest. The extent to which the poems drive the reader to the library is to *some* degree an indication of their validity as poems. The scholar can be motivated by money and promotions; the reader will be motivated by sheer interestingness.

There are other, more subtle problems, which the scholars and critics will discern. The influence of Auden is acknowledged frequently by Berryman, and we can hear it in the tone and theme of **"World-Telegram,"** an early poem which reports the contents of that newspaper on May 11, 1939. The flat ironic tone and the reportorial style allow the madness of the contents of a newspaper to seep through:

> News of one day, one afternoon, one time.
> If it were possible to take these things
> Quite seriously, I believe they might
> Curry disorder in the strongest brain,
> Immobilize the most resilient will,
> Stop trains, break up the city's food supply,
> And perfectly demoralize the nation.

Or in **"The Animal Trainer (2),"** I hear echoes of John Crowe Ransom:

> —The animals are coupling, and they cry
> 'The circus *is,* it is our mystery,
> It is a world of dark where animals die.'

> —Animals little and large, be still, be still:
> I'll stay with you. Suburb and sun are pale.

> —Animals are your distruction, and your will.

In **"Dream Song #8"** the voice is Berryman's, but the theme is Ransom's "Captain Carpenter," a favorite poem that Berryman often recited at readings. And doesn't one detect, despite Berryman's efforts to suppress his influence, overtones of T. S. Eliot's "Journey of the Magi" in **"The Moon and the Night and the Men?"**

> On the night of the Belgian surrender the moon rose
> Late, a delayed moon, and a violent moon
> For the English or the American beholder;
> The French beholder. It was a cold night,
> People put on their wraps, the troops were cold
> No doubt, despite the calendar, no doubt
> Numbers of refugees coughed, and the sight
> Or sound of some killed others. A cold night.

There are voices which Berryman worked to exorcise, but occasionally he quotes in a kind of tribute as in **"The Ball Poem"**:

> Soon part of me will explore the deep and dark
> Floor of the harbour.. I am everywhere,
> I suffer and move,. . . .

This is Whitman, a poet who greatly interested Berryman: "I am the man, I suffered, I was there."

One further example from **Delusions, Etc.,—"Scholars at the Orchid Pavilion."** Berryman recited the first stanza in an interview for the *Harvard Advocate* devoted to his work. The poem appears to be an "anachronistic gathering," a standard subject in Chinese painting in which philosophers, writers and painters from various periods are brought together in a painting. The poem seems to be set in the afterlife, a subject which Berryman has also written about elsewhere—notably in **"Dream Song #90."** In the first stanza, Mo-tsu, a 5th-4th century philosopher of the Sing State appears. He espoused altruism, universal love and pacifism rather than the traditional ancestor worship and reverence for parents. Thus—

Sozzled, Mo-tsu, after a silence, vouchsafed
a word alarming: 'We must love them all!'
Affronted, the fathers jumped.
'Yes' he went madly on and waved in quest of
his own dreadful subject. 'O the fathers'
he cried 'must not be all!'

It helps as well to know of the tradition to paint when
drunk. There were standard subjects for painting, but
the challenge was to drink and depend on one's
character and inner resources rather than one's skill.
"Great Wu" who pinches a serving girl, "forgetting his
later nature," is Wu Wang, founder of the Chou dynasty,
famous for his celibacy, because of the previous
dynasty's licentiousness. Ch'en Hung-shou was a later
painter, famous for his bamboo and his book on how to
paint. Ch'en seems to say that we must discriminate,
reserve our praise for masters, regardless of their time.
Three themes are intertwined in this poem—the "dreadful subject" of the fathers, referring to the suicide of
Berryman's own father, the lust of Wu, and the conception of a line of master artists, all obsessions of Berryman's developed singly and in unison in other poems.
If there is an actual painting on which this poem is
based, as in **"Winter Landscape,"** I have not found it
yet.

So, scholars will track down this sort of thing, and
many others. For instance, **"Dream Song #9"** is about
the Bogart movie, "High Sierra." In that poem, the
sheriff has "a p. a. echoing." In **"#77"** "Henry up / and
p. a. 'd poor thousands of persons on topics of grand /
moment to Henry . . ." The compression of "public address system" into the verb "p. a. 'd" is not easy to follow, but legitimate, I think, and links Henry's self-
admitted pomposity to the sheriff's demands to
surrender. Scholars will also have to learn something
about blues, astronomy, Freud, and a host of friends
private and famous.

2. IDIOM

In *Love and Fame,* Berryman quotes from Richard
Blackmur:

'The art of poetry
is amply distinguished from the manufacture of verse
by the animating presence in the poetry
of a fresh idiom: language

So twisted & posed in a form
that it not only expresses the matter in hand
but adds to the available stock of reality.'
I was never altogether the same man after *that.*

("Olympus")

Later in the book Berryman tells of reading Hart Crane
and Wallace Stevens to the English at Cambridge. "The
worthy young gentlemen are baffled. I explain, but the
idiom is too much for them." One commentator, Wil-

liam Martz, has used the word "style" as one of Berryman's obsessions, but "idiom" seems to be a more useful term, encompassing, as it does, Berryman's
complicated and sometimes "crushed" syntax, as well
as his mixtures of colloquial, literary and foreign
language, and baby talk. Berryman's idiom, Allen Tate
rightly observed, "derives from nobody else," and "cannot be imitated."

If Blackmur's words are taken exactly, "language so
twisted & posed . . . as to add to the available stock of
reality," we can partially understand Berryman's ambition. In *The Dispossessed* it occurs as a displacement of
direct objects from their usual position: "The turning
world / Brings unaware us to our enemies. . . ."
(**"Boston Common"**), and "Only I must forsake my
country's wrath / Who am earth's citizen, must human
blood / anywhere shed mourn. . . ." (**"The Pacificist's
Song"**), or displacement of the subject as well:
"Obstinate, gleams from the black world the gay and
fair, / My love loves chocolate, she loves also me, . . ."
(**"The Lightning"**). Compare this last example to
"Dream Song #16": "Golden, whilst your frozen
daiquiris / whir at midnight, gleams on you his fur / &
silky and black." The later usage of "gleams" is more
sophisticated, for "Henry's pelt" gleams "golden," "on
you," both predicate adjective and verb object.

Where the "idiom" works best, the abnormal syntax
creates new meanings and new emotional resonances
by creating a kind of suspense, as well, of course, as
new rhythms. In **"Dream Song #29,"** for instance—

He knows: he went over everyone, & nobody's miss-
ing.
Often he reckons, in the dawn, them up.
Nobody is ever missing.

The middle line is set like a jewel in the midst of the
surrounding, normal syntax. Not only the middle line,
but its surrounding lines deflate if it is rearranged into,
"He often reckons them up in the dawn," or some such
thing. The reader, as William Martz has said, must
become something of an actor in order to inflect the
words properly, and give them grammatical sense.

There are lines that continue to puzzle and may puzzle
for some time, may be discounted by critics as ineffectual tricks, but when the idiom works, it really works.
And of course the idiom is more than just tricky syntax;
developed forcefully in *Berryman's Sonnets* and later
in *Homage to Mistress Bradstreet,* the idiom becomes
consecutively more sophisticated in its diction and wit.
Take this example from **"Freshman Blues"** in **Love
and Fame**:

Thought much I then on perforated daddy,
daddy boxed in & let down with strong straps,
when I my friends' homes visited, with fathers
universal & intact.

This is more than just cuteness or a stab at fame, it is a way of dealing with topics too painful to otherwise handle, a way of coping with the world.

3. THEMES

John Berryman does not attempt to present a comprehensive intellectual system as other American poets have. His antecedent is Emily Dickinson rather than Walt Whitman; his materials are personal pain and fear; he does not attempt to systematically diagnose the world's ills. When asked what made the *Dream Songs* a single poem, he replied "personality—it's Henry. He thought up all these things over all the years. The reason I call it one poem is the result of my strong disagreement with Eliot's line, 'the impersonality of poetry . . .'"

The wealth of autobiographical material is tempting, even beguiling. In *Love and Fame* he reminds us in a poem with the teasing title, **"Message,"** "I am not writing an autobiography-in-verse my friends." / and "It's not my life. / That's occluded & lost." Earlier, in the *Dream Songs,* he has reminded us: "These Songs are not meant to be understood, you understand. / They are only meant to terrify & comfort." (**"#366"**). Certainly the poetic personality and the real personality have many points in common, perhaps are as nearly congruent as possible. That remains to be argued out. The place to begin is with the personality in the poems— what are its obsessions, its patterns, its dynamics?

Any single concept is inadequate, but for me, the word *couvade* provides a way in. It appears in **"Dream Song #124."** "Couvade was always Henry's favorite custom . . ." It refers to the custom among some tribes of the fathers going to bed and re-enacting the pains of his wife's birth labor. The dictionary also gives a meaning, from Middle French—"cowardly inactivity," and to brood over, to cover, as a bird her eggs. It seems to me that such a custom involves more than sympathy for the wife's pain (Berryman's doctor described him as a man of "cosmic sympathies"), but rather it means a participation in birth, from which men are cut off biologically, except in conception, when a different sort of feeling prevails. Couvade is a leaving of the self, but at the same time is a recognition of the self's need.

The theme can be seen in one of two stories Berryman published—both in *The Kenyon Review*—in 1945. **"The Imaginary Jew"** involves a young man who is wrongly accused of being a Jew, and hotly denies it, only to realize that his denial has made a victim of him:

> In the days following, as my resentment died, I saw that I had not been a victim altogether unjustly. My persecutors were right: I was a Jew. The imaginary Jew I was was as real as the imaginary Jew hunted down, on other nights and days, in a real Jew. Every murderer

strikes the mirror, the lash of the torturer falls on the mirror and cuts the real image, and the real and the imaginary blood flow down together.

The theme of our general guilt is picked up in an early poem, **"The Traveller,"** about a man of whom people say, "'That man / Will never become as we are, try as he can.'" Later, the ritual of Christian communion is "troublesome to imaginary Jews, / like bitter Henry." The situation is re-enacted many times, as in **"Dream Song #242,"** when a student weeps in Henry's office:

> go right ahead,' I assur-
> ed her, 'here's a handkerchief. Cry.' She did, I did.
>   When she got
> control, I said 'What's the matter—if you want to
>   talk?'
> 'Nothing. Nothing's the matter.' So.
> I am her.

This is the "nothing" of the couvade, in which no "real" labor pain is felt, the tears nevertheless are real, the condition real.

Earlier I cited a passage from **"The Ball Poem"** which also deals with something similar:

> . . . . I am everywhere,
> I suffer and move, my mind and my Heart move
> With all that move me, under the water
> Or whistling, I am not a little boy.

The boy has learned the "epistemology of loss"; what seems to be happening is that the voice of the poet is asserting that he too has been there, but that now he is a man. The assertiveness seems to undercut itself, however: if one had to pick a single phrase to describe Berryman's poetry, it would be "the epistemology of loss." Loss is never finished.

In the earlier poems, it has been observed, a persona is speaking, a voice of the poet but not really the poet's voice, as in *Homage to Mistress Bradstreet* and *The Dream Songs* and later. But looking back now, it is apparent that the boy is Berryman, whose "ultimate shocking grief" stems from his father's suicide symbolized by the lost ball. The event is the fixed point in his life to which Berryman again and again returns, as in the first *Dream Song*:

> All the world like a woolen lover
> once did seem on Henry's side.
> Then came a departure.
> Thereafter, nothing fell out as it might or ought.

The departure, the "irreversible loss" Berryman describes as Henry's, is most certainly his father's suicide.

What is lost is not only the father, but innocence, the fall into sin begins with this event. "Nothing is the matter," but something *is* the matter—possibly Berryman blames himself for his father's death—his couvade has crossed dangerous boundaries. For instance, in **"Dream Song #29"**:

> But never did Henry, as he thought he did,
> end anyone and hacks her body up
> and hide the pieces where they may be found.
> He knows: he went over everyone, & nobody's missing.

His very virtue is his undoing; his general guilt becomes unbearable.

How to survive? With "courage and kindness," and "children and high art." Concerning the religious poems of *Delusions, Etc.,* Berryman talked of a "God of rescue." I suspect that secretly he didn't believe he could be rescued, that what he was asking for was too much, that he had failed to accept the world as God made it. Most of us manage to survive easily, unrecognizing, while a few, like John Berryman, make art, while living on the verge of annihilation. It would be too simple a psychology to say he cultivated his affliction, though perhaps to those of us who survive easily, it might seem so. With his wild wit and his terrible anguish, for a long time John Berryman made permanent poetry for us, teetering always where it seems to me he had no choice but to be—on the edge.

J. M. Linebarger (essay date 1974)

SOURCE: Linebarger, J. M. "The Early Poetry." In *John Berryman,* pp. 29-51. Boston: Twayne Publishers, 1974.

[*In the following essay, Linebarger offers a thematic and stylistic overview of Berryman's early verse.*]

The first two collections of Berryman's early work—**"Twenty Poems,"** in *Five Young American Poets* (1940), and *Poems* (1942)—contain verse written in 1940 or earlier. Sixteen of the poems in these collections were reprinted in *The Dispossessed* in 1948, a convenient date to take as the end of the early period. With its useful introductory note unfortunately omitted, *The Dispossessed* was reprinted in the volume *Short Poems* (1957).

The fifty poems of *The Dispossessed* are arranged into five sections. The first of these has, the poet says, a "thematic" order (*The Dispossessed,* vii) but I am unable to discover it. Whatever theme the seven poems in this section share may have been deduced after they were composed, for the first four of them are reprinted

from the earlier collections and therefore were written before 1940. The following four sections of *The Dispossessed* are arranged "roughly [in] their order of writing" (*The Dispossessed,* vii). The twenty-four poems of sections II and III are dated 1940 or earlier, with the exception of **"Boston Common,"** which has for its setting and approximate date of composition February 1942. Section IV of the volume contains **"Canto Amor"** (dated 1944-45 by the phrase "my thirtieth year"), a group of nine poems called **"The Nervous Songs,"** and two poems written around 1947. Section V consists of seven poems written during 1947-48.

I THE EARLY POETRY: BORROWED VOICES

About one-third of the early poems, especially those written before 1940, were strongly influenced and sometimes dominated by the voices of other poets. In 1965, Berryman pinpointed the sources of this early style; first, he says, he imitated "Yeats, whom I didn't so much wish to resemble as to *be,* and for several fumbling years I wrote in what it's convenient to call 'period style,' the Anglo-American style of the 1930's, with no voice of my own, learning chiefly from middle and later Yeats and from the brilliant young Englishman W. H. Auden. Yeats . . . could not teach me to sound like myself (whatever that was) or tell me what to write about."[1]

The Yeats influence on the early poetry is seen in various devices. The basic trimeter line pattern of **"On the London Train"**[2] (*Short Poems,* 19-20) and **"The Apparition"** (**"Twenty Poems,"** 57) may have been learned from Yeats's "Easter 1916" or sections of "The Tower." The refrain, sometimes italicized as Yeats's usually were in his *Last Poems,* occurs in **"River Rouge: 1932"** (*Poems,* 7), in **"Thanksgiving: Detroit"** (*Poems,* 16), and most noticeably in **"White Feather"** (*Short Poems,* 54). The last is a retelling of a humorous and grotesque incident that occurred in Australia when a young lieutenant returns from the war after losing an eye. He is dressed in civilian clothes and is handed a white-feather, a symbol of cowardice, by a female passerby. He pops out his artificial eye and places it in the woman's hand, although he thinks at the time that, for all he or anyone else knows, every man is a coward. The refrain, *"The eye stared at the feather,"* is Yeatsian both in the directness of the image and in its suggestiveness.

Among other influences, a Yeats-like admiration for one's forebears is seen in **"Ancestor"** (*Short Poems,* 33-34), a poem that honors Berryman's great-grandfather, a Confederate general who fought at Shiloh, repudiated the Klan-ridden South, went into exile in Honduras, and finally returned home as a federal sheriff or marshal in blue uniform. We learn the ancestor's name—"Shaver"—in **"A Point of Age"**

(*Short Poems,* 9) and in **"Sonnet 76"** the poet would again write about him. Yeats's ambivalence toward man's physicality is mirrored in Berryman's two poems entitled **"The Animal Trainer"** (*Short Poems,* 42-45). Reminiscent of Yeats's "The Circus Animals' Desertion," Berryman's animals represent the sexuality, tension, and excitement that the poet at once despises and requires for the creation of his art. However, Yeats's influence is most pervasive in four meditative lyrics—**"Meditation," "At Chinese Checkers," "The Statue,"** and **"A Point of Age."** Three of these are divided into numbered stanzas in the Yeats manner, and all are based on the eight-line stanza, with various line lengths and rhymes, of Yeats's "In Memory of Major Robert Gregory" and other poems of his middle period.[3]

"Meditation" (**"Twenty Poems,"** 58-60) is based on the Yeatsian *ottava rima* stanza but adds a line to it. In the poem a young man who must be equated with the poet sits in his Cambridge room on a rainy day and recalls his boyhood at school, his dedication to his craft, and a disquieting love relationship. **"At Chinese Checkers"** (*Short Poems,* 37-41), written during the summer of 1939, is a clearer poem. In it, the poet plays the game of the title with three children and recalls his innocent childhood—when he played the same game with a friend named "Baynard" and the friend's sister, when he called out at night for his mother, and when he played football and chipped a tooth.[4] He feels now that something has been lost from those days of golden innocence, but he is unable to articulate exactly what it is.

"The Statue" (*Short Poems,* 4-5), written in New York in 1939, is the only one of the four meditations printed in all three of the collections of early poems. The statue, that of the explorer and scientist Alexander von Humboldt, is described by the poet as looking out over the people of the city—lonely clerks, cripples, misfits, sexual deviates, bums who have slept in the park all night, and strolling couples—all of whom are either unaware of the statue or indifferent to it. The poet associates himself with the statue in an awareness of time and death that others do not possess. The grotesques do not notice the sound of water fountains, even though "their happiness runs out like water. . . . / They trust their Spring; they have not seen the statue." The statue seems to symbolize not only a cynical awareness and resignation but also a kind of aristocratic pride that the poet shares. The people themselves resemble animals: the bums are figured as dogs who are turned out at morning; the lovers are seen as caged and anxious creatures.

Until the last stanza, the poem is impersonal and aloof. The poet's condescension to the bums and lovers, as well as his assumption of final wisdom while still in his middle twenties, is irritating. The final stanza concludes more satisfactorily, however, with the poet himself no longer superior to what he has described. He turns from the scene he has observed, notes the traffic lights and the buildings that lie between him and his own "dark apartment," and imagines himself there later in the evening. Spoken of in the third person he is the

> insignificant dreamer,
> Defeated occupant, [who] will close his eyes
> Mercifully on the expensive drama
> Wherein he wasted so much skill, such faith,
> And salvaged less than the intolerable statue.
>
> (*Short Poems,* 5)

The fourth Yeatsian meditation, **"A Point of Age"** (*Short Poems,* 8-12), is even wearier in its controlled despair. Written in Detroit in the spring of 1940, it looks backward for advice to Cotton Mather, Daniel Boone, Ethan Allen, and great-grandfather Shaver; but it expresses no hope for the present or the future. The language of the poem is sometimes borrowed from Yeats: the mind's changing "Images" may be taken from Yeats's "Among School Children"; and the windy storm that destroys great trees and the threatening birds of prey are the same as those in Yeats's symbology, where they foreshadow the downfall of great civilizations or are metaphors for the corruption of the modern age.

In some of the early poems both Yeats and Auden are operating behind the scenes. **"Letter to His Brother"** (*Short Poems,* 26-27) anti-fascistically refers to the concentration camp at Dachau but concludes more like Yeats's "Prayer for My Daughter" than a political poem: "May love, or its image in work, / Bring you the brazen luck to sleep with dark / And so to get responsible delight." The technique of slant rhyme ("laughed-left") in this poem and throughout Berryman's verse may have been learned from either Yeats or Auden, both masters of it. **"Desires of Men and Women,"**[5] a second poem of dual influence, first imagines the kind of aristocratic life that Yeats consistently praised—a great house with heirlooms, servants, and large, high-ceilinged rooms; a place of orderliness, peace, and the social amenities; a manor where the inhabitants follow hallowed custom throughout their daily lives. Such people embody and preserve the civil laws and civilization itself. They attend polite social affairs where they converse in French and behave impeccably. The poem has a line break, a familiar Yeats device; and it mentions a "Cinquecento" piece of jewelry, a word that recalls Yeats's "Quattrocento" in "Among School Children."

But the audience of the poem, the addressed "you," those in the present who dream of such a life, are not aristocrats; they are vulgar members of the middle class, and the poet scores them with an Audenesque sardonicism and irony and impersonality. He says that no one,

> my dears, would dream of you
> The half-lit and lascivious apartments
> That are in fact your goal, . . .
>   or dream of you the rooms,
> Glaring and inconceivably vulgar,
> Where now you are, where now you wish for life,
> Whence you project your naked fantasies.
>
> (*Short Poems,* 28)

An earlier and less successful poem of mixed parentage is **"The Trial,"** written in 1937. This fake-ancestral lament bemoans the decline of a conservative society. The first two stanzas echo Yeats's elegies for the past:

> The oxen gone, the house is fallen where
> Our sons stood, and the wine is spilt, and skew
> Among the broken walls the servants are
>
> Except who comes across the scorching field
> Historian. But where the wind is from
> That struck the mansion, great storms having failed,
>
> No man can say.

The third stanza begins to sound like Auden in its mixture of ancient implements and military sewage disposal: "Prosperous generations, scythe in hand, / Mapped the continents, murdered, built latrines" (**"Twenty Poems,"** 65).

An additional Auden touch is noticeable in an occasional brittle wit: a man dying is described as "graduating" from this life (**"The Statue,"** *Short Poems,* 5); a man killed in an auto accident had made a quick turn and suddenly "he became an angel / Fingering an unfamiliar harp . . ." (**"The Moon and the Night and the Men,"** *Short Poems,* 52); and a Botticelli goddess is called "Venus on the half-shell" (**"At Chinese Checkers,"** *Short Poems,* 41). More distracting than this wittiness are Audenesque lines that describe a general malaise in words of almost total abstraction:

> [This] day in history must hang its head
> For the foul letters many women got,
> Appointments missed, men dishevelled and sad
> Before their mirrors trying to be proud.
>
> (**"The Spinning Heart,"** *Short Poems,* 17)

What Berryman has called the "Auden climate" surrounds most of these early sociopolitical poems, though sometimes it is difficult to measure. Berryman once characterized poems written in that climate as being "ominous, flat, and social; elliptical and indistinctly allusive; casual in tone and form, frightening in import."[6]

"The Possessed"[7] (*Short Poems,* 22-23) and **"The Curse"** have all of these characteristics except "social." The first poem describes the arrival of night and the ghosts and the horror they bring. The narrator asks someone (perhaps himself) to feel guilty about his unspecified sins. Some vaguely dangerous attackers are said to be insistently climbing the stairs, and the speaker points out a knife that could be used to kill both "Heart & guilt" at once. But whether the weapon is to be used for suicide or for self-defense is not clear. Auden's "O What Is That Sound" is similar in its vagueness of setting, detail, and motive, and in the nightmarish horror it attempts to evoke. **"The Curse"** (**"Twenty Poems,"** 70) presents a man who stands at twilight beside a broken wall, and a Gothic house stands in the background. The descending darkness is compared to ghostlike sins that both threaten man and inspire him to evil acts. Only children, idiots, and the dead escape the "universal curse," that original tendency toward evil; and the children escape it only so long as they are young. The primary sin is war itself (the poem was written in 1938-39), but "war" may also be a metaphor for any kind of evil conflict between men.

Two of Berryman's prewar poems, **"Night and the City"** and **"Conversation,"** perfectly fit his definition of the Auden climate. The first of these continues as vaguely as it begins:

> Two men sat by a stone in what dim place
> Ravelled with flares in darkness they could find,
> Considering death. The older man's face
> Hollowed the hope out in the young man's mind. . . .
>
>   The air,
> Ironic, took their talk of time and cause
> Up to indifferent walls and left it there.
>
> (**"Twenty Poems,"** 66)

Similarly, **"Conversation"** (*Short Poems,* 31-32) never specifies its characters or their fears. The poem's basic metaphor is that of life as a voyage. But, in the prewar world, the ship has slipped anchor and is drifting aimlessly through a dense fog. There are discussions—or arguments—among the passengers, but all agree that they do not know where they are going. Food is running low, everyone is so frightened that he cannot sleep, and the darkness and the depths of the sea offer the only possible harbor—a place of death rather than safety. The real weakness of these two poems is their abstraction—we never feel that a specific conversation takes place in **"Conversation"** or that "two men" are actually present in **"Night and the City."**

Berryman did write two Audenesque poems that are more successful because they do specify a setting and clarify the causes of fear and despair. **"Nineteen Thirty-eight"** begins and concludes with the "great planes" that were beginning at the time to "swarm" like "germs" throughout the world. Successive stanzas refer to the assaults upon China by Japan, the takeover of Austria by Germany, the "island Dove" (England) allowing the "Eagle" of Germany to divide Czechoslovakia, the bombing of Spain by the Luftwaffe, and, finally, groups of surviving guerrillas in any or all of these countries who continue to fight for freedom. The last stanza is a powerful assertion that all men share in the guilt of war:

> The winter sky is fatal wings. What voice
> Will spare the aged and the dying year?
> His blood is on all thresholds, bodies found
> Swollen in swollen rivers point their fingers:
>   Criminal, to stand as warning.
>
> ("Twenty Poems," 69)

The "blood" is a misleading symbol: it seems to be like the blood of the Passover lamb, which identified the houses of the Israelites in Egypt; but in Berryman's poem the blood marks the thresholds of the guilty rather than the innocent.

"World-Telegram" similarly achieves its effect of sadness and horror by a calm recitation of specific facts taken from that New York newspaper of May 15, 1939[8]—a "Man with a tail" who is going to appear at the New York World's Fair, an accident, diplomatic conflicts among the world powers, a five-year-old Peruvian girl who has had a baby, machine guns at the coal mines in Kentucky, King George VI nearing Quebec, the imminent marriage of the film star Robert Taylor, and so on. Most of the details are recorded without alteration, and many of the words are directly from the newspaper. Dudley Fitts, in a generally negative review, still found "World-Telegram" to have "an assured grace and a *pietas*. . . ."[9] But the final lines of the poem are less effective than those which preceded them:

> If it were possible to take these things
> Quite seriously, I believe they might . . .
> Immobilize the most resilient will,
> Stop trains, break up the city's food supply,
> And perfectly demoralize the nation.
>
> (*Short Poems*, 30)

The passage is weakened by its use of the Briticisms "quite" and "perfectly" (which seem to be only padding), by the change of tone from factual to superior, and by the belaboring of the pessimism we have already been led to feel in preceding stanzas.

Four early sociopolitical poems are as absolutist as Auden could be in their assumption of truth and rectitude, but we would be unfair to attribute their manner wholly to Auden. Two of them are blatantly pro-labor and anticapitalist. "River Rouge: 1932" (*Poems*, 7) describes a strike, a lockout, and a demonstration that had taken place on March 7, 1932, at the Ford plant near Detroit. The police opened fire on the workers, killing three of them and wounding fifty. "Thanksgiving: Detroit" (*Poems*, 16) contrasts the workers and their enemies during another strike and lockout, one that occurred

after Berryman arrived in the city in 1939. In this poem the laborers ominously stand and wait in the streets while capitalists enjoy themselves elsewhere, "dancing, drinking, singing vainly." The phrase first means that the bourgeois are guilty of vanity; but, when it is twice repeated, it also comes to mean that their revelry is, or soon will be, ineffectual as a means of escape from the restless and sullen proletariat.

"The Dangerous Year," written on March 1, 1939, similarly attacks capitalists—not for opposing labor but for their greed and isolationism. The poem is a dialogue between the poet and a capitalist who speaks in the first-person plural. The capitalist speaks first, saying that he and his cohorts are vaguely troubled by a "Man of Fear" (Hitler, *Time* magazine's Man of the Year for 1938) and are aware of the conflicts throughout the world, in China and elsewhere; but they are certain that "we have the Atlantic to safeguard us: / No plane can reach our shore." An italicized line concludes the speaker's remarks, and the poet responds to them in words of doom:

> Forget the crass hope of a world restored
> To dignity and unearned dividends.
> Admit, admit that now the ancient horde
> Loosed from the labyrinth of your desire
>   Is coming as you feared.
>
> (*Poems*, 3)

Unlike Auden and most anticapitalists of the time, and in spite of his sympathy for labor, Berryman did not have a corresponding admiration for Communism. Perhaps because of his youth during the 1930's, he had escaped the typical view of liberal intellectuals that Communism was an effective force against Fascism and Nazism. That view was shattered when the Communists and Nazis signed a ten-year nonaggression pact on August 24, 1939, which permitted Hitler to invade Poland on September 1 and effectively begin World War II. Russia then invaded the Polish Ukraine on September 17, and in October it forced the Baltic states of Estonia, Latvia, and Lithuania to grant military bases there. "Communist" (*Poems*, 15), which refers to these events, sarcastically attacks both the Russian Communists and the now-disillusioned intellectuals who had trusted them. The form of the poem is the ballad, a form that Auden has parodied. "Communist" specifically parodies the anonymous "Lord Randal," a conversation between a mother and her son, a "handsome young man" who has been poisoned by his "truelove." In Berryman's poem, he is an "honest young man" whose mind has been poisoned by Communism.

One reviewer energetically praised *Poems*, the 1942 chapbook in which these four poems appeared, for "stirring up the right kind of protest and slinging a straight arrow at social and political corruption."[10] Necessarily these four self-righteous political poems seem dated, and Berryman chose not to reprint them in *The Dispossessed.*

The Yeats-Auden influence is, then, very strong in much of the early meditative or political verse. An examination of the basic subjects of the early poetry leads us to several poems in which Berryman was better able to harmonize the echoes of Yeats and Auden with his own voice, and sometimes to escape the echoes entirely.

II The Themes of the Early Poetry

In addition to sociopolitical concerns, most of the other themes that recur in Berryman's later work are evident by 1948: the nature of art, the conflict between faith and doubt; the academic life; friendship and love; dreams and madness; and, overshadowing all of these, a sense of loss—loss of innocence, love, friends, faith, sanity, or identity. Three of the best sociopolitical poems are **"1 September 1939," "The Moon and the Night and the Men,"** and **"Boston Common."** These are less acerbic in tone and broader in appeal than, say, **"The Dangerous Year."** Less willing to fix blame for the war, they convey instead a great sadness at its beginnings.

Although the poem shares the Auden climate, "1 September 1939" (*Short Poems,* 47) only superficially resembles Auden's **"September 1, 1939."**[11] Berryman, in his poem, is the man who sits on the seashore, tears off bits of cellophane, and helplessly ponders the invasion of Poland, the evacuation of children from London, and the Russian-German pact. The Russian "Bear" finds protection under the wings of the German "Eagle," and the other European nations are figured as small, frightened creatures. The lights of civilization seem to be going out as twilight descends; and the man begins to weep, imagining that Europe will itself be "dismembered" by the Luftwaffe in a manner similar to the cellophane that he has torn apart.

"The Moon and the Night and the Men" similarly presents the poet darkly observing "the night of the Belgian surrender" to Germany on May 28, 1940. He is playing chess with a friend but cannot keep his mind on the game. The two quote Paul-Henri Spaak, leader of the Belgian government-in-exile; and they discuss the future, a time when no man will be able to enjoy literature or the other arts, none will be able to determine his fate, none will be able to say what he thinks. The poet then quotes Henry Adams: "History is approaching a speechless end, / . . . [and] Adams was right." One reviewer feels that the idea is, "like the lines, too limp to live";[12] but the weakness in these lines is alleviated by the careful structure of the poem and by an almost incantatory effect of the repetition of "moon" and "cold," as here in the first stanza:

On the night of the Belgian surrender the moon rose
Late, a delayed moon, and a violent moon
For the English or the American beholder;
The French beholder. It was a cold night,
People put on their wraps, the troops were cold. . . .
                                        A cold night.

                                        (*Short Poems,* 52)

The significance of the next event in the poem, the death of a "stupid well-intentioned" motorist, is not clear until the final stanza in which the King of Belgium is also called "well-intentioned" and apparently stupid. Leopold III had been a "Roadmaker to hell" by proclaiming Belgium's neutrality in 1937, an unsuccessful move designed to avoid occupation by Germany. The poem last returns to the imagery of the first stanza as the war continues, "and the moon in the breast of man is cold." The symbols of moon-cold-death may be borrowed from García Lorca's *Blood Wedding* but are equally effective here.

A third political poem, **"Boston Common"** (*Short Poems,* 59-64), was written a few weeks after America had entered World War II. A Yeatsian meditation, it achieves a lofty power of its own. The poem is an attempt to define heroism; and it begins by praising Robert Gould Shaw, the Union hero who led the first regiment of Negro troops to fight in the Civil War. Shaw and nearly half his soldiers were killed in their attack in 1863 on Fort Wagner, South Carolina. The poet stands before the Saint-Gaudens monument to Shaw and his men and calls them "Immortal heroes" (stanza II). He is not being ironic in doing so, but he soon insists that the true hero is not a man of war and may even be the common and casual bum who has fallen asleep below Shaw's cenotaph (stanzas I, IV).

This man, the poet says, turns away from the glory of war and derides our worship of war heroes. Instead, he is imagined by the poet to admire men who may be of different religions, philosophies, or nationalities, but who work for peace. Such heroes, whatever their actual occupation, are figured as Candide-like tillers of the soil, taking care of their gardens and working only so that all mankind may enjoy the beauty and goodness of life (stanza XIV). Their work is called "violent," both because of the dedication and energy behind it and because it must at times result in armed conflict, as the examples in stanza XV make clear: Lincoln, Mao Tse-Tung, Teng Fa (an early associate of Mao's), and Tracy Doll (a labor leader imprisoned in Detroit in 1939).[13] The quality of their intention is what distinguishes the violence of these men from that of gloryseekers or aggressors; the poem implies that men like Lincoln and Mao fought wars only with the intent of securing peace—a paradox that **"Boston Common"** never adequately resolves.

The villain in the poem is aggressive and total war itself. War is compared with sex, a "Congress of adolescents, . . . / Bestial and easy, issueless" (stanza V). War is "issueless" in the sense that it does not resolve the issues and also because, in the metaphor, it has no offspring. War is a "brothel" where, instead of a marriage between the common man and the angel of truth and justice, the only kind of ceremony possible is one in which a "Hobbledehoy" of the air corps mounts his bomber. His moment of climax is his moment of death (stanza VII). The implied comparison of the young pilot aboard his metal bomber to Shaw astride his bronze stallion subtly alters the unalloyed praise for Shaw in stanzas II and III.[14]

The poet argues against the childish desire of some men to become war heroes by saying that, as often as not, officially recognized heroes are no more than "swine" (stanza VIII). He invokes the ghost of William James, the speaker at the dedication of the Shaw memorial in 1897, who repeats that such monuments are often simply "Accidents of history."[15] The ghost of James, which continues to speak to the poet, tells him that true heroes should perhaps have no memorials at all since men tend to forget their war heroes of the past (stanza IX). The poet agrees, imagining the many nameless and dead "defenders of our time, / From Spain and China, . . . / Leningrad, . . . Corregidor . . ." (stanza X). He has only respect for these men who were willing to die in defense of their homes, men who fought back with their knees or fingernails or any weapons at hand (stanza XI). He concludes that we might honor heroic action if we must, as he has honored Shaw; but his final command is for us and the common man, even the sleeping bum, to become "kicking" and "working" men (stanza XVI), like those in stanza XI who used their knees to defend themselves, or like those in stanza XV who labored for the common good.

"Boston Common," like the earlier meditations, may be too directly reminiscent of Yeats to project a "clearly identifiable voice,"[16] but its sensitive thought and its compassion are telling. Those readers who agree with Dudley Fitts that the "Yeatsian ancestry" of the poem is "unintegrated"[17] may prefer **"The Pacifist's Song"** (*Short Poems,* 76), written only two or three years later and entirely unlike Yeats. The poet, or his *persona,* is more explicitly pacifistic here than in **"Boston Common,"** saying that killing in war is murder, even a form of fratricide because all men are born of the Earth Mother. He insists that he is like other men in most ways, but cannot deny that he is pulled by some kind of lifeforce away from the murder of war; and, even though he is not guilty of such murder, he is visited in his nightmares by the horrid dead, their eyes empty and sad. When he awakens, he hears someone—or his conscience—telling him that he must not kill, that he must accept any suffering without resorting to violence. The poet concludes that he must ignore the patriotic insistence of his countrymen that he fight and kill, for

he has international sympathies; he rejects chauvinism and mourns the deaths of all men. The attitudes in this and the other sociopolitical poems persist throughout Berryman's later work: the sympathy for the underdog—for labor around 1940—tends to shift toward Jews and blacks; but the liberal, antitotalitarian, pacifistic stance remains the same.

The nature of art is one of the themes of **"Winter Landscape,"** the best of the early poems. A detailed description of Pieter Brueghel's sixteenth-century painting *Hunters in the Snow,* the poem is in blank verse and all in one slow sentence. It presents three hunters, carrying spears and accompanied by their hunting dogs. The group is returning to its village at dusk, and the men seem to be exhausted as they trudge through the snow, passing other townsfolk busy at play or at various tasks. Although the poem includes many minute details from the painting, it concentrates on the three hunters, men who

> Are not aware that in the sandy time
> To come, the evil waste of history
> Outstretched, they will be seen upon the brow
> Of that same hill: when all their company
> Will have been irrecoverably lost,
>
> These men, this particular three in brown
> Witnessed by birds will keep the scene and say
> By their configuration with the trees,
> The small bridge, the red houses and the fire,
> What place, what time, what morning occasion
>
> Sent them into the wood, a pack of hounds
> At heel and the tall poles upon their shoulders,
> Thence to return as now we see them and
> Ankle-deep in snow down the winter hill
> Descend, while three birds watch and the fourth flies.

(*Short Poems,* 3)

Berryman felt that this was his first poem which did not sound like "Yeats or Auden—or Rilke or Lorca or Corbière or any of my other passions of those remote days."[18] Several critics have praised the poem, and Robert Lowell has called it his "favorite Berryman poem" of the early period because of its "gentleness and delicacy and clarity."[19] Despite the apparent simplicity of **"Winter Landscape,"** it poses several difficulties. Berryman once complained that the poem is usually taken "for either a verbal *equivalent* to the picture or (like Auden's fine Brueghel poem, 'Musee des Beaux Arts,' written later) an *interpretation* of it. Both views I would call wrong. . . ."[20]

The poet directs us to an article by Arthur and Catherine Evans that posits the first view. These two aestheticians feel that the poet's intent is "to rival the peculiarly painterly exposition of an idea through a parallel reconstruction by means of verse."[21] Berryman agrees with several affinities discovered in the article and quotes from it: ". . . They say the poem's 'elabora-t[ive] sequence urged on by the sweeping carry-over lines' (they mean run-on)—within the stanza or between stanzas—preserves the same order of presentation and the same groupings of elements as the Brueghel composition. . . . Purposefully restricting himself to a diction as sober, direct, and matter-of-fact as the painter's treatment of scene and objects, Berryman so composes with it that he achieves an insistent and animated pattern of strong poetic effect.'"

But, Berryman, comments, "Nowhere is anything said as to what the poem is *about*. . . ." He then explains that the poem "dates from 1938-9 and was written in New York following two years' residence in England, during recurrent crises, with extended visits to France and Germany, especially one of the Nazi strongholds, Heidelberg. So far as I can make out, it is a war-poem, of an unusual negative kind. The common title of the picture is 'Hunters in the Snow' and of course the poet knows this. But he pretends not to, and calls their spears (twice) 'poles,' the governing resultant emotion being a certain stubborn incredulity—as the hunters are loosed while the peaceful nations plunge again into war."[22] These are wild and whirling words indeed. Berryman claims to have discovered, in writing **"Winter Land-scape,"** that "a poem's force may be pivoted on a miss-ing or misrepresented element in an agreed-on or imposed design. . . ."[23] But, without his comments, no reader of the poem could discover the missing element of war or his feelings about it. What Berryman seems to be saying is that the poem means, for him, something other than what it means to anyone else.

Even with the poet's comments, the poem does not seem to be a war poem of any kind. One critic claims that **"Winter Landscape"** fails entirely to "realize a meaningful theme. . . ."[24] Robert Lowell is closer to the truth in concluding that the poem reproduces the meaning of the penultimate stanza of Keats's "Ode on a Grecian Urn,"[25] the stanza that imagines the "little town . . . emptied of its folk, . . . silent." What Lowell has in mind is our sadness and desolation in the remem-brance of things past, and **"Winter Landscape"** does convey that. But it also suggests another theme of Keats's poem—art is long, life is short. As Berryman's poem states this thought, although all men die, "These men, this particular three in brown . . . will keep the scene . . . as now we see them. . . ." These men live, permanently, because they exist in an imperishable work of art.

Berryman's interest in pictorial art is one element in the **"Song of the Man Forsaken and Obsessed"** (*Short Poems,* 75). The artist who speaks is Paul Gaugin, the nineteenth-century Frenchman who gave up a business career and a family to live obscurely and to paint vividly in the Marquesas Islands. The theme of the poem is the obsession of the artist with his work and the necessary loneliness it brings.

The theme of the conflict between faith and doubt is seen most clearly in **"The Disciple"** (*Short Poems,* 6-7). Although the poet felt that Yeats saved him from the influence of T. S. Eliot,[26] this poem necessarily reminds us of Eliot's "Journey of the Magi."[27] **"The Disciple"** is a monologue spoken by an old man who recalls certain events in the life of Christ, events that he had witnessed years before. The poem tells us of Christ's raising of Lazarus, His compassion for the poor and the afflicted, His betrayal by Judas, and finally His crucifixion. It concludes with a stanza praising a faith that needs no reason to bolster it:

> I can tell you I saw then
> A terrible darkness on the face of men,
> [Christ's] last astonishment; and now that I'm
> Old I behold it as a young man yet.
> None of us now knows what it means,
> But to this day our loves and disciplines
> Worry themselves there. We do not forget.
>
> (*Short Poems,* 7)

The poem is, then, a hymn on the part of the *persona,* but it is not simply that. What is most notable about the speaker is his innocence. In the opening stanza of the poem, he remembers being deeply impressed by Christ's ability to make coins apparently disappear and to draw a piece of paper through a fire without its burning; but he finds the raising of Lazarus to be no more—or less—impressive than these tricks of legerdemain. Also, the speaker never mentions Christ's divinity, as if that were unimportant beside Christ's humane acts. And there are other difficulties. Ian Hamilton feels that such confu-sions reveal an ambivalence on the part of Berryman that makes it impossible to find the poem's "centre"; Hamilton wonders "whether Berryman isn't really floundering here."[28]

What bothers Hamilton is that Berryman seems to as-sent to the old man's faith in the final stanza; but, in the stanza immediately preceding it, he seems to ridicule such a faith by the use of a series of puns—"harboured" in the sense of "protecting from the law," "coppers" as policemen, "lifted" meaning stolen. Some of the puns Hamilton objects to do not occur in an earlier version of **"The Disciple"** (in **"Twenty Poems,"** 63-64); but their use in either version ought not necessarily lead us to conclude that Berryman is ridiculing the old man or his faith, or that he is, as Hamilton says, playing a "joke" on Christ or the policemen or himself.

The old man, in his naiveté, seems not to be aware of the puns. The poet's use of them, as well as our aware-ness of them, is a result of a greater sophistication on his part and ours. **"The Disciple"** becomes an ambitious attempt to present the pure faith of an elderly disciple and also to show an awareness of the doubt that of necessity arises in the modern world. The poet's attitude is ambivalent, expressing both faith and doubt; but there is no ridicule in it. The poem reminds us how simple faith is for the innocent, how difficult for others.

The subjects of the academic life, friendship, and love appear notably in three early poems. **"A Professor's Song"** (*Short Poems,* 71), one of the **"Nervous Songs,"** satirizes both the professor and the students in his literature class. The professor, who is most concerned about completing an historical survey of Alexander Pope, William Blake, Samuel Taylor Coleridge, and William Wordsworth, quotes a catch-phrase from "Kubla Khan" ("'That deep romantic chasm'") and misquotes the "Preface to the *Lyrical Ballads*" ("'A poet is a man speaking to men'"). He is irritated by his inattentive, sleepy-eyed students; and, when the bell rings, he dismisses them sardonically: "Until I meet you, then, in Upper Hell / Convulsed, foaming immortal blood: farewell." He is slyly accusing his students of the sins of incontinence that are punished in the Upper Hell of Dante's *Inferno,* but he is again inaccurate in having blood there.

"A Poem for Bhain" (*Short Poems,* 58), in tercets, was written for a friend who later, in 1940, died of cancer.[29] The poem, as simple and direct as **"Winter Landscape,"** is a forerunner of the many later poems written for or about the poet's friends. Perhaps less successful is **"Canto Amor,"** a "love song" dedicated to the poet's wife at the time the poem was written (*The Dispossessed,* vii). The poem is not at all direct and is not quite convincing in its joy. It concludes,

> Dance for this music, Mistress to music dear,
> more, that storm worries the disordered wood
> grieving the midnight of my thirtieth year
>
> and only the trial of our music should
> still this irresolute air, only your voice
> spelling the tempest may compel our good:
>
> Sigh then beyond my song: whirl & rejoice!
>
> (*Short Poems,* 67)

For some reason the poet seems less credible in poems praising his beloved than he is when dealing with the separation of lovers, as in **"Parting as Descent,"** a poem of 1938 or so. The poet is to catch a train at Waterloo but first spends a few minutes with his friend. When he must leave her, his departure is a journey to hell:

> The bitter coffee in a small café
> Gave us our conversation. When the train
> Began to move, I saw you turn away
> and vanish, and the vessels in my brain

> Burst, the train roared, the other travellers
> In flames leapt, burning on the tilted air
> Che si cruccia, I heard the devils curse
> And shriek with joy in that place beyond prayer.
>
> (*Short Poems,* 24)

The flames and the devils are from Dante; "Che si cruccia" ("he who torments himself") is from Canto XIX, line 31, of the *Inferno.*

The poet's fascination with dreams is seen as early as the vaguely nightmarish **"The Possessed"** (*Short Poems,* 22-23) and in the coolly clinical **"Desire Is a World by Night"** (*Short Poems,* 48-49), both written before 1940. One early poem, **"The Traveller"** (*Short Poems,* 13), seems to be a transcription of a dream. Usually these nightmarish poems imagine death, are populated by horses and devils, and express feelings of sin and guilt—as in **"Whether There Is Sorrow in the Demons"** (*Short Poems,* 82-83), a title that seems to be borrowed from Scholastic philosophy. This poem also suggests the theme that dominates Berryman's early work and remains important in *Berryman's Sonnets, Homage to Mistress Bradstreet, The Dream Songs,* and *Love & Fame*—the theme of loss.

"The Ball Poem" (*Short Poems,* 14) notes that learning about loss is, like the loss of innocence, a necessary part of maturation. The poet observes a boy playing with a ball that bounces out of his hands, down the street, and into the harbor. The poet says that, with the loss, the boy "senses first responsibility / In a world of possessions," and is being forced to learn the "epistemology of loss." The poet silently sympathizes with the boy, revealing that he too has encountered loss, in a Whitmanesque conclusion: "I am everywhere, / I suffer and move . . . / With all that move me, under the water / Or whistling, I am not a little boy." One phrase of the poem, "Balls will be lost always," may support Ian Hamilton's contention that Berryman's poems sometimes have disconcerting private jokes embedded in them; Berryman is elsewhere concerned with fears of castration, and the pun seems inescapable in **"The Ball Poem."** Whether or not the pun was intended, the poem suffers.

The archetypal loss for Berryman was his father's suicide in 1926, and two of the early poems, **"World's Fair"** and **"Fare Well,"** have that loss in their background. The first of these has the poet waiting beside a roller coaster for a girl to arrive. He has waited an hour, and his sudden recognition that she is not going to meet him reminds him of another kind of betrayal. He confuses autobiographical and literary memories. First, he is tormented by

> The inexhaustible ability of a man
> Loved once, long lost, still to prevent my peace. . . .

Childhood speaks to me in an austere face.
The Chast Mayd only to the thriving Swan
Looks back and back with lecherous intent, . . .
Middleton's grave in a forgotten place.

(*Short Poems,* 35)

The allusion is to Thomas Middleton's play *A Chast Mayd in Cheap-side* (1630) and the Swan Theater where it was performed.[30] The reference combines, in a complicated way, love lost with the loss of Berryman's father. In Middleton's play, Tim, a young Cambridge student, writes a letter to his parents, expressing his great love for both of them. In Berryman's poem, the memory of his father obsesses the poet but the grave, like Middleton's, is in "a forgotten place" because the poet had never returned to see it.[31] The "Chast Mayd" who looks longingly after a "thriving Swan" is Berryman's metaphor for the girl he awaits. She, like the unchaste maid in the play who tricks Tim into marriage, is interested only in a "thriving," successful young man. As the poet expected, his friend does not arrive; and he trudges off toward his apartment and his poetry and his "instructor"—the man who first instructed him in loss. **"Fare Well"** (*Short Poems,* 15) expresses a sense of loss more desperately; the poet despairs of ever remembering his father without undergoing a paroxysm of love and burning resentment. In this poem the phoenix becomes a symbol of the recurring grief. The poet tries to escape from the phoenix's pyre into a restful "snowbed"; the implication is that he will never escape his grief until he himself dies.

Besides the death of his father, the poet had another source for some of the early poems of loss. In 1947, he had the illicit love affair that drove him to severe mental disorder and eventually destroyed his first marriage. At the time, he considered "killing both himself and his mistress because she flatly refused to leave her husband and to marry him."[32] Section V of *The Dispossessed* and one poem in section IV, **"Surviving Love"** (*Short Poems,* 77), seem to have been written during this difficult time. The poet's feelings of madness and his sympathy for a friend who is undergoing similar psychological difficulties is revealed in **"A Winter-Piece to a Friend Away"** (*Short Poems,* 87-88). His father's death and his own impulse toward death inform **"The Long Home"** (*Short Poems,* 84-86).

The poet's feelings of loss—loss of stability, identity, and love—expand in the concluding and title poem of *The Dispossessed.* The sense of dispossession in it not only is personal but also extends to a view of the world itself in 1947. **"The Dispossessed"** (*Short Poems,* 94-95) is not, as the poet has claimed, "thoroughly mysterious"[33] but is indeed complex. The setting of the poem is an "empty" house where the poet is reading Luigi Pirandello's play *Six Characters in Search of an Author.* As he reads one line in the play ("'and something that..

that is theirs—no longer ours'"), he comes to an awareness that "old things," familiar and evil patterns of existence, continually recur. Simply stated, the patterns are political and personal—war and adultery.

The political implications of **"The Dispossessed"** were first pointed out by John Frederick Nims who, noting the references to German and Italian and recalling that both "Fuehrer" and "Duce" mean "Leader," suggested that the "flying arms" of the second stanza are airplanes and that the "umbrella" of the ninth stanza is a metonym for Neville Chamberlain.[34] The poet also mentions "Stalin," apparently comparing him to Hitler and Mussolini; and he compares all three of these villains to himself and to us, the readers of the poem: their weapons are also *"our* arms," and their story is "our story." No longer is the world a simple melodrama in which evil is easily recognized and overcome ("no hero rides"), for we are all guilty of involvement in war. As the poet explained in an essay in 1949,

> everybody is "guilty" of everything, and that is that. . . . Few men of reflection can be satisfied now with their actions and attitudes during the recent war. Well, we put that aside: the Enemy was clear, and moreover what happened (producing what is happening now) would have happened anyway, "It was done for us"—your modern intellectual is astonishingly fatalistic. This is the view generally taken, with a gain in uneasiness, of the use of the atomic bomb. But few men of reflection can be satisfied with their actions and attitudes *now.* Well, again the Enemy is clear (Stalin for Hitler), what is happening cannot be influenced by us, and so on.[35]

The poem also refers obliquely to the atomic bomb—the "weaponeer" arms it, the "cam" of a gunlike mechanism triggers it, and the "umbrella" cloud follows its explosion. (Combining cause and effect, the umbrella could also be Einstein's, mentioned in **"Dream Song #336."**) One result of the bomb's presence is that "Rarely a child sings now," a phrase that occurs in an earlier poem that tells of the death of a culture, **"The Song of the Young Hawaiian"** (*Short Poems,* 70).

The phrase "cam slid" in the eighth stanza of **"The Dispossessed"** is a connection between the political and the personal elements behind the poem, for the words occur in **"Sonnet 70"** as a sexual metaphor. Similarly, "the faceless fellow waving from her crotch" in **"The Dispossessed"** is the poet himself, who in **"Sonnet 98"** climbed up into a sycamore near his lover's house and there also compared her limbs with those of the tree. (The image is from Mallarmé's "Salut": *"De sirènes mainte à l'envers."*) The poet is "faceless" because he has lost his identity by engaging in the illicit love affair, just as the Father in *Six Characters* felt he was losing his when he spoke the line that opens Berryman's poem.

Two additional phrases reinforce the notion that **"The Dispossessed"** has the love affair behind it. The "Movement of stone within a woman's heart, / abrupt &

dominant" may refer either to his lover's leaving him or to his wife's discovery of the affair. The phrase "the spidery business of love" is echoed in **"Sonnet 88,"** where the poet's lover is figured as a spider who takes him for a victim. Speaking to women, the poet once said that in adultery, "You behave like a spider."[36] In **"The Dispossessed,"** the poet was observing the dark world situation and finding analogies between it and his own condition.

The themes of Berryman's early poetry remain fairly constant throughout his career; but he always tended to experiment in style. As we examine the style of the early poems, we shall determine which elements of it remain with the poet in his subsequent works.

III THE EARLY POETRY: THE SEARCH FOR A STYLE

Berryman's career was a "long, often back-breaking, search for an inclusive style. . . ."[37] By 1948, he had written in three fairly distinct styles: one is based on the Yeats-Auden influence, as in **"The Statue"** or **"Boston Common"**; the others are best illustrated by the first poem and the last of *The Dispossessed.* The 1939-40 poem **"Winter Landscape"** is impersonally quiet, relaxed, and graceful. It is consistent in tone and diction, orthodox in its blank verse, relatively clear in meaning. The 1947-48 poem **"The Disposesed"** is strikingly different. It is more personal, although veiled in its references to the poet's life; it is elliptical, strained, and excited; it mixes levels of diction, wrenches syntax, and is complex and allusive. The style of **"The Disposessed"** is similar to that of the contemporaneous *Sonnets* and, with them, is a forerunner of *Homage to Mistress Bradstreet* and of *The Dream Songs.*

We must not, however, oversimplify the poet's stylistic development by suggesting that between 1938 and 1948 it underwent an orderly progression. The Yeats-Auden influence was still in force even after the style of **"Winter Landscape"** had been developed; **"Boston Common"** was written about two years after that poem. And we can catch undigested bits of Auden's "September 1, 1939" as late as 1947 or so in **"Rock-Study with Wanderer"** (*Short Poems,* 79). **"New Year's Eve"** (*Short Poems,* 89-91) is Yeatsian in stanza form and Audenesque in its sardonic tone, although it was written about the same time (1947-1948) as **"The Dispossessed."** The 1938 poem **"Cloud and Flame"**[38] (*Short Poems,* 25) is as densely allusive and elliptical as **"The Dispossessed."** **"The Lightning"** (*Short Poems,* 78), a poem of 1947 or so, is as clear as **"Winter Landscape."**

The concurrency of various styles in the early period suggests that Berryman had not found any one style that would be expressive of himself. Indeed, we do not

get a clear picture of the poet from the early poems. Sometimes he seems cool and aloof; at other times, passionate and sympathetic; but in either case, he seems to be unwilling to speak about himself except obliquely. Although he disagreed with Eliot's view that poetry should be impersonal,[39] he was unable in the early poems to form a distinct poetic personality. He had not yet learned, as Yeats was forced to learn, that the subject of his poetry at its best was to be 'himself-as-himself' or as an "expressive personality."[40]

Berryman did find two devices in the early verse that would aid him later in overcoming his reticence about self. One, learned from Yeats or Pound, is the *persona,* as in **"The Disciple"** or **"The Nervous Songs,"** poems in which the speaker sometimes is and sometimes is not the poet himself. The second was the discovery in **"The Ball Poem"** that, as Berryman said in 1965, "a commitment of identity can be 'reserved,' so to speak, with an ambiguous pronoun. The poet himself is both left out and put in; the boy does and does not become him, and we are confronted with a process which is at once a process of life and a process of art. A pronoun may seem a small matter, but she matters, he matters, it matters, they matter. Without this invention . . . I could not have written either of the two long poems that constitute the bulk of my work so far."[41] The two long poems were *Homage to Mistress Bradstreet* and *77 Dream Songs.* The poet did not mention the *Sonnets,* still unpublished at the time he made these remarks in 1965. In the very personal *Sonnets,* the poet was able to overcome his natural reticence because, at the time he wrote them, he did not envision that they could ever be published.

Only one stylistic quality remains constant throughout the early poetry—the poet's craftsmanship. Sometimes, but not often, it seems to be merely a "delight in craftsmanship" (**"Twenty Poems,"** 47) for its own sake, as in the **"Letter to His Brother"** (*Short Poems,* 26-27), a poem in which a rhyme pattern (*abbacddc*) is counterpoised against a metrical pattern (5,4,5,5,5,4,5,5). Of course the early poems are not without an occasional weakness. William J. Martz has rightly attacked these lines for their triteness: "The summer cloud in summer blue / Capricious from the wind will run" (**"Cloud and Flame,"** *Short Poems,* 25).[42] He might also have noted the padding and the inversion in the second line, needed to achieve meter and a following rhyme. But to conclude, as Martz does, that Berryman's poetry generally is "sloppy in craft"[43] is absurd. Throughout his career Berryman was considered a "poet's poet,"[44] an epithet reserved for writers of superb technical control.

Notes

1. John Berryman, "One Answer to a Question," *Shenandoah,* XVII (Autumn 1965), 68.

2. Berryman explicated this poem fully in "A Note on Poetry," "Twenty Poems," pp. 45-48. ["Twenty Poems," *Five Young American Poets* (Norfolk, Conn., 1940); hereinafter cited internally]

3. Berryman, "One Answer," p. 72.

4. Cf. Dream Song 254, where the poet mentions being kicked in the face as he tackled a player at South Kent. [*The Dream Songs* (New York, 1969); hereinafter cited internally by Song number rather than by page.]

5. The poet has pointed out that the first line of this poem is a variation of Delmore Schwartz's "Tired and Unhappy, You Think of Houses" (*The Dispossessed,* vii). [*The Dispossessed* (New York, 1948). Reprinted in *Short Poems* (New York, 1967).]

6. "Waiting for the End, Boys," *Partisan Review,* XVV (Feb. 1948), 254.

7. When first collected, in "Twenty Poems," 75-76, the poem was titled "The Return."

8. The date that follows the poem, "11 May 1939," is incorrect.

9. Dudley Fitts, "Deep in the Unfriendly City," *New York Times Book Review,* June 20, 1948, p. 4.

10. Pearl Strachan, "The World of Poetry," *Christian Science Monitor,* Weekly Magazine Section, Oct. 3, 1942, p. 10.

11. According to Monroe K. Spears (*The Poetry of W. H. Auden* [New York, 1968], p. 356), Auden's poem was first published on Oct. 18, 1939. Berryman also seems to have written his poem very soon after the events; by its placement in *Poems,* it was written before "Communist," which is dated "October 1939" (*Poems,* 15). [*Poems* (Norfolk, Conn., 1940); hereinafter cited internally.]

12. Robert Fitzgerald, "Poetry and Perfection," *Sewanee Review,* LVI (Autumn 1948), 692.

13. Berryman furnished the information about Teng Fa and Tracy Doll in a letter to me dated June 27, 1971.

14. Berryman mentions "the mounted man" as an unrivaled "symbol for power" in his short story "The Imaginary Jew," p. 533.

15. Much of the poem's diction is from William James's speech, which can be found in *Memories and Studies* (New York, 1968), pp. 37-61.

16. Samuel French Morse, "Twelve Poets," *Virginia Quarterly Review,* XLIV (Summer 1968), 510.

17. Fitts, p. 4.

18. Berryman, "One Answer," p. 69. *cf.* Ezra Pound's "The Return."

19. Robert Lowell, "The Poetry of John Berryman," *New York Review of Books,* II (May 28, 1964), p. 3.

20. Berryman, "One Answer," p. 69. "Winter Landscape" was first published in *The New Republic,* CVIII (July 8, 1940); Auden's "Musee des Beaux Arts" first appeared in New Writing (Spring 1939). Spears, *The Poetry of W. H. Auden,* p. 348.

21. Arthur and Catherine Evans, "Pieter Bruegel and John Berryman: Two Winter Landscapes," *Texas Studies in Language and Literature,* V (Autumn 1963, 309.

22. Berryman, "One Answer," pp. 69-70

23. *Ibid.,* p. 70.

24. Martz, p. 18. [William J. Martz, *John Berryman,* University of Minnesota Pamphlets on American Writers, No. 85 (Minneapolis, 1969).]

25. Lowell, p. 3.

26. Berryman, "One Answer," p. 68.

27. Ian Hamilton first noted the similarity in "John Berryman," *London Magazine,* IV (Feb. 1965), 94.

28. *Ibid.,* p. 95.

29. The cause of Campbell's death is specified in Dream Song 88.

30. John Frederick Nims, "World's Fair," *Poetry: A Critical Supplement* (April 1948), p. 6.

31. Martz, p. 6.

32. *Ibid.,* p. 7.

33. John Berryman, *Poet's Choice,* ed. Paul Engle and Joseph Langland (New York, 1962), p. 135.

34. Nims, "The Dispossessed," *Poetry,* pp. 1-5.

35. John Berryman, "The State of American Writing: 1948," *Partisan Review,* XV (Aug. 1949), 857.

36. Berryman, as quoted in Howard, p. 76. [Jane Howard, "Whisky and Ink, Whisky and Ink," *Life* (July 21, 1967), p. 74.]

37. Lowell, p. 34.

38. The allusions in "Cloud and Flame" are to Swift, who because of his distaste for scholastic philosophy was permitted to graduate from Trinity College, Dublin, only by special arrangement; to John Cornford, a British poet killed in Spain in 1936; and to Thirkill (or Thurkill) the Sacrist who observed a statue of Christ bow its head before King Harold of England, indicating that Harold would be killed in the Battle of Hastings. *American Poetry,* ed. Gay Wilson Allen, Walter E. Rideout, and James K. Robinson (New York, 1965), n., p. 1075.

39. See John Berryman, "The Poetry of Ezra Pound," *Partisan Review,* XVI (April 1949), 389; and "An Interview with John Berryman," *Harvard Advocate,* CIII (Spring 1969), 5. The Pound article was intended as the introduction to *Ezra Pound: Selected Poems* (New York: New Directions, 1949), but it was rejected by Pound and by James Laughlin as being unsuitable for "young readers." In a letter to me dated June 27, 1971, Berryman wrote that his selection of Pound's poems may also have been discarded for the same reason—he is not certain, for he never looked at the published volume to see which poems it contains. New Directions is noncommittal on the matter.

40. Berryman, "The Poetry of Ezra Pound," p. 388.

41. Berryman, "One Answer," P. 71.

42. Martz, p. 17.

43. *Ibid.*

44. William Meredith, "Henry Tasting All the Secret Bits of Life: Berryman's *Dream Songs,*" *Wisconsin Studies in Contemporary Literature,* VI (Winter-Spring 1965), 27.

Selected Bibliography

PRIMARY SOURCES

1. POETRY

The Dispossessed. New York: William Sloane Associates, 1948.

"Twenty Poems," *Five Young American Poets.* Norfolk, Conn.: New Directions, 1940.

2. PROSE

"The Imaginary Jew," *Kenyon Review,* VII (Autumn 1945), 529-39.

"One Answer to a Question," *Shenandoah,* XVII (Autumn 1965), 67-76.

SECONDARY SOURCES

HOWARD, JANE. "Whisky and Ink, Whisky and Ink," *Life* LXIII (July 21, 1967), 67-76. A valuable source of biographical and personal information about the poet. Superior to most critical articles in literary judgments and selective quotations.

MARTZ, WILLIAM J. John Berryman. University of Minnesota Pamphlets on American Writers, No. 85. Minneapolis: University of Minnesota Press, 1969. Fullest analysis of Berryman's work to date. Adjudges Berryman's poems to be "uneven"; *The Dream Songs* are a "distinguished achievement" but considered inferior to *Homage.*

NIMS, JOHN FREDERICK. "The Dispossessed," "World's Fair," and "The Traveler," *Poetry: A Critical Supplement* (April 1948), pp. 1-6. Explication of the three poems with questions directed primarily to students.

Gary Q. Arpin (essay date 1978)

SOURCE: Arpin, Gary Q. "Late Poems." In *The Poetry of John Berryman,* pp. 87-100. Port Washington, N.Y.: National University Publications, 1978.

[*In the following essay, Arpin assesses the successes and failures of Berryman's later poetry.*]

Berryman did not stop writing dream songs after the publication of **His Toy, His Dream, His Rest**—"that admirable outlet" continued to attract him, apparently— but no new songs were added to the collected **Dream Songs** (1969), and most of his energies were being directed elsewhere. He was, at various times between 1968 and his death in 1972, working on a translation of Sophocles, a book on Shakespeare (on which he had been working, on and off, for decades), a life of Christ for children, and a novel, "'the first part of which was about a man trying to solve his inner problems, the second part about the sickness of the world today,'"[1] which was published unfinished as *Recovery* after his death. He was also, he declared in a press interview occasioned by his sharing the Bollingen award with Karl Shapiro, working on two books of poetry.[2] Short poems, but conceived from very early on as separate books. Not satisfied with the notion of simply writing lyrics, Berryman organized his short poems as he was writing them into a larger structure.

The first collection, **Love & Fame,** appeared in 1970, and shocked most critics. The jacket blurb announced "a style new for Berryman, new for anybody," and so indeed it seemed to be. Speaking in propria persona, Berryman bragged and strutted, alternately telling the reader how famous he was and what an active sex life he had. Falling on the ready-made pun, reviewers spoke, generally with distaste, of Berryman's name dropping and pants dropping. The book elicited not simply negative appraisals, but frequently hostile and mocking comments. The most hostile critics spoke of being "disgusted" by the subject matter; friendly critics worried that Berryman had lost his talent.

Berryman was himself unsure of the quality of this new collection. "They were so weird," he said, "so unlike all my previous work that I was a little worried"[3] before they were published. In the English edition and the second American edition, he "killed some of the worst poems,"[4] three "sexual" poems and three "political" poems.

At the same time, though, although he did not of course defend the quality of the poems, Berryman felt it necessary—once again—to correct some misconceptions, the most serious being the refusal to admit any irony into this bragging version of the search for love and fame. The book, he explained, was "a whole, each of the four movements criticizing backward the preceding, until Part 4 wipes out altogether all earlier presentations of the 'love' and 'fame' of the ironic title."[5] The book takes the form of the virtually mythic conversion narrative, the amoral youth discovering God and the error of his ways. Some reviewers noticed this (Jerome Mazzaro, principally, who compared the book to Augustine's *Confessions*[6]), but most did not. This was not entirely the fault of the reviewers, for Berryman relies on the progress of the book rather than on immediate irony to distance his "mature" self from his youth. The sequence is written by a man who has come to see the futility of the notions of "love" and "fame" that he had as a young man, but we seldom get a glimpse of that wiser man in the early sections. With a few exceptions, the early poems are straightforward and written from the point of view of the youth.

There is no noticeable irony, for example, in the description of Berryman's receiving a C in Professor Neff's course and almost not graduating from Columbia. His statement that receiving a C placed him "squarely in the middle of Hell" seems to be straightforward. "Is this," wrote Robert Phillips, "really sufficient impetus to place a soul 'squarely in the middle of Hell'?"[7] Of course it is not. But the problem, it seems to me, is cleared up in **"The Hell Poem"** in section 3. The contrast between this very real hell of "anguishes; / gnawings" and the egocentric youth's notion of hell in section 1 is extreme, and does indeed, as Berryman said, "wipe out" that early conception.

Berryman never claimed the status of a long poem for *Love & Fame,* but it must be read, as he said, as a whole. Indeed, the book is structurally more satisfying than Berryman's major long poem, ***The Dream Songs***, for there are few obtrusions into the narrative, and the story told is fairly clear. That story is not very different from the stories told in Berryman's other works. The book describes the development of a poetic sensibility struggling against both outer and inner obstacles. In his earlier work, though, much greater attention is paid to the outer obstacles—the mad culture the poet finds himself a part of—than is paid here. In *Love & Fame* there are some poems about American society, but what is most important about that society is Berryman's isolation from it. In school and at college he is, despite his efforts to the contrary ("I made at Columbia a point of being popular"[8]) an exile. His father's suicide separates him from the normal home life of his friends, and he is more comfortable in Harlem listening to blues singers than he is on Morningside Heights.

However, most of the obstacles in these early sections are inner. Berryman's own misconceptions and his own frightening lust are the real enemies. His ambition and his lust are related—they are both attempts to impose his massive ego on the world around him. His poetic drive and his sexual drive are brought together in **"Two Organs."** The first organ is feminine, Plato's uterus, which the young Berryman thinks he resembles:

> Plato's uterus, I say,
> an animal passionately longing for children
>
> and, if long unsatisfied after puberty,
> prone to range angrily, blocking the air passages
> & causing distress & disease.
> For 'children' read: big fat fresh original &
>   characteristic poems.
>
> [p. 16]

The second organ is masculine:

> An eccentric friend, a Renaissance scholar, sixty-odd,
> unworldly, he writes limericks in Medieval Latin,
> stood up in the rowboat fishing to take a leak
> & exclaimed as he was about it with excitement
>
> "I wish my penis was big enough for this whole lake!"
> My phantasy precisely at twenty:
> to satisfy at once all Barnard & Smith
> & have enough left over for Miss Gibbs's girls.
>
> [p. 17]

(Young Berryman, besides being a rake, is also a snob: he wishes to satisfy the Barnard and Smith girls before turning to their working class sisters at Katherine Gibb's Secretarial School). Both of these notions, both parts of Berryman's hermaphroditic drive, are wiped out in following sections, although it is his lust which brings him to the spiritual and emotional crisis that is at the center of the volume.

The beginning of this crisis is described in **"Damned."** The word is used seriously; this is not the undergraduate's hell of a C, but a true sense of emotional and spiritual damnation—**"The Hell Poem"** follows shortly. **"Damned"** describes the conception of Berryman's illegitimate child. In **"Her & It,"** the first poem in the volume, Berryman had said, rather cavalierly, "I'll bet she now has seven lousy children. / (I've three myself, one being off the record.)" This attitude—"seven lousy children"—changes during the course of the volume. In **"Message"** children are seen as being of central importance: "Children! Children! form the point of all. / Children & high art" (p. 57). Here, real children and poetic children, the offspring of "Plato's uterus," are equally important. The line should sound familiar, for the sentiment was for a long time a part of Berryman's work. But in **"Damned"** the child is not a form of solace, but a reminder of his adultery. The point of view in the poem shifts: there are several "Berrymans" in *Love & Fame,* and there are at least two here. In the first stanza Berryman's "mistress" (the poem seems to indicate that their relationship was limited to a single night; it was no doubt one of many such relationships) is pregnant. In the next three stanzas Berryman recalls the night of conception:

> She came again & again, twice ejecting me
> over her heaving. I turned my head aside
> to avoid her goddamned tears,
> getting in my beard.

> [p. 68]

This Berryman is simply a bastard. Turning his head "to avoid her god-damned tears," he is the logical result of the youthful Berryman who had thought only of self-gratification. It is this, I think, which makes Berryman a "damned" character. The Berryman of the following stanza is the Berryman of the present, the Berryman of the last line of the poem, and he is a very different man from the adulterer Berryman:

> I am busy tired mad lonely & old.
> O this has been a long long night of wrest.

The "long long night of wrest" in this marvelous couplet is metaphorical. It is Berryman's dark night of the soul, and one which has a way yet to go, through the darkness of **"Despair"** and the hell sequence.

"Despair" is one of the finest poems in the volume. It begins with flat statement, perfectly appropriate to its subject:

> It seems to be DARK all the time.
> I have difficulty walking.
> I can remember what to say to my seminar
> but I don't know that I want to.

> [p. 72]

The accretion of these bleak statements in the following two stanzas, one clipped sentence to a line, presents one of the most convincing depictions of despair in literature, one that is deepened by the contrast in the fourth stanza of a brief hope:

> Crackles! in darkness HOPE; & disappears.

The metrical regularity of the line—the only line of iambic pentameter (with a trochaic substitution in the first foot) in the poem—and the syntactic deviance print the brief lightning of hope on the mind. Even the typography emphasizes the contrast, the small capitals of HOPE balancing the small capitals of DARK in the first stanza. What provides this hope is his daughter: "I am in love with my excellent baby." The notion of love has changed radically from the beginning.

This notion is carried over into the institutional sequence which follows **"Despair."** The light of hope is provided by caring for someone outside of yourself, not

by avoiding their "goddamned tears." Thus, it is important that one of the first things we learn in **"The Hell Poem"** is "I like nearly all the rest of them too" (p. 73). Marjorie Perloff, in *The Poetic Art of Robert Lowell,* has compared Berryman's "hospital poems" with Lowell's, specifically contrasting "Waking in the Blue" with **"The Hell Poem."** After noting the similarities of the "surface features" in the two poems, Professor Perloff points out that an important difference between the two is that Lowell is a participant in what he describes and that he "moves toward some measure of self-insight and understanding," while Berryman, in a poem which suffers from an "arbitrariness of detail," is simply "a camera, recording what he perceives . . . as so much raw data."[9] Berryman is much like a camera in this poem, although I do not think, as we shall see, that this is a fault. The statement about "arbitrariness of detail," however, is not entirely accurate. While some of the details of the poem are arbitrary—simply setting the scene—others are, when the poem is read in context, significant. The statement that "They can't have matches," for example, takes on significance when one recalls the penultimate line of the preceding poem, **"Despair"**: "There are no matches" [in Berryman's spiritual darkness]. The matches are more a spiritual than a physical tinder.

One might also dispute Professor Perloff's statement that "the fact that 'It's all girls this time' doesn't really make much difference to the poet or, for that matter, to the reader,"[10] for in those girls Berryman is seeing the concrete results of the heartless behavior he had earlier so enthusiastically engaged in:

> It's all girls this time. The elderly, the men,
> of my former stays have given way to girls,
> fourteen to forty, raucous, racing the halls,
> cursing their paramours & angry husbands.

> [p. 74]

It is as if the younger Berryman's mistresses had come back to haunt him, "cursing their paramours" as he had once cursed them and their "goddamned tears"; the women blend with the "witches" of the following stanza. But there is a great difference in Berryman's attitude here, for he cares about these girls: "Will day glow again to these tossers, and to me?" This is the reason for Berryman's being like a camera in this poem: his attention is finally, after two and a half sections of self-preoccupation, directed as much outward as inward. In a sense, by merely asking the question he answers it, for care brings its own light with it. This is explicitly stated in the following poem, **"Death Ballad,"** which has the epigraph "I don't care," when Berryman tells the suicidal Tyson and Jo to

> take up, outside your blocked selves, some small thing
> that is moving

& wants to keep on moving
& needs therefore, Tyson, Jo, your loving.

[p. 76]

Caring is life, not caring is death, and Berryman's rebirth is a direct result of this discovery.

The course of "love" in this volume ends in the *Eleven Addresses to the Lord,* for Berryman discovers love not only in his family, as in his earlier works, but also in God. "I fell back in love with you, Father" (p. 95) echoes and wipes out the very first line of the volume: "I fell in love with a girl." But what of "fame"? It too, I think, is transformed—and radically so—by the end of the volume. The early Berryman's notion of "fame" is, like his notion of love, a form of ego-gratification, the imposition of his ego on the world around him. The "children" of "Plato's uterus" are described as "big fat fresh original & characteristic poems." "Original & characteristic": poems that would assert the poet's presence. The form that this assertion would take is more specifically described by a sentence quoted from R. P. Blackmur in **"Olympus"**:

> "The art of poetry
> is amply distinguished from the manufacture of verse
> by the animating presence in the poetry
> of a fresh idiom: language
> so twisted & posed in a form
> that it not only expresses the matter in hand
> but adds to the stock of available reality."

[18]

This is in fact an excellent description of Berryman's verse. But it is a description that is both implicitly and explicitly rejected at the end of *Love & Fame.* The notion of poetry and self-assertion is replaced by the notion of prayer and self-abnegation. Berryman's description of his "morning prayer" in the first of the *Eleven Addresses* is important: "It does not aim at eloquence." What is important in prayer is that it express "with precision everything that most matters." Berryman has moved, by section 4, from creation to the contemplation of creation. God is addressed as "Master of beauty, craftsman of the snowflake," and before such an artist Berryman humbles himself.

Berryman's religious poetry has been criticized, not so much as poetry, but for its lack of sincerity. "I am not convinced of the poet's repentance," wrote Robert Phillips, going on to say that "Berryman's Christian mystic, like the figure of Henry House, was yet another false one behind which to hide."[11] This seems unnecessary. The quality of Berryman's religious poems is uneven, but at his best Berryman was as good a religious poet as he was any other kind of poet. Some of the *Eleven Addresses to the Lord* are extraordinary. The third is perhaps the best. It begins:

Sole watchman of the flying stars, guard me
against my flicker of impulse lust: teach me
to see them as sisters & daughters. Sustain
my grand endeavors: husbandship & crafting.

and ends:

Cross am I sometimes with my little daughter:
fill her eyes with tears. Forgive me, Lord.
Unite my various soul,
sole watchman of the wide & single stars.

[88]

The contrast between the "flying stars" and "my flicker of impulse lust" caught up at the end as Berryman asks to be united as the "single stars" are, the play on "soul," implicit in the first line, explicit in the last two, and the simplicity of the language unite to make this an admirable poem. Without trying to be eloquent, it is: it says what must be said precisely.

Love & Fame is far from being the aesthetic botch that most reviewers found it to be. But this is not to say that it is Berryman's finest work. There is a problem with this "wiping out" strategy, for after the sensibility of the early poems is wiped out, there is very little left. There is very little stylistic attraction in the first two sections. Had the young Berryman been presented as a slightly more despicable character, the volume would have been improved. One will return to the unpleasant Berryman of **"Damned"** as one returns to some of Browning's monologues, for the monstrousness and the unattractive vitality of the poem; but most of the early poems present a sensibility without vitality. Young Berryman is not evil enough to attract, and, once or twice read, the anecdotes lose much of their power. The poems are necessary—the second half of the book depends upon them—but they are too often simply straw men, put up in order to be knocked down. The structure of the volume is satisfying, but the early components of that structure, by and large, are not.

In *Delusions, Etc.,* published posthumously but seen through proof by Berryman, there is a thematic unity of a sort, but no clear over-arching structure. When poems fail, and quite a few do, they do so on their own, without any narrative compensation. It is true that section 4, the only section with a title, is called **"Scherzo,"** but I would hesitate to claim a symphonic or sonata structure for the book. Individual sections are fairly well unified, but beyond that the book is more of a collection than were Berryman's earlier volumes. The full title of the book is *Delusions, Etc. of John Berryman,* but the delusions are not Berryman's alone. The chief delusion is man's thinking—the pride he takes in his rational faculties. Berryman's work had always been romanticist, and here that romanticism is quite blatant, but curiously mixed: at times Berryman sounds like Emerson, at other times like Melville.

"I don't try to reconcile anything," Berryman had approvingly quoted Ralph Hodgson, "this is a damned strange world";[12] and that is how Henry had ended, looking to Ralph Hodgson and not trying to reconcile "things and the soul." But the conflict that he had ended for Henry did not end for himself. Berryman *did* try to reconcile things: reason and faith, science and religion, the existence of evil and the notion of a benevolent God, and *Delusions, Etc.* is largely a record of that attempt. Hence, the Emersonian-Melvillian contrast: in some poems Berryman does seem to have reconciled these things, in others he recognizes, with pain, that he cannot.

"The passion for secrets," as Berryman describes it in **"Gislebertus' Eve,"** the Faustian desire *to know,* is at the center of the problem. In **"Year's End, 1970,"** Berryman had written:[13]

> Gislebertus: Eve deluded brought down on us Evil.
> How now shall we encounter His presence again?

He returns to Gislebertus's version of the Fall in **"Gislebertus' Eve"**:[14]

> She snaked out a soft
> small willing hand, curved her ivory fingers on
> a new taste sensation, in reverie over
> something other,
> sank her teeth in, and offered him a bite.
>
> I too find it delicious.

The diction here is nicely worked: Eve contains the serpent in her action, and the apple contains in its description the adman's "new taste sensation," the debasement of civilization that it will cause. The result of this fall is described in the third stanza:

> So now we see where we are, which is all-over
> we're nowhere, son, and suffering we know it,
> rapt in delusion. . . .

"Rapt in delusion" points to a familiar antinomy of Berryman's—the delusion is pleasant, and it is responsible for great human scientific accomplishments (Leonardo, Darwin, Freud, and Niels Bohr are mentioned). But it is nonetheless delusion, a point emphasized by several other poems in the volume.

Man's thinking—the scientific attitude taken by itself—is, Berryman says in **"A Usual Prayer,"** "eighteen-tenths deluded" (62). The notion that we can "know" the world around us by observing and thinking is simply not true. **"Certainty before Lunch"** explores this misconception:

> Ninety percent of the mass of the Universe
> (90%!) may be gone in collapsars. . . .

"May be"; but we cannot be certain that "collapsars" (black holes) even exist. The "may be" of the first stanza is answered by the "barely possible *may not* / BE" of the last. Thought cannot bring certainty; it can only point out probability (appropriately enough, Berryman is going for a walk with "the probability man"). The scientist is thus, ironically, for all of his rational thought and higher mathematics, forced to intuit the existence of black holes, just as the theologian must intuit the existence of God. Certainty can only be provided by an irrational leap of faith:

> My Lord, I'm glad we don't
> on x or y depend for Your being there.
> I know You are there. The sweat is, I am here.

We cannot argue the existence of God from the evidence of our senses; the gulf between "things and the soul" is impassable. God is "there," but "The sweat is, I am here," in a "flowerless April snow."

Elsewhere in the volume, though, in an implicitly transcendental manner, Berryman attempts to use science as the first step on the road to knowing God. When men intuit quasars, they must understand that this is God working through them. Science is properly used not as an end in itself, but as a springboard for the leap of faith; Berryman uses facts, as Whitman put it, to "enter by them to an area of my dwelling." Thus, scientific terminology becomes a source of metaphor for Berryman, one that is most evident in the first section of the volume, his "layman's winter mockup" of the Holy Office:

> I am like your sun, Dear, in a state of shear—
> parts of my surface are continually slipping past others,
> not You, not You. O I may, even, wave
> in crisis like a skew Wolf-Rayet star.
>
> [p. 5]

Here Berryman is using brief metaphysical conceits. The comparison of himself to the sun is appropriate, and although it is not developed very fully, it is developed enough to make it effective. The comparison to the Wolf-Rayet star, however appropriate it may be, is not effective, for the metaphor is not developed enough. A conceit demands elaboration, and here there is not even the minimal elaboration that there was in the comparison to the sun.

The scientific language in this section sometimes obtrudes, either because it is not sufficiently developed, as with the Wolf-Rayet star, or because there is too much of it, as in the first poem:

> Let us rejoice on our cots, for His nocturnal miracles
> antique outside the Local Group & within it
> & within our hearts in it, and for quotidian miracles
> parsecs-off yielding to the Hale reflector.
>
> [p. 3]

The point of the scientific language is to use it to transcend science; but such a fearful agglomeration of it emphasizes the science at the expense of the devotion and the poetry.

Over against the scientist stands the figure of the artist, who rises above mere thought:

> Thinking presides, some think now,—only presides—
> at the debate of the Instincts; but presides,
> over powers, over love, hurt-back.
> You grumbled: "Religion and Figured Bass are closed
>   concepts.
> Don't argue."
>
> [p. 22]

Beethoven is quoted in the poem ("Beethoven Triumphant") as describing himself as "brain-owner," but his art goes beyond the powers of thought:

> You made throats swallow
> and shivered the backs of necks.
> You made quiver with glee, at will; not long.
> This world is of male energy male pain.
>
> [p. 22]

As a result of this Beethoven achieves immortality, but it is the immortality of the artist—his "male energy," transformed into art, that lives in us. The elegy for the artist is one of Berryman's most familiar themes. But oddly enough, the four elegies in this volume do not quite fit with what I take to be the thematic significance of art in the book, which is that the goal of art is greater understanding of God. *"On parle toujours de l'art religieux,"* states one of the epigraphs, *"L'art est religieux."* This is the subject of one poem, **"Ecce Homo,"** in which the contemplation of a photograph of a painted crucifix leads Berryman to an understanding of Christ's humanity as well as his divinity. This aspect of art is not really touched on in the elegies. Beethoven's world and his immortality are "male energy male pain." These elegies are more reminiscent of *The Dream Songs* than *"l'art est religieux."* This does not hurt the poems themselves, of course, but it does weaken what little unity the volume has.

The use of scientific language is not the only aspect of linguistic experimentation in the volume; there are others, some quite effective, some unfortunate. The ability to juxtapose the formal and the colloquial, exhibited so successfully in *The Dream Songs,* is evident here as well. To place in the formal and solemn **"Minnesota Thanksgiving"** the word "Yippee!" is an audacious stroke and, I think, an effective one, as is the use of "hot diggity" in the poem to Emily Dickinson. But such experiments are not always successful. "Unknowable? perhaps not altogether," the subject of which is "Adonai of rescue," ends: "still / we're trans-acting with You" (p. 60). "Trans-acting" serves to vulgarize the poem's

subject, not to enliven it or bring it down to earth. "Yippee!" is the explosion of human, childlike, and perfectly charming enthusiasm; "trans-acting" strikes a false note—it sounds artificially informal and "hip," like "Are you running with me, Jesus?"

There are, indeed, some very weak poems in this collection. The book has been compared favorably with *Love & Fame,* in both reviews and criticism, but I must believe that this is due less to the poetry than to the attitude Berryman seemed to strike in each volume. In *Love & Fame* Berryman appeared to be a bragging oaf and the appearance hid the poetry. In *Delusions, Etc.* Berryman is "properly humble," and this too seems to have hidden the poetry, for the best one can say of the volume is that it is very uneven. The chief failure of the book, moreover, is not one of sensibility, but one of language—it is not that Berryman is too "confessional" or that his conversion is not convincing, but that his artistic experiments too frequently do not succeed.

When the language does work, as we have seen, it can be very effective. Perhaps the most successful poem in the book, though, is one in which the language calls the least attention to itself—**"He Resigns,"** in which the tone is flat, bleak, and despairing:

> Age, and the deaths, and the ghosts.
> Her having gone away
> in spirit from me. Hosts
> of regrets come & find me empty.
>
> I don't feel this will change.
> I don't want any thing
> or person, familiar or strange.
> I don't think I will sing
>
> any more just now;
> or ever. I must start
> to sit with a blind brow
> above an empty heart.
>
> [p. 40]

It is difficult to read this poem in light of Berryman's suicide. However, it is questionable psychology to read the poems as an adumbration of that act. It was written well before his suicide; he had written poems like it in the past; nevertheless, it expresses pure empty despair so well that we think we know that that's just how it felt and feels. But the artistry that helps to express that despair is highly wrought. The iambs of the repeated "I don't" phrases in the second stanza beat the feeling into the reader, as does the pyrrhic-spondaic combination, in the last stanza, of "with a blind brow." Furthermore, the "I don't" phrases emphatically illustrate the emptiness of the heart: "I don't feel"; "I don't want"; "I don't think." The enjambement, especially in the third line of the first stanza and the second line of the third stanza, leads one to an expectation and then immediately to the disappointment of that expectation—"Hosts": heavenly? no, "of regrets"; "start": a new beginning? yes, but the beginning, not of action, but of the end of action, "to sit." We believe that the poem is "real"—that is, that it is a direct and unmediated expression of intense despair—at least partly because of the strength of Berryman's craft. There is a distinction that must be made, even in these late, personal poems, between poet and man, between maker and subject. Berryman the poet has not been subsumed by Berryman the man. In all of these poems the emotion is worked, given form and order. Berryman was never a poet of "raw expression" (indeed, critics linking him with the Beats have overlooked this obvious fact), and even in *Delusions, Etc.* one must allow for the essential distinctions between the personality of the poet-in-the-poem and the personality of the poet. They are not completely discontinuous, but neither are they identical, and it is dangerous to argue across the barrier between them.

One fairly popular conception of the dangers inherent in confessional verse is that the poet, by seeking out the unsettling and self-destructive in himself, succeeds, not in controlling those feelings and putting them to the service of his art, but in allowing those feelings to control him. At least part of the responsibility for the rash of recent poet suicides, then, is to be laid both to the type of material the poets were concerned with and to the ultimate failure of their art. This might be true in certain cases, and one may look at *Delusions, Etc.* in this manner, but such a view would seem to me to be a great oversimplification. One must be very careful of the post hoc fallacy here. The relation between life and art—or at least Berryman's life and Berryman's art—is too complex to fit such a matrix. I cannot prove this, of course. To do so it would be necessary to conduct what scientists call a thought experiment—working out in one's mind (or in computer simulation) all of the results of all of the causes of both the life and the art. Nevertheless, I hope I have indicated enough evidence of the complexity of the relationships between Berryman's life and his art—even in these late poems—to call such a simple explanation into doubt.

There are both failures and successes of art in these late works. Despite the successes, however, both *Delusions, Etc.* and *Love & Fame* are overshadowed by the accomplishments of *Homage to Mistress Bradstreet* and *The Dream Songs.* It is hard to see how it could be otherwise. But I cannot argue from the weaknesses of many of these poems to a failure of life, or even a failure of talent, as many critics have—there are poems enough here to attest to the continuance of Berryman's gift. Moreover, what problems there are here are what might be termed positive problems—attempts to do with the language more than the language will successfully allow. Thus his failures here are not failures of character or even the failures of a dried-up talent, but

those of the experimentalist that Berryman was until the end, pushing the language around at times quite roughly, to use it in ways in which it had not been used before.

Notes

1. "Poet Berryman Killed in Plunge from Bridge," *Minneapolis Tribune,* 8 January, 1972, p. 3A, col. 2.

2. William Borders, "Berryman and Shapiro Share Award," *New York Times,* 6 January 1969, p. 36.

3. Peter Stitt, "The Art of Poetry, XVI," [*Paris Review* 14 (winter 1972)], 200.

4. "Scholia to Second Edition," *Love & Fame,* 2nd ed. (New York: Farrar, Straus & Giroux, 1972), page unnumbered.

5. Ibid.

6. Jerome Mazzaro, "False Confessions," *Shenandoah* 22 (winter 1971), 86-88.

7. Robert Phillips, *The Confessional Poets* (Carbondale, Ill.: Southern Illinois University Press, 1973), p. 100.

8. *Love & Fame,* 1st ed., p. 24.

9. Marjorie Perloff, *The Poetic Art of Robert Lowell* (Ithaca, N.Y.: Cornell University Press, 1973), p. 76.

10. Ibid., p. 178.

11. Phillips, 103-4.

12. "Afterword," in Theodore Dreiser, *The Titan* [New York: New American Library, 1965], p. 506.

13. "Year's End, 1970," *New York Times,* 1 January 1971, p. 22.

14. *Delusions, Etc.,* p. 33.

John Haffenden (essay date 1980)

SOURCE: Haffenden, John. "*Love & Fame* and Berryman's Luck." In *John Berryman: A Critical Commentary,* pp. 67-78. New York: New York University Press, 1980.

[*In the following essay, Haffenden addresses the prevailing critical view of* Love & Fame *as "little more than an act of personal catharsis."*]

Berryman described the subject of *Love & Fame* as 'solely and simply myself. Nothing else. A subject on which I am an expert . . . so I wiped out all the disguises and went to work.'[1] This is a clear statement of autobiographical intention; the poet has purged himself of earlier personae or masks, whether the poet-lover in **Berryman's Sonnets** and **Homage to Mistress Bradstreet** or **'Henry'** in **The Dream Songs**—'all the disguises'. Since the word 'disguises' suggests deception, it is reasonable to infer that **Love & Fame** would present the poet *in propria persona* speaking of a self formerly guarded or travestied. Berryman regarded the 'collection of lyrics' which constitute the volume as being unified 'because most of the poems are autobiographical, based on the historical personality of the poet'.[2] By 'historical' he meant a real, physical, space-time identity, not a fiction, except that the phrase 'based on' cautions us against reading the facts of the poems as forensic. Earlier Berryman had seemed to belie that statement with the words, 'I am not writing an autobiography-in-verse, my friends' (in the poem **'Message'**),[3] but he was more exactly disclaiming the possibility of total reconstruction. There seemed to him no hope of giving an account of the empirical truths either of character or of event, especially when the story was the partial one which makes up Parts I and II of **Love & Fame**—the six-year span from the ages of eighteen to twenty-four, covering the period of his education at Columbia College, New York, and Clare College, Cambridge. 'It's not my life,' he averred cannily. 'That's occluded and lost.'[4]

The structural principle of the sequence would appear to be simple; it functions by assessing the youth driven to two parallel ends—the pursuit of a series of girls (love as lust) and of fame both through scholarship and through poetry. It would appear further that the polemics of the sequence are conscious and deliberate, and work to demonstrate that the youth was misdirected when viewed in the light of the metaphysical and spiritual revelation which is the referent of Part IV of **Love & Fame**. Berryman accordingly does severe justice to his former self, the late adolescent of limited outlook and achievement. J. M. Linebarger says that in these poems Berryman 'has entirely mastered the reticence about himself that obscured some early poems and that led him to assume the mask of Henry'.[5] Linebarger laments too the lack of aesthetic distance involved in Berryman's 'descent into embarrassing self-revelation'.[6] I think that an important distinction is in question here, however, for Berryman lacks reticence only with regard to the surface detail, the gossipy or simply anecdotal subject matter of the poems. What is strikingly absent is the appearance of inwardness, perhaps because, as John Bayley has suggested, the sentiments have been 'cauterised by contrivance':[7] "Such a poetry has nothing of the *accidental* and inadvertent in it, no trace of genuine impurity".[8]

Berryman sees himself when young as a type of the lords who 'turn sonnet' in *Love's Labour's Lost* (I. ii. 173): temperament and circumstances drove him as much to expressions of love as to loving.

My love confused confused with after loves
not ever over time did I outgrow.
Solemn, alone my Muse grew taller.
Rejection slips developed signatures.[9]

The view may be condescending, but the sanctions which Berryman directs against his younger self do often reflect on himself at the time of writing.

The consensus of critical opinion has run to the view expressed by J. D. McClatchy: 'The naked trial of **Love & Fame,** its flattened style and obsessive details, make it the most exposed and intimate confessional collection—which is perhaps one factor contributing to the general puzzlement and disappointment which surrounded its publication.'[10] Even a more affirmative critic such as Peter Stitt has felt impelled to acknowledge the technical paucity of the more overtly autobiographical sections of the volume: 'The quality of the verse parallels this movement: the poems grow in power and technical mastery from the early ones, which are *prosaic, intentionally almost bad* [my italics], to the last eleven, which comprise a virtual tour de force.'[11]

One of the most sustained criticisms of the volume is by Ernest C. Stefanik, who argues well for the case that the volume involves 'a conscious disintegration and re-integration of personality'.[12] But his argument leads toward a statement about structure which is certainly over-schematic and in some ways slavish to Berryman: 'It proceeds from exuberance of language and scurrilous details to elegance of style and homage to the Lord. . . . John Berryman's pilgrimage is from unconsciousness to heightened awareness, from objective thinking to subjective faith.'[13] Stefanik seems undecided, however, about the very tone and thrust of the autobiographical passages of the sequence; his statements that 'Berryman exposes the past with the objectivity and candor of a disinterested observer'[14] and that 'the self-revelations are made by steady, harrowing degrees'[15] comport uneasily with the proposition that the poem is 'one written apparently in the immediacy of crisis—confusion, torment, and anguish; guilt, purgation, and epiphany'.[16] Even more uncritically, it would seem, he accepts the premise that the first two parts of **Love & Fame** are "self-parading"[17] and that the first three sections of **Love & Fame** constitute the poet's confession,[18] while suspending his task by claiming of the fourth and final part that 'no critical judgment is possible'.[19]

Another critic, Jonathan Galassi, sees no irony, self-criticism, or any other more positive form of self-apprehension, behind what he styles 'the histrionic self-advertisement of **Love & Fame**'.

Love and Fame is devoted like all Berryman's last work to the phantasies or delusions which dominated the poet's life . . . a passion for literary renown and an insatiable sexual urge inform this obsessive, regretful recollection of Berryman's youth . . . *Love and Fame* is an attempt at writing properly about the poet's own personality without the mediating device of an alterego . . . raw, unilateral self-scrutiny . . . the 'I' of these guilt-motivated recollections is often hysterically one-dimensional, hollow, and unreal. . . . In *Love and Fame,* the poet has blurred the distinctions we normally expect form, persona, and tone to make between what the writer feels and what he chooses to express. . . . Each poem is a new, uncorrected edition of the self, incomplete and failed because unchallenged and unamplified by another point of view.[20]

I have extrapolated what I take to be the burden of Galassi's argument, not because it marks an extreme point of view, but because it is all too representative. For many critics, it appears, Berryman accomplished in *Love & Fame* little more than an act of personal catharsis—'an attempt to neutralise his obsessions by glorifying them'[21]—which is beneath art.

Going beyond Stefanik's argument that one should perceive the thrust of the narrative line in the sequence, and that (for that purpose) 'the reader must first understand how the poems are brought into relation with one another',[22] it strikes me as equally important to discriminate the extent to which Berryman does actually contrive lyrics of a sufficient internal irony, and create a tension between subject and form. This is to acknowledge the act of imagination and crafting at work in the lyrics of the volume, and not merely to take their measure as artless and irresponsible acts of self-exploitation. The structure of *Love & Fame* was in no way predetermined but corresponds to a radical change in Berryman's outlook which took place during the period of composition. For that reason, the ironic structure of the work should be regarded as adventitious, not as prescriptive. It is well to bear in mind that the title *Love & Fame* is announced in the last poem of Part III of the book,[23] which was written before the **'Addresses to the Lord'** (Part IV) had even been conceived.

The lyrics of *Love & Fame* may perhaps be belittled for not fulfilling conventional expectations, for their loose anti-categorical prosody or their lax conversational idiom, even for the jargon (in **'Drunks'**, for instance) of phrases such as 'crawling with' and 'she turned out to have nothing on'.[24] Certain critics[25] have exaggerated the scatalogical interest to which the poems apparently appeal, and have undertaken the possibly fallacious procedure of levelling moral judgements at imaginative work. They are beguiled by the flagrant anecdotes, and fail to perceive the form of the poems. Tastelessness should be viewed, however, as a decoy for the psychological and emotional meaning which can be construed from the total form of each lyric. On the face of it, most of them make apparently inconsequential shifts

between constituent statements: the meaning must be derived from the relatedness of those statements. The weakest poems in the book (such as **'In & Out'**)[26] are those where the shifts are arbitrary and capricious, without serving a perceptible pattern. Berryman was himself well aware of the *forma* which the details of each poem were designed to fulfil. Reviewing the poem **'Transit',** for instance, he could find little sense of cogency and wrote 'mere damned rambling' on the manuscript; similarly, he thought that **'A Huddle of Need'** was 'poor', and **'Of Suicide'**, 'disordered'.[27] On the other hand, when studying the galley-proofs for the volume, he remarked 'a treat' against **'Drunks'** in the list of contents.

The poem **'Friendless'**[28] may be satisfactorily interpreted by paying high regard to points of strategic irony and structural meaning. The simple sense progression alone of the poem seems to yield little more than random reflections and historical recollections.[29]

> Friendless in Clare, except Brian Boydell
> a Dubliner with no hair
> an expressive tenor speaking voice
> who introduced me to the music of Peter Warlock
>
> who had just knocked himself off, fearing the return
> of his other personality, Philip Heseltine.

The poem situates the 'expressive' speaking voice of Brian Boydell against the 'voice of a lost soul moving', Philip Heseltine (who took the name Peter Warlock).[30] As Berryman understood it, the fictive Warlock killed himself because of a schizoid division from his real self. To that apparently disinterested observation Berryman juxtaposes his recollection that, when asked to read some modern American poetry to his fellow undergraduates, he discovered that the distinctive poetic voices of Stevens and Hart Crane did not register with the English ear. Worse: he remembers too that even W. B. Yeats signified so little to his contemporaries that they were unable to spell his name correctly.

> The Dilettante Society here in Clare
> asked me to lecture to them on Yeats
> and misspelt his name on the invitations.[31]

So precarious is self-identification, so unstable is fame, that the poet may well fear for his lack of personal voice or creative voice—for what he calls 'failure, or, worse, insignificance'—in the face of such object lessons in lost self-recognition and lost creative significance. The words 'voice' and 'fear' figure twice each in the poem, not necessarily as discrete: the one voice seems mostly to be direct speech, the other imaginative self-expression; the one fear is for sanity; the other, that of Berryman's anticipated failure to fulfil his vocation as poet. Berryman sees himself ironically in a context which condemns acknowledged masters—Stevens,

Crane, and Yeats—to incomprehension and neglect, and the success of a composer like Heseltine to the schism between his achievement and his real self. The bafflement which Berryman's contemporaries evince before the work of Stevens and Crane stands in adroit relation to his own failure to comprehend his burdensome sense of himself: that helplessness is signified by the plangent use of epanaphora in the last stanza:

> I gorge on Peek Freans and brood.
> I don't do a damned thing but read and write.
> I wish I were back in New York!
> I feel old, but I don't understand.

Similarly, the following poem, **'Monkhood'**,[32] is divided into two almost equal parts of five stanzas each; the first half appears to focus attention on Berryman's friend Patrick Barton, the second on Berryman himself. Berryman draws a terse portrait of his eccentric 'companion'[33] which seems little related to the almost exclusive self-appraisal of the second half of the poem. The point is that Barton's eccentricity is used to define the poet's own relative normality: 'And I think in my unwilling monkhood *I* have problems!'

Accordingly, in the second half, he sees himself as an object of attention and analysis, as defined either by himself, 'I knew I wasn't with it yet', or by others, 'Did even Eileen ever understand me sharper?' He recalls that another friend, Delmore Schwartz, had a 'gentle heart and high understanding of both the strengths and cripplings of men', but, in context, the praise is ironically self-gratifying, for it was the perceptive Schwartz who ('to my *pleasure* one day') imputed 'Satanic pride' to Berryman. The midpoint of the poem functions as an artistic and psychological axis about which Berryman balances two apparently contrasted modes of self-identification. In the first, Berryman reflects himself by association with the spectacle of a wayward friend; in the second, he expatiates more directly upon his own complex and unclassifiable behaviour, as the absorbing subject of speculation and self-inquiry.

> Will I ever write properly, with passion and exactness,
> of the damned strange demeanours of my flagrant
>   heart?
> and be by anyone anywhere undertaken?
> one *more* unanswerable question.

It is tactically appropriate that the poem modulates from historic present tense (the first five stanzas) through simple past tense (the next fourteen lines), and then back into a present tense (the last seven lines) which has canny reference to both historic and present predicaments. One meaning that emerges in the poem is that, *mutatis mutandis*, Berryman's understanding of himself remains partial and undeveloped, despite the strictly limited decisiveness about his younger self shown, for

example, in four statements which parallel the final stanza of 'Friendless', 'I never went . . . I knew I wasn't with it' (ll. 21-25).

Since both **'Friendless'** and **'Monkhood'** take personal isolation and literary unfulfilment for theme, it is important to observe that the syntax of the first line of **'Monkhood'** collapses two discrete and nonsequential ideas into one. The statement that 'I don't show my work to anybody' does not *require* the phrase 'I am quite alone'. In view of the fact that **'Monkhood'** proceeds to enlarge on a particular friendship, there seems to be an internal contradiction not unlike the contradiction in **'Friendless'** which holds that the poet is friendless (a word, strictly speaking, absolute and unqualifiable) 'except for Brian Boydell'. It should be understood that Berryman identified his failure as a poet with personal isolation; friendships such as those with Boydell or Barton did not signify on a level of permanent validity to him. They did not have access to what Berryman considered his real being, his creativity.

J. M. Linebarger has pointed out that *Love & Fame* 'is more limited than *The Dream Songs* in the kinds and intensity of its emotions'.[34] It may be that the fault, if it is one, is incurred because the basis of the lyrics is conceptual rather than perceptual. If they lack inwardness, that is to say, the poems lack vigour. The poet seems to coin what he calls 'fragrant scenes',[35] and responds to them (if at all) in a patronising or judgemental capacity. If such a view is taken, Berryman's vision of his younger self must be regarded as simplistic, involving his conscious mind much more than emotional empathy—largely because of the general law that 'memory is dissociated from the feelings that the original experience engendered'.[36]

An instance of such a dissociation from original experience may be found in the schematic poem **'Down & Back'**.[37] As the title suggests, the poet's observations are held to correlate with an emotional graph which begins in suspense, finds its nadir in one mode (sex), and its consequent zenith in another (scholarship). The poem is equally divided into two halves of twenty-four lines each (a count which takes the half-lines 28 and 29 as equal units, as Berryman clearly intended), the descent of the first half culminating in the line 'It was then I think I flunked my 18th Century', and resurgence charted in the second half. This swing from sexual frustration (the first five stanzas) results by implication in examination failure (stanza 6), for which Berryman compensates by earning academic acclaim. Such a swing is a simplistic structural device for the polemical purposes of the poem, with which the facts of the matter do not correspond so nicely. A number of falsehoods or just misrememberings were to Berryman's purpose in the poem, one of them being crucial.

As **'Down & Back'** states, Berryman studied so ill during the summer of 1934 that he failed an examination and consequently lost his scholarship, which then *de facto* prevented his return to college—purely for financial reasons. In truth, Dean Hawkes wrote cordially at the beginning of October to grant him leave of absence: 'I regret to learn that you are obliged to drop out of college for a little while. I enclose a leave of absence as you request and hope that we may see you back in school before long.'[38] The last twelve lines of the poem return to verisimilitude, including the facts that Berryman kept what he calls 'an encyclopedic notebook' and that he made 'an abridgement of Locke's essay' (which was even more concise than the 'hundred pages' he recalls),[39] but their effectiveness as a dénouement relies heavily on the earlier implication that he had been rusticated, as he euphemistically phrased it for the purposes of dramatic effect in these lines:

> The Dean was nice
> but thought the College & I should part company
> at least for a term, to give me 'time to think'
> & regroup my forces (if I'd any left).

—when his family's indigence alone had kept him from school. The Dean in fact granted him a year's leave of absence, but Berryman was able to return to college the next spring when his stepfather managed to make some money on the stock exchange. The poem gives the situation a more heroic cast than it actually took, being more precise as to artistic design than as to emotional rehearsal. Berryman's reconstitution of historical fact is climaxed with a sense of elation in the last two lines of the poem:

> My scholarship was restored, the Prodigal Son
> welcomed with crimson joy.

Far from being shameless and lacking reticence, the sentiment of the poem is as little self-purgation as it is *mauvaise honte*.

In other lyrics in Parts I and II of *Love & Fame* Berryman is equally ambiguous, as in **'Views of Myself'**[40] where (through double irony) his present self seems as arrogant as his past:

> I stand ashamed of myself;
> yes, but I stand. Take my vices alike
>
> with some my virtues, if you can find any.
> I stick up like Coriolanus with my scars
> for mob inspection.

Such a rationale for exposing his personal history contains a large proportion of continuing self-gratification. Similarly, **'Images of Elspeth'**[41] moves from the callow memory that he had been driven 'wild' by the girl's disclosure that she possessed photographs of herself in the nude, to the final line in which the poet continues to share that sense of ingenuous titillation: 'wishing I could lay my old hands somewhere on those snapshots.' A similar effect is betrayed through the use of the historic present tense in the poem **'Anyway'**,[42] which conveys the sense of immediacy of anticipation, of participation, or in the last stanza of **'Olympus'**, where, moved by the reflected glory of Mark Van Doren and Richard Blackmur, Berryman concludes:

> I have travelled in some high company since
> less dizzily.
> I have had some rare girls since but never one so
> philosophical
> as that same Spring (my last Spring there) Jean Bennett.[43]

The parallelism of 'high company' and 'rare girls' (Fame and Love respectively) is telling, for the poet concedes that they marked the limit of his impressionability and sexual involvement—'since' when, all else has seemed 'less'. More recent achievements have actually been as prestigious, but he himself (with a tenor that must be interpreted as wistful or envious) has lacked the capacity for surrender that he enjoyed in his last spring at Columbia. Similarly, in **'Tea'**, Berryman both relishes and regrets the reminiscence that

> By six-fifteen she had promised to stop seeing 'the
> other man'.
> I may have heard better news but I don't know when.[44]

In fact, many levels of significance are in play in the lyrics of *Love & Fame,* since the irony inherent in Berryman's mode of narration works at the expense not only of the *jeune premier* but also of the poet who unwittingly discloses his current weaknesses and predilections. 'Similar to the point of view of the Sonnets,' J. M. Linebarger says, 'this double view achieved by a man analyzing an earlier self is one of the pleasures of *Love & Fame.*'[45] The book is not an autobiography-in-verse only in the sense that, as Berryman himself admitted, it is not at the service of the truth of experiences. In **'Message'**,[46] he supplied the phrase which begins the second stanza—'Impressions, structures, tales'—after rejecting a draft version, 'Impressions, facts'. The change implicitly concedes the truth that he was not attempting verisimilitude.

A statement which has been taken as crucial to an understanding of the overall structure of *Love & Fame* is Berryman's own 'Afterword'[47] to the first English edition. Written in June 1971, at a time when Berryman chose to suppress a number of poems in the volume, including **'Thank You, Christine'** and **'To B—E—'**,[48] the 'Afterword' was, Berryman believed, an attempt ('little as I like to show my hand') to answer the 'uncomprehending' reception accorded the book by critics:

> It is—however uneven—a whole, each of the four
> movements criticizing backward the preceding, until

Part IV wipes out altogether all earlier presentations of the 'love' and 'fame' of the ironic title. . . . But the attack on these two notions begins in the opening poem.[49]

There is a sleight involved in the passage—whether a delusion, a rationalisation, or an untruth—which is radical. By arguing for the unity of the book, and by stating that the metaphysical—spiritual resolution of Part IV (**'Addresses to the Lord'**) is implicit even in the first poem of Part I—and hence, we must infer, in the succeeding poems of Parts I and II—Berryman tries to persuade both himself and his audience that the teleological development of the plot was predetermined, and not a matter of hindsight. R. Patrick Wilson bases a short article unquestioningly on that proposition: '. . . the 'stern religion' of the Addresses quenches the 'unwilling flame' of lust and pride. Berryman seems to be confessing his sins (rather than bragging about them) so that he might in good conscience begin his prayers.'[50]

The actual state of affairs differs markedly from such a view. In February and March 1970, Berryman had not yet experienced a moment of divine intervention in his life, and clearly relished the telling of the secular, lubricious autobiography of Parts I and II. The poems validated his present proud ambitions, and originally contained other stanzas of contemporaneous significance. As J. M. Linebarger says, many of the poems in *Love & Fame* achieve 'a delightful humor and irony by presenting the younger Berryman through the eyes of the older one'.[51] But certain of the poems show an older Berryman who is surely unregenerate, and as arrogant, as ambitious, as self-exalting, as the younger. It cannot be said that in such poems Berryman is simply lamenting his misspent youth. Stanza 13 of **'Shirley & Auden'**[52] was substituted at a late stage of composition for stanzas which included these lines:

Great now my power, which also I husband now
although I stake my life on one image.
I count on flowering into age.
(I'm 55) unlike my superiors Schubert

but Goya whose horror I almost emulate
and if K leaves me I could surely rival
Beethoven and his bangs
and deaf his final ecstasies

the most *promising* artist perhaps who has laboured:[53]

Taken in conjunction with line 64 of the published version—'I wonder if Shakespeare trotted to the jostle of his death'—it is evident that Berryman was proud of the implicit over-ambitious comparison.

By the time he came to write Part IV of the book—in a spirit of 'grave piety'[54]—he hoped that it might function as a palinode to the earlier poems, as Joel Conarroe observes in a judicious essay: 'My own sense is that the book can most helpfully be analysed in terms of its two halves, the second representing a total repudiation of the values inherent in the two sections that make up the first.'[55] In such a scheme, Part III of the volume may be seen to mark a transitional phase in Berryman's actual life, and consequently in the structure of the volume, ending no later than the first day of May 1970. It rehearses his sense of situation during the time he was undergoing treatment for alcoholism at St Mary's Hospital, a period when he was, though haggard, yet unreclaimed. It was only after many weeks that Berryman arrived at his wish to obviate or negate the swaggering mood among the earlier poems, when he reviewed unbound page proofs and wrote 'v. unpleasant! What ever made me think it anything else?' by the poem **'Thank you, Christine'**, and 'UGH' and 'disgusting' by **'To B—E—'**.[56] Berryman's 'Afterword' must accordingly have been conditioned by self-saving hindsight. This might have been discerned earlier, but it has been difficult for critics to perceive anything more than that the devotional sequence at the end of the book was expected to lend an ironic colouring to the earlier, more 'scurrilously' autobiographical poems: such simple, declarative lyrics seemed not otherwise sophisticated enough in themselves to suggest the play of a strong internal irony for which I have argued. The alternative to recognising and analysing the irony at work in those poems akin to **'Friendless'** is to interpret them as modes of naive wilfulness. In fact, they are lyrics not of artless candour, but of disingenuous and successful craft.

The different parts of *Love & Fame* correspond to the changes in Berryman's own spiritual development during the early months of 1970, and not to the plotting of a sequence of lyrics with a foregone thematic conclusion. It is certainly ironic that the volume may be judged very favourably on Berryman's own terms, as 'a whole, each of the four movements criticizing backward the preceding, until Part IV wipes out altogether all earlier presentations of the "love" and "fame" of the ironic title',[57] since its eventual and real success was contingent upon the luck of Berryman's real life.

Notes

1. An interview with John Berryman, Peter Stitt, 'The Art of Poetry XVI', *The Paris Review* no. 53 (Winter 1972), p. 200.

2. *Ibid.*, p. 199.

3. *Love & Fame* (London: Faber & Faber, 1971), p. 61.

4. Ibid.

5. J. M. Linebarger, *John Berryman* (New York: Twayne, 1974), p. 129.

6. Ibid.

7. John Bayley, 'John Berryman: A Question of Imperial Sway', in Rober Boyers (ed.), *Contemporary Poetry in America* (New York: Schocken Books, 1974), p. 71.

8. Ibid., p. 69.

9. 'Images of Elspeth', *Love & Fame,* p. 19.

10. J. D. McClatchy, 'John Berryman: The Impediments to Salvation', *Modern Poetry Studies* vol. 6 (Winter 1975), p. 266.

11. Peter Stitt, 'Berryman's Last Poems', *Concerning Poetry* vol. 6 (Spring 1973), p. 9.

12. Ernest C. Stefanik, 'A Cursing Glory: John Berryman's *Love & Fame*', *Renascence* vol. 25, pp. 115-16.

13. Ibid., p. 127.

14. Ibid., p. 121.

15. Ibid., p. 115.

16. Ibid., p. 116.

17. Ibid., p. 121.

18. Ibid., p. 126.

19. Ibid.

20. Jonathan Galassi, 'Sorrows and Passions of His Majesty the Ego', *Poetry Nation* no. 2, pp. 117-120.

21. Ibid., p. 119.

22. Stefanik, p. 115.

23. Final stanza of 'The Home Ballad', *Love & Fame,* p. 80.

24. *Love & Fame,* p. 22.

25. Edward Neill, for example, has called *Love & Fame* a 'morally chaotic work', in which Berryman's 'poetic integrity and authenticity' consists in what Neill has 'tentatively' defined 'as a fidelity to a kind of regressive complacency'. ('Ambivalence of Berryman: an Interim Report', *Critical Quarterly* vol. XVI, (Autumn 1974), pp. 275, 270.) Other notably pejorative notices include those by Robert Phillips, 'John Berryman's Literary Offenses', *The Confessional Poets* (Carbondale and Edwardsville: Southern Illinois University Press, 1973), pp. 92-106, and by Hayden Carruth, 'Love, Art and Money', *Nation,* 2 November 1970, pp. 437-8.

26. *Love & Fame,* pp. 31-33.

27. MSS., and the galley proofs to which I refer next, are located in the John Berryman Papers, Manuscripts Division, University of Minnesota.

28. *Love & Fame,* p. 49.

29. Cf. 'In all the looseness and plainness of *Love & Fame* there is not much successful intensity, but the anecdotes and reminiscences draw you forward at a great clip, keen to see how it all comes out.' (Clive James, 'Two Essays on John Berryman: (2) On *Love & Fame*', *The Metropolitan Critic,* London: Faber, 1974, p. 83.

30. Berryman met Brian Boydell, now Professor of Music at Trinity College, Dublin on 11 February 1937 (JB, letter to his mother, 14 February 1937, JBP). For a time Berryman became closely associated with what Boydell called their 'frightfully aesthetic/intellectual group' (letter Boydell to Haffenden, 13 July 1972), which gathered in his digs on Midsummer Common. On 22 February Boydell first played for Berryman the five records of *The Curlew,* Peter Warlock's melancholy settings for four of Yeats's early poems, 'O curlew, cry no more in the air', 'Pale brows, still hands and dim hair', 'The Withering of the Boughs' and 'I wander by the edge of this desolate lake', Berryman was convinced by the performance that the music needed to be heard in the dark. Peter Warlock was the pseudonym of Philip Heseltine, a mild, conscientious, melancholy man, who, adopting his other name, had assumed a role which was blustering mad, and amorous. As Peter Warlock, he managed difficult, extremely sad music of which *The Curlew* was the consummate type. Norman Stewart, who had been a friend of the composer's, told Berryman on this occasion that he felt Warlock had committed suicide at an early age from the realisation 'that Hazeltine [sic] would return and take possession from time to time throughout his lifetime'. Berryman liked Heseltine's music clearly because of its melancholy aestheticism, and because of what he took to be a bizarre and maudlin pose, a mask. '"The Curlew",' Berryman wrote, 'is beautiful but utterly despairing, the most desolate art I know.' (letter, JB to mother, dated 23 February 1937—actually, a chronicle letter running until 6 March, JBP.)

31. Andrew Chiappe asked Berryman to give the talk on Yeats on 16 January 1937 (letter, JB to mother, 17 January 1937, JBP). The invitations, signed by G. E. Hewan, gave notice that JB would speak on 'W. B. Yates'.

32. *Love & Fame,* pp. 50-1.

33. In view of Berryman's use of the word 'companion', it is interesting to learn from his contemporary account that he was utterly fascinated with the man, whom he first met at the beginning of March 1937:

   . . . 22 but very wise . . . Extraordinary modesty and the most destructive mind I've ever encountered; idea that no one is of the slightest value, but he is worth a little less than anyone else . . . I liked him extremely from the first, but very strange and uncannily silent in company he is. Constant delusions, terror of strangers and people: all, he thinks, believe him mad . . . He will unquestionably be insane in a few months if all continues, but I think it won't . . . Fantastic theories he has and devastating, some of them . . . one day a complete plan for criticism of the novel . . . the next the most profound despair. He was not at the university here but knew Witkenstein [sic], the metaphysician, well, and has been greatly influenced by him. There is a total lack of both conviction and pretension in all that he does. But I am certain that if his balance can be restored in the next year he may do great work. If not, he will infallibly kill himself. I would do all I can even if we were not, as we already are, *close friends* [my italics].

(Letter, JB to mother, 15 March 1937, JBP)

Berryman met Dylan Thomas, who figures only in the third line of the same poem ('This guy Dylan Thomas though is hotter than anyone we have in America'), at the same time, but was—then— much less struck by him than by Barton. Thomas was in Cambridge to give a reading at the Nashe Society: disciples gathered about him (as Berryman described to his mother, 'a mad group of people who chanted poetry and drank and argued till all hours' (letter to mother, 6 March 1937, JBP)) and celebrated with a binge that lasted literally for days—from 28 February to 5 March—at Mill Road where, in Katharine Fraser's absence, Thomas was staying. The celebrants included Patrick Barton and Andrews Wanning, who remembers one moment when Berryman, referring to Thomas, told him, 'Hush, the poet's asleep!' (Interview with Andrews Wanning, 11 March 1974.)

34. Linebarger, *John Berryman*, p. 127.

35. 'Images of Elspeth', *Love & Fame*, p. 19.

36. A phrase used by Roy Pascal to characterise St. Augustine's awareness of the problems of remembering (apropos of Book X of *The Confessions*), *Design and Truth in Autobiography* (London: Routledge & Kegan Paul), 1960, p. 69.

37. *Love & Fame*, pp. 23-4.

38. Letter, Dean Herbert E. Hawkes to JB, 2 October 1934. (College Papers, Office of the Registrar, Columbia University, hereafter cited as CP.)

39. Berryman's abridgement of Locke's *Essay Concerning Human Understanding* is 34 pages long ('College Papers', folder 1, JBP). In a published essay, he refers to it as 'a thirty-page digest'. ('Three and a Half Years at Columbia', in Wesley First (ed.), *University on the Heights* (New York: Doubleday and Co., 1969), p. 53.) In the same essay, he states that the notebook in question 'ran to several hundred pages'. Cf. letter. JB to Dean Hawkes, 'a 55,000-word overdue notebook' (16 January 1936, CP).

40. *Love & Fame*, p. 52.

41. Ibid., pp. 19-20.

42. Ibid., p. 43.

43. Ibid., p. 28.

44. Ibid., p. 55.

45. Linebarger, *John Berryman*, p. 132.

46. *Love & Fame*, p. 61. MS. draft in JBP.

47. Ibid., pp. 95-6. This 'Afterword' is substantially the same text as that of 'Scholia to Second Edition' (i.e. of the second American edition, 1972, pp. xiii-xiv), although the 'Scholia' curiously antedates the 'Afterword'.

48. *Love & Fame*, 1st edn. (New York: Farrar, Straus & Giroux, 1970, p. 48 and p. 52 respectively. 'To B—E—' is a poem of twenty lines in five equal stanzas; it is presumably titled on the model of certain of Byron's poems, or of Stephen Dedalus's address 'To E—C—' in Joyce's *A Portrait of the Artist as a Young Man*.

49. Loc. cit.

50. 'The Ironic Title of Berryman's *Love & Fame*', *Notes on Contemporary Literature* vol. 5, no. 4 (n.d.), p. 11. Wilson discusses too the possible sources for the title, whether the last line of Keats's sonnet, 'When I have fears, that I may cease to be', or l. 40 of Pope's 'Eloisa to Abelard'. Robert Phillips, in *The Confessional Poets* (Carbondale: Southern Illinois University Press, 1973, p. 98) remarks on the Keats possibility; Edward Mendelson ('How to Read Berryman's *Dream Songs*' in Robert B. Shaw (ed.), *American Poetry Since 1960* (Cheadle Hulme, Carcanet Press, 1973, p. 40), on the Pope context. C. D. Corcoran informs me that another possible source is l. 26 of George Herbert's poem 'The Thanksgiving' (see C. A. Patrides (ed.), *The English Poems of George Herbert* (London: Dent, 1974), p. 56), although it seems that none of these 'sources' are of necessary interpretative consequence, since the title is not obviously an allusion.

51. Linebarger, *John Berryman*, p. 132.

52. *Love & Fame*, p. 16.

53. MS. draft in JBP.

54. Interview with Berryman, *The Paris Review*, p. 201.

55. 'After Mr. Bones: John Berryman's Last Poems', *The Hollins Critic* vol. XIII, no. 4 (October 1976), p. 5.

56. Proofs in JBP.

57. *Love & Fame,* p. 95.

Elizabeth Davis (essay date 1983)

SOURCE: Davis, Elizabeth. "Berryman Saved from Drowning." In *On Poetry and Poetics,* edited by Richard Waswo, pp. 171-90. Tübingen, Germany: Gunter Narr Verlag, 1985.

[*In the following essay, originally presented as a paper in 1983, Davis provides a stylistic examination of Berryman's poem* Homage to Mistress Bradstreet *and examines the influences of Berryman's sonnets, his biography of Stephen Crane, and Nathaniel Hawthorne's* The Scarlet Letter *on the poem.*]

Throughout the critical literature on John Berryman, including the poet's remarks on his own work, **Homage to Mistress Bradstreet** is identified as the breakthrough in his career. The term implies a view of the career which is roughly contained in William Martz's remark that with this poem "the early Berryman becomes the later Berryman," a man who has achieved "poetic maturity" and, above all, "found his own voice." The early Berryman had not, and had suffered from all the evils of a secondary poet, slave on the one hand to his strong precursors and on the other to an ideal of originality for its own sake, lacking in subject matter, and given over to mannered peculiarities of style.[1] The breakthrough is especially impressive in Berryman's case since, as James Dickey once remarked, he was evidently a poet-made and not a poet-born. What sustained him through the long years of apprentice labor, when the poetry was often simply not good, was as much a commitment to poets as to poetry, a sense of shared calling and shared suffering which finds its supreme expression in the elegies of the Dream Songs.[2] *Mistress Bradstreet,* suggesting many forms in the course of its fifty-seven verses—invocation, dialogue, narrative, meditation—ends as an elegy.

In the title of the poem we find stated, ostensibly, both its central subject, an historical figure embodying the origin of a poetic tradition, and the contemporary poet's relation to it. In this sense the poem is "about" its own origins and occasion: about the meaning to the poet of a poetic precursor, about the problematic burden of what I would suggest is a specifically American past. In several different interviews and commentaries Berryman gave his own account of the genesis and progress of *Mistress Bradstreet,* never substantially changed though often elaborated. One version, from the *Paris Review* interview of 1970:

The situation with that poem was this. I invented the stanza in '48 and wrote the first stanza and the first three lines of the second stanza and then I stuck. . . . Then I stuck. I read and read and thought and collected notes and sketched for five years, until, although I was still in the second stanza, I had a mountain of notes and draftings—no whole stanzas, but passages as long as five lines. The whole poem was written in about two months, after which I was a ruin for two years.

Whereas he had been aware in beginning the Dream Songs that he was "embarked on an epic," Berryman says, "in the case of the Bradstreet poem I didn't know." This is something of a blueprint for "breakthrough": the beginning almost automatic, in unconsciousness, the arrest, the long and laborious gestation, the rush of creativity (or if you like, parturition) at the end, the all or nothing risk—two years of exhausted and depleted aftermath. The process is as much psychological as technical, and Berryman cited four "shocks" which set him going, two from life and two from literature. From his life: an operation undergone by his wife (he implies a hysterectomy; Eileen Simpson tells us otherwise), and a devastating experience in group therapy. From literature: a first reading of *The Adventures of Augie March,* which Berryman repeatedly called Bellow's "breakthrough," a rereading of Tolstoy's *Anna Karenina.*[3]

What interests me in this description of what we might call a compositional context is what Berryman omits from it, that is, the work he was engaged in in 1948 when he wrote those initial eleven lines: the sequence, begun in 1947 but not published until twenty years later as **Berryman's Sonnets,** and—in this he was quite drastically blocked—the biography of Stephen Crane which he had been commissioned to write in '45 and which was published in 1950. Each of these is of peculiar significance, I think, to **"Mistress Bradstreet."**

The connection with the *Sonnets* is the more obvious and has been often remarked. We now know, what very few did in 1953, that in '47 Berryman had an adulterous love affair with a woman named by him "Lise" and wrote a sonnet sequence commemorating it: eroticism, rebellion, defiance, a peculiarly Catholic sense of guilt, longing, a continuing suggestion, evidently picked up by the lady herself, that the whole enterprise exists in order to allow the poet occasion for his sonnets (the last lines of the final 115th announce their own dependence on the beloved's departure) and entry into the often-evoked literary tradition of Petrarch, Sidney, Spenser, Shakespeare, and so on.[4] Technically, the sonnets prepared Berryman for the new stanza invented for **"Bradstreet"** and sustained through great length: they were, in Martz's words, "good practice." But the connection is closer: lines attributed to Lise are now given to Anne Bradstreet (for instance, in 32.5, "I *want* to take you for my lover").[5] More important, this *secret* fact of the poet's personal and literary life adds special resonance to the title of his public work. A living mistress has departed and has been replaced by a dead poet, Mistress Bradstreet. The poet's relation to the latter is of wooing, really seduction, and in this sense the transformation of Anne Bradstreet in the poem includes the transformation of poet, "historical figure embodying the origin of a tradition," to adulteress.

The connections between the poem and the biography of Crane are subtler but actually, I think, closer. First, the prose work provided as much technical preparation of another sort as the sonnet sequence. It is, after all, a biography of a dead writer (a fiction writer occasionally a poet; Berryman is a poet occasionally a fiction writer): **"Mistress Bradstreet"** is, largely, a poetic biography of a dead writer presented as autobiography, or autobiographical monologue. And just as Berryman's poetic style was greatly influenced by Crane's prose (we recall his mention of other prose works as sources of poetic inspiration), so the prose of his own biography, in its occasionally circular or inverted syntax, in its imagery as well, can be heard in the poetic lines.[6] Second, Berryman's personal identification with Crane was, according to all evidence and accounts, extreme and traumatic, and we will have occasion to consider an even greater identification realized in the Bradstreeet poem. Finally, Berryman used his biography as an occasion to make his own, assertive revision of the American literary canon: Crane was in eclipse at this time, and the claims Berryman makes for his value and importance are so great as to have been ridiculed by contemporary reviewers as the most mindless kind of hyperbole.[7] This project also has something to do with Berryman's choice of Bradstreet as subject; or if, as he claimed, Bradstreet rather chose *him,* then with her service to him as subject.

Before turning to the critical question of the choice of subject, however, I should mention the intersections that exist between these two projects—the sonnets and the biography—since they do anticipate the central *temporal* "intersection" in the long poem. In **"Sonnet 22"** the poet imagines his mistress Lise "If not in white shorts," then in another age, the age and milieu of Crane's youth and more particularly, it seems to me, of his youthful novel *Maggie.* The final two lines contain a reference to "the *Red Badge* / Stevie's becoming known for" and end with the living lovers' return to their own time and place: "We drive home." **"Sonnet 99"** begins: "A murmuration of the shallow, Crane / Sees us," and ends with the question, "Does his wraith watch?" In other words, in the first instance the lovers "visit" the time of Crane; in the second, Crane—both wraith and, in an obvious implicit pun, water-bird— "visits" theirs. Berryman's imagination of the past (of

his literary past, we might say) seems spatial; he thinks in terms of visits, of the *exchange* of visits. The mirror-numbers 22 and 99 cannot, I think, be accidental.

To resume the question of choice: "the question," as Berryman wrote in 1965, "most put to me about the poem [of] why I chose to write about this boring high-minded Puritan woman who may have been our first American poet but is not a good one."[8] Perhaps the answers are suggested by these words. First of all, the Puritans *were* of historical interest to Berryman, and his own role as their historian was of crucial importance to him. (The term "historian," Whitman's designation of the poet, is one which Berryman cites with high approval at the expense of Eliot.) He was disgusted that "most critics" failed to recognize this dimension of his work and gratified when Robert Lowell pronounced it "the most resourceful historical poem in our literature."[9] And the facts of Bradstreet's history are convenient. The first edition of her poems published in England in 1650 was entitled *The Tenth Muse Lately Sprung Up in America*; evidently presenting the author as her own Muse, the title is peculiar for its time, but for Berryman's it seems a delightful anticipation: she is there, a point of origin, for the later poet to invoke.

First and late: here, I would suggest, is a crux in Berryman's choice of Bradstreet and in his relationship to her. Bradstreet's position in the American literary canon is as firmly fixed as Crane's was unstable. In terms of this canon she has what no other American poet can enjoy, that is, absolute priority. The priority has little or nothing to do with stature or quality:[10] it is based on what one might call the peculiarly American standard of having got there first. It is worth noting that had Berryman wished to discover an historical figure of greater literary stature he had a ready opportunity in Edward Taylor: excitement over the discovery of Taylor's manuscripts was a bare ten years old when Berryman began work, in a milieu where the event itself was of immediate impact. This is not what he wished.

We may speculate, as some critics have already done, that what Berryman wished was, indeed, a bad poet. "The endearing incompetence of her verse" Carol Johnson saw as a major part of her qualification as Muse.[11] "All this bald / abstract didactic rime I read appalled" the poet interrupts his Mistress in Stanza 12.[12] What, then, appeals? The weakness of Bradstreet as poet tends to some useful displacements of the homage itself. To pay homage to what is an essentially "academic" status of *first* American poet is, considered in a certain light, to *embrace* a burden, the poverty of the American tradition, the raw lowness of its origin, and in celebrating it to render it a blessing. This is in fact a characteristically Puritan strategy which could be applied to everything from religious persecution to the weather, from God's scourges of his chosen to the term

Puritan itself. In a powerful sense homage may fill a vacuum or even, as it were, reverse a judgment.[13] Homage is of course also displaced from poetic to other achievement, to the sheer physical survival of a pioneer woman, and more particularly, to that woman's person. She is from across the centuries the object of a sexual conquest which wins her away from her husband and her God and into the role of Muse/mistress. Sexual and literary mastery blend here: the twentieth-century poet's voice has priority in this poem, and from it emerges Bradstreet's, the "sourcing" of his own. Her stature comes from what Johnson has called "her subjection to superior praise," what I would elaborate as containment within a mastering voice which celebrates her priority—historical, hence negligible—while demonstrating its own—poetic, hence central.

This of course is an achievement of the entire poem, but the first "modulation" of the poet's voice into Bradstreet's (identified in Berryman's notes at 4.8) tells much about the initial move towards mastery. From stanza 4:

> . . . When the mouth dies, who misses you?
> Your master never died,
> Simon ah thirty years past you-
> Pockmarkt & westward staring on a haggard deck
> it seems I find you, young. I come to check,
> I come to stay with you,
> and the Governor, & Father, & Simon, & the huddled
>   men.

The modulation is evident in the single term "Father," which can only be Anne's; although the "I" of line 7 refers to the poet, the modulation creates some retrospectively ambiguous reverberations: whereas "I come to stay with you" announces the poet's movement back in time to Anne, it may also echo and answer his earlier address to her (3.4), "I think you won't stay," one which follows his first summons of Anne to *his* time. Throughout the poem, indistinct shiftings of reference in the "I . . . you" relationship create a sort of undertone of variations on the very theme of priority.[14] And there are further ambiguities in this stanza directly related to the theme of mastery. "Your master never died" is peculiar. "Simon ah thirty years past you," in apposition to master, echoes the reference to Simon in 1.1—"The Governor your husband lived so long"—but it also seems to repudiate it: the Governor did, finally, die. Here the timeless or out-of-time poet seems to "enter" the term master (crowding Simon out, as it were); or perhaps to join a series of those who have mastered the early poet by virtue of their aesthetic "care"—to fill a role that has never died. In the end "your Master" may be poetry itself, embodied in the present text.

The replacement of Simon by the poet (and poetry) has earlier begun. The assurance of 1.8—"Simon will listen while you read a Song"—is doubtfully contradicted in the following stanza, which we must cite in full.

> Outside the New World winters in grand dark
> White air lashing high thro' the virgin stands
> foxes down foxholes sigh,
> surely the English heart quails, stunned.
> I doubt if Simon than this blast, that sea,
> spares from his rigour for your poetry
> more. We are on each other's hands
> who care. Both of our worlds unhanded us. Lie stark.

The identification of Simon with the New England winter goes further than the rigorous deafness of each. We cannot ignore the strongly sexual overtones of lines 2-4: an evocation of winter; a suggestion of the shock of a ravished bride. There is also another sort of sexual possibility, that is, of castration, in "Both of our worlds unhanded us" to which I should like to return later. What I would suggest here is that literary mastery, apparently distinguished from the sexual in these lines (or, as in "Lie stark," frankly equated with it) is covertly associated with a different, somehow maimed sexuality that is shared by both true master and mastered.

To return to the modulating line of Stanza 4: the trio of authority in "the Governor, & Father, & Simon" contains peculiarities which anticipate a major aspect of Anne's narrative. The Governor, we know from both logic and history, can only be Winthrop, but the term is abstract and the only previous reference to The Governor has been to Simon (1.1). Curiously enough, Anne's father Thomas Dudley was also (after Winthrop, before Simon) Governor of Massachusetts. In other words, although the title in this context refers to one individual, it might refer to the other two named. Again, the abstraction of the reference to Father—admittedly, an intimate form of address which serves to distinguish the daughter/speaker—nevertheless permits a suggestion of the divine Father, as it also extends our sense of an interchangeability, or at least changeability, of title. The effect is rather of a *mélange*, from which emerges one image of thrice-fortified (patriarchal) Authority whose loftiness is accentuated further (even typographically) by the presence of "the huddled men."

One other telling example of this effect as it is sustained in the poem: in Stanza 12 the poet interrupts Anne's description of her tireless "Versing" to question her motive (line 5)—"To please your wintry father?" The lower case would suggest Thomas Dudley; the nature of the "abstract didactic rime," indeed of all Puritan verse, would suggest the Lord; the adjective "wintry" is Simon's. In fact, some reproach of Simon for being more a wintry father than a lover/husband may be implicit in the poet's rather testy attack on Anne as artist: "mistress neither of fiery nor velvet verse, on your knees / hopeful & shamefast, chaste, laborious, odd" (12.8, 13.1), if we take mistress in a double sense and chaste in an anachronistically narrow (e.g. virginal) one—both possibilities of the poet's "modern" voice.[15] In this instance Anne replies with an admission of past repinings, carried forward into present rebellion, against her God (13.8: "I found my heart more carnal and sitting loose from God"), her husband (14.4: "so-much-older Simon"), and her father (14.5: "so Father smiled"), united in the collective entity suggested in her phrase "Their will be done."

The "mastery" which Berryman's poem enacts depends, I would suggest, on the continuing presence, and subversion, of such a trinitarian "master-figure" combining the Puritan God (or such earthly agents of Divine power as John Cotton), the human father (or such public agents of patriarchal authority as the Governor), and the husband. And from the latter figure the expected sexual power or authority is eventually removed—appropriated, as I suggested above, by the seducer/poet who simultaneously transforms the nature of sexual mastery and identifies it with the explicitly *poetic*.

The nature of the appropriation is itself extremely complex. As we noticed of Stanza 2, the traditionally virile or aggressive sexual imagery associated with Simon is apparently left intact, while the poet appears associated with images perhaps emasculated or "feminized"; later, he comes forth "weak as a child, / tender & empty, doomed, quick to no tryst" (25.4-5). Such images of the poet suggest not just the child, I think, but the child victimized, doomed by the Father to annihilation. I am intrigued by the climactic detail Berryman selected for Anne's opening (and historically accurate) narrative of Stanzas 5 and 6, that is, the drowning of "young Henry Winthrop," son of the Governor of 4.8. Although one could argue that the proleptic appearance of a Henry in Berryman's work can only be coincidental,[16] the poet's later lament, which occurs during the central dialogue with Anne wherein he likens himself to a child—"I am drowning in this past"—seems to me to point squarely to identification with the drowned son. Berryman's life-long obsession with a (possibly apocryphal) incident when his own suicidal father threatened to drown him may lie behind the association.[17] Let us consider entire this crucial section of the poem, the stanzas following on Anne's bidding the poet to "Sing a concord of our thought," which conclude their final dialogue.

—Wan dolls in indigo on gold: refrain
my western lust. I am drowning in this past.
I lose sight of you
who mistress me from air. Unbraced
in delirium of the grand depths, giving away
haunters what kept me, I breathe solid spray.
—I am losing you.
Straiten me on.—I suffered living like a stain:

I trundle the bodies, on the iron bars,
over that fire backward & forth; they burn—
bits fall. I wonder if
I killed them. Women serve my turn.
—Dreams! You are good.—No.—Dense with

hardihood
the wicked are dislodged, and lodged the good.
In green space we are safe.
God awaits us (but I am yielding) who Hell wars.

Stanzas 33 and 34 are composed not of "concord," but of symbolic oppositions among the elements (earth, air, fire, and water) and between the temporal realms of history and eternity or, if we like, of the secular and the Divine. Again, in subtle contradiction of concord, the poet's associations seem as much private and personal as traditional. In the timeless realm of air, the mistress/ Muse Anne is joined to the Virgin Mother evoked by the Byzantine dolls (see Berryman's note to 33.1). "Drowning in this past" he prays to her for rescue. The "grand depths," both formless and yet "solid," suggest here a contrastingly secular and annihilating world of history. Like a delirious diver (see note to 33.5-6) he divests himself of "what kept me"—the female Spirit evoked above. Thus Anne's interruption "—I am losing you!" The depths are also implicitly masculine, for "*this* past" in which the poet is drowning is not, we realize in the end, the past of Anne who is losing him, from whom he is slipping away. Just as the drowning-image contains a seminal element of Berryman's autobiographical myth, so the poet's admission prepares the way for the sole, strictly self-referential or "autobiographical" confession in the long poem: "I suffered living like a stain." Whereas the simple past tense here places the poet in a "posthumous" mode (reviewing a life completed), the present tense in which he continues (34.1-4) calls forth the obsessive repetition of *dream.* (The subtle irony of Anne's consoling "Dreams! You are good" depends on an alteration of meaning, from dream as psychic reality to dream as idle phantom, which must be incomplete.) Interior and exterior histories merge here. The infernal image of 34.1-4 is at once radically interior and personal, in this dream sense, and wholly appropriate to the mid-century experience of war and holocaust. The strangely effective "Women serve my turn," both confession and threat, operates in a different sort of present. A seeming shift of reference from the dream-world to the ongoing circumstances of the "actual" life, the line jolts us into a revision of this poem, of the poet's relation to his subject. The emphatic opposition of the poet to the general "women" underlines, I think, a major aspect of the confession. Guilty within all these masculine spheres, of private and public history, of literary act, he is in a more fundamental sense *guilty of* the masculine. The poet's ventriloquist-identification with the Puritan woman is a self-rescue from the annihilating depths of the personal (time- and gender-bound) self and to its limitations as poetic subject.

Anne's answering image of consolation weds the eternal realm of faith with the spatial particularity ("dislodged . . . lodged") of the "green space" earth. But her consolation or absolution of the poet must be imperfect "(but I am yielding)" and it calls forth his own final confession of no-faith.

> —I cannot feel myself God waits. He flies
> nearer a kindly world; or he is flown.
> One Saturday's rescue
> won't show. Man is entirely alone
> may be. I am a man of griefs & fits
> trying to be my friend. And the brown smock splits,
> down the pale flesh a gash
> broadens and Time holds up your heart against my
>   eyes.

The sky—the realm of air—is empty, God is flown. But the earth, which is the woman's body, contains its own eternal spirit, which is joined to the poet's. The effect of the stanza's final three lines is multiple. In "Time holds up your heart *against* my eyes" we sense not so much a hungering vision filled as rather a blank one *screened*. The image is of shielding: the sky may remain as empty and godless as ever "in the present," but the poet has transformed time, consciousness, "heart," and is protected from that void. The image also recalls to me strongly the childbirth-stanza 19, "inverted" as it were. In this sense the poet is more than shielded by the mother-figure; he is able to "enter" her, not as lover but as offspring returned to its source. Poetically, identification is complete, and the voice of Anne continues uninterrupted through the close (Stanza 53) of the narrative part of the poem.

Such a reading of **"Mistress Bradstreet,"** wherein the poet usurps and replaces the father-husband, drowns or is emasculated as the son, and *becomes* the mother, may approach "intra-poetic relationships as parallels of family romance" in a manner rather too literal for criticism.[18] But Berryman's own invitations to such readings remain provocative, even imperative.

> The idea was not to take Anne Bradstreet as a poet-ess—I was not interested in that. I was interested in her as a pioneer heroine, a sort of mother to the artists and intellectuals who would follow her and play a large role in the development of the nation. People like Jefferson, Poe, and me.[19]

This is the hindsight of Berryman post *Dream Songs,* supplemented by the now heart-wrenching note of March, 1971 (after the final phrase quoted above) "Get the delusion." As he and his various biographers tell us, Berryman evidently organized his own, let's say psychoanalytic, version of his life—and of its poetic record *The Dream Songs* (his **"Song of Myself"**)—in relation to the fact of his father's suicide. According to Kenneth Connelly,

> This fact hangs like a fatal curse over the poem from beginning to end, dramatizing Henry's sense of rootlessness and confusion, heightening the temptation of death, and confronting him with the challenge not to betray his children as he has been betrayed.[20]

With the benefit of our own hindsight we might view the poet's strategy in **"Mistress Bradstreet,"** to identify with or become the mother, as an earlier, somehow liberating response to this parental challenge. In so becoming, the poet enables himself to rectify or reverse whatever inadequacies the maternal figure may suffer (or inflict) as precursor—a term we may take, I believe, in both familial and literary senses. To view Berryman's strategy in this way is, however, to render still more problematic the very notion of "mastery" which I've sought to explore.

Let us return to the point of identification with Bradstreet with which Berryman himself begins:

> We are on each others' hands
> who care. Both of our worlds unhanded us.

"One point of connection" between himself and his subject, as Berryman remarked, "being the almost insuperable difficulty of writing high verse in a land that cared and cares so little for it," the hint of emasculation in "unhanded" which I mentioned above is in keeping with the attitude of weakness and rejection in which each poet stands in relation to his community and culture. And the suggestion is equally appropriate to the different and opposite ways the two are unhanded by their respective worlds. In Puritan New England Bradstreet's writing was unwomanly, masculine. In Berryman's twentieth-century America, to be a poet—he had occasion to deplore this himself—was to be unmanned, feminized.[21] Given such sexual reversal, implicit in the very figure of the American poet, the seventeenth-century mother appears a kind of "weak father" to the twentieth-century offspring. It is the complex fate of the latter, the drama which **"Mistress Bradstreet"** enacts, that he must master, embrace, become, "complete" such a problematic precursor.

"A poem's force," Berryman wrote in 1965 (placing himself, to my mind, somewhere between Ernest Hemingway and Harold Bloom) "may be pivoted on a missing or misrepresented elements in an agreed-upon or imposed design."[22] Having begun my account of his break-through-poem by examining some elements missing from the poet's own account of its origins, let me conclude by proposing—in the spirit of Bloom's call for an "antithetical criticism"—an alternative, only superficially absent "strong" father to the work: that is, the Hawthorne of *The Scarlet Letter.* According to Bloom, the American poet differs notably from the British in his relation to the father:

> It seems true that British poets swerve from their precursors while American poets labor rather to "complete" their fathers. The British are more genuinely revisionists of one another, but we (or at least most of our post-Emersonian poets) tend to see our fathers as not having dared enough.[23]

Berryman, in the course of his acknowledgment of a Russian novelist's immediate influence on **"Mistress Bradstreet,"** remarks in passing on his "own" literary tradition:

> The only woman in American literature is Hester Prynne, and she is very good. I have great respect for her and the book, but Mistress Bradstreet is much more ambitious. It is very unlikely that it is better, but it attempts more.[24]

Hawthorne, in his ironically truthful, seriously fictive account of himself and the origins of his Romance, "The Custom House":

> While thus perplexed,—and cogitating, among other hypotheses, whether the letter might not have been one of those decorations which the white men used to contrive, in order to take the eyes of Indians,—I happened to place it on my breast. It seemed to me,—the reader may smile but must not doubt my word,—it seemed to me, then, that I experienced a sensation not altogether physical, yet almost so, as of burning heat; and as if the letter were not of red cloth, but red-hot iron. I shuddered, and involuntarily let it fall upon the floor.[25]

And Berryman's poetic "reply," which we have already had occasion to consider:

> And the brown smock splits,
> down the pale flesh a gash
> broadens and Time holds up your heart against my eyes.[26]

The surface connections between Berryman's Bradstreet and Hester Prynne are clear enough. I do not believe it is possible to link the terms "Puritan" and "adulteress" and *not* to think of Hawthorne's character: she is, as it were, the original. The "series of rebellions" which Berryman described as marking the theme of the poem—"each rebellion, of course . . . succeeded by a submission"—is very much the pattern of Hester's career. Indeed, the character described in Chapter XIII, "Another View of Hester," who, had it not been for her child, "might have come down to us in history, hand in hand with Anne Hutchinson, as the foundress of a religious sect . . . [who] might, and not improbably would, have suffered death from the stern tribunals of the period, for attempting to undermine the foundations of the Puritan establishment" carries rebellion, albeit speculative, to what would seem to be its limit. Inventing, Berryman makes Anne Hutchinson a friend of his Anne.[27] Given such links, Berryman's reference to Hester Prynne in the *Paris Review* interview seems inevitable.

But there are other, deeper connections which I think his more enthusiastic concern in that interview with Augie March and Anna Karenina may actively work to obscure. *The Scarlet Letter* is, after all, a fiction "about" its own and its author's precursors, about the burden of its American past. It represents in Hawthorne's work—in addition to being what we might call his own "breakthrough"—the synthesis of his active involvement with history with his great theme of inherited guilt, of the nature of good and evil *in historical time,* of the problematic relation of son to father explored in terms equally ambiguous of progress or declension.[28] In one sense Hawthorne confronts or comes to terms with the "stern and black-browed Puritans" evoked in "The Custom House" by assuming the badge or brand of the woman they victimized. It may be that the "Custom House" narrator's involuntary dropping of that brand symbolized for Berryman, as it has for other readers, a failure on Hawthorne's part of full, sympathetic identification with his heroine; his own ambition to "attempt more" seems to lie in this area. Berryman, as we've seen, enters or becomes the person of a woman doubly victimized: in the past by the hostile new world (which still victimizes him, through indifference and neglect); in the present by the poet himself, whose turn women serve.

What we must ask ourselves in the end is what is the nature of this second victimization: what turn *is* served for the poet? And here I think the perspective of *The Scarlet Letter* as precursor is most valuable, for from that perspective we can see, what may otherwise be less clear, the extent to which **"Mistress Bradstreet"** expresses, if not a yearning for religious faith, then a piercing lament at its loss and an attempt, through poetry, somehow to overcome it.

Let us recall briefly the trinitarian master-figure whose presence in **"Mistress Bradstreet"** serves the purpose of Anne's mild rebellion and the poet's subtler subversion. In a rather curious note on the composition of the poem Berryman, recalling "three occasions of special heat," mentions finally the "pleasant moment . . . when one night, hugging myself, I decided that her fierce dogmatic old father was going to die blaspheming, in delirium."[29] A clear enough gesture, it seems to me, of Oedipal rebellion (the image of Berryman hugging himself is mischievous and *boyish*), and an interesting conjunction of this conflict with the very issue of faith. But there is also, I would hazard, an element of self-identification with the old man dying in delirium by the poet "Unbraced / in delirium of the grand depths, giving away / haunters what kept me." In this sense the death is a kind of appropriation: I (poet) shall deprive you of your proper death and you (Father) shall suffer the death to which *I* am doomed.

But what we notice almost immediately in the poem, especially of the climactic confession of Stanza 35 and those that follow, is that such processes as rebellion and subversion are incomplete; indeed, they are ultimately reversed. The woman's "submission" is rather a triumph of achieved or *re*achieved faith (Stanzas 37-39) which emphasizes as much as it cures the gulf between her and her modern suitor. The interest of Anne's "bald / abstract didactic rime" must in the end be for him, more than its historical priority, its motivating subject: a "real" God Who is at the ontological center of her world and work. The dilemma of the modern poet of no-faith is that the motivating subject of his work must either be the self-swallowing abyss of his personal past or—if external to him—then lie in the faith of *another.* In so far as **Homage to Mistress Bradstreet** celebrates the faith of the subject, it acknowledges a doubly second-ary quality in itself. And against this secondary status the poet's strategy again seems to be one of appropria-tion. By making Anne Bradstreet the object of *his* faith and worship (and the subject of his poem) the poet empties the sky of her own God.

> O all your ages at the mercy of my loves
> together lie at once, forever or
> so long as I happen.

During the composition of **Mistress Bradstreet,** Eileen Simpson writes, Berryman, "in a state of manic excite-ment," was convinced that "he was having a religious experience, was on the point of conversion." He rid himself of the delusion, it seems, during a visit to the devoutly Catholic poet Robert Fitzgerald. Afterwards, the work went on in an atmosphere of even greater "nightmare."[30]

It may be that we gain some insight into the quality of this nightmare through contrast. In Chapter V of *The Scarlet Letter,* "Hester at Her Needle," we find a long passage on the effects on Hester's imagination of the "strange and solitary anguish of her life" in which our sense of an authorial self-reflexion is particularly strong. The effects themselves touch on Hawthorne's central themes—the evil of isolation from the community of men, the very different evils, of which Hester's "new sense" has given her appalled revelation, of the com-munity of guilt which all men share. The "loss of faith [which] is ever one of the saddest results of sin" is here, for Hester, a loss of faith not in God but in her fellow men; and it is a threatened or remembered loss, we sense, which the author himself struggles through by means of his character. It is at this point in the text that we are reminded of the symbolic moment recounted in "The Custom House":

> The vulgar, who, in those dreary old times, were always contributing a grotesque horror to what interested their imaginations, had a story about the scarlet letter which we might readily work up into a terrific legend. They averred, that the symbol was not mere scarlet cloth, tinged in an earthly dyepot, but was red-hot with infernal fire, and could be seen glowing all alight, whenever Hester Prynne walked abroad in the night-

time. And we must needs-say, it seared Hester's bosom so deeply, that perhaps there was more truth in the rumor than our modern incredulity may be inclined to admit.[31]

Just as his reference to the "*dreary* old times" is decid-edly ironic, so the author's apparent participation in "our modern incredulity" must be read aslant. In his relation to this incredulity or lack of faith, *and to the heroine who anticipates it,* it may well be that Haw-thorne enjoyed a greater freedom of the poet than his "dispossessed" literary descendant. His actual posses-sion of the Puritan past (strong traits of his ancestors' nature have intertwined themselves with his) permits him a rather privileged balance in the nineteenth-century present vis-à-vis both the past and the future. In feeling the former as a solid and weighty burden, in both participating in and liberating himself from it through Hester, Hawthorne permits himself an anticipation of the future which, if tainted with skepticism and irony, is nevertheless genuine and genuinely earned.

The "more" that Berryman's poem attempts seems to me, finally, a foredoomed willing-into-being of a burdensome past (the "present" of Anne's world against which she rebels, to which she finally submits) the real burden of which is its quality of absence. Thus, extreme identification with his heroine represents an attempted appropriation of a past from which he is—by the very fact of a literary ancestor like Hawthorne—all the more displaced. But the very hopelessness of the effort is the extraordinary power of **Homage to Mistress Bradstreet.** This is a poem which celebrates impossibilities. The impossibility of living in the faithless void of the present time, the impossibility of being an American poet at all—these are celebrated in this most American of poems in verse Berryman equalled but never surpassed. And it is the nearly impossible intensity of the poet's emotion—need, rage, longing, grief—that this verse contains, and that his Muse/mistress/subject is able to embody. Anne Bradstreet could, paradoxically, embody for Berryman the very weaknesses and absences from which his poetic effort had hitherto suffered—his breakthrough, at what he described as enormous cost; thereafter, **The Dream Songs** and Henry.

Notes

1. William J. Martz, *John Berryman,* University of Minnesota Pamphlets on American Writers, No. 85 (Minneapolis: University of Minnesota, Press, 1969), p. 34. Martz quotes Randall Jarrell on the early Berryman, pp. 8-9: "Doing things in a style all its own sometimes seems the primary object of the poem, and its subject gets a rather spasmodic treatment." For a provocative discussion of the distinction between "breakthrough" and "success" in Berryman's career see J. M. Linebarger, *John Berryman* (New York: Twayne Publishers, 1974), p. 73.

2. Quoted in Peter A. Stitt, "John Berryman: The Dispossessed Poet," *The Ohio Review* 15:2 (Winter 1974), 71. For a relevant discussion of Berryman's elegies see Douglas Dunn, "Gaiety & Lamentation: The Defeat of John Berryman," *Encounter* 43 (August 1974), 73.

3. Peter A. Stitt, "The Art of Poetry XVI," *The Paris Review,* 14 (Winter 1972), 195. (Hereafter *Paris Review*) Eileen Simpson's correction of Berryman's version and her own discussion of the origins and composition of the poem appear in her recent memoir, *Poets in Their Youth* (New York: Random House, 1982), Chapter IX, "Mistress Bradstreet," pp. 223-230 especially.

4. *Berryman's Sonnets* (New York: Farrar, Straus & Giroux, 1973). A recent treatment of the affair and its relation to the sonnets appears in John Haffenden, *The Life of John Berryman* (Boston: Routledge & Kegan Paul, 1982), Chapter 9, "Art and adultery, 1947," pp. 167-196.

5. For a fuller discussion of such interconnections see, for example, Joel Connaroe, *John Berryman: An Introduction to the Poetry* (New York: Columbia University Press, 1977), pp. 73 ff.

6. See Simpson pp. 188-89: "And he knew . . . how deeply Crane had entered his own soul. Crane's fiction, rather than his verse, had become a powerful influence on his poetry." She quotes in the same place Graham Greene's objections in a *New Statesman* review to Berryman's "tortured prose."

7. Berryman's sensitivity to the whole question of the canon and canon-making is evident throughout the biography and is of sufficiently self-revealing interest to warrant quotation at some length. From the chapter entitled "Crane's Art": "Since Dr. Johnson observed that a century was the term commonly fixed as the test of literary merit, authors have crowded each other out of sight more and more rapidly. The term cannot be now so long. An English critic says the present point is to write a book that will last just ten years; but a decade must be too short—fashion can catch up older trash than that. For Johnson, remember, the 'effects of favour' must have ended. Under our industry of literary scholarship, having to be kept supplied with subjects, survival is a more ambiguous condition than it used to be: one may stand to gain by overvaluing his author however meager, or his author's toe. Other conditions make a term difficult to fix. But Crane has been dead half a century, academic interest has avoided him as both peculiar and undocumented, and some of his work is still decidedly alive. This is long enough." *Stephen Crane* (New York: William Sloan Associates, 1950), p. 263.

8. "One Answer to a Question: Changes" in *The Freedom of the Poet* (New York: Farrar, Straus & Giroux, 1976), p. 328 (Hereafter "One Answer").

9. "'Song of Myself': Intention and Substance," *Freedom,* p. 230; "One Answer," p. 329.

10. Feminist critical revision has had its effect on Bradstreet's literary reputation. See for example Ann Stafford, *Anne Bradstreet: The Worldly Puritan* (New York: Burt Franklin, 1974) for a very positive assessment of Bradstreet's stature as a poet. Of especial interest in this context (the influence of Berryman's poem is paramount) is the postscript by Adrienne Rich to her Foreword to an edition of the poems ("Anne Bradstreet and her Poetry," in Jeannine Hensley, ed., *The Works of Anne Bradstreet,* Cambridge; Harvard University Press, 1967) which appears in *On Lies, Secrets and Silence* (New York: W. W. Norton, 1979).

11. Carol Johnson, "John Berryman and Mistress Bradstreet: A Relation of Reason," *Essays in Criticism* 14 (October, 1964), 388.

12. *Homage to Mistress Bradstreet* (New York: Farrar, Straus & Giroux, 1956). Future quotations will be identified by stanza and line numbers in the text.

13. In stressing the peculiarity of the American past, which in effect presents the modern poet with the burden of an absence, I mean implicitly to draw a contrast with, or at least to qualify, the argument put forth by Walter Jackson Bate in *The Burden of the Past and the English Poet* (London: Chatto & Windus, 1971). What Bate describes as "the writer's loss of self-confidence . . . [before] the rich heritage of past art and literature" is of course possible to *any* modern poet. But in a strictly national sense I would suggest that the American modern's dilemma is virtually reversed. It would be illuminating to consider in relation to Bate's work Berryman's whole relation to his literary past—less to Bradstreet and the tradition she represents than to his great Anglo-Irish predecessors, of whom he was an enthusiastic hero-worshipper. It is the very richness and complexity of such an inquiry which confines me to this parenthetical, footnoted suggestion.

14. In "One Answer" Berryman wrote, pp. 326-27: "The discovery here ["The Ball Poem"] was that a commitment of identity can be 'reserved,' so to speak, with an ambiguous pronoun. The poet himself is both left out and put in; the boy does and does not become him and we are confronted with a process which is at once a process of life and a process of art. A pronoun may seem a small matter, but she matters, he matters, it matters, they matter. Without this invention (if it is one—Rim-

baud's *'Je est un autre'* may have pointed my way, I have no idea now) I could not have written either of the two long poems that constitute the bulk of my work so far. If I were making a grandiose claim, I might pretend to know more about the administration of pronouns than any other living poet writing in English or American." Berryman continued to make such grandiose claims; see for instance William Heyen, "John Berryman: A Memoir and an Interview," *The Ohio Review* 15:2 (Winter 1974), 61-62.

15. Berryman's description of the two voices and their relation, and of his determination to avoid "pastiche," appears in Heyen, *loc. cit.*

16. Although Berryman gave his own account of the origin of Henry in a joke shared with his second wife, we must note (as he himself did) the prominence of the name in Crane's fiction: Henry Fleming of *The Red Badge of Courage,* for instance, Henry Johnson of "The Monster." See also *Paris Review,* p. 195.

17. See Simpson, pp. 60-61. Haffenden refers to the incident, pp. 24-26 *et passim.*

18. The allusion is to Harold Bloom, *The Anxiety of Influence* (London: Oxford University Press, 1973), p. 8. The extent to which the example and directives of this work might complicate the inquiry suggested above (note 13) must be taken as understood but, again, cannot be pursued here.

19. *Paris Review,* p. 195.

20. Kenneth Connelly, "Henry Pussycat. He Come Home Good," *Yale Review* 58 (Spring 1969), 424.

21. For instance in Jane Howard, "Whisky and Ink, Whisky and Ink," *Life* (July 21, 1967), 74, the complaint is paired with a telling indignation about the country's lack of *historical* sense: "Berryman resents the fact that in the U.S. poetry is considered effeminate, and finds it shameful that 'no national memory but ours could forget the fact that John Adams and Thomas Jefferson both died on the same day—the fourth of July in 1826.'"

22. "One Answer," p. 327.

23. Bloom, p. 68.

24. *Paris Review,* p. 197. Berryman also added to this remark the later footnote, "Get the delusion." When Berryman makes his claims for Crane's status as "master," the only American writers he names in comparison are Hawthorne and James. See *Stephen Crane,* pp. 283, 285.

25. Nathaniel Hawthorne, *The Scarlet Letter. An Authoritative Text, Backgrounds and Sources, Criticism,* ed. S. Bradley et al. (W. W. Norton, 1978), p. 28.

26. "One Answer," p. 328.

27. Hawthorne, p. 119. Anne Hutchinson's appearance in "Mistress Bradstreet" is worth remarking further. In the following lines—"Now Mistress Hutchinson rings forth a call—/ should she? many creep out at a broken wall—/ affirming the Holy Ghost / dwells in one justified. Factioning passion blinds / all to all her good, all—can she be exiled? / Bitter sister, victim! I miss you. /—I miss you, Anne / day or night weak as a child, / tender & empty, doomed, quick to no tryst." (24.6.-8, 21.1-5)—we notice that the climactic line in which Anne Bradstreet misses her sister victim serves as the occasion of the poet's interrupting to offer himself as *substitute*; the two possibilities, equivalent or alternative to "sister, victim," remain open.

28. One of the most striking instances in Hawthorne's work of this theme's surfacing to the point of self-reference occurs in the chapter "The Procession," which describes the symbolic pageant of soldiers, magistrates and churchmen before the assembled townspeople and marginals (Indians, sailors, one could add Hester, the author himself) on the day of the Governor's inauguration. In the course of an evidently rueful celebration of the spectacle the author remarks: "It was an age when what we call talent had far less consideration than now, but the massive materials which produce stability and dignity of character a great deal more. The people possessed, by hereditary right, the quality of reverence; which, in their descendants, if it survive at all, exists in smaller proportion, and with a vastly diminished force in the selection and estimate of public men. The change may be for good or ill, and is partly, perhaps, for both." Placing himself in the scene as a "thoughtful observer" (as is Hester), he places himself temporally as well at the end of a strain fostered by men "distinguished by a ponderous sobriety, rather than activity of intellect" (happily, for our purposes, the first of these men named is Anne's husband, Simon Bradstreet). His is the talent, the intellect unrecognized then; theirs the reverence unpossessed now—departed "for good or ill . . . for both," pp. 168-69.

29. "One Answer," p. 329.

30. Simpson, pp. 227-229. The last years of Berryman's life were marked by religious 'conversions' evidently willed, evidently failed in the end. Although the "great loss" Berryman located at the center of his life and of his character Henry is rightly taken to be that of the father by suicide, it is also true that from that event Berryman also dates—as he does in the *Paris Review* interview—the loss of his intense, boyhood faith. The faith

was devoutly Catholic, and Berryman's late attempt to embrace Judaism, like his earlier embrace of Calvinist Anne Bradstreet, suggests a search not just for faith but for orthodoxy. (One wonders about Berryman's reactions to the Catholic conversion of his friend Lowell, child of the Puritans; the situation seems oddly to mirror his own.) "The Bradstreet poem is very learned. There is a lot of theology in it," Berryman said in the *Paris Review* interview (p. 183). He meant it in the most serious sense, and we do him and the poem an injustice to psychologize it away.

31. Hawthorne, p. 67.

Michael Heffernan (essay date 1984)

SOURCE: Heffernan, Michael. "John Berryman: The Poetics of Martyrdom." In *Berryman's Understanding: Reflections on the Poetry of John Berryman,* edited by Harry Thomas, pp. 232-48. Boston: Northeastern University Press, 1988.

[*In the following essay, originally published in 1984, Heffernan asserts that* The Dream Songs *represents a paradigm of grief and loss, fragmentation, and spiritual desolation.*]

All the troubles of the time may enter the soul of a man and be mastered by creative innocence—that is the miracle of poetry. And they may enter the soul of a man and be mastered by the innocence of the heart—that is the miracle of sainthood.

—JACQUES MARITAIN

flame may his glory in that other place
for he was fond of fame, devoted to it,
and every first-rate soul
has sacrifices which it puts in play,
I hope he's sitting with his peers: sit, sit,
& recover & be whole.

—"Dream Song 157"

In his *Harvard Advocate* interview of 1968 John Berryman was asked about an "ulterior structure to *The Dream Songs,*" and he answered:

. . . there is none. *Il n'y en a pas!* There's not a trace of it. Some of the Songs are in alphabetical order; but, mostly, they just belong to areas of hope and fear that Henry is going through at a given time. That's how I worked them out.[1]

That may have the ring of a last word, so that the close reader attempting to expose the structure of *The Dream Songs,* like comparable treatments of the sonnets of Shakespeare, should quietly give up trying, perhaps after posting on his office door that lovely crack out of Berryman's poem on Blackmur (**"Olympus,"** from *Love & Fame*): "To be a *critic,* ah, / how deeper & more scientific."

Meantime the critic of *The Dream Songs* might ask a multitude of questions: Do *The Dream Songs* cohere mainly as poetry or as autobiography? Is Henry simply a version of Berryman, perhaps a photocopy? (Berryman denied this countless times, but does that matter?) Are they a bona fide long poem or a scattering of fragments shored against ruin? Do *The Dream Songs* mirror The Age or merely the pathetic case history of a blighted genius hagridden by alcohol and the curse of his father's suicide, predestined to his own self-destruction before he could see sixty? Is it possible for any poet, gifted and learned as Berryman so variously was, to attempt, achieve, and survive the making of a personal epic in an age as fractured and schizoid as the present? In short, did the making of *The Dream Songs* destroy their maker?

Possibly I am setting these questions forth mainly to grab some hand-hold on work that endlessly baffles and amazes. Adrienne Rich precluded a number of inquiries with a single statement that could scatter whole legions of exegetes: "*The Dream Songs* aren't literature, they are poetry; and poetry is real life"[2]—a view one might dismiss out of hand if Berryman himself had not supported it, indirectly, by his enthusiastic endorsement of Whitman's late argument as to his intentions in *Leaves of Grass*: "to put *a Person,* a human being (myself, in the latter part of the Nineteenth Century, in America) freely, fully and truly on record."[3] So poetry for Berryman *was* "real life," and the consequences of Rich's conclusion might be taken in full: "In a sense *The Dream Songs* want more than a linear reading. And in this, too, they are beyond literature."[4] And, necessarily, beyond criticism, at least of the literary variety.

Questions of order, unity, wholeness, nonetheless, keep begging to be dealt with, and with them the larger problem of the long poem in the twentieth century. Jacques Maritain has written a remarkable essay on "The Three Epiphanies of Creative Intuition," with an insightful passage on the "luck" of Dante: how he was lucky not only in the "innocence of his heart" and "the firmness of his religious faith" but in the perfect accident of his having come to life in an age pervaded by philosophical and theological stability:

I am thinking, here, of the heritage of culture received by Dante, and of the articulate universe of beliefs and values in which his thought dwelt. Dante wrestled with his time, which forced into exile the poet threatened with death. But as concerns the spiritual quality of the cultural heritage he was blessed by his time. Then the human mind was imbued with a sense of being, and nature appeared all the more real and consistent as it was perfected by grace. Being still turned toward wisdom, still permeated with rationality and mystery both of which descended from the Uncreate Word, still softened by the blood of the Incarnate Word, the universe of the late thirteenth century, with its ontological hierarchies mirrored in the hierarchies of intellectual disciplines, ensured to the intelligence and emotion of a poet, despite all the evil fevers, discords, crimes, and vices of the time, a state of integration and vitality that the modern man has lost.[5]

Despite their disparate containments of every sort of criminal and moral squalor, as well as the limits of imaginable sanctity, the cantos of the *Commedia* are rounded like a sphere through the unity of thirteenth-century Catholicism. Berryman's work may appear an exact twentieth-century antithesis: the work of an artist torn to pieces by personal loss of faith, directly consequent upon his father's self-slaughter, not to mention the less immediate but certainly as painful climate of life in a century of colossal warfare, rampant social unrest, and innumerable varieties of spiritual distress so general and endemic that one of its most widely read philosophers could announce, in the summary opening sentence of his most popular treatise: "There is but one truly serious philosophical problem, and that is suicide."

I want to suggest that *The Dream Songs* represent, through their cumulative portrayal of Henry's "plights & gripes," an open paradigm of grief and loss, fragmentation and spiritual collapse, that their author, as he worked through and beyond them, was obliged to transcend both as person and as poet. The totality of Berryman's spiritual program, his project of redemption, is not contained within the deliberately non-ulterior "structure" of the songs. Berryman wrote, in his last two books, a number of widely unappreciated poems that need to be studied side by side with *The Dream Songs* in order to put the poet of *The Dream Songs* in his own right perspective. Henry, as Berryman seems to have intended him, resides finally neither under our bootsoles nor somewhere off the edge of some planet on the table. By the end of the songs Henry is left where Berryman wanted him—alive and feeling, yet caught forever in his nest of hope and fear, his problems ultimately unresolved. Berryman himself admitted in his conversation with Richard Kostelanetz, that his lack of "solution" made *The Dream Songs,* as Henry's story, a virtual failure;[6] and, answering the *Advocate* students on the question of Henry "as the hero of a poem," he replied:

> Well, he's very brave, Henry, in that he keeps on living after other people have dropped dead. But he's a hopeless coward with regard to his actual death. That never comes out in the poem, but he is afraid of death.[7]

This problem of personal mortality connected for Berryman, as a long-term apostate longing to believe, with a far more terrifying problem in eschatology: the reality of Hell as a state of everlasting damnation. Berryman's thinking on the subject, informed in large degree by his reading of Origen's *De Principiis,* extended back a number of years before his well-documented conversion, his rediscovery, in May 1970, of a personal God

"interested in the individual life in the ordinary way."[8] Early in *The Dream Songs,* in **"Song 56,"** Berryman imagines Origen's Hell at the moment of *apocatastasis,* a time "known to God alone" when "the goodness of God through Christ will restore his entire creation to one end" and God will be "all in all," with even the demons brought into a state of virtue, if they desire it:[9]

> Hell is empty. O that has come to pass
> which the cut Alexandrian foresaw,
> and Hell lies empty.
> Lightning fell silent where the Devil knelt
> and over the whole grave space hath settled awe
> in a full death of guilt.

Henry is clearly dreaming or wishful-thinking, and the rest of the song moves toward irresolution and ambiguity as Henry, having imagined himself as a deer trapped by hunters closing on him with clubs, poses two virtual opposites in the vision of Hell emptied "in a full death of guilt" and the terrifying prospect of dying into a speechless silence like an animal. Berryman, for the moment, is testing out, from different angles, an idea which, some years later, he came to accept as a necessary article of his renewed faith, with its vision of a "God of rescue" devoted in the end to restoring His Creation. Berryman's need to absorb this as a personal and an artistic principle can be placed in a fuller context by an examination of a development in the later *Dream Songs.*

* * *

A moment of clarity happens in **"Song 324,"** **"An Elegy for W.C.W., the lovely man."** William Carlos Williams here appears as Henry's veritable antithesis:

> Henry in Ireland to Bill underground:
> Rest well, who worked so hard, who made a good
>   sound
> constantly, for so many years:
> your high-jinks delighted the continents & our ears:
> you had so many girls your life was a triumph
> and you loved your one wife.
>
> At dawn you rose & wrote—the books poured forth—
> you delivered infinite babies, in one great birth—
> and your generosity
> to juniors made you deeply loved, deeply:
> if envy was a Henry trademark, he would envy you,
> especially the being through.
>
> Too many journeys lie for him ahead,
> too many galleys & page-proofs to be read,
> he would like to lie down
> in your sweet silence, to whom was not denied
> the mysterious late excellence which is the crown
> of our trials & our last bride.

This homage to Williams may seem unusual at first, coming from a poet whose earliest masters were Yeats and Auden. James E. Miller has noticed the "metamorphosis" that took shape in Berryman's work during the late fifties, roughly contemporaneous with the publication of Ginsberg's *Howl* and its earliest impact, though Miller pinpoints Berryman's relatively late discovery of Walt Whitman as the turning point in his growth from the impersonal, highly derivative mold of his first poems.[10] It is certainly tempting to identify Whitman and his mid-century followers, among them Ginsberg and Williams, as generally responsible for Berryman's shift away from the tight stanzas of *The Dispossessed* and *Homage to Mistress Bradstreet* to the open stanzas of *The Dream Songs,* and Berryman himself emphasized his debt to Whitman in his *Paris Review* interview with Peter Stitt.[11] The problem of influence, direct or indirect, can be difficult to resolve. The rugged "personality" of Whitman in "Song of Myself" is finally not Henry's; neither does **"W.C.W., the lovely man,"** provide Berryman with much more than an invidious contrast to the lives of Henry and his friends. Williams represents for Henry, and for Berryman, a figure of grace and accomplishment, a completed master able in his old age to "crown" his labors in the craft with the brilliantly plain-spoken measures of "Asphodel, That Greeny Flower" and to renew his own imaginative vitalities with the further illuminations of the Unicorn Tapestries. Reviewing *Paterson Five* in 1959, Berryman wrote: "The gaiety of this old man is adorable."[12]

Counterpointing the celebration of Williams in **"Song 324"** is a disquieting sense of Henry's spiritual exhaustion: the elegy for Williams occurs as a bright surprise amid a large cluster of songs full of bitterness, desolation, and a more than usual air of hopelessness. Henry addresses Williams from a

> land of ruined abbeys,
> discredited Saints & brainless senators,
> roofless castles, enemies of Joyce & Swift,
> enemies of Synge,
>
> enemies of Yeats & O'Casey

> **("Song 321")**

Several songs earlier (**"309"**) Ireland has appeared a place of "fallen leaves and litter." Henry goes shopping and comes home with a book on the Easter Rising in which all of his "old heroes . . . spring back into action, fatuous campaigners / dewey with phantastic hope." The last stanza concludes:

> Phantastic hope rules Henry's war as well,
> all these enterprises are doomed, all human pleas
> are headed for the night.
> Wait the lime-pits for all originators,
> wounded propped up to be executed,
> afterward known as martyrs.

Enhancing this perception of the failure of political movements toward national renewal is Henry's aware-

ness of Ireland's religious heritage, both Christian and pre-Christian, equally "phantastic" for a country "full of con-men / as well as the lovely good" (**"Song 313"**):

> Saints throng these shores, & ancient practices
> continue in the dolmens, ruined castles
> are standard.
> The whole place is ghostly: no wonder Yeats believed
>   in fairies
> & personal survival. A trim suburban villa
> also is haunted, by me.
>
> Heaven made this place, also, assisted by men,
> great men & weird. I see their shades move past
> in full daylight.
> The holy saints make the trees' tops shiver,
> in the all-enclosing wind. And will love last
> further than tonight?

In the midst of the evidence of the blessed dead, Henry feels only "need need need" (**"Song 311"**); and, in **"Song 314"**:

> Penniless, ill, abroad, Henry lay skew
> to Henry's American fate, which was to be well,
> have money in the bank
> & be at home. He can't think what to do
> under this cluster of misfortune & hell. . . .

Set as it is ten songs later, the elegy for Williams details the pure achievement of one American poet whose "fate . . . was to be well, / have money in the bank / & be at home." Williams is also the accomplished person Henry would like to be, both as poet and lover. The placing of Berryman's homage to Williams in this section of generally dispirited songs sheds light on the nature of Henry's "hunger":

> Hunger was constitutional with him,
> women, cigarettes, liquor, need need need
> until he went to pieces.
> The pieces sat up & wrote.

> **("Song 311")**

Henry admires in Williams more than his life of "triumph," more than his love of one woman and his "being through." Unlike Yeats, whose "majestic Shade" (**"Song 312"**) fills Berryman with nearly speechless awe, Williams is Henry's more accessible idea of the poet who kept his life together, loved his "one wife" (despite his "many girls"), and finally produced, in his last years, poems that reveal a harmony of life and art. As of **"Song 324"**, Henry feels remote from such perfection: "Too many journeys lie for him ahead, / too many galleys & pageproofs to be read."

Forty songs later, on the verge of the final developments of *The Dream Songs,* Henry's tone approaches self-elegy as he explains what we can make of (and take from) "These Songs" now all but behind us:

> Chilled in this Irish pub I wish my loves
> well, well to strangers, well to all his friends,

seven or so in number,
I forgive my enemies, especially two,
races his heart, at so much magnanimity,
can it at all be true?

—Mr Bones, you on a trip outside yourself.
Has you seen a medicine man? You sound will-like,
a testament & such.
Is you going?—Oh, I suffer from a strike
& a strike & three balls: I stand up for much,
Wordsworth & that sort of thing.

The pitcher dreamed. He threw a hazy curve,
I took it in my stride & out I struck,
lonesome Henry.
These Songs are not meant to be understood, you
    understand.
They are only meant to terrify & comfort.
Lilac was found in his hand.

(**"Song 366"**)

The echo of Whitman in that last line seems obvious. Less obvious, and probably not intentional at all on Berryman's part, though certainly interesting to consider, is a parallel with the opening of Book III of Williams's "Asphodel, That Greeny Flower":

What power has love but forgiveness?
    In other words
            by its intervention
what has been done
        can be undone.
            What good is it otherwise?
Because of this
        I have invoked the flower
            in that
frail as it is
        after winter's harshness
            it comes again
to delect us.
        Asphodel, the ancients believed,
            in hell's despite
was such a flower.

Berryman's appreciation of the older poet's "mysterious late excellence" implies a response to Williams's final resolutions in terms of a poetry of love. Berryman's own post-*Dream Songs* development toward *Love & Fame* and *Delusions, Etc.* involved him in a series of love poems as important as any in his canon. These are the poems of his late-found and, I think, arguably genuine love for the Father he discovered in his last years to replace the earthly father who had abandoned him.

* * *

The loss accounted for in *The Dream Songs* is the traumatic loss both of the parent and of the vision, in an ultimate Father, of the object of true belief. Complicating his later poetry of conversion is a crucial difficulty, carried over from the songs: if I myself am

Hell, in the sense of Lowell's Miltonic line from "Skunk Hour," then how do I avoid Hell even though, in the end, I find my way toward acceptance of a "God of rescue"? In **"Eleven Addresses to the Lord,"** the sequence at the end of *Love & Fame,* Berryman begins to work out a resolution, at first tentative and speculative:

May be the Devil after all exists.
            . . . . .
Man is ruining the pleasant earth & man.
What at last, my Lord, will you allow?
Postpone till after my children's deaths your doom
if it be thy ineffable, inevitable will.

(**"Eleven Addresses,"** 2)

Gradually his assertions become surprisingly more confident, and confidential, addressing God as a friend, the way Hopkins did in "Thou Art Indeed Just, Lord," but without the irony:

Holy, & holy. The damned are said to say
"We never thought we would come into this place."
I'm fairly clear, my Friend, there's no such place
ordained for inappropriate & evil man.

Surely they fall dull, & forget. We too,
the more or less just, I feel fall asleep
dreamless forever while the worlds hurl out.
Rest may be your ultimate gift.

(**"Eleven Addresses,"** 5)

As lines like these reveal, Berryman had begun to implicate more thoroughly than ever into this work the writings of the early Christian Fathers, and especially those of Origen and, with special complexity, the martyrologist of St. Polycarp.

Two of the critics who have worked most closely with Berryman's late poems seem curiously indisposed to a precise exposition of the religious poems and their implications. While Peter Stitt describes the growth "in power and technical mastery" of **"Eleven Addresses to the Lord"** over the earlier poems in *Love & Fame,* he gives us hardly any actual detail from these important poems, transitional as they are to the crucial "Opus Dei" pieces in *Delusions, Etc.,* about which he has somewhat more to say, concluding that the word *if* in the clause "If He for me as I feel for my daughter" (**"Compline"**) lends the poem and the book both a sense of doubt and "an underlying ironic dimension." Stitt chooses to ignore the rest of **"Compline,"** with its important argument about Hell.[13]

Similarly, Ernest Stefanik has devoted considerable space to the religious element in Berryman's late work but, like Stitt, he elects to omit from discussion some of the more troubled passages. Writing in the pages of the Catholic journal *Renascence,* Stefanik argues that "***Love***

& Fame is not simply a collection of lyrics assembled under a common title . . . but a narrative that presents a self-portrait of the poet beginning his religious quest, his encounter with God and, concomitantly, with self. . . . Through his suffering and courage both as a ragged hero and as a foolish victim, he elicits and enlists the reader's sympathies as he reconstructs his past, confronts the unknowable in a meaningless world, and finally adopts a posture of Christian acceptance."[14] Stefanik's reading of *Love & Fame* is generally fair and useful, but he fails to grasp one of the most difficult statements in all of Berryman, the last sentence of the last poem of the book's final sequence, the **"Eleven Addresses."** Stefanik's problem is a tendency to traditionalize the nature of Berryman's "posture of Christian acceptance." Quoting only the last stanza of the brief #11, he writes: "Berryman is now able to accept the mutability of the world and the inevitability of God's will; and the final effect of the sequence unalterably moves toward an affirmation of the poet's being and a reversal of failure, concluding with a gesture of surrender to God's will."[15]

The "gesture of surrender" at the end of #11 needs to be placed not only in the context of the poem in its entirety but in the light of the evidence supplied by an examination of the poem's sources. Here is the poem:

> Germanicus leapt upon the wild lion in Smyrna,
> wishing to pass quickly from a lawless life.
> The crowd shook the stadium.
> The proconsul marvelled.

> "Eighty & six years have I been his servant,
> and he has done me no harm.
> How can I blaspheme my King who saved me?"
> Polycarp, John's pupil, facing the fire.

> Make too me acceptable at the end of time
> in my degree, which then Thou wilt award.
> Cancer, senility, mania,
> I pray I may be ready with my witness.

A relatively brief pursuit of references will reveal the text from which virtually everything in the first two stanzas came to hand: Kirsopp Lake's translation of "The Martyrdom of St. Polycarp, Bishop of Smyrna" in *The Apostolic Fathers,* vol. II, from the Loeb Classical Library. Polycarp suffered martyrdom about the year 155 during the proconsulship of Statius Quadratus, at Smyrna. According to the martyrology, "the most noble Germanicus" was martyred before him:

> and he fought gloriously with the wild beasts. For when the Pro-Consul wished to persuade him and bade him have pity on his youth, he violently dragged the beast towards himself, wishing to be released more quickly from their unrighteous and lawless life. So after this all the crowd, wondering at the nobility of the God-loving and God-fearing people of the Christians, cried out: "Away with the Atheists [i.e., the Christians]; let Polycarp be searched for."

Polycarp's hiding-place is searched out and he is brought, eventually, into the arena, where he is met by "a great uproar." Having tried to persuade Germanicus to "have pity on his youth," the Pro-Consul bids the aged Polycarp to "respect his age," to no avail; so

> when the Pro-Consul pressed him and said: "Take the oath [of allegiance to Caesar] and I let you go, revile Christ," Polycarp said: "For eighty and six years have I been his servant, and he has done me no wrong, and how can I blaspheme my King who saved me?"

Polycarp is bound to the stake and burned "for an oblation, a whole burnt offering made ready and acceptable to God."[16]

Berryman's borrowings from this text are remarkable for a number of reasons. They represent, for one, a considerable departure from his usual practice, especially in the second stanza, which is drawn virtually word for word from the Lake translation. The most interesting use of "The Martyrdom of St. Polycarp," however, is the precise association which Berryman brings to the word *witness* at the end of the poem (and the volume), a complex and disturbing meaning underscored by the translator's note at the beginning of the Loeb Library version, referring to the significance of Polycarp's martyrdom in terms of an etymology that Berryman would have been likely to take into account: "It is not clear whether *martyrion* ought to be translated 'martyrdom' or 'witness': there is an untranslatable play on the words."[17] It is surely this play on words that Berryman intended for the end of *Love & Fame.* "I pray I may be ready with my witness" (emphasizing *my* to associate more directly with Germanicus and Polycarp) involves a readiness to leap upon the wild lion or face the fire, to abandon the self in martyrdom whether from cancer, senility or, more problematically, mania. It was the last of these that Berryman suffered, praying to be made "acceptable at the end of time / in my degree." The eleventh of the **"Eleven Addresses to the Lord"** can be taken as a kind of palimpsest which itself embodies a metaphor of Berryman's struggle in the crosswinds of faith and self-destruction.

* * *

Berryman is at his prayers throughout *Delusions, Etc.* In the opening sequence, **"Opus Dei,"** based on the canonical hours, he prays especially

> not to be lost from You—
> if I could hear of a middle ground, I'd opt:

> a decent if minute salvation, sort of, on some fringe.
> I am afraid, afraid. Brothers, who if
> you are afraid are my brothers—veterans of fear—
> pray with me now in the hour of our living.

> **("Nones")**

Later, in the powerful **"Compline,"** Berryman turns again to Origen to verify his own version of the End of Time:

> If He for me as I feel for my daughter,
> being His son, I'll sweat no more tonight
> but happy hymn & sleep. I have got it made,
> and so have all we of contrition, for
>
> if He loves me He must love everybody
> and Origen was right & Hell is empty
> or will be at apocatastasis.
> Sinners, sin on. We'll suffer now & later
>
> but not forever, dear friends and brothers!

Berryman seems to have maintained this conviction through to the end of *Delusions, Etc.* **"The Facts & Issues,"** written the summer before his death, carries Berryman's view of God and hellfire beyond theodicy. It is not a well-made poem but rather an extended burst of loose free verse in which Berryman speaks once for all unmistakably in his own voice and person about the life he was beginning to find unbearable. Perhaps Adrienne Rich would be right about this one: it is beyond literature, beyond criticism, showing us finally how far Berryman had extended himself beyond his own capacity to stay in one piece:

> I really believe He's here all over this room
> in a motor hotel in Wallace Stevens' town.
> I admit it's weird; and *could*—or could it?—not be
>   so;
> but frankly I don't think there's a molecular chance of
>   that.
> It doesn't seem hypothesis. Thank heavens
> millions agree with me, or mostly do,
> and have done ages of our human time,
> among whom were & still are some very sharp cook-
>   ies.
> I don't exactly feel missionary about it,
> though it's *very* true I wonder if I should.
> I regard the boys who don't buy this as deluded.
> Of course they regard me no doubt as deluded.
> Okay with me! And not the hell with them
> at *all*—no!—I feel *dubious* on Hell—
> it's here, all right, but elsewhere, after? Screw that,
> I feel pretty sure that evil simply ends
> *for the doer* (having wiped him out,
> by the way, usually) where good goes on,
> or good *may* drop dead too: I don't think so:
> I can't say I have hopes in that department
> myself, I lack ambition just just there,
> I know that Presence says it's mild, and it's mild,
> but being what I am I wouldn't care
> to dare go nearer. Happy to be here
> and to have been here, with such lovely ones
> so infinitely better, but to me
> even in their suffering infinitely kind
> & blessing. I am a greedy man, of course,
> but I wouldn't want that kind of luck continued,—
> or even *increased* (for Christ's sake), & *forever?*
> Let me be clear about this. It is plain to me
> *Christ* underwent man & treachery & socks

> & lashes, thirst, exhaustion, the bit, for *my* pathetic &
>   disgusting vices,
> to make this filthy fact of particular, long-after,
> faraway, five-foot-ten & moribund
> human being happy. Well, he has!
> I am so happy I could scream!
> It's *enough!* I can't BEAR ANY MORE.
> *Let this be it.* I've *had* it. I can't wait.

The railing of the Washington Avenue Bridge was half a year away. William Meredith, who was with Berryman in Connecticut at the time of the poem's composition, has commented that **"The Facts & Issues"** "ends with the baffling spectacle of a man fending off torrents of a grace that has become unbearable. It is a heroic response to that crisis, as I think his death was too."[18] These last words bear a burden of proof that is truly outside the range of common criticism, but they state the case with startling offhandedness and plausibility. Berryman came to view himself, in his poetry, through Henry and beyond, as the hero of a work that had gradually, and terribly, become one with the life of its maker. "Happy to be here / and to have been here," and at peace with the idea of a God who would save even Satan, Berryman leapt upon his own wild lion and drew his life and his poem together into a triumph of self over circumstance. Suicide became for him a kind of martyrdom at the hands of forces darker and more ambiguous than the ones that stood Polycarp in the fire. As he wrote of the heroes of the Easter Rising:

> Wait the lime-pits for all originators,
> wounded propped up to be executed,
> afterward known as martyrs.

Risky as it may seem to suggest this, it is not impossible to think the same for the originator of Henry and his Songs. After I completed this essay in 1980, Eileen Simpson published her memoir, *Poets in Their Youth* (New York: Random House, 1982). Her "Afterword" (ch. 10) provides much useful detail from Berryman's last days. I agree, in spirit, with her final argument that "it was the poetry that kept [Berryman] alive," though largely in the sense that it was through his poetry that Berryman enabled himself to believe in an ongoing life for the soul despite bodily decrepitude and the imminent arrival of "his subtle foe." I do not believe, however, that Berryman killed himself, as Simpson suggests, because his muse had deserted him. On the contrary, Berryman had achieved, in his last poems, a synthesis through which the prospect of death, "ambiguous ahead," had positively become an accessible point of egress from "the wide hell in the world" (**"King David Dances"**—the final poem in *Delusions, Etc.*). Poetry became his consecrated ground.

Notes

1. *Harvard Advocate* 103, no. 1 (spring 1969): 5.

2. "Living with Henry," *Harvard Advocate* 103, no. 1 (spring 1969): 10.

3. See Berryman's 1957 essay "Song of Myself: Intention and Substance," *The Freedom of the Poet* (New York: Farrar, Straus and Giroux, 1976), p. 230.

4. "Living with Henry," p. 10.

5. *Creative Intuition in Art and Poetry* (New York: Pantheon Books, 1953), p. 318.

6. *Massachusetts Review* 11, no. 2 (spring 1970): 346.

7. *Harvard Advocate* 103, no. 1 (spring 1969): 6.

8. See John Haffenden's essay, "Drink as Disease: John Berryman," *Partisan Review* 44, no. 4 (1977): 576.

9. Origen, *On First Principles,* trans. G. W. Butterworth (New York: Harper & Row, 1966), pp. 52-88.

10. See the first chapter of *The American Quest for a Supreme Fiction: Whitman's Legacy in the Personal Epic* (Chicago: University of Chicago Press, 1979).

11. "I think the model in *The Dream Songs* was . . . 'Song of Myself'—a very long poem, about sixty pages. It also has a hero, a personality, himself. Henry is accused of being me and I am accused of being Henry and I deny it and nobody believes me. Various things entered into it, but that is where I started." *Paris Review* 53 (winter 1972): 90-91.

12. *The Freedom of the Poet,* p. 314.

13. "Berryman's Last Poems," *Concerning Poetry* 6, no. 1 (spring 1973): 9.

14. "A Cursing Glory: John Berryman's *Love & Fame,*" *Renascence* 25, no. 3 (spring 1973): 115.

15. Ibid., p. 126.

16. Harvard University Press, 1st printing 1913, pp. 317, 325, 331. All other extant translations differ significantly from Kirsopp Lake's.

17. Lake translation, p. 313.

18. "In Loving Memory of the Late Author of *The Dream Songs,*" reprinted in Richard J. Kelly's *John Berryman: A Checklist* (Scarecrow Press, 1972), p. xix.

Bo Gustavsson (essay date 1984)

SOURCE: Gustavsson, Bo. "The Poetics of *The Dream Songs.*" In *The Soul under Stress: A Study of the Poetics of John Berryman's* Dream Songs, pp. 45-75. Stockholm, Sweden: Uppsala, 1984.

[In the following essay, Gustavsson chronicles the composition of The Dream Songs *and considers the influence of Walt Whitman's* Leaves of Grass *on Berryman's collection.]*

The composition of *The Dream Songs* resembled the writing of *Homage to Mistress Bradstreet* in that Berryman first conceived the form for his chosen subject, and then he worked out the implications of his subject in a number of essays. Logically enough he thought that the poet who wanted to write a long poem first had to establish the form and the subject for his poem.[1] As with *Homage to Mistress Bradstreet,* the new poem dealt with his persona's life story, with the difference that, whereas the earlier work had dramatized the story of a past life, he set out in *The Dream Songs* to record the contemporary life of his persona Henry. When he started writing dream songs he knew that he was embarked on an epic,[2] but only gradually did he discover the structural organization for his work in progress. In 1955 the conception of *The Dream Songs* owed much to the example of the *Cantos.* Berryman's 1949 essay on Pound demonstrated that he found the *Cantos* especially inspiring on two accounts: first, the subject of the poem was the life of the modern poet; second, in method Pound relied on the drift of life while following loosely-held principles of organization.

As with the Bradstreet poem, however, it would take another four years before Berryman got started on his new poem. Perhaps, again like *Mistress Bradstreet,* he needed the "luck" of ordeal, as he expressed it in *The Paris Review* interview,[3] to really get into his new work. The ordeal that he faced this time was the divorce from his second wife Ann Levine. Over the next years Berryman wrote a great number of dream songs, but it was not until the summer of 1962 that he finally began ordering the contents of the book that appeared two years later as *77 Dream Songs.*[4] The nature of the work demanded this improvisational kind of composition since the poem recorded the ongoing life story of an individual. *The Dream Songs,* then, dealt with the life of the poet-persona, and the work depended more on the fortune of inspiration than on any pre-conceived scheme of organization. If the poem hereby gained in immediacy, there was perhaps a certain loss in the control of material; Berryman, however, willingly took this risk since he felt that the writing of a postmodern epic inevitably involved such a risk of failure.[5] Like the *Cantos,* the nature of *The Dream Songs* was exploratory, inasmuch as it was motivated by the search for knowledge and values in the mid-20th-century world. The direct expression of the poet's sensibility therefore took precedence over the esthetic will to order.

For *His Toy, His Dream, His Rest* Berryman followed the same procedure as before in that he continued writing dream songs while keeping in mind his structural notions for the poem. In the 1966 *Ivory Tower* interview he said that he would have to organize the remaining four Books of *The Dream Songs* out of the 181 songs written after the publication of *77 Dream Songs.*[6] He planned his long poem to include 161 songs closing with a song called **"My Heavy Daughter"** that eventually came to conclude *His Toy, His Dream, His Rest.* However, as a result of his stay in Ireland during the academic year 1966-1967, he wrote a great number of new songs which became Book VII when *His Toy* appeared the following year. Meanwhile Book VI had grown into the largest section of *The Dream Songs,* probably because of the tragic death of Berryman's close friend Delmore Schwartz in June 1966.[7] The new volume was in fact dedicated to "the sacred memory of Delmore Schwartz", and the fate of the artist in America became the major preoccupation of Book VI. From 1966 to 1968 Berryman's conception of his epic poem expanded from the originally planned 161 to 385 dream songs, and he had to change his plans considerably to be able to incorporate the new outspokenly autobiographical material. This development was not altogether unpredictable given the nature of his work: the recording of an individual's life in progress.

In *The Harvard Advocate* interview Berryman said that he modelled the dream songs on the songs of Yeats, adding that he regarded them as extended sonnets.[8] The dream songs consisted of three six-line stanzas, variously rhymed, with the metrical pattern 5-5-3-5-5-3. He first practiced this form in **"The Nervous Songs"** where he experimented with a series of personae for the purpose of expressing extreme states of mind. Furthermore, the dream song stanzas resembled the sestets of the Petrarchan sonnet that he adopted for his cycle of sonnets written in 1947. When he invented the dream song form he kept in mind the insights gained from his earlier writing while drawing inspiration from Yeats's lyrics in *Words for Music Perhaps.* Yeats employed a six-line stanza for his lyrics, and by speaking through a series of masks he could articulate violent feelings on the themes of love, death, religion, and politics. Similarly, Berryman probably intended his new poem to focus on the persona's exacerbated sensibility as man and artist living in the world of the mid-20th century. He thought that the content of art was emotionally "rebellious", while the form was "the servant of order".[9] Form then functioned as a means of channelling otherwise overpowering emotions.

Berryman's songs differed, however, from Yeats's in that they had no refrain and, since he was writing an epic instead of short lyrics, he chose a freer and more functional rhyme scheme. The Yeatsian metric combined iambic tetrameter and trimeter lines with the ballad stress meter. In his 1937 essay "A General Introduction for My Work", an important document for the understanding of the poetics of his late phase, Yeats declared that he sought to realize in his verse "the contrapuntal structure" of dramatic impassioned speech and traditional verse meters.[10] This ambition also came to inform the prosody of *The Dream Songs.* But, whereas Yeats's use of counterpointing was motivated by the doctrine of

the masks, Berryman appropriated the technique for the sake of expressing the contrasting sides of his own personality: on the one hand his deep melancholy and on the other his nervous vitality. The dream song stanza alternated pentameter and trimeter lines which allowed both for dramatic complication and narrative progression. And Berryman also kept the stanza open to the endless modifications imposed by his epic materials.

Berryman's discovery of his persona's name very much colored his original conception of this central figure. During a discussion of "intolerable names" with his second wife Anne Levine, he chose Mabel, while she decided on Henry.[11] From then on they affectionally called each other Mabel and Henry, and Berryman wrote the first dream song focusing on their relationship. But he soon made Henry into the single hero of the poem. The adoption of his own "intolerable" nickname for his persona's name revealed Berryman's intention to deal with those unpleasant aspects of his character and life that he had previously chosen to ignore or suppress. The persona would then serve as an imaginative version of himself for the purpose of coming to terms with difficult problems of living, and humor and irony would become important strategies. As his biographer notes, Berryman had the habit of reviewing his life, trying to put it in order, and in 1954 he kept a diary of strenuous dream-analysis that anticipated the use of the persona for *The Dream Songs.*[12] Indeed, he discovered in Henry a congenial means of self-investigation and self-expression. In the mid-fifties Berryman had established the form for his epic and general ideas about the subject: the life of his persona Henry. He was further to clarify and develop these ideas in two key essays from the late fifties: "'Song of Myself': Intention and Substance", written in 1957, and "From the Middle and Senior Generations", which appeared in the 1959 summer issue of *The American Scholar.* Only in 1959 did he feel certain enough about his method and aims to publish five unnumbered dream songs in the November 6 issue of *The Times Literary Supplement.*[13] Over the following years groups of songs appeared periodically in various American and British journals.

* * *

The posthumously published essay "'Song of Myself': Intention and Substance" documents Berryman's enthusiastic allegiance to a tradition of poetic theory and practice that coincided with his ambitions as a postmodern writer. This essay is crucial for an understanding of his poetics since, as he said in *The Paris Review* interview,[14] he set out in *The Dream Songs* to write the "Song of Myself" of his own age. He had lectured on Whitman for years, and the 1957 essay summarized his assessment of the American poet. The mid-fifties, in fact, saw a reappraisal of Whitman's achievement both among scholars and critics with such works as Gay

Wilson Allen's *The Solitary Singer* (1955) and Roger Asselineau's *L'Évolution de Walt Whitman* (1954). Many young poets also turned to Whitman for inspiration; indeed, the history of postmodernism began with this gradual reappropriation of the heritage of Walt Whitman. The 1960 collection of essays *Start with the Sun: Studies in the Whitman Tradition,* co-authored by James E. Miller Jr., Karl Shapiro, and Bernice Slote, testified to this reawakened interest in Whitman.[15] The book investigated Whitman's connections with D. H. Lawrence, Hart Crane, Dylan Thomas, Henry Miller, and William Carlos Williams. The introductory essay defined the Whitman tradition as the poetry of the whole man, both the emotions and the intellect, a poetry that, while taking into account the tragedy of life, was basically affirmative. And the project for this kind of poetry was to overcome man's sense of estrangement from himself and the universe, to search for the authentic life or "the supreme Fiction" in James E. Miller's use of Stevens' phrase.[16]

When Berryman wrote his essay in 1957, however, there were few signs of the cultural change under way. Charles Olson's experimentation at Black Mountain College remained largely unknown except to students and disciples. But the publication of *Howl* did predict the arrival of a new sensibility with Ginsberg's overt proclamation of himself as the heir of Whitman. Also in 1957 Robert Lowell was reworking his style along the lines of Williams' free verse, and Shapiro had already written but not published his perceptive essay on Whitman and Lawrence, "The First White Aboriginal". Berryman's essay belonged to this ambiance of excitement at discovering the relevance of a Whitmanian kind of poetry for the contemporary world. As Miller later argued, Berryman's and Lowell's renewal of their styles in the late fifties testified to the emergence of postmodernism.[17]

Since Berryman modelled **The Dream Songs** on "Song of Myself", in his opinion the epitome of *Leaves of Grass,* the investigation of Whitman's poetic enterprise in the 1957 essay had a direct bearing on the conception of his own epic poem. He thought that "Song of Myself" was "the greatest poem so far written by an American",[18] and his understanding of the poem determined the poetics of **The Dream Songs.** In order to understand Whitman's poem he focused on the central question of intention, whereby he also sought to clarify the goal of his own writing. He begins the essay by expressing his disagreement with the moderns' ambiguous judgment of Whitman, observing that their reservations derived from the fact that Whitman was a poet of life rather than a poet of culture.[19] Instead Berryman acknowledges him as a master of a new kind of poetry that has largely gone unappreciated. He notes that Whitman did not see his poem primarily as a work of art but rather as a work of life, and he suggests that

here lies the key to an understanding of "Song of Myself". In his *Paris Review* interview he calls the poem "a wisdom work, a work on the meaning of life and how to conduct it",[20] implying that Whitman's and his own epic were indeed so motivated. A favorite idea with Whitman was that in a time of crisis art would replace religion and philosophy as the only valid source of values. And Whitman thought that mid-19th-century America was going through such a time of crisis. Obviously, the idea of an art of crisis also appealed to Berryman.

Whitman formulated his theory of poetry in the prefaces to the succeeding editions of *Leaves of Grass* where he sought to justify his innovative writing by dwelling on his intentions. In his essay Berryman quotes the key statement of aims from the 1888 Preface, "A Backward Glance O'er Travel'd Roads": "'Leaves of Grass' has mainly been the outcroppings of my own emotional and personal nature—an attempt, from first to last, to put *a Person* [Whitman's italics], a human being (myself, in the latter part of the Nineteenth Century, in America), freely, fully, and truly on record".[21] This statement in effect summarizes the poetics that Whitman evolved out of Emerson's theorizing in the 1844 essay "The Poet", the urtext of postmodern poetry. Emerson here advocated the use of organic form, and he described the poet as the Adamic Namer who by the power of his imagination could invest men's lives with meaning. For Emerson, then, imagination served as the revelation of reality rather than as an escape from reality.

Whitman revolutionized the notion of poetics by basing his own poetics not on traditional esthetic principles but on the person of the poet who used art as means of realizing an ideal life. He thought that there was a correspondence between the poet's way of writing and his way of living, and in the 1855 Preface he sketched his ethical and epistemological kind of poetics. For his subject, the poet as Everyman, he adopted an open organic form and a free verse prosody. Berryman characterizes this new epic form as one of "*self-wrestling,* inquiry, and wonder",[22] a suitable form for the wisdom work that he thought "Song of Myself" to be and that he wanted to make **The Dream Songs.** Whitman saw life and art as a dual creative task: the creation of *Leaves* paralleled the creation of his own character and, in the end, as Roger Asselineau observed in *The Evolution of Walt Whitman,*[23] the book and the man became one. Whitman further thought that all great literature tended toward the moral and spiritual development of man. His project in *Leaves* was to present a representative individual, the poet, as the model for a new kind of man. In terms of the 1855 Preface the enterprise was to "indicate the path between reality and [men's] souls",[24] to inspire belief in the possibility of realizing the ideal life. This goal shaped the structure of "Song of Myself" according to the three declared purposes that Berryman's essay analyzes in detail. First was the national purpose dealing with the vision of a spiritual democracy, based on the ideals of liberty and equality. The second aim was religious, and it concerned the acquisition of a new religious sense, a true religion of life. Third was the metaphysical purpose, or the question of being, proposing the notion of time as a continuous present where past and future meet and coalesce. Berryman stresses the fact that "Song of Myself" is the record of a personality's growth in the present and that the structure conforms to that of a wisdom work. Whitman's vision includes not only the individual but also the state and ultimately the human race since he believed that American democracy represented a challenge to fulfill the history of civilization. Therefore Whitman in a sense inspired the postmoderns' endeavor to discover in personal experience those values and beliefs that could redeem their lives and times from the mentality of pessimism and alienation.

Berryman contrasts Whitman's personal theory of poetry, which sees the poet as a spiritual historian and inquirer concerned above all with urgent problems of living, with Eliot's impersonal theory holding that the poet is a craftsman, a maker of an autonomous and finished artwork. These differing theories, Berryman argues, give rise to the two opposing traditions in the 20th century: modern verse and postmodern verse. He declares his allegiance to the tradition inspired by Whitman because he wants an art that can deal with personal fate. When the Whitmanian poet articulates the reality of his own life he becomes in Emerson's terms a representative man who, by virtue of his imagination and candor, assumes the role of spokesman standing "among partial men for the complete man".[25] This notion of the poet as representative figure influenced Berryman's use of the persona; therefore Whitman's creation of the poet-persona for *Leaves of Grass* helps illuminate the problematic relation between author and persona in *The Dream Songs*. In his interviews Berryman made contradictory statements on this issue. On one occasion he claimed that there was indeed a close relation between himself and his persona; on another occasion he disclaimed any connection whatsoever; and in *The Paris Review* interview he explained somewhat cryptically that obviously he both was and was not Henry.

When Whitman published the first edition of *Leaves of Grass* he adopted a new identity, whereby he abandoned his given name Walter for his nickname Walt; Berryman in fact did the same thing when he wrote the first dream song about his persona Henry. Whitman's new identity enabled him to invest personal experience with universal significance, including his traumatic homosexuality, and so it immeasurably expanded his personality as representative spokesman. Berryman emphasizes that the Whitmanian poet is above all a voice, a medium

of expression "for himself and others; for others as *himself*".[26] By truthfully expressing what he feels and knows he says what others dare not or perhaps cannot say. Whitman's representativeness is characterized by a cosmic sense of identification with all existence, whose only limit on the one hand is God and on the other blind egotism. Like Whitman's poet, then, Henry functions as an imaginative extension of Berryman's personality, and the aim is to record the life of a representative individual in the mid-20th century. According to Whitman's formula that the personal is the universal, Berryman lets his own fate illustrate the conditions of life at mid-century. However, since he shares the pessimistic and sceptical temper of his age, his sense of representativeness differs from Whitman's idealism, although, as *Democratic Vistas* demonstrates, the older poet was well aware of the decay of American civilization. For Whitman, the idealistic vision in the end prevailed over his doubts and fears.

The Whitman essay taught Berryman two things that significantly clarified his conception of *The Dream Songs*. First, to use his persona as a means of expressing and generalizing his own life history according to the notion of the poet as a representative man. Second, to follow Whitman's revolution in the art of poetry by basing his poetics on the person of the poet. Whitman's enterprise "to put *a Person*, a human being (myself, in the latter part of the [Twentieth] Century, in America), freely, fully, and truly on record" then came to determine the poetics of *The Dream Songs*. In *Democratic Vistas* Whitman defined his poetry as the work of "personalism",[27] asserting that the task of culture and civilization was to further the realization of the human personality. In this sense the postmodern poets practiced different versions of personalism. In his 1971 interview for *The Chicago Daily News* Berryman made a statement about his aim in *The Dream Songs* that, as Miller observed,[28] paraphrased Whitman's statement from "A Backward Glance O'er Travel'd Roads": "The idea was, sort of, the way Whitman put his idea about 'Leaves of Grass'. The idea is to record a personality, put him through tests, to see what the hell he's up to, and through him, the country".[29] The intention was then to record a representative individual's growth of consciousness, a growth that in Whitman's terms involved the writing of a poetry of the body and the soul, or the whole man.

Two leading critics of Berryman's generation likewise called for the creation of a literature of the whole man. Randall Jarrell advocated the writing of a poetry of the conscious and the unconscious, while Philip Rahv argued for an art that was at once emotionally "redskin" and intellectually "paleface".[30] Berryman shared with Lowell this ambition to express fully his sensibility in art,[31] but, whereas Lowell devoted his whole poetic oeuvre to that goal, Berryman tried to realize it in one single work. The Whitmanian project to record fully the life of the poet therefore came to influence both the craft and the subject matter of *The Dream Songs,* while offering Berryman's version of a wisdom work for his age. At the center of the poem stands the persona Henry, whose fate is recorded. As in "Song of Myself" this fate has national, religious, and metaphysical implications since Henry is deeply involved with the destiny of American democracy on the one hand and with the problem of faith on the other; lastly he seeks to elucidate the meaning of personal history.

In the 1968 review-article "The Expansional Poet: A Return to Personality" Laurence Lieberman perceptively singled out John Berryman, James Dickey, and William Stafford as the practitioners of a new mode of writing that he called "expansional" poetry.[32] Lieberman's theorizing on this new mode helps us understand Berryman's project in *The Dream Songs*; furthermore, Berryman is here connected with the emergent postmodernist tradition. The expansional poet, Lieberman argues, strives to "deepen and intensify his total personality in his art".[33] The earliest exponent of this kind of poet was Theodore Roethke, who throughout his career wrote an imaginatively personal poetry. Lieberman cites Eliot's dictum of depersonalization from that central document of modernism "Tradition and the Individual Talent", insisting that the expansional poet, on the contrary, tries to liberate his sensibility and imagination by adopting a persona who can articulate the poet's whole range of experience. The persona therefore becomes the creative means of realizing a total personality, and the goal is greater self-knowledge and by implication a greater knowledge of human nature. The expansional poet employs a serial and cumulative form, and he gives priority to the free expression of his personality over the perfection of his art, since he regards poetry as an instrument of knowledge rather than as a specialized craft. Lieberman's essay in effect argues for Whitman's kind of poetry, which became the characteristic mode of postmodernism since the new poets made their own persons and lives the focus of their art.

* * *

In that other key essay from the late fifties "From the Middle and Senior Generations" Berryman sketched his own theory of poetry, a theory that accorded with his ambition to write a personal epic.[34] Here again he reveals his preoccupation with the state of American poetry by briefly discussing the contrast between what he calls the "Eastern" or modernist style and the "Western" or postmodernist style. Robert Lowell exemplifies an Easterner whose verse, before *Life Studies,* is formal, rhetorical, historical, religious, and impersonal. Berryman here reverses his earlier opinion of Lowell as the exemplar of a postmodern writer because of his allegiance to the Whitman tradition. The-

odore Roethke on the other hand practices the Western way of writing which is informal, colloquial, psychological, irreligious, and above all personal. Berryman sees Lowell as a poet of completed states and Roethke as a poet of process: the former's authority comes from tradition, whereas the latter's comes out of experience. He declares himself in favor of Roethke's Whitmanesque poetry of process where the poet strives to render directly his sense of reality.

In his essay Berryman further comments on the isolation of the poet in American society and, speculating on various motives for writing poetry, he asserts: "Poetry is a terminal activity, taking place out near the end of things, where the poet's soul addresses one other soul only . . . And it aims . . . at the reformation of the poet, as prayer does".[35] Art then becomes a way of dealing with situations of ordeal and, like the soul's outpourings in prayer, the goal is the acquisition of a new awareness, the gaining of the freedom to change one's life. Berryman here seems to refer to the notion of prayer as self-knowledge won through ordeal. Poetry assures a way of ordering and bringing meaning to life, a function traditionally undertaken by religion. The poet speaks to one person only, himself, another man, or ultimately God, since in his heroic encounter with his conditions of life he assumes the role of Everyman-Agonist whose identity comprises all other men. Like Roethke Berryman's authority of speech comes from personal experience, but, insofar as the experience of ordeal demands his whole will, mind, and imagination, he also draws on the knowledge and the sensibility of cultural history. Learning therefore serves to elucidate personal experience, but it never becomes an end in itself. For Berryman, as Donald Davie remarks in his review of *The Freedom of the Poet,*[36] the vocations of poet and scholar do indeed merge. Berryman sees in the careers of Yeats and Eliot a justification for his theory of poetry: both used poetry to come to terms with the crises of their lives, and both were able to renew themselves as men again and again through their art. Yeats and Eliot were then crisis poets who wrote out of a deep concern with moral and spiritual issues. Thus, although Berryman objected to Eliot's critical views, he gradually came to appreciate Eliot's achievement as a poet.

In his interviews Berryman further elaborates the theory of poetry that he outlined in his 1959 article. He reiterates the view that great art comes out of ordeal and crisis, whereby the poet's powers of survival are put to the test: "My idea is this: The artist is extremely lucky who is presented with the worst possible ordeal which will not actually kill him . . . Beethoven's deafness, Goya's deafness, Milton's blindness, that kind of thing".[37] If personal agony is a curse on the artist's life, it becomes a blessing for his art. Agony enables him to know his deepest feelings and so to state the disturbing truths of life, which makes him into an artist-agonist. Berryman here seems to echo Edmund Wilson's idea that there is a connection between genius and trauma, that all great artists have suffered some form of trauma that influences their work. In Berryman's case the ordeal that marked his life was the suicide of his father, and *The Dream Songs* represents his attempt to come to terms with the effects of that lifelong trauma.

The poetry of ordeal, however, poses great dangers for the poet both as man and artist since it literally involves his survival. The pressures on the poet may end in driving him into neurosis, or worse yet, into madness or suicide. He in a sense risks his sanity and life for the sake of his art by accepting the task as quester for values in a sceptical and apocalyptic age. Berryman was painfully aware of the high rate of mental breakdowns, alcoholism, and suicides among his contemporaries, and he blamed this state of affairs partly on American society and partly on the poets themselves. Still the rewards for the poet of personal crisis are great: because of his ability to survive ordeal he can assume the role as interpreter of life both for himself and others.

In his 1960 essay on Stephen Crane's short story "The Open Boat", Berryman makes a programmatic statement that in effect epitomizes his poetic theory: "The experience, and *only* the experience, of [life's] most dangerous and demanding ordeals fits man to do what it is most his duty and power to do: to *explain*—explain what [life] is, what man is, what matters".[38] As a record of crisis, then, *The Dream Songs* is a work of life, to adopt Berryman's terms for "Song of Myself", dealing with the poet's life situation, and as interpretation of experience the poem is a wisdom work on the problem of living in the 20th-century world. The kind of wisdom that Berryman envisions involves the individual's struggle with fate, a struggle that eventually turns into the means for a secular form of grace: through crisis the poet as Everyman-Agonist gains new awareness that enables him to change his life, to actively shape his destiny. The Crane essay approvingly quotes William Faulkner's belief, stated in the Nobel Prize Address, that "man will not merely endure: he will prevail . . . The poet's voice need not merely be the record of man, it can be one of the props, the pillars to help him endure and prevail".[39] In Berryman's opinion the major challenge for contemporary man is how to change his status as victim of history into that of responsible maker of history. Much of his criticism therefore deals with this crucial issue of freedom and fate.

The method of writing out of personal crisis, prescribed by Berryman's poetic theory, comes to determine the nature of *The Dream Songs* as a long poem. Like *Homage to Mistress Bradstreet* and the *Sonnets,* it is constructed from short lyrics, but, whereas the earlier

epic relates a completed life history from the past and the cycle of sonnets tends to depend on Petrarchan conventions, *The Dream Songs* represents Berryman's ambition to express fully the present life of his persona. His method therefore results in sequences of dream songs that record successive states of mind, and in this it recalls the procedure of the *Cantos*: to give expression to the poet's developing preoccupations and interests through the installments of his epic work in progress. In "One Answer to a Question: Changes" Berryman succinctly presents his understanding of the long poem under three headings: "1) a high and prolonged riskiness, 2) the construction of a world rather than the reliance upon one already existent which is available to a small poem, 3) problems of decorum most poets happily do not have to face".[40] The risk involved in the writing of this kind of open-ended epic is that the poet may not be able to finish his undertaking or, because of the many pressures on him, he may fall silent altogether. The world of the poem emerges with the telling of the persona's life story and, since he is dealing with such painfully personal material, there arise certain problems of decorum that he has to solve. What enables Berryman to resolve these problems is the notion of dream, implied by the title of his work, that he refers to in the Note to *77 Dream Songs.* His notion of dream concerns the persona's phantasmagoric sense of reality, and it allows for the full expression of his sensibility by freely mixing observations, fantasies, and sensations. This view of life as essentially a kind of phantasmagoria can be associated with the Freudian idea that dreaming represents the way the unconscious makes known forbidden thoughts and desires to the conscious mind.

The conception of the long poem as the record of the persona's sensibility in direct confrontation with his life circumstances owes of course a great deal to Whitman's redefinition of the epic for *Leaves of Grass,* a redefinition that Berryman approvingly comments on in his interviews. When Whitman read Edgar Allan Poe's criticism he realized that the traditional epic had become obsolete for the modern age. Poe advocated the replacement of the classical criterion of epic length as the highest achievement in literature with the romantic criterion of intensity. Since Whitman wanted to write a long personal poem he worked out a new conception of the genre, which he set forth in the 1855 Preface. His new kind of epic dealt with the present instead of the mythical past; the subject and the hero were the poet himself as representative man; the theme became the quest for valid values and beliefs rather than the justification of the ethos of a past civilization.[41] The view that Whitman derived from Poe of the long poem as a work of life, consisting of a series of intense lyrics that focused on the poet's states of mind, accords with Berryman's use of the form for *The Dream Songs.* His version, however, is significantly tempered by the confusions and uncertainties of the 20th century because he lacks the older poet's visionary beliefs in man and in democracy. Therefore the record of the poet's consciousness becomes all the more emotionally turbulent and intellectually urgent while unfolding the story of his life. As late as 1971, the year before his death, Berryman described both *The Dream Songs* and *Homage to Mistress Bradstreet* as "crisis poems" adding: "I am only interested in people in crisis. When I finish one, I enter on another".[42]

Why did Berryman feel compelled to construct a poetics based on the vision of people in crisis? Since he regarded the poet both as an individual and as a representative figure, personal reasons were compounded with historical ones. All his life Berryman suffered from the trauma of his father's suicide and the loss of his childhood faith. The feeling of being doomed to a life of agony was further strengthened by the shattering love affair of 1947, after which, as his biography demonstrates, his life became an endless series of miseries. The 20th century as he personally knew it saw the devastation of one world war followed by the frightening prospect of a nuclear holocaust. Moreover, the temper of scepticism and nihilism that the postmoderns inherited from the moderns, Eliot's vision of the anarchy and futility of this century's history, suffused all areas of life by mid-century. Because of their commitment to humane values and beliefs, the artists and the intellectuals found themselves in conflict with the Cold War spirit of conformity and materialism. The writings of Jarrell and Schwartz testified to the poet's difficult situation in mid-century America.[43] They felt that the poet as the man of sensibility and imagination had no place in the society of his time, a situation that turned him into the victim of his own hypersensitivity. In his essays from this period, Berryman worried about the future of American poetry, given the poet's difficult conditions of life. More important, however, he dwelt on the lack of a common morality, which in his view accounted for the decay of 20th-century civilization. History seemed indeed to confirm the fears qualifying Whitman's visionary optimism in *Democratic Vistas*: that rampant materialism would become the dominant creed of democracy.

The English critic A. Alvarez describes the situation of the postmodern artist in terms of the loss of four certainties that traditionally upheld artistic activity.[44] First, the Christian religion no longer offers any guidance in a secularized world, although the symbolism of the archetypal drama of salvation and damnation continues to inspire artists. Second, there is a general disenchantment with politics since all political idealism, whether of the right or the left, tends to end in some version of totalitarianism. The average citizen therefore adopts a cynical attitude to politics; he may believe in the democratic system but he does not believe in political ideals. If writers turn to political themes at all they celebrate the dissent of non-conformist individuals rather than dissent for ideological reasons. Third, artists have lost confidence in the relevance of the cultural tradition for dealing with the problems of the postwar world. The heroic endeavor of the moderns to recover the cultural past in order to revitalize the society of their time led only to the elitist estheticism of late modernism. Fourth, human reason itself proves inadequate as an instrument for ordering reality. The world-view presented by the scientist is tentative and provisional, the very antithesis of the logically ordered Newtonian universe that it has come to replace.

The disappearance of the traditional certainties of art forces the artist to adopt an attitude of radical worldliness that takes the form of a sceptical and non-idealistic survival. Alvarez characterizes this manner of survival as essentially Jewish, insofar as Judaism is the great secular religion whose foundation is not a belief in the afterlife but rather an ethic of respect, responsibility, and family piety. Contemporary artists therefore become imaginary Jews, as Berryman actually does in *The Dream Songs,* because they are trying to ascertain what values are to be found in everyday life. Their response to the crisis of 20th-century civilization becomes in Alvarez' terms an art of "Extremism", that is, an art that both in form and content reflects their historical predicament. The careers of Robert Lowell and John Berryman illustrate the best kind of extremist writing, arising from their courageous encounter with their life circumstances. Both use art as a means of discovering and creating their own identities, and this endeavor also has general implications given the conditions of life in the mid-20th century.

* * *

Berryman's Whitmanian enterprise to present fully the life of the poet in situations of crisis bears directly on the language and the prosody of *The Dream Songs*. Critics have rightly characterized the poem as a linguistic chaos, yet there is method in this chaos. *The Dream Songs* represents Berryman's attempt to express fully his sensibility while trying to elucidate his fate as man and artist in the 20th-century world. Expression therefore becomes part of characterization or, in Berryman's description of Crane's style, expression also becomes investigation.[45] In his Crane study he praises the American writer as one of the great stylists of the English language, describing Crane's style as the simultaneous presentation and investigation of his characters' lives. Berryman values Crane on the one hand for his ironic vision of human nature and on the other for his tragic vision of life. Crane's style is marked by a peculiar humor and irony, deriving from his honest recognition of the truths of life, which enables him both to sympathize with his characters and to criticize them. His tragicomic understanding of the human condition, then, is largely reflected in his style. Analogously, Berryman creates a language in *The Dream Songs* that seeks at once to express and to characterize the personality of Henry. This language represents his most ambitious application of the stylistic formula that he arrived at during the composition of the *Sonnets*: to invent a style that, in combining formal and colloquial qualities, is able to render fully his sensibility significantly tempered by a tragic view of life. What he attempts to do in *The Dream Songs* is to create a language that can articulate the shifting moods and attitudes experienced by an individual in a state of crisis. Thus Berryman, like other postmoderns, in a way carried on Wordsworth's and Whitman's reformation of the language and the verse of poetry by writing a poetry that became an essential part of his own life. This periodic reformation had earlier been accomplished by the great moderns who, in reaction against the rhetoric and the sentimentality of Victorian verse, called for a new idiom capable of articulating the modern spirit. By the 1950s poets once again felt the need to reform poetic language and prosody because they wanted to involve poetry in the life of the age.

Through the dual stylistic goal of expressing and exploring the personality of his persona, Berryman accommodates the modernist emphasis on intellect to the romantic preoccupation with feeling. However, for Berryman the combination of a vigorous mind and emotional spontaneity rather recalls the Elizabethan style and more specifically the late plays of Shakespeare. Throughout his career he worked on a critical biography of Shakespeare, and his abiding interest in the Elizabethan period is demonstrated by the fact that his collection of essays *The Freedom of the Poet* opens with the Elizabethans. The 1960 essay on Thomas Nashe's *The Unfortunate Traveller* discusses at length an exemplary practitioner of the Elizabethan style.[46] As a writer, Berryman argues, Nashe is an individualist who manages to write with his whole personality. He thinks as spontaneously as he feels, drawing freely on the different Renaissance styles for his own expressive needs. According to Berryman, Nashe is "one of the masters of English prose",[47] and he writes best under emotional pressure. Berryman opposes this individualistic kind of stylist to Eliot's dictum of impersonality in art. His assertion is that later writers to a large extent become the victims of the logic of grammarians and the conventions of literary taste, whereby they lose much of their own expressive powers.

The chief qualities of Nashe's style are improvisation and searching vigor; moreover, his active imagination manages to invest his experience with felt significance. Nashe exemplifies the enviable freedom of expression enjoyed by the individualist kind of writer. This freedom, Berryman declares, involves a protest against all forms of orthodoxy, whether religious, political, or

other. It is the freedom of an active sensibility whose fidelity to experience challenges all systematic modes of thinking. Indeed, Berryman thinks that the function of literature is to serve as a medium for the free expression of human sensibility, and he asserts that there is a need in contemporary writing for "the anti-categorical, and *ad hoc,* the flexible, the experimental".[48] The dream song style seeks precisely to approximate the freedom of expression mastered by the Elizabethans, and the aim is to present the whole living personality of the persona Henry.

In his review of *77 Dream Songs* Lowell discusses Berryman's stylistic development, declaring that his "writing has been a long, often back-breaking, search for an inclusive style, a style that could use his erudition, and catch the high, even frenetic, intensity of his experience, disgusts, and enthusiasm".[49] Lowell was in a good position to judge Berryman's lifelong search for an inclusive style since he himself shared this ambition, which in his case produced the long poem *Notebook* published in 1970. Here Lowell attempts to fuse art and life by writing a poem in diary form. He invents a blank verse variant of the sonnet, and, as he explains in the Afterthought,[50] the structure of the work is "intuitive in arrangement", following the progress of the poet's life. The writing conforms to the standards of realism but, when necessary, the mode changes into the fantastic and the surrealistic. It is relevant to comment here on Lowell's approach for, as Steven Gould Axelrod notes, Lowell probably modelled *Notebook* on *The Dream Songs.*[51] The poem constitutes Lowell's most ambitious endeavor to bring his whole personality into the writing of poetry; in fact, he here tries to compose a personal epic in the Whitman tradition.

What distinguishes the dream song style is the amazing range of dictions that Berryman commands: from formal and erudite speech, over colloquial speech, to slang, infantilisms, and various kinds of neologisms. This is not a contrived virtuosity; he needs this freedom of expression since he is writing a personal epic. The intention is to record the persona's direct responses to experience, those varying reactions of an individual under stress. Henry is an intellectual and a scholar, but he is also a man of feeling, *l'homme moyen sensuel,* who at times relapses into the reactions of a child or an adolescent. These habits of character have their distinctive idioms that together make up the linguistic personality of Henry. In freely expressing his changing reactions to experience he becomes the spokesman for the confusion and the anxiety of contemporary man. This is precisely the achievement of Berryman's style: it succeeds in faithfully articulating the sensibility of an individual who experiences to a heightened degree the predicament of living in the mid-20th-century world.

Berryman's use of dictions is reinforced by his technique of shifting pronouns, a technique that, as he observes in "One Answer to a Question: Changes", is fundamental to his notion of the persona.[52] Indeed, this technique is what enables him to explore the psychology of the whole personality. He suggests that Arthur Rimbaud's saying "Je est un autre" originally gave him the impulse to experiment with pronouns.[53] However, a more direct influence was probably Pound's mastery of multiple personae in the *Cantos*. If in **Homage to Mistress Bradstreet** Berryman employs shifting pronouns to indicate the relations between the poet and the persona, he fully develops the technique for **The Dream Songs** where he seeks to dramatize the complex nature of a single personality. By changing pronominal persons he can present the varying attitudes of involvement and detachment that the persona adopts towards his experience. These shifts of pronominal persons become component parts of Henry's personality, the purpose being to explore his Protean nature. Henry in fact contains many identities, and in his search for self-knowledge and self-renewal he must have the courage to act out the multiplicity of his own nature. Through the technique of shifting pronouns Berryman gains access to the expanded sense of personality that is necessary for his project of writing **The Dream Songs**. This epic enterprise therefore derives from the need to reexamine the nature of human personality, an ambition that Karl Malkoff sees as characteristic of the writings of the postmoderns.[54]

Stylistically Berryman establishes contexts for the understanding of the persona's experiences through allusions to cultural history. Learning is for him an urgently personal matter; indeed it becomes yet another resource in his efforts to cope with a strong sense of alienation. The moderns, on the other hand, use allusions as a means of objectifying their experience, since they believe in the authority of learning both as a literary technique and as a cultural asset. Their allusions therefore serve to universalize experience within the framework of Western myth, religion, and literature. As a postmodern poet Berryman is more versatile and heterodox, following Ezra Pound in extending his spectrum of allusions over both Eastern and Western civilizations. In **The Dream Songs** Berryman alludes to historical and fictional figures who either share the persona's predicament or have somehow solved the perennial problem of realizing one's fate as a human being. Indeed, Berryman suggests his own strategy for **The Dream Songs** when he notes in his review of *The Adventures of Augie March* that Bellow's allusive habit creates a new convention for American fiction, inasmuch as the technique introduces a series of ideal lives for Augie to emulate, while setting his story in legendary perspective.[55] Similarly, Berryman invokes figures from the history of civilization who illustrate ways of overcoming a personal sense of alienation. More often than not, however, he can only do so in an ironical or nostalgic mood since the ethos of the past no longer

can be realized in the world of the present. Still **The Dream Songs** is essentially motivated by the need to recover the possibility of actively shaping one's destiny in the manner of the exemplary figures from the history of the arts, religion, philosophy, and politics.

For Berryman the problem of realizing one's fate is intimately connected with the problem of suffering and evil; religion therefore becomes a major concern in his epic poem. In fact, he was preoccupied by the idea of a theodicy ever since the beginning of his career.[56] In **The Dream Songs** he finally undertakes the task of formulating a theodicy for his age, drawing on his wide knowledge of the theology and history of Christianity. Henry here assumes the role of a Job figure who through personal suffering can question the justice and love of God. On other occasions he laments, like the Jeremiah of Lamentations, the utter desolation of a world abandoned by God. He studies his favorite theologians, Augustine and Pascal, on the nature of evil, and he sees the early Christian martyrs and ascetics as exemplars of meaningful suffering. Henry would like to lead a Christian life, but he lacks the proper faith. However, he demonstrates a characteristic courage in that, although he fails to formulate a definite theodicy, he does not give up his search for faith. What more can be done by an honest man who lives in an irreligious age and yet longs for the certainties of religion?

The most conspicuous feature of the dream song style is without doubt Berryman's adoption of Negro dialect. When the interviewer for *Ivory Tower* asked him to describe the situation of his poem Berryman responded: "The basic situation is that of a modern man, early in middle age, pretending to be a Negro, that is to say, a minstrel in blackface, throughout, who has a friend who calls him Mr Bones . . . He endures and enjoys what is presented to him by contemporary American life".[57] In 1966 Berryman could not of course foresee that over the following years he would write a great number of new songs in which he gradually abandoned the Negro voice. Still, the dialect of the blues and the minstrel show have an important function in **The Dream Songs**. This kind of language enables Berryman to identify with the historical plight of blacks as a persecuted and discriminated people while he tries to acquire their virtues of survival, their peculiarly joyous stoicism. The blacks represent that form of heroism that Berryman most desires for himself: to be able to survive under all but intolerable circumstances. This concern with a morality of survival also explains his lifelong interest in Jewish history, as both Jews and blacks have succeeded in creating a distinctive culture out of their very powers of survival.[58] Thus he employs the language of the blues when he wants to give expression to more private moods of misery and loneliness, since the blues is an intensely personal kind of music, as LeRoi Jones shows in his *Blues People*.[59] The social and psychological predicament of blacks becomes for Berryman a paradigm for contemporary man's situation at a time when all traditional certainties are gone and the politics of fear and intolerance hold sway.

* * *

The prosody that Berryman creates for *The Dream Songs* is motivated, like his style, by the intention to write a personal epic. He develops his prosody from the combination of passionate utterance and traditional meter that Yeats first practiced in *Words For Music Perhaps.* This lifetime search for the means of expressing one's own sensibility in verse Yeats shared with William Carlos Williams, and both poets, in their different ways, influenced the experimentation of the postmoderns with prosodies that could render the poet's sense of experience. Berryman, on his part, realizes his lifelong ambition to express fully his prosodic personality by adopting traditional meters for his own purposes as an epic poet. The dream songs are therefore both controlled and free in distinctly new ways; the risk that Berryman associated with the writing of a long poem also involves the invention of an original prosody. The problem for the poet who wants to write a congenial verse is precisely how to accommodate the impulse toward freedom and spontaneity to the need for some kind of ordering principle. Berryman's solution is to let the dream song stanza, with its alternating pentameter and trimeter lines, assure the need for regularity, while the prosody serves to articulate his own personality.

As William Meredith suggests, Berryman's innovative versification can be connected on the one hand with his bohemianism and on the other with his love of decorum.[60] Meredith goes on to praise the accuracy of form that each poem achieves. Translated into prosodic terms the bohemianism takes the form of experimentation in the manner of the Emersonian meter-making argument, whereas the love of decorum manifests itself as reverence for the achievements of the history of prosody. Edwin Fussell justly sees these contrary impulses as the typical dilemma of the American poet: how to compromise between a natural bent toward innovation and an inescapable dependence on tradition.[61]

Since Berryman, like Yeats, is a stanzaic poet, he achieves basic control of his materials through the dream song stanza, whose regularity is what allows the amazing freedom of his versification. In *Love & Fame,* published in 1970, he goes a step further in that he relies on the quatrain as the sole ordering principle for his new conversational style, writing a kind of free verse. Berryman's virtuosity as a prosodist derives from the counter-pointing of his dramatic syntax with the verse pattern. He habitually varies the pentameter lines with hexameters and tetrameters and the trimeter lines with tetrameters and dimeters. The prosody freely mixes

iambic and trochaic rhythms, and this mixture of prosodic modes is what distinguishes the versification of *The Dream Songs.* The alternating, often clashing, rhythms of rising and falling feet dramatize a conflict between energetic, hopeful activity and elegiac, pessimistic resignation, a conflict that characterizes the mood of the dream songs. For the sake of greater intensity and emphasis he occasionally uses an accentual meter tending towards the spondee and sprung rhythm. The flexible metric of the dream songs then gives Berryman the freedom to blend iambics and trochaics at will and to introduce accentual lines when necessary. This kind of prosodic complexity matches the complexity of the subject matter of the poem: the recording of the poet's ongoing life story.

Dream songs 77 and 385 serve to illustrate Berryman's prosody since as summary poems they characterize the practice of *77 Dream Songs* and *His Toy, His Dream, His Rest,* while indicating the overall prosodic development of the work. "Song 77" demonstrates the flexibility of Berryman's metric and his ability to play variations on the verse pattern:

> Séedy Hénry róse up shý in de wórld
> & sháved & swúng his bárbells, dúded Hénry úp
> and p.á.'d poor thóusands of pérsons on tópics of
>   gránd
> móment to Hénry, áh to those léss & nóne.
> Wif a bóok of hís in eíther hánd
> he is strípt dówn to móve ón.
>
> —Come awáy, Mr Bónes.
>
> —Hénry is tíred of the wínter,
> & haírcuts, & a squéamish cómfy rúin-próne próud
>   nátional mínd, & Spríng (in the cíty so cálled).
> Hénry likes Fáll.
> Hé would be prepáred to líve in a wórld of Fáll
> for éver, impénitent Hénry.
> But the snóws and súmmers gríeve & dréam;
>
> thése fíerce & aíry occupátions, and lóve,
> ráved awáy so mány of Hénry's yéars
> it ís a wónder thát, with in éach hánd
> óne of his ówn mad bóoks and áll,
> áncient fíres for eýes, his héad fúll
> & his héart fúll, he's máking réady to move ón.

An average of three lines per stanza conform to the expected pattern except stanza 2 where only the fourth line is regular. This leaves ample room for Berryman's variations, and he achieves most freedom in the short third and sixth lines ranging from the dimeter to the pentameter. The song characteristically mixes trochaic and iambic-anapestic rhythms. When Henry breaks into hysteria in the long second line of stanza 2 the verse changes into strong stresses and sprung rhythm, still the normal beat persists in the background. The irregular second stanza is quite unusual for Berryman since he departs almost entirely from the metrical pattern, but he keeps securely within the framework of the six-line dream song stanza. The inversions and the ellipses of syntax interact with the verse to create the original music of the song, demonstrating Berryman's considerable skill as a syntactical prosodist. The song has only two full rhymes, while his preference for slant rhymes and assonantal rhymes clearly emerges, and so does his frequent use of alliterations. The diction shifts from colloquial language and Negro dialect to the use of a more formal speech. A typical neologism is the expression "p.a.'d" transforming a noun into a verb. For the sake of emphasis Berryman adds one line, the short seventh line, a strategy that he employs only in fifteen dream songs. The line also serves as part of the ongoing dialogue between the minstrel show characters Mr Bones and Mr Interlocutor.

"Song 385" concludes *His Toy, His Dream, His Rest* and again the mood is one of leave-taking and setting forth, but Henry has progressed from **"Song 77"** in that he now is rid of his anguished desperation, expressing instead a matured sense of commitment to life.

> My dáughter's héavier. Líght léaves are flýing.
> Éverywhere in enórmous númbers túrkeys wíll be dý-
> ing
> and óther bírds, all their wíngs.
> They néver gréatly fléw. Díd they wísh to?
> I should knów. Off awáy sómewhere ónce I knéw
> súch thíngs.
>
> Or góod Ralph Hódgson back thén díd, or dóes.
> The mán is déad whom Éliot praísed. My praíse
> fóllows and flóws too láte.
> Fáll is gríevy, brísk. Téars behínd the eýes
> álmost fáll. Fall cómes to ús as a príze
> to róuse us tóward our fáte.
>
> My hóuse is máde of wóod and it's máde wéll,
> únlike ús. My hóuse is ólder than Hénry;
> that's faírly óld.
> Íf there were a míddle gróund between thíngs and the
> sóul
> or íf the ský resémbled móre the séa,
> I wouldn't háve to scóld
>
>   my héavy dáughter.

The poem shows a greater conformity to the metrical pattern with an average of two variations per stanza. Obviously the emotions expressed here are not as overpowering as those in **"Song 77."** The iambic movement predominates but with frequent trochaic alternations. Noteworthy is the contrasting trochaic and anapestic rhythms which attest to a feeling wavering between mournfulness and hopefulness. Strong stresses and spondees add emphasis to the song's argument, for example "light leaves" in the first line and the two monosyllables of the sixth line. The rhyming is more regular, and the full rhymes create a sense of finality to the song. The last stanza, however, has only one full

rhyme which reinforces the concluding note of tragic uncertainty. Berryman dispenses with the rhetoric of dictions used elsewhere in *The Dream Songs*; instead he speaks directly in his own voice. Indeed, the disintegration into the many voices of Henry gradually gives way to the poet's unified voice in the last two Books. As a result the syntax becomes less fragmentary and elliptical. Thus, if the dramatic mode creates the complex prosody of *77 Dream Songs*, Berryman's shift to the narrative mode accounts for the comparatively more regular prosody of *His Toy, His Dream, His Rest.* Still the music of *The Dream Songs* remains a discordant music of conflicting feelings and moods, combining as it does hope and despair, euphoria and depression. What Berryman's prosody manages to do is to convey the changing emotional states of his persona Henry, a man of many moods and selves.

* * *

The dramatic mode of characterization employed in *The Dream Songs* is another important aspect of Berryman's exploration of the personality of Henry. Berryman adopts the two characters Mr Bones and Mr Interlocutor from the American minstrel show in order to present the drama of opposites within the human personality, which helps form the individual. In the classic minstrel show Mr Bones is a white man in blackface who plays on bone castanets, hence his name. Since he represents a caricature of the Negro, he dresses extravagantly and behaves in a boisterous and eccentric way. Mr Interlocutor, on the other hand, remains in whiteface, and among the company of minstrels he alone wears a dress suit. As the leader of the show he conducts the program of songs, dances, and skits. The two minstrels Mr Bones and Mr Interlocutor often engage in comic dialogue and, as Carl Wittke notes in his history of American minstrelsy, their relation resembles that of the traditional clown and the ringmaster.[62] In both cases the purpose is to dramatize the inevitable conflict between the man of emotion and intuition and the man of reason and logic. That Berryman sees Mr Bones and Mr Interlocutor as personifications of two conflicting attitudes towards life is borne out by the fact that he originally intended to use Daniel Emmett's description of the Virginia Minstrels as epigraph to *77 Dream Songs*: "We were all end-men, and interlocutors".[63] The two minstrel characters, then, allow Berryman a means of rendering the endless dialogue between head and heart that goes on within every man.

Berryman's dualistic conception of character is probably influenced by his analysis of Stephen Crane's method of characterization. Like early Greek comedy, Berryman argues in his Crane study, Crane's characterization presents a contest between the *Alazon* or Impostor and the *Eiron* or Ironical Man, and every person has his own *Alazon* and *Eiron*.[64] This fact explains Crane's peculiar humor and pathos, whereby he can at once sympathize with and criticize his characters. Since the context for this contest between Impostor and Ironical Man is the individual fate, his characterization proceeds from a tragicomic vision of man's struggle with his own nature in situations of ordeal. Insofar as the Interlocutor expresses a common-sense and fatalistic attitude to life, he shares this trait with the Ironical Man. Mr Bones, on the other hand, shows a certain affinity with the Impostor through his assertion of his many needs and desires. As some critics notice, in Freudian terms the two minstrels represent the superego and the id, the norms of the conscience and the drives of the unconscious. Since Berryman hints in his interviews that Mr Interlocutor also personifies death, there is the further association with the perennial conflict between Eros, or the instincts of life, and Thanatos, or the instincts of death, that according to Freud's *Civilization and Its Discontents* rules over both the individual and the social life.

Donald Davie observes in his review of *The Freedom of the Poet* that the two minstrel characters can also be associated with the figures of Don Quixote and Sancho Panza.[65] In the posthumously published essay "The Freedom of the Don", written around 1960, Berryman describes Don Quixote as a figure of failed idealism, more specifically the ideal of Christian humility.[66] Like Crane's Impostor and the minstrel Mr Bones, he is a comic and suffering man of unruly desire who actually lives out his pretension to be a knight errant. The Don is accompanied by the representative of practical common-sense folk wisdom, yet another Ironical Man or Mr Interlocutor, who serves as squire to his master, the knight. Berryman insists that Cervantes is above all a moralist who in his characterization explores moral issues; the Don and Sancho are both foolish and wise in their own special ways. He concludes that, like all great literature, the subject of Cervantes' masterpiece is the quest for freedom, or the human process of maturation. The master and his servant undergo a series of disastrous adventures in the Spain of the late 16th century, a Spain that is in rapid decline as an imperial power. Don Quixote and Sancho Panza then represent two failed characters in a world of great changes, and the parallels with the 20th century are of course numerous.

As Haffenden notes, Berryman further illuminates his method of characterization for *The Dream Songs* in his review of W. H. Auden's collection of essays *The Dyer's Hand*.[67] Berryman comments especially on "Balaam and His Ass", which he calls "the showpiece of the book".[68] Auden here discusses the master-servant relation in literature: Don Quixote and Sancho Panza, King Lear and the Fool, Don Juan and Leporello. He draws the conclusion that only through the technique of the master-servant relation is it possible to "present artisti-

cally a human personality in its full depth, its inner dialectic, its self-disclosure and self-concealment".[69] The two characters are at once inseparable and antithetical, and so they can serve to dramatize different sides of the human personality. Auden thinks that this kind of characterization derives from the psychological insight that the human personality has two contradictory wills. On the one hand men want the freedom to live their own lives and on the other they wish to serve others, to have a *telos* in their lives. Absolute freedom ends, however, in solipsism, while total service constitutes a form of masochistic death-wish. The conflict between these two wills determines the fate of the individual. For Auden the two contradictory wills of man can only be reconciled in the Christian *Agape*: the love of God.

Since Mr Bones and Mr Interlocutor express such differing attitudes to life, they can personify the perennial division within the human personality. Rational and stoic realism is set against pathetic and comic idealism; in Auden's terms, the will to service interacts with the will to freedom. Perhaps, in an age of scepticism, the dialogue between these differing stances towards life offers the only valid way of treating the problem of values. However, as the dramatic mode of *77 Dream Songs* shifts to the narrative mode of *His Toy, His Dream, His Rest,* the two knights of the burnt cork, the quixotic Mr Bones and the common-sense Mr Interlocutor, merge into the picaro-quest character. Though the emphasis is no longer on contrasting character types but rather on the active engagement with life circumstances, the aim remains the same: the persona's attempt to overcome a strong sense of alienation. The picaro-quest character manifests both realistic and idealistic qualities in his confrontation with the conditions of contemporary life, and this confrontation takes on general implications, inasmuch as Henry represents a unique Everyman.

* * *

Critics have debated over the structure of *The Dream Songs,* speculating on why the poem is divided into Books and according to what principles of organization. Where some find an underlying logical scheme, whether numerology or Hegelian epistemology, others see only formlessness and incoherence. However, I think that to approach the problem of structure it is first necessary to understand, as in the case of *Leaves of Grass,* the implications of the title of the poem. In his 1967 *Life* interview Berryman declares that his dream songs are neither dreams nor songs but what he calls "episodes" in the persona's ongoing life story.[70] The poems are then not literal dreams, as most critics assume; instead they represent metaphorically Henry's sense of life, although many songs do transcribe actual dreams. Berryman employs Freudian techniques and the symbolism of dream analysis when it suits his purpose to do so, yet overall the method is not Freudian. Robert Lowell perceptively remarks in his review of *77 Dream Songs* that the songs are not "real dreams but a waking hallucination in which anything that might have happened to the author can be used at random".[71] This kind of waking hallucination freely mixes observations, memories, and sensations, and the intention is to record fully Henry's way of experiencing reality. There is a parallel here with the Gothic mode of writing where the real freely mingles with the fantastic.

The Olive Schreiner epigraph to *77 Dream Songs* further emphasizes Berryman's metaphorical understanding of the title to his work: "But there is another method", and the quoted passage goes on, "the method of the life we all lead".[72] The quotation comes from the Preface to Olive Schreiner's classic novel *The Story of an African Farm* (1883), where she discusses her notion of two methods in art. First she mentions the traditional one of imposing esthetic order and coherence on experience, but then she goes on to specify the method that she prefers: to present directly the dreamlike absurdity and mystery of life. Berryman probably connects his epigraph with Schreiner's later work *Dreams* (1890), in which she employs dream allegories to express her vision of life. If the Schreiner epigraph announces the method of *The Dream Songs*, it more specifically applies to the mode of life phantasmagoria in *77 Dream Songs,* a mode that the Preface to *The Story of an African Farm* graphically describes: "Here nothing can be prophesied. There is a strange coming and going of feet. Men appear, and act and re-act upon each other, and pass away. When the crisis comes the man who would fit it does not return. When the curtain falls no one is ready . . . and what the name of the play is no one knows".[73] However, as Henry's sense of reality gradually changes from that of victim of fate to that of active agent of fate, the narrative mode comes more to the fore.

When Berryman comments on the structure of *The Dream Songs* in the interview for *The Paris Review,* he immediately associates *The Dream Songs* with "Song of Myself", asserting that like Whitman's poem the unity of his own poem derives from the personality of the poet.[74] He repeats this view in *The Harvard Advocate* interview while he yet again expresses his disagreement with Eliot's theory of impersonality, since he believes rather in Whitman's personal kind of poetry. The personality of the poet then gives unity to *The Dream Songs,* and as a result the structure becomes essentially narrative: the record of the poet's life story, a record that grows increasingly autobiographical as the poem progresses. However, Berryman also declares in his *Paris Review* interview that the structuring of *The Dream Songs* into books follows loosely-held philosophical and theological notions.[75] The poem's structure therefore is at once freely developing and thematically

ordered, both improvisational and schematic. The classic minstrel show offers a possible analogue inasmuch as here free improvisation alternates with a fixed program of songs and comedy. The interlocutor directs the loosely ordered first part, whereas the second part, the olio, consists of variety acts whose highlight is the hilarious stump speech delivered by one of the endmen, Mr Bones or Mr Tambo.[76] The stump speech opens the olio, and it corresponds perhaps to the Opus Posthumous section of *His Toy, His Dream, His Rest.* Anyway, the two volumes of dream songs show marked structural affinities with the two-part format of the minstrel show. Insofar as the poet's ongoing life story assures the narrative progression of *The Dream Songs,* its characteristic open-endedness, the search for meaning and values, in terms of Berryman's philosophical and theological notions, structures the epic materials of the work. According to Miller the goal of the Whitmanian personal epic is what he calls, adopting Wallace Stevens phraseology, "the quest for a supreme Fiction",[77] that is, the quest for new systems of values that concern both the individual and society. In Berryman's own formulation this kind of poetry aspires to become a wisdom work.

As Haffenden shows in his *Critical Commentary,* Berryman uses several working models for the structure of *The Dream Songs.* What the models share, however, is the paradigm of a wisdom work, inasmuch as they all tell the story of an initiation into the truths of life. These paradigmatic stories then help Berryman structure his "Survival-epic", as he came to call it.[78] The structuring of the poem owes perhaps most to Joseph Campbell's classic study of the journey of initiation, *The Hero with a Thousand Faces.*[79] Campbell sees in the mythologies and the religions of mankind a common pattern that he calls the "monomyth", which concerns the hero's search for knowledge about life on the road of trials following the three-part sequence of departure, initiation, and return. The goal of the monomyth is the hero's winning of the power to shape his own destiny and his returning with this wisdom to his culture. In this sense the Books of *The Dream Songs* consist of a series of initiatory journeys that Henry undertakes in his search for wisdom. Archbishop Carrington's analysis of the liturgical structure of St Mark in his *According to Mark* further reinforces the concept of the monomyth with elements from the Christian calendar year.[80] Seasonal ritual therefore assumes some importance in *The Dream Songs.* The other structural models used by Berryman, *The Iliad* and *The Divine Comedy,* rule much of the imagery and the symbolism of the poem. They furthermore give resonance to recurring key situations where Henry identifies alternately with the warrior Achilles or the traveller Dante.

Valuable for perceiving the special nature of Berryman's poem is the perceptive description of the structure of *Leaves of Grass* given by Asselineau in The *Evolution of Walt Whitman*. This description also helps us define the structure of **The Dream Songs** since, in Berryman's opinion, *Leaves* carries out on a larger scale the structural principles of his acknowledged model "Song of Myself": "*Leaves of Grass* was slowly shaped by the interaction of two different processes, the one of instinctive growth and the other of rational and deliberate construction".[81] Analogously, the recording of the poet's sensibility, his successive states of mind, results in the unpredictable and improvisatory character of **The Dream Songs,** while his need to understand his experiences demands a more deliberate ordering through themes, imagery, and symbolism. This seems to supply the appropriate structure for a poem that aspires at once to be a work of life and a work of wisdom.

Notes

1. [*Writers at Work:*] *The Paris Review Interviews IV,* p. 307.

2. *The Paris Review Interviews IV,* p. 310.

3. *The Paris Review Interviews IV,* p. 322.

4. Meredith, "In Loving Memory of the Late Author of *The Dream Songs*", *Virginia Quarterly Review,* p. 72.

5. "My Whiskers Fly: An Interview with John Berryman", *Ivory Tower,* pp. 15-16.

6. "My Whiskers Fly: An Interview with John Berryman", *Ivory Tower,* p. 15.

7. Arpin, *The Poetry of John Berryman,* p. 83.

8. "An Interview with John Berryman", *The Harvard Advocate,* p. 8.

9. Haffenden, *The Life of John Berryman,* p. 254.

10. *W. B. Yeats: Selected Criticism,* ed. by Norman Jeffares (London: Macmillan, 1964), p. 267.

11. *The Paris Review Interviews IV,* pp. 309-310.

12. Haffenden, *The Life of John Berryman,* pp. 247-248.

13. Ernest C. Stefanik Jr., *John Berryman: A Descriptive Bibliography* (Pittsburg: Univ. of Pittsburg Press, 1974), pp. 185-186.

14. *The Paris Review Interviews IV,* p. 307. In his *American Quest for a Supreme Fiction: Whitman's Legacy in the Personal Epic* (Chicago: The Univ. of Chicago Press, 1979) James E. Miller Jr. recognized the importance of this essay for *The Dream Songs,* but he did not elaborate the consequences for the poem's poetics. Miller's study is hereafter cited as *The American Quest.*

15. *Start with the Sun: Studies in the Whitman Tradition* (Lincoln: Univ. of Nebraska Press, 1960).

16. *The American Quest,* Ch. 12.

17. *The American Quest,* Ch. 1.

18. "'Song of Myself': Intention and Substance", *The Freedom of the Poet,* p. 227.

19. "'Song of Myself': Intention and Substance", *The Freedom of the Poet,* p. 230.

20. *The Paris Review Interviews IV,* p. 308.

21. "'Song of Myself': Intention and Substance", *The Freedom of the Poet,* p. 230. Miller also emphasizes the importance of this statement for an understanding of *Leaves of Grass* (*The American Quest,* p. 38).

22. "'Song of Myself': Intention and Substance", *The Freedom of the Poet,* p. 233.

23. *The Evolution of Walt Whitman: The Creation of a Personality* (Cambridge: The Belknap Press, 1960), pp. 15-16.

24. *Walt Whitman: Prose Works 1892,* ed. by Floyd Stovall, Vol. II (New York: New York Univ. Press, 1964), p. 439. Gay Wilson Allen writes in his *The New Walt Whitman Handbook* (New York: New York Univ. Press, 1975) that Whitman thought of democracy not primarily in terms of a political system but more as an experiment "in the development of individuals" (p. 130), and that to this end he called for a new kind of literature.

25. *The Selected Writings of Ralph Waldo Emerson,* ed. by Brooks Atkinson (New York: The Modern Library, 1964), p. 320.

26. "'Song of Myself': Intention and Substance", *The Freedom of the Poet,* p. 230.

27. *Walt Whitman: Prose Works 1892,* Vol. II, p. 391.

28. *The American Quest,* p. 238.

29. Joseph Haas, "Who killed Henry Pussy-cat? I did, says John Berryman, with love & a poem, & for freedom O", *Chicago Daily News,* February 6-7, 1971, p. 5.

30. See Philip Rahv's essay "Paleface and Redskin", rpt. in *Literature and the Sixth Sense* (London: Faber and Faber, 1970), pp. 1-6.

31. See the introduction to Steven Gould Axelrod's *Robert Lowell: Life and Art* (Princeton: Princeton Univ. Press, 1978).

32. Laurence Lieberman, "The Expansional Poet: A Return to Personality", *The Yale Review,* LVII (1968), 264.

33. "The Expansional Poet: A Return to Personality", *The Yale Review,* p. 264.

34. See "From the Middle and Senior Generations", *The Freedom of the Poet,* p. 310 ff.

35. *The Freedom of the Poet,* p. 312.

36. "Problems of Decorum: *The Freedom of the Poet*", *The New York Times Book Review,* April 25, 1976, p. 4.

37. *The Paris Review Interviews IV,* p. 322.

38. "The Open Boat", *The Freedom of the Poet,* p. 183.

39. "The Open Boat", *The Freedom of the Poet,* pp. 183-184.

40. "One Answer to a Question: Changes", *The Freedom of the Poet,* p. 330.

41. In his *American Quest* Miller summarizes Whitman's reconception of the epic in these terms (p. 36): "a long poem whose narrative is of an interior rather than exterior action, with emphasis on successive mental and emotional states; on a subject or theme not special or superior but common and vital; . . . focusing not on an heroic or semidivine individual but on the poet himself as representative figure, comprehending and illuminating the age; and whose awareness, insight, being—rather than heroic actions—involve, however obliquely, the fate of the society, the nation, the human race".

42. Meredith, "In Loving Memory of the Late Author of *The Dream Songs*", *Virginia Quarterly Review,* p. 77.

43. See Randall Jarrell's *A Sad Heart at the Supermarket* (New York: Atheneum, 1967) and *Selected Essays of Delmore Schwartz.*

44. A. Alvarez, *Beyond All This Fiddle* (London: Allen Lane, 1968), Ch. 1.

45. *Stephen Crane,* pp. 278-290.

46. See "Thomas Nashe and *The Unfortunate Traveller*", *The Freedom of the Poet,* p. 9 ff.

47. *The Freedom of the Poet,* p. 13.

48. *The Freedom of the Poet,* p. 18.

49. "The Poetry of John Berryman", *The New York Review of Books,* p. 3.

50. *Notebook* (New York: Farrar, Straus & Giroux, 1970), p. 262.

51. Axelrod, *Robert Lowell: Life and Art,* p. 194.

52. *The Freedom of the Poet,* pp. 326-327.

53. *The Freedom of the Poet,* p. 327.

54. See *Escape from the Self,* Ch. 1.

55. "A Note on *Augie*", *The Freedom of the Poet,* p. 223.

56. *The Paris Review Interviews IV,* p. 308.

57. "My Whiskers Fly: An Interview with John Berryman", *Ivory Tower,* p. 16.

58. In his two remarkable essays "The Development of Anne Frank" and "The Mind of Isaac Babel" Berryman explores this problem of survival in a hostile world. See *The Freedom of the Poet,* pp. 91-106 and 115-128.

59. See *Blues People: Negro Music in White America* (New York: William Morrow and Comp., 1963), Chs. 6 and 7.

60. "In Loving Memory of the Late Author of *The Dream Songs*", *Virginia Quarterly Review,* pp. 74-75.

61. *Lucifer in Harness: American Meter, Metaphor, and Diction* (Princeton: Princeton Univ. Press, 1973), pp. 39-45.

62. *Tambo and Bones: A History of the American Minstrel Stage* (Durham: Duke Univ. Press, 1930), p. 138.

63. "An Interview with John Berryman", *The Harvard Advocate,* p. 6.

64. *Stephen Crane,* pp. 278-280.

65. "Problems of Decorum: *The Freedom of the Poet*", *The New York Times Book Review,* p. 5.

66. See "The Freedom of the Don", *The Freedom of the Poet,* p. 144 ff.

67. Haffenden, *A Critical Commentary,* p. 48.

68. "Auden's Prose", *The New York Review of Books,* I (August 29, 1963), 19.

69. W. H. Auden, *The Dyer's Hand* (London: Faber and Faber, 1975), p. 110.

70. Jane Howard, "Whiskey and Ink, Whiskey and Ink", *Life,* 63 (July 21, 1967), 70.

71. "The Poetry of John Berryman", *The New York Review of Books,* p. 3.

72. Olive Schreiner, *The Story of an African Farm* (London: Hutchinson & Co., 1883), p. iii.

73. Schreiner, *The Story of an African Farm,* pp. iii-iv.

74. *The Paris Review Interviews IV,* p. 307.

75. *The Paris Review Interviews IV,* p. 307.

76. See Robert C. Toll, *Blacking-Up: The Minstrel Show in Nineteenth Century America* (New York: Oxford Univ. Press, 1974), pp. 51-56.

77. Miller, *The American Quest,* Ch. 12.

78. Haffenden, *A Critical Commentary,* p. 45.

79. Joseph Campbell, *The Hero with a Thousand Faces* (New York: Pantheon Books, 1949).

80. Philip Carrington, *According to Mark: A Running Commentary on the Oldest Gospel* (Cambridge: Cambridge Univ. Press, 1960).

81. Asselineau, *The Evolution of Walt Whitman,* p. 13.

Bibliography

I Works by John Berryman

"Auden's Prose". Rev. of *The Dyer's Hand,* by W. H. Auden. *The New York Review of Books,* I (August 29, 1963), 19.

Berryman's Sonnets. New York: Farrar, Straus & Giroux, 1967.

Delusions, Etc. of John Berryman. New York: Farrar, Straus & Giroux, 1972.

The Dispossessed. New York: William Sloane Associates, 1948.

The Dream Songs. New York: Farrar, Straus & Giroux, 1969.

Five Young American Poets. Ed. James Laughlin. Norfolk: New Directions, 1940, pp. 42-80.

The Freedom of the Poet. New York: Farrar, Straus & Giroux, 1976.

"From *The Black Book*". *Poetry,* 75 (January 1950), 192-196.

Henry's Fate and Other Poems, 1967-1972. Ed. John Haffenden. London: Faber and Faber, 1978.

His Toy, His Dream, His Rest. London: Faber and Faber, 1969.

Homage to Mistress Bradstreet. With Pictures by Ben Shan. New York: Farrar, Straus & Cudahy, 1956.

Love & Fame. London: Faber and Faber, 1971.

Poems. The Poet of the Month Series, ed. James Laughlin. Norfolk: New Directions, 1942.

Recovery/Delusions Etc. of John Berryman. New York: Dell Publishing Co., 1973.

77 Dream Songs. New York: Farrar, Straus & Giroux, 1964.

"The State of American Writing, 1948: Seven Questions". *Partisan Review,* 15 (1948), 855-894.

Stephen Crane. The American Men of Letters Series. New York: William Sloane Associates, 1950.

II Works on John Berryman

Alvarez, A. *Beyond All This Fiddle.* London: Allen Lane, 1968.

Arpin, Gary Q. *John Berryman: A Reference Guide.* Reference Guides in Literature No. 8. Boston: G.K. Hall & Co., 1976.

———. *The Poetry of John Berryman.* Port Washington: Kennikat Press, 1978.

Bailey, John. "On John Berryman". In *Contemporary Poetry in America: Essays and Interviews.* Ed. Robert Boyers. New York: Schocken Books, 1974, pp. 59-77.

Barbera, Jack V. "Shape and Flow in *The Dream Songs*". *Twentieth-Century Literature,* 22 (1976), 146-162.

Berg, Martin. "An Interview with John Berryman: A Truly Gentle Man Tightens and Paces". *The Minnesota Daily,* January 20, 1971, pp. 10, 14-15, 17.

Berndt, Susan G. *Berryman's Baedeker: The Epigraphs to The Dream Songs.* Rook Critical Monographs 2. Derry: The Rook Society, 1976.

Bewley, Marius. "Poetry Chronicle". Rev. of *Berryman's Sonnets. The Hudson Review,* XX (1967), 500-504.

Bogan, Louise. "Verse". Rev. of *77 Dream Songs. The New Yorker,* 40 (November 7, 1964), 238-243.

Brans, Jo. "Bones Bound, Henry Hero: A Reading of Berryman's First Dream Song". *John Berryman Studies,* 1, No. 4 (Fall 1975), 12-16.

Browne, Michael Denis. "Henry Fermenting: Debts to *The Dream Songs*". *The Ohio Review,* 15 (1974), 75-87.

Ciardi, John. "The Researched Mistress". Rev. of *Homage to Mistress Bradstreet. Saturday Review,* XL (March 23, 1957), 36-37.

Conarroe, Joel. *John Berryman: An Introduction to the Poetry.* Columbia Introductions to Twentieth-Century American Poetry. New York: Columbia Univ. Press, 1977.

"Congested Funeral: Berryman's New Dream Songs". Rev. of *His Toy, His Dream, His Rest. The Times Literary Supplement,* June 26, 1969, p. 680.

Connelley, Kenneth. "Berryman Henry Pussycat, He Come Home Good". Rev. of *His Toy, His Dream, His Rest. The Yale Review,* 58 (Spring 1969), 419-427.

Davie, Donald. "Problems of Decorum: *The Freedom of the Poet*". Rev. of *The Freedom of the Poet. The New York Times Book Review,* April 25, 1976, pp. 3-4.

Dodsworth, Martin. "John Berryman: An Introduction". In *The Survival of Poetry: A Contemporary Survey.* Ed. Martin Dodsworth. London: Faber and Faber, 1970, pp. 100-132.

Donoghue, Denis. "Berryman's Long Dream". Rev. of *His Toy, His Dream, His Rest. Art International,* XIII (March 20, 1969), 61-64.

Haas, Joseph. "Who killed Henry Pussy-cat? I did, says John Berryman, with love, & a poem, & for freedom O". *Chicago Daily News,* February 6-7, 1971, pp. 4-5.

Haffenden, John. *John Berryman: A Critical Commentary.* New York: New York Univ. Press, 1980.

———. *The Life of John Berryman.* Boston: Routledge & Kegan Paul, 1982.

Heyen, William. "John Berryman: A Memoir and an Interview". *The Ohio Review,* 15 (Winter 1970), 46-65.

Howard, Jane. "Whiskey and Ink, Whiskey and Ink". *Life,* 63 (July 21, 1967), 67-76.

Jarrell, Randall. "Verse Chronicle". Rev. of *The Dispossessed. The Nation,* CLXVII (1948), 80-81.

Kostelanetz, Richard. "Conversation with Berryman". *Massachusetts Review,* 11 (Spring 1970), 340-347.

Kunitz, Stanley. "No Middle Flight". Rev. of *Homage to Mistress Bradstreet. Poetry,* 90 (July 1957), 244-249.

Lieberman, Laurence. "The Expansional Poet: A Return to Personality". Rev. of *Berryman's Sonnets. The Yale Review,* LVII (1968), 258-271.

Linebarger, J. M. *John Berryman.* Twayne's United States Authors Series 244. Boston: Twayne Publishers, 1974.

Lowell, Robert. "The Poetry of John Berryman". Rev. of *77 Dream Songs. New York Review of Books,* II (May 28, 1964), 2-3.

Martz, William J. *John Berryman.* University of Minnesota Pamphlets of American Writers No. 85. Minneapolis: Univ. of Minnesota Press, 1969.

Mazzaro, Jerome. "Berryman's Dream World". Rev. of *His Toy, His Dream, His Rest. Kenyon Review,* XXXI (Spring 1969), 259-263.

McClelland, David et al. "An Interview with John Berryman". *The Harvard Advocate,* 103 (Spring 1969), 4-9.

Meredith, William. "Henry Tasting All the Secret Bits of Life: Berryman's *Dream Songs.*" Rev. of *77 Dream Songs. Wisconsin Studies in Contemporary Literature,* 6 (Spring 1965), 27-33.

———. "In Loving Memory of the Late Author of *The Dream Songs.*" *Virginia Quarterly Review,* 49 (1973), 70-78.

———. "Swan Songs". Rev. of *Love & Fame* and *Delusions, Etc. Poetry,* 122 (1970), 98-103.

Miller, Jr., James E. *The American Quest for a Supreme Fiction: Whitman's Legacy in the Personal Epic.* Chicago: The Univ. of Chicago Press, 1979.

Nims, John Frederick. "Homage in Measure to Mr Berryman". Rev. of *Homage to Mistress Bradstreet. The Prairie Schooner,* XXXII (Spring 1958), 1-7.

Pearson, Gabriel. "John Berryman: Poet as Medium". Rev. of *77 Dream Songs. The Review,* XV (April 1965), 3-17.

Porterfield, Jo R. "The Melding of a Man: Berryman, Henry, and the Ornery Mr Bones". *Southwest Review,* LVIII (Winter 1973), 30-46.

Simpson, Eileen. *Poets in Their Youth: A Memoir.* New York: Random House, 1982.

Sisson, Jonathan. "My Whiskers Fly: An Interview with John Berryman". *Ivory Tower* (October 3, 1966), 14-18, 34-35.

Stefanik, Jr., Ernest C. *John Berryman: A Descriptive Bibliography.* Pittsburg Series in Bibliography. Pittsburg: Univ. of Pittsburg Press, 1974.

Wasserstrom, William. "Cagey John: Berryman as Medicine Man". Rev. of *77 Dream Songs. Centennial Review,* 72 (Summer 1968), 334-354.

Writers at Work: The Paris Review Interviews. Ed. George Plimpton. Fourth Series. New York: The Viking Press, 1976.

III OTHER SECONDARY SOURCES

Allen, Gay Wilson. *The New Walt Whitman Handbook.* New York: New York Univ. Press, 1975.

Asselineau, Roger. *The Evolution of Walt Whitman: The Creation of a Personality.* Cambridge: The Belknap Press, 1960.

Auden, W. H. *The Dyer's Hand.* London: Faber and Faber, 1975.

Axelrod, Steven Gould. *Robert Lowell: Life and Art.* Princeton: Princeton Univ. Press, 1978.

Campbell, Joseph. *The Hero with a Thousand Faces.* The Bollingen Series XVII. New York: Pantheon Books, 1949.

Carrington, Philip. *According to Mark: A Running Commentary on the Oldest Gospel.* Cambridge: Cambridge Univ. Press, 1960.

The Selected Writings of Ralph Waldo Emerson. Ed. Brooks Atkinson. New York: The Modern Library, 1964.

Fussell, Edwin. *Lucifer in Harness: American Meter, Metaphor, and Diction.* Princeton: Princeton Univ. Press, 1973.

Jones, LeRoi. *Blues People: Negro Music in White America.* New York: William Morrow and Comp., 1963.

Lowell, Robert. *Notebook.* New York: Farrar, Straus & Giroux, 1970.

Malkoff, Karl. *Escape from the Self: A Study in Contemporary American Poetry and Poetics.* New York: Columbia Univ. Press, 1977.

Miller, Jr., James E. *The American Quest for a Supreme Fiction: Whitman's Legacy in the Personal Epic.* Chicago: The Univ. of Chicago Press, 1979.

Rahv, Philip. "Paleface and Redskin". In *Literature and the Sixth Sense.* London: Faber and Faber, 1970, pp. 1-6.

Schreiner, Olive. *The Story of an African Farm.* London: Hutchinson & Co., 1883.

The Selected Essays of Delmore Schwartz. Eds. Donald A. Dike and David H. Zucker. Chicago: The Univ. of Chicago Press, 1970.

Toll, Robert C. *Blacking-Up: The Minstrel Show in Nineteenth Century America.* New York: Oxford Univ. Press, 1974.

Walt Whitman: Prose Works 1892, Vol. II: Collect and Other Prose. Ed. Floyd Stovall. New York: New York Univ. Press, 1964.

Wittke, Carl. *Tambo and Bones: A History of the American Minstrel Stage.* Durham: Duke Univ. Press, 1930.

Kathe Davis (essay date winter 1985)

SOURCE: Davis, Kathe. "'Honey Dusk Do Sprawl': Does Black Minstrel Dialect Obscure *The Dream Songs?*" *Language and Style* 18, no. 1 (winter 1985): 30-45.

[*In the following essay, Davis considers the function of the black minstrel dialect in* The Dream Songs, *particularly in the poem "Big Buttons."*]

> But nakedness, woolen massa, concerns an innermost
>   atom.
> If that remains concealed, what does the bottom mat-
>   ter?
>
> —Wallace Stevens, "Nudity at the Capital"

John Berryman's **The Dream Songs** do not seem as strange now as they did at publication, when reviewers called them "garbled" and "confusing, impenetrable, distracting."[1] Strangeness is the judgment of an audience, and audiences learn and assimilate. The Songs have been rendered more comfortably familiar by repeated readings, by three introductory volumes on Berryman,[2] and by twenty years of scholarship (**77 Dream Songs** appeared in 1964, and the second volume of Songs, **His Toy, His Dream, His Rest,** in 1968).

Still, a great deal remains to be explained. It was the language of the **Songs** that most startled and bewildered readers. Berryman's style was perceived as so unusual as to constitute a separate "language": James Dickey felt at **The Dream Songs'** appearance "that the reader feels distinctly that he is having to learn—is, exhilaratingly, learning—a new language, a kind of Berryman Esperanto."[3] More recently, Joel Conarroe has discussed "Henryspeech, that queer language peculiar to this work" (116). Yet, though this "language" is the feature of the **Songs** probably most often mentioned in general, it is oddly enough the feature most neglected in its particulars. The blackface dialect has been widely mentioned, partly because it is the vehicle for the second most important character in **The Dream Songs,** Henry's antagonist and "friend, never named, who addresses him as Mr. Bones and variants thereof" (as Berryman explains in his introductory note to the second volume of **Songs**). But the dialect, though regularly named as a major factor in the **Songs'** oddity and difficulty, also has not been defined or described. Like the language of the **Songs** as a whole, it seems to be taken for granted even while being posed as problematic. Usually it is seen as part of Berryman's larger obscurantist tactics in **The Dream Songs.** In this view, the dialect represents the incomprehensible, the incoherent, the inarticulate, set forth in the poem as a reflection of or response to the incoherence and disorder of the modern world. As William Meredith says, "The world is acutely perceived, in all its wonderful incomprehensibility, in this dialect."[4] But the dialect's obscurity can scarcely convey this significance if it does not exist, and it does not: the blackface dialect obscures nothing in **The Dream Songs.**

Berryman himself felt that the dialect made the **Songs** simpler. He says of the "narrator":

> I didn't let him use fancy language. That was out. It didn't go with the blackface business. The diction is very limited. He doesn't have the language to discuss, for example, Heisenberg's theory of indeterminacy, or scholarly questions, or modern painting.[5]

Recognition that the dialect does not itself represent problems in comprehension, as I wish to demonstrate here, will permit us to move forward in our understanding of what the poem really aims at. Specifically, after glancing at the critical consensus on the role of blackface dialect in **The Dream Songs,** I would like to look at the dialect itself, to consider what it actually consists of and what purposes, as language, it does serve. **"Dream Song 2," "Big Buttons, Cornets: the advance,"** the first and in many respects the most important of the dialect Songs, provides the best illustration, and I will examine it in detail.

I should make it clear that I am not questioning the large importance of the black minstrelsy motif in the Songs. The Mr Bones friend (or Tambo, as Conarroe designates him) signals and expresses Berryman's identification with oppressed peoples in general and American blacks in particular; his social conscience, suffered as personal anguish; his demand that we acknowledge the whole Lawrentian darkness: sex, the unconscious, death. These and other thematic significances have been dealt with in detail, and sometimes very well, in several articles and again in the recent Berryman books. What I dispute is simply that the dialect creates linguistic difficulties in the *Songs,* which difficulties themselves serve thematic purposes.

I

A 1968 article by William Wasserstrom was the first to consider the dialect in any detail, and seems to have set the tone for later discussions.[6] Though good on the duplicity of minstrel-show irony, Wasserstrom considers the dialect deliberately incomprehensible—to whites—because it is a (sociologically motivated) code, "a kind of speech devised in order to hide true meaning from the Man, the enemy" (343). Therefore "its white (manifest) sense will be one thing and its black (latent) sense another" (344). He equates this sort of encoded or hidden meaning with the disguise of dreams: "In minstrelsy, then, Berryman found an exact analogue to dream" (344). But he then goes on to confuse nonrational order with disorder, hidden meaning with lack of meaning:

> it is Berryman's distinction that he alone plunges deep into some public sources of the primitive American imagination in search of a tradition which represents long immersion in and mastery of disjunction and disorder.
>
> (344)

As **"Dream Song 2"** illustrates, says Wasserstrom, this "disjunction and disorder" is mastered at the cost of comprehensibility:

> Cakewalk and masque, blues and slang—these bits and echoes do indeed banish meaning. Berryman's sense is virtually gone. Paradoxically, its very disappearance must be taken as a sign of the poet's achievement.
>
> (343)

The fullest elaboration of the idea that the dialect is thematically functional because incomprehensible appears in the influential *TLS* article, "The Life of the Modern Poet." According to that anonymous critic, Berryman "develops an expressive style out of the inarticulateness that fascinated him and that belongs to our time."[7] The dialect is said to express "Berryman's fears about the division of his own life between the eloquent public figure and the inarticulate hidden self." Both dialect and inarticulateness are ascribed to Henry, who is seen as having behind him Henry Johnson, the literally faceless hero of Stephen Crane's story "The Monster," who "talks in the deepest Southern accent,

with no regard for grammar."[8] But that accent is not heard in *The Dream Songs*—not, anyway, to the extent of obscuring anything.

II

Whatever real obscurity *The Dream Songs* manifest is far more largely a function of syntax than of diction. To the small extent that diction does present problems, it is not the diction of dialect.

Quantitatively, the dialect makes up only a small portion of the language of the Songs. The Songs that do use dialect mostly use it minimally, and even those few Songs that consist entirely of dialect are not incomprehensible on that account. There are only seventy-two Songs that use dialect, even including those that use only a single blackface word. Fewer than half of the dialect Songs (only thirty) use more than three or four dialect words. Only five Songs are entirely or almost entirely in dialect.

This small percentage might still constitute a significant barrier to understanding if the dialect were radically obscure, if it did "banish meaning" or even significantly hide it. But it does not. No commentator until now has felt obliged to specify the dialect's characteristics. The reason is the same one that accounts for the universal recognition of the dialect in the first place: we already know it. This is the stylized dialect of literary convention, bearing only a tangential relationship to actual black English.[9] As Meredith puts it, "Henry, being only an imaginary Negro, speaks mostly in blackface parody . . . the vaudeville dialect of Two Black Crows and Stepin Fetchit" (30). From Amos 'n' Andy and other latter-day derivatives of the minstrel show as well as from *Huckleberry Finn,* "Uncle Remus," and countless other popular stories, we are as familiar with this dialect as with any other literary convention. Now, Berryman's use of it may seem questionable if that literary and stage tradition is seen to represent a history of white expropriation.[10] Berryman made it clear that he meant the dialect to express himself as "imaginary Negro" in the same sense that he is "The Imaginary Jew" in his short story of that title, going beyond mere sympathy to an imaginative identification with oppressed peoples. (The story is based on an actual episode in which Berryman was unable to prove to a hostile audience that he was not Jewish. Similarly, while an undergraduate at Columbia, Berryman told a classmate that he had Negro blood, and then was apparently believed more fully and widely than he was quite prepared for.)[11] But Conarroe, for instance, feels that however "well-intended," Berryman's use of this "inflammatory" language is naive at best (104). On the other hand, the dialect's debased past need not limit its potential for more sensitive use. As Sterling Brown points out, "because conventionalized dialect poetry has these faults ["A few pat phrases, a few stock situations and characteristics, some misspelling"], dialect does not have to be dismissed as capable of only two stops, humor and pathos" (42). And the original Jim Crow was not a white imitation, but a crippled black man, as Arpin reminds us, like Rimbaud's "nigger" "one of 'the race that sang under torture'" (75).

In any case, Berryman was quite clearly not "operating in the dark" (Conarroe, 104), entirely ingenuous or ignorant of all negative implications. To the extent that the friend, in speaking the dialect, seems to partake of the Uncle Tom tradition associated with it, Henry fiercely opposes him: "—Uncle Tom, / sweep shut yo mouf" (**"DS [Dream Song] 60"**). The dialect can be depicted in print by varying degrees of variation from "standard" English, as the examples cited by Brown and others show: compare the lines from Paul Dunbar's "Song of Summer,"

> Tu'key gobbler gwine 'roun' blowin'
> Gwine 'roun' gibbin sass an' slack
>
> (Brown, 35)

or James Edwin Campbell's "dialect near to the Gullah speech of South Carolina" (Brown, 36):

> He put on he specs an' he use beeg wu'ds,
> He feel dee pu's [pulse] den he look mighty wise;
>
> (37)

The forms Berryman uses are never this extreme. The relative sparseness and the minor nature of the variations that constitute his "dialect" combine with our familiarity with the convention in general to minimize difficulties.

A look at these changes, at the features of the dialect as Berryman presents them, will demonstrate their minimal interference in understanding. The deviations can be handily categorized as "grammatical," in the schoolroom sense, lexical, and syntactic. In the first category, by far the most common feature is disagreement of number between subject and verb, which appears in more than fifty Songs: "I is," "you am," "we awaits," "Pascal drop in," and so on. (Related "ungrammaticalities" include the use of the present participle for the present tense form of the verb: "he wishing," "I figuring," "they placing." Another way to read these constructions is as missing the auxiliary "is," and the absence of some form of "to be" creates other "dialect" locutions: "*Some lady you make,*" "we free," "You [are] both.")

Be is also substituted for *is* sometimes: "what be wrong" and "he be cross." A redundant *be* is interpolated in one case: "if be you cares to say." Miscellaneous other unconventional but familiar verb uses sprinkle the Songs: "Man, I been thirsty," "he apologize," and "I see sank."

Less often than the verbs, other parts of speech are altered. Adjectives are used a few times instead of adverbs: "heavy bored," "this did actual happen," "he mutter spiffy," and "Freud was some wrong." "Them" is used instead of "those" half a dozen times, as in "them blue depths."

Sometimes pronouns are in the wrong case: "most of we," "us do," "will us." One nonstandard pronoun is used, "theirselves"; and twice reflexive pronouns are used colloquially: "I wish I had me some" and "fold us down."

One of the chief—and most familiar—features of Berryman's dialect is elision: dropped letters, especially the final -*g* ("soundin," "givin," "blowin," "totterin"), and run-together words. The dialect Songs are characterized mainly by these smaller omissions, indicated sometimes by an apostrophe, sometimes just by spelling. Several familiar instances are used, mostly just once each: "le's," "ev'ybody" and "yo," "ol'," "I don know" and "don'," "oursel's," "mysef," "agin," "jus," "spose," "o" and "a" (for "of"), "hafta," "donno," "gotta," and "gonna" (for a total of twenty-one). Some less familiar and consequently more questionable instances do occur, such as, "what's all about?" "wait'" (= "waiting"), "blinds'" (= "blinds is"), "'low" (= "allow"), and "thass."

Several other kinds of special (but conventional) pronunciation are also indicated by spelling: *de, dere,* and *dat* for *the, there,* and *that,* *wif* for *with,* and such variants as "afore," "sah," and "they'm."

Lexically, the dialect supplies even less that is out of the ordinary in the language of **The Dream Songs.** The special vocabulary of black speech (of either this century or last) might have been the source of obscurity as well as of real interest, had Berryman truly utilized it.[12] But he uses only terms that have been so completely assimilated into general speech as to be identifiable now as at most "colloquial": "ofays," "ornery," "clobber," "bugs um all," "cop my promise," "on the take." The most clearly blackface terms are "ol' Marster" and "we coons" in **"DS 51."**

The blackface Songs do often provide the occasion for Berryman neologisms, but these, while entertaining, offer no real resistance to understanding. Not genuinely new coinages, these are just slightly novel forms, or applications of familiar words: "so long agone," "too advancer" and "muching of which," "selving" (for "self"), "worsing" (for "worse"), and "othering" (for "others"), "choppering," and "horribles" (as a noun).[13]

Invented compound words hold real neologistic potential, but Berryman simply does not use them with a Joycean ingenuity, nor do they produce Joycean difficulties for the reader. The Songs offer only: "utility-man," "writer-man," and "pro-man"; "un-budge," "will-like," "excited-like," and "sick-house." The closest to obscure are two words that do not readily fit any classification: "backhanders" and "cave" used as a verb.[14] Apart from those, the vocabulary that can be laid at the door of dialect simply does not pose a problem.

Finally, there is syntax. Berryman's famous "crumpled" syntax is the greatest single source of obscurity in *The Dream Songs* in general. Some of the Songs using dialect words also display an unmistakably nonstandard syntax, but in locutions distinct from the dialectal vocabulary. In some half-dozen other blackface Songs, strange and difficult syntax incorporates dialects terms, but cannot itself be attributed to dialect (see **"DS 6," "11," "37," "114,"** and **"126"**). In those cases in which syntax is most clearly designed to achieve a dialect effect, it creates no obstacles to comprehension: "is stuffed, de world, wif feeding girls" (**"DS 4"**), and "Pinetop he . . ." (**"DS 68"**).[15]

III

If the dialect consists of such minor and nonobscurantist deviations from the norm, and if these appear so seldom, then what accounts for the apparently general impression of the blackface speech's disruptive power?

For one thing, in Berryman's hands the dialect displays much more varied features than quantity alone would suggest (as the examples above indicate), and that may contribute to the sense of the dialect's richness. Distribution is another important factor: few as the dialect words are, they are widely distributed. At least one or two appear in thirty-three of the first *77 Dream Songs* (and thirty-nine in the remaining *Songs*). Of those thirty-three, twenty use more than the isolated word or two, while only ten of the later Songs do, so that the dialect is concentrated toward the beginning of the book. Of the five Songs almost entirely in dialect, four are in the first seventy-seven (**"DS 2," "40," "60,"** and **"68"**; **"DS 220"** is the remaining one). Even within *77 Dream Songs,* the concentration is toward the beginning: of the first fifteen Songs, only four do not have at least an arguable trace. The upshot of all this is that the reader receives an initial impression of heavier dialect-use than the book really sustains. This impression begins with the second Song, which is almost entirely dialectal. When the Bones friend appears again in **"DS 4"** speaking dialect, he leads us to expect that half the Songs will represent him. While that expectation is not met—he does not reappear until Song 13—it lingers on. It is probably reinforced by the conspicuous dialect-features of the next Song, **"DS 5"** ("at odds wif de world . . .") and the similar verbal gestures of **"DS 6"** and **"7,"** and **"9"** through **"11."**

Finally, the impact is strong of those five all-dialect Songs (and the few others which use dialect fairly

heavily, such as **"DS 20,"** which sounds like the friend speaking, though it does not identify him: "When worst things got, how was you? Steady on?"). Although the dialect here is not any more obscure than elsewhere, the existence of whole patches of (more or less) unbroken dialect again helps to create a sense of the blackface speech's importance in the *Songs* as a whole.

IV

If the dialect does not obscure the *Songs,* for thematic purposes or otherwise, that leaves the question of what function it does serve, if any. It helps to create a character, of course (though its use is not restricted to the unnamed friend). It is one element among many in the complex of "deviant" or unusual language in the *Songs,* and serves the same general purposes. Arpin, for instance, considers that the "linguistic stew of the style" indicates Berryman's "important adaptation of the American tongue to the Symbolists' concern with the creation of a new language" (76-77). Certainly Berryman's experiments reflect his faith in the power of language not only to communicate, but also to shape our perceptions and hence our worlds. But the larger question of the function of his style as a whole deserve separate discussion, and is really beyond the scope of this essay. The function—*as language*—of the dialect specifically has not been discussed.

Robert Pinsky, alone among critics on Berryman, feels that the stylistic function of the dialect outweighs thematic ones: "that dialect is more a means toward a style than an end in itself (evoking the American South, or the stage, or Blacks)."[16] Comparing Berryman to Thomas Hardy and John Crowe Ransom, Pinsky maintains that all three poets employ a deflationary style to permit themselves to get away with a more grandiose rhetoric that they need to express the true breadth and depth of their emotional burdens, particularly their shared sense of loss. The "low" diction not only counterbalances loftier speech, however, but is also used in its place, to produce alternatives to the maudlin or bathetic. "In all them time" (**"DS 29"**), for instance, is superior to the failed drama or simple triteness of the standard speech it alters, "in all that time."

In general the dialect, with the whole comic tradition it invokes, is part of the bitter comedy that suffuses the entire *Dream Songs.* Linebarger compares their "seriocomic . . . tone" to that of black humor and the Theatre of the Absurd. He finds one explanation of that tone in Berryman's discussion of Stephen Crane's irony. Berryman introduces the antagonists of early Greek comedy, the Alazon or Imposter, and the Eiron or "ironical Man" (now familiar to us all, thanks to Northrop Frye). In Berryman's words, "after vauntings and pretensions, the Alazon is routed by the man who affects to be a fool" (Linebarger, 123). Now the ironic posture is of course defensive as well as offensive, and the doubleness of the role may well reflect a corresponding doubleness of attitude on the part of the author. As Berryman says of Crane, "this author is simultaneously *at war with* the people he creates and *on their side*—and displays each of these attitudes so forcibly that the reader feels he is himself being made a fool of" (Linebarger, 123; Berryman's emphasis).

If anything, the entire comment applies more accurately to Berryman than to Crane. Tambo plays the fool to undercut all pretension. But Henry as Mr Bones also plays a different sort of fool, though one with no less ironic force: the Prufrockian figure who is at once clown and dandy. Berryman's discussions of Eliot leave no doubt of the importance of Prufrock for him, and the antecedents of this aspect of the clown figure can be seen in the Symbolist and Decadent tradition of the dandy, the Wildean figure whose concern with perfecting his language and polishing his forms leads him to disdain being earnest about anything so quotidian as life. Like Prufrock, Henry stands at the border where clown merges into aesthete: "Mr Bones, you a clown" (**"DS 199"**). But uniquely he also faces *another* clown, who pierces aesthetic pretension and sardonically insists on the claims of life (and death).

More specifically, the dialect permits Berryman certain puns, or provides an excuse for them. For instance "will-like" in **"DS 366"** would seem by itself to mean "willful" or "strong-willed," but the context makes clear that another sort of will is in question: "You sound will-like, / a testament & such"—while the first meaning lingers as a pertinent suggestion. More rarely the dialect is the vehicle for almost Joycean portmanteaus: "I spose you got a lessen up your slave" (**"DS 84"**), "Back to lurk!" (**"DS 232"**), and "Muscle my whack" (**"DS 273"**) (changed in two stages from "break my back," as the hand-written first draft shows).[17] In **"DS 185,"** "The more I lessen to, the bore I hears," and in the same Song "blink" is substituted for "think": "Like it makes you blink, Mr Bones, of was & will?"—so that in effect both words are operative (and the pun on "will" continues).

Subject-verb disagreement also serves substantive functions. Like Berryman's famous "sliding" pronoun, a singular subject used with a plural verb, or vice versa, can indicate both the multiplicity of personality within one person, and the merger of personalities, which Berryman believed could be achieved through the power of a Whitmanian empathy. ("Both *Homage to Mistress Bradstreet* and *The Dream Songs* are built around the notion that individual identities can merge," Berryman said,[18] and his early **"The Ball Poem"** suggests the genesis of that conviction: "I am everywhere, / I suffer and move, my mind and my heart move / With all that move me.")

The plurality of selves within a single person suggested more or less explicitly by a locution like "Henry are baffled," is suggested less forcibly by lines like "He sleep up a short storm. / He wolf his meals, lamb-warm" (**"DS 96"**). Similarly, "you asks," "you offers," and "you has" reinforce the singularity of "you."

Finally, in a limited way the dialect serves Berryman's penchant for elision and ellipsis, for leaving things out. This tendency itself seems to have had several motives or impulses behind it. The main one is simply economy, and its corresponding emphasis on what is really important: "Write as short as you can, / in order, of what matters" (**"DS 54"**). Part of the dialect's appeal is that, like criminal argot, and for some of the same reasons, it is concise and pungent.[19]

V

Dream Song 2, **"Big Buttons, Cornets: the advance,"** is important because of its place at the head of the Songs and because of what it says. It provides a context for the use of dialect and, by implication, much of its rationale. The blackface epigraph to *The Dream Songs,* "Go in, brack man, de day's yo' own," comes from Carl Wittke's *Tambo and Bones,*[20] the early standard history of the minstrel show, which uses the same epigraph (become ironic "in the shift from front of book to front of book," as Gary Arpin points out [75]). Berryman's own copy of the book is only lightly marked and annotated, though he has jotted some dozen page numbers on the inside back jacket-flap. One of these is "Rice 175," the "Daddy Rice who sang and jumped 'Jim Crow' in Louisville in 1828 (London, 1836 and later)," as Berryman describes him in dedicating the Song to his memory. But that reference yields a history which, however intrinsically interesting, adds nothing to our understanding of *The Dream Songs* (any more than does Wasserstrom's recapitulation of it).

However, another passage in Wittke explains a good deal, and particularly the title:

> Whenever the minstrels came to town, their arrival was heralded by a street parade, in which the "silver" or "gold cornet band," gorgeously attired in colorful coats and trousers, big brass buttons and striking hats, led the procession through the streets of the town to the theatre, followed by the entire company.
>
> (145)

I had already marked this passage in my own copy of Wittke when I found confirmation of Berryman's use of it among his working papers: a note saying "The Parade (p. 145)" with "(poster, advance)" written immediately underneath. A few sketchy notations on the minstrel show format appear separately on the same sheet. An early draft of the poem shows that Berryman deleted "skyrockets" from the original title.

This poem, then, is the advance for and heralds the advance of the procession of Songs and characters that follows. It introduces the blackface friend (and the multitude of themes associated with him) just as Song 1 introduces Henry. Against **"DS 1"**'s (remembered or imagined) prelapsarian Henry singing in his Edenic tree, Song 2 sets fallen (but struggling) Henry in his hole: hell, grave, and womb.

Song of Myself supplies a passage which, given Whitman's centrality for Berryman,[21] may be fairly read as another gloss on the title:

> With music strong I come, with my cornets and my
>   drums,
> I play not marches for accepted victors only, I play
>   marches for conquered and slain persons.
>
> (Section 18)

The section continues in this vein, including the phrase "I beat and pound for the dead." Berryman's allusion is an implicit statement of intention, lavishly fulfilled in the Songs.

The first stanza of **"DS 2"** has less dialect than the following two. If it is obscure, it is because the entire stanza is an elaborate pun, like Cummings's extended double entendre: "She being Brand / -new; and you / know consequently a / little stiff . . . ," a modern conceit:

> The jane is zoned! no nightspot here, no bar
> there, no sweet freeway, and no premises
> for business purposes,
> no loiterers or needers.

The "advance" is a sexual advance—wished for, at least—as well as the advance of the book and an advance in the parade's quasimilitary sense. "Jane" is common enough slang for "woman" or "girl"; it is puzzling only because one hardly expects a woman to be "zoned." But that is precisely the poem's point (and the justification of the exclamation point). The poem was written Thanksgiving week of 1962, when Berryman was living in Providence, and "combines the frustration of finding all the bars legally closed on Thanksgiving Day itself with that of being black and lacking legal rights," in John Haffenden's interpretation.[22] That would explain the absence of people at which "Henry are baffled," but it rather misses the point of "The jane is zoned!": more than liquor is off limits. "There ought to be a law against Henry," Henry says in **"DS 4,"** and his friend assures him that there is. Here is that law in operation. Bafflement leads logically enough to the question opening the second stanza: "Arrive a time when all coons lose dere grip, / but is he come?" Assuming that the dialect here represents Henry rather than his friend, this is Henry as imaginary coon, trapped like the metaphorical "'possum treed" in **"DS 355"** and the literal "'coon treed" in **"DS 57."** As Gary Arpin nicely puts it, "In Henry's inverted, fallen world, Henry in a tree becomes Henry up a tree, Henry as a treed 'coon, a lynched 'coon."[23] (He is referring to the lynching scene in **"DS 10."** There "A vote would come / that would be no vote," in contrast to the vote here in **"DS 2."**) For someone in a tree, losing one's grip means falling out (as Henry does in **"DS 1,"** with its additional pun in "Thereafter nothing fell out as it might or ought." And Henry literally falls out of the tree at the end of **"DS 57."**) In this sense, we all lose our grip, and "all coons" is synonymous not just with all blacks but with all humankind, who likewise suffer. The inclusiveness of "all" also suggests that Henry means not just a grip on sanity, but his grip on the entire world: "We hafta *die*" (**"DS 36"**). (The personification of time as "he" causes time a little more to resemble the grim reaper.)

The remainder of the stanza may seem contradictory: is this "gal" a stripper, the same as the off-limits "jane"? And why does Henry invite her to dance, and instruct her to strip, if chastity is his aim? The manuscript version is a bit clearer: "Ol' strip, / ol' bank, skipping we, baby: we hang on." In other words, Henry is avoiding the act, rather than being avoided by the actress; the manuscript version makes it clear that it is Henry "hanging on" (not losing his grip) "one chaste evenin." He will dance "if them is all you seem to require"—that is, if dancing is the limit, if they stay within the zoning laws.

This uncharacteristic restraint arouses the friend's incredulity, but his half-derisive address, "Sir Bones, or Galahad," delineates another side of Henry's personality, the chivalric. When he is not lusting after maidens in distress (lust itself being the dragon), Henry fancies himself their rescuer, and this is an important aspect of his character as epic hero.

"Honey dusk do sprawl" is at the most literal level presumably a description of that twilight in which Henry finds himself, as so often in the *Songs,* unable legally to meet his "need need need." But metaphorically the line is the friend's explanation of why he finds it so "astonishin" that Henry should resist temptation. It is also a clear example of Berryman's "characteristic double syntax."[24] "Honey" sounds like a direct address, especially following "gal" and "sugar," and given Berryman's Shandean habit of addressing "pals" and "loves" throughout *The Dream Songs.* Then the line might be the friend's comment to the "gal" on Henry's lack of enlightenment. But the lack of a comma enforces the possibility that "honey" is an adjective. Read that way, "honey dusk" can refer to sexuality, sprawled even more generally over all. Either way, it is a bemusing sentence, "jauntily encompassing a Spenglerian darkness," as Hugh Kenner says of Robert Creeley.[25]

And either way, Henry's response is appropriate: "Hit's hard." Again the dialect provides the excuse for a pun. The remainder of that line, practicing the exuberance it recommends, has been regularly cited as an instance (for good or bad) of Berryman's nonsense: "Kinged or thinged, though, fling & wing." So I feel a bit diffident claiming understanding, but the line seems quite clear to me. In the unloveliness of paraphrase: our situation, life, is hard (or hits hard). But whether you are made to feel like a king or a thing (that is, whether you are celebrated or dehumanized), you should have a fling, spread your wings, in the parlance of popular songs. "Wing" also suggests "wing it," a winged bird (as "Fate winged me" in **"DS 42"**) and, in the context that supports "hoedown," also suggests the buck-and-wing, another minstrel-show dance.

The rough draft manuscript shows Berryman's change of "sing" to "wing." In fact, the end of the poem was originally quite different; the last three lines went:

> De only thing is: fling & ~~sing~~ wing
> When the worl' & ~~the gals~~ women sit down off from
>   you sad
> Fing is: don't get *mad.*

The revised ending brings the Song around again from the personal to the social, emphasizing that Henry's temporary virtue is operative at both levels: "yo legal & yo good." In railroad argot (*re:* "train" in the poem), "to wing her" means to set the emergency brakes, which is certainly what Henry is doing here (Mencken, 583). "Wings" is of course a multiply significant word in **The Dream Songs** as a whole.[26]

"Poll-cats" may be "cats" who vote, though the suggestion has been made that they are rather the collectors of the poll-tax, which would accord more closely with Linebarger's belief that "the pun on 'polecat and the 'hurrah, hurray' (from the song 'Dixie') are meant as attacks on a suppressive social system" (87). If one wishes to play the dictionary game (as Berryman often did), then it may not seem irrelevant that "poll" can also mean to cut hair or wool short, to crop or shear, to cut off the top (as of a tree: pollard), or to cut off or cut short horns.

". . . Are coming" refers to the parade to follow, but can also suggest a larger historical "coming." The whole complex provides a political meaning for "Big Buttons." "I votes in my hole" expresses the ambivalence of Henry's place in the world. He withdraws in a huff, as in the first Song—and "the isolation cells are the hole," in prison argot (Mencken, 580)—but then cannot resist putting in his word. He despairs of the world, particularly America, but not so completely that he stops offering criticism and advice: he votes. As in the "Op. Posth." Songs, he can't stay buried. Henry's ambiguity

about the role of citizen, especially the black citizen, is perfectly analogous to Berryman's about the role of the artist: he is modernistically rejected and rejecting while still aspiring to serve as spokesman and guide.

In this and a multitude of other ways Henry remains throughout the **Songs** "baffled" in almost the literal sense: confronted by a "maze of drink" (**"DS 339"**), by quotidian barriers and obstacles, and by the labyrinths of his own mind, "A mind like a house full of hidden stairways, trapdoors, sliding walls, and secret drawers."[27]

But Song 2, although beginning with Henry's having run up against one of those walls, moves on to a qualified celebration, "hurrah, hurray." Given that the blackface speech (in combination with some of the other verbal devices such as the nondialect slang used here) ameliorates precisely the chief fault of the **Songs**—their too single and unqualified tone of complaint—we can only conclude that, so far from obscuring **The Dream Songs** too much, the dialect does not "obscure" it enough. "Honey dusk do sprawl" may express as grim a vision as Song 1's "empty grows every bed," but the dialect, without reducing intelligibility, provides a levity we need to face the grave world.

Notes

1. "Congested Funeral: Berryman's New *Dream Songs,*" *Times Literary Supplement,* June 26, 1969, p. 680; and A. Alvarez, *Beyond All This Fiddle* (New York: Random House, 1969), p. 89.

2. J. M. Linebarger, *John Berryman* (New York: Twayne, 1974); Joel Conarroe, *John Berryman: An Introduction to the Poetry* (New York: Columbia Univ. Press, 1977); and Gary Q. Arpin, *The Poetry of John Berryman* (Port Washington, N.Y.: Kennikat Press, 1978). Subsequent references will be included in the text.

3. *Babel to Byzantium* (New York: Farrar, Straus, and Giroux, 1968), p. 199.

4. "Henry Tasting All the Secret Bits of Life: Berryman's *Dream Songs,*" *Wisconsin Studies in Contemporary Literature,* 6 (Winter-Spring 1965), 30.

5. Richard Kostelanetz, "Conversations with Berryman," *Massachusetts Review,* 11 (Spring 1970), 346. In all fairness it must be noted that despite this disclaimer, the narrator does discuss "antimatter" (DS 55), the "occlusion of a star" (DS 79), *and* modern art.

6. "Cagey John: Berryman as Medicine Man," *Centennial Review,* 12 (Summer 1968), 334-54.

7. *Times Literary Supplement,* February 23, 1973, p. 3.

8. *TLS*, February 23, 1973, p. 2. The heavy reliance on Crane is based on Berryman's having written a biography, *Stephen Crane* (1950; rpt. Cleveland: Meridian-World, 1962).

9. The features of actual black English are described in detail in J. L. Dillard, *Black English: Its History and Usage in the United States* (New York: Random House, 1972) and Geneva Smitherman, *Talkin and Testifyin: The Language of Black America* (Boston: Houghton Mifflin, 1977). Also see Walter A. Wolfram, *A Sociolinguistic Description of Detroit Negro Speech* (Washington, D.C.: Center for Applied Linguistics, 1969); Walt Wolfram and Nona H. Clarke, eds., *Black-White Speech Relationships* (Washington, D.C.: Center for Applied Linguistics, 1971); and William Labov, *Language in the Inner City: Studies in the Black English Vernacular* (Philadelphia: Univ. of Pennsylvania Press, 1972).

I owe thanks to Wiley Smith, Director of Kent State's Institute for African-American Affairs, for the advice and references he kindly supplied.

10. Both the expropriation and the dialect's role as the genuine expression of black life are underlined by Robert Bone in his preface to the reissue of Sterling Brown's 1937 study: *Negro Poetry and Drama* and *The Negro in American Fiction* (New York: Atheneum, 1972):

> In one of his favorite anecdotes, Sterling Brown tells the story of T. D. "Jim Crow" Rice [to whom Berryman dedicates DS 2], a white minstrel of the 1830's. One of his routines consisted of a shuffling clog dance, in which he impersonated a Negro hostler. "Legend has it that when he appeared in the sketch on a Cincinnati stage he was insistently encored, until a small voice from the wings whimpered, 'Gimme back mah clothes.'"

Brown cites James Weldon Johnson as his authority that this "mold established on the minstrel stage" (41) shaped the use of traditional dialect into a form that demeaned black life, even when that was portrayed by local colorists who supposed themselves sympathetic (Irwin Russell, J. A. Macon, Thomas Nelson Page) or by such black writers as Paul Laurence Dunbar or Johnson himself (Brown, n.p.).

LeRoi Jones (now Amira Imamu Baraka) provides a basis for finding a different set of implications altogether in the use of blackface dialect. As Wasserstrom points out, in *Blues People* (New York: Morrow, 1963) Jones claims that the black performers whom the white minstrels copied were *already* parodying white manners. "Whereas white minstrels in blackface merely exposed their own folly, Negro minstrels in blackface, anticipating Genet, created a black travesty of white burlesque

and thereby cut deep into the double life of both races" (Wasserstrom, 342).

11. In his *Harvard Advocate* interview (103, Spring 1969), Berryman summarized the circumstances of the short story, then explained, "Well, the Negro business—the blackface—is related to that. That is, I feel extremely lucky to be white, let me put it that way, so that I don't have that problem. Friends of mine—Ralph Ellison, for example, in my opinion one of the best writers in the country—he has the problem. He's black, and he and Fanny, wherever they go, they are black" (6).

12. The interested reader may refer to J. L. Dillard's *Lexicon of Black English: The Words the Slaves Made* (New York: Seabury, 1977).

13. In Songs 76, 99, 66, 194, 40, 114, and 28, respectively. There are also a number of adjectives formed by adding -*y* to nouns or verbs: "thinky," "relishy," "livey," and "bigoty" (DS 10 and 26, 84, 114, and 273).

14. Since I wrote this piece it has been pointed out to me that "backhanders" is not a neologism but a real word, meaning hard slaps to the face with the back of the hand. Certainly that fits the word in its *Dream Songs* context:

> 'O rare Ben Jonson'
> dictator too, & the thinky other Johnson
> dictator too, backhanders down of laws
>
> (DS 126)

The sense would seem to be that both men, as arbiters of taste and critics of renown who were not afraid of being dogmatic, were "handers down of laws," and their "laws" so powerfully put that they feel like "backhanders." That the reader may also be reminded of backhanded compliments, and of the backhand of tennis, may not be entirely irrelevant.

In the other curious construction, *cave* as a verb takes an infinitive:

> Somehow, when I make your scene,
> I cave to feel as if
> de roses of dawns & pearls of dusks, made up
> by some ol' writer-man, got right forgot
> & the greennesses of ours.
>
> (DS 50)

The use of the word is strange both semantically and syntactically, and no explanation is immediately derivable from the context. Perhaps we are to understand something like "cave in" (as a verb) in a metaphorical, emotional sense. *Cave* is a word with considerable resonance in the Songs, relating to the whole "hole" complex mentioned below. A cave is a primitive form of house, significant to "Henry House," who, in the house of his own body, searches for a further home, refuge, retreat. In DS 381 "Caveman Henry" would "rather have a house," but in 63 he envies bats their cave, described in womb terms: "lovely-chilly, dark, / ur-moist . . . / . . . crisisless, kid." In any case, this anomalous construction is the only instance of difficulty of that order in connection with the dialect in the Songs.

15. The most difficult such passage is in DS 194:

> —Try Dr. God, clown a ball,
> low come to you in the blue sad darkies' moans
> worsing than yours, too.

Even here the difficulty can not really be ascribed to the use of dialect. A comma after "blue" would resolve the syntactic ambiguity, and in fact, if all the words in the sentence are to be accounted for, the sentence must be read as if it did contain a comma. But the lack of a comma makes clear the play on "blue": that it can reinforce and intensify "sad" as well as meaning "dusk" or "dark." (With perhaps a gesture in the direction of "out of the blue"?) Having been stopped by the difficulty, the reader may then reflect on "darkies" as related to the dark of night that "blue" refers to. And since the blues is the expression of black sorrow, and stands in close relation to "moans" as both sound and emotion, the whole four-word phrase is almost fully interreferential.

16. *The Situation of Poetry: Contemporary Poetry and Its Traditions* (Princeton Univ. Press, 1976), p. 45.

17. A Kent State University Research Grant, an ACLS Grant-in-Aid, and the kindness of Kate Berryman permitted me to spend several months studying *The Dream Songs* manuscripts and related papers at the Manuscript Archives of the University of Minnesota Libraries. Mrs. Berryman also allowed me to spend some time perusing Berryman's private library, which is still in her home, where I saw the annotated copy of Wittke mentioned below.

18. "Changes," *Poets on Poetry,* ed. Howard Nemerov (New York: Basic Books, 1966), p. 94.

19. H. L. Mencken makes this point explicitly in his *The American Language* (New York: Knopf, 1936), p. 578. Berryman used slang quite deliberately, frequently consulting both Mencken and Eric Partridge's *A Dictionary of Slang and Unconventional English* (New York: Macmillan, 1937; 5th ed. 1961), as the marginal notes on his *Songs* manuscripts indicate. "Partridge / Mencken" appears in the margin next to "jane" in DS 2, for instance.

20. Durham, N.C.: Duke Univ. Press, 1930.

21. Whitman's importance to Berryman as both inspiration and model is attested to in Berryman's interview comments, his essay on Whitman in *The Freedom of the Poet* (New York: Farrar, Straus, and Giroux, 1976), and his references in *The Dream Songs* themselves (see DS 78, 234, and 279). These matters are discussed in detail, and any possible lingering doubts demolished, by James E. Miller, Jr., in his chapter on Berryman in *The American Quest for a Supreme Fiction: Whitman's Legacy in the Personal Epic* (Chicago: Univ. of Chicago Press, 1979).

22. "A Year on the East Coast: John Berryman, 1962-63," *Twentieth Century Literature,* 22 (May 1976), 138. He also confirms that Whitman would have been particularly on Berryman's mind at that time: that summer at Bread Loaf Berryman taught his course on "Deep Form" which "leaned heavily on Walt Whitman" (132), and taught it again at Brown that fall (141). This material has now been incorporated in slightly modified form in Haffenden's biography, *The Life of John Berryman* (New York: Routledge & Kegan Paul, 1982), pp. 304 ff.

23. "Forward to the End," *John Berryman Studies,* 4 (Fall 1975), 10.

24. The phrase is Gabriel Pearson's in "John Berryman—Poet as Medium," *The Review,* 15 (April), 14.

25. *A Homemade World: The American Modernist Writers* (New York: Morrow, 1975), p. 184. Kenner is referring specifically to "I Knew a Man": "The darkness surrounds us . . . what / can we do against it. . . ."

26. In "A Dying Fall Beneath the Music," *John Berryman Studies,* 9 (Fall 1976), 61-71, I discuss the many uses of the word, in connection with DS 385.

27. Eileen Simpson, *The Maze* (New York: Simon and Schuster, 1975).

Luke Spencer (essay date spring 1987)

SOURCE: Spencer, Luke. "'The pieces sat up & wrote': Art and Life in John Berryman's *Dream Songs*." *Critical Quarterly* 29, no. 1 (spring 1987): 71-80.

[*In the following essay, Spencer examines the unifying elements of* The Dream Songs, *contending that the collection "was converted from little more than a ragbag of transparently disguised confessions into a self-generating, self-completing object, the poem-as-life."*]

Commenting on John Berryman's *77 Dream Songs* in 1967, M. L. Rosenthal observed that 'the confessional movement . . . may be just about played out' and that '. . . its practitioners may be overindulging themselves if they think that every nuance of suffering brought out on the couch or in reverie is a mighty flood of poetic insight or the key to a new aesthetic'.[1] This was a radical qualification of the enthusiasm that had greeted collections such as Robert Lowell's *Life Studies* (1959) and Sylvia Plath's *Ariel* (1965). Rosenthal in America and A. Alvarez in England had been among the first to praise Lowell, Plath and Berryman for what was seen as a fierce new honesty about the most painful kinds of personal experience. To Alvarez such honesty came as a welcome corrective to the complacency of much post-war British poetry.[2] Yet, by 1967, Rosenthal was warning of the inadequacy of self-exposure as a creative principle. His brief discussion of *77 Dream Songs,* quoted above, accuses Berryman of sentimentality, attitudinising and a tendency to 'commandeer political themes too facilely or fashionably'.[3] These are perceptive judgements, but they do not sufficiently explain the shortcomings of the confessional mode as Berryman practiced it. To do that it is necessary to follow the growth of *The Dream Songs* beyond those first seventy-seven parts which prompted Rosenthal's anxieties. It is also necessary to examine, in more detail than Rosenthal was able to, the historical and cultural conditions in which 'to walk naked'[4] became such a seductive motivation for American poets.

John Haffenden records a comment by someone who was close to John Berryman in the early 1950s: '. . . his rages and tantrums and affairs were well known and gossiped about . . . "It's all part of my biography, that's all", he said once, when he was chasing some young woman around, and obviously embarrassing and hurting Eileen [his wife]'.[5] Not surprisingly, the speaker here was unimpressed by Berryman's off-hand self-justification. She probably didn't consider it enough to say that one's moral conduct happens with the impersonal force of a natural phenomenon—all part of the order (or disorder) of things and therefore to be fatalistically accepted. Probably she also caught in Berryman's words a note of hubris, an implication that its being part of *his* biography would excuse it, since he was someone who obviously merited a biography and whose lapses would come to seem venial when set against his creative achievements. To be sure, few of us would be fooled by such evasions—at least in other people. Yet what so clearly fails to persuade at the moral level has become a firmly established aesthetic defence of Berryman's most sustained piece of self-justification, *The Dream Songs.*

Commentators have tried many ways of detecting some overall narrative, thematic or chronological unity in *The Dream Songs,* but their best efforts have yielded poor results. Adrienne Rich's early review of *77 Dream Songs* still offers the most plausible approximation to a structural rationale: '. . . it is the identity of Henry . . . which holds the book together, makes it clearly a real book and not a collection of chance pieces loosely flung under one cover. None of the poems (except possibly the elegies) carries in isolation the weight and perspective that it does in relation to the rest; partly because the cumulative awareness of Henry is built from poem to poem'.[6]

Berryman's satisfaction with Rich's review[7] must have included a large admixture of relief that someone had found in the first batch of Songs a species of unity that already allowed for, if it did not actually anticipate, their projected expansion. Additional pieces of reminiscence, slapstick, lament or lucubration could henceforth be justified by invoking Henry's exfoliating biography. As Jack Vincent Barbera put it, 'The whole poem's "ultimate structure" is the ongoing and epic enterprise of probing and expressing that character—without, at the same time, developing some narrative action with a grand finale'.[8] Under the all-enabling rubric of 'dream' and 'songs' the sprawling continent of Henry's (i.e. Berryman's) psyche is opened up for a theoretically limitless series of lyrical explorations. What does not sing *of* Henry is sung *by* Henry. Every fragment is part of the 'House' that Henry is; it helps put flesh on the poem's 'Bones'.

The absence of any structural necessity beyond the unfolding of Henry's life and thoughts nevertheless caused Berryman a great deal of anxiety. His readiness to entertain any and every kind of theory about the poem's supposed structure[9] is evidence of a hankering for something more substantial than Henry House's biography on which to peg all those virtuoso performances. For one thing, where would it all end? The possibility of closure was ever-receding: the more Berryman spoke of finishing the Songs—let alone rounding them off satisfactorily—the more he was hag-ridden by a compulsion to go on with them: '. . . he was still writing Dream Songs at least as late as 1969—straining always to release himself from the terrible incubus of his inspiration'.[10] Haffenden insists on the helplessness of Berryman's situation, his inability to control his inspiration. **"Dream Song 26"** prefigures the only possible ultimate solution to this dilemma, 'I had a most marvellous piece of luck. I died'. Berryman's death, tragic as it was, authorised a last refinement of the argument for structural integrity. Joel Conarroe put it as succinctly as anyone: '. . . the Songs are built with pieces of the poet. At last there was no more'. If the demand for closure could not be satisfied by the dynamic of the poem alone, then reference to Berryman's life as the poem's ultimate *raison d'être* and organising principle would surely settle the issue. If Henry's existence was, by the poem's own dream-conventions, inexhaustible, his creator's was not. Henry could be buried and resurrected[11] along with his other vaudevillian transformations; Berryman's suicide was, in contrast, the most emphatic of conclusions: '. . . if anything *seals* the poem, it is not some larger closed structure—actual or implied—but Berryman's death'.[12] Thus *The Dream Songs* was converted from little more than a ragbag of transparently disguised confessions into a self-generating, self-completing object, the poem-as-life. To challenge the integrity of the poem would henceforth be like challenging the tragic truth of the life itself. Well-mannered critics could now safely concentrate on tracking down esoteric personal references and recondite scholarly allusions—activities far more congenial to most of them than raising awkward questions about structure and purpose.

Many strands of individualism, romanticism and formalism went into the making of the reified image of the poem-as-life; but more important than any of these was its ideological function in the marginalisation of the writer in American society after the Auden-inspired political engagement of the 1930s. For Berryman and his poetic generation (what Delmore Schwartz called 'the class of 1930') McCarthyism, cold war nationalism and the conditions of literary success itself foreclosed the option of a truly critical stance towards contemporary social reality.[13] Their only recourse was to an aggravated and inevitably destructive solipsism. The tensions which characterised their anguished marginality are everywhere present in *The Dream Songs,* challenging its claim to a mystified autonomy and problematising the notions of art and personal experience by which it seeks to validate its project.

To begin with, there is the issue of the poem's *manipulativeness,* raised perceptively by Edward Mendelson:

> Berryman is smart enough to realise that he presents himself in the least prepossessing manner he can imagine: his personal offensiveness is not accidental but entirely deliberate, for what he wants from his readers is their critical approval despite their personal disapproval, their assent despite their awareness of what they are assenting *to.* What Berryman hopes to enjoy is not the power to delight or enchant, but the power to control those who are both conscious and unwilling.[14]

I am not sure how complete a consciousness of motive and strategy is to be inferred from the word 'deliberate' here. Nor am I satisfied that most readers are 'unwilling' to accept the unsavoury details of Berryman's womanising, drunkenness and ambition. Nevertheless, the idea of the poem as a form of rape is a productive one and entirely consistent with the exploitative attitudes towards people, especially women,[15] which can be found throughout the sequence. 'It's all part of my biography' now becomes, in effect, 'It's all part of my poem', with precisely the same suggestion of inevitability. To be

sure, the poem-as-life requires unflattering revelations in the name of existential truth, but only so that we can be made to approve of them under the auspices of art.

A close look at some of the Songs will reveal how insistently the poem orchestrates our acquiescence in its most questionable—and least questioned—meanings.

> God bless Henry. He lived like a rat,
> with a thatch of hair on his head
> in the beginning.
> Henry was not a coward. Much.
> He never deserted anything; instead
> he stuck, when things like pity were thinning.
>
> So may be Henry was a human being.
> Let's investigate that.
> . . . We did; okay.
> He is a human American man.
> That's true. My lass is braking.
> My brass is aching. Come & diminish me, & map my
>   way.
>
> God's Henry's enemy. We're in business . . . Why,
> what business must be clear.
> A cornering.
> I couldn't feel more like it.—Mr Bones,
> as I look on the saffron sky,
> you strikes me as ornery.

(**"DS [Dream Song] 13"**)

The ideological assumptions which underpin the whole *Dream Songs* enterprise are very close to the surface here. Unregenerate individualism is given an easy victory over reductive sociological investigation. Human beings, especially American male human beings, are not to be mapped and diminished, even though they have their share of sexual frustrations (braking lasses) and financial hardships (aching brass). Henry may have lived like a rat, but when cornered by nosy researchers, or even a malign deity/destiny, he's ready to fight back. We are expected to take Henry's 'orneriness' as an instance of old-fashioned frontiersman-like independence coupled with new-style existentialist defiance. Homo Americanus can simultaneously fight his way out of sinister collectivist traps and negotiate the awkward corners on the high road of personal freedom. Questions of personal morality (cowardice, pity etc.) are glanced at only as authenticating evidence of honesty and courage. The real challenge of self-disclosure offered by the opening line is never taken up. Instead, the shock value of 'lived like a rat' is dissipated in the thinness of the reference to thinning hair. For the remainder of the Song the flow of self-praise is barely interrupted. The world may be short on pity and long on problems, but simply being himself will help Henry survive. Survival occupies a special place in the poem-as-life: it is a *sine qua non* of the poem's existence and a promise of its ultimate closure. Though the strength of purpose it implies is never set against the demands of constructive action, it confers a special authority on the experiences the poem records. Berryman commentators regularly pay fulsome tribute to Henry's tenacity while more or less ignoring the deficiency of moral being he works so hard to preserve.

The pattern of evasion is less obvious in **"Dream Song 14"**:

> Life, friends, is boring. We must not say so.
> After all, the sky flashes, the great sea yearns,
> we ourselves flash and yearn,
> and moreover my mother told me as a boy
> (repeatedly) 'Ever to confess you're bored
> means you have no
>
> Inner Resources.' I conclude now I have no
> inner resources, because I am heavy bored.
> Peoples bore me,
> literature bores me, especially great literature,
> Henry bores me, with his plights & gripes
> as bad as achilles,
>
> who loves people and valiant art, which bores me.
> And the tranquil hills, & gin, look like a drag
> and somehow a dog
> has taken itself & its tail considerably away
> into mountains or sea or sky, leaving
> behind: me, wag.

The first obstacle to a critical reading of this Song is that its overt issues are so dear to the hearts of postmodernist readers. Cynicism about the consolations of art, nature and social being is regarded as a virtual guarantee of authenticity, especially when it is combined with a wry belittlement of the self. After a blunt opening declaration the Song curls its lip successively at the pathetic fallacy, the American Dream (with its emphasis on 'Inner Resources'), other people, great literature and finally Henry himself, who is left with nothing but waggishness to mitigate his *taedium vitae*. In the first half of the Song the rhetoric of fastidious argumentation is deployed with measured irony ('After all . . . moreover . . . I conclude') and the break between stanzas one and two leaves an eloquent emptiness at the heart of that earnest advice about self-help. It is not until characteristic Henryisms like 'heavy bored' and 'Peoples bore me' are introduced that Berryman's general direction becomes clearer. There will be no examination of Henry's predicament in either its social or its psychological aspect: we are to be offered only the wholesale disparagement of Henry's miserable existence—the best of it along with the worst. Very well; we could perhaps make room for one more well-crafted statement of mid-century hopelessness. Yet even as a catalogue of shop-soiled commitments the Song disappoints. At the climax of its would-be confessional frankness Berryman's language discredits itself: 'Henry bores me, with his plights & gripes / as bad as achilles'. The decapitalised 'achilles' archly parades its cleverness under the flimsiest of anti-heroic cloaks. It makes a

feint of self-deprecation the better to court our complacent approval. And our approval is expected here because, though we are allowed a *frisson* of mockery, the classical reference winks to us its assurance that the enduring truths are still enduring. Great literature is politely parasitised for the terms of its token dismissal. Under the mask of irreverence reposes a very bland conservatism. The Song now stands revealed as no more than a poetic Feast of Fools in which established values are satirically inverted as a means of heading off the genuine questionings that lead to change.

Henry's mock-abasement is completed in the third stanza by the suggestion that he does not possess either the wholeness or the freedom of a dog that can at least control its own tail. Henry has a tail (tale) that wags him: he is a wag powerless to change the attachments that constitute his life. Many other Songs throughout the sequence end on a similar note of half-cheerful resignation to the incorrigible forces that shape Henry's destiny.[16] The poem-as-life is no more to be willed in any particular direction than the life itself. What Berryman called, in another Dream Song, 'the lines of nature & of will'[17] are forever bifurcated. The poor man's Achilles is the plaything of a fate more inscrutable than anything in the *Iliad*. He has surrendered his moral will to a reified image of his own inexorable biography: the poem-as-life is also the life-as-poem writing itself with no intervening human hand.

The sort of rhetorical manipulations I have discussed promote an idea of art and life as organic and mutually validating processes. Yet the fragmentariness and drift that the poem-as-life and life-as-poem try to deny ceaselessly declare their embarrassing presence:

> Hunger was constitutional with him,
> women, cigarettes, liquor, need need need
> until he went to pieces.
> The pieces sat up & wrote. They did not heed
> their piecedom but kept very quietly on
> among the chaos.
>
> **("DS 311,"** 7-12)

Interrogating Berryman's tragic posture we could choose to see those last three lines as an image not of heroic survival, but of a mutually impoverishing artlife relationship. Going further, we could regard the voracious appetite that paradoxically nourishes collapse as representing the poem's inability to achieve any principle of order beyond its sheer existential inclusiveness. In any case, it is fair to suppose that what would get written by pieces heedless of their 'piecedom' would itself be fragmentary. And this we can demonstrate from the Song; for, despite its tone of frankness, it blandly underwrites the derangement it takes the credit for criticising. The damaging consequences of piecedom to Henry's art and life are not engaged with at all. In fact, the Song ends with six lines about an imminent visit from an ex-mistress:

An old old mistress recently rang up,
here in Ireland, to see how Henry was:
how was he? delighted!
He thought she was 3000 miles away,
safe with her children in New York: she's coming at
    five:
we'll welcome her!

This abrupt change of subject in the final stanza is more than just an irritating failure to hold a serious issue in steady focus: it is an instance of hunger as a creative motivation. The 'constitutional' hunger that made Berryman a prodigious womaniser, smoker and boozer, when transferred from life to art, becomes an avidity for any stray item of memory or observation that can be corralled into the poem-as-life. It is a quantitative substitute for qualitative choice that Berryman found irresistible:

Pulling together Henry, somber Henry
woofed at things.
Spry disappointments of men
and vicing adorable children
miserable women, Henry mastered, Henry
tasting all the secret bits of life.

                                            ("DS 74," 16-21)

Henry's *soi-disant* mastery of life's recalcitrant materials comes from his weaving them together with the woof provided by the Songs. Every bit of life can thus, apparently, be subdued and enjoyed at will. Experience can be randomly repossessed as art. This is the very idea of a perfect reciprocity between art and life that the poem tries to impose on us. No matter how chaotic the life may be, it can be vindicated by an art made of that chaos itself. Berryman thinks he can reconstruct himself (pull himself together) and even penetrate the mysteries ('secret bits') of life in the simple act of recording his fragmentariness.

A more overt description of Henry at work gives strong support to the argument that Berryman conflates the drift of biography with the direction of art:

Tides of dreadful creation rocked lonely Henry
isolated in the midst of his family
as solitary as his dog.
In another world he'll have more to say of this, -
concepts came forward & were greeted with a kiss
in the passionate fog.

Lucid his project lay, beyond. Can he?
Loose to the world lay unimaginable Henry,
loose to the world,
taut with his vision as it has to be,
open & closed sings on his mystery
furled & unfurled.

Flags lift, strange chords lift to a climax. Henry
is past. Returning from his travail, he
he can't think of what to say.
The house's all about him, so is his family.

Tame doors swing upon his mystery
until another day.

                                            ("DS 260")

'Lonely . . . isolated . . . solitary', in a 'fog', Henry rocks on the tidal swells of his inspiration. Only from the imagined vantage-point of 'another world' can he envisage any possible detachment from his situation. In the meantime he must wait for 'concepts' to volunteer themselves for his embrace. Of course, he has a 'project' for the future, but can he complete it? (The next Song speaks of his writing—presumably of *The Dream Songs* itself—as 'habitual—life sentence—will he see it through?'). Significantly, 'Lucid' gives way to 'loose' as soon as the issue of completion is raised. Indeed, the sequence of adjectives throughout this stanza is an anthology of contradictions that offer themselves to us as fertile paradoxes adumbrating the 'mystery' of inspiration. But the ruse does not work. Despite the attempt at a consoling stasis in which positive and negative, active and passive, attributes hold each other in a mystified reciprocity of opposition, there is a perceptible, though unacknowledged, victory for drift. The assurances of lucidity and tautness are limply abstract compared with the (relatively) powerful images of befuddlement and involution. The process of creation is treated as something that happens as spontaneously as a lifting flag, as inexorably as a musical crescendo. But the supreme reification of what should be subject to human control is, once again, Henry's own life: 'Henry / is past.' His passive mediation in the reconstruction of life as art is over. Another day's quota of the poem-as-life is complete: 'Tame doors swing upon his mystery / until another day.' Is the tameness of the doors an unwitting image of Henry's submission to the muse of biography, or are the doors no more than a tragicomic segment of the mundane material world that Henry *can* control? Either answer points in the same direction.

'Henry under construction was Henry indeed' a late Song plausibly begins.[18] There can be no denying that Henry House is forever undergoing structural extension, improvement and repair. The trouble is that the whole edifice is built on sand, for there is no way out of the trap created by the poem-as-life. Life is vindicated by art which is vindicated by life which is vindicated by art . . . and so on, with no escape route to a social or historical perspective ('another world' indeed!) that might enable both to be radically re-examined. Denied a critical social function by the subjectivist prescriptions inscribed in post-war American culture, Berryman could either try to construct a public role for his biography, as Robert Lowell did, or he could try to close the circuit of art and private life altogether. He chose the second option, but not without uneasiness at its crippling limitations. Some of the most interesting Songs strain towards a recognition of public realities,[19] but Berryman could not resist for long the master-urge to submit to the limitless appetite of the poem-as-life. And here we must remind ourselves of a crucial aspect of the poem's manipulativeness: Berryman is as eager to impose a conviction of necessity upon himself as upon us. Though there are many traces of power-hunger and some of psychopathic tendencies in *The Dream Songs,* it is hardly conceivable that such a massive project of self-reconstruction should have been undertaken for the sole pleasure of fooling other people. Putting himself so relentlessly in the middle of the stage was both a symptom and an aggravation of Berryman's social marginality. American society could be very generous to its artists for not rocking the boat, but their sense of impotence could never be totally stifled:

> Seedy Henry rose up shy in de world
> & shaved & swung his barbells, duded Henry up
> and p.a.'d poor thousands of persons on topics of grand
> moment to Henry, ah to those less & none.

("**DS 77,**" 1-4)

Fellowships, prizes, lecture-tours, even a White House invitation, came Berryman's way in gratifying profusion. But a growing toll of burnt-out contemporaries was a reminder of the exorbitant price-tag:

> I'm cross with god who has wrecked this generation.
> First he seized Ted, then Richard, Randall, and now Delmore.
> In between he gorged on Sylvia Plath.
> That was a first rate haul. He left alive
> fools I could number like a kitchen knife
> but Lowell he did not touch.
>
> Somewhere the enterprise continues, not—
> yellow the sun lies on the baby's blouse—
> in Henry's staggered thought.
> I suppose the word would be, we must submit.
> *Later.*
> I hang, and I will not be part of it.

("**DS 153,**" 1-12)

All the poets in this list suffered from various combinations of alcoholism, depression and breakdown and Berryman clearly felt a special affinity with them as fellow victims of a malign fate. But what he, and they, experienced as fate was less inscrutable than they realised. Blaming 'god' left unexamined the cultural predicament that drove them so far into their already obsessional selves that they could not get out. By a predictable irony their deaths become in this Song more fragments for the shoring-up of Berryman's 'staggered thought'. Henry's non-submission to death, his hanging on, masks a hopeless fatalism before the scale and scandal of his generation's wreckage. Sheer survival fills the gap left by the absence of a critical engagement with destructive social forces.

Going to pieces was the definitive collective experience of Berryman's poetic generation. Reading the epic that

Berryman put together out of those pieces we should not look for the unity he tried so hard to create the semblance of for himself as much as for us. Instead we should trace the jaggedness of edges that do not fit and the broken contours of a design that could not fashion wholeness out of the mutual parasitism of art and an alienated private life. It is in such tormented areas of contemporary experience that the recuperation of art as a force for understanding and change might begin.

Notes

1. *The New Poets* (Oxford University Press, New York, 1967), p. 123.

2. See 'Beyond the gentility principle', introduction to *The New Poetry,* ed. A. Alvarez (Penguin, 1962 and frequently re-issued).

3. Rosenthal, *op. cit.,* pp. 119-22. On Berryman's treatment of political themes, see also: Luke Spencer, 'Politics and imagination in Berryman's *Dream Songs*', *Literature & History,* vol. 12, no. 1, pp. 38-47.

4. Alvarez's phrase, in *op. cit.,* p. 25.

5. *The Life of John Berryman* (Routledge & Kegan Paul, 1982), p. 219.

6. 'Mr Bones, he lives', *Nation,* CXCVIII (May 1964). Quoted in Haffenden, *op. cit.,* pp. 326-7.

7. Haffenden, *loc. cit.*

8. 'Shape and flow in *The Dream Songs*', *Twentieth Century Literature,* vol. XXII, no. 2 (1976), p. 155.

9. John Haffenden, *John Berryman: a Critical Commentary* (Macmillan, 1980), pp. 34-5.

10. Haffenden, *Life,* p. 318.

11. I refer to the 'Opus posthumous' section, nos. 78-91.

12. Barbera, *op. cit.*

13. See Christopher Lasch's *The Agony of the American Left* (André Deutsch, 1970), especially his comments on what he calls the 'wholesale defection . . . from social criticism' of American intellectuals after World War II. See also Saul Bellow's novel *Humboldt's Gift* (Secker & Warburg, 1975), in which Berryman's close friend Delmore Schwartz, thinly disguised as Humboldt, is presented as the victim of a 'business and technological America' that values its poets only to the degree that their self-destructive alienation confirms the power of 'American reality'.

14. 'How to read Berryman's *Dream Songs*', in *American Poetry Since 1960,* ed. Robert B. Shaw (Carcanet, 1973), p. 40.

15. Mendelson is good on Berryman's treatment of women as objects: *op. cit.,* pp. 39-40.

16. For example, Songs 5, 22, 62, 114, 133, 197, 257, 283, 310 and 357.

17. *Henry's Fate and Other Poems,* ed. Haffenden (Faber, 1978), p. 46.

18. *Ibid.,* p. 10.

19. Most notably, Songs 60, 66, 110, 162, 180, 181, 216 and 217.

Kathe Davis (essay date fall 1988)

SOURCE: Davis, Kathe. "The Freedom of John Berryman." *Modern Language Studies* 18, no. 4 (fall 1988): 33-60.

[*In the following essay, Davis views the themes of polarities and synthesis in the poems of* The Dream Songs *and explores the relationship between Berryman's critical work and his poetry.*]

I. "DOUBLE I SING"

"The middle generation," John Berryman called himself and his peers. As early as 1948 he was aware of the tensions built into their position between the great High Modernists and the younger generation we have since come to call postmodernist. Unlike Randall Jarrell, a close friend and important influence, Berryman did not make a name for himself as a critic, and early in his career gave up reviewing because so many prominent contemporary writers were his personal friends or acquaintances (or enemies). He derided what he called 'Rich Critical Prose' (**"DS [Dream Song] 170"**) from academic critics and reviewers alike ("When the mind dies it exudes rich critical prose"), and claimed to dislike theory. Nonetheless, his critical writing, mostly neglected so far, deserves closer attention. It holds up and hangs together; it is perceptive and funny. And though it is often idiosyncratic, it illuminates not only Berryman's own poetry—and life—but the difficult position of an entire generation of poets, caught between two opposing sets of literary values.

The first thing that must be said about Berryman's central thought is that it's not central. It tends to extremes. "There are two kinds of people," Henry James said (parodying his brother William's *Psychology*), "those who believe there are two kinds of people and those who don't." Berryman believed that there are two kinds of people, and he wanted to be both of them. He seems to have been temperamentally committed to trying to have it both ways. In his private life he tried for monogamy *and* promiscuity; world travel *and* serene

domesticity; alcoholic partying *and* disciplined productivity; scholarship *and* poetry writing, and so on. The same double tendency is clear in his poetic convictions. "A man must choose," says Yeats, but Berryman refused. He sought, if not exactly perfection of the life and of the work, at least a fullness of both, each in the other.

Such omniverousness can be dismissed as infantile, as the childish or neurotic refusal of the reality principle, of limitation and the necessity of making choices. On the other hand it could be argued that the imaginative reshaping of the world to forms more satisfactory than those of the "real" world is and always has been the business of literature. In any case, and whether we blame or praise Berryman for it, having it both ways was what he did, or tried to do, his entire life.

The language of doubleness recurs throughout his work and through the whole course of his career. "Double I sing," he declares, and everywhere refuses the either/or, grasping at the both/and. Further, both art and life are seen in terms of contradictory qualities: *The Dream Songs*' "Henry, goatish, reserved" (**"DS 297"**) sees the preservation of the forms of life in art for the dead—the catafalques of St. Patrick's in Dublin—as "tumultuous, serene" (**"DS 301"**).[1] He says in **"DS 325"** "I notice at this point a divided soul, / headed both fore & aft . . ." and **"DS 317"** refers to "his divided soul." The late, "open" *Love & Fame* speaks of "my double nature," and there in more or less his own voice he appeals to God to "unite my various soul."[2] He chooses Severance as the name of the protagonist of his late nakedly autobiographical "novel."[3] More specifically, in **"DS 49"** a contradictoriness in his personal qualities is remarked by his wife: "'Wastethrift': Oh one of cunning wives know that / he hoardy-squander." Likewise, Severance's wife comments on

> his polar positions: rebellion, awe. Both seemed built in, he was ready to defend both to the death. You had to have both. He saw damned little of either in most Americans at the moment: just cop-out or sheephood, no independence *or* emulation.

> (p. 66)

Berryman finds a similar polarity in his critical essay on "Thomas Nashe and the Unfortunate Traveller," where he conducts an argument about the impossibility of fitting Nashe into either of the available categories: "The split between journalist and imaginative writer, between 'nonfiction' and fiction, does not apply to him any better than it applies to Swift."[4] (In this as in so many of his critical views, Berryman anticipated the theory of our time, in direct contravention of that of his own. This may be the place to notice that he also took "criticism to be a branch of literature; I don't separate it out.")[5] From Nashe—and our reaction to him—Berryman draws a sizable generalization:

The larger truth might be we are uneasy *equally* with the enthusiastic and the censorious . . . while an Elizabethan was at home with both. . . . But our fundamental difficulty lies probably further on. . . . The real trouble is that . . . we are suspicious of anything that is not *wholly* pro or con: in a rambling-free Elizabethan structure we are unready for either violent praise or blame. Perhaps in literature we stand in some need, decidedly, of more of the anti-categorical, and *ad hoc*, the flexible, the experimental. . . .

(*FP* [*The Freedom of the Poet*], p. 18)

This list of what literature might need is a list of ways of being between. But, the Golden Mean notwithstanding, we tend to associate the middle with mediation and its pejorative connotations of compromise. Berryman wanted a synthesis that was not a compromise, and strove his entire life in the tradition of the Romantic dialectic. He tried to manage both polar positions simultaneously, but he also acknowledged the impossibility of doing so in both his art and life. Doubleness always holds the potential for dividedness, as we've already seen him noticing. If one's personal or poetic power is not enough to hold together opposing forces, and one hangs on to both (or all) of them, one flies apart. Berryman felt early the destructive potential of his characteristic tendency to opposed extremes. So a middle that is a place safely between, a place of moderation, becomes a desire for him, a home, a figure of achieved wholeness. The desire motivates the entire *Dream Songs,* appearing perhaps most poignantly in the final Song, where he laments the lack of "a middle ground between things and the soul."

In *The Dream Songs,* the doubleness, the dividedness, and the desire for an integrated and stable middle ground show up not only in what is said, but also in the form of the poem, and at every level: in the characters and their relations to each other (and to their author), the narrative (and lack of it), the diction, stanza form, and prosody (in the play of open form against a tight metrical "norm"). Overall *The Dream Songs* can be seen as a long exercise in following and not following modernist tenets, practices, and techniques. A good many of the critical arguments over the Songs derive from that fact. Like Nashe's, when the work was published it just wasn't classifiable in terms of the categories readily available at the time. The reasons come clear in the light of Berryman's critical ideas in general.

Berryman was not a theoretical thinker. He simply wasn't interested in theory as such. In the preface to *The Freedom of the Poet,* the volume of his collected criticism which he was in the process of assembling at the time of his death, he says, "I think my critical practice has attached itself to no school." He goes on then to list his teachers and influences, concluding, "My interest in critical *theory* has been slight" (p. x). (In another discussion of his own work, he says, "You may wonder whether I dislike aestheticians. I do" *FP*, p. 326). "The only theory that can be said to underlie Randall Jarrell's fiercely sympathetic retelling of human predicaments is the Freudian one, significantly a theory of life rather than a theory of art,"[6] says Helen Vendler. The same could be said of Berryman. He encountered literature as immediate and personal experience, and his critical writing communicates that experience—although it always does so by essentially formal means. But even though he was not interested in establishing a body of theoretical writing, never mind a system, his critical writing and comments over the years offer collectively a surprisingly coherent set of ideas about the nature and role of poetry and the poet. His ideas also modified and developed, naturally, in ways I will briefly consider. But over the forty years from 1932, when he entered Columbia University, until his death in 1972, his thinking remained remarkably consistent.

II. EMPATHY

In the first sentence of the first essay in *The Freedom of the Poet,* Berryman speaks of

those connexions, now illuminating, now mysterious, between the artist's life and his work, which interest an increasing number of readers in this century, and the existence of which is denied only by very young persons or writers whose work perhaps really does bear no relation to their lives, *tant pis pour eux.*

(*FP*, p. 3)

That was in 1952, when those "connexions" *were* beginning to interest an increasing number of readers. But by then Berryman had believed in their importance for almost twenty years, from long before the time when such ideas had begun to return to respectability.

Berryman discovered himself as a poet in the classroom of Mark Van Doren in his first year at Columbia. The following year he discovered a greater if remoter model: "I began work in verse-making as a burning, trivial disciple of the great Irish poet William Butler Yeats" (*FP*, p. 323). Yeats as modernist, declaring the priority of art and the necessity of choosing between "perfection of the life or of the work," did not attract Berryman. "To hell, by the way, with the mask," he declared at twenty-two.[7] But Yeats not only beautifully articulated the conflict; he also beautifully resolved it, and it is as the poet of the Unity of Being that he stood as a mentor-figure for Berryman. "For Berryman," says John Haffenden, "Yeats united action and contemplation as a complete man" (*L* [*The Life of John Berryman*], p. 87). At Cambridge on scholarship the year after receiving his B.A., Berryman hatched the plan of writing Yeats's biography. "While wary of over-estimating the importance of Yeats's life to his work, he did think that all biographical data were not only relevant, but also invaluable for him as a critic" (*L*, pp. 85-86). Berryman was impressed by the personal source and nature of Yeats's symbols. They helped to convince him of the relevance of biography generally, and virtually every essay in *Freedom* turns at least briefly to the life (whether known through the writing itself or biography) of the author under discussion for clarification and illumination.

The Eliotic High Modernism which was to hold sway for the next twenty-five or so years was already clearly formulated and firmly in place. So almost from the time that Berryman was aware that he *had* ideas about poetry, he found those ideas in conflict with the current orthodoxy. He was later glad: "Yeats somehow saved me from the then-crushing influences of Ezra Pound and T. S. Eliot" (*FP*, p. 324). However, he wasn't so saved as not to sound fairly orthodox in his poetry: in his own summary, "for several fumbling years I wrote in what it is convenient to call 'period style,' the Anglo-American style of the 1930's, with no voice of my own" (*FP*, p. 323). Even in 1948 the editor of *Poetry* magazine could identify him as "one of the better exemplars of what someone called the school that writes 'to be analyzed by Brooks & Warren.'"[8]

For these years his criticism may be a better index of his opinion than his poetry (although the early poems are not so unambiguously modernist as their mannerisms and an easy reading suggest; they are overdue for serious reconsideration). In 1940 he made his first book appearance with **"Twenty Poems"** in *Five Young American Poets* in the New Directions series, and two years later published his first volume, entitled simply **Poems.** But it was with *The Dispossessed*[9] that he achieved the beginnings of his characteristic voice(s), and a methodological breakthrough. Besides the significant title poem, the volume included Berryman's now most anthologized poem, **"The Ball Poem."** Here is the apparent genesis of the most important single principle animating Berryman's poetic practice for the length of his career. Writing a preface to the second edition of his 1970 volume *Love & Fame,* Berryman commented (with a characteristic feint at ingenuousness): "I notice it makes play with an obsession that ruled 'The Ball Poem' of 1942 as well as, later, *Homage to Mistress Bradstreet* (1948-1953) and *The Dream Songs* (1955-1968): namely, the dissolving of one personality into another without relinquishing the original." And again he insisted "Both *Homage to Mistress Bradstreet* and *The Dream Songs* are built around the notion that individual identities can merge."

These comments have been noticed and quoted often enough, but in conceptual isolation. **"The Ball Poem"** may be the most commented-upon of Berryman's early poems. What is usually discussed is the poem's presentation of loss, taken as Berryman's lifelong dominant theme. But what is at least as important in the poem is this business of merging identities, presented as a human response if not solution to loss. The merging is both source and result of a human sympathy that reaches beyond the confines of self to a full comprehension of another's sorrow.

The poem presents the utter innocent shock of a little boy whose playing ball has bounced irrecoverably into the water. That the poem trembles on the brink of bathos—"An ultimate shaking grief fixes the boy"—is deliberate, I think. The point is that the boy's emotion is unmediated by any expectation or experience, and his loss, trivial by adult standards, is for him momentarily absolute.

The poem emphasizes the difference between the adult poet observing and the little boy observed, and in fact ends "I am not a little boy." But the difference is emphasized to make a larger point than the difference in their understanding or loss. The poet possesses a power of empathy, or of identification with another, which goes beyond what we ordinarily call "empathy," which transcends that difference and permits him to partake of the experience of another individual. The poem concludes:

> Soon part of me will explore the deep and dark
> Floor of the harbor . . . I am everywhere,
> I suffer and move, my mind and my heart move
> With all that move me, under the water
> Or whistling, I am not a little boy.[10]

The paradox here is that what separates the poet from the little boy making his first acquaintance with loss is precisely the poet's mature capacity to identify so fully with others, including that little boy: "my mind and my heart move / With all that move me."

Such a claim may sound Whitmanian and overblown. But in fact the source is not Whitman but *The Tempest*. Miranda, describing to her father the shipwreck she has just witnessed, exclaims, "Oh! I have suffered / With those that I saw suffer." The additional resonance which allusion gives Berryman's lines is tempered by additional ambivalence. Miranda is inexperienced, like the boy innocent till now of the harshness of the world. A good part of the power of her famous line "O brave new world, that has such people in't," comes from the poignance of her sweet faith in the truth of appearance at the beginning of a play which in every way calls appearance into question, and along the way presents several varieties of human evil and folly. Yet she is not wrong: the shipwreck that would be her introduction to tragedy is a mere illusion, and the man with whom she falls in love as good as he is "brave." This perhaps is what saves from irony Berryman's speaker's use of her words.

Berryman may wish to emphasize the vulnerability that such a stand confers, but apparently he intends quite seriously and literally the avowal of shared pain. Of **"The Ball Poem"** he said:

> The discovery here was that a commitment of identity can be "reserved," so to speak, with an ambiguous pronoun. The poet himself is both left out and put in; the boy does and does not become him and we are confronted with a process which is at once a process of life and a process of art
>
> *(FP,* pp. 326-27)

Through the poet's perception of it, the boy's infant sorrow partakes of universal loss. So there is no irony in the *ubi sunt* echo created by the enjambment of the first line: "What is the boy now, who has lost his ball, / What, what is he to do?" Berryman quotes Miranda's line verbatim much later in his career, as one of the two epigraphs to *Recovery,* which is dedicated "To the Suffering Healers"—his doctors and attendants in the alcoholic hospital; but more generally the whole class of those who heal others by giving of themselves, among whom he wished to include poets. That novel's other epigraph is from John 7:16: "My doctrine is not mine." This, and the identification of *The Tempest* as "Shakespeare's second Redemptive work," point to the complex at the heart of Berryman's project. Redemption as self-transcendence through an identification with another, achieved through the agency of poetry: this was both his literary aim and his personal hope, until finally he gave up hope. The concept became more explicitly religious later in his life, though only marginally Christian until the very last. Berryman's idea of merging identities comes from a psychological notion of identification, which is essentially Romantic in origin, though complexly so, as will be seen.

James Engell, in his scholarly investigation into the roots of the Romantic ideal of *Einfühlung*—for which "empathy" was coined as a translation—has traced the link between sympathy and imagination back to the 1720's and James "Arbuckle's astonishingly original thought that the imagination is responsible not only for artistic and aesthetic pleasure but also for the ability to put oneself in the place of others."[11]

The function of this ability is multiple, for the Romantic generally as for Berryman. Says Engell,

> On a high philosophical plane, sympathy could be considered the cohesive force behind an organic view of the universe. Yet on a more manageable scale, sympathy also becomes that special power of the imagination which permits the self to escape its own confines, to identify with other people, to perceive things in a new way, and to develop an aesthetic appreciation of the world that coalesces both the subjective self and the objective other.[12]

It works in all these ways for Berryman. He was to develop and elaborate the concept, as we'll see, particularly in connection with his reading of Whitman, but according to his own later testimony concerning **"The Ball Poem,"** the idea's centrality was already apparent to him. His formulation may have begun with his intense involvement in drama, and especially Shakespeare.

Drama is the genre which most requires the author to move out of his own skin into an identification with other characters, and Shakespeare epitomized that ideal for the Romantics, as Engell hardly needs to point out. By the same token, drama is the most "impersonal" genre, a fact that simply illustrates the paradoxical nature of identification.

Berryman sees this clearly, as is apparent in his 1949 essay on Ezra Pound. There he says that the "perverse and valuable doctrine" of the impersonality of the poet, "associated in our time with Eliot's name, was toyed with by Goethe and gets expression in Keats's insistence that the poet 'has no identity—he is continually in, for, and filling some other body'" *(FP,* pp. 264-265). He goes on to declare the doctrine valuable for dramatic poetry, but "somewhat paradoxical" otherwise, partly because "It hides motive, which persists."

Drama had the greater part of Berryman's literary attention for years. He fell early and entirely under the spell of Shakespeare, who remained a lifelong subject of study. Haffenden records Berryman's comment as a graduate student at Cambridge in 1937, "It's awfully silly, I think, ever to do anything but read Shakespeare—particularly when we've only one lifetime" *(L,* p. 85). The following fall he wrote an exam that won him the Oldham Shakespeare Scholarship. For a long time he aspired to be a dramatist himself. While still an undergraduate he wrote an essay on Yeats's drama (1936; now the earliest essay collected in *The Freedom of the Poet*). He finds Yeats's plays trivial "considered in the tradition of English dramatic literature," and ascribes their failure to the fact that "Yeats's habit of mind is not dramatic but meditative" *(FP,* pp. 245 and 246). Over the years he began play after play himself, against mounting evidence that his own "habit of mind" was even less dramatic than Yeats's. His commitment to identity as a literary method is perhaps a vestige of that aspiration. He would begin with the idea of a character, usually historical, and plan to set that character forth in a play. He came closest to fulfilling that plan in **Homage to Mistress Bradstreet,** although that work is of course not only not a play, but an aggressively formal and "poetic" poem. Its innovative audacity is to have the poet-narrator "identify" with the protagonist in an actual seduction scene as well as merging with her more metaphysically.

It may be that his commitment to drama helped to keep Berryman's theoretical heterodoxy inconspicuous for so long. But it surfaced unmistakably in 1950, when he finally completed his critical biography of Stephen Crane.[13] That book is powerfully personal in at least two respects. It is psychoanalytical, probing with Freudian instruments the private motivations of the man who made the work—Berryman assumed the essentiality of the connection—and it is also obviously the work of an author who had identified strongly with his subject.

III. "WE DO NOT YET KNOW WHAT 'I' IS": WHITMAN

Berryman went on to identify with the poet who had made such identification his trademark. In 1954, as a visiting professor at the University of Iowa Writers' Workshop, Berryman "explicated Whitman's 'Song of Myself' at illuminating length . . . and managed to start a miniature Whitman revival at a time when the 'barbarci yawp' was regarded as mouthy, formless, and a poor risk in terms of New Critical analysis" (*L*, p. 239). Presumably on the basis of that work, he wrote the essay "'Song of Myself': Intention and Substance," completed in 1957 but not published until it appeared in *Freedom* in 1976.

Reviewing that volume, Donald Davie concluded,

> It cannot be denied that at some point in mid-career Berryman momentously shifted his stance toward his art and the experience his art fed upon, just as Lowell did with his "Life Studies" (1959). And the shift seems to have to do, not surprisingly, with that inescapable figure in every American poet's heritage, Walt Whitman.[14]

"Momentously shifted his stance" is too strong: rather than *shift*, Berryman's "stance toward his art and the experience his art fed upon" crystallized and clarified. But not to quibble: certainly the art itself changed. By 1955 Berryman had begun writing **Dream Songs** (well before *Life Studies,* as Lowell was the first to acknowledge), and these, while not the open or "naked" poetry they were often taken for, are still very different from the formal measures of **Homage.**

Those differences, and any change in Berryman's poetic "stance," probably have as much to do with the break-up of his eleven-year marriage at the end of the summer 1953, the following peripatetic year alone, and the ignominy of being jailed in the fall of 1954 for drunkenness in Iowa City (a town long inured to drunken poets), as it did with his reading of Whitman. Berryman lost his apartment and his job as a consequence of the arrest, and the episode assumed mythic proportions for him. He slunk off to the protection of Allen Tate at the University of Minnesota, where however he remained unemployed until the beginning

of the next semester. During that empty time (he turned 40 in October 1954) he recorded the dreams and intensive self-analysis that stand behind **The Dream Songs.**

But it remains true that in Whitman Berryman seems to have found confirmation and articulation of his own poetic aims, and in the process of explaining what Whitman is up to he lays out his own convictions, particularly regarding the poetic ego and its operations. Berryman's Whitman has been discussed elsewhere, and James E. Miller, Jr. has pointed out Berryman's use of Whitman as authority for his own opposition to "the long dominant New Critical theories."[15] There are further observations to be made, however. Most generally, Whitman provides a sanction for having it both ways, "both in and out of the game" (*Song of Myself,* Section 4).

More specifically, the title of Berryman's essay already implies the argument about which he is explicit in the text. First of all, the opposition to "intention and most of its romantic corollaries" was elegantly codified in Wimsatt and Beardsley's famous 1954 essay "The Intentional Fallacy." Their argument is that "The design or intention of the author is neither available nor desirable as a standard for judging the success of a work of literary art."[16] This remained the majority opinion well into the sixties. By overtly declaring his subject to be intention (or "motive, which persists"), Berryman set himself in deliberate and conspicuous opposition to the consciously anti-romantic, anti-expressionist criticism of his day. The second term of his title continues his opposition, for "substance"—or "content," to use the more familiar term—had also been rejected as a legitimate topic for critical discussion, except as it manifested itself in "form," that shaping which identified a work as "art," and from which content was supposed to be inseparable.

Whitman's purpose, he thinks, his "intention," is personal: to put the poet's self on record. This intention is only one of four that Berryman finds, the others being the national, the religious, and the metaphysical; but in fact each of those turns out to support the personal.

Berryman not only approves of this aggressive assertion of personality, but takes it for his own, as his often quoted comments on **The Dream Songs** make clear. "Ah—it's personality—it's Henry. . . . It has a plot. Its plot is the personality of Henry as he moves in the world."[17] And in a different interview: "The personality of Henry with his problems, his friends, and his enemies is why the thing came into being."[18] However, these declarations don't represent the simple-minded expressive or "confessional" doctrine that has been almost universally assumed to be their import. Indeed, almost the opposite is true. For one thing, Berryman is concerned not just with the personal self, but with the *idea* of selfhood. Further, in the romanticism he invokes, self-assertion turns inside-out to become something closer to self-abnegation. The personal is advocated and espoused, but the nature of that "personal" is negative. Whitman's self in particular Berryman sees as defining itself by including rather than excluding the world. Such inclusiveness is the opposite of self-expression as it is usually understood.

Throughout this essay he reads the expanding ego of "Song of Myself" as encompassing others, and the external world, only through a process of identification in which the ego is absorbed by the objects of its attention as much as they are absorbed by it. (By melding with the speaking subject these "objects" cease being distinct and opposed external objects. In the terms Buber has made familiar, the "I-it" relationship is transformed into an "I-Thou" relationship.) In this process, self-assertion becomes indistinguishable from self-effacement. Berryman emphasizes the escape from or transcendence of self that is involved for Whitman, and concludes that the self disappears altogether from the poem by the end.

Berryman begins with the observation that the self being asserted is far from simple, single, or unitary: "Whitman's poem has the form of a paean or exultation—'I celebrate myself'—unconditional, closed, reflexive. But this is misleading, for we do not yet know what 'I' is" (*FP*, p. 233). In Berryman's own work, and, he would probably want to claim, in the world at large, "we do not yet know what 'I' is." Berryman's whole career could almost be seen as an investigation into "what 'I' is," and at the end of his life he was still investigating, still pointing out that we don't know. But at this point in his essay he proceeds specifically to investigate the "I" of "Song of Myself."

After his "preamble," Berryman's essay proceeds to consider "substance" through a look at the form of the poem, discussing what most of us would call structure, and with a skill at close reading honed by his editorial work. He sees the poem as falling into four major "movements." His reading illustrates why he insists on the poem's negativity, in the sense of openness: "I take the work in fact to be one of Welcome, self-*wrestling,* inquiry, and wonder—conditional, open, astonished (not exulting as over an accomplished victory, but gradually revealing, puzzling, discovering)" (*FP*, p. 233). The first movement, the first five sections, "consists of a double invitation, from 'I,' or the human body, to the human soul and from 'I,' or the poet, to the reader" (*FP*, p. 233). He then quotes at considerable length to "emphasize in particular his extraordinary passages from helplessness through four stages of the jaunty to

solemnity and darkest, most grievous mystery, *back* to a sort of helplessness which yet proves consonant with the most exalted and persuasive confidence" (*FP*, p. 235).

"The Second Movement of the poem runs, I should say, through Section 19 and is concerned, after this prelude of the grass and death, with the 'I's' identifications *outward . . .*" (*FP*, p. 237).

The Third Movement (through Section 38) he considers to have "Being" for its theme. Negativity is present in these "triumphant explorations of experience" in that Berryman sees Whitman answering his own question of what a man is in two ways: "first, answers that are given as of the *Self*; second, answers that are given as *not* of the Self. Most of the famous passages occur in the first series, but the most intense reality, as a matter of fact, is experienced by him in the second series." Both sorts of answers fail for Whitman, becoming "intolerable," and Berryman sees him as "envisaging between them, with obvious envy, an entirely different kind of being, in the animals of Section 32" (*FP*, p. 237).

By the time Whitman reaches the famous line "I am the man, I suffer'd, I was there"—which from one angle can seem the poem's most distilled self-assertion—Berryman considers that "The self, of course, has disappeared, been put aside; the 'I' is now Soul only, the imagination." And he finds in the line probably "another Christ identification" (*FP*, p. 239). By the end of the "movement" (Section 38) "he becomes, in self-defense, a Self again." But then in the Fourth Movement, "addressed to his 'Eleves'—disciples," since he cannot travel their road for them, "the poet gradually withdraws."

IV. ART FOR USE

Berryman saw the dangers of the desire to escape, even though (or maybe because) it was a greater temptation for him than it had been for Whitman. So he is hard on those forms of transcendence that seem merely escapist, that deny or elude the life they are supposed to be transforming. That is the basis of his complaints against Rilke and Emerson. In Dream Song 3 he says startlingly "Rilke was a *jerk.*" This nearly heretical judgment is somewhat clarified in **"DS 294,"** dedicated to Adrienne Rich:

> I trust your detestation of Carlyle
> the evil way a genius can go.
> I hope you hate Carlyle
> & Emerson's insufferable essays,
> wisdom in every line, while his wife cried upstairs,
> disgusting Emerson & Rilke.

Among Berryman's unpublished papers is a note recording the same sentiment: "these hieratic jerks—Rilke for ex. O I *hate* Rilke." **"DS 3"** qualifies its name-calling with the afterthought "I admit his griefs & music / & titled spelled all-disappointed ladies." The note provides a gloss: "I don't deny his marvellous melody or his post-human sensitivity, but what is he based on? He can deal only w. cripples—"'Das lied des Idioten,' magical."[19]

Now, "Das lied des Idioten" is Rilke's own "Ball Poem." The poem's simple-minded speaker has the same innocence as the young boy in Berryman's poem, or the enisled Miranda. And his childish observations raise similar questions about possession and control:

> Ah, was ist das für ein schöner Ball;
> rot und rund wie ein Überall.
> Gut, dass ihr ihn erschuft.
> Ob der wohl kommt wenn man ruft?
>
> (Oh look at that beautiful ball over there:
> red and round as an Everywhere.
> Good that you made it be.
> If I call, will it come to me?)[20]

The childlike brightness with its unconscious freight of ominousness in the face of an incomprehensible world is presumably what Berryman found "magical." But the problem, apparently, is this character's remove from the sorts of perceptions and problems that confront most of us. And more generally, what Berryman has against Rilke, as against Emerson, is the pursuit of poetic transcendence at the expense of the quotidian, including the people, like Emerson's wife, who inhabit that daily life. Haffenden quotes a letter written late in 1954 or in 1955—that is, when Berryman was just beginning work on *The Dream Songs*—in which he censures "poets such as Rilke for displaying an unearthliness based on 'an elaborate and painfully self-satisfied fear of life':

> it is necessary to get down into the arena and kick around. . . . I like him when he was writing out of his active grief & awe, not these lay-sermons he sprayed around Europe instead of sleeping with people like a wicked but actual man. Love affairs on paper; ugh
>
> (*L*, p. 246)

Strong as his own escapist impulses were, Berryman recognized them for what they were, and himself pursued self-transcendence, or, better, self-reformation, in the hope of transforming his world rather than just being carried out of it. Even his late conversion was to what he called a "God of rescue": not a remote and extra-worldly spirit, but a concrete power of alteration in his immediate mundane activities. This (reluctant) commitment to lived life explains why he preferred Keats to the other English Romantics, and Keats' letters to his poetry. His lifelong objection to Eliot's "impersonality" was based at least partly on the escapist implications of that doctrine (and it will be remembered that "escape" is in fact the word Eliot uses: "Poetry is not a

turning loose of emotion, but an escape from emotion; it is not the expression of personality, but an escape from personality").[21] Against the Eliotic stance, then, Berryman argued the necessity of personality only to oppose escapism, not to oppose self-transcendence more generally.

Empathy is a form of removal from the limitation of oneself by which one does not "swing right along to the infinite nothing," as T. E. Hulme famously charged that romanticism did,[22] but rather remains grounded in human concerns. Against a perhaps more European tradition of Otherness experienced directly, through the immediate experience of the Holy by the isolate individual soul, Berryman stands Whitman's democratic American ideal of Otherness experienced literally in others, *e pluribus unum*.

V. THE REFORMATION OF THE POET

As it anchors the poet in the world, poetic sympathy anchors art in life. For Eliot, operating out of the Symbolist tradition, the effacement of the artist's personality is a consequence of the absolute commitment to art as technique, and therefore "the more perfect the artist, the more completely separate in him will be the man who suffers and the mind which creates."[23] Berryman simply couldn't buy that. At the same time, he saw that his own attitude toward the artistic process separated him from Whitman, as Whitman's set him in opposition to Eliot.

Even in his last and barest poetry, Berryman did not give up his awareness that art for life's sake is achieved through an art greater if possible than that exercised in the name of art for art's sake. He considered that, by contrast, Whitman's messianic vision of the poet's role took him toward something that wasn't finally art. Unlike most of his contemporaries, Berryman didn't underestimate Whitman's craft, and despite its title and its own declared intentions, his essay is a quite formal approach to "Song of Myself," with stretches of highly trained close reading or analysis.

But he sees that Whitman, however artful, finally comes down on the "wrong" side of the art-life question. Whitman entirely accepted Poe's pronouncement that "there can be no such thing as a long poem." He could nonetheless write "this poem of fifty pages" (*FP*, p. 227), Berryman thinks, because "he did not think of it as a poem at all. . . . he thought of it as a work of *life* . . ." (*FP*, p. 228).

By contrast, Berryman always thought of his own work, even at its most personal, as art. "I don't go that far," he said.[24] As a hard-working practising writer, he shared some part at least of Eliot's sense of the priority of craft: "You will have noticed that I have said nothing about my agonies and joys, my wives and children, my liking for my country, my dislike of Communist theory and practice, etc., but have been technical. Art is technical, too" (*FP*, p. 327).

He sees himself engaged in a double endeavor, "a process of life and a process of art," that seems contradictory only in the face of the absolute distinction between life and art which the critical establishment in this country was then insisting upon. Berryman's larger aim was to overthrow or simply deny that distinction, at least in its then-current terms, but his assault upon it from the side of art distinguishes him from his good gray precursor. On the one hand, Whitman was a conscious model: "I think the model in *The Dream Songs* was the other greatest American poem—I am very ambitious—'Song of Myself.'"[25] On the other hand, this is not as unequivocal as it sounds. For he also claimed Eliot as his model, and "the other greatest American poem" meant 'other than *The Waste Land*,' "the best long poem of the age" (*FP*, p. 327). "It is no good looking for models," he said in his 1969 National Book Award acceptance speech, "We want antimodels" (*L*, pp. 351-352). So Eliot was his antimodel. But then Whitman is also a kind of antimodel, though the relation is not so antithetical as that to Eliot.

As the disillusion of Henry's America stands in vivid and painful contrast to the potential of Whitman's, so the self which offers its identifications in *The Dream Songs* does so in a manner and even from motives markedly different from Whitman's. Consider the difference between Whitman's "I am large, I contain multitudes," and **"Dream Song 22," "Of 1826,"** with its catalogue of "I am's." Berryman's survey of common American humanity is a bitter satire ("I am the auto salesman and love you. / I am a teenage cancer, with a plan") aimed at his shallow countrymen who gather to celebrate, ostensibly, the founding of their country while ignorant of or indifferent to its real history and significance, such as the fact, presented obliquely in the last stanza, that Thomas Jefferson and John Adams both died on the same Fourth of July.

Despite Berryman's urge to understand other individuals, to comprehend them in the fullest sense of the word, his vistas are considerably less democratic than Whitman's. And his wavering faith in his fellow man is matched by similar doubts about the powers of his own selfhood.

The fundamental difference in attitude and approach is apparent in the rather neat contrast between Berryman's second epigraph, ". . . I am their musick," from Lamentations 3:63, a passage which begins:

> O Lord, thou hast seen my wrong: judge thou my cause.

> Thou hast seen all my vengeance and all their imaginations against me

—and Whitman's

> Were mankind murderous or jealous upon you, my
> brother, my sister?
> I am sorry for you, they are not murderous or jealous
> upon me,
> All has been gentle with me, I keep no account with
> lamentation,
> (What have I to do with lamentation?)
>
> > ("Song of Myself" 44)

By contrast, and for all that Berryman sings his elegies in a different key from Eliot's, the two are engaged in the same variety of poetic enterprise. **"DS 242"** begins, "about that me," and concludes with the statement about a student suffering from a grief she can't name: "I am her." The sympathetic identification sounds as personal and simply human as Whitman's or Miranda's. But it is art which has enabled Berryman to so identify. Similarly, the Berryman figure in Eileen Simpson's roman à clef *The Maze* says of his new book, the novel's counterpart of *Homage,* "I was as much Daphne as Flaubert was Emma. I'm still working my way out of it."[26]

In the post-Dream Song poem **"Beethoven Triumphant,"** the art itself is what is identified with:

> You force a blurt: Who was I /
> As I these tutti, am I this rallentando?
> This entrance of the oboe?
> > I am all these
> the sane man makes reply on the locked ward.[27]

Though Berryman's focus on art is modernist, the function of the art so focused-on is entirely different. Against the modernist insistence on the non-effectivity of art ("Poetry makes nothing happen"; "A poem should not mean / But be") he opposed an aggressive theory of art for use. The point of art's technicality, for him, is not to separate it from life but to move it closer to life and deeper into it. (The remark already quoted about art's technicality occurs in the same essay in which Berryman complains of the critics on his poem **"Winter Landscape,"** "Nowhere is anything said as to what the poem is *about,* nor is any interest expressed in that little topic" [*FP*, p. 325].)

"Dream Song 94" says "A hospital is where it all has a use, / so is a makar. . . ." "Makar" is an "archaic Scottish word for poet,"[28] which Berryman uses in two other Dream Songs.[29] There are ironies here: there's probably a sardonic note in the hospital comment. "That middle-sized wild man was ill," he says, and so he often was, and often hospitalized, so that he had, with unusual intensity, the usual feelings toward hospitals of mixed gratitude and hostility. Yet he seriously believed that poetry does serve a healing purpose—poets like doctors being "suffering healers." "Makar's" relation to *maker* suggests an aestheticist focus which ought to be exactly at odds with the assertion of poetry's utility, but again, that's Berryman's point: yes, art is technique, but technique in the service of something beyond itself.

If art is for use, of what use is it? First of all, for the audience, the artist's power of identification provides actual knowledge. Working a psychologically informed variation on the time-honored notion that fiction is "truer" than life (or that "the wish is the first truth about us," as Randall Jarrell put it), Berryman argues that art provides an insight into other persons that even those persons themselves cannot provide: "Most of us never get to know many other human beings very well, even our closest friends, even our husbands and wives, above all our children, even ourselves. Our experience of them is discontinuous, our attention uneven, our judgment and understanding uncertain." He is explaining here literature's advantage over life, even when the literature is drama, ordinarily considered the least psychologically revelatory of the genres. "Even when someone *wants* to reveal himself to another person, he is usually not very good at it, and probably most people spend most of their lives in self concealment; but self revelation is a large part of the creation of dramatic character" (*FP*, p. 64). Secondly, art is for both artist and audience an instrument of self-alteration. Through his art and its power of empathy the poet achieves a self-expansion, as we saw Whitman doing. He enacts the human potential for change, to engage in a self-transcendence that amounts finally, for Berryman, to an idea of personal redemption. His clearest statement of the aim of art occurs in a 1959 book review: "Poetry is a terminal activity, taking place out near the end of things, where the poet's soul addresses one other soul only, never mind when. And it aims—never mind *either* communication or expression—at the reformation of the poet, as prayer does" (*FP*, p. 312). This "freeing," as he called it, is then the chief function of art.

In enacting his own "reformation"—understood as freedom—the poet makes possibilities of reformation available to his readers as well. When an interviewer asked Berryman the portentous question, "Of what use do you think art is in the moral world?" Berryman's first reply was a flat "I don't know." And he said again, "I really don't know." But then without further prompting he went on to speak again of knowledge and change:

> It is absolutely certain that you can learn a great deal about life from the novels of Jane Austen. Or from the later novels of George Eliot, say *Middlemarch*. Or from the plays of Shakespeare; that's an example at the highest level. It's very clear that the conduct of someone who has really read the whole *Commedia* is likely to be altered.[30]

The idea that art, and particularly literature, provides "a freeing" runs long and deep through Berryman's

thought. Helen Vendler is exactly right in saying that in Henry Berryman found "some liberated dimension of himself."[31] The choice of *The Freedom of the Poet* as title for his one collection of criticism indicates the importance of the idea to him. Within that volume the term recurs, in titles especially, with a frequency that suggests that Berryman saw it as the unifying theme in his otherwise disparate inspections of literature over the years. The discussion there also make clear however that the liberation he has in mind is the very opposite of self-indulgence or "confessional" overflow. His freedom is achieved, as is always the case in art, through discipline.[32]

By freedom Berryman seems to have meant most largely and fundamentally fulfillment of human desire, freedom from the various toils of human life. Specifically, he imaged this liberty of spirit as a liberation from the constraints of various forms of selfhood. Though he was careful to avoid psychoanalytic jargon, he essentially accepted and agreed with the Freud of *Civilization and Its Discontents*.[33] In that work Freud provides in effect a psychological explanation for the experience of transcendence, and thus accounts for the sort of activity of the ego that Berryman observes in "Song of Myself."

Freud considers that "our present ego-feeling is . . . only a shrunken residue of a much more inclusive—indeed all-embracing—feeling which corresponded to a more intimate bond between the ego and the world about it" (p. 15)—the now famous "oceanic" feeling. We become individuals, then, "ourselves," only at the cost of becoming more limited. We cannot help but experience that selfhood *as* limitation, at least some of the time.

As Freud presents it, the ego's boundaries are by no means so clear or fixed as they seem, and are maintained only through constant effort. Although he doesn't emphasize the ego's flux, the implications of his statements provide Berryman with some sort of theoretical base for his ideas about "fluid identity." The power of identification already implies that the ego is not entirely confined within its usual boundaries (see Engell for a discussion of this issue as it affected Keats's developing thought, pp. 288-292). It was implicit, then, in Berryman's **"Ball Poem"** "discovery . . . that a commitment of identity can be 'reserved,' so to speak, with an ambiguous pronoun." The pronoun is a "shifter," in some grammatical terminologies, varying in its "reference" with the speaker and context. The self is a grammatical construct, and thereby open: "we do not yet know what 'I' is." Berryman's self-proclaimed mastery of pronouns was motivated by that recognition. In 1965, as "a man nearing fifty," and in the middle of writing *The Dream Songs,* Berryman opened the essay in which he discusses **"The Ball Poem"** with the declaration that

"I am less impressed than I used to be by the universal notion of a continuity of individual personality" (*FP*, p. 323). Jerry McGuire, who considers that Berryman "has hinted" (I would put it more strongly) that his own works are among those "that question the integrity of consciousness and the initiating role of the author," finds this process of undermining an integral narrator even in two early poems, where it is not complete, and traces its development to *The Dream Songs,* where he considers that Berryman's "earlier themes ["love, death, personal worth, and their combined shadow, time"] now recur always in this context of shifting consciousness."[34]

As Berryman explained that "context," "Henry, for instance, refers to himself as 'I,' 'he' and 'you,' so that the various parts of his identity are fluid. They slide, and the reader is made to guess who is talking to whom."[35] The personality that dissolves "into another without relinquishing the original" in *Love & Fame,* he explains, is "that of the nature poet omnipotent and that of the aging man deprived and powerless" (**"Scholia,"** n.p.). The passionate sense of identification is with himself, then, perhaps as the only means to Unity of Being. The situation is the same in *The Dream Songs,* he seems to say, except that there are more selves: "In the very long poem [*The Dream Songs*], of course, many personalities shift, reify, dissolve, survive, project—remaining one" (**"Scholia"**). The "one" they remain is however as ambiguous as the pronouns themselves. A conscious tension between the one and many is superimposed on the poem's conscious (and analogous) tension between life and art. Once again Berryman wanted to have it both ways. His "I" is different from Whitman's, then, even in its borderlessness. Dennis Donoghue, talking about the difference between the two poets' poetic lines—Whitman's extended and inclusive, Berryman's truncated and fragmented—says:

> Whitman's aesthetic implies that the self is the sum of its experiences, not the sum of its dissociated fragments. In Whitman the self is not dissociated, the self is deemed to be whole at any and every moment. The experiences are diverse; one experience follows upon another, the receiving self is enlarged. But the self is never understood as a fraction; it is always a whole number.[36]

In *The Dream Songs* decidedly the self is sometimes not a whole number:

> Hunger was constitutional with him,
> women, cigarettes, liquor, need need need
> until he went to pieces.

> (311)

It may even be true that "As his hold on his own personality becomes less secure, the poet is increasingly able to identify with the perilous lives of others."[37] And part of the motive in the drive toward self-transcendence

would seem to be pure escape, freedom from a self which manifests these dismaying tendencies. Yet even when fragmented, the self keeps on keeping on:

> The pieces sat up & wrote. They did not heed
> their piecedom but kept very quietly on
> among the chaos.

> (311)

If Whitman gave voice to "others as himself," he showed Berryman by inversion—a different sort of "anti-model" from Eliot—how to give voice to himself as others.

VI. DEATH

For a collection of poets' own favorite poems, Berryman chose an early work, **"The Dispossessed,"** written in 1947, and published the following year in a volume which used the same resounding title. "The notion of dispossession," Berryman says in his comment upon the poem, points in two "opposite directions . . . : the miserable, *put out of one's own,* and the relieved, saved, undevilled, de-spelled."[38]

Freedom from one's self has, like dispossession (or as a form of dispossession), two faces. If the ultimate human aim "is simply the programme of the pleasure principle,"[39] and this drive toward pleasure is at its most minimal a freedom from the pain of conflict, then the drive must finally be toward final stasis, the inorganic. So his own inexorable logic led Freud to conclude in *Beyond the Pleasure Principle* "The goal of all life is death."

For Berryman as for Freud creative activity, as a form of Eros, stands against death's unmaking, the chaos or formlessness that Berryman symbolizes (for personal reasons as well as traditional ones) as the sea: "for the grand sea awaits us, which will then us toss / & endlessly us undo" (**"DS 303"**). (A Barbados saying has it that "The sea ain' got no back door.") But the desire that creation satisfies, the freedom from the boundaries of a narrow ego armored against reality's assaults, is a desire that may also be satisfied by that different sort of dissolution. If the siren call of Eros cannot be met, Thanatos has a song of its own. So the two desires, initially separate and differently motivated, can meld into one longing for release, the sleep of dreams become inseparable from the sleep of death, "easeful Death," as our poetic tradition recognized long before Freud systematized its insights. Berryman found that melding in Shakespeare especially ("our little life is rounded with a sleep") and in Whitman. Certainly his own discussions of "freedom" assume the ultimate similarity of the drives toward pleasure and toward death.

In the Whitman essay he says, "we recognize as of psychological origin the profound dissatisfaction (no doubt sexual in character) that aims at *loss of identity,* in the poem, in two ways, through these identifications and through death—this is why death is a major subject" (*FP*, p. 232; his emphasis). Of "the magical interlude of the animals" in "Song of Myself," Berryman says that envy of animals (such as Rilke's) "expresses again, like death, a longing for escape from the human condition" (*FP*, p. 239). At the end of the poem he thinks "the poet gradually withdraws," as we've seen; and where the poet withdraws *to* is interesting: Section 52 "truly sounds like the speech-back-to-us of a being already elsewhere, *in* Happiness as a place. One might be surprised that he troubles to speak back, but this is his nature" (*FP*, p. 241).

He finds the same sort of longing for release in Shakespeare, and especially in Prospero's longing for escape—from passion, power, and responsibility specifically, from the self more generally. In "Shakespeare's Last Word," he speaks of

> . . . the thematic hammer in *The Tempest* of the word "free," the central word in the play. This is Shakespeare's word. It first appears as "Libertie," in Ariel's demand—which, with Prospero's promise, alluded to throughout and at last performed, is our metaphorical and dramatic instruction in the play's prime theme. But the constant words are "freedom," "free".
>
> (*FP*, p. 81)

"In the final line," he points out, "the final word, of the epilogue, Prospero asks the audience to set him 'free'" (*FP*, p. 82). He goes on then to discuss how Prospero *is* set free: "to be free of unruly and discreditable desire is the heart of the play's desire, and even in this does Prospero participate, released from the intoxications of hatred and might" (*FP*, p. 82).

A second essay on *The Tempest* supplies the volume with its title, "The Freedom of the Poet," though the essay, more biographical than the first, is actually less concerned with the issue of freedom. However, it closes with the same essential point:

> It is remarkable—in a work rich with the happiness of the exercise of supreme art—how often, and with what longing, *sleep* is invoked. . . . This longing—for release, for freedom—it is which resolves, I think, a genuine difficulty that I cannot truly remember any critic to have noticed: the coarse discrepancy, to appearance, between Prospero's reassurance, "be cheerefull Sir," to Ferdinand, and his celebrated, magnificent, apparently disillusioned and frightening forecast of universal dissolution that follows. But there is no discrepancy, and it is neither disillusioned nor frightening, this forecast—though not Christian either. It is radiant and desirous.
>
> (*FP*, pp. 86-87)

And he ends by quoting it.

What is unchristian is the finality of the "sleepe" that Prospero envisions, the fact that no celestial life afterward is imagined; "this insubstantiall Pageant faded" shall "Leaue not a racke behind." However, freedom is most fundamentally a religious concept for Berryman, and some tenets of Eastern religions, and even of Christianity, are closely akin to the idea as he understands it. He concerns himself with those connections in other of his discussions of freedom, and particularly in discussing Cervantes.

"The Freedom of the Don" is the other most important essay in *Freedom* besides the Whitman essay (and also not previously published. Giroux tentatively dates it 1960). Don Quixote was a signal book and character for Berryman, and especially for ***The Dream Songs,*** for which it provides some of the technique as well as part of the anti-heroic chivalry theme.

The essay calls our attention to Cervantes' "massive instruction to humility." "This word occurs again and again in Cervanticist criticism, with reason." The reason is that "If any virtue is more 'basic' in Cervantes's thought, it has yet to be discovered" (*FP*, p. 150). Glossing Sancho's goat story, Berryman finds a "philosophical" point: "abolition of self, a central tenet in Buddhism," and in support of which he tells a story of his own.[40] "The Christian counterpart," he argues, "is humility. The reader must be humble, as the author is" (*FP*, p. 152).

Not surprisingly, he finds *Don Quixote* to be a quest novel: "Quest, let's call the subject. It was Hamlet's also, and Oedipus', and King Lear's for freedom from the responsibilities of power, and Dante's in the Commedia." But his answer to his own question, "What is the quest for?" is a little more surprising. He digresses for a paragraph on the irrelevance of subject matter ("A magician stranded?—*The Tempest*. . . . Whales? a Puritan adultery?" (*FP*, p. 158). But then he confounds that (conventional) opinion with, not only the assertion that "the object of this quest is freedom," but the further claim that that same "topic" is the subject "of all art of which I have any knowledge." A large claim. It gains plausibility from his having already made clear that, as with Whitman, once again the freedom sought, so far from being personal and assertive, is negative, a matter finally of self-dissolution.

In the essay "The Development of Anne Frank," the focus is on growth, and the discussion ends with a discussion of freedom. Anne's "conversion" to adulthood from childhood in the forcing-house of the Annexe is compared to religious conversion, specifically Augustine's, and the *Diary* to his *Confessions* as documents which not merely recount the experience but make "the process itself available" (*FP*, p. 93).

Anne loses her superficial liberty, both physical freedom and the freedom of normal, gaily carefree girlhood, then evolves under "a special pressure" (*FP*, p. 93) to a higher level of it. "We began, then, with a certain kind of freedom, which is destroyed; we passed through a long enslavement, to the creation of a new kind of freedom" (*FP*, p. 106). This "new kind of freedom" is not simply the freedom of what he calls elsewhere in the essay "play of mind" (*FP*, p. 105), a trite freedom of imagination when the body is tethered. Rather she has enacted a permanent alteration in her self, a "reformation," through her writing (though, curiously, Berryman doesn't discuss the role the keeping of the diary itself played in the maturation process)—a conversion: she has become someone else. The process is not complete, or final, of course; it never is. When Anne fails, at the end, as Berryman thinks she does, it is not through death; death is not her loss of freedom. Her second freedom, he says, "is destroyed, too, or rather—not so much destroyed—as turned against itself" (*FP*, p. 106). He quotes then the last sentence in the last letter, or entry, in the diary: "[I] keep on trying to find a way of *becoming* what I would so like to be, and what I could be if . . . there weren't any other people living in the world." Says Berryman, "The italics of the lacerating verb are mine, but the desperate recognition that one must advance ("self-creation," in Whitehead's term) and that there are circumstances in which one cannot, and the accusing dots, are hers" (*FP*, p. 106).

Like Anne's conversion and like religious conversion, the artist's "reformation" is achieved through ordeal. Explaining that Anne "was forced to mature, in order to survive," Berryman is willing to generalize: "the hardest challenge, let's say, that a person can face without defeat is the best for him" (*FP*, p. 104). He then uses very similar language in talking with interviewers about art. He tells William Heyen, "Art is created out of ordeal and crisis. The greatest poem ever written was made by a fanatic who had to live in exile. The *Commedia*."[41] (A religious poem, one notes; perhaps *the* religious poem). Likewise he told Peter Stitt, "I do strongly feel that among the greatest pieces of luck for high achievement is ordeal. . . . My idea is this: the artist is extremely lucky who is presented with the worst possible ordeal which will not actually kill him."[42] And he ends that statement with the rather astonishing claim, "I hope to be nearly crucified."

Statements of this kind are no doubt what have led Berryman's biographer and so many reviewers and commentators, including Robert Lowell, into the understandable conviction that Berryman was self-consciously following the trajectory of a *poète maudit*.[43] He would seem to be operating in the post-Romantic, specifically symbolist tradition that takes art as religion's replacement. The idea seems explicit, in fact, in one of the four epigraphs to **Delusions, Etc.**: "*On parle toujours de 'l'art réligieux.' L'art est réligieux.*" (Peter Stitt ascribes the quotation to Paul Claudel.)[44] But his point is in a way just the opposite. Rather than there being a

religious art we can distinguish from secular art, *all* art is religious—not because it has replaced the religious function in a world in which God is known to be dead, but rather because art has the same aim as religion, and has had, all along. The poet may be something of a Christ figure in his suffering, but he is not a replacement, or alternative, to Christ, cast upon the altar of Art rather than religion. Rather his suffering, like Christ's own, serves the greater aim of redemption, of himself and of his fellow man. So his art *is* religious whether or not it is overtly "*l'art réligieux.*" For the same reason, the artist's suffering as Berryman understands it is categorically different from the self-gratifying suffering of the *poète maudit*. The examples of artists' ordeals that Berryman actually names are not Baudelairean agons, but "Beethoven's deafness, Goya's deafness, Milton's blindness, that kind of thing."[45] And ultimately even the sacrifice is in one sense not a sacrifice, in Berryman's version of artistic self-immolation, because the artist achieves personal redemption, that "freeing." Following the Biblical injunction, in losing himself he finds himself. That is why Berryman says of this reformation, "We may feel sorry for the society, as we do for a man who has never been in love, but hardly for the poet" (*FP*, p. 312).

Art's religious function *qua* art (poetry *qua* language), implicit in the entire Whitman essay, is explicit in the comment: "the Johannine *Logos* (God's self-revelation, in Christ—whose name is Word, as His Father's is I AM or Being) influenced Whitman's thought even more than his passion for grand opera, which dominates Section 26" (*FP*, p. 231). James Miller says of that same comment "Some readers will be surprised at such a theological interpretation of this section of 'Song of Myself.'"[46] He's no doubt right, but within the context of Berryman's thought as a whole, the collocation makes complete sense. That's why the reader's necessary "submission to the artist" (*FP*, p. 151) does not seem to him to contradict the artist's "abolition-of-self." He sees Whitman's secularism as a kind of ultimate religion: "It is clear that Whitman envisages a post-Christianity (and post-Buddhism, post-Hinduism) which will serve science and, *eventually* . . . egalitarianism" (*FP*, p. 229).

Although death can be understood as ultimate release, it is also ultimate human bondage ("we hafta *die*," **"DS 36"**), the greatest price of individuality or selfhood. Real freedom must be, or include, freedom from death. That freedom is one of the comforts religion provides, usually in Christianity's way, by denying it *as* death. In Christian doctrine, one dies and does not die. Berryman can't accept a simple idea of the soul's continuity, but turns to art for another version of death that is not death. He finds in *Song of Myself* "the attack upon time that characterizes all great poets" (*FP*, p. 234). To attack temporality is to attack death. Art as a stay against death, the permanence that counters the transience of human life, is of course one of the oldest topoi. Berryman incorporates that topos, but goes beyond it. (His frequent comparisons of poems to progeny, of artistic creation to childbearing, put a special emphasis on the role of both as our only forms of immortality.) Art seems for him almost coterminous with individuals, whether "fictional" (Henry) or "real" (Anne Bradstreet). Within the poem, the individual need not die. Not only, again, for the conventional reason that characters "live on" in fiction. Even within the works of art—where the character must after all be mortal to maintain human verisimilitude—he may yet both die and not die.

As we've seen, that's what Berryman considers happens to Whitman at the end of *Song of Myself*. In "The Freedom of the Don" he is even more explicit. Sancho, for one thing, is at the end of the book "restored to his original nothingness," Berryman says (*FP*, p. 157). Then, so is the Don. Having asserted that the novel's quest is for freedom, Berryman asks, "How is the Don's freedom arrived at, and in what does it consist?" (*FP*, p. 158). For one, the Don provides for Sancho the leadership he seeks: "freedom from inactivity—the proverbial Spanish vice" (*FP*, p. 158). A second freedom is consciousness:

> Throughout he *sees*: on p. 204 (of Cohen's translation) we understand at last: he is not taken in: he *sees what is* (what we see); but he also sees what is not—and it is in accord with the second that he acts,—and indeed isn't that what all Christians do? and all decent men? and everybody?
>
> (p. 158)

His final freedom is to be relieved of the burden of consciousness. The essay ends, "Then he is set free from that responsibility" (*FP*, p. 158).

In his brief essay on John Crowe Ransom's ballad "Captain Carpenter," Berryman points to the Christ comparison (while acknowledging Ransom's rejection of it) and then finds the Captain to be "Don Quixote, though, of course, transposed" (*FP*, p. 279). The remainder of the piece consists in an explanation of this comparison, or investigation, as he calls it, leading up to their similar deaths. Most readers of Cervantes, he says, will at the end of the novel "feel that the Don has died. But this is not quite so: he has both died and not died; one is shaken with an ambiguity only less mysterious than the corresponding event in *Oedipus at Colonus*."[47]

In a 1966 interview (**77 Dream Songs** had been published, but Berryman was still assembling Songs for the later volume), Berryman made the same reference, but this time in explicit comparison to his own character. In the last Dream Songs, he says, the subordinated voice of the poet proper returns,

leaving the fate of Henry, which has been discussed elaborately at many points earlier, in doubt—the way, if we now compare a chicken to a buffalo, I'm a chicken and Sophocles is a buffalo; the way in which Sophocles made mysterious the fate of Oedipus in *Oedipus at Colonus,* one of the reasons the play is so difficult to deal with: because Oedipus both dies and does not die.[48]

Earlier in the same interview he had talked at some length about Henry in the same connection:

> I would only say that at the end of the first book, **77 Dream Songs,** he disappears from the poem completely, and the whole fourth book, which is unpublished as yet, consists of *opus posthumous* songs, thirteen of them: Opus Posthumous Number One, and then just in case anybody thought I was kidding, Opus Posthumous Number Two, and Three, and so on up to Thirteen. Meanwhile there's a simulacrum of death earlier in the Dream Songs. But Henry is alive and well, in a certain sense, at the end of the seventh book. The work is far from being a comedy although parts of it are funny, but it's not a tragedy either. It's intended as descriptive.[49]

He would seem to want to put Henry in the end in a position like that of Whitman at the end of *Song of Myself*: ". . . a being already elsewhere, *in* Happiness as a place" (*FP*, p. 241). T. S. Eliot's J. Alfred Prufrock can likewise be understood as returned from "elsewhere," in Berryman's textbook presentation of what he calls "Prufrock's Dilemma."

> We have seen Prufrock already imagined as dead, the suggestion of the epigraph, and at the end of the poem he drowns. Here he thinks of himself as *come back*. Lazarus, perhaps, is the person whom one would most like to interview—another character from sacred history, not Christ's forerunner but the subject of the supreme miracles . . .—the one man who would tell us . . . what it is like.
>
> (*FP*, p. 274)

In the "Op. Post." Songs Henry, "the abominable & semi-mortal Cat" (**"DS 80"**), is explicitly compared to Lazarus (with perhaps glancing allusion to Sylvia Plath's also suicidal "Lady Lazarus," given the explicit mention of her in **"DS 172"** and **"187"**). What's funny and ironic is that, once resurrected, Henry's only thought is to return to the "cozy grave" (**"DS 82"**). He becomes (in Op. Posth. 14, the song added to the original arrangement), "Lazarus with a plan / to get his own back." "His own" is the ultimate version of that hole from which he voted in Song 2, womb and tomb, where he can enjoy, as Berryman thinks Whitman does, "a sort of helplessness which yet proves consonant with the most exalted and persuasive confidence" (*FP*, p. 235).

"The saved are different" (*FP*, p. 157). Whitman is saved, Oedipus is saved, the Don is saved. Prufrock, though hardly saved, does and does not drown. Guido de Montefeltro (whose words from the *Inferno* provide Prufrock's epigraph), in hell himself, gives Dante his information on the assumption that no one returns from hell, but Dante does just that, and is saved. These miracles are all accomplished by literature. Only in the work of art—or the holy book, the "wisdom work"—does the voice from beyond the grave come back to aid the living, come back to help them to achieve that "reformation" that is finally release from the self altogether.

Poetry is where you have it both ways, or, to be more accurate, where you both have it both ways and you don't. Henry both is and is not Henry because he is both Henry and an interested listener to Henry. (As Berryman said of Stephen Crane, he "was not only a man with truths to tell, but an interested listener to this man.")[50] He enables John Berryman both to be John Berryman, and not, because John Berryman is both John Berryman and Henry. Poetry both provides immortality and does not.

Of Henry's several deaths in *The Dream Songs,* the last one is the most final—in some ways; but it is also the most ambiguous and mysterious. **"Dream Song 382"** is untitled; it might be called "Berrymans Wake." It begins, "At Henry's bier let some thing fall out well," a request to counterbalance the lament that opens the Songs in **"DS 1"**: "thereafter nothing fell out as it might or ought." Here he imagines the scene as quiet and dignified, "everybody's mood / subdued, subdued," then there is a stanza break—"until the Dancer comes. . . ." In *Love & Fame* Berryman speaks to himself of himself at 21, "obscurely foreseeing / the hectic dancer of your delicious end."[51] Here she is, looking like Diane Wakoski in the 60's, "in a short short dress / hair black & long & loose, dark dark glasses, / uptilted face, / pallor & strangeness." When she appears "the music changes," she dances, "& she is free." She is free, and she comes to bring Henry's freedom. Momentarily—but only at the moment of Henry's destruction—the contradictions are embodied in a single figure. Just as Henry's "flashing & bursting tree" in **"DS 75,"** "unshedding bulky boleproud blue-green moist / thing," is a funny member of the same genus as Yeats's great-rooted blossomer, embodiment of the one and the many, so Berryman's Dancer, whatever else she may also be, is a relative of Yeats's dancer who cannot be told from the dance. Yeatsian echoes appear also in the final stanza's description of the Dancer's return "to the terrible gay / occasion hopeless & mad" (where the adjectives may refer either to the occasion or to the Dancer). The contradictions of "terrible gay" and "hopeless & mad" (at least if mad is understood as also Yeatsian and manic, as in "why should not old men be mad?"), Berryman's characteristic contradictions, are repeated in the rhymed endings of lines 16 and 17: "it's hell," and "all is well." The poem ends, "she dances Henry away." Henry is gone

from the Songs. He is mentioned once by the first-person speaker of the last two Songs (which both continue to play on meanings of "fall" and "fell"). But he has disappeared as an actor. He has both died and not died.

Berryman's own drive to self-destruction was so strong that suicide was as much a temptation to him as a threat, and it seems to have appealed to him increasingly as he grew older and wearier, as his sources of hope, his desperately renewed commitments to "the reformation of the poet," became more obviously delusory. Perhaps then when he jumped off his bridge, he thought of himself as being danced away to freedom. Maybe that's what accounted for the jaunty wave the local paper reported he gave to a horrified observer standing on the lower level of the bridge.

Roy Harvey Pearce, speaking of the defining differences of that post-modern poetry toward which Berryman and his contemporaries pointed the direction, says,

> I would not deny the dangers of the new poets' way. For striving toward the subject-to-subject relationship . . . can be an act so strained and desperate as to lead first to the homogenization and then to the annihilation of the sensibility. Expanding the definition of "man," exploring the definition to the utmost—this can lead to an act of suicide mistakenly made out to be a rite of passage.[52]

Whether suicide as rite of passage is a mistake or not is of course more than we know. (I happen to agree with Professor Pearce. But, still among the quick, we can hardly speak with authority.)

Robert Giroux, Berryman's friend, editor, and publisher, was likewise convinced that Berryman's suicide was a terrible mistake. In his preface to *The Freedom of the Poet,* Giroux tells how, when he visited Minneapolis for the new Berryman baby Sarah's christening, Berryman showed him "a sheaf of notes" for a project "entitled *Sacrifices.*" Giroux then gives verbatim a passage he copied out:

> An entirely new kind of freedom manifested in several ways, in retirement, in death, but invariably in a special retirement or death that contains as one of its chief meanings a repudiation of the earlier 'freedom.' There is a *conversion,* in short, if we can employ the term without either religious or psychoanalytic overtones. Someone is changed, simply, into someone else.

Giroux, feeling the inevitable guilt and grief, says "I still did not get the message, not until January 7, 1972, when I heard the incredible news of John's leap to his death from the high bridge over the Mississippi" (*FP,* p. ix). But he could spare himself, I think, at least if he were willing to accept the situation in Berryman's own terms. For the "message" of that passage is not simply that Berryman was planning (again or still) his own demise, but that he'd found a way to view that demise that freed him from its terror. The language is very like that he uses to describe Anne Frank, whose "conversion" is also a matter of becoming another person, creating for herself "a new kind of freedom" (*FP,* p. 106)—the same phrase he uses here. He followed the Freudian insight—that Eros and Thanatos are both opposites and not—to its ultimate conclusion. He went beyond "the earlier 'freedom'"—the poetic and Romantic beliefs in transcendence and/or the immortality of poetry, which are besides the religious the most usual defenses against the pall of Death's inevitability—to a conception of death that permitted him acceptance. It represented release to him, apparently, as to a Christian, but a profoundly unchristian release, like Prospero's (so that he could commit the unchristian act of taking his life himself).

Whether what Berryman experienced in dying may be termed a "conversion" or a rite of passage, in any further sense, the skeptical may properly doubt. I doubt it myself. But it was what he chose, his way of losing himself to find himself—to find freedom.

Notes

1. *The Dream Songs* (New York: Farrar, Straus & Giroux, 1969). All Dream Songs will hereafter be referred to in the text, by number.

2. *Love & Fame* (New York: Farrar, Straus & Giroux, 1970, second ed. 1972), pp. 85 and 82, respectively. Hereafter referred to in the text as *LF.*

3. *Recovery* (New York: Dell, 1973).

4. *The Freedom of the Poet* (New York: Farrar, Straus & Giroux, 1976), p. 18. Hereafter abbreviated in the text as *FP.*

5. Jonathan Sisson, "My Whiskers Fly: An Interview with John Berryman," *Ivory Tower,* October 3, 1966, p. 35.

6. *Part of Nature, Part of Us: Modern American Poets* (Cambridge: Harvard University Press, 1980, pp. 117-118.

7. *John Haffenden: The Life of John Berryman* (New York: Routledge & Kegan Paul, 1982), p. 84. Hereafter abbreviated in the text as *L.*

8. George Dillon, *Poetry* Magazine Papers, 1936-1953, Department of Special Collections, University of Chicago Library. My thanks to Sem C. Sutter and the Special Collections staff for their assistance, and to the Poetry Committee for permission to quote this passage.

9. (Norfolk, Conn.: New Directions, 1942), and (New York: Sloane, 1948) respectively.

10. *Short Poems* (New York: Farrar, Straus & Giroux, 1967), p. 14. Berryman's ellipses, as printed.

11. *The Creative Imagination: Enlightenment to Romanticism* (Cambridge: Harvard University Press, 1981), p. 145.

12. Engell, pp. 143-144.

13. *Stephen Crane* (New York: William Sloane Associates, 1950).

14. *New York Times Book Review,* quoted by James E. Miller, Jr., *The American Quest for a Supreme Fiction: Whitman's Legacy in the Personal Epic* (Chicago: University of Chicago, 1979), p. 9.

15. Miller, p. 237.

16. W. K. Wimsatt, Jr., and Monroe C. Beardsley, "The Intentional Fallacy," *The Verbal Icon: Studies in the Meaning of Poetry* (Lexington: University of Kentucky Press, 1954), p. 3.

17. "An Interview with John Berryman," Harvard *Advocate* 103 (Spring 1969), 5-6.

18. Sisson, p. 34.

19. Diary 1965-72. In the John Berryman archives in the Manuscript Archives of the University of Minnesota libraries. Quoted by permission of Kate Berryman.

20. *The Selected Poetry of Rainer Maria Rilke,* ed. and trans. by Stephen Mitchell (New York: Random House, 1982), pp. 18-19.

21. "Tradition and the Individual Talent," *Selected Essays, 1917-1932* (New York: Harcourt, Brace, and Co., 1932), reprinted in *Criticism: The Major Texts,* ed. Walter Jackson Bate (New York: Harcourt, Brace & World, 1952), p. 529.

22. "Classic and Romantic," *Speculations: Essays on Humanism and the Philosophy of Art,* ed. Herbert Read, 1924. Also reprinted in Bate, p. 566.

23. Bate, p. 527. Eliot explains, "For it is not the 'greatness,' the intensity, of the emotions, the components, but the intensity of the artistic process . . . that counts" (p. 528).

24. Peter Stitt, "The Art of Poetry XVI: John Berryman 1914-72," *Paris Review* 14 (Winter 1972), 192.

25. *Paris Review,* pp. 190-191.

26. (New York: Simon and Schuster, 1975), p. 81.

27. *Delusions, Etc.* (New York: Farrar, Straus & Giroux, 1972), p. 23.

28. J. M. Linebarger, *John Berryman* (New York: Twayne, 1974), p. 95.

29. The other two Songs are DS 43, where the manuscript shows the change from "poet," and DS 184, where Henry is "Failed as a makar."

30. Martin Berg, "A Truly Gentle Man Tightens and Paces: An Interview with John Berryman," *Minnesota Daily Magazine,* 20 Jan. 1971, p. 17.

31. *Part of Nature, Part of Us,* p. 120.

32. Interestingly enough, this concept of freedom, which from some angles might seem idiosyncratic or excessively romantic, has recently been given a sober, scholarly recommendation. In his Presidential Address to the Modern Language Association at the annual convention in December 1982, Wayne Booth offered as the central function of literary study something that sounds very like Berryman:

> As I see it now, my teachers and I, at every defensible stage of my story, were in the business of freeing ourselves into whatever was for us the next order of human awareness or understanding, the next step forward in our ability to join other minds, through language. . . . Whatever our terms for it, whatever our theories about how it happens or why it fails to happen more often, can we reasonably doubt the importance of that moment, at any level of study, when any of us— you, me, Malcolm X, my great-grandfather—succeeds in entering other minds, or "taking them in," as nourishment for our own?

> (*PMLA,* 98 [1983], 317-318)

33. Trans. James Strachey (New York: W. W. Norton, 1962). In a December 1969 letter to an enquiring graduate student, Berryman confirmed, "I have read most of Freud and have no doubt been greatly influenced by him especially his Civilizations & Its Discontents, wh. I've been lecturing on here off & on for the last 15 years" (Patricia Brenner, "John Berryman's *Dream Songs*: Manner and Matter," Diss. Kent State University 1970, p. 48, n. 3). Referring to the same student a year later in his *Paris Review* interview, he told Peter Stitt:

> She also thinks, and so do some other people, that the work is influenced by the later work of Freud, especially *Civilization and Its Discontents,* and that is very likely. For years I lectured on the book every year here at Minnesota, so I am very, very familiar with it—almost know it word for word.

> (p. 191)

34. "John Berryman: Making a Poem of the Self," *Modern Poetry Studies* X, 2-3 (1981), 176.

35. Jane Howard, "Whisky and Ink, whisky and ink," *Life* 63 (July 21, 1967), 76.

36. "Berryman's Long Dream," *Art International* 13 (March 1969), 62.

37. Martin Dodsworth, "John Berryman: An Introduction," *The Survival of Poetry* (London: Faber & Faber, 1970), p. 128.

38. *Poet's Choice,* ed. Paul Engle and Joseph Langland (New York: Delta Books, 1966), p. 136.

39. *Civilization and Its Discontents,* p. 23. Berryman seems to have relied on Freud's summary here of his reluctant progress toward belief in a death wish, rather than on Freud's earlier and more detailed presentation of the idea in *Beyond the Pleasure Principle.*

40. The Buddha was approached by a Brahmin bearing gifts in both hands. He said to the Brahmin, "Drop it!" and the Brahmin let fall the gift in his right hand. He came nearer. "Drop it!" said the Enlightened One, and the Brahmin let fall the gift in his left hand. He came closer, with empty hands. "Drop it!" the Buddha advised, and the Brahmin understood (pp. 151-2).

41. "John Berryman: A Memoir and an Interview," *The Ohio Review* 15 (Winter 1974), 60.

42. *Paris Review,* p. 207.

43. In her review of the biographies of Berryman and Lowell, Marjorie Perloff considers the contradictoriness as itself modernist, reflecting the modernist literary values of tension and paradox. Such a reading of their lives is ingenious and no doubt has some substance—though in Berryman's case at least emotional and intellectual inclusiveness derived more from his own immersion in Shakespeare, among other things, than from earlier Elizabethans filtered through Eliot. A more serious objection is that she presents both poets as more uncritically committed to the *poète maudit* model than the facts warrant. ("Poètes Maudits of the Genteel Tradition," *American Poetry Review,* May/ June 1983, pp. 32-38.)

44. "Berryman's Last Poems," *Concerning Poetry* 6 (Spring 1973), p. 9.

45. *Paris Review,* p. 207.

46. Miller, p. 237.

47. The comparison to Captain Carpenter is that at the end he seems totally dismembered, but in fact "along with his heart is *not* taken his tongue, so presumably he (the tradition, both of chivalry and Art) talks on, like Faulkner's Man in the Nobel Prize address" (*FP,* p. 281).

48. Sisson, p. 34.

49. Sisson, p. 17.

50. *Stephen Crane,* p. 277.

51. "Shirley and Auden," p. 8.

52. "The Burden of Romanticism: Toward the New Poetry," *Iowa Review* 2 (1971), 124-5.

Barbara Hardy (essay date spring 1991)

SOURCE: Hardy, Barbara. "Re-reading Berryman: Power and Solicitation." *English* 40, no. 166 (spring 1991): 37-46.

[*In the following essay, Hardy offers an assessment of Berryman's poetic oeuvre, maintaining that he "writes poetry which mixes what is admirable with what is intolerable."*]

The new edition of Berryman's *Collected Poems 1937-1971* does not include all the poems written, or even published, between these years.[1] It is described as a collection of those volumes arranged by the poet himself, with the exception of 9 poems published with 11 others as **'Twenty Poems'** in *Five Young American Poets* (1940), and **The Dream Songs** which have a volume to themselves. The poems in the posthumous volume **Henry's Fate and Other Poems** (1976) are omitted, because the poet was not responsible for the collection, though he had published some of them in magazines. Some are essential reading, including a group about fellow-alcoholics, some hitherto unpublished dream songs (not in the new edition of **Dream Songs**), some of his most individually desperate poems of despair and struggle against despair, including his last poem, written about not committing suicide, just before he did commit suicide, 'I don't. And I didn't. Sharp the Spanish blade . . .', and one of his better religious poems, **'Phase Four'.** Charles Thornbury's introduction to the **Collected Poems** quotes freely some suppressed poems from **Love & Fame** (1971), Berryman's most notoriously revelatory and indulgent book, usefully draws on the poet's own observations, has some good analysis of syntax and verse-craft, but stays close to Berryman's self-sympathy. It is interesting to have the chronological order of publication, determined by the poet, rearranged in the interest of compositional chronology, so that the original **Berryman's Sonnets,** (1967), now **Sonnets to Chris,** comes after the first volume, **The Dispossessed** (1948) and before **Homage to Mistress Bradstreet** (1953). This sonnet-sequence is revealed as the creative changepoint, taking the poet out of his early impersonal and austere imitations into the freer syntax, lexis, and dramatised passions of **Mistress Bradstreet** and the wild and inventive **Dream Poems,** which introduced Berryman the language-changer. Despite the exclusion of **Henry's Fate,** on the grounds that it was not chosen and arranged by the poet, Thornbury bases his selection of **Sonnets to Chris** (including the title) not on the author's designed 1967 publication, but on the typescript. These sonnets were published as **Berryman's Sonnets** twenty years or so after their composition, and the assertive and deceptive authorial title, unfortunately replaced by the typescript's title **Sonnets to Chris,** proclaims autobiographical rawness, closeness to life, and clandestine narrative. The poems accumulate a di-ary of desire and loss. They tell the story of a secret love-affair with allusive and fragmentary reticence and are more like George Meredith's sonnet-sequence *Modern Love* than the Renaissance sonnets they are often compared to and sometimes echo and emulate. After the narrative fullness and traditional discourse of **The Dispossessed** Berryman's lyric gift went underground to discover the roots of a new language, slangy and scholarly, cryptic and repetitive, indulgent and moral, declaring, not recollecting, passions in action. He finds a new compromise between naked and spontaneous-seeming utterance and disciplined craft, of which the poems are fully aware:

> How far upon these songs with my strict wrist
> Hard to bear down, who knows? None is to read
> But you: so gently . . . but then truth's to heed.

The same sonnet (47) speaks of 'Crumpling a syntax' and of using softening 'Stridor' for sexual persuasion. The hand-to-mouth lyrical narrative smashes the conventional (though also highly-compressed) language used in the first volume. Berryman finds that he is not Auden or Day Lewis. What is accomplished in these private or semi-private poems (which were not unaware of probable future publication, as **"Sonnet 87"** shows) is a relaxation of rhetoric. This love poetry combines startlingly inventive metaphor and structure with familiar banalities like 'I love you, darling', and such praise of grey eyes and golden hair as even linguistically ambitious lovers can't always avoid. (While rereading these sonnets, which I admired much more than when I read them in the sixties, when they seemed indulgently sloppy, I was reading an anthology of love-letters, few of which escaped banality, and they reminded me of Berryman). He draws on the everyday and everynight language of love-making's solicitation, erotic recall, and praise, to make a poetry of desire, remorse, and loss which transcends, contorts and dilapidates language. The contortions and dilapidations were there to stay, transforming his work. The obscurity of the later poetry also begins here, in the forms of an amorous phatic communion whose codes are hard to break. In an essay written for *The Survival of Poetry* (1970), Martin Dodsworth praised **Dream Songs** for helping 'to redeem an idea of literature consonant with our lives, and, like them, impure'. It is in the impurely kinetic and informal forms of daily jottings, knowing allusiveness, and private erotic address, that traditional syntax, lexis, and affective language are abandoned, for good.

Thornbury interestingly suggests that an impulse behind the next volume, **Homage to Mistress Bradstreet,** was the contemporaneous passion of **Sonnets to Chris**: a public mistress took the place of a secret one, history displaced autobiography. When we read **Mistress Bradstreet** immediately after the sonnets, there is indeed a visible shift from private present-tense poetry, written hand-to-mouth and day-to-day in longing and not-knowing, to a deliberated poetry made from scholarship, history, the texts and biography of another American poet, dead and a woman, and a reading of Gerald Manley Hopkins. One poem is very private, the other very public. But Berryman's public act of homage is erotic and possessive: the poem raises the continuing and difficult question of his sexism.

His habitual language about women is pluralising, possessive and stereotyped; 'my first wife', 'my second wife', 'my wives', 'girls', 'my good wife', 'my good gravid wife', 'every wife on the Eastern seaboard', and so on and so on. Like his élitism, snobbishness, conservatism, and implicit racism, his phallocratic assumptions are as unpleasant as they are pathetic. Hero shows himself victim at every count and boast. He said in *Dream Songs* (87), 'Them lady poets must not marry, pal' and rejects Emily Dickinson, in uningratiating jokiness, as an imaginary mistress '-fancy in Amherst bedding her'. But he fancies bedding Anne Bradstreet. He said he chose her as the first American poet, as a woman boldly espousing creativity, but also as a presence who solicited him. At least as important as the contrast between public and private mistress is the contrast between egocentric autobiographical narrative and a poetry which creates character to imagine otherness. Thornbury makes much of Berryman's adoption of a Keatsian concept of self-annihilation, but Berryman is almost always the least self-obliterating of poets. Neither Berryman nor Henry of the *Dream Songs* is a chameleon. The poet, and a few of his critics, insist that Henry is a dramatic character, but he is also very like the ego-clinging and ego-joking first person elsewhere in the poetry and prose. *Mistress Bradstreet* is important as his first and last essay at imagining another person, another gender, another life, another story. Its way of imagining is scarcely that of negative capability, though it is not self-projection either. It is erotic desire, a possessive urge, the embrace of elective affinity.

Here too the love sonnets have acted as instruction and rehearsal. The conventional poetry of desire grows into a more original and dramatic mode. There is an egocentric element in Berryman's feeling for Mistress Bradstreet: he unfairly and inaccurately belittles her poetry as bald and didactic, and observes in a note that her reading in Quarles and Sylvester was unfortunate—but what were the choices? He quotes and assimilates some of her words and images, but concentrates on her maternity and sexuality, not on her writing. He also puts himself into the poem, wooing the ghost as a profane love. But it is, directly and indirectly, obviously and subtly, a poem in love with otherness. In the process of creating Anne Bradstreet Berryman imagines love as complex creative need, imagines religious faith and suffering, birth and death and difference. Some poets—

Hardy and Lawrence—can love otherness but some, like Berryman, have to fall in love with it first. In his imagining of a woman, great emphasis is placed on the body, on sexuality, on fertility. There is a sense in which this sexual and textual possession of a historical woman poet is politically obnoxious. Berryman was imagining, here as elsewhere, in the restricted forms, feelings, and language of his acculturated middle-class American male gender. His desires shape the poem, and they are dominant, possessive, demanding procreation and gestation, enjoying the imagery and action of suffering, submissive and rapturous child-bearing. The poem is very much of its time, and it would probably be impossible for a male poet, as good as Berryman, to write anything like it now.

Erotic desire is not the only affect shaping the poem. Anne Bradstreet is deprecated as a poet, but imagined as a heroic character, suffering, travelling, settling, rebelling, a pilgrim father and not just a mother. The childbirth episode, where the woman is imagined with energetic physical particularity, has been praised by one of Berryman's best critics, Joel Connoroe: its sexism is compounded by a male critic's praise of a central passage 'to which everything in the poem is related, a stanza describing the moment of giving birth . . .'. But another equally powerful episode in the poem treats Anne Bradstreet's awareness of the recreating poet, unsettling the image of a conventionally restricted woman's role, socially and biologically determined. After her first child is born she feels 'in some ways . . . at a loss, / freer'; this sense of loss and freedom is followed by bereavement and then by the exile of Anne Hutchinson, a historical character fictitiously brought into the other Anne's story. Her exile is lamented, 'I miss you, Anne', and the words, as Thornbury observes, create an entry for the modern poet. 'I miss you, Anne' is the point of modulation, a shared apostrophe, and it is followed by words which could be spoken by Anne Bradstreet of herself or by the poet imagining her:

> —I miss you, Anne,
> day or night weak as a child
> tender & empty, doomed, quick to no tryst.

There follows a dialogue between the two poets, making good that affinity proclaimed at the beginning: 'We are on each other's hands / who care. Both of our worlds unhanded us'. Anne asks him to be kind, startlingly imagining him imagining her, 'you who leaguer / my image in the mist'. Perhaps she is the time-traveller, to whom he replies with one of the rarely subdued, passionate references to his personal life, reticently allusive and felt as a repressed force; 'Be kind you, to one unchained eager far & wild / and if, O my love, my heart is breaking, please / neglect my cries and I will spare you'. Berryman—or his surrogate poet - uses a reserved personal narrative as a means of creating his part in the dialogue, and uses dialogic form to tell by not telling, for a change. He too is a suffering person, like her, not just her maker. His articulate—barely articulate—awareness of the act of repression which makes the whole dramatic poem possible, alludes to his habitual egocentric bent, the sub-text of the love sonnets past and the dream songs to come and is at least as climactic as the childbed scene. It valuably creates her as creating him, in an imaginative reciprocity, remembering that she is a poet. They are both time-travellers now. He has criticised her for 'this bald / abstract didactic rime' which he 'read appalled / harassed for your fame / mistress neither of fiery nor velvet verse', but gives her credit for imagination equal to his own. He may offend by writing patronising verse for her which is not bald, abstract or didactic, and is fiery and velvet, but he does imagine her as an imagining woman, and also as his erotic equal, meeting his desire and in words also from **'Sonnets to Chris',** 'I *want* to take you for my lover'. She goes further and offers him her God, after he confesses guilt, 'I trundle the bodies. . . . / I wonder if / *I* killed them. Women serve my turn'. This woman is most subtly serving his turn and is allowed to patronise him and judge: 'Dreams! You are good' and 'God awaits us (but I am yielding) who Hell wars'. As the modern poet utters faith and a lack of faith, 'I cannot feel myself God waits. He flies / nearer a kindly world; or he is flown', she takes on his guilt and doubt, in a conversation of belief and confession, as well as desire. Berryman creates, across centuries, a dialogue which is metaphysical and ethical. His haunting brings with it, for both ghosts, a communication of values and passions, in a language and structure which is never bald, abstract, or didactic.

The poem pays homage to a Catholic, as well as a Puritan, poet, recalling in its deep structure that other great religious poem, strong in metaphor of stress, pain, and sea, 'The Wreck of the Deutschland', whose eight-line sprung rhythm stanza it recalls. Berryman is like Hopkins imagining the tall nun, and meditating through her suffering on the Passion, across gulfs of space. The gulfs here are gulfs of time, but the subduing of the poet's passion, the self-consciousness of the poetic act, and the tender admiring communion with a dead woman, make common ground. Each poem also contains a wonderfully sensuous, excursive imagining of Spring: for Hopkins it is 'the jay-blue heavens appearing / Of pied and peeled May! / Blue-beating and hoary-glow height . . .' and for Berryman it is the response to 'Talk to me' with 'It is Spring's New England, Pussy willows wedge / up in the wet. Milky crestings, fringed / yellow, in heaven . . .'. Berryman admired 'Father Hopkins' and wrote his meditation on the creative passion and death of a mother, a Puritan and anti-Catholic pilgrim fleeing England's religious restrictions, in response to Hopkins's homage to a nun, also on a voyage for religious liberty, a Catholic fleeing the Falk laws and also heading for America. For Hopkins, as for Berryman, the sustained, relatively long, narrative lyric was a complex act of meditation on otherness, the personal study of a text outside the personal life, a liberation into new poetry, and itself a new poetry.

After **Homage to Mistress Bradstreet** comes the return to self, Berryman at his most inclusive, wild, liberated, hit-and-miss, fiery and velvet, in the two sequences of **Dream Songs,** now collected into one volume. Virginia Woolf said she learnt her free and elastic language and form from the race and gallop and improvising immediacy of Byron's *Don Juan,* and from her own diary. (She conspicuously left out Joyce's *Ulysses,* which she seems not to have wanted to acknowledge). Berryman learnt his free and elastic language and form from his diary-poems, the love-sonnets, and also from the 'crumpled' syntax and self-interrupting, conversational language and form of Hopkins. Berryman was never again to write an equally impassioned and individual religious poetry, only the distressing banal language of willed desire, with no imagined object, in **Delusions.** But his language was freed to write about self, through the characters of the clown and blackface minstrel, Henry, and his straight man, the traditional Interlocutor of the minstrel show. (He is not so much Henry's critic as his male ego-extension, like Mrs. Gamp's Mrs. Harris reinforcing boasts and bravado: 'There ought to be a law against Henry. /—Mr. Bones: there is'.) Once more, there is a political barrier readers may not care to cross: there have been defences and explanations of the use of white minstrel dialect, suggestions that there is an anti-racist implication in this version of a disadvantaged people's language. But Berryman nowhere shows sympathy for the African-Americans within the **Dream Songs,** and I take the appropriation of dialect, like the adoption of Anne Bradstreet, as an insensitive mark of its history, not to be reasoned away. Henry's slangy and jokey dialect is in some ways like Lawrence's use of dialect in *Lady Chatterley's Lover,* a medium for wildness and freedom, not without sentimentality, but unlike Lawrence's idiom in its lisping infantilism. The humour isn't to be taken as ironic only: humour is a license as well as a self-critique, and Henry's humour is not ingratiating, especially in jokes about women and boobs and bores. Berryman insisted that Henry's whiteman's blackface was a mask, but it is more like a mirror, an image more common in Berryman than a mask. In **Dream Songs,** and in the much criticised **Love & Fame** (1971), Berryman writes what he did not want to call confessional poetry. It is less a confession than a grotesque boast, at worst, and raw cries for help, at best. 'Raw' is a misleading word if it's not qualified: Berryman became such a habitual craftsman, from the love sonnets onwards, that a rush and blurt of feeling finds form in subtly constructed music and narrative. Instant poetry came out crafted.

He often parades pride, arrogance and intellectual snob-bery, at the same time as he discovers brilliantly new and strange words or images for longing, hurt, effort, loneliness, despair, exhilaration. For instance, in *Dream Songs* (153), 'I'm cross with god who has wrecked this generation', he laments the loss of the gifted by bashing the ungifted. Admiration is followed by deprecation: 'He left alive / fools I could number like a kitchen knife'. The anguish of remorse has a similar habit of turning into and out of self-savouring. He somewhere compares himself with Coriolanus, which is both right and wrong. Right, because the poetry reveals a self-tormenting pride which makes for brittle vulnerability, and the undermining support of imagined male solidar-ity; wrong, because to see Coriolanus as mirror or mask should be to recognise, like Shakespeare, (whom Berry-man studied all his life) the destructiveness and self-destructiveness of phallocentricity. He can joke about Henry raging 'bright orange in a pine / if his young ladies were late' and declare 'Hunger was constitutional with him, / women, cigarettes, liquor-, need need need / until he went to pieces' but the self-critical taxonomist continues to make women into objects and classes and pluralities. Sexism and intellectual élitism meet. He can register, in *Love & Fame,* that 'worthy young gentlemen' in Cambridge are baffled by Wallace Stevens and Hart Crane, that Yeats's name is misspelt on an invitation, and that during a discussion of a production of *Love's Labour's Lost* he felt superiority—over a not too esoteric piece of knowledge:

> . . . a Garden production at Lord Horder's place
> down near Southampton's old estate in the Spring
>
> I don't think I said a word, although I knew
> (as probably no one else there did)
> the chance is good he wrote *Love's Labours*
> for the Earl and his friends down there in '93.

In the same poem he introduces one of his girls as 'the most passionate & versatile actress in Cambridge'. All this is Berryman at his most embarrassing. I don't ac-cept the explanation that the early parts of this sequence are deconstructed by the later; it is true that Berryman forces you to take the rough with the smooth, but the smooth does not erase the rough. The awful self-destructiveness, sometimes unaware, sometimes aware, seems to have had to be spelt out, spilt out, in order to spit out new words for helplessness and loneliness, part of the same stark story, part of the impure poetry:

> It seems to be DARK all the time.
> I have difficulty walking.
> I can remember what to say to my seminar
> but I don't know that I want to.
>
> ('Despair')

His experience of 'horribles' in this sequence, and elsewhere, can be articulated with a lyrical purity, as in the terrifying and piteous Dream Song **'Snow Line'**, 'It

was wet & white & swift and where I am / we don't know. It was dark and then / it isn't'. His shifts of tense and pronouns, category minglings, and cryptic avoid-ances of substantive and referend can make a passion-ate concentration of affect: 'There sat down, once, a thing on Henry's heart', 'Henry's pelt was put on sundry walls', and 'Animal Henry sat reading The Times Literary Supplement'. The incompletions of nar-rative and the misfitting juxtapositions register bewilder-ment, wildness, madness, mind and heart at the end of tether. The impurity in much of his writing is a juxtaposition of powerful and vivid affective utterances with raw materials, debris, bits we can't accept and digest. It is very tempting—perhaps especially for men—to romanticise such dislocations. What the reader is up against is not 'poetic' language yoked to 'unpoetic' language but articulated energy with inert language. But both vivid image and blunt prosaicism may be unpleas-antly indulgent and show-off or heartbreakingly feeble in need and begging. The less successful poetry of extremity is found in Berryman's religious prayers, un-berable to read, because they are desperately trying, and failing, to be individualised prayer. This is a failed poetry:

> Oil all my turbulence as at Thy dictation
> I sweat out my wayward works.
> Father Hopkins said the only true literary critic is
>   Christ.
> Let me lie down exhausted, content with that.
>
> ['**Eleven Addresses to the Lord**']

and from **'Matins'** in *Delusions*:

> Less were you tranquil to me in my dark
> just now than tyrannous. O some bore down
> sore with enticements—One abandoned me—
> half I swelled up toward—till I crash awake.

The evocations of Hopkins compound the inertness of language. In some poems the inertness is given a context, shown as a process of deadening, as in the last suicide poem from *Henry's Fate*, which hideously specifies, and frustrates, a fantasy of suicide, ending with the raw prose terror and misery of 'tomorrow's lectures / bad in themselves, the students dropping the course, 'The Administration hearing . . .'. In some of the hospital poems, too, the shifts from prose jotting or banal phrase to individuality and intensity patches an impure document, a failing message from a far-out verge. It is a poetry of emergency and extremity. No one can have written such singularly agonising poetry about alcoholism, about therapeutic and self-therapeutic effort, about the varieties of suffering that made up his 'own awful centre'.

This distressed poetry is experientially prolific and generative. Much of it is a poetry of appalling solicita-tion, not sublime or tragic but as repulsive and pitiable as self-pitying distress can be, outside poetry. Berryman writes poetry which mixes what is admirable with what is intolerable. To put so much of yourself into poetry is to break with traditional solaces and charms: the impurities of literature aren't always easy to take, like a beggar's stink. Berryman makes his constant reader shuttle between approaches and retreats, as he breaks down the poetry of desire. He is yesterday's poète maudit, neither to be dismissed nor romanticised.

Note

1. *Collected Poems 1937-1971*, edited by John Thornbury (Faber, 1990).

Ivy Schweitzer (essay date 1991)

SOURCE: Schweitzer, Ivy. "Puritan Legacies of Masculinity: John Berryman's *Homage to Mistress Bradstreet*." In *The Calvinist Roots of the Modern Era*, edited by Aliki Barnston, Michael Tomasek Manson, and Carol J. Singley, pp. 125-41. Hanover, N.H.: University Press of New England, 1997.

[*In the following essay, originally published in 1991, Schweitzer argues that* Homage to Mistress Bradstreet *is a historical poem in the sense that it should be thought of as "a document of the continuity of certain cultural constructions of masculinity, most particularly, Puritan legacies of masculinity."*]

> The discourse of man is in the metaphor of woman
>
> —Gayatri Spivak, "Displacement," 169

> Woman then stands in patriarchal culture as a signifier for the male other, bound by a symbolic order in which man can live out his fantasies and obsessions through linguistic command by imposing them on the silent image of woman still tied to her place as bearer, not maker, of meaning.
>
> —Laura Mulvey, *Visual and Other Pleasures*, 15

> The woman who is truly Spirit-filled will want to be totally submissive to her husband. . . . This is a truly liberated woman. Submission is God's design for women.
>
> —Beverly LaHaye, *The Spirit-Controlled Woman*, 71

In 1953 John Berryman published a long poem in *Partisan Review* about—of all things—the little-known colonial New England poet Anne Bradstreet. In an interview, Berryman claimed that he did not like Bradstreet's poetry but that he "fell in love with her; and wrote about her, putting myself in it" ("Interview" 7). Despite the work's confessional quality, Berryman insisted that **Homage to Mistress Bradstreet** was a historical poem and liked to quote Robert Lowell's pronouncement that it was "the most resourceful histori-

cal poem in our literature" ("Changes" 101). I will argue here that Berryman's poem is "resourceful" in its appropriation of the feminine for decidedly masculine and hegemonic purposes, and "historical" not in the way he and Lowell meant (and many readers have taken it), in its evocation of the "reality" of a figure in our country's colonial past, but as a document of the continuity of certain cultural constructions of masculinity, most particularly, Puritan legacies of masculinity.

In what ways, however, can we speak about "inheriting" cultural constructions of gender roles and expectations? David Rosen, in a recent study of the "changing fictions of masculinity" in English literature, argues for "a sense of the necessary instabilities of the idea of masculinity . . . and the need men have felt to stabilize the idea of masculinity from age to age" (215). Although I stress here that strategies and elements persist, I believe, in strong contradistinction to the mythopoetic views sparked by Robert Bly's work of the early 1990s, that masculinity, like femininity, is not transhistorical but is shaped by historical contexts and constructed by social and cultural forces; that there are multiple definitions of masculinity that are associated with particular cultural sites and manifested in specific social institutions, such as religious and political movements; and that the dynamic definitions of masculinity reflect as well as shape material conditions and especially relations of power. I agree with Rosen that "masculinity functions as a cultural and subcultural marker, working even within groups to define privileged loci of power" (221).

If gender roles are culture- and site-specific, can they be inherited? I would argue that our modern-day inheritance of Puritan legacies of masculinity is part of a particularly tenacious bequest of a specifically "American" set of ideologies—what the Protestant ethic has left to our modern era—that are also strongly linked to gender ideologies pervasive in the Western intellectual tradition.[1] In seeing John Berryman as one of many "inheritors" of Puritan legacies of masculinity, I do not mean to imply that he held their beliefs; Berryman struggled all his life with religious issues, and late in his life finally converted to Roman Catholicism. Nor do I mean that he was "Puritanical" in the conventional sense of that term. Given what we know of his personal life, he certainly was not. However, in his choice of Anne Bradstreet as subject, Berryman declares himself an "American" poet rooted in a tradition that has been deeply scored by Calvinist influences. When, for example, in an essay written in 1965, Berryman tried to answer the often-asked question of why, in his own words, "I chose to write about this boring high-minded Puritan woman who may have been our first American poet but is not a good one" ("Changes" 100), he sketches out a complicated, one might even say, Bloomian, relationship to Bradstreet as the personification of that American tradition. In doing so, he reenacts certain dynamics of the Puritan ideology of masculinity.

Berryman claims, first, that, in fact, he "did not choose her—somehow she chose me," thereby casting himself in the traditionally "feminine" position as the one chosen. We will look more closely at the gender politics at work in this remark. Next, he admits that "one point of connection, at any rate, [is] the almost insuperable difficulty of writing high verse at all in a land that cared and cares so little for it." Here, at least, he acknowledges Bradstreet's status as a poet attempting to write "high verse." Their shared rejection as poets is another ambivalent tie to the American "land." Despite this grudging and oblique acknowledgment of Bradstreet as poet, Berryman confesses he "was concerned with her, though, almost from the beginning, as a woman, not much as a poetess" ("Changes" 100). Aside from the condescending connotations of that last word, what can this mean?

I argue that the threat posed by the woman-as-poet, a magnification of the "ordinary" threat posed by "woman" in patriarchal culture, is revealed when Berryman, with seemingly nothing to fear from the long-dead and "boring poetess," grants her a power over his imagination but at the same time has to put her back into her "rightful" place, which is, as Laura Mulvey says above, "as bearer, not maker, of meaning." Ambivalently, he makes her both an object that he appropriates and his persona, with which he identifies. She is the means by which he, as Mulvey says, "can live out his fantasies and obsessions through linguistic command" of a silenced woman. In doing so, Berryman exhibits what poststructuralist feminist theorists identify in critical as well as textual practice as a masculine recuperation of "woman." Furthermore, these gestures and attitudes that Berryman expresses poetically about sexual difference and masculine entitlement also echo the attitudes of seventeenth-century Puritan New Englanders about the place of "woman," as well as their discursive use of the feminine.[2] While we can draw some conclusions pertinent to the work of John Berryman from the comparison, I also believe we can venture some more general speculations about the ongoing practices of contemporary ideologies of masculinity as well as masculine critical practice.

* * *

In an earlier study of self-representation in lyric poetry, I explored how the Puritan doctrines of conversion and salvation, understood and idiosyncratically applied in colonial New England in conjunction with the Massachusetts Bay's theocratic social and political arrangements, constituted a profoundly troubled and troubling set of paradigms for masculinity. Gender roles in Puritan New England were clearly demarcated and believed to be divinely imposed and biblically justified. Not just about individuals or individual behavior, they enmeshed people in an interlocking network of social and cultural structures. Men were the linchpins of the colonial New England social structure, which was organized as a patriarchal theocracy (Rotundo 11-12). Although Puritan doctrine taught men the necessity of learning to accept submission to superiors and to God, in a very broad way masculinity was identified with patriarchal order and public social power.

However, the discourse of Puritan piety as it developed in the New England colonies unsettled this easy identification. Puritan men and women were exhorted by their ministers, who promulgated a metaphorical understanding of the Song of Songs, to become the spiritual Brides of Christ, wooed by and betrothed to the divine and loving Bridegroom. This was the pervasive image for the saved soul. Would-be saints of both sexes had to quell the "masculine" aspects of their fallen selves—willfulness, independence, activity—and strove to achieve a redeemed state of "femininity" as passive vessels cleansed and receptive for the pouring in of divine grace. While females only had to go along with "nature" in accepting a submissive and obedient role in religious worship, males, understood by the Puritans as "naturally" willful, active, and assertive, spent their spiritual lives attempting to subjugate the very qualities their society told them they could not help but embody and were expected to manifest in daily life.[3]

Philip Greven, a historian of the period, bluntly summed up the dilemma that Puritanism posed: "for men to be saved they had to cease being masculine" (129). Furthermore, he suggests that the anxiety many Puritan males experienced as a result of the demand for spiritual feminization produced misogyny and a virulent rejection of effeminacy. Walter Hughes explores the implications of the "figurative homosexuality" that the religious discourse of salvation posed for Puritan males, as expressed in Puritan poetry (103). He finds that poets such as the eccentric Michael Wigglesworth and the more representative Edward Taylor are caught up in a vicious cycle. They struggle to discipline, humble, and feminize their willful selves and turn their errant desires toward an aggressive God. But once achieved, this spiritual triumph results in homosexual panic, self-loathing, and fear of annihilation. Wigglesworth, whose journal records in a secret code his sexual feelings for his male students, resolves his panic by allowing himself only masochistic pleasure in the transgressive loving of a male God. Taylor, in order to stave off his fears of being annihilated by submission to his divine Bridegroom, wildly multiplies the images of mutual objectification that he applies to himself and Christ, and so diffuses both desire and fulfillment into "a kaleidoscopic polysexual ecstacy" (120). Hughes is absolutely correct in pointing out how both poets, as many Puritan men of the time, suffered under the impossible psychic demands of rigorous Puritan doctrine. Yet, we must not forget that they also maintained important, visible public offices, were the pillars of their communities, headed households, and dominated religious and civic life. In other words, spiritual feminization or "figurative homosexuality," while causing private panic and suffering, are a productive part of the schizoid constellations of masculinity maintained by the Puritan patriarchal theocracy.

In fact, the constitution of male spiritual subjectivity by the occupation and/or appropriation of "feminine" positions not only empowered men but consolidated male power by effacing women and further marginalizing socially feminized others like Native Americans and enslaved people. In order to understand this, we need to look at colonial Puritan treatment of women and "woman." Although an essentialized notion of "woman" served as a figure for the regenerate Puritan soul, and womanly functions such as marrying, giving birth, and mothering were used to describe spiritual processes, real women and their biological and social functions were not elevated and ennobled by this use. Puritan women who fit the Pauline model were extolled, but the effect of approving women for being self-effacing would, presumably, be more and better self-effacement. In fact, only a certain scripturally defined and culturally approved notion of "woman" served as the typology of regenerate subjectivity. Carol Karlsen points out that "women who failed to serve men failed to serve God. To be numbered among God's elect, women had to acknowledge this service as their calling and *believe* they were created for this purpose" (166; her emphasis).

Karlsen is talking about the seventeenth century, but she outlines a lesson strategically embraced by Beverly LaHaye, an influential apologist of the 1980s for the New Right's "pro-family" agenda whose doublespeak about woman's place I quote as an epigraph.[4] In the seventeenth century, women like Anne Hutchinson, who swerved noticeably from the Pauline model of passivity, humility, and obedience (and today would be called "feminists"), were considered not just heretical but downright demonic. Governor John Winthrop summed up the prevailing attitude in his frequently cited comment on the tragedy of Anne Yale Hopkins, wife of the governor of Hartford, who allegedly wrote herself into insanity. "For," Winthrop concludes, "if she had attended her household affairs, and such things as belong to women, and not gone out of her way and calling to meddle in such things as are proper for men, whose minds are stronger, etc., she had kept her wits, and might have improved them usefully and honorably in the place God had set her" (*Winthrop's* 225). God set

woman in her *place,* a position subordinate to man, and as far as Winthrop was concerned, displacement spelled tragedy for women, chaos for society.

In the hands of Puritan theologians, the spiritualization of feminine imagery had the effect of erasing the earthly and fleshly femaleness from it. The male Puritan saint appropriated female imagery but only as a necessary phase on the way to the remasculinization offered by the Puritan conversion narrative, in which, ultimately, God adopts the saint as his son and heir, while woman/women disappear. According to the logic of conversion, all saints pass through a feminizing process. Brides become sons and heirs and are thus remasculinized, but they remain on the feminine side of the gender/power divide.[5] Edward Taylor makes as much clear in a rapturous contemplation of his many (subordinate) relationships to Christ, who, in assuming the masculine role, finally subsumes "Ev'ry thing":

> In us Relations all that mutuall are.
> I am thy Patient, Pupill, Servant, and
>   Thy Sister, Mother, Doove, Spouse, Son, and Heire.
>   Thou art my Priest, Physician, Prophet, King,
>   Lord, Brother, Bridegroom, Father, Ev'ry thing.
>
> (Med. 1.29.20-24)

Does the absence of "daughters" in this vision of heaven indicate that women also become "sons"? Finally, the paternal and patriarchal appropriation of the mother's role seems to be the point here. John Calvin, quoting John, emphasizes the logocentric—or more precisely, the phallogocentric—nature of faith in Christ, which grants "the privilege 'to become the Sons of God, even to them that believe in his name, which were born not of blood, nor of the will of the flesh, nor of the will of man, but of God' (John 1:12)" (465).[6]

It may be helpful to think about Puritan culture's discursive deployment of "woman" as a form of "gynesis," a concept articulated by feminist theorist Alice Jardine. Textually, gynesis designates "discourse *by, through, as* woman" (36); more generally, it is the effect produced when "woman" is employed as a figure in discourse, used as the vehicle of man's contemplation, as the Other who makes possible his apprehension of interiority and subjectivity. This process, according to Jardine and Gayatri Spivak, who analyzes the effects of gynesis in the thinking of Derrida, is at work in much of Western philosophical thought and recurs frequently in texts of a religious and literary nature (Jardine 63); for example, in the passage quoted above, Edward Taylor conspicuously figures himself as the feminized, and therefore, passive, receptive, and inferior partner in his spiritual marriage with Christ. Most recently, gynesis has been deployed in postmodernism's dismantling of the master narratives of patriarchal culture, including Puritanism. Thus, for example, because deconstruction rejects the notion of a fully conscious, transcendent subject, Derrida cannot speak as "man"; in order to deconstruct his centrality as illusory, he must speak deliberately as "woman," from a position of *displacement* (Spivak 173, 179). By understanding this conscious rhetorical move, deconstructive feminist theory enables us to see the phallogocentrism of Puritan thought and doctrine. In the light of Paul's metaphysics of gender and colonial New England's theo-patriarchal culture, Taylor's self-feminization can be understood as a form of spiritual empowerment that derives from his speaking from a seemingly disempowered feminine place.

In both cases, spiritually and critically, the male speaker gains power by appropriating a feminized position. How does this gynesis affect women? From the perspective of Puritan doctrine, as I argue above, women are ungendered by the logic of conversion and disappear. Culturally, female functions are appropriated and women as a class become the markers of cultural value, not the makers of culture. Critically, despite the crucial role Derridean thought has played for feminist and oppositional critical practice, a similar effect occurs. Postmodernism's privileging of the feminine does not imply a privileging of or even an equality for women, or a revaluation of our position socially or politically. In fact, as Barbara Johnson argues, in speaking from and thus occupying the place of "woman," male authors continue in reality to silence the sex to whom in theory they give voice (131). In her analysis of postmodern U.S. culture, Tania Modleski finds gynesis "deeply embedded in the American cultural tradition" (7) and traces a similar reinscription of female disempowerment in the thinking of several prominent postfeminist male critics. In their analyses, now de rigeur, of male power, these critics attempt "to reposition the struggle between feminism and the patriarchal tradition as a struggle inhering *in* that tradition" and thus confuse feminism and feminization (8). This "confusion" has been strategically deployed by some male critics to argue for the alleged "feminization" of the discipline and profession and is an example of how gynesis, despite its radical potential, is coopted to serve the interests of male-dominated culture.[7] In the following reading of *Homage,* I argue that Berryman harks back to Puritan attitudes in a gynetic identification with Bradstreet as "woman," which ultimately becomes a reactionary appropriation and erasure of women that reinscribes a patriarchal ideology of masculinity and, in some ways, prefigures the troubled privileging of the feminine of Berryman's postmodern literary and critical brethren.

* * *

In 1648, Anne Bradstreet's brother-in-law, John Woodbridge, took a manuscript of her poems to London and had them published without her knowledge or consent.

Though this was the first volume of poetry by a single author to come out of the New World, Woodbridge could not bring himself to name Bradstreet a poet. The title of the volume styles the unknown author as *The Tenth Muse, lately Sprung up in America.* But Bradstreet, whose own relationship with the nine sisters of antiquity was uneasy at best, knew that Muses are not poets. The Muse-poet relationship has always been a particularly vexed site of power relations.[8] Up until recently, and certainly in the seventeenth century, it was a rigorously heterosexual relation: muses were female, poets were male. Thus, in naming Bradstreet the "tenth muse," Woodbridge deliberately attempted to manage the threat of a woman quietly defying her culture's double messages about women's capabilities and roles by putting her back into a feminine place. He does this by attributing to her a status higher than that of mere poet, a mythic, even goddess-like, and controlling status. But every woman who has been put on a pedestal knows that this kind of deification is disarming, for it has the effect of denying her the status of subject, speaker, agent, or author.

Berryman employs a similar strategy in his "homage." His allegation that Bradstreet "chose" him suggests, in the spiritual/erotic language in which male poets traditionally addressed their earthly muses, that the power to choose was all on her side. But this courtly discourse is an ancient mode of equivocation. By calling his poem an "homage," he implies that he puts himself under obligation to a figure whom he reveres and also wants to flatter. But Berryman publicly denies his interest in Bradstreet's poetry and asserts instead his interest in her "as a woman"—an "interest" that becomes palpably sexual and manipulative in the middle section of the poem when the male poet's voice enters into dialogue with Bradstreet's voice. Abruptly, the male poet announces, "I have earned the right to be alone with you," to which the Bradstreet voice responds, "What right can that be? / Convulsing, if you love, enough, like a sweet lie" (27.6-8). It seems clear from her response, that "Bradstreet"—and thus her creator, Berryman—recognizes the "sweet lie" in her wooer's rhetoric. The tropes of courtly praise and the equivocal self-abnegation of an homage have always been a polite mask for sometimes illicit sexual desire and a pretext to sexual domination. Ironically, the response and resistance Berryman fashions for his "Bradstreet" indicate a self-consciousness about masculine strategies of domination. His desire to make them public does not, however, result in critique, but in reaffirmation of their effectiveness and his "rights" to them.

Like Bradstreet's brother-in-law's elevating her to the status of Muse, Berryman's equivocal "homage" recognizes and de-authorizes at the same time. The modern appropriation seems more insidious, however, because Berryman dismisses Bradstreet's poetic productions and then is free to raid and deploy them at will. Furthermore, his success in recreating Bradstreet can be measured by the number of critics who use his poem as a guide to Bradstreet's work. Hyatt Waggoner, for example, recommends reading Berryman's poem as an introduction to Bradstreet's poetry and to themes and images particularly "American" (8). Elizabeth Wade White, Bradstreet's most recent biographer, endorses Waggoner's recommendation because, she argues, the strangely wrenched syntax, psychological method, and historical setting of the poem seem to bring the woman and her environment eloquently to life. Neither seems disturbed by the ventriloquistic nature of her voice, the appropriation of her life, or the unsavory central action of the poem. They do not question the male poet's assumption that he can claim the right to be alone with "Bradstreet" because, like all the other Beatrices and Lauras of the male tradition, she is his creation, a figure who has sprung from his imagination and his desire, over whom—in the poetic sphere—he has total control. Berryman exercised this control by distorting the historical facts of Bradstreet's life to suit his own purposes.[9]

The sexual politics implied in the title are supported by the biographical context of Berryman's life and the poem's composition. Several critics argue that Berryman's *Homage* was motivated by the guilt he felt over his own compulsive adulterous affairs. Luke Spenser traces Berryman's ambivalent feelings about his strong-willed mother and her marital infidelities (354-55). Sarah Provost points out that the technical and creative breakthrough represented by *Homage* was preceded by another major work, *Sonnets to Chris,* which depict the poet at the mercy of a flamboyant woman called "Lise" with whom he had an obsessive and humiliating affair in 1947. Finally released from his compulsion to compose poetry to and about "Lise," he cast around for a subject that would allow him to fathom the tumultuous experience—in publishable form. In the middle of 1948 he wrote the first eleven lines of *Homage* but could go no further. For the next five years, he read and researched, finishing the poem in an anguished burst of creativity. Comparing the two works, Provost argues that the figure of Bradstreet is a tempered and pliant version of "Lise" (71). Thus, in his poetic rendition of the "real" affair, Berryman construed himself as the victim and fool, while in the later, "idealized" affair with his compliant creation he maintains rigorous control of events as well as his writing. Berryman's Bradstreet is, by contrast to "Lise" and the women poets crowding the postwar literary scene, the sign of an earlier version of masculine power, one that does not call into question traditional gender roles: intensely womanly, patient to a fault, and faithful. Not only is she the colonial foremother of "American" poetry, but she is also a woman deeply committed to motherhood, a fact that Berryman will appropriate as a metaphor for

male poetic creativity. For it is precisely the *difference* of gender that entices and challenges Berryman, a difference he wants to maintain, exploit, and transcend all at the same time.

But despite the importance of difference for Berryman's project, there exist complicating identifications between the modern male poet and the colonial female one. Several critics discuss this identification in terms of Yeatsian masks (Holden, Haffenden) and suggest that "Bradstreet is herself an antithetical self for the poet" (Mazzaro 125). Provost is surprised to discover that Bradstreet is both Berryman's idealized, quintessentially feminine mistress and the persona through which he projects his own struggles with guilt, creativity, and God. The notion of Yeatsian antithesis, however, does not adequately address the gender politics of Berryman's gynesis. Several aspects of the poem illustrate this gynesis and its connection to Puritan gynesis, especially Berryman's handling of the different voices and the means of their dialoguing. For example, at the very beginning, Berryman projects himself upon the deck of the *Arbella* as it landed in Boston harbor on a windy day in 1630. The poet's voice modulates into the Bradstreet voice through a repetition of first-person pronouns: "I come to check, / I come to stay with you, / and the Governor, & Father, & Simon, & the huddled men" (4.6-8). In the first line, the male poet imposes upon "Bradstreet" as yet another dominating, restraining male presence in her life in a hierarchy that is enumerated in the third line—governor, father, husband, males. This is only his first link with the Puritan patriarchy. In the middle line, the subject and object, "I" and "you," are ambiguous and in direct relation; this is the fleeting moment of identity that is dispelled by the lines surrounding it. Berryman then quotes Bradstreet's well-known words from a letter to her children that record her resistance and resignation to the Puritan and masculine direction of her fate: "my heart rose, but I did submit" (7.8). But again he acts in concert with Puritan governor, father, husband, males by having her embrace the conventional Puritan notion that women must suffer restraint as protection from the temptations of the devil, of heresy, as well as from the lure of their own impulses: "I must be disciplined, / in arms, against that one, and our dissidents, and myself" (11.7-8).

"Bradstreet's" patience and pliability are exaggerated; Berryman imagines her waiting dutifully in heaven for her husband, who outlived her by thirty years, and likewise waiting several centuries for him to "summon" her from the past (1.3-4; 3.2). Such exaggeration leads to a masochistic submission to male authority that the poem highly eroticizes in what amounts to a perverse celebration of female embodiment and a painful, futile awareness of the oppression that results. In recounting the arrangement of her marriage, she says "That year for my sorry face / so-much-older Simon burned, / so

Father smiled, with love. Their will be done" (14.3-5). This Christ-like obedience has a barely sublimated erotic energy, epitomized in her declaration of faith: "I kissed his Mystery" (14.8). Later in the poem, after "Bradstreet" has consented to the "affair" with the modern poet and is consumed with guilt and shame, she imagines her damnation and recalls the devil's promise to spare woman if she agrees to be his tool. But with a painful insight she realizes the uniformly oppressive nature of male power, and cries: "Father of lies, / a male great pestle smashes / small women swarming towards the mortar's rim in vain" (37.6-8). Here Berryman allows his character to recognize and condemn her oppressors while at the same time acknowledging her vulnerability; God, father, and devil coalesce into a looming phallic pestle that grinds helpless, ant-like women into a powder.[10] Her God is not paternally benevolent but sadistic, continually sending her physical chastisements to amend her errant soul. As she ages, and is beset with poor health, the death of children, the burning of her house, she says, "I look. I bear to look. Strokes once more his rod" (50.8), as God satisfies himself in a barely concealed display of phallic power. Yet she begs, "torture me, Father, lest not I be thine!" (39.1).

Berryman's gynesis of identity and difference is further illustrated by the manner in which the male poet enters "Bradstreet's" world. To do so he fantasizes that he must, like the Puritan fathers (including Bradstreet's own father), displace a very powerful, masculine, and thus threatening, female friend: Anne Hutchinson. Hutchinson was the woman most feared by the early Puritan leadership, and her defeat gave them the opportunity to further restrict female visibility and speech. In a tactical move, Berryman portrays Hutchinson as Bradstreet's closest friend, though their sisterhood is based not on strength or resistance, but on the experience of victimization. Though there is little historical basis for this friendship, the connection allows Berryman to replay the repressive authoritarianism of the Puritan fathers. As "Bradstreet" mourns Hutchinson's isolation and exile, crying, "Bitter sister, victim, I miss you," the voice of the male poet interrupts her and the first dialogue of the seduction ensues, their voices alternating, beginning with the male poet's:

> —I miss you, Anne,
> day or night weak as a child,
> tender & empty, doomed, quick to no tryst.
> —I hear you. Be kind, you who leaguer
> my image in the mist.
> —Be kind you, to one unchained eager far & wild
>
> and if, O my love, my heart is breaking, please
> neglect my cries and I will spare you. Deep
> in Time's grave, Love's, you lie still.
> Lie still.
>
> (25.3-26.4)

Echoing her words of empathy, implying a previous acquaintance, and playing upon her "motherly" instincts by comparing himself in his weakness to a child, he imposes his own projected need between the two women. Berryman's note to this passage is illuminating. Speaking of the male poetic voice, he says, "He is enabled to speak, at last, in the fortune of an echo of her—and when she is loneliest (her former spiritual adviser having deserted Anne Hutchinson, and this her closest friend banished), as if she had summoned him; and only thus, perhaps, is she enabled to hear him." The fantasy at work here—a familiar one—is the heterosexist displacement of strong female associations and female desire for abusive male attention. Notice that the male voice comes into speech as an "echo" of the female voice's need, "as if *she* had summoned *him*" (my emphasis), and as if the continuation of his attentions is dependent on her desires. A *fantasy* of female power (voice, desire) underlies this effacing gynetic appropriation and display of linguistic male power.[11]

Despite his ostensible "need," Berryman barely conceals his aggression toward women in the poem. The above passage contains a pattern of words the male poet uses repeatedly, as does his Puritan antecedent John Winthrop, to put woman back in her place. Describing his vision of Bradstreet at rest in "Time's grave," he notes her peacefulness—"you lie still"—and advises her (against his own urgings) to dismiss his suit and "Lie still"—that is, remain peacefully at rest in the past. The word "still" also occurs three times in stanza one and twice in the final stanza. It suggests remaining in a place, motionless, like a still pool or fixed like a "still" photograph, silent, subdued, or hushed, quiet and tranquil. As an adverb "still" describes an on-going condition. The conflation of adjectival and adverbial meanings calls up Keats's strangely applicable and subliminally sinister invocation of his Grecian urn, "Thou still unravish'd bride of quietness." At the same time as the male poet imagines "Bradstreet" peaceful and silent in the past and wants her to remain that way as a source of constancy for him, he is maneuvering to drag her into the tumult of adulterous passion, unquiet speech, and breach of faith. When "still" is applied to the verb "lie," the gentle imperative "Lie still" takes on threatening implications of enforced silence or immobility and continuing deception; recall "Bradstreet"'s earlier recognition of the "sweet lie" of "convulsing" love.

The threat surfaces more openly when "Bradstreet" fulfills the poet's ambivalent desires and asks to be touched, kissed, talked to. Then, in what Berryman describes as "an only half-subdued aria-stanza" ("Changes" 101), his love song takes on explicitly aggressive forms:

> —It is Spring's New England. Pussy willows wedge
> up in the wet. Milky crestings, fringed

yellow, in heaven, eyed
by the melting hand-in-hand or mere
desirers single, heavy-footed, rapt,
make surge poor human hearts. Venus is trapt—
the hefty pike shifts, sheer—
in Orion blazing. Warblings, odours, nudge to an
    edge—

                    (31.1-8)

The erotically charged, wet, and burgeoning world of New England spring fills the poet's heart at the moment he achieves his conquest. But this fades rapidly into a threatening nightsky world with intimations of conflict between Venus, the goddess of love, formerly a menacing carnivorous plant, and Orion, a mythic giant and hunter who terrorized the sisters known as the Pleiades and was eventually slain by Artemis. Venus, who once slyly trapped men in her "engines" (see Bradstreet's "An Elegy upon . . . Philip Sidney," l. 27), is now herself trapped by Orion's sharp pikes, and the stars have become weapons. By the end of this stanza, love is a prisoner and the sounds and smells of nature that "rapt" Bradstreet and brought her a glimpse of heaven (see her "Contemplations" ll. 8-15), bring the lovers to a dangerous precipice.

In the course of their bizarre intimacy, the male poet confesses to murderous feelings and an unrestrained "western lust" that fills his mind with images of Nazi atrocities: "I trundle the bodies, on the iron bars, / over that fire backward & forth; they burn; / bits fall. I wonder if / *I* killed them. Women serve my turn" (33.2; 34.1-4).[12] "Dreams!" responds his generous mistress; "You are good," she tells him despite all evidence to the contrary, and prays to her God for "mercy for him and me" (34.5; 39.3). Still, he is torn by unbelief. While she can affirm that "God awaits us," he is despondent. "I cannot feel myself God waits" (34.8-35.1), he admits, expressing the dark heart of his fears, which leads to an unexpected enactment of a ritual mutilation of the woman's body:

           Man is entirely alone
may be. I am a man of griefs & fits
trying to be my friend. And the brown smock splits,
down the pale flesh a gash
broadens and Time holds up your heart against my
    eyes.

                    (35.4-8)

While the speaker doesn't quite believe that the world is devoid of God ("may be"), he implies that he is far from any source of meaning. The next image, a kind of caesarian birth performed on "Bradstreet"'s brown-smocked body by "Time," images forth the effects of his wrenching doubt. Perhaps her faith is unbelievable; perhaps she, his creation, is unbelievable, and he requires visual evidence, her heart—seat of her emotions and faith—delivered up to him. There is also a

sense in which time measures her heart (faith) against his eyes (skepticism) and finds him wanting. The excision of her heart, a violation of her body and metaphorical theft of her soul, can be read as an emblem of how in his doubt he has forced her open in an "unnatural" birth where her sex becomes a Christ-like gash, a wound, yet still the only way to her heart, her faith, to that which he does not and cannot possess except through violence. To be loved and known, woman must be sacrificed.

By contrast, Berryman has "Bradstreet" narrate her bodily decline and impending death in sexual terms that contradict the forced, adulterous opening: "Light notes leap, a beckon, swaying / the tilted, sickening ear within. I'll—I'll—/ I am closed & coming. Somewhere! I defile / wide as a cloud, in a cloud, / unfit, desirous, glad—" (53.4-8). In an ecstasy of eschatological desire, her body seems to evaporate into the air. But the male poet retains his relentless preoccupation with her body, and reserves for himself the details of her burial, sending her off with imagery alternately tender and grotesque:

    —You are not ready? You áre ready. Pass,
as shadow gathers shadow in the welling night.
Fireflies of childhood torch
you down. We commit our sister down.
One candle mourn by, which a lover gave,
the use's edge and order of her grave.
Quiet? Moisture shoots.
Hungry throngs collect. They sword into the carcass.

                    (54.1-8)

The movement here is resolutely downward, and the emphasis falls on "Bradstreet"'s deceased body, not on transcendence or her released soul. The contradictory image of fireflies "torching" her to her final rest captures his need to return her to a childlike status, diminutive and fanciful—a small body that glows intermittently. Distancing himself, his voice takes on the detached tones of a preacher addressing mourners. Then, with a kind of Marvellian glee, he watches as the "hungry throngs" of worms pierce her body. Marvell's mistress was more "coy," but her body was just as indispensable to satisfy the poet's lust for power, immortality, song.

However, just as "Bradstreet"'s imaginary body is the locus for the male poet's aggression, it provides her with an identity and power he covets. According to Berryman's own account, "the moment of the poem's supreme triumph" is the birth of "Bradstreet"'s first child ("Changes" 101), a passage that must be set against the forced birth cited above. The tension, rhythm, and emotions accelerate in an extended, hallucinatory description of labor:

            everything down
hardens I press with horrible joy down
my back cracks like a wrist

      . . . . .

> I work thrust I must free
> now I all muscles & bones concentrate
> what is living from dying?
>
> Then, just as she can no longer endure,
>
> it passes the wretched trap whelming and I am me
>
> drencht & powerful, I did it with my body!
> One proud tug greens Heaven. Marvellous,
> unforbidding Majesty.
> Swell, imperious bells. I fly.
> Mountainous, woman not breaks and will bend:
> sways God nearby: anguish comes to an end.
> Blossomed Sarah, and I
> blossom. . . .
>
> (19.5-7; 20.1-3; 20.8-21.1-8)

In this irreducibly female and quintessentially feminine experience, "Bradstreet" finds herself competent, powerful, and blessed by God. Through motherhood, "Bradstreet" eludes the trap of sinful love. Her refuge from the harsh and oppressive world is her "Beloved household" (22.1) where her delight in her children reenforces her sense of identity: "When by me in the dusk my child sits down / I am myself," she declares peacefully, echoing the declaration of selfhood through birth: "I am me . . . I did it with my body!" (42.1-2). By comparison, "The proportioned, spiritless poems accumulate. / And they publish them / away in brutish London, for a hollow crown" (42.6-8). Literary notoriety for woman is barbarous, worldly. Here, Berryman reimposes on "Bradstreet" the same split that male-dominated Puritan culture imposed on creative women, and that Bradstreet's poetic productions belie: the split between procreativity and artistic creativity. For, in the end, "Evil dissolves, & love, like foam; / that love. Prattle of children powers me home" (39.6-7). "That love" is the adulterous, evil love with which she is tempted; her mother-love allows her to resist her "demon-lover's" blandishments and return to domestic fidelity and religious hope.[13]

In the poem's coda, "Bradstreet" 's resistance to temptation and her achievement of identity are contrasted to the poet's damning declaration of selfhood, in which he ruefully admits to being corrupt and dark:

> I am a closet of secrets dying,
> races murder, foxholes hold men,
> reactor piles wage slow upon the wet brain time.
>
> (55.6-8)

Resonating suggestively with the gender politics at work in the poem, this passage associates the male poet's own moral corruption and spiritual emptiness with the decline of modern, postwar society, the rabidity of racist nationalism, and the abuse of nuclear power. This declaration of male subjectivity is rife with the corruptive effects of what is repressed and undisclosed. The masculine psyche is a "closet" whose secret contents are ultimately destructive on a personal as well as a broader political level. In Bradstreet's times, a "closet" was a small private room to which one retreated for private religious meditation; however, we cannot ignore the contemporary connotation of the term, which suggests that Berryman understood that the effects of gynesis were not merely personal but more broadly cultural: to make real women invisible and unthreatening, thereby reenforcing male dominance and facilitating homosocial male bonding.

The triumph of body, will, and faith here is woman's. Despite the male poet's relentless imposition of control, he can only experience these triumphs by appropriating them. In fact, Bradstreet had the children *and* the poems; after much suffering and doubt, she achieved a hard-won faith. Furthermore, "Lise" left Berryman to return to her husband and child (Provost 77). Berryman recreates Bradstreet not simply as an object of love or lust but also as a wishful recreation of himself, empowered by the physical exertion of birth, which he can only experience vicariously, as the "couvade" of poetic creation.[14] By inhabiting her body, he can imagine the "proud tug" that "greens Heaven," and the unqualified love that overcomes devious lust. By speaking through her voice he can try on the beliefs he cannot sustain in his own world, quieting his own doubts with a faith that would elude him for many years. In a note he typed up for the ending of *Homage,* he explained, "Upon her turn away from evil, with her help, *he* finally turns" (qtd. in Haffenden 28; Berryman's emphasis). And by projecting his shameful desires onto her, and watching her agony and redemption, the male poet can exorcise his guilt publicly and be expiated. Despite homages and honorifics, and the trappings of Puritanism, modernism, or postmodernism, female visibility, independence, and agency are once again sacrificed for the spiritual, critical, and rhetorical advancement of the male.

Notes

I would like to thank the editors for their helpful comments, and Dana Nelson for her astute reading and suggestions.

1. See Bordo for a discussion of Descartes's determining "flight to objectivity," "a compensatory turning toward the *paternal* for legitimation through external regulation, transcendent values, and the authority of law," and away from "the *maternal*—the immanent realms of earth, nature, the authority of the body" (58).

2. Spenser, whose analysis of the poem appeared in 1994 (well after my initial reading in *Work* but remarkably close to mine), makes a similar argument. Though he finds "many moments of dra-

matic power, even empathy" with the Puritan woman's experience, "there is also a current of feeling that seeks to colonize Anne Bradstreet as a 'mistress,' with as much rhetorical insistence as Bradstreet's fellow (male) colonists established their authority over Massachusetts" (356).

3. For a more complete discussion, see Schweitzer, *Work,* especially chapter 1.

4. Compare Winthrop's remarks to the General Court of Massachusetts: "a true wife accounts her subjection her honor and freedom, and would not think her condition safe and free, but in her subjection to her husband's authority" (*Winthrop's* 239).

5. See Romans 8:15-17. "Sonship," Samuel Willard said, proceeds from "our Marriage to Christ; so that by becoming his Spouse . . . we are made the Children of God" (qtd. in Morgan, *Puritan* 165).

6. This point is echoed in Rotundo's conclusion. For more on the suppression or negation of woman in Puritanism, see Ong and, from the perspective of French postmodernism, Jean-Joseph Goux, who argues that "*the* founding fantasy" of Western culture is "the active negation of the Mother" (qtd. in Jardine 32).

7. Jardine differentiates between contemporary instances of gynesis and concludes that the Anglo-American version is reactionary, concerned primarily with reenforcing the status quo (231-36). This supports my argument about Berryman's gynesis; however, Jardine anchors her speculation in the different symbolic economies constructed by Protestant democracies and a Catholic monarchy. Berryman's later conversion to Catholicism complicates any simple or reductive attribution of ideological content.

8. DeShazer surveys the literary history of the Muse of male as well as female poets. See pp. 1-44.

9. See Holden, who catalogues the discrepancies between the poem's historical claims and Berryman's major source for Bradstreet's life and circumstances, the already semifictional biography by Helen Campbell, *Anne Bradstreet and her Time* (1891). For other critical views that do not condemn Berryman's effacing procedures, see C. Johnson; Provost, who (eerily echoing Winthrop's attitudes about women) says the finale of *Homage* "restores the woman to her proper place . . . serv-[ing] to further, rather than hinder, the poet's work" (73); and Rich's reversal of her 1967 claim that *Homage* is a great poem. For feminist interpretations, see Watts, who calls the poem "macho" (34 n.4); Ostriker, who concludes "that Berryman created, out of his own yearning, a

lover-anima-muse figure who would never be seen as a colleague, collaborator, or equal" (26-27); and Gilbert and Gubar, who also find that despite Berryman's ostensible reverence for Bradstreet he, like fellow poets Roethke and Lowell who celebrate female contemporaries, has "made a critical gesture that suggests some measure of hostility toward literary women" (158).

10. No one has pointed out that this startling image without the gender specificity occurs in Bradstreet's poetry and prose, for example, in her letter to her children: "when I have been in sickness and pain, I have thought if the Lord would but lift up the light of His countenance upon me, although He ground me to powder, it would be but light to me" (*Works* 243), and in Meditation 19: "Corn, till it have past through the mill and been ground to powder, is not fit for bread. God so deals with his servants: he grinds them with grief and pain til they turn to dust, and then are they fit manchet for his mansion" (*Works* 275).

11. In an interview, Berryman comments: "I decided to tempt her. I could only do this in a fantasy; the problem was to make the fantasy believable" (Stitt 196).

12. Between *Sonnets* and *Homage,* Berryman worked on a series of poems concerning victims of the Holocaust entitled *The Black Book,* which he abandoned because the topic was too painful. During this period he also had recurring dreams in which he killed women (Provost, 70, 78; Haffenden 19).

13. Berryman describes the voices' dialogue as "a sort of extended witch-seductress and demon-lover bit" ("Changes" 101).

14. Berryman's wife at the time, Eileen Simpson, records in her memoir that when Berryman finished the passage on Bradstreet's delivery, he threw himself down and said, "Well, I'm exhausted. I've been going through the couvade. The little monster nearly killed *me*" (226). Provost points out that accounts of Berryman's creative process repeatedly compare it to birth-throes. She argues that the "children" he wanted were his poems, birthed as women birth children, but at their expense (76). Mancini analyzes Berryman's "couvade consciousness" from an "archetypal" perspective and thus ignores the gender politics. I agree with Friedman, who argues that "Men's use of the metaphor [of childbirth] begins in distance from and attraction to the Other" and appears to be a "tribute to woman's special generative powers" but is ultimately "an appropriation of women's (pro)creativity [because it] subtly helps to perpetuate the confinement of women to procreation" (84).

Works Cited

Berryman, John. "Changes." *Poets on Poetry*. Ed. Howard Nemerov. New York: Basic, 1966. 94-103.

Bordo, Susan R. *The Flight to Objectivity: Essays on Cartesianism and Culture*. Albany: State of U of New York P, 1987.

Bradstreet, Anne. *The Works of Anne Bradstreet*. Ed. and introd. by Jeannine Hensley. Cambridge: Harvard UP, 1967.

DeShazer, Mary K. *Inspiring Women: Reimagining the Muse*. New York: Pergamon, 1986.

Friedman, Susan Stanford. "Creativity and the Child-birth Metaphor: Gender Difference in Literary Discourse." *Feminist Studies* 13.1 (1987): 49-82. Rpt. in *Speaking of Gender*. Ed. Elaine Showalter. New York: Routledge, 1989. 73-100.

Gilbert, Sandra M., and Susan Gubar. *The War of the Words*. New Haven: Yale UP, 1988. Vol. 1 of *No Man's Land: The Place of the Woman Writer in the Twentieth Century*. 3 vols.

Haffenden, John. *John Berryman: A Critical Commentary*. New York: New York UP, 1980.

Holden, Alan. "Anne Bradstreet Resurrected." *Concerning Poetry* 2 (1969): 11-18.

Jardine, Alice. *Gynesis: Configurations of Woman and Modernity*. Ithaca: Cornell UP, 1985.

Johnson, Carol. "John Berryman and Mistress Bradstreet: A Relation of Reason." *Essays in Criticism* 14 (1964): 338-96.

Mancini, Joseph, Jr. "John Berryman's Couvade Consciousness: An Approach to His Aesthetics." *Recovering Berryman: Essays on a Poet*. Ed. Richard J. Kelly and Allan K. Lathrop. Ann Arbor: U of Michigan P, 1993. 169-78.

Morgan, Edmund S. *The Puritan Family: Religion and Domestic Relations in Seventeenth-Century New England*. New York: Harper, 1965.

Ong, Walter J. *In the Human Grain: Further Explorations of Contemporary Culture*, New York: Macmillan, 1967.

Ostriker, Alicia Suskin. *Stealing the Language: The Emergence of Women's Poetry in America*. Boston: Beacon, 1986.

Provost, Sarah. "Erato's Fool and Bitter Sister: Two Aspects of John Berryman." *Twentieth Century Literature* 30 (Spring 1984): 69-79.

Rich, Adrienne. "Anne Bradstreet and Her Poetry." Bradstreet ix-xxi.

Rotundo, E. Anthony. *Manhood: Transformations of Masculinity from the Revolution to the Modern Era*. New York: Basic, 1993.

Schweitzer, Ivy. *The Work of Self-Representation: Lyric Poetry in Colonial New England*. Chapel Hill: U of North Carolina P, 1991.

Simpson, Eileen. *Poets in Their Youth*. New York: Random, 1982.

Spenser, Luke. "Mistress Bradstreet and Mr. Berryman: The Ultimate Solution." *American Literature* 66 (June 1994): 353-66.

Stitt, Peter A. "The Art of Poetry XVI." *Paris Review* 53 (1972): 177-207.

Watts, Emily Stipes. "'The posy UNITY': Anne Bradstreet's Search for Order." *Puritan Influences in American Literature*. Ed. Emory Elliot. Urbana: U of Illinois P, 1979. 23-27.

Winthrop, John. *Winthrop's Journal: "History of New England" 1630-1649*. Ed. James Kendall Hosmer. Vol. 2 New York: Scriber's Sons, 1908. 2 Vols.

John Roe (essay date April 1999)

SOURCE: Roe, John. "Huffy Henry and Crazy Jane: *The Dream Songs* in Ireland." *Symbiosis* 3, no. 1 (April 1999): 26-40.

[*In the following essay, Roe examines the influence of W. B. Yeats on Berryman's* The Dream Songs.]

In the middle to late nineteen-sixties, the **Dream Songs** began to make an impact on the discerning public and at last the rewards and recognition that Berryman had long sought, and incessantly spoke about in his poems, began to be his. He was able to take stock and pause for a sabbatical year, 1966-67, which he decided to spend in Ireland.

> They wanted to know whether   his sources of inspira-
> tion
> might now be Irish: I cried out 'of course'
> & waved him off with my fountain pen.
>
> ("**DS 342**")[1]

Why Ireland? The simple and convenient answer is that Ireland is the home of Yeats; and home-coming, of a kind, was what Berryman professed as a motive (or one of his motives):

> After thirty Falls I rush back to the haunts of Yeats
> & others, with a new book in my briefcase
> four times too large:
> all year I must in terminal debates

with me say who is to lives & who to dies
before my blessed discharge.

                                    ("DS 281")

And again,

I seem to be Henry then at twenty-one
steaming the sea again   in another British boat
again, half mad with hope:
with my loved Basque friend[2] I stroll the topmost
    deck
high in the windy night, in love with life
which has produced this wreck.

                                    ("DS 283")

The second time around, and this time full of foreboding, Berryman sails towards that Irish fog and hauntings and mystery;[3] towards the encounter with the ghost of Yeats waiting for him like an aged Cuchulain with his large club of formal rhetoric.

The Irish poet had been *the* influence on the young Berryman, 'Yeats whom I did not so much wish to resemble as to *be*.'[4] He had taught Berryman the capacious discipline of the eight-line stanza, which had informed so many of the poems in early collections like *The Dispossessed*; and he had saved Berryman from 'the then-crushing influences of Ezra Pound and T. S. Eliot,' but at the cost of overwhelming our youthful, impressionable American with his own 'gorgeous and seductive rhetoric' (*Freedom of the Poet* 324-5). Finally in the 1953 poem *Homage to Mistress Bradstreet* Berryman gained his freedom, Hopkins literally helping to spring him from Yeats's influence and direct him towards his own voice. Any final encounter now with the spirit or conjured presence of Yeats was bound to be complicated, as Berryman foresaw—not just a simple thank-you but also something of a have-at-you:

I have moved to Dublin to have it out with you,
majestic shade, You whom I read so well
so many years ago,
did I read your lesson right? did I see through
your phases to the real? your heaven, your hell
did I enquire properly into?

For years then I forgot you, I put you down,
ingratitude is the necessary curse
of making things new:
I brought my family to see me through,
I brought my homage & my soft remorse,
I brought a book or two

only, including in the end your last
strange poems made under the shadow of death
Your high figures float
again across my mind and all your past
fills my walled garden with your honey breath
wherein I move, a mote.

                                    ("DS 312")

This is both a salute, an *ave atque vale* kind of address, and a confrontation. But it is a confrontation in the

Yeatsian manner, that is, it is measured, sonorous, and stately; relatively free of the idiomatic usage which itself registers the degree to which Berryman had slipped the Yeatsian knot while having absorbed as much as he needed of Yeats's stanzaic structures. What you mainly find in Berryman's middle years is a man writing as if inspired, as if in a fever-fit of despair, the words crowding in thick and fast, but with all the structural discipline, built up over twenty to thirty years, in place and containing the seemingly irrepressible, random, chaotic energy. Let me as an example of this, try out the following comparison between a Yeats poem and one by Berryman on the subject of Passion versus Scholarship, especially viewed from the rueful, reflective vantage of middle age. Yeats and Berryman were at a comparable point around the fifty mark when they wrote these poems. The first is Yeats's 'The Scholars' with its sardonic opening:

Bald heads forgetful of their sins,
Old, learned, respectable bald heads
Edit and annotate the lines
That young men, tossing on their beds,
Rhymed out in love's despair
To flatter beauty's ignorant ear.

All shuffle there; all cough in ink;
All wear the carpet with their shoes;
All think what other people think;
All know the man their neighbour knows.
Lord, what would they say
Did their Catullus walk that way?

How do you bring this poem up to date without succumbing to its sonorities, which even in Yeats's hands threaten to make it just a bit portentous (always the danger of high rhetoric), and which pose a deadly threat to his imitators (as the maturing Berryman discovered)? The answer most likely comes in an early *Dream Song* ("35"), which carries the title *MLA,* and attacks the annual conference somewhat in Yeats's spirit (though not in manner) and particularly in the spirit of Edmund Wilson who published his damning 'Fruits of the MLA' essay a few years later in *The New York Review of Books* (1968). The poem refers to Sir Wilson, whom I take, then, to be Edmund Wilson,[5] saluted in the guise of a scholar-knight (as opposed to an academic professional):

Hey, out there!—assistant professors, full,
associates,—instructors—others—any—
I have a sing to shay.
We are assembled here in the capital
city for Dull—and one professor's wife is Mary—
at Christmastide, hey!

and all of you did theses or are doing
and the moral history of what we were up to
thrives in Sir Wilson's hands—
who I don't see here—only deals go screwing
some of you out, some up—the chairmen too
are nervous, little friends—

a chairman's not a chairman, son, forever,
and hurts with his appointments; ha, but circle—
take my word for it—
though maybe Frost is dying—around Mary;
forget your footnotes on the old gentleman;
dance around Mary.

("DS 35")

For Catullus Berryman gives us Robert Frost, an anti-Academy poet if ever, who was then about to die (see **"DS 37"** which commemorates his actual death). But as well as death there is necessarily birth. One professor's wife is Mary, a clear inspiration of delight and desire in Berryman and any of the others who still have some feeling. But it doesn't stop there—not if this is Christmas and she is called Mary. Is Mary's husband a professor of Carpentry, perhaps? The poem's pointedly ironic frame extends nicely to include an impression of all those MLA participants going to be taxed.

Would Yeats have approved of Berryman's manner, even though he rides out in the same protesting spirit to give passionate fight to the forces of age and stultification? Yeats most likely would have deplored the calculated indecorum of the voice Berryman adopts, especially his painfully accurate rendering of a man whose candour depends on having had a drink too many ('I have a sing to shay'). This way of speaking strays well outside the bounds of formal rhetoric to which Yeats, even at his most vituperative, always held. What that address to the shade of Yeats does is to assert how much Berryman has repudiated his influence, even in the process of absorbing it—rejecting the poetic father. The Poundian dictum, 'Make it new,' to which the line in **"Dream Song 312"** refers, is not so simple as its bold declaration supposes. Berryman speaks of the necessary curse of ingratitude, to which we might add the implied word 'filial'. Pound's presence in the words just quoted perhaps indicates a further way in which Old Ez helped Berryman put his adulation of Yeats into perspective. Pound was infamously no respecter of persons, especially when the subject in question was inclined to be a little pompous. Berryman visited the 'cracked' and broken Pound in the hospital at St. Elizabeth where they discussed Yeats's poetry among other things, and he records an instance of Pound's typically scurrilous wit:

> He urged me to stay on and on . . . insisted on getting the Yeats photograph from his room, and quoted in very good brogue a parody-epitaph 'Under bare Ben Bulben's bum . . .'—and waved from the barred window—'Ha!'[6]

Pound's predilection for infantile expression in his battle to subvert the increasingly authoritative reputations of his peers, notably Eliot and Yeats, corresponds well with, perhaps even inspires, Berryman's Freudian, father-felling stance. The calculated infantilisms in the speech of *The Dream Songs* are often defiantly, irreverently Poundian, and that and Berryman's Freudian habit of perceiving relationships emphasise at how primitive and irrational a level he sees essential conflicts taking shape. Though saved originally by Yeats from the 'crushing influence' of Pound, Berryman doubtless found in his re-encounter with the distraught, shattered Ezra of St. Elizabeth something which in turn helped liberate him from Yeats: an impish, under-your-skin irritant, which formed no part of the Yeatsian poetic armoury, but which contributed to that suppleness of idiom Berryman developed to express perfectly the themes and issues of a later age.

Throughout *The Dream Songs,* then, Berryman addresses more than one shade; the principal ghost or spectre is of course that of his own father 'who shot his heart out in a Florida dawn' (**"DS 384"**) when the poet was only twelve. **"DS 384"** attempts a final encounter with the father just as in **"DS 312"** he attempts to confront the poetic father Yeats. There are of course many other references, submerged or apparent, throughout; and the poet's feelings towards his father fluctuate from grief to guilt and anger. There is also the further possible relationship, for those who see *The Dream Songs* as a theodicy, of God the Father to his Son.[7] The attempt to absorb and finally fight free of Yeats stylistically seems to mirror Berryman's attempt to resolve matters with his natural father. So exact and obvious is the parallel that Berryman appears to have been conducting it deliberately along Freudian lines.[8]

The presence in the *Songs* of the natural, self-immolating father gives a special personal dimension to the enterprise. Symbols, masques, everything that imposes order and impersonality on the emotions, dissolve in the messiness of the life lived with its unresolved questions, unfinished encounters. 'Dream' for Berryman does not signify the 'cold snows' of formal resolution but the heat of impulse, terror, hauntings, the disorganization of random emotions: in a word 'nightmare', made only bearable by its farcicalness. Berryman recognizes that everything he had learnt from Yeats had to be shed—or at least 'crumpled' (to use a favourite Berrymanism) to yield a new sort of rhetorical compound capable of expressing the condition he now found himself living. One stylistic insight came in the middle of the Bradstreet poem where he conceived of the idea of a sexual encounter with Anne across the centuries (*The Freedom of the Poet,* 329). This in turn became part of his attempt to break through the inhibitions which so far had kept him in thrall to his predecessors and mentors. The new, confident recklessness with which he thumbed his nose at the very models which had served him can be summed up in a single line:

> I held all solid, then I let some jangle.

("DS 198")

As *The Dream Songs* enter the final Irish phase, in which Berryman attempts to bring some sort of overall closure to bear, a larger reflective sweep can be discerned. The *Songs* remain consistently within a continuing loose narrative, capable of accommodating day-to-day events or ideas as they crop up—the sort of *ad hoc* pattern which seems to have impressed Lowell enough to try out his own version in *Notebook*. But he is making them form something less random than this. He had always had in mind an epic, with the implications of homecoming, or at least significant finish. Epic models, then? Within Ireland he finds another and natural one, beloved of Yeats, and that is Spenser, the creator of Faery Land. Berryman had invoked Spenser earlier, in a Quixotic chivalric fashion (in that same defiantly 'jangling' song):

> How tiresome Spenser's knights, their grave wounds
>   overnight
> annealed, whilst Henry with one broken arm
> deep in hospital lay
> with real pain between shots from light to light
> ten lights, two specialists, where nurses swarm
> day after achieveless day.

("DS 198")

In the Irish section this kind of humour seems more diffused, more gentle and whimsical, as in the invocation of Spenserian values in the following address to the aptly named Valerie Trueblood, a loyal friend and admirer, chastely standing as a transatlantic muse (she seems, a rare enough occurrence, not to have had an affair with Berryman). Spenser's Petrarchan element furnishes a Laura figure:

> My lady is all in green, for innocence
> I am in black, a terror to my foes
> who are numerous & strong.
> I haven't lost a battle yet but I am tense
> for the first losing. I wipe blood from my nose
> and raise up my voice in song.
>
> Hard lies the road behind, hard that ahead
> but we are armed & armoured & we trust
> entirely one another.
> We have beaten down the foulest of them, lust,
> and we pace on in peace, like sister & brother,
> doing that to which we were bred.

("DS 315")

The lady, in true Petrarchan fashion, is not his wife. Raising up your voice in song is something you can do easily in a pub in Dublin, and Berryman heard and joined in on such singing. He was especially friendly with Ronnie Drew, one of the singers of the folk-music group, the Dubliners, in a song of whose comes the refrain, 'like sister and brother.' In turn Ronnie Drew attended a poetry reading Berryman gave while in Dublin (Haffenden 345). Berryman who found in Yeats the staunchest defendant of high culture also drew on low

or popular culture for his inspiration;[9] and this reminds us of Berryman's varied opposition to Yeats and Yeatsian values. The lesson of *The Faerie Queene* is one of humility, especially for gentlemen. Did Yeats know humility? Did he need to know it? Berryman's fiercest reproof of the arrogance of Yeats, as he saw it, comes in his tribute to that former knight and irreducible gentleman Roger Casement.

Berryman shows impatience, indeed, in the late, Irish, Section VII, with what he sees as Yeats's extraordinary lack of insight into the condition of his compatriot, Casement, whose 'queer' plight qualifies him as one of the benighted figures of the *Dream Songs*:

> . . . the note from my bank this morning was stampt
>   with Sir Roger Casement,
> no 'Sir,' just the portrait & years:
> about whom Yeats was so wrong
> This distinguisht & sensitive man lived in the grip
> of a homosexual obsession, even the 'tools' of native
>   policemen excited him.

("DS 334")

The tragedy of Casement was greater than that of merely being homosexual: during the First World War he was convicted of treason by the British, and executed (while being stripped of his knighthood). To an uncanny extent Casement's fate in this war, though grimmer finally, corresponded to that of Pound in the Second, a comparison that may well have occurred to Berryman that year in Ballsbridge where he composed so many of the final songs. Like Pound, and like Berryman himself, Casement 'lived in the grip' of a self-destructive obsession which none of them was able to control. The matter of Casement, then, 'about whom Yeats was so wrong,' and whose plight Berryman understood intuitively, leads him further in the same Song to comment with remarkable dismissiveness on the want of humanity in his former poetic mentor:

> Yeats knew nothing about life: it was all symbols
> & Wordsworthian egotism.

But the basis of Berryman's reproach is more complex than might at first appear. Yeats must have thought he had done rather well by Casement; after all he wrote two poems in his memory, blaming first those perjurers who had 'blackened his good name', and then John Bull himself for his collective ill-treatment of nobler, weaker peoples. Yeats wrote these poems in response to a then recent book by W. J. Maloney who disputed the authenticity of Casement's diary revelations of extensive homosexual activities.[10] The press had got hold of extracts of the diaries and mention of them undoubtedly made an impact on public opinion, though they were not referred to during the trial. Yeats accepted Maloney's argument that the 'diaries' were the product of governmental foul play:

I say that Roger Casement
Did what he had to do,
He died upon the gallows
But that is nothing new.
Afraid they might be beaten
Before the bench of Time
They turned a trick by forgery
And blackened his good name.[11]

However, Casement's recent biographer Brian Inglis takes a different view from Maloney and argues for the genuineness of the publication. While acknowledging there is some room for doubt, Inglis shows fairly conclusively that a forgery on the scale required would have been hard to pull off, and he finds the evidence for Casement's homosexuality to be irrefutable. The official release of the documents in 1956 dampened the case for forgery.[12]

Why, though, should Berryman take it out on Yeats for his defence of the memory of Casement, whether ill-informed or not? It would be quite inappropriate to read into the words 'blackened his good name' the implication that Yeats would have deplored Casement's homosexuality had it been proven at the time, for he expressly said to Dorothy Wellesley that it was a thing of no account.[13] But it is only possible, Berryman impatiently seems to be saying, to hold such a generous attitude from a position of moral superiority, in which case tolerance is a privilege practised by those unassailed by self-doubt or unvisited by fears over past actions. Such liberality, though well-intentioned, lacks insight, and—more damagingly—its heart is uninvolved. For Berryman, by contrast, Casement's human qualities are inseparable from his 'queerness'; it is the mark of his sensitivity that he is prey to an obsession. Acknowledging his kinship with Casement—for the latter's sexual deviancy read the other's alcoholism—Berryman is right down there with him (like Pound in his Pisan cage) looking up angrily at Yeats who in declaiming his high rhetoric merely enlists Casement in another 'cause.' This ultimate, and surprising, reproach of Yeats (especially given his peace-making with the shade of the great poet which Berryman performs in the beautiful **"Dream Song 312"**) only proves how much it mattered to him that poets should know about the abject, humiliating (especially *publicly* humiliating) depths of suffering before they presumed to speak of it. In the course of that long heart-to-heart with Pound at St. Elizabeth Berryman had perhaps drawn closer to him than even he then knew. There are, however, ways in which Yeats too came near to Pound, though in thinking rather than in suffering.

For in dealing with the question of Yeats and political causes it may be relevant to consider Conor Cruise O'Brien's controversial yet, to my mind, judicious assessment of implications of fascism in Yeats, in his essay 'Passion and Cunning', published in an important

centenary volume which appeared the year before Berryman set sail to Ireland, and which he almost certainly would have known.[14] Indeed, the occasion of Yeats's centenary was an obvious extra stimulus for Berryman to choose Ireland as the place for his sabbatical. Berryman nowhere mentions it in the context of Yeats on Casement, but O'Brien's essay spells out clearly and to the discomfort of Yeatsian admirers the pitfalls of high-mindedness, especially in the 1930s. The enlistment of Casement in the attack on British foreign policy comes very close, according to O'Brien, to declaring an admiration for the political situation in Germany under Hitler.[15] Even sympathetic biographers such as Joseph Hone reveal the degree to which his friends felt anxious over the political rantings of Yeats at this point. It is curious, too, that Yeats who was so silent about Casement at the time of his trial, and who also wrote those worried, reflective poems about the Easter Uprising (hardly poems of endorsement for Sinn Fein) should become so vituperative in the mid 1930s, especially in view of events on the Continent. Maloney's book, from which Yeats drew inspiration, is as much a piece of anti-British propaganda as it is an attempt to right an old injustice. While at first glance it is hard to see Yeats's championing of Casement in the negative light in which Berryman perceives it, it may well be that Berryman is signalling—in the abbreviated, semaphore fashion of so many of the Songs—something akin to O'Brien's disquiet over Yeats's 'vision' at the period of the Casement poems. Sometimes the fractured, unstable, degenerate personality is a more certain reminder of human value than the pure-minded figure of blameless deportment. Hitler, after all, was incorruptible.

A further, apparently disparaging observation on Yeats occurs in **"Dream Song 331"**:

Yeats listened once, he found it did him good.

The context is more sympathetic than this single line suggests; nonetheless, it is a curiously impatient remark from someone who had once wanted to be Yeats—all the more so for not being explained. Berryman makes more positive references to Yeats than bad, but as late as the posthumous volume, *Henry's Fate,* we find him saying:

Young men (young women) ask about my 'roots,'—
as if I were a *plant.* Yeats said to me,
with some pretentiousness, I felt even then,
'London is useful, but I always go back

to Ireland, where my roots are.'[16]

But there is also something slightly evasive in the poem's final abrupt retort:

O really I don't care where I live or have lived.
Wherever I am, young Sir, my wits about me,

memory blazing, I'll cope & make do.

At what does memory blaze? Could the anger include Yeats for having had it too easy, especially in his childhood? By contrast Berryman could only look back with unhappiness at *his* early 'roots'. If we ask where the association of Yeats and Wordsworth comes from (see the Casement Song), we find the answer most likely in these lines from 'The Tower,' in which Yeats recalls his boyhood in the manner of Wordsworth in *The Prelude*:

> Never had I more
> Excited, passionate, fantastical
> Imagination, nor an ear and eye
> That more expected the impossible—
> No, not in boyhood when with rod and fly,
> Or the humbler worm, I climbed Ben Bulben's back
> And had the livelong summer day to spend.
>
> (*Poems* 194)

Such lines conjure a very different recollection of childhood from that recalled by Berryman, confronted with his father's violent death when he was still only a boy. But in its opening statement the same poem gives Berryman something he can share:

> What shall I do with this absurdity—
> O heart, O troubled heart—this caricature,
> Decrepit age that has been tied to me
> As to a dog's tail?
>
> (*Poems* 194)

Here is Yeatsian humility and self-loathing, but rendered as always with rhetorical dignity. Both poets experience a similar despair at the passing of life, the end of sexual adventure which they look back upon with mingled guilt and pride (perhaps more guilt in the case of Berryman), and they are equally capable of giving passionate voice to such themes. But the language, the voice, is different, for Berryman, in the *Dream Songs,* has moved decisively away from Yeatsian decorum. Crazy Jane speaks to the Bishop in his own voice sounding like one half of a Petrarchan-Augustinian dialogue:

> I met the Bishop on the road
> And much said he and I.
> 'Those breast are flat and fallen now
> Those veins must soon be dry;
> Live in a heavenly mansion,
> Not in some foul sty.'
>
> 'Fair and foul are near of kin,
> And fair needs foul,' I cried.
>
> (*Poems* 259)

Compare this with the voice of the protesting female Berryman reproduces in one of the early *Dream Songs*:

> . . . she was heard at last, haughtful & greasy,
> to bawl in that low bar:
> 'You can biff me, you can bang me, get it you'll never.
> I may be only a Polack broad but I don't lay easy.
>
> (**"DS 15"**)

In these words lie so many things that make up the difference between the two poets: the acknowledgment of racial difference, questions of miscegenation, the changing attitude towards women; and as we read on in the *Dream Songs* comes the involvement of the United States in global politics, including its wars with Asian peoples which develop as a theme in Section VII (to say nothing of the complex role of blackspeak on the home front). In quoting his Polack broad, Berryman makes it clear that he can have no truck with Yeats's habit of seeing the Irish peasantry as one element in the construction of his myth of Faeryland.

Nonetheless, Faeryland of the Spenser-Yeats variety achieves something of a presence in the last Irish section, and it comes sometimes in the form of a suffering heroine desperately awaiting rescue at the hands of a Guyon or Calidore:

> Cold & golden lay the high heroine
> in a wilderness of bears. His spirit fled
> upon this apparition.
>
> (**"DS 291"**)

The lines 'Cold & golden lay the high heroine / in a wilderness of bears' recur twice more in **"DS 302"** and **"372"**; they continue in a transformed, heroic manner the poet's obsessiveness over the sufferings of women, a theme that goes all the way back to a dramatic early lyric such as **'The Song of the Tortured Girl'** (1948). Given the mythological shaping of the formula, as here, it seems clear to me that Berryman is drawing upon the Yeats-Spenser picture to develop and finally draw to a conclusion some of the matters that have haunted him throughout his poetic career. Why not invoke the ghosts of Faeryland to lay other ghosts to rest? Although Berryman registers his opposition to Yeats, and indeed his distaste for him, at one level, at another he seems to return to him as a kindred spirit and mentor who can teach what is required. But it is less easy for Berryman to undertake the Spenserian role of disciplined, questing knight than it was for Yeats who, kept perpetually at arm's length by Maud Gonne, was able to serve her in the imagination as an heroic figure. In contrast, those beasts and bears—'salvages'—of the Spenserian undergrowth were too familiar to Berryman as manifestations of himself in the grip of lust. Granted that the terms of Spenser's psychomachia allow the allegory of the poet/reader's doing battle with his own dark forces, Berryman had caused too much havoc in his personal relations, and experienced too much self-disgust at his own lack of will, to feel easy with the poetic nobility of the enterprise. If, saving Valerie Trueblood in his mind, he were to see himself in the shape of the bear who is pawing her, what else might his spirit do but flee? Significantly, the *Dream Songs* seem unable to do more than reiterate fitfully the desolate, haunting refrain of the 'cold & golden . . . high heroine,' presumably beyond rescue in her wilderness of bears.

While pursuing a determinedly epic path, the *Dream Songs* threaten always to end in an impasse. Mock-heroic is a proven, traditional means of renewing the life of the heroic poem, and Berryman exploits its comic possibilities accordingly: if Spenser's knights bleed profusely from their wounds, then let our hero suffer a humble nose-bleed in return ('I wipe blood from my nose,' **"DS 315"***)*. But the gravity of the sequence, given that so many of the Songs concern themselves with Eros's counterpart, death, requires greater ballast than the jauntiness of parody alone. A particular break-through seems to me to occur when he drops down from the high, cold wilderness into the element of the sea, in which Yeats rehearsed so many conflicts successfully. The sea in her tidal surges is conventionally understood as a source of renewal—of life certainly, but of style also—and this capacity shows through in the successful merging of the two poets' idioms. This I find to be most marked in his great quasi-mythological Song (sub-titled **'The Armada Song' ("DS 361")**) which for me reads like a re-casting of something like 'Cuchulain's Fight with the Sea.' In Berryman's Song the 'invulnerable tide' takes the form of Spanish sailors, their cause in ruins and yet their potency intact as they emerge from the sea to renew themselves and claim against the odds the favours of the victorious. Through and beyond Yeatsian Celtic myth may be that of Cronus castrating his father Uranus and throwing his genitals into the waves, which in turn produces the birth of Venus-Aphrodite. Yet this too Yeats supplied in that beautiful, majestic stanza in 'A Prayer for my Daughter' (1919):

> Helen being chosen found life flat and dull
> And later had much trouble from a fool,
> While that great Queen, that rose out of the spray,
> Being fatherless could have her way
> Yet chose a bandy-leggèd smith for man.
> It's certain that fine women eat
> A crazy salad with their meat
> Whereby the Horn of Plenty is undone.

> (*Poems* 188)

The point here is that Yeats facilitates Berryman's use of mythology. The American poet's voice is slangy, demotic, mischievous; but it has a resonance which Yeats would recognize and which at this late stage of the game Berryman has come to ask from the only poet who could have given it to him.[17] Yeats's expression 'crazy salad', though as always subordinate to the majestic dignity of his voice, prepares idiomatically for the free-wheeling language of scurrilous Henry, while thematically the wildness and unpredictability of sexual preferences, especially those of women, point towards **'The Armada Song'** as a Yeatsian poem re-made by Berryman:

> They came ashore with erections
> & laid the Irish maidens in large numbers

> then in 1588.
> Spaniards are vile and virile.
> History is after all a matter of fumbles.
> Man's derelictions, man's fate,

> is a matter of sorry record. Somehow the prizes
> come at the wrong times to the proper people
> & vice versa.
> The great ships, confused in tempest,
> drove on the shoals. Accepting ladies
> crowded the northern shore.

> In they plunged, in half-armour, with their strength
> returned to the personal. Philip's on his own.
> These fragrant maidens
> are good to a man out of the sea, at length,
> in a new world, and each new man, alone,
> made up his own destiny.

> **("DS 361")**

This is not just parody, or mock-heroic; the last stanza is bidding for something more ambitious. Let us call it a democratic poem in the Yeatsian grand manner—not something Yeats would have thought worth doing, but nonetheless something that could not have been done without his example. Or if not democratic, perhaps the aristocracy of the humble. That is closer to something Yeats took seriously, and Berryman shows in his way how it may be achieved. Berryman absorbed his Irish poetic father fully, and then expunged and repudiated him; but he was always there to be recalled (hence the sabbatical voyage to Ireland), and this last phase of the *Dream Songs* declares a positive re-engagement with the voice of Yeats.

Notes

1. John Berryman, *The Dream Songs* (New York: Farrar, Strauss, and Giroux, 1969). All quotations from the *Dream Songs* (*DS*) are taken from this edition.

2. The friend was Pedro—or Pierre—Donga, a 'journalist and political caricaturist.' The friendship was one of those short-lived youthful enthusiasms which quickly give way to changing circumstances. See Paul Mariani, *Dream Song: the Life of John Berryman* (Amherst: University of Massachusetts Press; 2nd ed., 1996), 58-69. Donga—a Spaniard remembered at sea during a second voyage, this time to the country of Yeats—possibly helped inspire Berryman to write 'The Armada Song' (*DS* 361). See the discussion below.

3. 'The whole place is ghostly: no wonder Yeats believed in fairies / and personal survival' (*DS* 313).

4. 'One Answer to a Question: Changes,' in *The Freedom of the Poet* (New York: Farrar, Strauss & Giroux, 1976), 324.

5. For his opinion of Wilson at about the time he wrote the Song, consider the following statement

in a letter to Berryman's mother, dated 3 March 1963: 'I wrote to Edmund Wilson yesterday, to my mind the most remarkable American man of letters surviving, and ill, in Cambridge' (in *We Dream of Honour: John Berryman's Letters to his Mother,* ed. Richard J. Kelly, New York & London: W. W. Norton, 1988, 353). Berryman also dedicated *Dream Song* 58 to Wilson and his wife Elena.

6. In John Haffenden, *Life of John Berryman* (London: RKP, 1982), 214.

7. See Berryman's interview with Peter A. Stitt, 'The Art of Poetry,' in *Paris Review,* 16 (Winter, 1972), 176-207.

8. Berryman's absorption of Freudian theory is well documented. See his application of Freud to Eliot's poetry and to Conrad's 'darkness' in the essays 'Prufrock's Dilemma' and 'Conrad's Journey' in *The Freedom of the Poet,* 270-78 and 107-14.

9. The title *Dream Songs* was confirmed, incidentally, by Berryman's hearing the Everly brothers singing 'Dream, Dream, Dream' on a café jukebox (Mariani, 334).

10. *The Forged Casement Diaries* (Dublin & Cork: Talbot Press, 1936).

11. *W. B. Yeats: the Poems,* ed. Richard J. Finneran (London: Macmillan, 1983), 305-06.

12. Brian Inglis, *Roger Casement* (London: Hodder and Stoughton, 1973), 373-88.

13. 'If Casement were a homosexual, what matter?' *The Letters of W. B. Yeats,* ed. Allan Wade (London: Rupert Hart-Davis, 1954), 884.

14. Conor Cruise O'Brien, 'Passion and Cunning: an Essay on the Politics of W. B. Yeats', in *In Excited Reverie: A Centenary Tribute to William Butler Yeats 1865-1939,* ed. A. Norman Jeffares and K. G. W. Cross (London: Macmillan, 1965), 207-78. O'Brien includes the essay in his more recent volume (which takes its title from the Yeats essay), *Passion and Cunning* (London: Weidenfeld and Nicholson, 1988).

15. O'Brien's essay caused a furore among the poet's admirers because he went so far as to envisage Yeats as co-operating with the Nazis in an eventual occupation of Ireland: 'Meanwhile in Ireland one would have expected to see him at least a cautious participant, or ornament, in a collaborationist régime' (*In Excited Reverie,* 273). O'Brien later and under pressure tried to exculpate himself from such a statement, but not altogether convincingly. See *Passion and Cunning* (1988), 'Introduction' (10). Berryman, of course, does not express this

view of Yeats but takes the more traditional approach to him as being dreamily unaware. Imagining Yeats's comportment before a firing-squad, Berryman despairingly conjectures that he would have been so out of touch with reality 'not [to] have been scared, like you and me' (*DS* 334).

16. *Henry's Fate & Other Poems, 1967-72* (London: Faber, 1977), 58.

17. One might suggest Pound as an alternative, especially given the attention paid to him above; but Berryman's relationship to Pound was not one of reaction, and he already resembled him in coming to Europe to find older, established accents to measure against his own.

Ernest J. Smith (essay date summer 2000)

SOURCE: Smith, Ernest J. "John Berryman's 'Programmatic' for *The Dream Songs* and an Instance of Revision." *Journal of Modern Literature* 23, nos. 3-4 (summer 2000): 429-39.

[*In the following essay, Smith investigates the function of Berryman's extensive notes on the composition of* The Dream Songs, *arguing that they "offer invaluable insight into his method, concerns, and intent."*]

Among John Berryman's papers at the University of Minnesota Libraries Manuscripts Division is a series of rough, sporadic notes kept by the poet as he was working on his major project, *The Dream Songs.*[1] At times headed with the word "programmatic," these notes are both conceptual and analytic, laying out the plan and organization of the long sequence of poems and critiquing the progress and quality of the individual Dream Songs as they were written. Throughout his career, Berryman used notes to plan future projects in both poetry and prose, many of which never reached completion. However, with each of his major poems, *Homage to Mistress Bradstreet* (1953) and *The Dream Songs,* Berryman's extensive notes, while not systematic in form or clearly collated by the author, offer invaluable insight into his method, concerns, and intent.

Berryman began writing Dream Songs in 1955, and the notes for them seem to have begun around the same time. While most of the roughly twenty-five pages of notes are undated, one of the most crucial documents, a page headed "form," bears the date "1955? '56?" in the upper right corner. The question marks, which also appear on various dated manuscript pages of poems, indicate that Berryman occasionally reviewed his work and attempted to date it. This is the case throughout the archive, even with some of the many scraps of paper containing a single or a few lines of poetry, random thoughts which occurred to the writer as he worked, or very broad ideas for projected works. Some of these fragments are specifically dated by day, month, and year, others undated, while still others bear tentative dates of a year followed by a question mark, as with the "form" page. Apparently never organized by their author, the Dream Song notes fall randomly amidst the draft and manuscript pages of both the published and unpublished Songs. While some of the notes reflect back over the poems which had been organized for the first volume, indicating that they date to the early-to-mid 1960s, many belong to the 1955-1960 period, when Berryman conceived and began writing the sequence. As he found his form and voice and became more comfortable with his new technique, the notes decrease in frequency. But, conversely, as the manuscript of *77 Dream Songs* takes shape during the early 1960s, the notes increasingly take on a therapeutic function, a means for the poet to reassure himself that his book-in-the-making has a discernible form, as well as an overall unity, both thematically and technically.

The page headed "form" and dated 1955-56 is almost certainly the earliest page of notes.[2] The first Dream Song which Berryman wrote, one ultimately excluded from the collection, was drafted on 12 August 1955, and the plan for a volume of the Songs conceived nine days later.[3] In these notes on the form of his new undertaking, Berryman envisions a group of twenty five to thirty poems, comprising "a *whole book,* or the major part of one." He instructs himself to "ad lib," but to make "each a *poem,* w. a title, subj., theme." Of course these plans changed as the work progressed, for the Dream Songs when published contained few titled poems, and both the poet, and eventually the book's reviewers, would question how well some of the individual Songs stood alone as poems. Even on this earliest sheet of notes, Berryman anticipates what will become his ongoing concern with unity, as well as the possible need to interrelate the individual poems, by noting that the poems should be "inevitably semicontra-puntal." He wanted to have the "stronger work to [toward] either *coarse* or *soft,*" with "*less* obviously-lyricism." Looking to his earlier work for a possible model, he turned to the nine **"Nervous Songs"** of *The Dispossessed* (1948), in which he had used an array of voices within a regular form, three six-line stanzas. But according to the 1955-56 notes, the new poems were to employ "a *much* 'rougher' & more 'brilliant'" technique than their predecessors, with "damned serious *humour,*" a combined "gravity of matter" and "gaiety of manner." As if urging himself to experiment with content and form, he writes: "Do anything crazy, & see how it feels & sounds, & *builds.*"

The problem of form in a long poem made up of individual lyrics continued to obsess the poet, even after he had decided on organizing and publishing a group of seventy five (ultimately seventy seven) poems as the first volume. Berryman's later notes question whether his book will be held together by "Accumulation *or* Thematic Dev't [development] of themes," themes that he identified as art, death, politics, illness, sex, paranoia.[4] Aside from the thematic strands of unity, Berryman considered using more conventional techniques, such as the "unity of *the year* (seasons, but dreamlike)," to bind the sequence. In notes dated April 1958, he reflected that after nearly three years at work on the project, "I have not yet got the *journey, action, structure*[.]" Again reviewing his earlier work, he realized that it had taken him nearly five years to develop these strands in **Homage to Mistress Bradstreet.** Even then, "unbelievably stupid" reviewers had gone so far awry as to the "*plot & voices*" of that poem, that this time he had better "have *a clear narrative-&-meditative line.*" Revisiting his notes for the Bradstreet poem, as well as his journals and notebooks of self-analysis, might afford even more material for the Songs, he noted, but the major concern at this stage was organization and unity. Hence, he reminded himself to "restrict composition" to a poem every few days, and to "spend most of that time on construction," planning ahead.

This two-page set of notes was composed while the poet was in the hospital, as was a three-page set found in the same folder and dated February 1959. Periods of recuperation from physical and mental exhaustion—brought on by the self-abuse that Berryman put himself through while writing the poems—offered a chance to reflect, organize, plan. These two sets are the longest, and among the most detailed, of any notes pertaining to *The Dream Songs.* For sheer quantity of words on the page, they are rivaled only by the early notes and by one other page, dated November 1958, the mid-point between the two sets composed during his hospitalization.

In the notes dated February 1959, Berryman listed other literary works which might offer possible models for organizing his own sprawling text.

> The only poems I know are Dante & Homer & *Job.* Study *PL* [*Paradise Lost*], then *Aeneid,* & *Faust* even. Tillyard's *Epic Poem*; Bowra's. Study structure of Sh'n [Shakespearean] trag. What the reader—modern X [Christian]—can take[.] Allow in the direction (only) of "Song of Myself."

In fact, Berryman was very well read in all of these works. Much of his life was devoted to Shakespearean scholarship, and his essay on "Song of Myself" is arguably his most crucial critical work, offering extensive insight into his own attempt at a long, personal poem, while the Book of Job was a text he hoped someday to translate.[5] Among his papers are various sets of notes made during his extensive reading of epic poems during the early stages of Dream Song composition, and at one point he speculated that his study might produce a major essay or at least a university course on the epic form. Berryman termed his own epic "modern, subjective" and listed the modes for the poem as "comedy, farce, tragedy, satire, testament, diary, phillipic, prayer." Studying the structure of epic, as well as laying out themes or modes shared by these poems and by his own, was one of his preliminary methods of planning his own poem's organization. Next to these vertical lists of themes or modes, he could list the individual Dream Songs which, although they would not appear consecutively in the book, clustered around what Berryman hoped would be unifying axes. Ultimately, however, his notes indicate that the Songs would primarily use thematic strands for overall unity more than for strict organization of groups of poems, with central themes recurring intermittently throughout the sequence, rather than appearing in poems placed consecutively in the sequence. The order and movement of the poems would follow the picaresque hero, Henry, on his "Quest" and "Self-quest" in what would be essentially a "survival-epic."

> The poem "ought" to be organized in (narrative or implicit) "actions"—if I can do it, if it seems truly *suitable* to the stuff—like pieces of a novel (scenic, panoramic, monologue) or Books of *The Iliad,* or Cantos.

Eventually the poems would find their way into books or "large parts"; in spite of his own recurring misgivings, Berryman would later feel that the most astute reviews of *77 Dream Songs* were those which emphasized the character of Henry as the poem's main organizing principle.[6]

If reviewers and readers had problems with Berryman's Songs when they appeared, the reservations more often than not concerned the odd language of the poems, the gnarled syntax, minstrel dialect, and shifting pronoun usages. Berryman's notes show that his overall schema for the language of the poem developed and evolved as he continued to compose and that it helped him clarify the effect he wished to achieve with the sequence of poems. Early on, on a page of notes in which he refers to the first Dream Song that he had written, he conceives of the project as being "like a *series* of dreams, some funny etc, bitter but some, and esp. Late on in the series, designed to lift the reader *out of the world.*"[7] To this end, the main point of emphasis concerning language in the notes is on flexibility and experimentation. Again comparing the Songs to the Bradstreet poem, Berryman anticipates that "the *language* is going to be just as difficult a probl.," but nonetheless he urges himself to "*play* more" and to make the stanzas of the new poem "infinitely more varied." Whereas his *Homage to Mistress Bradstreet* employed "archaism," the new poem would incorporate "kid-talk."[8] At various points in his notes, Berryman refers to the use of a "recurring

child-tone" which he wanted for particular Dream Songs; again, the initial Song offers an example.[9] In this poem about a "jolly old man" and his sworn lover, the poet employs the neologism "childness" as a sort of antidote to adulthood, and in one analysis of that poem he notes that the work is meant simultaneously to suggest a return to childhood and a movement toward having a child.[10]

Part of the strategy in using baby talk or childlike language in *The Dream Songs* is to vary the tone within the sequence. The language of Berryman's early work shows the influence of both Yeats and Shakespeare in its combination of vigor and stateliness, but with the Songs he wished to shed any overt signs of influence. Thus, in comparison to his earlier work, the Dream Songs would "avoid too high a key" and be careful to "drop key" regularly.[11] Although the influence of *The Waste Land* is one that Berryman consistently downplayed, he clearly did share Eliot's philosophy that the long poem should move by means of alternating passages of intensity and relaxation, a constantly varying music. "Work *toward* the Big ones," Berryman instructed himself, repeating the earlier idea of experimenting to see how the poem "builds." On the same page of notes, he lists side by side "the need to vary, the need to continue" and "prob's [problems] of diction & rhythm." To a great extent, the ordering and subsequent reordering of individual poems into sections or books within the projected volume seem to have been driven by the issue of pace and tonal variance. Gathering twelve early Songs to send out as a group, Berryman noted that he still had not determined the central action of the poem as a whole, but he was able to catalogue the tones of the individual poems as he had arranged them: "paranoiac intensity; high wit; crazy humor; rhet. [rhetorical] splendour; pathos; beauty; FORCE; SHORTNESS; darkness, violence; vista (biog. Relig. & geogr.) [biographical, religious, and geographical]; PRIDE; agony." As more and more Songs were written in the coming years, and when some of the initial reviews criticized the seeming chaos of *77 Dream Songs,* he would again make lists of the varied tones and themes which he intended to unify the sequence as a whole.

One particular technique which Berryman initially wished to experiment with was the use of multiple voices, especially those of women. On the early "form" sheet, he notes that "many" of the Songs would be "about women," and after writing his first Dream Song he envisioned a second major character for the poem, a woman named Mabel, Henry's companion or wife. Henry and Mabel were the pet names that Berryman and his second wife used for each other, and as he planned the Dream Songs, he saw the poems as "partly, a sort of history of *marr.* [marriage]—1) a desired one 2) a *real* one."[12] On this same page of notes, he advises himself to use quotations from *"women's speech,"* both real and imagined. Later, in the February 1959 hospital notes, he would speculate that even though he was not a great admirer of Joyce, "the organization of Molly's soliloquy" might be of use as he attempted to shape the poem. Of course, Berryman had some experience in using the voices of women, having published **"The Song of the Tortured Girl,"** one of the **"Nervous Songs,"** as well as *Homage to Mistress Bradstreet.* But as he wrote, Mabel failed to materialize as a character or voice and was replaced by a nameless second character whose function is to talk to Henry. However, the voices and presence of women play a major role in the Songs, ranging from Henry's mother in Song 14 and the self-described "Polack broad" of 15, to the tearful lady of 242 and the "heavy daughter" of 385, among others. Often the object of Henry's lust, love, or even incredulity, as with the virgin Mary, other women animate individual poems, and the term "women" often appears in the lists of themes compiled by Berryman as he chronicled the Dream Songs in his notes.

Among the aspects of style and technique, much of the notation on the Songs has to do with his concern over the poem's diction, especially the problem of diction in relation to rhythm. At one point, Berryman undertook a very detailed line-by-line analysis of the "jolly old man" Song, the poem which, although never published, nonetheless sparked the entire project and receives so much attention in the poet's notes. His full-page critique identifies the number of beats in each line, the wide range of metrical feet occurring in each, and then offers a description of the type of diction employed in each line, language described with terms such as "nursery; elevated; casual-high; fold-domest. [domestic]; tough; lyric; clowning; exalted-famil. [familiar]; crude."[13] These varied levels of diction correlate with the multiple tones that Berryman sought, ranging from tragedy to comedy or even farce, and then to testament or prayer. Concerned that the tragic aspect of the poem—which at one time he considered subtitling "The tragical history of Henry"—might overpower its other keys, he advised himself that "an admixture of non-despair [is] needed, & in fact ecstasy." The trajectory of each major part should be downward, but rise toward the end, ending either "in the kind of *doubt* Homer goes in for," "a large, smooth-muscled ceremonial section," or even *gladly.*"

Finding some of the individual poems "not striking enough," Berryman undertook to catalogue all of the potential clichés in the sequence, particularly "stylistic cliches" taking the form of particular adjectives or verbs which he tended to couple with Henry's name, in the manner of Homeric epithets. Two examples which he listed are "seedy" and "muttered," along with simple words such as "once," "down," and 'come," language that he feared was overly common. At the same time,

he rationalized that "the poem's Decorum wants simple rime (& *none*) as well as simple diction." He then began what would be one of the many studies of rhyme in his manuscript, finding most of his rhyme words monosyllabic. Apparently Berryman, like most of his readers, found the rhymes so perfectly unobtrusive that he had to reassure himself that they were actually present, as he wished them to be.

Berryman's major breakthrough in his notes on the Songs' language was the creation of a second major character and voice in the poem. Among the folders of unpublished Dream Songs is a collection of notes dated 10 November 1958, containing a block of writing—placed between two sets of lines meant to find their way in Dream Songs—labeled "NEW: the nameless interlocutor who calls him [Henry] 'Mr. Bones.'"[14] Berryman tells himself to make this figure the "2nd *real character*" of the poem, Mabel now being projected as the third. He is to be Henry's "confidant," having been first an "*enemy,* then *friend.*" They will talk and "debate, abt the proposed adventure, & its early details, etc, as betw. Don Q & SP." Drawing a circle around the name "Mr. Bones," Berryman notes simply, "STUDY." "Mr. Bones" was a name drawn from minstrel shows, which Berryman studied primarily through Carl Wittke's *Tambo and Bones* (1930), the source for one of the epigraphs to *77 Dream Songs.* But Berryman never wrote about Wittke's early historical study and never produced an essay on minstrel shows or their significance to the language and methods of his Songs. The brief 1958 note remains the poet's most extensive comment on the genesis of the interlocutor. Although Berryman would later be quite disconcerted by critics' and readers' confusion over the name "Mr. Bones," their failure to understand that it referred to Henry and not to his friend, the poet himself made a similar mistake on a note dated 6 April 1960. On this page he wrote, in a large scrawl, "'Mr. Bones' is *Death,* Henry's *friend*—who at the end takes him offstage."[15] Despite the slip, this note clarifies that the name "Mr. Bones" is meant, in itself, to carry chilling associations; the voice of the nameless End-man, as Berryman would later call him, serves as a reminder of mortality. Death is one of the most prominent themes of the poem, but the presence of this patient, indulgent ferryman renders Henry's existence all the more tenuous. The second voice is, as Berryman told a Harvard audience in 1962, "a Job's comforter. He's a friend you would not want, anywhere. He's nothing but censorious, witty, and hostile, and so on, except for rare moments."[16]

Still, Berryman appears to have had some trouble deciding how to employ the interlocutor, at one point asking himself, "how many *is* his friend in, & in what roles, & to what extent?"[17] On the same page, he worries about forcing Henry into too many individual poems: "Be v. careful how I Henrify *poems*—NEVER *try* to pull into series. Lean the other way. Make, in fact, a key representative list of perfectly characteristic ones." Berryman's various lists of "characteristic" Dream Songs take the form of central themes identified in the sequence, followed by either the number or the opening words of poems which concern these themes. The lists make for interesting groupings of Songs and highlight the unity within the series, that unity which Berryman needed to reiterate to himself during the early stages of composition. For instance, one clustering of poems from *77 Dream Songs* reads: "liquor: 5, 63, (49); conflict: 1, 50; paranoia: 52, 74, 8, 43, 16; death 33-39, 21, 68; self-love: 71, 75, 67; sex: (2), 3, 4, 69; politics: 22-3; 59; travel: 5, 73; relig.: 46-8, 17, 55, 66." These "registers," as Berryman called them, were one of the main methods of organizing and ordering the suitcase full of poems which he had amassed by the early 1960s, a tool for maintaining thematic coherence in a poem with a constantly fluctuating tone and frame of reference.

*   *   *

One example of the process by which Berryman's extensive revision of individual Dream Songs illustrates his "programmatic" is the second poem in the sequence, **"Big Buttons, Cornets: the advance."** The title, one of only a handful given to individual Songs, refers to the attire and announcement of minstrels entering a theatre. It would seem that among the *77 Dream Songs* published in 1964, this was one of the last to take shape, for what appears to be the earliest of the many draft versions of the poem (at least six are extant), is headed "1st typed version, 6 Sept '63." Berryman's extensive reworking of the poem took place quickly; what I believe to be the fourth draft, the only other dated version, bears "rev. 16 Sept" in its lower-right corner. Taken as a whole, Berryman's revisions of the poem underscore his urge to make the language of *77 Dream Songs* jazzier, "rougher," more "crazy," to utilize minstrelsy, humor, and the alternating voices of Henry and his unnamed friend as ballast for Henry's hurt and outrage.

"Big Buttons" is the first instance in *The Dream Songs* of Henry's posturing as a minstrel and his attempting what he considered the dialect of the disenfranchised African-American.[18] By 1963, Berryman had researched the minstrel show, compiling a rough page of notes which referred to the "unsolemn" funeral parade, jazz, traditions of whiteface and blackface performance, burlesques of Shakespeare, "pop gems" from opera, and various types of minstrel shows of the early century as possible influences on his Songs. Placing **"Big Buttons"** as the second Dream Song establishes both the convention of Henry in blackface and the edgy, lusty language of the unconscious that so distinguishes the sequence. Many of Berryman's revisions over the

course of the six surviving drafts attempt to interject additional slang into the poem's language, while at the same time making it less direct, more oblique. The first stanza of the poem, in what I believe is the first draft, reads:

> The jane is zoned! no nightclub here, no bar
> there, no sweet freeway, and no premises
> for business purposes,
> no loiterers, no beggars. Henry are
> baffled. Has everybody gone to Maine,
> electric' shut down?[19]

Consider, in contrast, the final version of the same stanza, as it appears in *Dream Songs*:

> The jane is zoned! no nightspot here, no bar
> there, no sweet freeway, and no premises
> for business purposes,
> no loiterers or needers. Henry are
> baffled. Have ev'ybody head for Maine,
> utility-man take a train?[20]

With the exception of the final line, Berryman's changes in this stanza seem subtle. But by revising "nightclub" to "nightspot," "beggars" to "needers," and "gone to" to "head for," Berryman makes Henry's voice more that of the participant than of the observer. The plural verb "have" in line five, paralleling the preceding "Henry are," and the elision of the syllable in "ev'ybody," brings the poem closer to the language of the street corner. This loosening of diction, rendering the Song as a product of Henry's psyche, is no doubt part of what Berryman had in mind when he wrote of "Henrifying" the poems. We see this in other instances of elided syllables, the dropping of the final letter in words ending *-ing*, enhanced alliteration and assonance (Henry / head; baffled / have), and revisions which amplify the poetry's rough music or achieve the type of "simple rime" which concludes stanza one in the final version. Attention to the conventions of rhythm and rhyme was clearly among Berryman's concerns as he wrote and revised Dream Songs. His revision of the final line here creates a simple, almost comic rhyme and, at the same time, amplifies the music of the stanza by extending the meter. The tetrameter line now falls but one foot short of the iambic pentameter, the predominant meter running through the poem. Cutting back the meter by one foot enforces the image of the closed-down town without abruptly ending the stanza with a forgettable line, as in the first draft. The image of the "utility-man" leaving via train is more "striking" and memorable, made more so by the blues-like rhyme.

Other changes in the poem also have to do with sound qualities. In the second stanza, Berryman creates an internal rhyme by revising the opening phrase from "Come in a time" to "Arrive a time," and changes "a blue, a shuffle" to "one blue, one shuffle," thereby threading an *-o* sound through the entire stanza. In the final stanza, "Honey hours sprawl" becomes "Honey dusk do sprawl," providing a sharper image of the time of evening, alliteration within the line, and a rhyme-echo ("do") with the "yo" and "you" from the preceding line. But as with most of the Dream Songs, these prosodic elements are inconspicuous, overshadowed by the sheer strangeness of the poem's language.

Nowhere is that odd language more on display than in the poem's final stanza, in which, for the first time in the sequence, Berryman introduces the voice of Henry's friend. What I contend is the first draft of that stanza reads:

> —Sir Bones, or Galahad astonishing
> yo' legal & yo' good. Does you feel well?
> Honey hours sprawl.
> —Hit's hard. De only thing is: fling & sing,
> when the worl' & the gals sit down off from you sad.
> Fing is: don't get *mad*.

By the time of publication, the final stanza reads rather differently:

> —Sir Bones, or Galahad: astonishin
> yo legal & yo good. Is you feel well?
> Honey dusk do sprawl.
> —Hit's hard. Kinged or thinged, though, fling & wing.
> Poll-cats are coming, hurrah, hurray.
> I votes in my hole.[21]

Where the revisions to the first three lines here fit into the larger pattern of pushing toward a jazzier street language, it is in the final three lines of the poem, constituting Henry's response to the interlocutor, that Berryman makes his most extensive changes. The only language unit that remains constant throughout all six drafts is Henry's opening phrase, "Hit's hard," words ambiguous enough, with their dual suggestion of not only "it's hard," but also "it *hits* hard." What follows, however, strikes me as one of the most obscure passages in the entire poem. The initial version is clear enough, reiterating Henry's sense of being wronged by the world, a theme established by the first Dream Song. When such injustice hits, Henry advises himself, a spontaneous blues shuffle ("fling & sing") would be a more advisable response than outrage. By the fourth draft, Berryman has begun to lighten the mood in these closing lines. This fourth version reads:

> —Hit's hard. Carled or earled, though, fling & wing,
> when the worl' & women sit down from you, had.
> Fing is: don jump *mad*.

This draft eliminates repetition ("thing is" / "Fing is"), suggests the range of Henry's possible positions on the social scale ("Carled or earled"), and has some fun with language. Two drafts later, however, Berryman pencils in extensive changes on a typescript, including a complete rewriting of the final two lines, simultaneously

capturing Henry's manic humor and his paranoia: "Poll-cats are coming, hurrah, hurray. / I votes in my hole." At a stroke, Berryman has excised the element of self-pity while intensifying the sense of fear and isolation, all the while maintaining the Song's blackface humor. But the handwritten revision also reveals that Berryman considered other versions of the final line. While changing "Pole" to "Poll" was the only last-minute change in the penultimate line, Berryman's first sixth-draft casting of the final line was "vote in yr [your] favourite hole," which he then amended to "I votes in my favourite hole." Underlining "favourite" with the wavy line he used to designate words which he felt might need revising, he listed "deep-in" and "secret" as possible alternatives. Above the two words, which he placed in the right margin, he wrote: "(mother)."

The unusual, highly strained relationship between Berryman and his overbearing, provocative mother is perhaps best chronicled in their voluminous correspondence.[22] The suicide of Berryman's father (John Allyn Smith) when the boy was seven, the remarriage of his mother almost immediately afterward, and the changing of the son's name from John Allyn Smith, Jr. to John Angus McAlpin Berryman were events that haunted the poet for the remainder of his life. His mother's constant revision of her theory of the suicide did not help matters. Both in formal psychiatric analysis and in his extensive attempts to write out analyses of his own dreams, Berryman explored his familial relations, including what, according to Berryman's diaries, his psychiatrist called "a heavy incest barrier," engendered at least in part by a "provocative mother."[23] Berryman's obscure and tangled dream analyses suggest that he felt part of his fascination with incest had to do with a subconscious desire to reunite with the lost father.[24] Repeatedly, he questions which of the two parents is the object of his imagined sexual union. There is no firm evidence that Berryman was involved in any literal incestuous relationship, but both the poet and many of those closest to him during his life noted that his mother frequently addressed and treated him more like a lover than a son. More than once, Berryman speculated that his own tendency to womanize had its roots in his mother's promiscuity. The reference to his mother in the final draft version of Dream Song 2 suggests that Berryman may have consciously imbedded a private sexual reference in the poem's final line, a line whose primary connotation enforces the sense of Henry's paranoia, his retreat, through alcohol and sex, from social participation. Berryman astutely analyzed his own psychological struggle with this complex in a dense three-page unpublished text, apparently an outline for a projected longer essay, which he titled "The Incest Taboo and the Concept of Virginity." In this prose draft, he proposes that

> . . . the misconceptions in the mod [modern] mind abt
> the real meaning of incest are so great that we are

ourselves in danger of carrying on incestuous unions in the form of negative *participatins* [sic] *mystiques* without knowing it; and, indeed, much neurosis is itself the result of such psychol [psychological] tho not necess phys [physical] unions.[25]

This "real meaning," he goes on to explain, has to do with the fact that those instinctive desires (in Biblical terms, he notes, the Flesh) cannot be satisfied in the spirit (or the Word). Many of the three hundred eighty-five published Dream Songs enact just such a transformation, giving voice to hidden, even unconscious desires, turning them into art.

Notes

1. The first volume of Dream Songs is *77 Dream Songs* (Farrar, Straus and Giroux, 1964). The second volume is *His Toy, His Dream, His Rest* (Farrar, Straus and Giroux, 1968). These are brought together in *The Dream Songs,* (Farrar, Straus and Giroux, 1969). All quotations from and references to the published Dream Songs are from this volume. References to unpublished Dream Songs are identified in footnotes.

2. All quotations from Berryman's notes in this paragraph are taken from the Berryman Papers, Box 5, folder 5, labeled "Published Poetry: *77 Dream Songs,* University of Minnesota Libraries Manuscripts Division. My thanks to Alan Lathrop, Curator, for his assistance while I consulted the archive. I owe a special thanks to Berryman's wife, Kate Donahue, for allowing me access to Berryman's papers, and for her permission to quote from the unpublished material.

3. See Paul Mariani, *Dream Song: The Life of John Berryman* (William Morrow, 1990), pp. 298-99, as well as John Haffenden, *The Life of John Berryman* (London: Ark, 1982), pp. 250 ff.

4. All quotations in this paragraph are from the Berryman Papers, Box 1, folder 2, titled "Unpublished Dream Songs." Many of the notes in this folder are dated 1958 or 1959.

5. The bulk of Berryman's published criticism, including the essay "'Song of Myself': Intention and Substance," is collected in the posthumously-published *The Freedom of the Poet* (Farrar, Straus, Giroux, 1976). Some of the Shakespeare criticism has recently been collected and edited by John Haffenden in *Berryman's Shakespeare* (Farrar, Straus, Giroux, 1999).

6. In particular, see Adrienne Rich's review of *77 Dream Songs,* "Mr. Bones, He Lives," *The Nation* (25 May 1964), pp. 538 ff.

7. Berryman Papers, Box 5, folder 5, "Published Poetry: *77 Dream Songs.*

8. Berryman Papers, Box 1, folder 2, "Unpublished Dream Songs."

9. Although he excluded this poem from the collection, it did appear in the journal co-founded by Berryman's friend Saul Bellow, *The Noble Savage,* I (1960), p. 119.

10. Berryman Papers, Box 5, folder 5, "Published Poetry: *77 Dream Songs.*"

11. All quotations in this paragraph are from the Berryman Papers, Box 5, folder 11, "Published Poetry: *77 Dream Songs*", and Box 1, folder 2, "Unpublished Dream Songs."

12. Berryman Papers, Box 5, folder 5, "Published Poetry: *77 Dream Songs.*

13. Quotations in the next two paragraphs are from the Berryman Papers, Box 1, folder 2, "Unpublished Dream Songs," and Box 5, folders 5 and 11, *77 Dream Songs.*"

14. Berryman Papers, Box 2, folder 16, "Unpublished Dream Songs."

15. Berryman Papers, Box 5, folder 11, "Published Poetry: *77 Dream Songs.*" All quotations in the next two paragraphs, unless otherwise noted, are from this folder.

16. Berryman made this remark during a reading at Harvard's Poetry Room in 1962. Audiotape from *The Poet's Voice: Poets Reading Aloud and Commenting Upon Their Works,* selected and edited by Stratis Haviaras.

17. All quotations in this paragraph are from the Berryman Papers, Box 5, folder 11, "Published Poetry: *77 Dream Songs.*"

18. For an interesting poetic response to this attempt, see Michael S. Harper's poem "Tongue Tied in Black and White," in *Images of Kin: New and Selected Poems* (University of Illinois Press, 1977).

19. The six drafts of the poem are found in the Berryman Papers, Box 5, folder 11, "Published Poetry: *77 Dream Songs.*"

20. *Dream Songs,* p. 4.

21. *Dream Songs,* p. 4.

22. See *We Dream of Honour: John Berryman's Letters to His Mother,* ed. Richard J. Kelly (Norton, 1988). For more general information, see the Mariani and Haffenden biographies.

23. Berryman Papers, Diaries 1958-1964.

24. The dream analyses date mainly to the 1950s, concurrent with the initial composition of Dream Songs. The extensive notes and analyses of his

dreams, which Berryman at least briefly considered a possible literary project in its own right, are collected under the title "St. Pancras Braser" in the Berryman Papers.

25. Berryman Papers, Box 1, folder 2, "Unpublished Dream Songs."

FURTHER READING

Bibliography

Arpin, Gary Q. *John Berryman: A Reference Guide.* Boston: G. K. Hall & Co., 1976, 158 p.
    Provides a bibliography of Berryman's works and secondary criticism.

Biographies

Haffenden, John. *The Life of John Berryman.* Boston: Routledge & Kegan Paul, 1982, 451 p.
    Offers a thorough biography of Berryman.

Mariani, Paul. *Dream Song: The Life of John Berryman.* New York: William Morrow and Company, Inc., 1990, 519 p.
    Provides a full-length study of Berryman's life and work.

Criticism

Blake, David Haven. "Public Dreams: Berryman, Celebrity, and the Culture of Confession." *American Literary History* 13, no. 4 (winter 2001): 716-36.
    Surveys the "confessional poets" of the 1950s.

Bloom, James D. *The Stock of Available Reality: R. P. Blackmur and John Berryman.* Lewisburg, Penn.: Bucknell University Press, 1984, 216 p.
    Contrasts the work of Berryman and R. P. Blackmur.

Djos, Matts. "John Berryman's Testimony of Alcoholism: Through the Looking Glass of Poetry and the Henry Persona." In *The Languages of Addiction,* edited by Jane Lilienfeld and Jeffrey Oxford, pp. 193-203. New York: St. Martin's Press, 1999.
    Considers the impact of Berryman's lifelong struggle with alcoholism on his "Henry" poems.

Frost, Carol. "Berryman at Thirty-Eight: An Aesthetic Biography." *New England Review* 16, no. 3 (summer 1994): 36-53.
    Evaluates Berryman's career at its mid-point.

———. "The Poet's Tact, and a Necessary Tactlessness." *New England Review* 20, no. 3 (summer 1999): 196-204.
    Elucidates Berryman's poetic style.

Johnson, Manly. "John Berryman: A Note on the Reality." *World Literature Today* 64, no. 3 (summer 1990): 422-25.
    Investigates the real-life experiences that influenced Berryman's poetry.

Kelly, Richard J., and Alan K. Lathrop, eds. *Recovering Berryman: Essays on a Poet.* Ann Arbor, Mich.: The University of Michigan Press, 1993, 303 p.
    Presents a number of critical essays on Berryman's poetry.

Spencer, Luke. "Mistress Bradstreet and Mr. Berryman: The Ultimate Seduction." *American Literature* 66, no. 2 (June 1994): 353-66.
    Discusses Berryman's critique of Anne Bradstreet.

Thornbury, Charles. "John Berryman and the 'Majestic Shade' of W. B. Yeats." *Yeats* 3 (1985): 121-72.
    Offers a thorough account of Yeats's profound influence on Berryman.

White, Roberta. "John Berryman's Anne." In *The Anna Book: Searching for Anna in Literary History,* edited by Mickey Pearlman, pp. 27-35. Westport, Conn.: Greenwood Press, 1992.
    Considers the persona of Anne Bradstreet in Berryman's *Homage to Mistress Bradstreet.*

Additional coverage of Berryman's life and career is contained in the following sources published by Thomson Gale: *American Writers*; *Concise Dictionary of American Literary Biography, 1941-1968*; *Contemporary Authors,* **Vols. 13-16, 33-36R;** *Contemporary Authors Bibliographical Series,* **Vol. 2;** *Contemporary Authors New Revision Series,* **Vol. 35;** *Contemporary Authors Permanent Series,* **Vol. 1;** *Contemporary Literary Criticism,* **Vols. 1, 2, 3, 4, 6, 8, 10, 13, 25, 62;** *Dictionary of Literary Biography,* **Vol. 48;** *DISCovering Authors Modules: Poets*; *Encyclopedia of World Literature in the 20th Century,* **Ed. 3;** *Literature Resource Center*; *Major 20th-Century Writers,* **Eds. 1, 2;** *Poets: American and British*; *Reference Guide to American Literature,* **Ed. 4; and** *World Poets.*

Anne Carson
1950-

Canadian poet and essayist.

INTRODUCTION

A scholar of Greek language and literature, Carson is
known for her unique, genre-bending blend of poetry
and prose, fiction and nonfiction. She claims the study
of Classics as her true calling and profession; however,
her published works of poetry—prose poems and novels
in verse—have earned her critical acclaim as well as
numerous awards and honors. Carson's style is an
unparalleled combination of lyricism, essay, unmetered
verse, blurred genre lines, and startling contrasts of
character and situation.

BIOGRAPHICAL INFORMATION

Carson was born June 21, 1950, in Toronto, Ontario,
Canada. She was raised Roman Catholic and lived in
small towns around the province of Ontario. Carson
studied Latin in high school, which was a normal course
of study at that time. Her Latin teacher knew ancient
Greek and, when Carson expressed interest, offered to
teach it to her during lunch hours. Carson continued to
study Latin and Greek at the University of Toronto but
frustrations with the university system caused her to
drop out after the first year and take a job. She
reenrolled the following year but dropped out again to
attend commercial art school for a year. After that, Carson returned to the University of Toronto and completed
her bachelor's degree. She then studied abroad at the
University of St. Andrews in Scotland with Greek
scholar Kenneth Dover and earned her master's degree
in Classics. She returned again to the University of Toronto and completed her Ph.D. in 1980. Her doctoral
dissertation on Sappho was the foundation for her first
published work, a book-length essay titled *Eros the Bittersweet* (1986). Carson is very quiet about her personal
life, preferring her writing to be the focus of attention.
She has admitted in interviews to having two desks at
home, one for her creative work and one for her
academic work. What is known about her life since college is that she is divorced and has suffered the loss of
her whole family: her father, mother, and brother, all of
whom died from a variety of causes. In a rare autobiographical revelation, Carson penned the moving and
dedicatory "Appendix to Ordinary Time" for her mother,
published at the end of *Men in the Off Hours* (2000).

Carson has worked as an instructor at many colleges
and universities around North America, including the
University of Calgary, Princeton University, Emory
University, and McGill University. She has been the
recipient of many awards. *Glass, Irony, and God* won
her the QSPELL Poetry Prize in 1996 and was also a
finalist for the Forward Prize in Britain. Carson was
awarded the Lannen Literary Award for poetry in 1996
and the Pushchart Prize in 1997. *Autobiography of Red*
won her a second QSPELL Poetry Prize in 1988 and
was a finalist for both the National Book Critics Circle
Award and the T. S. Eliot Prize for Poetry. She was also
granted a Guggenheim Fellowship in 1998. In 2000 she
received the Griffin Poetry Prize and was nominated for
the Governor General's Award for *Men in the Off Hours.*
That same year, Carson was awarded the prestigious
MacArthur Foundation "genius" grant. For *The Beauty
of the Husband,* she was awarded the T. S. Eliot Prize
for Poetry and was a finalist for the Lenore Marshall
Poetry Prize. Carson is sometimes thought to be a U.S.
poet because she has spent so much time working and

publishing in the States. She is currently a professor of Classics, comparative literature, and English at the University of Michigan.

MAJOR POETIC WORKS

After five volumes of poetry, Carson still considers herself more of a visual artist than a writer, telling *Publishers Weekly* interviewer Stephen Burt, "I didn't write very much at all until I guess my twenties because I drew. I just drew pictures, and sometimes wrote on them when I was young, but mostly I was interested in drawing. I never did think of myself as a writer!" In fact, the poems in her first book of poetry, *Short Talks* (1992), were originally intended as captions for her drawings. In 1995 she published *Plainwater,* a collection of essays and poems that began Carson's evasion of categorical classification in earnest. This collection includes, among other forms, verbal photographs, mock interviews, and mini lectures. *Glass, Irony, and God,* another collection of essays and poems, was also published in 1995. This collection contains one of Carson's most noteworthy and critically examined pieces, "The Glass Essay," a poem about a woman who is devastated at the end of a love affair. These genre-blending lyrical books, which draw on classical themes and philosophy, immediately began to earn Carson acclaim. *Autobiography of Red* (1998) is a "novel in verse" retelling the ancient story of the tenth labor of Herakles: the slaying of red-winged Geryon. Carson tells this tale in a modern setting that is nevertheless imbued with magic and mythology. Geryon falls in love with selfish, hedonistic Herakles and is drawn deep into a love triangle from which Geryon finally emerges, scathed but alive. *Men in the Off Hours* is a collection of poems juxtaposing historical and literary figures in unusual combinations and situations. Her most recent book of poetry, *The Beauty of the Husband* (2001), has elicited considerable critical attention. Another novel in verse, *The Beauty of the Husband* tells the story of a wife struggling with her husband's repeated infidelities.

CRITICAL RECEPTION

Plainwater was published in the same year as her second, highly-acclaimed poetry and essay collection, *Glass, Irony, and God.* The success of *Glass, Irony, and God,* and particularly the poem "The Glass Essay," quickly overshadowed critical study of *Plainwater.* In his Introduction to *Eros the Bittersweet,* Guy Davenport claims "The Glass Essay" as "a poem richer than most novels nowadays." Adam Phillips, writing for *Raritan,* and Jeff Hamilton, writing for the *Denver Quarterly,* have both examined Carson's work in *Plainwater* as well as *Glass, Irony, and God.* Phillips praises Carson's stylistic and thematic choices as well as her wit, scholarship, and form. Hamilton also praises Carson's inventiveness and intelligence, declaring "How do we talk

about what hasn't been done before?" However, not all critics have been so taken with Carson's work. Mark Halliday, examining *Autobiography of Red* for the *Chicago Review,* expresses discontent with the novel's modern elements and with Carson's choice to compose her novel in verse, stating that "the versification also has an arbitrary quality." Writing for *Parnassus,* Mark Scroggins explores *Glass, Irony, and God, Men in the Off Hours,* and *The Beauty of the Husband.* He disdains Carson's use of the "essay poem," claiming that "the fact that it's broken into verse lines doesn't make it any less an essay." Scroggins also disparages her lyricism, calling her poetic lines "unmusical" and prosey. In anticipation of such critical assessments, Davenport contends that "Anne Carson's eyes are original. We are not yet used to them and she may seem unpoetic, or joltingly new, like Whitman or Emily Dickinson in their day," and notes that her poems "are the remarks of a speaker who remains silent until there's something to be said, something that has been processed in the heart and brooded over in the imagination and is not to be further processed in rhyme or meter."

PRINCIPAL WORKS

Poetry

Short Talks 1992
Glass, Irony, and God 1995
Plainwater: Essays and Poetry 1995
Autobiography of Red: A Novel in Verse 1998
Men in the Off Hours 2000
The Beauty of the Husband: A Fictional Essay in 29 Tangos 2001

Other Major Works

Eros the Bittersweet: An Essay (essay) 1986
Economy of the Unlost: Reading Simonides of Keos with Paul Celan (nonfiction) 1999
If Not, Winter: Fragments of Sappho [translator] (poetry) 2002

CRITICISM

Guy Davenport (essay date 1995)

SOURCE: Davenport, Guy. Introduction to *Glass, Irony, and God,* by Anne Carson, pp. vii-x. New York: New Directions, 1995.

[*In the following essay, Davenport discusses Carson's up-and-coming presence as a poet, as well as her skill in essay writing and philosophy.*]

Anne Carson begins her *Eros the Bittersweet* (1986), a book about love and learning, with a fragment of Kafka's in which *ein Philosoph* tries to catch spinning tops, "for he believed that the understanding of any detail, that of a spinning top for instance, was sufficient for the understanding of all things." *War die kleinste Kleinigkeit wirklich erkannt, dann war alles erkannt.* Our planet spins on its axis; atoms spin; the liveliest equilibrium seems to require vertigo. An earlier *Philosoph* who also liked to be around playing boys thought that Eros, himself a boy, was necessary to philosophy, a *love* of learning. Behind Kafka's *Der Kreisel,* half a page long, are Greek boys tossing knucklebones, watched by Sokrates, who knows that as long as they are playing their minds are spinning and alive and open to intelligent questioning.

What we learn from *Eros the Bittersweet* while being spun alive by its brilliance is that its author is a philosopher of much cunning and an agile reader, a scholar with a mind as fresh as a spring meadow, no dust anywhere on her. Classicists tend to be a sprightly lot. Erasmus was as charming a person as God makes them. A. E. Housman, now that we know his secret life, vied with Norman Douglas for being the last authentic pagan. My first Greek teacher, James Nardin Truesdale, had swum, mother-naked, many laps of the pool in the Duke gym, before he met our eight o'clock class. At our very first meeting he strode in and said in the voice of a drill sergeant that the first letter of the Greek alphabet is *alpha,* the second *beta,* the third *gamma.*

My second text by Anne Carson was an article in a learned journal, "Echo with No Door on Her Mouth: A Notional Refraction through Sophokles, Plato, and Defoe." Defoe! There are classicists whose writing is just short of terrifying to read (Zuntz, Kirk, Cunningham, and Page for starters). Bringers of the Law down from Olympos are stern and earnest men, and they carry a cane to deal with Eros should he show his impudent face. Yet it is precisely the classicists who see our culture as one among many (Greece, like ancient Israel, was a traffic circle of belligerently different peoples, and Rome was a United States of meddlers in all the affairs of the world) and who are least embarrassed by the pagan topsoil in which our culture still grows its garden.

The past for the classicist is simply another room in the house, as familiar as any other. Jane Harrison grew up with a county father who intrepidly, for grace before meals, said, "For what we are about to receive, may the Lord be truly thankful." Both Zeus and Yahweh would have seen nothing askew in this prayer, and little Jane grew up to be a diligent explicator of Greek ritual. In Anne Carson's poetry we are everywhere looking into depths, through transparences of time and place. As with Virginia Woolf, she gives us scenes—moors, rooms, orchards, deserts—in which vivid action holds our attention.

Poets distinguish themselves by the way they see. A dull poet is one who sees fashionably or blindly what he thinks poets see. The original poet sees with new eyes, or with imported vision (as with Eliot seeing like Laforgue or Pound like the Chinese). Anne Carson's eyes are original. We are not yet used to them and she may seem unpoetic, or joltingly new, like Whitman or Emily Dickinson in their day. She writes in a kind of mathematics of the emotions, with daring equations and recurring sets and subsets of images. As with Matthew Arnold, truth and observation are more important than lyric effect or coloring. If a good line happens, it happens. Anne Carson's poems are like notes made in their pristine urgency, as fresh and bright as a series of sudden remarks. But they are the remarks of a speaker who remains silent until there's something to be said, something that has been processed in the heart and brooded over in the imagination and is not to be further processed in rhyme or meter.

The poem called **"Book of Isaiah"** may give us a clue as to the circuits of Anne Carson's genius. This is a poem that reminds us of Shulamith Hareven's *Navi* (*Prophet*) in its ability to imagine archaic theology and the deeply primitive *feel* of ancient Judaism. Both Hareven and Carson can enter Old Testament ways of thought and narrative, Hareven into the *numen*, Carson into the human (and even witty) narrative eccentricities of biblical style, a gathering into what sounds like history of disparate events, an oral tradition written down by different chroniclers without regard for sequence or consistency. Carson's Isaiah and Carson's God are both authentically biblical, no libel anywhere. They look wonderfully strange because we were rarely taught to read the bible with an honest mind.

I had begun discovering Anne Carson's poems about the same time as James Laughlin, who knows a poet when he sees one. He alerted me to "a poem about God that you have to read." Sitting at his back window at Meadow House in Connecticut, from which he observes his flock of sheep and where he writes his own poems and keeps in touch with hundreds of writers whom he has come to know in sixty years of publishing ("the Godfather of Modernism," Andréi Codrescu calls him), Laughlin's knowing eye saw Anne Carson for what she is: a real poet whose poems are unfailingly memorable. Hence this book, which I gather wasn't easy to come by. And then this inadequate introduction, as Laughlin thought "she needs explaining." I don't think she needs explaining at all, but Laughlin has lived through the slow acceptance of his New Directions poets—three decades for William Carlos Williams to advance from smalltown doctor who wrote poems between patients, and whom Laughlin was discerning and brave enough to publish, to Old Master—and wants to speed things up. There are probably beguiling ways of going about this far better than anything I might do (I know nothing of Anne Carson except her writing and the stray fact that she is also a fancier of volcanoes and paints them erupting).

The test of poetry, however, is easy. Read **"The Glass Essay,"** a poem richer than most novels nowadays. See how in its utter clarity of narration it weaves and conflates one theme with another, how it works in the Brontës as daimons to preside over the poem and to haunt it, how it tells two strong stories with Tolstoyan skill, how it reflects on its themes in subtle and surprising ways. This is a boldly new kind of poem, but neither its boldness nor its novelty make it good. It is good because of its truth and the sensibility of its telling. These qualities maintain from poem to poem, though no two poems are alike. Anne Carson's powers of invention are apparently infinite. The range of her interests is from horizon to horizon.

It has been the spirit of the arts for most of the century to dare new forms. Joyce's daring is evident on every page he wrote; so are Pound's and Cummings's. Sometimes the daring was more for its own sake (as with about half of Gertrude Stein and much of Picasso) than toward a technique useful to others. Anne Carson's daring succeeds. She is among those who are returning poetry to good strong narrative (as we might expect of a classicist). She shifts attention from repeating stanzaic form (which came about when all poems were songs) to well-contoured blocks of phrases: analogues of paragraphs in prose. Prose will not accommodate Carson's syncopations, her terseness, her deft changes of scene.

She writes philosophy and critical essays that are as beautiful and charming as good poetry; it is not surprising that her poems are philosophical—in the old sense, when from Herakleitos (if his fragments are from a poem) to Lucretius, and even longer (Bernardus, Dante, Cavalcanti), poetry was a way to write philosophy. When Sokrates took Sappho's desire for the young and fused it with the process of learning, sublimating it and disciplining it with stoic restraint, he gave the genius of the West a philosophical idea that lasted almost two thousand years. Desire is now a medical and sociological problem. The god Eros and his mother Aphrodita are outlaws again, a new puritanism descends, but there are still poets—Anne Carson is among them—who allow Eros his dominion and can tell us that while prophets sleep, the asters in the garden unload their red thunder into the dark.

Adam Phillips (essay date fall 1996)

SOURCE: Phillips, Adam. "Fickle Contracts: The Poetry of Anne Carson." *Raritan* 16, no. 2 (fall 1996): 112-19.

[*In the following essay, Phillips appraises Carson's* Plainwater *and* Glass, Irony, and God, *concluding that the "artful, tenacious voices of Carson's writing continually astonish by what she dares to consider."*]

When an interviewer for the *Village Voice* asked Anne Carson how often she wrote—not always the most interesting question—Carson also told him *where* she wrote: "anywhere all the time in the margins of anything to hand. Everyday yes regardless." If "yes" here is a moment's hesitation in her Beckettian sentence, the sense is that almost nothing stops her. Writing in the margins, whether that entails squeezing oneself in, or randomly expanding a text, shows a certain regard for boundaries and for bodies—if only of words—the twin preoccupations of all Carson's writing and about which she is unfailingly interesting. She makes the formal considerations of writing—where you do it, in essays, or poems, or on the margins of other peoples's words—seem as urgent as bodily needs. Even if you are all over the place, you have to have a place to be all over; and in language that place is form. The poems, essays, and quirky enigmatic parables that make up these two books are enquiries into the nature of profusion.

There is, though, no visionary gush about Carson's witty writing, obsessed as it is by overflow, and a complementary sense that all our notions of tempering excess are a mere tribute to something that may have been pictured all wrong. Concluding the essay "The Gender of Sound," the brilliant coda to **Glass, Irony, and God,** she writes:

> Lately, I have begun to question the Greek word *sophrosyne.* I wonder about this concept of self-control and whether it really is, as the Greeks believed, an answer to most questions of human goodness and dilemmas of civility. I wonder if there might be another idea of human order than repression, another notion of human virtue than self-control, another kind of human self than one based on dissociation of inside and outside. Or indeed another human essence than self.

It is not easy to wonder these days about such things without sounding cute or disingenuous. But the assurance of her tone, and the pacing of her curiosity, convince the reader that he is in on the beginning of something and that we are, indeed can only be, amateurs in our frank wish to appraise the big questions. It is as though we are overhearing someone being intrigued. One of the many exhilarating things about Carson as a writer is the sheer enigma and momentum of her ambition, if only to herself. Her questions bemuse her, but because she is the least knowing or supercilious of writers—one of the very few writers who can be ironic without sounding arch—she seems to collapse the distinction between innocence and experience. If these are both topical and perennial issues that she is wondering about—what must we be assuming a self to be if we use words like *self-control*—then her handling of them in her poetry and poetic fictions is both dramatic and puzzling.

It is as if the continual risk (and temptation) of self-exposure is made bewildering by the possibility that there may be "another human essence than self." This is the mystery that the heroes and heroines and narrators of her poems are always being initiated into. They are always discovering something in themselves that doesn't seem quite human, that leaves them on edge, teetering at the limits of the available stories. Sometimes she calls this an ahuman quality of experience, the sacred; and sometimes we know what she means (that, say, the uncanny is that which we could never be canny enough about; or that language is merely an attempted cure for the demonic). "What is so terrible," she asks in *Plainwater,* as though it was a mock dare, "about stepping off the end of a story?" Because for Carson ends are always edges, there is no closure; there is only translation, or flight. The stories she tends to step off the edge of are, in various unusual combinations, Greek myths (and their ethos), Psychoanalysis, and the prodigal modernism of Gertrude Stein. But stories, essentially for Carson, are for stepping off. That, for better and for worse, is what we can't help doing with them. "Shapes of life," she writes in **"The Anthropology of Water"** (in *Plainwater*), "change as we look at them, change us for looking."

* * *

Carson's first book, *Eros, The Bittersweet* (1986) is like a primer of erotic paradoxes, a work, in one sense, of traditional classical scholarship, but staged as thirty-four brief essays or excursions with titles like "Gardening for Fun and Profit," "Then Ends Where Now Begins," and "The Sidestep." Immensely informed and wacky, like its hero, the book straddles its necessary contradictions with logic and verve. "Desire then," Carson writes, laying it out for us, "is neither inhabitant nor ally of the desirer." Foreign to her will, it forces itself irresistibly upon her from without. "Eros is an enemy. Its bitterness must be the taste of enmity. That would be hate." This is itself irresistible; it has the inevitability of a proof, but it describes a phenomenon that Carson insists is fundamentally unintelligible. In this book, Eros makes distinctions—here, between love and hate—only to blur them. Paradoxically, Eros, by putting us in a terrible muddle, also shows us the difference between the familiar and the strange. You knew who you were; you fall in love; it ruins what you thought was your life. Everything may now be a mess, but that mess is the new, or the unknown. Carson seems both to relish these erotic zigzags, and to be terrorized by them. Indeed, how could it be otherwise given both the subject matter, and what Carson seems to be doing to and with the whole notion of traditional, classical scholarship by exposing a certain Olympian earnestness. The book, in other words, seems to be written by both Eros and one of his victims, and then edited by a serious scholar. Carson is nowhere more tricky or difficult to place than in her singular amusements. And in this extraordinary book she introduces us to a sensibility—of both the author and her subject—that is essentially a sense of humor.

But Carson was not, in this book, a happy (i.e. convinced) irrationalist; neither a Nietzschean nor a glamorizer of Woman as a dark continent, positions more similar than they at first seem. So she could celebrate, in Eros, Socrates' wisdom as "a power to see the difference between what is known and what is unknown." For Carson this is Eros in action, the power of love as a craving for something—knowledge, a person, or the knowledge that another person exists—that makes a difference visible and by doing so intimates the possible infinity of such differences, the sheer horror and exhilaration of how different we can be from ourselves. This is the trauma, the weird rationality of Eros, that love is a ridiculous disfiguring. Its logic is the breaking of forms.

With its calculated attentiveness to etymologies, the really very idiosyncratic classical scholarship that informs virtually all Carson's work is of a piece with her appetite for formal constraints. She is attracted to what form itself is used to do—to make formlessness both possible and invidious, to give a kind of shape to shape—one that makes it thereby intelligible. "Rembrandt wakens you," she writes in one of her dazzling "Short Talks" in *Plainwater,* "just in time to see matter stumble out of its forms." If this is apparently unthinkable, it is also an emblematic possibility that haunts Carson's writing, a glimpse of a new kind of birth (the "Short Talk" is entitled **"On The End,"** and is a brief commentary on Rembrandt's *The Three Crosses*). "Matter" here is a creature, and it is the stumbling that Carson wants to get at, to articulate. She is continually staging situations in which we are faced with the unimaginable, in which old familiar selves won't work, and something else has to come into play. "Think what it means," she writes in **"The Fall of Rome: A Travellers Guide"** (in *Glass, Irony, and God*), "to be a stranger / and to walk into the word 'Live!'" In Carson's writing people are characteristically in shock. They've been interrupted. They've been woken up just in time to see something that doesn't make sense.

Her figures for the inevitable turbulence of form are Eros, Woman, and the Journey as heroic quest or pilgrimage. The traditional gravity and permanence of forms—and these just mentioned figures in particular—is insisted upon because, to use one of Carson's winning words, forms are "leaky"; the quest makes the hero promiscuous. What we are prepared for is not what we end up having to deal with. All our means of containing ideas turn out to be preemptive strikes. In a fascinating essay not included in these books, "Putting Her In Her Place: Women, Dirt and Desire," Carson writes of women being, for the ancient Greeks, "intimate with formlessness and the unbounded in their alliance with the wet, the wild and raw nature." So ancient wedding rites were "contrived to bring the inviolate bride into contact with her bridegroom, to touch what was untouchable, to veil and seal what was an exposed pore, to civilize and purify what was wild and polluted." These desperate measures, in Carson's view, are a means of insulation at all costs. The world is a wedding for Carson, but the wedding is a momentary and inadequate means of averting catastrophe. The ancient marriage rites she describes with such homey, scarifying wit in this essay are a kind of working model or blueprint for the peril and necessity of literary (among other) forms. The characters in Carson's writing are continually sealing themselves up and then finding themselves unsealed. For Carson this is a virtual definition of relationship. So the essays, enigmatic parables, and weirdly luminous poems in these books are about form as damage-limitation, and about relationships between people as quite starkly the violation of forms. ("To touch across boundaries means serious, dangerous leakage.") Carson is not melancholic, not staving off emotional entropy, but rather, fascinated by leakage. And because leakage is everywhere—in the offing, as it were—we are always overexposed, always giving ourselves away in the joke we call language. Carson is a Freudian, if only in her sense that all language is the language of love, the language of self-betrayal.

Because she is so adept at exposing exposure—"TV is made of light, like shame"—she is unusually alert to hidden complicities. So there is often a connection or a distinction, a link, that her narrators are trying to clarify, as though they were involved in some ongoing translation. ("Translating ancient Greek," Carson says in her *Village Voice* interview, "is a process of lustration that I couldn't do without.") Because she is both chatty and incisively literary, she can make the most plangent distinctions sound almost wry. "Is this a law?" she writes in her poem **"TV Man: Sappho."** "No, a talent. To step obliquely / where stones are sharp. / Vice is also sharp. / There are laws against vice. / But the Shock stays with you." You make necessary, literary, tactful distinctions when you do something as ordinary as walk over sharp stones; but the difference between a law and a tale, and a law and a virtue, can be a difference of kind, not of degree—the kind of difference scandals can be made of. The law—like Carson's ancient marriage rite—is there to remind you of everything it can't do: It can't stop bad things from happening, nor the shock after they have happened. It leaks. It has a secret, and secretive affinity with all it pretends to control. It is underwritten by its own impossibility. "And the first rule is," she writes in **"The Life Of Towns"** (*Plainwater*), "The love of chance." A rule is a form of love, but a love for an intermediate object. Rules are broken to be made.

* * *

In Carson, all the rituals of form are first and foremost an expression of their own limitations, the sign of what leaks out of them. She's often interested, as a result, in

what people are trying not to be, how their acts depend upon how they clean up their acts—are the way they clean up their acts. In one of her "Short Talks" in *Plainwater* called **"On Sylvia Plath,"** she dramatizes this as an excerpt of what Plath's mother could not, or was not able to say about her daughter's poetry:

> Did you see her mother on television? She said plain, burned things. She said I thought it an excellent poem but it hurt me. She did not say jungle fear. She did not say jungle hatred wild jungle weeping chop it back chop it. She said self-government she said end of the road. She did not say humming in the middle of the air what you came for chop.

Plain burned things are the raw things that have been overcooked. The mother is sensible, engages our sympathy, but the unspoken voice of the mother is genuinely incoherent, speaking a cartooned madness, at one with her daughter's disarray. For the mother to speak like that, to expose that voice on television, would have implicated her in the artful savage dismay of her daughter's poetry. It is the disavowal of involvement, the refusal or rupture of implication that Carson closes in on. The mother seals up the daughter in the language of commonplace sentiment ("it hurt me"). If every writer has the scene of a crime to which they keep returning, this is Carson's: the moment when one person imposes upon another the specious civility of distance. She writes with a terrible lucidity about these scenes of disentanglement, in which people reassert, or insist upon their purity:

> Not enough spin on it,
> he said of our five years of love.
> Inside my chest I felt my heart snap into two pieces
>
> which floated apart. By now I was so cold
> it was like burning. I put out my hand
> to touch his. He moved back.
>
> I don't want to be sexual with you, he said. Everything
>   gets crazy.
> But now he was looking at me.
> Yes, I said as I began to remove my clothes.
>
> Everything gets crazy. When nude
> I turned my back because he likes the back.
> He moved onto me.
>
> Everything I know about love and its necessities
> I learned in that one moment
> when I found myself
>
> thrusting my little burning red backside like a baboon
> at a man who no longer cherished me.
> There was no area of my mind
>
> not appalled by this action, no part of my body
> that could have done otherwise.
>
>   (from **"The Glass Essay"**)

Like Mrs. Plath, the man here, whom Carson calls "Law," uses a casual throwaway formula ("not enough spin on it") to remove himself from the scene. If Carson shows us the devastations of too-ordinary language, she also shows us how the couple begin to impersonate their own impersonality. His cheerful, sporty cliché prompts her, as if by magic, to turn into another thing. Naked would have been very different from nude, as would *my* back be different from *the* back, making you wonder, as it does, what exactly he likes the back of, or wants to see the back of. There is the horror here of impossible redress, and the sheer bafflement of what looks like shame but what Carson sees as quite other than self-exposure. The poem continues:

> But to talk of mind and body begs the question.
>
> Soul is the place,
> stretched like a surface of millstone grit between
>   body and mind,
> where such necessity grinds itself out.
>
> Soul is what I kept watch on all that night.

Not a vale of soul-making but a mill of soul-making. One's fate is as irresistible and perverse as a perfect seduction—"no part of my body . . . / could have done otherwise"—but one is not ground down but ground out. Carson's staunch, visionary commitment to "another human essence than self" frees her from the bad faith, the bad poetry of pathologizing her actions.

Without a self there is nothing to confess, but there may be more daunting things to describe. The artful, tenacious voices of Carson's writing continually astonish by what she dares to consider. "You can learn to seem rational," she writes in **"The Anthropology of Water,"** ruefully perhaps. Her writing makes us wonder how we learn to be irrational, or whether we just are.

Jeff Hamilton (essay date summer/fall 1997)

SOURCE: Hamilton, Jeff. "This Cold Hectic Dawn and I." *Denver Quarterly* 32, nos. 1 & 2 (summer/fall 1997): 105-24.

[*In the following essay, Hamilton examines Carson's* Plainwater *and* Glass, Irony, and God, *describing her work as "discursive, self-conscious, highly intelligent."*]

These two books [**Plainwater: Essays and Poetry** and **Glass, Irony, and God**] by the Canadian poet and classicist Anne Carson accomplish the enormous task of re-imagining the border between the meditative lyric and the autobiographical narrative poem. How do we talk about what hasn't been done before? Averse to the unsettling hybrid forms among the books' eleven pieces,

some readers may decide Carson doesn't write poems. Formally, her work ranges from prose poem to verse novel, generically from satire to scholarly essay, with a dollop of confession to garnish them. The lyric commodity some of our most venerable journals have on offer is, for the moment at least, outside Carson's range. As she tells us in **Plainwater,** she has "no talent for lyrical outpourings." Her work moves all around—one wants to say it is all about—that single stanza, sincere and lyric account of personal experience at least one journal calls Poetry. In fact, however, it would be more accurate to say that Carson's work is about the quality of the poem such lyrics commodify: the voice—a sounding so intimate to us as we read silently that we refrain at first from giving it any but the most figurative status. (We call it the voice whether or not we're reading aloud.) The titles Carson gives her two books may be descriptive of just this subject.

Carson's work is discursive, self-conscious, highly intelligent—yet in our poetry culture the revolt against self-consciousness is in full charge, and I suspect these poems cannot overcome it. Is it possible to write a poem about the voice that isn't vulnerable to the charges of subject-mongers who despise whatever smacks of poetry about poetry? Indeed, from Michael Palmer to Louise Glück it has been done successfully, charge what thou wilt. Poetry in English contains multitudes, certainly, but this fact by itself gets to be a problem for a poet like Carson who asks, for starters, whether the voice can be represented—within a poem, within a picture, within a political system—and if not, then what chance does any poet have of finding again a central place within the tribe? The poet of "Song of Myself," in his own time far from being this central poet, rather sings about the problem of poetic voice. We get the thing confused. Will the voice find itself increasingly subjugated into representative, typical identity positions? Carson's first two books appear in a moment when the poets of identity politics, who at least have a politically engaged audience, and the avant garde, with no audience outside the academy but armed with their hallowed rationale in the idea of progress, have almost nothing to say to one another. In her omnibus review of women poets in *Poetry,* Sandra M. Gilbert lumps Carson's books in with poets as disparate in their work as Julia Alvarez, Janet Lewis, Linda Pastan, and Alice Fulton, and then says not a word about the feminism of these writers, but rather insensately plots them on a spectrum of "memory and desire"—*Eliot's* phrase, of all things, with our poets of identity politics on the memory side and the formal experimenters Fulton and Carson holding down Eliot's desire. Surely this is academic. That Gilbert, a credentialed feminist, can't discuss the political meaning of Carson's work in the pages of *Poetry* suggests how right Whitman was to claim the crisis over poetic voice has vista—we're still in that crisis. Carson's approach to the problem of subject matter is fascinating, though I suspect it will be welcomed more warmly by the reader who is not a poet—someone Riding and Graves called "the plain reader"—than among practitioners.

Each of the poems in these two books would seem to have subject enough, something you could catalogue: In one, the newly found fragments of a pre-Socratic philosopher-poet are presented along with his discoverer's commentary and an interview with the beleagured and post-humous ancient. In another, one of several travelogues, the diary of a North American tourist in Spain emerges as a failed conversion narrative, with stations punctuated by scriptural reference from the literature of Buddhism. A dog narrates the story of Anna, the muse of a painter commissioned to do a group portrait of philosophers attending a phenomenology conference in Perugia. An ethnographer copies down the "short talks" of three old women working in the fields. A suitably anonymous narrator offers a new redaction of the first forty chapters of Isaiah. Several pieces anatomize the aftermath of a love affair gone bad.

Subject matter, yes. Yet on the surface, at least, these eleven pieces, three or four themselves booklength, don't look like poems. Often they are presented as fake books, with introductions, tables of content and epigraphs. For instance, the following is an introduction to something called **"The Anthropology of Water"**:

> Water is something you cannot hold. Like men. I have tried. Father, brother, lover, true friends, hungry ghosts and God, one by one all took themselves out of my hands. Maybe this is the way it should be—what anthropologists call "normal danger" in the encounter between cultures. It was an anthropologist who first taught me about danger. He emphasized the importance of using *encounter* rather than (say) *discovery* when talking about such things. "Think of it as the difference," he said, "between believing what you want to believe and believing what can be proved." I thought about that. "I don't want to believe anything," I said. (But I was lying.) "And I have nothing to prove." (Lying again.) "I just like to travel into the world and stop, noticing what is under the sky." (This, in fact, is true.) Cruelly at this point, he mentioned a culture he had studied where true and false virgins are identified by ordeal of water [. . .]

Several pleasures that can be had from reading Carson are on display in this excerpt. A winning precociousness characterizes the speaker, whose intellectual curiosity is the instrument of comic chaos in her romantic life. The irony masks a more desperate motive, however; Carson can't help exposing the costs of the speaker's irresistible comic timing. There's a playful enactment in Carson's narration of the way the voice performs the self's claims vocally, deliciously floating them aloud as a way of divining truth from lie. All the

mental ear hears the interior voice say will seem true, as they screw up the courage to speak. The integrity Carson's poetic voice achieves in this short passage comes from its movement of thought, a compression as lively in the narrator's refusal to tell us *how* the anthropologist taught her about danger as in her agile shift from the interior voice of judgement "(This, in fact, is true)" to the more narrator-like "Cruelly, at this point. . . ." What the anthropologist so cruelly responds to in what the narrator said outright is perhaps no more than that the subject he changes does so inevitably, as a function of human differences, in this case between men and women, which the narrator would prefer to think of as genius, or poetry. The poet's distance from her narrator is a waggish joke on our assumption that they are one and the same. Carson gets off this gag again and again.

Carson's poems have subject matter then, but only a nominal one; the secret subject of the passage just quoted is borne by the movement of thought, by what gets left out in the hurry to go on. Writer, narrator, dramatic speaker: Carson insists on being all three, and nearly never at once, so that to stay with her we have to tune in to the motive of her shifting attentions. What makes Carson's prose movement so often such a hoot is that, whatever her subject matter, she's always got her mind on what the characters in Preston Sturges movies used to call Topic A. For these characters it was sex, and for Carson, too, but with the added and dreadful implication in Carson of the loss of the self's integrity in the face of the beloved.

This loss of self, of which love is the model, the voice can represent only at the cost of its own integrity: writer, narrator, dramatic speaker, and *if* all at once, then always one dominant. I suspect Carson feels that, in order to keep her secret subject comic—that is, tolerable—she must give up something as a poet; often, verse. Or put another way, let us suppose that Carson feels the prose essay is her native form and it's only her feminist emulation, along with her deepest cherishments as a reader, that draw her into verse. As a reader she's often in evidence with her epigraphs from canons both East and West, an avocation she makes light of by tagging her narrators with scholarly epithets. Scholars write prose, however, so her insecurities as a verse writer may rhyme conveniently with her political passion in those decisions which resist her discursive mastery in prose—her glib comic timing. Throughout the following—one of the prose travelogues in which the speaker is making a cross-country trip with her lover, a Chinese anthropologist she refers to as the emperor—but particularly in the last sentence, her timing is expert:

> In camping, cryptic rituals of the lost tribe confront the anthropologist. I am learning to read a map. There are many small numbers. I navigate us across Kansas and

into a large ruined area where crumbled fenders and auto parts are lying about. It is hard to find the exit. "Women don't know maps, I never met a woman who could read a map," says the emperor. Well I haven't been a woman for long, I will keep working on maps. They imitate reality in somewhat the same way sex does desire, curtly. *Make me your fuck boy,* I hear one of us whispering in the midst of dark tent nights—where do I go for a map into that country?

She gets her laugh, but too much of so fond a thing as a Carson punchline can slur into the banter of a hundred Maureen Dowd-type newspaper columnists, with their damned foothold in Yankee sanity. At this point in her work Carson seems to understand the risk of being a crowd pleaser, and if nothing else the length of **"Anthropology of Water"**—130 pages—secures the reader's sense of the narrator's desperately comic repetition. Perhaps aficionadoes of travel narrative will bring more patience to this work than I do. In any case, what can't be overlooked about Carson's prose is the way its values transform her verse, for were she not quite conscious of this herself she would not have included essay and verse under one cover.

We need some explanation of Carson's funkiness as a poet. As a maker of free verse, Carson can hardly live without her catty and satirical repose toward the tradition. Of course she's part of a conversation going on since Whitman between prose, verse and poetry. When she steals verse compression for her prose, the movement of voice typifies one kind of exchange poetry often makes with prose:

"Short Talk on Van Gogh"

The reason I drink is to understand the yellow sky, the great yellow sky, said Van Gogh. When he looked at the world he saw the nails that attach colors to things and he saw the nails were in pain.

This is terrific, so we don't haggle over distinctions about what to call it; if anyone asks we say it's a prose poem. The issue gets trickier, however, when verse steals prosiness and the thief risks being called a versifier. It is a commonplace to observe about a verse line that when it lopes beyond five metrical feet it begins to lose its mnemonic function. When Carson writes a series of lines like the following, from the verse novel **"Canicula di Anna,"**

Some of Perugino's early works
were extensive frescoes
for the Ingesati fathers in their convent
(destroyed shortly thereafter in the siege of Florence).

she risks the accusation that she versifies (or fails to versify) an art history paper. Yet this last line of prose permits a slight shift of tone, from the informative to the pedantic, which, when often enough struck, becomes amusingly exposed, thematic—one strain within a

shrewd orchestration of themes the novel manages. Cattily, then, as in *Plainwater*'s other work of verse, **"The Life of Towns,"** Carson risks a rather mordant relation to the tradition. Most of the verse in these two volumes merely critiques the blank verse line of our tradition, pilfering here and there by now-abandoned formal ideas that serve the cause of Carson's satire. Unless we read **"The Glass Essay,"** a booklength autobiographical poem from *Glass, Irony, and God,* we gain from these volumes no sense of Carson's singular engaged response to the debate in this century over the relation of the free verse line to the blank verse tradition.

This isn't at all to regret the persnickity irony of a poem like **"Canicula di Anna,"** Carson's brilliant and deadpan parody of a certain obsolescent kind of high brow romanticism. She may get her title from Pound's observation about an Umbrian landscape he knew well: "the dry earth pants against the canicular heat." The tip-off came when I realized Carson's novel seemed to be narrated by a typical panter of another kind—a dog, who obsesses about his master as a painter might his muse. The muse of a painter visiting Perugia to paint a portrait of the attendees to a phenomenology conference, the "Anna" of the title is a scholar who misses more than one of the sessions. Her absurd death, "the aeroplane / . . . exploded near Milan / by newsmen / simulating a terrorist incident," gives Anna the quality of an Antonioni heroine, whose affectless manner inscrutably seems part her own motive, part her creator's. In any case, the tone of this speaker's voice is so ripe one doesn't know whether to keep looking or pick it:

"Do not hinge on me," Anna says.
"If you want my advice,
do not hinge at all."
One of our many discussions of freedom.
Anna goes dancing
with a phenomenologist
who is also a captain
in the military
(reserves).
When he sees some of his philosophy students
(to whom he refers as "the enlisted men")
dancing,
he retreats to the bar.
Anna dances joyously on alone.
I do not dance.
A dog has a choice.

The point of view might be painter or dog, given the evidence here, though if it's a dog then it's one trained in art history, who meditates elsewhere on the technologies of paint and on the Perugian master Perugino. "In perspective / he applied / the novel rule / of two centers of vision"—the two in Carson's case being dog and painter, we suppose, though the narrator refers to Perugino. The narrator is a kind of monster searching for his Master, howling feverishly, as is a dog's, or a man's, prerogative. Anna, however, can be neither dog nor man—she's just chosen as the object of commentary.

If the lines above would have us ask who the speaker is, then we might take it that the novel wants us to meditate on why it's in verse. For Carson the issues are bound up. She closes *Glass, Irony, and God* with an essay on "The Gender of Sound," which argues that the classical aversion to sounds that could not be rationally referred to something in the world was a form of gynophobia. (A howl is just such a sound.) That "gynophobia" is the only word that will do here Carson suggests by opening her essay with the anecdote from *A Moveable Feast* in which Hemingway quits the anteroom of Gertrude Stein and Alice Toklas in horror at the lover's names the lesbians call each other behind a closed door within Hemingway's hearing (Namely, Pussy). In the world of **"Canicula di Anna,"** "Wild dogs, mouths dripping with such bloody / syllables, ebb and run over the ocean / floor down there" (in the underground section of Perugia). The syllables that aren't yet words are linked to women's menstrual blood, probably the "sacred filth" in the passage that follows. In a moment of solidarity with his muse, the narrator allows that to categorize is to name in public and admits:

> To categorize
> is to clarify, often.
> But not invariably.
> Sacred filth, for example,
> constitutes an ancient category
> distressing to scholars
> and other men of freedom
> in the present day.
> One continuous howl
> by now . . .
> Sound
> that shines up as a laugh
> and sounds like blood
> is another troublesome,
> ancient
> category.

The lapideous footfall of verse lines that sound this howl will seem unassuming at first to the reader plummeting down the page, with only occasional landings at single-word lines and section breaks. (There are 53 sections.) The line here is more a unit of mass than weight, as though space, and not, as conventionally, silence, were being asked to carry the burden of the poet's irony. Over 860 lines, the effect of such movement is surprisingly enchanting, and the mis-steps of this verse novel, if there are mis-steps, aren't in the verse-making. The tension between the vertical pull of short lines and the sectional intervals works beautifully to permit the narrator to be as smart as the poet likes (the dog has his day); Carson's novel contains a surfeit of ideas. Yet so many thematic elements are in the air, the movement of voice so extended in order to keep them up there, that occasionally I hear the acrobat's

irony freefall into the safety net of thesis statements, for example in section 46:

> The beloved's innocence
> brutalizes the lover.
> As the singing of a mad person
> behind you on the train
> enrages you,
> its beautiful
> animal-like teeth
> shining amid black planes
> of paint.
> As Helen
> enrages history.
>
> *Senza uscita.*

The themes here have everything to do with the scholar's work on "The Gender of Sound," surely why she includes the essay in a volume of poems. The compression of thought in these lines characterize her prose movement as much as it does her verse, as we have seen. Indeed, some readers will no doubt envy Carson's reluctance to see scholar's and poem's argument out of plumb. Nonetheless, Carson's use of the short line here doesn't howl as it should. The thesis-like texture of thought moving in swelling rhythms (i.e., the way the same number of words per line swell in syllable counts of 2-3-5-5: "of paint. / As Helen / enrages history. // *Senza uscita*") tries to hold the tone steady as we plummet down the page through abstractions that lose something of their ironic subsistence when asked to resolve thematic strains in this way. At the novel's parodic best, the jagged rhythms that owe to prose their tonal grit need no such resolution.

Still, as a free verse poet Carson's ranginess and poise is more evident in **"Canicula di Anna"** than in **"The Life of Towns,"** the other verse sequence in *Plainwater.* If the speed-bump rhythms of the former owe something to a free verse line tradition beyond Mina Loy's "Anglo-Mongrels and the Rose," the experimental cadence and punctuation of **"The Life of Towns"** would be unthinkable without Gertrude Stein's little-read 1957 poem, *Stanzas in Meditation.* Carson herself suggests the comparison, and not only by drawing on the poems of antiquity to argue for Stein's contribution to a feminist poetics in "The Gender of Sound." Several years ago when **"The Life of Towns"** was chosen for a volume of *The Best American Poetry* series, she published the following author's note: "The poem is part of an ongoing war with punctuation; we fought to a standstill here." For those who have struggled to understand the meaning of Stein's great essay "Poetry and Grammar," this would ring a bell, for Stein tells us there that from early in her life her temperament required that writing sentences should go on and on; that the sentences' only relation to time be happenstantial; that the sentences' periodization occur "beside" the fact of its going on. In other words, Stein conceived of sentences spatially, as a kind of allegorical terrain on which plot—the succession of referential events called words—could *happen into* relation with non-referential events like punctuation, syntax, and the space between words. These grammatical events had a powerful life-force for Stein; when later in her development she realized that, as she says, periods "might come to have a life of their own and commence breaking things up in arbitrary ways," she was not being fanciful. Nor is Carson when she tells us she is in "an ongoing war with punctuation; we fought to a standstill here." She's surprisingly candid about presenting herself as an heir to Gertrude Stein. (Indeed, why not cipher the equation that The Life of Towns + heir = "a life of t[heir] own"?)

Maybe it's toilsome that Carson performs Stein's experiment from *Stanzas in Meditation*'s "Winning His Way" sequence, but Carson provides a kind of rationale earlier in **Plainwater** when her ethnographer tells us: "I began to copy out everything that was said. The marks construct an instant of nature gradually, without the boredom of a story. I emphasize this. I will do anything to avoid boredom." If there's a scholar's earnestness to Carson's imitation, then there's a sensualist's dread of passivity, too. Those "marks" she refers to are letters, extensive things that avoid the boredom of story provided someone constructs of them "an instant of nature." Similarly, **"The Life of Towns"** is a sequence of single stanza sections, each line end-stopped with a period, the sections "Towns" which, as the introduction informs us, ". . . are the illusion that things hang together somehow, my pear, your winter. I am a scholar of towns, let God commend that . . . A scholar is someone who takes a position." The position the scholar of towns takes toward Stein is that while Stein uses the period freely throughout the syntactical unit we recognize as a sentence—

> And so. Now. A poem.
> Is in. Full swing.
> A narrative poem. Is commencing.
> A poem. Entitled.
> Winning his way.
> A poem. Of poetry.
> And friendships.

—Carson's scholar uses the period only as end-stop, so that the tension between line and sentence is more clearly isolated, exposed:

> "Town of Bathsheba's Crossing"
>
> Inside a room in Amsterdam.
> Rembrandt painted a drop of life inside.
> The drop he painted Rembrandt's stranger.
> Dressed as a woman rippling.
> With nakedness she has.
> A letter in her hand she is.
> Travelling.
> Out of a thought toward us.

> Her foam arrives.
> Before her even when he.
> Paints Rembrandt's stranger.
> As Rembrandt he shows.
> Him bewildered and tousled.
> As if just in.
> From journeys.
> On tracks and sideroads.

In the prose introduction to this sequence the scholar of towns defines her vocation as one "from which position, certain lines become visible. You will think I'm painting the lines myself; it's not so. I merely know where to stand to see the lines that are there." The poet's insistence on lines, on verse, on turning, comes not from drama's jealousy of picture, even though poetic use of the term "lines" borrows from the technology of vision. (Carson is herself a painter.) What the scholar has in mind when she says "lines" can perhaps be recognized by turning **"Town of Bathsheba's Crossing"** into a 12-line, six sentence poem in fairly regular iambic tetrameter:

> "Town of Bathsheba's Crossing"
>
> Inside a room in Amsterdam
> Rembrandt painted a drop of life
> Inside the drop he painted. Rembrandt's
> Stranger dressed as a woman.
> Rippling with nakedness, she has
> A letter in her hand. She is
> Travelling out of a thought toward us.
> Her foam arrives before her.
> Even when he paints Rembrandt's
> Stranger as Rembrandt he shows him
> Bewildered and tousled, as if just in
> From journeys on tracks and side roads.

If we were to encounter this in some notebook of Carson's, it would seem no more than a fairly conventional painting poem—Victorian scholars call it an ecphrasis. Nothing to it except the first sentence, an essentialist thesis about painting: that life is *in*—in Amsterdam, in a drop of paint—as it might be applied to the Rembrandt. For if it is not *in*, life might otherwise find itself *beside,* as Stein saw her own attraction to periods "beside" their having "had to exist." Were one to agree that periods "live," couldn't they go anywhere? And if so, then what does "where the period goes" mean? What you will, Stein would say, since fixing the meaning of a sentence is one linguistic activity that "goes on." But while any isolated sentence can mean different things, only paragraphs and stanzas have the emotional force that encourages the consensus of more than a single reader. If a poet's "voice" functions in the disambiguating force of stanzas, then the force of Carson's successive end-stopped lines may similarly interrupt the reader's hurry to get to the end of grammatical and syntactic events we call a sentence. We don't need to regard the concensus, or lack of ambiguity, as anything more than a necessary illusion, she suggests. Her sequence, **"The Life of Towns,"** are single stanza sections, or towns, which "are the illusion that things hang together somehow." The trick is only on the page: Readers accustomed to anticipating the end of the sentence across verse lines (more likely the further the tradition strays from blank verse) will read Carson's sequence hearing at once the metrical line and sentence underneath it (my version heightens those two components), their convergence a vanishing point toward which one must take a position. Carson cleverly recognizes a verse equivalent to the vanishing point in a reader's sense of the vertical and horizontal pulls that are the perceptual drag of reading verse. A kind of inner syntax, running idle, wants always to speed up the phrase so that it will become pure sound, a theme—an acceleration corrected for in the tension between line and sentence. By using end-stops to distend the horizontal drag of the line and frequent short lines to compensate vertically, Carson manages to restore to the verse line the spatial texture it had before prose values in verse began to resolve all tensions in favor of a vertical acceleration that makes narrative succession of everything. She will do anything, her ethnographer tells us, to avoid boredom.

"The Life of Towns"'s experiment with the line's spatial texture has no truck with boredom, then, but probably nets no more than the result of most experiments: information, in Carson's case symptomatic of her anxiety with narrative, and with the blank verse line perhaps we would associate with Frost—information more practical in poems other than those so staked on the dazzle of the writer's formal invention. No doubt sheer brilliance takes us a long way in Carson, where a droll concept enshrined in the title **"The Truth About God,"** or an intellectual burlesque carried on in **"Mimnermos: The Brain-Sex Paintings,"** can outflank whatever sympathetic interest her voice elicits in poems with a more conventional form. The range of its formal invention makes *Plainwater* the more substantial of the two collections under review, yet by measure of its improvisation on the meditative form, **"The Glass Essay"** (from *Glass, Irony & God*) seems the benchmark of Carson's achievement so far.

"The Glass Essay" sustains meditation; its genre is the autobiographical relation—once properly a "confessional" poem. The subject is again, nominally, love, or sex, a blue note the poem hits only long enough to sneak us the sense that the real subject hides elsewhere. The speaker has come home to visit her mother and her institutionalized father after the failure of a five-year love affair. We know little of her but that she is a reader—an avid fan of the Bronte sisters, she's rereading *Wuthering Heights*. When at the outset she offhandedly tells us "I can hear little clicks inside my dream. / Night drips its silver tap / down the back. / At 4 A.M. I wake. Thinking // of the man who / left in September. His name is Law," all that saves the lines

from profound unimpressiveness is the writer's coy disguise of the lover as a personification. And when by the end of the poem the speaker ventures such weather reports as "Gradually I understood that these were naked glimpses of my soul," or "I had become entirely fascinated with my spiritual melodrama,"—droll utterances that might have been overheard at some Cheeverish late sixties cocktail party, and prose enough to chasten any lyric compression—she gets away with it because the "I" has been placed into a series of relations (with her mother, her lover, her father, her psychotherapist, Emily Bronte, and Bronte scholars) that distance the reader from the confessions the speaker would make. Without this slight mediation, pages upon pages of this speaker would be pure dreariness. For quite unlike her more satirical poems, where the speaker is often typed (scholar, painter, tv director), in **"The Glass Essay"** Carson produces this distance without her customary irony, and this makes characterizing the poem's voice all the more fascinatingly difficult.

The dramatic motive for the confession appears to be that when Law attempted to leave her,

. . . I put out my hand
to touch his: He moved back.

I don't want to be sexual with you, he said. Everything
  gets crazy.
But now he was looking at me.
Yes, I said as I began to remove my clothes.

Everything gets crazy. When nude
I turned my back because he likes the back.
He moved onto me.

Some of the humiliation the "I" undergoes for our delectation is sieved off in Carson's exposure of the lines' more loaded terms. So, for example, the speaker's father has "got crazy" some years before this moment of humiliation; the speaker offers too a running essay on the naked and the nude, of which visions she keeps her therapist apprised:

Nude #1 Woman alone on a hill.
She stands into the wind.

It is a hard wind slanting from the north.
Long flaps and shreds of flesh rip off the woman's
  body and lift
and blow away on the wind . . .

The conventional, gothic language of this vision sounds a lot like Emily Bronte, a fact of which the therapist, named Dr. Haw to rhyme with Law, seems lugubriously unaware when she advises the speaker to ignore the visions. That the writer circulates the language of mortification and spirit throughout the speaker's account without putting a kind of ironic "shock quotes" around it permits us to enter freely that space between

Carson and speaker; to read those gothic conventions as Carson's characters read them in the literary texts they love. Indeed, between the beloved and the therapist's rhyming names, the pratfalling advice of those close to her, and the speaker's gothic fixation on moors and self-flagellation, there's something loopy right on the surface of her conflict. Below the surface something tells us she quite seriously faces a spiritual crisis to which the writer does not encourage us to feel superior.

Not unlike Susan Howe, whose drift back and forth between prose and verse is similarly fascinating, Carson's political passion, her feminism, permits her to double the speaker's spiritual crisis with a literary historical meditation on the domestication of women's voices. A section early in the poem informs us of a textual crux in one of Emily Bronte's poems, "Tell me, whacher, is it winter?" where her male editors have regularized "whacher" as "whether" (though in my edition it's "watcher"). Whacher, pronounceable as "whacker" and "wake her" (as well as "wager") resists utterance, and is therefore a fascinating portmanteau, a word, the speaker argues, Bronte used to address herself:

> To be a whacher is not in itself sad or happy,
>
> although she uses these words in her verse
> as she uses the emotions of sexual union in her novel,
> grazing with euphemism the work of whaching.
>
> But it has no name.
> It is transparent.
> Sometimes she calls it Thou.

There are names for things, things that have no name, and names that mean nothing but to those who know them—the portmanteau lovers use. "Thou" is another version of the ideal self the lover sees in the beloved—the lover and beloved personae Carson has chosen to study since her first book, *Eros: The Bittersweet* (1986), a study of Sappho and the Platonic representations of love. Commenting there on the impassivity of the "thou," Carson argued that to use the word "constitutes [for the lover] a glimpse of a new possible self. Could she realize that self, she too would be 'equal to the gods' amidst desire; to the degree that she fails to realize it, she may be destroyed by desire. Both possibilities are projected on a screen of what is actual and present by the poet's tactic of triangulation." The craft of Carson's autobiographical confession is precisely in the cause of such a "triangulation." Can the lapidary spaces of the 19th century novel be reproduced in belatedly modern meditative verse? Carson wants not to tell a story, but to show the slippage between categories like poetry, verse, and prose; the self, the other, and the act of love by which that relation gets represented. She writes with the lucky sense of assurance that there's something erotic in the moment a poem listens for a voice like Emily Bronte's (or listens to itself):

> . . . in between the neighbor who recalls her
> coming in from a walk on the moors
> with her face "lit up by a divine light"
>
> and the sister who tells us
> Emily never made a friend in her life,
> is a space where the little raw soul
>
> slips through.

That the space the speaker finds for Emily Bronte's whaching is "in between" and not "aside from" the disparate perceptions of neighbor and sister depends on the eros of the lover-scholar reading about her and seeing the difference "between" the two perceptions. The "in between" is inutterable, like the "soul" the speaker "kept watch on all that night. / Law stayed with me // . . . caressing and singing to one another in our made-up language."

It's a poem of astonishing clarity—and intellectual density. Reading it, I had the sense that the poet was in the midst of these spaces she'd made saying, This can be done and how surprising—lucky, really, that it hasn't been. A certain gravity, too, in choosing to suss out the meaning of one's luck. She shows us things we don't often see—the way, for example, the erotic space of a poem's voice is similar to the adult language of non-verbal expression we first notice when our parents flee from the inadequacy of words. This kind of erotic charge is enacted again later in the poem by Carson's conduction of a space across which narration and imitation, narrator and writer, behold one another. The speaker remembers her father's flirtation with the mother within the child's hearing: "I stared at the back of her head waiting for what she would say. / Her answer would clear this up. // But she just laughed a strange laugh with ropes all over it." Like the earlier non-response of the therapist ("Haw" itself suggests a non-verbal language—a laugh), the mother's non-response allows the daughter a perception of space across which "soul slips":

> She was talking on the telephone in the kitchen.
> Well a woman would be just as happy with a kiss on
>   the cheek
> most of the time but YOU KNOW MEN
>
> she was saying. Laugh.
> Not ropes. Thorns.
> I have arrived at the middle of the moor . . .

The movement of thought in these lines enacts an encounter between Carson the writer and Carson the confessant. If I seem to address various components of a single function, then such are the nimble antennae that is the voice in Carson's work. The narrator is responsible to the story told, and to her listener; while Carson's more writerly imitation wants us to suffer an experience that hasn't yet been narrated into understanding, for example the eleven-year old girl's listening in on a mother's telephone conversation. Our speaker locates herself dramatically between the writer's cunning and the narrator's responsibility. What seems important in the passage just cited is the way the first line, a line of narration, abuts a space shared by the second line imitating the mother's voice which (since there are no quotation marks) for a moment we may even mistake for the narrator's commentary—one kind of movement, then, is our shifting perception of this mistake. Think of it as a space within which imitative idioms like "YOU KNOW MEN," with its three beat terminal irony, and narrative exposition (an unarticulated yet clear enough history of the mother's sexual disappointment) can intersect, rendering the speaker helpless but to submit to the (second) line even as it gallops prosaically to the end of the page; the speaker's only recourse is the laconic, and painfully precise narrator's idiom, "she was saying"—which by now is unnecessary to the story being told but which nonetheless provides us with essential information about how the speaker understands the mother's confidence. Our speaker is reduced to taking the writer's dictation across the lines' caesuras and uttering one word accounts of the sense she can make of it (Laugh. Not ropes. Thorns.), each one less the language of the mother's moment and more the language of the poem's voice.

Carson's work raises certain questions: Must a speaker be always so subjugated? Can the voice be represented? If so then the poem suggests that the subject of the representation hides. From this hiding place in the poem, we go on to hear a narrator who accepts the rescue of projecting herself into Emily Bronte's world ("I have arrived at the middle of the moor") and offers an interpretation of Bronte's poem, "I'll come when thou art saddest." In doing so she is certainly the scholar-lover of Bronte's work, an authorial stand-in witnessing in *Wuthering Heights* and, as all lovers do, the slippage between an actual and an ideal self in the beloved. Yet she is also a speaker, the dramatic subject of an encounter between the poem's narrative and imitative functions. We get a glimpse of her at that vanishing point; we might say the speaker both witnesses this slippage and *is* it. While on one level the enactment I have just described allows the speaker to say "It is a shock to realize that this low, slow collusion / of master and victim within one voice / is a rationale / for the most awful loneliness of the poet's hour," as though the lines described the poet's mastery of the victimized eleven year old's voice; on another level the speaker is referring here to Bronte's relationship to the "Thou," that transparency (we recall) it is to "whacher." Like eros, "whacher" is properly thought of as a verb, as a movement across space, a "soul slips." The movement approximates closely a classical notion of what a poem does—it catches or traps the soul in something, as in a mirror. In what follows, the "she" might as easily refer

to (the poet) Carson and the "I" to Bronte; though by the speaker's lights, it's the contrary:

> She has reversed the roles of thou and Thou
> not as a display of power
>
> but to force out of herself some pity
> for this soul trapped in glass,
> which is her true creation.
>
> Those nights lying alone
> are not discontinuous with this cold hectic dawn.
> It is who I am.

While the speaker seems modestly to claim her literary ancestry through Bronte's poem, on another more astonishing level the lines claim that Bronte's true creation is the "I"—a "trapped" moment of infinite reproducibility. We might say a glass essay would try to make such a mirror transparent, and that if it succeeded, it would achieve that "triangulation" which is "the poet's tactic." I for one believe she's done it.

For the moment, at least, this meditation in glass on the subjugated voice and the mastery we honor with the epithet "poem" is essential reading. It's tonic for those of us made weary by poems with an ahistorical narrator who comes on like a paper mache angel with a tale of victimization. When such narrators are then disavowed, called "personae" by writers like Sharon Olds, it's morally tedious, indeed. The way a subject secrets itself in the form of the speaker's address to the reader can't be accounted for by changing the site of the romantic poem from the hillside at sunrise to the dinner table when dad sticks his hand up the waitress's dress. It's only our insistence that we live in the world that can defeat such convenient typing, and force the poet to listen. With **"The Glass Essay,"** Carson makes the reader matter.

Anne Carson and John D'Agata (interview date 1997)

SOURCE: Carson, Anne, and John D'Agata. "A _____ with Anne Carson." *Iowa Review* 27, no. 2 (1997): 1-22.

[*In the following interview, Carson shares with D'Agata some of her personal history, her philosophy on writing, and a glimpse of the process behind the composition of* Autobiography of Red.]

Near a river one Sunday morning, Anne Carson shrugged. I asked her for her thoughts about her family life, about where she grew up in Canada, about the effects of winter on her writing. She curled herself into a black ball of skirt and told me: "Fondly"; "Same town as the Cowboy Junkies"; "I like snow and I like white and I like pain-freezing cold and the way voices sound in hockey rinks."

Anne Carson is a professor of classics at McGill University in Montreal. Long a distinguished scholar of Greek, she has only recently received acclaim for her "creative" work as well—we write *"creative"* because Anne Carson's scholarship is as lucid as her poetry and essays, her essays and poetry as sharp as her scholarship. Indeed, the two are, for many readers, indistinguishable, although Carson often acknowledges using two different desks in two separate rooms of her house for her two kinds of writing—"scholarship" and "poetry."

The recipient of fellowships from the Lannan and Rockefeller Foundations, two Residency Fellowships to the Banff School of Fine Arts, and two McGill International Travel Awards, Carson has also served as a consultant to "The Nobel Legacy," a series of Public Broadcasting programs on the conflicting values of science and humanism. In 1986, Princeton published her groundbreaking work of Greek scholarship titled *Eros the Bittersweet: An Essay.* Then came the book-length essay **Short Talks** (Brick Books, 1992), and most recently have come **Plainwater** (Knopf, 1995) and **Glass, Irony, and God** (New Directions, 1995). A new work, *Greed: Simonides,* will appear in 1998.

In print for over a decade now, Anne Carson has given only one other interview: "The interview to end all interviews—almost four hours we talked! More of a conversation, really. I don't think anything could top it. Do you want to start?" Anne Carson and I met on the steps outside of The University of Iowa's Museum of Art in Iowa City, beside the Iowa River. She was on campus to give a reading at the Iowa Writers' Workshop. Her eighth. Ever.

[D'Agata]: *Have you avoided interviews?*

[Carson]: I think I would avoid them if possible.

Why?

It's like finding a good conversation—how often does that happen? No, I don't like them. I don't like thinking about myself, I don't like thinking about who I am. It's like watching yourself walk. You inevitably stumble.

It would interfere with your writing process?

I don't think about writing theoretically. Always when I do it stops that line of exploration. I don't know. It stops something of the energy of the process, of the not knowing what you're doing, whatever it is you're exploring.

Is that the form itself? Is that the form of the essay?

Well, it leads to the form, I think, by searching around what's not known. It informs what you want to say. It sort of has to circulate because if you knew what you wanted to do then that would be that.

Then what form would that be if you knew what you were going to do?

If one were to just do it? I guess then it would be a treatise.

Okay. Back in time. Let's start with education.

Education? Yes, I was educated.

Well, I mean, what happened after high school? For example.

I went to the same place for all of university. The University of Toronto.

What was your major study?

Classics. I went to Scotland for one year for my Masters, and then to graduate school.

Did you first start classics in high school?

I did, oddly. Because my Latin teacher in grade thirteen (we have an extra grade that you don't) knew Greek and offered to teach me Greek during the lunch hour. So we did that for a year.

Wow.

It was a little amazing. Her name was Alice Cowan. She subsequently went to Africa—and disappeared. I mean from my scan.

Why classics in high school? Why did you study it? Did you choose it or was it mandatory?

No, we had an option. We could take Latin or typing. And I took Latin, and then I regretted it and did typing the second year, but then went back to Latin.

So you're who you are because you didn't want to take typing?

No, I wouldn't say it that baldly. I like Latin. And it seemed the article of an educated gentleman. You know, you're really searching for your own roots here, John.

What?

You're trying to decide whether you should go back to classics because you dropped it in college.

How do you know?

I can just tell.

I am not.

Okay. I guess you'd know.

Anyway. Would you have gone on to study classics in college if you had only studied Latin in high school and not Greek as well?

I probably would have. I like Latin, and you can start Greek in university easily.

Is that entirely what you focused on in college, or did you have other majors and interests?

No, I never studied anything else at all.

Really?

Greek is so good, after you discover it there's no point doing anything else. It's really the best language in the world. It's better than Latin. Latin is good, but Latin is sort of a mathematics of thought whereas Greek is an art. It's just amazing. The day I finally come to the end of Greek I guess I won't go on doing it. But it hasn't ended yet.

You never had English literature courses in college?

Well, I think I took a survey of English literature. Our first year we had to do a survey, which was really awful. I couldn't see any point to that. We did some Milton, and I remember I didn't like him. And I didn't see any point in studying a language as a subject.

You mean other than Greek.

Well, yes. Something with some depth, you know? [pause] Well, I guess that's not fair. English is probably a very reasonable thing to study, but it seemed to me I could do that without special expertise. I could just take my mind and study Milton if I wanted to, whereas Greek I couldn't.

So all of these English writers whom you seem to know so much about, that knowledge just comes out of—

It's fake. Totally fake. I note down the odd quote when I happen upon it, but I don't know much about English. Really shockingly little about English.

Is everything you want to read in English with a critical or theoretical mind automatically filtered through what you know about Greek?

No, I think it's more parallel. Although the English side of it is just anecdotal information. It gives me a way of reading without focusing on anything. And sometimes I go and look up stuff.

So even when you were in Scotland you weren't studying English?

Nope. Greek.

And because that's where all the best Greek scholars are?

One of them was, actually. At the time, believe it or not. When I graduated from college I felt incompetent in Greek to do anything significant, so I thought the way to get competent was to study with a hard person. The hardest person in Greek was in Scotland at the time. I wrote to him and asked if I could study with him. They had this program at St. Andrew's for one year. He invited me and so I went to study Greek metrics with him.

He?

Kenneth Dover. He was truly terrifying.

And this was when?

1975-76.

Right after college?

Well, I dropped out of college after the first year, partly because of that Milton stuff and other things that seemed of little importance. I went to work, and then I went back to university for a second year, and dropped out again. Then I went to art school.

Oh!

Which was even more boring, but not because of art. It was "advertising" art. I thought I wanted to get into the work force expeditiously, so I went for a year to get a certificate. We spent a year designing cereal boxes. It was horrible. So I went back to university and stayed in for the last two years. Then Scotland. Then back to Toronto for the Ph.D. And then I got some jobs.

Princeton, right?

Calgary first, then Princeton.

Is Eros the Bittersweet *a version of your dissertation?*

Yes.

That's amazing.

It's juicy, yes. I still sometimes look at it with wonder. It was like following a path through the woods. I still enjoy reading it. I think partly because I had done so much work on the whole subject, the dissertation just made the book that much easier. The dissertation was this big [fingers inches apart] and when you think about anything for that long you get a whole lot of patterns and thoughts set that you haven't articulated but are ready to travel along. So that was nice. I really enjoyed doing that.

What keeps you interested in classics?

It's just intrinsically interesting. It just seems to me the best thing in the world.

Suppose I haven't the foggiest. Explain to me what's intrinsic about it.

When you're traveling around in Greek words, you have a sense that you're among the roots of meanings, not up in the branches.

Why?

I don't know. Because they're pure, they're older, they're original.

Even though there are older languages?

But they're not older in a continuous line. Well, maybe. Who knows? But as far as we can take any language back there is always a thing called Greek. And you can feel that sense of beginning from these people who were stumbling around in the world saying, "The name for this is blank and it's just the right name for it." More reality in the words. They just shine right out at you.

That's interesting.

It's insatiable! Once you experience it it's addictive. Germans know this. That's why all those German guys keep going back and inventing philosophical terms out of Greek. It's qualitative, there's more life there.

Others would call it being closer to the garden. Smack under the tree, even.

I'm not interested in using vegetable metaphors. It's more like mining to me. Mining metaphors work like the texture of the experience, like the ore of language.

The first human impulse to name. Is Greek the closest we can get to things?

I think so. Though I'm not sure that linear time is more than a metaphor. It's really the quality of those words that's exciting. They are early. We value earliness, we call it original.

Hmm.

You're hesitating because you don't want to admit that you should go back to relearn Greek.

No. Get off that. I'm thinking about this really beautiful argument in Eros the Bittersweet *about Sappho and friends being so close to their own origins. You say in there that it's no wonder so much of this early writing*

is love poetry, and no wonder so many of these love poems are so great. You say it's because there's perhaps no true lover suggested—no guy or gal that's literally intended in the poems—but instead that the real lover and recipient of this desire is language itself. At least I think that's what you say.

Isn't that profound? See, you can have those kinds of ideas when you're young. So, yes, okay. That's good. I think I still believe that. Sappho is the best example, in my experience, of that original thing coming into the world. It's precious. It's like if you had a world of people who couldn't see colors and that world were just a black and white TV to them. Then someone came into the world and clicked on color. It's that much different reading the words we have in English compared to those in Greek. They're turned around, the Greeks. Homer talks about how people are situated in time. He says they have their backs to the future, facing the past. If you have your face to the past, you just look at the stuff that's already there and take what you need. It's not the same as us, facing the future, where we have to think about that [points behind] then turn around and get it and bring it here, bring it in front of us. So I think for someone like Sappho it's not a question, it's just original. It's what's there. It's a part of being.

When did you start writing?

Second grade.

So is any of that in **Plainwater**?

Not as such. I just remember writing in second grade every Friday afternoon. It was such a pleasure. We'd draw a picture then write on it and tell what it was.

Why was that pleasurable?

How could it not be pleasurable?

Okay. When did you turn professional, then?

I always wrote in little notebooks. I don't know. I'm not really interested in finding my beginnings.

You told me once that you keep two desks in your office. One for classical scholarship, one for creative writing. So obviously you're very conscious of having one part of your life be academic and one artistic. When did this start?

That method?

Well no, not the method but the writing. There's a big difference between having a desk for one thing and a desk for another, and just having a notebook that you occasionally dip into.

True. I guess after—. Well maybe I don't know that. I guess after *Eros,* after I wrote the *Eros* book. It was possibly the last time I got those two impulses to move in the same stream—the academic and the other. After that, I think I realized I couldn't do that again.

You could?

No. Couldn't. Because I had developed a more mature method.

By separating them out on two desks?

Yes.

Some people would say you're still doing it, though, that you're still working with both in the same stream. That there's no suggestion of two desks at work.

No.

No?

How does the dissertation compare to Eros*? Is it as lyrical?*

No. It follows a much more rigorous academic framework. All of the imaginative sections had to be forced into an appendix. There was an appendix on the brain, for example, wherein I argued that the acquisition of literacy had an effect on the formation of the frontal lobes of the brain in ontogenetic development in human beings. I read medical textbooks on neural pathologies and I ended up with a preposterous theory, but worked out in standard academic ways. When my dissertation director read it, he said, "Maybe this should go in an appendix." So we chiseled it out of the middle of my argument and relegated it safely to the end. This was before I had two tables. The two tables helped avoid those bonsai-shaped appendices.

But between the bonsai and the two tables was Eros the Bittersweet. *You did manage it.*

It was my last flailing at holiness, so to speak, trying to make the psyche come together into one stream. It's what's called an essay also.

And it worked. I mean, it worked. That's what I'm trying to point out.

But in the way that if you're not any good at doing high jumps and you decide you're just going to try it until you go up there and do one perfect high jump, it worked, yes. But I couldn't go back and do another such jump. It was a one-time thing.

All right.

I'm sure of this. Intuitively. It may not make any sense. But—

It's just fascinating to hear you say this because there are readers who would swear that you're absolutely still doing it.

If feels different to me. For example?

For example, a tiny essay of yours appeared in VLS *called "Economy," about Simonides and Cèlan. Just as an example. They're a lot of "ideas" in there, even if you don't think they're legitimate. On the popular front, though, like for the* Village Voice, *it's a sophisticated one-page argument. Plus it's gorgeous prose.*

I guess I'm thinking about the academic part of those frameworks. I know what went into *Eros the Bittersweet*—all the footnotes and bibliographies and research—even if it was only in the dissertation and never made it into the book. That's not what went into the "Economy" essay. Probably the same amount of mental energy went into it but not through those same channels. So perhaps it's a good thing that it doesn't show up in the final product. But I can't go back, that's what I'm saying. I can't come back together to replicate *Eros.*

Why? Why can't you come back together?

I just can't. It's partly a function of age. You can do things when you're young that you can't do when you're older. You can't get simple again. Simple in a good sense, I mean. If you were to get out the essays you wrote in high school, some of them would strike you as profound and you'd wish you could do that now, but you can't do that now. Stuff goes down river and it gets dirty. You can't do clean things when you're old.

People still call **"The Glass Essay,"** *for example, brilliant literary criticism and a brilliant poem, together in one form, in one consistent voice. I'm just saying that you might be the only one who thinks otherwise. Just let me say that. Just take it.*

Well. Then, it must be true.

You know what I mean.

But, you see, this is another aspect of not knowing what you're doing when you're doing it. Here we are theorizing about something. Watching ourselves walk. So maybe these are the limits of that process. Maybe this is where it breaks down. Where it ends. Of course it would be encouraging if what you say is true. I'm just not sure it is.

Have you ever studied writing with anyone?

No.

Do you have readers?

No. I used to, but I don't know what to do with their comments. I thought about keeping them and making a separate work out of them so that they wouldn't go to waste.

A lot of your work, when I read it, feels very formal to me.

Hmm. Okay, sounds good.

But I'm not sure what that form is. I mean, I can't tell where it comes from, either in the essays or your poetry.

Well, that's because it arises out of the thing itself. They aren't forms that are from somewhere, they're just in there. You have to mess around until you find your form at the beginning, and once you find it you just follow it.

Does that also include facts in form? You told me earlier that you're more interested in an intriguing set of facts rather than a story, and that what you create when you write is more of a nexus for the facts, some kind of narrative, some kind of anecdote or scenario to fit them into. Does your form then originate out of those facts that you discover and become fascinated with?

I think it does. I think if we take facts to mean stuff in the world, like the way a lake is is a fact, yes.

Is that what the form is trying to do?

Yes, I think so. I think that that is a pure moment, when you see that a fact has a form, and you try to make that happen again in language. Form is a rough approximation of what the facts are doing. Their activity more than their surface appearance. I mean, when we say that form imitates reality or something like that it sounds like an image. I'm saying it's more like a tempo being covered, like a movement within an event or a thing.

*Looking at most of your collected essays, just structurally or typographically, I see a lot of fragmented narratives. Especially those in **Plainwater**. Is that the effect of lots of facts at work?*

Facts are a substitute for story. Facts are useful to me because I don't have any stories in my head, so in the absence of story you can always talk about facts to fill the time. Right? I don't know what it has to do with fragmentation, though. What do you mean by a "fragment"?

Well, I don't mean that the narrative is fragmented, I mean the essays, with all their sections, work like . . . collage, maybe.

Oh, I see. Okay. Well that's a true insight, I've always thought of it as painting. Painting with thoughts and facts.

Which is something that a straight narrative can't do?

I would think not. Because in a straight narrative you'd have too many other words, too many other words that aren't just the facts. You're too busy trying to get from one fact to another by standard methods: *and; but; oh, no; then I was in this room; because; that's Patti.* These aren't facts; they're hard to paint.

That's interesting. Because if your passion is coming out of Greek and the rootedness of Greek, fragmentation seems like it'd be closer to the thing than a straight narrative, which as you say imposes too much of Writer onto the facts.

Right. The meaning is all padded, costumed in normalcy. I think probably my painting notion comes out of dealing with classical texts which are, like Sappho, in bits of papyrus with that enchanting white space around them, in which we can imagine all of the experience of antiquity floating but which we can't quite reach. I like that kind of surface.

Who influences you?

Um, probably Homer the most. Homer is the most amazing thing in the world, in every way. I think everyone should read Homer a lot. Also presently I've been reading a lot of Cèlan. He's clarifying. There are other people but Homer is primal.

I think this might be sidestepping official interviewer protocol, but I'll bring it up anyway. I once wrote you a letter, kind of fan mail, I guess, asking whether you had writing students at McGill and what your writing process was like. When you wrote back you said, "I have never taught writing nor would I ever essay to do so. Not teachable."

Well that's true.

Is that because you've never had a writing teacher and had to find your way on your own?

I guess so. I don't think I would know how to go about it. It seems a completely individual thing. Completely idiosyncratic.

Do you ever comment on people's stuff?

With reluctance. Because, again, I don't know what to say. I have to grade all the time in classics and I hate it. Because my only experience of getting to a way of writing when I want to write is to break rules or change categories or go outside where they say the line is, so how am I going to say to somebody else, "Now, here is the line"? It's dishonest. All I can do is say, "Find the line and go someplace else," which is not helpful. But I understand it is taught. I mean, it's taught here, right? So it must be teachable. I just don't understand how. Unless we mean by "teaching writing" just getting together and having insights about what literature is.

This question might annoy you but I want to ask it just because it's hot.

Why don't you move, it's cool in the shade. You're in the sun partly.

No I mean hot at—. Do you know what I'm talking about? Is that a joke?

No. Are you hot?

No, it's nice in the sun.

Oh. Okay. I'm a very literal person. "It's hot." Does that mean this is a fashionable question?

It's an essay question, so . . . yeah. It's trendy to talk about, I think. In that same letter you sent me—

It must have been creepy for you to get this letter.

Are you kidding?

Well I must have been so discouraging.

No. I loved it. I was honored.

Well that's nice.

So, in that same letter you explained to me your understanding of the essay. You said it was "an attempt to reason and tell," "to have something to say and to do so." Which I find interesting, especially as a student in one of these new graduate programs in nonfiction because there's constant chatter about what the essay is, and there's a very strong claim that the essay comes out of Montaigne.

Hmm.

Rather than, say, Cicero, or maybe somebody even older whom you'd probably know.

Not too much older. Plutarch, maybe. But, okay, Cicero.

And those are really two different worlds. I mean, you get in Montaigne a mind willing to change its mind and change the facts within an essay, or essay to essay, or from edition to edition of the same essay.

Which is more like autobiography dressed up as community.

Yeah. And this seems to be used to justify the memoir craze in the U.S. at the moment, which really seems kind of—

Appalling.

Well. Yes. And I think Montaigne lets us take very literally this sense of the essay as an attempt, a trial, or experiment. Which makes the essay a process rather than a product. And you don't get that in Cicero.

No.

I mean, he knows what he's going to say before he takes out his reed.

Yes.

So your quote—"to have something to say and to do so"—lands you more in that camp than in Montaigne's, I think.

Thank you.

Is that because of your academic background or is it an aesthetic choice?

I find that idea of the essay as self-exploration kind of creepy. Because when you write an essay you're giving a gift, it seems to me. You're giving this grace, as the ancients would say. A gift shouldn't turn back into the self and stop there. That's why facts are so important, because a fact is something already given. It's a gift from the world or from wherever you found it. And then you take that gift and you do something with it, and you give it again to the world or to some person, and that keeps it going. It's hard to talk about these things because I realize as I talk about them that the way I think about them comes from the way the ancients talk and think about language, which is different from the way we do. Because they have this word for grace, *charis*, which means grace in the reciprocal sense of coming and going. It's both a gift given and a gift received. The Greeks used the word for the grace of a poem, the charm that makes it a poem and makes you want to remember it. So for them to make a poem is to make something that will be so charming that it will be a gift that the world wants to receive and also give back precisely because it's so good. And that reciprocation keeps going and makes culture have substance, a coming and going. A memoir that goes back into me doesn't contribute to that exchange at all. These things that people are writing nowadays seem to me self-circling. A form of therapy. It's a way of writing without having to have any facts, so it's also just lazy. But disrespectful, mostly, which is more important than lazy, because in order to just concentrate on yourself you really have to do a lot of ignoring of the world. The world is constantly giving things to you that you could be giving back.

Then what about the autobiographical element in your writing? How autobiographically are we as readers meant to take that "I" of yours?

Just a part of the facts in the world. You know, like I'm a set of facts, the river's another set, these steps are another set—and just use them all in some kind of democratic fashion. I don't know how autobiographical I am.

I think you're hedging.

No, I'm not. That's a big space, the "I."

Okay. Next question. A friend asked me to ask you something.

Does this mean you're not responsible for it?

Yes, definitely. So, she asks, "Why do you choose to be erotically shocking at times?"

I don't know. It's something to do. Maybe it's a way of lifting the erotic material slightly separate from the rest of what you're saying.

Making it shocking does that?

Yes. It puts an electricity around it, as erotic experiences have around them. She would be a hard interviewer, your friend.

Probably. Well, more up front, at least. Now. In essays like "Kinds of Water," the "I" reads specifically as an individual pilgrim. But there's also a sense of Pilgrim throughout it. You know, of an "I" speaking generally, on behalf of all questers. How do you respond to that, to this idea of a more generalized voice, especially in light of Jorie Graham's announcement last night at your reading that "We love Anne Carson because we find in her the universal voice that we once lost"?

I tuned-out before she said that. I can't listen to people talking about me.

Well you should have because it was beautiful.

No.

Anyway. That's what she said.

Yes. That's what she said, and I guess we have to confront it now. [pause] In the essay about pilgrims it's true. Sections begin with "Pilgrims . . ." and then generalize about them as a category.

And end that way, too.

Yes, right. So it must have been something I wanted to do there. But probably it was endemic to that experience. I don't think that that happens too much elsewhere. I mean, I don't think I say, "Swimmers . . . dah dah dah" and then expound on them. So—

But it's in other works, too, like "Short Talks." There's a lack of an "I" there. There's certainly a strong voice, but there's no self in there. I don't think there is.

Oh, I see. So you think it's a mechanism for avoiding the self?

Well, I don't know.

Let's see. Well, in "Short Talks" there was a definite effort on my part to avoid the autobiographical impulse. That's true. I wanted those each to be a short kind of dance.

Maybe even as pictures of things, as you've said?

Okay, right. Pictures of themselves. That's all I know about that, though.

Is there a difference between essays and poetry?

You know, I see all those questions you have about that on your sheet there, but I just haven't the faintest idea. This is one of those things I just couldn't know unless I was finished doing it. And I'm not. So—

Let me ask this: Do you see the form in your head first?

Yes.

Do you sometimes try something as an essay and then rework it or revise it into a poem and find it works better that way, or vice versa?

Well, there's a novel I've written that was all prose at first and very thick. Then I thought, "What if I break these lines up a bit? Maybe they'd move along more smartly." So now the novel's in verse. But when I'm writing, usually I mush around first with the form, and if I don't get it in a few days then I don't try to write the thing because I can't begin without a form.

Davenport said something interesting about this in his introduction to Glass, Irony, and God.

And I didn't read it. I was tempted, though.

Well I'll tell you what he said—

No, don't.

No? [pause] Well then I may have to ask a hard question to compensate.

Okay. Ask a hard question.

Okay.

Okay. Even though you didn't listen to Jorie Graham's intro last night, and even though you don't read reviews of your stuff, or read Davenport's thing, I'm wondering what you think accounts for what seems like the sudden and kind of overwhelming response people have had to your work recently.

Am I supposed to know this?

No. But I'm asking you to. I know it's embarrassing, but I'm the one asking the question and hereby forcing you to respond, so it won't look bad in print. Trust me. It'll be my fault.

[pause] I was just talking with someone about John Ashbery and how I can never understand anything he writes. That's frustrating to me. I think that there's a sense that people are lost, especially in so-called creative writing in America today.

And you think that's why we're responding to you?

I think yes. I think people like to be told something that they can get, you know? I mean otherwise it's like giving a person a gift that they can't unwrap. That's cruel. And so I guess writing is a kind of gift that can be undone in different ways by different people. John Ashbery may be beyond that claim.

And the "universal voice"?

I think it arises out of compassion, you know? People are just out there struggling to make sense of life. You have to give them something they can use. It's only polite to do that.

Finally—

Finally. Yes?

Volcanoes?

Oh, volcanoes! Well, it was winter. I broke my knee. I had to stay in a lot, so I started painting. At the time it seemed the obvious subject to paint. I realize there's a narrative gap there. My paint collection at the time included only red and yellow acrylic. And I had black ink. But I also just like volcanoes. They're a lot in the novel, too. The boy in the novel goes to South America and visits volcanoes, in fact he flies over them. He has wings. Also, when I first started to do the paintings my

friend in Montreal said, "Oh, good. You're dealing with your anger." And I said, "What anger!" So there's that, too. Does that help?

Yeah. Thanks.

Good. Now turn that off.

Mark Halliday (review date 1999)

SOURCE: Halliday, Mark. "Carson: Mind and Heart." *Chicago Review* 45, no. 2 (1999): 121-27.

[*In the following review, Halliday assesses Carson's* Autobiography of Red *with ambivalence both toward the poet's choice to compose a novel in verse and the modern elements she added to this old story.*]

The first thing I read by Anne Carson blew me away. It was **"The Glass Essay"** (in *Glass, Irony, and God,* 1995), a thirty-eight-page poem narrated by a woman devastated by the collapse of a love affair. The woman tries to understand her despair, and to imagine a livable response to it, by contemplating the mysteriously heroic loneliness of Emily Brontë. The poem combines intelligence and passion in a rare way; it's a combination you suddenly realize you're terribly hungry for. The effect calls to mind some great mid-length poems—Wordsworth's "Resolution and Independence," Whitman's "Out of the Cradle Endlessly Rocking," Bishop's "Crusoe in England," Bidart's "Confessional"—I feel **"The Glass Essay"** stands up in such company. It made me wonder if the best living poet in English could turn out to be a Canadian Professor of Classics.

But then I found my reactions to other poetry and prose by Carson were tentative and fuzzy; the passionate cogency of **"The Glass Essay"** seemed to appear only in scattered passages. Still, I approached *Autobiography of Red* with high hopes.

Carson's "novel in verse" tells the story of Geryon from boyhood to age twenty-two. Geryon is an extremely sensitive and precocious boy who has a charming and affectionate but ineffectual mother; an inattentive athletic father; and an oppressive older brother. They live on an unspecified island. Realistic contemporary details establish the time as the late twentieth century. Meanwhile, there is a mythic dimension to the story, which is included in the matter-of-fact manner of Latin American magical realism. Geryon, who from childhood consciously identifies with the Geryon of Greek mythology (a monster slain by Herakles in the hero's tenth labor), has a completely red body, with red wings growing from his back like the monster. His wings are not merely psychological (when Geryon first goes to school, his mother "neatened his little red wings and pushed him out the door"), and yet they play no role in the plot until the end, and even then their plot-function is oblique and unconvincing. The wings serve to remind us of the radical strangeness of Geryon among other people; Geryon becomes a metaphor for the deeply sensitive self, the self who will always endure a sense of profoundly embarrassed difference from others.

Geryon survives sexual abuse at the hands of his older brother. Then at the age of fourteen he meets a charismatic boy named Herakles who is sixteen. Infatuation is instantaneous: "it was one of those moments / that is the opposite of blindness. / The world poured back and forth between their eyes once or twice." (They meet as Herakles is getting off "the bus from New Mexico"—from New Mexico to where? Soon we are told that "Herakles' hometown of Hades / lay at the other end of the island about four hours by car," and there is a volcano in it. Carson's geography is teasingly unmappable.) Geryon's love for Herakles is soon requited sexually, though Herakles cannot match the soul-tearing totality of Geryon's adoration. Against his mother's wishes, Geryon goes to Hades with Herakles. They talk with Herakles' grandmother, discuss photography (Geryon's creative interest), and visit the volcano. (Here as in other writing, Carson is fascinated by volcanoes: vast molten intensity hidden beneath outward calm, waiting for expression which will be frenzied, destructive, and beautiful.) Geryon returns home, knowing he can't rely on Herakles' love (Herakles has in fact uttered the inevitable "we'll always be friends"). Later Herakles phones and mentions a new boyfriend, and tells Geryon "I want you to be free."

The next thing we know, Geryon is twenty-two and has decided to fly to Buenos Aires—apparently because Herakles is there, though when they meet it happens by chance. Geryon yearns for Herakles as before, but Herakles has a new Peruvian lover named Ancash. The three young men make a tense sexual triangle, dominated by the hedonistic Herakles who is adored by the other two. The drama of desire and jealousy produces charged moments, but the ending is anticlimactic; the three visit a volcano in Peru, and Geryon has yet another opportunity to ponder the infinity of lava-like passion in finite hearts, but by this time he has already realized that his love for Herakles has burned out.

Carson's verse novel is willfully whimsical and delightedly peculiar. While some images are garishly symbolic (the wings, the volcanoes, Geryon's camera which captures "the flashes in which a man possesses himself"), many other images seem casually tossed in. Carson evokes Buenos Aires and Lima vividly, for example, but never convinces us that *Autobiography of Red* especially needed to unfold in those two cities rather than any other two.

The versification also has an arbitrary quality. Each of the forty-seven sections of the narrative moves down the page in alternating long lines and short lines, but no regular meter is observed, and most of the line breaks are not interesting as such. However, the lineation does help us feel the fierce loadedness of Carson's style.

>   . . . He saw the doorway
> the house the night the world and
> on the other side of the world somewhere Herakles
>   laughing drinking getting
> into a car and Geryon's
> whole body formed one arch of a cry—upcast to
>   that custom, the human custom
> of wrong love.

Carson's decision to write a novel in verse involves, of course, the desire for both the cause-and-effect momentum of narrative and the cherished luminous moments of poetry. Carson does achieve narrative momentum often—yet the story she tells turns out to be so strangely simple, despite oddities of detail, that all in all *Autobiography of Red* feels like a lyric poem fanatically extended. This is because Carson is so devoted to the emotional fluctuations of her protagonist; one feels that her favorite moments are those when Geryon broods in beautifully tortured solitude.

"*Jealous of My Little Sensations*"—this is the title Geryon gives to a photograph in his autobiography; the phrase is consciously ironic (Geryon is capable of observing his own emotionality intelligently), yet the reader may still feel there's too much truth in the phrase, and that it refers too aptly to Geryon's creator.

It's a question of whether the following passage strikes you as thrilling or febrile, penetrating or histrionic:

> He hugged his overcoat closer and tried to
>   assemble in his mind Heidegger's
> argument about the use of moods.
> We would think ourselves continuous with the
>   world if we did not have moods.
> It is state-of-mind that discloses to us
> (Heidegger claims) that we are beings who have
>   been thrown into something else.
> Something else than what?
> Geryon leaned his hot forehead against the
>   filthy windowpane and wept.
> *Something else than this hotel room*
> he heard himself say and moments later he was
>   charging along the hollow gutters
> of Avenida Bolivar.

More than half of Carson is a flaming romantic, and proud of it. She experiences the world as a realm where passions far exceed opportunities for expression and fulfillment, exceed the capacity of mere flesh to contain them, while remaining always the most important realities. She is startlingly unembarrassed by the idea that this romanticism is essentially adolescent. "SPIRIT

RULES SECRETLY ALONE THE BODY ACHIEVES NOTHING / is something you know / instinctively at fourteen and can still remember even with hell in your head / at sixteen." Though Geryon does experience sexual love, still the hero he reminds me of is the intolerably sensitive virginal Holden Caulfield.

The purple (or red, as Carson prefers) romanticism is thinly camouflaged by a scholarly framework around the verse novel. I haven't mentioned this till now because it is much less crucial than it seems at first. Carson the Professor of Classics begins her book with a brief homage to Stesichoros, an ancient poet who "released being" by shedding Homeric formulas and wielding adjectives with passionate metaphorical freshness. Stesichoros wrote a long poem about Geryon; only fragments of it survive; Carson's verse novel can be taken as an effort to imagine the poem Stesichoros might have written if he and his Geryon lived today.

That's a mildly interesting premise—or is it only whimsical? Adam Kirsch, reviewing *Autobiography of Red* in *The New Republic* (May 18, 1998), was stern about Carson's learned references:

> They are ostentatiously announced and then simply left behind; any or all of them could be dropped without significantly damaging the Geryon narrative. Their purpose, then, is only to call attention to themselves; and it is the sterility of this learning, not the learning itself, that is injurious to poetry, and gives Carson's allusions a stale air of pedantry and puzzle.

Kirsch argues persuasively, yet I think "sterility" is misleading. When Carson wraps her scenes in classical (or otherwise bibliographical) accoutrements, I think she's not so much teasing us as desperately trying to keep us from staring too directly at her. That is, I think the references to Stesichoros are among Carson's ambivalent gestures toward concealing the intimately confessional energy of her tale.

The homosexuality of the main characters seems another such gesture. Nothing in the plot depends on the lovers being homosexual rather than heterosexual. Like the red wings, homosexuality seems to be serving Carson as a metaphor for the queerness of any deep spirit in the material world. Though we are told that Geryon writes his autobiography, it's hard not to feel that Carson has herself in mind with the first word of her book's title.

Is it okay for a heterosexual woman to use male homosexuality as a metaphor for her own loneliness? If I'm right about the essential irrelevance of homosexuality in *Autobiography of Red,* then how should we feel about it? Well, when a writer tries to inhabit imaginatively the experience of others who are differently situated in relation to mainstream culture (or "relatively disempowered"—we tiptoe through these minefield phrases), we can call it empathy or we can call it appropriation. Sometimes we feel the attempt is wonderfully vital and transcendently human (that's how I feel about Jarrell's "Next Day," and Faulkner's Benjy); but sometimes we feel it is ostentatious, opportunistic, arrogant. I'm not sure what I think in this case. I prefer never to side with the correctness police, yet I suspect that if I were gay, my reaction to *Autobiography of Red* might be not just quizzical but skeptical.

To what extent is Geryon an alter ego, a male disguise for Anne Carson in her youth? We can't know. In her prose memoir "Just For the Thrill: An Essay on the Difference Between Women and Men" (in *Plainwater,* 1995) Carson experimentally offers links between gender and emotion (as she does more logically in her essay "The Gender of Sound")—for example: "Time has a gender; I suppose you know this. For example, the first afternoons of a love affair are some of the longest in a woman's life." "What is it men want? They talk of pleasure. They go wild, then limp, then fall asleep. Is there something I'm not getting?" But the extreme vulnerability and extreme monogamous devotion and endless hunger ascribed to women also characterize Geryon. Carson sounds a lot like Geryon when she writes: "Even now it is hard to admit how love knocked me over. I had lived a life protected from all surprise, now suddenly I was a wheel running downhill, a light thrown against a wall, paper blown flat in the ditch." Geryon's desolation when betrayed by Herakles has in its genealogy some phases of Carson's memoir.

> To desire and be desired, what could be simpler? A woman cannot tell a simple story, my father used to say. Well here is what it looks like on the videotape. You see desire go traveling into the total dark country of another soul, to a place where the cliff just breaks off. Cold light like moonlight falling on it.

Carson's imagined videotape is like Geryon's magical photos of the spirit.

The problem for both hero and author is to create a combination of mind and heart, a self that integrates intellect and passion without vitiating either. Carson fears this can't finally be done, which must be why she is willing to let her scholarship seem only a thorny armor to cover, unconvincingly, the molten innerness.

In a poem about another male persona, Antonin Artaud, Carson says "He felt God pulling him out through his own cunt"—a statement which seems to repudiate gender distinctions with violent confidence—and then: "The drawback of being mad was that he could not both be so and say so." Two desires are considered contradictory, the desire to live in passion and the desire to describe it.

So is Anne Carson a polarized personality, in whom intellect and emotion are segregated so that each becomes overreaching? Well, she lures any reader down this path of playing psychoanalyst. She challenges us to see how her erudition fits valuably with her crimson romanticism. The episode in which Geryon thinks about Heidegger, quoted earlier, begins with this isolated line: "Under the seams runs the pain." I do think erudition and romanticism are successfully stitched together in the passage I quoted, and in **"The Glass Essay"** I think the co-presence of mind and heart is so real that we needn't call it stitching.

Stepping back from Carson's work, I feel wary but hopeful. What will this smart, ambitious, peculiar writer achieve in years ahead? There's a double wariness: the erudition could turn out to be (as regards the poetry), upon reflection, more of a flourishing than a nourishing; the passion might turn out to be too floody. But a hopefulness: Carson is more interesting than many a more manageable writer. Anyone who could write **"The Glass Essay"** has earned my attention for a long while.

Mark Scroggins (essay date 2002)

SOURCE: Scroggins, Mark. "Truth, Beauty, and the Remote Control." *Parnassus* 26, no. 2 (2002): 127-45.

[*In the following essay, Scroggins argues that Carson's poetry, particularly in* Men in the Off Hours *and* The Beauty of the Husband, *is enigmatic and unmusical.*]

Never short of cheek, Ezra Pound printed the following three lines, ellipses and all, as a complete poem in his 1916 collection *Lustra*:

>   Spring. . . .
>   too long. . . .
>   Gongula. . . .
>
>   ("Papyrus")

"Papyrus" is of course a (barely) plausible translation of what remains of three lines from one of Sappho's poems, preserved on a scrap of parchment (not papyrus) first transcribed and published in 1902. ("Gongula," who also appears in Fragment 211, is Sappho's heart-throb of the moment.) There's an idealism involved in speaking of Sappho's "poems," because none of them, save for a single twenty-eight line lyric, now exists complete. Groups of lines, clumps of words, and lone letters—quoted by classical grammarians and critics, or made out by turn-of-the-century German scholars peering themselves blind—are all we have of the seventh century BC.

And yet, as Guy Davenport writes, these "mere words and phrases . . . were once a poem, and, like broken statuary, are strangely articulate in their ruin."[1] Certainly many twentieth-century poets have found them so. Where the Romantics had embraced Winckelmann's

notion of Periclean culture as the apex of beauty and grace, the modernists made space at the table for Sappho's fragments, stripped of the padding and conjectural reconstructions within which Victorian translators had swaddled them. There was a new respect for the fragment, a fascination we can see not only in "Papyrus" but in, for instance, Rilke's "Archaic Torso of Apollo" and the "fragments" Eliot shores against his ruin at the close of *The Waste Land*. The classical fragment, dating from "the springtime of the world,"[2] comes into its own in the modernist period, and it's no surprise that so many of the modern poets—Pound, Cummings, H. D., Zukofsky—were classicists of an unorthodox stripe who revolted against philology, the deadening Germanic discipline in which Pound had been trained at Penn. These were poems, after all. If some silly University of Chicago classicist couldn't recognize *Homage to Sextus Propertius* as an adaptation rather than a translation, how could he see the poetic energy that radiated from three words of a Sappho fragment?

Following squarely in this tradition, Anne Carson launched her meteoric career—she has won a basketful of prizes, sold quite a few books, been profiled in *The New York Times Magazine,* and is writing her way through a multi-volume contract with Knopf—with a meditation (mostly) on Sappho called *Eros the Bittersweet: An Essay* (1986). Suddenly, out of the drab woods of classical scholarship—those stolid Clarendon editions of Greek medical texts, those sociological examinations of burial practices—sprang this glittering nymph of a little book, thirty-six brief chapters dwelling on, caressing, unravelling erotic desire as Sappho and her contemporaries conveyed it. In limpid, pointed prose, *Eros the Bittersweet* shows the power of desire to unseat reason, to loosen limbs, to destroy cities. By the time I've gotten to the last page, where Carson rests her case—

> It is a high-risk proposition, as Sokrates saw quite clearly, to reach for the difference between the known and the unknown. He thought the risk worthwhile, because he was in love with wooing itself. And who is not?

—I'm willing to forgive the inflated rhetorical question and count myself in.

Part of the appeal of *Eros the Bittersweet* is that while it treats of fragments and may seem, on the surface, to be (in the manner of Pound's choppy *Guide to Kulchur*) rather fragmentary itself, in fact there's a logical order behind the dips, swoops, and veers of these aphoristic mini-essays. The book began as a doctoral dissertation—Carson being, as everyone knows, a classics professor by trade—and the traditional argumentative structure of the academic paper still lurks behind its modular form. Each two- to nine-page chapter builds upon the ones before it, and Carson sets observations, speculations, and interpretations upon each other in a balanced and seemingly inescapable progression.

Yet can the same be generally said, *mutatis mutandis,* of her poetry? For here too Carson is irresistibly drawn to fragments, even if she refuses to acknowledge it. In a hilarious *Iowa Review* interview with John D'Agata—who, armed with all the slings and arrows of an MFA vocabulary, seems as frustrated as his subject—Carson, when asked about "fragmented narratives," impatiently responds, "What do you mean by a 'fragment'?" She'd rather speak of "painting with thoughts and facts." At the same time, she would have her poems manifest a quality known to the Greeks as *charis,* which she defines for D'Agata as follows:

> The Greeks used the word for the grace of a poem, the charm that makes it a poem and makes you want to remember it. So for them to make a poem is to make something that will be so charming that it will be a gift that the world wants to receive and also give back precisely because it's so good.[3]

But how does a poem achieve this grace, this memorability, when the poet is so attracted to the fragmentary, the broken, the enigmatic bit? What sorts of "charm"—if any—is Carson able to conjure out of her shards of language and emotion?

* * *

Carson's favorite trick over the years has been to juxtapose elements, usually taken from sources that are widely disparate, either culturally, temporally, or both. Sometimes such juxtaposition seems to serve a didactic purpose; more often, it just elicits a pleasant shock of the strange (a shock which often doesn't survive multiple readings). **"The Glass Essay,"** the longest poem of Carson's second collection *Glass, Irony, and God* (1995), manages to give us at once a seemingly autobiographical narrative and a meditation on the works and lives of the Brontë sisters. For *Autobiography of Red* (1998), her "novel in verse," Carson went back to the fragments of the seventh-century BC poet Stesichoros and refashioned his narrative of the monster Geryon so that Geryon becomes pretty much your average backpack-carrying, artistically inclined, self-consciously gay teenager—burdened, incidentally, by being winged, bright red, and in love with a Don Juan named Herakles.

All this, needless to say, is very modernist indeed, not very different from what Joyce did when he plopped Odysseus down in 1904 Dublin in the person of a petit-bourgeois Jewish ad canvasser, or what Eliot did when he had Tiresias play peeping Tom to the amours of a bored typist and a repulsive office clerk. But the strategy has served Carson well enough, and she continues to

experiment with it in *Men in the Off Hours.* In the twinned poems **"Hokusai"** and **"Audubon,"** she contrasts the two painters, one Japanese, the other American. (Our approval is meant to go to Hokusai, because he doesn't have to kill and wire up his tigers to paint them, as Audubon his birds.) In **"Lazarus (1st draft),"** the resurrected brother of Mary and Martha quotes *War and Peace.* In **"Hopper: Confessions,"** short poems responding to Edward Hopper paintings are counterpointed with passages from St. Augustine's *Confessions.*

But such overlaid perspectives are freshest in Carson's **"TV Men,"** parts of which first appeared in *Glass, Irony, and God.* The sequence has been expanded and made more complex in *Men in the Off Hours,* and now it even has a pseudo-epigraph: "TV makes things disappear. Oddly the word comes from Latin *videre* 'to see.' (Longinus, *de Sublimitate,* 5.3)." (That, I take it, is a joke, though a rather labored one: Part Five of *On the Sublime* has only one section.)

While at least some of these poems were inspired by Carson's experience working with Boston public television on a series about Nobel Prize winners, she admits not owning a set and seems to sport the standard intellectual disdain for the medium: It boils complex issues down to sound-bites, it promotes flashy images over intelligent discourse, it turns our youth into couch-bound lotus-eaters, and so forth. But Carson's approach has less to do with TV as experienced by a regular viewer than with how it produces its shiny, ephemeral illusions. **"TV Men: Hektor"** (*Glass, Irony, and God*) lays down portentous one-liners ("TV is ugly, like the future," "TV is inherently cynical. It speaks to the eye, but the mind has no eye," "TV is loud, yet we do not awake") as it transports the Trojan hero to Death Valley, where he is being filmed in his own death scene:

> He had constructed throughout Troy a system of gutters,
> which ran along both sides of every street,
> squared with stone
>
> in alternating blocks of polished and unpolished agate.
> Waters ran quietly out of Troy.
> Now Hektor worries
>
> that stains on the back of his clothing will be visible
> from the helicopter as he turns
> to run.

W. H. Auden might have chuckled; in his 1969 poem "Moon Landing," he noted that "Hector / was excused the insult of having / his valor covered by television."

In the later, more fully realized poems of the sequence, Carson takes the odd distancings and awkward dissonances inherent to her conception of television and uses them as jumping-off points. In some poems, she explores the juxtapositions that occur between image and voice-over in documentaries. **"TV Men: Tolsroy"** crosscuts a narrative of moments in the novelist's life (often interior) with the visuals (often not "visual" at all) over which that narrative might be spoken:

> A curiously tender man and yet
> even after their marriage he
> called his desire to kiss her
> "the appearance of Satan."
>
> *Her in right profile against the light, all the music in*
> *the room streams toward the blue frosty window.*

In other poems, she worries the relationship between life and script, the accidental or nefarious telescoping involved in cramming experience and thought into a twenty-inch screen and a thirty-minute time slot. Antigone, walking behind her father, the blind Oedipus, pauses to deliver a forty-two-second speech into the microphone. "For sound-bite purposes," the director notes, "we had to cut Antigone's script from 42 seconds to 7 . . ." The resulting six lines, cobbled together out of the original fourteen, are indeed more sound-bite-worthy:

> *Other things I like: a lot of money!*
> *The way we live, light and shadow are ironic.*
> *Projects? yes: physics. Anarchy. My father.*
> *Here, twist a bit off.*
> *Freedom is next.*
>
> **("TV Men: Antigone *(Scripts 1 and 2)*")**

There's one of Carson's judgments on television: from Sophokles to Jerry Springer.

The most striking of these video odes is **"TV Men: Lazarus,"** which spreads itself over three sections. The first is a "voiceover" from the Director of Photography, who is both a technician and something of a theorist; he knows what TV is all about, "how the pull is irresistible. The pull to handle horrors / and to have a theory of them." He is about to film Christ's raising of Lazarus from the dead, and while not entirely sure of the theological implications of that resurrection ("if / God's gift is simply random, well / for one thing / it makes a / more interesting TV show"), he knows the Platonic implications of his own medium: "Lazarus is an imitation of Christ,"

> As TV is an imitation of
> Lazarus. As you and I are an imitation of
> TV. Already you notice that
> although I am merely
> a director of photography,
>
> I have grasped certain fundamental notions first
>   advanced by Plato,
> e.g. that our reality is just a TV set

inside a TV set inside a TV set, with nobody watching
but Sokrates,
who changed
the channel in 399 B.C.

But the director is not interested in repetition, how Christ's resurrection will reply that of Lazarus, nor in the "Before and after"—there won't be any "home videos of Lazarus / in short pants," or "footage of Mary and Martha side by side on the sofa / discussing how they manage / at home / with a dead one sitting down to dinner." Instead, his documentary will focus "entirely on this moment, the flip-over moment" of resurrection:

> I put tiny microphones all over the ground
> to pick up
> the magic
> of the vermin in his ten fingers and I stand back to
>   wait
> for the miracle.

That final detail—"the vermin in his ten fingers"—succeeds, to some degree, in making the entire monologue come alive, redeeming it from the director's irredeemable vulgarity (not to mention the flat, prosaic lines in which he speaks).

Would that Carson could sustain the balance of **"Director of Photography: Voiceover"** in the middle section of the poem. **"Lazarus Standup"** attempts to narrate the experience of being raised from the dead, a tall order that Carson isn't quite up to. She falls into overheated metaphor, a hyperbolic miming of the "blooming, buzzing confusion" of sensation that leads up to an embarassing climax, deflated not nearly enough by the director's voice: "We know the difference now / (life or death) / For an instant it parts our hearts. / *Someone take the linen napkin off his face,* / says the director quietly." The final, ekphrastic section, "Giotto Shot List," consists of four looks at Giotto's Lazarus fresco in the Scrovegni chapel. "Giotto," Carson writes, addressing Lazarus, "slips / you / sideways into time." Lazarus's eyes "have the power of the other world. Barely open, / narrow shock slits / whose gaze is directed—simply, nowhere." The painting is described lovingly, even painfully, and with an intensity Carson denies the video medium.

It's hard not to read a moral here, and a rather obvious one at that: TV may capture the moment as it happens, and it may be where the money gets made, but when it comes to real miracles, give me that old-time religion of Renaissance frescoes. One can't help feeling that Carson is looking at television from only one end of the tube. In her fascination with the fractious goings-on that take place behind the camera and in the script doctor's office, she overlooks the oddly seamless reality that the medium presents to viewers on their couches. She's less the restaurant critic assessing the andouille than the health inspector wrinkling her nose at what goes into the casings. (Inevitably, in some future installment of **"TV Men,"** Carson will latch onto the remote control, the magic wand that zaps us through thirty worlds a minute, and I'm not sure whether to look forward to that moment with pleasure or trepidation.)

As mixed as the results may be, one has to admire Carson's originality and audacity in taking television production as a formal model. In fact, this is just one example of her refusal to be bound by generic conventions. She seems determined to make every form she touches new, to twist it out of the expected. One hesitates to call Carson a formalist—there's not a sonnet to be found in her books, nor a ghost of meter (though one turns up a very occasional rhyme)—but her work shows a continual fascination with casting ideas into different forms.

The seven little "Epitaphs" sprinkled through *Men in the Off Hours,* for example, have the brevity, shapeliness, and conceptual snap that we associate with the genre, yet they entirely resist the specificity, the human connection it demands. **"Epitaph: Zion"** paints in shades of Celan—

> Murderous little world once our objects had gazes.
>   Our lives
>   Were fragile, the wind
> Could dash them away. Here lies the refugee breather
>   Who drank a bowl of elsewhere.

—While **"Epitaph: Thaw"** flirts with early Auden at his most Edward Learish, in the process pointing up Carson's fondness for the awkward and the faux-naïf:

> Little clicks all night in the back lane there blackness
>   Goes leaking out the key.
> "It twindles," said Father to April on her
>   Anvil of deep decree.

Another form that Carson extensively tinkers with—or perhaps eviscerates—in *Men in the Off Hours* is the essay poem. (Like *Glass, Irony, and God,* the book also includes a traditional essay, "Dirt and Desire: Essay on the Phenomonology of Female Pollution in Antiquity," reprinted from a scholarly venue and trailing a cloud of footnotes. So far as I'm concerned, Carson should keep such work out of her poetry books.) **"Essay on What I Think About Most"** is pretty much what its title claims: a little essay on "Error / and its emotions," beginning with Aristotle's claim that metaphor "causes the mind to experience itself // in the act of making a mistake" and then musing over a computational error in an Alkman poem. The fact that it's broken into verse lines doesn't make it any less an essay, a brief bit of expository writing. Its follow-up poem, however, **"Essay on Error (2nd Draft)"** is something else altogether, a brief, enigmatic monologue by an unnamed poet:

It is also true I dream about soiled suede gloves.
And have done so
since the day I read
in the third published volume of Freud's letters
(this was years after I stopped seeing him)
a sentence which I shall quote in full.
Letter to Ferenczi 7.5.1909:
"He doesn't look a bit like a poet except for the
    lashes."
Freud hesitates to name me
but
let me tell you
that was no
pollen stain.
Here
I could paraphrase Descartes
The hand that busy instrument
or just let it go.
After all
what are you and I compared to him?
Smell of burnt pastilles.
I still remember the phrase every time I pass that spot.

Who speaks here? What was that yellow stain on those suede gloves? Above all, who has made the "error"? I don't have a problem with the poem's esoteric references, but I'm not running to the library to check out Freud's letters or thumbing through my Descartes, either; the poem's learning seems no more than a nimbus of teasing mystery. Carson might call this an "essay" all she wants, but it has nothing to do with anything Cicero or Plutarch pioneered. (As she tells D'Agata, her idea of the essay is on the Ciceronian model, "to have something to say and to do so"; she has no time either for Montaigne's self-revelations or his recursive ramblings.[4]) **"Essay on Error (2nd Draft)"** is a fragment of speech, half of a long-distance telephone conversation. It belongs on the same shelf as Pound's "Papyrus" or Eliot's "Prufrock." One reason Carson's poem isn't in the same league as Eliot's, however, is her mostly inert, unmusical lines. She has no gift for rhythm, and her unsubtle line breaks—"but / let me tell you" or "Here / I could paraphrase Descartes"—read like an undergraduate's touching attempts to jazz up a piece of prose.

Finally, *Men in the Off Hours* also includes several translations, if one can call them that. When Carson translates Sappho or Archilochos in *Eros the Bittersweet,* she seems more interested in getting across Greek word order than in recreating poems; her versions of Sappho aren't a patch on Davenport's or Mary Barnard's. In *Men in the Off Hours,* however, she joins the ranks of iconoclastic modernist translators. Pound covered his tail by calling his Propertius an "Homage." Zukofsky was less shy—the zany, slangy, phonetic transliterations he (in collaboration with his wife Celia) did of Catullus were meant "to breathe the 'literal' meaning" of the *Carmina.* Carson ups the ante in **"Catullus: Carmina,"** where she adapts fifteen of Catullus's lyrics in a manner that would give my high school

Latin teacher conniption fits. "Passer Deliciae Meae Puellae," where the poet moans about the attention his beloved is giving her sparrow (rather than him), becomes a grim, slightly perverse contemporary snapshot:

> On her lap one of the matted terriers.
> She was combing around its genitals.
> It grinned I grinned back.
> It's the one she calls Little Bottle after Deng Xiaoping.

The old chestnut **"Odi et Amo"** ("I hate and love. Why I do so, perhaps you ask. I know not, but I feel it, and am in torment," in F. W. Cornish's stolid translation) becomes a Dick Higgins-like Fluxus piece:

> Hate hate hate hate hate hate hate hate hate. Hate
> hate hate hate hate hate hate love hate.
> Love love love love love love love love love love.
> Love love love love love love love love love love.
> Why why why why why why why why why why.
> Why why why why why I why why why why why.
> I I I I I I I I I I I I I I I I I I I I I I I I I I I I I I I I I I.
> I I I I I I I I I I I I I why I I I I I I I I I I I I I I I.

That, I fear, wears less well on each rereading. Far more compelling is Carson's reduction of **"Si Quisquam Mutis Gratum Acciptumve Sepuleris"**—a lovely poem in which Catullus comforts his friend Calvus on the death of his wife—down to a *Cathay*-like flutter of words:

> As tree shapes from mist
> Her young death
> Loose
> In you.

* * *

Carson's determination to explode and splice forms is even more pronounced in her most recent book, *The Beauty of the Husband,* which is provocatively subtitled "a fictional essay in 29 tangos." Not surprisingly, the book isn't really an essay at all, but rather a narrative poem in twenty-nine sections, or "tangos." "The word 'tango,'" María Susana Azzi gushes in the liner notes to yet another Astor Piazzola recording, "conjures up images of Buenos Aires, of a dimlylit dance floor, the smoke of a cigarette curling up into the air, a beautiful woman in the arms of a man, surrendering to a rhythm that is at once love and dream, pain and reality."[5] Carson is briefer: "A tango (like a marriage) is something you have to dance to the end." The poet may be less prone to imaginative flights than Azzi (and most everybody else who's written on the dance), but Azzi's images fit *The Beauty of the Husband* pretty well: While it may not feature romance or trance, there's love, pain, and a woman's "surrender" to a rhythm—a rhythm of desire, which in the poem is inextricable from the rhythm of marriage.

The rest of the book's dust-jacket copy (aside from the definition of "tango") reads as follows: "*The Beauty of the Husband* is an essay on Keats's idea that beauty is truth, and is also the story of a marriage." The relationship of Keats to *The Beauty of the Husband* is worth pondering, though I doubt I've worked it out. The tangos are introduced with little quotations from Keats, some of them from the odes but most from the dreary piecework tragedy *Otho the Great* and the ham-fisted, unfinished satire *The Jealousies: A Faery Tale, by Lucy Vaughan Lloyd of China Walk, Lambeth* (better known as "The Cap and Bells"). Many of those quotations are, in the best Susan Howe style, deleted lines and questionable readings, and frankly, only God and Carson know their relationship to the tangos they introduce. And of course to speak of "Keats's idea that beauty is truth" is to open a whole other can of worms. Strictly speaking, Keats didn't say that—the Grecian urn did. What Keats himself said, in his letter to Benjamin Bailey of November 22, 1817, was, "I am certain of nothing but of the holiness of the Heart's affections and the truth of Imagination—What the imagination seizes as Beauty must be truth—whether it existed before or not—for I have the same Idea of all our Passions as of Love they are all in their sublime, creative of essential Beauty." One could read through a whole shelf of critical studies arguing out the implications of this statement, along with a few other passages in which Keats addresses the truth/beauty business, but Carson is interested in a far more concrete sense of beauty. As the longsuffering Wife of her poem says,

> . . . why did I love him from early girlhood to late
>   middle age
> and the divorce decree came in the mail?
> Beauty. No great secret. Not ashamed to say I loved
>   him for his beauty.
> As I would again
> if he came near. Beauty convinces. You know beauty
>   makes sex possible.
> Beauty makes sex sex.

To summarize in the quickest and nastiest fashion, *The Beauty of the Husband* tells the story, largely from the point of view of the Wife, of a marriage in which the Husband is the sort of serial adulterer whose dalliances derive their savor from being committed in spite of the enamored and madly patient spouse to whom he always eventually returns. His attraction lies neither in his brains nor in his character, but in his "beauty"—this is all we know, and all we need to know.

The poem's narrative (the Wife, by the way, eventually shakes off this inexplicably attractive schmuck, if not his memory) is matter for a Jeanette Winterson novel, or a *New Yorker* short story. It is sturdily told, and at times reaches rather frightening emotional pitches. One scene unfolds in a hotel room in Athens, where the Husband has taken the Wife "after three years of separation . . . for adoration, for peace," but still must "telephone New York every night from the bar / and speak to a woman / who thought he was over on 4th Street / working late." Tuuhere is a confrontation, an argument, and then, just as the two have reached an impasse (the Wife's mind running over Parmenides), "His nose begins to bleed."

> Then blood runs down over his upper lip, lower lip, chin.
> To his throat.
> Appears on the whiteness of his shirt.
> Dyes a mother-of-pearl button for good,
> blacker than a mulberry.
> Don't think his heart had burst. He was no Tristan
> (though he would love to point out that in the common version
> Tristan is not false, it is the sail that kills)
> yet neither of them had a handkerchief
> and that is how she ends up staining her robe with his blood,
> his head in her lap and his virtue coursing through her
>
> as if they were one flesh.
> Husband and wife may erase a boundary.
> Creating a white page.
>
> But now the blood seems to be the only thing in the room.
>
> If only one's whole life could consist in certain moments.
> There is no possibility of coming back from such a moment
> to simple hatred,
> black ink.
>
> If a husband throws the dice of his beauty one last time, who is to blame?

As a narrative climax, and as the crossing-point of a number of interlinked images and motifs—the nosebleed, the sail from *Tristan and Isolde,* the white page and black ink—this is a gripping passage. But, as with far too much of Carson's work, it falls short as poetry. For one thing, I'm not fond of Carson's propensity for emphasizing her line breaks with syntactically uncalled-for full stops ("Creating a white page."). It calls attention to the generally loose lineation of the verse, which might well be chopped-up prose. In her interview with D'Agata, Carson speaks of "a novel I've written that was all prose at first and very thick. Then I thought, 'What if I break these lines up a bit? Maybe they'll move along more smartly.' So now the novel's in verse."[6] Breaking up one's prose is an efficient way of producing poems, I suppose, but the finished product is often stillborn. (Read a few pages of late MacDiarmid, for instance.) I'm an anti-Laodicean here: If you choose to write in lines, you ought to make damn sure those lines are doing every bit of work for you they can.

And then there's the matter of melopœia, the music of the language. Carson's lines have a ruthless clarity, a simplicity that is sometimes graceful Shaker and sometimes just plain rude Puritan. The best Guy Davenport can say for Carson's poetic language, in his introduction to *Glass, Irony, and God,* is that "truth and observation are more important than lyric effect or coloring. If a good line happens, it happens." In *The Beauty of the Husband,* the sans-serif type seems almost to emphasize the resolute prosiness of the phrasing:

> They are both serious.
> Their seriousness wracks her.
> People who can be serious together, it goes deep.
> They have a bottle of mineral water on the table between them
> and two glasses.

Many of the "tangos" trudge forward in this clipped voice, reserving their moment of lyricism for a final sucker punch:

> A cold ship
>
> moves out of harbor somewhere way inside the wife
> and slides off toward the flat gray horizon,
>
> not a bird not a breath in sight.

There is a moment of magic here—a very brief one—but too often we're left scanning the flat gray horizon of the language for some glimpse of bright plumage that never shows up.

Despite its generally undistinguished language, *The Beauty of the Husband* offers a number of pleasurable moments, some quite modernist and others more traditional. There are the eight quirky elegiacs quoted by the Wife in Tango XXVI (out of her manuscript, she explains, of 5,820!):

> This Wind at Night carrying it all over the Sky like Quartets
> 　Or Dido surviving between Lightning Sets
> Against this Wall, the way Brothers tear at
> 　one another's Heads with their Love, it fought

There are subtly repeated leitmotifs: Kutuzov and Napoleon at the Battle of Borodino, Keats's scratching a bit of misspelled graffiti on a window and prefiguring his own name "writ in water." There is the sheer pleasure of learning things, or having known things repeated in a new, seductive manner: the varieties of European and American grapes in Tango VI, the rape of Persephone in Tango IX, the minutiae of Nahum Tate's revision of *King Lear* in Tango XXI, the appalling details of the Battle of Epipolai (413 BC) in Tango XXV. And throughout the poem, as through much of *Men in the Off Hours,* there is a compressed emotional intensity that seems able to find its outlet only in intellectual statement.

The story doesn't so much end as peter out. The Wife, older and wiser, returns to the Keats saw: "To say Beauty is Truth and stop, / Rather than to eat it. / Rather than to want to eat it. This was my pure early thought." Like Persephone or Eve, however, she has been unable to resist the object of desire. A painter named Ray, who works in a diner, eats mashed potatoes for breakfast, enjoys speaking in rhyme, and has been both her confidant and the Husband's, has the penultimate word, and a banal one it is:

> Well life has some risks. Love is one. Terrible risks.
> Ray would have said
> Fate's my bait and bait's my fate.
> *On a June evening.*
> Here's my advice,
> hold.
>
> Hold beauty.

But that's not all. A final, unnumbered tango gives us the voice of the Husband:

> Some tangos pretend to be about women but look at
>   this.
> Who is it you see
> reflected small
> in each of her tears.
>
> Watch me fold the page now so you think it is you.

This final turn, where the villain steps forward and announces that he's been the central character all along, is too clever by half. We've already been shown the Husband's monstrous self-centeredness in a dozen ways—why this last twist of the knife? And that metafictional gambit—Dear Reader, look into your own heart and find yourself in this story—simply doesn't ring true.

Perhaps my specific dissatisfaction with **The Beauty of the Husband**—apart, that is, from my general disquiet with the texture of Carson's verse—rests ultimately with that blunt, totalizing "beauty." *Eros the Bittersweet,* when it addressed the complex, social, and often baffling experience of desire, did so in a thorough and nunaced manner; it took very few conceptual shortcuts. **The Beauty of the Husband** explains all of its anguishes through the simple ideogram of "beauty," and in the end "beauty" can't stand up as an explanation of the erotic complications Carson's poem dramatizes. *Eros the Bittersweet* analyzed—painstakingly, painfully—Sappho's triangulated desire, where the lover's desire for the beloved is sparkled and fuelled by the presence of a competitive other. Here, that relationship has become a bad old-fashioned love triangle.

Carson has been schooled by the earliest—and still the keenest—dissectors of the heart in the Western tradition, whose pain, lust, and clarity are still sometimes aglow in her lines; we hear those antique frustrations echoing, even through the static and montage of our own era. As Carson's televised Sappho laments, worried that the changing foliage of the Place de la Concorde will cause continuity problems in the videoplay in which she's acting,

> You cannot erase.
> Is this a law?
>
> No, a talent. To step obliquely
> where stones are sharp.
> Vice is also sharp.
> There are laws against vice.
> But the shock stays with you.

> **("TV Men: Sappho")**

"You cannot erase." You may smash them into fragments to be reassembled into an Absolut vodka ad, or you may clip and telescope them into a Ken Burns documentary, but the maxims, epitaphs, and cries of stymied desire of Carson's archaic precursors will not be erased. Her own poems are mosaics of such desire, scrambled by the video snow of arbitrary juxtaposition and muffled by the bluntness of her language. If she can imbue her verse with some of the grace and music of her ancestors, then perhaps her poems as well can be acts of *charis,* "the charm that makes it a poem and makes you want to remember it."

Notes

1. Guy Davenport, *7 Greeks* (New York: New Directions, 1997), 13.

2. *7 Greeks,* 5.

3. John D'Agata, "A _____ With Anne Carson," *Iowa Review* 27.2 (1997), 17.

4. "A _____ With Anne Carson," 16-17.

5. Trans. Richard Haney-Jardine, from Yo-Yo Ma, *Soul of the Tango: The Music of Astor Piazolla,* Sony SK 63122, 1997.

6. "A _____ With Anne Carson," 20.

Andre Furlani (essay date spring 2003)

SOURCE: Furlani, Andre. "Reading Paul Celan with Anne Carson: 'What Kind of Withness Would That Be?'" *Canadian Literature/Littérature canadienne,* no. 176 (spring 2003): 84-104.

[*In the following essay, Furlani explores Paul Celan's considerable influence on Carson, which reaches far beyond Carson's examination of Celan in* Economy of the Unlost.]

1

In a 1996 interview Anne Carson said, "I've been read-ing a lot of Celan. He's clarifying" (D'Agata 19). To fellow Montreal poet-professor Mary di Michele she later listed Celan with Dickinson, Pessoa and Stein among primary influences: "Economy and devotion interest me in these writers" (di Michele 9). An unpublished recent lecture, "If Body Is Always Deep but Deepest at its Surface: Translation as Humanism," is devoted in part to Celan's poem *Weggebeizt* ("Etched Away"), which she reads as a translation of his wife Gisèle Lestrange's etchings. In 1999 she published *Economy of the Unlost: Reading Simonides of Keos with Paul Celan,* using the Bronze Age Greek poet as a means to explore the epitaphic quality of Celan's verse. Her poetic engagement with Celan's legacy is equally involved. For her adversaries this marks Carson as a mere epigone. David Solway, another Montreal poet and teacher, writes that what Carson does "has been done before, done better and done authentically—for example, by Akhmatova as by Celan" (Solway 25).

Carson's close attention to Celan's work could not, however, be confused with mere emulation. While Car-son is indebted to Formalist doctrines important to Celan,[1] their affinities are limited. The discrepancies between the poets are not of the kind she would pretend to discount. She is of secular Protestant extraction, raised in post-war prosperity in English Canada, and Professor of Classics at McGill University. Her scholar-ship is influenced by feminist theory while her poetry reflects closest engagement not only with the Bronze Age Greek lyric poets but with Gertrude Stein. Celan in contrast was reared in modest circumstances in an observant Jewish family in what until recently had been the Habsburg city of Czernowitz, in the Bukovina region of Romania. His parents perished in a German concen-tration camp while he was conscripted into a Romanian labour camp. Freed, he translated Russian texts into Romanian and studied Romance languages before flee-ing to the West in 1947. He settled in Paris, where he lectured on German literature at the École Normale Supérieure until, after years of impaired mental health, he committed suicide in 1970. Philosophically oriented toward phenomenology, Celan experimented in a poetry that adapts Biblical cadences and themes to modernist strategies, exploiting the plasticity of German to craft a neologistic, elliptical and intensely suggestive idiom, whereby he recast a mother tongue undone by the Shoah.

Carson is frequently comic, self-consciously allusive and quotidian where Celan is elegiac, oblique and portentous. The ancient language she studied most closely was Greek, he Hebrew. His most conspicuous stylistic debt is to French surrealism and German expressionism, hers to Stein and American collage art.

He is a poet of Orphic concentration and sombre musicality while she is expansive, whimsical and prosaic. And in contrast to the introspective lyric typi-cal of Celan, Carson's characteristic mode is narrative.

Both poets have nevertheless been vilified for writing gnomic poetry, indeed for not writing poetry at all. Most gravely, both have been accused of writing someone else's work: the widow of Yvan Goll charged Celan in 1953 with pilfering her husband's verse; in a recent diatribe David Solway charges Carson with pilfering both from Celan and Celan scholar John Fel-stiner (whose *Paul Celan: Poet, Survivor, Jew* describes the devastating consequences of the scandal on Celan). Carl Hohoff took up Clare Goll's accusations and in 1955 published an article similar to Solway's, setting what he alleged were incriminating passages side by side before condemning Celan as a charlatan and second-rate imitator of a master poet's style. The Alsa-tian Goll, like Celan a German-speaking Jew who lived in Paris, had forged ties to surrealism, as would Celan later, and wrote (again like Celan) of Jewish dislocation and isolation. Both were polyglots who earned their liv-ings in part by translating. (Goll, much of whose work is in French, translated *Ulysses* into German.) Celan's first major verse translation was of Goll's work.

Affinities between Celan's work and Carson's are easy to discern, as easy indeed as those between Goll's and Celan's. Goll's precedent obviously strengthened Celan's confidence in techniques he had developed in his first book, *Sand aus den Urnen,* published before he was introduced to Goll in 1949. Translating three col-lections of Goll's poetry in the early 1950s, while writ-ing the poems collected in 1955 in *Von Schwelle zu Schwelle* (the book which revived cries of plagiarism), permitted Celan to venture an encounter with the elder poet—one in a sense strengthened by Goll's death in 1950. Celan's precedent has analogously strengthened Carson's confidence in techniques she appears to have developed prior to making an encounter with the poet. (Her remark to Di Michele quoted above suggests that Carson began reading Celan in the mid-1990s, by which time she had published her first two books of poetry.) She probably honed her appreciation of Celan, just as Celan honed his of Goll, by translating the poet, as is reflected in the poems of *Men in the Off Hours,* composed while she was preparing *Economy of the Un-lost,* lectures that include a number of her versions of his poetry.

Rather than the proprietorial terms Solway uses with the peremptory self-assurance of a bailiff, Carson's involvement in Celan's work might more faithfully be understood in the complementary terms Celan and Car-son themselves apply to their creative engagements. In *Begegnung* (encounter) Celan found a term primitive to neat discriminations between exposure, reading, translation, and influence—indeed, in its aura of spiritualized tangibility, primitive to the distinction between presence and absence, even between life and death. The site of encounter offered him a margin of licence, where converged the yearning for self-effacement in, and the desire for self-enlargement by means of, the other's vitality. Neither masochistic self-denial nor vampiric exploitation was involved in cooperation with these guides to his own powers.

Behind this protocol of engagement stands another, perhaps decisive encounter: that with Martin Buber, before whom Celan is said to have knelt, the master's books in hand, when this philosopher of the spirituality immanent in all verbal exchange visited Paris in 1960. Buber, preserver of communal tales and translator of scripture, proposes that the truth-telling function of language inheres not in articulation per se but in dialogue—in *Begegnung*. (Indeed Buber had come to Paris from Munich, where he had been honoured for his efforts to re-establish dialogue between Germans and Jews, concerning which Celan questioned him [see Felstiner 161].)

The fullest expression of this notion Celan reserves for "*Der Meridian*," which like almost all of his few essays was written for a direct encounter, here an address in Darmstadt upon receiving the 1960 Georg Büchner Prize. He calls poetry a "leading to encounter": "*das Gedicht zur Begegnung Führende*" (61). He asked his Darmstadt audience, "*Aber steht das Gedicht nicht gerade dadurch, also schon hier, in der Begegnung—im Geheimnis der Begegnung?*" [Yet does not the poem precisely thereby stand, even here, in encounter—in the mystery of encounter?] (55). He stresses how his readings open spaces where the encountered grant access to a utopian ground of origin; the encounters of poetry prove "*eine Art Heimkehr*" [a kind of homecoming] (60). They finally make the poet tangible to himself: "*Ich bin* [. . .] *mir selbst begegnet*" [I am myself encountered] (59). The degree of fostering reciprocity and eagerly undertaken encroachment involved in *Begegnung* renders it immune to anxieties of plagiarism as of anxieties of influence. Celan assumes no mere Poundian "pact" with the precursor but consent (recall him kneeling before Buber), indeed mutuality (as when Goll responded to the gift of *Sand aus den Urnen* by returning to writing poems in German, indeed a German suggestive of Celan's innovations). Such contact is of course unverifiable—a genuine "*Geheimnis*" (mystery). *Begegnung* thus operates rather as a "supreme fiction" in Wallace Stevens's terms, an enabling myth redeemed by the faith with which it is made to serve the exigencies and ideals of craft. It permits Celan as well to recover the classical and medieval ideal of the poet as member of a guild or sodality, and to extend it into the domain of reception, by inclusion of the reader and translator.

Begegnung furnishes a metaphysical recuperation of conditions most other poets (including Carson) can safely assume—those of home, community, audience—but which were unavailable to Celan, an orphaned stateless émigré in France writing in German, language of the murderers. What Celan shows—and Carson grasps—is this wider "mystery of encounter." In *Economy of the Unlost,* where she invokes this phrase, Carson approvingly stresses Celan's view of poetry as encounter between I and You: "The properly invisible nature of otherness guarantees the mystery of our encounters with it, pulls out of us the act of attention that may bring 'some difference' to light here" (71-72).[2] It is in these terms that she would attempt to meet him, and it is in these terms that one might usefully attempt to meet both.

In a section of **"The Truth about God"** called "God's Christ Theory," Carson acknowledges the theological enigma of "withness" (*Glass* 51): how is God "with" Christ, how is Christ "with" us? She returns to this conundrum in the preface to *Economy of the Unlost*:

> Think of the Greek preposition πρός. When used with the accusative case, this preposition means "toward, upon, against, with, ready for, face to face, engaging, concerning, touching, in reply to, in respect of, compared with, according to, as accompaniment for." It is the preposition chosen by John the Evangelist to describe the relationship between God and The Word in the first verse of the first chapter of his Revelation:
>
> πρὸς θεόν
>
> "And The Word was with God" is how the usual translation goes. What kind of withness is it?
>
> (viii)

She proposes no answers but, placed toward the end of her preface to a book subtitled "Reading Simonides of Keos with Paul Celan," the question invites us to rethink notions of literary propinquity. Despite the mischievous pedantry with which she coins the word, "withness" stands as Carson's earnest attempt to adapt *Begegnung* to her uses: a term both cheeky and solemn, comical and sacramental. Almost every denotation of the accusative πρὸς suggests a shade of Celan's *Begegnung* and furnishes a model of contact corresponding to Carson's encounter with the poet: Celan is with Carson, who responds by approaching, engaging, touching, replying to, respecting, and accompanying Celan's work within and by means of her own.

2

Carson has attended to Celan's techniques in small ways as well as large. There are, for instance, the sonorous repetitions when writing of death, as in **"Catullus;** *Carmina"*:

One carries.
One carries.
One carries it.

(***Men*** 38)

This compares with Celan's "Matière de Bretagne":

Du
du lehrst
du lehrst deine Hände
du lehrst deine Hände du lehrst
du lehrst deine Hände
                              schlafen.

(*Gedichte* [1: 172])

[You / you teach / you teach your hands / you teach
your hands you teach / you teach your hands / to sleep.]

There is the mundane chain of noun phrases mounting
into mystery, as in the description of Orvieto in **"The
Fall of Rome"**:

On top
arises
a pedestal of volcanic rock.
On top of the rock is a word.

(***Glass*** 96)

Celan too makes abrupt transitions from elementary
particulars to metaphysical statement, a device which
permits both poets to hypostatize abstractions, treating
mental constructs as objects. This, after all, is precisely
what the builders and artists of Orvieto did, "shaping
the word / into a cathedral" (***Glass*** 96). In *"Ich hörte
sagen"* ("I heard say") "word" and "stone" are bonded
in much the same way:

Ich hörte sagen, es sei
im Wasser ein Stein und ein Kreis
und über dem Wasser ein Wort
das den Kreis um den Stein legt.

(1: 85)

[I heard say, there was / in the water a stone and a
circle / and over the water a word / which lays the
circle about the stone.]

Celan's own poem about a medieval Italian cathedral,
"Assisi," works similarly to describe St. Francis as the
church's first builder:

Umbrische Nacht
Umbrische Nacht mit dem Silber von Glocke und Ölb-
latt.
Umbrische Nacht mit dem Stein, den du hertrugst.
Umbrische Nacht mit dem Stein.

(1: 108)

[Umbrian night / Umbrian night with the silver of
churchbell and olive leaf. / Umbrian night with the
stone that you bore there. / Umbrian night with the
stone.]

One may hear both poems in **"Lazarus (First Draft)"**:
"Inside the rock on which we live, another rock" (***Men***
21). In places the echo approximates allusion: "Hard,
darling, to be sent behind their borders. / Carrying a
stone in each eye" (**"Mimnermos,"** *Plainwater* 6). *"Die
Offenen tragen / den Stein hinterm Aug"* [The open
ones bear / the stone behind the eye] (*"Rebleute gra-
ben,"* "Vintners Dig," Celan, *Gesammelte* 123). Carson
adapts Celan's literalized tropes, fusing an often unpar-
ticularized object with its figurative connotations. Thus
Francis is both a Christ bearing not a cross but a stone,
and a Christian Sisyphus (mythic builder of Corinth), as
well as church-builder. Carson's "rock" meanwhile is
both the earth and the earth's resistance to us; "another
rock" is both Lazarus's tomb and the deliverance
implied in his resurrection.

Carson follows Celan's practice of rendering nouns ad-
jectively, as in **"Hopper;** *Confessions***"**: "You on the
other hand creature whitely Septembered" (***Men*** 58).
Compare this with the untitled late lyric beginning
"Eingejännert / in der bedornten / Bahme" [Januaried /
into the bethorned / rock recess] (2: 351). Arbitrary
temporal divisions become agents, acting as psychological states with the sanction and force of seasons.

Sanctioned in part by the recovery of the Anglo-Saxon
kenning in Doughty, Hopkins, Pound and Joyce, Carson
exploits Celan's most distinctive lexical device, the
neologistic compound. A section of **"Catullus:** *Carmina***"** ends: "So then I grew old and died and wrote
this. / Be careful it's worldsharp" (***Men*** 40). A convincing compound is both an arranged marriage and an
elopement. It is calculating and coerced yet should appear an unsanctioned flight into new possibility. The
dictionary refuses to recognize the union, but this verbal
infringement, though a defiance of linguistic propriety,
is also an enlargement of the properties of language.
Indeed this wilful aberration becomes the lexical
embodiment of encounter: a model not of assimilation
or integration but of equipoise, exchange and cooperation. Neologisms are unnaturalized compounds, the two
elements retaining their integrity even while generating
unforeseen combinations. Carson writes that neologisms
"raise troubling questions about our own verbal mastery.
We say 'coinages' because they disrupt the economic
equilibrium of words and things that we had prided
ourselves on maintaining. A new compound word in
Celan, for example, evokes something that now suddenly seems real, although it didn't exist before and is
attainable through this word alone. [. . .] It has to
invent its own necessity" (*Economy* 134). If Carson's
Orvieto cathedral is an affirming word (it proclaims
"the word 'Live!'" [***Glass*** 96]) upon "volcanic rock,"
speech in Celan strives to do the same with vastly more
compromised materials: *"Wortaufschüttung, vulkanisch,*
/ meerüberrauscht" [Wordheapings, volcanic, / sea-
overswept] (2: 29). Such compounds suggest a tumultu-

229

ous semantic exuberance difficult to separate from violence. The compound itself, be it Carson's "day-wolf" (**Men** 19) or Celan's "*Schneetrost*" [snow-comfort] (*Gesammelte* 105) is a heaping-up of words, where incompatibility conceals profound secret affinities.

Celan routinely appeals to an unidentified auditor, a "you" both intimate and unknown—a mobile token of company ghostly, domestic, and readerly. Carson sometimes invokes this auditor as well. A section of "Kinds of Water: An Essay on the Road to Compostela" begins: "Your voice I know. It had me terrified. When I hear it in dreams, from time to time all my life, it sounds like a taunt—but dreams distort sound, for they send it over many waters" (**Plainwater** 175). This disembodied voice, generalized yet specific, intimate yet unsettling, belongs to the awry logic of the dream. It is one of what Celan calls "sleepshapes," the oneiric "you" appearing in Celan's late poem "*Alle die Schlafgestalten*":

> *Alle die Schlafgestalten, krystallin,*
> *die du annahmst*
> *im Sprachshatten*
>
> *ihnen*
> *führ ich mein Blut zu*
>
> (*Gesammelte* 76)

[All the sleepshapes, crystalline, / which you assumed / in the speechshadow // to them / I lead my blood]

Carson comments on this poem: "Whoever 'you' are, you are placed at the beginning and end of the poem, to enclose the poet in the middle and make his existence possible for him in two essential ways: for you take on shapes that he can understand and you give him a place for his grief" (*Economy* 70). Carson's rhetoric here arrestingly conspires with Celan's to affirm the vital reality of "you." "You" sheds its quotation marks, becoming the subject of her direct address as of Celan's. You thus give her as much as him understanding and a place for grief.

In the Büchner Prize address Celan calls the poem a "*Flaschenpost*" or message in a bottle:

> *Gedichte sind auch in dieser Weise unterwegs; sie halten auf etwas zu. Worauf? Auf etwas Offenstehendes, Besetzbares, auf ein ansprechbares Du vielleicht, auf eine ansprechbare Wirklichkeit.*
>
> (*Meridian* 39)

[Poems are also in this way en route: they are making for something. For what? For something standing open, engageable, for an addressable You perhaps, for an addressable reality.]

In "*Die Silbe Schmerz*" ("The Syllable Pain") he writes:

> *Es gab sich Dir in die Hand:*
> *ein Du, todlos,*
> *an dem alles Ich zu sich kam.*
>
> (1: 280)

[There appeared in your hand: / a You, deathless, / in which all things I came to itself.][3]

The You is both potentially a solipsistic projection and an idealization by which the shards of identity may textually reassemble.[4] For Carson it can be an enigmatic but enabling alterity, as in **"Kinds of Water."** This text culminates in the intercession of an unidentified, perhaps imaginary you, who rescues the pilgrim from an intangible menace: "Your action is simple. You take hold of my paws and cross them on my breasts as a sign that I am one who has been to the holy city and tasted its waters, its kinds" (**Plainwater** 187). Carson's Compostela echoes Celan's Assisi; she makes a pilgrimage along the Camino bearing psychic equivalents to St. Francis's stone. Within the logic of "withness" the "you" who meets her at the "holy city" acts on the speaker of the poem as Celan acts on the poet, extending protection and conferring a sanction.

This "you" even becomes, however obliquely, Celan himself. In **The Beauty of the Husband,** the narrator's unfaithful husband has travelled with her to Athens to promote a reconciliation. Noticing her sadness, he asks, "why in your eyes—" but she deflects his attention by requesting tea. While he fetches drinks she is reminded of a line of poetry: "why sadness? This flowing the world to its end. Why in your eyes—" (**Beauty** 98). The lines derive from an epistolary poem sent to Celan in a letter dated March 10, 1958 by the expatriate German Jewish poet Nelly Sachs:

> *Warum diese Traurigket?*
> *Dieses Welt-zu Ende-fließen?*
> *Warum in deinen Augen*
> *das perlende Licht daraus Sterben sich zusammensetzt?*
>
> (*Briefwechsel* 16)

[Why this sadness? / This world-to-end-flowing? / Why in your eyes the pearling light of which dying consists?]

"Your eyes" are, in the context of this uncollected poem, Celan's. (He reciprocated four years later with an epistolary poem inspired by their first meeting, "*Zürich, Zum Storchen,*" in which the "you" is its dedicatee, whose words close the poem.) Celan thus surreptitiously enters Carson's own poem, with uncanny repercussions:

> It is a line of verse. Where has it stepped from. She searches herself. Waiting.
> Waiting is searching.
> And the odd thing is, waiting, searching, the wife suddenly knows
> something about her husband.

The fact for which she has not searched
jerks itself into the light
like a child from a closet.

(***Beauty*** 98)

By a kind of portentous happenstance, recollection of a passage from the sibling-tender correspondence between Celan and Sachs precedes—induces?—an insight into the protagonist's failed marriage. The figurative "light" in an Athens hotel room is also *das perlende Licht* of death in Celan's eyes. (He indeed would drown himself in the Seine in 1970, less than a month before Sachs's own death in Stockholm from cancer.)

Carson can however praise in Celan powers which, in her own poetry, come under scrutiny. "*Sprich—/ Doch scheide das Nein nicht vom Ja*" ("Speak—/ But split the No not from Yes," as she translates it), Celan writes in "*Sprich Auch Du*" ("Speak You Too") (1: 135). Of the line Carson notes, "yet the German word order does split *das Nein* from *Ja* by the negative adverb *nicht*. In between No and Yes Celan places the poet's power to cancel their difference, his licence to double the negative of death" (*Economy* 109). The catechistic ending of *Economy of the Unlost* suggests compliance with Celan's imperative: "Is stammering a waste of words? Yes and No" (134). Yet, when the unfaithful husband returns with tea to the Athens hotel room in ***The Beauty of the Husband,*** and his wife confronts him with the truth mysteriously linked to Nelly Sachs's poem to Celan, this capacity proves a bedevilment. The wife's accusations can be parried easily because "he was holding Yes and No together with one hand" (***Beauty*** 100). The ability to align affirmation and negation grants a terrible immunity to the mercurial husband. Celan's imperative can thus be exploited meanly, to deflect calls to account.

The cycle of epitaphic verses in ***Men in the Off Hours*** are particularly Celanesque. Terse, brittle and oracular, they measure frail human possibilities against the annihilating prodigies of superhuman and subhuman force. "Epitaph: Annunciation" reads:

Motion swept the world aside, aghast to white nerve
nets.
    Pray what
Shall I do with my six hundred wings? As a blush
feels
    Slow, from inside.

(***Men*** 14)

The world reduced and vulnerable, the objects in it precisely denoted yet enigmatic, occasionally being specifically yet perplexingly numbered: all this is characteristic of Celan.[5] And the body utterly exposed, whittled away:

Hohles Lebensgehöft. Im Windfang
die Leer-

geblasene Lunge
blüht. Eine Handvoll
Schlafkorn
weht aus dem wahr-
gestammelten Mund
hinaus zu den Schnee-
gesprächen.

(2:42)

[Hollow life's-farmstead. In the draught-screen / the empty- / blown lung / blossoms. A handful of / sleep-grain / wafts from the true- / stammered mouth / to the snow- / conversations.]

A wind that germinates as it denudes, a body that signals truths through—and by means of—its decay: these are redemptive paradoxes dear to Carson. The "six hundred wings" constitutes a curiously baffled whole celestial hierarchy of powers, or an outrageous proliferation of Rilke's angelic orders in the *Duino Elegies*. Rather than complementing the claim made in the first phrase, each of the subsequent three phrases confounds its sense, the confusion operating as well at the level of grammar. Within a more conventional syntax Celan's compounds accumulate a similar pressure on sense. Something, however briefly, is nevertheless being retrieved from oblivion and rehabilitated, its validity suggested by the very instability and disorder of its expression.

At the end of **"The Glass Essay"** the poet, abruptly and inexplicably reconciled to the loss of love, approaches in a vision what appears to be a Yeatsian figure of decline, a tattered coat upon a stick:

It could have been just a pole with some old cloth at-
    tached,
but as I came closer
I saw it was a human body

trying to stand against winds so terrible that the flesh
    was blowing off the bones.
And there was no pain.
The wind

was cleansing the bones.
They stood forth silver and necessary.

(***Glass*** 38)

Here is a hollow life's farmstead where, as in Celan, germination defies the void, and inarticulate sounds make valid speech. The sterilizing blast inadvertently disperses the seed in Celan, and it purifies in Carson.

As in Celan, the wind is a devastation in Carson's **"Epitaph: Zion,"** which recounts an even more costly deliverance:

Murderous little world once our objects had gazes.
    Our lives
        were fragile, the wind

could dash them away. Here lies the refugee breather who drank a bowl of elsewhere.

(Men 9)

That refugee from annihilating violence could be Celan himself, a survivor who in exile remained fragile, and who tasted "elsewhere" both as an ideal (Zion) and a dislocation (Austria and France).

In *Economy of the Unlost* Carson asserts that, from Simonides to Celan, epitaphs provide, even while restricted to mere inscription, a mode of redemption:

> Salvation occurs, through the act of attention that forms stone into memory, leaving a residue of greater life. I am speaking subjectively. There is no evidence of salvation except in a cold trace in the mind. But this trace convinces me that the beautiful economic motions of Simonides' epitaphic verse capture something essential to human language, to the give and take of being, to what saves us.
>
> (95)

Carson proposes that, though the poet composed only one explicit epitaph ("*Grabschrift für François*" ["Epitaph for François"], for his infant), the spirit of Celan's verse is epitaphic. An epitaph is a speaking stone, is the dead speaking or addressed, thus a mode of encounter. She invokes "*Grabschrift*" as evidence that the poet "does seem at times to have entertained the notion that the dead can save the living" (95).

Carson is responsive to Celan's curiously devout lack of faith. She is a secular poet preoccupied with belief—indeed, as the quotation above suggests, with soteriology. Though her opera libretto *Decreation* may echo the works Gertrude Stein wrote for Virgil Thompson, the subject is the Christian mystic Simone Weil. (The unpublished recent lecture "Decreation" focusses on Weil and other female apophatic mystics, including Marguerite Porete.) To Mary di Michele Carson claimed that "a fundamental motive of thinking and making stuff [. . .] is worship. That is, apprehension of some larger-than-oneself thing. And that is what is missing from a great deal of modern thought" (di Michele 9). She cites Celan as an exception.

Exasperated worship characterizes Celan's relations with God, and some of Carson's finest poems, such as **"The Book of Isaiah,"** describe just such a state. Her emphasis however frequently falls on the verbal formulas and the gendered constructions of faith, while the tone is often comic and acerbic. Celan's encounters with the émigré German Jewish poet Nelly Sachs, who remained devout, suggest how a poetics of *Begegnung* could allow him to enter into states alien to him. After a six-year correspondence they first met on Ascension Day 1960, near the Zürich Minster, the talk turning naturally enough to theology. Celan's notes record the

conversation: "*4h Nelly Sachs, allein. 'Ich bin ja gläubig.' Als ich darauf sage, ich hoffte, bis zuletzt lästern zu können: Man weiß ja nicht, was gilt*" ["4 o'clock, Nelly Sachs, alone. 'I am indeed a believer.' When I replied that I hoped to be able to blaspheme to the very end: One just doesn't know what counts"] (*Briefwechsel* 41). Three days later Celan wrote "*Zürich, Zum Storchen*," based on their exchange. The poem begins by invoking the multiplicity of identities convoked in the second-person singular pronoun: "*Vom Zuviel war die Rede, vom / Zuwenig. Von Du / und Aber-Du*," where the hyphenated pronoun can mean "Again-You," "Yet-You," or literally "But-You: "The talk was of Too Much, of / Too Little. Of You / and Yet-You" (214).

> *Von deinem Gott war die Rede, ich sprach*
> *gegen ihn, ich*
> *ließ das Herz, das ich hatte,*
> *hoffen:*
> *auf*
> *sein höchstes, umröcheltes, sein*
> *haderndes Wort—*
>
> (1: 214)

[The talk was of your God, I spoke / against him, I / let the heart that I had / hope: / for / his highest, rattling, his / quarrelling word—]

The interlocutor replies, "*Wir / wissen ja nicht, weißt du, / wir / wissen ja nicht, was gilt*" [we / just don't know, you know, / we just don't know, what counts] (214-15). The *Du* and *Aber-Du* converge in the knowing ignorance of the plural personal pronoun. For emphasis Celan isolates the pronoun on its own lines. What "we" know, in this variation on the Delphic wisdom of Socrates, is that we do not know—and as in Plato's Socratic dialogues this is knowledge of a high order. Between manuscript draft (see facsimile, *Briefwechsel* 43) and publication three years later in *Die Niemandsrose*, Celan had removed the quotation marks initially placed around the Sachsian interlocutor's reply, thereby reinforcing further the pronominal fusion and the validity of its utterance. Indeed the speaker has entered into a relation of witness with his interlocutor. Doubt of God becomes doubt of one's own capacity to judge of such a matter, as expressed in a strategy of verbal convergence.

Even Celan's most nihilistic poems tend to hypostatize the void. The very gap left by God's disappearance is made to assume deific agency. From its Biblical title on, "Psalm" proclaims this paradoxical mode of metaphysical renewal:

> *Niemand knetet uns wieder aus Erde und Lehm,*
> *niemand bespricht unsern Staub.*
> *Niemand.*
>
> *Gelobt seist du, Niemand.*
> *Dir zulieb wollen*

wir blühn.
Dir entgegen.
Ein Nichts
waren wir, sind wir, werden
wir bleiben, blühend:
di Nichts-, die
Niemandsrose.

(Celan 2: 225)

[No one kneads us again from earth and clay, / no one conjures our dust. / No one. // Praised be you, No one. / For your sake we want / to bloom. / Towards / you. // A nothing / we were, are we, will / we remain, blooming: / the Nothing-, the / No one's rose.]

Solemnly cadenced, its very occasion the paradox of apophatic belief, "Psalm" finds its metaphysical compensations in their absence. In **"God's Beloveds Remain True,"** a section of "The Truth about God," Carson catalogues the outrages perpetrated on human beings as though—but only as though—they coincided with divine providence:

Our hope is a noose.
We take our flesh in our teeth.
The autumn blows us as chaff across the fields.
We are sifted and fall.
We are hung in a void.
We are shattered on the ocean.
We are smeared on the darkness.
We are slit and drained out.
Little things drink us.
We lie unburied.
We are dust.
We know nothing.
We can not answer.
We will speak no more.
BUT WE WILL NOT STOP.
For we are the beloveds.
We have been instructed to call this His love.

(**Glass** 47)

Here is another Niemandsrose or No one's rose, whose abjection is not the result of an absolute desolation. No more than Celan's is Carson's the Darwinian abyss of mere chance. Celan's Griffel is not only a "pistil" but also a "stylus" or "slate pencil," which inscribes the text ("purple-word") of a song chanted, psalm-like, beyond the ravages of unredeemed nature. The densely figurative language of "Psalm" and **"God's Beloveds Remain True"** acts as a credential, signalling specifically human resources to which the poets defiantly, on behalf of us all, "remain true." Our "dust" in Carson is no more conjured than Celan's "Staub"; we know in Carson no more than we do in "Zürich, Zum Storchen," but as in Celan negations culminate in concealed affirmations: "WE WILL NOT STOP."[6]

Where Celan's slippery levels of irony, however, are metaphysical (rooted in negative theology), Carson's are primarily historical. Stress falls not on the inimical effects of nature or on doctrines of deliverance from it, but on the historical conviction that such a deliverance exists. "We are the beloveds," "instructed" to understand even our despair as evidence of divine favour. This instruction of course derives from the Book of Job and Rabbinical and Patristic exegesis (most influentially Origen's) of the Song of Songs, by which the "beloved" Shulamite is by turns identified allegorically with Israel, the Church, and the soul in union with God. Celan repeatedly evokes the same Biblical texts and exegetical tradition.[7] Carson however emphasizes the gendered binaries of Judeo-Christian doctrine (see such other sections of the poem as "God's Woman" and "God's Stiff," which immediately precede this one), thereby undermining its validity in historical terms. That "we have been instructed to call this His love" is a sardonic incongruity. Human perseverance begins to seem a Beckettian endgame rather than a desert exodus to some redeeming Canaan. "Psalm" consequently reads both as more astringent and more consolatory than **"The Truth about God."** "We sang" and, in the reading, are singing still some primary psalm of praise. In Carson, we are, on the other hand, passive and very possibly hoodwinked pupils of the agents of an apathic deity. This she presents not as a transcendent destiny but as a curious historical imperative. Her poems often ask why we construct and maintain, despite their futility, narratives of this kind. Her series of "TV Men" poems explore, for instance, the role of mass media in reinforcing the passivity and ignorance that help to perpetuate such narratives. Her poems express an aghast fascination with pain and with the metaphysical rationalizations of its causes.

A later section of **"The Truth about God,"** "God's Christ Theory," is characteristic in deflating its own tentative metaphysical assertions by showing their conflict with history. The poem reads as an urbane and canny response to one of Celan's best-known poems, "Tenebrae":

God had no emotions but wished temporarily
to move in man's mind
as if He did: Christ.

(**Glass** 51)

Celan's poem concerns the limitations inherent in the scheme Carson describes, for what can a deathless, apathic deity truly know of human suffering ($\pi\acute{\alpha}\theta o\varsigma$, passion) or of death (the Passion)?

Not passion but compassion.

Com—means "with."
What kind of withness would that be?

(**Glass** 51)

Unlike her phrasing of this question in the preface to Economy of the Unlost, here the question is dubious, indeed facetious: God cannot "feel with" (exhibit compassion toward) his mortal surrogate.

As God translates himself into Jesus, and *com* translates into "with," so the poem translates the "theory" of "God's Christ Theory" into its application, Jesus becoming now an all-too-human friend:

> Translate it.
> I have a friend named Jesus
> from Mexico.
>
> His father and grandfather are called Jesus too.
> They account me a fool with my questions about
>   salvation.
> They say they are saving to move to Los Angeles.
>
> (***Glass*** 51)

The poet's friend in Jesus is not some Baptist projection of a personal saviour but an economic migrant whose notion of salvation is deflatingly secularized, his New Jerusalem contracted into Los Angeles. Jesus is a mere moniker, a mobile token of merely vestigial religious implication, like the name "city of angels" itself. One saves not oneself but one's money. The poem thus mocks the theological and etymological concerns of its opening stanzas. For a modernist poet these men would be passive participants in a social order intent on their physical, moral and spiritual displacement in order to advance the mercantile and imperialistic aims of an urban, secular, international elite. Carson invites a different response by dramatizing a dialectic in which the poet's judgment enjoys no priority. The local and contemporary challenge and even overturn speculation. Carson yields to the authority of history. By contrast, in Celan—and this signals his continuity with German modernism—history ultimately furnishes temporal indices of metaphysical facts.

His "*Tenebrae*" shows this:

> *Windshief gingen wir hin,*
> *gingen wir hin, uns zu bücken*
> *nach Mulde und Maar.*
>
> *Zur Tränke gingen wir, Herr.*
>
> *Es war Blut, es war,*
> *was du vergossen, Herr.*
>
> *Es glänzte.*
>
> *Es warf uns dein Bild in die Augen, Herr.*
> *Augen und Mund stehn so offen und leer, Herr.*
>
> *Wir haben getrunken, Herr.*
> *Das Blut und das Bild, das im Blut war, Herr.*
>
> *Bete, Herr.*
> *Wir sind nah.*
>
> (1: 163)

[Askew we went forth, / we went forth, to bend ourselves / toward hollow and ditch. // To the watering-place we went, Lord. // It was blood, it was, / what you shed, Lord. // It gleamed. // It cast your image into our eyes, Lord. / Eyes and mouth stand so open and empty, Lord. // We have drunk, Lord. / The blood and the image that was in the blood, Lord. // Pray, Lord. / We are near.]

Hans-Georg Gadamer argues that even so scabrously irreverent a poem, in which death establishes our unity with Jesus at the expense of any faith in transcendence, ultimately reaffirms Christian teaching: "By taking seriously and accepting it as the destiny of human beings beyond all hope and comfort, the poem approaches the ultimate intention of the Christian doctrine of the incarnation" (176). From its inversion of Friedrich Hölderlin's "Patmos" ("*Nah is, und schwer zu fassen, der Gott*": "Near is, and hard to grasp, the Lord" [Hölderlin 177]), to its faith not in the Resurrection but in commonality in suffering, "*Tenebrae*" is anything but a novel restatement of Christian doctrine. For Gadamer, who does not consider the poet's relation to the Crucifixion in terms of his Judaism, "it is precisely this martyrdom upon which our unity with him [the Lord] and our closeness to him rests" (195). For Celan, however, the basis of any such unity would be the Lord's forsaken state, from which human witnesses alone could rescue him.

"*Tenebrae*" hovers between blasphemy and compassion, whereby the poet may share in the Crucifixion as one mortal witnessing the final suffering of another. The "withness" that puzzles Carson and provokes her wry scepticism is in "*Tenebrae*" transferred from God to the Creation: We are with the Lord, rather than God being with us. Shared destitution is the basis of a new covenant between crucified and witnesses, one which excludes God. By drinking from this blood sacrifice we acquire the sanction to receive, rather than to utter, a very different Lord's prayer. Here is the prayer of a nonpractising Jew (whose wife was the daughter of a pious Catholic, aristocratic French family), recovering from the crucified Jew a mode of reverence at odds both with Judaism (as in the defiance of the kosher law against ingesting blood) and with Christian teaching.

In Carson and Celan God is chillingly remote and unappeasable, yet fulfilment of divine providence depends on human intercession.[8] Such intercession must however not be confused with union. Celan's religious poetry is in the tradition of the lyric petition, of private prayer made public, inaugurated by the Psalms. They are intimate, searching, helpless. Carson by contrast is often cheeky and self-disparaging. **"My Religion"** announces "My religion makes no sense / and does not help me / therefore I pursue it" (***Glass*** 39). This non sequitur is a comic variation on a Kierkegaardian paradox. She then speculates that, for all our blind contortions of piety,

God may simply have wanted "some simple thing" that struggles in vain to communicate itself. In an echo of Donne's sonnet "Batter My Heart," Carson feels the thought of this simple thing "battering" against the walls of our unnecessarily complex conceptions of the divine: "It batters my soul / with its rifle butt" (40). The agent of violence is not God but an intellectual image of thwarted divine yearning.

Carson's **"The Book of Isaiah"** again presents God as deficient, because yearning, who finds completion only in human acquiescence to his (compromised) power. The poem includes other Celanesque elements, from the neologism "worldsheet" ("Inside Isaiah God saw the worldsheet burning" [*Glass* 107]), to a phrase reworked from the "*Grabschrift für François*"; when Isaiah refuses to praise God, God responds by projecting before him a vision of global conflagration: "All the windows of the world stood open and burning" (114). The image opens Celan's epitaph on the death of his infant son, quoted in full in *Economy of the Unlost*: "*Die beiden Türen der Welt / stehen offen*" (1: 105). Carson translates the phrase as "The two doors of the world / stand open" (*Economy* 86). Whereas Celan describes the doors of birth into, and death out of, the house of life, Carson describes windows onto unredeemed human suffering. The conflagration is part of God's tactic to tempt Isaiah with the role of deliverer: "I tell you Isaiah you can save the nation" (*Glass* 115). While he hesitates Isaiah has another, more immediate vision, of God's curious susceptibility:

> The wind was rising, God was shouting.
> You can strip it down, start over at the wires, use
>   lions! use thunder! use what you see—
> Isaiah was watching sweat and tears run down God's
>   face.
>
> (115)

The fire projected and the effort exerted to win his prophet's submission exact a toll on God's all-too-human body. Not only Adam must sustain himself by the sweat of his brow; not only the angel who appeared before Jacob must wrestle with a mortal. Divine lack however does not imply divine impotence, and God retains in Carson as in Celan a terrible (because confused) elemental power. This violence secures a harsh covenant:

> Okay, said Isaiah, so I save the nation. What do you
>   do?
> God exhaled roughly.
> I save the fire, said God.
> Thus their contract continued.
>
> (115)

Carson's are not the plagiarisms of an unscrupulous admirer or mere borrowings for effect but encounters, efforts to overcome the formidable hindrances to passage through an alien yet exemplary body of work. Carson has, like any poet who admires his work, heard herself addressed in Celan's "*Du*," and she has answered, indeed as had Sachs, with poetic messages placed in the very bottles in which she received his. This encounter is for Carson as close an approach to "withness" as a poet may achieve: a humble and compassionate proximity, free of paternalistic anxieties regarding precedence or derivation, and inseparable finally from a higher devotion. Here is an approach toward, an engagement with, a reply to and an accompanying of Celan, rather than a plundering.

Does Carson take from Celan?

Yes and No.

Notes

1. "Yes, the estrangement, the discomfiting of the reader, has some deep purpose I'm not quite aware of. It comes and goes in my writing; it comes and goes as an emotion," Carson states in an interview, suggesting that her intentions resemble those of Gertrude Stein: "to defamiliarize and therefore cause a friction of mind and spirit in the taking up of the page into the reader's mind" (Irvine 82-83). In a later interview she says, à propos the title *Men in the Off Hours*, "If you can get your mind at an angle—you'll notice this in teaching, that when students are suddenly a little displaced from what they thought they thought, they begin to actually think. But that angle is hard to get to" (Deslauriers and Cantwell 5).

2. "Some difference" quotes her translation of the phrase μεταβουλία δέ τις φανείν Ζεῦ πάτερ, ἐκ σεο ("may some change of mind appear from you, father Zeus") from Simonides' Danaë fragment.

3. The italicized first person singular pronoun translates Celan's capitalization of it.

4. "*Sharben*," or "shards," is how Celan characterizes mankind in "*Vor Mein*"—"Before My" (*Gesammelte* 81).

5. See for example "*Einmal*" and "*In den Flüßen nördlich der Zukunft*" ("Once" and "In the rivers north of the future") (1: 107 and 14).

6. "The interesting thing about a negative, then," Carson writes in *Economy of the Unlost*, "is that it posits a fuller picture of reality than does a positive statement" (102).

7. The iconography of The Song of Songs, where roses and thorns proliferate, is unmistakable in "*Psalm*": e.g., "I am the rose of Sharon, and the lily of the valley. As the lily among thorns, so is

my love among the daughters" (2: 1-2). This underscores the poem's oblique fidelity to Judaism. *"Todesfuge"* ("Death-Fugue") meanwhile alludes directly to the Biblical book: *"Dein aschenes Haar Schulamith"*—"your ashen hair Shulamite" (1: 41).

8. Among Celan's modern precursors this notion is elaborated upon in Rilke's prose cycle *Geschichten vom lieben Gott,* but it can be traced at least as far back as Angelus Silenius (Johannes Scheffler) in, for example, the couplet *"Gott lebt nicht ohne mich"* ("God does not live without me").

Works Cited

Carson, Anne. *The Beauty of the Husband.* New York: Knopf, 2001.

———. *Economy of the Unlost.* Princeton, N.J.: Princeton UP, 1999.

———. *Glass, Irony, and God.* New York: New Directions, 1995.

———. *Men in the Off Hours.* New York: Knopf, 2000.

———. *Plainwater.* New York: Knopf, 1995.

Celan, Paul. *Der Meridian und andere Prosa.* Frankfurt am Main: Suhrkamp Verlag, 1983.

———. *Gedichte* I. Frankfurt am Main: Suhrkamp Verlag, 1975.

———. *Gedichte* II. Frankfurt am Main: Suhrkamp Verlag, 1975.

———. *Gesammelte Werke.* Vol. 3. Frankfurt am Main: Suhrkamp Verlag, 1986.

Celan, Paul and Nelly Sachs. *Briefwechsel.* Ed. Barbara Wiedeman. Frankfurt am Main: Suhrkamp, 1993.

D'Agata, John. "A Talk with Anne Carson." *Brick* 12:3 (1996): 14-22.

Deslauriers, Marguerite and Michael Cantwell. "A Conversation with Anne Carson." *McGill in Focus* (Spring 2001): 3-5.

di Michele, Mary. "Interview with Anne Carson." *The Matrix Interviews.* Montreal: DC Books, 2001: 7-12.

Felstiner, John. *Paul Celan: Poet, Survivor, Jew.* New Haven: Yale UP, 1995.

Gadamer, Hans-Georg. *Gadamer on Celan.* Ed. and trans. Richard Heinemann and Bruce Krajewski. Albany: State U of New York P, 1997.

Hölderlin, Friedrich. *Werke, Briefe, Dokumente.* Ed. Friedrich Beißner. München: Winkler Verlag, 1963.

Irvine, Dean. "Dialogue without Sokrates: An Interview with Anne Carson." *Scrivener* 21 (1997): 80-87.

Solway, David. "The Trouble with Annie." *Books in Canada* 30.1 (July 2001): 24-6.

Monique Tschofen (essay date spring 2004)

SOURCE: Tschofen, Monique. "'First I Must Tell about Seeing': (De)monstrations of Visuality and the Dynamics of Metaphor in Anne Carson's *Autobiography of Red." Canadian Literature/Littérature canadienne,* no. 180 (spring 2004): 31-50.

[*In the following essay, Tschofen examines Carson's use of metaphor and layers of meaning in* Autobiography of Red *and investigates the mythological, historical, and literary backgrounds of Carson's characters.*]

> It is in fact upon the world of things needing to be uncovered that the world of merely visible things keeps exerting its pressure.
>
> (Simonides fr. 598, trans. Carson, *Economy* 60)

1. A METAPHOR OF METAPHOR

Anne Carson excavates and resurrects Geryon, the red monster with wings, in her "novel in verse," ***Autobiography of Red.*** Her portrait of a monster who makes photographic portraits offers a dense meditation on two related terms—vision and revision—that are key to Carson's implicit, yet consistent theorization of the relationships between language and images.

Carson claims she was a painter before she was a creative writer. Recalling the "rhapsodic" moment in an art class that she took as a child in which she was allowed to write a "kind of legend" on one of her images, she has explained that her first book of poetry, ***Short Talks,*** was originally intended to be a set of drawings with lengthy titles: "Nobody liked the drawings so I expanded the titles into the talks" (Interview). Despite the fact that her movement into poetry appears to have been initiated by the erasure of her work as a visual artist, traces of her interest in art appear throughout her writings. To read the body of her work is to be immersed in an exquisite frenzy of the visible in which inscription, painting, photography, film, and television collide in one textual space. Yet it would be a mistake to think that Carson's engagement with the visual reflects her simple assent to a notion with some currency in contemporary cultural studies, namely that cultural history has led to a dominance of visual media over verbal activities of speech, writing, textuality, and reading, and that this dominance comes at the expense of other sensory modalities (Mitchell, *Picture* 16). Reviving such "tactics of imagination" (*Eros* 69) as monstrous structures and language while she bounces between antiquity and the contemporary moment, in *Autobiography* Carson pictures a monster's pictures in order to lead us away from the world of merely visible things and into "the counterworld behind the facts and inside perceived appearances" (*Economy* 60). It would also be a mistake to confuse Carson's interest in the visual with the disengaged, disembodied vision Norman Bryson associates with the aoristic mode that has dominated Western painting and philosophy. Carson's archaeological excavation and resurrection of the monster Geryon recovers a subordinate history of deictic practices within philosophy and art from antiquity to the present day, which "create and refer to their own perspective" (Bryson 88). In this revisionary "counterworld," signification is playfully carnal. Fascinated with their own genesis and development, the alternative forms of cultural practice Carson uncovers inscribe the spatiality and the temporality of both the producer and the receiver. So, although it might look like Carson sets her sights on the graphic, especially the photographic and cinematographic, her focus is wider, on "the act that Simonides calls λὸγος [*logos*] and defines as 'a picture of things' for it contains visibles and invisibles side by side, strangeness by strangeness" (Carson, *Economy* 68).

At the heart of Carson's investigation into *logos* lies metaphor, one of the chief "subterfuges" by which the visual domain may be introduced into the verbal arts (Bal 3). As Umberto Eco puts it, metaphor conflates two images: two things become different from themselves and yet remain recognizable (96). Metaphor is not merely ornamental. It is also a cognitive instrument:

> And thus the metaphor posits ('posits' in a philosophical sense, but also in a physical sense, as 'in *putting before the eyes*,' το ηρὸ ὀμμάτωνηοιεῖν a proportion that, wherever it may have been deposited, was not before the eyes; or it was before the eyes and the eyes did not see it, as with Poe's purloined letter. To point out, or teach how to see, then.
>
> (102)

What does metaphor point out or teach us how to see? asks Eco. Not the real itself, but rather a knowledge of the "dynamics of the real" (102). The best metaphors, he suggests, are those that point out the cultural process of semiosis (102).

Carson's red-winged photographer is one of these best metaphors. As a figure uniting strangeness with strangeness, her monster is an icon of the things that lie just beyond our physical vision (past the edge of our maps, on the other side of our waking state). Her monster is also a symbolic tool by which she probes the secrets of perception, temporality, and language. Because Carson's monster refers to nothing phenomenally real,

because he is a purely figurative sign, he can be understood as a metaphor of metaphor itself (Williams 12). That Carson develops the metaphor of the monster as a metaphor of metaphor in order to demonstrate language's power of "making and begetting" is no small thing, since, as the philosophers have long insisted, "metaphor seems to involve the usage of philosophical language in its entirety" (Derrida, "White" 209).

Carson has written extensively about the workings of metaphor. Before focusing on the way her metaphor of monstrosity is both visionary and revisionary, it is useful to turn to one of her poems, **"Essay on What I Think About Most,"** where she claims that "From the true mistakes of metaphor a lesson can be learned. // Not only that things are other than they seem, / and so we mistake them, / but that such mistakenness is valuable. / Hold onto it, Aristotle says, / there is much to be seen and felt here" (**Men** 31). Referring to Aristotle's discussion of metaphor in the *Rhetoric*, Carson argues that the trope demonstrates novel and valuable ways of feeling as well as of seeing. Her injunction via Aristotle to "hold" onto mistakenness and "feel" it is made possible because of the operations of metaphor, of course, but what is important about this particular metaphor is its emphasis on the sensory. As she sheds light on both the participatory and embodied dimensions of our thinking made possible by metaphor, Carson issues a challenge to the difficult legacy of Cartesian dualism.

2. MONSTROUS GENRES

Technically, ***Autobiography of Red*** is not an autobiography, nor really, as the subtitle suggests, is it "A Novel in Verse." Working with the fragments of a lyric poem about the monster Geryon from the sixth century B.C.E. poet Stesichoros of Himnera called the *Geryoneis,* Carson locates the work in a larger literary history and explicates its importance, translates it into English, and finally adapts its core elements to create an extended novelistic narrative. The central portions of the ***Autobiography,*** then, take the form of a *Künstlerroman,* but one that doubles an earlier telling of the same "cross section of scenes, both proud and pitiful" (6) of a monster struggling with human things like family and fate. To this mirrored image of mythic narrative materials, Carson adds a framing apparatus of prefaces and appendices that, through citation, also repeat earlier commentary on the Geryon matter (6). Generically, the text refuses to blend its constituent parts. Juxtaposing the scholarly and the lyrical, the narrative and the journalistic, this is a hybrid text, what Judith Halberstam describes as a "stitched body of distorted textuality" (33).

That Carson refuses to blend the different genres into a more coherent structure recalls a debate in classical aesthetics in which the ideal text was figured through a visual metaphor as a healthy, intact, symmetrical, beautiful, static body, while writing that failed to live up to the ideal was figured as a monstrous body. Writers like Longinus and Horace imply that there is something devastatingly counterproductive, even self-annihilating, about a text that, "like a sick man's dreams," risks monstrous combinations (Horace 128). When contemporary reviewers have on occasion complained that Carson's combinations of the poetic with the scholarly are "unproductive" and give it a "stale air of pedantry and puzzle" (Kirsch), they seem to be blind to the fact that Carson's mission in this text—to resurrect *a monster* and demonstrate the powers of revision—hinges on her deliberate mating of disparate things. Form, content, and purpose could not be less at odds than they are here.

3. Revisioning Geryon

Just as **Autobiography of Red** is an assemblage of disparate genres, Carson's monster Geryon is a composite pieced together from fragments which originate elsewhere. To understand what Geryon demonstrates in Carson's work, it is important to trace the origins and history of the various elements which combine to form him.

Though Carson never mentions this incarnation of Geryon explicitly, it is not difficult to uncover the fact that Geryon was a significant, though marginal, figure in Canto XVII (the half-way point) of Dante's *Inferno*. Many of Carson's interests in the relationship between vision and visuality and poetic language reflect and refract Dante's. Described as a vile monster whose stench fills the world, Dante's Geryon carries Virgil and Dante on his back down to Malebolge, the eighth level of hell where the sin of Fraud is punished. Dante's Geryon is depicted as a figure of duplicity, "fraud's foul emblem" ("*imagine di froda*") (XVII 6). His sight fills the poet with terror but also with a sense of liberation, because, as the vehicle permitting the continuation of the poet's journey, the monster represents the very instruments of deceitfulness and lying that the poet must use. When Dante recounts that Geryon's back and breasts and both sides are "painted with designs of knots and circles" more coloured in field and figure than any cloth ever woven by a Tartar or Turk or the nets loomed by Arachne (XVII 13-15), it is clear that the monster is to be perceived as an emblem of an aesthetic fraud, an "image" (*imagine*) of the kind of lying performed by the pictorial art of poetry (XVII 6). Compared to a boat, a beaver, an eel, a falcon, and an arrow, Dante's Geryon is connected with motion, and this too allies him with the poet's tools. Du Marsais's definition of metaphor (which is indebted to Aristotle's definition) as "a figure by means of which the proper, literal meaning of a word is transported" facilitates an understanding of the analogy between monster and metaphor conveyed

with Geryon's flight (Derrida, "White" 234). A consideration of Geryon's mobility—his ability to "transport," both literally and figuratively—leads to a consideration of another kind of mobility in Dante's text that is important to Carson: the mobility of the gaze of the viewer. In his depiction of Geryon, Dante makes a distinction between appearances and essences, between parts and wholes. His Geryon is an "image" of fraud, but in this image, appended to the trunk of a serpent and the paws of an animal, is the face of a just man, outwardly kind ("*La faccia sua era faccia d'uom giusto, / tanto benigna avea di fuor la pelle*") (XVII 10-11). In order not to be deceived by the contradictory parts of the image, the beholder (the poet and also the reader) of such a hybrid composite must learn a way of seeing that is mobile enough to apprehend the whole, and powerful enough to penetrate the surface. Like Dante, Carson is interested in the ethics and aesthetics of fraud, and so when she transports Dante's Geryon into contemporary narrative, the monster also brings with him Dante's concerns about the poetic lie that can transport us, and about ways of seeing that can carry us past the surface of appearances.

Carson's Geryon initially knows nothing about lies, but notices quickly that words dissemble and dis-assemble: divorced from their literal meanings, words keep coming apart or cracking in half (26, 62). Herakles' rhetoric is particularly treacherous for Geryon. His promises are slippery, moving for instance from statements about intimacy—"we'll always be friends" (62)—to distancing—"we're true friends you know that's why I want you to be free" (74). Geryon begins his autobiography trying to put together the pieces of this fractured world of language, first with glue (34), then by adding a corrective in the form of a happier ending to a story he has written (38), but he soon abandons these palliative measures and makes the very paradox of the power and fragility of language the subject of his photographs.

If Geryon's connection to Dante's monster foregrounds a theory of poetic lying, Carson further develops this theory in the highly convoluted syllogistic exercise she offers as "Appendix C" to the main body of the narrative of **Autobiography.** Here she suggests that as an integral part of stories, lies set things into motion. (Elsewhere, Carson suggests that lies make possible the continuation of story: "everytime you see I would have to tell the whole story all over again or else lie so I lie I just lie who are they who are the storytellers who can put an end to stories" [**Plainwater** 25-26].) Trespassing the boundaries between reality and the imagination (something monsters in stories also do), lies operate logical reversals, and in each reversal is the possibility of a return. The imagery Carson develops around her discourse on lies is dynamics: we are "in reverse"; we will "go along without incident"; we will "meet Stesichoros on our way back"; we will "be taken downtown by the police for questioning" (*Autobiography* 19-20). Her argument, if one can be stitched together, is that while we are thus transported by the lie (or by its kin, metaphor), we can either be eyewitnesses to a landscape that, because of the lie, looks inside out, or we can be blinded. In effect, both of these propositions mean the same thing: we learn to see in ways that exceed the merely visible world (19-20). The monster Geryon thus offers Carson a point of entry into an argument about the ethical, cognitive, and perceptual possibilities unleashed by language.

The scene in Dante's *Inferno* in which the monster Geryon appears is one of the text's most dramatic because of the sense of narrative visualization enabled by Geryon's flight. Robert Hollander remarks on the cinematic quality of Dante's prose in Canto XVII, all the more notable since it would be several centuries before the technologies of the cinema would be invented:

> In his innovative description of flight, Dante offers a cinematic succession of images designed to establish a "perspective vision" for the architectural complex of the eighth circle where, as we shall see, the variation in Dante's original topography with its "pouches," "ridges" and "bridges" requires—in modern terms—a clarity and precision of camera angles, depth of field, lighting and dimension. From Dante's timid aerial look down from Geryon's back into the pit below to numerous and even risky positionings on the little bridges to catch sight of a particular sinner, the narrator becomes even more insistent in his techniques of the "zoom to close-up," . . . the "wide pan" . . . and the "aerial shot" . . . making the reader at times even conscious of the "stage directions" of this visualization.

In Carson's hands, this proto-cinematic inheritance of "perspective vision" makes its appearance in her translation of Stesichoros's fragments which offers, as she puts it,

> a tantalizing cross section of scenes, both proud and pitiful, from Geryon's own experience. We see his red boy's life and his little dog. A scene of wild appeal from his mother, which breaks off. Interspersed shots of Herakles approaching over the sea. A flash of the gods in heaven pointing to Geryon's doom. The battle itself. The moment when everything goes suddenly slow and Herakles' arrow divides Geryon's skull. We see Herakles kill the little dog with His famous club.
>
> (*Autobiography* 6)

Observe the language demarcating scenes, fade outs, zooms, crane shots, and slow motion. Carson sees in Stesichoros's fragments, just as she also sees in Dante's scene of flight, a juxtaposition of different points of view in quick succession. She further develops this inheritance of (proto-)cinematic strategies with the disjunctions and collisions (Sergei Eisenstein would say "conflicts") that generate the motion of *Autobiography.*

Zooming in on emotionally laden moments, as well as slowing down the motion and jumping between scenes, Carson's montage techniques celebrate all forms of juxtaposition. She sets up conflicts between genres such as between the narrative and the appendices; between events and their duration (Eisenstein 39), such as when Geryon contemplates the ascent of the rapist up the stairs as slow as lava (Carson 48); between matter and viewpoint (Eisenstein 54), such as when Geryon's contemplation of philosophic problems leads him to write, "I will never know how you see red and you will never know how I see it" (Carson 105); and between the frame of the shot and the subject (Eisenstein 40), such as when Geryon takes "a number / of careful photographs but these showed only the shoes and socks of each person" (72). Carson's insight is to construct a genealogy of the origins of a way of thinking in two separate time frames at once, modern and ancient. Cinematic montage sets two images side by side so that the things become different from themselves and yet remain recognizable. So too does metaphor. Through Dante, then, Carson's monster Geryon puts before our eyes the history of the apparatus (that is, the mental machinery) of a visual language upon which both literary and cinematic practices rely.

Dante, however, is not the only poet to write about Geryon, the monster with wings. Carson is explicit about the more ancient sources she and Dante draw upon. In traditional Greek mythology, Geryon, "most powerful of all men mortal," is a minor character who figures in Herakles' tenth labour. As traditionally narrated in such texts as Apollodorus's *The Library* (2.10), Hesiod's *Theogony* (979-83), and Pausanias's *Description of Greece* (1.35.7 and 4.36.3), the story is full of slaughter and bloodshed, "framed as a thrilling account of the victory of culture over monstrosity" (Carson 6). As an alternative to this rather excessive story of masculine power, Carson resurrects the version told in the fragments of Stesichoros's lyric *Geryoneis*. According to Carson, Stesichoros's revision of the myth reverses the roles of protagonist and antagonist and thus shifts the point of view. Because we see things through his eyes, the monster becomes the character with whom we sympathize, and so the hero's qualities of masculine courage and zeal begin to appear monstrous. Instead of controlling and containing the monstrous sign, Stesichoros sets it loose.

4. FRAGMENTS

Fragmentation and recombination are the key principles in the composition and arrangement of Carson's monstrous text. The composition of the sections of *Autobiography* as a whole, their stark juxtapositions and seemingly random ordering, mimics the material decomposition of the principal interior text, Stesichoros's *papyrae,* over time. Carson explains:

the fragments of the *Geryoneis* itself read as if Stesichoros had composed a substantial narrative poem then ripped it to pieces and buried the pieces in a box with some song lyrics and lecture notes and scraps of meat. The fragment numbers tell you roughly how the pieces fell out of the box. You can of course keep shaking the box.

(6-7)

The textual fragments in Stesichoros's (and Carson's) box are ripped and torn, and, as if Carson wishes to underline that these are proper to monsters, they are shaken around with "meat." The image is striking. Just what is going on with all this red meat? If red is a "matter of the body," red meat is even more so (Derrida, *Secret* 100). Red meat is the very stuff we are made of, where we feel our pleasures and our pains. It is what feeds us, and what we are turned into when we die. This complex ambiguity is what Carson, in her commitment to a material, embodied deictic practice which has the potential to topple Cartesian abstraction, wishes to address when she invites us to manipulate the box and pull out and examine the fragments: "'Believe me for meat and for myself,' as Gertrude Stein says. Here. Shake" (7).

5. "What Difference Did Stesichoros Make?"

The association of monsters with language is, according to David Williams, "a profound, longstanding one that simultaneously reveals something of our historical conception of monstrosity as well as an ambivalence toward language itself" (61). His argument that the language of the monstrous is parasitic, feeding at the margins and limits of conventional languages "so as to gain the power to transcend these analytic discourses," helps explain the work of Carson's monster. Williams explains that "true to its etymology (monstrare: to show)," monstrous language "points to utterances that lie beyond logic" (10). The title of Carson's first chapter—"Red Meat: What Difference Did Stesichoros Make?"—poses a question that follows from a statement in which neither the logical nor the syntactic relationship between these two parts is visible. Carson thus directs us to a place just beyond our range of experiences, perceptions, and modalities of understanding, where the juxtaposition of discrepant things lets us see and feel what was not before our eyes or what we could not already see.

What difference did Stesichoros make? Carson singles out two major "differences" that Stesichoros has made to literary history. Stesichoros's first contribution is tropic. According to Carson, Stesichoros unleashed the adjective from the fixity of the Homeric epithet, and thus "released being" (5). Homeric epithets tend to be straightforward: "In the epic world, being is stable and particularity is set fast in tradition. When Homer men-

tions blood, blood is *black*. [. . .] Death is *bad*. Cowards' livers are *white*" (4). Then Stesichoros came along, and "suddenly there was nothing to interfere with horses being *hollow hooved*. Or a river being *root silver*. Or a child *bruiseless*. [. . .] Or killings *cream black*" (5). Where in epic, adjectives are used to put things in their place and keep them there, in the lyric world that Stesichoros unleashes, adjectives are used to bring to things spectacular depths and dazzling ambiguities. To move from the "black" of "blood" to the "cream black" of "killings," for instance, is to leave behind the metonymic—a logic where connections are based on association—and to enter a realm of metaphor—a logic in which connections are limited only by the imagination. This new metaphoric logic is dynamic; in it, dramatic reversals and returns are possible. It also invites a complex and carnal sensory engagement, and this is how it connects with the first part of the proposition "red meat."

Stesichoros's adjectives are synaesthetic. His poetic language joins together two images in terms that belong to one or more differing perceptual modes or senses. The connotations and meanings of the images change, depending on which senses the reader considers. The seemingly simple image of killings as "cream black," for instance, juxtaposes the tactile with the visual—the texture with the colour of blood—just as it invokes the sense of taste, contrasting an image of richness and sustenance with an image of rot and putrescence. One "difference" Stesichoros makes is thus to find a way of using language that invites us to perceive with all of our bodily senses—to make us feel. Another "difference" has to do with how his use of language relates to the way we think. Just as the image formed by Stesichoros's adjectives invokes specific sensory experiences, so too does it let us picture the processes of cognition and perception themselves. The rhetorical trope used here, the oxymoron, puts together two contradictory qualities that risk cancelling each other out. "Cream black" qualifies the noun "killing" through this type of cancellation, in effect performing a sort of "killing" on the level of language itself. Carson's writings frequently return to what she calls "iconic grammar" (*Economy* 52), that is, to statements that do what they say. Such use of language as a "synthetic and tensional" unit that "reenacts the reality of which it speaks," she says, requires "a different kind of attention than we normally pay to verbal surfaces" (52). The difference Stesichoros makes, then, is to expand the communicability of language. He lets us see that words say but that they also show, that they make us think, but they also make us feel.

According to Carson, Stesichoros's second contribution to literary history is narrative. Just as he unleashed words from the weight of the past, so too did he unleash story, completely altering the assessment of important mythological figures. In addition to the poet's revision of the "Geryon Matter" in the *Geryoneis,* Stesichoros turned his attentions to the origins of the Trojan War. After writing a poem about Helen of Troy that replicated the tradition of whoredom "already old by the time Homer used it," Stesichoros went blind (Carson, *Autobiography* 5). According to the *Testimonia* of Plato, Isokrates, and Suidas, his blindness occurred because Helen herself was furious at the slander. To regain his sight, Stesichoros wrote his famed palinode, or "counter-song," which recanted the poem he had just written: "No it is not the true story. / No you never went on the benched ships. / No you never came to the towers of Troy" (Carson, *Autobiography* 17). There is a perfect symmetry to the story; the palinode lets the heroine off, and she, in turn, lets the poet off. The story can thus be read as an allegory, with obvious appeal to a writer like Carson, about the power words have to transform the real.

If Stesichoros's contribution to literary history is to "undo the latches" (5) on the level of syntax, unleashing the adjective from its fixity in epic diction and, on the level of narrative, abandoning the oppressive sets of traditional assumptions about characters such as Helen of Troy and Herakles and Geryon, exactly what "difference" does Anne Carson's writing make? Like Stesichoros, Carson works to "release being," but against the directional image she uses to explain Stesichoros's work, in which all the substances in the world go "floating up" (5), Carson posits a bi-directional image to explain her own work—bouncing (3). "Words bounce," Carson explains, and (echoing Gertrude Stein) she elaborates: "Words, if you let them, will do what they want to do and what they have to do" (3). This is a playful metaphor, but it involves a very serious kind of engagement. Words bounce when they connect with other words and with the people who use them. When a speaker picks up a word, she alters its velocity and trajectory forever. When a speaker catches a word, he holds history itself in his hands for an instant, and when he redirects that word, he lets go a different future. A dual movement in which time is dismembered and remembered thus infuses all of Carson's work. On one hand, Carson shows us ways to break free from the constraints of the past; on the other hand, she asks us to connect with it. Her image of words bouncing and connecting offers a brilliant corollary to her proposition of monstrous fragmentation and rupture. Resuscitative and vital, this image linking past and present recalls Carson's discussion elsewhere of two ancient practices: the *symbolon,* the concrete token of a gift, which "carries the history of the giver into the life of the receiver and continues it there" (*Economy* 18), and the monument, which has the purpose of "insert[ing] a dead and vanished past into a living present" (73). Re-presentation is thus posited as the point of connection that reunites the subject with the other, the object world, and history.

6. PICTURING ESCAPE

Despite the prevalence of narrative traditions which seek to suppress monstrous otherness, monsters can "evoke potent escapist fantasies; the linking of monstrosity with the forbidden makes the monster all the more appealing as a temporary egress from constraint" (Jeffrey Cohen 17). Carson's *Autobiography* celebrates all forms of egress and escape. In the five prefatory parts of the text and the concluding interview, Carson allies her work with that of writers who have shown how to break free from the ideological restraints of traditions, and who have revealed how linguistic and syntactical experiments can widen the possibilities for thought and expression. In the main body of the narrative, her own transformations of the Geryon matter further frame activities of revision in terms of freedom. The central difference between Carson's and other versions of Geryon's story has to do with the ending. The slaughter and bloodshed are gone, and in its place is the agony of passion and longing drawn out over time. Traditionally a figure intimately associated with death and the dead, Carson's Geryon lives well past forty (36, 60).

A comparison can better show the nature and the extent of Carson's revisions. We can begin *hors texte* with one of Stesichoros's fragments, translated by David Campbell, telling of how Herakles slaughters Geryon:

> in silence he thrust it cunningly into his brow, and it cut through the flesh and bones by divine dispensation; and the arrow held straight on the crown of his head, and it stained with gushing blood his breastplate and gory limbs; and Geryon drooped his neck to one side, like a poppy which spoiling its tender beauty suddenly sheds its petals.
>
> (77)

When Carson translates this fragment in the prefatory part of *Autobiography of Red,* she reveals a greater sensitivity to the poetic quality of the adjectives. Though more dense than Campbell's translation, these images remain tragic:

> XIV. Herakles' Arrow
>
> Arrow means kill It parted Geryon's skull like a comb Made
> The boy neck lean At an odd slow angle sideways as when a
> Poppy shames itself in a whip of Nude breeze.
>
> (13)

What in Campbell's translation suggests passivity— "drooping" his neck, "shedding" its petals—becomes, in Carson's translation, active and erotically charged— "sham[ing]" itself in a "whip of Nude breeze." Carson prepares us here to envision Geryon's strength rather than his weakness.

In the actual "Romance" section of *Autobiography of Red,* Carson presents the most radical changes to the fragment. The core metaphors and imagery remain, but the context has shifted. Red, the dominant colour, is now explicitly linked with *eros* (and I think the implicit punning on arrows is intentional) rather than *thanatos,* sex rather than slaughter:

> The smell of the leather jacket near
> his face [. . .]
> sent a wave of longing as strong as a colour through
>   Geryon.
> It exploded at the bottom of his belly.
> Then the blanket shifted. He felt Herakles' hand move
>   on his thigh and Geryon's
> head went back like a poppy in a breeze
>
> (118-9)

Having separated the mythic cause ("arrow") from its effect (the boy "neck lean"), Carson overlays a more carnal logic in which the phallus (which presumably is like an arrow) provokes sexual ecstasy (Geryon's head, back "like a poppy in a breeze").

Carson also transforms the weapon, which in the traditional versions of his story cuts Geryon's life short, into a metaphor for time and continuity. Geryon's favourite question, one to which he returns again and again, concerns the substance of time: what is time made of? Different answers present themselves: "Time isn't made of anything. It is an abstraction / Just a meaning that we / impose upon motion" (90); "Much truer / is the time that strays into photographs and stops" (93). In a discussion about this topic of time, so obviously relevant to a character marked from birth by a powerful fate, we find the arrow, transmuted into a harpoon:

> Fear of time came at him. [. . .]
> he felt its indifference roar over
> his brain box. An idea glazed along the edge of the
>   box and whipped back
> down into the canal behind the wings
> and it was gone. A man moves through time. It means
>   nothing except that,
> like a harpoon, once thrown he will arrive.
>
> (81)

The simile retains a classical, quasi-tragic fatalism; a man moves inevitably towards his future just as a harpoon moves to its target. Notice, however, that in this version, there is no mention of what precisely his fate is. The transposition is subtle, but highly relevant. Instead of being represented as the victim of an arrow, Geryon is now figured as that arrow, moving through time towards a future that, though frightening, remains open.

Rather than wrap the story up and impose an ending of any sort, the narrative leaves us *in medias res,* with Geryon and his antagonists, Herakles and Ancash, paus-ing to ponder the beauty of fire. Time itself might be rushing, but the protagonist, reconciled with his enemies, is now immune to it: "We are amazing beings / Geryon is thinking. We are neighbors of fire. / And now time is rushing towards them / where they stand side by side with arms touching, immortality on their faces, / night at their back" (146). With this inconclusive conclusion, Carson has linked Geryon back to his beginnings as the "mighty son of immortal Khrysaor and Kallirhoe" (Campbell 67). And this is what Carson's bewildering syllogistic exercise in "Appendix C" prophesies for all who dare to step into the labyrinth with monsters, revisioning storytelling and lies: "we are now in reverse and by continuing to reason this way are likely to arrive back at the beginning" (19). The way Carson leads us to this picture of immortality is noteworthy. Rather than seeking to transcend time or erase the traces of its passing, Carson's archaeological method, by excavating layer upon layer of past meanings, explicitly foregrounds the temporal. She encourages us to disinter the genesis and metamorphosis of each monstrous image she puts before our eyes, and in so doing, invites us to renew its life.

7. GERYON'S PHOTOGRAPHY

Carson's portrait of the monster Geryon casts him as a photographer who specializes in portraits. The medium of photography provides an answer to his perennial question regarding the nature of time: "Much truer / is the time that strays into photographs and stops" (93). Geryon's musings on time and photography begin when he sees a photograph of a volcanic eruption taken by Herakles' grandmother, entitled "Red Patience," which "has compressed / on its motionless surface / fifteen different moments of time, nine hundred seconds of bombs moving up / and ash moving down / and pines in the kill process" (51), and when he hears the story of Lava Man, the only survivor of the volcano, who was a prisoner in the local jail. As a creature of reversals destined to go back to the beginning and revise his own ending, it is only natural that Geryon is compelled by the paradox of the form (it introduces motion into stasis and yet compresses the movement of time into an instant) as well as by the themes of this picture and the story that frames it: "identity memory eternity" (149).

Geryon's insights into the medium develop from these conceptual origins. He realizes that "Photography is disturbing [. . .] / Photography is a way of playing with perceptual relationships" and brings this realization into his practice (65). Many of Geryon's autobiographical photographs are technically impossible; framed by evocative titles and descriptions, they appear to picture things that cannot be seen with the eyes. Often, they are synaesthetic, linking what are usually discrete sensory phenomena: "this page has a photograph of some red rabbit giggle tied with a white rib-

bon. / He has titled it 'Jealous of My Little Sensations'"
(62). Occasionally, their object is unreal, belonging
somewhere between dreamspace and prehistory: "He
had dreamed of [. . .] creatures that looked like young
dinosaurs [. . .] [that] went crashing / through under-
bush and tore / their hides which fell behind them in
long red strips. He would call / the photograph 'Human
Valentines'" (131). In both of these instances, Geryon's
photographs manage to capture and make permanent
the fleeting and transient, repeating "what could never
be repeated existentially" (Barthes 4).

Additionally, Geryon's photographs involve complex
intertextual negotiations of abstractions. In seventh
grade, we are told, Geryon "began to wonder about the
noise that colors make":

> Roses came
> roaring across the garden at him.
> He lay on his bed at night listening to the silver light
>   of stars crashing against
> the window screen. Most
> of those he interviewed for the science project had to
>   admit they did not hear
> the cries of the roses
> being burned alive in the noonday sun. Like horses,
>   Geryon would say helpfully,
> like horses in war. No, they shook their heads. [. . .]
> The last page of his project
> was a photograph of his mother's rosebush under the
>   kitchen window.
> Four of the roses were on fire.
> They stood up straight and pure on the stalk, gripping
>   the dark like prophets
> and howling colossal intimacies
> From the back of their fused throats.

                                                    (84)

Geryon's acute perceptions of the noises of colour
belong to a commonplace of the *Künstlerroman*,
highlighting the qualities that will make the protagonist
into a real artist. His attention to this particular form of
synaesthesia, moreover, allies Geryon closely with artists such as Wassily Kandinsky and perhaps foreshadows
Geryon's gradual turning from the representational to
the abstract. (Kandinsky claimed he heard sound
whenever he saw colours, and suggested that abstraction most effectively reveals the "inner sounds" of a
picture [273].)

The most rhapsodic part of the "photograph" lies in the
development of its legend. The density of the different
moments compressed in the explanatory frame in which
Geryon attempts to translate the meaning of his image
through an analogy—"like horses in war" (84)—is
characteristic of Carson's vast intertextual reaching.
Carson's Geryon returns to his origins when he draws
this image of horses in war from the very papyrus fragments Carson draws from to tell his story. Horses appear twice in Stesichorus's *Geryoneis,* and in both

instances they are linked to chilling images of suffering.
In fragment S22, horses are connected to sounds and
the limits of the speakable: "(things speakable) and
things unspeakable [. . .] untiring and un- [. . .] painful strife [. . .] battles and slaughterings of men [. . .]
piercing (cries?); [. . .] of horses [. . .]" (Campbell
81). Fragment S50 sets horses within an image of tearing—"[. . .] (all?) [. . .] horse(s) [. . .] was torn,"
while the next very brief fragment, S53, seems to announce the location of the scene of tearing: "war" (85).

Geryon's explanation of the photo connects to other
histories as well. Within the frame of modern art, the
phrase "horses in war" conjures Pablo Picasso's painting of the agony of the Spanish Civil War, *Guernica*
(1937), just as the dramatic movements of silver crashing against the screen evoke the swirling motions in
Van Gogh's *Starry Night* (1889). Likewise, within the
frame of contemporary theory, Geryon's impossible
photograph with its explanatory legend conjures the
origins of structuralist linguistics. Geryon offers a verbal
explanation in the form of a Saussurean punning for
those who are not able to "hear" the noises compressed
in these paintings. In the *Cours de linguistique générale,*
Ferdinand de Saussure refers to the horse to demonstrate
that language is arbitrary, that nothing but a social
agreement links concepts (represented in the body of
his text as pictures) to sound patterns. An understanding
of Saussurean linguistics sheds light on the primary
logical connection that leads Geryon from "roses" to
"horses," namely a transposition of sounds rather than
any translation of concepts. Geryon's connections
between two seemingly visual images, the rose and the
horse, demonstrate the invisible workings of language.

In Geryon's enigmatic photograph, the roses are on fire;
distances shift as Carson brings additional images
together to reveal their kinship. The contours of Moses'
burning bush from the book of Exodus—a sign of God
made visible—are apparent in Geryon's rose bush,
especially since the flowers themselves grip the "dark
like prophets." Geryon's photo also recalls the image of
"fire and roses" in "Little Gidding," the fourth of T. S.
Eliot's *Four Quartets* (223). In this poem about revisiting a "familiar compound ghost" (217), Eliot's burning
roses are ambiguous emblems of time's passing and are
used to conjure both endings—"Dust [from the ashes of
a burnt rose] in the air suspended / Marks the place
where a story ended" (216)—and beginnings—"All
manner of things shall be well / when [. . .] / the fire
and the rose are one" (223). For both Eliot and the
book of Exodus, burning is linked to continuity rather
than destruction; Moses' bush is miraculously untouched
by the fire, while in Eliot's poem, the fire prompts
renewal. Thus connoting endurance and eternity, the
burning roses offer a fitting corrective to the devastation
connoted by the image of horses in war. It should be
apparent that the complex metaphorical framing

provided by Geryon's "helpful" explanations is essential to the meaning of the untitled piece. Whether or not their sources are located intertextually in words or pictures, what is at stake in the analogies Geryon lays out as part of the frame is a perspective on those constant themes "identity memory eternity" (149).

Situated just past the limits of the visible, Geryon's photographs refuse to show merely what has been seen. Instead, they "show seeing" itself (Mitchell). This seeing, however, is planted firmly on the side of *logos,* and is firmly committed to the revisionary. Through Geryon, Carson shows seeing inflected through an implicit critique of violence. Presenting reversals—like photo negatives—of the usual tropes of violence, the portraits of *Autobiography* revise the way we look at heroism and victimhood. This seeing is also inflected through a critique of disembodied vision. The portraits' synaesthetic qualities and the ways their meaning emerges from a mediation of word and image guarantee that their meaning climbs up inside and vibrates through the whole body. Finally, this seeing is inflected through a commitment to a dialectic of flux and duration. Carson believes that the image produced by a single phrase can compress an infinity of moments of time on its surface, and that an archaeological excavation of the past can animate what has been buried and even bring new things to life.

8. REACHING TO KNOW

Through the deft strategies of revision and reversal made possible by Geryon's impossible photographic portraits, Carson's *Autobiography* brings us to "one of those moments / that is the opposite of blindness" in which nothing less than "the world" passes back and forth between our eyes (*Autobiography* 39). Clearly, in this image of an epiphany shared by two observers, she wishes to conjure more than mere physical sight, which extends "only to the surface of bodies" (*Economy* 50). Carson's interests are in the red meat, in what lies unseen underneath surfaces and appearances.

In her other more properly scholarly writings, Carson has explicitly developed a theory that remains only implicit in *Autobiography* about the hazards of understanding seeing as something we do only with our eyes. In *Economy of the Unlost,* she recalls Simonides' famous fragment in which he says "the word is a picture of things" (*Economy* 47). Against a reading of the phrase as a commitment to put words to the service of the visible world, Carson argues that Simonides means to conjure words' power to "point beyond themselves toward something no eye can see no painter can paint" (51). From her analysis of Simonides' fragment, Carson makes it possible to arrive at an understanding that reality is twofold (19): visible and invisible worlds rest side by side (45). "The way to know" this dual reality, she

echoes elsewhere in a poem, "is not by staring hard" (*Men* 11). The invisible world, simply put, is not accessible to the eyes or to the arts that restrict their gaze to the surface of things. Instead, using an image that brings together body and mind, she stipulates that to know, one must "reach—/ mind empty / towards that thing you should know // until you get it" (11).

Reaching is what Carson does when she dips into the materials of a dead and vanished past and inserts it into the living present (*Economy* 73) and what she does when she mates disparate things in the body of her text. It is what Carson asks her readers to do as they try to locate the connective tissues that bridge the spaces between the different segments she has positioned side by side. More important, as she demonstrates in the poetic legends to the portraits in Geryon's autobiography, reaching is all around us: it is the work of metaphoric language. Buried here beneath Carson's invitation to reach is a reference to Aristotle, who, in *On Metaphor,* writes that "All men by their nature reach out to know" (*Eros* 70). How can metaphor activate the kind of knowing that is conveyed in this image of reaching? Why is such reaching necessary in the first place?

In *Eros the Bittersweet,* Carson takes us to a moment in cultural history when our perceptual abilities were reoriented away from the audio-tactile and towards the visual—the moment of alphabetization:

> As the audio-tactile world of the oral culture is transformed into a world of words on paper where vision is the principal conveyor of information, a reorientation of perceptual abilities begins to take place within the individual.
>
> (43)

One consequence of the new demands placed on vision, Carson suggests, is a global desensorialization of word and reader, and the introduction of distancing in the communication act:

> Literacy desensorializes words and reader. A reader must disconnect himself from the influx of sense impressions transmitted by nose, ear, tongue and skin if he is to concentrate upon his reading. A written text separates words from one another, separates words from the environment, separates words from the reader (or writer) and separates the reader (or writer) from his environment. Separation is painful.
>
> (50)

Metaphor and other virtuoso "tactics of imagination" (69) which "shift distances" from far to near (73) work against this separation.

Metaphor connects words to each other, to their environment, and to the reader or writer. Metaphor also connects reader and writer to each other. (Ted Cohen explores this notion when he argues that metaphor cultivates intimacy and community [6].) Metaphoric thinking is cognitive and imaginative, but it also is sensory and conveys powerful feeling (Ricoeur 154). It is dynamic, introducing motion into stasis and duration into flux, just as it fragments experiences and then reconnects them in new ways. And even more important, metaphor is liberating. As David Williams puts it, metaphor "jars the mind by disordering our expectations. . . . At the same time, we enjoy it . . . because while it disturbs, metaphor also frees the mind from its habitual course" (41). As a monstrous (that is hybrid, disorderly, and powerful) practice, metaphor demonstrates "what is proper to man" (Derrida, "White" 246).

Long ago, Carson argues in **Autobiography,** a poet named Stesichoros broke free from a restrictive cultural logic where connections were based on contiguity and association and entered into the realm of metaphor, where connections were limitless. In so doing, he undid "the latches" and "released being" (**Autobiography** 5). This connective gesture, one that Geryon repeats with every metaphor-driven image in his "autobiography," one that Carson repeats as she re-envisions this story about the things a monster can demonstrate, is one we can repeat every time we allow words and their deferral, which is "beautiful," "foiled," and "endless" (*Eros* 29), to take us to the edge. Outside things are mortal, Carson shows us in **Autobiography of Red,** but the realm of metaphoric language connects us back to time and thus to duration. Outside things can only be known through their surfaces, but the realm of metaphoric language lets us get to their meat and in so doing, can restore our own embodied pleasures. In response to a question about "a sort of concealment drama going on in [his] work" in the "Interview" staged with Stesichoros at the end of **Autobiography,** Stesichoros offers to tackle the question of "blindness" (147). "First," he insists, "I must tell about seeing" (147). And this is the point Carson's study of metaphor intends to make: until we understand that telling sets seeing into motion, we will remain blind to the world of things needing to be uncovered. Poetic telling invites us to bridge the gaps between the disparate things we see and lets us reach beyond "outside" things to connect with immortality itself.

Works Cited

Alighieri, Dante. *The Inferno of Dante.* Trans. Robert Pinsky. New York: Farrar, 1994.

Apollodorus. *The Library.* Trans. Sir James George Frazer. 2 vols. Loeb Classical Library. Cambridge: Harvard UP, 1921.

Bal, Mieke. *The Mottled Screen: Reading Proust Visually.* Trans. Anna-Louise Milne. Stanford: Stanford UP, 1997.

Barthes, Roland. *Camera Lucida: Reflections on Photography.* Trans. Richard Howard. New York: Hill, 1981.

Bryson, Norman. *Vision and Painting: The Logic of the Gaze.* New Haven: Yale UP, 1983.

Campbell, David A., ed. and trans. *Greek Lyric III: Stesichorus, Ibycus, Simonides, and Others.* Cambridge: Harvard UP, 1991.

Carson, Anne. *Eros the Bittersweet.* Normal, IL: Dalkey Archive, 1998.

———. *Autobiography of Red: A Novel in Verse.* New York: Vintage, 1998.

———. *Economy of the Unlost: Reading Simonides of Keos with Paul Celan.* Princeton: Princeton UP, 1999.

———. Interview with Shelly Pomerance. *All in a Weekend.* 21 Jul. 2002. CBC Montreal, Radio One. 12 Nov. 2002 <http://www.montreal.cbc.ca/allinaweekend/>.

———. *Men in the Off Hours.* New York: Knopf, 2000.

———. *Plainwater: Essays and Poetry.* Toronto: Vintage, 2000.

Cohen, Jeffrey. *Monster Theory.* Minneapolis: U of Minnesota P, 1996.

Cohen, Ted. "Metaphor and the Cultivation of Intimacy." Sacks 1-10.

Derrida, Jacques. "White Mythology: Metaphor in the Text of Philosophy." *Margins of Philosophy.* Trans. Alan Bass. Chicago: U of Chicago P, 1982. 207-71.

Derrida, Jacques and Paule Thévenin. *The Secret Art of Antonin Artaud.* Trans. Mary Ann Caws. Cambridge: MIT, 1998.

Eco, Umberto. *Semiotics and the Philosophy of Language.* Bloomington: Indiana UP, 1986.

Eisenstein, Sergei. *Film Form and Film Sense.* Ed. and trans. Jay Leyda. Cleveland: Meridian, 1967.

Eliot, T. S. "Little Gidding." *Collected Poems 1909-1962.* London: Faber, 1974. 214-23.

Ferrucci, Franco. *The Poetics of Disguise: The Autobiography of the Work in Homer, Dante, and Shakespeare.* Trans. Ann Dunnigan. Ithaca: Cornell UP, 1980.

Halberstam, Judith. *Skin Shows: Gothic Horror and the Technology of Monsters.* Durham: Duke UP, 1995.

Hesiod. *The Homeric Hymns and Homerica.* Trans. Hugh G. Evelyn-White. Loeb Classical Library. Cambridge: Harvard UP, 1982.

Hollander, Robert. "Dante's Virgil: A Light that Failed." *Lectura Dantis* 4 (Spring 1989). 12 Nov. 2002 <http://www.brown.edu/Departments/Italian_Studies/LD/numbers/04/hollander.html>.

Horace. "The Art of Poetry." *Literary Criticism: Plato to Dryden.* Ed. Allan H. Gilbert. Detroit: Wayne State UP, 1967. 128-43.

Kandinsky, Wassily. "From 'The Problem of Form.'" *Modernism: An Anthology of Sources and Documents.* Ed. Vassiliki Kolocotroni, Jane Goldman, and Olga Taxidou. Chicago: U of Chicago P, 1998. 270-75.

Kirsch, Adam. Rev. of *Autobiography of Red* by Anne Carson. *New Republic* 18 May 1998: 37-41.

Longinus. "On Literary Excellence." *Literary Criticism: Plato to Dryden.* Ed. Allan H. Gilbert. Detroit: Wayne State UP, 1967. 146-98.

Mitchell, W. J. T. *Picture Theory.* Chicago: U of Chicago P, 1994.

———. "Showing Seeing: a Critique of Visual Culture." *Journal of Visual Culture* 1.2 (2002): 165-81.

Pausanias. *Description of Greece.* Trans. W. H. S. Jones and H. A. Ormerod. 4 vols. Loeb Classical Library. Cambridge: Harvard UP, 1918-35.

Ricoeur, Paul. "The Metaphoric Process as Cognition, Imagination, and Feeling." Sacks 141-58.

Sacks, Sheldon, ed. *On Metaphor.* Chicago: U of Chicago P, 1979.

Saussure, Ferdinand de. "Nature of the Linguistic Sign." *Modern Criticism and Theory.* Ed. David Lodge. London: Longman, 1988. 10-15.

Williams, David. *Deformed Discourse: The Function of the Monster in Mediaeval Thought and Literature.* Montreal: McGill-Queen's UP, 1999.

FURTHER READING

Criticism

Burt, Stephen. "Poetry without Borders." *Publishers Weekly* 247, no. 14 (3 April 2000): 56-7.
    Presents a brief interview with Carson.

Carson, Anne, and Kevin McNeilly. "Gifts and Questions: An Interview with Anne Carson." *Canadian Literature/Littérature Canadienne,* no. 176 (spring 2003): 12-25.
    Discusses, among other topics, the notion of writing for an audience.

Davenport, Guy. "Eros the Bittersweet." *Grand Street* 6, no. 3 (spring 1987): 184-91.
    Discusses Carson's verse "essay," *Eros the Bittersweet.*

McNeilly, Kevin. "Five Fairly Short Talks on Anne Carson." *Canadian Literature/Littérature Canadienne,* no. 176 (spring 2003): 6-10.
    Ruminates on some aspects of Carson's oeuvre.

Rae, Ian. "'Dazzling Hybrids': The Poetry of Anne Carson." *Canadian Literature/Littérature Canadienne,* no. 166 (autumn 2000): 17-41.
    Compares Carson to Gertrude Stein, among others.

Wahl, Sharon. "Erotic Sufferings: *Autobiography of Red* and Other Anthropologies." *Iowa Review* 29, no. 1 (1999): 180-92.
    Notes that Carson's work gives off a feeling of "tenderness."

Additional coverage of Carson's life and career is contained in the following sources published by Thomson Gale: *American Writers Supplement,* Vol. 12; *Contemporary Authors,* Vol. 203; *Contemporary Literary Criticism,* Vol. 185; *Dictionary of Literary Biography,* Vol. 193; *Literature Resource Center*; and *Poetry for Students,* Vol. 18.

Donald Justice
1925-2004

(Full name Donald Rodney Justice) American poet, essayist, memoirist, librettist, and short story writer.

INTRODUCTION

Although he was not a prolific writer, Justice's well-crafted and understated poetry earned him several major awards, including the Pulitzer Prize in 1979 for his *Selected Poems*. Justice is known for his attention to form and language, his use of rhyme and meter, his ability to master many poetic forms, and his experimental methods of writing. Although critical assessments of his work vary, he is considered by many to be one of the most significant American poets of the twentieth century.

BIOGRAPHICAL INFORMATION

Justice was born on August 12, 1925, in Miami, Florida. In 1945 he received a B.A. from the University of Miami and a M.A. in English from the University of North Carolina in 1947. He studied under Yvor Winters at Stanford University in 1948. He then attended the prestigious Writer's Workshop at the University of Iowa, where he received his Ph.D. in 1954. At Iowa he worked under influential poets such as John Berryman, Robert Lowell, and Karl Shapiro. Justice taught several promising writers at Iowa, such as Mark Strand, Charles Wright, and Jorie Graham. He was a professor at the University of Iowa, Syracuse University, the University of California, and other universities before settling at the University of Florida. He retired in 1992 but continued to write and publish essays and poetry. He received several awards for his verse, including the Lamont Poetry Selection, a nomination for the National Book Award, the Pulitzer Prize, the Bollingen Prize, and awards from the Rockefeller and Guggenheim foundations and the National Endowment for the Arts. He died of pneumonia on August 6, 2004.

MAJOR WORKS

The Summer Anniversaries (1960), Justice's first collection of verse, focuses on the poet's childhood experiences in Miami and explores familial and community

relationships. Critics praise the poems for being nostalgic without becoming maudlin or melodramatic. They also note his experimentation with form, particularly his interest in difficult poetic structures such as the sestina and villanelle. He was awarded the Lamont Poetry Selection for this work. In his next collection, *Night Light* (1967), Justice shifted his attention to his adult experiences but continued his exploration with poetic form. Commentators note the influence of William Carlos Williams on these verses. Justice's poetic experimentation reached new levels in *Departures* (1973), in which he created poems by placing words on cards and then shuffling them to create poems by chance. Published in 1995, *New and Selected Poems* features fifteen new poems as well as work spanning three decades. The poems in this work illustrate the defining characteristics of Justice's poetic oeuvre, show his propensity to explore various poetic forms, and touch on his major themes, including sorrow, loss, nostalgia, and vulnerability. His last collection of verse,

Collected Poems (2004), includes previously published poems as well as ten new poems written during the last ten years of his life.

CRITICAL RECEPTION

Critical reaction to Justice's poetry has been mixed. Commentators view him as a formalist poet who did not conform to the tenets of modern verse, which is characterized by its personal and emotional tone and unstructured form. Some critics compare him unfavorably to his contemporaries, particularly the Beat and Black Mountain poets, and deride his poetry as uninspired, passive, and lacking vitality and passion. Other critics commend his poetry for its economy of expression, attention to detail, technical skill, and nostalgic tone. Moreover, they assert that the subtlety and simplicity of his poetry is an effective way to evoke emotion and connections between readers. Critics note the influence of musical compositions as well as such poets as Wallace Stevens and William Carlos Williams on Justice's verse; commentators also detect parallels between Justice and the British poet Philip Larkin. Commenting on the negative criticism of Justice's work, critic Bruce Bawer maintains that Justice's unpopularity is "a reflection not of any failing in the work itself but of the manifold moral and cultural failures of an age in which it has been Justice's peculiar honor to be the apotheosis of the unfashionable poet."

PRINCIPAL WORKS

Poetry

The Summer Anniversaries 1960
A Local Storm 1963
Night Light 1967
Sixteen Poems 1970
From a Notebook 1971
Departures 1973
Selected Poems 1979
Tremayne 1984
The Sunset Maker: Poems/Stories/A Memoir (poetry, short stories, memoir) 1987
A Donald Justice Reader: Selected Poetry and Prose (poetry and essays) 1991
New and Selected Poems 1995
Poems to Go 1995
Orpheus Hesitated beside the Black River: Poems, 1952-1997 1998
Collected Poems 2004

Other Major Works

Platonic Scripts (essays) 1984
The Death of Lincoln (libretto) 1988
Oblivion: On Writers and Writing (essays) 1998

CRITICISM

Donald Justice, Gregory Fitz Gerald, and William Heyen (interview date winter 1973-1974)

SOURCE: Justice, Donald, Gregory Fitz Gerald, and William Heyen. "Falling into Place: A Conversation with Donald Justice," edited by Philip L. Gerber and Robert J. Gemmett. *Prairie Schooner* 47, no. 4 (winter 1973-1974): 317-24.

[*In the following interview, Justice discusses aspects of his poetry, the stylistic development of his verse, and his creative process.*]

A native of Florida and graduate of the Universities of North Carolina and Iowa, Donald Justice has published two collections of poems. The first book, ***The Summer Anniversaries*** (1960), was the Lamont Poetry Selection; it was followed by ***Night Light*** (1967). Another volume, ***Sixteen Poems*** has been published recently by Iowa's Stone Wall Press. Currently at Iowa Univ., Mr. Justice has been affiliated with Syracuse and UC Irvine.

The present conversation results from Mr. Justice's appearance in March, 1970, on the *Writers Forum* series at the State University of New York, Brockport. With him appear Gregory Fitz Gerald, Director of the Forum, and William Heyen, author of *Depth of Field*.

The editors are both of the English Department at Brockport. Mr. Gerber has published critical volumes on Robert Frost and Theodore Dreiser, and Mr. Gemmett is the author of *William Beckford,* forthcoming in Twayne's English Authors Series.

The conversation begins with Mr. Justice reading his **"Here in Katmandu"**:

> We have climbed the mountain,
> There's nothing more to do.
> It is terrible to come down
> To the valley
> Where, amidst many flowers,
> One thinks of snow,

As, formerly, amidst snow,
Climbing the mountain,
One thought of flowers,
Tremulous, ruddy, with dew,
In the valley.
One caught their scent coming down.

It is difficult to adjust, once down,
To the absence of snow.
Clear days, from the valley,
One looks up at the mountain.
What else is there to do?
Prayerwheels, flowers!

Let the flowers
Fade, the prayerwheels run down.
What have these to do
With us who have stood atop the snow
Atop the mountain,
Flags seen from the valley?

It might be possible to live in the valley,
To bury oneself among flowers,
If one could forget the mountain,
How, setting out before dawn,
Blinded with snow,
One knew what to do.

Meanwhile it is not easy here in Katmandu,
Especially when to the valley
That wind which means snow
Elsewhere, but here means flowers,
Comes down,
As soon it must, from the mountain.

[*Fitz Gerald*]: *Why did you use Katmandu as the locale for the poem you just read?*

[Justice]: Katmandu is a city in Nepal, the starting point of the expedition which originally conquered Mt. Everest. I got my information out of the movie that was made about the expedition, a film which impressed me very much with its visual magnificence. It seemed to be providing images for a poem, and so I tried to use them in a way that touched a subject I was interested in.

[*Fitz Gerald*]: *Were you interested in human aspiration?*

Yes, that's a way of putting it. Being born in flat country—Florida—and reading books about climbing: all that probably had more to do with the poem than any largish abstraction would. You might say that geography provides metaphors for the human. But if any of my poems moralize, as I suppose some of them unavoidably do, **"Here in Katmandu"** moralizes on the theme of failure and success. You wanted to conquer Everest, you did it, and then, either you felt an emptiness, or you didn't like what you came back to. But you didn't like what you had found in the process either.

[*Fitz Gerald*]: *And then there's the sense of let-down in descending from any heights, or from any emotional experience of that magnitude?*

That's the underlying theme which the word "down" keeps emphasizing.

[*Heyen*]: *Would you say that the voice of this poem is typical of your work?*

I hope that most of my poems have something of what I could recognize as my own voice, whether other people could or not. It's a voice that is pitched somewhat impersonally, which is usually the way I speak in poems.

[*Heyen*]: *Do you see the unity of your work as residing within the individual poems, or within your books as a whole?*

If there is unity, I think you'll find it within the individual pieces. I can't imagine planning out a whole book, and making it coherent and unified before I have written any of the work. I know that other people have been able at times to approximate something like that kind of organization, but I couldn't. Sometimes, however, the poems seem to fall into place together by themselves. You may write several poems without seeing a relationship; then once you have finished them, you recognize that they are truly connected. You learn something.

[*Fitz Gerald*]: *What are the strings of connection in* **The Summer Anniversaries?**

I am still a little surprised to find out how many of the poems in **The Summer Anniversaries** deal with childhood or memory, because I didn't set out to write a whole gathering of poems that dealt with these subjects. Once I had written some of them, I saw that this was happening. I don't, then, usually say, "Well, I've written poems on this subject, and it seems to be working, I'll write more on it." I'm afraid I'm incapable of planning that much in advance.

[*Heyen*]: *You do have a poem in* **Night Light** *called "Early Poems," in which you say, "How fashionably sad my early poems are." Are you speaking of your own self there, or is it a persona talking?*

I think it's my own voice, but it's a voice which is meant to be ironic, at least this is one way of reading the poem. It means to be saying that I'm putting aside, or even putting down the early poems: "The rhymes, the meters, how they paralyze." While I say that, the later poem itself is strictly metering and strictly rhyming, which ought to be some sign that there is an irony involved even in the thrusting aside or putting down what were earlier my concerns.

[*Fitz Gerald*]: *Are there any changes other than stylistic between your early work and your later poems?*

I don't recognize any really profound changes, though there may be some. My more recent poems do feel different to me as I'm writing them. As I compare them with my early poems, I see the subject of childhood has mostly disappeared. The formal apparatus of the poems, which I'm immensely concerned with, is quite different. Since form and content operate together, what's being said is necessarily going to sound and actually be a little different, too. When I began to learn something about writing, I was interested in the forms that others had demonstrated could be used, and could be used interestingly. My interest in very ingenious and elaborate forms is connected somewhat with the desire that seems to be natural with me: to displace the self from the poem—not to remove it entirely, but to displace it, in some degree. A fairly elaborate apparatus of form does just that.

[*Fitz Gerald*]: *Do you spend a considerable amount of time revising your work?*

A good deal of revision, yes, usually because I'm not always lucky the first time through a poem, and I want to make it better. I do restrain myself when writing, particularly by leaving out things. If it doesn't sound good, even though it seemed at one point an important part of the argument or presentation of a scene, then I'd be inclined to leave it out. It's a poem after all, and it wants to sound good.

[*Heyen*]: *Are you worried about the personal element in poetry?*

Not as far as my own poems are concerned. I think that whatever character or temperament I have unavoidably enters the better poems and so I don't find myself taking a lot of trouble trying to get myself in. I go to far more trouble trying to leave myself out.

[*Heyen*]: *Certainly your poetry isn't as personal as, say,* Heart's Needle *by W. D. Snodgrass.*

Heart's Needle is a fine book, with many fine poems in it. You probably know that essay Snodgrass wrote after the book came out. It contains a passage, which I might try paraphrasing, to the effect that we who were brought up in that generation were raised on a criticism which showed us how really to examine a poem and understand it, or even how to put it together, but that time has passed now; the final test is sincerity. Now that is a different kind of poetry from what I naturally write, but it's the kind he naturally writes, and he writes it very well.

[*Fitz Gerald*]: *You have done a good deal of teaching of poetry in workshops. What do you feel the relationship of the workshop is in general to contemporary poetry?*

Many poets I know have been in workshops, for better or for worse, both on the receiving end and the giving end. I find it very often a fine situation, but not always. One of the great things, though, is that you gather a community of persons with like interests, doing similar things, teaching each other either on purpose or by accident. It was helpful. To me, certainly. And I could mention some others—some who might be reluctant to admit it. It never has been fashionable to admit it, which strikes me sometimes as a rather snob attitude.

[*Fitz Gerald*]: *You spoke earlier about creating new forms of your own. Could you describe something of what you've been doing recently in this line?*

I don't, myself, want to use the term "organic form"— that's been batted about too much, it seems to me—and anyhow that isn't quite the way I look at it. But the forms do make themselves up as the poems get written. Is that too nebulous a description?

[*Heyen*]: *There's a sense in which our study of literature has become an attempt to try to enunciate for ourselves the relationship between the thing that is said and the way it is said, and how these two finally merge. It's almost impossible to talk about it; it's something you feel, I suppose.*

Yes. It is very hard to express. If a poem comes out as good, then there was no other way it could have been said. We have that kind of faith.

[*Fitz Gerald*]: *When you were speaking of* **"Here in Katmandu,"** *you said the poem "moralizes about the theme of failure and success." Does this imply that didacticism is returning to contemporary poetry?*

All the poets I know now certainly try to avoid sounding at all didactic in their poems, though not necessarily in their criticism. Very much to the contrary there, of course. At the same time, in the last seven or eight years, some poets have turned on occasion to making direct statements on public topics and world events. Twenty years ago this was very rare. So we have something with what seems to be a didactic tinge to it; but it's not what a literary handbook would label as didacticism.

[*Fitz Gerald*]: *Then you would not assent to the notion that much of contemporary poetry is unmoral?*

I'd say that much of it is undidactic. That doesn't mean that it may not have a moral passion in it, or a moral view of that part of the world which it enters.

[*Fitz Gerald*]: *To what extent does a poet's own ethos enter into his work?*

I don't think this ethos, as you call it, can be left out. It's not anything the poet has to be much concerned about getting into his poems. If his poems are honest and good poems, this ethos will automatically appear in what he writes.

[*Fitz Gerald*]: *It's implicit rather than explicit?*

It can be made explicit. Bly and Merwin come to mind, for instance: the statements made in their poems with moral weight are made usually by means of images. That seems to me an indirect way of making a statement with moral energy in it. I prefer it for that reason. When Robert Bly reads, the impromptu comments he intersperses between the poems during the reading are of a far different nature than the poems themselves—much more didactic, seeming to have a more direct and even a simpler moral fervor to them. The poems are somewhat distanced by their becoming objects of artistic interest to him and his audience. I suggest images as a mechanism for making statements that have moral weight, but without sounding as if one is speaking from a platform.

[*Heyen*]: *It is odd, though, that Bly does use the word "political" to describe his poems.*

Yes, there's an interesting piece he wrote about political poetry in which he quotes a Neruda poem as an example of great political poetry. If I remember this right, it's a poem filled with surreal images. There seems for Bly—and this may be true of a good deal of poetry that is being written now—that the surreal or the semi-surreal image has somehow got involved in the current of literary history and in the current of politics. They have somehow got together—it's fascinating.

[*Heyen*]: *What we're trying to say is that we sense in a book such as your **Night Light** the essential spirit of the time in which we are living. Yet the titles of your poems are not directly topical.*

There's one topical poem of mine that now seems dated to me. It was a poem written in February, 1965, within two weeks after the initial full-scale bombing raids in North Vietnam, which upset me very much. It's called **"To the Hawks."** It's dedicated to three political figures who according to the newspapers then were among the outspoken hawks. None of them is any longer in the administration. It turned out that one of them was a milder hawk than the others. But as I understood it in February, 1965, this was the way it seemed, and I somehow couldn't help writing at that point. Within the last eight or ten years, the possibility of writing about public events has seemed for me more likely in poems. Other poets have shown the way—Bly is one of them.

[*Fitz Gerald*]: *You've written a poem called **"The Assassination."** This is a poem about the death of John Kennedy, isn't it?*

No, it's about the assassination of Robert Kennedy. Somehow I wasn't prepared to write about John Kennedy's death. Things have to happen two or three times for me before I begin to catch on. By the time John Kennedy's brother was assassinated, I felt something of what assassination was like, what it could mean to me. Also I had a television set, so I could see the events in an immediate and rather scary way. So I thought—I feel something about this; I have something to say about it; maybe this is a public event I could write about. It wasn't laid out in a machine-like way, but I did feel I could write a poem about it. Because I usually approach things indirectly, I just didn't want merely to say, "Well, isn't it terrible?" I was also interested in the notion of playing around with chance, partly because of my acquaintance with John Cage. So about this time I started writing words down on three-by-five note cards, which happened to be lying around the house. And writing down sentence models—syntax blanks or abstracts—on another set of cards. Once the cards had been shuffled, I found several sentences that I could then complete with a word from the other stack. Then with some changing later on, I managed to approach this subject which I found hard to approach directly. To aim chance in the right direction, I filled cards with words I heard on several TV news broadcasts. I'm sorry if that description is not too clear, but the process was both complicated and improvised. In any case, the result was the following poem, dated June 5, 1968:

It begins again, the nocturnal pulse.
It courses through the cables laid for it.
It mounts to the chandeliers and beats there, hotly.
We are too close. Too late, we would move back.
We are involved with the surge.

Now it bursts. Now it has been announced.
Now it is being soaked up by newspapers.
Now it is running through the streets.
The crowd has it. The woman selling carnations
And the man in the straw hat stand with it in their
     shoes.

Here is the red marquee it sheltered under;
Here is the ballroom, here
The sadly various orchestra led
By a single gesture. My arms open.
It enters. Look, we are dancing.

[*Fitz Gerald*]: *The central image hidden there is blood, is it not?*

Yes, that's what runs through the poem. I think it does until perhaps the last couple of very short sentences.

[*Heyen*]: *Have you written many poems using the chance method you describe?*

I think about three and a half.

[*Heyen*]: *Do you plan to write more?*

I've tried shuffling the cards some more, but I haven't had any luck.

[*Heyen*]: *But what does it enable you to do?*

To put it simply, it frees the imagination. I don't tell myself I have to accept what chance determines. There are poets who *will* accept whatever comes up in the cards. I reserve the right for final approval of what chance tells me to say.

Donald Justice and the *Ohio Review* (interview date spring 1975)

SOURCE: Justice, Donald, and the *Ohio Review*. "The Effacement of Self: An Interview with Donald Justice." *Ohio Review* 16, no. 3 (spring 1975): 40-63.

[*In the following interview, Justice discusses his poetic development, the style and structure of his work, and the role of emotion in his poems.*]

[*Ohio Review*]: *I would like to hear you talk about what you think is the change between where you were with the first book,* **Summer Anniversaries,** *and where you've come to with the latest,* **Departures.** *The poems are formally different, of course, but what about the change in the presence of Don Justice in the poems?*

[Justice]: The very nature of the question makes it hard for me to judge that. I can speak of intentions. I haven't ever intended to put myself directly into the poems, not in any of the poems I've written. I've always felt it was an author's privilege to leave himself out if he chose—and I chose, contrary to the choice of certain friends and contemporaries. I suppose I must have been acting originally under the powerful influence of early essays by Eliot in that, and, insofar as it was a conscious choice, seeking the—I've forgotten the phrase—"the effacement of the personality." The self. I have in my poems conscientiously effaced my self, I think, if not my personality. But I might be the last to know if I could be recognized as a person in the poems or not. I am often speaking in some imagined or borrowed voice. That is the way I see it, anyway, when I'm working on poems. I may be writing about things I know personally, even intimately, but to a certain degree I want to be pretending otherwise.

I understand that, but I was thinking about the obvious topographical difference—the simple fact that so many more of them speak in the assumed first person, whatever the character, and even—well, let's say in the poem "**Variations on a Text by Vallejo.**"

Yes, that's true, I do assume it there . . .

Which I find a tremendously moving, powerful poem.

Well, thank you, but the Vallejo itself is powerful and moving, and I was moved to try to borrow some of its power, I suppose. Because that is a case, I think, of a borrowed voice. And borrowing the voice allows me, it seems, to speak of myself more directly, more objectively because the voice is not mine. Not simply mine. Probably more than other poets I know, I play games in my poems (as I do in my life), and one of the unwritten rules of the game for me, as I like it played, is that you can risk this much personality or that much confession if the voice is promised to be that of someone else to start with. Even without my recognizing it at the time of writing, that may be one of the reasons I can get pretty literary in choice of subjects, in taking off from other people's texts. There is something in the works of others, I suppose, that gets to me personally, that affords me another perspective, the objectivity and distance I like, so that it is as if I could say to myself, let me use his experience as an image of my own, and I won't have to use mine. But using his turns out to be another experience for me, so it really *will* be mine in the end. I'm not making that very clear, I guess, but it must be a sort of psychological mechanism. I think it works that way. A defense mechanism.

Okay. Does that borrowing occur in "**Absences**" *and* "**Presences**" *too?*

"**Absences,**" as far as I know, is not a borrowed voice, not beyond the first phrase, at least. "**Presences,**" as one may easily recognize, is a borrowing from Vallejo again, but a less open borrowing and therefore not acknowledged.

Well, granting and assuming that there is a borrowed voice in some of these more personal-seeming poems, I wonder what you think of the different kind of poetry that you're generating and creating by the simple use of that, as distinct from a more objective kind, a more distant poetry that you were writing fifteen years ago.

Some of the poems in my second book, *Night Light,* are probably more objective transcriptions of what would appear to be reality than anything I can remember, offhand, in the first book, or than most of the things in the latest book, *Departures.* I don't know quite how that came about, but I have wanted, as many poets must have, to try all kinds of things in writing, and I wouldn't be satisfied with, say, finding a formula for writing a poem and then doing it a second time, except perhaps in a short series of related poems, with the end already in sight; or, if I were, I'd rather not *know* that I was doing it. I would like to write different kinds of things all the time. I do think *Departures* is different from *Sum-*

mer Anniversaries or from *Night Light,* and both the second and third books are, I like to think, developments, even improvements upon, *departures* from, the first book, which was largely, I believe, apprentice work. It proved to me, if not to anyone else, that I could go through the motions of writing poems. I take the motions seriously enough, but more as a demonstration of . . .

Some of those formal sestinas in there, I think, testify in part . . .

Yeah, well, I love sestinas, though not my own particularly. I have no objection to the sestina as an imposed form or anything of the sort, and if I could write a sestina easily tonight when I go home, I'd do so, but having done it already I'd have to think the new one would be different somehow. I don't know. Which may be why I won't do it, not tonight, anyhow. Two of the four I attempted in that first book—the last ones I did—resemble each other on the surface—**"A Dream Sestina"** and **"Sestina on Six Words by Kees."** They came about in different ways, and so I can think of them as different. But the other two are really variations on a sestina base, as it were.

"Here In Katmandu" starts off being a perfect one, but then it changes . . .

What I called it at the time was a free-verse sestina, because the lines varied considerably in length and toward the end I changed an end-word or two. I wanted to make a pun on "Katmandu" out of the end-word *do.*

I believe you changed the pattern, even, somewhere along the line.

Maybe. I know I did in **"A Dream Sestina,"** because the first ten lines or so of that were dreamed in a real dream and in the second stanza I simply got the order of the end-words wrong, a natural enough mistake for anybody asleep to make, so I had to work it out from there when I woke up. I didn't want to change the "mistake."

But do I understand you right in thinking that part of what you said is that this is not necessarily a one-way street: in other words you come from, say, your apprentice work to the present, but not in a necessarily evolutionary way—developmental, yes, but not necessarily evolutionary?

I think that's true. That's my own sense of it. There are single poems, perhaps even groups of poems, or poems in a certain style, that I would be willing to put aside, but I wouldn't want to be too harsh on any phase of what I've done just because it was this instead of that. There's a way in which, since it's mine, I like it all.

Doesn't everybody feel that way? No, I don't look on it as progress, which would be the term to describe an evolution. If anything, it's more a simple process of continual change and not a progress toward any foreseeable goal of perfection. Partly it must be in response to the pressures in what you might even call the culture of the time, you know. I think most people are sensitive to fashions, literary fashions, and I believe I have been too. I don't feel guilty about it.

But isn't part of that change from the first book to the second and the third due to your reading of certain Spanish poets?

They certainly were an influence on some of the poems in the third book, yes.

I was thinking of "The Man Closing Up," for example.

That's from the French, of course, a sort of leap I take from Guillevic's poem. No, I couldn't have written that poem without having read some Guillevic, even though it happened to be written without my having a copy of his poems around. I remembered his poem. I had translated it very roughly one afternoon, about, oh, ten months before I sat down to write my own version, and of course without planning at the time to write a poem from it, and I remembered something about it. I certainly remembered the *strong* sense of a definite style that Guillevic had given me. And I was interested in seeing if I could do something similar in style in my own language, in English.

That was really my question: what is it that you found in the translation of, let's say, French?

I thought I found in some poets various possibilities for style which I had not found in American and English poets or in myself. But I hope the styles I saw corresponded somehow to things in myself, and potentially in the language. Not altogether foreign. I'm not *sure* that that's so.

This may be dumb, but what do you mean by style? If we were talking about prose, I'd think I'd have a better sense . . .

Well. There were certain features of style in Guillevic, for instance, in the poems of his that I liked, which I had not seen handled in the same way by American or English poets. He did write in the skinny line, the short line, which a lot of American poets have done, but he did not sound at all like William Carlos Williams, which most skinny-line poems in English tend to do, or did until a few years ago. He used particulars, for example, but did not make a big point of it. They might appear or they might not. And he used plain language and, I suppose, even some somewhat slangy turns of phrase, which might make him resemble Williams, but the total effect of the way he put all these together was so unlike Williams that it was refreshing, not that I don't admire Williams himself greatly. I suppose, now that I think of it, I was interested in the fact that his poems looked as if they should sound like Williams and they didn't. There was a sort of challenge to me to find out what the secret of that was, and I tried to invent or duplicate that kind of effect for myself, for, as far as I know, the first time in English and for, as far as I know, up to this point, the last time, too. For better or worse.

But in those poems in the second book, and I think this is true of many things in **Departures,** *there's a lot more breathing room, a lot more—the current cliché is "open-endedness." Let's say there's a very clear sense of silence surrounding the poems. And inside the poems, too.*

That's true. I used to try to put in all the logical steps, and all the connections, and to try to finish the statement with a conclusion. I was thinking, before coming over here tonight, that I used to be more certain about things in my youth than I am now. Whatever changes may have taken place may be related to that—some principle of uncertainty. Most poems written in 1970, say, were more like that—more "open-ended"—than most poems written in 1950, and it may simply be that I was going along with the tide of the time. But I am generally more wary of "statement" now, of announcing any conclusions, in verse *or* prose, than I was when starting out—in 1952.

Despite your still-professed interest in the sestina (which I believe I have, too), nonetheless, you don't write many sestinas.

No, I haven't written any for, oh, nearly twenty years.

And your commitment to that kind of formal pattern certainly seems less than it once was.

As to commitment, yes. I have been interested not in what passes for organic form, which I have never understood as applied to literature, but in finding what I would prefer to acknowledge as literary forms, perhaps ones that have not been much used before, however. One of the reasons for my interest in poems in other languages, for instance, was a result, I believe, of the illusion of perceiving in them literary forms which I had not encountered in English. Now, I don't mean something that you could call, say, a sonnet. Take an example. I like to talk specifically, when I can. There's a section of an Alberti poem about his early school days called "Collegio, S.J." I first encountered it in translation in *Modern European Poetry,* and then I read it in Spanish, and I noticed that the translator had altered what seemed to me a crucial part of the syntactical form of the poem, an alteration which, to my mind, very drastically changed the rhetorical force of the original construction. There had been an address to the sea in the poem, at the beginning of the last paragraph: "O Sea," he says, or just "Sea"—I've forgotten now what he says in Spanish. And the translator had put this at the *beginning* of the poem, and just such a simple shift as that seemed to me to eliminate a great virtue in the original text, in which, for line after line, maybe fifteen lines—I don't remember the exact figures—Alberti had been addressing something or someone, you didn't know who or what. It was very mysterious and engaging, and suddenly he says, "Sea, you used to come up to our classroom"—whatever it is he says there. And I thought that was a magical moment, which the translator had obliterated. In the interest of clarity, perhaps. Well, I was interested in seeing if that postponement of the apostrophe, as at the least a small syntactical or rhetorical form, truly had the inherent power I suspected, and if what I thought I found there in the Spanish might also be used in English. I think I found that it could be. That kind of thing—small things often—but that sort of thing is one way in which I think I was borrowing from foreign poets, things that are more rhetoric or structure than content or attitude.

As long as we're talking about form and things, here's one of those impossible questions I wanted to ask you. What determines a line in unmetered verse, do you think?

That does appear to depend on whim, and I think you might say the duty of the poet is to enforce his whim, so that it comes close to being a principle. And one that can be perceived. Otherwise, I find it boring to see the text broken up as lines. Many free-verse poets, obviously, have broken lines according to phrase length, according to phrase division. That would seem to me the most conventional way of doing it. Much of Stevens's free verse seems to me to divide by phrase. And that's a reasonable method of proceeding. Others have not— Williams often did not break by phrase, as we commonly understand it. He had some other rhythm, I suppose, in his mind or ear, and yet I believe that his aberrant line divisions—aberrant in the sense that they do not obey the phrase length, the phrase division— seem in many poems to reach toward the level of principle, to be perceptible as significant. Other poets have broken lines in order to be witty. Williams does this sometimes, consciously or not—to get a double sense out of either the last word or the first phrase in the next line. Marvin Bell used to do that frequently in his earlier poems, and Creeley has done that some. Other people have done it. I find it difficult to understand the mystique of line lengths obeying the breath, by rules. I just don't understand that, though some people seem to. I should think, in that case, that if the poet lived long enough and developed emphysema, his lines would become shorter, more ragged, more desperate. Fewer.

It suggests that Creeley is terribly asthmatic.

I didn't mean to suggest that. But he is being, I believe (I think I can say this without prejudice), willful and arbitrary with his line divisions, and he must know it. *He does* know it, I'm sure. Yet some of his poems do, I think, reach toward suggesting, or better, demonstrating, a perceptible principle in this business of the line. Must free verse be something in which anything goes? I think the things that go are things which you can see as going much in the same way, from line to line, or even, in the body of a poet's work, from poem to poem, so that you can say about the work of X, "Oh, I see. His lines go like this," and in the work of Y, "Oh, his lines go like that." If a universal principle for free verse were ever discovered—but that's inconceivable, isn't it?

When you say it's according to a poet's whim, that does somehow suggest, not just arbitrariness, but almost capriciousness.

Surely all of us must have read many poems which seemed absolutely capricious in their manipulation of line length, at least, if nothing else. That might by paradox become principle, perhaps, but I don't think so. Some people don't care, you know, and that's almost their principle, I think. I wouldn't want to mention names. I prefer a poem to be organized.

What does that mean?

First, to have an apprehensible structure. Something that if you were required by law to do so you could describe in other words. Not something merely felt, which I think is likely to be illusion, but something which three reasonable people could all agree had indeed been happening.

I don't understand what would be the difference between saying you establish something as a principle within a poem and saying that you found the physical form for the spiritual event or idea or impulse in the poem. Would they be the same thing?

I suppose they could be, if I could understand the second option, but, you see, I just have a kind of mental block there. I can't understand how the physical could represent the spiritual. It may be that I have that kind of difficulty because I don't believe in the spiritual. You know, there is a power in the obvious. That which is hidden I can't see. That may be because I was brought up as a Southern Baptist and lost my faith.

Well, the containing and ordering of energy, would that be the same thing?

That sounds pretty good to me, yes. But again, you might ask the question, "What would the ordering be?"

Where does it come from? That's really the question.

I don't think it comes from some source exterior to the operations of the mind or to the syntactical potential of the language.

Denise Levertov has made the statement somewhere that experience has a pattern, has an order, and that the problem of the poet is to find that.

She *undoubtedly* must believe that. She's an honest woman, but whatever pattern my experience has, I can't find it. My experience, my life, may have a certain pattern to it, but if so, it would be so simple to describe that it would be a great bore to describe it, even to bother to mention it. And I'm interested in other matters anyhow. One thing: I'm just not that interested in imposing my sense of self, of my discoveries about the essence of life on others. I don't like to think of myself as a propagandist or an evangelist.

In other words, understatement is to you, practically, a religious principle.

Yes.

Nevertheless, when one reads the first book and the second book and the third book and sees, maybe not an evolutionary growth, but certainly sees your developmental kind of change, one can still perceive, I think, a kind of unity of voice, or sensibility, which, in fact, is saying something. Maybe not something "spiritual," but nevertheless it has about it certain means, certain content, certain things to say.

I hope so. It seems to me I can see that, sometimes while working on something, but I'm not sure, and I wouldn't want to force it.

But what is being said? By **Departures,** *it seems to me, you are, obviously, not only deepening whatever it is that makes up your concern, but, to use Mark Strand's word, it is getting "darker." Is that just a function of age?*

Oh, I think it probably is, to tell the truth. One could make moral and philosophical . . . One could say that one has seen deeply into the heart of things, but I'm not sure that's so. Most people, I believe, become sadder as they grow older. And there's plenty of reason to.

Yes. But there is clearly a self being revealed there, even if one is not, in fact, being forced at the reader.

Yes, sure. I probably was too quick to dismiss the self before. If one has enough character, it's going to show in spite of one's attempts to disguise it, as an actor playing a role can be recognized from role to role, even though the name of the character he's playing has changed, or the age of the character, the setting, *et cetera*. Something about his own character is going to be visible, or he lacks strength as an actor, and will not get many jobs, and those will be small ones. Given that (and it's the sort of thing one has to have faith in), believing that one's character is there, then it seems to me you can stop worrying about it. And it will show up. If it doesn't, then you throw the poem away. Or others will. So I feel nervous about fingering the self too much, or about others who do. I think it's something that *won't* disappear.

Would you agree that it has become more visible in your work by the third book, through its own reticence, perhaps?

Well, it's possible that it has. If so, I don't see that it has done so *because* I've been trying to withdraw. That seems contradictory, offhand.

Well, I think in a very paradoxical sense the withdrawing is a presence. With the understanding and the reticence the self becomes more and more exposed.

I began to think toward the end of writing those poems, that the effacement of the self could become or had already become a pose, and I wouldn't want to play around with it too much longer. I threw away some pieces on that theme—a total effacement at last, the pose abandoned. I think some kind of pose is probably being struck in most poems, though. But one of the poses that I prefer to strike is of not striking a pose. It gets pretty elaborate if you start to articulate it. You know what I mean.

* * *

One of the things I'd like to talk about out of this kind of conversation is really a difficult, but serious and fundamental matter: namely the source of poetry, the source of the impulse *of poetry, maybe in general but particularly in your own poetry. I think you have always had a profound strain of melancholy in your poems, right from the outset. And I wonder, what seems to you to be the source of the poems, the impulse for poetry? Is it loss, that essential presence of time in our perception, the sense that even at the moment of being, we know it's passing?*

Something like that, I'm sure. True for me, maybe for others. So far as I can psychologize it, one of the motives for writing is surely to recover and hold what would otherwise be lost totally—memory or experi-

ence. Put very simply, so that one might not wholly die. Sometimes I think of poetry as making things, you know. Common enough, surely. And I would like to have made some nice things. And in those nice things to have got something I would not like to have forgotten: probably involving my own experience, but perhaps that of others. I'd like to think I could write dramatically about other people, not just the damned self all the time. I like looking at old photographs very much, and I. . . . It's not a very high-class analogy—but I would like it if, not directly, but in a similar way, some of the poems I've tried to write were treasurable in the sense that I *know* a photograph can be treasurable. Treasured.

Would you say that your attitude, your feeling, your attitude toward *your feeling about what you've written and made would be to say, "these I made" rather than "these I was?"*

Oh, I would certainly prefer that articulation.

Let me ask you this: do you think, do you feel that when you're working on one particular poem, you leave out a good deal more than you put in (certainly I feel I'm doing that) but also that in the process you're getting more of that poem in.

Well, what does get in can be more accurately perceived by virtue of the exclusion of those things which did not pertain. I like to try, although I think it's very hard to do—and I don't try to do it so much in life as distinct from art—but I would like to make as much sense out of things as possible. And not to go through art, even if I may be obliged to go through life, confused. I would like to make efforts toward clarity and perceptions truly registered, and . . .

So your poems are an instrument to that end?

Language itself is for me—when I'm being very careful with it, as I am when I'm writing. Talking isn't. Talking is for social intercourse and pleasure, too, but I think the pleasure is of a different order. For one thing, it can last, it can be repeated.

You think that's why you write slowly?

Well, yes, I think that's one of the reasons, sure. I do like to get things right. I don't care nearly so much in conversation. Or in interviews.

I'm just wanting somehow to talk more fundamentally about the distinction between the poet as ongoing poem, which several people live their lives and writing as these days; and the poet as a filter, organizer, register of experience. I think the American classical poetical differentiation is between a Whitman and a Dickinson esthetic.

I think that makes sense, and obviously, I would belong to Dickinson's "closed room."

* * *

After **Departures** *what happens?*

I don't know. I really don't know and I'm not as excited about not knowing as probably I should be. But I—if I write anything more, it will probably be either a reversion to the formal, perhaps even the absolutely formal, or else a number of dignified prose sentences, one after the other. I really don't think I'll write many more poems in the mode—or modes—of *Departures* or *Night Light* or *Summer Anniversaries.* I wouldn't find that very fascinating to do, and so I—insofar as I'm looking for anything—I'm looking for a way to do something a little different that would still be natural to me. For instance, one of the reasons the formal possibility interests me a little now is that I feel that the poems in *Summer Anniversaries,* some of which were quite formal, were just, for me, demonstrations to myself that I *could* do something. I now think that I could handle those things better. And it might be worth doing, for myself, if not for anyone else. But I'm not sure about that—just about all I've written since *Departures* has been a long libretto and a few epigrams, a few fragments. Fragments appeal to me—there's an inevitable pathos about them. Which may be an unacknowledged reason for the appeal of so much that's chaotic in art nowadays, unfinished. I might write another libretto, then, or a few more epigrams. Certainly more fragments.

You think you're getting more interested in the theater, then?

I would be if I could be. I would write a play tomorrow if I could, but I don't think I could. When one starts out in life—isn't this true for all of you? It was for me—one thinks the possibilities are infinite. There is nothing you couldn't do. But as time passes, some of the possibilities, obviously, fall away. And you probably can't do them any longer. You might have been able to had you started twenty years before. Really getting immersed, as I got immersed in writing poems, things choose you. I wanted most to write music. I've said that before.

You were a pianist?

I played the piano and a few other instruments, not all that well, but I did study composition for, oh some while in late adolescence. With Carl Ruggles, incidentally—a fine teacher. He wanted me to study with Hindemith at one time. I may have shown some promise but at some essential point I doubted. My sense of

rhythm came into question, I think. And so I sort of stopped. I'd always been writing a little—words, I mean—and I turned to that. But I regret the music.

Who were your poetry teachers?

I was in classes with several people. Let's see. The first one must have been Winters. I was already trying to write poems, of course, and had gone to Stanford because Winters was there, and I stayed there a year. The next poetry class I was in was conducted by Paul Engle here at Iowa. And while I was a student here, classes I was a member of were taught by Karl Shapiro and Robert Lowell and John Berryman. All of them in some sense were teachers of mine. Stevens was too—though just through a book. One of the reasons I'm skeptical about whatever reputation I have as a teacher is that there is an obvious sense in which teachers don't teach directly—the classes provide the occasion for doing what you would be doing otherwise or anywhere. I learned some things from all those men, I'm sure, but it's very hard for me to know exactly what, except that I think I did learn more about meters from being around Winters than I would have caught onto by myself, or so quickly.

I'd like to go back with you just a second to something you said a moment ago. I was intrigued by what you said, that after **Departures** *you didn't know where you would go, maybe to write formal poems, or a series of dignified prose sentences, statements. I wondered why.*

Because that would be something that I haven't done before, and I think it would be a possibility for writing that would be interesting enough to make me try it. I've tried doing it some in private lately. And the first alternative—the strictly formal—because, as I say, I don't think I got it quite right the first time and would like to give myself a second chance.

I was thinking of that second alternative. I understand the first one. Do you find many experiments with the prose poem nowadays interesting?

No, not very. There was a period when the prose poem did interest me, when not very many people had been doing it. Now the form of the prose poem or the kind of prose poem most people have written in America in the last ten, fifteen years is, as far as I can see, just about used up. The ones that may be interesting right now are of a type that my mind just isn't given to making up—little prose fables. They're different from the standard nineteenth-century French prose poem, which most of the prose poems in America I read and enjoyed really took off from. No, I'm not interested in the prose poem specifically. I wrote a couple—actually I wrote more than a couple but I published only three, I guess: two in a book and one in a magazine. And that was about it.

Why do you think it has been fascinating to a number of people the last ten years?

Partly because it's different from the poem organized by lines. It looks different, it gives you different chances for putting words together. And also, to be candid, I think it's probably easier. And it may be a way of being honest about things. You could divide most of the prose poems I've seen up into lines, and they would look like poems. But it's a modest pleasure to be honest in this way and say, "Well, but that would just be for the show of it, to divide this poem up into lines. I'm just going to put it down here in a natural-looking way and make no pretensions about it." I like that attitude, but I think it's been done enough now so that I'm not interested in it for myself.

Do you think it has been part of, at its best, an experimenting on the frontiers of trying to find out when you cease to write poetry, what poetry can be?

It may well have been for some writers. I don't see it that way as a part of American literary history. It's just another thing that people were doing. I'm not sure that it has very much importance at all. I think it will probably be an occasional thing for your average American poet. I think it should be an option available to anyone. But it has no serious, as far as I can see, no serious importance as something apart from whatever else poets have tried.

Nor any discovery importance beyond itself?

As far as I can tell, the French discovered it in the middle of the nineteenth century and that was that.

I would be interested in knowing just exactly what you think of emotion in poems, or what you think the place of emotion is or how it works in poems.

I no longer know. At one time I thought I did, and I used to say that I didn't think it had any place in poems, but I'm far less certain about that now. I think probably emotion *does* belong in poetry. But just how much and just where? The question might better be, how to keep it out? I really don't know. As I was saying, I'm much less certain about some things now than I used to be. Someone once told me: "I just gave this poetry reading to a high school (I think it was a high school) and before I was through reading the kids were in tears." And that appalled me. I thought that was, I really thought that morally wrong. I've never wanted myself to move people in that physical way through whatever emotion there may be, properly or not, in poetry. I guess I like to think of poems as, ideally, objects of contemplation. Objects, first, of contemplation rather than of action. Action would include the weeping of an audience.

Are not you yourself sometimes moved to tears by poems?

No.

You never have been, by anybody's?

No. And I hope I can say that at the very end as I say it now.

"I never wept." Last words, "I never wept."

Yes. I have been moved close to tears by dramatic occasions, but . . .

You have been moved by poems, emotionally, surely.

Yes, some interior psychological motion, which may have been emotion, yes. But physical evidence was missing.

I'm interested in that. A person can weep inside.

I did come close to weeping many years ago at a play called *A Hatful of Rain* when Shelley Winters picked up the phone and said "Police, I want to report a junkie," pause, "my husband. . . ." Then the second time I can remember coming close to tears was another dramatic occasion, the movie—what is the name of it?—the movie with Shirley Booth and Burt Lancaster . . .

Come Back, Little Sheba.

Come Back, Little Sheba. And again, by coincidence perhaps, it was when Shirley Booth picked up the phone to call her parents and say something like "Doc's at it again." And I thought, maybe emotional responses of a gross physical sort were tied for me exclusively to the telephone, and I didn't understand that. I still don't understand it. But those were the first two times in my life since about the age of twelve that I can remember being close to tears. And then last year I saw a performance of a little opera by Hindemith and Thornton Wilder called *The Long Christmas Dinner,* and there was something about the staging of it which moved me *very* close to tears. The people, when they died, walked down some steps into the audience. They're dying all through the opera—it was a play first and then made into an opera—and somehow when they would take that first step down into the audience, some little thing in the corner of my eye would quiver. And I found that so interesting, partly just to observe my own reaction because it was so rare, that I went back to see it the second night it was being performed, and the same thing happened. Every step, practically, boom! Something happened in the corner of my eye. But it's a very rare thing, which is one of the reasons I bother to mention it. I am, I hope, stoic.

Do you think poems have an emotional dimension?

Most poetry has what you could call, very simply, content, subject matter—people and events—as novels do. Events like death, love, the death of love, the love of death: I would like to associate the emotion I may be feeling when reading a poem or writing a poem with the event which itself is associated with, or evokes, the emotion. And I do feel the pleasure of recognition or the excitement of being startled that can be aroused by some language in some poetry now and then, or a sense of admiration or envy, when suddenly a word is very surprising or very revealing, or when a phrase is memorable and you're not going to forget it. I don't know if I'd call that emotion or not. I think of that, in part at least, as an intellectual reaction, which is not quite the same thing as an emotional reaction, though the two may be tied together.

Well then you would say of "Absences" that there is an intellectual concept that's behind that?

The poem? I think that the poem is an intellectual construction—as I look at it anyway. But what I refer to throughout that poem is events, rather indirectly sometimes, but events, or people; and emotions are associated with these events, these people.

Well, I don't think it's possible to deal with events or people without the emotional possibilities.

I use a word in there that I suppose, for me, is loaded with about as much emotion as a word is likely to be for me, the word "palms." And for me that's a very rich word because of, for one thing, the childhood associations with the palms around where I grew up, and partly it has become richer for me because it now exists *only* in memory—there are no palms in Iowa City—and, furthermore, the palms in Miami happen to be dying. And they always seemed like a really visible physical symbol of—if there is such a thing—something spiritual to me. There is a beauty in palms, I think, perhaps because of childhood associations, and then also because—you know, even this is an intellectual or literary association—Mallarmé uses palms in a beautiful and surprising place in one of his poems, and don't think I didn't think of that when I thought of using the word "palms," too. I'm loaded down with self-consciousness. But mainly its associations for me are with childhood, as I think is more or less spelled out in the poem.

But it seems to me the poem "Absences" is all about emotion. I mean, it seems to me it is emotion.

It's one of the most emotional poems, I guess, I ever wrote. Some people seem to like it, perhaps for that reason.

But I think its content is emotional and that all of the things you have selected in it, your inclusions, are there because of the emotion that they are adequate to and accurate representations of.

All right, okay. That seems fair enough to me, yes. I wouldn't have put the cereus in, for instance, if I hadn't felt serious about it. And yet emotion tends to disappear for me, I think, when much show is made of it.

You wouldn't go as far as to say only technique endures? As opposed to Pound's own emotion.

Well, no, I wouldn't, now that you cite me that exemplary observation. I wouldn't dare.

Oh, of course you would dare, if you believed it.

You know, in Pound's work—I don't know it as well as many people do—but it seems to me that his technique may last at least as long as the emotion. So I think cases might alter circumstances. Circumstances might alter cases? How does that go? Anyway, with some poets, it might be that the technique is indeed what endures. And I don't think that's a judgment involving value or hierarchies. A normal reaction might be to think, oh yes, those whose technique only endures are the lesser poets. I'm not sure that's the case.

But isn't technique at the service of something? Almost by definition—I wouldn't say almost—*in fact by definition.*

Well, maybe so.

Technique, the practice of doing something.

Maybe so.

Well, let's go back to "the impulse to poetry." What is the technique at the service of? Recording fact or moment? Rescuing from oblivion? Embodying the emotional reality of an experience? Consider your poem "Landscape with Little Figures." That poem would seem to be a good example of your sense of enriching the content of a poem by leaving out. But actually what is left out of that poem is still completely apprehensible in the emotional aura of a *time and* a *place—and even, one assumes, of your life.*

Yes, that's good, if you get that sense from it.

But why is that good?

Well, because it is . . . Let me try to say this right. It is good (if it is) because it had to be through the verbal construction rather than the facts of experience that it came to seem so, and therefore the purpose of the poem, or one of the purposes of the poem, reaches its end, is successful in that way, in that it does something of what it set out to do. I think it does that by equivalence, though—that's not a very clear way of putting it—but I think it operates—as many poems do—like this: I go through these motions in the poem and thereby you see, yes, it *is* as if such and such *were* so, or as if such and such were to be felt. I don't think the correspondence between what is felt or seen by a reader can possibly be the same as what I first knew, but I have, as it were, mediated between the reader and what could only be known to me by way of these lines, these words and phrases. Partly to conceal, really, rather than to reveal. I'm talking about A in the poem, say, and in truth I'm thinking B. But I'm talking about A so that *you* can feel or see C. That's too complicated a way to try for such a simple little point, but. . . .

It's a kind of poetry by deflection.

That's a better way of putting it, a simpler way. I'm not really talking straight in that poem—even in that poem, simple and childlike as it may seem.

I'm too dense to understand what you mean by that. I don't understand what you mean when you say that the emotion was excluded. I don't understand.

I haven't looked at that poem in a long time, but I think I remember it.

I want to read it to you.

Well, no, I think I remember it well enough to know that it pretends to be talking about the change that took place in a certain neighborhood, and it . . .

I think it is *talking about that.*

Yes, okay. That's its ostensible subject matter, that's the vehicle for the emotion. And the place, this neighborhood, has changed, sadly. Things are not as they were. And I think that's a kind of image for a secret subject which I don't announce in the poem. And don't intend to announce now.

Don't you think that all *poems do that?*

Yes. A lot of poems *are* like that.

But isn't the point that the emotion appropriate to the one you do not directly announce is also the emotion that you endow that "as if" thing with? In other words, that emotion is present. You simply use another vehicle to express that . . .

Okay. Yes. I think all this we're saying is really what I was trying to get at with my elaborate A B C's.

But my point is that that emotion is not excluded in any sense, and it is not denied. A moment, a particular example of it from your private experience, is perhaps not rendered as the vehicle for us to apprehend, true . . .

Yes, that may be unimportant. That's true. But I would like to insist that my own private view of it *is* left out, whether it matters that it's left out or not. Although I do know where the neighborhood was, you know. I'm using something true to fake with. And you can't see it there anymore, you know. That's true, too.

But don't you think anyone who would read that poem would know it's not about a neighborhood? Anyone who's sophisticated enough to read . . .

Maybe so, maybe I'm just simple-minded about my own work. I'm not trying to be funny. But I always thought if I said, say, Rivershore Drive, people would think I meant Rivershore Drive, whereas I felt that I had preserved a secret since I really didn't mean Rivershore Drive. Apparently people must have been reading me all along and knowing that I didn't mean anything like Rivershore Drive.

What I'm wanting to suggest, really, finally, through my posing of questions on this is, tentatively, that the real subject matter of this poem (as, maybe, in many other poems of yours and other people), is that emotion.

You may be right.

Not another thing . . .

You may be right, but I would feel obliged to maintain that insofar as that was true I was unaware of it. I thought I was dealing with other materials. That is, I thought I was dealing with the raw materials of language and rhythm. Usually, when I'm working with a poem, it is such matters as those that I am consciously thinking of. Of choosing among a hoard of words, adjusting rhythms, little things like that.

But you choose for feel, too, don't you?

Probably I would tend to choose, ordinarily, a word richer in what could conveniently be called emotional association than a word poorer, though I've made other choices, words poor in association, on purpose. So it's not always the one thing. But that is, at least, what my conscious mind, when I'm working on a poem, is dealing with. Just the simple raw materials of language and rhythm. I think most words you use in poetry are unavoidably full of content, and so you're dealing with content, too. But that, for me, has always seemed secondary. Now I may be fooling myself.

Do you think there can be any difference between content and subject matter?

No, no, I meant only subject matter, content, whatever term is used. You see, all I want to claim is that, for me, in the process of working, what my conscious mind was attending to was something other than the subject matter, at least primarily. And I'm not trying to boast that it was so or apologize for the fact that it was so, just to describe the case.

Don't you think that's inevitable? That if, in fact, you knew what it was, you couldn't write it or couldn't deal with it or you wouldn't want to, that it would be solved?

For me, that is so.

I think that's certainly true for me, too.

It is? Well, I'm glad to hear it. You know, sometimes it's nice to exchange the sense of things with other people because, don't you ever have the feeling that you're the only one who is screwed up in that particular way?

Exactly, Oh, yes. But I think we're all screwed up in that way. Still, to pursue this point, it does seem to me that that's what the poem is groping toward and after, and that whatever else you're doing, all the skill that you're bringing to bear is, finally, to enable that subject matter to find a local habitation, a home.

You know, ever since I mentioned the word "photograph" earlier, just casually—I had never thought of it that way before—I've been thinking in the back of my mind that it would be a pleasure to write a series of poems which simulated photographs, which really did make up a little album. I don't know. I realized as soon as I said the word some minutes ago that probably none of my poems resembled photographs at all and maybe it would be good to be more direct about it instead of round-about, and, I don't know, maybe I'll try to write some of those.

Let me ask you this question, not in any reductive way at all! I'd like it to kind of open out and see how willing you would be to go a little farther with it. Robert Bly said somewhere, sometime, something to the effect that American poets are too concerned with form, or have been too concerned with form, historically. Now, leaving Robert Bly aside, what do you think of that? As, not only a poet but as a teacher of poets, a conductor of workshops, much involved at the center of the development of American poetry and as an observer of American poetry: what do you think of that?

I think it's partly true and partly not true. It's an exaggeration, it's a propaganda point. There have been brief periods in American literary history, I'm sure, when there has been too much absorption with obvious form. And then—since you did mention Bly as a source for the opinion—one of the times when that was probably true was when he was maturing, as it was of the time when I was maturing. Same period.

Well, I think maybe he said "technique." Excuse me.

Or technique, yes. Things probably do move (later they seem to have moved, when you look back at them) in terms of reactions to what came just before. Another commonplace. And if around 1950 most poets were writing in quatrains, say, it would be natural as a historical process, as a literary process, to stop writing quatrains after a while and to say we were writing too many quatrains, or paying too much attention to technique or to form—whatever term one chose—and to go in another direction. To keep changing—that's probably healthy in the literary life of a culture, as I *definitely* believe it is healthy in the life of a person to keep changing. I'm unsatisfied with the work of most poets who early found a formula and then reproduced it over again. And I think it would be a sign of deadening in the culture of a nation if a formula were found and simply articulated thereafter into eternity. You know, things are going to change. So I think if that were said specifically of twenty years ago he would have to be right; if he were speaking of, say, 1970, he would be wrong. That's all. Poets were *not,* in 1970, too much concerned with form.

I think I sense in that a certain dissatisfaction with an insufficient attention to technique. Am I right?

Yes. Or else . . .

That you think, in other words, that it has gone too far the other way, the reaction.

Yes, I think the time will come, may even now be upon us, for a healthy reaction in the other direction, perhaps not ever to the extent that right after the war we experienced. Literary fashions! The changing generations! It's funny to have watched so much of it, both from the sidelines and as a player of the game. Nostalgic, like watching old movies. There are several poems in ***Departures*** which sort of twit the younger generation and the older lookers-on as well—a little double-sided. **"The Telephone Number of the Muse"** means to operate both ways. The last lines of **"Self-Portrait as Still Life"** announces my position on that, if I have one. Probably, you know, with experience, it begins to seem that nobody has *all* the right of it. There are things to be said on too many sides.

What has been gained by American poetry in, say, the reaction against the extreme formalism of the fifties? What's been gained?

Certain things are obvious. A broadening of subject matter, for one thing, which is a curious accompaniment to the destruction of form. An opening up of subject matter, I believe. And also more fluency. The syntax of poetry being written in 1950, to take the same exemplary year, the syntax tended to be very self-conscious, convoluted, elaborate, restrictive, though sometimes the poems were indeed interesting compositions. Now poets can, it seems to me, be more fluent, easy-going, natural, can say more things. I'm trying to speak of what seem to be virtues. I think a vice that's arisen—oh, there are several obvious vices, no doubt—is so great a lack of formal awareness or concern that an unattractive, an actively unpleasant chaos results, a total abandonment of what I would call, very simply, organization. Order, to be more high-toned. And this, then, is not only absent but prized for being absent, which I cannot go along with. And also—to use a popular term these days—a certain type of "inwardness." Inwardness may be fine for some, but it really can be a drag to others, including me. I mean, I am at least as interested in plain fact as I am in the mystical speculations of X, Y, and Z. And there has been a great outpouring of inwardness, and of a sort that almost always goes in the direction of the mystical, and none of that really is at all interesting to me. Against fashion, I know, but there has been a great deal more self-indulgence of that kind in the poetry of 1970 than in the poetry of 1950. So it seems things balance out. Some good, some not so good.

Do you think as a part of that fluency that poets are able to write a more American language and rhythm?

That's probably true. Some poets were already able to. But more poets prize it now than formerly, and that is a gain, if we are to think in evolutionary terms.

Is it possible to write an American line, an American diction, an American language, in toto, in traditional forms?

Obviously, since it has been done by Robert Frost, for one. He didn't always do it, but, my God, he did it in so many lines that to imagine that it's impossible seems to me ridiculous, if you can read and if you can hear. Sure, Robert Frost did it. Not many others have done it, not so often, so aptly and so expressively. I wouldn't want to sound like Robert Frost in many of my poems. Who would? But he certainly did *that*. If that's the assigned task, he completed it successfully.

* * *

You say in the note in **Departures** *that certain of the poems come, in part, from chance methods. What do you mean by that?*

Well, first to the "in part." Those, I believe, who really commit themselves to chance in the various arts would go all the way and let chance govern. So, the "in part"

is meant to say that I only go so far with it, or that I'm not really a Cage, obviously enough; I like elegance, as he once told me, and the Cage methods do not necessarily result in elegance. But I was interested in finding a further means of keeping myself distant. And I thought it would be interesting to simulate a small computer without actually using one, and so I wrote words onto a great number of note cards, words which I had taken from passages of poems I admired. My own taste, in other words, was involved in the preparations, so that I might think of whatever result was to come as mine, somewhat mine. Thus the "in part": not giving myself totally to the gods of chance. If I were doing that, I could simply open a book, any book, and just take the words down. I can see I haven't explained this very clearly. Anyway, here is what I went through in trying to get in touch with chance: I wrote down on note cards a lot of words from poems or passages I liked. I chose a good number of sentences which interested me as sentences, as syntactical forms, or passages I liked, and I wrote these down on another set of note cards. I divided the word cards up into three groups, nouns, verbs, and adjectives, from which I thought I could generate any other parts of speech necessary to deal with the sentences. I then shuffled the sentence cards, as I called them, and dealt myself a sentence, you might say, and where the sentence called for a noun, I shuffled the noun cards and dealt myself a noun. And where it called for a verb, the same. And so on. And I found in working around with this that chance wasn't all that good to me the first time through, so on some large sheets of paper I would try filling in each sentence three times. Then I would have what seemed a multitude of choices, but actually a workable limit, and having three words to choose from in each place in each sentence, that meant I could generate a number of sentences from each sentence card, and I could go on for as many sentences as I wanted to. By then I might have quite a few lines and I found that when things were going well, when I was being dealt winning hands, you might say, the sentences seemed to cohere to some degree; and where they cohered to a lesser degree than I approved of, I was willing to violate chance and impose myself, to make connections or to leave things out. The first few times I tried it I was running a hot streak, and I thought that I had found a way to write poems forever, one I could give to friends even, but now, well . . . well, I'm not all that much . . .

Only your closest *friends.*

Yes. I'm not all that much for increasing the world's population of poems, so I guess I would have restricted it to a few. But then the more I tried it the less productive it became. I had made my first set of cards in Syracuse and after exhausting that first set I made up another out in California. And that second set exhausted itself much more quickly than the first, so I haven't tried it a third time. Anyway, I realized fairly soon that it wasn't the solution to the problem of writing poems. But I like some of the results and in any case I would only keep whatever results seemed true and not just lucky. I wasn't going to surrender myself totally to chance. I wanted esthetic choice. I reserved the right to do my own work. But it seemed to me—one of the ways I like to think of it is that it seemed to me to simulate the actual working of the imagination. I mean, one does have an accumulated store of words and some notions of what interesting sentences would be like; and with this process you didn't have to wait, didn't have to do that dull sort of beginning work, or you did it in a different way, so therefore it seemed stimulating and interesting. And I certainly must have come up with some lines and some images that I would never have gotten otherwise with the very hardest work. For a while there I felt I could go out there and say to the gods that don't exist, "Give me something."

Gerald L. Bruns (essay date fall 1980)

SOURCE: Bruns, Gerald L. "Anapostrophe: Rhetorical Meditations upon Donald Justice's 'Poem.'" *Missouri Review* 4, no. 1 (fall 1980): 71-6.

[*In the following essay, Bruns elucidates his reaction to Justice's "Poem" and poetry in general.*]

> This is so important because it has to do with the question of a writer to his audience. One of the things I discovered in lecturing was that gradually one ceased to hear what one said one heard what the audience hears one say, that is the reason that the oratory is practically never a master-piece very rarely and very rarely history, because history deals with people who are orators who hear not what they are not what they say but what their audience hears them say. It is very interesting that letter writing has the same difficulty.
>
> —Gertrude Stein, "What Are Master-Pieces and Why Are There So Few of Them" (1936)

I

> This poem is not addressed to you.
> You may come into it briefly,
> But no one will find you here, no one.
> You will have changed before the poem will.

This poem ["**Poem**"] is not addressed to me, but it was not written except to teach me the meaning of its disregard. Its message could not have been more swift and deadly. I know that poems do not mean what they say, and that this poem is not addressed to me except in cunning plainness, yet I am allowed to figure in it only briefly, the phantom of apostrophe, with barely enough time to wander among the poem's relations before turning these odd transparent colors. No doubt anyone may

enter this poem, so free and easy is it among its new favorites, but toward me it obtains a strange and chaste decorum. I find that enter yes I may, but I am coolly received and soon a servant appears and asks not at all quietly will I be remaining long, yet if I commit quickly everything to memory surely then it will be mine, having not surrendered itself, to be sure, but let us say selected its place among my inward and fanciful possessions. Cacodaemonic poem! It forms part of my self-possession but nothing, alas, of my self-regard. The poem is not addressed to me, resists each of my careful advances, but it has claimed some unaccountable portion, has made itself mine but oddly in my most alien part. The other bad news is that I was one time the handsome contemporary of this poem, but now you will hardly recognize me. No doubt I am restored now and again to regular sources of dignity, but the poem remains itself, aristocratically reserved, I will not say in the special instance before me absolutely unfaded before or against the aging of its pages, but there is no mistaking its graceful carriage and the clarity of its rule. For my part I suffer ceaseless and furious daily revision, my author seems not to know what to say, nor art nor purpose attend his actions, I am addressed to no one. I cry out unpredictably. I will one day idly stop, bereft of an ending, whereas this nettlesome poem will until the angels die recline in its most masterful repose. It is something in which I could hide, no one will think to find me here.

II

> Even while you sit there, unmovable,
> You have begun to vanish. And it does not matter.
> The poem will go on without you.
> It has the spurious glamor of certain voids.

The poem seems not to imagine my agitation and the quick elusive motions as I read. I have begun to vanish, but chiefly in principle; in reality I struggle to maintain a full economy of desire. I propose, therefore, that no one, not even the poet, can explain why this poem refuses to take me into its confidence. Can't you see that it simply wishes to be rid of me, the common and the gentle reader, and so it conspires with certain handy devices to disguise my presence? I am the you in the poem who is not addressed, and who is therefore abolished as by uncreating discourse. You have begun to vanish, it says—this is not impressive. Once I heard a hypnotist use these very words. You have begun to vanish, he said, and now you have faded completely into nothingness. The audience was restless and uncomprehending, the hypnotist was French. Only a few of us could imagine the poor subject's dumb alarm when the empty mirror was placed before him. I could see written in his face the sudden colossal story of his disappearance, but then the hypnotist recalled him with an odd word and by God there he was, or anyhow there the other one of him was: as though to confirm his self-possession he began making faces. The hypnotist looked at him wearily. No one applauded because, of course, no one could be sure anything had happened. There was only a momentary and generally second-hand sense of dispensation. Dogs and monkeys routinely confront empty mirrors, that which is odorless being also naturally invisible. To make it sound systematic a philosopher will say that the appearance or disappearance of anything is indifferent to its reality. At all events the poem will proceed alone, much like the image that consumed but did not reflect the interest of its companion.

III

> It is not sad, really, only empty.
> Once perhaps it was sad, no one knows why.
> It prefers to remember nothing.
> Nostalgias were peeled from it long ago.

You are being addressed, not me, on the subject of mind or memory, music or history, the expression on her face, the famous onion of regret, the poet's heart, his word and the failure to keep it, skepticism. A poem grows sooner or later isolated from its occasion, hence the lover's lapse into anaesthetic song. A certain melancholy obtains the more keenly for being unaccountable—or, what is more likely, this is what the poet would like her to believe, you can tell he's aching for her still. The poem, for its part, indifferently survives, full of reserve and discretion: we don't even know her name, whether she returned to that obscure town, what it was that brought them to this pass, how they used to goad one another into painful confessions. All of that is behind us now, the subject of poetry and forgetfulness. Looking at her now you would not have guessed that her eyes were heartbreaking even to strangers. I have only seen a photograph of her, taken, of course, when she was much younger, long before the trip to Canada that ended in hysteria and recrimination. Now everything is quiet. I prefer it this way. You will think me needlessly subtle, but really I'm able to remember nothing of the events that concern you. It's certain I'm not the person appealed to in this document. The authorities will vouch for me.

IV

> Your type of beauty has no place here.
> Night is the sky over this poem.
> It is too black for stars.
> And do not look for any illumination.

Every poem must have its dark lady, owing mainly to the odd business of the dragon's teeth. As with most things in the beginning there was lucid song and a life lived in someone's trust. Radiant transcendental creatures talking the night away—no one thought much about them. Every misunderstanding produced a terrific

laugh, and every word the poet sang had a story behind it. Then, with everyone pretending not to notice, it went to pieces. Things affected an indifferent or guarded behavior and memory grew self-willed and marvelous. You couldn't enter a conversation without someone tugging at you for explanations. I swear to you I never used to think twice about meaning what I said, but I've learned how the animals have wrong names which it is all right to use and right ones that can take a piece out of your tongue. That's partly why I have this difficulty with my speech, and why under the aegis of night I take counsel of dissembling and concealment—and why it is I have this problem with a poem. Unanswerable style! It is useless to think on it. The natural inclination of meaning is to steal away under the cover of darkness. Poetry is not so lustrous as she is vulnerable, as, for example, to time, which can steal away the meaning of any utterance. What if there is no such thing as meaning except in the caverns of the alphabet? The poet speaks, and his words disperse like galaxies simultaneously in all directions, momentarily they fill some of the voices I carry with me for business reasons; he writes, however, and meanings scurry every which way, nor shall we set eyes on many of them again, although we know precisely where they are.

V

> You neither can nor should understand what it means.
> Listen, it comes without guitar,
> Neither in rags nor any purple fashion.
> And there is nothing in it to comfort you.

It may be, of course, that ways lie open for me to understand this poem. Methods are everywhere at hand, inexpensive and easy to learn, portable at least, hence I may advance more or less in this poem's direction, having failed to get there on my own. It is method that stems the flow of reason and memory. Suppose, therefore, that this poem is not about itself but is rather a frightful precursor of that which passes understanding? The way is therefore open to ask: When it arrives, this impassable poem, what will it resemble, or will it be secretly sublime, addressing itself in everyday expressions yet growing more impassive as it draws more near? Perhaps it is already upon us, not a very popular piece of work, being stealthy, by turns daemonic and divine, nor will it teach for money, it is of the middle style and a Good Physician, in its language we find not our comfort but our misery and our cure, it will not be put to the test, it will prove the undoing of many, nor shall we escape its vengeance, especially not those who disseminate theories, nor those who customarily speak to the matter at hand, nor those who cultivate the language of distraction, nor those who will lie merely to gain your attention. Suppose, on the other hand, its theme is befuddlement and the dispossession of faculties? I would not come near such a poem. I would conduct myself irreproachably in order to bear witness against it, showing greater forbearance, for example, among my own kind. I need hardly say how much I would refuse to hear word of it, thoughtfulness ought not to be incurred in its behalf. Yet consider what would recoil to my benefit were it given to me to understand as, in a sense, it was? What would it mean for me to possess the meaning of a poem not addressed to you? Would you not be uncertain of your progress? Would you not mutter among yourselves, we do not know the origin of his teachings? Consider, however, the history we've had with precursors, it's been nothing but anguish and embarrassment, we're still looking for the way to be done with them. Turn away from this poem, don't listen to it.

VI

Close your eyes, yawn. It will be over soon.
You will forget the poem, but not before
It has forgotten you. And it does not matter.
It has been most beautiful in its erasures.

What does she see when she shuts her eyes? Woods and green things growing, to be sure, and Troy finally—*finally!*—on the verge of being taken, but it does not matter. What she sees is perhaps no more than part of the poem which is not written, part of some terrible self-intimacy that fires the poet most darkly and compels him to revise, part of that which beguiles me into these absurd unwanted readings, availing not and mattering not, frequently to the alarm of those who maintain an interest in my welfare. It has erased me from its memories, I see no reason to let this upset me—tell me, what could it have remembered in any case? The agony of composition, you will say, words of superior and lamented meaning, that astonishing rendition that cries to us even now and whose wild voice came within seconds of breaking Plato's heart. But don't you see that he was determined from the beginning to reserve that portion to himself? For this the art of writing gained its considerable reputation. It enabled him to work in silence and without witnesses, and to obliterate now this line, now that, leaving only so much behind to assure us that something we should never understand had taken place. It was shrewd, I can tell you, in its way a master-work. You may as well return his papers, they will show what he thought worth writing, not what he wanted to remember. But I am not finished with him, not by any means. One day he'll forget himself, that daunting self-possession will fail him, he will give himself away. In the heat of some unforeseen composition he'll rehearse those lines, thinking them new evidence of originality. Then we'll have him.

VII

O bleached mirrors! Oceans of the drowned!
Nor does it matter what you think.
These are not my words now.

This poem is not addressed to you.

A mirror is a sanctum of higher conversation. A clock will tell you what time it is, and a map will advise you as to the better or the proven way, but a mirror is contemplative. O speculum mentis! Every once in a while I will consult a mirror on some minor or idle point only to catch a reflection of the sun. The first time it happened I was beside myself. Blinded by my own brilliance, I thought. Later I reflected that it was merely the momentary radiance of self-regard. The mirror did not dispute these reflections, perhaps it silently acknowledged their pastoral utility, but it was made clear that I had got it wrong. Do not bring expectations to a mirror; you must listen to it with an ear for uncertainty and remote connection. Sequor non inferior, it will say; or, Every idea contains within itself the semblance of its reality. Or, again: Οἶνος γὰρ ανθρώποις δίοπτρον. It is painful to consider this self-sufficiency, which naturally diminishes the prerogatives of reason, and also the pleasures of authorship. Years ago a mirror said to me: Only once was I left in the dark; it was that damnable Maimonides. Sometimes I will watch a mirror for days, wondering what it knows. The answer is: there are no depths to it. It is not any sort of reservoir, its vast mobile spaces conceal nothing, if you rap your knuckles against it, it will say tap tap and then, invariably, break into gales of laughter. It refuses to be fathomed. Its words do not originate anywhere; they are not addressed to you.

Michael Ryan (essay date winter 1984)

SOURCE: Ryan, Michael. "Flaubert in Florida." *New England Review and Bread Loaf Quarterly* 7, no. 2 (winter 1984): 218-32.

[*In the following essay, Ryan explores the defining characteristics of Justice's verse.*]

The unusual technical variety of Donald Justice's poetry issues from his consistent refusal to repeat himself, though such "rich refusals" are indicative of an invariable temperament woven into the fabric of the poetry like "God in the universe, present everywhere and visible nowhere," a temperament as relentless as Flaubert's in its insistence on perfect objectivity. Since his first poems, the unmistakeable impression of that famous signature has been just underneath Justice's own: the painstaking search for *le mot juste*, that particular mixture of razor intelligence, cold eye, disaffection, and hermeticism. Justice would agree with Flaubert that "Poetry is as precise as geometry," but would probably note with irony that we now know that even basic axioms can only be proved within closed systems. Each of Justice's poems is a closed system.

Formal limits, conventional or invented, are in his view connected to the nature of language. Only by means of such limits can a world which is always threatening to dissolve be focussed and "fixed"—as he says of the effect of meter—by achieving form (it would be characteristic if he chose the word "fixed" in this context for both of its meanings: "stabilized" *and* "rectified"). At the same time, a formal exercise is sterile unless it uncovers some rich, unavoidable secret. Flaubert kept a stuffed, green parrot on his writing desk to remind himself of the irrational—the same writing desk on which he composed the sentence "Poetry is as precise as geometry." For both Flaubert and Justice, the work does not resolve this paradox so much as embody it, as if concurrent, conflicting desires for the wholly mysterious and the wholly comprehensible can be satisfied only in and by the work itself.

Justice's green parrot appears in **"Tales From A Family Album,"** caged but alive—fed by an "aunt" who, the speaker says, never "overcame her fears, yet missed no feeding, / Thrust in the crumbs with thimbles on her fingers." This is the sort of elaborate literary joke Justice delights in, and it sometimes generates lines and even whole poems. In **"The Mild Despair of Tremayne,"** "mordancies of the armchair" is obviously a take-off from Stevens's "complacencies of the pegnoir"; in **"Variations On A Text By Vallejo,"** Donald Justice dies in Miami on a sunny Sunday, instead of Cesar Vallejo in Paris on a rainy Thursday. And in **"The Summer Anniversaries"** (recast completely in Justice's *Selected Poems* from the opening poem in his first volume), when the poet-at-age-ten exclaims "O brave new planet!—/ And with such music in it," we are probably expected to understand that, in contrast to Miranda in *The Tempest* ("O brave new world, / That hath such people in't!"), this particular child *prefers* music.

But the allusiveness pervading Justice's poems is less an act of criticism (as it was for Pound) or a structural principle (as it was for Eliot), than simply a way of working, of getting the poem onto the page, for a writer who is "loaded down with self-consciousness." This description of Justice is his own, from an interview that appeared in the Spring, 1975 issue of *The Ohio Review*; he talks there about this way of working as "borrowing the voice":

> borrowing the voice allows me, it seems, to speak of myself more directly, more objectively because the voice is not mine. Not simply mine. Probably more than other poets I know, I play games in my poems (as I do in my life), and one of the unwritten rules of the game for me, as I like it played, is that you can risk this much personality or that much confession if the voice is promised to be that of someone else to start with. Even without my recognizing it at the time of writing, that may be one of the reasons I can get pretty literary in choice of subjects, in taking off from other people's texts. There is something in the works of others, I suppose, that gets to me personally, that affords me another perspective, the objectivity and distance I like, so that it is as if I could say to myself, let me use his experience as an image of my own, and I won't have to use mine. But using this turns out to be another experience for me, so it really *will* be mine in the end.

This doesn't account for all, or nearly all, of Justice's poems—since 1975, he has written most often about private experiences, past and present, with his usual detachment yet without "borrowing the voice." But the passage illustrates the paradoxical cast of mind ("the objectivity and distance *I like*") that determines how his poems are made. And they are, above all, *made,* whether from their external forms inward or from their emotional centers outward (as in the poems Justice starts with another poet's "experience as an image of [his] own"). The hazards and limitations of this way of working are obvious but if as a consequence we rarely feel that "he *had* to write about the subject he took, and in that way" (one of Eliot's main criteria for "a great writer"), the poet's distance may be compensated by the poem's immediacy. Given ideal skill, a poet certainly argues implicitly for a particular kind of poetry by writing his own poems the way he does, but he also writes the way he does simply because he hasn't any other choice. Stevens put it better when he said, "I write the way I do not because it pleases me, but because no other way pleases me." The particular character of Justice's style—its unusual lucidity and perfect decorum—may be his response to his temperament as well as a reflection of it. How can a person for whom "emotion tends to disappear when much show is made of it" (another self-description) still write poetry? Justice's style is his answer to this question.

This, then, is Justice's signature, too: the poet's emotion is withheld while the poem's material is presented. The opposite has often been true in American poetry since 1959, the *annus mirabilis* of confessional poetry with Lowell's *Life Studies* and Snodgrass's *Heart's Needle.* Justice and Snodgrass were students at Iowa during the fifties, and Lowell taught there briefly. *Heart's Needle,* Snodgrass's first volume, won the Pulitzer Prize in 1960; Justice's first volume, **The Summer Anniversaries,** appeared the same year. It shows Justice writing, if anything, *against* the confessional impulse, as he has ever since. The passion animating Justice's work has always been a passionate restraint, even a passion *for* restraint. In this way, it resembles Elizabeth Bishop's, but Justice tends much more to irony which can in one mood turn bitter (see **"Sonatina in Green"**) and, in his dominant mood, he is more attracted to possibilities for menace. Like Bishop for most of her life, Justice has been known as a "craftsman" and "a poet's poet." His poems invite this, as if, like some people, they would rather be respected than loved. At first glance, they may appear "cold," "traditional," or, as an acquaintance of mine described them, "sturdy"—to prefer modest accomplishment to ambitious failure. This is not endearing to a Romantic age. Like *Madame Bovary,* Justice's poetry goes to a great deal of trouble not to ask the reader to complete it. He tells us, twice, in **"Poem"**: "This poem is not addressed to you," and, moreover, "it does not matter what you think" (there is a negation in almost every line). Not exactly a Whitmanian embrace.

Yet Justice's relentless insistence on clarity, on realizing the subject within the borders of the poem, amounts to a consideration of the reader which to my mind is the greatest consideration. In a literary atmosphere which has indulged obscurity as "brilliance," Justice's style, were it a matter of choice, would represent an act of moral courage. If this style proceeds from traditional assumptions about language, it nonetheless may make new poetry by going deeper into old, rich veins and by fusing alloys of old and new, of English and European traditions.

Ingmar Bergman, whose films were a springboard for one of Justice's poems (**"A Dancer's Life"**), once said in an interview that the best camera angle is usually the one where the audience doesn't notice the camera. Justice certainly aims for such transparency, to present the subject seemingly without his intervention in "the best words in the best order." As a consequence, each word is required to have a fresh, rational use and placement, and decorum and wit are therefore elevated to major poetic virtues.

So the worst of Justice's poetry suffers from "virtuosity," never from other common contemporary maladies of sloppiness, over-writing, sentimentality, opacity, or tin ear. When Justice's poems fail, it is usually because they are eviscerated by self-conscious irony, mannerism, and literary poses of spiritual exhaustion that derive ultimately from the poetry of Flaubert's contemporaries and that have already resurfaced in every possible guise in English poetry over the last hundred years. As the graffito says, ennui is boring. And as Eudora Welty says in her beautiful essay on Henry Green: "Virtuosity, unless it move the heart, goes at the head of the whole parade to dust." Adding immediately, "With Henry Green we always come back to this: this work is so moving." The extraordinary distillation that can be the main virtue of Justice's style leaves nothing for us to care about when the subject is too removed or attenuated or literary to begin with.

Consequently, Justice's poems are best when it does seem that "*he* had to write about the subject he took, and in that way" (changing Eliot's emphasis from *had* to *he*), when his style seems a discipline to contain his urgency, a way to make the subject pervade the poem, as if (as in Eliot's poetry) such powerful emotion had

to be powerfully muted in order to be objectively realized. These subjects, invariably, are a challenge to Justice's control, because of their richness or mystery, or—perhaps "despite" the writer—his personal investment in them.

Here is one of the earliest (and shortest) of these poems, from ***The Summer Anniversaries,*** dating from about 1959:

"A MAP OF LOVE"

> Your face more than others' faces
> Maps the half-remembered places
> I have come to while I slept—
> Continents a dream had kept
> Secret from all waking folk
> Till to your face I awoke,
> And remembered then the shore,
> And the dark interior.

This is the closest thing to a love poem in Justice's ***Selected Poems***—the only other "beloved" addressed directly is a dressmaker's dummy—although there are other poems about sexual love, most often treated ironically. There's no irony in **"A Map Of Love,"** even if the poem begins with a characteristic qualification or deflation ("more than others' faces") that will be the business of this particular poem to overcome. This sort of deflation is the given when Justice picks up his pen; here it is explicit rather than assumed, which may account in part for this poem's effectiveness. The beloved's presence is barely felt, but the poem is not about her—it's about what she provokes, what takes place in the internal territory of the speaker's psyche. Thus the title (revised—and improved—from **"Love's Map"**), which is the governing trope.

Though this conceit is inventive enough, and its handling graceful enough, the main pleasure of the poem comes, at least to me, from how it presents its information in one sentence draped across trochaic tetrameter couplets. The poetry is more in this, the poem's enactment—the relationship of syntax, rhythm, and content—than in its paraphraseable ideas. "Your face" in the sixth line, for example, causes one of the few disjunctions between metrical and rhetorical stress in the poem, and we feel it as a slight dissonance, a subconscious emphasis, at an important moment in the drama. Marvell showed how the tetrameter couplet could be used in a serious poem by enjambing frequently; Justice does this, and in addition truncates the last six lines to seven syllables each, so that he's not locked into using feminine rhymes (e.g., faces-places), which in couplets tend after a while to become comic. The two middle rhyming pairs (slept-kept, folk-awoke) have a hard, clipped sound, which sets us up for another variation at the end (shore-interior), a soft, half-rhyme on the final, weakly-stressed syllable. This is Justice's main currency: subtle effects solidly based in the arrangement of the language, the organization of the poem. Metrically, the last line consists of two weaker stresses flanking two strong ones, again a *slight* variation within the established pattern of a four-stress line in which the first and last stresses are at least as strong as the others. The syntax of the sentence, besides organizing the elements of the plot, acquires a clarity and ease at the end which is in contrast with the knots and inversion in the middle. The last line, of course, is like "the click of the closing box"; it wants to gather and culminate all that has preceded it, and it does. The speaker's shock of recognition is dramatized by the syntax; what is discovered (in the Platonic sense, "remembered") comes last: "the dark interior." We not only understand this shock, we feel it, literally, because of the variations in the sound, rhythm, and syntax.

This feeling, of course, is fused by the words of the poem to our understanding, our "memory" of having discovered "the dark interior" through another. Such effects may be most easily traced in poems in fixed forms because the pattern of rhythm and rhyme is roughly identifiable, but the sound and syntax of free verse must work analogously or it probably isn't verse at all. The extraordinary palpability of Justice's poems derives as much from the clarity of their shapes as of their subjects, but subject and shape are of course inextricable in language that simultaneously has sound, syntax, and meaning. Since we pay attention primarily to meaning, the sound and syntax subliminally influence the way we receive it, but the sound and syntax—separately and in combination—also make complicated, protean shapes of their own that the reader may not attend to, but which work on him nonetheless. For Justice, however, at least in 1964, a poem by its nature calls for "a different sort of attention on the part of both writer and reader":

> If in a novel the great event is likely to be a death or wedding, in a poem it may well be a sentence, a line, a phrase, or just possibly a single word.

This was the sort of attention encouraged by New Criticism; if current academic criticism is any indication, such attention has almost disappeared from the reading, if not the writing, of poetry. The poets included in *New Poets of England and America* (1957), most of them born in the twenties, were brought up on the assumptions of New Criticism, but almost all of them discarded these assumptions as "academic" within a few years of the anthology's publication. Though Justice was also influenced by the proliferation of translation in the sixties, and himself edited an anthology of *Contemporary French Poetry,* he never underwent the complete turnaround of a Merwin or Rich. Reading Justice's *Selected Poems* in chronological sequence, as it's happily arranged, no careful reader would confuse a poem from the late sixties with one written ten years earlier

or ten years later; the volume as a whole presents even Justice's poetic development with unusual clarity. Yet the attention to "a sentence, a line, a phrase, or just possibly a single word," which he could have learned from Yvor Winters at Stanford in 1948, is the constant in Justice's *Selected Poems* from the oldest poems to the most recent.

What makes the book interesting as a volume, however, is the sense of Justice's testing his assumptions and experimenting with them, from poem to poem. So, if in 1964 (in an essay called "The Writing of Poetry," also quoted above) he wrote:

> In a good short poem a fine sense of relations among its parts is felt, word connecting with word, line with line: as with a spider web, touch it at any part and the whole structure responds.

—which could be an excerpt from the most orthodox New Critical text (and is surely behind the writing of **"A Map of Love"**)—at about the same time he could also write a poem which challenges such structural ideas:

"THE SUICIDES"

If we recall your voices
As softer now, it's only
That they must have drifted back

A long way to have reached us
Here, and upon such a wind
As crosses the high passes.

Nor does the blue of your eyes
(Remembered) cast much light on
The page ripped from the tablet.
. . . . .

Once there in the labyrinth,
You were safe from your reasons.
We stand, now, at the threshold,

Peering in, but the passage,
For us, remains obscure; the
Corridors are still bloody.
. . . . .

What you meant to prove you have
Proved—we did not care for you
Nearly enough. Meanwhile the

Bay was preparing herself
To receive you, the for once
Wholly adequate female

To your dark inclinations;
Under your care the pistol
Was slowly learning to flower

In the desired explosion,
Disturbing the careful part

And the briefly recovered

Fixed smile of a forgotten
Triumph; deep within the black
Forest of childhood that tree

Was already rising which,
With the length of your body,
Would cast the double shadow.
                    . . . . .

The masks by which we knew you
Have been torn from you. Even
Those mirrors, to which always

You must have turned to confide,
Cannot have recognized you,
Stripped, as you were, finally.

At the end of your shadow
There sat another, waiting,
Whose back was always to us.
                    . . . . .

When the last door had been closed,
You watched, inwardly raging,
For the first glimpse of your selves
Approaching, jangling their keys.

Musicians of the black keys,
At last you compose yourselves.
We hear the music raging
Under the lids we have closed.

If the overall structure of **"The Suicides"** does not seem much like a spider web, the poem nonetheless makes as much sense as **"A Map of Love,"** even if sense does derive largely from the "relations among its parts." The conceit of **"A Map of Love"** causes the sequence of images to acquire a kind of momentum like that in problem-solving, and, in retrospect, we see that their order and relationship is fixed and necessary (map-shore-interior). In **"The Suicides,"** the sections seem to be in an appropriate order, and we especially feel the "lastness" of the last section, but the images from section to section don't lock into a connecting logic of their own. The high passes of section one, for example, have nothing to do with the mirrors of section four, and, in fact, a main source of pleasure in the poem is the multiplicity and variety of its figures.

Then how does the poem hold together? There are "spider webs" in **"The Suicides,"** but they are within the sections and not among them, so this represents only what might be called the poem's "secondary" structure. The effect of this sectioning is to let in more air, which is—and this indicates Justice's expertise—sorely needed because of the nature of the subject. And the subject, as it turns out, is less the suicides, the people who died, than the reaction of the living, the opacity of self-destruction. In spite of their differences, **"The Suicides"** and **"A Map of Love"** are identical in

this one way: just as the presence of the beloved is distilled in the earlier poem, the suicides are barely felt because the poem is not about them but about the connection of their act of self-destruction to the living.

This is also the connection that holds the poem together. The grace and ingenuity of **"The Suicides"** becomes apparent when one notices the placement of the we-you pronouns, and the variety of ways they are yoked, syntactically and dramatically. This address—of a kind of representative "we" to an equally, if oppositely, representative "you"—pervades the poem, but Justice modulates it continuously, causing it to be absorbed into little dramas, putting a little more weight now upon the "we" (as in the second section), now upon the "you" (as in the third). As a structuring device, this allows much more range than the development of a single conceit. The poem seems at once various and unified, fluid and solid.

Each section of **"The Suicides"** begins with the we-you address, cast in terms of drama or statement or some combination of the two. This is necessary structural work, but never seems obtrusive or repetitious:

If *we* recall *your* voices
as softer now . . .

* * *

Once there in the labyrinth,
You were safe from your reasons.
We stand, now, at the threshold . . .

* * *

What *you* meant to prove *you* have
Proved—*we* did not care for *you*
Nearly enough.

* * *

The masks by which *we* knew *you*
Have been torn from *you*.

Probably part of our pleasure in the poem comes from the variety, efficiency and inventiveness with which this structural work is accomplished, whether we are aware of its being accomplished or not. We're reminded at the beginning of each section that the poem is addressed to the suicides, and this focusses each section's elaboration of its figures while these elaborations keep the focus on the suicides from being unbearably constricted. The result is a pattern of departure and return, a movement in the mind thinking about the suicides, away and back, the response preferred and the one compelled.

The last section is a kind of coda to this movement. It's a formal *tour de force*, the end words of the first stanza mirrored in the second: closed, raging, yourselves, keys; keys, yourselves, raging, closed. The form mimics the balance and opposition of the "we" and "you" through-out the poem. The first stanza is given to the suicides, and is a wholly dramatic rendering of their first moments after death. And the second stanza belongs to the "we," the living, once again addressing the suicides (though for the first time with an epithet: "Musicians of the black keys"). Drama and direct address, the representative "you" and the representative "we," departure and return—the opposites previously combined in the poem are here isolated, presented in separate stanzas. Yet they are linked through the form, the end words locking into place a closure that the previous sections avoid. The connection between the "we" and the "you," the living and the dead—as in **"A Map of Love"**—is more felt than spoken, and felt primarily through the poem's form and structure. And of course it's no accident that the emotional climax of the poem occurs at a moment when the form is most disciplined.

"The Suicides" is one of Justice's earliest poems in syllabics, which he used frequently in the mid-sixties, and in which he did some of his best work (**"The Suicides," "The Tourist From Syracuse," "Hands"**) and, curiously, some of his worst (**"In The Greenroom," "At A Rehearsal of** *Uncle Vanya*," **"To The Hawks"**). The former group are in seven syllable lines, and the latter in five, and it's as if the shorter line is too constricted. But the syllabic line, even as Justice uses it, has no prosodic identity in English; it doesn't provide a measure (since the duration of each syllable is variable) but simply an arbitrary restriction to an otherwise free verse. Justice no doubt became interested in syllabics through his translation of French—in which the syllable *is* the measure—and it may have given him a way to write a line that is closer to speech than did his earlier metrical line on his way to writing free verse with its own rhythmical identity.

A good book could be written on how Justice uses free verse that would also be a manual of prosody for contemporary poetry. Invariably, the line acts as a tensioning device against the syntax of the sentence, which both discloses its prose rhythm and makes it into something else. One of the best examples, **"Men at Forty,"** also dates from the mid-sixties, when Justice was working primarily with the syllabic line. The poem consists of five stanzas and five sentences, and it gives me great pleasure to watch how the sentences fall into the stanzas and across them, and how the sentence is cut on the phrase to uncover its rhythm and cut against the phrase for the sake of the poetry.

"MEN AT FORTY"

Men at forty
Learn to close softly
The doors to rooms they will not be

Coming back to.

At rest on a stair landing,
They feel it
Moving beneath them now like the deck of a ship,
Though the swell is gentle.

And deep in mirrors
They rediscover
The face of the boy as he practices tying
His father's tie there in secret

And the face of that father,
Still warm with the mystery of lather.
They are more fathers than sons themselves now.
Something is filling them, something

That is like the twilight sound
Of the crickets, immense,
Filling the woods at the foot of the slope
Behind their mortgaged houses.

The basic prosodic principle at work here is one Justice learned from his lifetime study of meter: the establishment of a pattern and variation on it. The first two lines must be cut on the phrase in order for the third to have any effect cut against it (reinforced by the triplet rhyme: forty-softly-be). And this applies to the first two sentences each snugly fitting a stanza, a pattern varied by the last three sentences in the last three stanzas. The breaks between stanzas three and four and stanzas four and five also seem articulate, almost part of the content, as does the fact that the statement embedded in the fourth stanza is one sentence and one line.

"Men at Forty" has all the clarity of shape of the most formal poem because it *is* a most formal poem. Justice's most effective writing has often taken the form of free verse because it has caused an even greater fidelity to the subject. This is what I mean by "palpability": it is as if the thing itself were given to us to hold in our hands; it is a quality of lucidity in the choice of words and their organization, the language honed to a fine transparency.

And the sun will be bright then on the dark glasses of
    strangers
And in the eyes of a few friends from my childhood
And of the surviving cousins by the graveside,
While the diggers, standing apart, in the still shade of
    the palms,
Rest on their shovels, and smoke,
Speaking in Spanish softly, out of respect.

                    * * *

The breast of Mary Something, freed from a white
    swimsuit,
Damp, sandy, warm; or Margery's, a small caught
    bird—

                    * * *

And here comes one to repair himself at the mirror,
Patting down damp, sparse hairs, suspiciously still
  black,
Poor bantam cock of a man, jaunty at one a.m.,
  perfumed, undiscourageable . . .

The tone, of course, varies, and the kinds of "things" presented, and the uses made of them. But, as in **"Men at Forty,"** this quality of Justice's style seems to be what allows him to bring over into language something which we did not have before.

Like so many of Justice's poems, the donnée of **"Men at Forty"** can be traced to a literary source; in this case, to Wallace Stevens's "Le Monocle de Mon Oncle":

If men at forty will be painting lakes
The ephemeral blues must merge for them in one,
The basic slate, the universal hue.
There is a substance in us that prevails.

The figure of Flaubert probably shades into the large figure of Wallace Stevens in the background of Justice's work, and it would be hard not to be overshadowed by it. Justice shares many of Stevens's beliefs, and lack of them; poetry is certainly "a conscious activity" for Justice, and he probably learned from Stevens that poems can conceal as well as reveal. But one does not feel in Justice's work that it is "a sanction of life," except perhaps a life in memory. The "Supreme Fiction," the "magnificent fury," the "blessed rage for order" that animates Stevens's poetry at its best—in short, the ambition in his work to encompass life and even to replace it—is not part of Justice's temperament or intention. This may be only Justice's reading of history or literary history, but it informs the poems he has written. As he says in **"Homage to the Memory of Wallace Stevens"**: "The *the* has become an *a.*" However, those who have read Justice as a Stevens epigone have read him badly.

"Men at Forty" is also illuminated by what Justice does *not* take from "Le Monocle de Mon Oncle," namely, the subject of a sexual relationship in middle age. This absence is an undercurrent in Justice's poem, the absence of anyone else except in memory, the absence of connection.

And this, I think, is Justice's main subject, though most often it appears only implicitly—characteristically enough—in poems about memory, about an almost Edenic childhood. Though the child is "happily ignored," and knows "the pleasures of certain solitudes," Justice's myth of childhood is pervaded by a sense of community, of a proper, workable, social role not available to the adult *poète maudit,* even a tenured *poète maudit.* What the childhood actually was—and a number of Justice's poems refer to a serious childhood

disease—is less important than the fact of its being remembered, because the very act of remembering is a gesture of identity in a dissolving world.

"How hard it is to live with what you know and nothing else"—this line is Camus's, and one from which Justice would certainly excise the first two words. But it begins to describe the stark discipline of Justice's poetry and the boundaries of its spirit, and tells me why I sometimes find it moving even if, as he has said, he would not have it so. It is a poetry of isolation, composed in exile, most often—not so paradoxically—with the help of other poems, knowingly, sometimes even "rationally" (while employing "chance methods"), always moving toward the consolations of memory and form. I think my favorite poem of Justice's is my favorite because this implicit condition is made explicit and is written about directly. It is, in this sense, both uncharacteristic and, for me at least, central to his work. The poem was composed as one of a pair of companion pieces (the other is entitled **"Absences"**), and it "borrows the voice" of Cesar Vallejo's "Agape." Both of these contexts may enrich our reading of the poem, but I think I begin to see the heart of Justice's work when it is stripped of them:

"PRESENCES"

Everyone, everyone went away today.
They left without a word, and I think
I did not hear a single goodbye today.

And all that I saw was someone's hand, I think,
Thrown up out there like the hand of someone drown-
  ing,
But far away, too far to be sure what it was or meant.

No, but I saw how everything had changed
Later, just as the light had; and at night
I saw that from dream to dream everything changed.

And those who might have come to me in the night,
The ones who did come back but without a word,
All those I remembered passed through my hands like
  clouds—

Clouds out of the south, familiar clouds—
But I could not hold onto them, they were drifting
  away,
Everything going away in the night again and again.

Mark Jarman (essay date 1984)

SOURCE: Jarman, Mark. "Ironic Elegies: The Poetry of Donald Justice." *Pequod* nos. 16-17 (1984): 104-09.

[*In following essay, Jarman views Justice's poems as ironic elegies.*]

Donald Justice is the most mordant poet we have in this country today. I can think of no living American counterpart whose poetry has his ironic bite. If he has any contemporary with a similar style and vision, it is Britain's own uniquely caustic poet, Philip Larkin. My aim here is not to develop all the parallels between these two, but to develop the most distressing one: one that certainly exists and is most distressing is that neither poet is as greatly appreciated in his own country as many poets who are less gifted and less unique.

The paltry number of reviews which have appeared for Justice's Pulitzer Prize winning *Selected Poems* and the narrowness of their scope is an indication of this nearsightedness. Some of the daft conclusions of the book's reviewers are additional evidence. In *Parnassus,* Vernon Young, making a point that American poets, as they begin to dry up, return to their families and childhoods for subjects, a silly enough notion, suggests that Justice is guilty of this, too; and "in quiet desperation" is writing odes to himself "way back there in that swimming hole of innocence or terror." Obviously, Young has not read Justice's recent poem **"First Death"** with a subtlety equal to the poet's. But we lose faith in a critic who does not recognize a variation on a pantoum, "In the Attic," when he sees one.

All the same, the irony of history tastes bitterly of a certain mindless optimism that the best will be known for its true worth in its time. In fact, new fields of approval have been chalked and happy teams are lining up to be counted as the children of Whitman and Dickinson, our pair of odd and newly found parents. Justice is not there. He would not go were he invited. Besides, he would only make the spectators and participants uncomfortable.

"POEM"

This poem is not addressed to you.
You may come into it briefly,
But no one will find you here, no one.
You will have changed before the poem will.

Even while you sit there, unmovable,
You have begun to vanish. And it does not matter.
The poem will go on without you.
It has the spurious glamor of certain voids.

It is not sad, really, only empty.
Once perhaps it was sad, no one knows why.
It prefers to remember nothing.
Nostalgias were peeled from it long ago.

Your type of beauty has no place here.

"Poem," from this third book *Departures,* has been pointed to as an example of Justic's minimalism. Yet to call this minimalist is to ignore the complexities of the poem's tone, its modulations between an apparent *froideur* and an underlying hostility. The speaker seduces the reader with indifference, even anticipating the reader's skepticism, while offering phrases that are

nearly precious because they are so delectable, like the eighth and twelfth lines above, and then claiming to be doing no such thing.

Listen, it comes without guitar,
Neither in rags nor any purple fashion.
And there is nothing in it to comfort you.

There is irony in this seduction, and its irony occasions reason for the poem's strength: the poet is writing an elegy for his reader. Murmuring all the while, he puts the bite on in the penultimate stanza.

Close your eyes, yawn. It will be over soon.
You will forget the poem, but not before
It has forgotten you. And it does not matter.
It has been most beautiful in its erasures.

Then, in the final stanza, after a mocking exclamation on the lost reader's behalf, the most cutting shift of all is made, ending the poem with a repetition of the first line like an unheeded warning.

O bleached mirrors! Oceans of the drowned!
Nor is one silence equal to another.
And it does not matter what you think.
This poem is not addressed to you.

This is a singular accomplishment and a singular recognition of the inevitable effacement of a poet's readers and hence of his work and himself. It is singular especially for a poet commonly thought of as narcissistic. Such labelling apparently issues from the mirror-motif in Justice's work, but the mirror as a love object, to mix my own metaphors a moment, is a red herring; for as Justice has implied in **"Fragment: To a Mirror,"** the mirror itself is merely a "half of nothingness."

Emphasis on a possibly narcissistic quality misleads the critic, who thus overlooks a more essential role Justice returns to in his most significant poems—that of the elegist. Throughout his thirty year career his mordancy and his ear for the musical lament have made a fortuitous union. While **"Poem"** has been their most original product, each elegy before and since has reflected its origins in them, from the opening lines of **"On the Death of Friends in Childhood"** ("We shall not ever meet them bearded in heaven, / Nor sunning themselves among the bald of hell') to **"Early Poems"** ("The rhymes, the meters, how they paralyze") to **"Variations on a Test by Valllejo"** ("I will die in Miami in the sun"), an elegy for himself ironically recasting Vallejo's famous self-fulfilling prophecy. As the originality of approach has grown, so has the irony of mourning. What a critic like Young mistakes for improverishment of subject matter in Justice's recent poetry is actually a taking on of a newly recognized challenge in certain childhood concerns.

One of these recent poems is **"First Death."** A complexly formal elegy of three parts, each of eight rhymed couplets sounds simple and balladic while moving deftly between acatelectic and catelectic iambic tetrameter. In the last part, the speaker sits beside his mother at his grandmother's funeral.

> The stiff fan stirred in mother's hand.
> Air moved, but only when she fanned.
>
> I wondered how could all her grief
> Be squeezed into one small handkerchief.
>
> There was a buzzing on the sill.
> It stopped, and everything was still.
>
> We bowed our heads, we closed our eyes
> To the mercy of the flies.

The boy Rimbaud, taking aim at the foolery and righteousness around him, never displayed Justice's subtlety, and yet Rimbaud did better than anyone else. Justice's poetic tone is more like Mamillius' teasing of his mother's ladies-in-waiting ("I learned it out of women's faces"). What memory has retrieved here is the beginning of a way of seeing that will set the boy apart. Here mordancy fixes the coloring of this vision as it shows both the small irony of the mother's tears and the great one of the attendant flies.

The condensation of Justice's bitterness since his first book *Summer Anniversaries,* which critics seem to prefer and long for with unpeeled nostalgia, may be a reason he is so poorly understood. For in this condensation there has been a slight separation, too. Nothing in **"First Death"** is quite as acrid as **"Unflushed Urinals."**

> Seeing them, I recognize the contempt
> Some men have for themselves.
>
> This man, for instance, zipping quickly up, head
>   turned,
> Like a bystander innocent of his own piss.

One wonders at the consideration of form by critics who, thinking form is troublesome, believe they need not mention it but in footnotes. The first line break here leaves us with a (spine tingling) ambiguity, as do the first two words of the third line. This is how Justice pays attention to the form within the form or the seemingly formless. Yet, the more elegiac recent poems appear in a less fluorescent light. **"Thinking about the Past"** has the fragmentary brilliance of a broken bundle of mirrors.

> Certain moments will never change, nor stop being—
> My mother's face all smiles, all wrinkles soon;
> The rock wall building, built, collapsed then, fallen;
> Our upright loosening downward slowly out of tune—
> All fixed into place now, all rhyming with each other.
> The red-haired girl with wide mouth—Eleanor—
> Forgotten thirty years—her freckled shoulders, hands.
> The breast of Mary Something, freed from a white
>   swimsuit,

> Damp, sandy, warm; or Margery's, a small, caught
>   bird—
> O marvellous early cigarettes! O bitter smoke, Benton
>   . . .
> And Kenny in wartime whites, crisp, cocky,
> Time a bow bent with his certain failure.
> Dusks, dawns; waves; the ends of songs . . .

Here, might we be reminded not of Rimbaud but of Laforgue? Had he lived beyond the age of 27, the author of "Complainte de l'Oubli des Morts," might have written, with this ironic forgiveness of things, of the world where the dead hardly go out anymore, except in poems. For unpleasant and unhappy as they seem, our elegies in Justice's hands record our failures. "What of the dead?" we ask. And out of the importunate, raging wind, Justice, like Laforgue, answers with the irony I have feebly tried to describe, simply, "They travel. . . ."

The self-effacement of the elegist is traditional, at least since Milton sang of his friend, the drowned poet Edward King, "For Lycidas is dead, dead ere his prime, / Young Lycidas, and hath not left his peer." The irony with which Justice effaces himself is noted by William Logan in his essay on the poet in *Crazyhorse* 20, for it makes him "a modern turned inside out: confession is silenced, revelation masked, statement disavowed." This irony certainly does make Justice modern, but the twist it puts on the tradition is what makes him individual.

Justice's complexity of tone requires a quality of attention on the part of a reader that is hard to give; in fact, it is hard to describe what we hear, except by quoting the poem itself or, as Randall Jarrell once said, just pointing. I think we hear the voice of a supremely skeptical romantic, not a cynic, but an ironic elegist who, in his paradoxical largess, can sing not only of your death, mine and his own; he can even sing of the death of his own poetic gift.

"The Telephone Number of the Muse"

> I call her up sometimes, long distance now.
> And she still knows my voice, but I can hear,
> Beyond the music of her phonograph,
> The laughter of the young men with their keys.
> I have the number written down somewhere.

Mary Gosselink De Jong (essay date 1985)

SOURCE: De Jong, Mary Gosselink. "'Musical Possibilities': Music, Memory, and Composition in the Poetry of Donald Justice." *Concerning Poetry* 18, nos. 1 & 2 (1985): 57-66.

[*In the following essay, De Jong investigates the influence of music on Justice's poetry.*]

For centuries authors, composers, and critics have been exploring the parallels between the "sister arts" of music and literature. As Calvin S. Brown dryly observes, the study of musico-literary correspondences holds "a fatal attraction for the dilettante, the faddist and the crackpot."[1] To suggest, then, that Pulitzer-Prize-winning poet Donald Justice has been influenced by music is to incur a certain risk. Being called a faddist or a dilettante would fracture no bones, only pride, and an academic becomes accustomed to being thought a crackpot, by students if not by colleagues and social acquaintances. Still, one would prefer other epithets. Moreover, influence cannot be proved, not even (or especially not?) by a writer's own statements about his or her art. In the case of Justice, it is unlikely that absolute "proof" of musical influence would help us to interpret his poems. But an awareness of his use of "musical possibilities"[2] does afford insights into the composing process; it does enhance the reader's experience of Justice's poetry. As a writer and writing teacher, Justice is much concerned with the way in which a work takes shape. His commitment to the appropriate form—the characteristic feature of his poetry[3]—and his use of certain structures, techniques, and metaphors may be traced to his early and continuing interest in music.

Justice has stated that in his youth he "played the piano and a few other instruments," studied musical composition, and aspired to be a composer.[4] Recently asked by an interviewer whether music has influenced his poetry, he replied that it probably has, but he could not specify how. After speaking of poetic and musical rhythms as "roughly analogous," he continued, "There would be a common sensibility in composing music and writing poems; the same sort of . . . creative desire would obviously lie behind virtually any of the arts. But music and poetry are the two that I would know most about from personal experience. In both there is the same kind of joy in working something out. . . ."[5] In another interview, while making the point that poems are not developed only from subjects, Justice again compared composing music and writing poetry. Poetry has various sources, he said, "just as a composition in music may come from merely fooling around. Or from thinking: This time I'll try D minor; or, I like what Handel wrote just there, I think I'll try some variations on it."[6]

His interest in music is immediately obvious in certain titles—**"White Notes," "Sonatina in Green," "Variations for Two Pianos."** In the latter poem he treats pianist Thomas Higgins as a hero for bringing art to the wilderness of Arkansas. Playing Mozart for "his pupils, the birds," Higgins taught them trills and attacks they could not otherwise have learned. But he has moved away, "taking both his pianos," and "There is no music now in all Arkansas."[7] Though his poem is whimsical and well as elegiac, it records a real loss and testifies to Justice's regard for the beauty and order of art.

He is a virtuoso of the sound effects commonly called "musical": rhyme, assonance, consonance, and other kinds of repetition. To be sure, many poets—Algernon Charles Swinburne and Edward Lear, for example—have charmed the ear, but poems should not be called "musical" simply because they are euphonious.[8] One of Justice's fortes is the structural and thematic use of sound patterns. **"Beyond the Hunting Woods,"** composed of two fifteen-line stanzas, is unrhymed, but oral performance brings out recurring consonants and vowels in the end-words:

> I speak of that great house
> Beyond the hunting woods,
> Turreted and towered
> In nineteenth-century style,
> Where fireflies by the hundreds
> Leap in the long grass,
> Odor of jessamine
> And roses, canker-bit,
> Recalling famous times
> When dame and maiden sipped
> Sassafras or wild
> Elderberry wine,
> While far in the hunting woods
> Men after their red hounds
> Pursued the mythic beast.
>
> I ask it of a stranger,
> In all that great house finding
> Not any living thing,
> Or of the wind and the weather,
> What charm was in that wine
> That they should vanish so,
> Ladies in their stiff
> Bone and clean of limb,
> And over the hunting woods
> What mist had maddened them
> That gentlemen should lose
> Not only the beast in view
> But Belle and Ginger too,
> Nor home from the hunting woods
> Ever, ever come?[9]

This repetition, pleasing in itself, tightens each stanza and links it with the other, for certain vowels (short i, long i) are used throughout. **"Presences"** illustrates his use of repetition to unify a work as well as enact its meaning:

> Everyone, everyone went away today.
> They left without a word, and I think
> I did not hear a single goodbye today.
>
> And all that I saw was someone's hand, I think,
> Thrown up out there like the hand of someone drowning,
> But far away, too far to be sure what it was or meant.
>
> No, but I saw how everything had changed
> Later, just as the light had; and at night
> I saw that from dream to dream everything changed.

And those who might have come to me in the night,
The ones who did come back but without a word,
All those I remembered passed through my hands like
   clouds—

Clouds out of the south, familiar clouds—
But I could not hold onto them, they were drifting
   away,
Everything going away in the night again and again.[10]

The recurrence of words and images corresponds with the paradoxical constancy of loss and change; it conveys the presence of absence. In his essay, "Meters and Memory" Justice speaks of poetic meters as having no organic relationship to the sense of the poem but functioning to make it orderly.[11] Like a composer of music, he has made such structural use of repetition and variation; as a poet, he can use these techniques to create and convey meaning.

During the 1960s many American poets rather noisily abandoned rhyme and other literary conventions, arguing that poetry must be "natural," "sincere," not "artificial." Justice's first book, *The Summer Anniversaries* (1960), which appeared at the beginning of this poetic revolution, includes a number of sonnets and sestinas. He did not repudiate literary tradition even when it was fashionable to do so, but in the last twenty years he has developed a repertoire of open forms, some departing from established ones, many assuming the shape of their subjects. Some are reminiscent of musical structures. **"Dreams of Water"** (*NL* [*Night Light*], 16-17), for instance, has three ten-line 'movements' linked by theme but different in mood; they might be marked *Riposato, Misterioso,* and *Scherzando.* The titles and subtitles of certain poems ask us to think of them as musical compositions: "Variations on a Theme from James," "Improvisations on themes from Guillevic," "Variations on a Text by Vallejo," and his two "Sonatinas." With such titles he acknowledges influences, indicates how we may perceive a poem and the relations between its parts, and presents his work as his contribution to the common enterprise of Art. Epigraphs, allusions, and endnotes identifying his sources associate his work with that of composers and performers in various art-forms.

Justice's poetic statements about his art are often expressed in terms of another medium—sometimes painting, more often music. Richard Howard has called "Thus," first published more than twenty years ago, Justice's "artistic credo."[12] The narrator says that his key "must be minor. / B minor, then, as having passed for noble / On one or two occasions." His one theme, "with variations," will be "spoken outright by the oboe / Without apology of any string" and "without overmuch adornment." Not for him "the major resolution of the minor, / Johann's great signature"; he has no pretensions to the grand style (*TSA* [*The Summer Anniversary*], 29). The ironic stance and subdued voice are characteristic; some critics have spoken of Justice as a "low-keyed" poet. His one theme, by no means minor, is change—on this he has worked many variations.[13]

"Sonatina in Green," subtitled "for my students," assesses the state of contemporary poetry. Iconoclastic, undisciplined novices who burst into the muse's "boudoir" are contrasted with "We few with the old instruments, / Obstinate, sounding the one string." For the young, art is "ecstatic" utterance, Bacchic revelry; for their elders it means "playing upon worn keys," enamored of a rich literary past and their own accomplishments but not unaware that modern audiences may have no ear for the music of another time. Both kinds of poet, he implies, think too much of themselves as performers. Seeking publicity and publication, they do not really respect their art: "There has been traffic enough / In the boudoir of the muse" (*D* [*Departures*], 42-43). A highly respected teacher of writing, Justice suggests here what he makes explicit elsewhere, that a number of contemporary poets are indifferent craftsmen with too little concern for *making* the memorable poem.[14] (He has called poetry readings "a kind of vaudeville," "show-biz rather than art."[15]) By speaking of poets as musicians, he asks us to recognize them as performers and reminds us of the ancient unity of poetry and music—not held 'sacred' by many of today's poets.

The most evocative of his poems about art, **"Sonatina in Yellow,"** explores the relationship between memory and the creative imagination. Justice has stated that the writer's subject "seems always to be involved, in one way or another, with memory" and remarked that some of his own most profound memories are accompanied by music.[16] **"Sonatina in Yellow"** dramatizes the creative process of a pianist, Justice's figure for the poet. Stimulated by a yellowed photography album, he relives a moment from his childhood. He sits at his instrument thinking of and trying to forget the past. But the forgetting is "an exercise requiring further practice." Fingering the keys as he tries to suppress a memory, he seems to hear it as "a difficult exercise, played through by someone else." The recollection assumes a definite shape: the hot, quiet room; the summer sunlight; he is a child; his father, risen from the dead, wakes from a nap, speaks. . . . In the last stanza, which Justice has called the poem's "coda,"[17] the artist comes back to himself at the keyboard. He realizes that in reliving, as it were rehearsing, the long-past drama and its attendant emotions, he has also been shaping it: for the creative mind, to remember is not merely to recall. Wishing to hear the 'music' he has been composing, he says, "Repeat it now, no one was listening. / Repeat it, the air, the variations." The man remembers; the artist makes. **"Sonatina in Yellow"** closes with these lines: "So your hand moves, moving across the keys, / And slowly the keys grow darker to the touch" (*D,* 44-45). His father is dead, his youth is gone, the evening of his own life approaches; but in descending into memory he has discovered, controlled, and preserved a part of his past. The poet, then, has not merely experienced and expressed emotion: he has made something. The final image of dark keys is particularly rich for readers familiar with other poems by Justice.

The former pianist uses keys and scales to represent moods and phases of development. **"Absences"** contemplates descending scales played on "the white keys of a childhood piano," snowflakes, drooping flowers, and other luminous and delicate things that can be kept only in memory—or art (*D,* 51). If white keys are associated with innocence and loss, black keys suggest the complexity of mature experience. In **"Anniversaries,"** a poem tracing the speaker's loss of certainty about his own destiny, the narrator recalls how unlike other seventeen-year-olds he was: while they played kickball, he pondered the neurosis of the governess in *The Turn of the Screw* and spent a year "lost / Somewhere among the black / Keys of Chopin . . . / Fingering his ripe heart" (*TSA,* 4).

Piano keys suggest another kind of self-expression in **"The Suicides."** The narrator muses on the life-long masquerade of acquaintances who surprised everyone by destroying themselves. They made certain that their friends would not really know them—yet they must have always been secretly furious at not being known and accepted for what they were. Speaking for their survivors, the narrator addresses the suicides, now in their coffins, as "musicians of the black keys," as if they were pianists—then, more chillingly, as if, being no longer human, they are boxed-up pianos angrily playing themselves for only themselves in death as they did in life: "At last you compose yourselves. / We hear the music raging / Under the lids we have closed" (*NL,* 54). Eyes, cases, and selves are locked shut forever. Who can know the meaning of lives whose music is so muffled?

Justice uses the keys image again in **"Homage to the Memory of Wallace Stevens,"** a tribute to a master and farewell to operatic poetry. Human activities and natural processes proceed in a world without Stevens; poets no longer imitate his "French words and postures." Yet "The poet practicing his scales / Thinks of you as his thumbs slip clumsily under and under, / Avoiding the darker notes" (*D,* 40). Again the association of music, poetry, and memory. Here the "darker notes" suggest a level of creativity that only the artist with skill, experience, and courage can attempt. Apprentice pianists—and poets—must practice.

For Justice, poetry, music, and the other fine arts are means for making sense of experience.[18] The artist does

this for himself and his audience by composing. A poetic form "fixes" an occurrence, insight, or emotion so that it may be apprehended.[19]

Justice is convinced that it is not the poet's business to expose himself in verse or other media.[20] His association of the composing process with memory and music has apparently influenced his own techniques of composition and certainly given him a way of writing about his past and his art while maintaining aesthetic distance. A mature artist enjoying the benefits of his early finger exercises, Justice plays the white keys and the black.

Notes

1. "Comparative Literature," *Georgia Review,* 13 (1959), 175. Brown's *Music and Literature: A Comparison of the Arts* (1948: rpt. Athens, GA: Univ. of Georgia Press, 1963) is the classic comparative study. For a current bibliography of work in the field see Steven P. Scher, "Literature and Music," in *Interrelations of Literature,* ed. Jean-Pierre Barricelli and Joseph Gibaldi (New York: Modern Language Assn., 1982), pp. 225-50.

2. Justice uses the quoted phrase in "An Interview with Donald Justice," *Iowa Review,* 11 (1980), 8, while stating that he has imitated musical sounds and structures (the sonatina, blues songs). Justice wrote the libretto for Edward Miller's opera *The Young God.*

3. Greg Simon, "'My Still to Be Escaped From': The Intentions of Invisible Forms," *American Poetry Review,* 5 (1976), 30-31; Thomas Swiss, "The Principle of Apprenticeship: Donald Justice's Poetry," *Modern Poetry Studies,* 10 (1980), 44-58.

4. "The Effacement of Self: An Interview with Donald Justice," *Ohio Review,* 16 (1975), 52.

5. "An Interview with Donald Justice," *Missouri Review,* 4 (1980), 41-42.

6. *Iowa Review,* p. 16.

7. *Night Light,* rev. ed. (Middletown, CT: Wesleyan Univ. Press, 1981), p. 25; hereafter cited in the text as *NL.*

8. On the use of "musical" in literary criticism, see John Hollander, "The Music of Poetry," *Journal of Aesthetics and Art Criticism,* 15 (1956), 232-44; Northrop Frye's introduction to *Sound and Poetry* (New York: Columbia Univ. Press, 1957), pp. ix-xiii: and Steven Paul Scher, "How Meaningful is 'Musical' in Literary Criticism?," *Yearbook of Comparative and General Literature,* 21 (1972), 52-56. Justice himself has remarked, ". . . I think 'musical' as a critical term referring to effects of sound in poetry is much overused, abused even" (*Iowa Review,* p. 8).

9. Copyright © 1956 by Donald Justice. Rpt. from *The Summer Anniversaries* (Middletown, Conn.: Wesleyan Univ. Press, 1960), pp. 22-23, hereafter cited in the text as *TSA*. Rpt. by permission of Weslyan Univ. Press. "Beyond the Hunting Woods" first appeared in *The New Yorker*.

10. *Departures* (New York: Atheneum, 1973), p. 52; hereafter cited in the text as *D*. Rpt. with the permission of Atheneum Publishers, Inc.

11. *Antaeus*, 30/31 (1978), 314-20, rpt. in *The Structure of Verse: Modern Essays on Prosody*, ed. Harvey Gross (New York: Ecco Press, 1979), pp. 269-76. In "Boysenberry Sherbet," a review of *Departures*, Irvin Ehrenpreis mentions Justice's use of repeated words, syllables, and images (including guitars and pianos) as "iterative and musical designs"; he refers to the "musical modulation" of remembering and forgetting in "Sonatina in Yellow" (*New York Review of Books*, 22 [16 Oct, 1975], 3-4). To my knowledge, the musical qualities of Justice's work have not been discussed elsewhere in print.

12. *Alone with America: Essays on the Art of Poetry in the United States since 1950*, enlarged ed. (New York: Atheneum, 1980), p. 296.

13. Justice recently stated that "Thus" "didn't really represent the way I felt about the case" (*Iowa Review*, p. 4)—referring, I suggest, to the narrator's statement that the oboe *announces* his theme. In the same interview he said that he could not remember ever writing "directly" about a subject of great significance for him (p. 5; see also p. 8, where he speaks again of writing about a subject "indirectly, from an angle," and *Ohio Review*, pp. 57-59).

14. *Iowa Review*, pp. 15-16; *Ohio Review*, pp. 47-48, 60-61.

15. *Missouri Review*, pp. 59, 60.

16. "Meters and Memory," p. 271; *Iowa Review*, p. 7.

17. *Iowa Review*, p. 5. In this interview he discussed his interest in musical structures, particularly as he composed "Sonatina in Yellow": "I'd played many sonatinas on the piano, [but] I didn't know what a sonatina in poetry would be until I had tried to write one. . . . I think it's as close as anybody's been able to get to a musical form in poetry—musical form, that is, so far as the structural outline goes" (p. 9). He went on to speak of modeling this "Sonatina" after the "abstract structure" of a musical form.

18. *Ohio Review*, pp. 50-51.

19. "Meters and Memory," pp. 271-72; *Fifty Contemporary Poets: The Creative Process*, ed. Alberta T. Turner (New York: Longman, 1977), p. 154.

20. *Ohio Review*, pp. 41-42, 48-50. See also his "Baudelaire: The Question of HIs Sincerity: Or, Variations on Several Texts by Eliot," *Texas Quarterly*, 1 (1958), 36-41.

Bruce Bawer (essay date 1992)

SOURCE: Bawer, Bruce. "'Avec une élégance grave et lente': The Poetry of Donald Justice." In *Certain Solitudes: On the Poetry of Donald Justice*, edited by Dana Gioia and William Logan, pp. 7-18. Fayetteville: The University of Arkansas Press, 1997.

[*In the following essay, originally published in 1992, Bawer examines the negative critical reaction to Justice's poetry and maintains that his unpopularity is "a reflection not of any failing in the work itself but of the manifold moral and cultural failures of an age in which it has been Justice's peculiar honor to be the apotheosis of the unfashionable poet."*]

On the American poetry scene these days, the only thing rarer than a fine poem is a negative review. Yet reviewers of Donald Justice, who has written some of the finest poems of our time, have often been not only negative but surprisingly hostile. Calvin Bedient, assessing Justice's 1979 **Selected Poems** in the *Sewanee Review*, described him as "an uncertain talent that has not been turned to much account." Wrote Gerald Burns: "**Selected Poems** reads like a very thin Tennessee Williams—little poems about obscure Florida people and architecture. . . . As a *career* his, though honest, does not quite make the ascent to poet from racket." And Alan Hollinghurst, appraising the same volume for *The New Statesman*, complained that Justice's poems lacked "vitality . . . urgency . . . colour and surprise," that they suffered from "lassitude," "a weary passivity," and "a habit of elegance which cushions meaning," and that the poems, "formal but *fatigués* . . . create the impression of getting great job-satisfaction without actually doing much work."

What has Justice done to deserve such attacks? Well, he was imprudent enough to publish his first book at a time when the Beats were at the height of their popularity and when many readers were unable to see, in his low-decibel traditional verses, anything but an absence of the "vitality" and "urgency" that they admired in the Beats and in the recognized non-Beat camps of the day: the Black Mountain poets, the New York poets, the confessionalists. Nor did Justice necessarily appeal to the academic admirers of his fellow traditionalists Richard Wilbur and Anthony Hecht; for it was, and is, in the nature of a certain kind of postwar academic critic to feel very much at home with the poems of a Wilbur or a Hecht—many of which seem, by their intricacy and impersonality, to solicit critical attention—while feeling uncomfortable with a plainer and more personal poet such as Justice, to whose sublime and delicate music such a critic may well be deaf and to whose conspicuous and compassionate interest in people's lives and feelings he may be constitutionally incapable of responding except by reflexively and defensively dismissing the poet as sentimental.

Nor has Justice gone out of his way to endear himself to the poetry world. While many poets of his generation have distributed enthusiastic blurbs like Halloween candy, Justice has committed the grave error of saying what he really thinks about his contemporaries. In the interviews collected in *Platonic Scripts,* he scorns the vapid, glibly romantic *idées reçues*—*"Nature is good . . . government is bad . . . [poetry is] good for the Soul"*—that form the contemporary Poets' Code; in a time when poets pay more attention to politics than to aesthetics, Justice declares that poems should not be didactic; in a time when one of the major prerequisites for an American poet seems to be an endless capacity for self-righteousness about his vocation, Justice observes stingingly that poets today "act as if they believed there were something almost sacred in the name of *poet.*" While other poets hesitate to step on toes, he refers bluntly to the "so-called poetry of the Beats," dismisses terms like Olson's "organic form" as so much pretentious blather, and is "appalled" by poets who brag about moving young people to tears, saying that such things are "morally wrong" and that poems should properly be "objects of contemplation." Ultimately, the dismissive reviews of Justice's **Selected Poems** are a reflection not of any failing in the work itself but of the manifold moral and cultural failures of an age in which it has been Justice's peculiar honor to be the apotheosis of the unfashionable poet.

Justice's poetry is, it must be said, understated. (He once agreed with an interviewer who remarked that "understatement is to you, practically, a religious principle.") But it does not lack vitality and urgency. What it lacks, rather, are the vulgarity, hysteria, conceit, anarchism, and morbid fixation on madness, drug abuse, grubby sex, and the like that characterize the most extreme Beat and confessional verses and that some readers, alas, equate with vitality and urgency. The urgency of Justice's finest verse is of a thoroughly different order. It is the urgency of deeply controlled feeling about loss and mortality, about the inevitable passing of time and the irrevocable pastness of the past. And while a table of contents that includes such titles as **"Sonnet to My Father"** and **"Tales from a Family Album"** and **"On the Death of Friends in Childhood"** might well strike many a critic as a firm guarantee of a poet's sentimental leanings, Justice's poems are delivered from sentimentality by honest feeling, careful observation, and fresh expression—and by a seemingly

stoical resistance to grief. In an age of emotional exhibitionism, Justice rises, time and again, beyond his particular circumstances toward the level of tragic myth. To be sure, many a line from a Justice poem might indeed sound maudlin in other contexts, such as the closing line of one poem: "But already the silent world is lost forever." Yet such a line is maudlin only if it strikes one as false and easy, as having been forced onto a poem rather than having grown out of it. Such is not the case here. On the contrary, the poem positions the reader perfectly for the line, so that it seems true and heartfelt, the inevitable terminus of a very real emotional journey; the poem, in other words, captures with extraordinary precision the tenor of a mind and the rhythms of its thought, and the concluding line comes as the natural reflection on all that has gone before.

It is, to be sure, misleading to speak of Justice's poetry as if it were all of an ilk. His first book, **The Summer Anniversaries** (1960), established the intelligent, composed, and pensive voice with which he is most frequently identified—and established, too, his independence from the accepted poetic modes of the day. For many of his contemporaries, notably his teacher Robert Lowell (whose pivotal *Life Studies* had appeared a year earlier), the breakthrough to using autobiographical material in poetry was coupled with a break with form, a rejection of virtuosity as the ultimate poetic value in favor of sincerity; but though many of the poems of **The Summer Anniversaries** patently concern people and places that are of great personal significance for the poet, none of the poems is in free verse; Justice refuses to join Lowell, Snodgrass, Sexton, et al., in emphasizing sincerity at the expense of formal artistry ("Now that is simply not the kind of poetry I write," he once told an interviewer apropos of Snodgrass). Justice distinguishes between writing about himself, which he tries not to do ("I've always felt it was an author's privilege to leave himself out if he chose," he has said, citing with approval Eliot's now-unfashionable theory of the impersonality of the poet), and writing about people and places that have been important to him. Indeed, though his family and friends proliferate in **The Summer Anniversaries,** Justice attempts to restrict himself to the role of the observer and chronicler, and when he *is* present (or, more accurately, when there is an *I* in the poem that one tends to identify with the poet), he does his best to objectify his experience, to place mythic elements in the foreground, and to exclude the irrelevantly personal.

Justice has said that poems, at their best, transform a subjective experience into an object not unlike a treasured family photograph, an object that preserves a precious moment for readers of present and future generations as well as for the later refreshment of one's own memory, and he has expressed the hope that "some of the poems I've tried to write were treasurable in the sense that I *know* a photograph can be treasurable. Treasured." ("I like it," he has said of his poem **"First Death,"** "because it records something otherwise lost.") Rather than write subjective, anti-literary, free-verse effusions in the manner of the Beats or the confessional poets, then, he seeks to create timeless, unapologetically literary objects—*made* objects ("I think of poetry as making things")—that preserve selected encounters, observations, and reflections. More than one interviewer has seemed bemused by Justice's traditional bent, by his habit of constant revision and his devotion to established forms; one interlocutor even asked if he ever felt the need to "free yourself from this restraint or control?" Justice's reply: "I don't think I feel the need to let go. Nowadays people may think of that as a flaw. I don't." Critics routinely praise the "courage" of an Allen Ginsberg; but there is more pluck in Justice's firm "I don't" than in all of Ginsberg's *Collected Poems.*

Formal though they are, though, Justice's poems do not recall what he has called the "hard, thuddy iambic pentameter line" of Lowell's dense, formal verses in *Lord Weary's Castle* any more than they recall the more relaxed free-verse rhythms of *Life Studies* and after. Rather, his poems exhibit a limpid lyricism, a gracefully flowing music. Trained in his early years as a pianist, Justice himself makes reference to the musicality of his poems, prefacing his volume **The Sunset Maker** with several tempo markings from major modern composers: "Sec et musclé" (Milhaud), "Avec une élégance grave et lente" (Debussy), "broadly singing" (Carl Ruggles). Justice's most representative poems do tend to display these characteristics: they are dry, muscular, elegant, grave, and slow (one might mark them *piano* and *andante*), with a fine, smooth, and austere melodic line, as it were, reminiscent of many a modern French composer.

Justice is, moreover, a poet who, even as he pays tribute to the radiant possibilities of human experience and the natural world, associates unalloyed wonder and joy at these things with the innocence of childhood, characterizing life, in **"To a Ten-Months' Child,"** as a state that one enters from a "remote . . . kingdom" and, in **"Song,"** describing a glorious dawn with awe and saying that "all that day / Was a fairy tale / Told once in a while / To a good child." To Justice, growing up is a matter of recognizing that life is not the perfectly sublime affair that one may have believed it to be in one's early years: in **"The Snowfall,"** he refers to the "terrible whispers of our elders / Falling softly about our ears / In childhood, never believed till now." The innocence of joy and the terror of knowledge are also themes of the memorable **"Sonnet,"** in which the innocents are not children but Adam and Eve:

> The walls surrounding them they never saw;
> The angels, often. Angels were as common

> As birds or butterflies, but looked more human.
> As long as the wings were furled, they felt no awe.
> Beasts, too, were friendly. They could find no flaw
> In all of Eden: this was the first omen.
> The second was the dream which woke the woman:
> She dreamed she saw the lion sharpen his claw.
> As for the fruit, it had no taste at all.
> They had been warned of what was bound to happen;
> They had been told of something called the world;
> They had been told and told about the wall.
> They saw it now; the gate was standing open.
> As they advanced, the giant wings unfurled.

Both in its vision of man and his world and in its means of imparting that vision, this poem is vintage Justice. With one stunning final image—an image that is all the more effective for the quiet simplicity with which it is presented and for the omission of any reference to Adam and Eve's reaction to it—Justice makes one feel the terror of the knowledge that comes to all of us when we move beyond the complacent bliss of childhood: the knowledge of our mortality, of the world's imperfection, and of our separation from the awful, winged majesty of God and His angels. The irony here, a familiar one in Justice's poetry, is that though the happiness of a child, or of Adam and Eve in Eden, is untainted by the adult's bitter knowledge, it is only in that state of knowledge, born of loss, that the irreclaimable joys of creation can be fully appreciated.

A reader of **"Sonnet"**—and of the numerous poems in which Justice refers to saints and angels and heaven—might be excused for concluding that he is a religious man. Yet though he was raised as a Southern Baptist, Justice has said that he lost his faith as a young man. "I don't believe in the spiritual," he declared flatly in a 1975 interview. "You know, there is a power in the obvious. That which is hidden I can't see." Yet in these secular times, Justice has a remarkable sense of what one cannot describe as anything other than the sanctity of the quotidian (he writes in **"Unflushed Urinals"** of "The acceptingness of the washbowls, in which we absolve ourselves!"); to him, sin and grace manifestly remain vital concepts, and life, for all its deficiencies, has its moments of sublime radiance.

His second and third collections find Justice in territory that one doesn't necessarily think of as his own. These are books of experiment, in which Justice wanders afield from the disciplined forms and elegant musicality of his debut volume to try his hand at blank verse, syllabic verse, and free verse. Both books also contain a number of verses inspired not by personal experience but by the work of other poets; since such poems as **"The Telephone Number of the Muse"** suggest that Justice felt abandoned by the Muse, one presumes that imitation and experiment were his way of keeping busy at his craft during her supposed absence. And indeed, though they are far from unaccomplished, the poems of

Night Light (1967, revised 1981) and *Departures* (1973) represent something of a loosening, a thinning out, a descent into the fine but familiar from the serene and singular music of *The Summer Anniversaries.*

The models for the poems in these two volumes come from all over the map. There is a pair of **"American Sketches"** written in imitation of William Carlos Williams (to whom they are dedicated); there is a poem entitled **"After a Phrase Abandoned by Wallace Stevens"**; and there are several elliptical, portentous poems, with wildly different line lengths and short, clipped sentences, in imitation of Lorca and Vallejo. These poems, surreal and often deliberately disjointed and fragmentary, are quite admirable of their kind, but they strike one as being very much against the grain of Justice's own native music, which typically casts its spell by means of clear and coherent imagery, elegant and supple language, and delicate variations on the iambic line. Justice's Lorcaesque poems, by contrast, tend to be too metrically varied, too expressionistic, and too loosely conversational in tone and rhythm to satisfy a lover of Justice's best work; conversely, there may well be too much in these poems of Justice's to satisfy an ardent admirer of Vallejo or Lorca. The bottom line is that Justice's gently responsive sensibility and strong sense of control don't really lend themselves to the jagged rhythms and erratic thought patterns of a Lorca-type poem; to read Justice's Lorcaesque poems, in fact, is a bit like hearing an opera singer do *Showboat*: it's not great opera and it's not great Kern. Nonetheless, both books show a side of Justice that one cannot but admire: namely, Justice the astute and sensitive student of his art, who has never lost the essential humility, and the willingness to learn, of the earnest young painter copying an Old Master canvas in a museum.

In the new poems included in the Pulitzer Prize-winning *Selected Poems* (1979), Justice leaves Lorca and company behind and writes in what might be described as a sharper, more seasoned version of his *Summer Anniversaries* voice. Indeed, one of the finest poems in *Selected Poems* is **"The Summer Anniversaries,"** an alternate version of **"Anniversaries,"** the opening poem in his debut volume. The poem charts the speaker's growth from a ten-year-old who, though wheelchair-bound, glories in the bounties of the earth—

> I thought it absurd
> For anyone to have quarreled
> Ever with such a world—
> O brave new planet!—
> And with such music in it.

—to a twenty-one-year-old who sees a balloon "veer crazily off" and compares it to himself, "All sense of direction gone," to a thirty-year-old who watches

> Through the window beside my desk
> Boys deep in the summer dusk

> Of Iowa, at catch,
> Toss, back and forth, their ball.
> Shadows begin to fall.
> The colors of the day
> Resolve into one dull,
> Unremarkable gray,
> And I watch them go in from their play[,]
> Small figures of some myth
> Now, vanishing up the path.

With extraordinary concision and effectiveness, the poem captures in turn the child's naive enthusiasm about life, the adolescent's confusion and romantic self-pity, and the adult's preoccupation with the prosaic business of existence, which, when he notices young people at all, causes him to think of them—and of his own younger self—as if they were part of some half-remembered legend. The poem is a splendid example, too, of Justice's genius for distancing: as much as any sonnet of Donne, it represents not an indulgence in personality but an escape from personality's restrictions; the specifics take on a symbolic weight, and one does not find oneself wondering (as one does with much confessional verse) about the poem's degree of autobiographical accuracy. (The poem is reminiscent, in particular, of Donne's "A Valediction: Of Weeping," in which three round objects—a ball, a tear, and the earth—are connected imagistically; here, similarly, Justice connects three round objects—a wheelchair wheel, a balloon, a ball—all emblems of the cycle of life.)

The Sunset Maker (1987) displays the music of Justice's poetry at its most elevated and austerely beautiful. In this volume, which contains not only twenty-five poems but two stories and a prose memoir, Justice is more than ever a poet of things past and passing, lamenting his incalculable losses and tendering his most cherished memories—mostly of his parents and of his childhood piano teachers—in language replete with allusions to the fragile beauty of music, to the ever-shifting light and shadow of nature ("The sun seems not to move at all, / Till it has moved on"), and to the tenets and typology of Christianity, with its assurance of an eternal and omnipresent deity (after rain, Justice writes in **"Mule Team and Poster,"** the sun returns, "Invisible, but everywhere present, / and of a special brightness, like God"). The echoes of Stevens are more multitudinous than ever: if a line like "Mordancies of the armchair!" (in **"Tremayne"**) brings to mind "Sunday Morning," a reference to "the last shade perhaps in all of Alabama" (in **"Mule Team and Poster"**) recalls "Anecdote of the Jar." As in earlier volumes, Justice takes somber note of the contrast between the real world and childhood's fanciful view of it, noting that the world a child dreams "is the world we run to from the world."

For the Justice of *The Sunset Maker,* the chief function of art is to preserve what little it can of life. Perhaps the book's two most idiosyncratic items are the poem **"The Sunset Maker"** and its pendant, a story entitled "Little Elegy for Cello and Piano"; both works concern the speaker's friendship with a recently deceased and largely forgotten composer named Eugene Bestor, who survives only in a six-note phrase remembered by the speaker:

> The hard early years of study, those still,
> Sequestered mornings in the studio,
> The perfect ear, the technique, the great gift
> All have come down to this one ghostly phrase.
> And soon nobody will recall the sound
> These six notes made once or that there were six.

It is to be hoped—not only for his sake, but for that of American poetry—that Justice's work will be more widely remembered than that of the fictional Bestor. Certainly there is more than one phrase in Justice's verse—plain, unaffected, and gently apocalyptic—that haunts the memory: "Darkness they rise from, darkness they sink back towards," "It is the lurch and slur the world makes, turning," "To shine is to be surrounded by the dark." Justice is the poet of a world in which loss is ubiquitous, sorrow inevitable, and adult joy always bittersweet, a world in which the genuinely heroic act, for a literary artist, is not to thrash about uncontrollably, raising a manic and ugly din, but to fashion a body of work whose beauty and poise and gravity in the face of life's abomination may, one trusts, help it to endure.

Clive Watkins (essay date fall 1993)

SOURCE: Watkins, Clive. "Some Reflections on Donald Justice's Poem 'After a Phrase Abandoned by Wallace Stevens.'" *Wallace Stevens Journal* 17, no. 2 (fall 1993): 236-44.

[*In the following essay, Watkins examines the influence of Wallace Stevens's verse on "After a Phrase Abandoned by Wallace Stevens."*]

> The alp at the end of the street
> Occurs in the dreams of the town.
> Over burgher and shopkeeper,
> Massive, he broods,
> A snowy-headed father
> Upon whose knees his children
> No longer climb;
> Or is reflected
> In the cool, unruffled lakes of
> Their minds, at evening,
> After their day in the shops,
> As shadow only, shapeless
> As a wind that has stopped blowing.

> Grandeur, it seems,
> Comes down to this in the end—
> A street of shops
> With white shutters
> Open for business . . .

> —Donald Justice[1]

In the course of a recent essay on Donald Justice, the poet and critic Dana Gioia discusses his short poem **"After a Phrase Abandoned by Wallace Stevens"** as an illustration of "the unusual manner in which [Justice] uses borrowed material to generate new poems," a device Gioia designates "generative quotation." Justice's poem, he says, bears

> a family resemblance to Stevens' work. Justice not only borrows the opening line from his Hartford master. He also employs Stevens' characteristic dialectic between the sublime and the quotidian suggested by the borrowed phrase. Moreover, Justice uses some Stevensian stock characters, the burgher and the shopkeeper. But no sooner has Justice established this Stevensian scene in the three opening lines than he liberates the town from the elder poet's metaphysics. . . . He postulates no Stevensian struggle with abstractions of reality. Rather than transforming his observations into the premises of a supreme fiction, Justice accepts the loss of mythic consciousness as a condition of modern life. Justice even celebrates—despite the touch of irony in the last stanza—the functional beauty of the burghers' workaday world.[2]

While Gioia usefully draws attention to the fact that **"After a Phrase Abandoned by Wallace Stevens"** is built from recognizably Stevensian elements, he underestimates, I believe, the subtlety of Justice's appropriations. Indeed, in some respects, Gioia simplifies Stevens, too. Stevens' theater of types, for instance, is more various than Gioia's reference to "stock characters" implies and while the image of the mountain is important throughout Stevens' writing, so is the image of the father, which Justice uses very much as Stevens might have. The resulting dialogue, in which Justice's poem draws close to and yet keeps at a distance from its literary ancestor, is more interesting—but also more equivocal—than Gioia in his brief remarks was able to explore.

As many have observed, one of Stevens' favorite devices is to heap up definitions or descriptive phrases, sometimes so prolifically that the phrases grow out of one another in a dizzying and ambiguous way and seem in danger of losing touch with the original impulse of the series. There are traces of this in Justice's poem. The alp, which is first of all described as a "snowy-headed father," becomes (alternatively or in addition) a reflection. This image spawns a third, since the mountain is reflected "As shadow only" "In the cool, unruffled lakes of / Their minds." Indeed, a fourth variation emerges, for the "shadow" is "shapeless / As a wind that has stopped blowing." The syntax here functions in much the same way as the syntax in section II of **"The Auroras of Autumn,"** with its exploration of the various whitenesses visible in the beach-scene, though a more apposite analogue (because of its mountain image and its anthropomorphism) is the following passage from **"Chocorua to Its Neighbor"**:

V

He was a shell of dark blue glass, or ice,
Or air collected in a deep essay,
Or light embodied, or almost, a flash
On more than muscular shoulders, arms and chest,
Blue's last transparence as it turned to black,

VI

The glitter of a being, which the eye
Accepted yet which nothing understood,
A fusion of night, its blue of the pole of blue
And of the brooding mind, fixed but for a slight
Illumination of movement as he breathed.[3]

In the blurring of the boundary between the imagined and the real, another characteristically Stevensian effect appears. Indeed, this duality is indicated by the opening two lines of the poem, where the alp is presented as having a double existence—as an external physical object "at the end of the street" and as a property existing also in the insubstantial realm of dreams. This duality is reinforced by what follows, for inasmuch as it "broods" "Over burgher and shopkeeper," the alp is clearly a geographical feature; "reflected / In the cool, unruffled lakes of / Their minds," however, the alp is a mental phenomenon, too. Justice's use of active and passive verbs embodies this ambiguity. The alp "broods" over the inhabitants of the town, which may or may not indicate their consciousness of him as an active presence in their world; alternatively (or, again, in addition), he is passively "reflected" in their minds, whose very stillness allows this to take place. As the alp recedes into metaphor, the vehicle in this chain of metaphors comes to acquire more immediacy than the tenor, creating a circular pattern in which properties introduced ostensibly to describe the effect the alp has on the minds of the town's inhabitants ("lake" and "shadow" and "wind") are precisely properties we might reasonably expect to encounter in the physical world that alp and street seem to occupy: "lake" and "shadow" and "wind" belong, so to speak, both to the inner and the outer landscapes.

The syntactical rhythms, too, are fittingly Stevensian, miming the process by which thought improvises its own utterance. The placement of the adverbial phrases "at evening, / After their day in the shops," which might have come more naturally after "reflected," suggests that they had just that moment sprung into the speaker's mind; and the second phrase has the air of a further, unpremeditated elaboration, prompted by its predeces-

sor. The line-break after "shapeless," by delaying the surprise of the final simile, contributes to this improvisatory effect. Such meshings of inner and outer and the transformations that result constitute, of course, one of Stevens' major themes, but, as **"Domination of Black"** and **"The Poem That Took the Place of a Mountain"** from the opposite ends of his writing life illustrate, Justice has borrowed from Stevens not merely one of his characteristic themes: he has taken over also a characteristic manner of developing them.

In order to "place" what he regards as Justice's habitual practice, Gioia proposes a four-fold classification of quotation—generative, decorative, emphatic, and contrapuntal. It is a classification that, though suggestive, is hardly precise. As Gioia's own argument demonstrates, for instance, Justice's use of Stevens' phrase is not merely "generative," a means of leaping off into his own poem. **"After a Phrase Abandoned by Wallace Stevens"** must be read—intertextually— against the background of Stevens' own work; but though he comments on the apparent and superficial echo of Auden's "Fish in the Unruffled Lakes,"[4] Gioia ignores the allusion to Stevens' elegy for George Santayana, "To an Old Philosopher in Rome." Particularly relevant are these lines:

It is a kind of total grandeur at the end,
With every visible thing enlarged and yet
No more than a bed, a chair and moving nuns. . . .

(*CP* [*The Collected Poems of Wallace Stevens*] 510)

Given the explicit attribution that the title of Justice's poem makes and the prominence of the poem in Stevens' later work, it does not seem unreasonable to suspect a deliberate allusion here, but even if the parallel is fortuitous, reading the final section of Justice's poem in the light of this passage illuminates both it and, by contrast, Stevens.

Echoing a passage from his 1948 essay "Imagination as Value," Stevens presents his Harvard mentor as pausing at the close of his life on the "threshold of heaven," "As if the design of all his words takes form / And frame from thinking and is realized" (*CP* 511). By a kind of conscious artistry, his life and death have been composed so as to combine the actual with the transcendent. (Earlier, Stevens has told us that "The life of the city never lets go, nor do you / Ever want it to. It is part of the life in your room" [*CP* 510].) In the same essay, Stevens had defined the imagination as "the power of the mind over the possibilities of things," and in a later passage he spoke of how, by the operation of the imagination, "The world is no longer an extraneous object, full of other extraneous objects, but an image. In the last analysis, it is with this image of the world that we are vitally concerned" (*NA* [*The Necessary Angel*] 136, 151). The citizens of Justice's "town" have likewise composed for themselves an image of the world, a particular life whose design maintains an ambiguous stance towards the mountain / father in whose shadow they live. How far, in fact, have they turned away from the transcendent and how far does it continue to affect their lives?

At one level, as Gioia indicates, the poem seems to say that true grandeur is not to be found in the inhuman splendor of a mountain: it is to be found in the world that men and women fashion for themselves in their everyday lives. In this sense, the poem repudiates the anthropomorphism by which the mountain is turned into a "snowy-headed father." A feeling of loss remains, however, generated in part by the way the images in the first section are handled and in part by the way the poem distorts the Santayana poem even as it echoes it.

For, as Gioia notes, it is the citizens who have abandoned the alp. There is no evidence that the mountain, though massive and snowy-headed, has ceased to care for his "children"; nor would such disproportionate attributes (size and age) necessarily imply in a human father any lack of fondness. We are invited, in fact, to feel pathos towards the neglected mountain, an invitation the poem only partly rejects. The note of pathos is sounded early in the poem through its very first verb, "Occurs," with its implication that the impact of the alp on the inner life of the town is almost casual and insignificant (as if the phrase "Occurs in" were shadowed by the ghost idiom "occurs to"). Perhaps we should simply understand that the "children," in growing older, have left behind the habit of demonstrating their affection by climbing on their father's knee. It is a sign of their independence—something that underpins their commercial life; and though he continues to appear in their dreams and to be reflected in their minds, he is no longer permitted to have an overt place in their lives. The collocation of "cool" and "unruffled" strengthens this sense of controlled feeling.

An early analogue for this ambivalence occurs in Stevens' journal for 18 April 1904. During the train journey back to New York from Tompkins' Cove after one of his long and solitary walks, he considered

> how utterly we have forsaken the Earth, in the sense of excluding it from our thoughts. There are but few who consider its physical hugeness, its rough enormity. It is still a disparate monstrosity, full of solitudes + barrens + wilds. It still dwarfs + terrifies + crushes. The rivers still roar, the mountains still crash, the winds still shatter. Man is an affair of cities. . . . Somehow, however, he has managed to shut out the face of the giant from his windows. But the giant is there, nevertheless.
>
> (*L* [*Letters of Wallace Stevens*] 73)

The opening lines of Justice's second section can be read as commentary on "It is a kind of total grandeur at the end," where "at the end" indicates that Santayana's

death is the culmination of a lifetime of philosophical and aesthetic effort. In one sense, the corresponding phrase in Justice—"in the end"—implies that high-flown talk of "grandeur" (of the kind adumbrated by Stevens) can be reduced to something quite ordinary—a street of shops open for business. The phrase "comes down to" re-reinforces this reductive interpretation with its sense of decline from some realm of higher values. Indeed, there is a general movement in the poem from high places—the alp is massive and broods "Over burgher and shopkeeper"—through the intermediate level of the "cool, unruffled lakes," to a point of apparent rest in the small town at the foot of the mountain, though perhaps the three dots with which the poem concludes imply a continuing movement in the same direction. Much depends on how we read that little phrase "it seems" ("Grandeur, it seems . . ."), with its ambiguous note of regret. To whom does it seem that grandeur comes down to quotidian reality in the end? To the inhabitants? To the "speaker"?—And whose is the regret? Whether we attribute the anthropomorphic representation of the mountain as father to the "speaker" or to the inhabitants, its effect is to project a nostalgia for a lost (or at least attenuated) sense of the sublime.

An interesting parallel is afforded by "The American Sublime" of 1935. "But how does one stand"—the poem asks—"To behold the sublime? . . . How does one feel?"

> One grows used to the weather,
> The landscape and that;
> And the sublime comes down
> To the spirit itself,
>
> The spirit and space.

—an account which veers from dismissiveness ("grows used to," "and that") towards an apparent assertion of transcendence ("spirit and space"), immediately undercut by Stevens with a bitterness typical of many of his poems of this period:

> The empty spirit
> In vacant space.

The poem ends with two questions—

> What wine does one drink?
> What bread does one eat?
>
> (*CP* 130-31)

—questions whose frustration and despair relate to both body and spirit. Though the burghers of Justice's poem may appear to have responded with an equable worldliness to such questions and to have rejected the sublime, I believe Justice leaves these issues more open than Gioia allows.

What the last five lines indicate, perhaps, is the separation Stevens himself made between the imaginative and professional aspects of his own life. Gioia suggests that

"Without mocking Stevens' fixation on the loss of religious faith, Justice quietly moves beyond this late Romantic concern to create a poem of contemporary consciousness" (54), but this is to underestimate both the variousness of Stevens' work and the degree to which it developed over a long life of writing. In particular, it is to underestimate the complexity of his poetic transactions with parent figures, both mothers and fathers, from his earliest poems onward, something to which Justice "quietly" and perceptively alludes.

Justice, then, plays with themes and procedures characteristic of Stevens. In its diction, however, and in the patterns of its verse, **"After a Phrase Abandoned by Wallace Stevens"** distinguishes itself sharply from Stevens' customary practice.

Viewed across the great expanse of his output, Stevens' diction is very various, encompassing words of all sorts, from the formal to the colloquial, including the native and the foreign—and nonce and nonsense words, too. Despite this variety, it is dominated by words of Latin or Romance origins, as any random opening of *The Collected Poems* or *Opus Posthumous* demonstrates. It is such words and their traditional associations with serious literary discourse that establish, directly and by contrast, the lexical extremes within which Stevens' poems function. Frequently Stevens plays different levels of diction off against one another, sometimes creating an effect of disconcerting rhetorical instability; typically, it is by such slippages of register that his meanings are enacted. In "Late Hymn from the Myrrh-Mountain," for instance, a poem of similar length to Justice's, the resounding title is followed immediately by the mocking "Unsnack your snood, madanna. . . ." Then, after the lyrical simplicity of "Already the green bird of summer has flown / Away," we are led into a passage of more elevated language:

> These are not
> The early constellations, from which came the first
> Illustrious intimations—uncertain love,
>
> The knowledge of being, sense without sense of time.

The poem ends with a return to directness and the simple notation of physical details presaging a bleaker season:

> Take the diamonds from your hair and lay them down.
>
> The deer-grass is thin. The timothy is brown.
> The shadow of an external world comes near.
>
> (*CP* 349-50)

The distribution of words with Greek, Latin, or Romance origins conforms to the degree of "lift" in the language. The overall proportion of such words is typical of Stevens and, moreover, considerably higher than the proportion in Justice's poem. Apart from "grandeur," which he deliberately undercuts, the words of Latin or Romance origin which Justice employs can all be regarded, in terms of frequency, as part of the common stock. Though such expressions do, of course, occur in Stevens—for instance, in "Late Hymn from the Myrrh-Mountain," "place" and "colors"—rarer words (such as "artifice" and "intimations") play a significant role in his effects. By contrast, Justice's diction is chaster and its rhetoric altogether cooler and more level than we might have expected from Stevens, had he developed a poem of his own from this abandoned fragment.

As to its verse patterns, **"After a Phrase Abandoned by Wallace Stevens"** superficially resembles such poems as "Winter Bells" or "The Common Life." Like them, it is written in short, nonmetrical lines set out in unequal sections. The proportion of poems in *The Collected Poems* and *Opus Posthumous* with these features is, however, small—less than 9%. What is more, poems with these formal features are confined almost entirely to *Harmonium*. To this extent, "Winter Bells" or "The Common Life" (from *Ideas of Order* and *Parts of a World*) are themselves untypical, for in the later volumes Stevens relies increasingly on blank verse or its less rigorous derivatives. Thus, in its overall formal shape, Justice's poem holds itself at a distance from its thematic forebears.

A closer examination reveals another non-Stevensian feature—the "strong" enjambment that occurs in "the cool, unruffled lakes of / Their minds." Where, in his metrical verse, Stevens leaves a form-word suspended across an enjambment, such suspensions almost always resolve themselves into notionally stressed syllables, as, for instance, in these lines from "Evening without Angels"—

> Sad men made angels of the sun, and of
> The moon they made their own attendant ghosts.
>
> (*CP* 137)

Or these from section II of "Esthétique du Mal"—

> and in
> Its own hallucination never sees. . . .
>
> (*CP* 315)

Metrical resolution—though not always to stressed syllables—also tends to occur in verse that, though not strictly metrical itself, is haunted by the ghost of the iambic, as happens in "Anecdote of Canna":

> Huge are the canna in the dreams of
> X, the mighty thought, the mighty man . . .
>
> (*CP* 55)

and—with a greater sense of unresolved tension—in "So-And-So Reclining on Her Couch":

the flux

Between the thing as idea and
The idea as thing. . . .

(*CP* 295)

In his free-verse poems, however, Stevens prefers to organize his line endings so that they coincide with the patterns of his syntax, and metrically unresolved suspensions of form-words occur only in a tiny handful of cases. There are, for instance, the striking, one-word lines in "Earthy Anecdote" ("And") and in "Metaphors of a Magnifico" ("Are"). There is another odd suspension in another early poem, "Architecture" (in *Opus Posthumous*):

Pass the whole of life earing the clink of the
Chisels of the stone-cutters cutting the stones.

(*OP* [*Opus Posthumous*] 37)

These instances apart, however, Stevens seems not to have allowed himself such unresolved suspensions in his nonstanzaic free verse and only very infrequently indeed in his stanzaic free verse. Thus, the "strong" enjambment in "the cool, unruffled lakes of / Their minds" is also, it seems, untypical.

How far, then, should we regard **"After a Phrase Abandoned by Wallace Stevens"** as a pastiche? For instance, if, through some accident of transmission, Justice's poem were to disappear from view to turn up again (without its title) in a hundred years as "a previously lost poem by Stevens, recently discovered," should we be able—purely from internal evidence—to detect the mistake? Though Justice's poem clearly reflects, in its theme and procedures, important aspects of Stevens' practice, other aspects—notably lexical and prosodic features—distinguish it from its imaginative antecedents. After all, as Justice himself makes clear in his unassuming title, **"After a Phrase Abandoned by Wallace Stevens"** must be read in the shadow of Stevens' own opus.

Notes

1. Donald Justice, "After a Phrase Abandoned by Wallace Stevens," *Selected Poems: Donald Justice* (New York: Atheneum, 1979), 38. The phrase "the alp at the end of the street" comes from a Stevens notebook entitled "From Pieces of Paper." See George S. Lensing's edition of the notebook in *Wallace Stevens: A Poet's Growth* (Baton Rouge: Louisiana State University Press, 1986), 167.

2. Dana Gioia, "Tradition and an Individual Talent," *Verse* (University of St. Andrews, Scotland) 8/9 (Winter/Spring, 1992): 50-58.

3. Wallace Stevens, *The Collected Poems of Wallace Stevens* (New York: Alfred A. Knopf, 1954), 297; hereafter cited as *CP*. References to Stevens' *The*

Necessary Angel: Essays on Reality and the Imagination (New York: Vintage, 1951) will be cited as *NA; Letters of Wallace Stevens,* sel. and ed. Holly Stevens (New York: Alfred A. Knopf, 1966) as *L;* and *Opus Posthumous,* rev. ed., ed. Milton J. Bates (New York: Alfred A. Knopf, 1989) as *OP.*

4. The first two stanzas of this famous lyric distinguish humans, burdened by morality and time, from the beasts, which, existing in a purely physical universe, are free from such concerns. In the last stanza, the speaker rejoices that his lover ("my swan"), who has "All the gifts that to the swan / Impulsive Nature gave, / The majesty and pride," should have added his "voluntary love"; that is, that he should have exercised his peculiarly human power of emotional election. On this reading, it is hard to find any link of meaning between source and apparent echo—which is why, no doubt, Gioia assigns it to the category "decorative." Read as echo, it contributes only its own surface: the phrase sits snugly inside Justice's text, and indeed it is only as echo that it obtrudes at all. Inasmuch as it does obtrude, drawing one's attention purposelessly aside, it might just as validly be described as a blemish, an unresolved—and unresolvable—element entering the poem from an alien universe of language and thematic concerns.

Walter Martin (essay date 1997)

SOURCE: Martin, Walter. "Arts of Departure." In *Certain Solitudes: On the Poetry of Donald Justice,* edited by Dana Gioia and William Logan, pp. 37-47. Fayetteville: The University of Arkansas Press, 1997.

[*In the following essay, Martin discusses the relationship between translation, imitation, and creation in Justice's verse.*]

". . . it should be remembered that the author was several different persons during the course of writing, which covered many years."

I

In one of several modestly revealing comments about translation scattered through the interviews in *Platonic Scripts,* Donald Justice says, "Certainly you don't want to imitate. I don't want to imitate poets who write in other languages any more than I would want to imitate poets who write in my language; but I can perhaps learn something intangible from them." Only a poet who had spent much of his life teaching and learning from teachers—Winters, Berryman, Lowell—would put it that way, perhaps. Justice is a man for whom translation, difficult as it is, is never enough. Poets of original and genuine inspiration, driven to express themselves, incapable of holding back from doing so, have seldom been content to find equivalents for other men's verses, even when that was their honest and only intention.

II. TAIN'T WHAT A MAN SEZ, BUT WOT HE MEANS THAT THE TRADUCER HAS GOT TO BRING OVER.

"I am not unaware, of course, that there are many readers who take persistent pleasure in deprecating everything and that they will vent their spleen on this work too," said Saint Jerome. "It is difficult when you are following another man's footsteps, to keep from going astray somewhere. . . . If I translate word for word, the result is ludicrous; if I am forced to change the words or rearrange them, it will look as though I had failed in my duty as a translator." This is where the trouble starts, and the treason in the well-known equation, *traduttore traditore.*

The ideal translator is not traitor but arbitrator, bent on reconciling the conflicting claims of two languages, each competing for the reader's attention. In the business of settling differences by give-and-take, by trade-off, by compromise, he is a go-between who must make the ever-more-delicate decisions upon which the life of the text depends. There are many good reasons why the translation of poetry should not be attempted, many reasonable explanations for why the attempt is bound to fail. "'Tis much like dancing on ropes with fettered legs: a man may shun a fall by using caution; but the gracefulness of motion is not to be expected; and when we have said the best of it, 'tis but a foolish task; for no sober man would put himself into danger for the applause of escaping without breaking his neck." Thus Dryden, chiding Ben Jonson for adopting the metaphrastic method in his version of the *Art of Poetry* (1640). The metaphrast turns his author from one tongue to another, word by word and line for line, and to Dryden such a method was self-defeating. Had not Horace himself cautioned, *Nec verbum verbo curabis reddere fidus / Interpres*?

Paraphrase, as exemplified by Waller in his fourth book of the *Aeneid* (1658), seemed a more sensible solution to the ancient dualism of Beauty versus Fidelity. Such a translation, "with latitude, where the author is kept in view . . . so as never to be lost, but his words are not so strictly followed as his sense; and that too is admitted to be amplified, but not altered," became Dryden's own ideal and the modus operandi for his transformations of Horace, Ovid, Juvenal, and Virgil. The method of the paraphrast was not the opposite of metaphrastic procedure. It was seen as the common-sense compromise between hard-line Jonsonian literalism and the dreaded excesses of Mr. Cowley in his eccentric and

extravagant versions, or perversions, of Pindar. His *imitations,* that is, of Pindar in the *Pindarique Odes* (1656).

In an *imitation,* the translator "(if now he has not lost that name) assumes the liberty, not only to vary the words and sense, but to forsake them both as he sees occasion; and taking only some general hints from the original, to run division on the groundwork as he pleases." Cowley in his own preface justifies having "taken, left out, and added what I please" by asserting that a man would be thought mad if he translated Pindar literally, assuring us that "it does not at all trouble me that the Grammarians [pedants] perhaps will not suffer this libertine way of rend'ring foreign Authors, to be called Translation; for I am not so much enamour'd of the Name Translator, as not to wish rather to be Something Better, tho' it want yet a Name." To which Dryden's reply was that *imitation,* so-called, was nothing less than profanation of the dead.

III. THAT SERVILE PATH THOU NOBLY DOST DECLINE, / OF TRACING WORD FOR WORD AND LINE FOR LINE.

We take a more generous attitude to the outrage of *imitation* nowadays, thanks to some notable successes by modern practitioners. "*Qui n'est successivement ravi et outré, s'il garde un œil pour le latin, par ce que VALÉRY a fait des Bucoliques?*" asks Pierre Leyris, himself a distinguished translator of Hopkins and Eliot. Exasperation and delight—are they not what we have come to expect from the great imitators, whether a Pope or a Pound? The squawking that greeted Pound's *Propertius* and Lowell's *Imitations* were one and the same. Now they are taught in the classroom; the alert learn something intangible from them, as we know from the example of Justice.

At Iowa in the fall of 1953 he took a translation course from Lowell: "We as a class, went through about two-thirds of those poems [in *Imitations*] . . . I was surprised to see them show up later in his book. It was his work; his own voice is all too recognizable in those versions, but we had been privileged to have a sort of preview." When the book appeared eight years later, its dust jacket carried this disclosure: "Mr. Lowell calls this unusual collection of poetry 'a book of versions and free translations.' His intention is not to make a literal rendering of a poem written in another tongue, but to try to create from the original a poem which is successful *in English*. At times there are wide departures from the originals, yet he usually stays quite close. Though they are 'imitations,' the imitator is unmistakably Robert Lowell."

Lowell's own introduction continues the apologia by suggesting that the reader set aside prior notions of these particular foreign poets altogether, at least on first reading, and listen instead to the *sequence,* "one voice running through many personalities," which he hopes will have "something equivalent to the fire and finish" of the originals. He confesses that he has been "reckless with literal meaning, and labored hard to get the tone," which "is of course everything." Or rather—backpedaling here—he has labored to get "*a* tone, for *the* tone is something that will always more or less escape transference to another language and cultural moment. I have tried to write live English and to do what my authors might have done if they were writing their poems now and in America." Then the credo: *I believe that poetic translation . . . must be expert and inspired, and needs at least as much technique, luck and rightness of hand as an original poem.* Expertise and inspiration having licensed him to make new poems based on Sappho, to strip Villon, take Hebel out of dialect, cut Hugo's "Gautier" in half, unclot Mallarmé, lop a third off Rimbaud's "Drunken Boat," add stanzas to Rilke, shift lines by Villon, move sections, change images, alter meter and intent—"And so forth!"

This was *running division on the ground-work* with a vengeance, and to modern "Grammarians" an act of cavalier insouciance and indecency. Perverse as translation and unpalatable as poetry.

IV. The idea of translation in general embodied here—it is an idea only and by no means intended to achieve the status of a theory—is that meaningful versions of poems in one language can exist in another. These are neither word-for-word prose versions nor "imitations," though each of these kinds of translation can serve a useful purpose.

Contemporary French Poetry, coedited by Alexander Aspel and Donald Justice, appeared in 1965. Aspel chose the poets to be translated; Justice, the twenty-four young translators—Edmund Keeley, Charles Wright, Mark Strand, and W. D. Snodgrass among them. Justice wrote a "Note on the Translations" from which the above is extracted.

The book was further evidence of America's fascination with an ideal of French verse. (A lopsided affair, one might add, since, apart from the awkward piety toward Poe, the French have never shown any enthusiasm for American poetry.) It contains straightforward renditions of work by members of the so-called "middle generation," survivors of surrealism, the great-great-grandchildren of Rimbaud and Baudelaire. What seemed daring in its day now seems outdated. This goes for much of the English as well, a mild-mannered Esperanto that rarely gets out of line, the translatorese that smothered all too many poems in the sixties and beyond. One exception, a poem by Philippe Jaccottet

entitled *"La Traversée,"* is worth quoting in full to show what Justice could accomplish when fettered by the triple constraints of rhythm, rhyme, and syllable count.

"La Traversée"

Ce n'est pas la Beauté que j'ai trouvée ici,
ayant loué cette cabine de seconde,
débarqué à Palerme, oublié mes soucis,
mais celle qui s'enfuit, la beauté de ce monde.

L'autre, je l'ai peut-être vue en ton visage,
mais notre cours aura ressemblé à ces eaux
qui tracent leurs grands hiéroglyphes sur les plages
au sud de Naples, et que l'été boit aussitôt,

signes légers que l'on récrit sur les portières . . .
Elle n'est pas donnée à nous qui la forçons,
pareils à des aventuriers sur les frontières,
à des avares qui ont peur de la rançon.

Elle n'est pas non plus donnée aux lieux étranges,
mais peut-être à l'attente, au silence discret,
à celui qui est oublié dans les louanges
et simplement accroît son amour en secret.

"The Crossing"

It is not Beauty I've discovered here—
having reserved this cabin, second-class,
landed at Palermo, forgot my care—
but the world's beauty only, which will pass.

I may have seen that other in your face,
but we are like these waters moving on,
that on the beaches south of Naples trace
great hieroglyphs, and are by summer gone,

faint signs, inscribed again on portières . . .
She is not given us who force our way,
who would adventure out on her frontiers,
misers, who fear the ransom we must pay.

She is not given to any foreign place,
although to waiting and to silence she may be,
to one forgotten in the midst of praise,
who simply tends his love, and secretly.

Elective affinity is the one indispensable element in the art of translation. If the poet is beguiled by the features he finds reflected in his original, he may do a good job. If not, not. This particular example—Justice as metaphrast—is about as far from the notion of *imitatio* as one could get. Lowell himself had come to the conclusion that meter had something to do with fidelity in translation, that a metrical version may well "turn out to be more accurate, for some queer reason," and that theory is tested here. The result is a poem, metrical, accurate, that would not have seemed out of place in *The Summer Anniversaries.* (Indeed, Alexander Aspel's assessment of the poems of Jaccottet—also born in 1925—sounds oddly clairvoyant when read with

Justice's own later work in mind: "A feeling of frailty, shadow, and void in a secretly threatened reality underlies Jaccottet's reaction to the world. His diction has a limpid quality, an ease in motion and a light grace producing effects of transparency and discreet serenity. . . . Jaccottet is not a poet of self-confession or mere self-assertion.")

V. FRENCH AND ENGLISH CONSTITUTE THE SAME TONGUE.

In 1973 the Stone Wall Press published a letterpress edition of 150 copies of *The Man Closing Up*, which included both a "translation" and an "improvisation." This curious amalgam takes off in two directions from a long French original by Guillevic, *"L'Homme qui se ferme,"* preceded by this note:

> Sitting in a cafeteria one afternoon in the spring of 1964, I made a first draft of the translation. About a year later, in another city, late one night, I happened to recall Guillevic's poem and, having neither the French text nor my version of it at hand to consult, began to improvise off fragments recollected from the original, almost as if I were remembering a tune, or tunes. The city was Miami, and a certain desolate stretch of the bay there and a memory of an old lighthouse on Key Biscayne entered into this new poem, which was finished in an hour or two, the quickest writing I have ever done. . . .

The translation, at 171 lines chopped into twenty-one irregular segments, is the most ambitious of Justice's sight readings. Like a latter-day, more laconic Prufrock, ill at ease in the purgatory of the natural world, the man closing up "holds in his hand / Something threatening. / He hopes that some day / He will know what to do with it." A generic enigma, the stick-figure of a man in a scale model, with a craving for dead leaves, a knack for calculation, and little else. *Chacun ses monstres* . . . against which he has "cooked up / His little song."

> Much like the man
> Who, naked, would put on the skin of a stag
> Still warm from the last chase.
>
> And speaks like someone
> Who'd have something to say
> From the center.
>
> It remains to be seen what to make of it,
> Of what he says.

Justice's delicately balanced equivalent—impossible to quote effectively—is a long snake of upended dominoes.

The "improvisation" had already appeared in *Night Light* (1967) (there titled **"The Man Closing Up"** and subtitled "Improvisations on themes from Guillevic"), severed from the translation in which it began. The man closing up is seen in close-up, coming to life, a human figure in a seascape, pinpointed in the note. Unfolding so that it can be read alongside the translation (the book is ingeniously constructed), the improvisation is more vivid, more desperate, a scenario of claustrophobic deprivation:

> There is a word for it,
> A simple word,
> And the word goes around.
>
> It curves like a staircase,
> And it goes up like a staircase,
> And it *is* a staircase,
>
> An iron staircase
> On the side of a lighthouse.
> All in his head.
>
> And it makes no sound at all
> In his head,
> Unless he says it.
>
> Then the keeper
> Steps on the rung,
> The bottom rung,
>
> And the ascent begins.
> Clangorous,
> Rung after rung.
>
> He wants to keep the light going,
> If he can.
>
> But the man closing up
> Does not say the word.

"Probably more than other poets I know, I play games in my poems (as I do in life), and one of the unwritten rules of the game for me, as I like it played, is that you can risk this much personality or that much confession if the voice is promised to be that of someone else to start with. . . ."

VI. BLOOD BROUGHT TO GHOSTS . . .

Transformations and re-creations abound in *Departures* (published in the same year as *The Man Closing Up*), a work of inspired ventriloquism. They multiply in ***The Sunset Maker*** and the two volumes of selections, most notably in the experiments based on Baudelaire.

"MIAMI, FLORIDA, C. 1936"

Je n'ai pas oublié, voisine de la ville,	a
Our new house on the edge of town	a
Notre blanche maison, petite mais tranquille;	a
Looks bare at first, and raw. A pink	b
Sa Pomone de plâtre et sa vieille Vénus	b
Plaster flamingo on one leg	c

Dans un bosquet chétif cachant leurs membres nus,	b
Stands preening by the lily pond.	d
Et le soleil, le soir, ruisselant et superbe,	c
And just as the sun begins to sink	b
Qui, derrière la vitre où se brisait sa gerbe,	c
Into the Everglades beyond,	d
Semblait, grand œil ouvert dans le ciel curieux,	d
It seems to shatter against the pane	e
Contempler nos dîners longs et silencieux,	d
In little asterisks of light,	f
Répandant largement ses beaux reflets de cierge	e
And on our lids half-closed in prayer	g
Sur la nappe frugale et les rideaux de serge.	e
Over the clean blue willowware.	g

In *Departures,* Lorca and Vallejo make cameo appearances, along with four ancient Chinese, not to mention Anon, author of a well-known Old English riddle. There is even a departure from another man's translation: "1971" remodels John Batki's version of Attila József, transposing it, stars and all, from Hungary to America.

The fascination with Guillevic centers on questions of technique: "Just to read him seemed to constitute a kind of discovery for me. I had, for a while, the ambition to translate that *style,* as it were, into American verse. . . . What I tried to do, once I found a style in another language which was to me of great interest, was to put it into American." And, "I suppose, now that I think of it, I was interested in the fact that his poems looked as if they should sound like Williams and they didn't. There was a sort of challenge to me to find out what the secret of that was, and I tried to invent or duplicate that kind of effect for myself."

There were other inventions, including several from the work of Rafael Alberti. "I've taken three different poems by Alberti and modeled an English poem on them. Not in what Lowell calls an imitation, and not a translation, not an adaptation. . . ." Again, the technical challenge—*la difficulté vaincue*—provides the starting point for these reworkings, some characteristic of the structure of the originals that catches his eye. And the care with which Justice distances his own enterprise from Lowell's is worth noting.

To imitate is to ape and follow suit, parrot and take after. To depart from is to vary and change, swerve and diverge. On a sliding scale of strategies for transformation, departure is a natural step beyond the notion of imitation. The original poet and the original poem slowly vanish as the Justice version comes into focus. The task of the translator becomes something new, "Something Better, 'tho it want yet a Name."

A method not without dangers and temptations. The temptation, of course, is to smash and grab, to plagiarize and purloin another man's inspiration, run off with his muse. And the danger is that one's translation may cast a shadow over the foreign poem, as Santayana's immaculate conversion of Gautier's *"L'Art"* exceeds its original. *A translator is to be like his author*—Dr. Johnson speaking—*it is not his business to excel him.* Hence the modesty of Justice, and the tact, the scrupulous tracking of origins and sources, the giving of credit where credit is due, even to the dead, especially to the dead. This eases the dangers if it does not erase them.

Andrew Hudgins (essay date summer 2002)

SOURCE: Hudgins, Andrew. "Homage: Donald Justice." *Southern Review* 38, no. 3 (summer 2002): 654-61.

[*In the following essay, Hudgins offers an appreciation of Justice's verse.*]

I have heard Don Justice read his poems at least nine times over four decades in five different states. One of those readings, at Bread Loaf in 1985, was the best I've ever heard. In a hushed yet firm and clear voice, Don read with a musician's attentiveness to rhythm that approached, but never became, chant. The poems, which I knew backwards and forwards, edged toward pure music, while expanding their emotional and intellectual reach. It was a magical moment.

Before I ever heard Don read, I knew his work on the page, and when I first heard it aloud the voice that spoke it was mine. I read the poems over and over, enjoying how fluidly they floated off my tongue. I can't now remember exactly when I first read Don's work, but I know *Night Light* (1967) was the first of his books I owned. My copy is a third printing, from 1968. To give a sense of how long ago that was other than in mere years, my copies of *Night Light* and *The Summer Anniversaries* cost $2.45 and my copy of *Departures* $2.95. Those sums were more expensive then, and not just financially. When I was in high school and college, my parents did not allow me to have a checking account, and the few bookstores in Montgomery, Alabama, did not carry poetry more contemporary than Robert Frost, Robert Service, and Helen Steiner Rice. To obtain a book written by a living poet, I had to track down a publisher's address, hand over to my mother money I had earned from my job at Solomon Brothers Dry Goods, and convince her that I was not ordering anything profane. She then grudgingly wrote a check to Wesleyan University Press. Months would pass, and then books by James Dickey, Robert Bly, James Wright, and, later, Donald Justice showed up in the mailbox. My first infatuation to slip from those padded envelopes was Dickey. I loved the raw, unapologetic southern redneck macho of it, at least partially because I worried that loving poetry meant I was a homosexual in some way I didn't understand. Such were the terrors of the time, or at least my terrors of the time. And I loved the fact that Dickey's was my South, not the aristocratic South that the Fugitives, most of them, both disdained and embodied. But soon the very things that drew me to Dickey drove me away, and a new envelope arrived, with *Night Light* in it, a book I knew nothing about except that it was published by Wesleyan. It was both a revelation and a relief to find a contemporary poet who coolly refused the yearning and the straining of romanticism, a poet who, without lapsing into coldness, shared Eliot's understanding of the impersonality of art.

In an interview Justice cites elegance as the characteristic he most admires in poetry, and that's the quality that Richard Howard, in an early review, found to be the signal virtue of Don's own poetry. But it's a very American kind of elegance—classical in its clarity, rationality, and emphasis on perfection of form without being rigid, stultifying, or programmatic. Don's poetry is precise without calling overt attention to its precisions. The language is natural American speech that does not make an issue of its naturalness. And I loved how Don wrote in both free and formal verse, bringing the resources of the one to the other. Don's **"Here in Katmandu"** is so gracefully written in free-verse lines that I would be ashamed to say how many times I read it before I realized it was a sestina.

For my last three years in college and the year after I graduated, I stayed overnight with an elderly man, a retired opera singer, four times a week. After I emptied his bedpan and helped him into bed, I sat at his desk and copied poems I admired into a series of notebooks with black marbleized covers. Most of *Night Light, The Summer Anniversaries,* and *Departures* are in those notebooks, in my still unformed hand, blocky and labored. I simply wanted to claim those poems. I wanted them in my hand, and I wanted my hand to move the way their author's had in fashioning them. This was not an homage but an Emersonian claiming. I wanted them to be useful for me. I wanted them to be mine.

* * *

In an interview in *Platonic Scripts,* Justice is asked, "What poets do you think influenced you?" He replies, "Practically all the poets in all the anthologies in all the

languages . . ." I might have rolled my eyes at this had I read it before taking a class with Don in the spring of 1982. At the first or second meeting, he assigned Matthew Arnold's essay about touchstones and asked us to bring in for the next class our ten touchstones. I don't remember most of my list. It included the opening and closing sections of Robert Lowell's "After the Surprising Conversions," a passage from Alexander Pope's *Essay on Man,* and perhaps Philip Larkin's "The Old Fools," which I was much taken with around that time. I also included one obscene limerick that, for a couple of months, I repeated to anyone who would listen. Just one item on my list caused Don to hesitate: "Who is this coming up from the wilderness, leaning on her beloved?" It was perhaps unfair to include it, but the line haunted me then. I walked around town repeating it maddeningly, like a pop song stuck in my head. I woke up in the middle of the night chanting it. Don recognized the line as biblical, narrowed it down to the Old Testament, then paused for a split second before venturing that it came from *The Song of Songs.* He was of course right. But that is not the impressive part. There were about fifteen students in the class, each with ten touchstones from a variety of literatures, and a good number of them from the obscurities of the poetry of the moment. I was able to identify significantly fewer than half of my classmates' touchstones. Don identified them all.

Don's astonishing knowledge of poetry is matched by his perfect pitch. The poet Henri Coulette once assured me that Don is the only poet he'd ever known who could hear the syllabic count in lines as they were read aloud. That is a skill I find almost impossible to believe, as marvelous to me as knowing that dogs can hear those high-pitched whistles that are silent to the human ear.

To my ear, Don's rhythms have learned much from Eliot and the poets Eliot learned from, though Don's poems are in most ways more musical. Here is the end of Eliot's "Little Gidding":

> Through the unknown, remembered gate
> When the last of the earth left to discover
> Is that which was the beginning;
> At the source of the longest river
> The voice of the hidden waterfall
> And the children in the apple-tree
> Not known, because not looked for
> But heard, half heard, in the stillness
> Between two waves of the sea.
> Quick now, here, now, always—
> A condition of complete simplicity
> (Costing not less than everything)
> And all shall be well and
> All manner of thing shall be well
> When the tongues of flame are in-folded
> Into the crowned knot of fire
> And the fire and the rose are one.

If you were to drain the religious sensibility from this passage, you would also have to give up the consolations of the belief that "All manner of thing shall be well" and the triumphant—and critically controversial—rhetoric, as well as the symbolism of the fire and the rose becoming one. But if you preserved the downwardly spiraling rhythm of the passage while adjusting it for an austere sensibility that did not admit the consolations of God and an afterlife, you might get something like Don's **"Pale Tepid Ode"**:

> Not with the vague smoke
> In the curtains,
> Not with the pigeons or doves
> Under the eaves,
> Nevertheless you are there, hidden,
> And again you wake me,
> Scentless, noiseless,
> Someone or something,
> Something or someone faithless,
> And that will not return.
>
> Undiscovered star,
> That fade and are fading,
> But never entirely fading,
> Fixed,
> And that will not return.
>
> Someone, someone or something,
> Colorless, formless,
> And that will not return.

It is, I think, a purer lyric than Eliot's, one that strives for elegance and disdains the power that both enlarges and blemishes Eliot's great passage. In Eliot, the muscularity of the vision leads to necessary if awkward qualifiers, qualifiers that sound clumsily legalistic, in their exactitudes: "Is that which was . . ." and "not less than." Don's ode strives for a lyrical perfection unmarred by the complexities of a vision, theological or not. It integrates into itself as many allusions as Eliot does, but more seamlessly. It's hard not to hear Shakespeare in that "fixed" star. I also detect Whitman's "noiseless, patient spider" that "launch'd forth filament, filament, filament, out of itself, / Ever unreeling them, ever tirelessly speeding them." With Don's "pigeons or doves / Under the eaves," I hear Yeats's "The brawling of a sparrow in the eaves"—though of course English poetry contains enough doves, pigeons, and sparrows to fill a dovecote the size of the Royal Albert Hall. From one of his fine essays, we know that Don admires Walter Savage Landor. Am I wrong, I wonder, to hear in Don's ode Landor's habit of exploiting reversal as lyric repetition while using it to expand the emotional and intellectual range of the poem, as he does in **"Late Leaves"**?

> The leaves are falling; so am I;
> The few late flowers have moisture in the eye;
> So have I too.
> Scarcely on any bough is heard
> Joyous, or even unjoyous, bird
> The whole wood though.
>
> Winter may come: he brings but nigher
> His circle (yearly narrowing) to the fire

> Where old friends meet.
> Let him; now heaven is overcast,
> And spring and summer both are past,
> And all things sweet.

Certainly Landor's restrained and classical pondering of age and loss recounted with a lyrical dying fall must have struck a chord with Justice. And one can also hear in the ode a rhythm that is taken in a different direction in the early poems of Wallace Stevens—say, "Peter Quince at the Clavier" or "The Place of the Solitaires":

> Let the place of the solitaires
> Be a place of perpetual undulation.
>
> Whether it be in mid-sea
> On the dark, green water-wheel,
> Or on the beaches,
> There must be no cessation
> Of motion, or of the noise of motion,
> The renewal of noise
> And manifold continuation;
>
> And, most, of the motion of thought
> And its restless iteration,
> In the place of the solitaires,
> Which is to be a place of perpetual undulation.

If you were more modest in temperament and softer-voiced than Stevens, you might, in emulating these lines, tone down their noise and restlessness, and change the peremptory tone of the opening and the formal flourishes of the old-fashioned subjunctive mood. If so, you might get a poem that in its circling and falling rhythms was very like **"Pale Tepid Ode."**

More tentatively, I hear behind Don's poem the water-drop song from *The Waste Land,* and more tentatively yet these lines from W. H. Auden's "The Question":

> Till, losing memory,
> Bird, fish, and sheep are ghostly,
> And ghosts must do again
> What gives them pain. . . .
>
> Shall memory restore
> The steps and the shore,
> The face and the meeting place. . . .
>
> Can love remember
> The question and the answer,
> For love recover
> What has been dark and rich and warm all over?

Does "Bird, fish, and sheep are ghostly / And ghosts must do again / What gvies them pain" prefigure the ghostly, haunted repetitions of **"Pale Tepid Ode"**?

Because we know from Don's own note that **"Cool Dark Ode,"** one of two companion pieces to **"Pale Tepid Ode,"** was "loosely modeled on a poem by Rafael Alberti," I can propose with more confidence that Alberti is also deliberately echoed in **"Pale Tepid Ode."** Mark Strand's translation of "Song of the Luckless Angel" goes this way:

You are what moves:
water that carries me,
that will leave me.

Look for me in the wave.

What moves and doesn't return:
wind that in shadows
dies down and rises.

Look for me in the snow.

What nobody knows:
the floating earth
that speaks to nobody.

Look for me in the air.

These influences, if they are influences, are so smoothly integrated into a unique voice, a voice instantly recognizable as Don's, that I wonder if I'm really hearing them—them and the many other echoes that haunt my ear but drift away as I try to name them.

But there's one more source to consider, one I've been holding back so I could isolate and mull over other possibilities. In a short essay called "The Invention of Free Verse," Don finds in Ezra Pound's "Cino," the fourth poem in *Personae,* "an unmistakable little musical motif, scarcely if ever heard before in English verse." The lines he cites are lines four through twelve of a fifty-six-line poem:

> Lips, words, and you snare them,
> Dreams, words, and they are as jewels,
> Strange spells of old deity,
> Ravens, night, allurement:
> And they are not;
> Having become the souls of song.
>
> Eyes, dreams, lips, and the night goes.
> Being up the road once more,
> They are not.

Cino, Pound's speaker, is going to turn his back on women, he says, and sing of the sun. After these nine lines, as Don points out, the poem reverts to the rhythms of the '90s. But even this fascinating passage is mired in the language of that era; none of the words and little

of the tone would surprise, say, Ernest Dowson. To my ear, Don has a finer sense of the appropriate subject matter for the rhythm.

Have I, in searching for influence, overburdened Don's lovely lyric? I don't think so. Don's ear is so fine and his knowledge of poetic rhythm so vast that it's impossible to rule out any likely possibility.

It is a truism that reading Pound, Eliot, and Joyce provided the poets and critics of their generation with a wide-ranging classical education. Reading Don Justice has provided two generations of students with an education in the music of poetry, and in a particularly American form of poetic elegance.

FURTHER READING

Criticism

Hoy, Philip. *Donald Justice in Conversation with Philip Hoy.* London: Between the Lines, 2001, 130 p.
> Provides a fresh, book-length interview with Justice.

Justice, Donald. *Platonic Scripts.* Ann Arbor: University of Michigan Press, 1984, 225 p.
> Offers interviews and essays by Justice.

————, David Hamilton, and Lowell Edwin Folsom. "An Interview with Donald Justice." *Iowa Review* 11, nos. 2-3 (spring-summer 1980): 1-21.
> Presents an interview with Justice.

Sheridan, Michael. Review of *Selected Poems,* by Donald Justice. *New Letters* 48, no. 1 (fall 1981): 114-16.
> Reviews *Selected Poems* and surveys Justice's overall body of work.

St. John, David. "Scripts and Water, Rules and Riches." *Antioch Review* 43, no. 3 (summer 1985): 309-19.
> Discusses and contrasts Justice and Howard Moss.

Wright, Charles. "Homage to the Thin Man." *Southern Review* 30, no. 4 (autumn 1994): 741-44.
> Discusses some of Justice's influences.

Additional coverage of Justice's life and career is contained in the following sources published by Thomson Gale: *American Writers Supplement,* Vol. 7; *Contemporary Authors,* Vols. 5-8R; *Contemporary Authors New Revision Series,* Vols. 26, 54, 74, 121, 122; *Contemporary Literary Criticism,* Vols. 6, 19, 102; *Contemporary Poets,* Ed. 7; *Contemporary Southern Writers; Dictionary of Literary Biography Yearbook 1983; DISCovering Authors Modules: Poets; Encyclopedia of World Literature in the 20th Century,* Ed. 3; *Literature Resource Center; Major 20th-Century Writers,* Ed. 2; and *Poetry for Students,* Vol. 14.

The Heights of Macchu Picchu

Pablo Neruda

The following entry presents criticism of Neruda's poem *Las alturas de Macchu Picchu* (1946; *The Heights of Macchu Picchu*). For discussion of Neruda's complete poetic works, see *PC,* Volume 4.

INTRODUCTION

Widely regarded as one of the most important Latin American poets of the twentieth century, Neruda is noted for his innovative methods of versification and influential contribution to modern poetry. His writing is generally categorized by scholars into several periods, ranging from his early, traditional works to his spontaneous surrealist poetry of the 1930s to the simple, direct, and political verse of his later years. The twelve-part poetic sequence entitled *Las alturas de Macchu Picchu* (*The Heights of Macchu Picchu*), considered one of Neruda's exceptional literary accomplishments, is generally thought to inaugurate his late period. First published in 1946 and later incorporated as the second section of his definitive 1950 version of the *Canto general,* the poem has typically been viewed as a turning point in Neruda's development as a poet. Its earlier portions encapsulate the metaphysical vision and lyrical use of language exemplified in Neruda's two-volume *Residencia en la tierra* (1933 and 1935; *Residence on Earth*), while the poem's later cantos adumbrate the predominately political sensibility that would distinguish his writing of the 1950s to early 1970s. Overall, the *Canto general* is typically regarded as one of Neruda's major achievements, and *The Heights of Macchu Picchu* is perceived as its visionary evocation and thematic core. The sequence itself, inspired by Neruda's visit to the Incan ruins alluded to in its title, concerns the poet's imaginative pilgrimage in search of meaning and an elusive human unity spanning the past, present, and future.

BIOGRAPHICAL INFORMATION

Born Ricardo Neftalí Reyes in Parral, Chile, in 1904, Neruda moved with his family at the age of three to Temuco, a rainy region of the South American country that would later feature prominently in his verse. He began publishing poetry at fifteen years of age, and in

1921 took part in a poetry contest at the annual Spring Festival in Santiago for which he received first prize. Around this time he first published poems under the pen name "Pablo Neruda." In 1924 Neruda entered the University of Chile in Santiago to study poetry. That same year he established a national reputation with the publication of *Veinte poemas de amor y una canción desesperada* (*Twenty Love Poems and a Song of Despair*), a work since esteemed as a masterpiece of Hispanic erotic poetry. Other significant works followed in the 1920s, including the experimental *Tentativa del hombre infinito* (1926).

In honor of his various achievements, Neruda was appointed to the Chilean diplomatic service in 1927 as consul to Burma, and would later serve in Ceylon and the Dutch East Indies. While in the Far East, Neruda experienced a period of loneliness and frustration, and began writing pieces for the first volume of *Residence on Earth,* a continuing cycle that established him as a leading figure in Spanish-language literature. When Neruda returned to Chile in 1933, he was reassigned to Buenos Aires, Argentina, and befriended poet Federico Garcia Lorca and other Spanish writers of the Generation of 1927. During this time he continued to compose the introspective, metaphysical verse that forms his *Residencia* cycle.

Neruda's life and poetry took an abrupt political turn following the outbreak of the Spanish Civil War in 1936. He published *España en el corazón* (*Spain in the Heart*), an impassioned tribute in verse dedicated to the cause of Spanish loyalists, in 1937. His increasingly outspoken involvement with leftist politics in the subsequent period culminated in his expulsion from the Chilean diplomatic service in 1943. That year, he visited the ruined Incan city located high in the Peruvian Andes known as Machu Picchu (which Neruda spells "Macchu Picchu"). The trip inspired *The Heights of Macchu Picchu,* which Neruda completed by the fall of 1945 and submitted to the Venezuelan journal *Exprésion* for publication the following year.

The poem was subsequently integrated into Neruda's epic work, *Canto general de Chile,* a collection (extensively revised between its original appearance in 1943 and its final version in 1950) that features 340 poems concerned with the natural, cultural, and political history of Latin America. With this volume, Neruda renounced his work written prior to 1937 and proclaimed himself a populist poet. He was elected to the Chilean Senate in 1946. Later indicted for treason due to his open condemnation of Chile's president Gabriel González Videla, Neruda was forced to flee his homeland in 1949. He traveled extensively over the next several years while completing revisions to the *Canto general.* Welcomed throughout the communist world, Neruda enjoyed his newfound international notoriety and was eventually permitted to return to Chile in 1953.

High points of his later poetic career include the playfully sardonic *Odas elementales* (1954; *Elementary Odes*) and *Estravagario* (1958; *Extravagaria*), as well as several volumes of didactic, political verse. A member of the Chilean Communist Party since 1945, Neruda emerged as a nominee for the presidency of Chile in 1970 but withdrew after the five parties that made up Chile's political left decided to endorse Salvador Allende. While serving as Ambassador to France under Allende's government, Neruda was honored with the Nobel Prize for literature in 1971. He died of cancer two years later. Since his death, numerous critics have endorsed Neruda as a major figure in world literature, and Neruda's poetic compositions from all phases of his career continue to elicit commentary.

MAJOR THEMES

Critics typically view *The Heights of Macchu Picchu* as the lyrical record of Neruda's spiritual journey in search of the fundamental truths of humankind. Relying on the central symbol of a pilgrimage to the ruins of the pre-Columbian Inca civilization, the poem moves through twelve cantos, progressing from an awareness of the fundamental futility of modern existence to the discovery of a meaningful transcendence of isolation, social disorder, and even death through fraternal love and human solidarity. Within the dozen individual sections that make up the sequence, Neruda confronts a collection of themes including the significance of death, the transience of life, the cyclical renewal of nature, the alienation and loneliness of urban existence, the elusiveness of truth, and the deceptiveness of surface appearances.

In the opening lines of the poem, Neruda invokes the image of an empty net cast through city streets, a net that retrieves nothing. He presents a world of chaos, disintegration, and emptiness. In the poem's second canto, nature imagery features prominently, representing what Robert Pring-Mill has called "the enduring values of self-perpetuating nature," which is the source of the essential qualities Neruda demonstrates are lacking in the dislocated lives of modern city-dwellers. With the poem's third canto, Neruda continues the process of contrasting the senseless toil of urban life with the limitless vitality of nature, relying on a profusion of nature and elemental imagery. Canto four reinforces themes of death, loneliness, and isolation, counterbalanced by the potentialities of love, both erotic and filial. The sequence reaches its pessimistic nadir in the short, surrealistic fifth canto, which presents scenes of contemporary life in stasis and despair, recounting the shallowness of modern existence.

With canto six, *The Heights of Macchu Picchu* features its first major turning point as Neruda ascends through the Peruvian jungle to the ruined Inca citadel. Speaking to the sleeping city, Neruda begins to travel backward in time, mingling history and nature as he evokes an epoch before the native inhabitants of South America came into contact with European explorers. In canto seven, Neruda begins to study the nature of this pre-Columbian people, addressing the men who died while constructing Machu Picchu. Section seven closes, "a life of stone after so many lives," highlighting the transience of human existence against the centuries-long endurance of the city's stone foundation. Canto eight contains Neruda's questions to the city itself, a poetic interrogation into the elusive essence of a dead people. Canto nine shifts from the interrogative mode to one of incantation, and offers an almost liturgical enumeration of metaphorical names for the city. It ends by calling Machu Picchu a "wellspring of stone."

The beginning of canto ten presents a second turning point in the work as Neruda imaginatively reconstructs the human history of this Inca city. Drawing connections between ancient and modern people, Neruda asks if the inhabitants of Machu Picchu suffered, five centuries or more ago, from the same tedium of existence that afflicts contemporary men and women. He wonders if slaves were used to build these ruins, and if so, how many died in this labor? The final portions of the section concentrate on these workers as Neruda looks beyond the stones to the men and women who once lived among them. Canto eleven introduces the theme of brotherhood and Neruda's poetic search for "the old forgotten human heart." In the poem's final canto, Neruda offers an exhortation to the vanished workers of Machu Picchu, asking them to release their pain, silence, and struggle. "Raise to be born with me, brother," he writes, "Speak through my words and my blood." The poem closes, then, with a theme of humanitarianism, expressing the poet's celebration of love for his fellow human beings.

CRITICAL RECEPTION

The Heights of Macchu Picchu is frequently cited by scholars as among Neruda's finest works of poetry, and as a central piece in his development as a writer. Neruda himself, in discussing the poem, once remarked that it reflected "a new stage in my style and a new direction in my concerns." Commentators have tended to agree with this statement. In their view, cantos one through five of the poem offer a reprise of Neruda's earlier poetry, especially the lyrical and metaphysical pieces of his well-regarded *Residencia* collections. Teeming with imagery, these early portions of the sequence remind scholars of Neruda's innovative capacity as a lyric poet.

The latter cantos of *The Heights of Macchu Picchu*, particularly its final three movements, have traditionally been more troubling to commentators. Following the poet's evocation of time and place at Machu Picchu, the poem begins to shift, as Neruda himself was to do, from metaphysical to social and political concerns. In the wake of this shift, commentators have located the poem's closing humanitarian vision, a worldview akin to that demonstrated in Neruda's collection *Spain in the Heart.* Yet with their more prosaic style, cantos ten through twelve of *The Heights of Macchu Picchu* have indicated to critics the fundamental social and political themes that would dominate Neruda's late poetry. In particular, scholars have discerned an adumbration of Neruda's coming ideological devotion to the idea of human solidarity associated with communist political philosophy. Most critics, however, have hesitated to reduce *The Heights of Macchu Picchu* to mere political content. Instead, they have praised the essential

complexity and ambiguity of Neruda's poem as a search for human truth. While these qualities have made *The Heights of Macchu Picchu*, like much of Neruda's poetic work, difficult to translate, they remain some of the most compelling aspects of one of the poet's outstanding achievements in verse.

PRINCIPAL WORKS

Poetry

La canción de la fiesta 1921

Crepúsculario 1923

Veinte poemas de amor y una canción desesperada 1924; also published as *Twenty Love Poems and a Song of Despair,* 1969

Tentativa del hombre infinito 1926

*Residencia en la tierra: 1925-1931 1933

Homenaje a Pablo Neruda de los poetas españoles: tres cantos materiales 1935; also published as *Tres cantos materiales: Three Material Songs,* 1948

*Residencia en la tierra: 1931-1935 1935

†España en el corazón 1937

Las furias y las penas 1939

Canto general de Chile: Fragmentos 1943

Nuevo canto de amor a Stalingrado 1943

Las alturas de Macchu Picchu 1946; also published as *The Heights of Macchu Picchu,* 1966

Tercera Residencia, 1935-1945 1947; also published as *Residence on Earth,* 1973

Que despierte el leñador! 1948; also published as *Peace for Twilights to Come!,* 1950

‡Canto general 1950

Let the Splitter Awake and Other Poems 1950

Los versos del capitán 1952; also published as *The Captain's Verses,* 1972

Poesía política: discursos politicos. 2 vols. 1953

Odas elementales 1954; also published as *Elementary Odes,* 1961

Las uvas y el viento 1954

Nuevas odas elementales 1956

Oda a la tipografía 1956

Obras completas 1957

Estravagario 1958; also published as *Extravagaria,* 1972

Cien sonetos de amor 1959; also published as *One Hundred Love Sonnets,* 1986

Odas: al libro, a las Americas, a la luz 1959

Canción de gesta 1960; also published as *Song of Protest,* 1976

§Memoríal de Isla Negra. 5 vols. 1964; also published as *Isla Negra: A Notebook,* 1980

Bestiary/Bestiario: A Poem 1965

Arte de pájaros 1966; also published as *Art of Birds*, 1985

Nocturnal Collection: A Poem 1966

La barcarola 1967

Twenty Poems 1967

We Are Many 1967

Aún 1969; also published as *Still Another Day*, 1984

A New Decade: Poems, 1958-1967 1969

Pablo Neruda: The Early Poems 1969

Antología popular 1972 1972

Cuatros poemas escritos en Francia 1972

Geografía infructuosa 1972

New Poems, 1968-1970 1972

El mar y las campanas 1973; also published as *The Sea and the Bells*, 1988

La rosa separada: obra póstuma 1973; also published as *A Separate Rose*, 1985

El corazón amarillo 1974; also published as *The Yellow Heart*, 1990

Defectos escogidos 1974

Elegía 1974; also published as *Elegy*, 1983

Five Decades: A Selection: Poems, 1925-1970 1974

Jardín de invierno 1974; also published as *Winter Garden*, 1986

Libro de las preguntas 1974; also published as *The Book of Questions*, 1991

Oda a la lagartija 1974

Late and Posthumous Poems, 1968-1974 1988

Neruda's Garden: An Anthology of Odes 1995

The Essential Neruda: Selected Poems 2004

Other Major Works

El habitante y su esperanza (prose) 1925

Anillos [with Tomás Lago] (prose) 1926

Prosas de Pablo Neruda (prose) 1926

Homenaje a García Lorca (prose) 1939

La crisis democratica de Chile (essay) 1947; also published as *The Democratic Crisis of Chile* 1948

Viaies (prose) 1955

Fulgor y muerte de Joaquín Murieta (play) 1967; also published as *Splendor and Death of Joaquín Murieta*, 1972

La copa de sangre (poetry and prose) 1969

Discurso pronunciado con occasión de la entrega del premio Nobel de literatura, 1971 (lecture) 1972; also published as *Toward the Splendid City: Nobel Lecture*, 1974

Confieso que he vivido: memorias (memoirs) 1974; also published as *Memoirs*, 1977

Cartas a Laura (letters) 1978

Para nacer he nacido (poems, essays, and lectures) 1978; also published as *Passions and Impressions*, 1982

El río invisible (poetry and prose) 1980

*These works were published in one volume as *Residencia en la tierra (1925-1935)* in 1944, and in English with other poems in one volume as *Residence on Earth and Other Poems* in 1946.

†This work, translated as *Spain in the Heart,* appears in *Residence on Earth and Other Poems.*

‡This work includes *Las alturas de Macchu Picchu.*

§This work was originally published in five volumes: *Donde nace la lluvia* (Vol. 1), *La luna en el laberinto* (Vol. 2), *El fuego cruél* (Vol. 3), *El cazador de raices* (Vol. 4), and *Sonata critica* (Vol. 5).

CRITICISM

James Wright (review date June 1968)

SOURCE: Wright, James. "'I Come to Speak for Your Dead Mouths.'" *Poetry* 112, no. 3 (June 1968): 191-94.

[*In the following review, Wright admires Nathaniel Tarn's English translation of* The Heights of Macchu Picchu *and summarizes the content of Neruda's poem.*]

By this time it is clear to everybody who has ever heard of him that Neruda is a very great poet.

It is the folly of Americans to assume that to say as much is to say that a man is a great man, worthy of worship, a relief to us in our frantic and temporary deaths.

But a great poet is a disturbance. If poetry means anything, it means heart, liver, and soul. If great poetry means anything, anything at all, it means disturbance, secret disturbance, that can be disposed of in public, as the pharmacist's delivery of prescription disposes of lonely midnight day-dreams. But that cannot be so easily disposed of privately, as the insomniac discovers that the soporific provides him with sleep only to follow the hand of sleep into a land of secret wakening, nightmare, or illumination, that he wished to escape in the first place. It is bad enough to be miserable; but to be happy, how far beyond shock it is. To be alive, with all one's unexpected senses, and yet to face the fact of unhappiness.

There is a critic in the English language whose nobility and spaciousness allowed him to make the statement about poetry that can in turn allow us to cherish what is great. It is a statement about Shakespeare, and it applies to Neruda's poem *The Heights of Macchu Picchu.* In his preface to the works of Shakespeare, Dr. Johnson wonders why we should care about a poet after he has been dead for more than a hundred years. After all the envious reviewers are dead, something lives. How do we know it lives? We love it. It is alive. It is all we have. But why? Why do we love it? What is alive?

It combines a flowering in language with a cold pruning of form. Great poetry folds personal death and general love into one dark blossom.

I don't know why you read it, but I read it because I like it. I want poetry to make me happy, but the poetry I want should deal with the hell of our lives or else it leaves me cold. Why should I care? Why should I let it touch me?

Here is Johnson's remark on great poetry, which on this particular occasion happens to be Shakespeare:

> Nothing can please many or please long but just representations of general nature. Particular manners can be known to few, and few only can judge how nearly they are copied. The irregular combinations of fanciful invention may delight awhile, by that novelty of which the common satiety of life sends us all in quest. But the pleasures of sudden wonder are soon exhausted, and the mind can only repose on the stability of truth.

Neruda's abundance is clear in every country whose citizens care about poetry. He is too huge to handle in an essay, but I think we should try to identify his genius in a single poem.

Neruda wrote *The Heights of Macchu Picchu* in the fall of 1945. In 1943 he had returned to Chile, and it is very odd to reflect that on that return from his travels as Chilean consul-general in Mexico, a "triumphal journey, on which he found himself acclaimed in capital after capital by huge crowds" (in the words of Professor Robert Pring-Mill, whose introduction is one of the most valuable features in this volume), he should have written this great poem. He had achieved fame, all right. And we know what fame is. Milton has told us. It is an infirmity. But Neruda responded as follows.

In a sequence of twelve poems, the poet tells how he had spent his early life wandering in the cities of his country, sick to death of his loneliness, longing for love. The love he longed for was partly sexual, and this love had already been achieved and celebrated in the *Twenty Poems* that made his poetic reputation (by the way, the best English version of these love poems can be found in the neglected masterpiece, Kenneth Rexroth's *Thirty Spanish Poems of Love and Exile,* published by City Lights Books). But Neruda's love is human, and human love is a hell. Coming home, acclaimed, he responded by grieving over his failure to achieve a fulfillment of love with the living. And yet they were cheering him! Imagine. He is a very great poet. Instead of writing an Ode to His Readers, he composed the *Macchu Picchu.*

But how can that be? Macchu Picchu, the big city of the Incas, was dead. And the people who built it were dead.

No, they were living in the modern cities of Chile. They were also living in Cleveland, as we know. (If we are sane.)

Neruda couldn't find them in Cleveland, or in Santiago.

So he ascended.

I would paraphrase Neruda's argument as follows: Appalled by loneliness I sought my human brothers among the living; I do not really object to their death, as long as I can share with them the human death; but everywhere I go among the living I find them dying each by each a small petty death in the midst of their precious brief lives. So I ascended to the ancient ruins of the city of Macchu Picchu in the Andes; and there I found that, however the lives of my human brothers may have suffered, at least they are all now dead together. Look at the gorgeous things they have made. But wait a moment. Weren't their lives just as petty and grotesquely fragmented as the very people who die early and pointlessly in the modern cities where I have just been celebrated? Yes, they were. And therefore I love the poor broken dead. They belong to me. I will not celebrate the past for its perfect power over the imperfect living. "I come to speak for your dead mouths." The silent and nameless persons who built Macchu Picchu are alive in Santiago de Chile. The living are the living, and dead the dead must stay.

In conveying this idea, Neruda writes twelve poems that move from his despair in the living cities to his ascent to the city of the dead, and thence to his invocation of the dead who, in his poetry, are the living. As Professor Pring-Mill remarks, the poet's ascent through space is also an ascent backwards through time. In fact, that is the form of the poem; to discover the living in the past is to discover the living in the present. The image which fulfills this grieving discovery is enclosed in a passage which, in the words of Mr. Tarn, seems to me tragic and beautiful.

> Let me have back the slave you buried here;
> Wrench from these lands the stale bread
> of the poor, prove me the tatters
> on the serf, point out his window.
> Tell me how he slept when alive,
> whether he snored,
> his mouth agape like a dark scar
> worn by fatigue into the wall.

The translation of Neruda into English is a problem which has engaged several poets. One of the most effective of these is Mr. H. R. Hays, whose version of **"Walking Around"** remains, to me, one of the greatest poems in the modern American language. Mr. Clayton Eshleman has also done a Neruda notable for its daring and force. Now we have Mr. Nathaniel Tarn, the gifted English poet. He has tried to solve the most difficult poem by Neruda which involves not only the stylistic and imaginative brilliance of the great poet's language but also his formal mastery of these elements which enables Neruda to illuminate for us some of the meanings of life. Although personally I would hem and haw over this and that detail of Mr. Tarn's translation, I have to confess that I think it is a beautiful poem in the English language, worthy of the noble and spacious poem which identifies Neruda as one of the precious few great masters of our time and of any time.

Kay Engler (essay date summer 1974)

SOURCE: Engler, Kay. "Image and Structure in Neruda's *Las alturas de Macchu Picchu.*" *Symposium* 28, no. 2 (summer 1974): 130-45.

[*In the following essay, Engler evaluates the symbolic structure of* The Heights of Macchu Picchu, *analyzing archetypal metaphors of apocalyptic and demonic worlds in the poem.*]

It is generally conceded that after *Residencia en la tierra* (1933-35), Pablo Neruda's finest work is *Las alturas de Macchu Picchu,* written in 1943 following the poet's first visit to the fabulous lost city of the Incas, first published in 1946 and later included in his *Canto general* (1950). *Las alturas de Macchu Picchu* is important not only because of its intrinsic literary merit, but also because, as critics have pointed out, it represents a key to Pablo Neruda's evolution as a poet. For example, Hernán Loyola has pointed out in *Ser y morir en Pablo Neruda* that *Las alturas de Macchu Picchu* is "[un] poema-sintesis . . . [cuya] significación radica en el hecho de reflejar el punto culminante de una encrucijada dialéctica, la resolución final de una etapa del proceso interior que venía viviendo Neruda, y, al mismo tiempo, la apertura de una nueva etapa."[1]

Amado Alonso's now classic *Poesía y estilo de Pablo Neruda* stands alone as an invaluable guide to the study of the first stage of Neruda's poetic development, the surrealist period of *Residencia en la tierra* (1933-35). Criticism of Neruda's later works has tended to be thematic rather than stylistic, a tendency which perhaps reflects the change in Neruda's poetry itself toward a more prosaic, less hermetic style. The criticism which exists on *Las alturas de Macchu Picchu* is either vague and impressionistic (Loyola,[2] de Lellis,[3] Larrea[4]) or thematic (Rodriguez-Fernandez,[5] Montes[6]). Robert Pring-Mill's brief introduction to Nathaniel Tarn's English translation of the poem stands as an exception.

Pring-Mill outlines the basic structure of the work and comments briefly on the poem's imagery.[7] What follows is an attempt to expand on Pring-Mill's introduction, to study carefully and in depth the nature of the imagery and the metaphorical structure of the work.

The poet Pablo Neruda enters the world of Macchu Picchu with a two-fold inheritance from the past: the shattering experience of a world of chaos and disorder recorded in his *Residencia en la tierra* and *Tercera residencia,* and the kinship in human suffering experienced in the Spanish Civil War and recorded in *España en el corazón.* The poems of *Residencia,* in themselves, exhibit a spiritual duality: between a material world in chaos and disintegration and the plenum of nature and matter, of the vegetal universe which presages life and well-being; between the poet's horror at the insignificance and vulnerability of the individual human being confronted with the totality of Being and his longing to be a part of that Being; between the poet's awareness of his own discordant, disintegrating self and his search for meaning; between his profound tenderness and concern for human sorrow, fragility and weakness and his simultaneous repugnance before a distorted humanity, before what human weakness has wrought: a world which suffocates man and nature's full potentiality.

In reality, *España en el corazón* adds a third dimension. Neruda abandons, for the moment, the problem of his relationship with the material world and turns instead to the problem of his relationship with his fellow men. Probing behind the world of objects, of material things, he touches on the material basis of human fraternity: a common bond of suffering willfully toward a certain end. As Luis Monguió states: "Neruda suddenly saw himself no longer estranged, but 'reunited'— not with accidents of matter, in blind processes of cosmic fatality, as before, but with men in processes of will."[8]

In the twelve poems of *Las alturas de Macchu Picchu* Neruda reflects and actually re-lives the earlier stages of his poetry. Macchu Picchu thus becomes the center of a complex web of associations which are only fully resolved in the context of his other works. The basic structure of the poem follows the dual vision established in the *Residencias.* The final resolution of the conflict, however, is profoundly influenced by the humanitarian vision of *España en el corazón.* Within the framework of the *Residencias,* the poem is a continuation of the poet's search for the individual's place in the universe and of the aesthetic used to convey that search. At the same time, the poem is an attempt to fit the metaphysics and aesthetics of the *Residencias* into the somewhat narrower social and historical framework of *España en el corazón.* Within the context of the *Canto general,* an epic-like work which explores the nature of Latin American history and culture, *Las alturas de Macchu*

Picchu stands at the thematic center of the search for historical reality.

Las alturas de Macchu Picchu and the ***Canto general*** of which it is a part stand as a monumental and grandiose effort to encompass the universal, to integrate the whole of reality. Macchu Picchu, symbolically and in a very real sense, offers the poet a kind of Archimedean point, beyond time and space, from which to survey the whole of being and to perceive the dimensions of its meaning. At the same time, Macchu Picchu stands at the center of reality past and present, temporal and eternal, particular and universal. It is, in Neruda's words, the destination of time, "dirección del tiempo,"[9] the destination of all things, the center of meaning, the point from which all makes sense. The central paradox of Macchu Picchu, above and beyond the world, yet standing at its existential center, is the principle around which the poem is structured. On the heights of Macchu Picchu, existence is made eternal, the particular becomes universal, many are made one, being is completed.

Neruda achieves this integral vision of reality through the use of metaphor. Interwoven patterns of image and metaphor establish Macchu Picchu as the center of an apocalyptic world where total identification is possible. The nature of metaphor itself, as explained by Northrop Frye in his *Anatomy of Criticism,* is the basis for the construction of an apocalyptic world, "the imaginative conception of the whole of nature as the content of an infinite and eternal living body."[10] As Frye explains, metaphor, in its purest and most poetic form, is a matter of the simple juxtaposition of images. Here it operates as the intuition of reality, following the associative patterns of lyricism. On the descriptive level, it operates as a simile in which both the verbal structure (the image itself) and the phenomena to which it is related (the reality behind the image) are present. On the formal, or conceptual, level where images function as ideas (in Frye's words, "where symbols are images or natural phenomena conceived as matter or content") (p. 124), metaphor operates as an analogy of natural proportions. There are four terms (two of which have a common member) implicit in the two images which make up the metaphor. Frye's example is "The hero was a lion," in which courage is the element common to both hero and lion. Finally, on a symbolic level, the metaphor may operate as a concrete universal. If the images used in the metaphor have been established through literary tradition or through the conscious effort of the poet within the confines of his work as archetypes, the metaphor unites, at the same time, individual images and the associative clusters to which they belong. Within the realm of the poetic imagination, metaphor knows no limits beyond those of human desire and fear. Here all things may be compared. In Frye's words, "The literary universe [. . .] is a universe in which everything is potentially identical with everything else. . . . All poetry . . . proceeds as though all poetic images were contained within a single universal body" (pp. 124-25). For Frye, the function of metaphor, then, rests on the concept of identity. Metaphor is the process of identifying two or more independent forms, of placing them within a larger enveloping context which nevertheless allows them to retain their individuality. As he states, "Identity is the opposite of similarity or likeness, and total identity is not uniformity, still less monotony, but a unity of various things" (p. 125).

The metaphors and images of a poem are interwoven in the form of a myth that gives structure and meaning to the work. Myth which takes the form of two contrasting worlds of total metaphorical identification, one desirable and the other undesirable, is, in Frye's terminology, "undisplaced." "Displaced" myth suggests implicit mythical patterns in a world more closely related to human experience. The two contrasting worlds are present, but in less extreme form (p. 139). The apocalyptic world presents the categories of reality in the form of the ultimate of man's ideals: the eternal oneness of Being. This is accomplished through the use of the archetypal metaphor, the concrete universal, identical with the others and with each individual in it. The source Frye uses in his discussion of undisplaced myth, the vision of apocalypse, is, of course, the Bible. In the apocalyptic world of the Bible, the divine, human, animal, vegetable and mineral worlds undergo complete metaphorical identification in the person of Christ. He sees the following pattern in the apocalyptic world of the Bible:

> divine world = society of gods = One God
> human world = society of men = One Man
> animal world = sheepfold = One Lamb
> vegetable world = garden or park = One Tree (of life)
> mineral world = city = One Building, Temple, Stone.
>
> (p. 141)

Christ, who is both one God and one Man, the Lamb of God, the Tree of Life, or the Vine of which we are the branches, the Stone on which the temple is built, unites all, metaphorically and existentially.

The demonic world, on the other hand, is "the presentation of the world that desire totally rejects: the world of nightmare, bondage and pain and confusion. . . ." (p. 147). While the apocalyptic world presents the total identity, the oneness of being, the demonic world presents a world of chaos, disintegration, sterility. The demonic world is often a cruel parody of the apocalyptic world: here there is no meaning; rather there is a sense of human remoteness and futility; there is no possibility of fulfillment for the individual; there is no eucharistic communion, but cannibalism, or mutual destruction. The vegetable world is represented as nature gone wild or having destroyed itself (a desert). The city is a ruin, a waste land. The fire of purgation and cleansing has become the fire of hell, or has gone out. Water has become the water of death, or is identified with spilt blood.

These metaphorical patterns are, in themselves, static. Yet they seldom occur in isolation, and when both are present, a dialectical tension is established which pulls the reader toward "the metaphorical and mythical un-displaced core of the work" (p. 151). The relationship of these co-existent structures has traditionally been represented in the static conception of a heaven (apocalyptic world) above, a hell (demonic world) beneath, and a cyclical cosmos or order of nature between. Yet when seen as a dialectic (movement from one structure to another within the narrative of the poem), the relationship is a dynamic one, involving two fundamental movements: a cyclical movement within the order of nature and a dialectical movement from that order into the apocalyptic world above or the demonic world below.

The top half of the cycle, or the movement of ascent, is what Frye calls "the analogy of innocence;" the lower half, or the movement of descent, "the analogy of experience" (p. 151). The function of the analogies of innocence and experience is "the adaptation of myth to nature," a way of dealing with life as process. As Frye explains it, "The apocalyptic and demonic worlds, being structures of pure metaphorical identity, suggest the eternally unchanging, and lend themselves very readily to being projected existentially as heaven and hell, where there is continuous life, but no process of life" (p. 158). Through the analogies of innocence and experience single images and patterns of images come to reflect process, the cyclical movement of the natural world.

Neruda, in *Las alturas de Macchu Picchu,* makes use of the traditional structures of archetypal imagery which Frye describes, yet modifies them substantially in fashioning his own original vision. The work itself consists of twelve poems of varying length and metrical form, in imitation of the calendar year, twelve lunar cycles in one solar cycle. The first five poems establish the conflict between the apocalyptic and demonic worlds, and introduce the poet as the center of conflict, the point of maximum tension. The presence of Macchu Picchu is not made explicit until the sixth poem (coincident with the summer solstice in the sixth month), which is the high point of the work: here on the heights of Macchu Picchu the abolishment of the demonic world and the realization of the apocalyptic world is possible. The next three poems examine more fully the meaning of Macchu Picchu, a subtle process which results, in the tenth poem, in a second major turning point in the work: here the realization of the

apocalyptic world the poet had longed for since the early years of the *Residencias,* and which at last seemed possible on the heights of Macchu Picchu, fails to be reconciled with the humanitarianism of *España en el corazón.* In the poems which follow, the meaning of Macchu Picchu changes, and the poet turns to the only possible basis for oneness with being: love for one's fellow human beings. The crisis is hinted at in the eighth poem (the waning of summer in the eighth month), is more openly suggested in the ninth month (coincident with the autumnal equinox) and takes overt form only in the tenth poem (coincident with the fullness of autumn and the coming of winter, the falling away of the outer foliage, revealing the bare branches of the trees). In the final poems, the poet celebrates his symbolic death and rebirth, the birth of a new vision (coincident with the end of the old cycle and the beginning of a new one).

In *Las alturas de Macchu Picchu,* both the apocalyptic and demonic worlds have been brought within the sphere of the natural order: the apocalyptic world, in large measure, is but a projection of the ascendant half of the cycle; the demonic world, of the descendent half of the cycle. The cyclical nature of the cosmos becomes an ideal in itself, so that the poet shows great fear of anything which threatens to disturb that cycle, to break down the order of the universe. Neruda's apocalyptic world is a self-contained, self-perpetuating, contracting universe where the cyclical movement has a centripetal force, drawing everything up into itself. It is a universe of elemental forces working in harmony. The projected opposite, of course, is a self-destructive, disintegrating universe where the cyclical movement has a centrifugal force which eventually unravels into nothingness, a world of alienation of being from being. It is a world of discord in which elemental forces have been seriously disrupted by the presence of man.

Neruda's vision of paradise is one of eternal spring and summer: the earth in a time of conception, creation, growth, and the bearing of fruit; man in the springtime of his existence, in the fullness of his being in oneness with the universe at the dawn of human civilization. Neruda's apocalyptic vision would make not only the world of creation but the very act of creation, the process of life, eternal: the moment must be made eternal, every individual act and being must be, at the same time, the Act of Creation and the One Being. "Entre la primavera y las espigas" (p. 2) the poet searches for "la eterna veta insondable / que antes toqué en la piedra o en el relámpago que el beso desprendía" (p. 8). The truth will be found in the eternal moment of creation.

Neruda's metaphors thus seek to eternalize both the product and the process of creation. The vegetable world provides the traditional symbol of the sheaf of wheat and the original symbol of wheat as "una historia ama-rilla / de pequeños pechos preñados (que) va repitiendo un número / que sin cesar es ternura en las capas ger-minales" (p. 8). This image of wheat implies a collec-tive identity which is shared by all the individual grains, together repeating endlessly the yellow history of the grain. The flower is both stamen, jasmine, and the act of pollination itself. Water, traditionally a symbol of the life force, is at once the source or spring, and an end-less current of rushing water. Neruda captures both concepts in a single metaphor of life eternal as "corri-ente como agua de manantial encadenado" (p. 8). The self-perpetuation of the world of vegetation extends to the mineral world as well, as seen in this metaphor which clearly identifies the two worlds: ". . . la flor a la flor entrega el alto germen / y la roca mantiene su flor diseminada / en su golpeado traje de diamante y arena" (p. 6). The rocks, too, create themselves over and over again throughout time in a myriad of different forms which nevertheless retain something of their original identity.

This is the world of genesis: the center of creation, the source of life, the beginning of time. Paradise is "la pa-tria nupcial," "lo más genital de lo terrestre," el oro de la geología" (p. 2). As an apocalyptic world, a projec-tion of the poet's desires, it stands at the summit of the ascendant half of the mythical cycle. As the source of meaning of the myth, its roots are buried deep in the center of that world. For Neruda, this paradise is "un mundo como una torre enterrada" (p. 2), an explicit reference as well to Macchu Picchu, where the realiza-tion of the apocalyptic world is possible.

The demonic world of the poem is one of waning life, autumn fading into winter. It is drawn, not from the harmony of the natural world in the fullness of its be-ing, but from the discord of the world of modern civilized man, who is alienated from the elemental forces of nature and from himself. This is a world of daily death, small sorrows, in a natural world gone awry, destroyed by man. It is a surface world which has no roots. The Tree of Life has become "el miserable ár-bol de las razas asustadas" (p. 8), and man appears as the dead or dying leaves of a dying tree. Wheat, as a symbol of being, is not "una historia amarilla / de pe-queños pechos preñados" (p. 8), but "el maíz (que) se desgranaba en el inacabable / granero de los hechos perdidos" (p. 12). The water of life has stopped flow-ing, and stands as "lágrimas en el océano / como es-tanques de frío" (p. 6). The brilliant light of paradise has gone out like "(una) lámpara / que se apaga en el lodo del suburbio" (p. 12).

In direct contrast to the self-perpetuating apocalyptic world, the demonic world is self-destructive. While nature perpetuates itself eternally, man destroys it:

> Si la flor entrega el alto germen
> y la roca mantiene su flor diseminada
> en su golpeado traje de diamante y arena,
> el hombre arruga el pétalo de luz que recoge
> en los determinados manantiales marinos
> y taladra el metal palpitante en sus manos.
>
> (p. 6)

In the process, man destroys himself as well by alienat-ing himself from the natural world. He reduces himself to the status of one of his own poor creations:

> Y pronto, entre la ropa y el humo, sobre la mesa hun-dida,
> como una barajada cantidad, queda el alma:
> cuarzo y desvelo, lágrimas en el océano
> como estanques de frío.
>
> (p. 6)

swept away by the elemental forces of nature like "ropas dispersas hijas del otoño rabioso" (p. 8), lost in the ocean of time.

In human terms, love, "el más grande amor" (p. 2), the life force of the apocalyptic world, has turned to hate, the destructive force of the demonic world. Com-munion, symbolized in the sheaf of wheat, the vine, the leaves of the tree of life, has turned to mutual destruc-tion and exploitation: "La cólera ha extenuado / la triste mercancía del vendedor de seres" (p. 6). The soul, imprisoned by man's material and social inventions, is killed by hate. It is killed, tortured by "papel y odio" (p. 6), submerged "en la alfombra cotidiana," torn to shreds by "las vestiduras hostiles del alambre" (p. 6).

In essence, the demonic world is a cruel and tragic parody of the apocalyptic world. In the demonic world, the hand of creation which would have implanted the life force appears as "un guante que cae" (p. 2); the sun as the source of life in the universe appears as "una larga luna" (p. 2), a far away moon, a pale echo of the sun. The life force, in man, has been rendered impotent, like "días de fulgor vivo en la intemperie de los cuer-pos" (p. 2). The fullness of the natural world has been violated in "(los) estambres agredidos de la patria nup-cial" (p. 2). The cyclical cosmos has broken down, like "noches deshilachadas hasta la última harina" (p. 2). In total opposition to the apocalyptic world of eternal creation, the demonic world of modern man is defined by his "inexistencia herida" (p. 18). It is a world where both the product and the process of creation have been destroyed.

Life in both the apocalyptic and demonic worlds is defined negatively, in terms of the kind of death with which it ends. Death in the apocalyptic world is as magnificent and elemental as the world of which it is a part. Because it is an intimate part of the cycle of life, it is represented as "ancho mar," "la sal invisible de las olas" (an extension of the symbol of the sea as the source of life), or as "los totales números de la noche" (the working out of the calculus of the universe) (p. 16). Death comes like "un ave de plumas férreas" (p. 22), or "un galope de claridad nocturna" (p. 16), a sudden and unique event of earth-shaking proportions: "lo que su invisible sabor diseminaba / era como mitades de hundimientos y altura / o vastas construcciones de viento y ventisquero" (p. 16). It is a sudden sharp point in time and space: "férreo filo," la angostura del aire" (p. 16), where man, at the moment of death, comes "al estelar vacío de los pasos finales / y a la vertiginosa carretera espiral" (p. 16), leading to the void and then to the center of creation once more.

Death in the demonic world has, like life itself, disintegrated into "un pequeño otoño [. . .]: la muerte de mil hojas" (p. 16). Life falls away in slow daily death; "El ser como el maiz se desgranaba en el inacabable / granero de los hechos perdidos, de los acontecimientos miserables" (p. 16). Man awaits his daily death: "una muerte pequeña, polvo, gusano [. . .] una pequeña muerte de alas gruesas" (p. 12). Death has been killed by dying: "los pobres dolores [. . .] mataban la muerte" (p. 22). It is no longer described in terms of the natural world, but in terms of man's world of which it is now a part. The poet, invoking Death of the apocalypse, offers an implicit condemnation of the other death:

> Nunca llegaste a hurgar en el bosillo, no era
> posible tu visita sin vestimenta roja:
> sin auroral alfombra de cercado silencio:
> sin altos o enterrados patrimonios de lágrimas.
>
> (p. 16)

But Death, killed by dying, has become "todas las falsas muertes y las resurrecciones sin tierra, sin abismo" (p. 16). The final struggle between Life and Death can never take place, for men have weakened "esperando su muerte, su corte muerte diaria" (p. 12). Death is now "un pobre pétalo de cuerda exterminada / un átomo del pecho que no vino al combate / o el áspero rocío que no cayó en la frente." (p. 22). Unlike Death in the apocalyptic world which is a part of the eternal cycle of life, death and rebirth, this death "Era lo que no pudo renacer, un pedazo / de la pequeña muerte sin paz ni territorio: un hueso, una campana que morían en él (el hombre)" (p. 22). In the demonic world, death, like life, has been stripped of all potentiality for fulfillment. Within man, who is but a skeleton of his former self, toll the bells for his own death.

In the opening lines of the poem, the poet represents himself as being suspended between the two worlds, like an empty net, sifting experience but finding nothing: "Del aire al aire, como una red vacía / iba yo entre las calles y la atmósfera" (p. 2). Drained by the surface of existence, the poet turns inward and downward in search of the apocalyptic world of his desires, "un mundo como una torre enterrada" (p. 2):

> más abajo, en el oro de la geología,
> como una espada envuelta en meteoros,
> hundí la mano turbulenta y dulce
> en lo más genital de lo terrestre.
>
> (p. 2)

The poet's hand, as the medium of contact with the object of his desire, becomes a symbol of the desire itself. The intensity and nature of the desire is indicated in the metaphor of the hand as "una espada envuelta en meteoros." The sword of his desire thrusts upward to the paradise above, is enveloped in the meteors of heaven. Yet at the same time the direction of the desire is inward and downward, as the verb "hundir" indicates. The contact with the goal would be decisive, complete; the desire would be surrounded by its goal: the hand sunk into the center of the earth. Verbs conveying the concept of sinking or descending through time and space into a center or holding onto solid matter abound in the early poems of the work, all indicating the desire of the poet to become one with the self-contained universe.

The spatial notion of the site, or the place, upon which to rest his hand becomes symbolic of his goal. But reaching out, grasping for something to hold onto, he finds only that which is dead, blown away by the winds:

> No pude asir sino un racimo de rostros o de máscaras
> precipitadas, como anillos de oro vacío,
> como ropas dispersas hijas de un otoño rabioso
> que hiciera temblar el miserable árbol de las razas
>   asustadas.
>
> (p. 8)

He cannot find the place of eternal spring:

> No tuve sitio donde descansar la mano
> y que, corriente como agua de manantial encadenado,
> o firme como grumo de antracita o cristal,
> hubiera devuelto el calor o el frío de mi mano exten-
>   dida.
>
> (p. 8)

The poet's hands become "manos manantiales" (p. 18), like his desire searching for the source. But man, "el pobre roedor de calles espesas" (p. 12), dying his daily death, "fue cerrando paso y puerto para que / no tocaran mis manos manantiales su inexistencia herida" (p. 18). Yet even turning within, the poet's hands in search of springs find nothing more, and the poet himself is seen as a directionless wanderer, dying his own small death: ". . . sin lámpara, sin fuego / sin pan, sin piedra, sin silencio, solo, / rodé muriendo mi propia muerte" (p. 18). Yet still seeking, the poet raises "las vendas del yodo" (p. 22) of the soul's wounds, sinks his hands one last time into "los pobres dolores que mataban la muerte" (p. 22), but finds nothing, only a cold wind blowing through the interstices of his soul: "y no encontré en la herida sino una racha fría / que entraba por los vagos intersticios del alma" (p. 22).

This, the end of the fifth poem, is the lowest point of the work as a whole. Suddenly, in the sixth poem, the poet, and the rhythm of the work as a whole, leap suddenly upward. The first verb of the first line of the sixth poem marks the moment of change: "Entonces en la escala de la tierra he subido / entre la atroz maraña de las selvas perdidas / hasta ti, Macchu Picchu" (p. 26). Here, on the heights of Macchu Picchu, all seems to make sense: the apocalypse has come. Here the two parallel lines of the human and natural worlds have met and are eternalized: "En ti, como dos líneas paralelas, / la cuna del relámpago y del hombre / se mecían en un viento de espinas" (p. 26). In Macchu Picchu, heaven and earth, sea and sky, human and eternal time meet, for Macchu Picchu is "madre de piedra" (earth), "espuma de los condores" (heaven), "Alto arrecife" (sea), "de la aurora humana" (sky) (p. 26). For Neruda, "Ésta fue la morada, éste es el sitio" (p. 26). Was and is are as one, the dwelling place has become the eternal site.

Here the cycle of the seasons went on interrupted: "Aquí los anchos granos del maíz ascendieron / y bajaron de nuevo como granizo rojo" (p. 26). This was the golden age of innocence: "Aquí la hebra dorada salió de la vicuña / a vestir los amores, los túmulos, las madres, / el rey, las oraciones, los guerreros" (p. 26). Men knew peace and communion with his fellow men and with the natural world around him. Men slept in the eagle's nest and trod the night with feet of thunder. They knew the stones of the earth: "y tocaron las tierras y las piedras hasta reconocerlas en la noche o la muerte" (p. 28), as the stones knew their touch. The vestige of man is still present: "Miro las vestiduras y las manos, / el vestigio del agua en la oquedad sonora, / la pared suavizada por el tacto de un rostro [. . .]" (p. 28), though he and his civilization are gone: "porque todo: ropaja, piel, vasijas, / palabras, vino, panes, / se fue, cayó a la tierra" (p. 28). The poet feels himself a part of this world, for as a man, the presence of man in Macchu Picchu is his presence. The walls of the city were softened "por el tacto de un rostro / que miró con mis ojos las lámparas, / que aceitó con mis manos las desaparecidas maderas" (p. 28).

Death came, not with the furious winds of autumn which sweep away all in their path, but "con dedos / de azahar sobre todos los dormidos" (p. 28). The winds are like "suaves huracanes de pasos / lustrando el solitario recinto de la piedra" (p. 28). What endures is not the fragile presence of individual men, but "the collective permanence those men created."[11] They, through their creation, endure, becoming a part of nature in the process.

The next poem continues to establish the contrast between what endures and what vanishes. Echoing an earlier tendency, Neruda again defines by opposites, defining what endures by the manner of death. The death of the men of Macchu Picchu was "la verdadera, la más abrasadora / muerte . . ." (p. 32). Their death is made nobler by having been a collective one. These men are "muertos de un solo abismo, sombras de una hondonada, / la profunda . . ." (p. 32), who fell, not as dry leaves, but like the whole of autumn in a single death. Individual men and their customs collapsed like weak threads. What remains is "una permanencia de piedra y de palabra" (p. 32). The Word, symbol of creation, is made eternal in stone. Macchu Picchu appears as a chalice, a communion symbol in itself, raised on high by the collective effort of men. It is the life of many in one, rendered eternal in stone. It is "la rosa permanente, la morada" (p. 34), the oneness of creation everlasting; "el alto sitio de la aurora humana" (p. 34), the place, the dawn of human existence the poet was seeking.

Here, at the end of the seventh poem, we catch only a glimpse of the final resolution of the conflict of the work. The symbol of the chalice is an ambiguous one. It of course suggests the transubstantiation of forms of life, the communion of being in the Eucharist. Yet the symbol alone and in the context of the poem suggests something of sacrifice, of spilt blood. The chalice of Macchu Picchu was lifted "en las manos / de todos, vivos, muertos, callados, sostenidos / de tanta muerte, de tanta vida un golpe / de pétalos de piedra." (p. 32). Macchu Picchu is a life of stone after so many lives, a crucible forged at what price?

The poet recovers his impetus briefly at the beginning of the eighth poem, yet fatefully introduces the third element, "amor americano," which will change the course of the work. The first stanzas have a tone of exhilaration. The poet invites his other self to rise with him in adoration of the secret stones of Macchu Picchu, to witness nature in the grandeur of its being: "Sube conmigo, amor americano, / Besa conmigo las piedras secretas" (p. 38). Yet the poet soon introduces a discordant note, viewing himself as "el hijo ciego de la nieve" (p. 38), blinded by the brilliance of the world of Macchu Picchu. He begins to question the meaning of this world: "qué idioma traes a la oreja apenas / desarraigada de la espuma andina?" (p. 28). His thoughts turn implicitly from the created, the act of creation, to the creator, from Macchu Picchu to the men who created it, and the price they paid. He questions his own purpose in coming there and the meaning he has taken from it.

Love must stay away from the border world of earth and heaven: "Amor, amor, no toques la frontera, / no adores la cabeza sumergida" (p. 42). The poet would avoid the confrontation with time: "deja que el tiempo cumple su estatura / en su salón de manantiales rotos" (p. 42), and would return once more to the valley, a new level: "Mantur estalla como un lago vivo / o como un nuevo piso de silencio" (p. 42). His love of man must remain within: "Ven a mi propio ser, al alba mía, / hasta las soledades coronadas" (p. 42), for "El reino muerto vive todavía" (p. 42): the kingdom of death survives, the fallen kingdom haunts him still. On the face of time falls the shadow of human hunger and vulnerability: "Y en el Reloj la sombra sanguinaria / del condor cruza como una nave negra" (p. 42).

The ninth poem has proved to be the most difficult for critics to handle. Juan Larrea sees the poem's similarity to religious litany, but his deep prejudice against Neruda and his poetry prevents him from understanding the real value and function of the images Neruda employs and from seeing the stylistic and thematic importance of the ninth poem in the work as a whole. Larrea begins to examine the initial metaphors, one by one, but finds them vague, absurd and arbitrary, having nothing to do with the reality of Macchu Picchu: "Las palabras se suceden sin otra razón que la vagamente surrealista y dícese que reaccionaria de la arbitrariedad."[12]

The ninth poem stands as an incantation, an invocation of the apocalypse, a prayer for its realization and paradoxically, in metaphors which show paradise turned against itself, a lament for the impossibility of its realization. It consists of 72 metaphors arranged in 43 twelve-syllable lines, which together evoke the presence of Macchu Picchu. Here, in explicit form, is Macchu Picchu as the incarnation of the apocalyptic world of total metaphorical identification.

In the construction of his apocalyptic world in Macchu Picchu, Neruda fully exhausts the potential of metaphor, formally and functionally. Neruda's metaphors are never explicitly of the A is B type, for the A member, Macchu Picchu, is only implicitly present. The second member of the comparison is usually of the form noun + *de* + noun or noun + adjective (rosa de piedra, escala torrencial) which often unite opposites. The Metaphor of the poem as a whole is accomplished by mere juxtaposition of images (individual metaphors). Both serve a quadruple function in the poem: the intuition or emotional experience of reality through poetic association; the representation of reality through description; the conception of reality on a level where image functions as idea; and the interpretation of reality on a level where image functions as symbol.

Neruda's metaphors of Macchu Picchu function as the concrete universals of which Frye spoke. Each image represents a particular world—human, divine, animal, vegetable, mineral—which together form the oneness of Being. Macchu Picchu joins together the vegetable world (viña, polen, rosa, planta, árbol), the animal world (águila, serpiente, caballo, paloma, abeja), the mineral world (hierro, piedra, granito, cuarzo, amaranto), the human (párpado, cabellera, cinturón, manos, dentadura), and the heavenly (cielo, alturas, estrellas). In Macchu Picchu is joined the undisciplined life force (manantial, vendaval, catarata, temporal, volcán, ola, ráfaga) and man's attempts to control it (bastión, escala, muralla, techumbre, torre, ventana, techo, cúpula, catedral); the formless vastness (luz, vapor, noche, nieblas, bruma) and man's attempt to understand it (geometría, libro, arquitectura).

Each metaphor serves as the center of a complex web of associations and in turn is woven into the complex web of associations which is Macchu Picchu itself. A close examination of several of these epithets will suffice to show how the individual metaphor functions in creating the total Metaphor: (1) "aguila sideral" (p. 46): The eagle (representative of the animal world) flying high, reaches the stars (world of the heavenly bodies). Macchu Picchu itself reaches the height of the stars. The poet's ideal stands above the real world, reaching the level of the heavens. (2) "viña de bruma" (p. 46): The vine represents the fullness of the vegetal universe; it appears in the mist where water, the current of life, is in a state of suspicion in the air, enveloping the vine. The vine is a common communion symbol (the source of wine, spilt blood), yet it appears wrapped in the mists, the mysterious nature of the Eucharist. On a purely representational level, the dark stones of Macchu Picchu appear as vine leaves enveloped in mist on a dark night. (3) "escala torrencial" (p. 46): The stairway, a creation of man, made of stone, appears as a torrent of water. Water the life force, appears frozen in time, eternal. (4) "polen de piedra" (p. 46): The pollen of the vegetal world (agent of germination) has turned to stone. The process of creation is made eternal. (5) "témpano entre las ráfagas labrado" (p. 46): Interaction of water and wind on the cold heights have made Macchu Picchu an iceberg. Like the buried tower, its roots extend unseen far below the surface to the center of creation. (6) "muralla por los dedos suavizada" (p. 48): The stone walls of Macchu Picchu are softened by human fingers. The eternity of stone and the finitude of man are one.

The eternal refrain of permanence—stone, granite, rock—runs throughout the poem: "polen de piedra [. . .], pan de piedra [. . .], rosa de piedra [. . .], manantial de piedra [. . .], luz de piedra [. . .], vapor de piedra [. . .], libro de piedra [. . .], lámpara de granito [. . .]" (p. 46) as the poet evokes the apocalyptic world of oneness. Yet a disturbing note in a minor key jarrs the ear in a series of ambiguous images: "paloma endurecida" (p. 50), "manos de puma, roca sangrienta" (p. 48), "nivel sangriento" (p. 50), "luna arañada" (p. 52), "volcán de manos (p. 52), "catarata oscura" (p.

52); and other less ambiguous metaphors: "piedra amenazante" (p. 52), "dirección del tiempo" (p. 52).

The menacing stones overwhelm the poet at last, and in the next poem the subdued questioning breaks into full view: "Piedra en la piedra, el hombre, dónde estuvo? / Aire en el aire, el hombre, dónde estuvo?" (p. 56). Turning against Macchu Picchu, he demands:

> Macchu Picchu, pusiste
> piedras en la piedra, y en la base, harapo?
> Carbón sobre carbón, y en el fondo la lágrima?
> Fuego en el oro y en él, temblando el rojo
> goterón de la sangre?
>
> (pp. 56-58)

Neruda abandons the "rosa abstracta" (p. 58) of Macchu Picchu because he cannot bear the thought of the human suffering required:

> Antigua America, novia sumergida,
> . . .
> también, también tus dedos,
> los que la rosa abstracta y la línea del frío, los
> que el pecho sangriento del nuevo cereal trasladaron
> hasta la tela de materia radiante, hasta las duras cav-
>   idades,
> también también, America enterrada, guardaste en lo
>   más bajo,
> en el amargo intestino, como un aguila, el hambre?
>
> (p. 58)

His vision of paradise was too abstract, too European (remember "alguien que me esperó entre violines encontró un mundo como una torre enterrada" (p. 2)) and cannot be reconciled with his all too real love for his fellow men, past and present, and his concern for their suffering: "Déjame olvidar, ancha piedra, las piedras del panal, / y de la escuadra déjame hoy resbalar / la mano sobre la hipotenusa de áspera sangre y silicio" (p. 62).

His vision now must be consistent with that he brought with him from *España en el corazón.* He seeks not the collective permanence of the past, but "Juan Cortapiedras, hijo de Wiracocha, / Juan Comefrio, hijo de estrella verde, / Juan Piesdescalzos, nieto de la turquesa [. . .]" (p. 62). The abstract "Sube conmigo, amor americano" of the eighth poem has become, in the last poem, "Sube a nacer conmigo, hermano" (p. 66). His hand now grasps the hand of his brother. Neruda, who once spurned the trembling cup of human sorrows in favor of the stone chalice of Macchu Picchu, now asks the men of Macchu Picchu: "traed a la copa de esta nueva vida / vuestros viejos dolores enterrados" (p. 66). Not the abstract stone rose, but the real blood of his brothers, spilt in sacrifice, and now coursing through his veins, is the source of communion.

The style of the work changes considerably in the last three poems. Neruda now uses the prosaic style of *España en el corazón,* almost totally devoid of metaphor or complicated syntax. Like the style, the final vision of *Las alturas de Macchu Picchu* is that of *Tercera residencia,* where the poet has said: "Yo de los hombres tengo la misma mano herida, / yo sostengo la misma copa roja, / igual asombro enfurecido."[13]

Neruda at last abandons the apocalyptic vision which had haunted him since the early years of *Residencia en la tierra.* He no longer projects his desires on a world of paradise, a near-divine world, but upon the human world about him. The religious imagery of the last poem suggests his acceptance, instead, of the vision of the humanitarianism of a very human Christ. The poet asks his fellow men to reveal their sorrows, expressed in terms of the sorrows of Christ, and offers himself as a kind of substitute Christ figure who will express their sorrows for them and through whom communion is possible: "Yo vengo a hablar por vuestras bocas muertas [. . .] / Apegadme los cuerpos como imanes. / Acudid a mis venas y a mi boca. / Hablad por mis palabras y mi sangre" (p. 70).

Notes

1. Hernán Loyola, *Ser y morir en Pablo Neruda* (Santiago, Chile: Editora Santiago, 1967) p. 197.

2. As cited above.

3. Mario J. deLellis, *Pablo Neruda* (Buenos Aires: Editorial "La Mandrágora," 1957).

4. Juan Larrea, *Del surrealismo a Machupicchu* (Mexico: Juaquín Mortiz, 1967).

5. Mario Rodriguez Fernández, "El tema de la muerte en 'Alturas de Macchu Picchu' de Pablo Neruda," *Anales de la Universidad de Chile* (julio-septiembre de 1964): 23-50.

6. Hugo Montés, "Acera de Alturas de Macchu Picchu," *Mapocho* 2 No. 3 (1964): 202-209.

7. Robert Pring-Mill, Preface to *The Heights of Macchu Picchu,* by Pablo Neruda, trans. by Nathaniel Tarn, (New York: Farrar, Straus and Giroux, 1966) pp. vii-xix.

8. Luis Monguió, Introduction to *Selected Poems of Pablo Neruda,* a bilingual edition edited and translated by Ben Belitt (New York: Grove Press, 1961) p. 22.

9. Neruda, *The Heights of Macchu Picchu,* p. 52.

10. Northrop Frye, *An Anatomy of Criticism: Four Essays* (New York: Atheneum, 1966), p. 119.

11. Pring-Mill, *op. cit.,* p. xvi.

12. Larrea, *op. cit.,* p. 145.

13. Pablo Neruda, "Reunión bajo las nuevas banderas," in *Obras completas* (Buenos Aires: Losuda, 1967) I, 270.

Agnes Gullón (review date autumn 1975)

SOURCE: Gullón, Agnes. "Pablo Neruda at Macchu Picchu." *Chicago Review* 27, no. 2 (autumn 1975): 138-45.

[*In the following review, Gullón assesses the thematic sweep of* The Heights of Macchu Picchu, *concentrating on the poem's subject of the search for an all-encompassing human unity.*]

The painter of outdoor art allows the pedestrian who passes by the moving figures of a mural to merge momentarily with them, or at least to walk with them side by side. Bustling along a city street, brushing against others who form the real mass mirrored in such a mural, one comes eerily close to mistaking one's footsteps for those of the painted feet, the sidewalk for the wall. Yet this shifting identity barely shocks, because the mural after all is meant to depict us, the nameless many; all of us in private and perhaps secret worlds, but each able to stop to ask or give the time, or name the street.

The poet who would unite us attempts quite a bit more. Neruda achieves this fusion in *Alturas de Macchu Picchu,* the dozen poems set like an island in the vast sea of his *Canto general.* And I would like to stop there, where this synthesis of souls finds its most dramatic expression, to consider the genius of his poetry.

Just to read this sequence of poems is to reach great heights. Its surge of life—the poet's, the earth's, mankind's—makes a formal analysis seem somehow inappropriate to me. Their spirit balks at that sort of treatment.

So I propose instead to trace that spirit, or follow in its path, with stops along the way.

> From the air to the air, like a net
> empty,
> I moved through the streets and the atmosphere,
>   arriving and leaving
> at the coming of fall, the scattered money
> of the leaves, and between spring and tassels,
> what the greatest love, as if into a glove
> falling, gives us like a long moon.

The opening lines happen in the air and suggest movement everywhere: from place to place, from the motion of the net to the heart, from season to season, from one expanse (of leaves) to another (of love). Comparisons are irresistible from the outset, because the poet carries ever-forming correspondences with him on his journey. This first stanza introduces Neruda's sense of himself as a creature susceptible to sensations embracing the subjective in the cosmic; a creature whose humanity derives so intimately from the earth he inhabits that a certain confusion of essences occurs. A transmigration of sorts, and one that the poet records in a language of materials, as the second stanza shows:

> Days of brilliancy I live in the unshelteredness
> of bodies: steel converted
> to the silence of acid:
> nights unravelled to the final flour:
> assaulted stamens of the nuptial land.

Bodies, steel, acid, nights, stamens: how life palpitates in each is what the poet catches in a stream of language heading for incoherence, collecting in its currents whatever drops in. And Neruda's perception is incredibly fine, picking up significance in matter usually appreciated only by geologists. The quantity of such geological detail can be a bit excessive in some of the *Canto general,* recalling a too thickly vegetated area where the tangles and knots of branches strike one more than the trees and plants themselves. In *Macchu Picchu* there is more restraint, less fixation on this aspect of nature, and I think the book benefits from it. The broad theme, that of attaining union with all men, undoubtedly lent more structure to the compositions.

There is a cosmic intensity throughout, an intermittent awareness of totality that gives the miniscule a special importance, one I would call Blakean were it not for the inevitable associations with mysticism. Neruda is no mystic, certainly. But his vision of the earth, of its evolution and engendering of man with his own peculiar, tragic history, makes the terrestrial sacred. Neruda loves the earth as Lorca did: not its rose gardens and seascapes alone, but first its minute creatures and basic elements—ants, seeds, sand, quartz, water, air, and of course stone, which in *Macchu Picchu* later dominates. Poetry, as Neruda often said, is like the dew, the disappearing essence that profiles the earth at dawn. And on his climb—soon an ascent—the most earthly matter accompanies him. In poem 2 he says:

> And soon, between clothes and smoke, on the table
>   sunken
> like a shuffled quantity, lies the soul:
> quartz and sleeplessness, tears in the ocean
> like pools of cold

Isolation, complexity, and disorder are the facets of man's soul that Neruda feels have always existed. He starts his journey with this awareness and seeks assurance that there is at least some continuity, some kind of unity:

> I wanted to pause and look for the eternal abysmal
>   vein
> I had already touched in stones or in the flash of
> lightning that gave off a kiss.

Touching, more than seeing, hearing, smelling or tasting, is the sense which discovers most in this book, and it is understandable that tactile qualities should attract

Neruda as he explores part of the earth. What gives this book its peculiar radiance is that the poet never abandons his faith in touching, even when he is trying to 'touch' what is completely intangible: a thread of continuity from primitive to present man. The link, he suggests, is the earth; knowing and loving the only live presence which our forebears also experienced. The rest is dead: beliefs, artifacts, entire races of people, countries. . . . Architecture, whether mental or physical, is destructible, leaving only ruins to be studied, whereas the earth in obeying a cosmic order lives on. The substance of man, throughout its changes, is what the poet hopes to find. At the end of poem 2 he asks:

> What was man? In what part of his open conversation
> near shops and whistling, in which of his metallic
>   movements
> lived the indestructible, the unperishing—life?

The question is an ancient one, probably predating its first written formulation, and inevitably leads not to an answer but to a consciousness of death, the refinement of which prepares us for venturing an answer. Consciousness of mortality marks the next three poems (3,4,5), where Neruda faces the power of death in its many guises, especially the "short daily death," and he faces the issue dramatically rather than philosophically, thus making it personal. In poem 4 the poetic voice no longer narrates; it addresses death directly, and the dialogue is a prelude to other dialogues with successive interlocuters. Whether consciously adopted or not, the technique is adroit, for it eliminates a rhetorical atmosphere. If Neruda had begun *Alturas de Macchu Picchu* by addressing other men (to whom the poems are eventually dedicated), our entrance into the text could not but have seemed facile and unprivate. Dealing with the most intimate area of each man, the soul, the poet must tread questioningly. This for me is one of the book's supreme achievements: Neruda reveals a prodigious amount about his soul, respects the mystery of others and gradually fuses us all in a vision of mankind. Neruda the lyricist has triumphed over Neruda the politician, the latter of whom in lesser poems makes immediate assumptions about what we are or should be, but who supplies only stereotypes. The issue is pertinent, I believe, for too often the political and the poetical have been mistaken in Pablo Neruda. Political implications may be detected in these poems, true; but politics is not necessary, nor even relevant really.

To return to the technical question of the introduction of dialogue, it is curious that Neruda speaks first to death, then to a place (the location, Macchu Picchu), then to the multifarious life of the South American continent (down to its minerals), and finally, decisively, to fellow man ("*hermano*"). Progressing from the abstract to an increasingly human life dramatizes the final unity between individuals. Musically, the movement is from an orchestration to a duo, a duo that symbolizes the linking of any man with any man. As the participants in the poetic dialogue change, so do the grammatical moods used; the indicative is preferred until the poet asks for company in poem 8, where the imperative (not at all mandatory) takes over: "Come, miniscule life," is how he urges living organisms from below to rise with him, revealing his very human desire to reach the heights in warm company, not solitary triumph. The message runs throughout Neruda's poetry and perhaps helps to explain its author's popularity today, when swarming technological inventions threaten our senses and, by extension, our sentiments. The ascent is an escape from all in contemporary life which separates us.

The poet states at the beginning of poem 6 that he has climbed to the "high city of scaled stones" out of "the atrocious tangle of lost jungles," and it is there—with arriving, "here"—that he feels the full impact of the cosmos he has experienced intermittently until now:

> Here man's feet rested at night
> next to the eagle's feet in high bloodthirsty
> lairs, and at dawn
> they tread with the feet of the thunder on rarified snow
> and they touched the earth and stones
> until they could recognize them at night or in death.

An almost erotic magic. Neruda envisions primitive man secure even amidst danger and extremes, conquering the peaks of the earth as surely as the eagle and the thunder. The images of their feet contacting the earth transmit the power and closeness of the three—man, eagle, thunder. Like a pre-Columbian sculptor, Neruda insistently exaggerates hands, feet, eyes. Through the torrential metaphors that characterize his poetry, these three features recur again and again, as if obeying an instinct, or a wish to keep alive in verse the first South American man.

At the summits death reappears, this time historically, as the end of a civilization which Neruda presents as a falling: "all that you were fell: customs, worn out / syllables, masks of dazzling light." But although he is made conscious of death again, he is also on the verge of discovering the "eternal vein" he has been seeking; it is the stone, the material that has outlived catastrophes and recorded past for future:

> But a permanence of stone and word:
> the city like a glass was raised in the hands
> of all, live, dead, silent, sustained
> by so much death, a wall, by so much life a blow
> of petals of stone: the permanent rose, the dwelling:
> this Andean reef of glacial colonies.

With this view of Macchu Picchu, we are ready for the synthesis given five lines further:

> the high site of man's dawn:
> the highest vessel that ever contained silence:
> a life of stone after so many lives.

These three lines depict the counterpart for all the life of the present below. Whereas no shape can contain the numerous, diverse lives and "short daily deaths," the wandering and anguish of the cities,—in sum, the palpitating presences Neruda describes—the lost Andean colony is like a vessel of stone whose petrification suggests at once former life, and lives, and their death.

The sight of the "glacial colonies" coincides with a sudden shift in Neruda's style. It is here in poem 8 that the imperative is introduced and his language becomes much tighter, more direct. Is the change inspired by the change in nature's panorama? (With the meandering, there is a more discursive style; with the arrival, condensation.) Whatever the cause, the effect is an artistic contraction which is accentuated in poem 9, where conventional syntactical orders vanish and are replaced by an exhaustive inventory of images ordered in a distinct way. The images are issued either one per line or are neatly grouped, two per line. Such form comes as a mild shock: Neruda's language usually flows, yet here it is abruptly locked into rhythms whose regularity suggests a litany. These lines are a sample of the symmetrical accentuation (two stresses per clause), more striking in the original Spanish:

> Triangular tunic, pollen of stone.
> Lamp of granite, bread of stone.
> Mineral serpent, rose of stone.

This type of verse contrasts with another, which is built on a single image rather than a pair and does not follow a strict pattern of accentuation; there are usually three stresses per line, but the distribution is not as symmetrical:

> Regime of the claw provoked.
> Gale withstood by the slope.
> Immobile turquoise waterfall.

Forty-three such lines are packed together, and conventional transitions are absent. At first reading, the poem is like a stone wall: so full of content (literally speaking) that meaning cannot be penetrated. It is a poem of pure impact, perhaps the effect of Macchu Picchu on the poet's imagination. Instead of exploring and wondering as he first did, or addressing some entity in his mind, the poet now stops and names; he regresses to the most primitive type of discourse: the utterance, which in this context hardly seems like utterance because of the profusion of metaphors. At this peak in his imagery, the poet captures the spatial, temporal, material, and spiritual complexity suggested by the ruins of Macchu Picchu.

And just as the poetic language has become concentrated, so has the matter described. Stone becomes in poem 9 the beginning, middle and end of human life. Present as primary rock, it is also the statues, walls and hand-carved objects preserving man's past. Seeing the stone remains of human labors in a rocky panorama where no one has survived calls to mind the power and durability of this first solid form of the creative rhythm (air→fire→water→stone). The harmony achieved by the poet is impressive: his wandering and climbing stopped, he fixates at the summits on the only solid element—stone—and the modifications in his verbal expression register his adjustment to the surroundings.

Confrontation with this world of stone intensifies the poet's awareness of man's precarious essence in a cosmic scheme where the elements seem so firmly established. Poem 10 opens with:

> Stone in stone, man, where was he?
> Air in air, man, where was he?
> Time in time, man, where was he?
> Were you also the little broken piece
> of the unfinished man, of an empty eagle
> that through the streets of today, in the tracks,
> through the leaves of a dead fall
> is hammering his soul into his grave?
> The poor hand, and foot, the poor life . . .

The spell has been broken. The cryptic assemblage in stone has provoked a single plaintive question: "Where was he?", which is perhaps the same as asking "Where am I?" No answer is offered, nor could it be, considering the beliefs of the questioner. Because Neruda, an incessant traveller in his own lifetime, never quenched his thirst for "the place." (An earlier book of poems hinted in its own title at this preoccupation: ***Residence on Earth.***)

In the magnificent poem 10, Neruda's perceptions of matter are transfused by his awareness of orders of which matter is merely a vestigial reminder. He is at once dazzled by the real spectacle of Macchu Picchu and intent on getting beyond, to the men lost in it:

> I interrogate you, salt of the roads,
> show me the spoon, let me, architecture,
> gnaw with a stick at the stamens of stone,
> climb all the steps of air up to the void,
> scratch the entrails until I touch man.

Into the realm of the untouchable and indeed, the intangible, Neruda persists in his quest: to touch, even in disappearing matter, man. His insistently physical probing reveals a poet convinced of the power of every atom of life on the earth and determined to stay close to the organic matter that nourishes him.

The impact of the summits on Neruda is reproduced in the poetry, which transports us to that "confused splendor." And for the poet, there must have been a considerable struggle to both record his diverse impressions and manage his verbal material so as to create in us the illusion of finding that supreme reality at the summits: a sense of feeling for other men. There is evidence of this tension in the middle of poem 11:

> Let me forget, wide stone, and powerful proportion,
> the transcendent measurement, the stone of the
>   honeycomb,
> and from the staff let me today slide
> my hand long the hypotenuse of stiff blood and hair-
>   shirt.

Faced with the "powerful proportion"—massive stone, the past disintegrating the present—Neruda's wish for unity is momentarily endangered: the scale is too enormous to be captured or shared. His perspective, unlike the sophisticated perspective of an elaborate camera designed to control visual fields, is that of the poor human eye, overcome by the summits and all they suggest to his spirit. So he pleads, almost humbly, for a chance to know, at these real and figurative altitudes, with his senses: "let me slide my hand . . .". Touching continues to be as important as speaking.

And his speech, which has been a confessing, telling, wondering, asking, inviting and uttering, becomes in the last line of poem 11 simply talking: "come up to be born with me, brother." The sentence is repeated as the opening line of the final poem, where it becomes a gentle urging, showing a simplicity and compassion that echo through poem 12. It is here that Neruda explicitly states his poetic purpose: "I come to speak for your dead mouths." He, the living, hopes to perpetuate those gone; and as poet, hopes to unite us with them. He offers his words and his body to join men. The closing line of *Alturas de Macchu Picchu* is:

> Speak through my words and blood.

A testimony to Pablo Neruda's concept of art and life.

Dieter Saalman (essay date winter 1977)

SOURCE: Saalman, Dieter. "The Role of Time in Pablo Neruda's *Alturas de Macchu Picchu*." *Romance Notes* 18, no. 2 (winter 1977): 169-77.

[*In the following essay, Saalman examines the metaphysics of time presented in* The Heights of Macchu Picchu, *comparing it with that of T. S. Eliot's* Four Quartets.]

Pablo Neruda's **Alturas de Macchu Picchu** represents one of the numerous examples in modern literature dealing with the metaphysics of time. In this respect Robert Pring-Mill in his introduction to Nathaniel Tarn's English translation of the **Alturas** points to a striking similarity between the temporal concepts espoused in Neruda's epic and T. S. Eliot's *Four Quartets*.[1] "Time present and time past are both perhaps present in future time, and time future contained in time past."[2] It is according to this notion that the Chilean poet laureate conceives his experience in the Peruvian highlands of that which constitutes the essence of life. In turning his attention to the "muertos de un solo abismo"[3] to discover authentic being, "una vida de piedra después de tantas vidas" (*OC* [*Obras completas*] I, 341), he subscribes to the motto "sube a nacer conmigo, hermano" (*OC* I, 347) thereby destroying the moment of death, that brief interval which separates inauthentic living from the undivided existence beyond the confines of time. In resurrecting the spirit that animated the "esclavos" which at a specific point in time dwelt in the mountain retreat, the poet is able to surmount the fixation in time imposed by historical circumstance. He succeeds in liberating the quintessential qualities of the former inhabitants from their temporal limitations while experiencing their attributes as a personal revelation and, by the same token, making them accessible to present and future generations. Time, therefore, becomes "unredeemable," to quote Eliot, "if all time is eternally present" (*CP* [*Collected Poems 1902-1962*], p. 175), i.e. if past, present, and future merge into an omniscient mind. Then and only then the temporal divisions cease to exist given the fact that "time past and future time what might have been and what has been point to one end, which is always present" (*CP*, p. 176). This idea of time, the attempt to remove the need for its "redemption" awakens in Neruda the desire to transform the historical moment to which "el antiguo ser, servidor, el dormido . . . un cuerpo, mil cuerpos, un hombre, mil mujeres" (*OC* I, 346) belong, into a span of timeless infinity:

> Deja que el tiempo cumpla su estatura
> en su salón de manantiales rotos,
> . . .
> Ven a mi propio ser, al alba mía,
> hasta las soledades coronadas.
>
> El reino muerto vive todavía.
>
>   (*OC* I, 343)

The spatial ascent toward Macchu Picchu and the simultaneous backward movement within the historical perspective, "desde la altura hasta el final del tiempo" (*OC* I, 341), in the rarified atmosphere of this Nerudian 'magic mountain' culminate in that point where there is, as Eliot expresses it, "neither arrest nor movement . . . neither descent nor decline" (*CP*, p. 177), the instant in which the poet discovers the answer to his searching question: "Tiempo en el tiempo," i.e., chronological time as an alien notion foisted by man upon eternal time, "el hombre, dónde estuvo?" (*OC* I, 345). The answer lies beyond the "tela de materia radiante," it is "el viejo corazón del olvidado" which Neruda describes as "un ave mil años prisionera . . ." (*OC* I, 346). The apotheosis of his experience on the mountain can be compared to Eliot's "Erhebung," i.e., exaltation "without motion, concentration without elimination . . ." (*CP,* p. 178). Such consciousness man owes to history or, to place the historical aspect in a wider context, to the reconstituting power of memory, "for liberation—not less of love but expanding of love beyond desire, and so liberation from the future as well as the past. . . . History may be servitude, history may be freedom" (*CP,* p. 205). Such is the basic intent of Neruda's journey to the citadel of the Incas. The "madrépora del tiempo sumergido" (*OC* I, 344), a symbol of psychological time submerged in timelessness, serves as the catalyst of a metamorphosis by means of the word which transforms "history as servitude," i.e. the erecting of the monument at the expense of those who sacrificed their lives in performing their duty, into "history as freedom" by invoking the presence of the builders of Macchu Picchu in the final section. "The time of death" which for Eliot is every moment ". . . shall fructify in the lives of others" (*CP,* p. 197). Neruda's entire effort has thus been directed toward releasing the liberating forces of history in the absolute sense of tearing down the falls of time thereby transcending the historical accident which gave birth to Macchu Picchu and raising the history of the Incas to the level of the saga of the entire South American humanity from its inception past the present into an all-encompassing consciousness "del tiempo subterráneo":

Macchu Picchu . . .
. . .
Devuélveme el esclavo que enterraste!

[Canto X]

Dame la mano desde la profunda
zona de tu dolor diseminado.
. . .
A través de la tierra juntad todos
los silenciosos labios derramados
y desde el fondo habladme toda esta larga noche,
como si yo estuviera con vosotros anclado,
contadme todo . . .
. . .
y dejadme llorar, horas, días, años,
edades ciegas, siglos estelares.

([Canto XII], *OC* 1, 345-48)

By plunging "la mano turbulenta y dulce en lo más genital de lo terrestre" (*OC* I, 335) the Chilean displays that "consciousness of the past" which for Eliot is the distinctive mark of the true poet.[4] In surrendering his personality to a poetic invocation of the "viejos dolores enterrados" (*OC* I, p. 347) Neruda undergoes a process of "depersonalization" (*SE* [*Selected Essays 1917-1932*], p. 7) which reduces the role of the poet to that of a mere "medium," (*SE,* pp. 7 und 9) an impersonal

spokesman for the vanished craftsmen of the Inca fortress: "Yo vengo a hablar por vuestra boca muerta" (*OC* I, p. 347). Such is the nature of Eliot's theory of an "impersonal" poetry, his conception of the poet "set . . . among the dead," (*SE,* p. 4) in "the present moment of the past" (*SE,* p. 11) continually renouncing in an act of "selflessness and self-surrender" (*CP,* p. 198) his own impure feelings in favor of those "significant" emotions (*SE,* p. 11) which originate in the poem itself, for Neruda in the very poetic substance that is Macchu Picchu. Like Eliot in *The Dry Salvages* the Chilean is made to realize that the sufferings of the preceding generations have a more permanent value than the individual observer's own petty agonies. Penetrating "behind the assurance of recorded history . . . the torment of others remains" for him "an experience unqualified, unworn by subsequent attrition" (*CP,* p. 195). In view of the foregoing the *Alturas* can truly be regarded as a genuine embodiment of Eliot's credo that "poetry is not a turning loose of emotion, but an escape from emotion; . . . not the expression of personality, but an escape from personality" (*SE,* p. 10), a fact borne out by Neruda's concluding exhortation in acting as the official mouthpiece for the former inhabitants of the citadel:

Acudid a mis venas y a mi boca.

Hablad por mis palabras y mi sangre.

(*OC* 1, 348)

The author thus confronts the archaeological wonder of Peru as living testimony of his own past—"sentí que yo mismo había trabajado allí en alguna etapa lejana cavando surcos, alisando peñascos"[5]—having an immediate bearing on the present as well as the future and, by implication, heralding the possibility of forging the intermingling time currents into a unified realm. As Eliot expresses it:

Here the impossible union
Of spheres of existence is actual,
Here the past and future
Are conquered, and reconciled,

(*CP,* p. 199)

Consequently, the landscape of lamentation that is "antigua América, novia sumergida" (*OC* I, 346) bestows a new sense of confidence in mankind and a rekindled feeling of dignity upon the poet:

. . . una permanencia de piedra y de palabra:
la ciudad como un vaso se levantó en las manos
de todos, vivos, muertos, callados, sostenidos
de tanta muerte, un muro, de tanta vida un golpe
de pétalos de piedra: . . .

el alto sitio de la aurora humana.

(*OC* 1, 341)

In conjuring up the vision of those who left their indelible imprint on Machu Picchu and in perpetuating their presence by means of the poetic expression, Neruda endowes their heritage with an enduring configuration. For according to Eliot it is "only by the form, the pattern" (*CP*, p. 180) that their essence can be rescued from "the aspect of time caught in the form of limitation between un-being and being" (*CP*, p. 181). Their 'Sein' guaranteed through the ever-lasting qualities of the 'logos' is the equivalent of "coexistence," "the end precedes the beginning, and the end and the beginning were always there before the beginning and after the end. And all is always" (*CP*, p. 180). Descending toward the very heart of "la rosa permanente, la morada" (*OC* I, 341) which is defined in the *Oda al edificio* as "la rosa colectiva . . . el edificio de todos los hombres" (*OC* I, 1049),[6] the poet perceives the "footfalls" that "echo in the memory" of Eliot (*CP*, p. 175). Unlike the latter, however, he does not fail to unlock "the door . . . into the rose-garden" of those vanished scenes and faces which emerge as a spiritual transfiguration of their former being. By establishing an intellectual communion between himself and the minds of the deceased and by speaking on their behalf Neruda portrays a cyclical notion of existence inasmuch as he is "born with the dead" (*Ibid.*, p. 208). Hence every poem of his represents, in Eliot's words, "an end and a beginning . . . an epitaph" as well as the promise of a new dawn of life. (*Ibid.*)

Death has, therefore, lost its traditionally frightening aspect. For the Chilean, "un poeta más cerca de la muerte que de la filosofía,"[7] the affirmation of life and the acceptance of death coincide to the extent that death is considered an indispensable complement to life. Neruda's own confession in regard to his sojourn in the Peruvian Andes throws a most revealing light on the existential significance of the Inca fortress when he states: "En la soledad de las ruinas la muerte no puede apartarse de los pensamientos."[8] He firmly adheres to the view that death must be incorporated into man's intellectual universe as a positive step toward mankind's spiritual renewal, as evinced in the following passage from *Viajes*:

> Hay una sola enfermedad que mata, y ésa es la vida. Hay un solo paso, y es el camino hacia la muerte. . . . Si al nacer empezamos a morir . . . si la vida misma es una etapa patética de la muerte . . . no integramos la muerte en nuestra cotidiana existencia, no somos parte perpetua de la muerte, ¿no somos lo más audaz, lo que ya salió de la muerte? . . . Si ya hemos muerto, si venimos de la profunda crisis, perderemos el temor de la muerte. Si el paso más grande de la muerte es el nacer, el paso menor de la vida es el morir.[9]

Such interdependence of life and death promulgated with persuasive conviction is an absolute prerequisite for the realization of Eliot's dictum that "history may be freedom," or liberation from the superficial straitjacket of external events:

> The inner freedom from the practical desire,
> The release from action and suffering, release from the inner
>
> And the outer compulsion . . .
>
> (*CP*, p. 177)

Death now assumes the characteristics of a historical phenomenon in the sense that the recognition of the truly timeless nature of death is equated with man's ability to restore the essential continuity of historical phenomena thereby transcending the observer's own temporal fixation. The 'search of absolute time lost,' the experience of a "vendaval sostenido en la vertiente" (*OC* I, 344) bereaves history of its empirical context, of its life-death dichotomy and accentuates its non-temporal qualities with death as an everpresent reality. It is in these quintessential attributes that Neruda finds the "dirección del tiempo," its substance laid bare. (*Ibid.*)

To the extent that only its eternal verities are retained by the poet, the duration of history as a succession of fundamental truths is preserved. This, in turn, assures the continuum of human existence as an uninterrupted endeavour to find the noumenal behind the representational. Thus Neruda sees in the recollection of things past the only guarantee of the unity and perpetuity of man's self and, coincidentally, of the society of which he forms a part. Although he engages in an effort to break out of his own "fixity" (*CP*, p. 177) in a given historical situation through a return to the past, he nevertheless regards the degree to which a poet is able to convey the spirit of his age as the very basis of his obligation to humanity. In this respect, Eliot's attitude toward time and history illustrates quite convincingly the stance taken by the Chilean:

> This historical sense, which is a sense of the timeless as well as of the temporal and of the timeless and of the temporal together, is what makes a writer traditional. And it is at the same time what makes a writer most acutely conscious of his place in time, of his own contemporaneity
>
> (*SE*, p. 4)

It is true that Neruda reaches "the still point of the turning world" (*CP*, p. 177)," the point of intersection of the timeless with time" which Eliot defines as "an occupation for the saint" (*CP*, p. 198). But Neruda manages to escape the dubious distinction of becoming patron saint of timelessness for its own sake by fusing the moments of personal and historical experience into a new vision of the human race. "A people without history is not redeemed from time," asserts Eliot, "for history is a pattern of timeless moments" (*CP*, p. 208). As far as the South American is concerned, the conventional antithesis of the temporary versus the permanent has thus been resolved in favor of the ineffable properties of historical time. These enduring characteristics survive beyond the "trascendente medida" in the "hipotenusa de áspera sangre y cilicio" (*OC* I, 346) embodied in the right angle of each rock in its sublime beauty pointing toward that propitious constellation in human history when the "dos líneas paralelas, la cuna del relámpago y del hombre se mecían en un viento de espinas," i.e., the two lineages of permanence and transitoriness are fused into a timeless condition of eternal presence: "Este fué la morada, éste es el sitio" (*OC* I, 339).

Completely aware of and fully responsible to the needs of society, Neruda identifies his poetic vocation with the fate of the Latin American nations in a very tangible sense. He sees his own destiny as well as that of the peoples of his continent inextricably bound to the notion of time in recognition of the fact that for him as for Eliot "time the destroyer is time the preserver" (*CP*, p. 195), because "only in time can the moment in the rose-garden" of Macchu Picchu "be remembered" forever (*CP*, p. 178). Even if he succeeds quite admirably in objectifying the Marxist ideological bias of his work largely on account of the expressive power of his poetic language, the basic social intentions of the *Alturas* characterize it nevertheless as an 'œuvre' whose prime purpose is to serve in a very immediate way the human community, in whose fertile historical soil the roots of the epic are ineradicably embedded. History for Pablo Neruda is now and South America[10]—"esa inmensidad de América que es Macchu Picchu"[11]—since it is "only through time" that "time is conquered," as Eliot acknowledges in the *Four Quartets* (*CP*, p. 178), only through an active search for the lasting values of the temporal can the fleeting and deadly nature of time be overcome. In celebrating the "cabeza sumergida" (*OC* I, 343) Neruda at the same time magnifies existence as being sustained by the closely intertwined dual fountainheads of life and death which together assure authentic being. If man is able to detemporalize time, at least for a brief moment of epiphanal revelation, death becomes devoid of its mortal attributes, and both time and death submerge in a consciousness expanding beyond the limits of the heightened instant of awareness:

> . . . Not the intense moment
> Isolated, with no before and after,
> But a lifetime burning in every moment
> And not the lifetime of one man only
> But of old stones . . .
>
> (*CP*, p. 189)

Notes

1. Pablo Neurda, *The Heights of Macchu Picchu,* Translated by Nathaniel Tarn (New York, 1967), p. XVI.

2. T. S. Eliot, *Collected Poems 1902-1962* (New York, 1970), p. 175. Cited in the text as *CP*.

3. Pablo Neruda, *Obras completas,* Vol. I (Buenos Aires, 1968), 340. Cited in the text as *OC* I.

4. T. S. Eliot, *Selected Essays 1917-1932* (New York, 1932), p. 6. Cited in the text as *SE*.

5. Hernán Loyola, *Ser y morir en Pablo Neruda: 1918-1945* (Santiago, 1967), p. 194.

6. See Robert Pring-Mill in his introduction to Nathaniel Tarn's translation, p. XVI.

7. E. Rodríguez Monegal, *El viajero inmóvil* (Buenos Aires, 1966), p. 83.

8. Loyola, p. 195.

9. Pablo Neruda, *Obras completas,* Vol. II (Buenos Aires, 1968), 14.

10. Cf. T. S. Eliot: ". . . History is now and England" (*CP*, p. 208).

11. Comment by Pablo Neruda quoted in Margarita Aguirre, *Genio y figura de Pablo Neruda* (Buenos Aires, 1964), p. 157.

Salvatore Bizzarro (essay date 1979)

SOURCE: Bizzarro, Salvatore. "*Alturas de Macchu Picchu.*" In *Pablo Neruda: All Poets the Poet,* pp. 76-87. Metuchen, N.J.: The Scarecrow Press, Inc., 1979.

[*In the following essay, Bizzarro interprets* The Heights of Macchu Picchu *as reflective of Neruda's shift from surrealist to socialist poet and surveys the thematic progression of the twelve-part work from lyric to political poem.*]

Section II of the *Canto general, Alturas de Machu Picchu,* is a political and historical interpretation of America. The lost city of the Incas[1] serves as the setting which symbolizes the destiny of the American man, from his beginning to the present. As a man committed to a political ideology, the poet has a definite set of norms to follow, a system of values that looks to social revolution as a base from which to change the world. *Alturas de Machu Picchu* reflects the social and political themes in the poetry of Pablo Neruda.

To understand the total message of this section of the *Canto general,* it is important to consider some biographical details. In August, 1940, Neruda was appointed Chilean consul-general in Mexico, where he spent the next three years. His reputation as a poet had grown steadily during this time, and his poetry seemed to express the suffering and aspirations of all Latin

Americans. His return to Chile in October, 1943, was a triumphant journey and he found himself acclaimed by large crowds in country after country. It was during this journey that Neruda visited Machu Picchu, which inspired the poem he composed in Isla Negra two years later.

The year 1945 was very significant in the life of the poet: he obtained the Premio Nacional de Literatura; he officially became a member of the Communist Party; he was elected senator from the provinces of Tarapaca and Antofagasta (northern Chile) with the backing of the working classes; and he legally changed his name from Ricardo Neftalí Reyes to Pablo Neruda. In September of this same year, during a rest from a period of intense political activities, Neruda finished *Alturas de Machu Picchu.* He had recently returned from a tour of the north of Chile, where he had witnessed the miserable conditions in the nitrate and copper mines. The poverty he found everywhere, and his direct contact with the proletariat, reminded him of his responsibilities as a poet engaged politically since the beginning of the Spanish Civil War. This preoccupation of putting his art at the service of social realism, to voice his solidarity with the working people of Latin America, is once again reflected—as Neruda himself has admitted—in Section II of the *Canto general.*[2]

The central symbol of *Alturas de Machu Picchu* is a journey: the poet's ascent to the ruins of the lost citadel high up in the Peruvian Andes, where the past seems to come together with the present. This journey is a kind of pilgrimage through human life in search of meaningful truth. Neruda explores both his inner world and the past of the American man. When the poet reaches Machu Picchu, its heights turn out to be the place from which all existence is explained, including his own.

The ideology of *Alturas de Machu Picchu* can be explained in terms of Neruda's adherence to a political philosophy and to the discipline of the Communist Party. In the 12 poems that make up the sequence, we can follow the change which occurred in Neruda's work: the poet of anguish and solitude becomes the poet of human solidarity; the metaphysical poetry and the surrealist images of *Residencia en la tierra* are replaced by the simple exhortation typical of his social poetry.

Alturas de Machu Picchu is perfectly structured and represents a synthesis of Neruda's earlier works. The first five poems of the sequence recapitulate images, settings, and themes which are common to the poetry he composed prior to **"Reunión bajo las nuevas banderas"**: the interminable flux of time; isolation and the longing to communicate; earth, wind and air; sexual love and death; the longing to discern order in life; the loneliness and the attempt to find a significant identity and establish a relationship with the rest of mankind. The sixth poem reveals the name of Machu Picchu for the first time. The poet has reached the summit and can see and understand the world beneath him. The last six poems move from the abstract to the concrete: we have a description of Machu Picchu, and an evocation of the aborigines who built the city of stone, and of America, buried under the ruins. Section II ends with an exhortation. The militant poet calls his American brothers to join him. In their past, and in the future ahead, he has found the meaningful truth he was seeking.

The social and political themes in *Alturas de Machu Picchu* are expressed explicitly in the last three poems of the sequence, as we shall see. Neruda's journey begins with a profusion of surrealistic images which do not state but suggest:

> From air to air, like an empty net,
> I walked through streets and vapor, arriving and send-
> ing forth
> in the coming of autumn the offered coins of leaves,
> and, between the spring and ears of wheat,
> that which the greatest love, as though caught within a
> fallen glove,
> gives us like a stretched moon.
>
> (Days of live radiance in the inclemency
> of bodies: weapons converted
> to the silence of acid:
> nights frayed down to the last flour:
> assaulted stamens of the nuptial land.)
>
> Someone who awaited me amid the violins
> found a world like a buried tower
> sinking its spiral deeper than all
> the harsh sulphur-colored leaves:
> and deeper yet, in a layer of gold,
> like a sword swathed in meteors,
> I sank a turbulent and tender hand
> to the most visceral parts of the earth.
>
> I placed my forehead amid deep waves,
> I descended, like a drop, into sulphuric peace,
> and, like a blind man, I returned to the jasmine
> of our spent human spring.
>
> Del aire al aire, como una red vacía,
> iba yo entre las calles y la atmósfera, llegando y des-
> pidiendo,
> en el advenimiento del otoño la moneda extendida
> de las hojas, y entre la primavera y las espigas,
> lo que el más grande amor, como dentro de un guante
> que cae, nos entrega como una larga luna.
>
> (Días de fulgor vivo en la intemperie
> de los cuerpos: aceros convertidos
> al silencio del ácido:
> noches deshilachadas hasta la última harina:
> estambres agredidos de la patria nupcial.)
>
> Alguien que me esperó entre los violines
> encontró un mundo como una torre enterrada
> hundiendo su espiral más abajo de todas

las hojas de color de ronco azufre:
más abajo, en el oro de la geología,
como una espada envuelta en meteoros,
hundí la mano turbulenta y dulce
en lo más genital de lo terrestre.

Puse la frente entre las olas profundas,
descendí como una gota entre la paz sulfúrica,
y, como un ciego, regresé al jazmín
de la gastada primavera humana.

[*OC* (*Obras completas*) 312][3]

This opening section shows us Neruda seeking inward and downward for a concealed "vein of gold," then sinking lower still in the more "visceral" depths of the earth in a blind search to rediscover our "exhausted human springs."[4] Although there are many indefinite allusions in the poem—"del aire al aire," or "alguien que me esperó entre los violines"—to which a precise meaning cannot be affixed, the idea of a journey is conveyed clearly by the verbal forms "iba," "descendí," "regresé." Following the poet's itinerary in the next four poems, we shall see that he comes face to face with death before he is able to gain knowledge of the meaning of life.

The second fragment of *Alturas de Machu Picchu* contrasts the order found in nature with the disorder found in man:

Flower to flower surrenders its seed
and rock maintains its scattered flower
in a battered dress of diamond and sand,
man crumples the petals of the light he gathers
in the fixed origins of the sea,
and pierces the palpitating metal in his hands.
And soon, between clothes and smoke, upon the
    sunken table,
the soul remains like a shuffled deck . . .

Si la flor a la flor entrega el alto germen
y la roca mantiene su flor diseminada
en su golpeado traje de diamante y arena,
el hombre arruga el pétalo de la luz que recoge
en los determinados manantiales marinos
y talandra el metal palpitante en sus manos.
Y pronto, entre la ropa y el humo, sobre la mesa hun-
    dida,
como una barajada cantidad queda el alma . . .

[*OC* 313]

Nature is self-perpetuating, rich and fecund in its cycles, sprouting on fertile soil and even in the rocks. Man, on the other hand, loses his freedom to the world of objects until he becomes aware that his own soul is left impoverished.

The poet longs for truth, the kind of truth he had once perceived in a stone. But he cannot find it in the urban centers he has left behind, where he sees the empty faces of men who like robots go to their factories, their department stores, their mechanized tasks. He asks:

What was man? In what part of his empty talk
among his shops and sirens, in which of his metallic
    movements
lived the indestructible, the undying, life?

Qué era el hombre? En que parte de su conversación
    abierta
entre los almacenes y los silbidos, en cual de sus mov-
    imientos metálicos
vivía lo indestructible, lo imperecedero, la vida?

[*OC* 314]

The answer to this question does not appear in the three subsequent poems, which deal with two facets of death: one, great and noble like the essence of life, which cannot be found in the cities; the other, less impressive and miserable, which hovers in congested metropolitan centers.

The latter is the subject of the third poem. In this fragment Neruda looks at modern man's withering existence: seeing it gradually husked off the cob like maize, in a humiliating process, and not proudly scythed away with a single stroke. Neruda looks at man's life as a wasting death "in a black cup." The image of the black cup—as Robert Pring-Mill has pointed out—"prepares the way for the contrasting image of Machu Picchu as a 'permanence of stone . . . raised like a chalice'."[5]

In the fourth poem, Neruda uses sea imagery to depict a more noble death: as the tide is at the ebb, reaching its lowest point, so man's existence fades away. This inevitable death is the same Neruda portrays in the poems of *Residencia en la tierra.* What is disconcerting is not man's doubt about the afterlife, but the belief that death is the total negation of man's existence. The theme of love for one's fellow men is also introduced in this fragment, but the love remains unrealizable as long as all the poet sees of them is their daily deaths.

Neruda visualizes his own insignificant death in an empty mood, which recalls the anguish of his earlier work:

I went, then, street by street, river by river,
city by city, bed by bed,
my salt mask passing through a desert,
till in the last miserable houses, without lamp, without
    fire,
without bread or stone or silence, alone,
I rolled, dying of my own death.

Entonces fui por calle y calle y río y río,
y ciudad y ciudad y cama y cama,
y atrovesó el desierto mi máscara salobre
y en las últimas casas humilladas, sin lámparas, sin
    fuego,
sin pan, sin piedra, sin silencio, sólo,
rodé muriendo de mi propia muerte

[*OC* 315]

The last verse announces a very definite and degrading death. This is reflected in the reiteration of the concept of dying, the alliteration, and the use of the verb "rodar," "to roll," more adequate in expressing the motion of an object than that of a person.

Using a series of surrealistic images, Neruda defines death in the short fifth poem of the sequence:

> It was not you, solemn death, bird of iron plumage
> that the poor inheritor of such dwellings
> carried among his hasty rations, under vacuous skin:
> it was, instead, a pitiful strand of old rope:
> inner strength which did not come forth,
> harsh dew that didn't turn to sweat.
> That which could not be reborn, a particle
> of insignificant death, without peace or grave:
> a bone or a bell that died from within.
>
> I lifted the bandages of iodine and sank my hands
> in the feeble pains that killed death
> and found nothing in the wound save a cold gust of
>   wind
> that entered and chilled the nebulous crevices of my
>   soul.
>
> No eras tú, muerte grave, ave de plumas férreas,
> la que el pobre heredero de las habitaciones
> llevaba entre alimentos apresurados, bajo la piel vacía:
> era algo, un pobre pétalo de cuerda exterminada:
> un átomo del pecho que no vino al combate
> o el áspero rocío que no cayó en la frente.
> Era lo que no pudo renacer, un pedazo
> de la pequeña muerte sin paz ni territorio:
> un hueso, una campana que morían en él.
>
> Yo levanté las vendas del yodo, hundí las manos
> en los pobres dolores que mataban la muerte,
> y no encontré en la herida sino una racha fría
> que entraba en los vagos intersticios del alma.

[OC 316]

Its conclusion refers to modern life, described in the last two verses with nothing in its wounds except cold gusts of wind that chill one's soul. We have reached the lowest point of the entire sequence. After the poet has identified himself with his past, and with the sufferings of the American man, he is ready to ascend to the heights of Machu Picchu.

Just as **"Reunión bajo las nuevas banderas"** represents a break in Neruda's poetic evolution, incorporating his earlier work and presenting it from a social perspective, so fragment six of *Alturas de Machu Picchu* represents a break within the poem, embodying the content of the preceding fragments and preparing the way for Neruda's social and political message.

As Neruda climbs upward in space toward the heights, the poem itself seems to rise:

> Then up the ladder made of earth I climbed
> through vast undergrowth of lost jungle
> until I touched you, Machu Picchu.

> High city of stepped stone,
> a dwelling at last
> not hidden in mundane sleeping garments.
> In you, like two parallel lines,
> the cradle of lightning and of man
> rocked in a wind of thorns.
>
> Mother of stone, sperm of condor.
>
> High reef of human dawn.
>
> Spade lost in primordial sand.
>
> Entonces en la escala de la tierra he subido
> entre la atroz maraña de las selvas perdidas
> hasta ti, Machu Picchu.
>
> Alta ciudad de piedras escalares,
> por fin morada del que lo terrestre
> no escondió en las dormidas vestiduras.
> En ti, como dos líneas paralelas,
> la cuna del relámpago y del hombre
> se mecían en un viento de espinas.
>
> Madre de piedra, espuma de los cóndores.
>
> Alto arrecife de la aurora humana.
>
> Pala perdida en la primera arena

[OC 316]

As he reaches the summit, he looks back in time towards the moment when the city was erected. Suddenly past and present seem to make sense—a sense which later on will turn out to be the reunification of the Inca world with contemporary American man. The two parallel lines that meet symbolize the death of insignificant men and the permanence of the citadel. Machu Picchu brings back to life an ancient kingdom, with its triangular structures and simple architecture. This is the location where the "maize grew high," and where the vicuña fleece was woven. But all that was transitory has disappeared and what endures is the city of stone collectively built by the men of the past.

The contrast between what endures and what has vanished is emphasized in the seventh poem. The death of the men who built Machu Picchu is depicted as being nobler because it was a collective experience. What these men left behind was a city "raised like a chalice in all those hands," whose permanence is symbolized by the image of an "everlasting rose."

Neruda sees in the death of these men a built-in lesson for the future, and he identifies himself with them. His search for noble death has also been the search for a more significant existence in their company. The poet's journey upward in space and backward in time does not end with the discovery of Machu Picchu living its enduring "life of stone." For the next two poems, Neruda exalts the city with powerful lyricism.

The eighth poem takes us a step further in the past. It is a vivid evocation of pre-Columbian man and of nature. Neruda summons his American ancestor with a call of love:

> Arise with me, American love.
>
> Kiss with me the secret stones.
>
> . . .
>
> Come to my very being, to my own dawn.
>
> Sube conmigo, amor americano.
>
> Besa conmigo las piedras secretas.
>
> . . .
>
> Ven a mi propio ser, al alba mía

[OC 318, 320f]

In these verses there is already an indication of the more personal summons to his past brothers, which we find in poem XI.

The ninth poem of the sequence is a solemn chant to Machu Picchu, written mostly in hendecasyllables and describing the site with 84 epithets. Not one single verb appears in this fragment, which is composed in the style of a liturgical litany, with an abundance of repetitive phrases:

> Triangular tunic, pollen of stone.
>
> Lamp of granite, bread of stone.
>
> Mineral serpent, rose of stone.
>
> Buried ship, source of stone.
>
> Horse of the moon, light of stone.
>
> Equinoctial quadrant, vapor of stone.
>
> Final geometry, book of stone.
>
> Túnica triangular, polen de piedra.
>
> Lámpara de granito, pan de piedra.
>
> Serpiente mineral, rosa de piedra.
>
> Nave enterrada, manantial de piedra.
>
> Caballo de la luna, luz de piedra.
>
> Escuadra equinoccial, vapor de piedra.
>
> Geometría final, libro de piedra

[OC 320]

The entire poem is a "crescendo" culminating in the last two lines, which orient our thoughts towards the multitude of men who carried gigantic stones to build the city.

The last major turning point of **Alturas de Machu Picchu** comes in the tenth fragment. We are dealing here with a social poetry that has a clear political aim. The poet once again turns to man, the true subject of this section of the *Canto general.* He compares the men of the past with those of the present, and wonders whether the Incas, responsible for the grandeur of Machu Picchu, may not perhaps have been like urban men today, erecting the city on a base of human suffering. He asks:

> Stone within stone, and man, where was he?
> Air within air, and man, where was he?
> Time within time, and man, where was he?
>
> Piedra en la piedra, el hombre, dónde estuvo?
> Aire en el aire, el hombre, dónde estuvo?
> Tiempo en el tiempo, el hombre, dónde estuvo?

[OC 321]

If slaves built the city with stone upon stone, in what conditions did they live? Were starvation and human exploitation as common in ancient America as in modern America?

In the last two fragments, Neruda abandons his passive attitude which had characterized poems I to X. He rises before the ruins and demands that the dead slaves be returned to him. He becomes the active poet who wants to rescue the humble man, whose name, Juan, is the same as that of the earth (**"La tierra se llama Juan,"** Section VIII of the *Canto general*). This Juan is a worker who descends from Viracocha, the legendary Father of the Incas. The association of a Spanish name with an Indian name symbolizes the union of the two races, who had been enemies before. The product of these two races is the American man.

In the last poem of the sequence Neruda wants to be the spokesman of all men who died building Machu Picchu, so that they may rise again to birth, as his brothers. He wants to be the link between past and present so that he can build a better future for America. "Sube a nacer conmigo, hermano" is the call of the militant poet who wants to identify himself with the workers:

> Farmer, weaver, silent shepherd,
> tamer of tutelar guanacos:
> mason of the daring scaffold:
> bearer of Andean tears:
> jeweler with crushed fingers:
> tiller trembling among seeds:
> potter amid spilled clay:
> bring to the cup of this new life
> your ancient, buried sorrows
>
> . . .

sharpen the knives you put away. . . .

Labrador, tejedor, pastor callado:
domador de guanacos tutelares:
albañil del andamio desafiado:
aguador de las lágrimas andinas:
joyero de los dedos machacados:
agricultor temblando en la semilla:
alfarero en tu greda derramado:
traed a la copa de esta nueva vida
vuestros viejos dolores enterrados.

. . .

afilad los cuchillos que guardasteis. . . .

[*OC* 324]

The call to violence in the last verse cited, and the concluding exhortation of the poem, clearly show the political aim of *Alturas de Machu Picchu.* The poet abandons the initial pessimism and becomes involved in a social struggle for justice:

Give me silence, water, hope.

Give me struggle, iron, volcanoes.

Let bodies press against me like magnets.

Come swiftly to my veins and to my mouth.

Speak through my words and through my blood.

Dadme el silencio, el agua, la esperanza.

Dadme la lucha, el hierro, los volcanes.

Apegadme los cuerpos como imanes.

Acudid a mis venas y a mi boca.

Hablad por mis palabras y mi sangre

[*OC* 324]

Thus ends Section II of the *Canto general.* In the space of 12 short fragments we have followed Neruda's journey, which has symbolically linked him to the American man in a fraternal bond.

Notes

1. Machu Picchu was rediscovered, after nearly four centuries of abandon, by the American explorer Hiram Bingham in 1911, following three earlier unsuccessful expeditions which had begun in 1906. See his book, *Lost City of the Incas,* 3d ed. (New York: Duell, Sloan, and Pearce, 1948).

2. In an interview I had with the poet in his house in Isla Negra, on December 22, 1968, Neruda emphasized the connection between events that touched his life in 1945 and his composition of *Alturas de Machu Picchu,* which indicate a definite political orientation in his work.

3. The interested reader should turn to Nathaniel Tarn's delightful translation of *Alturas de Machu Picchu* in its entirety. See note 4.

4. Pablo Neruda, *The Heights of Macchu Picchu,* translated by Nathaniel Tarn with a Preface by Robert Pring-Mill (London: Jonathan Cape, 1966), p11.

5. *Ibid.*

John Felstiner (essay date 1980)

SOURCE: Felstiner, John. "Translating *Alturas de Macchu Picchu.*" In *Translating Neruda: The Way to Macchu Picchu,* pp. 151-200. Stanford, Calif.: Stanford University Press, 1980.

[*In the following excerpt, Felstiner considers the process of rendering* The Heights of Macchu Picchu *into English verse and investigates the thematic and stylistic material of the poem's early cantos.*]

FROM VOICE TO VOICE

Perhaps the real "original" behind any translation occurs not in the written poem, but in the poet's voice speaking the verse aloud. Roger Caillois was lucky to be there that day in 1945, for as "litany followed upon invective and grief upon anger," he was hearing in Neruda's voice the formal and the emotional components of *Alturas de Macchu Picchu.* In more specific ways, a translator may also pick up vocal tones, intensities, rhythms, and pauses that will reveal how the poet heard a word, a phrase, a line, a passage. To get from the poet's voice into another language and into a translator's own voice is the business of translation. It depends on a moment-by-moment shuttle between voices, for what translating comes down to is listening—listening now to what the poet's voice said, now to one's own voice as it finds what to say. [I have used three recordings as aids in translating and interpreting. One is an Odeon recording of (I believe) 1955: Neruda's voice is often sonorous, slow, laden with emotion. The other, on tape, may be his earlier recording from 1947 (Santiago: Ibero-américa). In any case, it is a far more harsh, urgent, and compelling rendition. The third, probably from 1966, is a Caedmon recording, CDL 51215.]

In order to go between but not get between the author and the reader, a translator constantly makes local choices in diction and phrasing that tune the new version as it goes. With *Alturas de Macchu Picchu* in particular, the choices matter because this poem marked "a new stage in my style and a new direction in my concerns," as Neruda said.[1] But newness emerges from what came before. Into Neruda's long poem may have fed anything from his life up until August 1945—childhood, love, travel, politics, previous writings. A knowledge of these things should feed into the translator's work as well, if only to bring about some lexical echo, or shift in tone, or emphatic rhythm that shows what the newness actually consists of. This [essay] recounts in detail the process of making an English version of *Alturas de Macchu Picchu*—that is, of creating yet another stage, another direction for the poem itself.[2]

To make a new version is to reimagine the original poem, and in this process the translator develops particular affinities with the author: a shared historical or philosophical perspective, a parallel emotional impetus, a kindred linguistic task. Occasionally one great poet translates another and brilliantly proves the affinity. Rilke translated Valéry's "Cimetière marin" into German with "an equivalence I scarcely thought could be achieved," he said; "my resources so corresponded with his great, glorious poems that I have never translated with such sureness and insight."[3] Or in the ultimate case, Samuel Beckett makes faithful but firsthand versions of Beckett's French—they are just what he would say in English.[4] When the translator is other than a great poet, those emotional and linguistic affinities are put to the test: each choice, each rendering attempts to realize in English what the author has said—that is, both to comprehend and to make actual. This is the heart of the process, this twofold incitement. Sometimes it strains the language of translation, whose words must keep to an original and yet set their own pace too. But often enough a happy chance will render the original fully and at the same time let the English verse do what it wants to.

The translator becomes obsessively alert to words, as certain of them spring into relief from the page or from the poet's recorded voice. Perhaps an ambiguous term in *Alturas de Macchu Picchu* occurred in earlier poems or prose in such a way as to clarify its present usage. In translating as prolific a writer as Neruda, one builds up a kind of concordance from work to work. A number of weighted words turn up more than once in *Alturas de Macchu Picchu*: *manantial* ("spring," "source"), *hundir* ("to sink," "plunge"), *entregar* ("to give up," "hand over"), and others become familiar tokens that keep their meaning. One can hear something slightly different in each context, but maybe those shadings signify less than the pattern and the resonance that emerge in translating the word identically as often as possible. There can be no hard-and-fast rules for deciding between the demands of the original and those of the translation. So I write from within the Spanish and without, feeling for the pulse and pressure of Neruda's verse but also keeping a distance at which my new version becomes just that—a new version of the story now discernible in both poems. What follows, then, is a

close account of the translator's basic activity, the to-and-fro movement between Spanish and English.

CANTOS I, II: "THE EXHAUSTED HUMAN SPRING"

Opening the first half of the poem, the stage before his life brought him to Macchu Picchu, Neruda draws us right into that life, saying where he has been and when, how he has acted, and what he has missed so far. But with all that, his syntax and imagery still unfold somewhat obscurely:

> Del aire al aire, como una red vacía,
> iba yo entre las calles y la atmósfera, llegando y des-
>   pidiendo,
> en el advenimiento del otoño la moneda extendida
> de las hojas, y entre la primavera y las espigas,
> lo que el más grande amor, como dentro de un guante
> que cae, nos entrega como una larga luna.

Even a close, practically word-for-word rendering requires a dozen decisions (some of them made while thinking out these paragraphs) that affect the sense and movement of the passage:

> From the air to the air, like an empty net,
> I went on through streets and thin air, arriving and
>   leaving behind,
> at autumn's advent, the coin handed out
> in the leaves, and between spring and ripe grain,
> the fullness that love, as in a glove's
> fall, gives over to us like a long-drawn moon.

Other translations begin "From air to air."[5] Though it is often possible to drop the definite article when translating Neruda, here I think his opening movement belongs to "the air" we all live in. That movement also needs a protracted rhythm. He is dragging the air, as it were, searching his surroundings for something, coming to the fruits of summer and autumn but then leaving them behind.

The syntax of these lines has troubled readers and translators,[6] since *llegando y despidiendo* could make an independent unit, "arriving and saying goodbye." But *despedir* may have a stronger transitive meaning here, "dismiss" or "renounce." Perhaps "leaving behind" splits the difference between saying goodbye and renouncing. To settle then on *la moneda* ("the coin") as the object of *despedir,* a comma between *otoño* and *la moneda* would help: "leaving behind, / at autumn's advent, the coin." No editions have a comma there, but Neruda does pause markedly in two phonograph recordings (the third is noncommittal). So despite the pun, I think we see him leaving behind or forsaking the season's generosity, what the leaves and what love have to give. Not to relate him to them would ignore the emptiness of his net, the very need that set him writing this poem. In *Veinte poemas de amor* (1924) Neruda had said, "I cast my sad nets in your oceanic eyes."[7] That yearning for fulfillment, baffled for so many years, becomes the initial memory in **Alturas de Macchu Picchu**—a memory of failing to connect with nature and humankind.

Some of the translator's choices in these lines have a more local significance. Neruda's *moneda extendida,* the "extended" coin, calls not only for a visual image but also for a figurative sense, as in coin "handed out." And when love *nos entrega* (literally, "delivers to us"), which in the first of the **Veinte poemas de amor** suggests passive surrendering, Neruda's verb here can carry as well an active sense of giving. The phrase "give over" blends both ideas and also modulates away from the trivial rhyme of "glove" with "love." Within this same figure, the preposition *dentro* ("within") poses a more crucial question. If the fullness of love comes *dentro de un guante que cae,* literally "within a glove that falls," does it somehow come within the glove itself or—a more compelling thought—within a moment, "as in a glove's fall"? Neruda locates this experience, like the swelling calabashes of "Galope muerto" twenty years before, in high summer, "between spring and ripe grain." This is the kind of love we are offered but seldom grasp. It can concentrate and reveal itself in a moment, yet extend *como una larga luna,* "like a long-drawn moon"—*larga* implying duration rather than distance, as in *ese sonido ya tan largo,* "that sound so drawn out now," from "Galope muerto." In that poem Neruda perceived a kind of consummation that could seem a moment's doing yet stretch on endlessly. Both nature and passion gave him instances of it. Then **Alturas de Macchu Picchu** subjected that consummation to the demands of history.

After Neruda's "empty net" drifts through the streets, reaching then leaving behind seasons of ripeness, a sudden parenthesis interposes four images of forceful passion:

> (Días de fulgor vivo en la intemperie
> de los cuerpos: aceros convertidos
> al silencio del ácido:
> noches deshilachadas hasta la última harina:
> estambres agredidos de la patria nupcial.)

These images, with each phrase bearing four marked stresses, need the directest possible conveyance into English:

> (Days of live brilliance in the storm
> of bodies: steels transmuted
> into silent acid:
> nights raveled out to the final flour:
> battered stamens of the nuptial land.)

The figures surge up into Neruda's narrative from a deeper stratum than the lines around them. They all imagine a passion that is now only latently possible—is too brilliant, too consuming to take form yet as a clause or sentence. The last line, *estambres agredidos de la patria nupcial,* "battered stamens of the nuptial land," poses problems in translation. For one thing, "fatherland" or even "homeland" at the end would dissipate the rhythm too much—why is it that English has nothing but compound words for this idea? And *estambres* can mean either "stamens" or "threads," which are both germane to the poem. Italian and French have cognates that retain both meanings, but the English word "stamen" has lost the root sense of "thread," and a choice must be made. Whereas "threads" would pick up "raveled" from the previous line, "stamens" does better by bringing out a regenerative potential in the "nuptial" land. But then why such violence in *agredidos* ("assaulted," "injured")? The previous figures embody a memory and a hope of sexual passion; in "battered stamens of the nuptial land" Neruda may momentarily be envisioning the damaged lives at Macchu Picchu and their difficult rebirth.

Following the parenthesis occurs a change of tense that can easily get lost in translation. Before, Neruda had said *iba yo,* "I was going" or "I went on" rather than "I went" through streets and air. Now he moves from the imperfect into a full sentence with preterite forms, *hundí, descendí, regresé,* "I plunged . . . dropped down . . . went back." The change marks a departure: from a drifting to a willed descent. Canto I, then, not only sets in motion the imagery of fruitless wandering but also imagines a decisive journey that will not actually occur until Canto VI—an ascent that requires descending because the site is buried, sunken out of consciousness. Having spoken of a *patria nupcial,* Neruda in this opening canto enters "a world like a buried tower," *un mundo como una torre enterrada.* Both *patria* and *torre* will come back later as epithets for Macchu Picchu, and the "human spring" Neruda seeks in this canto is echoed when he calls the city "High reef of the human dawn" (VI). In his beginning, Neruda's words prefigure his end.

Canto I also sets the poem's coordinates in time and space. Through the unfulfilling streets and seasons Neruda moves horizontally, but after imagining "days of live brilliance" he drops vertically like a buried tower, a sinking spiral, a sword, a plunging hand (the same verb, *hundir,* can yield both sinking and plunging in this sentence). *Hundí la mano turbulenta y dulce / en lo más genital de lo terrestre,* "I plunged my turbulent and gentle hand / into the genital quick of the earth." It seems a semantic windfall that the best rendering of *dulce,* "gentle," softens the sound of "turbulent" and then chimes etymologically with "genital." As for *lo más genital* (literally "the most genital"), "the genital quick" tunes up Neruda's Spanish slightly—I hope he would approve the change. Every quest is sexual, it seems, and so Neruda thinks of penetrating to some progenitive source beneath earth and ocean, even more purposefully here than in "Entrance into Wood." Because the source has been spent or forgotten, his descent along the vertical axis must also take him back in time, "back . . . to the jasmine / of the exhausted human spring." In the Caedmon recording, Neruda misreads *jazmín* ("jasmine") as *jardín,* as if it were the "garden" of the exhausted human spring, and that odd slip corroborates his return to some lost Eden. The *primavera humana,* being a natural as well as a historical source, may justify in translation the pun on "spring" as a fountain. Or perhaps that word needs capitalizing, so that other meanings of "spring" do not obscure Neruda's search for a season of renewal and rebirth.

His search has the elements of a mythic or ritual procedure, a spellbound underworld and undersea descent. To mark that quality throughout the canto's final lines, I give them more rhythmic shape than English free verse usually has, establishing an iambic pentameter base and varying it with anapests and dactyls:

> and deeper yet, in geologic gold,
> like a sword sheathed in meteors
> I plunged my turbulent and gentle hand
> into the genital quick of the earth.

> I bent my head into the deepest waves,
> dropped down through sulfurous calm
> and went back, as if blind, to the jasmine
> of the exhausted human spring.

Neruda himself recited much of the poem in an incantatory tone and rhythm, as if conscious that only a heightened utterance would carry him on this journey.

Having gone back to the "human spring," he begins Canto II, *Si la flor a la flor*—echoing the poem's opening, *Del aire al aire*—and then goes on to show why the human spring is exhausted. The trouble lies in our dissonance with nature:

> Si la flor a la flor entrega el alto germen
> y la roca mantiene su flor diseminada
> en su golpeado traje de diamante y arena,
> el hombre arruga el pétalo de la luz que recoge
> en los determinados manantiales marinos
> y taladra el metal palpitante en sus manos.

> While flower to flower gives up the high seed
> and rock keeps its flower sown
> in a beaten coat of diamond and sand,
> man crumples the petal of light he picks
> in the deep-set springs of the sea
> and drills the pulsing metal in his hands.

The equation between natural and human existence, which is lyric poetry's main source of metaphor, carries an inescapable logic: instead of crumpling the flower, "man" (*el hombre*) should conform to the example of nature's regenerative process. Neruda's clauses by their very placement reveal the crux of his method. Flowers give, but man crumples: what's broken is the metaphoric connection sought so avidly in Neruda's love poems. That is, human life should be embodying and enacting metaphors from nature.

In translating *la flor entrega,* "flower gives up," it is worth echoing Canto I, where love *nos entrega,* "gives over to us": our own generousness and nature's ought to coincide. By the same token Neruda's next line is crucial: *y la roca mantiene su flor diseminada.* Across the word *flor* a tensile arc gives shape to the line, connecting two verbs whose meanings might be opposed: *mantener* ("maintain") and *diseminar* ("disseminate"). What holds them together is the idea that giving does not entail loss, that in spending passion and energy one need not lose substance or identity. Neruda's political exertions from 1936 to 1945 taught him this, and now on the way to Macchu Picchu he can put it in a single line.

That word *mantiene* marks Neruda's first use of the root *tener,* "to hold," which will occur in critical ways throughout the poem. Whether as "maintain," "sustain," "contain," or "detain," the root implies a dynamic form—some kind of matter or energy held in, yet holding its own. In translation, short Germanic verbs seem better than the Latinate words for holding this line's tensile shape: "and rock keeps its flower sown." "Sown" also lends a stronger sound and rhythm to the whole passage than "disseminated," and "keeps" has the sense of at once containing and prolonging. The rock that "keeps its flower sown" can give us intimations of Macchu Picchu, a stone structure that may have kept life stirring within it.

Since this first half of **Alturas de Macchu Picchu** essentially recapitulates the experience of Neruda's twenties, images of denatured life from his earlier poems keep turning up. The "clothing hung from a wire" in **"Walking Around"** can be seen here in "clothes and smoke" and "hostile trappings of the wire." The *amapola* ("poppy"), a frequent symbol for passion in his love poems, appears now in a striking figure from Canto II, where Neruda asks:

> quién guarda sin puñal (como las encarnadas
> amapolas) su sangre?

> who (like the crimson poppy) keeps
> no dagger to guard his blood?

In the earlier love poems it was usually enough to say something like "the color of poppies sits on your brow." Here, human and physical nature remain disjunct. Societal anxiety closes parentheses around the poppy, nature's example of passionate openness. More specifically, the word "guard" implies that we would lose less through openness than through constraint; that we might thrive within organic forms of existence rather than rigid forms of control.

In Canto II, nature provides the touchstone for sexual and social acts though not yet for political existence. The passage beginning "How many times in the city's winter streets" drifts with no verb through four long lines of loveless human scenes until *me quise detener,* "I wanted to stop." *Detener* ("stop," "pause," "arrest"), a common verb, was one Neruda often used revealingly. "Galope muerto" finds him *deteniéndose*—"in what's immobile, holding still, to perceive"—and in "Sonata y destrucciones" he is *detenido,* a journeyer "held" between shadows and wings. His prose also uses the word at important moments: in Spain "my poetry paused" amidst the anguish, and then "roots and blood began to rise through it"; and going home in 1943, he says, *Me detuve,* "In Peru I stopped and climbed to the ruins of Macchu Picchu."[8] Here in Canto II the verb *detener* interrupts a frustrating horizontal movement, what Eliot's *Four Quartets* calls "the waste sad time / stretching before and after," and creates, in Eliot's words, a "point of intersection of the timeless / with time":[9]

> me quise detener a buscar la eterna veta insondable
> que antes toqué en la piedra o en el relámpago que el
>   beso desprendía.

> I wanted to stop and seek the timeless fathomless vein
> I touched in a stone once or in the lightning a kiss
>   released.

Eliot's word "timeless" (for *eterna*) helps in translation, since both poets conceived of profound and heightened experience along a vertical axis, out of time. And because Spanish has another word for human veins (*vena*), my translation relies on "fathomless" to locate this mineral *veta* underground or perhaps undersea. In wanting to stop in mid-career and to descend, the poet recalls some early joy and anticipates in "a stone" some future one.

Right after Neruda recalls the stone and "the lightning a kiss released," an extended vision arises, showing what that vital touch was and what it might be like again. This vision arises between parentheses, as if caught and held against the stream of daily experience:

> (Lo que en el cereal como una historia amarilla
> de pequeños pechos preñados va repitiendo un número
> que sin cesar es ternura en las capas germinales,
> y que, idéntica siempre, se desgrana en marfil
> y lo que en el agua es patria transparente, campana
> desde la nieve aislada hasta las olas sangrientas.)

These lines, as the translator comes to realize, develop no main clause: beginning *lo que* ("that which"), they form a kind of instantaneous subliminal flash depicting what the poet stopped to seek:

> (Whatever in grain like a yellow history
> of small swelling breasts keeps repeating its number
> ceaselessly tender in the germinal shells,
> and identical always, what strips to ivory,
> and what is clear native land welling up, a bell
> from remotest snows to the blood-sown waves.)

Moving through progressive verb forms, a present tense, and the verb "is," this passage never resolves into a main verb but remains in suspension. Life given over to time and change ("history," "repeating," "ceaselessly," "germinal") is not exhausted, but through that very change keeps its form ("grain," "breast," "number," "shell").

The key phrase is the strangest, *idéntica siempre,* and needs close rather than interpretive translation. Tarn says that the grains shell "always the same way," but I think Neruda means they are "identical always": no matter how much generation the germ of life goes through, it keeps its essential identity, it remains one and the same.[10] Like the parenthesis in Canto I, which closes with "battered stamens of the nuptial land," this parenthesis closes with a presage of the mountain site: *y lo que en el agua es patria transparente, campana / desde la nieve aislada hasta las olas sangrientas.* No English verse could equal the way Neruda's *ah*-sounds move through *agua* to the *patria transparente,* then into the roundedness of *campana,* and finally resonate throughout the landscape of the last line. I have played with the sense a little to get rhyming vowel sounds— "clear native land welling up, a bell / from remotest snows to the blood-sown waves"—though that mixture may be somewhat rich.

The parenthesis closes and Neruda's narrative voice now returns, in the past tense again, saying he could not "touch," he could only "grasp" hollow faces or masks. In this alienation, he imagines finding some responsive touch in a place that will be either "running" or "firm":

> No tuve sitio donde descansar la mano
> y que, corriente como agua de manantial encadenado,
> o firme como grumo de antracita o cristal,
> hubiera devuelto el calor o el frío de mi mano exten-
>   dida.

> I had no place to rest my hand,
> none running like linked springwater
> or firm as a chunk of anthracite or crystal
> to give back the warmth or cold of my outstretched
>   hand.

The translation can, like the original, enrich its language by association: "my outstretched hand" reaches back to "the coin handed out in the leaves" in Canto I, as well as forward to moments when Neruda's hand will touch the city's stones and reach for the men who dwelt there. A place "running like linked springwater" will be found in Canto IX's epithet for the city, "wellspring of stone," *manantial de piedra,* and my word "linked," instead of the literal "chained" for *encadenado,* will again be heard when Neruda says to the Indian workers in Canto XII, "Tell me everything, chain by chain, link by link." I choose "linked" in Canto II because the word suggests controlling yet releasing a life-giving source: it anticipates the Incas' ingeniously stepped conduits and irrigation runnels at Macchu Picchu, which link the levels of the city, harmonizing hard natural fact with human need. One more phrase in this passage, *No tuve sitio,* also looks ahead through the poem as if through the years. Here Neruda says, "I had no place" to rest, and the need for one is so sharp that it carries through to Canto VI, where he will announce simply: *éste es el sitio,* "this is the place."

CANTOS III, IV, V: "WHAT COULD NOT BE REBORN"

Because this poem prepared a new stage in his work, it "came out too impregnated with myself," Neruda said. "The beginning is a series of autobiographical recollections. I also wanted to touch for the last time there upon the theme of death."[11] He said this after being exiled as a Communist between 1948 and 1952, during which time he was welcomed throughout the Soviet orbit and in China, saw **Canto general** translated into twenty-five languages, and felt persuaded that poetry's task was to hearten the common struggle.[12] These conditions made him sensitive to the poem's subjective, dispirited vein. Yet it is hard to imagine **Alturas de Macchu Picchu** without Neruda's presence, particularly the constantly inquiring force of his voice.

"What was man?," Neruda cries at the close of Canto II, and the next canto opens with another figure from nature:

> Lives like maize were threshed in the bottomless
> granary of wasted deeds . . .
> and not one death but many deaths came each man's
>   way.

What troubles Neruda most about this way of living, which feels like a "lamp snuffed out in suburban mud, a petty fat-winged death," is that such dwindling and death have no communal matrix, no shared vision, no common *logos* to redeem them. "Alone," he says in Canto IV, "I roamed round dying of my own death." Even the workers whom he evokes fairly strongly, "the drover, the son of seaports, the dark captain of the plow," remain isolated as *cada ser* or *cada uno* or *cada hombre*: "each being," "each one," "each man." One can question whether Neruda's vision really is shared commonly. In translating, it is hard to see *hijo* ("son" or "child"), *uno,* and *hombre* as generic rather than gender-

linked: this canto does not suggest that for women, as for drovers and sailors and farmers, "their dismal weariness each day was like / a black cup they drank down trembling."

Canto IV opens with *La poderosa muerte.* Whether a "powerful," "mighty," "irresistible," or "overmastering" death, as translators have heard it,[13] it is in any case the "one death," which Canto III opposed to the "many deaths" that isolated men die day after day. By complex figures of speech—death was like salt in the waves, like sinking and height—Neruda connects this *poderosa muerte* to other ideas in the poem. It is not simply that his writing runs to figures of speech, but that in those figures he evolves the deeper-than-narrative structure of his poem, particularly through words the translator has noticed and will come upon again:

> La poderosa muerte me invitó muchas veces:
> era como la sal invisible en las olas,
> y lo que su invisible sabor diseminaba
> era como mitades de hundimientos y altura.
>
> The mightiest death invited me many times:
> like invisible salt in the waves it was,
> and what its invisible savor disseminated
> was half like sinking and half like height.[14]

The literal sense of *diseminaba* seems called for (and enriches the sound) in this instance. Along with its corrosiveness, salt has enhancing and preserving qualities, and these fit Neruda's idea of a death that sustains the potential for rebirth. In Canto XII, for instance, he will say to the buried American, "Give me your hand out of the deep / region seeded by all your grief"—your *dolor diseminado.* The analogy in Canto IV imagines death *como mitades de hundimientos y altura*—literally, "like halves of sinkings and height." The available verse translations miss Neruda's drift, I think. Belitt's "height, or the ruin of height, a plenitude halved" eludes my understanding, and Tarn's "fragments of wrecks and heights" skirts the exact sense of *mitades* ("halves"), the idea that death is a whole made up equally of what sinking and height connote.[15] The image of sinking need not have negative force, as Belitt and Tarn imply; for Neruda it leads to the deep pole, the basis, the root. The words *hundir* and *altura* take various forms both early and late in the poem, suggesting that an encounter with Macchu Picchu involves the full scale of what we can experience: from the unconscious to the spirit, from sexual earthiness to transcendent ecstasy, from past to future, from death to renewal.

Even when a profuse and vaguely symbolic imagery in **Alturas de Macchu Picchu** makes translating uncertain, it is well to trust rather than paraphrase Neruda, for a logic usually underlies what he says. In the poem's opening image he had stopped wandering through the streets to sink into earth and sea. Now in "suburban mud" or "cluttered streets" (III) he looks for the dimension that people lack, crying out to it *ancho mar, oh muerte!,* "broad sea, oh death!" (IV). Then a little later he says: *quise nadar en las más anchas vidas, / en las más sueltas desembocaduras.* The choice of rendering *anchas* again as "broad"—"I wanted to swim in the broadest lives, / in the openest river mouths"—indicates that life can have great breadth, like that of death.

Neruda is seeking a consummation in the "openest river mouths" and the undifferentiated primal element from which life emerged and to which it returns. A source for this idea can be found in some impressions he sent from Ceylon to a Chilean newspaper in 1929, during the period these early cantos represent. He was talking about the effect of Hindu belief on life in the Orient:

> Origin and duration are antagonistic states: original being is still immersed in spontaneousness, in the creative and destructive element, while day-to-day lives go on abandoned, deprived of beginning or end. With no loss of itself, and losing itself, being goes back to its creative origin, "like a drop of seawater to the sea," says the *Katha Upanishad.*[16]

In 1929, trying to find some meaning in his own day-to-day life, Neruda saw this potential immersion in the primal sea of being as "a source of impossible and fatal obscurities." But what he called "duration" or daily life had by 1945 come to be in need of "its creative origin." Having seen so many abandoned, deprived lives around him, and seeking to recover an American genesis, Neruda at Macchu Picchu felt impelled to plunge his hand or sink like a drop through earth and sea to the human spring.

The poet's "turbulent and gentle hand," from Canto I, now in Canto IV has found men denying him as if he made a Christ-like demand on them: they shut themselves off "so I would not touch / with my streaming hands their wound of emptiness," *para que no tocaran / mis manos manantiales su inexistencia herida.* There seems no good way to specify in translation the recurrent image of *manantial* ("source," "spring"), as here in *manos manantiales,* though Tarn's "divining fingers" hits on an ingenious solution. As "streaming hands" they could easily be Walt Whitman's hands touching his fellow creatures or dressing the wounded, and in fact another passage, from Canto V, also begins much like Whitman:

> I lifted the iodine bandages, plunged my hands
> into meager griefs that were killing off death,
> and all I found in the wound was a cold gust
> that passed through loose gaps in the soul.

It begins like Whitman, at least, but ends more like Eliot, whose vision of urban and suburban spiritlessness in *Four Quartets*—"men and bits of paper, whirled by the cold wind / . . . Wind in and out of unwholesome lungs"—is strikingly akin to Neruda's.[17]

Eliot would never play the healing or suffering servant of humanity as Whitman and Neruda do, and they in turn could hardly live with Eliot's austere deprecation of sensuality. Yet Neruda's and Eliot's ideas share similar forms, if they differ in substance and tone. Eliot's sense of a "darkness to purify the soul," where "the darkness shall be the light"[18] (which in fact derives from the Spanish mystic San Juan de la Cruz), resembles Neruda's vision of death as a "gallop of nighttime clarity" (IV), except that Neruda's paradox seems homemade, instinctive. And in Canto V Neruda's formula for the empty human shuffle around him—*Era lo que no pudo renacer,* "It was what could not be reborn"—might well be translated by Eliot's fine discrimination of what keeps humankind from spiritual rebirth: "that which is only living / Can only die."[19] What distinguishes Neruda from Eliot, at least in ***Alturas de Macchu Picchu,*** is that finally he aims at a secular rebirth and makes himself the agent of it.

CANTOS VI, VII: "LIVING, DEAD, SILENCED, SUSTAINED"

Entonces—in Neruda's recordings the word is weighted, slow, sonorous:

> Entonces en la escala de la tierra he subido
> entre la atroz maraña de las selvas perdidas
> hasta ti, Macchu Picchu.

Our word "then" sounds too thin and brief for such a crucial moment. "Then, then" (depending on how it's spoken) might get a dramatic emphasis at this point, but once one begins such compensating for an adequate English rendering, the door opens too wide.

> Then on the ladder of the earth I climbed
> through the lost jungle's tortured thicket
> up to you, Macchu Picchu.

This is the watershed of the poem, as of Neruda's entire poetry, and it makes a beautifully timed cadence. For *hasta ti, Macchu Picchu,* I am tempted to say "up to thee, Macchu Picchu," to preserve the Spanish form used with one's intimates or when praying to God. Even without that archaism in English, we can hear Neruda speaking to Macchu Picchu in the directly personal way he spoke a canto earlier to death: "Solemn death it was not you," *No eras tú, muerte grave.* He may feel equally close to both and may also in some way mean to identify the two.

Another small semantic event in Canto VI's opening lines has larger implications that might go unnoticed or remain vague without the specific focus that occurs in translation. Neruda climbs *en la escala de la tierra,* "on the ladder of the earth," and immediately invokes Macchu Picchu as *Alta ciudad de piedras escalares*—High city of laddered stones," as a Spanish ear might hear the phrase, though "stepped" or "scaled" describes the actual construction more closely. By echoing *escala* in *escalares,* Neruda makes the cut stone and the earth congruent with each other. A human construction conforms superbly to raw, ineluctable nature: this is what gives Macchu Picchu its mythic aura. [In 1929 in Ceylon, Neruda visited the site of Sigiriya, a ruined palace built in A.D. 477 atop a granite rock of great height. His impressions of the place, written for the Santiago newspaper *La Nación* (Nov. 17, 1929) and entitled "Ceylán espeso" ("Dense Ceylon"), show some of the same imagery and ideas that emerged from his visit to Macchu Picchu: "The grey shells of slender stone capitals buried for twenty centuries loom up among the plants; demolished statues and stairways, immense pools and palaces that have returned to the soil, their progenitors now forgotten. . . . In the center of dense jungle, an abrupt, immense hill of rock, barely accessible by insecure, dangerous steps cut in the great stone; on its height the ruins of a palace and the marvelous Sigiriyan frescos intact despite the centuries . . . everywhere the ruins of what disappeared, covered by plant growth and oblivion." The entire article is reprinted in Juan Loveluck, ed., "Neruda en *La Nación* (1927-1929): prosa olvidada," *Anales de la Universidad de Chile,* 129, nos. 157-60 (Jan.-Dec. 1971), 78.] The physical site and the city do exhibit this conformity in the way the steep, rocky slopes give rise to flights of stone steps and mortarless walls as smooth as the day they were fitted. Unlike the urban scene in **"Walking Around,"** with its "hideous intestines hanging from the doors of houses I hate," Neruda finds stone buildings that fuse the primordial presence of the Andes with the aspirations of an indigenous people.

That fusion of nature and history explains another image from the beginning of Canto VI. *En ti,* Neruda says to the site,

> En ti, como dos líneas paralelas,
> la cuna del relámpago y del hombre
> se mecían en un viento de espinas.

> In you like two lines parallel,
> the cradles of lightning and man
> rocked in a wind of thorns.

Tarn interestingly chooses the figurative sense of *línea* and has two "lineages" issuing in one "cradle both of man and light." His choice of "light" for Neruda's *relámpago* ("lightning flash") tends to assimilate this image to a biblical genesis. "Lightning," on the other hand, not only recalls Neruda's glimpse of ecstasy in Canto II, "the lightning a kiss released," but finds a dazzling, threatening energy at the cradle of a cosmos more secular than biblical. Neruda's cradles identify Macchu Picchu as a remote source of both natural and human phenomena, of "lightning and man." In the scheme of *Canto general* (1950), Neruda used *Alturas*

de Macchu Picchu as the second of fifteen books, thus placing it far back in the epic's chronology. It follows directly upon the poems about untouched minerals, wild plants, solitary birds, and invisible Arauco, and it comes before the third book, *The Conquistadors.* In effect, then, Macchu Picchu occurs between a Creation and the first human cataclysm. It stands suspended, untouched (as was indeed the case) by the incursions of history.

The poet in Canto VI continues invoking this place with honorific yet pointed epithets:

> Mother of stone, spume of condors.
> High reef of the human dawn.
> Spade lost in the primal sand.

Catalogs of attributes are a vital convention in medieval oral poetry: addressed to a god, a ruler, a sacred place, they establish the qualities or powers that a people value. Here Neruda, whose emphatic, alliterated lines sound rather like Anglo-Saxon verse, reinforces Macchu Picchu's twofold aspect as a human construction and a fact of nature by calling to the "Mother of stone" alongside the "spume of condors." His second epithet does much the same: "High reef of the human dawn"—a natural metaphor for a primal history. But if he sees the city as a reef, long-lasting and visible, he also imagines it as a spade lost in the sand: Macchu Picchu appears emergent and yet buried. In Neruda's next line the verb tenses embody a similar double vision: *Ésta fué la morada, éste es el sitio,* "This was the dwelling, this is the place." *Sitio* could of course be translated as "site," but that risks giving it a merely archaeological significance. The past tense balanced against the present and the matching half-lines divide Macchu Picchu's genius equally between the city that people formerly dwelt in and the natural site a poet now announces.

Neruda's assurance that past and present time can fuse through the poet's agency takes even more concrete form later in Canto VI, in a particular sequence of tenses:

> Miro las vestiduras y las manos,
> el vestigio del agua en la oquedad sonora,
> la pared suavizada por el tacto de un rostro
> que miró con mis ojos las lámparas terrestres,
> que aceitó con mis manos las desaparecidas
> maderas.

As it happens, the first-person, present-tense *miro* ("I look at") takes only a change in accent to become, three lines later, the third-person past, *miró* ("looked at"). English cannot quite match that economy:

> I look at clothes and hands,
> the trace of water in an echoing tub,
> the wall brushed smooth by the touch of a face
> that looked with my eyes at the lights of earth,
> that oiled with my hands the vanished
> beams.

Using one English verb for *miro* and *miró* helps in recognizing Neruda's presence as both a pilgrim now and a native then. Tarn varies the verb, saying "I gaze" and then "a face that witnessed," because "gaze" has a strength that is needed here and "witness" has suggestive overtones. Neruda's kind of witness can also gain from simplicity and immediacy. His double residence at Macchu Picchu, in the present and the past, can bear every possible emphasis in translation, for it matters vitally to him. (In his urgency Neruda even says that the face not only looked, it also "oiled.") He recited these lines passionately, putting unusual stress on *mis ojos* and *mis manos*: "that looked with *my eyes*," "that oiled with *my hands*."

This emphasis also clarifies Neruda's surprising use of *porque* ("because") in the very next line. Why does he look at the trace of water, the vanished beams, the wall brushed by "a face / that looked with my eyes"?

. . . porque todo, ropaje, piel, vasijas,
palabras, vino, panes,
se fué, cayó a la tierra.

. . . because everything, clothing, skin, jars,
words, wine, bread,
is gone, fallen to earth.

Having for years let my translation of *porque todo . . . se fué* remain as "for everything . . . is gone," I now see it fails to intensify the logic of Neruda's statement. Precisely "because" every rudiment of that previous life is now gone, he says "my" eyes long ago looked and "my" hands worked. We may not want to assent to that illusion, but it fosters a crucial idea. Unless renewed in the person of the poet, these beams, jars, and wine remain utterly lost to us now. To redeem the past, to translate it over the centuries into his own eyes and hands, requires an act of imagination—not, as ultimately for Eliot, an act of religious faith. Neruda does allow a hint of resurrection (or transubstantiation) by including *palabras, vino, panes,* "words, wine, bread," among the things we may have lost. Tarn calls the *panes* "loaves," giving a more specific Christian coloring to Neruda's redemptive mission.

To translate *panes* as "loaves," the way Tarn does, and in the next canto *vaso* ("glass" or "vessel") as "chalice," accentuates an already difficult question. Neruda has been faulted for making use of his Spanish Catholic heritage while at the same time lamenting the Conquest, and no doubt that is a real split in him as in many Latin Americans.[20] In **Alturas de Macchu Picchu,** I think he deliberately highlights neither Christian nor indigenous imagery because he is addressing a general audience, both Latin and American. It is also held against him that he speaks for pre-Columbian peoples while ignoring present-day Indians—another tendency in countries such as Peru and Mexico. He calls up slaves from the Inca past without a word for modern Quechua speakers, but here again I believe he does so to be heard by modern workers in general, for whose plight he finds a deep basis at Macchu Picchu.

Notes

1. "Algo sobre mi poesía y mi vida," *Aurora* (Santiago), 1 (July 1954), 10-21, p. 13.

2. Studies of *Alturas de Macchu Picchu* may be found in Hernán Loyola, *Ser y morir*; Frank Riess, *The Word and the Stone*; Emir Rodríguez Monegal, *El viajero inmóvil*; Jaime Concha, "El descubrimiento del pueblo en la poesía de Neruda"; Mario Rodríguez Fernández, "El tema de la muerte en *Alturas de Macchu Picchu* de Pablo Neruda," *Anales de la Universidad de Chile,* 131 (July-Sept. 1964), 23-50; Hugo Montes, "Acerca de *Alturas de Macchu Picchu*," *Mapocho* (Santiago), 2, no. 6 (1964), 120-34; Leonidas Morales T., "Estructura mítica de *Alturas de Macchu Picchu*," *Estudios Filológicos* (Univ. Austral, Valdivia, Chile), 1 (1964), 167-83; Juan Loveluck, "*Alturas de Macchu Picchu*: Cantos I-V," *Revista Iberoamericana* (Pittsburgh), 39, nos. 82-83 (Jan.-June 1973), 175-88; Cedomil Goić, "*Alturas de Macchu Picchu*: la torre y el abismo," *Anales de la Universidad de Chile,* 129, nos. 157-60 (Jan.-Dec. 1971), 153-65; Robert Pring-Mill, Preface to *The Heights of Macchu Picchu,* trans. Nathaniel Tarn, pp. vii-xix. See also the excellent bibliography on recent studies of Neruda: Enrico Mario Santí, "Fuentes para el conocimiento de Pablo Neruda, 1967-1974," in *Simposio Pablo Neruda,* ed. Isaac Jack Lévy and Juan Loveluck (Columbia, So. Carolina: Las Américas, 1975), pp. 355-82. My discussion here uses the text of *Alturas de Macchu Picchu* from *OC*. That text differs from other versions in the spacing of verse paragraphs and from the first magazine version in punctuation and in the omission of one line (see pp. 174, 197). In Canto VIII, I follow earlier editions in spacing separately the third line from the end. The poem's full texts are printed in this book so that a line ending with a period at the base of a page marks a stanza break (Canto IX has no stanzas).

3. *Letters of Rainer Maria Rilke: 1910-1926,* trans. Jane Bannard Greene and M. D. Herter Norton (New York: Norton, 1969), pp. 279, 318-19. A more recent example of affinity between a poet-translator and a poet may be found in Clayton Eshleman's introduction to César Vallejo, *The Complete Posthumous Poetry,* trans. Clayton Eshleman and José Rubia Barcia (Berkeley: Univ. of California Press, 1979).

4. See Hugh Kenner, "Beckett Translating Beckett: Comment C'est," *Delos,* 5 (1970), 194-211.

5. Waldeen's translation in *Let the Rail Splitter Awake and Other Poems,* trans. Joseph M. Bernstein et al.; Angel Flores's translation, "Summits of Macchu Picchu," in *The World's Best,* ed. Whit Burnett; Nathaniel Tarn, *The Heights of Macchu Picchu.*

6. Tarn says "I came / lavish, at autumn's coronation, with the leaves' / proffer of currency," which seems to lose the sense of *despedir* (*The Heights of Macchu Picchu,* p. 3).

7. *Obras completas* (*OC*), I, 87.

8. *Confieso,* pp. 204, 229.

9. "Burnt Norton," V; "The Dry Salvages," V.

10. See Neruda's 1933 lyric, "Unidad": "There is something dense, unified, deeply seated, / repeating its number, its identical sign"—*su señal idéntica*; *OC,* I, 173.

11. "Algo sobre mi poesía," p. 13.

12. For translations, see the bibliography in *OC,* III, 1067-1106.

13. Angel Flores, "Summits of Macchu Picchu; H. R. Hays, in *Twelve Spanish American Poets*; Nathaniel Tarn, *The Heights of Macchu Picchu*; and Ben Belitt, in *Selected Poems of Pablo Neruda.*

14. I am indebted to Flores's translation for the construction of the last line.

15. Belitt, *Selected Poems of Pablo Neruda,* p. 123.

16. Quoted in Jaime Alazraki, "Para una poética de la poesía póstuma de Pablo Neruda," in *Simposio Pablo Neruda,* ed. Isaac Jack Lévy and Juan Loveluck, p. 63.

17. "Burnt Norton," III.

18. *Ibid.*; "East Coker," III.

19. "Burnt Norton," V.

20. Gordon Brotherston, *Latin American Poetry: Origins and Presence.* Cambridge: Cambridge University Press, 1975, pp. 51-53.

Manuel Durán and Margery Safir (essay date 1981)

SOURCE: Durán, Manuel, and Margery Safir. "The Public Poet." In *Earth Tones: The Poetry of Pablo Neruda,* pp. 74-114. Bloomington: Indiana University Press, 1981.

[*In the following excerpt, Durán and Safir study* The Heights of Macchu Picchu *within the epic, lyrical, political, and thematic contexts of Neruda's* Canto general.]

In *Canto General,* Neruda returns to look at his own land. The lyrical and the political poetic forms present in *Spain in My Heart* are extended and expanded, this time to embrace the epic, a collective and historical vision of an entire continent, in which immediate feelings and events are replaced by a broader, all-encompassing vision of America. Neruda had not chosen to become a political poet in Spain; he had been forced into it by the events he witnessed there. As Selden Rodman quotes him: "Nobody has ever *asked* me to write a political poem. If the subject didn't touch me, I couldn't. I haven't written a poem about intervention in the Dominican Republic, for instance, but I am free to write one. Poets like T. S. Eliot and Saint-John Perse are not free to. They are hobbled by conventions. Their conventions inhibit them, tell them that such a subject must wait a hundred years to be usable. After a hundred years the blood will be washed away by the rain. I prefer the blood to the rain . . . I do not believe in social realism. That label, that way of looking at things, is prefabricated. I want to taste the wine before it is bottled."[1]

In the same way, Neruda did not choose to become an epic poet; he was forced into it by the social reality of his country and his continent. As Neruda defined the poet's role: "Our volcanoes and our rivers have been so far mired upon the dry lines of textbooks. Let their fire and their fertility be given to the whole world by our poets. We are the chroniclers of a retarded birth."[2] *Canto General* means general song, and in his *Canto General* Neruda simply recognizes and accepts the role he sees as belonging to the Latin American poet. He sees a need for a poetry that will express the vision, history, and goals of a people, a poetry that can connect past, present, and future around the destiny of millions of human beings. For this poetry, Neruda necessarily turns to the epic tradition.

Although often associated with the classics, the epic has, in reality, never disappeared altogether from the world of poetry; it was very much alive during the medieval period and later. Dante, in his *Divine Comedy,* was often an epic poet, as was Milton in *Paradise Lost.* Epic poetry was present during the Enlightenment and surfaced at random during the nineteenth century, as in Victor Hugo's "Les Châtiments" or "Napoléon le Petit," written in political exile and inspired by a violent opposition to Napoleon III. The examples of Mickiewicz in Poland and Petöfi in Hungary are equally significant, if less well known. When political poetry transcends the specific moment that gave it birth, when specific personalities are subsumed in a vast panorama, this poetry can no longer be called strictly political. It becomes patriotic, in the best sense of this much-abused word, and finally epic. It deals with the destiny of societies, peoples, and cultures, and it tries to come to grips with the eternal problem of man's role on earth and his place in the world of the future. Neruda's *Canto*

General—not all of it, to be sure, but enough of it—belongs to this privileged category. In it the role of the poet in today's world is redefined and exalted.

Neruda's erotic poetry and his Nature poetry are primarily lyrical, *Spain in My Heart* is both lyrical and political, and *Canto General* is lyrical, political, and epic. It should be understood that we are here using the word *epic* in a generic way that defines poetry by its content and that does not demand strict adherence to formal structures or meters associated with the classical epic. *Epic* here is used to reflect the fact that *Canto General* is no longer only Neruda's immediate and emotional vision of the world. In the *Canto,* Neruda presents his history of the American continent, a history that describes the very beginning of the continent, its geography and flora and fauna before the existence of man, that goes on to catalogue its violent history of conquest, and ends by dealing with current political figures and problems, and with the life of the poet himself. It is the scope and attitude of the poem that classify it as epic, rather than any adherence to classical rules of epic form. And it is above all the poet's place in the poem that establishes this classification, for here Neruda rises to become the epic bard of the Americas.

Throughout much of *Canto General,* Neruda is no longer the single individual Pablo Neruda or his poetical projection or persona. He is the spokesman and chronicler for an entire people, he is the voice of the South American continent, much as his greatly admired predecessor, Walt Whitman, saw himself as the voice of the North American continent. [Emir Rodríguez Monegal has stressed this relationship between the two poets in a seminar at Yale University, "Neruda and Whitman."] It is a break with the poetical themes of the Old World in order to establish a poetry, a vision, a mythology for the New World. In the Heroic Age of Greece, the chronicler of such vast histories, the epic bard, his disciples and imitators already "were marked as men possessing peculiar qualities of memory and vision. In fact, the purveyors and refurbishers of popular tradition concerning gods and heroes, they were credited with being able, by special inspiration, to transcend the limitations of sense . . . and to rescue the past from oblivion, restoring it to life and moving their hearers to pity and fear."[3] This is precisely Neruda's stance in much of *Canto General.* It is the poet as epic bard who evokes the past and imbues it with palpitating life, who takes history and makes it immediate, almost journalistic in its presence. The poet is here as chronicler, observer, participant, and actor, and, above all, as the voice of a collectivity, a voice possessing all the special powers of evocation and creation of drama that form part of the magic of the classical epic bard.

And like that of the classical bard, Neruda's vision of history is not unlyrical. It is, in fact, more often personal than objective. The historical vision of *Canto General* has often been criticized on these grounds, especially for its simplistic division into black and white, good and evil, hero and villain. The vision *is* simplistic on the historical level. In it there are stars and scoundrels, and the line between them is implacably drawn: Nature, the indigenous American population, the common man of America are the heroes; the invaders, first the Spaniards and later the United States with its multinational corporations, are the villains. The heroes are too perfect, the common man, long-suffering, righteous, is elevated in Whitmanesque fashion to larger-than-life virtue; the Spaniards, in contrast, are presented as having no virtue. Even the imposition of their language (which the poet himself is forced to employ to communicate his rejection of it) is seen as a destructive rape of the indigenous and authentic American heritage. It is not only on this level that Neruda's historical vision is arbitrary. Certain political leaders, among them González Videla of Chile, are singled out for castigation, while others, like Trujillo, who were guilty of much greater crimes, are generally overlooked. Neruda seeks to present an epic of the South American continent, yet he largely ignores huge sections of that continent, most particularly the multiple spaces and personalities of Brazil. The poet's vision of the United States is likewise arbitrary. He defines the United States as an "outsider" in the Americas and ignores its very real accomplishments in order to focus exclusively on its imperialistic role in South America. Even in his narrow focus on the United States and his diatribe against modern invaders—the United Fruit Company and other multinational corporations—Neruda's vision is nearsighted and simplistic. As Emir Rodríguez Monegal has pointed out, Neruda singles out the United States, not only because it had in fact a large presence in South America, but also because Neruda was a strict Soviet-style Communist when he wrote the *Canto,* and as such, he shared the cold-war attitude toward the "Colossus to the North." But in this historical vision limited by ideology, other exploiters, true invaders in the Americas—France, Holland, and England all had colonies in Latin America at the time Neruda wrote—are strangely excluded from mention.[4]

Yet to acknowledge the personal and even inaccurate historical nature of Neruda's vision is not to lessen its impact as an epic work. In his *Satyricon,* Petronius makes clear that even for the classical epic bard historical accuracy is not a requisite or even the goal: "Things actually done are not to be put into verses, for historians treat them far better; instead . . . the free spirit is to rush; so there is evidenced rather the vaticination of a raging mind than the testimony of scrupulous statement by witnesses."[5] In other words, in presenting a personal vision of history, Neruda is well within the epic tradition. And in this tradition heroes and villains are customarily overdrawn. The heroism of El Cid, for example, and his generosity and his loyalty are matched only by the cowardice, niggardliness, and fickle ingratitude of the king he serves. In the epic, heroes are indeed heroes and villains are indeed villains. Neruda's treatment of the native American population and the invading Spaniards and North Americans follows that practice.

The ideological and propagandistic overtones of much of *Canto General* are also in the epic tradition. Ruling monarchs and noblemen often commissioned epic poetry to be written for the express purpose of presenting a particular version of historical or contemporary political events. The epic was used as a propaganda vehicle: the great deeds of former heroes were recounted in order to excite patriotic fervor and nationalistic zeal. The epic became the vehicle for putting forth a certain vision of reality, particularly in times of war, in order to spur on the listening public, to inspire its listeners to make great sacrifices and to perform acts of valor in the name of the realm. Neruda's often one-sided ideological vision may fail as history, but once again, it does not fail as epic poetry. On the contrary, it forms part of the popular epic tradition. Like Vergil's *Aeneid,* it "is deliberately conceived . . . to give meaning to the destiny of a people, asserting the implications of their history and recognizing the significance of contemporary events in relation to the past."[6]

Canto General, while largely an epic work, repeats the creative pattern established in Neruda's more lyrical works: it grew out of personal experience. Political activism and disillusion brought forth *Canto General.* After the disaster in Spain, Neruda returned to Chile. As chronicled earlier in discussing Neruda's erotic poetry, the 1940s were for Neruda a time of active political involvement followed by acute disappointment. Neruda had been elected a Senator in 1945, the same year that he joined the Communist Party. It was the Party that encouraged his writing of the *Canto,* which he had begun years earlier, and, in 1947, it was again the Party that gave Neruda leave from his parliamentary duties so he could devote himself fully to the *Canto.* He returned to the Senate, however, in 1947 and a year later made a blistering attack—"I Accuse"—on the government. Suddenly, Neruda found himself an "enemy of the State," forced to go underground and ultimately into exile. "But even in hiding," Rodríguez Monegal notes, "he continues writing that *Canto General* which will be converted inevitably into a weapon of political battle, not only in Chile, but internationally."[7]

What had been intended to be a history of Neruda's native land, a general song of Chile, became the epic of an entire continent. The finished work of these days of political battle was published in 1950. It is one of the few works of modern poetry to attempt in one volume a sweeping chronicle which spans time and space, history and geography to form a self-contained vision of a continent, its land and its people. It is divided into fifteen principal sections. Each section has a defined subject and tone, and each must be at least briefly considered for the reader to begin to grasp the scope and greatness of the work, for its fame rests not only on the excellence of many individual poems contained in it, but above all on the vastness of its vision, unique in modern poetry.

The first section portrays the birth of the American continent. If the epic is the basic model for the *Canto* in its entirety, in this first section, another ancient model prefigures and gives definition to the poet's words: the Bible. Like the Bible, and using verse forms and literary devices imitative of Biblical models, *Canto General* begins with a genesis. Nature is presented in its raw state, without the presence of man. Neruda goes back to the origins, to the chaotic world where twilight reminds us of the hues of the iguana's skin and monkeys in their frenzied flight among the trees seem to weave a thread of erotic violence. We witness the flight of a cloud of butterflies, we wade in the night of the alligator, surrounded by snouts moving out of the slime. We hear a clatter of armor, we catch a glimpse of huge primitive animals turning and twisting in the misty shadows. The jaguar appears and disappears, a phosphorous streak, faster than our eye can catch it. The eyes of the puma seem to blaze endlessly in the night, like the eyes of Blake's tiger; the "alcoholic eyes of the jungle," Neruda writes, burn in his head (**"Some Beasts"**). Badgers rake the river beds, red-toothed, ready for the final assault; below, surrounded by the vastness of water, as a dot in the circle of a continent, drenched in the ritual mud, rapacious and religious, the gigantic coiled anaconda appears.

Neruda introduces this virginal state of Nature with lines whose imagery and contrasts will hold constant for the entire *Canto*:

> Before the wig and frock-coat
> were the rivers, arterial rivers;
> were the mountains, on whose frayed wave
> the condor or the snow seemed fixed:
> there was humidity and thicket, thunder
> still without name, the planetary plains.

> ["**Love America,**" *A Lamp on this Earth*]

Here the opposition present throughout the long epic is established. The "wig and frock-coat" represent the conquerors, the Spaniards who will be the invading force in this primeval garden. They are the "after" and they are designated by artificial trappings—false hair and man-made clothing to hide the naked reality of the body—which clash with the Nature they penetrate. The "before" is the eternal inheritance of America, what is lasting and authentic, America's roots, its rivers, its mountains, the condor, the native bird of the Andes. The poet's "before" is even before the invasion of language to categorize and limit, by naming; there is thunder before there is the word to designate it and separate it from the primal unity. In Neruda's portrait, Nature predates not only "civilized," artificial and invading man, but also language, the vehicle of social organization.

The verse is free, matching the motion of creation, the palpitation of unrestricted existence. This sense of active creation is reinforced by the mixing of natural elements: the mountains are described in terms of water, a "frayed wave," and the condor, a symbol of flight, is related to snow and transformed into an immobile statue which seems to almost form part of the "frayed wave," awaiting its moment of creation to soar into space. In the *Residence* poems, Neruda's mixture of natural elements in his metaphors signified a world in disorder; here it signifies a world before man's order, and it takes on a positive value. The metaphorical confusion of elements heightens the sense of a world just awakening; the elements seem alive and express a sense of becoming in an almost pantheistic universe where there are no divisions, only flowing, all-encompassing oneness and unity.

To describe America's genesis, Neruda employs poetic techniques like those Whitman used in *Leaves of Grass,* which have their origin in the Hebraic poetry of the Bible: the use of constructive parallels, a system of thought balance in which a verse cannot stand alone, but is dependent on the following verse to complete its thought; rapid enumeration characteristic of inspired speech; reiteration in varying form, and extensive alliteration, both designed to produce rhythm within the free verse and an almost chanting, hypnotic quality to the lines. Neruda's choice of verbs is also worth noting. The poet says the rivers "were." He could have said "there were rivers," but instead he chooses to give the rivers independent being; they were, they existed, they had life. This verb choice makes the rivers alive and immediate. It transforms them into quivering veins that reflect the "before," the "In the beginning" theme.

The entire first section of the *Canto* is devoted to this "before," to the raw, untamed Nature of the American continent. It is perhaps Neruda's greatest Nature poetry:

A new perfume spread out and out
filling through every pore in the earth
the living lungs, turning them into smoke and
  fragrance.
Wild tobacco was lifting into dawn
its rosebush of imagined atmosphere.
As a spear, as a sword ending in fire,
corn came out: its slim vertical statue
lost its kernels and was born again,
its flour was broadcast, it cradled

dead bodies under its roots, and later
from its cradle it witnessed
the slow growth of the vegetal gods.

["**Vegetations,**" *A Lamp on this Earth*]

In these lines, Nature exists on its own, the long enumeration of the variety of American vegetation becoming reminiscent at times of Andrés Bello's neoclassical ode to the richness of the Americas. And Neruda's genesis is specifically American. In it, only the lands, the minerals, the reptiles, birds, and mammals of the Americas are described. What is striking, moreover, in this genesis is that God is absent from the vast panorama. The animals spring to life within a tropical or arid landscape; they display their strength and their beauty among vast rivers—the Amazon, the Orinoco—and many-hued skies. The condor, both king and assassin, lonely friar of the skies, hurricane among the birds of prey, flies on and on over sharp summits and rivers of shadow. Fireflies send down their droplets of phosphor. This unfolding of mineral riches, vast jungles, birds is an autonomous, unmotivated, undirected surge of life. No Jehovah orchestrates from above the explosion of natural forces.

The particular symbolic value given to Nature in the opening of the *Canto* is the poet's own personal vision. It is he who assigns it a positive value, even where its more violent aspects are portrayed, in order to then set up the contrast with the men of "wigs and frockcoats" who will violate it. And it is he who presents the unfolding of Nature independent of any theological origin. Nonetheless, this vision, while personal, is no longer always strictly lyrical in its projection of Nature. It does not reflect the poet's immediate emotional state, as did the chaotic ruins of the Orient in the *Residence* poems. Now the poet is able to transcend the actual in order to arrive at a sweeping historical vision in which virginal Nature is the genesis, the point of departure in the destiny of a continent, the matrix for the man of Nature, the indigenous man of America, its sole legitimate heir.

Only after the raw continent has been described and all its vegetation, animal population, rivers, and minerals have been enumerated does this man of Nature appear as a central force in the poem. He *is:*

like a vessel of clay it came,
this mineral race, man
carved out of stones and thin air,
clean like a drinking vessel, full of music.

["**The Men,**" *A Lamp on this Earth*]

Mayas, Incas, Araucanians, the Indian tribes of Mexico, Central America, and South America are listed one after another. Through the continual repetition of key images the poet makes it clear that the Indians are the only authentic possessors of the land. Earth, clay, air, copper, and stone are the raw elements of America, and these are also the key words used to designate the Indian. The male Indian is evoked as a "young warrior of shadow and copper," and the female as the maternal "nuptial plant . . . alligator mother, metallic dove" (**"Love America"**). Whether male or female, the indigenous American is described in earth tones; the copper of his body, the stone of his tools, artifacts, and cities, the earth from which he alone springs are metaphorically related to the strength or gentleness of America's native plants and animals. The Indian is the genuine offspring of Nature, the son of America; this authentic, indigenous, natural man is contrasted always with the inauthentic, artificial man of wigs and clothing, the rapacious invador, the *conquistador.*

We have noted that in Neruda's presentation of the Nature of the American continent, no divinity is present as the source of life. The same is true when man appears. Once again, it is in this fashion that Neruda's genesis departs from its Biblical model. In the Bible, as in the *Canto,* man is surrounded by mystery and fear, by vast forces he cannot control. But in the Bible man copes with the awe of Nature, of knowledge, of his own destiny by making a pact with God, a pact which—through Abraham, Noah, Moses—has to be clarified and renewed from time to time. The ensuing dialogue between man and God constitutes the central part of the Bible, both the Old and the New Testaments, and forms also the core of the Biblical interpretation of the universe. When man appears in Neruda's poem, however, Jehovah remains absent from the heavens. Neruda is not about to fall back on Christian eschatology and theology. Nonetheless, the poet knows that mistakes, even disasters, can occur when man no longer understands the huge forces that surround him. In his own personal and secular way, he intuitively grasps the Biblical message that the pact between man and the forces of Nature, History, Destiny has to be established and reestablished, written and reinforced, time and again.

Such a pact is at the center of section II of *Canto General.* The genesis of section I closes with the appearance of man, and section II brings forth the "I" of the poet in one of Neruda's most acclaimed works, *Heights of Macchu Picchu*:

> From the air to the air, like an empty net,
> I went among the streets and the atmosphere, arriving
> and saying good-bye, . . .

> [*Heights of Macchu Picchu,* I]

The poet, adopting the persona of the American man, walks among the ruins of the great Inca city, Machu Picchu, built high into the mountains near Cuzco in Peru as a last, and vain, retreat from the onslaught of the invading Spanish conquerors. It is a poem of symbolic death and of resurrection in which the poet himself participates as actor, beginning as a lonely voyager and ending with the manifestation of his full commitment to the collectivity, to the American indigenous people, their Indian roots, their past and their future.

Neruda had visited the Inca city in 1943. Unlike most other Indian ruins where only one or two individual structures, fragments of the whole, remain, Machu Picchu is a complete city. Hidden until one is virtually within the city itself, it suddenly appears, spreading before the viewer an entire urban landscape, tier on tier and row on row of terraced stone, an incredible sight to come upon in the remote and silent mountain terrain. One is compelled to imagine hordes of people going about their daily lives; it is this strong sense of human presence, even more than the vast stone, which strikes awe in the modern visitor to the city. Like others before and after him, Neruda in 1943 was open to this sense of awe and to the shadows of the city, whose mystery and allure penetrate in interstitial fashion. What sets Neruda apart is not his sensibility, his reaction to the contact with Machu Picchu—the city calls forth that response from everyone who sees it—but his ability to convert this personal experience into a collective rebirth for an entire people. *Heights of Macchu Picchu,* written in the same year he joined the Communist Party, is perhaps Neruda's finest blending of the lyrical with the epic.

The hero of the poem is the "I" of the narrator. The poet explores the cosmos, penetrates the earth to its secret chambers, ascends toward light from the roots through the stems of plants, identifies with the stones of the huge sacred city. The poet as primitive man, as prophet and, ultimately, as semi-divinity, soaring through space and through history, brings the reader with him on an incredible voyage, an adventure to the end of the earth. A strange poetic time machine allows the poet to swim upstream in the flow of time, finding Nature, man, history, visions of the future.

A similar kind of movement is also present, of course, in the Bible and in Dante's *Divine Comedy.* Yet once again, Neruda's poem achieves epic scope and majestic rhythm without embracing theology. The Bible and Dante's work are the only kind of epic poetry that could have been produced by a deeply religious people or man. *Heights of Macchu Picchu* is perhaps the only poetry that could have been produced by a poet who no longer believes in God; it may also be the only kind of poetry fully comprehensible to the readers of our time, of an era that has been described more than once as the "post-Christian era." A Bible without Jehovah, a *Divine Comedy* without Vergil, Beatrice, Satan, and the Trinity. This is the sort of epic and philosophical vision Neruda offers.

In this vision, the poet experiences a vertical descent into the heart of matter:

> I placed my forehead among the deep waves,
> I descended like a drop among the sulphurous peace,
> and, like a blind man, I went down back to the jasmine
> of mankind's worn-out primeval spring.
>
> [*Heights of Macchu Picchu,* II]

The attitude toward matter, the dark flow of time, the mysterious and violent spring of mankind is one thing that separates the poet from Dante. Neruda stresses what Dante chooses largely to ignore, the presence of matter, both inorganic and organic, as the inescapable reality. The poet touches stone, earth, roots, trees, rain, clouds, space. He is here, as elsewhere, the poet of "heroic matter," and each line, each metaphor brings this matter closer to human experience, specifically to human sexuality:

> deeper and deeper, in the gold of geology,
> like a sword wrapped in meteors,
> I sank my tempestuous sweet hand
> into the most genital recesses of the earth.
>
> [*Heights of Macchu Picchu,* II]

The tale that is slowly, serenely, majestically unfolded in Neruda's lines is the tale of the poet, alone, face to face with the vastness of matter. Dialogue is absent in this tale: we hear only the poet's voice, sometimes clearly, at other times muffled as in a dream or stream of consciousness. Both the Bible and Dante's work are, in contrast, rich in dialogue. Abraham, Noah, Job actually hear God's voice and respond to it, the patriarchs and prophets speak and are answered; Dante's dialogue with the inhabitants of the three vertically organized kingdoms fills out memorable pages of his book. Neruda, too, has his questions, but here, there is no God or gods beside him or above him. He will reach the high stone pinnacles of the sacred city, Machu Picchu, a city built by men to the greater glory of their gods, but the gods are departed. No mention is made of the divine forces that moved the Incas to haul huge stones in order to build the sacred city as a last refuge from the advance of the Spaniards and the religion they would impose. Only the stones remain, only an echo of the ancient fervor, the old faith.

Yet it would be a mistake to think that the poet's questions go unanswered. The dialogue between a poet and the world of matter, space, time cannot be defined except on terms established in the poem itself. In the *Book of Job,* God's answer to Job's anguished question is not the logical, expected one. Rather, God displays His awesome presence, His infinite power as a rebuke to the finite, ultimately self-centered questions Job asks. In Neruda's poem, the answer given is also in irrational or superrational language, an answer given by a Power that is at the same time the Power of Light and of Darkness:

> All-powerful death invited me many times:
> its words were like salt hidden in the waves
> and what its invisible fragrance suggested
> were fragments of wrecks and heights
> or vast structures of winds and snowdrifts.
>
> I had come to the steely edge of the blade, the narrowest
> channel of wind, the shroud of field and stone,
> the interstellar void of ultimate steps
> and the vertiginous spiral way:
> but not through wave on wave dost thou reach us,
>   thou vast sea of death
> yet rather like a gallop of twilight
> or like the comprehensible mathematics of the dark.
>
> [*Heights of Macchu Picchu,* II]

The poet can travel vast distances, dive into the deepest seas of matter and history, because he is a visionary poet, endowed with all the powers such poets have. In this particular case Neruda makes full use of a special sort of poetic language, one associated with the surrealist school, the only modern school of art and poetry that has tried to come to terms with infinity. We find constantly the jarring juxtaposition of nouns and adjectives that are unexpectedly brought together, the strange metaphors that create a link between two aspects of reality no one else thought could be similar.

The poet's magic boots have taken him first down into the earth, through seas of darkness. Now he will go up the ladder. Climbing, the poet goes through thickets toward the tall city rocked in a wind of thorns, the city that is like a spade buried in primordial sand, the city made out of stone and the foam of condors, the abandoned city where the grains of corn grew to the heavens to fall again like red hail, up where men trod the thinning mist. And the poet beckons his reader:

> Climb up with me, American love.
>
> Kiss these secret stones with me . . .
> Love, love, until the night full of cliffs,
> from the musical flint of the Andes
> descends toward the dawn's red knees,
> come out and contemplate the snow's blind son.
>
> [*Heights of Macchu Picchu,* VIII]

Echoes, sounds, chords, voices out of the mist come forth. There is a double presence of which we become aware, the overwhelming presence of Nature in all its power, and the ghostly presence of ancient men, of men who came to terms with Nature many centuries ago. Both presences fuse in a moment of love and recognition, and the past becomes as well the present. And here, the quasi-surrealist imagery of earlier verses gives way to a clear statement:

> Come to my very being, to my own dawn,
> climb toward crowned solitudes.

The fallen kingdom goes on living.

[*Heights of Macchu Picchu,* VIII]

And again:

We face a permanence: the stone, the word, endure:
the city upraised like a vase in our hands,
all the hands together, the living, the dead, the quiet,
death's fullness holds us here, a high wall, the full-
        ness
of so much life is like a blow falling
a blow of petals of flint, an enduring rose, a dwelling:
all this in a stone reef, in a glacier in the Andes.

[*Heights of Macchu Picchu,* VII]

What the poet finds in his vertical pilgrimage is not
God or the gods but something perhaps more moving,
the traces of a destroyed civilization, the ashes of a
ruined kingdom, its priests, its women, its children, its
slaves. Everywhere the footprints of man are present,
everywhere matter has been penetrated. Within a confusion of splendor and hope, the night of stone and hunger
recedes. It is no longer the wide rivers and the shiny
boulders of the first contact with Nature that occupy the
poet. Beneath each stone the poet now senses a presence from the past, the presence of a lost brother. And
the initial loneliness of the poem evolves toward
exhilaration and joy. The gods may have vanished, but
the presence of man endures. The ghosts invoked by
the poet are the humble ghosts of laborers, slaves,
everyday men and women:

John Splitstone, son of Wiracocha,
John Coldbody, heir of a green star,
John Barefoot, grandson to the turquoise,
come up to be reborn with me, as my own brother.

[*Heights of Macchu Picchu,* XI]

Come up to be born again, brother.
Give me your hand from the deep
recess of your scattered grief . . .
I am here to speak for your dead lips.

[*Heights of Macchu Picchu,* XII]

Identity and brotherhood are the key words of the
poem's climactic end. Only thus are the ancient ghosts
placated, not only the haunting figures of the ancient
dwellers of these American lands, but also the half-
seen, frightful ghosts of Neruda's *Residence* poems,
ghosts that were only a reflection, in a dark mirror, of
the poet's own isolation and despair.

Another word for "brotherhood" is "communion." Communion is identity, companionship within a common
goal. The future takes over, it overwhelms with its light
the dark night of the past. The poet has identified with
his ancestors, he *is* his ancestors. He asks them to link
their limbs, their memories, their lips, and from the bottom of a long night he listens to their voices as if he,

the poet, were anchored to their bodies. He wants to
hear every tale, every life story, step by step, he wants
to receive from their hands each one of their tools, their
knives, "a river of yellow sun rays," "a river of buried
tigers." He asks for tears, for silence, for water and
hope:

Give me the struggle, the iron, the volcanoes.
Cleave your bodies to mine like magnets.
Flow into my veins, into my mouth.
Speak through my words and through my blood.

[*Heights of Macchu Picchu,* XII]

In *Heights of Macchu Picchu,* the poet has come into
contact with death and with resurrection. It is the
kindling of an identification and a commitment of
solidarity with America's past, present, and future. It is
also a rebirth for Neruda's own poetic sytle. When the
poet is alone in the initial lines of this poem, the images are difficult, often depending on the radical
juxtaposition characteristic of surrealism. As the poet
moves toward his commitment to the collectivity,
however, as he calls out to common ancestors, he speaks
a language they can comprehend. The obscure and
unexpected imagery of the early lines then gives way to
the simple, easily understood language of Neruda's
later poetry, making *Heights of Macchu Picchu* the
death and regeneration as well of a form of poetic
expression. It is one of Neruda's most important works
of poetry. Like Neruda's days earlier in war-torn
Madrid, the visit to Machu Picchu and the poem it
inspired come close, on multiple levels, to achieving a
kind of mystical communion and rebirth of purpose.

Toward Veracruz a murderous wind is blowing.
It is there that horses are brought to the shore.
The ships are thick with claws
and with red beards from Castile.
There come the Arias, the Reyes, the Rojas and Mal-
        donados,
the sons of Castilian poverty,
the ones that knew about hunger in winter
and knew all about lice in country inns.

[**"They Arrive at the Mexican Sea,"** *The Conquistadors*]

Notes

1. Quoted by Selden Rodman, *Tongues of Falling
   Angels* (New York: Grove Press, 1975), p. 69-70.

2. Quoted by Emir Rodríguez Monegal, *El viajero
   inmóvil: introducción a Pablo Neruda.* (Buenos
   Aires: Losada, 1966), p. 142.

3. *Princeton Encyclopedia of Poetry and Poetics,* ed.
   Alex Preminger (Princeton: Princeton University
   Press, 1972), p. 242.

4. Rodríguez Monegal, p. 238ff.

5. *Satyricon,* Loeb Classics ed., p. 297.

6. *Princeton Encyclopedia*, p. 243.

7. Rodríguez Monegal, p. 235.

Enrico Mario Santí (essay date 1982)

SOURCE: Santí, Enrico Mario. "Prophecy of Writing." In *Pablo Neruda: The Poetics of Prophecy,* pp. 104-75. Ithaca, N.Y.: Cornell University Press, 1982.

[*In the following excerpt, Santí probes the relationship between* The Heights of Macchu Picchu *and the Western literary tradition of prophetic and allegorical verse.*]

Critics have often noted the strong Dantean echo in *Alturas* and throughout *Canto General,* but the exact implications of this relationship still await a reading that does not betray its complexity.[1] We should note, as a first step, that the echo of *Purgatorio,* the *cantica* of the celebration of art and of poetry, serves as a bridge for the poem's revision of literary history and alters retrospectively our perception of the first half of the poem. The events there, in which the speaker wanders through a dark forest of alienation and falls into a total descent, amount in effect to an analogue of the *Inferno.* In his famous prologue scene, we should recall, Dante dramatizes the bankruptcy of Neoplatonic philosophical ascents in the pilgrim's failure to climb, in a first attempt, "il dilettoso monte" (the delectable mountain). In Plato's *Republic,* for example, the philosopher is the one who knows, and his knowledge consists of realizing the deceptiveness of the flickering shadows on the sides of the cave. It is this knowledge that, for Plato, redeems the philosopher and defines his ascent as the unchaining of the mind from the fetters of the body. By having the pilgrim fail at this purely intellectual ascent, Dante in effect rewrites Plato's metaphoric or philosophical itinerary of the mind, thus requiring that it become an internal spiritual process, cleansed of all pride, as a descent or turning upside down of the earlier philosophical scheme.[2] The pilgrim's failed attempt is a fall into the wilderness or spiritual ruin, akin to Adam's, which Dante describes with the metaphorical scheme that Neruda exploits in his own poem: "mentre ch'i *ruinavo* in basso loco" (while I fell back to the lower place) (l. 61; my italics). In the *Purgatorio,* only after descending through the depths of Hell and emerging from its bottom, does the pilgrim ascend. The ascent, at this point in the allegory, signifies a moral purgation of the cardinal sins, which are inscribed, with seven *P's* (for *peccatum,* offense) on the pilgrim's forehead. Each of these letters, in turn, is erased as the pilgrim climbs, with the aid of several agents, the seven terraces of Mount Purgatory and at last gains the summit where the earthly paradise is lodged: "Qui fu inocente l'umana radice / qui primavera sempre ed ogni fruto" (Here the

human root was innocent / here was always spring and always fruit) (*Purgatorio,* XXVIII, ll. 142-43). It could be said that the two ascents, the abortive journey of the prologue and the successful climb of the *Purgatorio,* provide the dramatic underpinning of the entire *Commedia.* For, as Charles Singleton has shown, much of the poem's significance rests on the difference between the two attempts: one simply an ascent, the other an ascent that succeeds.[3]

We could regard Neruda's use of Dante as a condensed rearrangement of the *Commedia*'s three *cantiche.* Excluding the prologue, cantos II through V correspond to the descent of the *Inferno,* VI through IX to the ascent of the *Purgatorio,* and X through XII to the *Paradiso.* One need not press this general correspondence, of course, to realize that Neruda's poem principally refers to the *Purgatorio.* Besides being suggested in the reference to altitude in Neruda's title, the second *cantica* is suggested in the seven cantos that make up the latter half of the poem (cantos VI through XII), which evoke the seven terraces of Mount Purgatory. In both poems, Dante's and Neruda's, the ascent signifies the central experience of purgation; but the motives for the ascent differ. Whereas in the *Commedia* the pilgrim expiates the sins of moral blindness, in *Alturas* he atones for the errors of cultural alienation, a blindness that has kept him from seeing the true way of pre-Columbian origins. This difference explains each pilgrim's vision: Dante discovers, at the summit of Mount Purgatory, the Garden of Eden, while Neruda, high atop the Andes, looks upon a garden made of ruins, the spectacle of historical signs. Dante adopted the scheme of prophetic ascent both in reaction to earlier philosophical tradition and in borrowing from pertinent biblical passages and patristic tradition.[4] After Dante, of course, the tradition of ascent is so widespread that one need not refer to its original model. It includes, among others, the Renaissance ascents of Petrarch, St. John of the Cross, and Camões, the Romantic prospects in Rousseau, Wordsworth, Schiller, and Nietzsche, and the modern and postmodern versions by Thomas Mann and Jack Kerouac. It is clear, in any case, that *Alturas* belongs to this tradition and that it constitutes a modern, secular version of the *peregrinatio,* the parable of the Prodigal Son's long journey toward home, which M. H. Abrams describes as "an education in experience which culminates on the level of intellectual maturity . . . [and] in which the protagonist finally learns who he is, what he was born for and the implicit purpose of all he has endured on the way."[5]

Still, it is in reference to the *Purgatorio* that Neruda's revision achieves its greatest significance. The least obvious meaning, perhaps, is related to the rewriting of *Residencia en la tierra,* whose temporal argument now is amended by the pressures of purgatorial experience. Whereas time in *Residencia* dispersed the self into fragments that could be rescued only by an aesthetic project, the purgatorial scheme of **Alturas** posits a teleological thrust that lends time a moral urgency. Besides providing a "realm of possibility, where the spiral topography summarizes spiritual motives,"[6] purgatorial time translates the speaker into the human community, turning his aesthetic gratification to ethical care and his temporal fear to historical trust. Moreover, Neruda's use of Dante's topography obliquely makes Machu Picchu a site of earthly redemption. If we recall further details of Dante's imaginary geography, Mount Purgatory was an island at the farthest remove from Jerusalem, the city located at the center of the world according to the description of Ezekiel 5:5. In the medieval conception, the antipodes formed the diametrical obverse of the Northern Hemisphere and occupied a fourth, condemned space, separated from Adam and Christ by an impassable ocean, which did not fit the trinitary geography that was upheld by the church fathers. *Inferno* XXXIV, in particular, provides the geological allegory of the Southern Hemisphere's origin as the hollow made by the earth's flight as it sought to avoid contact with Satan during his fall. A mountain island was thus formed as the earth's bowels rushed upward toward the south, and there deposited, atop the only land in the lower hemisphere, the earthly paradise. Thus in a gesture ultimately intended as a metaphorical redemption of the antipodes, Dante locates Eden, the scene of man's fall, at a point directly opposite Jerusalem, the scene of man's redemption: "contraposto a quel che la gran secca / coverchia e sotto 'l cui colmo consunto / fu l'uom che nacque e visse senze pecca" (Opposite that where spreads the continent / of land, underneath whose meridian perished / The man who sinless came and sinless went).[7]

It takes no particularly scientific mind to deduce that what medieval geography called the antipodes is what today we know as the Western Hemisphere. As Edmundo O'Gorman has shown, in a definitive contribution to historiography, the antipodes were the mythical prefiguration of the New World, an *orbis alterius* whose existence was "invented" before it was actually discovered.[8] A trenchant revisionary pattern thus emerges with Neruda's metaphorical association of Machu Picchu with Purgatory. By locating in concrete space what in Dante is but a figure derived from theological tradition, Neruda confronts the West with its own otherness and makes it stumble upon the fiction it once expelled. Not only does this gesture have the effect of bringing paradise down to earth in order to show us, through a meditation on ruins, its necessarily historical meaning, but it rescues the very concept of "New World" from the stigma to which the antipodes doctrine condemned it. Machu Picchu's physical permanence goes beyond the redemption of an American space from theological

fallenness to dissolve the figurative opposition between Jerusalem and the earthly paradise within a scheme of concrete human history.[9]

Neruda's recourse to Dante, then, is intended both to exalt Machu Picchu and to emphasize the poem's redemptive act. This redemption takes place . . . within and through a dense network of texts that duplicates, at the level of reading, the historical revision proposed by the poem. For this reason it becomes all the more significant that critics who noted this strong Dantean echo should have suggested the influence of Rubén Darío's "Visión" (1907), an overtly Dantean poem that describes the symbolist poet's ascent to a realm of pure poetry.[10] In adducing this influence, Neruda's critics assumed Darío's mediation of Dante almost as if to suggest that one must justify the *Commedia*'s passage through Latin American literary history before taking note of Neruda's own statement. Juan Larrea, for example, thought Darío's echo so strong that he collated the two poems and denounced Neruda's virtual quotations as further proof of his betrayal of an Americanist sensibility.[11] Yet the link between the two poems, I submit, is part of a revisionary strategy that includes Darío's Romantic tradition as well as Dante. For contrary to Larrea's defense, Darío's poem eschews all geographical reference for a world of pure poetry in which the *Paradiso* represents the symbolist ideal of nonrepresentation. Larrea's defense of Darío on the precise grounds that his poem rejected becomes, in fact, all the more puzzling in view of the fact that Neruda's revision challenges Darío's nonmimetic reading by opposing the importance of the *Purgatorio* (the only one of the three *cantiche* that takes place in time) to the ostensible superiority of the *Paradiso*.[12]

It is not in reference to Darío, however, that we can best detect Neruda's challenge to Romanticism, but in reference to José María Heredia and his "En el teocalli de Cholula" (On the Pyramid of Cholula) (1820), whose synthesis of visionary perspective and lamentation over a ruin make it even more clearly an antecedent. The setting for Heredia's ode, a *locus classicus* of Americanist poetry, is a ruined pre-Columbian pyramid on which the poet sits in meditation. What begins as a pre-Romantic argument on the analogy of self and landscape soon turns into the typical Neoclassical tirade against tyranny and superstition. However much Heredia may have intended this poem as an allegory of contemporary Mexican politics, its focus on Indian ruins as the vehicle for abuse stigmatized them as the vestiges of a barbarous civilization whose time was past. Underlying Heredia's poem is a providential ideology that views the ruins as a lesson on pagan instincts and implicitly justifies the virtual annihilation of Indian culture that occurred during the Conquest. Even the most cursory comparison between the two poems reveals how Neruda inverts Heredia's prejudice in order to defend that culture's historical significance: "permanencia de piedra y de palabra" seems to be a distant response to Heredia's "Muda y desierta / ahora te ves, pirámide" (Silent and deserted / you find yourself now, pyramid) with which the ruins are condemned.[13]

Heredia's Christian argument is also heir to the providential vision that permeates much of the earlier poetry of ruins, in which the fall of Rome was seen as a sign of divine justice. Rodrigo Caro's "Canción," for example, ends with an invocation of San Geroncio, Itálica's prelate and martyr, a poignant ending that suggests that the ruins attest to God's wrathful vengeance. The same theme recurs in at least one other famous ruins poem, Juan de Arguijo's "A Cartago," which adduces a temporal parallel between the ruins' lesson on antiquity and their future witnessing of Christ's Second Coming.[14] This mixture of praise and moral condemnation generally reflects the Renaissance ambivalence toward the ancient past: its physical accomplishments were revered while its pagan values were condemned. But what on the surface appears to be mere thematic coincidence is actually the appearance of a major biblical topos, *occidit urbis,* the fall of the city, which not only clarifies Heredia's argument but provides a rhetorical clue to the prophetic message of *Alturas.* Ruins, in the Old Testament, symbolize God's retribution for Israel's transgression of its covenant as a chosen people. The prophets repeatedly interpret the physical devastation of Jerusalem, whether by military or natural disaster, as God's wrathful response to Israel's apostasy, to the spiritual waywardness that is manifest in its recurrent fall into idolatry. As the architectural metaphor stands throughout the Bible for confidence in God and obedience to his commands, so ruins symbolize Israel's waywardness and disobedience.[15] One can hardly exaggerate, then, the rhetorical importance of this imagery for the redemptive scheme of Neruda's poem. The ruins motif provides a discreet contrast between this biblical metaphor for apostasy and Machu Picchu's cultural faithfulness. Indeed, Machu Picchu's historical meaning lies precisely in the fact that it symbolizes cultural sameness, another meaning of the "permanence" invoked in canto VII. Though discreet, the difference is pointed enough to convey, within the poem's redemptive argument, both the undeserved punishment to which Machu Picchu was subjected and the profound injustice to which its inhabitants fell victim.

From the poetry of ruins, to Dante, to Heredia and Darío, to the Old Testament, the poem's revisionary scope thus coincides with the speaker's access to cultural self-awareness as a Latin American. One cannot miss the paradox inherent in this strategy as the Western library is called upon to represent, with all its authority, the unspoiled signs of pre-Columbian culture. How valid, one might ask, is the claim to Latin American self-awareness if it can be voiced only through Western literary traditions? Would not the adoption of these texts, as rhetorical strategies, signal instead a literary self-consciousness that preempts any such claim? If the pilgrim truly atones for cultural error, and if the literary revisions indeed constitute a conversion, how can such a densely allusive text become the vehicle for authentic change? None of these questions can be answered with the handy dialectical formulas of the "tradition and originality" type, for the poem poses nothing less than the possibility of subverting the imperialism of Western literary history. Nor can one ignore the truly problematic nature of these allusions. For if gaining access to Machu Picchu's meaning allows Latin America to wipe the slate clean of all Western prejudice and make a new beginning, then it would seem that the speaker's conversion ought to deny all Western signs, including the very allusions that form (and subvert) his own writing. When Neruda recalls his first visit to Machu Picchu and says that all other ruins seemed bookish in comparison, he implies that neither Machu Picchu nor his poem were bookish. But then why write an allegory, the most bookish or overtly fictional of literary texts?

Paradox, then, may well be the figure that describes the poem's rhetorical tension, its seemingly outrageous claim for cultural immediacy, but it is paradox, nevertheless, that lends coherence to its argument and forms the core of its statement on history. The answer (although not the solution) to this apparent impasse is provided by the next two cantos, in which the speaker, now converted to his new allegiance, takes up the task of translating the ruins' silent message. Indeed, translation seems to be the best description not only for the dramatic movement of the next two cantos, but for the speaker's insistence on seeing beyond the reified matter of the ruins and achieving a redemptive interpretation. The first step in this poetics of translation[16] is the summoning of "amor americano," Machu Picchu's genius of place. Neruda's alliterative name, we should note, poetically motivates the two words and valorizes *americano* through *amor.* More important, the series of imperatives throughout the canto, of which "sube" is the first, shifts the tone from passive description to restrained urgency. Whether the invitation to climb addresses only the genius of place or includes the speaker as well is left unclear. The ambiguity, at any rate, is significant. By using the present tense of the same verb that in canto VI was used in the present perfect ("Entonces en la escala de la tierra *he subido*") (I, 335), another instance of narrative disruption is suggested. This time, however, the shift in tense conveys the specifically temporal nature of the disruption, a distinction that in context emphasizes its link to the poem's cultural allegory. As the ruined landscape proved earlier to be a projection of the speaker's internal state, so now his pilgrimage turns out to be a necessary illusion—he has been there all along. That is, as an allegory the poem has unfolded an atemporal awareness of cultural values as a "successive mode capable of engendering duration."[17] The recurrent disruptions, of which this latest one is perhaps the most revealing, expose the illusionary quality of duration. And while such exposure may redefine the manner of the conversion, it does not invalidate what is ultimately an epistemological adjustment in the speaker. What it does threaten is the status of the cultural allegory, which is thereby implied to be just as illusionary. That is, the notion of process is retained symbolically despite the disappearance of the hierarchy of values and objectives.

Whatever the further implications of these disruptions may be, they occur as the speaker evokes, in the word's precise etymological sense of calling forth, the genius of place. And his second plea, "Besa conmigo las piedras secretas" (Kiss with me the secret stones) (I, 337), conveys the desire to decipher the ruins jointly. Similarly, the Urubamba River, the apostrophe to which dominates the canto, embodies the genius itself as it magically flies pollen back to its point of origin. The topos of *genius loci,* as Geoffrey Hartman has shown, is intrinsically related to "vision and prophecy: to determining the destiny of an individual or nation." Moreover, to invoke the genius of landscape prepares us, as we shall see, for "a deeper, ceremonial merging of the poet's spirit and the spirit of place."[18] The Urubamba is presented as a guardian genius and also, therefore, as a historian who, like the Muse of epic poetry, will disclose to the poet the history of the site. To this end the canto suggests the river's eloquence by setting up a contrast between its thunderous "plata torrencial" (torrential silver) and "sonoro pedernal andino" (sonorous Andean flint), on the one hand, and the "silencio del cajón serrano" (silence of the mountain strongbox), on the other (I, 337-38). Language, indeed the motivated language of poetry itself (as the lingering recurrence of "Amor, amor" suggests), constitutes the genius' infusing spirit, whose "minúscula vida," a pointed antidote to the earlier "pequeña muerte," the speaker summons for the first of two times in the canto. And as the apostrophe to the river—called Wilkamayu, its Indian name—is about to begin in the fifth stanza, he has already become the blind man ("el hijo ciego de la nieve" [the blind son of the snow]) (I, 338) anticipated in the prologue.

The apostrophe, in the next five stanzas, assumes this linguistic motif as part of the speaker's investigation into the causes of Machu Picchu's ruin:

> Oh, Wilkamayu de sonoros hilos,
> cuando rompes tus truenos lineales
> en blanca espuma, como herida nieve,
> cuando tu vendaval acantilado
> canta y castiga despertando al cielo,
> qué idioma traes a la oreja apenas
> desarraigada de tu espuma andina?

> Quién apresó el relámpago del frío
> y lo dejó en la altura encadenado,
> repartido en sus lágrimas glaciales,
> sacudido en sus rápidas espadas,
> golpeando sus estambres aguerridos,
> conducido en su cama de guerrero,
> sobresaltado en su final de roca?

> Qué dicen tus destellos acosados?
> Tu secreto relámpago rebelde
> antes viajó poblado de palabras?
> Quién va rompiendo sílabas heladas,
> idiomas negros, estandartes de oro,
> bocas profundas, gritos sometidos,
> en tus delgadas aguas arteriales?

> Quién va cortando párpados florales
> que vienen a mirar desde la tierra?
> Quién precipita los racimos muertos
> que bajan en tus manos de cascada
> a desgranar su noche desgranada
> en el carbón de la geología?

[I, 338-39]

O Wilkamayu of sonorous threads, / when you break your linear thunders / in white froth, like wounded snow, / when your steep storm / sings and punishes awaking the sky, / what language do you bring to the ear hardly / uprooted of your Andean froth? / Who imprisoned the lightning of the cool air / and left it chained on the height, / scattered about in its glacial tears, / shaken in its rapid swords, / striking its battle-scarred fabric, / led out in its warrior's bed, / assailed in its rock's end? / What do your vexed glimmers say? / Your secret, rebellious lightning, / did it once travel full of words? / Who's breaking frozen syllables, / black languages, gold standards, / deep mouths, subdued screams, / in your thin arterial waters? / Who's cutting down floral eyelids / that come to look from the ground? / Who rushes the dead clusters / that descend in your cascade's hands / to scatter their scattered night / in the coal of geology?

We must read this apostrophe in connection with the earlier references to silence as the speaker turns to the river in an effort to gather information that the ruins themselves cannot yield. By thus alternating inquiries into the river's eloquence with those into the site's violent past, the canto suggests a crucial link between language and historical reconstruction. And yet the Urubamba's embodiment of eloquence constitutes an analogy between language and the river's flow, which, like the movement of history itself, will not be arrested and must be understood in its ability to unsettle all stable meanings. For this reason the speaker gives up the goal of finding a specific culprit when he realizes that any attempt at historical reconstruction must face up to the precarious nature of such knowledge. More pointedly, he avoids the temptation of nostalgic idolatry ("no toques la frontera / ni adores la cabeza sumergida" [don't touch the facade / or revere the drowned head]), which would turn the Indian past into a mere fetish, and argues instead for an authentic temporality that faces up to the risks of historicity:

> deja que el tiempo cumpla su estatura
> en su salón de manantiales rotos,
> y, entre el agua veloz y las murallas,
> recoge el aire del desfiladero,
> las paralelas láminas del viento,
> el canal ciego de las cordilleras,
> el áspero saludo del rocío,
> y sube, flor a flor, por la espesura,
> pisando la serpiente despeñada.

[I, 339]

> let time accomplish its height / in its room of broken water, / and, between rapid water and the walls, / gather the canyon's air, / the wind's parallel layers, / the blind channel of the mountain range, / the dew's rough greeting, / and arise, flower by flower, through the thickness, / trampling the flung serpent.

To time's erosion the speaker opposes time's own sediment, the cumulative layering that yields, metaphorically at least, Machu Picchu's "stature." Physical decay, that is, cannot be divorced from historical significance because ruins are the place where matter and morality interact. It is therefore to the narrow space somewhere between the river's eloquence and the walls' silence ("entre el agua veloz y las murallas") that the speaker directs the genius of place in a second summons to climb. This second summoning parallels the later imperative in the penultimate stanza,

> Ven a mi propio ser, al alba mía,
> hasta las soledades coronadas.
> El reino muerto vive todavía.

[I, 339]

> Come to my own being, to the dawn of me, / up to the crowned solitudes. / The dead kingdom still lives,

which urges the genius of place to join in the poet's rebirth. One cannot simply gloss over this climax. Poetic renewal is shown here to coincide with the last stage in the poetics of translation, a self-investiture that can be described only as a linguistic access to prophecy. Like the singer amid mute objects in **"Galope muerto,"** the prophet sets out to speak on behalf of the ruins, even as the specter of death, symbolized by the condor, threatens to cut that project short: "Y en el Reloj la sombra sanguinaria / del cóndor cruza como una nave negra" (And in the Clock the bloody shadow / of the condor crosses like a black ship) (I, 339). The symbolic bird was prefigured in cantos III and V, but its ominous reappearance against the background of the allegorical "Reloj" harks farther back, to the temporal anxieties of *Residencia en la tierra*. Besides giving a sense of urgency to the prophet's task, the bird's appearance at this juncture serves to demystify any illusions of immortality that might have been implanted by the preceding self-investiture.

It is at this point, then, that canto IX, the intriguing catalogue that Larrea disliked, completes the ecphrastic sequence of cantos VII and VIII. If we have in fact identified in this sequence the various stages of a poetics of translation, then canto IX must be its resulting text. The paratactic catalogue of nominal phrases, especially following a prophetic summoning, suggests a kind of mantic song flowing from a state of ecstasy. Moreover, as Felstiner notes, many of the words in the canto—*ciega, escala, párpado, polen, serpiente, rosa, manantial, muralla,* and so on—are taken from the earlier narrative, as if in an attempt to gather scattered fragments.[19] The catalogue thus translates silence onto poetic presence in the form of a series of descriptions which amounts to a metaphorical reconstruction of the city. The compacting of eighty-one metaphors into one single column, as if it were a stone block, creates a spatial illusion that attests to the translation's success. We cannot miss the specifically visual effect of this ecphrastic mimesis, the result of writing or script (as opposed to the effect of a voice) which in turn depends on the experience of reading. It is the writing/reading metaphor that ultimately guarantees the indelibility of the ruins' message. Instead of merely speaking for them, the prophet now *writes* on their behalf: *verba volant, scripta manent* (words fly, writings remain).

The implications of this metaphor are crucial. In terms of the poem's statement on history, it signals Machu Picchu's access to Western consciousness as embodied in the institution of writing and its role in the production of historical record. Such access reverses in effect the historical obliteration of Inca culture, which, unlike its Mesoamerican counterparts, had no system of writing. Moreover, the poem shows this historical access to be linked to a process of translation by which the past is transformed, with all its attendant revisions, into the present. It is the act of translation, in fact, that provides the culmination to the earlier revision of literary history by becoming the figure that adopts Western signs as part of a new beginning. And yet it would be naive simply to assume this metaphor as a recuperative process—a healing agency, that is—whose access to historical consciousness would render the ruins present. On the contrary, writing and history appear to be linked in the poem in their common erosion of unmediated presence. Canto IX, in this sense, constitutes a turn against referentiality, against the reality of the ruins, which signals textual autonomy. Not only does the language of the canto violate (as Larrea aptly complained) both empirical reality and cultural propriety, but it offers a verbal analogue whose formal qualities compete with the real Machu Picchu. Besides providing an impeccable ecphrasis, for example, the canto occupies a position in the poem which corresponds to the midpoint of the ascent, halfway between the initial encounter in canto VI and the end of the poem in canto XII. In addition, were we to pursue the specific echo of Dante we would find that, besides alluding to the magical number associated with Beatrice in *La vita nuova,* the ninth canto corresponds to the midpoint of Dante's own ascent, the fourth terrace of Purgatory, where the cardinal sin of acedia or spiritual sloth is cleansed. Acedia, which in Dante means spiritual sloth due to insufficiency of love, is the medieval name for melancholy, which was the "fuel" of prophetic vision in the poetics of *Residencia en la tierra.*[20] Thus the oblique allusion to *Residencia* within the context of the new poetics of translation itself involves a discreet rewriting that raises the canto above its empirical source.

It is on writing as spacing, then, on the irruptive and irreducible marks that displace presence and significance, that the poem's writing metaphor rests. The poem's translation of silence into language, of historical obliteration into consciousness, itself deconstructs those Western metaphysical assumptions that underlie such concepts as translation and consciousness. Writing as spatial difference, that is, exposes the sign's inherent lack and its need to be supplemented by an endless chain of other signs. And far from being confined to the ecphrasis of canto IX, spacing is everywhere implied by the poem's allegory, which observes a code *outside* the text, as well as by its dense allusive texture, as if supplementing its own ontological lack through other literary texts.[21] It is the difference implied, finally, by the very title of the poem, which not only changes *ruinas* to *alturas,* but also changes *Machu* to *Macchu,* Neruda's own spelling for the Quechua word for "old."

Starting with the poem's publication in 1946 and throughout all four editions of his *Obras Completas,* Neruda ignored the traditional spelling and wrote the name of the site with four *c*'s instead of three. Critics have noticed, though never explained, the unorthodox spelling, and recently it so disturbed one Chilean scholar in particular that, in an edited anthology of poems about Machu Picchu, he changed it to make it conform to the traditional spelling employed by the other authors.[22] No Quechua dictionary, to be sure, recognizes Neruda's spelling. And while anthropologists report that there are several variants for the orthography of *picchu,* they note a single and consistent one for *machu.*[23]

My point has less to do with the need to observe a "correct" spelling than with this error, so to speak, as an index of the poem's writing metaphor. Neruda's rewriting, we should note, improves visually an otherwise unsymmetrical name. The extra letter in the first word (Machu) supplies a typographical symmetry which, besides conveying a cognate link, points to a numerical correspondence between the twelve letters of the new title and the poem's twelve cantos. As such, the altered name reflects a cosmic balance similar to that of an hourly or monthly cycle and thereby attempts

to correct the imbalance of the traditional spelling. In so doing, the new spelling unwittingly mirrors and magnifies the arbitrariness that subverts all attempts to transcribe the sounds of any Amerindian language. In fact, it would be a mistake to speak of a "misspelling," for what is involved here is the very basis of determining Machu Picchu's "proper" name and, beyond that, of the "proper" in general. Indeed, Neruda's disrupting orthography may be but one more turn in the ongoing controversy surrounding the name "Machu Picchu," which anthropologists have long suspected to be a misnomer.[24] By thus suspending semantic depth, by becoming a nonsign of the impossibility of significance, the supplementary letter short-circuits referentiality and points to a *different* place. More crucial still, the extra *c* can be nothing but a written sign, an inaudible mark (at least in Spanish pronunciation) which must be read, experienced visually, in writing, not unlike the column of metaphors in the ninth canto. The extra letter constitutes the pure movement of differentiation with which writing displaces presence, empirical experience, and which results in a disjunction, a *décalage* of referentiality, the gap that Larrea attempted to close in his violent rewriting.

We may regard the final three cantos as enacting the consequences of this writing metaphor. In the tenth canto, for example, after the subversion of Machu Picchu's presence, the speaker undertakes a radical demystification of the ruins. In language that recalls the first half of the poem, he questions whether the original inhabitants could have escaped the alienation he endured then:

> Fuiste también el pedacito roto
> de hombre inconcluso, de águila vacía
> que por las calles de hoy, que por las huellas,
> que por las hojas de otoño muerto
> va machacando el alma hasta la tumba?
> La pobre mano, el pie, la pobre vida . . .
> Los días de luz deshilachada
> en ti, como la lluvia
> sobre las banderillas de la fiesta,
> dieron pétalo a pétalo de su alimento oscuro
> en la boca vacía?
>   Hambre, coral del hombre,
> hambre, planta secreta, raíz de los leñadores,
> hambre, subió tu raya de arrecife
> hasta esta altas torres desprendidas?

> [I, 341]

Were you also the little broken piece / of inconclusive man, of empty eagle / which through today's streets, through the tracks, / through dead autumn's leaves / goes on crushing the soul to the grave? / The poor hand, the foot, the poor life . . . / Did the days of tattered light / in you, like rain / over feast-day banners, / give petal by petal of its dark food / in the empty mouth? / Hunger, human coral, / hunger, secret plant, woodcutters' root, / hunger, did your line of reefs climb up / to these high disjointed towers?

The apostrophe marks a stage of unillusioned awareness of human limits beyond the promises of history, as if the speaker attempted to ward off the delusions of cultural discovery that are sustained by the allegory. Besides posing Machu Picchu's significance in terms of death, the profuse self-quotations in the first stanza therefore amount to yet another exposure that unmasks the successive illusions of allegorical discourse. While the adjectives in "águila vacía" and "luz deshilachada," for example, recall salient images of the prologue, other phrases—"calles de hoy," "hojas del otoño muerto," "machacando el alma" virtually quote from the descriptions of an urban wasteland in the second canto. This unmasking of temporal duration culminates in "Hambre, coral del hombre," a line whose pun exposes the uncanny closeness of human nature to human lack beyond historical redemption. The self-quotations thus dramatize, at the level of reading, the speaker's demystified awareness of history. As the allegory is once again shown to be of fictive duration, history is exposed as the (albeit necessary) illusion of progress. For this reason, "hambre," human lack and desire, becomes the recurrent metaphor for demystified knowledge throughout the speaker's interrogation, which seeks to acquire factual knowledge beyond the distorting laws of archaeology.

Whether in fact the ruins harbor this knowledge remains an open question, as demonstrated by the suspension of an answer at the end of canto X and the opening lines of canto XI, which abandon the issue altogether:

> A través del confuso esplendor,
> a través de la noche de piedra, déjame hundir la mano
> y deja que en mí palpite, como un ave mil años pri
> sionera,
> el viejo corazón del olvidado!
> Déjame olvidar hoy esta dicha, que es más ancha que
> el mar,
> porque el hombre es más ancho que el mar y que sus
> islas,
> y hay que caer en él como en un pozo para salir del
> fondo
> con un ramo de agua secreta y de verdades sumergi
> das.
> Déjame olvidar, ancha piedra, la proporción ponde
> rosa,
> la trascendente medida, las piedras del panal
> y de la escuadra, déjame hoy resbalar
> la mano sobre la hipotenusa de áspera sangre y cilico.

[I, 342]

Through the confused splendor, / through the night of stone, let me plunge my hand / and let beat in me, like a bird a thousand years imprisoned, / the old heart of the forgotten! / Today let me forget this happiness, which is wider than the sea, / because man himself is wider than the sea and its islands, / and one must fall in it as in a well in order to emerge from the bottom / with a branch of secret water and submerged truths. / Let me forget, wide stone, the powerful proportion, /

the transcendent measure, the honeycomb stones / and those cut square, today let me slip / my hand over the hypotenuse of rough blood and silicon.

The speaker plunges his hand, thus repeating the prologue ("hundí la mano turbulenta y dulce"), into "confuso esplendor," the metaphor for his own perplexity, as if leaping over the conceptual problems that are entailed in the preceding demystification for the sake of identifying with the ancient past. Except that by this point in the allegory that past has been acknowledged to be death itself, a meaning hinted at in the simile "como un *ave* mil años prisionera." Further details in the canto emphasize the subtle use of the symbol here, but we must for the moment read this acknowledgment within the context of a renunciation. The tone of the passage is one of imperative pleading, as if the speaker were struggling to wrench himself from the opposite extremes of skepticism and self-deception. The imperatives, for example, signal in succession his renunciation of both a demystified questioning and the ruins' aesthetic lure, while their respective objects ("*hundir* la mano," "*resbalar* la mano") mark the identity and difference between the two gestures. Halfway between, as if pointing to the space of the allegory, an overt allusion to Dante's inverted route from the bottom of Hell to the entrance of Mount Purgatory accounts for both.[25] Its strategic placement, within the context of renunciation, conveys the intermediate position that the poem assumes in regard to both mythical faith and demystified knowledge.

The poem opts, instead, in a profoundly dialectical move, for the alternative of a vision:

> Cuando como una herradura de élitros rojos, el cóndor
> furibundo
> me golpea las sienes en el orden del vuelo
> y el huracán de plumas carniceras barre el polvo som
> brío
> de las escalinatas diagonales, no veo a la bestia veloz,
> no veo el ciego ciclo de sus garras,
> veo el antiguo ser, servidor, el dormido
> en los campos, veo un cuerpo, mil cuerpos, un hom
> bre, mil mujeres
> bajo la racha negra, negros de lluvia y noche,
> con la piedra pesada de la estatua:
> Juan Cortapiedras, hijo de Wiracocha,
> Juan Comefrío, hijo de estrella verde,
> Juan Piesdescalzos, nieto de la turquesa,
> sube a nacer conmigo, hermano.

[I, 342-43]

When, like a horseshoe of red wing cases, the furious condor / batters my temples in his flight / and the hurricane of butcher feathers sweeps the somber dust / of the diagonal stairways, I don't see the nimble bird, / I don't see the blind cycle of its talons, / I see the ancient being, servant, the sleeper / in the fields, I see a body, a thousand bodies, one man, a thousand women, / under the black gust, black with rain and night, / with the statue's heavy stone: / Juan Stonecutter, son of Wiracocha, / Juan Coldeater, son of green star, / Juan Barefoot, grandson of the turquoise, / rise and be born with me, my brother.

The condor's assault, which has been threatened since the end of the eighth canto, fuses this negative symbol with the positive implications of the metaphor. The entire passage is made up of a single sentence whose initial adverb ("Cuando") dominates the temporal significance of the bird's beating against the speaker's temples—the site of poetic imagination. The attendant storm, moreover, casts the contest as a cosmic struggle that is resolved in the speaker's inability to see the assailant and later in his vision of a massive resurrection. One must note that the specific terms of the resolution—the poem's insistence on demonstrating a shift in the speaker's perception—do not allow for a simple reversal of terms: it is not so much that death becomes transubstantiated, in the precise sense of changing into a mystical body, as that the speaker can no longer recognize it as death. What suggests this change is the language employed in the description, which, in addition to emphasizing the specifically visual character of the scene, conveys a revision of **Residencia** in the discarded images of "polvo sombrío" and "ciego ciclo." The resurrection must be understood, then, as a trick of vision stemming from the meditation on death, a death that, though authentically acknowledged, is nonetheless transcended for the explicit purpose of yielding a poetic statement on history. In a move clearly designed to disclose the fictionality that permeates the canto, the speaker assigns allergorical surnames to the resurrected, who are thus born in the poet's naming.

The last canto in particular upholds this acknowledgment of death by forestalling any idealized return of the dead in the series of "No volverás" (You will not return). The renewed summons to rise and be born ("Sube a nacer conmigo, hermano") therefore refers to their future existence in language and, more specifically, in writing. As the dead extend their hands "desde la profunda zona" (from the depths) and look upon the speaker "desde el fondo de la tierra" (from the bottom of the earth), the symbolic nature of their kinship is further reinforced. This figurative meaning reaches a first climax in the image of "copa de esta nueva vida" (cup of this new life), which identifies the poem as a testament designed to redeem all the suffering endured in the convulsions of history. The Christian resonance of the image echoes the earlier "copa negra" (I, 173) and the "vaso" (I, 337), both of which prefigure this "copa," in addition to anticipating the more pointed "os crucificaron" (they crucified thee) later in the same stanza.[26] By the time the prophet announces, in a second climax, "Yo vengo a hablar por vuestra boca muerta" (I am going to speak through your dead mouth), we must view this "vocalization," as Rodríguez Monegal sug-

gests, in its precise sense of *vox populi,* a commonplace figure that enhances the text's rhetorical presence.[27] This speech takes place, moreover, on behalf of the dead ("boca *muerta,*") an acknowledgment that is reinforced by later references to "silenciosos labios" (silent lips) and the recurrent "desde el fondo." As Felstiner notes, by this time the prophet has literally become a translator of silence and death.[28]

As the poem is brought to a close, once the prophet has suffered the victim's history, he sees himself as iron that is drawn to the magnetic dead: "Apegadme los cuerpos como imanes" (Let your bodies stick to me like magnets) (I, 334). The metaphor implicitly valorizes the poem's discourse as the fulcrum for otherwise scattered fragments. The elements of the last two lines, which invoke the speaker's blood and mouth, are inversely related, as if conjuring the figure of the cross, the ultimate sacrificial symbol, in the covenant with which the poem ends: "Acudid a mis venas y a mi boca. / Hablad por mis palabras y mi sangre" (Succour my veins and my mouth. / Speak through my words and my blood) (I, 344).

Notes

1. See Goić, *"Alturas de Macchu Picchu,"* p. 155. Roberto Fernández Retamar noted the Dantean echo in his "Prologue" to Pablo Neruda, *Poesias* (Havana: Casa de las Américas, 1965). Perhaps the earliest to notice the presence of Dante was Sarandy Cabrera, "Primera teoría del *Canto General,"* *Número,* 13-14 (1951), 189-95.

2. For this background see John Freccero, "Dante's Prologue Scene," *Dante Studies,* 84 (1966), 1-25. Giuseppe Mazzotta argues that Dante's detour from the abstractions of Neoplatonism must in addition be read in relation to the turn to history that is signaled by the pilgrim's encounter with Vergil and the historical world of the Aeneid. See *Dante, Poet of the Desert: History and Allegory in the Divine Comedy* (Princeton: Princeton University Press, 1979), pp. 152-57.

3. *"De exitu Israel de Aegypto,"* in *Dante: A Collection of Critical Essays,* ed. John Freccero (Englewood Cliffs, N.J.: Prentice-Hall, 1970), p. 110.

4. For Dante's biblical sources see Carol V. Kaske, "Mount Sinai and Dante's Mount Purgatory," *Dante Studies,* 89 (1971), 1-18.

5. *Natural Supernaturalism: Tradition and Revolution in Romantic Literature* (New York: Norton, 1971), pp. 193-94. For a partial reading of the tradition of ascent, see Marjorie H. Nicolson, *Mountain Gloom and Mountain Glory* (Ithaca: Cornell University Press, 1959).

6. Ricardo J. Quiñones, *The Renaissance Discovery of Time* (Cambridge: Harvard University Press, 1972), p. 72.

7. I quote from *La Divina Commedia,* ed. C. H. Grandgent and rev. Charles S. Singleton (Cambridge: Harvard University Press, 1972), p. 307. For the sources of Dante's geographical/logical allegory, see John G. Demaray, *The Invention of Dante's Commedia* (New Haven: Yale University Press, 1974), pp. 154-68; Rodolfo Bernini, "Origine, sito, forma e dimensioni del Monte del Purgatorio e dell'Inferno dantesco," *Rendiconti della Reale Accademia di Lincei,* 5th ser., 25 (1916), 1015-1129; and Edward R. Moore, "The Geography of Dante," in *Studies of Dante,* 3d ser., *Miscellaneous Essays* (1903; rpt. New York: Greenwood Press, 1968), pp. 109-43.

8. *The Invention of America: An Inquiry into the Historical Nature of the New World* (Bloomington: Indiana University Press, 1961).

9. It could be shown, of course, that Neruda's text remains partially blind to Dante's own historical interpretation of Eden, which in *Purgatorio* appears as "a place of radical ambiguity . . . that shatters its seemingly idyllic quality" (Mazzotta, *Dante,* p. 114).

10. The echo of Darío is mentioned by Goić, "*Alturas de Macchu Picchu,*" p. 155, and Larrea, *Del surrealismo,* pp. 176-79. The text of the poem appears in Rubén Darío, *Poesías Completas,* ed. Alfonso Méndez Plancarte and Antonio Oliver Belmás (Madrid: Aguilar, 1968), pp. 720-22.

11. Larrea, *Del surrealismo a Machupicchu,* pp. 179.

12. Ibid., p. 178. Larrea, moreover, grants Darío the revision of Dante which he denies Neruda (see p. 176). But in doing so he reveals that his reading of Darío is colored by his reading of Neruda.

13. José María Heredia, *Poesías completas,* ed. Angel Aparicio Laurencio (Miami: Universal, 1970), p. 195.

14. See Elias Rivers, ed. *Renaissance and Baroque Poetry of Spain,* pp. 350-51; and Juan de Arguijo's sonnet: "Ejemplo cierto fue en la edad pasada, / y será fiel testigo a la futura, / del fin que ha de tener la más segura / Pujanza vanamente confiada" (True example it was in times gone by, / and will be faithful witness in future times, / to the end that awaits the surest / ambition, vainly self-confident) (p. 143).

15. For a striking contrast see Isaiah 28:16 ("Behold, I lay in Zion for a foundation, a stone, a tried stone, a precious corner stone, a sure foundation: he that believeth shall not make haste"), in contrast to Isaiah 25:2 ("For thou hast made of a city an heap; of a defenced city a ruin, a palace of strangers to be no city"). "The foundation stone," according to J. Lindblom, "means confidence in Yaweh, the walls mean justice and confidence and righteousness. . . . Those who understood and practised this religion would be saved from ruin, while the "scoffers,' those who made lies their refuge, would perish" (*Prophecy in Ancient Israel* [Philadelphia: Fortress Press, 1962], pp. 342-43). For a different reading in terms of the theme of *fiat justitia, pereat mundus,* see Abraham J. Heschel, *The Prophets* (New York: Harper & Row, 1955), pp. 279-306. The motif appears in both St. Augustine (*The City of God,* XV, 4) and Orosius (*History against the Pagans,* V, i) as a scheme of salvation history. More recently it reappears as a political metaphor. See especially C. F. Volney, *Les ruines, ou Méditations sur les révolutions des empires* (1791), and the examples cited in Goldstein, *Ruins and Empire.*

16. I borrow the term from John Freccero, "Medusa: The Letter and the Spirit," *Yearbook of Italian Studies,* 1 (Florence, 1962), 17, who uses it in contrast to a "poetics of reification."

17. De Man, "Rhetoric of Temporality," p. 207.

18. "Romantic Poetry and the Genius Loci," in *Beyond Formalism: Literary Essays, 1958-1970* (New Haven: Yale University Press, 1970), pp. 314-22.

19. John Felstiner, *Translating Neruda,* p. 180.

20. See Fritz Saxl, Erwin Panofsky, and Raymond Klibansky, *Saturn and Melancholy* (London: Thomas Nelson, 1964), pp. 75-81, for a discussion of the medieval view of melancholy, based primarily on St. Thomas (*Summa Theologiae,* Prima, q. lxiii, art. 2). In *Purgatorio,* the fourth terrace corresponds to Canto XVIII, where the slothful are made to run continually around the terrace. For the mystic significance that Dante attaches to the number 9 (the square of 3, or the Trinity), see *La vita nuova,* especially sections 2 and 3: *The Portable Dante,* ed. Paolo Milano (New York: Viking Press, 1947), pp. 547-51.

21. For this view of writing as spacing see Jacques Derrida, *Positions,* trans. Alan Bass (1972; Chicago: University of Chicago Press, 1981): "This interweaving, this textile, is the *text* produced only in the transformation of another text. . . . Spacing designates *nothing,* nothing that is, no presence at a distance; it is the index of an irreducible exterior, and at the same time of a *movement,* a displacement that indicates an irreducible alterity" (pp. 26, 81). The term "allegory" itself designates a discourse of otherness

(from Greek *allos,* other, and *agouerein,* to say), as defined by Isidore of Seville: "Nam allegoria dicitur ab *alleon,* graece, quod in latinum dicitur *alienum*" (Allegory comes from the Greek *alleon,* what in Latin is said as *alienum,* other) (*Etymologiarum sive Originem Libri XX,* ed. W. M. Lindsay [Oxford: Clarendon, 1966], I, xxxviii, 220. For a brilliant discussion of the affinity of writing and allegory in terms of a "play of otherness," see Benjamin, *Origin of German Tragic Drama,* pp. 159-67.

22. See *Machu Picchu en la poesía,* ed. Hugo Montes (Santiago de Chile: Nueva Universidad, 1972). Pring-Mill adds: "The proper spelling of the place name is 'Machu Picchu,' since the first word does not contain the Quechua guttural represented by the second *c* of Picchu" (*Pablo Neruda: A Basic Anthology,* [Oxford: Dolphin, 1975], p. xxxiii).

23. Luis E. Valcárcel, *Machu Picchu* (Buenos Aires: Eudeba, 1964), p. 7. The name in Quechua means the fully grown or old peak, in distinction to Huayna Picchu, the half-grown or young peak, which stands alongside the site of the ruins. In current use *machu* and *huayna* mean grandfather and young man, respectively, and are also used figuratively as comparative terms to distinguish visually the height of Andean peaks.

24. For a meditation on the "proper name" as the sign of deceptive self-presence, see Jacques Derrida, *Of Grammatology,* trans. Gayatri Chakravorty Spivak (1967; Baltimore: Johns Hopkins University Press, 1976), pp. 101-18. According to Hiram Bingham, the ruins took the name of the mountain "because when we found them no one knew what to call them" (*The Lost City of the Incas* [New York: Duell, Sloan, 1948], p. viii). This "misnomer theory," so to speak, has been challenged by José Uriel García [see "Machu-Picchu" *Cuadernos Americanos,* 106 (1961), 161-251], who cites both the testimony of French archaeologist Charles Wiener (in his *Pérou et Bolivie* [Paris: Hachette, 1880]) and an eighteenth-century notarial record to uphold the ancient name. Still, neither document settles the crucial issue of whether the name refers to the ruins or the mountain, and Uriel García is forced to admit, in reference to the motley group of witnesses who figure in the latter document: "One wonders whether all these people truly knew about the marvelous, hidden, dead city" (p. 180). It is interesting to note that Neruda visited Machu Picchu in the company of Uriel García, then a senator from Cuzco, as he states in the interview "Pablo Neruda habla," *El Siglo* (Santiago de Chile), December 5, 1943, p. 12. The two must have known each other at least since 1939, when Neruda spoke at a dinner in his honor:

"Discurso en homenaje a Uriel García," *Qué Hubo* (Santiago de Chile) 30 (January 2, 1940). For a revealing discussion of Uriel García's possible influence on Neruda, see Felstiner, *Translating Neruda,* pp. 143-44. Uriel García's essay seems to have been part of a series that included "Sumas para la historia de Cuzco I-III," in *Cuadernos Americanos,* 104 (1959), 133-51, 140-61, and 152-86. The challenge to this "misnomer theory" has been taken up anew by Simone Waisbard, *Machu Picchu: Cité perdue des Incas* (Paris: Robert Laffont, 1974), pp. 155-64, published in English as *The Mysteries of Machu Picchu* (New York: Avon, 1974), pp. 121-29.

25. See especially *Inferno XXXIV.* For a discussion of inversion as a metaphor of knowledge, see John Freccero, "Infernal Inversion and Christian Conversion (*Inferno XXXIV*)," *Italica,* 42 (1965), 35-41.

26. The source of this image is Christ's words in Luke 22:20: "Esta copa es el nuevo pacto en mi sangre que por vosotros se derrama" (This cup is the new testament in my blood, which is shed for you). This passage is also part of the Eucharist liturgy in the Catholic mass.

27. See *Neruda: El viajero inmóvil,* pp. 455-63. For the pertinence of the topic, see Walter J. Ong, *The Presence of the Word* (New Haven: Yale University Press, 1967), pp. 180-92.

28. *Translating Neruda,* p. 178.

Bibliography

Books

Benjamin, Walter. *The Origin of German Tragic Drama.* Trans. John Osborne. 1928; London: NLB, 1977.

Felstiner, John. *Translating Neruda: The Way to Macchu Picchu.* Stanford: Stanford University Press, 1980.

Goldstein, Laurence. *Ruins and Empire: The Evolution of a Theme in Augustan and Romantic Literature.* Pittsburgh: University of Pittsburgh Press, 1977.

Larrea, Juan. *Del surrealismo a Machupicchu.* Mexico City: Joaquín Mortiz, 1967.

Rivers, Elias, ed. *Renaissance and Baroque Poetry of Spain.* New York: Dell, 1965.

Rodríguez Monegal, Emir. *Neruda: El viajero inmóvil.* 1966; 2d rev. ed. Caracas: Monte Avila, 1977.

Essays and Articles

Goić, Cedomil. "*Alturas de Macchu Picchu*: La torre y el abismo." *Anales de la Universidad de Chile,* 157-60 (1971), 153-66.

Man, Paul de. "The Rhetoric of Temporality." In *Interpretation: Theory and Practice,* ed. Charles S. Singleton, pp. 173-209. Baltimore: Johns Hopkins University Press, 1969.

Marjorie Agosin (essay date 1986)

SOURCE: Agosin, Marjorie. "*Canto General*: The Word and the Song of America." In *Pablo Neruda*, pp. 58-74. Boston: Twayne Publishers, 1986.

[*In the following excerpt, Agosin concentrates on the theme of death temporarily transcended through brotherhood in* The Heights of Macchu Picchu *and calls the poem a turning point in Neruda's poetic career.*]

The pre-Columbian genesis with the earth and men that emerge from it are the protagonists of the first section of the *Canto general.* In the second, and perhaps the most important section of the *Canto,* there is a change in the cast of characters. Now it is the poet, the lyrical speaker, who narrates from the perspective of his own emotion and from his own chaos. These sections constitute a founding voice of an American reality.

Several motifs predominate throughout this poem that alone could be a self-sufficient unit. From cantos 1 through 5 the lyrical I appears as a traveler or pilgrim who speaks of a past. According to the majority of critics, the awareness of this past is linked to all the earlier poetry of Neruda, especially the *Residence* cycle. The tone of these initial verses transports us back to a past recently traversed and then speaks of a new present:

> Del AIRE al AIRE, como una red vacía,
> iba yo entre las calles y la atmósfera, llegando y despidiendo,
> en el advenimiento del otoño la moneda extendida
> de las hojas, y entre la primavera y las espigas,
> Lo que el más grande amor, como un guante
> que cae nos entrega como una larga luna.

> (From AIR to AIR, like an empty net,
> dredging through streets and ambient atmosphere, I came
> lavish, at autumn's coronation, with the leaves
> proffer of currency and between spring and wheat ears
> that which a boundless love, caught in a gauntlet fall,
> grant us like a long-fingered moon.)

The poet, trapped in a routine stay on earth where man simply exists, wanders about, directionless, amid "clothing and smoke." Then he once again asks rhetorical questions, as he did in the *Residences*:

> ¿Qué era el hombre? ¿En qué parte de su conversación abierta
> entre los almacenes y los silbidos, en cuál de sus movimientos metálicos

> vivía lo indestructible, lo imperecedero, la vida?

> (What was man? In what layer of his humdrum conversation,
> among his shops and sirens, in which of his metallic movements
> lived on imperishably the quality of life?)

(section 1, p. 8)

These questions serve as a preamble to one of the most significant sections of the *Canto general,* the meditations on death and temporality. The third section speaks of a "small death" that could mean dying slowly day by day:

> cada día una muerte pequeña, polvo
> gusano, lámpara
> que se apaga en el lodo del suburbio,
> una pequeña muerte de alas gruesas
> entraba en cada hombre como una corta lanza.

> (each day a little death: dust
> maggot, lamp
> drenched in the mire of suburbs,
> a little death with fat wings
> entered into each man like a short blade.)

(section 2, p. 12)

After these five preambles to the description of the remote past, the poet, overcome by the meditation on death, and immersed in a journey of interior quest, ascends to the lost city of Macchu Picchu, in the forgotten jungles of a vanished civilization. But this culture also was annihilated and had its own death, not the personal one described in stanzas one to five, not the death of the city, but "true death," that which annihilates an entire people.

Here we have the essential juxtaposition established in *The Heights of Macchu Picchu,* configured by two movements, the descent toward the individual conscience of a past and the ascent toward the future:

> Entonces en la escala de la tierra he subido
> entre la atroz maraña de las selvas perdidas
> hasta tí, Macchu Picchu.

> (Then up the ladder of the earth I climbed
> through the barbed jungle thickets
> until I reached you, Macchu Picchu.)

(section 6, p. 26)

In this ascent to the pre-Columbian citadel the poet reaches the culminating moment of the poem. In the ruins of a lost city, on the threshold of a sleeping past, the poet outlines with great clarity what has been enunciated in the previous five cantos: the "small death" that alluded to the social conventions of every day and the other death that cuts us off from our history and our past. The death of a people gives him the courage to regenerate himself in the "spent human spring" and to speak for all men.

The poet knows instinctively that the transcendence of one's own death is reached through others, through the history of those men buried and rediscovered in Macchu Picchu. That life among the stones was interrupted for a while and over it another history arose. Those who, like the ancient Egyptians, sculpted these stones and built this city were plain men, the makers of the true history of America:

> Mírame desde el fondo de la tierra,
> labrador, tejedor, pastor callado
>
> (Look at me from the depths of the earth
> tiller of fields, weaver, reticent shepherd)
>
> (section 12, p. 66)

Paradoxically, it is a dead city, in ashes and ruins, a city of the past, that Neruda uses to tell the history of America and of his own self.

The idea of brotherhood is established when the lyrical speaker addresses "tú, hombre" and "tú, lector" ("you, man" and "you, reader") inviting us all to climb that path that he himself took when a mysterious prophetic voice bade him ascend. In this union with other men who lived in these ruins, the life of the poet and the life of those who could not speak or tell the past are permanently merged.

In section 7 the lyrical speaker proclaims the mission already established in the first canto of **"La lámpara en la tierra."** He wishes to hear the secret voices of those who cannot speak. Neruda, then, speaks to the dead in their tombs, a call that in poem 12 is made more explicit: "Mostrádme vuestra sangre y vuestro surco. Decidme aquí fui castigado" ("Show me your blood and your furrow. Say to me here I was scourged") (section 12, p. 67). His words resonate not only with the literary tradition of mythological voyages to the underworld but with Dante's *Inferno*.

The last stanza of **The Heights of Macchu Picchu** is a synthesis of the entire poem. The poet, now at one with a geographical space, raises his voice to vindicate his past and his present:

> Dadme el silencio, el agua, la esperanza.
> Dadme la lucha, el hierro, los volcanes.
> Apegadme los cuerpos como imanes.
> Acudid a mis venas y a mi boca.
> Hablad por mis palabras y mi sangre.
>
> (And give me silence, give me water, hope.
> Give me the struggle, the irons, the volcanoes.
> Let bodies cling like magnets to my body.
> Come quickly to my veins and to my mouth.
> Speak through my speech and through my blood.)
>
> (section 12, p. 70)

The line "Speak through my words and my blood" brings to a close the journey of the pilgrim lost within himself.

The Heights of Macchu Picchu is a poem that represents a transnational American cultural identity that is a turning point in Neruda's artistic and political career. The poem was composed in 1945, two years after Neruda's visit to Macchu Picchu, an indication that the poem was the fruit of prolonged meditation.

Donald L. Shaw (essay date 1988)

SOURCE: Shaw, Donald L. "Interpretations of *Alturas de Macchu Picchu*." *Revista Interamericana de Bibliografía/Inter-American Review of Bibliography* 38, no. 2 (1988): 186-95.

[*In the following essay, Shaw questions prior critical estimations of* The Heights of Macchu Picchu *that have avoided the ambiguity of the poem's final cantos, arguing that Neruda used Machu Picchu not principally as a symbol of human redemption, but rather as an image linking the human present and past.*]

Neruda's **Alturas de Macchu Picchu,** the second section of **Canto General,** has deservedly been the subject of much critical writing. Enrico Mario Santí prefaces his detailed interpretation of the poem with a long list of items consulted[1] up to and including some from 1981, a list which appears to be exhaustive except for the omission of María M. Solá's *Poesía y política en Pablo Neruda. Análisis de Canto General* (Río Piedras, Puerto Rico: University of Puerto Rico Press, 1980, and Peter R. Beardsell, "*Hombre planetario and Alturas de Macchu Picchu,*" BHS, LIV, 1977, 21-28.

Little of major importance on **Alturas** seems to have appeared since. A sampling of the most serious critical writings listed by Santí, including his own chapter, reveals an initial category of critics like Robert Pring-Mill[2] and Hernán Loyola[3] who emphasize the contrast between the negativity of cantos I-V followed by the achievement of "collective permanence" (Pring-Mill, p. xvi) in canto VII, but signally fail to do justice to the remaining cantos. Loyola, in fact, after dedicating almost twenty pages to the first seven cantos, dismisses the last five in a page and a half.

A second category of critics includes Dieter Saalmann,[4] who recognizes the importance of the last five cantos of the poem but fails to perceive the extent to which they modify the apparently triumphant tone of canto VII. His view (p. 171) that the last cantos illustrate "a metamorphosis by means of the word which transforms 'history as servitude' . . . into 'history as freedom'" is tricked out with notions borrowed from T. S. Eliot (a dangerous figure to compare ideologically with a poet who was at this time moving ever closer to a Marxist orientation). It conceals behind a screen of rhetorical assertions an unwillingness to face the ambiguity of the later part of *Alturas.* Alongside Saalmann we may set Kay Engler[5] who actually perceives that "Neruda abandons the 'rosa abstracta' of Macchu Picchu because he cannot bear the thought of the human suffering required" (p. 143) and that the emphasis then shifts to his concern for the sacrifice of its builders. But, despite the mention of "Structure" in her title, she ignores the crucially important structural contrast that this abandonment creates, and like Loyola, devotes little more than a page to the last cantos.

A third category of critics includes Cedomil Goić, Santí and John Felstiner. Unlike Juan Larrea,[6] who regards the last part of the poem, with its apostrophe to the workers of the past, as mere demagogy, or Noé Jitrik,[7] whose essay eludes any attempt to interpret the possible meaning of the *vaivén* which he posits in the last cantos, these critics face the issue more or less squarely. Goić[8] refers correctly to "la ambigüedad del monumento contemplado [Macchu Picchu], que suscita tan variados como contradictorios movimientos en el ánimo del poeta" (p. 63) and insists on "el rechazo de los aspectos que no sean la directa vinculación con los enterrados." Whereas Engler suggests that in the last cantos Neruda wants communion with the workers of the past and "offers himself as a kind of substitute Christ figure who will express their sorrows for them" (p. 144), which is a rather selective account of the poet's role in the canto, Goić goes beyond this and, in consonance with his interpretation of *Alturas* as an elegy, sees the last cantos as the traditional *consolatio.* The poet does not merely participate in the sorrows and sufferings of the ancient Indians, but in some sense triumphs over their death by preserving their memory and dignifying them poetically. The city of Macchu Picchu itself, given such a reading, is incomplete as a monument to meaningful, collective "poderosa muerte," as distinct from the "pequeña muerte" of modern man which is insignificant and meaningless. Only when Neruda's poem evokes the toiling and suffering masses who built the city is the monument complete.

Goić's article is of major importance in that it emphasizes a progress in the poem beyond the joyful contemplation of

una permanencia de piedra y de palabra

beyond

la rosa permanente, la morada

of canto VII. A process of thought which after *celebrating* Macchu Picchu, both at the Latin American level as a source of American identity, and at the universal level as a symbol of the triumph of the collectivity over individual death, goes on to *question* that celebration.

This is what is missing in the interpretations of Pring-Mill, Loyola and others. But Goić seems over-ready to suggest that the end of the poem can be readily reconciled to the first seven cantos and to smooth over the contradiction to which he himself alludes. Felstiner[9] traces that contradiction to the fact that the phrase

El reino muerto vive todavía

is not the climax of canto VIII but is followed by the final sinister reference to "la sombra sanguinaria del cóndor" with which the canto actually ends. This, he points out, "reminds us that the dead realm still lives in a threatened time." Later he observes cogently (p. 185) that in the last cantos the emphasis of the poem shifts significantly from *Alturas* to *entraña* and from exaltation to anger. Nevertheless, Felstiner, like Goić, feels that despite the shift which becomes explicit in canto X, the two parts of the poem fit together: "one vision responds to the other" (p. 184). More than that, he asserts: "If Neruda did not turn on the city in this way, demanding to forget the unforgettable structure of it, *Macchu Picchu* would remain a powerful but conventional meditation" (p. 189). As it is, "la poderosa muerte" of the long-dead masses is in some sense complemented or redeemed. "Sube a nacer conmigo": in renewing himself, the poet would bring others to a kind of rebirth" (p. 191) calling them back collectively. Like Engler, Felstiner sees Neruda's final stance as Christ-like.

The problem with this approach is that it does not do full justice to the last canto with its commands to the long-dead builders of Macchu Picchu:

afilad los cuchillos que guardásteis

and

dadme la lucha.

Although Felstiner makes a coy reference to "revolutionary jargon," he plays down this aspect of the end of the poem, despite the fact, which he acknowledges, that not only the theme changes but also the form. The densely figurative language of the early cantos, cognate with that of the *Residencias,* has suddenly given way to a much more directly comprehensible mode of poetic discourse aimed at immediate communication. The motivation for this important shift is plainly ideological. It cannot be explained except in terms of a thematic shift from the metaphysical to the implicitly political. Goić, for his part, recognises this, pointing specifically to the harnessing of the religious references in *Alturas* to "una visión política y no transcendental del hombre" (p. 159), and later mentions Neruda's "escatológico sentido de la historia en que se redimen las contradicciones sociales en el paraíso de los trabajadores" (p. 161). But he seems reluctant to develop this recognition in relation to the final cantos.

Santí takes quite a different tack. In total contrast to the accepted consensus, he appears to argue (pp. 141-3) that the thrust of cantos six and seven is not positive at all; that "la poderosa muerte" of the Inca toilers presents no contrast to "la pequeña muerte" of modern man. For him the symbolism of Macchu Picchu is no more than an effect of self-delusion. The real point of contact between the two forms of death is not contrastive but re-emphatic: "individual mortality, as portrayed in the first half of the poem" appears "insignificant in comparison with the magnitude of cultural annihilation." For Santí, there is no comfort in cantos VI and VII but only an "insight that refuses to surrender any negative knowledge." He goes on, in the face of considerable evidence, to insist on the "radically negative meaning" (p. 144) of the central cantos and on the "pervasive nihilism" (p. 146) of Neruda's vision which they express. It follows that, for this critic, the final cantos confirm the impossibility of any redemption by the word such as Goić had postulated.

If I have understood his argument correctly, Santí emphasises the fact that Macchu Picchu survives as a *ruin,* rather than the fact of the survival itself. Brushing aside Neruda's own comments on his poem as "anxious, self-serving, though perhaps unconscious strategies to rewrite a text perhaps proved too bewildering or too embarrassing in its contradictions to be left on its own" (p. 172), Santí denies that the end of the poem refers us to "the comfortable stability of cultural identity," that is, to Neruda's identification of himself with the American past (along with his confidence in the power of poetry to redeem it).

My own view is that by affirming (p. 170) that in the last resort the language of *Alturas de Macchu Picchu* does not interact with "a safely external referent that would provide an unequivocal principle of explanation," but instead "maneuvers an enigmatic play among signs or texts," Santí reads into the end of the poem an unnecessary complexity which conflicts totally with the shift in poetic expression, from the more difficult to the more immediately expressive, which we have noted.

The foregoing remarks are designed to suggest certain conclusions about the current criticism of *Alturas de Macchu Picchu.* What, in fact, is the presente situation? Ever since the illuminating article by Juan Loveluck[10] on the first five cantos, we have been in possession of a coherent and generally accepted account of the first part of the poem, the meditation on death in the context of modernity. Sporadic difficulties, of course, remain. How are we to explain, for instance, the two similies at the end of stanza one of the first canto:

> lo que el más grande amor, como dentro de un guante
> que cae, nos entrega como una larga luna?

But in general the line of thematic development is clear. Similarly, in cantos VI and VII we can, with the assistance of the critics so far mentioned, readily perceive the contrasting presentation of Macchu Picchu and its builders in terms of collective death and symbolic permanence, as against the trivial contingency of modern death. The difficulties begin with canto VIII, which no critic has so far interpreted convincingly (what is the "potencia aciaga" which Goić tantalizingly mentions, and which the Urubamba seems to symbolize? What revelation does the poet want from the river in response to his [unanswered] questions?). The litany in canto IX is also mysterious. Is it simply a laudatory expansion of the poet's earlier description of Macchu Picchu as:

> una vida de piedra,

as its climax:

> Ola de plata, dirección del tiempo

seems to imply; or do the images which are applied to the city sometimes deliberately portend the thematic shift which is about to overtake the poem, as when Neruda calls it

> roca sanguinaria

using an adjective applied not long before to the shadow of the condor, associated with death? If, as I think we should, we see the litany as containing elements which foreshadow the final cantos, and therefore as to some degree ambiguous, how are we to handle the concept of ambiguity when we come to the last part of the poem?

Not, surely, as Santí does. But equally, not by trying to explain it away. The last part of *Alturas de Macchu Picchu* is genuinely disconcerting for several reasons. Fist of all because of the unexpected way in which, after exalting the city, Neruda (in Felstiner's words) "turns on" it. There is no way in which we can ignore the contradiction at this point. If Macchu Picchu really represents "collective permanence," the sacrifices by which that triumph over individual deaths is achieved necessarily must take second place. If, on the other hand, the price which was paid for the "permanencia de piedra" was too high, what becomes of canto VII? We have to recognize here a thematic discrepancy which the efforts of even the most favourably inclined critics are powerless to resolve and which to some extent flaws the poem as a literary artefact. We do not make the transition easily from Macchu Picchu as the redemptive symbol of human permanence to the poet as "Christ-like" redeemer.

It is possible, however, that Neruda thought of the poem in terms of a quasi-dialectical process. The city, by itself, the original fount of inspiration for the poem, is, as we have seen, inadequate as a symbol of redemption from death, however moving and exalting the contemplation of it as a work of human hands may be. It is only when the act of contemplation generates the *word,* poetry, when the inanimate inspires the animate, that redemption becomes possible. The two elements of the process are inseparable. The city is meaningless until symbolic meaning is conferred upon it by the poem. Conversely, the poem could not have come into being without the existence of the city. Only by meditating on Macchu Picchu both as a positive and as a negative symbolic referent, can the poet eventually reach the point (the resolution of the antithesis) at which he can present himself as possessed of the redeeming voice.

A second disconcerting feature of the last cantos of *Alturas de Macchu Picchu* is the way in which Neruda not only incorporates indirect references to a range of "Western" (white) literary texts to figure forth an original American message (Santí, p. 171), but also the way in which he regularly has recourse to Christian and eucharistic imagery (crucifiction, stigmata, the chalice, bread and blood, and so on) within what Goić correctly perceives as a strictly non-Christian frame of reference.

Given these features, how should we approach the last three cantos of *Alturas*? A suitable point of departure is the contrast in canto IX between two descriptions of Macchu Picchu:

> Lámpara de granito, pan de piedra

on the one hand, and:

> Madrépora del tiempo sumergido

on the other. The first two images relate unequivocally to the central section of *Alturas,* that which exalts Macchu Picchu as a symbol of triumph over death and of American identity. Every reader of the *Veinte poemas de amor* recognizes *lámpara* as one of Neruda's most positive symbols. Similarly *pan* here is an obvious eucharistic reference: Macchu Picchu represents the bread of life, the nourishment of the spirit to Latin Americans with any consciousness of historical tradition. But *madrépora* is quite a different sort of image. It alludes to the well-known fact that coral reefs grow by the accretion of the skeletons of stony coral as each tiny organism dies. The reference now is not backward to the central section of *Alturas,* but forward to canto X:

> Hambre, coral del hombre

The city implicitly grew by the accretion of the bones of its dead builders as they fell in successive generations from undernourishment. That is why, later in canto IX, the city is described as:

> cerezo de alas negras

combining another familiar positive symbol, that of the cherry tree, with the sinister implications of black pinions, recalling the condor-symbol of death. In this sense canto IX contains clues, to be picked up by the alert reader, which point the way to the shift in the last three cantos of *Alturas de Macchu Picchu.* The opening of canto X questions in their entirety the assumptions of cantos VI and VII. The poet is assailed by the realization that the lives of the builders of Macchu Picchu may have been no different from those of modern man; their "días de la luz deshilachada" no different from the "noches deshilachadas" which the twentieth-century poet had endured in canto I. The glorious:

> Alto arrecife de la aurora humana

of canto VI has suddenly turned into the *arrecife* of canto X, the coral reef created out of the heaped up skeletons. The "tantas vidas" of canto VII, which gave rise to an eternal "vida de piedra" have become the ragged downtrodden slaves of canto X. The "pared suavizada por el tacto de un rostro" of canto IV has become:

> el muro
> El muro, el muro!

the granite-hard pillow of the exhausted and famished slave-labourer.

Despite the fact that much of canto X is phrased in the form of questions, the remaining two cantos make it clear that they are purely rhetorical. They are not expressive of doubt, but are in reality more emphatic kinds of statement, in which the interrogative form primarily expresses the poet's initial unwillingness to pursue this unwelcome line of thought. For it is a line of thought which contaminates one of the cradles of Latin American identity with concepts of oppression and misery. But once started on it, Neruda pursues it to the end. The pattern of alternating ascent and descent which runs right throught *Alturas* reappears in the last two cantos. In canto XI the poet turns deliberately away from the city of Macchu Picchu perched high on its mountain top. He calls on the spirit of love of America, which has silently accompanied him from the opening of the poem, and which was to provide the introduction to *Canto general* as a whole, to allow him to forget "esta dicha," the exaltation which imbued cantos six and seven, and plunge into the depths of humanity, to re-emerge with "un ramo de agua secreta," a hidden fount of suppressed and hitherto overlooked truths. The return of the image of the condor, that is, of death, leads the poet to exclaim that he no longer sees it abstractly (as he had implicitly done in the meditation on death and on the collective triumph over it earlier in the poem). Now he sees it concretely in terms of the deaths of real human individuals, the ancient Inca serfs, bowed under the black reinstorm of death, in terms of the three Juans, the representatives of the exploited masses.

The rhetorical questions of canto X are answered in canto XII, the climax of the poem. Macchu Picchu *was* built on human suffering: "vuestros viejos dolores enterrados," "vuestra sangre;" its stone is "la piedra en que caisteis," its wood is "la madera en que os crucifi-caron." The overseer's whip and the executioner's axe have replaced the "anchos granos del maíz" and the "hebra dorada de la vicuña" as the appropriate objects to be associated with the walls and buildings of Macchu Picchu. The cost of the city in human sweat, blood and lives is unbearable to think of and the poet longs to mourn for that terrible cost longer than the city itself has existed:

> dejadme llorar, horas, días, años,
> edades ciegas, siglos estelares.

Here then, at the end of the poem, the city as *madrépora* confronts the city as *morada,* the political vision confronts the metaphysical vision: thesis and antithesis. Can there be a synthesis? There can. Despite Santí's tortuous attempt at the end of his chapter on *Alturas* to protect his revisionist reading of the poem from the platitudes of earlier criticism about the redeeming effects of poetry, he himself recognizes the poem as (in some qualified sense at least) "a testament designed to redeem all the suffering endured" (p. 168). Saalmann's attempt to see this redemption in terms of Eliot's temporal concepts in the *Four Quartets,* earlier alluded to in this connection by Pring-Mill, is wholly unconvincing. Santí is right in placing the emphasis in the first place squarely on Neruda's acknowledgement that the death of the masses who built Macchu Picchu is in one sense absolute:

> No volverás del fondo de las rocas
> No volverás del tiempo subterráneo
> No volverá tu voz endurecida
> No volverán tus ojos taladrados.

The triumph of the collectivity over death, symbolized by Macchu Picchu in canto VI is utterly contradicted by these bleak words. Only when the whole basis of society has been changed, Neruda's final canto implies, can that contradiction be overcome. Not the least disappointing aspect of Solá's all too brief comments on *Alturas* in her book on Neruda's political stance in *Canto general* is that she entirely fails to bring out this crucially important point. The view of Engler and Felstiner that Neruda here becomes "a kind of substitute Christ figure who will express their sorrows for them" (Engler, p. 142), or that he undertakes "a Christ-like assumption of reponsibility" (Felstiner, p. 197) seems to place a heavier burden on the wording of canto XII than it can actually bear. Where those critics who have discussed canto XII at all have fallen short is in emphasizing the poet's redemptive role to the point of all but identifying him with Christ, instead of directing attention to what Neruda actually says about the redemptive role of poetry (in a totally *human* context). Beardsell, for example. writes: "he will bring their [the ancient workers'] burdens into the present; he will be inspired by them and be given their hope. And he will also seek, by voicing their sufferings, to vindicate them, as though to bring atonement for the injustices they

underwent were in some way to remove the burden of injustice in the present world" (p. 27). This hardly goes far enough. What it is essential to notice at this point is not so much that Neruda offers himself as a spokesman for the toilers of the past, but *what it is* that they are invited to call upon him to transmit:

> traed a la copa de esta nueva vida
> vuestros viejos dolores enterrados.
> Mostradme vuestra sangre . . .
> y la madera en que os crucificaron,
>   . . . los látigos pegados
> a través de los siglos en las llagas
> y las hachas de brillo ensangrentado . . .
> contadme todo, cadena a cadena
> eslabón a eslabón . . .

This is not the call of Christ to "come unto me all ye that labor and are heavy laden and I will give you rest." It is the language of the social poet that Neruda had become after his experiences in Spain during the civil war and during his political campaigns. Poetry is for him now less a metaphysical exploration of the human condition than a contributory factor in helping to change that condition. Only by helping to dynamize the modern struggle (in which Neruda had so recently been engaged both in Spain and in his senatorial campaign in northern Chile), by reminding the workers of today about the age-long sufferings of the workers of yesterday can the dead of Macchu Picchu contribute to the new collective task. We know that to marxists there is no survival after death except as part of the eternal collectivity. One lives on in others engaged in the common upward struggle. Transcendence can only be achieved by participating in that struggle. This is what underlies the conclusion of *Alturas.* By contributing the story of their sufferings through the mouth of the poet, the workers of Macchu Picchu will assist in the task of raising the level of historical (and hence political) awareness of the readers, and thus achieve in the here and now of the 20th century a renewal of life. It is this, surely, that is implicit in the call to the shades of the past to join vicariously in the fray:

> afilad los cuchillos que guardásteis
> ponedlos en mi pecho y en mi mano
> . . . Dadme la lucha, el hierro, los volcanes . . .

Felstiner makes the wrong decision (which he himself admits is a risky one) in concluding that Neruda "wants to suffer the knives, not use them" (p. 196). "Put them in my breast" (not "drive them into my breast") means no more than "give me the passionate will to use them." Similarly, one may interpret "volcanes" in the sense of the sudden explosions of revolutionary energy necessary to sustain "la lucha." The final canto of *Alturas* postulates an ideal two-way process. Not just, as Engler, Felstiner, Beardsell and others have noticed, one in which the poet proposes himself as the mouthpiece for the toilers of the past, but also one in which they must supply the theme of his song. If Neruda adopts in any sense at all a Christ-like stance here, it is the stance of

Christ as "hijo de hombre" as in Roa Bastos's famous left-wing novel.[11]

To conclude: *Alturas de Macchu Picchu* marks a major transition in Neruda's poetry. Despite the implication of "Explico algunas cosas," in 1937, that a change had already overtaken his work, it was not until after his return to the New World, his stay in Mexico and his senatorial campaign amid the workers of Tarapacá and Antofagasta, that the crucial moment arrives. As Loyola remarks (p. 198), the poem looks both backward and forward: "es una compleja condensación de revisiones (hacia el pasado) y de propósitos (hacia el futuro)." With only slight exaggeration one may say that the clearest sign of the shift is the change in poetic expression between cantos IX and X from the more hermetic kind of discourse we associate with the *Residencias* to the more direct—ideologically inspired—mode of expression of much of *Canto general.* In the context of *Alturas* itself, this coincides with a shift from the elegy, in which a single poetic voice speaks for itself, to the ode or hymn, a collective statement, whose *persona* is that of the collectivity. Thematically, as we have seen, the shift is from the metaphysical to the political. This is not an easy transition, as Carpentier realized in *El siglo de las luces,* when he came to the recognition that the Revolution's social ideology was not enough in itself to fulfil man's deeper yearning for survival. Neruda's response to the difficulty is two-fold. On the one hand the ancient collectivity is shown to have left its enduring monument at Macchu Picchu. But that monument, however impressive, is, as Santí emphasizes, a dead ruin. Moreover, it may be a monument to servitude. To that extent, its relationship with "lo que pudo renacer" of canto V is at least ambiguous. On the other hand, therefore, the poem's climax postulates the poet's ability to recall the workers of the past, from the dead, so that they may survive death and collaborate actively with the future, dynamizing the impulse to progress through the story of their wrongs and sufferings. This was destined to become one of the major threads binding together the rest of *Canto general.* Not for nothing does Neruda say to Fray Bartolomé de las Casas in "Los libertadores" II:

> Te mostraré las cartas, el tormento
> de mi pueblo . . .
> Te mostraré los antiguos dolores

It is through this possibility that the toilers of the past can, in a sense, live again through a form of participation in the struggles of the present. To interpret *Alturas de Macchu Picchu* correctly, we must understand that it is not in the end the "permanencia de piedra" that matters to Neruda, but the hope (or dream) of establishing a living link with the past which, in a dialectical relationship with the present, will help to forge the future.

Notes

1. Enrico Mario Santí, *Pablo Neruda: The Poetics of Prophecy* (Ithaca: Cornell University Press, 1982), 106-107.

2. Robert Pring-Mill, *Preface to The Heights of Macchu Picchu,* translated by Nathaniel Tarn (New York: Farrar, Straus and Giroux, 1967), vii-xix.

3. Hernán Loyola, *Ser y morir en Pablo Neruda, 1918-1845* (Santiago, Chile: Editora Santiago, 1967), 197-242.

4. Dieter Saalman, "The Role of Time in Pablo Neruda''s *Alturas de Macchu Picchu,*" *Romance Notes,* 18:2, 1977, 169-77.

5. Kay Engler, "Image and Structure in Neruda's *Las [sic] alturas de Macchu Picchu,*" *Symposium,* 28:2, 1974, 130-45.

6. Juan Larrea, *Del surrealismo a Macchu Picchu* (México: Joaquín Mortiz, 1967), 161.

7. Noé Jitrik, "*Alturas de Macchu Picchu,*" *Nueva Revista de Filología Hispánica,* 26:2, 1967, 510-55.

8. Cedomil Goić, "*Alturas de Macchu Picchu,* la torre y el abismo," *Anales de la Universidad de Chile,* CXXIX, 157-60, 1971, 153-65.

9. John Felstiner, *Translating Neruda* (Stanford, California: Stanford University Press, 1980), 179.

10. Juan Loveluck, "*Alturas de Macchu Picchu,* I-V," *Revista Iberoamericana,* 39, 1973, 175-88.

11. Augusto Roa Bastos, *Hijo de hombre* (1st ed.; Buenos Aires: Editorial Losada, 1960).

Jill Kuhnheim (essay date 2002)

SOURCE: Kuhnheim, Jill. "Quests for Alternative Cultural Antecedents: The Indigenism of Pablo Neruda, Ernesto Cardenal, and Gary Snyder." In *Pablo Neruda and the U.S. Culture Industry,* edited by Teresa Longo, pp. 61-81. New York: Routledge, 2002.

[In the following excerpt, Kuhnheim focuses on The Heights of Macchu Picchu *as a work concerned with Latin American identity by examining the role of indigenous cultures in the poem.]*

Las alturas de Macchu Picchu (The Heights of Macchu Picchu) is one of the best known and most anthologized set of poems from Pablo Neruda's *Canto general.* First published in 1946 in the *Revista nacional de cultura* (Caracas, Venezuela), its twelve parts comprise the second section of the *Canto.* This famous set of poems has been read in terms of the personal transformation of Neruda, in contrast to the poetry of the *Residencias,* and as an affirmation of history through the speaker's contemplation of the ruins of Incan civilization. It has been read as an example of Neruda's Marxist, materialist politics and as an example of a politics of language, through which the poet enters a larger debate about cultural authenticity. At Machu Picchu the contemporary Spanish American speaker delves into an indigenous past, and his evocation of the Indian is central to all that happens in the poem, providing him with a means to transcend and transform modern life. In this way, Neruda participates in the indigenist tradition, representing Indian life from a non-Indian perspective. Focusing on the Indian in the *Canto general* highlights the strategies Neruda employs to make the Native representative of American identity.

Many aspects of Neruda's portrait of native life continue the romantic, mythified vision of the Indian that has been of fundamental importance to defining national identity in the region. Connected to self definition in the nineteenth century,[1] *indigenismo* continued in the early twentieth century. It has not disappeared in the late twentieth century. It has changed, becoming linked to the realm of identity politics. The focus of indigenist discourse has shifted from an earlier concern with issues of economics, class, and the possibility or impossibility of integration, evidenced in writing from the first half of the twentieth century, to ethnicity, race, and agency. At the turn of the millennium, Indian people increasingly appropriate indigenist discourse in their societies and use it to gain a social voice, and to attempt to change society and their position in it, in part through the affirmation of their own identities.[2] There is not one Indigenism, but many, and a range of receptions to and redeployments of these discourses as well.

Neruda published *Las alturas de Macchu Picchu* 53 years ago; writing as a non-Indian he incorporates indigenous elements into a regional perspective in order to redefine his culture. He, like the other authors I will consider here, speaks from *outside* of an autochthonous community. His romantic, unself-conscious use of the Indian may appear to be a nostalgic and artificial appropriation of the Native, suspect to contemporary readers. Yet, while recognizing its limitations, Neruda's struggle to find an American ethic through his appreciation and revalorization of Native cultures has a power and merit that resonates across the continent. His perspective is a step in an on-going process, for his 1946 poems antecede a series of similar redefinitions of dominant culture through the marginal—in South, Central, and North America as well. . . .

"La lámpara en la tierra" (Light on earth), the first section of the *Canto general,* sets up the importance of the Indian in this text. Neruda rewrites an originary myth, combining elements from Genesis and echoing formal aspects of the Bible (as Enrique Mario Santí notes in his edition of the poem, p. 103), with traces of

Indigenous versions of the creation of the world, such as the Mayan *Popol Vuh* (human beings are first modeled in mud, nature is animate). The introductory section, "Amor América (1400)," is narrated by the voice of pre-America, an autochthonous speaker who identifies himself as, "*Yo, incásico del légamo*" (I, Incan from the mud) (135) yet who walked among *flores zapotecas* (Zapotecan flowers) (140). He is Incan yet able to wander far from his territory, a supernatural Indian who, perhaps, embodies many Indian identities. He speaks of the past of this place: "*Tierra sin nombre, sin América, / estambre equinoccial, lanza de púrpura, / tu aroma me trepó por las raíces / hasta la copa que bebía, hasta la más delgada / palabra aún no nacida de mi boca*" (original italics, ll 43-47).[3] He is penetrated by this place, by nature, as he awaits his speaking future.

The use of italics here separates this speaker from the one who follows in the poems, the speaker who names animals, birds, rivers, minerals, men. He catalogues the variety of tribes on the continent: caribe, araucana, inca, anahuac, zapoteca, tarahumara, tarasco, azteca, maya, guaraní—by no means a complete list, but one that offers some idea of the human diversity and calls attention to the irony of the name "Indian," a misnomer resulting from Spanish colonialization that falsely unites disparate cultural identities. This speaker assumes an adamic function, naming the American world and, like the introductory "I," we find again that nature is the origin of his speech. He exhorts the river:

> Pero háblame, Bío Bío,
> son tus palabras en mi boca
> las que resbalan, tú me diste
> el lenguaje, el canto nocturno
> mezclado con lluvia y follaje.
>
> (I, ll 58-62)[4]

In addressing the river, he animates it, seeking to recover some lost, original language accessible through nature.

The *yo poético* speaks to different places and groups in **"La lámpara en la tierra"** but in each instance receives no response. This repressed dialogic aspect culminates in the last poem, in which he observes an Indian presence: "En el fondo de América sin nombre / estaba Arauco entre las aguas" (In the background of unnamed America / was the Araucanian among the waters) (I, ll 97-98). At the same time, near the end of the poem, he addresses a "tú," imploring him or her to look and listen while he reiterates that there is no one there:

> No hay nadie. Mira las piedras.
> Mira las piedras de Arauco.
> No hay nadie, sólo son los árboles.
> Sólo son las piedras, Arauco.
>
> (I, ll 127-30)[5]

The last line makes it clear that the addressee is the Araucanian himself; a missing other or interlocutor. Like the reader, he is at once present and absent, discovered and undiscovered, for he is hailed yet does not appear. This evocation of the Araucanian can be read as the emblematic presence of the past, an indigenous past that Neruda will also address in "Alturas." The Araucanian may also be a figure for absence ("No hay nadie"), an absence that will respond in the subsequent section through the poetic speaker, "Yo vengo a hablar por vuestra boca muerta" ("I come to speak through your dead mouth") (II, XII, 1406), lending an authentic voice to Neruda's poetic discourse on and to America.

Neruda's use of the indigenous is continually complex, as are ensuing readings of this element in his work. Recounting the critical debate surrounding *Alturas de Macchu Picchu,* Enrique Mario Santí inevitably confronts the broader problem of cultural authenticity. This problem is an element in the long struggle in the nineteenth and twentieth centuries to demonstrate that Latin American literature and cultural production is not only a European derivative, but that it possesses its own originality. Santí engages the terms of the dichotomy imitation-original as he explains that when, in a 1943 debate, Spaniard Juan Ramón Jiménez accused Neruda of "artificial Indigenism," he was, in fact, putting his finger on the "rhetorical impasse of the modern Latin American writer" (*Pablo Neruda: The Poetics of Prophecy* 112). In the mid-twentieth century, "once direct claims to the pre-Columbian, non-Western past are no longer possible," he says, "it would seem that the writer can no longer assume cultural difference [necessary to evade the accusation of imitation and assert an American singularity] without succumbing to bad faith. A bit like modesty, Americanism seems to share the fate of an aporia: the moment you say you have it, you've lost it" (112). Santí's masterful reading of *Alturas* extends Jiménez's opposition of the West and the rest, and finds that this cycle of poems uses Western signs to found an "original culture" through its "subversion of the Western library" (171). Neruda's writing, in effect, moves America from a "scriptless marginality" (175) to a "new textual theater, or scene of writing" (177). In his reading, Santí shifts the locus of Neruda's project from an overt politics to a politics of writing.

Posing the problem in terms of a politics of writing reinforces the opposition between Western and non-Western cultures and defines the work of Neruda's poem in relation to concepts such as cultural originality, authenticity, and, implicitly, these terms' opposite: imitation. Some ideas in the recent work of Roberto Schwartz illuminate what is obscured in this shift—the question of the validity of these categories themselves. In his essay, "Brazilian Culture: Nationalism by Elimination," Schwartz proposes that the hierarchical relations between center and periphery, model and imitation, which have been theoretically undone in the work of Foucault and Derrida, have begun breaking down "cultural dazzlement [with the model, the center] in the underdeveloped countries" (7). Still, Schwartz argues, these philosophical changes:

do not go to the heart of a problem which is essentially practical in character. . . . If theory remains at this level, it will continue to suffer from the same limitations, and the radicalism of an analysis that passes over efficient causes will become in its turn largely delusive. The inevitability of cultural imitation [by underdeveloped of overdeveloped countries] is bound up with a specific set of historical imperatives over which abstract philosophical critiques can exercise no power.

(7)

This contrast between original and copy is not a real opposition, according to Schwartz, for "the painfulness of an imitative civilization is produced not by imitation—which is present at any rate—but by the social structure of the country" that "presents as a national characteristic what is actually a malaise of the dominant class" (15). The real issue is who is excluded from the universe of contemporary culture. Not Neruda, Jiménez, or Santí, of course, but the poor, whose numbers in the majority of Latin American countries include a disproportionate percentage of indigenous people. It is the subaltern, the underclass, who need to gain access to the "terms of contemporary life" and Schwartz proposes that their exclusion is obscured by the false problem of imitation (15). Significantly, this situation is also apparent in Neruda's scheme in *Alturas de Macchu Picchu,* for his speaker confronts his indigenous past in order to claim an American identity, but also to create a historical sense of class solidarity. The indigenous people function as metaphor for workers and the dispossessed.

This is apparent in various sections of *Alturas* where the absent workers, like the submerged past, are made present metonymically. In Canto VI, we see their ubiquitous hands, so frequently associated with labor and production in Neruda's work: "Miro las vestiduras y las manos, / el vestigio del agua en la oquedad sonoro" ("I see the garments and hands, / the vestige of water in the sonorous cavity") (l. 149-50). Indeed, Canto IX forms a wall of writing as Santí demonstrates, not only to formally compete with the real Machu Picchu (161), but also to incorporate a series of images of human industry, workers' products and their presence. This is a "Muralla por los dedos suavizada" ("wall smoothed by fingers") (1. 275) and natural images are joined with terms that consistently refer to human productivity: *pan, campana, libro, nave, estatua, patria* (bread, bell, book, ship, statue, county). The walls embody human presence: "Piedra en la piedra, el hombre, ¿dónde estuvo?" ("Stone upon stone, Man, Where was he?") (Canto X, 1.306) as the speaker later pleads with the site: "Devuélveme el esclavo que enterraste" ("Return to me the slave you buried") (1.332). In Canto XI the vision of the laborers becomes quite explicit:

> veo el antiguo ser, servidor, el dormido
> en los campos, veo un cuerpo, mil cuerpos, un hombre,
> mil mujeres,
> bajo la racha negra, negros de lluvia y noche,
> con la piedra pesada de la estatua:

Juan Cortapiedras, hijo de Wiracocha,
Juan Comefrío, hijo de estrella verde,
Juan Piesdescalzos, nieto de la turquesa,
sube a nacer conmigo, hermano.

(l. 371-78)[6]

The workers are present and are designated with surnames that describe their condition, as well as approximating some Native American graphic surnames. But their first names (in this case, literally Christian names) are not indigenous, they are the generic "Juan." Neruda embeds evidence of the colonial situation in his naming and also signals that the laborial role is significantly linked to the indigenous one as he summons these people from the past.

This emphasis on the worker has undoubtably been clear to most readers of **Alturas de Macchu Picchu.** I return to it now in order to highlight how Santí's emphasis on the problem of writing signals something else. Let me clarify my stance—I don't take issue with Santí's fine reading of Neruda, for he convincingly demonstrates that the problem of writing and American identity *is* textualized in **Alturas de Macchu Picchu.** What I want to do here is to briefly historicize Neruda's relationship to the problem of cultural authenticity via writing and the Indigenous and to situate Santí's reading of it in terms of subsequent theoretical ideas.

The critic's interest in the relation between metropolitan and peripheral writing and the problem of cultural authority signals that writing is a privileged category here. Writing allows Neruda to enter into and/or to compete with the canon. At the same time it signifies the paradoxical status of Latin American writing in relation to canonical discourse; Neruda's work participates in the avant-garde questioning of the role of art as institution in bourgeois society while it shows signs of its struggle to be included in that institution. Many commentaries on the **Canto general** mention Neruda's revision of the lyric with his prosaic style, his creation of a new epic poetry that revises yet inserts itself into the tradition of the classics (Bello, Ercilla, Pound, Whitman); this is the "rhetorical impasse" that Santí finds paradigmatic in the poem. Yet in Santí's reading, certain elements, such as the worker and the indigene, are subsumed into the broader allegorical assertion of the problem of writing. I find that reading **Alturas de Macchu Picchu** as primarily a poem about writing and cultural authority reduces its reach and translates its multiple radical trajectories into a single issue that can be assimilated into the Western academy. It directs our view away from the social structure. It also continues the move whereby cultures are seen as statically polarized rather than dynamic, in flux.

Notes

1. Domingo Faustino Sarmiento's manipulation of the idea of the Indian in relation to the Argentine state is an obvious and striking example of this. In poetry, his countryman Esteban Echeverría's romantic poem "La cautiva" offers another emblematic example as do Uruguayan José Zorrilla de San Martín's "Tabaré" and Mexican José Joaquín de Pesado's "Cantos de Nezahuacóyotl."

2. Some recent studies that discuss the effects of Indian appropriation of the term "indigenismo" are Guillermo Delgado P.'s "Ethnic Politics and the Popular Movement" (in *Latin America Faces the Twenty-First Century: Reconstructing a Social Justice Agenda.* Eds. Susanne Jonas and Edward J. McCaughan. Boulder: Westview Press, 1994: 77-88), and Marcia Stephenson's, "The *Taller de Historia Oral Andina*: Forging an Indigenous Counterpublic Sphere in Bolivia," unpublished manuscript.

3. *Land without a name, without America, / equinoctial thread, purple lance, / your aroma climbed up through my roots / up to the tree-top that drank, up to the most tenuous / word still unborn from my mouth.* All translations are my own, unless otherwise indicated.

4. But speak to me, Bío Bío, / yours are the words in my mouth / those that slip, you gave me / language, the nocturnal song / mixed with rain and foliage.

5. There is no one. Look at the stones. / Look at the Araucanian's stones. / There is no one, there are only trees. / There are only rocks, Araucanian.

6. I see the ancient being, a servant, sleeping in the fields / I see a body, a thousand bodies, a man, a thousand women, / under the black wind, black from rain and night, / with the statue's heavy stone: / John Stonecutter, son of Wiracocha / John Coldeater, son of green star, / John Barefoot, grandson of turquoise, / come up to be born with me, brother.

Works Cited

Santí, Enrique Mario, ed. *Canto General.* By Pablo Neruda. 1950. Madrid: Ediciones Cátedra, S.A., 1990.

———. *Pablo Neruda: The Poetics of Prophecy.* Ithaca and London: Cornell UP, 1982.

Schwartz, Roberto. "Brazilian Culture: Nationalism by Elimination." *Misplaced Ideas: Essays on Brazilian Culture.* London: Verso, 1992:1-18.

FURTHER READING

Criticism

Jara, René. "Pablo Neruda (1904): A Centennial Greeting." In *Pablo Neruda and the U.S. Culture Industry,* edited by Teresa Longo, pp. 179-222. New York: Routledge, 2002.

Includes a summary of the thematic progression of *The Heights of Macchu Picchu,* viewing the poem as an encapsulation of human existence.

Karen, Sonja. "Neruda's *Canto general* in Historical Context." *Symposium* 32, no. 3 (fall 1978): 220-35.
Characterizes Neruda's *Canto general* as a political work with little lyrical content aside from *The Heights of Macchu Picchu.*

Méndez-Ramírez, Hugo. "The Indigenous Theme and the Search for Roots." In *Neruda's Ekphrastic Experience: Mural Art and* Canto General, pp. 68-122. Cranbury, N.J.: Associated University Presses, 1999.
Describes Neruda's use of indigenous Latin American identity and culture in his poetry—particularly in his *Canto general*—while making brief mention of *The Heights of Macchu Picchu.*

Pring-Mill, Robert. Preface to *Pablo Neruda: The Heights of Macchu Picchu,* translated by Nathaniel Tarn, pp. 7-13. London: Jonathan Cape, 1966.
Summarizes Neruda's life and the content of *The Heights of Macchu Picchu,* describing the work as a "pilgrimage through human life in search of meaningful truth."

Riess, Frank. "The Poet and the Collectivity." In *The Word and the Stone: Language and Imagery in Neruda's* Canto General, pp. 1-42. Oxford: Oxford University Press, 1972.
Considers the *Canto general* as Neruda's definitive work, and recounts its thematic movement from private and personal emotion to a general and

integral vision of humanity in its sections *La lámpara en la tierra* and *The Heights of Macchu Picchu.*

Rosman, Silvia N. "The Poetics of Politics and the Politics of the Poet: Experience and Testimony in Pablo Neruda." In *Pablo Neruda and the U.S. Culture Industry,* edited by Teresa Longo, pp. 126-37. New York: Routledge, 2002.
Probes subjects of cultural authenticity, collective responsibility, and political engagement with regard to *The Heights of Macchu Picchu.*

Santí, Enrico Mario. "*Canto general*: The Politics of the Book." *Symposium* 32, no. 3 (fall 1978): 254-75.
Studies the prophetic mode and near-apocalyptic vision of the *Canto general,* categorizing the function of *The Heights of Macchu Picchu* as an "epic invocation" to the volume.

Tarn, Nathaniel. "Archaeology, Elegy, Architecture: A Poet's Program for Lyric." *Sub-Stance* 28, no. 1 (1981): 3-24.
Outlines an aesthetic theory of lyric poetry, using *The Heights of Macchu Picchu* as an illustrative example of elegy.

Teitelboim, Volodia. "Personal and Extrapersonal Meaning of Machu Picchu." In *Neruda: An Intimate Biography,* translated by Beverly J. DeLong-Tonelli, pp. 259-62. Austin: University of Texas Press, 1991.
Calls *The Heights of Macchu Picchu* "an American poetic manifesto" that reinforces Neruda's political and cultural affiliations at the middle of his literary career.

How to Use This Index

The main references

```
Calvino, Italo
    1923-1985 ....... CLC 5, 8, 11, 22, 33, 39,
                                73; SSC 3, 48
```

list all author entries in the following Gale Literary Criticism series:

AAL = *Asian American Literature*
BG = *The Beat Generation: A Gale Critical Companion*
BLC = *Black Literature Criticism*
BLCS = *Black Literature Criticism Supplement*
CLC = *Contemporary Literary Criticism*
CLR = *Children's Literature Review*
CMLC = *Classical and Medieval Literature Criticism*
DC = *Drama Criticism*
HLC = *Hispanic Literature Criticism*
HLCS = *Hispanic Literature Criticism Supplement*
HR = *Harlem Renaissance: A Gale Critical Companion*
LC = *Literature Criticism from 1400 to 1800*
NCLC = *Nineteenth-Century Literature Criticism*
NNAL = *Native North American Literature*
PC = *Poetry Criticism*
SSC = *Short Story Criticism*
TCLC = *Twentieth-Century Literary Criticism*
WLC = *World Literature Criticism, 1500 to the Present*
WLCS = *World Literature Criticism Supplement*

The cross-references

```
See also CA 85-88, 116; CANR 23, 61;
DAM NOV; DLB 196; EW 13; MTCW 1, 2;
RGSF 2; RGWL 2; SFW 4; SSFS 12
```

list all author entries in the following Gale biographical and literary sources:

AAYA = *Authors & Artists for Young Adults*
AFAW = *African American Writers*
AFW = *African Writers*
AITN = *Authors in the News*
AMW = *American Writers*
AMWR = *American Writers Retrospective Supplement*
AMWS = *American Writers Supplement*
ANW = *American Nature Writers*
AW = *Ancient Writers*
BEST = *Bestsellers*
BPFB = *Beacham's Encyclopedia of Popular Fiction: Biography and Resources*
BRW = *British Writers*
BRWS = *British Writers Supplement*
BW = *Black Writers*
BYA = *Beacham's Guide to Literature for Young Adults*
CA = *Contemporary Authors*
CAAS = *Contemporary Authors Autobiography Series*
CABS = *Contemporary Authors Bibliographical Series*
CAD = *Contemporary American Dramatists*
CANR = *Contemporary Authors New Revision Series*
CAP = *Contemporary Authors Permanent Series*
CBD = *Contemporary British Dramatists*
CCA = *Contemporary Canadian Authors*
CD = *Contemporary Dramatists*
CDALB = *Concise Dictionary of American Literary Biography*
CDALBS = *Concise Dictionary of American Literary Biography Supplement*
CDBLB = *Concise Dictionary of British Literary Biography*

CMW = St. James Guide to Crime & Mystery Writers

CN = Contemporary Novelists

CP = Contemporary Poets

CPW = Contemporary Popular Writers

CSW = Contemporary Southern Writers

CWD = Contemporary Women Dramatists

CWP = Contemporary Women Poets

CWRI = St. James Guide to Children's Writers

CWW = Contemporary World Writers

DA = DISCovering Authors

DA3 = DISCovering Authors 3.0

DAB = DISCovering Authors: British Edition

DAC = DISCovering Authors: Canadian Edition

DAM = DISCovering Authors: Modules

   DRAM: Dramatists Module; **MST:** Most-studied Authors Module;

   MULT: Multicultural Authors Module; **NOV:** Novelists Module;

   POET: Poets Module; **POP:** Popular Fiction and Genre Authors Module

DFS = Drama for Students

DLB = Dictionary of Literary Biography

DLBD = Dictionary of Literary Biography Documentary Series

DLBY = Dictionary of Literary Biography Yearbook

DNFS = Literature of Developing Nations for Students

EFS = Epics for Students

EXPN = Exploring Novels

EXPP = Exploring Poetry

EXPS = Exploring Short Stories

EW = European Writers

FANT = St. James Guide to Fantasy Writers

FW = Feminist Writers

GFL = Guide to French Literature, Beginnings to 1789, 1798 to the Present

GLL = Gay and Lesbian Literature

HGG = St. James Guide to Horror, Ghost & Gothic Writers

HW = Hispanic Writers

IDFW = International Dictionary of Films and Filmmakers: Writers and Production Artists

IDTP = International Dictionary of Theatre: Playwrights

LAIT = Literature and Its Times

LAW = Latin American Writers

JRDA = Junior DISCovering Authors

MAICYA = Major Authors and Illustrators for Children and Young Adults

MAICYAS = Major Authors and Illustrators for Children and Young Adults Supplement

MAWW = Modern American Women Writers

MJW = Modern Japanese Writers

MTCW = Major 20th-Century Writers

NCFS = Nonfiction Classics for Students

NFS = Novels for Students

PAB = Poets: American and British

PFS = Poetry for Students

RGAL = Reference Guide to American Literature

RGEL = Reference Guide to English Literature

RGSF = Reference Guide to Short Fiction

RGWL = Reference Guide to World Literature

RHW = Twentieth-Century Romance and Historical Writers

SAAS = Something about the Author Autobiography Series

SATA = Something about the Author

SFW = St. James Guide to Science Fiction Writers

SSFS = Short Stories for Students

TCWW = Twentieth-Century Western Writers

WLIT = World Literature and Its Times

WP = World Poets

YABC = Yesterday's Authors of Books for Children

YAW = St. James Guide to Young Adult Writers

Literary Criticism Series
Cumulative Author Index

Andrade, Carlos Drummond de ..... **CLC 18**
See Drummond de Andrade, Carlos
See also EWL 3; RGWL 2, 3
Andrade, Mario de .... **TCLC 43**
See de Andrade, Mario
See also DLB 307; EWL 3; LAW; RGWL
2, 3; WLIT 1
Andreae, Johann V(alentin)
1586-1654 .... **LC 32**
See also DLB 164
Andreas Capellanus fl. c. 1185- .... **CMLC 45**
See also DLB 208
Andreas-Salome, Lou 1861-1937 ... **TCLC 56**
See also CA 178; DLB 66
Andreev, Leonid
See Andreyev, Leonid (Nikolaevich)
See also DLB 295; EWL 3
Andress, Lesley
See Sanders, Lawrence
Andrewes, Lancelot 1555-1626 .... **LC 5**
See also DLB 151, 172
Andrews, Cicily Fairfield
See West, Rebecca
Andrews, Elton V.
See Pohl, Frederik
Andreyev, Leonid (Nikolaevich)
1871-1919 .... **TCLC 3**
See Andreev, Leonid
See also CA 104; 185
Andric, Ivo 1892-1975 .... **CLC 8; SSC 36;**
TCLC 135
See also CA 81-84; 57-60; CANR 43, 60;
CDWLB 4; DLB 147; EW 11; EWL 3;
MTCW 1; RGSF 2; RGWL 2, 3
Androvar
See Prado (Calvo), Pedro
Angelique, Pierre
See Bataille, Georges
Angell, Roger 1920- .... **CLC 26**
See also CA 57-60; CANR 13, 44, 70; DLB
171, 185
Angelou, Maya 1928- ... **BLC 1; CLC 12, 35,**
64, 77, 155; PC 32; WLCS
See also AAYA 7, 20; AMWS 4; BPFB 1;
BW 2, 3; BYA 2; CA 65-68; CANR 19,
42, 65, 111, 133; CDALBS; CLR 53; CP
7; CPW; CSW; DA; DA3; DAB;
DAC; DAM MST, MULT, POET, POP;
DLB 38; EWL 3; EXPN; EXPP; LAIT 4;
MAICYA 2; MAICYAS 1; MAWW;
MTCW 1, 2; NCFS 2; NFS 2; PFS 2, 3;
RGAL 4; SATA 49, 136; WYA; YAW
Angouleme, Marguerite d'
See de Navarre, Marguerite
Anna Comnena 1083-1153 .... **CMLC 25**
Annensky, Innokentii Fedorovich
See Annensky, Innokenty (Fyodorovich)
See also DLB 295
Annensky, Innokenty (Fyodorovich)
1856-1909 .... **TCLC 14**
See also CA 110; 155; EWL 3
Annunzio, Gabriele d'
See D'Annunzio, Gabriele
Anodos
See Coleridge, Mary E(lizabeth)
Anon, Charles Robert
See Pessoa, Fernando (Antonio Nogueira)
Anouilh, Jean (Marie Lucien Pierre)
1910-1987 . **CLC 1, 3, 8, 13, 40, 50; DC**
8, 21
See also CA 17-20R; 123; CANR 32; DAM
DRAM; DFS 9, 10, 19; EW 13; EWL 3;
GFL 1789 to the Present; MTCW 1, 2;
RGWL 2, 3; TWA
Anselm of Canterbury
1033(?)-1109 .... **CMLC 67**
See also DLB 115
Anthony, Florence
See Ai

Anthony, John
See Ciardi, John (Anthony)
Anthony, Peter
See Shaffer, Anthony (Joshua); Shaffer,
Peter (Levin)
Anthony, Piers 1934- .... **CLC 35**
See also AAYA 11, 48; BYA 7; CA 200;
CAAE 200; CANR 28, 56, 73, 102, 133;
CPW; DAM POP; DLB 8; FANT; MAI-
CYA 2; MAICYAS 1; MTCW 1, 2; SAAS
22; SATA 84, 129; SATA-Essay 129; SFW
4; SUFW 1, 2; YAW
Anthony, Susan B(rownell)
1820-1906 .... **TCLC 84**
See also CA 211; FW
Antiphon c. 480B.C.-c. 411B.C. .... **CMLC 55**
Antoine, Marc
See Proust, (Valentin-Louis-George-Eugene)
Marcel
Antoninus, Brother
See Everson, William (Oliver)
Antonioni, Michelangelo 1912- .... **CLC 20,**
144
See also CA 73-76; CANR 45, 77
Antschel, Paul 1920-1970
See Celan, Paul
See also CA 85-88; CANR 33, 61; MTCW
1; PFS 21
Anwar, Chairil 1922-1949 .... **TCLC 22**
See Chairil Anwar
See also CA 121; 219; RGWL 3
Anzaldua, Gloria (Evanjelina)
1942-2004 .... **CLC 200, HLCS 1**
See also CA 175; 227; CSW; CWP; DLB
122; FW; LLW 1; RGAL 4; SATA-Obit
154
Apess, William 1798-1839(?) .... **NCLC 73;**
NNAL
See also DAM MULT; DLB 175, 243
Apollinaire, Guillaume 1880-1918 .... **PC 7;**
TCLC 3, 8, 51
See Kostrowitzki, Wilhelm Apollinaris de
See also CA 152; DAM POET; DLB 258;
EW 9; EWL 3; GFL 1789 to the Present;
MTCW 1; RGWL 2, 3; TWA; WP
Apollonius of Rhodes
See Apollonius Rhodius
See also AW 1; RGWL 2, 3
Apollonius Rhodius c. 300B.C.-c.
220B.C. .... **CMLC 28**
See Apollonius of Rhodes
See also DLB 176
Appelfeld, Aharon 1932- ... **CLC 23, 47; SSC**
42
See also CA 112; 133; CANR 86; CWW 2;
DLB 299; EWL 3; RGSF 2
Apple, Max (Isaac) 1941- .... **CLC 9, 33; SSC**
50
See also CA 81-84; CANR 19, 54; DLB
130
Appleman, Philip (Dean) 1926- .... **CLC 51**
See also CA 13-16R; CAAS 18; CANR 6,
29, 56
Appleton, Lawrence
See Lovecraft, H(oward) P(hillips)
Apteryx
See Eliot, T(homas) S(tearns)
Apuleius, (Lucius Madaurensis)
125(?)-175(?) .... **CMLC 1**
See also AW 2; CDWLB 1; DLB 211;
RGWL 2, 3; SUFW
Aquin, Hubert 1929-1977 .... **CLC 15**
See also CA 105; DLB 53; EWL 3
Aquinas, Thomas 1224(?)-1274 ..... **CMLC 33**
See also DLB 115; EW 1; TWA

Aragon, Louis 1897-1982 .... **CLC 3, 22;**
TCLC 123
See also CA 69-72; 108; CANR 28, 71;
DAM NOV, POET; DLB 72, 258; EW 11;
EWL 3; GFL 1789 to the Present; GLL 2;
LMFS 2; MTCW 1, 2; RGWL 2, 3
Arany, Janos 1817-1882 .... **NCLC 34**
Aranyos, Kakay 1847-1910
See Mikszath, Kalman
Aratus of Soli c. 315B.C.-c.
240B.C. .... **CMLC 64**
See also DLB 176
Arbuthnot, John 1667-1735 .... **LC 1**
See also DLB 101
Archer, Herbert Winslow
See Mencken, H(enry) L(ouis)
Archer, Jeffrey (Howard) 1940- .... **CLC 28**
See also AAYA 16; BEST 89:3; BPFB 1;
CA 77-80; CANR 22, 52, 95; CPW; DA3;
DAM POP; INT CANR-22
Archer, Jules 1915- .... **CLC 12**
See also CA 9-12R; CANR 6, 69; SAAS 5;
SATA 4, 85
Archer, Lee
See Ellison, Harlan (Jay)
Archilochus c. 7th cent. B.C.- .... **CMLC 44**
See also DLB 176
Arden, John 1930- .... **CLC 6, 13, 15**
See also BRWS 2; CA 13-16R; CAAS 4;
CANR 31, 65, 67, 124; CBD; CD 5;
DAM DRAM; DFS 9; DLB 13, 245;
EWL 3; MTCW 1
Arenas, Reinaldo 1943-1990 .. **CLC 41; HLC**
1
See also CA 124; 128; 133; CANR 73, 106;
DAM MULT; DLB 145; EWL 3; GLL 2;
HW 1; LAW; LAWS 1; MTCW 1; RGSF
2; RGWL 3; WLIT 1
Arendt, Hannah 1906-1975 .... **CLC 66, 98**
See also CA 17-20R; 61-64; CANR 26, 60;
DLB 242; MTCW 1, 2
Aretino, Pietro 1492-1556 .... **LC 12**
See also RGWL 2, 3
Arghezi, Tudor .... **CLC 80**
See Theodorescu, Ion N.
See also CA 167; CDWLB 4; DLB 220;
EWL 3
Arguedas, Jose Maria 1911-1969 .... **CLC 10,**
18; HLCS 1; TCLC 147
See also CA 89-92; CANR 73; DLB 113;
EWL 3; HW 1; LAW; RGWL 2, 3; WLIT
1
Argueta, Manlio 1936- .... **CLC 31**
See also CA 131; CANR 73; CWW 2; DLB
145; EWL 3; HW 1; RGWL 3
Arias, Ron(ald Francis) 1941- .... **HLC 1**
See also CA 131; CANR 81; DAM MULT;
DLB 82; HW 1, 2; MTCW 2
Ariosto, Ludovico 1474-1533 ... **LC 6, 87; PC**
42
See also EW 2; RGWL 2, 3
Aristides
See Epstein, Joseph
Aristophanes 450B.C.-385B.C. .... **CMLC 4,**
51; DC 2; WLCS
See also AW 1; CDWLB 1; DA; DA3;
DAB; DAC; DAM DRAM, MST; DFS
10; DLB 176; LMFS 1; RGWL 2, 3; TWA
Aristotle 384B.C.-322B.C. .... **CMLC 31;**
WLCS
See also AW 1; CDWLB 1; DA; DA3;
DAB; DAC; DAM MST; DLB 176;
RGWL 2, 3; TWA
Arlt, Roberto (Godofredo Christophersen)
1900-1942 .... **HLC 1; TCLC 29**
See also CA 123; 131; CANR 67; DAM
MULT; DLB 305; EWL 3; HW 1, 2; LAW

Armah, Ayi Kwei 1939- . **BLC 1; CLC 5, 33, 136**
See also AFW; BRWS 10; BW 1; CA 61-64; CANR 21, 64; CDWLB 3; CN 7; DAM MULT, POET; DLB 117; EWL 3; MTCW 1; WLIT 2

Armatrading, Joan 1950- .... **CLC 17**
See also CA 114; 186

Armitage, Frank
See Carpenter, John (Howard)

Armstrong, Jeannette (C.) 1948- .... **NNAL**
See also CA 149; CCA 1; CN 7; DAC; SATA 102

Arnette, Robert
See Silverberg, Robert

Arnim, Achim von (Ludwig Joachim von Arnim) 1781-1831 ..... **NCLC 5; SSC 29**
See also DLB 90

Arnim, Bettina von 1785-1859 ...... **NCLC 38, 123**
See also DLB 90; RGWL 2, 3

Arnold, Matthew 1822-1888 ..... **NCLC 6, 29, 89, 126; PC 5; WLC**
See also BRW 5; CDBLB 1832-1890; DA; DAB; DAC; DAM MST, POET; DLB 32, 57; EXPP; PAB; PFS 2; TEA; WP

Arnold, Thomas 1795-1842 .... **NCLC 18**
See also DLB 55

Arnow, Harriette (Louisa) Simpson
1908-1986 .... **CLC 2, 7, 18**
See also BPFB 1; CA 9-12R; 118; CANR 14; DLB 6; FW; MTCW 1, 2; RHW; SATA 42; SATA-Obit 47

Arouet, Francois-Marie
See Voltaire

Arp, Hans
See Arp, Jean

Arp, Jean 1887-1966 .... **CLC 5; TCLC 115**
See also CA 81-84; 25-28R; CANR 42, 77; EW 10

Arrabal
See Arrabal, Fernando

Arrabal, Fernando 1932- ... **CLC 2, 9, 18, 58**
See Arrabal (Teran), Fernando
See also CA 9-12R; CANR 15; EWL 3; LMFS 2

Arrabal (Teran), Fernando 1932-
See Arrabal, Fernando
See also CWW 2

Arreola, Juan Jose 1918-2001 .... **CLC 147; HLC 1; SSC 38**
See also CA 113; 131; 200; CANR 81; CWW 2; DAM MULT; DLB 113; DNFS 2; EWL 3; HW 1, 2; LAW; RGSF 2

Arrian c. 89(?)-c. 155(?) .... **CMLC 43**
See also DLB 176

Arrick, Fran .... **CLC 30**
See Gaberman, Judie Angell
See also BYA 6

Arrley, Richmond
See Delany, Samuel R(ay), Jr.

Artaud, Antonin (Marie Joseph)
1896-1948 .... **DC 14; TCLC 3, 36**
See also CA 104; 149; DA3; DAM DRAM; DLB 258; EW 11; EWL 3; GFL 1789 to the Present; MTCW 1; RGWL 2, 3

Arthur, Ruth M(abel) 1905-1979 ..... **CLC 12**
See also CA 9-12R; 85-88; CANR 4; CWRI 5; SATA 7, 26

Artsybashev, Mikhail (Petrovich)
1878-1927 .... **TCLC 31**
See also CA 170; DLB 295

Arundel, Honor (Morfydd)
1919-1973 .... **CLC 17**
See also CA 21-22; 41-44R; CAP 2; CLR 35; CWRI 5; SATA 4; SATA-Obit 24

Arzner, Dorothy 1900-1979 .... **CLC 98**

Asch, Sholem 1880-1957 .... **TCLC 3**
See also CA 105; EWL 3; GLL 2

Ascham, Roger 1516(?)-1568 .... **LC 101**
See also DLB 236

Ash, Shalom
See Asch, Sholem

Ashbery, John (Lawrence) 1927- .. **CLC 2, 3, 4, 6, 9, 13, 15, 25, 41, 77, 125; PC 26**
See Berry, Jonas
See also AMWS 3; CA 5-8R; CANR 9, 37, 66, 102, 132; CP 7; DA3; DAM POET; DLB 5, 165; DLBY 1981; EWL 3; INT CANR-9; MTCW 1, 2; PAB; PFS 11; RGAL 4; WP

Ashdown, Clifford
See Freeman, R(ichard) Austin

Ashe, Gordon
See Creasey, John

Ashton-Warner, Sylvia (Constance)
1908-1984 .... **CLC 19**
See also CA 69-72; 112; CANR 29; MTCW 1, 2

Asimov, Isaac 1920-1992 ..... **CLC 1, 3, 9, 19, 26, 76, 92**
See also AAYA 13; BEST 90:2; BPFB 1; BYA 4, 6, 7, 9; CA 1-4R; 137; CANR 2, 19, 36, 60, 125; CLR 12, 79; CMW 4; CPW; DA3; DAM POP; DLB 8; DLBY 1992; INT CANR-19; JRDA; LAIT 5; LMFS 2; MAICYA 1, 2; MTCW 1, 2; RGAL 4; SATA 1, 26, 74; SCFW 2; SFW 4; SSFS 17; TUS; YAW

Askew, Anne 1521(?)-1546 .... **LC 81**
See also DLB 136

Assis, Joaquim Maria Machado de
See Machado de Assis, Joaquim Maria

Astell, Mary 1666-1731 .... **LC 68**
See also DLB 252; FW

Astley, Thea (Beatrice May)
1925-2004 .... **CLC 41**
See also CA 65-68; 229; CANR 11, 43, 78; CN 7; DLB 289; EWL 3

Astley, William 1855-1911
See Warung, Price

Aston, James
See White, T(erence) H(anbury)

Asturias, Miguel Angel 1899-1974 .... **CLC 3, 8, 13; HLC 1**
See also CA 25-28; 49-52; CANR 32; CAP 2; CDWLB 3; DA3; DAM MULT, NOV; DLB 113, 290; EWL 3; HW 1; LAW; LMFS 2; MTCW 1, 2; RGWL 2, 3; WLIT 1

Atares, Carlos Saura
See Saura (Atares), Carlos

Athanasius c. 295-c. 373 .... **CMLC 48**

Atheling, William
See Pound, Ezra (Weston Loomis)

Atheling, William, Jr.
See Blish, James (Benjamin)

Atherton, Gertrude (Franklin Horn)
1857-1948 .... **TCLC 2**
See also CA 104; 155; DLB 9, 78, 186; HGG; RGAL 4; SUFW 1; TCWW 2

Atherton, Lucius
See Masters, Edgar Lee

Atkins, Jack
See Harris, Mark

Atkinson, Kate 1951- .... **CLC 99**
See also CA 166; CANR 101; DLB 267

Attaway, William (Alexander)
1911-1986 .... **BLC 1; CLC 92**
See also BW 2, 3; CA 143; CANR 82; DAM MULT; DLB 76

Atticus
See Fleming, Ian (Lancaster); Wilson, (Thomas) Woodrow

Atwood, Margaret (Eleanor) 1939- ... **CLC 2, 3, 4, 8, 13, 15, 25, 44, 84, 135; PC 8; SSC 2, 46; WLC**
See also AAYA 12, 47; AMWS 13; BEST 89:2; BPFB 1; CA 49-52; CANR 3, 24, 33, 59, 95, 133; CN 7; CP 7; CPW; CWP; DA; DA3; DAB; DAC; DAM MST, NOV, POET; DLB 53, 251; EWL 3; EXPN; FW; INT CANR-24; LAIT 5; MTCW 1, 2; NFS 4, 12, 13, 14, 19; PFS 7; RGSF 2; SATA 50; SSFS 3, 13; TWA; WWE 1; YAW

Aubigny, Pierre d'
See Mencken, H(enry) L(ouis)

Aubin, Penelope 1685-1731(?) .... **LC 9**
See also DLB 39

Auchincloss, Louis (Stanton) 1917- .. **CLC 4, 6, 9, 18, 45; SSC 22**
See also AMWS 4; CA 1-4R; CANR 6, 29, 55, 87, 130; CN 7; DAM NOV; DLB 2, 244; DLBY 1980; EWL 3; INT CANR-29; MTCW 1; RGAL 4

Auden, W(ystan) H(ugh) 1907-1973 . **CLC 1, 2, 3, 4, 6, 9, 11, 14, 43, 123; PC 1; WLC**
See also AAYA 18; AMWS 2; BRW 7; BRWR 1; CA 9-12R; 45-48; CANR 5, 61, 105; CDBLB 1914-1945; DA; DA3; DAB; DAC; DAM DRAM, MST, POET; DLB 10, 20; EWL 3; EXPP; MTCW 1, 2; PAB; PFS 1, 3, 4, 10; TUS; WP

Audiberti, Jacques 1899-1965 .... **CLC 38**
See also CA 25-28R; DAM DRAM; EWL 3

Audubon, John James 1785-1851 . **NCLC 47**
See also ANW; DLB 248

Auel, Jean M(arie) 1936- .... **CLC 31, 107**
See also AAYA 7, 51; BEST 90:4; BPFB 1; CA 103; CANR 21, 64, 115; CPW; DA3; DAM POP; INT CANR-21; NFS 11; RHW; SATA 91

Auerbach, Erich 1892-1957 .... **TCLC 43**
See also CA 118; 155; EWL 3

Augier, Emile 1820-1889 .... **NCLC 31**
See also DLB 192; GFL 1789 to the Present

August, John
See De Voto, Bernard (Augustine)

Augustine, St. 354-430 .... **CMLC 6; WLCS**
See also DA; DA3; DAB; DAC; DAM MST; DLB 115; EW 1; RGWL 2, 3

Aunt Belinda
See Braddon, Mary Elizabeth

Aunt Weedy
See Alcott, Louisa May

Aurelius
See Bourne, Randolph S(illiman)

Aurelius, Marcus 121-180 .... **CMLC 45**
See Marcus Aurelius
See also RGWL 2, 3

Aurobindo, Sri
See Ghose, Aurabinda

Aurobindo Ghose
See Ghose, Aurabinda

Austen, Jane 1775-1817 ...... **NCLC 1, 13, 19, 33, 51, 81, 95, 119, 150; WLC**
See also AAYA 19; BRW 4; BRWC 1; BRWR 2; BYA 3; CDBLB 1789-1832; DA; DA3; DAB; DAC; DAM MST, NOV; DLB 116; EXPN; LAIT 2; LATS 1:1; LMFS 1; NFS 1, 14, 18, 20; TEA; WLIT 3; WYAS 1

Auster, Paul 1947- .... **CLC 47, 131**
See also AMWS 12; CA 69-72; CANR 23, 52, 75, 129; CMW 4; CN 7; DA3; DLB 227; MTCW 1; SUFW 2

Austin, Frank
See Faust, Frederick (Schiller)
See also TCWW 2

Baraka, Amiri 1934- .... **BLC 1; CLC 1, 2, 3, 5, 10, 14, 33, 115; DC 6; PC 4; WLCS**
See Jones, LeRoi
See also AFAW 1, 2; AMWS 2; BW 2, 3; CA 21-24R; CABS 3; CAD; CANR 27, 38, 61, 133; CD 5; CDALB 1941-1968; CP 7; CPW; DA; DA3; DAC; DAM MST, MULT, POET, POP; DFS 3, 11, 16; DLB 5, 7, 16, 38; DLBD 8; EWL 3; MTCW 1, 2; PFS 9; RGAL 4; TUS; WP

Baratynsky, Evgenii Abramovich
1800-1844 .... **NCLC 103**
See also DLB 205

Barbauld, Anna Laetitia
1743-1825 .... **NCLC 50**
See also DLB 107, 109, 142, 158; RGEL 2

Barbellion, W. N. P. .... **TCLC 24**
See Cummings, Bruce F(rederick)

Barber, Benjamin R. 1939- .... **CLC 141**
See also CA 29-32R; CANR 12, 32, 64, 119

Barbera, Jack (Vincent) 1945- .... **CLC 44**
See also CA 110; CANR 45

Barbey d'Aurevilly, Jules-Amedee
1808-1889 .... **NCLC 1; SSC 17**
See also DLB 119; GFL 1789 to the Present

Barbour, John c. 1316-1395 .... **CMLC 33**
See also DLB 146

Barbusse, Henri 1873-1935 .... **TCLC 5**
See also CA 105; 154; DLB 65; EWL 3; RGWL 2, 3

Barclay, Alexander c. 1475-1552 .... **LC 109**
See also DLB 132

Barclay, Bill
See Moorcock, Michael (John)

Barclay, William Ewert
See Moorcock, Michael (John)

Barea, Arturo 1897-1957 .... **TCLC 14**
See also CA 111; 201

Barfoot, Joan 1946- .... **CLC 18**
See also CA 105

Barham, Richard Harris
1788-1845 .... **NCLC 77**
See also DLB 159

Baring, Maurice 1874-1945 .... **TCLC 8**
See also CA 105; 168; DLB 34; HGG

Baring-Gould, Sabine 1834-1924 ... **TCLC 88**
See also DLB 156, 190

Barker, Clive 1952- .... **CLC 52, 205; SSC 53**
See also AAYA 10, 54; BEST 90:3; BPFB 1; CA 121; 129; CANR 71, 111, 133; CPW; DA3; DAM POP; DLB 261; HGG; INT CA-129; MTCW 1, 2; SUFW 2

Barker, George Granville
1913-1991 .... **CLC 8, 48**
See also CA 9-12R; 135; CANR 7, 38; DAM POET; DLB 20; EWL 3; MTCW 1

Barker, Harley Granville
See Granville-Barker, Harley
See also DLB 10

Barker, Howard 1946- .... **CLC 37**
See also CA 102; CBD; CD 5; DLB 13, 233

Barker, Jane 1652-1732 .... **LC 42, 82**
See also DLB 39, 131

Barker, Pat(ricia) 1943- ...... **CLC 32, 94, 146**
See also BRWS 4; CA 117; 122; CANR 50, 101; CN 7; DLB 271; INT CA-122

Barlach, Ernst (Heinrich)
1870-1938 .... **TCLC 84**
See also CA 178; DLB 56, 118; EWL 3

Barlow, Joel 1754-1812 .... **NCLC 23**
See also AMWS 2; DLB 37; RGAL 4

Barnard, Mary (Ethel) 1909- .... **CLC 48**
See also CA 21-22; CAP 2

Barnes, Djuna 1892-1982 .... **CLC 3, 4, 8, 11, 29, 127; SSC 3**
See Steptoe, Lydia
See also AMWS 3; CA 9-12R; 107; CAD; CANR 16, 55; CWD; DLB 4, 9, 45; EWL 3; GLL 1; MTCW 1, 2; RGAL 4; TUS

Barnes, Jim 1933- .... **NNAL**
See also CA 108, 175; CAAE 175; CAAS 28; DLB 175

Barnes, Julian (Patrick) 1946- . **CLC 42, 141**
See also BRWS 4; CA 102; CANR 19, 54, 115; CN 7; DAB; DLB 194; DLBY 1993; EWL 3; MTCW 1

Barnes, Peter 1931-2004 .... **CLC 5, 56**
See also CA 65-68; CAAS 12; CANR 33, 34, 64, 113; CBD; CD 5; DFS 6; DLB 13, 233; MTCW 1

Barnes, William 1801-1886 .... **NCLC 75**
See also DLB 32

Baroja (y Nessi), Pio 1872-1956 .... **HLC 1; TCLC 8**
See also CA 104; EW 9

Baron, David
See Pinter, Harold

Baron Corvo
See Rolfe, Frederick (William Serafino Austin Lewis Mary)

Barondess, Sue K(aufman)
1926-1977 .... **CLC 8**
See Kaufman, Sue
See also CA 1-4R; 69-72; CANR 1

Baron de Teive
See Pessoa, Fernando (Antonio Nogueira)

Baroness Von S.
See Zangwill, Israel

Barres, (Auguste-)Maurice
1862-1923 .... **TCLC 47**
See also CA 164; DLB 123; GFL 1789 to the Present

Barreto, Afonso Henrique de Lima
See Lima Barreto, Afonso Henrique de

Barrett, Andrea 1954- .... **CLC 150**
See also CA 156; CANR 92

Barrett, Michele .... **CLC 65**

Barrett, (Roger) Syd 1946- .... **CLC 35**

Barrett, William (Christopher)
1913-1992 .... **CLC 27**
See also CA 13-16R; 139; CANR 11, 67; INT CANR-11

Barrett Browning, Elizabeth
1806-1861 ... **NCLC 1, 16, 61, 66; PC 6, 62; WLC**
See also BRW 4; CDBLB 1832-1890; DA; DA3; DAB; DAC; DAM MST, POET; DLB 32, 199; EXPP; PAB; PFS 2, 16; TEA; WLIT 4; WP

Barrie, J(ames) M(atthew)
1860-1937 .... **TCLC 2, 164**
See also BRWS 3; BYA 4, 5; CA 104; 136; CANR 77; CDBLB 1890-1914; CLR 16; CWRI 5; DA3; DAB; DAM DRAM; DFS 7; DLB 10, 141, 156; EWL 3; FANT; MAICYA 1, 2; MTCW 1; SATA 100; SUFW; WCH; WLIT 4; YABC 1

Barrington, Michael
See Moorcock, Michael (John)

Barrol, Grady
See Bograd, Larry

Barry, Mike
See Malzberg, Barry N(athaniel)

Barry, Philip 1896-1949 .... **TCLC 11**
See also CA 109; 199; DFS 9; DLB 7, 228; RGAL 4

Bart, Andre Schwarz
See Schwarz-Bart, Andre

Barth, John (Simmons) 1930- ... **CLC 1, 2, 3, 5, 7, 9, 10, 14, 27, 51, 89; SSC 10**
See also AITN 1, 2; AMW; BPFB 1; CA 1-4R; CABS 1; CANR 5, 23, 49, 64, 113; CN 7; DAM NOV; DLB 2, 227; EWL 3; FANT; MTCW 1; RGAL 4; RGSF 2; RHW; SSFS 6; TUS

Barthelme, Donald 1931-1989 ... **CLC 1, 2, 3, 5, 6, 8, 13, 23, 46, 59, 115; SSC 2, 55**
See also AMWS 4; BPFB 1; CA 21-24R; 129; CANR 20, 58; DA3; DAM NOV; DLB 2, 234; DLBY 1980, 1989; EWL 3; FANT; LMFS 2; MTCW 1, 2; RGAL 4; RGSF 2; SATA 7; SATA-Obit 62; SSFS 17

Barthelme, Frederick 1943- ...... **CLC 36, 117**
See also AMWS 11; CA 114; 122; CANR 77; CN 7; CSW; DLB 244; DLBY 1985; EWL 3; INT CA-122

Barthes, Roland (Gerard)
1915-1980 .... **CLC 24, 83; TCLC 135**
See also CA 130; 97-100; CANR 66; DLB 296; EW 13; EWL 3; GFL 1789 to the Present; MTCW 1, 2; TWA

Bartram, William 1739-1823 .... **NCLC 145**
See also ANW; DLB 37

Barzun, Jacques (Martin) 1907- ..... **CLC 51, 145**
See also CA 61-64; CANR 22, 95

Bashevis, Isaac
See Singer, Isaac Bashevis

Bashkirtseff, Marie 1859-1884 .... **NCLC 27**

Basho, Matsuo
See Matsuo Basho
See also PFS 18; RGWL 2, 3; WP

Basil of Caesaria c. 330-379 .... **CMLC 35**

Basket, Raney
See Edgerton, Clyde (Carlyle)

Bass, Kingsley B., Jr.
See Bullins, Ed

Bass, Rick 1958- .... **CLC 79, 143; SSC 60**
See also ANW; CA 126; CANR 53, 93; CSW; DLB 212, 275

Bassani, Giorgio 1916-2000 .... **CLC 9**
See also CA 65-68; 190; CANR 33; CWW 2; DLB 128, 177, 299; EWL 3; MTCW 1; RGWL 2, 3

Bastian, Ann .... **CLC 70**

Bastos, Augusto (Antonio) Roa
See Roa Bastos, Augusto (Antonio)

Bataille, Georges 1897-1962 .... **CLC 29; TCLC 155**
See also CA 101; 89-92; EWL 3

Bates, H(erbert) E(rnest)
1905-1974 .... **CLC 46; SSC 10**
See also CA 93-96; 45-48; CANR 34; DA3; DAB; DAM POP; DLB 162, 191; EWL 3; EXPS; MTCW 1, 2; RGSF 2; SSFS 7

Bauchart
See Camus, Albert

Baudelaire, Charles 1821-1867 . **NCLC 6, 29, 55; PC 1; SSC 18; WLC**
See also DA; DA3; DAB; DAC; DAM MST, POET; DLB 217; EW 7; GFL 1789 to the Present; LMFS 2; PFS 21; RGWL 2, 3; TWA

Baudouin, Marcel
See Peguy, Charles (Pierre)

Baudouin, Pierre
See Peguy, Charles (Pierre)

Baudrillard, Jean 1929- .... **CLC 60**
See also DLB 296

Baum, L(yman) Frank 1856-1919 .. **TCLC 7, 132**
See also AAYA 46; BYA 16; CA 108; 133; CLR 15; CWRI 5; DLB 22; FANT; JRDA; MAICYA 1, 2; MTCW 1, 2; NFS 13; RGAL 4; SATA 18, 100; WCH

Baum, Louis F.
See Baum, L(yman) Frank

Baumbach, Jonathan 1933- .... **CLC 6, 23**
See also CA 13-16R; CAAS 5; CANR 12, 66; CN 7; DLBY 1980; INT CANR-12; MTCW 1

Bausch, Richard (Carl) 1945- .... **CLC 51**
See also AMWS 7; CA 101; CAAS 14; CANR 43, 61, 87; CSW; DLB 130

Baxter, Charles (Morley) 1947- . **CLC 45, 78**
See also CA 57-60; CANR 40, 64, 104, 133; CPW; DAM POP; DLB 130; MTCW 2

Baxter, George Owen
See Faust, Frederick (Schiller)

Baxter, James K(eir) 1926-1972 .... **CLC 14**
See also CA 77-80; EWL 3

Baxter, John
See Hunt, E(verette) Howard, (Jr.)

Bayer, Sylvia
See Glassco, John

Baynton, Barbara 1857-1929 .... **TCLC 57**
See also DLB 230; RGSF 2

Beagle, Peter S(oyer) 1939- .... **CLC 7, 104**
See also AAYA 47; BPFB 1; BYA 9, 10, 16; CA 9-12R; CANR 4, 51, 73, 110; DA3; DLBY 1980; FANT; INT CANR-4; MTCW 1; SATA 60, 130; SUFW 1, 2; YAW

Bean, Normal
See Burroughs, Edgar Rice

Beard, Charles A(ustin)
1874-1948 .... **TCLC 15**
See also CA 115; 189; DLB 17; SATA 18

Beardsley, Aubrey 1872-1898 .... **NCLC 6**

Beattie, Ann 1947- ..... **CLC 8, 13, 18, 40, 63, 146; SSC 11**
See also AMWS 5; BEST 90:2; BPFB 1; CA 81-84; CANR 53, 73, 128; CN 7; CPW; DA3; DAM NOV, POP; DLB 218, 278; DLBY 1982; EWL 3; MTCW 1, 2; RGAL 4; RGSF 2; SSFS 9; TUS

Beattie, James 1735-1803 .... **NCLC 25**
See also DLB 109

Beauchamp, Kathleen Mansfield 1888-1923
See Mansfield, Katherine
See also CA 104; 134; DA; DA3; DAC; DAM MST; MTCW 2; TEA

Beaumarchais, Pierre-Augustin Caron de
1732-1799 .... **DC 4; LC 61**
See also DAM DRAM; DFS 14, 16; EW 4; GFL Beginnings to 1789; RGWL 2, 3

Beaumont, Francis 1584(?)-1616 .. **DC 6; LC 33**
See also BRW 2; CDBLB Before 1660; DLB 58; TEA

Beauvoir, Simone (Lucie Ernestine Marie Bertrand) de 1908-1986 .... **CLC 1, 2, 4, 8, 14, 31, 44, 50, 71, 124; SSC 35; WLC**
See also BPFB 1; CA 9-12R; 118; CANR 28, 61; DA; DA3; DAB; DAC; DAM MST, NOV; DLB 72; DLBY 1986; EW 12; EWL 3; FW; GFL 1789 to the Present; LMFS 2; MTCW 1, 2; RGSF 2; RGWL 2, 3; TWA

Becker, Carl (Lotus) 1873-1945 ..... **TCLC 63**
See also CA 157; DLB 17

Becker, Jurek 1937-1997 .... **CLC 7, 19**
See also CA 85-88; 157; CANR 60, 117; CWW 2; DLB 75, 299; EWL 3

Becker, Walter 1950- .... **CLC 26**

Beckett, Samuel (Barclay)
1906-1989 .. **CLC 1, 2, 3, 4, 6, 9, 10, 11, 14, 18, 29, 57, 59, 83; DC 22; SSC 16, 74; TCLC 145; WLC**
See also BRWC 2; BRWR 1; BRWS 1; CA 5-8R; 130; CANR 33, 61; CBD; CDBLB 1945-1960; DA; DA3; DAB; DAC; DAM DRAM, MST, NOV; DFS 2, 7, 18; DLB

13, 15, 233; DLBY 1990; EWL 3; GFL 1789 to the Present; LATS 1:2; LMFS 2; MTCW 1, 2; RGSF 2; RGWL 2, 3; SSFS 15; TEA; WLIT 4

Beckford, William 1760-1844 .... **NCLC 16**
See also BRW 3; DLB 39, 213; HGG; LMFS 1; SUFW

Beckham, Barry (Earl) 1944- .... **BLC 1**
See also BW 1; CA 29-32R; CANR 26, 62; CN 7; DAM MULT; DLB 33

Beckman, Gunnel 1910- .... **CLC 26**
See also CA 33-36R; CANR 15, 114; CLR 25; MAICYA 1, 2; SAAS 9; SATA 6

Becque, Henri 1837-1899 .... **DC 21; NCLC 3**
See also DLB 192; GFL 1789 to the Present

Becquer, Gustavo Adolfo
1836-1870 .... **HLCS 1; NCLC 106**
See also DAM MULT

Beddoes, Thomas Lovell 1803-1849 .. **DC 15; NCLC 3, 154**
See also DLB 96

Bede c. 673-735 .... **CMLC 20**
See also DLB 146; TEA

Bedford, Denton R. 1907-(?) .... **NNAL**

Bedford, Donald F.
See Fearing, Kenneth (Flexner)

Beecher, Catharine Esther
1800-1878 .... **NCLC 30**
See also DLB 1, 243

Beecher, John 1904-1980 .... **CLC 6**
See also AITN 1; CA 5-8R; 105; CANR 8

Beer, Johann 1655-1700 .... **LC 5**
See also DLB 168

Beer, Patricia 1924- .... **CLC 58**
See also CA 61-64; 183; CANR 13, 46; CP 7; CWP; DLB 40; FW

Beerbohm, Max
See Beerbohm, (Henry) Max(imilian)

Beerbohm, (Henry) Max(imilian)
1872-1956 .... **TCLC 1, 24**
See also BRWS 2; CA 104; 154; CANR 79; DLB 34, 100; FANT

Beer-Hofmann, Richard
1866-1945 .... **TCLC 60**
See also CA 160; DLB 81

Beg, Shemus
See Stephens, James

Begiebing, Robert J(ohn) 1946- .... **CLC 70**
See also CA 122; CANR 40, 88

Begley, Louis 1933- .... **CLC 197**
See also CA 140; CANR 98; DLB 299

Behan, Brendan (Francis)
1923-1964 .... **CLC 1, 8, 11, 15, 79**
See also BRWS 2; CA 73-76; CANR 33, 121; CBD; CDBLB 1945-1960; DAM DRAM; DFS 7; DLB 13, 233; EWL 3; MTCW 1, 2

Behn, Aphra 1640(?)-1689 .. **DC 4; LC 1, 30, 42; PC 13; WLC**
See also BRWS 3; DA; DA3; DAB; DAC; DAM DRAM, MST, NOV, POET; DFS 16; DLB 39, 80, 131; FW; TEA; WLIT 3

Behrman, S(amuel) N(athaniel)
1893-1973 .... **CLC 40**
See also CA 13-16; 45-48; CAD; CAP 1; DLB 7, 44; IDFW 3; RGAL 4

Belasco, David 1853-1931 .... **TCLC 3**
See also CA 104; 168; DLB 7; RGAL 4

Belcheva, Elisaveta Lyubomirova
1893-1991 .... **CLC 10**
See Bagryana, Elisaveta

Beldone, Phil "Cheech"
See Ellison, Harlan (Jay)

Beleno
See Azuela, Mariano

Belinski, Vissarion Grigoryevich
1811-1848 .... **NCLC 5**
See also DLB 198

Belitt, Ben 1911- .... **CLC 22**
See also CA 13-16R; CAAS 4; CANR 7, 77; CP 7; DLB 5

Belknap, Jeremy 1744-1798 .... **LC 115**
See also DLB 30, 37

Bell, Gertrude (Margaret Lowthian)
1868-1926 .... **TCLC 67**
See also CA 167; CANR 110; DLB 174

Bell, J. Freeman
See Zangwill, Israel

Bell, James Madison 1826-1902 .... **BLC 1; TCLC 43**
See also BW 1; CA 122; 124; DAM MULT; DLB 50

Bell, Madison Smartt 1957- ...... **CLC 41, 102**
See also AMWS 10; BPFB 1; CA 111, 183; CAAE 183; CANR 28, 54, 73, 134; CN 7; CSW; DLB 218, 278; MTCW 1

Bell, Marvin (Hartley) 1937- .... **CLC 8, 31**
See also CA 21-24R; CAAS 14; CANR 59, 102; CP 7; DAM POET; DLB 5; MTCW 1

Bell, W. L. D.
See Mencken, H(enry) L(ouis)

Bellamy, Atwood C.
See Mencken, H(enry) L(ouis)

Bellamy, Edward 1850-1898 ..... **NCLC 4, 86, 147**
See also DLB 12; NFS 15; RGAL 4; SFW 4

Belli, Gioconda 1948- .... **HLCS 1**
See also CA 152; CWW 2; DLB 290; EWL 3; RGWL 3

Bellin, Edward J.
See Kuttner, Henry

Bello, Andres 1781-1865 .... **NCLC 131**
See also LAW

Belloc, (Joseph) Hilaire (Pierre Sebastien Rene Swanton) 1870-1953 .... **PC 24; TCLC 7, 18**
See also CA 106; 152; CLR 102; CWRI 5; DAM POET; DLB 19, 100, 141, 174; EWL 3; MTCW 1; SATA 112; WCH; YABC 1

Belloc, Joseph Peter Rene Hilaire
See Belloc, (Joseph) Hilaire (Pierre Sebastien Rene Swanton)

Belloc, Joseph Pierre Hilaire
See Belloc, (Joseph) Hilaire (Pierre Sebastien Rene Swanton)

Belloc, M. A.
See Lowndes, Marie Adelaide (Belloc)

Belloc-Lowndes, Mrs.
See Lowndes, Marie Adelaide (Belloc)

Bellow, Saul 1915- . **CLC 1, 2, 3, 6, 8, 10, 13, 15, 25, 33, 34, 63, 79, 190, 200; SSC 14; WLC**
See also AITN 2; AMW; AMWC 2; AMWR 2; BEST 89:3; BPFB 1; CA 5-8R; CABS 1; CANR 29, 53, 95, 132; CDALB 1941-1968; CN 7; DA; DA3; DAB; DAC; DAM MST, NOV, POP; DLB 2, 28, 299; DLBD 3; DLBY 1982; EWL 3; MTCW 1, 2; NFS 4, 14; RGAL 4; RGSF 2; SSFS 12; TUS

Belser, Reimond Karel Maria de 1929-
See Ruyslinck, Ward
See also CA 152

Bely, Andrey .... **PC 11; TCLC 7**
See Bugayev, Boris Nikolayevich
See also DLB 295; EW 9; EWL 3; MTCW 1

Belyi, Andrei
See Bugayev, Boris Nikolayevich
See also RGWL 2, 3

Bembo, Pietro 1470-1547 .... **LC 79**
See also RGWL 2, 3

Benary, Margot
See Benary-Isbert, Margot

Benary-Isbert, Margot 1889-1979 .... **CLC 12**
See also CA 5-8R; 89-92; CANR 4, 72;
CLR 12; MAICYA 1, 2; SATA 2; SATA-
Obit 21

Benavente (y Martinez), Jacinto
1866-1954 .... **HLCS 1; TCLC 3**
See also CA 106; 131; CANR 81; DAM
DRAM, MULT; EWL 3; GLL 2; HW 1,
2; MTCW 1, 2

Benchley, Peter (Bradford) 1940- .. **CLC 4, 8**
See also AAYA 14; AITN 2; BPFB 1; CA
17-20R; CANR 12, 35, 66, 115; CPW;
DAM NOV, POP; HGG; MTCW 1, 2;
SATA 3, 89

Benchley, Robert (Charles)
1889-1945 .... **TCLC 1, 55**
See also CA 105; 153; DLB 11; RGAL 4

Benda, Julien 1867-1956 .... **TCLC 60**
See also CA 120; 154; GFL 1789 to the
Present

Benedict, Ruth (Fulton)
1887-1948 .... **TCLC 60**
See also CA 158; DLB 246

Benedikt, Michael 1935- .... **CLC 4, 14**
See also CA 13-16R; CANR 7; CP 7; DLB
5

Benet, Juan 1927-1993 .... **CLC 28**
See also CA 143; EWL 3

Benet, Stephen Vincent 1898-1943 ..... **PC 64;**
SSC 10; TCLC 7
See also AMWS 11; CA 104; 152; DA3;
DAM POET; DLB 4, 48, 102, 249, 284;
DLBY 1997; EWL 3; HGG; MTCW 1;
RGAL 4; RGSF 2; SUFW; WP; YABC 1

Benet, William Rose 1886-1950 ..... **TCLC 28**
See also CA 118; 152; DAM POET; DLB
45; RGAL 4

Benford, Gregory (Albert) 1941- ..... **CLC 52**
See also BPFB 1; CA 69-72, 175; CAAE
175; CAAS 27; CANR 12, 24, 49, 95,
134; CSW; DLBY 1982; SCFW 2; SFW
4

Bengtsson, Frans (Gunnar)
1894-1954 .... **TCLC 48**
See also CA 170; EWL 3

Benjamin, David
See Slavitt, David R(ytman)

Benjamin, Lois
See Gould, Lois

Benjamin, Walter 1892-1940 .... **TCLC 39**
See also CA 164; DLB 242; EW 11; EWL
3

Ben Jelloun, Tahar 1944-
See Jelloun, Tahar ben
See also CA 135; CWW 2; EWL 3; RGWL
3; WLIT 2

Benn, Gottfried 1886-1956 .. **PC 35; TCLC 3**
See also CA 106; 153; DLB 56; EWL 3;
RGWL 2, 3

Bennett, Alan 1934- .... **CLC 45, 77**
See also BRWS 8; CA 103; CANR 35, 55,
106; CBD; CD 5; DAB; DAM MST;
MTCW 1, 2

Bennett, (Enoch) Arnold
1867-1931 .... **TCLC 5, 20**
See also BRW 6; CA 106; 155; CDBLB
1890-1914; DLB 10, 34, 98, 135; EWL 3;
MTCW 2

Bennett, Elizabeth
See Mitchell, Margaret (Munnerlyn)

Bennett, George Harold 1930-
See Bennett, Hal
See also BW 1; CA 97-100; CANR 87

Bennett, Gwendolyn B. 1902-1981 .... **HR 2**
See also BW 1; CA 125; DLB 51; WP

Bennett, Hal .... **CLC 5**
See Bennett, George Harold
See also DLB 33

Bennett, Jay 1912- .... **CLC 35**
See also AAYA 10; CA 69-72; CANR 11,
42, 79; JRDA; SAAS 4; SATA 41, 87;
SATA-Brief 27; WYA; YAW

Bennett, Louise (Simone) 1919- .... **BLC 1;**
CLC 28
See also BW 2, 3; CA 151; CDWLB 3; CP
7; DAM MULT; DLB 117; EWL 3

Benson, A. C. 1862-1925 .... **TCLC 123**
See also DLB 98

Benson, E(dward) F(rederic)
1867-1940 .... **TCLC 27**
See also CA 114; 157; DLB 135, 153;
HGG; SUFW 1

Benson, Jackson J. 1930- .... **CLC 34**
See also CA 25-28R; DLB 111

Benson, Sally 1900-1972 .... **CLC 17**
See also CA 19-20; 37-40R; CAP 1; SATA
1, 35; SATA-Obit 27

Benson, Stella 1892-1933 .... **TCLC 17**
See also CA 117; 154, 155; DLB 36, 162;
FANT; TEA

Bentham, Jeremy 1748-1832 .... **NCLC 38**
See also DLB 107, 158, 252

Bentley, E(dmund) C(lerihew)
1875-1956 .... **TCLC 12**
See also CA 108; DLB 70; MSW

Bentley, Eric (Russell) 1916- .... **CLC 24**
See also CA 5-8R; CAD; CANR 6, 67;
CBD; CD 5; INT CANR-6

ben Uzair, Salem
See Horne, Richard Henry Hengist

Beranger, Pierre Jean de
1780-1857 .... **NCLC 34**

Berdyaev, Nicolas
See Berdyaev, Nikolai (Aleksandrovich)

Berdyaev, Nikolai (Aleksandrovich)
1874-1948 .... **TCLC 67**
See also CA 120; 157

Berdyayev, Nikolai (Aleksandrovich)
See Berdyaev, Nikolai (Aleksandrovich)

Berendt, John (Lawrence) 1939- ...... **CLC 86**
See also CA 146; CANR 75, 93; DA3;
MTCW 1

Beresford, J(ohn) D(avys)
1873-1947 .... **TCLC 81**
See also CA 112; 155; DLB 162, 178, 197;
SFW 4; SUFW 1

Bergelson, David (Rafailovich)
1884-1952 .... **TCLC 81**
See Bergelson, Dovid
See also CA 220

Bergelson, Dovid
See Bergelson, David (Rafailovich)
See also EWL 3

Berger, Colonel
See Malraux, (Georges-)Andre

Berger, John (Peter) 1926- .... **CLC 2, 19**
See also BRWS 4; CA 81-84; CANR 51,
78, 117; CN 7; DLB 14, 207

Berger, Melvin H. 1927- .... **CLC 12**
See also CA 5-8R; CANR 4; CLR 32;
SAAS 2; SATA 5, 88; SATA-Essay 124

Berger, Thomas (Louis) 1924- .. **CLC 3, 5, 8,**
11, 18, 38
See also BPFB 1; CA 1-4R; CANR 5, 28,
51, 128; CN 7; DAM NOV; DLB 2;
DLBY 1980; EWL 3; FANT; INT CANR-
28; MTCW 1, 2; RHW; TCWW 2

Bergman, (Ernst) Ingmar 1918- ...... **CLC 16,**
72
See also CA 81-84; CANR 33, 70; CWW
2; DLB 257; MTCW 2

Bergson, Henri(-Louis) 1859-1941 . **TCLC 32**
See also CA 164; EW 8; EWL 3; GFL 1789
to the Present

Bergstein, Eleanor 1938- .... **CLC 4**
See also CA 53-56; CANR 5

Berkeley, George 1685-1753 .... **LC 65**
See also DLB 31, 101, 252

Berkoff, Steven 1937- .... **CLC 56**
See also CA 104; CANR 72; CBD; CD 5

Berlin, Isaiah 1909-1997 .... **TCLC 105**
See also CA 85-88; 162

Bermant, Chaim (Icyk) 1929-1998 ... **CLC 40**
See also CA 57-60; CANR 6, 31, 57, 105;
CN 7

Bern, Victoria
See Fisher, M(ary) F(rances) K(ennedy)

Bernanos, (Paul Louis) Georges
1888-1948 .... **TCLC 3**
See also CA 104; 130; CANR 94; DLB 72;
EWL 3; GFL 1789 to the Present; RGWL
2, 3

Bernard, April 1956- .... **CLC 59**
See also CA 131

Bernard of Clairvaux 1090-1153 .. **CMLC 71**
See also DLB 208

Berne, Victoria
See Fisher, M(ary) F(rances) K(ennedy)

Bernhard, Thomas 1931-1989 ..... **CLC 3, 32,**
61; DC 14
See also CA 85-88; 127; CANR 32, 57; CD-
WLB 2; DLB 85, 124; EWL 3; MTCW 1;
RGWL 2, 3

Bernhardt, Sarah (Henriette Rosine)
1844-1923 .... **TCLC 75**
See also CA 157

Bernstein, Charles 1950- .... **CLC 142,**
See also CA 129; CAAS 24; CANR 90; CP
7; DLB 169

Bernstein, Ingrid
See Kirsch, Sarah

Beroul fl. c. 1150- .... **CMLC 75**

Berriault, Gina 1926-1999 .... **CLC 54, 109;**
SSC 30
See also CA 116; 129; 185; CANR 66; DLB
130; SSFS 7,11

Berrigan, Daniel 1921- .... **CLC 4**
See also CA 33-36R, 187; CAAE 187;
CAAS 1; CANR 11, 43, 78; CP 7; DLB 5

Berrigan, Edmund Joseph Michael, Jr.
1934-1983
See Berrigan, Ted
See also CA 61-64; 110; CANR 14, 102

Berrigan, Ted .... **CLC 37**
See Berrigan, Edmund Joseph Michael, Jr.
See also DLB 5, 169; WP

Berry, Charles Edward Anderson 1931-
See Berry, Chuck
See also CA 115

Berry, Chuck .... **CLC 17**
See Berry, Charles Edward Anderson

Berry, Jonas
See Ashbery, John (Lawrence)
See also GLL 1

Berry, Wendell (Erdman) 1934- ... **CLC 4, 6,**
8, 27, 46; PC 28
See also AITN 1; AMWS 10; ANW; CA
73-76; CANR 50, 73, 101, 132; CP 7;
CSW; DAM POET; DLB 5, 6, 234, 275;
MTCW 1

Berryman, John 1914-1972 ... **CLC 1, 2, 3, 4,**
6, 8, 10, 13, 25, 62; PC 64
See also AMW; CA 13-16; 33-36R; CABS
2; CANR 35; CAP 1; CDALB 1941-1968;
DAM POET; DLB 48; EWL 3; MTCW 1,
2; PAB; RGAL 4; WP

Bertolucci, Bernardo 1940- ...... **CLC 16, 157**
See also CA 106; CANR 125

Berton, Pierre (Francis Demarigny)
1920-2004 .... **CLC 104**
See also CA 1-4R; CANR 2, 56; CPW;
DLB 68; SATA 99

Bertrand, Aloysius 1807-1841 .... **NCLC 31**
See Bertrand, Louis oAloysiusc

Blom, Jan
See Breytenbach, Breyten
Bloom, Harold 1930- .... **CLC 24, 103**
See also CA 13-16R; CANR 39, 75, 92, 133; DLB 67; EWL 3; MTCW 1; RGAL 4
Bloomfield, Aurelius
See Bourne, Randolph S(illiman)
Bloomfield, Robert 1766-1823 ..... **NCLC 145**
See also DLB 93
Blount, Roy (Alton), Jr. 1941- .... **CLC 38**
See also CA 53-56; CANR 10, 28, 61, 125; CSW; INT CANR-28; MTCW 1, 2
Blowsnake, Sam 1875-(?) .... **NNAL**
Bloy, Leon 1846-1917 .... **TCLC 22**
See also CA 121; 183; DLB 123; GFL 1789 to the Present
Blue Cloud, Peter (Aroniawenrate)
1933- .... **NNAL**
See also CA 117; CANR 40; DAM MULT
Bluggage, Oranthy
See Alcott, Louisa May
Blume, Judy (Sussman) 1938- .... **CLC 12, 30**
See also AAYA 3, 26; BYA 1, 8, 12; CA 29-32R; CANR 13, 37, 66, 124; CLR 2, 15, 69; CPW; DA3; DAM NOV, POP; DLB 52; JRDA; MAICYA 1, 2; MAICYAS 1; MTCW 1, 2; SATA 2, 31, 79, 142; WYA; YAW
Blunden, Edmund (Charles)
1896-1974 .... **CLC 2, 56**
See also BRW 6; CA 17-18; 45-48; CANR 54; CAP 2; DLB 20, 100, 155; MTCW 1; PAB
Bly, Robert (Elwood) 1926- .... **CLC 1, 2, 5, 10, 15, 38, 128; PC 39**
See also AMWS 4; CA 5-8R; CANR 41, 73, 125; CP 7; DA3; DAM POET; DLB 5; EWL 3; MTCW 1, 2; PFS 6, 17; RGAL 4
Boas, Franz 1858-1942 .... **TCLC 56**
See also CA 115; 181
Bobette
See Simenon, Georges (Jacques Christian)
Boccaccio, Giovanni 1313-1375 ... **CMLC 13, 57; SSC 10**
See also EW 2; RGSF 2; RGWL 2, 3; TWA
Bochco, Steven 1943- .... **CLC 35**
See also AAYA 11; CA 124; 138
Bode, Sigmund
See O'Doherty, Brian
Bodel, Jean 1167(?)-1210 .... **CMLC 28**
Bodenheim, Maxwell 1892-1954 .... **TCLC 44**
See also CA 110; 187; DLB 9, 45; RGAL 4
Bodenheimer, Maxwell
See Bodenheim, Maxwell
Bodker, Cecil 1927-
See Bodker, Cecil
Bodker, Cecil 1927- .... **CLC 21**
See also CA 73-76; CANR 13, 44, 111; CLR 23; MAICYA 1, 2; SATA 14, 133
Boell, Heinrich (Theodor)
1917-1985 ..... **CLC 2, 3, 6, 9, 11, 15, 27, 32, 72; SSC 23; WLC**
See Boll, Heinrich
See also CA 21-24R; 116; CANR 24; DA; DA3; DAB; DAC; DAM MST, NOV; DLB 69; DLBY 1985; MTCW 1, 2; SSFS 20; TWA
Boerne, Alfred
See Doeblin, Alfred
Boethius c. 480-c. 524 .... **CMLC 15**
See also DLB 115; RGWL 2, 3
Boff, Leonardo (Genezio Darci)
1938- .... **CLC 70; HLC 1**
See also CA 150; DAM MULT; HW 2

Bogan, Louise 1897-1970 .... **CLC 4, 39, 46, 93; PC 12**
See also AMWS 3; CA 73-76; 25-28R; CANR 33, 82; DAM POET; DLB 45, 169; EWL 3; MAWW; MTCW 1, 2; PFS 21; RGAL 4
Bogarde, Dirk
See Van Den Bogarde, Derek Jules Gaspard Ulric Niven
See also DLB 14
Bogosian, Eric 1953- .... **CLC 45, 141**
See also CA 138; CAD; CANR 102; CD 5
Bograd, Larry 1953- .... **CLC 35**
See also CA 93-96; CANR 57; SAAS 21; SATA 33, 89; WYA
Boiardo, Matteo Maria 1441-1494 .... **LC 6**
Boileau-Despreaux, Nicolas 1636-1711 . **LC 3**
See also DLB 268; EW 3; GFL Beginnings to 1789; RGWL 2, 3
Boissard, Maurice
See Leautaud, Paul
Bojer, Johan 1872-1959 .... **TCLC 64**
See also CA 189; EWL 3
Bok, Edward W(illiam)
1863-1930 .... **TCLC 101**
See also CA 217; DLB 91; DLBD 16
Boker, George Henry 1823-1890 . **NCLC 125**
See also RGAL 4
Boland, Eavan (Aisling) 1944- .. **CLC 40, 67, 113; PC 58**
See also BRWS 5; CA 143, 207; CAAE 207; CANR 61; CP 7; CWP; DAM POET; DLB 40; FW; MTCW 2; PFS 12
Boll, Heinrich
See Boell, Heinrich (Theodor)
See also BPFB 1; CDWLB 2; EW 13; EWL 3; RGSF 2; RGWL 2, 3
Bolt, Lee
See Faust, Frederick (Schiller)
Bolt, Robert (Oxton) 1924-1995 .... **CLC 14**
See also CA 17-20R; 147; CANR 35, 67; CBD; DAM DRAM; DFS 2; DLB 13, 233; EWL 3; LAIT 1; MTCW 1
Bombal, Maria Luisa 1910-1980 .... **HLCS 1; SSC 37**
See also CA 127; CANR 72; EWL 3; HW 1; LAW; RGSF 2
Bombet, Louis-Alexandre-Cesar
See Stendhal
Bomkauf
See Kaufman, Bob (Garnell)
Bonaventura .... **NCLC 35**
See also DLB 90
Bond, Edward 1934- .... **CLC 4, 6, 13, 23**
See also AAYA 50; BRWS 1; CA 25-28R; CANR 38, 67, 106; CBD; CD 5; DAM DRAM; DFS 3, 8; DLB 13; EWL 3; MTCW 1
Bonham, Frank 1914-1989 .... **CLC 12**
See also AAYA 1; BYA 1, 3; CA 9-12R; CANR 4, 36; JRDA; MAICYA 1, 2; SAAS 3; SATA 1, 49; SATA-Obit 62; TCWW 2; YAW
Bonnefoy, Yves 1923- . **CLC 9, 15, 58; PC 58**
See also CA 85-88; CANR 33, 75, 97; CWW 2; DAM MST, POET; DLB 258; EWL 3; GFL 1789 to the Present; MTCW 1, 2
Bonner, Marita .... **HR 2**
See Occomy, Marita (Odette) Bonner
Bonnin, Gertrude 1876-1938 .... **NNAL**
See Zitkala-Sa
See also CA 150; DAM MULT
Bontemps, Arna(ud Wendell)
1902-1973 ... **BLC 1; CLC 1, 18; HR 2**
See also BW 1; CA 1-4R; 41-44R; CANR 4, 35; CLR 6; CWRI 5; DA3; DAM MULT, NOV, POET; DLB 48, 51; JRDA; MAICYA 1, 2; MTCW 1, 2; SATA 2, 44; SATA-Obit 24; WCH; WP

Boot, William
See Stoppard, Tom
Booth, Martin 1944-2004 .... **CLC 13**
See also CA 93-96; 188; 223; CAAE 188; CAAS 2; CANR 92
Booth, Philip 1925- .... **CLC 23**
See also CA 5-8R; CANR 5, 88; CP 7; DLBY 1982
Booth, Wayne C(layson) 1921- .... **CLC 24**
See also CA 1-4R; CAAS 5; CANR 3, 43, 117; DLB 67
Borchert, Wolfgang 1921-1947 .... **TCLC 5**
See also CA 104; 188; DLB 69, 124; EWL 3
Borel, Petrus 1809-1859 .... **NCLC 41**
See also DLB 119; GFL 1789 to the Present
Borges, Jorge Luis 1899-1986 ... **CLC 1, 2, 3, 4, 6, 8, 9, 10, 13, 19, 44, 48, 83; HLC 1; PC 22, 32; SSC 4, 41; TCLC 109; WLC**
See also AAYA 26; BPFB 1; CA 21-24R; CANR 19, 33, 75, 105, 133; CDWLB 3; DA; DA3; DAB; DAC; DAM MST, MULT; DLB 113, 283; DLBY 1986; DNFS 1, 2; EWL 3; HW 1, 2; LAW; LMFS 2; MSW; MTCW 1, 2; RGSF 2; RGWL 2, 3; SFW 4; SSFS 17; TWA; WLIT 1
Borowski, Tadeusz 1922-1951 .... **SSC 48; TCLC 9**
See also CA 106; 154; CDWLB 4; DLB 215; EWL 3; RGSF 2; RGWL 3; SSFS 13
Borrow, George (Henry)
1803-1881 .... **NCLC 9**
See also DLB 21, 55, 166
Bosch (Gavino), Juan 1909-2001 ..... **HLCS 1**
See also CA 151; 204; DAM MST, MULT; DLB 145; HW 1, 2
Bosman, Herman Charles
1905-1951 .... **TCLC 49**
See Malan, Herman
See also CA 160; DLB 225; RGSF 2
Bosschere, Jean de 1878(?)-1953 ... **TCLC 19**
See also CA 115; 186
Boswell, James 1740-1795 ... **LC 4, 50; WLC**
See also BRW 3; CDBLB 1660-1789; DA; DAB; DAC; DAM MST; DLB 104, 142; TEA; WLIT 3
Bottomley, Gordon 1874-1948 ..... **TCLC 107**
See also CA 120; 192; DLB 10
Bottoms, David 1949- .... **CLC 53**
See also CA 105; CANR 22; CSW; DLB 120; DLBY 1983
Boucicault, Dion 1820-1890 .... **NCLC 41**
Boucolon, Maryse
See Conde, Maryse
Bourdieu, Pierre 1930-2002 .... **CLC 198**
See also CA 130; 204
Bourget, Paul (Charles Joseph)
1852-1935 .... **TCLC 12**
See also CA 107; 196; DLB 123; GFL 1789 to the Present
Bourjaily, Vance (Nye) 1922- .... **CLC 8, 62**
See also CA 1-4R; CAAS 1; CANR 2, 72; CN 7; DLB 2, 143
Bourne, Randolph S(illiman)
1886-1918 .... **TCLC 16**
See also AMW; CA 117; 155; DLB 63
Bova, Ben(jamin William) 1932- ...... **CLC 45**
See also AAYA 16; CA 5-8R; CAAS 18; CANR 11, 56, 94, 111; CLR 3, 96; DLBY 1981; INT CANR-11; MAICYA 1, 2; MTCW 1; SATA 6, 68, 133; SFW 4
Bowen, Elizabeth (Dorothea Cole)
1899-1973 . **CLC 1, 3, 6, 11, 15, 22, 118; SSC 3, 28, 66; TCLC 148**
See also BRWS 2; CA 17-18; 41-44R; CANR 35, 105; CAP 2; CDBLB 1945-

Breton, Andre 1896-1966 .. **CLC 2, 9, 15, 54; PC 15**
See also CA 19-20; 25-28R; CANR 40, 60; CAP 2; DLB 65, 258; EW 11; EWL 3; GFL 1789 to the Present; LMFS 2; MTCW 1, 2; RGWL 2, 3; TWA; WP

Breytenbach, Breyten 1939(?)- .. **CLC 23, 37, 126**
See also CA 113; 129; CANR 61, 122; CWW 2; DAM POET; DLB 225; EWL 3

Bridgers, Sue Ellen 1942- .... **CLC 26**
See also AAYA 8, 49; BYA 7, 8; CA 65-68; CANR 11, 36; CLR 18; DLB 52; JRDA; MAICYA 1, 2; SAAS 1; SATA 22, 90; SATA-Essay 109; WYA; YAW

Bridges, Robert (Seymour)
1844-1930 .... **PC 28; TCLC 1**
See also BRW 6; CA 104; 152; CDBLB 1890-1914; DAM POET; DLB 19, 98

Bridie, James .... **TCLC 3**
See Mavor, Osborne Henry
See also DLB 10; EWL 3

Brin, David 1950- .... **CLC 34**
See also AAYA 21; CA 102; CANR 24, 70, 125, 127; INT CANR-24; SATA 65; SCFW 2; SFW 4

Brink, Andre (Philippus) 1935- . **CLC 18, 36, 106**
See also AFW; BRWS 6; CA 104; CANR 39, 62, 109, 133; CN 7; DLB 225; EWL 3; INT CA-103; LATS 1:2; MTCW 1, 2; WLIT 2

Brinsmead, H. F(ay)
See Brinsmead, H(esba) F(ay)

Brinsmead, H. F.
See Brinsmead, H(esba) F(ay)

Brinsmead, H(esba) F(ay) 1922- ...... **CLC 21**
See also CA 21-24R; CANR 10; CLR 47; CWRI 5; MAICYA 1, 2; SAAS 5; SATA 18, 78

Brittain, Vera (Mary) 1893(?)-1970 . **CLC 23**
See also BRWS 10; CA 13-16; 25-28R; CANR 58; CAP 1; DLB 191; FW; MTCW 1, 2

Broch, Hermann 1886-1951 .... **TCLC 20**
See also CA 117; 211; CDWLB 2; DLB 85, 124; EW 10; EWL 3; RGWL 2, 3

Brock, Rose
See Hansen, Joseph
See also GLL 1

Brod, Max 1884-1968 .... **TCLC 115**
See also CA 5-8R; 25-28R; CANR 7; DLB 81; EWL 3

Brodkey, Harold (Roy) 1930-1996 .. **CLC 56; TCLC 123**
See also CA 111; 151; CANR 71; CN 7; DLB 130

Brodsky, Iosif Alexandrovich 1940-1996
See Brodsky, Joseph
See also AITN 1; CA 41-44R; 151; CANR 37, 106; DA3; DAM POET; MTCW 1, 2; RGWL 2, 3

Brodsky, Joseph . **CLC 4, 6, 13, 36, 100; PC 9**
See Brodsky, Iosif Alexandrovich
See also AMWS 8; CWW 2; DLB 285; EWL 3; MTCW 1

Brodsky, Michael (Mark) 1948- .... **CLC 19**
See also CA 102; CANR 18, 41, 58; DLB 244

Brodzki, Bella ed. .... **CLC 65**

Brome, Richard 1590(?)-1652 .... **LC 61**
See also BRWS 10; DLB 58

Bromell, Henry 1947- .... **CLC 5**
See also CA 53-56; CANR 9, 115, 116

Bromfield, Louis (Brucker)
1896-1956 .... **TCLC 11**
See also CA 107; 155; DLB 4, 9, 86; RGAL 4; RHW

Broner, E(sther) M(asserman)
1930- .... **CLC 19**
See also CA 17-20R; CANR 8, 25, 72; CN 7; DLB 28

Bronk, William (M.) 1918-1999 .... **CLC 10**
See also CA 89-92; 177; CANR 23; CP 7; DLB 165

Bronstein, Lev Davidovich
See Trotsky, Leon

Bronte, Anne 1820-1849 ..... **NCLC 4, 71, 102**
See also BRW 5; BRWR 1; DA3; DLB 21, 199; TEA

Bronte, (Patrick) Branwell
1817-1848 .... **NCLC 109**

Bronte, Charlotte 1816-1855 ...... **NCLC 3, 8, 33, 58, 105; WLC**
See also AAYA 17; BRW 5; BRWC 2; BRWR 1; BYA 2; CDBLB 1832-1890; DA; DA3; DAB; DAC; DAM MST, NOV; DLB 21, 159, 199; EXPN; LAIT 2; NFS 4; TEA; WLIT 4

Bronte, Emily (Jane) 1818-1848 ... **NCLC 16, 35; PC 8; WLC**
See also AAYA 17; BPFB 1; BRW 5; BRWC 1; BRWR 1; BYA 3; CDBLB 1832-1890; DA; DA3; DAB; DAC; DAM MST, NOV, POET; DLB 21, 32, 199; EXPN; LAIT 1; TEA; WLIT 3

Brontes
See Bronte, Anne; Bronte, Charlotte; Bronte, Emily (Jane)

Brooke, Frances 1724-1789 .... **LC 6, 48**
See also DLB 39, 99

Brooke, Henry 1703(?)-1783 .... **LC 1**
See also DLB 39

Brooke, Rupert (Chawner)
1887-1915 ..... **PC 24; TCLC 2, 7; WLC**
See also BRWS 3; CA 104; 132; CANR 61; CDBLB 1914-1945; DA; DAB; DAC; DAM MST, POET; DLB 19, 216; EXPP; GLL 2; MTCW 1, 2; PFS 7; TEA

Brooke-Haven, P.
See Wodehouse, P(elham) G(renville)

Brooke-Rose, Christine 1926(?)- ..... **CLC 40, 184**
See also BRWS 4; CA 13-16R; CANR 58, 118; CN 7; DLB 14, 231; EWL 3; SFW 4

Brookner, Anita 1928- .. **CLC 32, 34, 51, 136**
See also BRWS 4; CA 114; 120; CANR 37, 56, 87, 130; CN 7; CPW; DA3; DAB; DAM POP; DLB 194; DLBY 1987; EWL 3; MTCW 1, 2; TEA

Brooks, Cleanth 1906-1994 . **CLC 24, 86, 110**
See also AMWS 14; CA 17-20R; 145; CANR 33, 35; CSW; DLB 63; DLBY 1994; EWL 3; INT CANR-35; MTCW 1, 2

Brooks, George
See Baum, L(yman) Frank

Brooks, Gwendolyn (Elizabeth)
1917-2000 ... **BLC 1; CLC 1, 2, 4, 5, 15, 49, 125; PC 7; WLC**
See also AAYA 20; AFAW 1, 2; AITN 1; AMWS 3; BW 2, 3; CA 1-4R; 190; CANR 1, 27, 52, 75, 132; CDALB 1941-1968; CLR 27; CP 7; CWP; DA; DA3; DAC; DAM MST, MULT, POET; DLB 5, 76, 165; EWL 3; EXPP; MAWW; MTCW 1, 2; PFS 1, 2, 4, 6; RGAL 4; SATA 6; SATA-Obit 123; TUS; WP

Brooks, Mel .... **CLC 12**
See Kaminsky, Melvin
See also AAYA 13, 48; DLB 26

Brooks, Peter (Preston) 1938- .... **CLC 34**
See also CA 45-48; CANR 1, 107

Brooks, Van Wyck 1886-1963 .... **CLC 29**
See also AMW; CA 1-4R; CANR 6; DLB 45, 63, 103; TUS

Brophy, Brigid (Antonia)
1929-1995 .... **CLC 6, 11, 29, 105**
See also CA 5-8R; 149; CAAS 4; CANR 25, 53; CBD; CN 7; CWD; DA3; DLB 14, 271; EWL 3; MTCW 1, 2

Brosman, Catharine Savage 1934- ..... **CLC 9**
See also CA 61-64; CANR 21, 46

Brossard, Nicole 1943- .... **CLC 115, 169**
See also CA 122; CAAS 16; CCA 1; CWP; CWW 2; DLB 53; EWL 3; FW; GLL 2; RGWL 3

Brother Antoninus
See Everson, William (Oliver)

The Brothers Quay
See Quay, Stephen; Quay, Timothy

Broughton, T(homas) Alan 1936- ..... **CLC 19**
See also CA 45-48; CANR 2, 23, 48, 111

Broumas, Olga 1949- .... **CLC 10, 73**
See also CA 85-88; CANR 20, 69, 110; CP 7; CWP; GLL 2

Broun, Heywood 1888-1939 .... **TCLC 104**
See also DLB 29, 171

Brown, Alan 1950- .... **CLC 99**
See also CA 156

Brown, Charles Brockden
1771-1810 .... **NCLC 22, 74, 122**
See also AMWS 1; CDALB 1640-1865; DLB 37, 59, 73; FW; HGG; LMFS 1; RGAL 4; TUS

Brown, Christy 1932-1981 .... **CLC 63**
See also BYA 13; CA 105; 104; CANR 72; DLB 14

Brown, Claude 1937-2002 ... **BLC 1; CLC 30**
See also AAYA 7; BW 1, 3; CA 73-76; 205; CANR 81; DAM MULT

Brown, Dee (Alexander)
1908-2002 .... **CLC 18, 47**
See also AAYA 30; CA 13-16R; 212; CAAS 6; CANR 11, 45, 60; CPW; CSW; DA3; DAM POP; DLBY 1980; LAIT 2; MTCW 1, 2; NCFS 5; SATA 5, 110; SATA-Obit 141; TCWW 2

Brown, George
See Wertmueller, Lina

Brown, George Douglas
1869-1902 .... **TCLC 28**
See Douglas, George
See also CA 162

Brown, George Mackay 1921-1996 ... **CLC 5, 48, 100**
See also BRWS 6; CA 21-24R; 151; CAAS 6; CANR 12, 37, 67; CN 7; CP 7; DLB 14, 27, 139, 271; MTCW 1; RGSF 2; SATA 35

Brown, (William) Larry 1951-2004 . **CLC 73**
See also CA 130; 134; CANR 117; CSW; DLB 234; INT CA-134

Brown, Moses
See Barrett, William (Christopher)

Brown, Rita Mae 1944- .... **CLC 18, 43, 79**
See also BPFB 1; CA 45-48; CANR 2, 11, 35, 62, 95; CN 7; CPW; CSW; DA3; DAM NOV, POP; FW; INT CANR-11; MTCW 1, 2; NFS 9; RGAL 4; TUS

Brown, Roderick (Langmere) Haig-
See Haig-Brown, Roderick (Langmere)

Brown, Rosellen 1939- .... **CLC 32, 170**
See also CA 77-80; CAAS 10; CANR 14, 44, 98; CN 7

Brown, Sterling Allen 1901-1989 ...... **BLC 1; CLC 1, 23, 59; HR 2; PC 55**
See also AFAW 1, 2; BW 1, 3; CA 85-88; 127; CANR 26; DA3; DAM MULT, POET; DLB 48, 51, 63; MTCW 1, 2; RGAL 4; WP

Brown, Will
See Ainsworth, William Harrison

Brown, William Hill 1765-1793 .... **LC 93**
See also DLB 37

DAC; DAM MST, NOV, POP; DLB 2, 8, 16, 152, 237; DLBY 1981, 1997; EWL 3; HGG; LMFS 2; MTCW 1, 2; RGAL 4; SFW 4

Burton, Sir Richard F(rancis) 1821-1890 .... **NCLC 42**
See also DLB 55, 166, 184

Burton, Robert 1577-1640 .... **LC 74**
See also DLB 151; RGEL 2

Buruma, Ian 1951- .... **CLC 163**
See also CA 128; CANR 65

Busch, Frederick 1941- ... **CLC 7, 10, 18, 47, 166**
See also CA 33-36R; CAAS 1; CANR 45, 73, 92; CN 7; DLB 6, 218

Bush, Barney (Furman) 1946- .... **NNAL**
See also CA 145

Bush, Ronald 1946- .... **CLC 34**
See also CA 136

Bustos, F(rancisco)
See Borges, Jorge Luis

Bustos Domecq, H(onorio)
See Bioy Casares, Adolfo; Borges, Jorge Luis

Butler, Octavia E(stelle) 1947- .. **BLCS; CLC 38, 121**
See also AAYA 18, 48; AFAW 2; AMWS 13; BPFB 1; BW 2, 3; CA 73-76; CANR 12, 24, 38, 73; CLR 65; CPW; DA3; DAM MULT, POP; DLB 33; LATS 1:2; MTCW 1, 2; NFS 8; SATA 84; SCFW 2; SFW 4; SSFS 6; YAW

Butler, Robert Olen, (Jr.) 1945- ...... **CLC 81, 162**
See also AMWS 12; BPFB 1; CA 112; CANR 66; CSW; DAM POP; DLB 173; INT CA-112; MTCW 1; SSFS 11

Butler, Samuel 1612-1680 .... **LC 16, 43**
See also DLB 101, 126; RGEL 2

Butler, Samuel 1835-1902 .... **TCLC 1, 33; WLC**
See also BRWS 2; CA 143; CDBLB 1890-1914; DA; DA3; DAB; DAC; DAM MST, NOV; DLB 18, 57, 174; RGEL 2; SFW 4; TEA

Butler, Walter C.
See Faust, Frederick (Schiller)

Butor, Michel (Marie Francois)
1926- .... **CLC 1, 3, 8, 11, 15, 161**
See also CA 9-12R; CANR 33, 66; CWW 2; DLB 83; EW 13; EWL 3; GFL 1789 to the Present; MTCW 1, 2

Butts, Mary 1890(?)-1937 .... **TCLC 77**
See also CA 148; DLB 240

Buxton, Ralph
See Silverstein, Alvin; Silverstein, Virginia B(arbara Opshelor)

Buzo, Alex
See Buzo, Alexander (John)
See also DLB 289

Buzo, Alexander (John) 1944- .... **CLC 61**
See also CA 97-100; CANR 17, 39, 69; CD 5

Buzzati, Dino 1906-1972 .... **CLC 36**
See also CA 160; 33-36R; DLB 177; RGWL 2, 3; SFW 4

Byars, Betsy (Cromer) 1928- .... **CLC 35**
See also AAYA 19; BYA 3; CA 33-36R, 183; CAAE 183; CANR 18, 36, 57, 102; CLR 1, 16, 72; DLB 52; INT CANR-18; JRDA; MAICYA 1, 2; MAICYAS 1; MTCW 1; SAAS 1; SATA 4, 46, 80; SATA-Essay 108; WYA; YAW

Byatt, A(ntonia) S(usan Drabble)
1936- .... **CLC 19, 65, 136**
See also BPFB 1; BRWC 2; BRWS 4; CA 13-16R; CANR 13, 33, 50, 75, 96, 133; DA3; DAM NOV, POP; DLB 14, 194; EWL 3; MTCW 1, 2; RGSF 2; RHW; TEA

Byrd, Willam II 1674-1744 .... **LC 112**
See also DLB 24, 140; RGAL 4

Byrne, David 1952- .... **CLC 26**
See also CA 127

Byrne, John Keyes 1926-
See Leonard, Hugh
See also CA 102; CANR 78; INT CA-102

Byron, George Gordon (Noel)
1788-1824 ..... **DC 24; NCLC 2, 12, 109, 149; PC 16; WLC**
See also BRW 4; BRWC 2; CDBLB 1789-1832; DA; DA3; DAB; DAC; DAM MST, POET; DLB 96, 110; EXPP; LMFS 1; PAB; PFS 1, 14; RGEL 2; TEA; WLIT 3; WP

Byron, Robert 1905-1941 .... **TCLC 67**
See also CA 160; DLB 195

C. 3. 3.
See Wilde, Oscar (Fingal O'Flahertie Wills)

Caballero, Fernan 1796-1877 .... **NCLC 10**

Cabell, Branch
See Cabell, James Branch

Cabell, James Branch 1879-1958 .... **TCLC 6**
See also CA 105; 152; DLB 9, 78; FANT; MTCW 1; RGAL 4; SUFW 1

Cabeza de Vaca, Alvar Nunez
1490-1557(?) .... **LC 61**

Cable, George Washington
1844-1925 .... **SSC 4; TCLC 4**
See also CA 104; 155; DLB 12, 74; DLBD 13; RGAL 4; TUS

Cabral de Melo Neto, Joao
1920-1999 .... **CLC 76**
See Melo Neto, Joao Cabral de
See also CA 151; DAM MULT; DLB 307; LAW; LAWS 1

Cabrera Infante, G(uillermo) 1929- . **CLC 5, 25, 45, 120; HLC 1; SSC 39**
See also CA 85-88; CANR 29, 65, 110; CD-WLB 3; CWW 2; DA3; DAM MULT; DLB 113; EWL 3; HW 1, 2; LAW; LAWS 1; MTCW 1, 2; RGSF 2; WLIT 1

Cade, Toni
See Bambara, Toni Cade

Cadmus and Harmonia
See Buchan, John

Caedmon fl. 658-680 .... **CMLC 7**
See also DLB 146

Caeiro, Alberto
See Pessoa, Fernando (Antonio Nogueira)

Caesar, Julius .... **CMLC 47**
See Julius Caesar
See also AW 1; RGWL 2, 3

Cage, John (Milton, Jr.)
1912-1992 .... **CLC 41; PC 58**
See also CA 13-16R; 169; CANR 9, 78; DLB 193; INT CANR-9

Cahan, Abraham 1860-1951 .... **TCLC 71**
See also CA 108; 154; DLB 9, 25, 28; RGAL 4

Cain, G.
See Cabrera Infante, G(uillermo)

Cain, Guillermo
See Cabrera Infante, G(uillermo)

Cain, James M(allahan) 1892-1977 .. **CLC 3, 11, 28**
See also AITN 1; BPFB 1; CA 17-20R; 73-76; CANR 8, 34, 61; CMW 4; DLB 226; EWL 3; MSW; MTCW 1; RGAL 4

Caine, Hall 1853-1931 .... **TCLC 97**
See also RHW

Caine, Mark
See Raphael, Frederic (Michael)

Calasso, Roberto 1941- .... **CLC 81**
See also CA 143; CANR 89

Calderon de la Barca, Pedro
1600-1681 .... **DC 3; HLCS 1; LC 23**
See also EW 2; RGWL 2, 3; TWA

Caldwell, Erskine (Preston)
1903-1987 .... **CLC 1, 8, 14, 50, 60; SSC 19; TCLC 117**
See also AITN 1; AMW; BPFB 1; CA 1-4R; 121; CAAS 1; CANR 2, 33; DA3; DAM NOV; DLB 9, 86; EWL 3; MTCW 1, 2; RGAL 4; RGSF 2; TUS

Caldwell, (Janet Miriam) Taylor (Holland)
1900-1985 .... **CLC 2, 28, 39**
See also BPFB 1; CA 5-8R; 116; CANR 5; DA3; DAM NOV, POP; DLBD 17; RHW

Calhoun, John Caldwell
1782-1850 .... **NCLC 15**
See also DLB 3, 248

Calisher, Hortense 1911- ..... **CLC 2, 4, 8, 38, 134; SSC 15**
See also CA 1-4R; CANR 1, 22, 117; CN 7; DA3; DAM NOV; DLB 2, 218; INT CANR-22; MTCW 1, 2; RGAL 4; RGSF 2

Callaghan, Morley Edward
1903-1990 ..... **CLC 3, 14, 41, 65; TCLC 145**
See also CA 9-12R; 132; CANR 33, 73; DAC; DAM MST; DLB 68; EWL 3; MTCW 1, 2; RGEL 2; RGSF 2; SSFS 19

Callimachus c. 305B.C.-c.
240B.C. .... **CMLC 18**
See also AW 1; DLB 176; RGWL 2, 3

Calvin, Jean
See Calvin, John
See also GFL Beginnings to 1789

Calvin, John 1509-1564 .... **LC 37**
See Calvin, Jean

Calvino, Italo 1923-1985 .... **CLC 5, 8, 11, 22, 33, 39, 73; SSC 3, 48**
See also AAYA 58; CA 85-88; 116; CANR 23, 61, 132; DAM NOV; DLB 196; EW 13; EWL 3; MTCW 1, 2; RGSF 2; RGWL 2, 3; SFW 4; SSFS 12

Camara Laye
See Laye, Camara
See also EWL 3

Camden, William 1551-1623 .... **LC 77**
See also DLB 172

Cameron, Carey 1952- .... **CLC 59**
See also CA 135

Cameron, Peter 1959- .... **CLC 44**
See also AMWS 12; CA 125; CANR 50, 117; DLB 234; GLL 2

Camoens, Luis Vaz de 1524(?)-1580
See Camoes, Luis de
See also EW 2

Camoes, Luis de 1524(?)-1580 . **HLCS 1; LC 62; PC 31**
See Camoens, Luis Vaz de
See also DLB 287; RGWL 2, 3

Campana, Dino 1885-1932 .... **TCLC 20**
See also CA 117; DLB 114; EWL 3

Campanella, Tommaso 1568-1639 .... **LC 32**
See also RGWL 2, 3

Campbell, John W(ood, Jr.)
1910-1971 .... **CLC 32**
See also CA 21-22; 29-32R; CANR 34; CAP 2; DLB 8; MTCW 1; SCFW; SFW 4

Campbell, Joseph 1904-1987 .... **CLC 69; TCLC 140**
See also AAYA 3; BEST 89:2; CA 1-4R; 124; CANR 3, 28, 61, 107; DA3; MTCW 1, 2

Campbell, Maria 1940- .... **CLC 85; NNAL**
See also CA 102; CANR 54; CCA 1; DAC

Campbell, (John) Ramsey 1946- ..... **CLC 42; SSC 19**
See also AAYA 51; CA 57-60; 228; CAAE 228; CANR 7, 102; DLB 261; HGG; INT CANR-7; SUFW 1, 2

Chopin, Katherine 1851-1904
See Chopin, Kate
See also CA 104; 122; DA3; DAC; DAM MST, NOV

Chretien de Troyes c. 12th cent. - .. **CMLC 10**
See also DLB 208; EW 1; RGWL 2, 3; TWA

Christie
See Ichikawa, Kon

Christie, Agatha (Mary Clarissa)
1890-1976 .. **CLC 1, 6, 8, 12, 39, 48, 110**
See also AAYA 9; AITN 1, 2; BPFB 1; BRWS 2; CA 17-20R; 61-64; CANR 10, 37, 108; CBD; CDBLB 1914-1945; CMW 4; CPW; CWD; DA3; DAB; DAC; DAM NOV; DFS 2; DLB 13, 77, 245; MSW; MTCW 1, 2; NFS 8; RGEL 2; RHW; SATA 36; TEA; YAW

Christie, Philippa .... **CLC 21**
See Pearce, Philippa
See also BYA 5; CANR 109; CLR 9; DLB 161; MAICYA 1; SATA 1, 67, 129

Christine de Pizan 1365(?)-1431(?) .... **LC 9**
See also DLB 208; RGWL 2, 3

Chuang Tzu c. 369B.C.-c.
286B.C. .... **CMLC 57**

Chubb, Elmer
See Masters, Edgar Lee

Chulkov, Mikhail Dmitrievich
1743-1792 .... **LC 2**
See also DLB 150

Churchill, Caryl 1938- .... **CLC 31, 55, 157; DC 5**
See Churchill, Chick
See also BRWS 4; CA 102; CANR 22, 46, 108; CBD; CWD; DFS 12, 16; DLB 13; EWL 3; FW; MTCW 1; RGEL 2

Churchill, Charles 1731-1764 .... **LC 3**
See also DLB 109; RGEL 2

Churchill, Chick
See Churchill, Caryl
See also CD 5

Churchill, Sir Winston (Leonard Spencer)
1874-1965 .... **TCLC 113**
See also BRW 6; CA 97-100; CDBLB 1890-1914; DA3; DLB 100; DLBD 16; LAIT 4; MTCW 1, 2

Chute, Carolyn 1947- .... **CLC 39**
See also CA 123; CANR 135

Ciardi, John (Anthony) 1916-1986 . **CLC 10, 40, 44, 129**
See also CA 5-8R; 118; CAAS 2; CANR 5, 33; CLR 19; CWRI 5; DAM POET; DLB 5; DLBY 1986; INT CANR-5; MAICYA 1, 2; MTCW 1, 2; RGAL 4; SAAS 26; SATA 1, 65; SATA-Obit 46

Cibber, Colley 1671-1757 .... **LC 66**
See also DLB 84; RGEL 2

Cicero, Marcus Tullius
106B.C.-43B.C. .... **CMLC 3**
See also AW 1; CDWLB 1; DLB 211; RGWL 2, 3

Cimino, Michael 1943- .... **CLC 16**
See also CA 105

Cioran, E(mil) M. 1911-1995 .... **CLC 64**
See also CA 25-28R; 149; CANR 91; DLB 220; EWL 3

Cisneros, Sandra 1954- .... **CLC 69, 118, 193; HLC 1; PC 52; SSC 32, 72**
See also AAYA 9, 53; AMWS 7; CA 131; CANR 64, 118; CWP; DA3; DAM MULT; DLB 122, 152; EWL 3; EXPN; FW; HW 1, 2; LAIT 5; LATS 1:2; LLW 1; MAICYA 2; MTCW 2; NFS 2; PFS 19; RGAL 4; RGSF 2; SSFS 3, 13; WLIT 1; YAW

Cixous, Helene 1937- .... **CLC 92**
See also CA 126; CANR 55, 123; CWW 2; DLB 83, 242; EWL 3; FW; GLL 2; MTCW 1, 2; TWA

Clair, Rene .... **CLC 20**
See Chomette, Rene Lucien

Clampitt, Amy 1920-1994 .... **CLC 32; PC 19**
See also AMWS 9; CA 110; 146; CANR 29, 79; DLB 105

Clancy, Thomas L., Jr. 1947-
See Clancy, Tom
See also CA 125; 131; CANR 62, 105; DA3; INT CA-131; MTCW 1, 2

Clancy, Tom .... **CLC 45, 112**
See Clancy, Thomas L., Jr.
See also AAYA 9, 51; BEST 89:1, 90:1; BPFB 1; BYA 10, 11; CANR 132; CMW 4; CPW; DAM NOV, POP; DLB 227

Clare, John 1793-1864 .. **NCLC 9, 86; PC 23**
See also DAB; DAM POET; DLB 55, 96; RGEL 2

Clarin
See Alas (y Urena), Leopoldo (Enrique Garcia)

Clark, Al C.
See Goines, Donald

Clark, (Robert) Brian 1932- .... **CLC 29**
See also CA 41-44R; CANR 67; CBD; CD 5

Clark, Curt
See Westlake, Donald E(dwin)

Clark, Eleanor 1913-1996 .... **CLC 5, 19**
See also CA 9-12R; 151; CANR 41; CN 7; DLB 6

Clark, J. P.
See Clark Bekederemo, J(ohnson) P(epper)
See also CDWLB 3; DLB 117

Clark, John Pepper
See Clark Bekederemo, J(ohnson) P(epper)
See also AFW; CD 5; CP 7; RGEL 2

Clark, Kenneth (Mackenzie)
1903-1983 .... **TCLC 147**
See also CA 93-96; 109; CANR 36; MTCW 1, 2

Clark, M. R.
See Clark, Mavis Thorpe

Clark, Mavis Thorpe 1909-1999 ...... **CLC 12**
See also CA 57-60; CANR 8, 37, 107; CLR 30; CWRI 5; MAICYA 1, 2; SAAS 5; SATA 8, 74

Clark, Walter Van Tilburg
1909-1971 .... **CLC 28**
See also CA 9-12R; 33-36R; CANR 63, 113; DLB 9, 206; LAIT 2; RGAL 4; SATA 8

Clark Bekederemo, J(ohnson) P(epper)
1935- .... **BLC 1; CLC 38; DC 5**
See Clark, J. P.; Clark, John Pepper
See also BW 1; CA 65-68; CANR 16, 72; DAM DRAM, MULT; DFS 13; EWL 3; MTCW 1

Clarke, Arthur C(harles) 1917- .... **CLC 1, 4, 13, 18, 35, 136; SSC 3**
See also AAYA 4, 33; BPFB 1; BYA 13; CA 1-4R; CANR 2, 28, 55, 74, 130; CN 7; CPW; DA3; DAM POP; DLB 261; JRDA; LAIT 5; MAICYA 1, 2; MTCW 1, 2; SATA 13, 70, 115; SCFW; SFW 4; SSFS 4, 18; YAW

Clarke, Austin 1896-1974 .... **CLC 6, 9**
See also CA 29-32; 49-52; CAP 2; DAM POET; DLB 10, 20; EWL 3; RGEL 2

Clarke, Austin C(hesterfield) 1934- .. **BLC 1; CLC 8, 53; SSC 45**
See also BW 1; CA 25-28R; CAAS 16; CANR 14, 32, 68; CN 7; DAC; DAM MULT; DLB 53, 125; DNFS 2; RGSF 2

Clarke, Gillian 1937- .... **CLC 61**
See also CA 106; CP 7; CWP; DLB 40

Clarke, Marcus (Andrew Hislop)
1846-1881 .... **NCLC 19**
See also DLB 230; RGEL 2; RGSF 2

Clarke, Shirley 1925-1997 .... **CLC 16**
See also CA 189

Clash, The
See Headon, (Nicky) Topper; Jones, Mick; Simonon, Paul; Strummer, Joe

Claudel, Paul (Louis Charles Marie)
1868-1955 .... **TCLC 2, 10**
See also CA 104; 165; DLB 192, 258; EW 8; EWL 3; GFL 1789 to the Present; RGWL 2, 3; TWA

Claudian 370(?)-404(?) .... **CMLC 46**
See also RGWL 2, 3

Claudius, Matthias 1740-1815 .... **NCLC 75**
See also DLB 97

Clavell, James (duMaresq)
1925-1994 .... **CLC 6, 25, 87**
See also BPFB 1; CA 25-28R; 146; CANR 26, 48; CPW; DA3; DAM NOV, POP; MTCW 1, 2; NFS 10; RHW

Clayman, Gregory .... **CLC 65**

Cleaver, (Leroy) Eldridge
1935-1998 .... **BLC 1; CLC 30, 119**
See also BW 1, 3; CA 21-24R; 167; CANR 16, 75; DA3; DAM MULT; MTCW 2; YAW

Cleese, John (Marwood) 1939- .... **CLC 21**
See Monty Python
See also CA 112; 116; CANR 35; MTCW 1

Cleishbotham, Jebediah
See Scott, Sir Walter

Cleland, John 1710-1789 .... **LC 2, 48**
See also DLB 39; RGEL 2

Clemens, Samuel Langhorne 1835-1910
See Twain, Mark
See also CA 104; 135; CDALB 1865-1917; DA; DA3; DAB; DAC; DAM MST, NOV; DLB 12, 23, 64, 74, 186, 189; JRDA; LMFS 1; MAICYA 1, 2; NCFS 4; NFS 20; SATA 100; SSFS 16; YABC 2

Clement of Alexandria
150(?)-215(?) .... **CMLC 41**

Cleophil
See Congreve, William

Clerihew, E.
See Bentley, E(dmund) C(lerihew)

Clerk, N. W.
See Lewis, C(live) S(taples)

Cleveland, John 1613-1658 .... **LC 106**
See also DLB 126; RGEL 2

Cliff, Jimmy .... **CLC 21**
See Chambers, James
See also CA 193

Cliff, Michelle 1946- .... **BLCS; CLC 120**
See also BW 2; CA 116; CANR 39, 72; CD-WLB 3; DLB 157; FW; GLL 2

Clifford, Lady Anne 1590-1676 .... **LC 76**
See also DLB 151

Clifton, (Thelma) Lucille 1936- .... **BLC 1; CLC 19, 66, 162; PC 17**
See also AFAW 2; BW 2, 3; CA 49-52; CANR 2, 24, 42, 76, 97; CLR 5; CP 7; CSW; CWP; CWRI 5; DA3; DAM MULT, POET; DLB 5, 41; EXPP; MAICYA 1, 2; MTCW 1, 2; PFS 1, 14; SATA 20, 69, 128; WP

Clinton, Dirk
See Silverberg, Robert

Clough, Arthur Hugh 1819-1861 ... **NCLC 27**
See also BRW 5; DLB 32; RGEL 2

Clutha, Janet Paterson Frame 1924-2004
See Frame, Janet
See also CA 1-4R; 224; CANR 2, 36, 76, 135; MTCW 1, 2; SATA 119

Clyne, Terence
See Blatty, William Peter

Cobalt, Martin
See Mayne, William (James Carter)

Cook, Michael 1933-1994 .... **CLC 58**
See also CA 93-96; CANR 68; DLB 53
Cook, Robin 1940- .... **CLC 14**
See also AAYA 32; BEST 90:2; BPFB 1;
CA 108; 111; CANR 41, 90, 109; CPW;
DA3; DAM POP; HGG; INT CA-111
Cook, Roy
See Silverberg, Robert
Cooke, Elizabeth 1948- .... **CLC 55**
See also CA 129
Cooke, John Esten 1830-1886 .... **NCLC 5**
See also DLB 3, 248; RGAL 4
Cooke, John Estes
See Baum, L(yman) Frank
Cooke, M. E.
See Creasey, John
Cooke, Margaret
See Creasey, John
Cooke, Rose Terry 1827-1892 ...... **NCLC 110**
See also DLB 12, 74
Cook-Lynn, Elizabeth 1930- .... **CLC 93;**
NNAL
See also CA 133; DAM MULT; DLB 175
Cooney, Ray .... **CLC 62**
See also CBD
Cooper, Anthony Ashley 1671-1713 .. **LC 107**
See also DLB 101
Cooper, Dennis 1953- .... **CLC 203**
See also CA 133; CANR 72, 86; GLL 1; St.
James Guide to Horror, Ghost, and Gothic
Writers.
Cooper, Douglas 1960- .... **CLC 86**
Cooper, Henry St. John
See Creasey, John
Cooper, J(oan) California (?)- .... **CLC 56**
See also AAYA 12; BW 1; CA 125; CANR
55; DAM MULT; DLB 212
Cooper, James Fenimore
1789-1851 .... **NCLC 1, 27, 54**
See also AAYA 22; AMW; BPFB 1;
CDALB 1640-1865; DA3; DLB 3, 183,
250, 254; LAIT 1; NFS 9; RGAL 4; SATA
19; TUS; WCH
Cooper, Susan Fenimore
1813-1894 .... **NCLC 129**
See also ANW; DLB 239, 254
Coover, Robert (Lowell) 1932- ...... **CLC 3, 7,**
15, 32, 46, 87, 161; SSC 15
See also AMWS 5; BPFB 1; CA 45-48;
CANR 3, 37, 58, 115; CN 7; DAM NOV;
DLB 2, 227; DLBY 1981; EWL 3;
MTCW 1, 2; RGAL 4; RGSF 2
Copeland, Stewart (Armstrong)
1952- .... **CLC 26**
Copernicus, Nicolaus 1473-1543 .... **LC 45**
Coppard, A(lfred) E(dgar)
1878-1957 .... **SSC 21; TCLC 5**
See also BRWS 8; CA 114; 167; DLB 162;
EWL 3; HGG; RGEL 2; RGSF 2; SUFW
1; YABC 1
Coppee, Francois 1842-1908 .... **TCLC 25**
See also CA 170; DLB 217
Coppola, Francis Ford 1939- ... **CLC 16, 126**
See also AAYA 39; CA 77-80; CANR 40,
78; DLB 44
Copway, George 1818-1869 .... **NNAL**
See also DAM MULT; DLB 175, 183
Corbiere, Tristan 1845-1875 .... **NCLC 43**
See also DLB 217; GFL 1789 to the Present
Corcoran, Barbara (Asenath)
1911- .... **CLC 17**
See also AAYA 14; CA 21-24R, 191; CAAE
191; CAAS 2; CANR 11, 28, 48; CLR
50; DLB 52; JRDA; MAICYA 2; MAIC-
YAS 1; RHW; SAAS 20; SATA 3, 77;
SATA-Essay 125
Cordelier, Maurice
See Giraudoux, Jean(-Hippolyte)

Corelli, Marie .... **TCLC 51**
See Mackay, Mary
See also DLB 34, 156; RGEL 2; SUFW 1
Corinna c. 225B.C.-c. 305B.C. ...... **CMLC 72**
Corman, Cid .... **CLC 9**
See Corman, Sidney
See also CAAS 2; DLB 5, 193
Corman, Sidney 1924-2004
See Corman, Cid
See also CA 85-88; 225; CANR 44; CP 7;
DAM POET
Cormier, Robert (Edmund)
1925-2000 .... **CLC 12, 30**
See also AAYA 3, 19; BYA 1, 2, 6, 8, 9;
CA 1-4R; CANR 5, 23, 76, 93; CDALB
1968-1988; CLR 12, 55; DA; DAB; DAC;
DAM MST, NOV; DLB 52; EXPN; INT
CANR-23; JRDA; LAIT 5; MAICYA 1,
2; MTCW 1, 2; NFS 2, 18; SATA 10, 45,
83; SATA-Obit 122; WYA; YAW
Corn, Alfred (DeWitt III) 1943- .... **CLC 33**
See also CA 179; CAAE 179; CAAS 25;
CANR 44; CP 7; CSW; DLB 120, 282;
DLBY 1980
Corneille, Pierre 1606-1684 ... **DC 21; LC 28**
See also DAB; DAM MST; DLB 268; EW
3; GFL Beginnings to 1789; RGWL 2, 3;
TWA
Cornwell, David (John Moore)
1931- .... **CLC 9, 15**
See le Carre, John
See also CA 5-8R; CANR 13, 33, 59, 107,
132; DA3; DAM POP; MTCW 1, 2
Cornwell, Patricia (Daniels) 1956- . **CLC 155**
See also AAYA 16, 56; BPFB 1; CA 134;
CANR 53, 131; CMW 4; CPW; CSW;
DAM POP; DLB 306; MSW; MTCW 1
Corso, (Nunzio) Gregory 1930-2001 . **CLC 1,**
11; PC 33
See also AMWS 12; BG 2; CA 5-8R; 193;
CANR 41, 76, 132; CP 7; DA3; DLB 5,
16, 237; LMFS 2; MTCW 1, 2; WP
Cortazar, Julio 1914-1984 ... **CLC 2, 3, 5, 10,**
13, 15, 33, 34, 92; HLC 1; SSC 7, 76
See also BPFB 1; CA 21-24R; CANR 12,
32, 81; CDWLB 3; DA3; DAM MULT,
NOV; DLB 113; EWL 3; EXPS; HW 1,
2; LAW; MTCW 1, 2; RGSF 2; RGWL 2,
3; SSFS 3, 20; TWA; WLIT 1
Cortes, Hernan 1485-1547 .... **LC 31**
Corvinus, Jakob
See Raabe, Wilhelm (Karl)
Corwin, Cecil
See Kornbluth, C(yril) M.
Cosic, Dobrica 1921- .... **CLC 14**
See also CA 122; 138; CDWLB 4; CWW
2; DLB 181; EWL 3
Costain, Thomas B(ertram)
1885-1965 .... **CLC 30**
See also BYA 3; CA 5-8R; 25-28R; DLB 9;
RHW
Costantini, Humberto 1924(?)-1987 . **CLC 49**
See also CA 131; 122; EWL 3; HW 1
Costello, Elvis 1954- .... **CLC 21**
See also CA 204
Costenoble, Philostene
See Ghelderode, Michel de
Cotes, Cecil V.
See Duncan, Sara Jeannette
Cotter, Joseph Seamon Sr.
1861-1949 .... **BLC 1; TCLC 28**
See also BW 1; CA 124; DAM MULT; DLB
50
Couch, Arthur Thomas Quiller
See Quiller-Couch, Sir Arthur (Thomas)
Coulton, James
See Hansen, Joseph

Couperus, Louis (Marie Anne)
1863-1923 .... **TCLC 15**
See also CA 115; EWL 3; RGWL 2, 3
Coupland, Douglas 1961- .... **CLC 85, 133**
See also AAYA 34; CA 142; CANR 57, 90,
130; CCA 1; CPW; DAC; DAM POP
Court, Wesli
See Turco, Lewis (Putnam)
Courtenay, Bryce 1933- .... **CLC 59**
See also CA 138; CPW
Courtney, Robert
See Ellison, Harlan (Jay)
Cousteau, Jacques-Yves 1910-1997 .. **CLC 30**
See also CA 65-68; 159; CANR 15, 67;
MTCW 1; SATA 38, 98
Coventry, Francis 1725-1754 .... **LC 46**
Coverdale, Miles c. 1487-1569 .... **LC 77**
See also DLB 167
Cowan, Peter (Walkinshaw)
1914-2002 .... **SSC 28**
See also CA 21-24R; CANR 9, 25, 50, 83;
CN 7; DLB 260; RGSF 2
Coward, Noel (Peirce) 1899-1973 . **CLC 1, 9,**
29, 51
See also AITN 1; BRWS 2; CA 17-18; 41-
44R; CANR 35, 132; CAP 2; CDBLB
1914-1945; DA3; DAM DRAM; DFS 3,
6; DLB 10, 245; EWL 3; IDFW 3, 4;
MTCW 1, 2; RGEL 2; TEA
Cowley, Abraham 1618-1667 .... **LC 43**
See also BRW 2; DLB 131, 151; PAB;
RGEL 2
Cowley, Malcolm 1898-1989 .... **CLC 39**
See also AMWS 2; CA 5-8R; 128; CANR
3, 55; DLB 4, 48; DLBY 1981, 1989;
EWL 3; MTCW 1, 2
Cowper, William 1731-1800 ..... **NCLC 8, 94;**
PC 40
See also BRW 3; DA3; DAM POET; DLB
104, 109; RGEL 2
Cox, William Trevor 1928-
See Trevor, William
See also CA 9-12R; CANR 4, 37, 55, 76,
102; DAM NOV; INT CANR-37; MTCW
1, 2; TEA
Coyne, P. J.
See Masters, Hilary
Cozzens, James Gould 1903-1978 . **CLC 1, 4,**
11, 92
See also AMW; BPFB 1; CA 9-12R; 81-84;
CANR 19; CDALB 1941-1968; DLB 9,
294; DLBD 2; DLBY 1984, 1997; EWL
3; MTCW 1, 2; RGAL 4
Crabbe, George 1754-1832 .... **NCLC 26, 121**
See also BRW 3; DLB 93; RGEL 2
Crace, Jim 1946- .... **CLC 157; SSC 61**
See also CA 128; 135; CANR 55, 70, 123;
CN 7; DLB 231; INT CA-135
Craddock, Charles Egbert
See Murfree, Mary Noailles
Craig, A. A.
See Anderson, Poul (William)
Craik, Mrs.
See Craik, Dinah Maria (Mulock)
See also RGEL 2
Craik, Dinah Maria (Mulock)
1826-1887 .... **NCLC 38**
See Craik, Mrs.; Mulock, Dinah Maria
See also DLB 35, 163; MAICYA 1, 2;
SATA 34
Cram, Ralph Adams 1863-1942 ..... **TCLC 45**
See also CA 160
Cranch, Christopher Pearse
1813-1892 .... **NCLC 115**
See also DLB 1, 42, 243

Cynewulf c. 770- .... **CMLC 23**
  See also DLB 146; RGEL 2
Cyrano de Bergerac, Savinien de
  1619-1655 .... **LC 65**
  See also DLB 268; GFL Beginnings to
  1789; RGWL 2, 3
Cyril of Alexandria c. 375-c. 430 . **CMLC 59**
Czaczkes, Shmuel Yosef Halevi
  See Agnon, S(hmuel) Y(osef Halevi)
Dabrowska, Maria (Szumska)
  1889-1965 .... **CLC 15**
  See also CA 106; CDWLB 4; DLB 215;
  EWL 3
Dabydeen, David 1955- .... **CLC 34**
  See also BW 1; CA 125; CANR 56, 92; CN
  7; CP 7
Dacey, Philip 1939- .... **CLC 51**
  See also CA 37-40R; CAAS 17; CANR 14,
  32, 64; CP 7; DLB 105
Dacre, Charlotte c. 1772-1825? ... **NCLC 151**
Dafydd ap Gwilym c. 1320-c. 1380 ..... **PC 56**
Dagerman, Stig (Halvard)
  1923-1954 .... **TCLC 17**
  See also CA 117; 155; DLB 259; EWL 3
D'Aguiar, Fred 1960- .... **CLC 145**
  See also CA 148; CANR 83, 101; CP 7;
  DLB 157; EWL 3
Dahl, Roald 1916-1990 .... **CLC 1, 6, 18, 79**
  See also AAYA 15; BPFB 1; BRWS 4; BYA
  5; CA 1-4R; 133; CANR 6, 32, 37, 62;
  CLR 1, 7, 41; CPW; DA3; DAB; DAC;
  DAM MST, NOV, POP; DLB 139, 255;
  HGG; JRDA; MAICYA 1, 2; MTCW 1,
  2; RGSF 2; SATA 1, 26, 73; SATA-Obit
  65; SSFS 4; TEA; YAW
Dahlberg, Edward 1900-1977 .. **CLC 1, 7, 14**
  See also CA 9-12R; 69-72; CANR 31, 62;
  DLB 48; MTCW 1; RGAL 4
Daitch, Susan 1954- .... **CLC 103**
  See also CA 161
Dale, Colin .... **TCLC 18**
  See Lawrence, T(homas) E(dward)
Dale, George E.
  See Asimov, Isaac
Dalton, Roque 1935-1975(?) ..... **HLCS 1; PC
  36**
  See also CA 176; DLB 283; HW 2
Daly, Elizabeth 1878-1967 .... **CLC 52**
  See also CA 23-24; 25-28R; CANR 60;
  CAP 2; CMW 4
Daly, Mary 1928- .... **CLC 173**
  See also CA 25-28R; CANR 30, 62; FW;
  GLL 1; MTCW 1
Daly, Maureen 1921- .... **CLC 17**
  See also AAYA 5, 58; BYA 6; CANR 37,
  83, 108; CLR 96; JRDA; MAICYA 1, 2;
  SAAS 1; SATA 2, 129; WYA; YAW
Damas, Leon-Gontran 1912-1978 .... **CLC 84**
  See also BW 1; CA 125; 73-76; EWL 3
Dana, Richard Henry Sr.
  1787-1879 .... **NCLC 53**
Daniel, Samuel 1562(?)-1619 .... **LC 24**
  See also DLB 62; RGEL 2
Daniels, Brett
  See Adler, Renata
Dannay, Frederic 1905-1982 .... **CLC 11**
  See Queen, Ellery
  See also CA 1-4R; 107; CANR 1, 39; CMW
  4; DAM POP; DLB 137; MTCW 1
D'Annunzio, Gabriele 1863-1938 ... **TCLC 6,
  40**
  See also CA 104; 155; EW 8; EWL 3;
  RGWL 2, 3; TWA
Danois, N. le
  See Gourmont, Remy(-Marie-Charles) de

Dante 1265-1321 .... **CMLC 3, 18, 39, 70; PC
  21; WLCS**
  See also DA; DA3; DAB; DAC; DAM
  MST, POET; EFS 1; EW 1; LAIT 1;
  RGWL 2, 3; TWA; WP
d'Antibes, Germain
  See Simenon, Georges (Jacques Christian)
Danticat, Edwidge 1969- .... **CLC 94, 139**
  See also AAYA 29; CA 152, 192; CAAE
  192; CANR 73, 129; DNFS 1; EXPS;
  LATS 1:2; MTCW 1; SSFS 1; YAW
Danvers, Dennis 1947- .... **CLC 70**
Danziger, Paula 1944-2004 .... **CLC 21**
  See also AAYA 4, 36; BYA 6, 7, 14; CA
  112; 115; 229; CANR 37, 132; CLR 20;
  JRDA; MAICYA 1, 2; SATA 36, 63, 102,
  149; SATA-Brief 30; WYA; YAW
Da Ponte, Lorenzo 1749-1838 .... **NCLC 50**
Dario, Ruben 1867-1916 .... **HLC 1; PC 15;
  TCLC 4**
  See also CA 131; CANR 81; DAM MULT;
  DLB 290; EWL 3; HW 1, 2; LAW;
  MTCW 1, 2; RGWL 2, 3
Darley, George 1795-1846 .... **NCLC 2**
  See also DLB 96; RGEL 2
Darrow, Clarence (Seward)
  1857-1938 .... **TCLC 81**
  See also CA 164; DLB 303
Darwin, Charles 1809-1882 .... **NCLC 57**
  See also BRWS 7; DLB 57, 166; LATS 1:1;
  RGEL 2; TEA; WLIT 4
Darwin, Erasmus 1731-1802 .... **NCLC 106**
  See also DLB 93; RGEL 2
Daryush, Elizabeth 1887-1977 ...... **CLC 6, 19**
  See also CA 49-52; CANR 3, 81; DLB 20
Das, Kamala 1934- .... **CLC 191; PC 43**
  See also CA 101; CANR 27, 59; CP 7;
  CWP; FW
Dasgupta, Surendranath
  1887-1952 .... **TCLC 81**
  See also CA 157
**Dashwood, Edmee Elizabeth Monica de la
  Pasture** 1890-1943
  See Delafield, E. M.
  See also CA 119; 154
da Silva, Antonio Jose
  1705-1739 .... **NCLC 114**
Daudet, (Louis Marie) Alphonse
  1840-1897 .... **NCLC 1**
  See also DLB 123; GFL 1789 to the Present;
  RGSF 2
d'Aulnoy, Marie-Catherine c.
  1650-1705 .... **LC 100**
Daumal, Rene 1908-1944 .... **TCLC 14**
  See also CA 114; EWL 3
Davenant, William 1606-1668 .... **LC 13**
  See also DLB 58, 126; RGEL 2
Davenport, Guy (Mattison, Jr.)
  1927-2005 .... **CLC 6, 14, 38; SSC 16**
  See also CA 33-36R; CANR 23, 73; CN 7;
  CSW; DLB 130
David, Robert
  See Nezval, Vitezslav
Davidson, Avram (James) 1923-1993
  See Queen, Ellery
  See also CA 101; 171; CANR 26; DLB 8;
  FANT; SFW 4; SUFW 1, 2
Davidson, Donald (Grady)
  1893-1968 .... **CLC 2, 13, 19**
  See also CA 5-8R; 25-28R; CANR 4, 84;
  DLB 45
Davidson, Hugh
  See Hamilton, Edmond
Davidson, John 1857-1909 .... **TCLC 24**
  See also CA 118; 217; DLB 19; RGEL 2
Davidson, Sara 1943- .... **CLC 9**
  See also CA 81-84; CANR 44, 68; DLB
  185

Davie, Donald (Alfred) 1922-1995 .... **CLC 5,
  8, 10, 31; PC 29**
  See also BRWS 6; CA 1-4R; 149; CAAS 3;
  CANR 1, 44; CP 7; DLB 27; MTCW 1;
  RGEL 2
Davie, Elspeth 1919-1995 .... **SSC 52**
  See also CA 120; 126; 150; DLB 139
Davies, Ray(mond Douglas) 1944- ... **CLC 21**
  See also CA 116; 146; CANR 92
Davies, Rhys 1901-1978 .... **CLC 23**
  See also CA 9-12R; 81-84; CANR 4; DLB
  139, 191
Davies, (William) Robertson
  1913-1995 .... **CLC 2, 7, 13, 25, 42, 75,
  91; WLC**
  See Marchbanks, Samuel
  See also BEST 89:2; BPFB 1; CA 33-36R;
  150; CANR 17, 42, 103; CN 7; CPW;
  DA; DA3; DAB; DAC; DAM MST, NOV,
  POP; DLB 68; EWL 3; HGG; INT CANR-
  17; MTCW 1, 2; RGEL 2; TWA
Davies, Sir John 1569-1626 .... **LC 85**
  See also DLB 172
Davies, Walter C.
  See Kornbluth, C(yril) M.
Davies, William Henry 1871-1940 ... **TCLC 5**
  See also CA 104; 179; DLB 19, 174; EWL
  3; RGEL 2
Da Vinci, Leonardo 1452-1519 ..... **LC 12, 57,
  60**
  See also AAYA 40
Davis, Angela (Yvonne) 1944- .... **CLC 77**
  See also BW 2, 3; CA 57-60; CANR 10,
  81; CSW; DA3; DAM MULT; FW
Davis, B. Lynch
  See Bioy Casares, Adolfo; Borges, Jorge
  Luis
Davis, Frank Marshall 1905-1987 ...... **BLC 1**
  See also BW 2, 3; CA 125; 123; CANR 42,
  80; DAM MULT; DLB 51
Davis, Gordon
  See Hunt, E(verette) Howard, (Jr.)
Davis, H(arold) L(enoir) 1896-1960 . **CLC 49**
  See also ANW; CA 178; 89-92; DLB 9,
  206; SATA 114
Davis, Natalie Z(emon) 1928- .... **CLC 204**
  See also CA 53-56; CANR 58, 100
Davis, Rebecca (Blaine) Harding
  1831-1910 .... **SSC 38; TCLC 6**
  See also CA 104; 179; DLB 74, 239; FW;
  NFS 14; RGAL 4; TUS
Davis, Richard Harding
  1864-1916 .... **TCLC 24**
  See also CA 114; 179; DLB 12, 23, 78, 79,
  189; DLBD 13; RGAL 4
Davison, Frank Dalby 1893-1970 ..... **CLC 15**
  See also CA 217; 116; DLB 260
Davison, Lawrence H.
  See Lawrence, D(avid) H(erbert Richards)
Davison, Peter (Hubert) 1928- .... **CLC 28**
  See also CA 9-12R; CAAS 4; CANR 3, 43,
  84; CP 7; DLB 5
Davys, Mary 1674-1732 .... **LC 1, 46**
  See also DLB 39
Dawson, (Guy) Fielding (Lewis)
  1930-2002 .... **CLC 6**
  See also CA 85-88; 202; CANR 108; DLB
  130; DLBY 2002
Dawson, Peter
  See Faust, Frederick (Schiller)
  See also TCWW 2, 2
Day, Clarence (Shepard, Jr.)
  1874-1935 .... **TCLC 25**
  See also CA 108; 199; DLB 11
Day, John 1574(?)-1640(?) .... **LC 70**
  See also DLB 62, 170; RGEL 2
Day, Thomas 1748-1789 .... **LC 1**
  See also DLB 39; YABC 1

Dent, Lester 1904-1959 .... **TCLC 72**
See also CA 112; 161; CMW 4; DLB 306;
SFW 4

De Palma, Brian (Russell) 1940- ...... **CLC 20**
See also CA 109

De Quincey, Thomas 1785-1859 ..... **NCLC 4, 87**
See also BRW 4; CDBLB 1789-1832; DLB
110, 144; RGEL 2

Deren, Eleanora 1908(?)-1961
See Deren, Maya
See also CA 192; 111

Deren, Maya .... **CLC 16, 102**
See Deren, Eleanora

Derleth, August (William)
1909-1971 .... **CLC 31**
See also BPFB 1; BYA 9, 10; CA 1-4R; 29-
32R; CANR 4; CMW 4; DLB 9; DLBD
17; HGG; SATA 5; SUFW 1

Der Nister 1884-1950 .... **TCLC 56**
See Nister, Der

Der Stricker c. 1190-c. 1250 .... **CMLC 75**

de Routisie, Albert
See Aragon, Louis

Derrida, Jacques 1930-2004 .... **CLC 24, 87**
See also CA 124; 127; CANR 76, 98, 133;
DLB 242; EWL 3; LMFS 2; MTCW 1;
TWA

Derry Down Derry
See Lear, Edward

Dersonnes, Jacques
See Simenon, Georges (Jacques Christian)

Desai, Anita 1937- .... **CLC 19, 37, 97, 175**
See also BRWS 5; CA 81-84; CANR 33,
53, 95, 133; CN 7; CWRI 5; DA3; DAB;
DAM NOV; DLB 271; DNFS 2; EWL 3;
FW; MTCW 1, 2; SATA 63, 126

Desai, Kiran 1971- .... **CLC 119**
See also BYA 16; CA 171; CANR 127

de Saint-Luc, Jean
See Glassco, John

de Saint Roman, Arnaud
See Aragon, Louis

Desbordes-Valmore, Marceline
1786-1859 .... **NCLC 97**
See also DLB 217

Descartes, Rene 1596-1650 .... **LC 20, 35**
See also DLB 268; EW 3; GFL Beginnings
to 1789

Deschamps, Eustache 1340(?)-1404 .. **LC 103**
See also DLB 208

De Sica, Vittorio 1901(?)-1974 .... **CLC 20**
See also CA 117

Desnos, Robert 1900-1945 .... **TCLC 22**
See also CA 121; 151; CANR 107; DLB
258; EWL 3; LMFS 2

Destouches, Louis-Ferdinand
1894-1961 .... **CLC 9, 15**
See Celine, Louis-Ferdinand
See also CA 85-88; CANR 28; MTCW 1

de Tolignac, Gaston
See Griffith, D(avid Lewelyn) W(ark)

Deutsch, Babette 1895-1982 .... **CLC 18**
See also BYA 3; CA 1-4R; 108; CANR 4,
79; DLB 45; SATA 1; SATA-Obit 33

Devenant, William 1606-1649 .... **LC 13**

Devkota, Laxmiprasad 1909-1959 . **TCLC 23**
See also CA 123

De Voto, Bernard (Augustine)
1897-1955 .... **TCLC 29**
See also CA 113; 160; DLB 9, 256

De Vries, Peter 1910-1993 ..... **CLC 1, 2, 3, 7, 10, 28, 46**
See also CA 17-20R; 142; CANR 41; DAM
NOV; DLB 6; DLBY 1982; MTCW 1, 2

Dewey, John 1859-1952 .... **TCLC 95**
See also CA 114; 170; DLB 246, 270;
RGAL 4

Dexter, John
See Bradley, Marion Zimmer
See also GLL 1

Dexter, Martin
See Faust, Frederick (Schiller)
See also TCWW 2

Dexter, Pete 1943- .... **CLC 34, 55**
See also BEST 89:2; CA 127; 131; CANR
129; CPW; DAM POP; INT CA-131;
MTCW 1

Diamano, Silmang
See Senghor, Leopold Sedar

Diamond, Neil 1941- .... **CLC 30**
See also CA 108

Diaz del Castillo, Bernal
1496-1584 .... **HLCS 1; LC 31**
See also LAW

di Bassetto, Corno
See Shaw, George Bernard

Dick, Philip K(indred) 1928-1982 ... **CLC 10, 30, 72; SSC 57**
See also AAYA 24; BPFB 1; BYA 11; CA
49-52; 106; CANR 2, 16, 132; CPW;
DA3; DAM NOV, POP; DLB 8; MTCW
1, 2; NFS 5; SCFW; SFW 4

Dickens, Charles (John Huffam)
1812-1870 .... **NCLC 3, 8, 18, 26, 37, 50, 86, 105, 113; SSC 17, 49; WLC**
See also AAYA 23; BRW 5; BRWC 1, 2;
BYA 1, 2, 3, 13, 14; CDBLB 1832-1890;
CLR 95; CMW 4; DA; DA3; DAB; DAC;
DAM MST, NOV; DLB 21, 55, 70, 159,
166; EXPN; HGG; JRDA; LAIT 1, 2;
LATS 1:1; LMFS 1; MAICYA 1, 2; NFS
4, 5, 10, 14, 20; RGEL 2; RGSF 2; SATA
15; SUFW 1; TEA; WCH; WLIT 4; WYA

Dickey, James (Lafayette)
1923-1997 ... **CLC 1, 2, 4, 7, 10, 15, 47, 109; PC 40; TCLC 151**
See also AAYA 50; AITN 1, 2; AMWS 4;
BPFB 1; CA 9-12R; 156; CABS 2; CANR
10, 48, 61, 105; CDALB 1968-1988; CP
7; CPW; CSW; DA3; DAM NOV, POET,
POP; DLB 5, 193; DLBD 7; DLBY 1982,
1993, 1996, 1997, 1998; EWL 3; INT
CANR-10; MTCW 1, 2; NFS 9; PFS 6,
11; RGAL 4; TUS

Dickey, William 1928-1994 .... **CLC 3, 28**
See also CA 9-12R; 145; CANR 24, 79;
DLB 5

Dickinson, Charles 1951- .... **CLC 49**
See also CA 128

Dickinson, Emily (Elizabeth)
1830-1886 ... **NCLC 21, 77; PC 1; WLC**
See also AAYA 22; AMW; AMWR 1;
CDALB 1865-1917; DA; DA3; DAB;
DAC; DAM MST, POET; DLB 1, 243;
EXPP; MAWW; PAB; PFS 1, 2, 3, 4, 5,
6, 8, 10, 11, 13, 16; RGAL 4; SATA 29;
TUS; WP; WYA

Dickinson, Mrs. Herbert Ward
See Phelps, Elizabeth Stuart

Dickinson, Peter (Malcolm de Brissac)
1927- .... **CLC 12, 35**
See also AAYA 9, 49; BYA 5; CA 41-44R;
CANR 31, 58, 88, 134; CLR 29; CMW 4;
DLB 87, 161, 276; JRDA; MAICYA 1, 2;
SATA 5, 62, 95, 150; SFW 4; WYA; YAW

Dickson, Carr
See Carr, John Dickson

Dickson, Carter
See Carr, John Dickson

Diderot, Denis 1713-1784 .... **LC 26**
See also EW 4; GFL Beginnings to 1789;
LMFS 1; RGWL 2, 3

Didion, Joan 1934- . **CLC 1, 3, 8, 14, 32, 129**
See also AITN 1; AMWS 4; CA 5-8R;
CANR 14, 52, 76, 125; CDALB 1968-
1988; CN 7; DA3; DAM NOV; DLB 2,

173, 185; DLBY 1981, 1986; EWL 3;
MAWW; MTCW 1, 2; NFS 3; RGAL 4;
TCWW 2; TUS

di Donato, Pietro 1911-1992 .... **TCLC 159**
See also CA 101; 136; DLB 9

Dietrich, Robert
See Hunt, E(verette) Howard, (Jr.)

Difusa, Pati
See Almodovar, Pedro

Dillard, Annie 1945- .... **CLC 9, 60, 115**
See also AAYA 6, 43; AMWS 6; ANW; CA
49-52; CANR 3, 43, 62, 90, 125; DA3;
DAM NOV; DLB 275, 278; DLBY 1980;
LAIT 4, 5; MTCW 1, 2; NCFS 1; RGAL
4; SATA 10, 140; TUS

Dillard, R(ichard) H(enry) W(ilde)
1937- .... **CLC 5**
See also CA 21-24R; CAAS 7; CANR 10;
CP 7; CSW; DLB 5, 244

Dillon, Eilis 1920-1994 .... **CLC 17**
See also CA 9-12R, 182; 147; CAAE 182;
CAAS 3; CANR 4, 38, 78; CLR 26; MAI-
CYA 1, 2; MAICYAS 1; SATA 2, 74;
SATA-Essay 105; SATA-Obit 83; YAW

Dimont, Penelope
See Mortimer, Penelope (Ruth)

Dinesen, Isak ..... **CLC 10, 29, 95; SSC 7, 75**
See Blixen, Karen (Christentze Dinesen)
See also EW 10; EWL 3; EXPS; FW; HGG;
LAIT 3; MTCW 1; NCFS 2; NFS 9;
RGSF 2; RGWL 2, 3; SSFS 3, 6, 13;
WLIT 2

Ding Ling .... **CLC 68**
See Chiang, Pin-chin
See also RGWL 3

Diphusa, Patty
See Almodovar, Pedro

Disch, Thomas M(ichael) 1940- ... **CLC 7, 36**
See Disch, Tom
See also AAYA 17; BPFB 1; CA 21-24R;
CAAS 4; CANR 17, 36, 54, 89; CLR 18;
CP 7; DA3; DLB 8; HGG; MAICYA 1, 2;
MTCW 1, 2; SAAS 15; SATA 92; SCFW;
SFW 4; SUFW 2

Disch, Tom
See Disch, Thomas M(ichael)
See also DLB 282

d'Isly, Georges
See Simenon, Georges (Jacques Christian)

Disraeli, Benjamin 1804-1881 ... **NCLC 2, 39, 79**
See also BRW 4; DLB 21, 55; RGEL 2

Ditcum, Steve
See Crumb, R(obert)

Dixon, Paige
See Corcoran, Barbara (Asenath)

Dixon, Stephen 1936- .... **CLC 52; SSC 16**
See also AMWS 12; CA 89-92; CANR 17,
40, 54, 91; CN 7; DLB 130

Dixon, Thomas 1864-1946 .... **TCLC 163**
See also RHW

Djebar, Assia 1936- .... **CLC 182**
See also CA 188; EWL 3; RGWL 3; WLIT
2

Doak, Annie
See Dillard, Annie

Dobell, Sydney Thompson
1824-1874 .... **NCLC 43**
See also DLB 32; RGEL 2

Doblin, Alfred .... **TCLC 13**
See Doeblin, Alfred
See also CDWLB 2; EWL 3; RGWL 2, 3

Dobroliubov, Nikolai Aleksandrovich
See Dobrolyubov, Nikolai Alexandrovich
See also DLB 277

Dobrolyubov, Nikolai Alexandrovich
1836-1861 .... **NCLC 5**
See Dobroliubov, Nikolai Aleksandrovich

Dobson, Austin 1840-1921 .... **TCLC 79**
See also DLB 35, 144
Dobyns, Stephen 1941- .... **CLC 37**
See also AMWS 13; CA 45-48; CANR 2, 18, 99; CMW 4; CP 7
Doctorow, E(dgar) L(aurence)
1931- .... **CLC 6, 11, 15, 18, 37, 44, 65, 113**
See also AAYA 22; AITN 2; AMWS 4; BEST 89:3; BPFB 1; CA 45-48; CANR 2, 33, 51, 76, 97, 133; CDALB 1968-1988; CN 7; CPW; DA3; DAM NOV, POP; DLB 2, 28, 173; DLBY 1980; EWL 3; LAIT 3; MTCW 1, 2; NFS 6; RGAL 4; RHW; TUS
Dodgson, Charles L(utwidge) 1832-1898
See Carroll, Lewis
See also CLR 2; DA; DA3; DAB; DAC; DAM MST, NOV, POET; MAICYA 1, 2; SATA 100; YABC 2
Dodsley, Robert 1703-1764 .... **LC 97**
See also DLB 95; RGEL 2
Dodson, Owen (Vincent) 1914-1983 .. **BLC 1; CLC 79**
See also BW 1; CA 65-68; 110; CANR 24; DAM MULT; DLB 76
Doeblin, Alfred 1878-1957 .... **TCLC 13**
See Doblin, Alfred
See also CA 110; 141; DLB 66
Doerr, Harriet 1910-2002 .... **CLC 34**
See also CA 117; 122; 213; CANR 47; INT CA-122; LATS 1:2
Domecq, H(onorio Bustos)
See Bioy Casares, Adolfo
Domecq, H(onorio) Bustos
See Bioy Casares, Adolfo; Borges, Jorge Luis
Domini, Rey
See Lorde, Audre (Geraldine)
See also GLL 1
Dominique
See Proust, (Valentin-Louis-George-Eugene) Marcel
Don, A
See Stephen, Sir Leslie
Donaldson, Stephen R(eeder)
1947- .... **CLC 46, 138**
See also AAYA 36; BPFB 1; CA 89-92; CANR 13, 55, 99; CPW; DAM POP; FANT; INT CANR-13; SATA 121; SFW 4; SUFW 1, 2
Donleavy, J(ames) P(atrick) 1926- .... **CLC 1, 4, 6, 10, 45**
See also AITN 2; BPFB 1; CA 9-12R; CANR 24, 49, 62, 80, 124; CBD; CD 5; CN 7; DLB 6, 173; INT CANR-24; MTCW 1, 2; RGAL 4
Donnadieu, Marguerite
See Duras, Marguerite
Donne, John 1572-1631 ... **LC 10, 24, 91; PC 1, 43; WLC**
See also BRW 1; BRWC 1; BRWR 2; CD-BLB Before 1660; DA; DAB; DAC; DAM MST, POET; DLB 121, 151; EXPP; PAB; PFS 2, 11; RGEL 3; TEA; WLIT 3; WP
Donnell, David 1939(?)- .... **CLC 34**
See also CA 197
Donoghue, P. S.
See Hunt, E(verette) Howard, (Jr.)
Donoso (Yanez), Jose 1924-1996 ... **CLC 4, 8, 11, 32, 99; HLC 1; SSC 34; TCLC 133**
See also CA 81-84; 155; CANR 32, 73; CD-WLB 3; CWW 2; DAM MULT; DLB 113; EWL 3; HW 1, 2; LAW; LAWS 1; MTCW 1, 2; RGSF 2; WLIT 1
Donovan, John 1928-1992 .... **CLC 35**
See also AAYA 20; CA 97-100; 137; CLR 3; MAICYA 1, 2; SATA 72; SATA-Brief 29; YAW

Don Roberto
See Cunninghame Graham, Robert (Gallnigad) Bontine
Doolittle, Hilda 1886-1961 . **CLC 3, 8, 14, 31, 34, 73; PC 5; WLC**
See H. D.
See also AMWS 1; CA 97-100; CANR 35, 131; DA; DAC; DAM MST, POET; DLB 4, 45; EWL 3; FW; GLL 1; LMFS 2; MAWW; MTCW 1, 2; PFS 6; RGAL 4
Doppo, Kunikida .... **TCLC 99**
See Kunikida Doppo
Dorfman, Ariel 1942- .... **CLC 48, 77, 189; HLC 1**
See also CA 124; 130; CANR 67, 70, 135; CWW 2; DAM MULT; DFS 4; EWL 3; HW 1, 2; INT CA-130; WLIT 1
Dorn, Edward (Merton)
1929-1999 .... **CLC 10, 18**
See also CA 93-96; 187; CANR 42, 79; CP 7; DLB 5; INT CA-93-96; WP
Dor-Ner, Zvi .... **CLC 70**
Dorris, Michael (Anthony)
1945-1997 .... **CLC 109; NNAL**
See also AAYA 20; BEST 90:1; BYA 12; CA 102; 157; CANR 19, 46, 75; CLR 58; DA3; DAM MULT, NOV; DLB 175; LAIT 5; MTCW 2; NFS 3; RGAL 4; SATA 75; SATA-Obit 94; TCWW 2; YAW
Dorris, Michael A.
See Dorris, Michael (Anthony)
Dorsan, Luc
See Simenon, Georges (Jacques Christian)
Dorsange, Jean
See Simenon, Georges (Jacques Christian)
Dorset
See Sackville, Thomas
Dos Passos, John (Roderigo)
1896-1970 ... **CLC 1, 4, 8, 11, 15, 25, 34, 82; WLC**
See also AMW; BPFB 1; CA 1-4R; 29-32R; CANR 3; CDALB 1929-1941; DA; DA3; DAB; DAC; DAM MST, NOV; DLB 4, 9, 274; DLBD 1, 15; DLBY 1996; EWL 3; MTCW 1, 2; NFS 14; RGAL 4; TUS
Dossage, Jean
See Simenon, Georges (Jacques Christian)
Dostoevsky, Fedor Mikhailovich
1821-1881 .. **NCLC 2, 7, 21, 33, 43, 119; SSC 2, 33, 44; WLC**
See Dostoevsky, Fyodor
See also AAYA 40; DA; DA3; DAB; DAC; DAM MST, NOV; EW 7; EXPN; NFS 3, 8; RGSF 2; RGWL 2, 3; SSFS 8; TWA
Dostoevsky, Fyodor
See Dostoevsky, Fedor Mikhailovich
See also DLB 238; LATS 1:1; LMFS 1, 2
Doty, M. R.
See Doty, Mark (Alan)
Doty, Mark
See Doty, Mark (Alan)
Doty, Mark (Alan) 1953(?)- .... **CLC 176; PC 53**
See also AMWS 11; CA 161, 183; CAAE 183; CANR 110
Doty, Mark A.
See Doty, Mark (Alan)
Doughty, Charles M(ontagu)
1843-1926 .... **TCLC 27**
See also CA 115; 178; DLB 19, 57, 174
Douglas, Ellen .... **CLC 73**
See Haxton, Josephine Ayres; Williamson, Ellen Douglas
See also CN 7; CSW; DLB 292
Douglas, Gavin 1475(?)-1522 .... **LC 20**
See also DLB 132; RGEL 2
Douglas, George
See Brown, George Douglas
See also RGEL 2

Douglas, Keith (Castellain)
1920-1944 .... **TCLC 40**
See also BRW 7; CA 160; DLB 27; EWL 3; PAB; RGEL 2
Douglas, Leonard
See Bradbury, Ray (Douglas)
Douglas, Michael
See Crichton, (John) Michael
Douglas, (George) Norman
1868-1952 .... **TCLC 68**
See also BRW 6; CA 119; 157; DLB 34, 195; RGEL 2
Douglas, William
See Brown, George Douglas
Douglass, Frederick 1817(?)-1895 ..... **BLC 1; NCLC 7, 55, 141; WLC**
See also AAYA 48; AFAW 1, 2; AMWC 1; AMWS 3; CDALB 1640-1865; DA; DA3; DAC; DAM MST, MULT; DLB 1, 43, 50, 79, 243; FW; LAIT 2; NCFS 2; RGAL 4; SATA 29
Dourado, (Waldomiro Freitas) Autran
1926- .... **CLC 23, 60**
See also CA 25-28R; 179; CANR 34, 81; DLB 145, 307; HW 2
Dourado, Waldomiro Freitas Autran
See Dourado, (Waldomiro Freitas) Autran
Dove, Rita (Frances) 1952- . **BLCS; CLC 50, 81; PC 6**
See also AAYA 46; AMWS 4; BW 2; CA 109; CAAS 19; CANR 27, 42, 68, 76, 97, 132; CDALBS; CP 7; CSW; CWP; DA3; DAM MULT, POET; DLB 120; EWL 3; EXPP; MTCW 1; PFS 1, 15; RGAL 4
Doveglion
See Villa, Jose Garcia
Dowell, Coleman 1925-1985 .... **CLC 60**
See also CA 25-28R; 117; CANR 10; DLB 130; GLL 2
Dowson, Ernest (Christopher)
1867-1900 .... **TCLC 4**
See also CA 105; 150; DLB 19, 135; RGEL 2
Doyle, A. Conan
See Doyle, Sir Arthur Conan
Doyle, Sir Arthur Conan
1859-1930 .... **SSC 12; TCLC 7; WLC**
See Conan Doyle, Arthur
See also AAYA 14; BRWS 2; CA 104; 122; CANR 131; CDBLB 1890-1914; CMW 4; DA; DA3; DAB; DAC; DAM MST, NOV; DLB 18, 70, 156, 178; EXPS; HGG; LAIT 2; MSW; MTCW 1, 2; RGEL 2; RGSF 2; RHW; SATA 24; SCFW 2; SFW 4; SSFS 2; TEA; WCH; WLIT 4; WYA; YAW
Doyle, Conan
See Doyle, Sir Arthur Conan
Doyle, John
See Graves, Robert (von Ranke)
Doyle, Roddy 1958(?)- .... **CLC 81, 178**
See also AAYA 14; BRWS 5; CA 143; CANR 73, 128; CN 7; DA3; DLB 194
Doyle, Sir A. Conan
See Doyle, Sir Arthur Conan
Dr. A
See Asimov, Isaac; Silverstein, Alvin; Silverstein, Virginia B(arbara Opshelor)
Drabble, Margaret 1939- ...... **CLC 2, 3, 5, 8, 10, 22, 53, 129**
See also BRWS 4; CA 13-16R; CANR 18, 35, 63, 112, 131; CDBLB 1960 to Present; CN 7; CPW; DA3; DAB; DAC; DAM MST, NOV, POP; DLB 14, 155, 231; EWL 3; FW; MTCW 1, 2; RGEL 2; SATA 48; TEA
Drakulic, Slavenka 1949- .... **CLC 173**
See also CA 144; CANR 92

Drakulic-Ilic, Slavenka
See Drakulic, Slavenka

Drapier, M. B.
See Swift, Jonathan

Drayham, James
See Mencken, H(enry) L(ouis)

Drayton, Michael 1563-1631 .... **LC 8**
See also DAM POET; DLB 121; RGEL 2

Dreadstone, Carl
See Campbell, (John) Ramsey

Dreiser, Theodore (Herman Albert)
1871-1945 .... **SSC 30; TCLC 10, 18, 35, 83; WLC**
See also AMW; AMWC 2; AMWR 2; BYA 15, 16; CA 106; 132; CDALB 1865-1917; DA; DA3; DAC; DAM MST, NOV; DLB 9, 12, 102, 137; DLBD 1; EWL 3; LAIT 2; LMFS 2; MTCW 1, 2; NFS 8, 17; RGAL 4; TUS

Drexler, Rosalyn 1926- .... **CLC 2, 6**
See also CA 81-84; CAD; CANR 68, 124; CD 5; CWD

Dreyer, Carl Theodor 1889-1968 ...... **CLC 16**
See also CA 116

Drieu la Rochelle, Pierre(-Eugene)
1893-1945 .... **TCLC 21**
See also CA 117; DLB 72; EWL 3; GFL 1789 to the Present

Drinkwater, John 1882-1937 .... **TCLC 57**
See also CA 109; 149; DLB 10, 19, 149; RGEL 2

Drop Shot
See Cable, George Washington

Droste-Hulshoff, Annette Freiin von
1797-1848 .... **NCLC 3, 133**
See also CDWLB 2; DLB 133; RGSF 2; RGWL 2, 3

Drummond, Walter
See Silverberg, Robert

Drummond, William Henry
1854-1907 .... **TCLC 25**
See also CA 160; DLB 92

Drummond de Andrade, Carlos
1902-1987 .... **CLC 18; TCLC 139**
See Andrade, Carlos Drummond de
See also CA 132; 123; DLB 307; LAW

Drummond of Hawthornden, William
1585-1649 .... **LC 83**
See also DLB 121, 213; RGEL 2

Drury, Allen (Stuart) 1918-1998 .... **CLC 37**
See also CA 57-60; 170; CANR 18, 52; CN 7; INT CANR-18

Druse, Eleanor
See King, Stephen (Edwin)

Dryden, John 1631-1700 ..... **DC 3; LC 3, 21, 115; PC 25; WLC**
See also BRW 2; CDBLB 1660-1789; DA; DAB; DAC; DAM DRAM, MST, POET; DLB 80, 101, 131; EXPP; IDTP; LMFS 1; RGEL 2; TEA; WLIT 3

du Bellay, Joachim 1524-1560 .... **LC 92**
See also GFL Beginnings to 1789; RGWL 2, 3

Duberman, Martin (Bauml) 1930- ..... **CLC 8**
See also CA 1-4R; CAD; CANR 2, 63; CD 5

Dubie, Norman (Evans) 1945- .... **CLC 36**
See also CA 69-72; CANR 12, 115; CP 7; DLB 120; PFS 12

Du Bois, W(illiam) E(dward) B(urghardt)
1868-1963 ..... **BLC 1; CLC 1, 2, 13, 64, 96; HR 2; WLC**
See also AAYA 40; AFAW 1, 2; AMWC 1; AMWS 2; BW 1, 3; CA 85-88; CANR 34, 82, 132; CDALB 1865-1917; DA; DA3; DAC; DAM MST, MULT, NOV; DLB 47, 50, 91, 246, 284; EWL 3; EXPP; LAIT 2; LMFS 2; MTCW 1, 2; NCFS 1; PFS 13; RGAL 4; SATA 42

Dubus, Andre 1936-1999 ..... **CLC 13, 36, 97; SSC 15**
See also AMWS 7; CA 21-24R; 177; CANR 17; CN 7; CSW; DLB 130; INT CANR-17; RGAL 4; SSFS 10

Duca Minimo
See D'Annunzio, Gabriele

Ducharme, Rejean 1941- .... **CLC 74**
See also CA 165; DLB 60

du Chatelet, Emilie 1706-1749 .... **LC 96**

Duchen, Claire .... **CLC 65**

Duclos, Charles Pinot- 1704-1772 .... **LC 1**
See also GFL Beginnings to 1789

Dudek, Louis 1918-2001 .... **CLC 11, 19**
See also CA 45-48; 215; CAAS 14; CANR 1; CP 7; DLB 88

Duerrenmatt, Friedrich 1921-1990 ... **CLC 1, 4, 8, 11, 15, 43, 102**
See Durrenmatt, Friedrich
See also CA 17-20R; CANR 33; CMW 4; DAM DRAM; DLB 69, 124; MTCW 1, 2

Duffy, Bruce 1953(?)- .... **CLC 50**
See also CA 172

Duffy, Maureen 1933- .... **CLC 37**
See also CA 25-28R; CANR 33, 68; CBD; CN 7; CP 7; CWD; CWP; DFS 15; DLB 14; FW; MTCW 1

Du Fu
See Tu Fu
See also RGWL 2, 3

Dugan, Alan 1923-2003 .... **CLC 2, 6**
See also CA 81-84; 220; CANR 119; CP 7; DLB 5; PFS 10

du Gard, Roger Martin
See Martin du Gard, Roger

Duhamel, Georges 1884-1966 .... **CLC 8**
See also CA 81-84; 25-28R; CANR 35; DLB 65; EWL 3; GFL 1789 to the Present; MTCW 1

Dujardin, Edouard (Emile Louis)
1861-1949 .... **TCLC 13**
See also CA 109; DLB 123

Duke, Raoul
See Thompson, Hunter S(tockton)

Dulles, John Foster 1888-1959 .... **TCLC 72**
See also CA 115; 149

Dumas, Alexandre (pere)
1802-1870 .... **NCLC 11, 71; WLC**
See also AAYA 22; BYA 3; DA; DA3; DAB; DAC; DAM MST, NOV; DLB 119, 192; EW 6; GFL 1789 to the Present; LAIT 1, 2; NFS 14, 19; RGWL 2, 3; SATA 18; TWA; WCH

Dumas, Alexandre (fils) 1824-1895 ...... **DC 1; NCLC 9**
See also DLB 192; GFL 1789 to the Present; RGWL 2, 3

Dumas, Claudine
See Malzberg, Barry N(athaniel)

Dumas, Henry L. 1934-1968 .... **CLC 6, 62**
See also BW 1; CA 85-88; DLB 41; RGAL 4

du Maurier, Daphne 1907-1989 .. **CLC 6, 11, 59; SSC 18**
See also AAYA 37; BPFB 1; BRWS 3; CA 5-8R; 128; CANR 6, 55; CMW 4; CPW; DA3; DAB; DAC; DAM MST, POP; DLB 191; HGG; LAIT 3; MSW; MTCW 1, 2; NFS 12; RGEL 2; RGSF 2; RHW; SATA 27; SATA-Obit 60; SSFS 14, 16; TEA

Du Maurier, George 1834-1896 ..... **NCLC 86**
See also DLB 153, 178; RGEL 2

Dunbar, Paul Laurence 1872-1906 ... **BLC 1; PC 5; SSC 8; TCLC 2, 12; WLC**
See also AFAW 1, 2; AMWS 2; BW 1, 3; CA 104; 124; CANR 79; CDALB 1865-1917; DA; DA3; DAC; DAM MST, MULT, POET; DLB 50, 54, 78; EXPP; RGAL 4; SATA 34

Dunbar, William 1460(?)-1520(?) .... **LC 20**
See also BRWS 8; DLB 132, 146; RGEL 2

Dunbar-Nelson, Alice .... **HR 2**
See Nelson, Alice Ruth Moore Dunbar

Duncan, Dora Angela
See Duncan, Isadora

Duncan, Isadora 1877(?)-1927 .... **TCLC 68**
See also CA 118; 149

Duncan, Lois 1934- .... **CLC 26**
See also AAYA 4, 34; BYA 6, 8; CA 1-4R; CANR 2, 23, 36, 111; CLR 29; JRDA; MAICYA 1, 2; MAICYAS 1; SAAS 2; SATA 1, 36, 75, 133, 141; SATA-Essay 141; WYA; YAW

Duncan, Robert (Edward)
1919-1988 .... **CLC 1, 2, 4, 7, 15, 41, 55; PC 2**
See also BG 2; CA 9-12R; 124; CANR 28, 62; DAM POET; DLB 5, 16, 193; EWL 3; MTCW 1, 2; PFS 13; RGAL 4; WP

Duncan, Sara Jeannette
1861-1922 .... **TCLC 60**
See also CA 157; DLB 92

Dunlap, William 1766-1839 .... **NCLC 2**
See also DLB 30, 37, 59; RGAL 4

Dunn, Douglas (Eaglesham) 1942- .... **CLC 6, 40**
See also BRWS 10; CA 45-48; CANR 2, 33, 126; CP 7; DLB 40; MTCW 1

Dunn, Katherine (Karen) 1945- .... **CLC 71**
See also CA 33-36R; CANR 72; HGG; MTCW 1

Dunn, Stephen (Elliott) 1939- .... **CLC 36**
See also AMWS 11; CA 33-36R; CANR 12, 48, 53, 105; CP 7; DLB 105; PFS 21

Dunne, Finley Peter 1867-1936 ...... **TCLC 28**
See also CA 108; 178; DLB 11, 23; RGAL 4

Dunne, John Gregory 1932-2003 ..... **CLC 28**
See also CA 25-28R; 222; CANR 14, 50; CN 7; DLBY 1980

Dunsany, Lord .... **TCLC 2, 59**
See Dunsany, Edward John Moreton Drax Plunkett
See also DLB 77, 153, 156, 255; FANT; IDTP; RGEL 2; SFW 4; SUFW 1

Dunsany, Edward John Moreton Drax Plunkett 1878-1957
See Dunsany, Lord
See also CA 104; 148; DLB 10; MTCW 1

Duns Scotus, John 1266(?)-1308 ... **CMLC 59**
See also DLB 115

du Perry, Jean
See Simenon, Georges (Jacques Christian)

Durang, Christopher (Ferdinand)
1949- .... **CLC 27, 38**
See also CA 105; CAD; CANR 50, 76, 130; CD 5; MTCW 1

Duras, Claire de 1777-1828 .... **NCLC 154**

Duras, Marguerite 1914-1996 . **CLC 3, 6, 11, 20, 34, 40, 68, 100; SSC 40**
See also BPFB 1; CA 25-28R; 151; CANR 50; CWW 2; DLB 83; EWL 3; GFL 1789 to the Present; IDFW 4; MTCW 1, 2; RGWL 2, 3; TWA

Durban, (Rosa) Pam 1947- .... **CLC 39**
See also CA 123; CANR 98; CSW

Durcan, Paul 1944- .... **CLC 43, 70**
See also CA 134; CANR 123; CP 7; DAM POET; EWL 3

Durfey, Thomas 1653-1723 .... **LC 94**
See also DLB 80; RGEL 2

Durkheim, Emile 1858-1917 .... **TCLC 55**

Durrell, Lawrence (George)
1912-1990 ...... **CLC 1, 4, 6, 8, 13, 27, 41**
See also BPFB 1; BRWS 1; CA 9-12R; 132; CANR 40, 77; CDBLB 1945-1960; DAM NOV; DLB 15, 27, 204; DLBY 1990; EWL 3; MTCW 1, 2; RGEL 2; SFW 4; TEA

Eliot, Dan
See Silverberg, Robert

Eliot, George 1819-1880 ...... **NCLC 4, 13, 23, 41, 49, 89, 118; PC 20; SSC 72; WLC**
See Evans, Mary Ann
See also BRW 5; BRWC 1, 2; BRWR 2; CDBLB 1832-1890; CN 7; CPW; DA; DA3; DAB; DAC; DAM MST, NOV; DLB 21, 35, 55; LATS 1:1; LMFS 1; NFS 17; RGEL 2; RGSF 2; SSFS 8; TEA; WLIT 3

Eliot, John 1604-1690 .... **LC 5**
See also DLB 24

Eliot, T(homas) S(tearns)
1888-1965 ...... **CLC 1, 2, 3, 6, 9, 10, 13, 15, 24, 34, 41, 55, 57, 113; PC 5, 31; WLC**
See also AAYA 28; AMW; AMWC 1; AMWR 1; BRW 7; BRWR 2; CA 5-8R; 25-28R; CANR 41; CDALB 1929-1941; DA; DA3; DAB; DAC; DAM DRAM, MST, POET; DFS 4, 13; DLB 7, 10, 45, 63, 245; DLBY 1988; EWL 3; EXPP; LAIT 3; LATS 1:1; LMFS 2; MTCW 1, 2; NCFS 5; PAB; PFS 1, 7, 20; RGAL 4; RGEL 2; TUS; WLIT 4; WP

Elizabeth 1866-1941 .... **TCLC 41**

Elkin, Stanley L(awrence)
1930-1995 .. **CLC 4, 6, 9, 14, 27, 51, 91; SSC 12**
See also AMWS 6; BPFB 1; CA 9-12R; 148; CANR 8, 46; CN 7; CPW; DAM NOV, POP; DLB 2, 28, 218, 278; DLBY 1980; EWL 3; INT CANR-8; MTCW 1, 2; RGAL 4

Elledge, Scott .... **CLC 34**

Elliott, Don
See Silverberg, Robert

Elliott, George P(aul) 1918-1980 .... **CLC 2**
See also CA 1-4R; 97-100; CANR 2; DLB 244

Elliott, Janice 1931-1995 .... **CLC 47**
See also CA 13-16R; CANR 8, 29, 84; CN 7; DLB 14; SATA 119

Elliott, Sumner Locke 1917-1991 ..... **CLC 38**
See also CA 5-8R; 134; CANR 2, 21; DLB 289

Elliott, William
See Bradbury, Ray (Douglas)

Ellis, A. E. .... **CLC 7**

Ellis, Alice Thomas .... **CLC 40**
See Haycraft, Anna (Margaret)
See also DLB 194; MTCW 1

Ellis, Bret Easton 1964- ...... **CLC 39, 71, 117**
See also AAYA 2, 43; CA 118; 123; CANR 51, 74, 126; CN 7; CPW; DA3; DAM POP; DLB 292; HGG; INT CA-123; MTCW 1; NFS 11

Ellis, (Henry) Havelock
1859-1939 .... **TCLC 14**
See also CA 109; 169; DLB 190

Ellis, Landon
See Ellison, Harlan (Jay)

Ellis, Trey 1962- .... **CLC 55**
See also CA 146; CANR 92

Ellison, Harlan (Jay) 1934- ... **CLC 1, 13, 42, 139; SSC 14**
See also AAYA 29; BPFB 1; BYA 14; CA 5-8R; CANR 5, 46, 115; CPW; DAM POP; DLB 8; HGG; INT CANR-5; MTCW 1, 2; SCFW 2; SFW 4; SSFS 13, 14, 15; SUFW 1, 2

Ellison, Ralph (Waldo) 1914-1994 .... **BLC 1; CLC 1, 3, 11, 54, 86, 114; SSC 26, 79; WLC**
See also AAYA 19; AFAW 1, 2; AMWC 2; AMWR 2; AMWS 2; BPFB 1; BW 1, 3; BYA 2; CA 9-12R; 145; CANR 24, 53; CDALB 1941-1968; CSW; DA; DA3; DAB; DAC; DAM MST, MULT, NOV;

DLB 2, 76, 227; DLBY 1994; EWL 3; EXPN; EXPS; LAIT 4; MTCW 1, 2; NCFS 3; NFS 2; RGAL 4; RGSF 2; SSFS 1, 11; YAW

Ellmann, Lucy (Elizabeth) 1956- ..... **CLC 61**
See also CA 128

Ellmann, Richard (David)
1918-1987 .... **CLC 50**
See also BEST 89:2; CA 1-4R; 122; CANR 2, 28, 61; DLB 103; DLBY 1987; MTCW 1, 2

Elman, Richard (Martin)
1934-1997 .... **CLC 19**
See also CA 17-20R; 163; CAAS 3; CANR 47

Elron
See Hubbard, L(afayette) Ron(ald)

El Saadawi, Nawal 1931- .... **CLC 196**
See al'Sadaawi, Nawal; Sa'adawi, al-Nawal; Saadawi, Nawal El; Sa'dawi, Nawal al-
See also CA 118; CAAS 11; CANR 44, 92

Eluard, Paul .... **PC 38; TCLC 7, 41**
See Grindel, Eugene
See also EWL 3; GFL 1789 to the Present; RGWL 2, 3

Elyot, Thomas 1490(?)-1546 .... **LC 11**
See also DLB 136; RGEL 2

Elytis, Odysseus 1911-1996 .... **CLC 15, 49, 100; PC 21**
See Alepoudelis, Odysseus
See also CA 102; 151; CANR 94; CWW 2; DAM POET; EW 13; EWL 3; MTCW 1, 2; RGWL 2, 3

Emecheta, (Florence Onye) Buchi
1944- .... **BLC 2; CLC 14, 48, 128**
See also AFW; BW 2, 3; CA 81-84; CANR 27, 81, 126; CDWLB 3; CN 7; CWRI 5; DA3; DAM MULT; DLB 117; EWL 3; FW; MTCW 1, 2; NFS 12, 14; SATA 66; WLIT 2

Emerson, Mary Moody
1774-1863 .... **NCLC 66**

Emerson, Ralph Waldo 1803-1882 . **NCLC 1, 38, 98; PC 18; WLC**
See also AAYA 60; AMW; ANW; CDALB 1640-1865; DA; DA3; DAB; DAC; DAM MST, POET; DLB 1, 59, 73, 183, 223, 270; EXPP; LAIT 2; LMFS 1; NCFS 3; PFS 4, 17; RGAL 4; TUS; WP

Eminescu, Mihail 1850-1889 .. **NCLC 33, 131**

Empedocles 5th cent. B.C.- .... **CMLC 50**
See also DLB 176

Empson, William 1906-1984 ... **CLC 3, 8, 19, 33, 34**
See also BRWS 2; CA 17-20R; 112; CANR 31, 61; DLB 20; EWL 3; MTCW 1, 2; RGEL 2

Enchi, Fumiko (Ueda) 1905-1986 ..... **CLC 31**
See Enchi Fumiko
See also CA 129; 121; FW; MJW

Enchi Fumiko
See Enchi, Fumiko (Ueda)
See also DLB 182; EWL 3

Ende, Michael (Andreas Helmuth)
1929-1995 .... **CLC 31**
See also BYA 5; CA 118; 124; 149; CANR 36, 110; CLR 14; DLB 75; MAICYA 1, 2; MAICYAS 1; SATA 61, 130; SATA-Brief 42; SATA-Obit 86

Endo, Shusaku 1923-1996 ..... **CLC 7, 14, 19, 54, 99; SSC 48; TCLC 152**
See Endo Shusaku
See also CA 29-32R; 153; CANR 21, 54, 131; DA3; DAM NOV; MTCW 1, 2; RGSF 2; RGWL 2, 3

Endo Shusaku
See Endo, Shusaku
See also CWW 2; DLB 182; EWL 3

Engel, Marian 1933-1985 .... **CLC 36; TCLC 137**
See also CA 25-28R; CANR 12; DLB 53; FW; INT CANR-12

Engelhardt, Frederick
See Hubbard, L(afayette) Ron(ald)

Engels, Friedrich 1820-1895 .. **NCLC 85, 114**
See also DLB 129; LATS 1:1

Enright, D(ennis) J(oseph)
1920-2002 .... **CLC 4, 8, 31**
See also CA 1-4R; 211; CANR 1, 42, 83; CP 7; DLB 27; EWL 3; SATA 25; SATA-Obit 140

Enzensberger, Hans Magnus
1929- .... **CLC 43; PC 28**
See also CA 116; 119; CANR 103; CWW 2; EWL 3

Ephron, Nora 1941- .... **CLC 17, 31**
See also AAYA 35; AITN 2; CA 65-68; CANR 12, 39, 83

Epicurus 341B.C.-270B.C. .... **CMLC 21**
See also DLB 176

Epsilon
See Betjeman, John

Epstein, Daniel Mark 1948- .... **CLC 7**
See also CA 49-52; CANR 2, 53, 90

Epstein, Jacob 1956- .... **CLC 19**
See also CA 114

Epstein, Jean 1897-1953 .... **TCLC 92**

Epstein, Joseph 1937- .... **CLC 39, 204**
See also AMWS 14; CA 112; 119; CANR 50, 65, 117

Epstein, Leslie 1938- .... **CLC 27**
See also AMWS 12; CA 73-76, 215; CAAE 215; CAAS 12; CANR 23, 69; DLB 299

Equiano, Olaudah 1745(?)-1797 . **BLC 2; LC 16**
See also AFAW 1, 2; CDWLB 3; DAM MULT; DLB 37, 50; WLIT 2

Erasmus, Desiderius 1469(?)-1536 ..... **LC 16, 93**
See also DLB 136; EW 2; LMFS 1; RGWL 2, 3; TWA

Erdman, Paul E(mil) 1932- .... **CLC 25**
See also AITN 1; CA 61-64; CANR 13, 43, 84

Erdrich, Louise 1954- .... **CLC 39, 54, 120, 176; NNAL; PC 52**
See also AAYA 10, 47; AMWS 4; BEST 89:1; BPFB 1; CA 114; CANR 41, 62, 118; CDALBS; CN 7; CP 7; CPW; CWP; DA3; DAM MULT, NOV, POP; DLB 152, 175, 206; EWL 3; EXPP; LAIT 5; LATS 1:2; MTCW 1; NFS 5; PFS 14; RGAL 4; SATA 94, 141; SSFS 14; TCWW 2

Erenburg, Ilya (Grigoryevich)
See Ehrenburg, Ilya (Grigoryevich)

Erickson, Stephen Michael 1950-
See Erickson, Steve
See also CA 129; SFW 4

Erickson, Steve .... **CLC 64**
See Erickson, Stephen Michael
See also CANR 60, 68; SUFW 2

Erickson, Walter
See Fast, Howard (Melvin)

Ericson, Walter
See Fast, Howard (Melvin)

Eriksson, Buntel
See Bergman, (Ernst) Ingmar

Eriugena, John Scottus c.
810-877 .... **CMLC 65**
See also DLB 115

Ernaux, Annie 1940- .... **CLC 88, 184**
See also CA 147; CANR 93; NCFS 3, 5

Erskine, John 1879-1951 .... **TCLC 84**
See also CA 112; 159; DLB 9, 102; FANT

Eschenbach, Wolfram von
See Wolfram von Eschenbach
See also RGWL 3

Fecamps, Elise
   See Creasey, John
Federman, Raymond 1928- .... **CLC 6, 47**
   See also CA 17-20R, 208; CAAE 208;
   CAAS 8; CANR 10, 43, 83, 108; CN 7;
   DLBY 1980
Federspiel, J(uerg) F. 1931- .... **CLC 42**
   See also CA 146
Feiffer, Jules (Ralph) 1929- ...... **CLC 2, 8, 64**
   See also AAYA 3; CA 17-20R; CAD; CANR
   30, 59, 129; CD 5; DAM DRAM; DLB 7,
   44; INT CANR-30; MTCW 1; SATA 8,
   61, 111
Feige, Hermann Albert Otto Maximilian
   See Traven, B.
Feinberg, David B. 1956-1994 .... **CLC 59**
   See also CA 135; 147
Feinstein, Elaine 1930- .... **CLC 36**
   See also CA 69-72; CAAS 1; CANR 31,
   68, 121; CN 7; CP 7; CWP; DLB 14, 40;
   MTCW 1
Feke, Gilbert David .... **CLC 65**
Feldman, Irving (Mordecai) 1928- ..... **CLC 7**
   See also CA 1-4R; CANR 1; CP 7; DLB
   169
Felix-Tchicaya, Gerald
   See Tchicaya, Gerald Felix
Fellini, Federico 1920-1993 .... **CLC 16, 85**
   See also CA 65-68; 143; CANR 33
Felltham, Owen 1602(?)-1668 .... **LC 92**
   See also DLB 126, 151
Felsen, Henry Gregor 1916-1995 ..... **CLC 17**
   See also CA 1-4R; 180; CANR 1; SAAS 2;
   SATA 1
Felski, Rita .... **CLC 65**
Fenno, Jack
   See Calisher, Hortense
Fenollosa, Ernest (Francisco)
   1853-1908 .... **TCLC 91**
Fenton, James Martin 1949- .... **CLC 32**
   See also CA 102; CANR 108; CP 7; DLB
   40; PFS 11
Ferber, Edna 1887-1968 .... **CLC 18, 93**
   See also AITN 1; CA 5-8R; 25-28R; CANR
   68, 105; DLB 9, 28, 86, 266; MTCW 1,
   2; RGAL 4; RHW; SATA 7; TCWW 2
Ferdowsi, Abu'l Qasem 940-1020 . **CMLC 43**
   See also RGWL 2, 3
Ferguson, Helen
   See Kavan, Anna
Ferguson, Niall 1964- .... **CLC 134**
   See also CA 190
Ferguson, Samuel 1810-1886 .... **NCLC 33**
   See also DLB 32; RGEL 2
Fergusson, Robert 1750-1774 .... **LC 29**
   See also DLB 109; RGEL 2
Ferling, Lawrence
   See Ferlinghetti, Lawrence (Monsanto)
Ferlinghetti, Lawrence (Monsanto)
   1919(?)- ..... **CLC 2, 6, 10, 27, 111; PC 1**
   See also CA 5-8R; CANR 3, 41, 73, 125;
   CDALB 1941-1968; CP 7; DA3; DAM
   POET; DLB 5, 16; MTCW 1, 2; RGAL 4;
   WP
Fern, Fanny
   See Parton, Sara Payson Willis
Fernandez, Vicente Garcia Huidobro
   See Huidobro Fernandez, Vicente Garcia
Fernandez-Armesto, Felipe .... **CLC 70**
Fernandez de Lizardi, Jose Joaquin
   See Lizardi, Jose Joaquin Fernandez de
Ferre, Rosario 1938- ...... **CLC 139; HLCS 1;**
   SSC 36
   See also CA 131; CANR 55, 81, 134; CWW
   2; DLB 145; EWL 3; HW 1, 2; LAWS 1;
   MTCW 1; WLIT 1

Ferrer, Gabriel (Francisco Victor) Miro
   See Miro (Ferrer), Gabriel (Francisco
   Victor)
Ferrier, Susan (Edmonstone)
   1782-1854 .... **NCLC 8**
   See also DLB 116; RGEL 2
Ferrigno, Robert 1948(?)- .... **CLC 65**
   See also CA 140; CANR 125
Ferron, Jacques 1921-1985 .... **CLC 94**
   See also CA 117; 129; CCA 1; DAC; DLB
   60; EWL 3
Feuchtwanger, Lion 1884-1958 .... **TCLC 3**
   See also CA 104; 187; DLB 66; EWL 3
Feuerbach, Ludwig 1804-1872 ..... **NCLC 139**
   See also DLB 133
Feuillet, Octave 1821-1890 .... **NCLC 45**
   See also DLB 192
Feydeau, Georges (Leon Jules Marie)
   1862-1921 .... **TCLC 22**
   See also CA 113; 152; CANR 84; DAM
   DRAM; DLB 192; EWL 3; GFL 1789 to
   the Present; RGWL 2, 3
Fichte, Johann Gottlieb
   1762-1814 .... **NCLC 62**
   See also DLB 90
Ficino, Marsilio 1433-1499 .... **LC 12**
   See also LMFS 1
Fiedeler, Hans
   See Doeblin, Alfred
Fiedler, Leslie A(aron) 1917-2003 ..... **CLC 4,**
   13, 24
   See also AMWS 13; CA 9-12R; 212; CANR
   7, 63; CN 7; DLB 28, 67; EWL 3; MTCW
   1, 2; RGAL 4; TUS
Field, Andrew 1938- .... **CLC 44**
   See also CA 97-100; CANR 25
Field, Eugene 1850-1895 .... **NCLC 3**
   See also DLB 23, 42, 140; DLBD 13; MAI-
   CYA 1, 2; RGAL 4; SATA 16
Field, Gans T.
   See Wellman, Manly Wade
Field, Michael 1915-1971 .... **TCLC 43**
   See also CA 29-32R
Field, Peter
   See Hobson, Laura Z(ametkin)
   See also TCWW 2
Fielding, Helen 1958- .... **CLC 146**
   See also CA 172; CANR 127; DLB 231
Fielding, Henry 1707-1754 .... **LC 1, 46, 85;**
   WLC
   See also BRW 3; BRWR 1; CDBLB 1660-
   1789; DA; DA3; DAB; DAC; DAM
   DRAM, MST, NOV; DLB 39, 84, 101;
   NFS 18; RGEL 2; TEA; WLIT 3
Fielding, Sarah 1710-1768 .... **LC 1, 44**
   See also DLB 39; RGEL 2; TEA
Fields, W. C. 1880-1946 .... **TCLC 80**
   See also DLB 44
Fierstein, Harvey (Forbes) 1954- ..... **CLC 33**
   See also CA 123; 129; CAD; CD 5; CPW;
   DA3; DAM DRAM, POP; DFS 6; DLB
   266; GLL
Figes, Eva 1932- .... **CLC 31**
   See also CA 53-56; CANR 4, 44, 83; CN 7;
   DLB 14, 271; FW
Filippo, Eduardo de
   See de Filippo, Eduardo
Finch, Anne 1661-1720 .... **LC 3; PC 21**
   See also BRWS 9; DLB 95
Finch, Robert (Duer Claydon)
   1900-1995 .... **CLC 18**
   See also CA 57-60; CANR 9, 24, 49; CP 7;
   DLB 88
Findley, Timothy (Irving Frederick)
   1930-2002 .... **CLC 27, 102**
   See also CA 25-28R; 206; CANR 12, 42,
   69, 109; CCA 1; CN 7; DAC; DAM MST;
   DLB 53; FANT; RHW

Fink, William
   See Mencken, H(enry) L(ouis)
Firbank, Louis 1942-
   See Reed, Lou
   See also CA 117
Firbank, (Arthur Annesley) Ronald
   1886-1926 .... **TCLC 1**
   See also BRWS 2; CA 104; 177; DLB 36;
   EWL 3; RGEL 2
Fish, Stanley
   See Fish, Stanley Eugene
Fish, Stanley E.
   See Fish, Stanley Eugene
Fish, Stanley Eugene 1938- .... **CLC 142**
   See also CA 112; 132; CANR 90; DLB 67
Fisher, Dorothy (Frances) Canfield
   1879-1958 .... **TCLC 87**
   See also CA 114; 136; CANR 80; CLR 71,;
   CWRI 5; DLB 9, 102, 284; MAICYA 1,
   2; YABC 1
Fisher, M(ary) F(rances) K(ennedy)
   1908-1992 .... **CLC 76, 87**
   See also CA 77-80; 138; CANR 44; MTCW
   1
Fisher, Roy 1930- .... **CLC 25**
   See also CA 81-84; CAAS 10; CANR 16;
   CP 7; DLB 40
Fisher, Rudolph 1897-1934 .... **BLC 2; HR 2;**
   SSC 25; TCLC 11
   See also BW 1, 3; CA 107; 124; CANR 80;
   DAM MULT; DLB 51, 102
Fisher, Vardis (Alvero) 1895-1968 .... **CLC 7;**
   TCLC 140
   See also CA 5-8R; 25-28R; CANR 68; DLB
   9, 206; RGAL 4; TCWW 2
Fiske, Tarleton
   See Bloch, Robert (Albert)
Fitch, Clarke
   See Sinclair, Upton (Beall)
Fitch, John IV
   See Cormier, Robert (Edmund)
Fitzgerald, Captain Hugh
   See Baum, L(yman) Frank
FitzGerald, Edward 1809-1883 ...... **NCLC 9,**
   153
   See also BRW 4; DLB 32; RGEL 2
Fitzgerald, F(rancis) Scott (Key)
   1896-1940 ... **SSC 6, 31, 75; TCLC 1, 6,**
   14, 28, 55, 157; WLC
   See also AAYA 24; AITN 1; AMW; AMWC
   2; AMWR 1; BPFB 1; CA 110; 123;
   CDALB 1917-1929; DA; DA3; DAB;
   DAC; DAM MST, NOV; DLB 4, 9, 86,
   219, 273; DLBD 1, 15, 16; DLBY 1981,
   1996; EWL 3; EXPN; EXPS; LAIT 3;
   MTCW 1, 2; NFS 2, 19, 20; RGAL 4;
   RGSF 2; SSFS 4, 15; TUS
Fitzgerald, Penelope 1916-2000 . **CLC 19, 51,**
   61, 143
   See also BRWS 5; CA 85-88; 190; CAAS
   10; CANR 56, 86, 131; CN 7; DLB 14,
   194; EWL 3; MTCW 2
Fitzgerald, Robert (Stuart)
   1910-1985 .... **CLC 39**
   See also CA 1-4R; 114; CANR 1; DLBY
   1980
FitzGerald, Robert D(avid)
   1902-1987 .... **CLC 19**
   See also CA 17-20R; DLB 260; RGEL 2
Fitzgerald, Zelda (Sayre)
   1900-1948 .... **TCLC 52**
   See also AMWS 9; CA 117; 126; DLBY
   1984
Flanagan, Thomas (James Bonner)
   1923-2002 .... **CLC 25, 52**
   See also CA 108; 206; CANR 55; CN 7;
   DLBY 1980; INT CA-108; MTCW 1;
   RHW

Francis, Lord Jeffrey
See Jeffrey, Francis
See also DLB 107
Frank, Anne(lies Marie)
1929-1945 .... **TCLC 17; WLC**
See also AAYA 12; BYA 1; CA 113; 133;
CANR 68; CLR 101; DA; DA3; DAB;
DAC; DAM MST; LAIT 4; MAICYA 2;
MAICYAS 1; MTCW 1, 2; NCFS 2;
SATA 87; SATA-Brief 42; WYA; YAW
Frank, Bruno 1887-1945 .... **TCLC 81**
See also CA 189; DLB 118; EWL 3
Frank, Elizabeth 1945- .... **CLC 39**
See also CA 121; 126; CANR 78; INT CA-
126
Frankl, Viktor E(mil) 1905-1997 ...... **CLC 93**
See also CA 65-68; 161
Franklin, Benjamin
See Hasek, Jaroslav (Matej Frantisek)
Franklin, Benjamin 1706-1790 .... **LC 25;
WLCS**
See also AMW; CDALB 1640-1865; DA;
DA3; DAB; DAC; DAM MST; DLB 24,
43, 73, 183; LAIT 1; RGAL 4; TUS
**Franklin, (Stella Maria Sarah) Miles
(Lampe)** 1879-1954 .... **TCLC 7**
See also CA 104; 164; DLB 230; FW;
MTCW 2; RGEL 2; TWA
Franzen, Jonathan 1959- .... **CLC 202**
See also CA 129; CANR 105
Fraser, Antonia (Pakenham) 1932- . **CLC 32,
107**
See also AAYA 57; CA 85-88; CANR 44,
65, 119; CMW; DLB 276; MTCW 1, 2;
SATA-Brief 32
Fraser, George MacDonald 1925- ...... **CLC 7**
See also AAYA 48; CA 45-48, 180; CAAE
180; CANR 2, 48, 74; MTCW 1; RHW
Fraser, Sylvia 1935- .... **CLC 64**
See also CA 45-48; CANR 1, 16, 60; CCA
1
Frayn, Michael 1933- . **CLC 3, 7, 31, 47, 176**
See also BRWC 2; BRWS 7; CA 5-8R;
CANR 30, 69, 114, 133; CBD; CD 5; CN
7; DAM DRAM, NOV; DLB 13, 14, 194,
245; FANT; MTCW 1, 2; SFW 4
Fraze, Candida (Merrill) 1945- .... **CLC 50**
See also CA 126
Frazer, Andrew
See Marlowe, Stephen
Frazer, J(ames) G(eorge)
1854-1941 .... **TCLC 32**
See also BRWS 3; CA 118; NCFS 5
Frazer, Robert Caine
See Creasey, John
Frazer, Sir James George
See Frazer, J(ames) G(eorge)
Frazier, Charles 1950- .... **CLC 109**
See also AAYA 34; CA 161; CANR 126;
CSW; DLB 292
Frazier, Ian 1951- .... **CLC 46**
See also CA 130; CANR 54, 93
Frederic, Harold 1856-1898 .... **NCLC 10**
See also AMW; DLB 12, 23; DLBD 13;
RGAL 4
Frederick, John
See Faust, Frederick (Schiller)
See also TCWW 2
Frederick the Great 1712-1786 .... **LC 14**
Fredro, Aleksander 1793-1876 .... **NCLC 8**
Freeling, Nicolas 1927-2003 .... **CLC 38**
See also CA 49-52; 218; CAAS 12; CANR
1, 17, 50, 84; CMW 4; CN 7; DLB 87
Freeman, Douglas Southall
1886-1953 .... **TCLC 11**
See also CA 109; 195; DLB 17; DLBD 17
Freeman, Judith 1946- .... **CLC 55**
See also CA 148; CANR 120; DLB 256

Freeman, Mary E(leanor) Wilkins
1852-1930 .... **SSC 1, 47; TCLC 9**
See also CA 106; 177; DLB 12, 78, 221;
EXPS; FW; HGG; MAWW; RGAL 4;
RGSF 2; SSFS 4, 8; SUFW 1; TUS
Freeman, R(ichard) Austin
1862-1943 .... **TCLC 21**
See also CA 113; CANR 84; CMW 4; DLB
70
French, Albert 1943- .... **CLC 86**
See also BW 3; CA 167
French, Antonia
See Kureishi, Hanif
French, Marilyn 1929- .. **CLC 10, 18, 60, 177**
See also BPFB 1; CA 69-72; CANR 3, 31,
134; CN 7; CPW; DAM DRAM, NOV,
POP; FW; INT CANR-31; MTCW 1, 2
French, Paul
See Asimov, Isaac
Freneau, Philip Morin 1752-1832 .. **NCLC 1,
111**
See also AMWS 2; DLB 37, 43; RGAL 4
Freud, Sigmund 1856-1939 .... **TCLC 52**
See also CA 115; 133; CANR 69; DLB 296;
EW 8; EWL 3; LATS 1:1; MTCW 1, 2;
NCFS 3; TWA
Freytag, Gustav 1816-1895 .... **NCLC 109**
See also DLB 129
Friedan, Betty (Naomi) 1921- .... **CLC 74**
See also CA 65-68; CANR 18, 45, 74; DLB
246; FW; MTCW 1, 2; NCFS 5
Friedlander, Saul 1932- .... **CLC 90**
See also CA 117; 130; CANR 72
Friedman, B(ernard) H(arper)
1926- .... **CLC 7**
See also CA 1-4R; CANR 3, 48
Friedman, Bruce Jay 1930- ...... **CLC 3, 5, 56**
See also CA 9-12R; CAD; CANR 25, 52,
101; CD 5; CN 7; DLB 2, 28, 244; INT
CANR-25; SSFS 18
Friel, Brian 1929- .... **CLC 5, 42, 59, 115; DC
8; SSC 76**
See also BRWS 5; CA 21-24R; CANR 33,
69, 131; CBD; CD 5; DFS 11; DLB 13;
EWL 3; MTCW 1; RGEL 2; TEA
Friis-Baastad, Babbis Ellinor
1921-1970 .... **CLC 12**
See also CA 17-20R; 134; SATA 7
Frisch, Max (Rudolf) 1911-1991 ... **CLC 3, 9,
14, 18, 32, 44; TCLC 121**
See also CA 85-88; 134; CANR 32, 74; CD-
WLB 2; DAM DRAM, NOV; DLB 69,
124; EW 13; EWL 3; MTCW 1, 2; RGWL
2, 3
Fromentin, Eugene (Samuel Auguste)
1820-1876 .... **NCLC 10, 125**
See also DLB 123; GFL 1789 to the Present
Frost, Frederick
See Faust, Frederick (Schiller)
See also TCWW 2
Frost, Robert (Lee) 1874-1963 .. **CLC 1, 3, 4,
9, 10, 13, 15, 26, 34, 44; PC 1, 39;
WLC**
See also AAYA 21; AMW; AMWR 1; CA
89-92; CANR 33; CDALB 1917-1929;
CLR 67; DA; DA3; DAB; DAC; DAM
MST, POET; DLB 54, 284; DLBD 7;
EWL 3; EXPP; MTCW 1, 2; PAB; PFS 1,
2, 3, 4, 5, 6, 7, 10, 13; RGAL 4; SATA
14; TUS; WP; WYA
Froude, James Anthony
1818-1894 .... **NCLC 43**
See also DLB 18, 57, 144
Froy, Herald
See Waterhouse, Keith (Spencer)

Fry, Christopher 1907- .... **CLC 2, 10, 14**
See also BRWS 3; CA 17-20R; CAAS 23;
CANR 9, 30, 74, 132; CBD; CD 5; CP 7;
DAM DRAM; DLB 13; EWL 3; MTCW
1, 2; RGEL 2; SATA 66; TEA
Frye, (Herman) Northrop
1912-1991 .... **CLC 24, 70**
See also CA 5-8R; 133; CANR 8, 37; DLB
67, 68, 246; EWL 3; MTCW 1, 2; RGAL
4; TWA
Fuchs, Daniel 1909-1993 .... **CLC 8, 22**
See also CA 81-84; 142; CAAS 5; CANR
40; DLB 9, 26, 28; DLBY 1993
Fuchs, Daniel 1934- .... **CLC 34**
See also CA 37-40R; CANR 14, 48
Fuentes, Carlos 1928- .. **CLC 3, 8, 10, 13, 22,
41, 60, 113; HLC 1; SSC 24; WLC**
See also AAYA 4, 45; AITN 2; BPFB 1;
CA 69-72; CANR 10, 32, 68, 104; CD-
WLB 3; CWW 2; DA; DA3; DAB; DAC;
DAM MST, MULT, NOV; DLB 113;
DNFS 2; EWL 3; HW 1, 2; LAIT 3; LATS
1:2; LAW; LAWS 1; LMFS 2; MTCW 1,
2; NFS 8; RGSF 2; RGWL 2, 3; TWA;
WLIT 1
Fuentes, Gregorio Lopez y
See Lopez y Fuentes, Gregorio
Fuertes, Gloria 1918-1998 .... **PC 27**
See also CA 178; 180; DLB 108; HW 2;
SATA 115
Fugard, (Harold) Athol 1932- . **CLC 5, 9, 14,
25, 40, 80; DC 3**
See also AAYA 17; AFW; CA 85-88; CANR
32, 54, 118; CD 5; DAM DRAM; DFS 3,
6, 10; DLB 225; DNFS 1, 2; EWL 3;
LATS 1:2; MTCW 1; RGEL 2; WLIT 2
Fugard, Sheila 1932- .... **CLC 48**
See also CA 125
Fukuyama, Francis 1952- .... **CLC 131**
See also CA 140; CANR 72, 125
Fuller, Charles (H.), (Jr.) 1939- .... **BLC 2;
CLC 25; DC 1**
See also BW 2; CA 108; 112; CAD; CANR
87; CD 5; DAM DRAM, MULT; DFS 8;
DLB 38, 266; EWL 3; INT CA-112;
MTCW 1
Fuller, Henry Blake 1857-1929 .... **TCLC 103**
See also CA 108; 177; DLB 12; RGAL 4
Fuller, John (Leopold) 1937- .... **CLC 62**
See also CA 21-24R; CANR 9, 44; CP 7;
DLB 40
Fuller, Margaret
See Ossoli, Sarah Margaret (Fuller)
See also AMWS 2; DLB 183, 223, 239
Fuller, Roy (Broadbent) 1912-1991 ... **CLC 4,
28**
See also BRWS 7; CA 5-8R; 135; CAAS
10; CANR 53, 83; CWRI 5; DLB 15, 20;
EWL 3; RGEL 2; SATA 87
Fuller, Sarah Margaret
See Ossoli, Sarah Margaret (Fuller)
Fuller, Sarah Margaret
See Ossoli, Sarah Margaret (Fuller)
See also DLB 1, 59, 73
Fuller, Thomas 1608-1661 .... **LC 111**
See also DLB 151
Fulton, Alice 1952- .... **CLC 52**
See also CA 116; CANR 57, 88; CP 7;
CWP; DLB 193
Furphy, Joseph 1843-1912 .... **TCLC 25**
See Collins, Tom
See also CA 163; DLB 230; EWL 3; RGEL
2
Fuson, Robert H(enderson) 1927- .... **CLC 70**
See also CA 89-92; CANR 103
Fussell, Paul 1924- .... **CLC 74**
See also BEST 90:1; CA 17-20R; CANR 8,
21, 35, 69, 135; INT CANR-21; MTCW
1, 2

Gontier, Fernande 19(?)- .... **CLC 50**

Gonzalez Martinez, Enrique
See Gonzalez Martinez, Enrique
See also DLB 290

Gonzalez Martinez, Enrique
1871-1952 .... **TCLC 72**
See Gonzalez Martinez, Enrique
See also CA 166; CANR 81; EWL 3; HW
1, 2

Goodison, Lorna 1947- .... **PC 36**
See also CA 142; CANR 88; CP 7; CWP;
DLB 157; EWL 3

Goodman, Paul 1911-1972 ..... **CLC 1, 2, 4, 7**
See also CA 19-20; 37-40R; CAD; CANR
34; CAP 2; DLB 130, 246; MTCW 1;
RGAL 4

GoodWeather, Harley
See King, Thomas

Googe, Barnabe 1540-1594 .... **LC 94**
See also DLB 132; RGEL 2

Gordimer, Nadine 1923- ...... **CLC 3, 5, 7, 10,
18, 33, 51, 70, 123, 160, 161; SSC 17,
80; WLCS**
See also AAYA 39; AFW; BRWS 2; CA
5-8R; CANR 3, 28, 56, 88, 131; CN 7;
DA; DA3; DAB; DAC; DAM MST, NOV;
DLB 225; EWL 3; EXPS; INT CANR-28;
LATS 1:2; MTCW 1, 2; NFS 4; RGEL 2;
RGSF 2; SSFS 2, 14, 19; TWA; WLIT 2;
YAW

Gordon, Adam Lindsay
1833-1870 .... **NCLC 21**
See also DLB 230

Gordon, Caroline 1895-1981 . **CLC 6, 13, 29,
83; SSC 15**
See also AMW; CA 11-12; 103; CANR 36;
CAP 1; DLB 4, 9, 102; DLBD 17; DLBY
1981; EWL 3; MTCW 1, 2; RGAL 4;
RGSF 2

Gordon, Charles William 1860-1937
See Connor, Ralph
See also CA 109

Gordon, Mary (Catherine) 1949- .... **CLC 13,
22, 128; SSC 59**
See also AMWS 4; BPFB 2; CA 102;
CANR 44, 92; CN 7; DLB 6; DLBY
1981; FW; INT CA-102; MTCW 1

Gordon, N. J.
See Bosman, Herman Charles

Gordon, Sol 1923- .... **CLC 26**
See also CA 53-56; CANR 4; SATA 11

Gordone, Charles 1925-1995 .. **CLC 1, 4; DC
8**
See also BW 1, 3; CA 93-96; 180; 150;
CAAE 180; CAD; CANR 55; DAM
DRAM; DLB 7; INT CA-93-96; MTCW
1

Gore, Catherine 1800-1861 .... **NCLC 65**
See also DLB 116; RGEL 2

Gorenko, Anna Andreevna
See Akhmatova, Anna

Gorky, Maxim .... **SSC 28; TCLC 8; WLC**
See Peshkov, Alexei Maximovich
See also DAB; DFS 9; DLB 295; EW 8;
EWL 3; MTCW 2; TWA

Goryan, Sirak
See Saroyan, William

Gosse, Edmund (William)
1849-1928 .... **TCLC 28**
See also CA 117; DLB 57, 144, 184; RGEL
2

Gotlieb, Phyllis (Fay Bloom) 1926- .. **CLC 18**
See also CA 13-16R; CANR 7, 135; DLB
88, 251; SFW 4

Gottesman, S. D.
See Kornbluth, C(yril) M.; Pohl, Frederik

Gottfried von Strassburg fl. c.
1170-1215 .... **CMLC 10**
See also CDWLB 2; DLB 138; EW 1;
RGWL 2, 3

Gotthelf, Jeremias 1797-1854 .... **NCLC 117**
See also DLB 133; RGWL 2, 3

Gottschalk, Laura Riding
See Jackson, Laura (Riding)

Gould, Lois 1932(?)-2002 .... **CLC 4, 10**
See also CA 77-80; 208; CANR 29; MTCW
1

Gould, Stephen Jay 1941-2002 .... **CLC 163**
See also AAYA 26; BEST 90:2; CA 77-80;
205; CANR 10, 27, 56, 75, 125; CPW;
INT CANR-27; MTCW 1, 2

Gourmont, Remy(-Marie-Charles) de
1858-1915 .... **TCLC 17**
See also CA 109; 150; GFL 1789 to the
Present; MTCW 2

Gournay, Marie le Jars de
See de Gournay, Marie le Jars

Govier, Katherine 1948- .... **CLC 51**
See also CA 101; CANR 18, 40, 128; CCA
1

Gower, John c. 1330-1408 .... **LC 76; PC 59**
See also BRW 1; DLB 146; RGEL 2

Goyen, (Charles) William
1915-1983 .... **CLC 5, 8, 14, 40**
See also AITN 2; CA 5-8R; 110; CANR 6,
71; DLB 2, 218; DLBY 1983; EWL 3;
INT CANR-6

Goytisolo, Juan 1931- .... **CLC 5, 10, 23, 133;
HLC 1**
See also CA 85-88; CANR 32, 61, 131;
CWW 2; DAM MULT; EWL 3; GLL 2;
HW 1, 2; MTCW 1, 2

Gozzano, Guido 1883-1916 .... **PC 10**
See also CA 154; DLB 114; EWL 3

Gozzi, (Conte) Carlo 1720-1806 .... **NCLC 23**

Grabbe, Christian Dietrich
1801-1836 .... **NCLC 2**
See also DLB 133; RGWL 2, 3

Grace, Patricia Frances 1937- .... **CLC 56**
See also CA 176; CANR 118; CN 7; EWL
3; RGSF 2

Gracian y Morales, Baltasar
1601-1658 .... **LC 15**

Gracq, Julien .... **CLC 11, 48**
See Poirier, Louis
See also CWW 2; DLB 83; GFL 1789 to
the Present

Grade, Chaim 1910-1982 .... **CLC 10**
See also CA 93-96; 107; EWL 3

Graduate of Oxford, A
See Ruskin, John

Grafton, Garth
See Duncan, Sara Jeannette

Grafton, Sue 1940- .... **CLC 163**
See also AAYA 11, 49; BEST 90:3; CA 108;
CANR 31, 55, 111, 134; CMW 4; CPW;
CSW; DA3; DAM POP; DLB 226; FW;
MSW

Graham, John
See Phillips, David Graham

Graham, Jorie 1951- .... **CLC 48, 118; PC 59**
See also CA 111; CANR 63, 118; CP 7;
CWP; DLB 120; EWL 3; PFS 10, 17

Graham, R(obert) B(ontine) Cunninghame
See Cunninghame Graham, Robert
(Gallnigad) Bontine
See also DLB 98, 135, 174; RGEL 2; RGSF
2

Graham, Robert
See Haldeman, Joe (William)

Graham, Tom
See Lewis, (Harry) Sinclair

Graham, W(illiam) S(idney)
1918-1986 .... **CLC 29**
See also BRWS 7; CA 73-76; 118; DLB 20;
RGEL 2

Graham, Winston (Mawdsley)
1910-2003 .... **CLC 23**
See also CA 49-52; 218; CANR 2, 22, 45,
66; CMW 4; CN 7; DLB 77; RHW

Grahame, Kenneth 1859-1932 ...... **TCLC 64,
136**
See also BYA 5; CA 108; 136; CANR 80;
CLR 5; CWRI 5; DA3; DAB; DLB 34,
141, 178; FANT; MAICYA 1, 2; MTCW
2; NFS 20; RGEL 2; SATA 100; TEA;
WCH; YABC 1

Granger, Darius John
See Marlowe, Stephen

Granin, Daniil 1918- .... **CLC 59**
See also DLB 302

Granovsky, Timofei Nikolaevich
1813-1855 .... **NCLC 75**
See also DLB 198

Grant, Skeeter
See Spiegelman, Art

Granville-Barker, Harley
1877-1946 .... **TCLC 2**
See Barker, Harley Granville
See also CA 104; 204; DAM DRAM;
RGEL 2

Granzotto, Gianni
See Granzotto, Giovanni Battista

Granzotto, Giovanni Battista
1914-1985 .... **CLC 70**
See also CA 166

Grass, Guenter (Wilhelm) 1927- ... **CLC 1, 2,
4, 6, 11, 15, 22, 32, 49, 88; WLC**
See Grass, Gunter (Wilhelm)
See also BPFB 2; CA 13-16R; CANR 20,
75, 93, 133; CDWLB 2; DA; DA3; DAB;
DAC; DAM MST, NOV; DLB 75, 124;
EW 13; EWL 3; MTCW 1, 2; RGWL 2,
3; TWA

Grass, Gunter (Wilhelm)
See Grass, Guenter (Wilhelm)
See also CWW 2

Gratton, Thomas
See Hulme, T(homas) E(rnest)

Grau, Shirley Ann 1929- .... **CLC 4, 9, 146;
SSC 15**
See also CA 89-92; CANR 22, 69; CN 7;
CSW; DLB 2, 218; INT CA-89-92;
CANR-22; MTCW 1

Gravel, Fern
See Hall, James Norman

Graver, Elizabeth 1964- .... **CLC 70**
See also CA 135; CANR 71, 129

Graves, Richard Perceval
1895-1985 .... **CLC 44**
See also CA 65-68; CANR 9, 26, 51

Graves, Robert (von Ranke)
1895-1985 .. **CLC 1, 2, 6, 11, 39, 44, 45;
PC 6**
See also BPFB 2; BRW 7; BYA 4; CA 5-8R;
117; CANR 5, 36; CDBLB 1914-1945;
DA3; DAB; DAC; DAM MST, POET;
DLB 20, 100, 191; DLBD 18; DLBY
1985; EWL 3; LATS 1:1; MTCW 1, 2;
NCFS 2; RGEL 2; RHW; SATA 45; TEA

Graves, Valerie
See Bradley, Marion Zimmer

Gray, Alasdair (James) 1934- .... **CLC 41**
See also BRWS 9; CA 126; CANR 47, 69,
106; CN 7; DLB 194, 261; HGG; INT
CA-126; MTCW 1, 2; RGSF 2; SUFW 2

Gray, Amlin 1946- .... **CLC 29**
See also CA 138

Gryphius, Andreas 1616-1664 .... **LC 89**
See also CDWLB 2; DLB 164; RGWL 2, 3
Guare, John 1938- .... **CLC 8, 14, 29, 67; DC 20**
See also CA 73-76; CAD; CANR 21, 69, 118; CD 5; DAM DRAM; DFS 8, 13; DLB 7, 249; EWL 3; MTCW 1, 2; RGAL 4
Guarini, Battista 1537-1612 .... **LC 102**
Gubar, Susan (David) 1944- .... **CLC 145**
See also CA 108; CANR 45, 70; FW; MTCW 1; RGAL 4
Gudjonsson, Halldor Kiljan 1902-1998
See Halldor Laxness
See also CA 103; 164
Guenter, Erich
See Eich, Gunter
Guest, Barbara 1920- .... **CLC 34; PC 55**
See also BG 2; CA 25-28R; CANR 11, 44, 84; CP 7; CWP; DLB 5, 193
Guest, Edgar A(lbert) 1881-1959 ... **TCLC 95**
See also CA 112; 168
Guest, Judith (Ann) 1936- .... **CLC 8, 30**
See also AAYA 7; CA 77-80; CANR 15, 75; DA3; DAM NOV, POP; EXPN; INT CANR-15; LAIT 5; MTCW 1, 2; NFS 1
Guevara, Che .... **CLC 87; HLC 1**
See Guevara (Serna), Ernesto
Guevara (Serna), Ernesto 1928-1967 .... **CLC 87; HLC 1**
See Guevara, Che
See also CA 127; 111; CANR 56; DAM MULT; HW 1
Guicciardini, Francesco 1483-1540 ..... **LC 49**
Guild, Nicholas M. 1944- .... **CLC 33**
See also CA 93-96
Guillemin, Jacques
See Sartre, Jean-Paul
Guillen, Jorge 1893-1984 . **CLC 11; HLCS 1; PC 35**
See also CA 89-92; 112; DAM MULT, POET; DLB 108; EWL 3; HW 1; RGWL 2, 3
Guillen, Nicolas (Cristobal) 1902-1989 .... **BLC 2; CLC 48, 79; HLC 1; PC 23**
See also BW 2; CA 116; 125; 129; CANR 84; DAM MST, MULT, POET; DLB 283; EWL 3; HW 1; LAW; RGWL 2, 3; WP
Guillen y Alvarez, Jorge
See Guillen, Jorge
Guillevic, (Eugene) 1907-1997 .... **CLC 33**
See also CA 93-96; CWW 2
Guillois
See Desnos, Robert
Guillois, Valentin
See Desnos, Robert
Guimaraes Rosa, Joao 1908-1967 .... **HLCS 2**
See Rosa, Joao Guimaraes
See also CA 175; LAW; RGSF 2; RGWL 2, 3
Guiney, Louise Imogen 1861-1920 .... **TCLC 41**
See also CA 160; DLB 54; RGAL 4
Guinizelli, Guido c. 1230-1276 ...... **CMLC 49**
Guiraldes, Ricardo (Guillermo) 1886-1927 .... **TCLC 39**
See also CA 131; EWL 3; HW 1; LAW; MTCW 1
Gumilev, Nikolai (Stepanovich) 1886-1921 .... **TCLC 60**
See Gumilyov, Nikolay Stepanovich
See also CA 165; DLB 295
Gumilyov, Nikolay Stepanovich
See Gumilev, Nikolai (Stepanovich)
See also EWL 3
Gump, P. Q.
See Card, Orson Scott

Gunesekera, Romesh 1954- .... **CLC 91**
See also BRWS 10; CA 159; CN 7; DLB 267
Gunn, Bill .... **CLC 5**
See Gunn, William Harrison
See also DLB 38
Gunn, Thom(son William) 1929-2004 . **CLC 3, 6, 18, 32, 81; PC 26**
See also BRWS 4; CA 17-20R; 227; CANR 9, 33, 116; CDBLB 1960 to Present; CP 7; DAM POET; DLB 27; INT CANR-33; MTCW 1; PFS 9; RGEL 2
Gunn, William Harrison 1934(?)-1989
See Gunn, Bill
See also AITN 1; BW 1, 3; CA 13-16R; 128; CANR 12, 25, 76
Gunn Allen, Paula
See Allen, Paula Gunn
Gunnars, Kristjana 1948- .... **CLC 69**
See also CA 113; CCA 1; CP 7; CWP; DLB 60
Gunter, Erich
See Eich, Gunter
Gurdjieff, G(eorgei) I(vanovich) 1877(?)-1949 .... **TCLC 71**
See also CA 157
Gurganus, Allan 1947- .... **CLC 70**
See also BEST 90:1; CA 135; CANR 114; CN 7; CPW; CSW; DAM POP; GLL 1
Gurney, A. R.
See Gurney, A(lbert) R(amsdell), Jr.
See also DLB 266
Gurney, A(lbert) R(amsdell), Jr. 1930- .... **CLC 32, 50, 54**
See Gurney, A. R.
See also AMWS 5; CA 77-80; CAD; CANR 32, 64, 121; CD 5; DAM DRAM; EWL 3
Gurney, Ivor (Bertie) 1890-1937 ... **TCLC 33**
See also BRW 6; CA 167; DLBY 2002; PAB; RGEL 2
Gurney, Peter
See Gurney, A(lbert) R(amsdell), Jr.
Guro, Elena (Genrikhovna) 1877-1913 .... **TCLC 56**
See also DLB 295
Gustafson, James M(oody) 1925- ... **CLC 100**
See also CA 25-28R; CANR 37
Gustafson, Ralph (Barker) 1909-1995 .... **CLC 36**
See also CA 21-24R; CANR 8, 45, 84; CP 7; DLB 88; RGEL 2
Gut, Gom
See Simenon, Georges (Jacques Christian)
Guterson, David 1956- .... **CLC 91**
See also CA 132; CANR 73, 126; DLB 292; MTCW 2; NFS 13
Guthrie, A(lfred) B(ertram), Jr. 1901-1991 .... **CLC 23**
See also CA 57-60; 134; CANR 24; DLB 6, 212; SATA 62; SATA-Obit 67
Guthrie, Isobel
See Grieve, C(hristopher) M(urray)
Guthrie, Woodrow Wilson 1912-1967
See Guthrie, Woody
See also CA 113; 93-96
Guthrie, Woody .... **CLC 35**
See Guthrie, Woodrow Wilson
See also DLB 303; LAIT 3
Gutierrez Najera, Manuel 1859-1895 .... **HLCS 2; NCLC 133**
See also DLB 290; LAW
Guy, Rosa (Cuthbert) 1925- .... **CLC 26**
See also AAYA 4, 37; BW 2; CA 17-20R; CANR 14, 34, 83; CLR 13; DLB 33; DNFS 1; JRDA; MAICYA 1, 2; SATA 14, 62, 122; YAW
Gwendolyn
See Bennett, (Enoch) Arnold

H. D. .... **CLC 3, 8, 14, 31, 34, 73; PC 5**
See Doolittle, Hilda
H. de V.
See Buchan, John
Haavikko, Paavo Juhani 1931- .. **CLC 18, 34**
See also CA 106; CWW 2; EWL 3
Habbema, Koos
See Heijermans, Herman
Habermas, Juergen 1929- .... **CLC 104**
See also CA 109; CANR 85; DLB 242
Habermas, Jurgen
See Habermas, Juergen
Hacker, Marilyn 1942- ...... **CLC 5, 9, 23, 72, 91; PC 47**
See also CA 77-80; CANR 68, 129; CP 7; CWP; DAM POET; DLB 120, 282; FW; GLL 2; PFS 19
Hadewijch of Antwerp fl. 1250- ... **CMLC 61**
See also RGWL 3
Hadrian 76-138 .... **CMLC 52**
Haeckel, Ernst Heinrich (Philipp August) 1834-1919 .... **TCLC 83**
See also CA 157
Hafiz c. 1326-1389(?) .... **CMLC 34**
See also RGWL 2, 3
Hagedorn, Jessica T(arahata) 1949- .... **CLC 185**
See also CA 139; CANR 69; CWP; RGAL 4
Haggard, H(enry) Rider 1856-1925 .... **TCLC 11**
See also BRWS 3; BYA 4, 5; CA 108; 148; CANR 112; DLB 70, 156, 174, 178; FANT; LMFS 1; MTCW 2; RGEL 2; RHW; SATA 16; SCFW; SFW 4; SUFW 1; WLIT 4
Hagiosy, L.
See Larbaud, Valery (Nicolas)
Hagiwara, Sakutaro 1886-1942 .... **PC 18; TCLC 60**
See Hagiwara Sakutaro
See also CA 154; RGWL 3
Hagiwara Sakutaro
See Hagiwara, Sakutaro
See also EWL 3
Haig, Fenil
See Ford, Ford Madox
Haig-Brown, Roderick (Langmere) 1908-1976 .... **CLC 21**
See also CA 5-8R; 69-72; CANR 4, 38, 83; CLR 31; CWRI 5; DLB 88; MAICYA 1, 2; SATA 12
Haight, Rip
See Carpenter, John (Howard)
Hailey, Arthur 1920- .... **CLC 5**
See also AITN 2; BEST 90:3; BPFB 2; CA 1-4R; CANR 2, 36, 75; CCA 1; CN 7; CPW; DAM NOV, POP; DLB 88; DLBY 1982; MTCW 1, 2
Hailey, Elizabeth Forsythe 1938- ..... **CLC 40**
See also CA 93-96, 188; CAAE 188; CAAS 1; CANR 15, 48; INT CANR-15
Haines, John (Meade) 1924- .... **CLC 58**
See also AMWS 12; CA 17-20R; CANR 13, 34; CSW; DLB 5, 212
Hakluyt, Richard 1552-1616 .... **LC 31**
See also DLB 136; RGEL 2
Haldeman, Joe (William) 1943- .... **CLC 61**
See Graham, Robert
See also AAYA 38; CA 53-56, 179; CAAE 179; CAAS 25; CANR 6, 70, 72, 130; DLB 8; INT CANR-6; SCFW 2; SFW 4
Hale, Janet Campbell 1947- .... **NNAL**
See also CA 49-52; CANR 45, 75; DAM MULT; DLB 175; MTCW 2
Hale, Sarah Josepha (Buell) 1788-1879 .... **NCLC 75**
See also DLB 1, 42, 73, 243

Howard, Maureen 1930- .... **CLC 5, 14, 46, 151**
See also CA 53-56; CANR 31, 75; CN 7; DLBY 1983; INT CANR-31; MTCW 1, 2
Howard, Richard 1929- .... **CLC 7, 10, 47**
See also AITN 1; CA 85-88; CANR 25, 80; CP 7; DLB 5; INT CANR-25
Howard, Robert E(rvin)
1906-1936 .... **TCLC 8**
See also BPFB 2; BYA 5; CA 105; 157; FANT; SUFW 1
Howard, Warren F.
See Pohl, Frederik
Howe, Fanny (Quincy) 1940- .... **CLC 47**
See also CA 117, 187; CAAE 187; CAAS 27; CANR 70, 116; CP 7; CWP; SATA-Brief 52
Howe, Irving 1920-1993 .... **CLC 85**
See also AMWS 6; CA 9-12R; 141; CANR 21, 50; DLB 67; EWL 3; MTCW 1, 2
Howe, Julia Ward 1819-1910 .... **TCLC 21**
See also CA 117; 191; DLB 1, 189, 235; FW
Howe, Susan 1937- .... **CLC 72, 152; PC 54**
See also AMWS 4; CA 160; CP 7; CWP; DLB 120; FW; RGAL 4
Howe, Tina 1937- .... **CLC 48**
See also CA 109; CAD; CANR 125; CD 5; CWD
Howell, James 1594(?)-1666 .... **LC 13**
See also DLB 151
Howells, W. D.
See Howells, William Dean
Howells, William D.
See Howells, William Dean
Howells, William Dean 1837-1920 ... **SSC 36; TCLC 7, 17, 41**
See also AMW; CA 104; 134; CDALB 1865-1917; DLB 12, 64, 74, 79, 189; LMFS 1; MTCW 2; RGAL 4; TUS
Howes, Barbara 1914-1996 .... **CLC 15**
See also CA 9-12R; 151; CAAS 3; CANR 53; CP 7; SATA 5
Hrabal, Bohumil 1914-1997 ...... **CLC 13, 67; TCLC 155**
See also CA 106; 156; CAAS 12; CANR 57; CWW 2; DLB 232; EWL 3; RGSF 2
Hrotsvit of Gandersheim c. 935-c. 1000 .... **CMLC 29**
See also DLB 148
Hsi, Chu 1130-1200 .... **CMLC 42**
Hsun, Lu
See Lu Hsun
Hubbard, L(afayette) Ron(ald)
1911-1986 .... **CLC 43**
See also CA 77-80; 118; CANR 52; CPW; DA3; DAM POP; FANT; MTCW 2; SFW 4
Huch, Ricarda (Octavia)
1864-1947 .... **TCLC 13**
See also CA 111; 189; DLB 66; EWL 3
Huddle, David 1942- .... **CLC 49**
See also CA 57-60; CAAS 20; CANR 89; DLB 130
Hudson, Jeffrey
See Crichton, (John) Michael
Hudson, W(illiam) H(enry)
1841-1922 .... **TCLC 29**
See also CA 115; 190; DLB 98, 153, 174; RGEL 2; SATA 35
Hueffer, Ford Madox
See Ford, Ford Madox
Hughart, Barry 1934- .... **CLC 39**
See also CA 137; FANT; SFW 4; SUFW 2
Hughes, Colin
See Creasey, John
Hughes, David (John) 1930- .... **CLC 48**
See also CA 116; 129; CN 7; DLB 14

Hughes, Edward James
See Hughes, Ted
See also DA3; DAM MST, POET
Hughes, (James Mercer) Langston
1902-1967 ..... **BLC 2; CLC 1, 5, 10, 15, 35, 44, 108; DC 3; HR 2; PC 1, 53; SSC 6; WLC**
See also AAYA 12; AFAW 1, 2; AMWR 1; AMWS 1; BW 1, 3; CA 1-4R; 25-28R; CANR 1, 34, 82; CDALB 1929-1941; CLR 17; DA; DA3; DAB; DAC; DAM DRAM, MST, MULT, POET; DFS 6, 18; DLB 4, 7, 48, 51, 86, 228; EWL 3; EXPP; EXPS; JRDA; LAIT 3; LMFS 2; MAICYA 1, 2; MTCW 1, 2; PAB; PFS 1, 3, 6, 10, 15; RGAL 4; RGSF 2; SATA 4, 33; SSFS 4, 7; TUS; WCH; WP; YAW
Hughes, Richard (Arthur Warren)
1900-1976 .... **CLC 1, 11**
See also CA 5-8R; 65-68; CANR 4; DAM NOV; DLB 15, 161; EWL 3; MTCW 1; RGEL 2; SATA 8; SATA-Obit 25
Hughes, Ted 1930-1998 . **CLC 2, 4, 9, 14, 37, 119; PC 7**
See Hughes, Edward James
See also BRWC 2; BRWR 2; BRWS 1; CA 1-4R; 171; CANR 1, 33, 66, 108; CLR 3; CP 7; DAB; DAC; DLB 40, 161; EWL 3; EXPP; MAICYA 1, 2; MTCW 1, 2; PAB; PFS 4, 19; RGEL 2; SATA 49; SATA-Brief 27; SATA-Obit 107; TEA; YAW
Hugo, Richard
See Huch, Ricarda (Octavia)
Hugo, Richard F(ranklin)
1923-1982 .... **CLC 6, 18, 32**
See also AMWS 6; CA 49-52; 108; CANR 3; DAM POET; DLB 5, 206; EWL 3; PFS 17; RGAL 4
Hugo, Victor (Marie) 1802-1885 .... **NCLC 3, 10, 21; PC 17; WLC**
See also CA 28; DA; DA3; DAB; DAC; DAM DRAM, MST, NOV, POET; DLB 119, 192, 217; EFS 2; EW 6; EXPN; GFL 1789 to the Present; LAIT 1, 2; NFS 5, 20; RGWL 2, 3; SATA 47; TWA
Huidobro, Vicente
See Huidobro Fernandez, Vicente Garcia
See also DLB 283; EWL 3; LAW
Huidobro Fernandez, Vicente Garcia
1893-1948 .... **TCLC 31**
See Huidobro, Vicente
See also CA 131; HW 1
Hulme, Keri 1947- .... **CLC 39, 130**
See also CA 125; CANR 69; CN 7; CP 7; CWP; EWL 3; FW; INT CA-125
Hulme, T(homas) E(rnest)
1883-1917 .... **TCLC 21**
See also BRWS 6; CA 117; 203; DLB 19
Humboldt, Wilhelm von
1767-1835 .... **NCLC 134**
See also DLB 90
Hume, David 1711-1776 .... **LC 7, 56**
See also BRWS 3; DLB 104, 252; LMFS 1; TEA
Humphrey, William 1924-1997 .... **CLC 45**
See also AMWS 9; CA 77-80; 160; CANR 68; CN 7; CSW; DLB 6, 212, 234, 278; TCWW 2
Humphreys, Emyr Owen 1919- .... **CLC 47**
See also CA 5-8R; CANR 3, 24; CN 7; DLB 15
Humphreys, Josephine 1945- ..... **CLC 34, 57**
See also CA 121; 127; CANR 97; CSW; DLB 292; INT CA-127
Huneker, James Gibbons
1860-1921 .... **TCLC 65**
See also CA 193; DLB 71; RGAL 4
Hungerford, Hesba Fay
See Brinsmead, H(esba) F(ay)

Hungerford, Pixie
See Brinsmead, H(esba) F(ay)
Hunt, E(verette) Howard, (Jr.)
1918- .... **CLC 3**
See also AITN 1; CA 45-48; CANR 2, 47, 103; CMW 4
Hunt, Francesca
See Holland, Isabelle (Christian)
Hunt, Howard
See Hunt, E(verette) Howard, (Jr.)
Hunt, Kyle
See Creasey, John
Hunt, (James Henry) Leigh
1784-1859 .... **NCLC 1, 70**
See also DAM POET; DLB 96, 110, 144; RGEL 2; TEA
Hunt, Marsha 1946- .... **CLC 70**
See also BW 2, 3; CA 143; CANR 79
Hunt, Violet 1866(?)-1942 .... **TCLC 53**
See also CA 184; DLB 162, 197
Hunter, E. Waldo
See Sturgeon, Theodore (Hamilton)
Hunter, Evan 1926- .... **CLC 11, 31**
See McBain, Ed
See also AAYA 39; BPFB 2; CA 5-8R; CANR 5, 38, 62, 97; CMW 4; CN 7; CPW; DAM POP; DLB 306; DLBY 1982; INT CANR-5; MSW; MTCW 1; SATA 25; SFW 4
Hunter, Kristin
See Lattany, Kristin (Elaine Eggleston) Hunter
Hunter, Mary
See Austin, Mary (Hunter)
Hunter, Mollie 1922- .... **CLC 21**
See McIlwraith, Maureen Mollie Hunter
See also AAYA 13; BYA 6; CANR 37, 78; CLR 25; DLB 161; JRDA; MAICYA 1, 2; SAAS 7; SATA 54, 106, 139; SATA-Essay 139; WYA; YAW
Hunter, Robert (?)-1734 .... **LC 7**
Hurston, Zora Neale 1891-1960 .... **BLC 2; CLC 7, 30, 61; DC 12; HR 2; SSC 4, 80; TCLC 121, 131; WLCS**
See also AAYA 15; AFAW 1, 2; AMWS 6; BW 1, 3; BYA 12; CA 85-88; CANR 61; CDALBS; DA; DA3; DAC; DAM MST, MULT, NOV; DFS 6; DLB 51, 86; EWL 3; EXPN; EXPS; FW; LAIT 3; LATS 1:1; LMFS 2; MAWW; MTCW 1, 2; NFS 3; RGAL 4; RGSF 2; SSFS 1, 6, 11, 19; TUS; YAW
Husserl, E. G.
See Husserl, Edmund (Gustav Albrecht)
Husserl, Edmund (Gustav Albrecht)
1859-1938 .... **TCLC 100**
See also CA 116; 133; DLB 296
Huston, John (Marcellus)
1906-1987 .... **CLC 20**
See also CA 73-76; 123; CANR 34; DLB 26
Hustvedt, Siri 1955- .... **CLC 76**
See also CA 137
Hutten, Ulrich von 1488-1523 .... **LC 16**
See also DLB 179
Huxley, Aldous (Leonard)
1894-1963 .... **CLC 1, 3, 4, 5, 8, 11, 18, 35, 79; SSC 39; WLC**
See also AAYA 11; BPFB 2; BRW 7; CA 85-88; CANR 44, 99; CDBLB 1914-1945; DA; DA3; DAB; DAC; DAM MST, NOV; DLB 36, 100, 162, 195, 255; EWL 3; EXPN; LAIT 5; LMFS 2; MTCW 1, 2; NFS 6; RGEL 2; SATA 63; SCFW 2; SFW 4; TEA; YAW
Huxley, T(homas) H(enry)
1825-1895 .... **NCLC 67**
See also DLB 57; TEA

Jacobs, W(illiam) W(ymark)
1863-1943 .... **SSC 73; TCLC 22**
See also CA 121; 167; DLB 135; EXPS;
HGG; RGEL 2; RGSF; SSFS 2; SUFW
1

Jacobsen, Jens Peter 1847-1885 .... **NCLC 34**

Jacobsen, Josephine (Winder)
1908-2003 .... **CLC 48, 102; PC 62**
See also CA 33-36R; 218; CAAS 18; CANR
23, 48; CCA 1; CP 7; DLB 244

Jacobson, Dan 1929- .... **CLC 4, 14**
See also AFW; CA 1-4R; CANR 2, 25, 66;
CN 7; DLB 14, 207, 225; EWL 3; MTCW
1; RGSF 2

Jacqueline
See Carpentier (y Valmont), Alejo

Jacques de Vitry c. 1160-1240 ...... **CMLC 63**
See also DLB 208

Jagger, Mick 1944- .... **CLC 17**

Jahiz, al- c. 780-c. 869 .... **CMLC 25**

Jakes, John (William) 1932- .... **CLC 29**
See also AAYA 32; BEST 89:4; BPFB 2;
CA 57-60, 214; CAAE 214; CANR 10,
43, 66, 111; CPW; CSW; DA3; DAM
NOV, POP; DLB 278; DLBY 1983;
FANT; INT CANR-10; MTCW 1, 2;
RHW; SATA 62; SFW 4; TCWW 2

James I 1394-1437 .... **LC 20**
See also RGEL 2

James, Andrew
See Kirkup, James

James, C(yril) L(ionel) R(obert)
1901-1989 .... **BLCS; CLC 33**
See also BW 2; CA 117; 125; 128; CANR
62; DLB 125; MTCW 1

James, Daniel (Lewis) 1911-1988
See Santiago, Danny
See also CA 174; 125

James, Dynely
See Mayne, William (James Carter)

James, Henry Sr. 1811-1882 .... **NCLC 53**

James, Henry 1843-1916 .... **SSC 8, 32, 47;**
TCLC 2, 11, 24, 40, 47, 64; WLC
See also AMW; AMWC 1; AMWR 1; BPFB
2; BRW 6; CA 104; 132; CDALB 1865-
1917; DA; DA3; DAB; DAC; DAM MST,
NOV; DLB 12, 71, 74, 189; DLBD 13;
EWL 3; EXPS; HGG; LAIT 2; MTCW 1,
2; NFS 12, 16, 19; RGAL 4; RGEL 2;
RGSF 2; SSFS 9; SUFW 1; TUS

James, M. R.
See James, Montague (Rhodes)
See also DLB 156, 201

James, Montague (Rhodes)
1862-1936 .... **SSC 16; TCLC 6**
See James, M. R.
See also CA 104; 203; HGG; RGEL 2;
RGSF 2; SUFW 1

James, P. D. .... **CLC 18, 46, 122**
See White, Phyllis Dorothy James
See also BEST 90:2; BPFB 2; BRWS 4;
CDBLB 1960 to Present; DLB 87, 276;
DLBD 17; MSW

James, Philip
See Moorcock, Michael (John)

James, Samuel
See Stephens, James

James, Seumas
See Stephens, James

James, Stephen
See Stephens, James

James, William 1842-1910 .... **TCLC 15, 32**
See also AMW; CA 109; 193; DLB 270,
284; NCFS 5; RGAL 4

Jameson, Anna 1794-1860 .... **NCLC 43**
See also DLB 99, 166

Jameson, Fredric (R.) 1934- .... **CLC 142**
See also CA 196; DLB 67; LMFS 2

James VI of Scotland 1566-1625 .... **LC 109**
See also DLB 151, 172

Jami, Nur al-Din 'Abd al-Rahman
1414-1492 .... **LC 9**

Jammes, Francis 1868-1938 .... **TCLC 75**
See also CA 198; EWL 3; GFL 1789 to the
Present

Jandl, Ernst 1925-2000 .... **CLC 34**
See also CA 200; EWL 3

Janowitz, Tama 1957- .... **CLC 43, 145**
See also CA 106; CANR 52, 89, 129; CN
7; CPW; DAM POP; DLB 292

Japrisot, Sebastien 1931- .... **CLC 90**
See Rossi, Jean-Baptiste
See also CMW 4; NFS 18

Jarrell, Randall 1914-1965 .... **CLC 1, 2, 6, 9,**
13, 49; PC 41
See also AMW; BYA 5; CA 5-8R; 25-28R;
CABS 2; CANR 6, 34; CDALB 1941-
1968; CLR 6; CWRI 5; DAM POET;
DLB 48, 52; EWL 3; EXPP; MAICYA 1,
2; MTCW 1, 2; PAB; PFS 2; RGAL 4;
SATA 7

Jarry, Alfred 1873-1907 .... **SSC 20; TCLC 2,**
14, 147
See also CA 104; 153; DA3; DAM DRAM;
DFS 8; DLB 192, 258; EW 9; EWL 3;
GFL 1789 to the Present; RGWL 2, 3;
TWA

Jarvis, E. K.
See Ellison, Harlan (Jay)

Jawien, Andrzej
See John Paul II, Pope

Jaynes, Roderick
See Coen, Ethan

Jeake, Samuel, Jr.
See Aiken, Conrad (Potter)

Jean Paul 1763-1825 .... **NCLC 7**

Jefferies, (John) Richard
1848-1887 .... **NCLC 47**
See also DLB 98, 141; RGEL 2; SATA 16;
SFW 4

Jeffers, (John) Robinson 1887-1962 .. **CLC 2,**
3, 11, 15, 54; PC 17; WLC
See also AMWS 2; CA 85-88; CANR 35;
CDALB 1917-1929; DA; DAC; DAM
MST, POET; DLB 45, 212; EWL 3;
MTCW 1, 2; PAB; PFS 3, 4; RGAL 4

Jefferson, Janet
See Mencken, H(enry) L(ouis)

Jefferson, Thomas 1743-1826 . **NCLC 11, 103**
See also AAYA 54; ANW; CDALB 1640-
1865; DA3; DLB 31, 183; LAIT 1; RGAL
4

Jeffrey, Francis 1773-1850 .... **NCLC 33**
See Francis, Lord Jeffrey

Jelakowitch, Ivan
See Heijermans, Herman

Jelinek, Elfriede 1946- .... **CLC 169**
See also CA 154; DLB 85; FW

Jellicoe, (Patricia) Ann 1927- .... **CLC 27**
See also CA 85-88; CBD; CD 5; CWD;
CWRI 5; DLB 13, 233; FW

Jelloun, Tahar ben 1944- .... **CLC 180**
See Ben Jelloun, Tahar
See also CA 162; CANR 100

Jemyma
See Holley, Marietta

Jen, Gish .... **AAL; CLC 70, 198**
See Jen, Lillian
See also AMWC 2

Jen, Lillian 1956(?)-
See Jen, Gish
See also CA 135; CANR 89, 130

Jenkins, (John) Robin 1912- .... **CLC 52**
See also CA 1-4R; CANR 1, 135; CN 7;
DLB 14, 271

Jennings, Elizabeth (Joan)
1926-2001 .... **CLC 5, 14, 131**
See also BRWS 5; CA 61-64; 200; CAAS
5; CANR 8, 39, 66, 127; CP 7; CWP;
DLB 27; EWL 3; MTCW 1; SATA 66

Jennings, Waylon 1937- .... **CLC 21**

Jensen, Johannes V(ilhelm)
1873-1950 .... **TCLC 41**
See also CA 170; DLB 214; EWL 3; RGWL
3

Jensen, Laura (Linnea) 1948- .... **CLC 37**
See also CA 103

Jerome, Saint 345-420 .... **CMLC 30**
See also RGWL 3

Jerome, Jerome K(lapka)
1859-1927 .... **TCLC 23**
See also CA 119; 177; DLB 10, 34, 135;
RGEL 2

Jerrold, Douglas William
1803-1857 .... **NCLC 2**
See also DLB 158, 159; RGEL 2

Jewett, (Theodora) Sarah Orne
1849-1909 .... **SSC 6, 44; TCLC 1, 22**
See also AMW; AMWC 2; AMWR 2; CA
108; 127; CANR 71; DLB 12, 74, 221;
EXPS; FW; MAWW; NFS 15; RGAL 4;
RGSF 2; SATA 15; SSFS 4

Jewsbury, Geraldine (Endsor)
1812-1880 .... **NCLC 22**
See also DLB 21

Jhabvala, Ruth Prawer 1927- . **CLC 4, 8, 29,**
94, 138
See also BRWS 5; CA 1-4R; CANR 2, 29,
51, 74, 91, 128; CN 7; DAB; DAM NOV;
DLB 139, 194; EWL 3; IDFW 3, 4; INT
CANR-29; MTCW 1, 2; RGSF 2; RGWL
2; RHW; TEA

Jibran, Kahlil
See Gibran, Kahlil

Jibran, Khalil
See Gibran, Kahlil

Jiles, Paulette 1943- .... **CLC 13, 58**
See also CA 101; CANR 70, 124; CWP

Jimenez (Mantecon), Juan Ramon
1881-1958 .... **HLC 1; PC 7; TCLC 4**
See also CA 104; 131; CANR 74; DAM
MULT, POET; DLB 134; EW 9; EWL 3;
HW 1; MTCW 1, 2; RGWL 2, 3

Jimenez, Ramon
See Jimenez (Mantecon), Juan Ramon

Jimenez Mantecon, Juan
See Jimenez (Mantecon), Juan Ramon

Jin, Ha .... **CLC 109**
See Jin, Xuefei
See also CA 152; DLB 244, 292; SSFS 17

Jin, Xuefei 1956-
See Jin, Ha
See also CANR 91, 130; SSFS 17

Joel, Billy .... **CLC 26**
See Joel, William Martin

Joel, William Martin 1949-
See Joel, Billy
See also CA 108

John, Saint 10(?)-100 .... **CMLC 27, 63**

John of Salisbury c. 1115-1180 ..... **CMLC 63**

John of the Cross, St. 1542-1591 .... **LC 18**
See also RGWL 2, 3

John Paul II, Pope 1920- .... **CLC 128**
See also CA 106; 133

Johnson, B(ryan) S(tanley William)
1933-1973 .... **CLC 6, 9**
See also CA 9-12R; 53-56; CANR 9; DLB
14, 40; EWL 3; RGEL 2

Johnson, Benjamin F., of Boone
See Riley, James Whitcomb

Junger, Ernst
See Juenger, Ernst
See also CDWLB 2; EWL 3; RGWL 2, 3
Junger, Sebastian 1962- .... **CLC 109**
See also AAYA 28; CA 165; CANR 130
Juniper, Alex
See Hospital, Janette Turner
Junius
See Luxemburg, Rosa
Just, Ward (Swift) 1935- .... **CLC 4, 27**
See also CA 25-28R; CANR 32, 87; CN 7;
INT CANR-32
Justice, Donald (Rodney)
1925-2004 .... **CLC 6, 19, 102; PC 64**
See also AMWS 7; CA 5-8R; CANR 26,
54, 74, 121, 122; CP 7; CSW; DAM
POET; DLBY 1983; EWL 3; INT CANR-
26; MTCW 2; PFS 14
Juvenal c. 60-c. 130 .... **CMLC 8**
See also AW 2; CDWLB 1; DLB 211;
RGWL 2, 3
Juvenis
See Bourne, Randolph S(illiman)
K., Alice
See Knapp, Caroline
Kabakov, Sasha .... **CLC 59**
Kabir 1398(?)-1448(?) .... **LC 109; PC 56**
See also RGWL 2, 3
Kacew, Romain 1914-1980
See Gary, Romain
See also CA 108; 102
Kadare, Ismail 1936- .... **CLC 52, 190**
See also CA 161; EWL 3; RGWL 3
Kadohata, Cynthia 1956(?)- ..... **CLC 59, 122**
See also CA 140; CANR 124
Kafka, Franz 1883-1924 ... **SSC 5, 29, 35, 60;**
TCLC 2, 6, 13, 29, 47, 53, 112; WLC
See also AAYA 31; BPFB 2; CA 105; 126;
CDWLB 2; DA; DA3; DAB; DAC; DAM
MST, NOV; DLB 81; EW 9; EWL 3;
EXPS; LATS 1:1; LMFS 2; MTCW 1, 2;
NFS 7; RGSF 2; RGWL 2, 3; SFW 4;
SSFS 3, 7, 12; TWA
Kahanovitsch, Pinkhes
See Der Nister
Kahn, Roger 1927- .... **CLC 30**
See also CA 25-28R; CANR 44, 69; DLB
171; SATA 37
Kain, Saul
See Sassoon, Siegfried (Lorraine)
Kaiser, Georg 1878-1945 .... **TCLC 9**
See also CA 106; 190; CDWLB 2; DLB
124; EWL 3; LMFS 2; RGWL 2, 3
Kaledin, Sergei .... **CLC 59**
Kaletski, Alexander 1946- .... **CLC 39**
See also CA 118; 143
Kalidasa fl. c. 400-455 .... **CMLC 9; PC 22**
See also RGWL 2, 3
Kallman, Chester (Simon)
1921-1975 .... **CLC 2**
See also CA 45-48; 53-56; CANR 3
Kaminsky, Melvin 1926-
See Brooks, Mel
See also CA 65-68; CANR 16
Kaminsky, Stuart M(elvin) 1934- ..... **CLC 59**
See also CA 73-76; CANR 29, 53, 89;
CMW 4
Kamo no Chomei 1153(?)-1216 .... **CMLC 66**
See also DLB 203
Kamo no Nagaakira
See Kamo no Chomei
Kandinsky, Wassily 1866-1944 .... **TCLC 92**
See also CA 118; 155
Kane, Francis
See Robbins, Harold
Kane, Henry 1918-
See Queen, Ellery
See also CA 156; CMW 4

Kane, Paul
See Simon, Paul (Frederick)
Kanin, Garson 1912-1999 .... **CLC 22**
See also AITN 1; CA 5-8R; 177; CAD;
CANR 7, 78; DLB 7; IDFW 3, 4
Kaniuk, Yoram 1930- .... **CLC 19**
See also CA 134; DLB 299
Kant, Immanuel 1724-1804 ..... **NCLC 27, 67**
See also DLB 94
Kantor, MacKinlay 1904-1977 .... **CLC 7**
See also CA 61-64; 73-76; CANR 60, 63;
DLB 9, 102; MTCW 2; RHW; TCWW 2
Kanze Motokiyo
See Zeami
Kaplan, David Michael 1946- .... **CLC 50**
See also CA 187
Kaplan, James 1951- .... **CLC 59**
See also CA 135; CANR 121
Karadzic, Vuk Stefanovic
1787-1864 .... **NCLC 115**
See also CDWLB 4; DLB 147
Karageorge, Michael
See Anderson, Poul (William)
Karamzin, Nikolai Mikhailovich
1766-1826 .... **NCLC 3**
See also DLB 150; RGSF 2
Karapanou, Margarita 1946- .... **CLC 13**
See also CA 101
Karinthy, Frigyes 1887-1938 .... **TCLC 47**
See also CA 170; DLB 215; EWL 3
Karl, Frederick R(obert)
1927-2004 .... **CLC 34**
See also CA 5-8R; 226; CANR 3, 44
Karr, Mary 1955- .... **CLC 188**
See also AMWS 11; CA 151; CANR 100;
NCFS 5
Kastel, Warren
See Silverberg, Robert
Kataev, Evgeny Petrovich 1903-1942
See Petrov, Evgeny
See also CA 120
Kataphusin
See Ruskin, John
Katz, Steve 1935- .... **CLC 47**
See also CA 25-28R; CAAS 14, 64; CANR
12; CN 7; DLBY 1983
Kauffman, Janet 1945- .... **CLC 42**
See also CA 117; CANR 43, 84; DLB 218;
DLBY 1986
Kaufman, Bob (Garnell) 1925-1986 . **CLC 49**
See also BG 3; BW 1; CA 41-44R; 118;
CANR 22; DLB 16, 41
Kaufman, George S. 1889-1961 ...... **CLC 38;**
DC 17
See also CA 108; 93-96; DAM DRAM;
DFS 1, 10; DLB 7; INT CA-108; MTCW
2; RGAL 4; TUS
Kaufman, Sue .... **CLC 3, 8**
See Barondess, Sue K(aufman)
Kavafis, Konstantinos Petrou 1863-1933
See Cavafy, C(onstantine) P(eter)
See also CA 104
Kavan, Anna 1901-1968 .... **CLC 5, 13, 82**
See also BRWS 7; CA 5-8R; CANR 6, 57;
DLB 255; MTCW 1; RGEL 2; SFW 4
Kavanagh, Dan
See Barnes, Julian (Patrick)
Kavanagh, Julie 1952- .... **CLC 119**
See also CA 163
Kavanagh, Patrick (Joseph)
1904-1967 .... **CLC 22; PC 33**
See also BRWS 7; CA 123; 25-28R; DLB
15, 20; EWL 3; MTCW 1; RGEL 2
Kawabata, Yasunari 1899-1972 ..... **CLC 2, 5,**
9, 18, 107; SSC 17
See Kawabata Yasunari
See also CA 93-96; 33-36R; CANR 88;
DAM MULT; MJW; MTCW 2; RGSF 2;
RGWL 2, 3

Kawabata Yasunari
See Kawabata, Yasunari
See also DLB 180; EWL 3
Kaye, M(ary) M(argaret)
1908-2004 .... **CLC 28**
See also CA 89-92; 223; CANR 24, 60, 102;
MTCW 1, 2; RHW; SATA 62; SATA-Obit
152
Kaye, Mollie
See Kaye, M(ary) M(argaret)
Kaye-Smith, Sheila 1887-1956 .... **TCLC 20**
See also CA 118; 203; DLB 36
Kaymor, Patrice Maguilene
See Senghor, Leopold Sedar
Kazakov, Iurii Pavlovich
See Kazakov, Yuri Pavlovich
See also DLB 302
Kazakov, Yuri Pavlovich 1927-1982 . **SSC 43**
See Kazakov, Iurii Pavlovich; Kazakov,
Yuri
See also CA 5-8R; CANR 36; MTCW 1;
RGSF 2
Kazakov, Yury
See Kazakov, Yuri Pavlovich
See also EWL 3
Kazan, Elia 1909-2003 .... **CLC 6, 16, 63**
See also CA 21-24R; 220; CANR 32, 78
Kazantzakis, Nikos 1883(?)-1957 .... **TCLC 2,**
5, 33
See also BPFB 2; CA 105; 132; DA3; EW
9; EWL 3; MTCW 1, 2; RGWL 2, 3
Kazin, Alfred 1915-1998 ..... **CLC 34, 38, 119**
See also AMWS 8; CA 1-4R; CAAS 7;
CANR 1, 45, 79; DLB 67; EWL 3
Keane, Mary Nesta (Skrine) 1904-1996
See Keane, Molly
See also CA 108; 114; 151; CN 7; RHW
Keane, Molly .... **CLC 31**
See Keane, Mary Nesta (Skrine)
See also INT CA-114
Keates, Jonathan 1946(?)- .... **CLC 34**
See also CA 163; CANR 126
Keaton, Buster 1895-1966 .... **CLC 20**
See also CA 194
Keats, John 1795-1821 ...... **NCLC 8, 73, 121;**
PC 1; WLC
See also AAYA 58; BRW 4; BRWR 1; CD-
BLB 1789-1832; DA; DA3; DAB; DAC;
DAM MST, POET; DLB 96, 110; EXPP;
LMFS 1; PAB; PFS 1, 2, 3, 9, 17; RGEL
2; TEA; WLIT 3; WP
Keble, John 1792-1866 .... **NCLC 87**
See also DLB 32, 55; RGEL 2
Keene, Donald 1922- .... **CLC 34**
See also CA 1-4R; CANR 5, 119
Keillor, Garrison .... **CLC 40, 115**
See Keillor, Gary (Edward)
See also AAYA 2; BEST 89:3; BPFB 2;
DLBY 1987; EWL 3; SATA 58; TUS
Keillor, Gary (Edward) 1942-
See Keillor, Garrison
See also CA 111; 117; CANR 36, 59, 124;
CPW; DA3; DAM POP; MTCW 1, 2
Keith, Carlos
See Lewton, Val
Keith, Michael
See Hubbard, L(afayette) Ron(ald)
Keller, Gottfried 1819-1890 .... **NCLC 2; SSC**
26
See also CDWLB 2; DLB 129; EW; RGSF
2; RGWL 2, 3
Keller, Nora Okja 1965- .... **CLC 109**
See also CA 187
Keller, Jonathan 1949- .... **CLC 44**
See also AAYA 35; BEST 90:1; CA 106;
CANR 29, 51; CMW 4; CPW; DA3;
DAM POP; INT CANR-29

Kingsley, Sidney 1906-1995 .... **CLC 44**
See also CA 85-88; 147; CAD; DFS 14, 19;
DLB 7; RGAL 4

Kingsolver, Barbara 1955- . **CLC 55, 81, 130**
See also AAYA 15; AMWS 7; CA 129; 134;
CANR 60, 96, 133; CDALBS; CPW;
CSW; DA3; DAM POP; DLB 206; INT
CA-134; LAIT 5; MTCW 2; NFS 5, 10,
12; RGAL 4

Kingston, Maxine (Ting Ting) Hong
1940- .... **AAL; CLC 12, 19, 58, 121;
WLCS**
See also AAYA 8, 55; AMWS 5; BPFB 2;
CA 69-72; CANR 13, 38, 74, 87, 128;
CDALBS; CN 7; DA3; DAM MULT,
NOV; DLB 173, 212; DLBY 1980; EWL
3; FW; INT CANR-13; LAIT 5; MAWW;
MTCW 1, 2; NFS 6; RGAL 4; SATA 53;
SSFS 3

Kinnell, Galway 1927- ..... **CLC 1, 2, 3, 5, 13,
29, 129; PC 26**
See also AMWS 3; CA 9-12R; CANR 10,
34, 66, 116; CP 7; DLB 5; DLBY 1987;
EWL 3; INT CANR-34; MTCW 1, 2;
PAB; PFS 9; RGAL 4; WP

Kinsella, Thomas 1928- .... **CLC 4, 19, 138**
See also BRWS 5; CA 17-20R; CANR 15,
122; CP 7; DLB 27; EWL 3; MTCW 1, 2;
RGEL 2; TEA

Kinsella, W(illiam) P(atrick) 1935- . **CLC 27,
43, 166**
See also AAYA 7, 60; BPFB 2; CA 97-100,
222; CAAE 222; CAAS 7; CANR 21, 35,
66, 75, 129; CN 7; CPW; DAC; DAM
NOV, POP; FANT; INT CANR-21; LAIT
5; MTCW 1, 2; NFS 15; RGSF 2

Kinsey, Alfred C(harles)
1894-1956 .... **TCLC 91**
See also CA 115; 170; MTCW 2

Kipling, (Joseph) Rudyard 1865-1936 . **PC 3;
SSC 5, 54; TCLC 8, 17; WLC**
See also AAYA 32; BRW 6; BRWC 1, 2;
BYA 4; CA 105; 120; CANR 33; CDBLB
1890-1914; CLR 39, 65; CWRI 5; DA;
DA3; DAB; DAC; DAM MST, POET;
DLB 19, 34, 141, 156; EWL 3; EXPS;
FANT; LAIT 3; LMFS 1; MAICYA 1, 2;
MTCW 1, 2; RGEL 2; RGSF 2; SATA
100; SFW 4; SSFS 8; SUFW 1; TEA;
WCH; WLIT 4; YABC 2

Kirk, Russell (Amos) 1918-1994 .. **TCLC 119**
See also AITN 1; CA 1-4R; 145; CAAS 9;
CANR 1, 20, 60; HGG; INT CANR-20;
MTCW 1, 2

Kirkham, Dinah
See Card, Orson Scott

Kirkland, Caroline M. 1801-1864 . **NCLC 85**
See also DLB 3, 73, 74, 250, 254; DLBD
13

Kirkup, James 1918- .... **CLC 1**
See also CA 1-4R; CAAS 4; CANR 2; CP
7; DLB 27; SATA 12

Kirkwood, James 1930(?)-1989 .... **CLC 9**
See also AITN 2; CA 1-4R; 128; CANR 6,
40; GLL 2

Kirsch, Sarah 1935- .... **CLC 176**
See also CA 178; CWW 2; DLB 75; EWL
3

Kirshner, Sidney
See Kingsley, Sidney

Kis, Danilo 1935-1989 .... **CLC 57**
See also CA 109; 118; 129; CANR 61; CD-
WLB 4; DLB 181; EWL 3; MTCW 1;
RGSF 2; RGWL 2, 3

Kissinger, Henry A(lfred) 1923- ..... **CLC 137**
See also CA 1-4R; CANR 2, 33, 66, 109;
MTCW 1

Kivi, Aleksis 1834-1872 .... **NCLC 30**

Kizer, Carolyn (Ashley) 1925- ... **CLC 15, 39,
80**
See also CA 65-68; CAAS 5; CANR 24,
70, 134; CP 7; CWP; DAM POET; DLB
5, 169; EWL 3; MTCW 2; PFS 18

Klabund 1890-1928 .... **TCLC 44**
See also CA 162; DLB 66

Klappert, Peter 1942- .... **CLC 57**
See also CA 33-36R; CSW; DLB 5

Klein, A(braham) M(oses)
1909-1972 .... **CLC 19**
See also CA 101; 37-40R; DAB; DAC;
DAM MST; DLB 68; EWL 3; RGEL 2

Klein, Joe
See Klein, Joseph

Klein, Joseph 1946- .... **CLC 154**
See also CA 85-88; CANR 55

Klein, Norma 1938-1989 .... **CLC 30**
See also AAYA 2, 35; BPFB 2; BYA 6, 7,
8; CA 41-44R; 128; CANR 15, 37; CLR
2, 19; INT CANR-15; JRDA; MAICYA
1, 2; SAAS 1; SATA 7, 57; WYA; YAW

Klein, T(heodore) E(ibon) D(onald)
1947- .... **CLC 34**
See also CA 119; CANR 44, 75; HGG

Kleist, Heinrich von 1777-1811 ...... **NCLC 2,
37; SSC 22**
See also CDWLB 2; DAM DRAM; DLB
90; EW 5; RGSF 2; RGWL 2, 3

Klima, Ivan 1931- .... **CLC 56, 172**
See also CA 25-28R; CANR 17, 50, 91;
CDWLB 4; CWW 2; DAM NOV; DLB
232; EWL 3; RGWL 3

Klimentev, Andrei Platonovich
See Klimentov, Andrei Platonovich

Klimentov, Andrei Platonovich
1899-1951 .... **SSC 42; TCLC 14**
See Platonov, Andrei Platonovich; Platonov,
Andrey Platonovich
See also CA 108

Klinger, Friedrich Maximilian von
1752-1831 .... **NCLC 1**
See also DLB 94

Klingsor the Magician
See Hartmann, Sadakichi

Klopstock, Friedrich Gottlieb
1724-1803 .... **NCLC 11**
See also DLB 97; EW 4; RGWL 2, 3

Kluge, Alexander 1932- .... **SSC 61**
See also CA 81-84; DLB 75

Knapp, Caroline 1959-2002 .... **CLC 99**
See also CA 154; 207

Knebel, Fletcher 1911-1993 .... **CLC 14**
See also AITN 1; CA 1-4R; 140; CAAS 3;
CANR 1, 36; SATA 36; SATA-Obit 75

Knickerbocker, Diedrich
See Irving, Washington

Knight, Etheridge 1931-1991 ... **BLC 2; CLC
40; PC 14**
See also BW 1, 3; CA 21-24R; 133; CANR
23, 82; DAM POET; DLB 41; MTCW 2;
RGAL 4

Knight, Sarah Kemble 1666-1727 .... **LC 7**
See also DLB 24, 200

Knister, Raymond 1899-1932 .... **TCLC 56**
See also CA 186; DLB 68; RGEL 2

Knowles, John 1926-2001 ... **CLC 1, 4, 10, 26**
See also AAYA 10; AMWS 12; BPFB 2;
BYA 3; CA 17-20R; 203; CANR 40, 74,
76, 132; CDALB 1968-1988; CLR 98; CN
7; DA; DAC; DAM MST, NOV; DLB 6;
EXPN; MTCW 1, 2; NFS 2; RGAL 4;
SATA 8, 89; SATA-Obit 134; YAW

Knox, Calvin M.
See Silverberg, Robert

Knox, John c. 1505-1572 .... **LC 37**
See also DLB 132

Knye, Cassandra
See Disch, Thomas M(ichael)

Koch, C(hristopher) J(ohn) 1932- .... **CLC 42**
See also CA 127; CANR 84; CN 7; DLB
289

Koch, Christopher
See Koch, C(hristopher) J(ohn)

Koch, Kenneth (Jay) 1925-2002 .... **CLC 5, 8,
44**
See also CA 1-4R; 207; CAD; CANR 6,
36, 57, 97, 131; CD 5; CP 7; DAM POET;
DLB 5; INT CANR-36; MTCW 2; PFS
20; SATA 65; WP

Kochanowski, Jan 1530-1584 .... **LC 10**
See also RGWL 2, 3

Kock, Charles Paul de 1794-1871 . **NCLC 16**

Koda Rohan
See Koda Shigeyuki

Koda Rohan
See Koda Shigeyuki
See also DLB 180

Koda Shigeyuki 1867-1947 .... **TCLC 22**
See Koda Rohan
See also CA 121; 183

Koestler, Arthur 1905-1983 ... **CLC 1, 3, 6, 8,
15, 33**
See also BRWS 1; CA 1-4R; 109; CANR 1,
33; CDBLB 1945-1960; DLBY 1983;
EWL 3; MTCW 1, 2; NFS 19; RGEL 2

Kogawa, Joy Nozomi 1935- ...... **CLC 78, 129**
See also AAYA 47; CA 101; CANR 19, 62,
126; CN 7; CWP; DAC; DAM MST,
MULT; FW; MTCW 2; NFS 3; SATA 99

Kohout, Pavel 1928- .... **CLC 13**
See also CA 45-48; CANR 3

Koizumi, Yakumo
See Hearn, (Patricio) Lafcadio (Tessima
Carlos)

Kolmar, Gertrud 1894-1943 .... **TCLC 40**
See also CA 167; EWL 3

Komunyakaa, Yusef 1947- .. **BLCS; CLC 86,
94; PC 51**
See also AFAW 2; AMWS 13; CA 147;
CANR 83; CP 7; CSW; DLB 120; EWL
3; PFS 5, 20; RGAL 4

Konrad, George
See Konrad, Gyorgy

Konrad, Gyorgy 1933- .... **CLC 4, 10, 73**
See also CA 85-88; CANR 97; CDWLB 4;
CWW 2; DLB 232; EWL 3

Konwicki, Tadeusz 1926- .... **CLC 8, 28, 54,
117**
See also CA 101; CAAS 9; CANR 39, 59;
CWW 2; DLB 232; EWL 3; IDFW 3;
MTCW 1

Koontz, Dean R(ay) 1945- .... **CLC 78**
See also AAYA 9, 31; BEST 89:3, 90:2; CA
108; CANR 19, 36, 52, 95; CMW 4;
CPW; DA3; DAM NOV, POP; DLB 292;
HGG; MTCW 1; SATA 92; SFW 4;
SUFW 2; YAW

Kopernik, Mikolaj
See Copernicus, Nicolaus

Kopit, Arthur (Lee) 1937- ...... **CLC 1, 18, 33**
See also AITN 1; CA 81-84; CABS 3; CD
5; DAM DRAM; DFS 7, 14; DLB 7;
MTCW 1; RGAL 4

Kopitar, Jernej (Bartholomaus)
1780-1844 .... **NCLC 117**

Kops, Bernard 1926- .... **CLC 4**
See also CA 5-8R; CANR 84; CBD; CN 7;
CP 7; DLB 13

Kornbluth, C(yril) M. 1923-1958 .... **TCLC 8**
See also CA 105; 160; DLB 8; SFW 4

Korolenko, V. G.
See Korolenko, Vladimir Galaktionovich

Korolenko, Vladimir
See Korolenko, Vladimir Galaktionovich

Leibniz, Gottfried Wilhelm von
　　1646-1716 .... **LC 35**
　　See also DLB 168
Leimbach, Martha 1963-
　　See Leimbach, Marti
　　See also CA 130
Leimbach, Marti .... **CLC 65**
　　See Leimbach, Martha
Leino, Eino .... **TCLC 24**
　　See Lonnbohm, Armas Eino Leopold
　　See also EWL 3
Leiris, Michel (Julien) 1901-1990 ..... **CLC 61**
　　See also CA 119; 128; 132; EWL 3; GFL
　　1789 to the Present
Leithauser, Brad 1953- .... **CLC 27**
　　See also CA 107; CANR 27, 81; CP 7; DLB
　　120, 282
le Jars de Gournay, Marie
　　See de Gournay, Marie le Jars
Lelchuk, Alan 1938- .... **CLC 5**
　　See also CA 45-48; CAAS 20; CANR 1,
　　70; CN 7
Lem, Stanislaw 1921- ...... **CLC 8, 15, 40, 149**
　　See also CA 105; CAAS 1; CANR 32;
　　CWW 2; MTCW 1; SCFW 2; SFW 4
Lemann, Nancy (Elise) 1956- .... **CLC 39**
　　See also CA 118; 136; CANR 121
Lemonnier, (Antoine Louis) Camille
　　1844-1913 .... **TCLC 22**
　　See also CA 121
Lenau, Nikolaus 1802-1850 .... **NCLC 16**
L'Engle, Madeleine (Camp Franklin)
　　1918- .... **CLC 12**
　　See also AAYA 28; AITN 2; BPFB 2; BYA
　　2, 4, 5, 7; CA 1-4R; CANR 3, 21, 39, 66,
　　107; CLR 1, 14, 57; CPW; CWRI 5; DA3;
　　DAM POP; DLB 52; JRDA; MAICYA 1,
　　2; MTCW 1, 2; SAAS 15; SATA 1, 27,
　　75, 128; SFW 4; WYA; YAW
Lengyel, Jozsef 1896-1975 .... **CLC 7**
　　See also CA 85-88; 57-60; CANR 71;
　　RGSF 2
Lenin 1870-1924
　　See Lenin, V. I.
　　See also CA 121; 168
Lenin, V. I. .... **TCLC 67**
　　See Lenin
Lennon, John (Ono) 1940-1980 .. **CLC 12, 35**
　　See also CA 102; SATA 114
Lennox, Charlotte Ramsay
　　1729(?)-1804 .... **NCLC 23, 134**
　　See also DLB 39; RGEL 2
Lentricchia, Frank, (Jr.) 1940- .... **CLC 34**
　　See also CA 25-28R; CANR 19, 106; DLB
　　246
Lenz, Gunter .... **CLC 65**
Lenz, Jakob Michael Reinhold
　　1751-1792 .... **LC 100**
　　See also DLB 94; RGWL 2, 3
Lenz, Siegfried 1926- .... **CLC 27; SSC 33**
　　See also CA 89-92; CANR 80; CWW 2;
　　DLB 75; EWL 3; RGSF 2; RGWL 2, 3
Leon, David
　　See Jacob, (Cyprien-)Max
Leonard, Elmore (John, Jr.) 1925- . **CLC 28,
　　34, 71, 120**
　　See also AAYA 22, 59; AITN 1; BEST 89:1,
　　90:4; BPFB 2; CA 81-84; CANR 12, 28,
　　53, 76, 96, 133; CMW 4; CN 7; CPW;
　　DA3; DAM POP; DLB 173, 226; INT
　　CANR-28; MSW; MTCW 1, 2; RGAL 4;
　　TCWW 2
Leonard, Hugh .... **CLC 19**
　　See Byrne, John Keyes
　　See also CBD; CD 5; DFS 13; DLB 13

Leonov, Leonid (Maximovich)
　　1899-1994 .... **CLC 92**
　　See Leonov, Leonid Maksimovich
　　See also CA 129; CANR 74, 76; DAM
　　NOV; EWL 3; MTCW 1, 2
Leonov, Leonid Maksimovich
　　See Leonov, Leonid (Maximovich)
　　See also DLB 272
Leopardi, (Conte) Giacomo
　　1798-1837 .... **NCLC 22, 129; PC 37**
　　See also EW 5; RGWL 2, 3; WP
Le Reveler
　　See Artaud, Antonin (Marie Joseph)
Lerman, Eleanor 1952- .... **CLC 9**
　　See also CA 85-88; CANR 69, 124
Lerman, Rhoda 1936- .... **CLC 56**
　　See also CA 49-52; CANR 70
Lermontov, Mikhail Iur'evich
　　See Lermontov, Mikhail Yuryevich
　　See also DLB 205
Lermontov, Mikhail Yuryevich
　　1814-1841 .... **NCLC 5, 47, 126; PC 18**
　　See Lermontov, Mikhail Iur'evich
　　See also EW 6; RGWL 2, 3; TWA
Leroux, Gaston 1868-1927 .... **TCLC 25**
　　See also CA 108; 136; CANR 69; CMW 4;
　　NFS 20; SATA 65
Lesage, Alain-Rene 1668-1747 .... **LC 2, 28**
　　See also EW 3; GFL Beginnings to 1789;
　　RGWL 2, 3
Leskov, N(ikolai) S(emenovich) 1831-1895
　　See Leskov, Nikolai (Semyonovich)
Leskov, Nikolai (Semyonovich)
　　1831-1895 .... **NCLC 25; SSC 34**
　　See Leskov, Nikolai Semenovich
Leskov, Nikolai Semenovich
　　See Leskov, Nikolai (Semyonovich)
　　See also DLB 238
Lesser, Milton
　　See Marlowe, Stephen
Lessing, Doris (May) 1919- ... **CLC 1, 2, 3, 6,
　　10, 15, 22, 40, 94, 170; SSC 6, 61;
　　WLCS**
　　See also AAYA 57; AFW; BRWS 1; CA
　　9-12R; CAAS 14; CANR 33, 54, 76, 122;
　　CD 5; CDBLB 1960 to Present; CN 7;
　　DA; DA3; DAB; DAC; DAM MST, NOV;
　　DFS 20; DLB 15, 139; DLBY 1985; EWL
　　3; EXPS; FW; LAIT 4; MTCW 1, 2;
　　RGEL 2; RGSF 2; SFW 4; SSFS 1, 12,
　　20; TEA; WLIT 2, 4
Lessing, Gotthold Ephraim 1729-1781 . **LC 8**
　　See also CDWLB 2; DLB 97; EW 4; RGWL
　　2, 3
Lester, Richard 1932- .... **CLC 20**
Levenson, Jay .... **CLC 70**
Lever, Charles (James)
　　1806-1872 .... **NCLC 23**
　　See also DLB 21; RGEL 2
Leverson, Ada Esther
　　1862(?)-1933(?) .... **TCLC 18**
　　See Elaine
　　See also CA 117; 202; DLB 153; RGEL 2
Levertov, Denise 1923-1997 .. **CLC 1, 2, 3, 5,
　　8, 15, 28, 66; PC 11**
　　See also AMWS 3; CA 1-4R, 178; 163;
　　CAAE 178; CAAS 19; CANR 3, 29, 50,
　　108; CDALBS; CP 7; CWP; DAM POET;
　　DLB 5, 165; EWL 3; EXPP; FW; INT
　　CANR-29; MTCW 1, 2; PAB; PFS 7, 17;
　　RGAL 4; TUS; WP
Levi, Carlo 1902-1975 .... **TCLC 125**
　　See also CA 65-68; 53-56; CANR 10; EWL
　　3; RGWL 2, 3
Levi, Jonathan .... **CLC 76**
　　See also CA 197

Levi, Peter (Chad Tigar)
　　1931-2000 .... **CLC 41**
　　See also CA 5-8R; 187; CANR 34, 80; CP
　　7; DLB 40
Levi, Primo 1919-1987 ...... **CLC 37, 50; SSC
　　12; TCLC 109**
　　See also CA 13-16R; 122; CANR 12, 33,
　　61, 70, 132; DLB 177, 299; EWL 3;
　　MTCW 1, 2; RGWL 2, 3
Levin, Ira 1929- .... **CLC 3, 6**
　　See also CA 21-24R; CANR 17, 44, 74;
　　CMW 4; CN 7; CPW; DA3; DAM POP;
　　HGG; MTCW 1, 2; SATA 66; SFW 4
Levin, Meyer 1905-1981 .... **CLC 7**
　　See also AITN 1; CA 9-12R; 104; CANR
　　15; DAM POP; DLB 9, 28; DLBY 1981;
　　SATA 21; SATA-Obit 27
Levine, Norman 1924- .... **CLC 54**
　　See also CA 73-76; CAAS 23; CANR 14,
　　70; DLB 88
Levine, Philip 1928- .. **CLC 2, 4, 5, 9, 14, 33,
　　118; PC 22**
　　See also AMWS 5; CA 9-12R; CANR 9,
　　37, 52, 116; CP 7; DAM POET; DLB 5;
　　EWL 3; PFS 8
Levinson, Deirdre 1931- .... **CLC 49**
　　See also CA 73-76; CANR 70
Levi-Strauss, Claude 1908- .... **CLC 38**
　　See also CA 1-4R; CANR 6, 32, 57; DLB
　　242; EWL 3; GFL 1789 to the Present;
　　MTCW 1, 2; TWA
Levitin, Sonia (Wolff) 1934- .... **CLC 17**
　　See also AAYA 13, 48; CA 29-32R; CANR
　　14, 32, 79; CLR 53; JRDA; MAICYA 1,
　　2; SAAS 2; SATA 4, 68, 119, 131; SATA-
　　Essay 131; YAW
Levon, O. U.
　　See Kesey, Ken (Elton)
Levy, Amy 1861-1889 .... **NCLC 59**
　　See also DLB 156, 240
Lewes, George Henry 1817-1878 ... **NCLC 25**
　　See also DLB 55, 144
Lewis, Alun 1915-1944 .... **SSC 40; TCLC 3**
　　See also BRW 7; CA 104; 188; DLB 20,
　　162; PAB; RGEL 2
Lewis, C. Day
　　See Day Lewis, C(ecil)
Lewis, C(live) S(taples) 1898-1963 .... **CLC 1,
　　3, 6, 14, 27, 124; WLC**
　　See also AAYA 3, 39; BPFB 2; BRWS 3;
　　BYA 15, 16; CA 81-84; CANR 33, 71,
　　132; CDBLB 1945-1960; CLR 3, 27;
　　CWRI 5; DA; DA3; DAB; DAC; DAM
　　MST, NOV, POP; DLB 15, 100, 160, 255;
　　EWL 3; FANT; JRDA; LMFS 2; MAI-
　　CYA 1, 2; MTCW 1, 2; RGEL 2; SATA
　　13, 100; SCFW; SFW 4; SUFW 1; TEA;
　　WCH; WYA; YAW
Lewis, Cecil Day
　　See Day Lewis, C(ecil)
Lewis, Janet 1899-1998 .... **CLC 41**
　　See Winters, Janet Lewis
　　See also CA 9-12R; 172; CANR 29, 63;
　　CAP 1; CN 7; DLBY 1987; RHW;
　　TCWW 2
Lewis, Matthew Gregory
　　1775-1818 .... **NCLC 11, 62**
　　See also DLB 39, 158, 178; HGG; LMFS
　　1; RGEL 2; SUFW
Lewis, (Harry) Sinclair 1885-1951 . **TCLC 4,
　　13, 23, 39; WLC**
　　See also AMW; AMWC 1; BPFB 2; CA
　　104; 133; CANR 132; CDALB 1917-
　　1929; DA; DA3; DAB; DAC; DAM MST,
　　NOV; DLB 9, 102, 284; DLBD 1; EWL
　　3; LAIT 3; MTCW 1, 2; NFS 15, 19;
　　RGAL 4; TUS

Longfellow, Henry Wadsworth
1807-1882 .... **NCLC 2, 45, 101, 103; PC 30; WLCS**
See also AMW; AMWR 2; CDALB 1640-1865; CLR 99; DA; DA3; DAB; DAC; DAM MST, POET; DLB 1, 59, 235; EXPP; PAB; PFS 2, 7, 17; RGAL 4; SATA 19; TUS; WP

Longinus c. 1st cent. - .... **CMLC 27**
See also AW 2; DLB 176

Longley, Michael 1939- .... **CLC 29**
See also BRWS 8; CA 102; CP 7; DLB 40

Longus fl. c. 2nd cent. - .... **CMLC 7**

Longway, A. Hugh
See Lang, Andrew

Lonnbohm, Armas Eino Leopold 1878-1926
See Leino, Eino
See also CA 123

Lonnrot, Elias 1802-1884 .... **NCLC 53**
See also EFS 1

Lonsdale, Roger ed. .... **CLC 65**

Lopate, Phillip 1943- .... **CLC 29**
See also CA 97-100; CANR 88; DLBY 1980; INT CA-97-100

Lopez, Barry (Holstun) 1945- .... **CLC 70**
See also AAYA 9; ANW; CA 65-68; CANR 7, 23, 47, 68, 92; DLB 256, 275; INT CANR-7, -23; MTCW 1; RGAL 4; SATA 67

Lopez Portillo (y Pacheco), Jose
1920-2004 .... **CLC 46**
See also CA 129; 224; HW 1

Lopez y Fuentes, Gregorio
1897(?)-1966 .... **CLC 32**
See also CA 131; EWL 3; HW 1

Lorca, Federico Garcia
See Garcia Lorca, Federico
See also DFS 4; EW 11; PFS 20; RGWL 2, 3; WP

Lord, Audre
See Lorde, Audre (Geraldine)
See also EWL 3

Lord, Bette Bao 1938- .... **AAL; CLC 23**
See also BEST 90:3; BPFB 2; CA 107; CANR 41, 79; INT CA-107; SATA 58

Lord Auch
See Bataille, Georges

Lord Brooke
See Greville, Fulke

Lord Byron
See Byron, George Gordon (Noel)

Lorde, Audre (Geraldine)
1934-1992 .. **BLC 2; CLC 18, 71; PC 12**
See Domini, Rey; Lord, Audre
See also AFAW 1, 2; BW 1, 3; CA 25-28R; 142; CANR 16, 26, 46, 82; DA3; DAM MULT, POET; DLB 41; FW; MTCW 1, 2; PFS 16; RGAL 4

Lord Houghton
See Milnes, Richard Monckton

Lord Jeffrey
See Jeffrey, Francis

Loreaux, Nichol .... **CLC 65**

Lorenzini, Carlo 1826-1890
See Collodi, Carlo
See also MAICYA 1, 2; SATA 29, 100

Lorenzo, Heberto Padilla
See Padilla (Lorenzo), Heberto

Loris
See Hofmannsthal, Hugo von

Loti, Pierre .... **TCLC 11**
See Viaud, (Louis Marie) Julien
See also DLB 123; GFL 1789 to the Present

Lou, Henri
See Andreas-Salome, Lou

Louie, David Wong 1954- .... **CLC 70**
See also CA 139; CANR 120

Louis, Adrian C. .... **NNAL**
See also CA 223

Louis, Father M.
See Merton, Thomas (James)

Louise, Heidi
See Erdrich, Louise

Lovecraft, H(oward) P(hillips)
1890-1937 .... **SSC 3, 52; TCLC 4, 22**
See also AAYA 14; BPFB 2; CA 104; 133; CANR 106; DA3; DAM POP; HGG; MTCW 1, 2; RGAL 4; SCFW; SFW 4; SUFW

Lovelace, Earl 1935- .... **CLC 51**
See also BW 2; CA 77-80; CANR 41, 72, 114; CD 5; CDWLB 3; CN 7; DLB 125; EWL 3; MTCW 1

Lovelace, Richard 1618-1657 .... **LC 24**
See also BRW 2; DLB 131; EXPP; PAB; RGEL 2

Lowe, Pardee 1904- .... **AAL**

Lowell, Amy 1874-1925 ... **PC 13; TCLC 1, 8**
See also AAYA 57; AMW; CA 104; 151; DAM POET; DLB 54, 140; EWL 3; EXPP; LMFS 2; MAWW; MTCW 2; RGAL 4; TUS

Lowell, James Russell 1819-1891 ... **NCLC 2, 90**
See also AMWS 1; CDALB 1640-1865; DLB 1, 11, 64, 79, 189, 235; RGAL 4

Lowell, Robert (Traill Spence, Jr.)
1917-1977 .... **CLC 1, 2, 3, 4, 5, 8, 9, 11, 15, 37, 124; PC 3; WLC**
See also AMW; AMWC 2; AMWR 2; CA 9-12R; 73-76; CABS 2; CANR 26, 60; CDALBS; DA; DA3; DAB; DAC; DAM MST, NOV; DLB 5, 169; EWL 3; MTCW 1, 2; PAB; PFS 6, 7; RGAL 4; WP

Lowenthal, Michael (Francis)
1969- .... **CLC 119**
See also CA 150; CANR 115

Lowndes, Marie Adelaide (Belloc)
1868-1947 .... **TCLC 12**
See also CA 107; CMW 4; DLB 70; RHW

Lowry, (Clarence) Malcolm
1909-1957 .... **SSC 31; TCLC 6, 40**
See also BPFB 2; BRWS 3; CA 105; 131; CANR 62, 105; CDBLB 1945-1960; DLB 15; EWL 3; MTCW 1, 2; RGEL 2

Lowry, Mina Gertrude 1882-1966
See Loy, Mina
See also CA 113

Loxsmith, John
See Brunner, John (Kilian Houston)

Loy, Mina .... **CLC 28; PC 16**
See Lowry, Mina Gertrude
See also DAM POET; DLB 4, 54; PFS 20

Loyson-Bridet
See Schwob, Marcel (Mayer Andre)

Lucan 39-65 .... **CMLC 33**
See also AW 2; DLB 211; EFS 2; RGWL 2, 3

Lucas, Craig 1951- .... **CLC 64**
See also CA 137; CAD; CANR 71, 109; CD 5; GLL 2

Lucas, E(dward) V(errall)
1868-1938 .... **TCLC 73**
See also CA 176; DLB 98, 149, 153; SATA 20

Lucas, George 1944- .... **CLC 16**
See also AAYA 1, 23; CA 77-80; CANR 30; SATA 56

Lucas, Hans
See Godard, Jean-Luc

Lucas, Victoria
See Plath, Sylvia

Lucian c. 125-c. 180 .... **CMLC 32**
See also AW 2; DLB 176; RGWL 2, 3

Lucretius c. 94B.C.-c. 49B.C. .... **CMLC 48**
See also AW 2; CDWLB 1; DLB 211; EFS 2; RGWL 2, 3

Ludlam, Charles 1943-1987 .... **CLC 46, 50**
See also CA 85-88; 122; CAD; CANR 72, 86; DLB 266

Ludlum, Robert 1927-2001 .... **CLC 22, 43**
See also AAYA 10, 59; BEST 89:1, 90:3; BPFB 2; CA 33-36R; 195; CANR 25, 41, 68, 105, 131; CMW 4; CPW; DA3; DAM NOV, POP; DLBY 1982; MSW; MTCW 1, 2

Ludwig, Ken .... **CLC 60**
See also CA 195; CAD

Ludwig, Otto 1813-1865 .... **NCLC 4**
See also DLB 129

Lugones, Leopoldo 1874-1938 .... **HLCS 2; TCLC 15**
See also CA 116; 131; CANR 104; DLB 283; EWL 3; HW 1; LAW

Lu Hsun .... **SSC 20; TCLC 3**
See Shu-Jen, Chou
See also EWL 3

Lukacs, George .... **CLC 24**
See Lukacs, Gyorgy (Szegeny von)

Lukacs, Gyorgy (Szegeny von) 1885-1971
See Lukacs, George
See also CA 101; 29-32R; CANR 62; CDWLB 4; DLB 215, 242; EW 10; EWL 3; MTCW 2

Luke, Peter (Ambrose Cyprian)
1919-1995 .... **CLC 38**
See also CA 81-84; 147; CANR 72; CBD; CD 5; DLB 13

Lunar, Dennis
See Mungo, Raymond

Lurie, Alison 1926- ..... **CLC 4, 5, 18, 39, 175**
See also BPFB 2; CA 1-4R; CANR 2, 17, 50, 88; CN 7; DLB 2; MTCW 1; SATA 46, 112

Lustig, Arnost 1926- .... **CLC 56**
See also AAYA 3; CA 69-72; CANR 47, 102; CWW 2; DLB 232, 299; EWL 3; SATA 56

Luther, Martin 1483-1546 .... **LC 9, 37**
See also CDWLB 2; DLB 179; EW 2; RGWL 2, 3

Luxemburg, Rosa 1870(?)-1919 ..... **TCLC 63**
See also CA 118

Luzi, Mario 1914- .... **CLC 13**
See also CA 61-64; CANR 9, 70; CWW 2; DLB 128; EWL 3

L'vov, Arkady .... **CLC 59**

Lydgate, John c. 1370-1450(?) .... **LC 81**
See also BRW 1; DLB 146; RGEL 2

Lyly, John 1554(?)-1606 .... **DC 7; LC 41**
See also BRW 1; DAM DRAM; DLB 62, 167; RGEL 2

L'Ymagier
See Gourmont, Remy(-Marie-Charles) de

Lynch, B. Suarez
See Borges, Jorge Luis

Lynch, David (Keith) 1946- ...... **CLC 66, 162**
See also AAYA 55; CA 124; 129; CANR 111

Lynch, James
See Andreyev, Leonid (Nikolaevich)

Lyndsay, Sir David 1485-1555 .... **LC 20**
See also RGEL 2

Lynn, Kenneth S(chuyler)
1923-2001 .... **CLC 50**
See also CA 1-4R; 196; CANR 3, 27, 65

Lynx
See West, Rebecca

Lyons, Marcus
See Blish, James (Benjamin)

Lyotard, Jean-Francois
1924-1998 .... **TCLC 103**
See also DLB 242; EWL 3

Lyre, Pinchbeck
See Sassoon, Siegfried (Lorraine)

Lytle, Andrew (Nelson) 1902-1995 ... **CLC 22**
See also CA 9-12R; 150; CANR 70; CN 7;
CSW; DLB 6; DLBY 1995; RGAL 4;
RHW

Lyttelton, George 1709-1773 .... **LC 10**
See also RGEL 2

Lytton of Knebworth, Baron
See Bulwer-Lytton, Edward (George Earle
Lytton)

Maas, Peter 1929-2001 .... **CLC 29**
See also CA 93-96; 201; INT CA-93-96;
MTCW 2

Macaulay, Catherine 1731-1791 .... **LC 64**
See also DLB 104

Macaulay, (Emilie) Rose
1881(?)-1958 .... **TCLC 7, 44**
See also CA 104; DLB 36; EWL 3; RGEL
2; RHW

Macaulay, Thomas Babington
1800-1859 .... **NCLC 42**
See also BRW 4; CDBLB 1832-1890; DLB
32, 55; RGEL 2

MacBeth, George (Mann)
1932-1992 .... **CLC 2, 5, 9**
See also CA 25-28R; 136; CANR 61, 66;
DLB 40; MTCW 1; PFS 8; SATA 4;
SATA-Obit 70

MacCaig, Norman (Alexander)
1910-1996 .... **CLC 36**
See also BRWS 6; CA 9-12R; CANR 3, 34;
CP 7; DAB; DAM POET; DLB 27; EWL
3; RGEL 2

MacCarthy, Sir (Charles Otto) Desmond
1877-1952 .... **TCLC 36**
See also CA 167

MacDiarmid, Hugh .... **CLC 2, 4, 11, 19, 63;**
PC 9
See Grieve, C(hristopher) M(urray)
See also CDBLB 1945-1960; DLB 20;
EWL 3; RGEL 2

MacDonald, Anson
See Heinlein, Robert A(nson)

Macdonald, Cynthia 1928- .... **CLC 13, 19**
See also CA 49-52; CANR 4, 44; DLB 105

MacDonald, George 1824-1905 .... **TCLC 9,**
113
See also AAYA 57; BYA 5; CA 106; 137;
CANR 80; CLR 67; DLB 18, 163, 178;
FANT; MAICYA 1, 2; RGEL 2; SATA 33,
100; SFW 4; SUFW; WCH

Macdonald, John
See Millar, Kenneth

MacDonald, John D(ann)
1916-1986 .... **CLC 3, 27, 44**
See also BPFB 2; CA 1-4R; 121; CANR 1,
19, 60; CMW 4; CPW; DAM NOV, POP;
DLB 8, 306; DLBY 1986; MSW; MTCW
1, 2; SFW 4

Macdonald, John Ross
See Millar, Kenneth

Macdonald, Ross ..... **CLC 1, 2, 3, 14, 34, 41**
See Millar, Kenneth
See also AMWS 4; BPFB 2; DLBD 6;
MSW; RGAL 4

MacDougal, John
See Blish, James (Benjamin)

MacDougal, John
See Blish, James (Benjamin)

MacDowell, John
See Parks, Tim(othy Harold)

MacEwen, Gwendolyn (Margaret)
1941-1987 .... **CLC 13, 55**
See also CA 9-12R; 124; CANR 7, 22; DLB
53, 251; SATA 50; SATA-Obit 55

Macha, Karel Hynek 1810-1846 .... **NCLC 46**

Machado (y Ruiz), Antonio
1875-1939 .... **TCLC 3**
See also CA 104; 174; DLB 108; EW 9;
EWL 3; HW 2; RGWL 2, 3

Machado de Assis, Joaquim Maria
1839-1908 .... **BLC 2; HLCS 2; SSC 24;**
TCLC 10
See also CA 107; 153; CANR 91; DLB 307;
LAW; RGSF 2; RGWL 2, 3; TWA; WLIT
1

Machaut, Guillaume de c.
1300-1377 .... **CMLC 64**
See also DLB 208

Machen, Arthur .... **SSC 20; TCLC 4**
See Jones, Arthur Llewellyn
See also CA 179; DLB 156, 178; RGEL 2;
SUFW 1

Machiavelli, Niccolo 1469-1527 ... **DC 16; LC**
8, 36; WLCS
See also AAYA 58; DA; DAB; DAC; DAM
MST; EW 2; LAIT 1; LMFS 1; NFS 9;
RGWL 2, 3; TWA

MacInnes, Colin 1914-1976 .... **CLC 4, 23**
See also CA 69-72; 65-68; CANR 21; DLB
14; MTCW 1, 2; RGEL 2; RHW

MacInnes, Helen (Clark)
1907-1985 .... **CLC 27, 39**
See also BPFB 2; CA 1-4R; 117; CANR 1,
28, 58; CMW 4; CPW; DAM POP; DLB
87; MSW; MTCW 1, 2; SATA 22; SATA-
Obit 44

Mackay, Mary 1855-1924
See Corelli, Marie
See also CA 118; 177; FANT; RHW

Mackay, Shena 1944- .... **CLC 195**
See also CA 104; CANR 88; DLB 231

Mackenzie, Compton (Edward Montague)
1883-1972 .... **CLC 18; TCLC 116**
See also CA 21-22; 37-40R; CAP 2; DLB
34, 100; RGEL 2

Mackenzie, Henry 1745-1831 .... **NCLC 41**
See also DLB 39; RGEL 2

Mackey, Nathaniel (Ernest) 1947- .... **PC 49**
See also CA 153; CANR 114; CP 7; DLB
169

MacKinnon, Catharine A. 1946- .... **CLC 181**
See also CA 128; 132; CANR 73; FW;
MTCW 2

Mackintosh, Elizabeth 1896(?)-1952
See Tey, Josephine
See also CA 110; CMW 4

MacLaren, James
See Grieve, C(hristopher) M(urray)

Mac Laverty, Bernard 1942- .... **CLC 31**
See also CA 116; 118; CANR 43, 88; CN
7; DLB 267; INT CA-118; RGSF 2

MacLean, Alistair (Stuart)
1922(?)-1987 .... **CLC 3, 13, 50, 63**
See also CA 57-60; 121; CANR 28, 61;
CMW 4; CPW; DAM POP; DLB 276;
MTCW 1; SATA 23; SATA-Obit 50;
TCWW 2

Maclean, Norman (Fitzroy)
1902-1990 .... **CLC 78; SSC 13**
See also AMWS 14; CA 102; 132; CANR
49; CPW; DAM POP; DLB 206; TCWW
2

MacLeish, Archibald 1892-1982 ... **CLC 3, 8,**
14, 68; PC 47
See also AMW; CA 9-12R; 106; CAD;
CANR 33, 63; CDALBS; DAM POET;
DFS 15; DLB 4, 7, 45; DLBY 1982; EWL
3; EXPP; MTCW 1, 2; PAB; PFS 5;
RGAL 4; TUS

MacLennan, (John) Hugh
1907-1990 .... **CLC 2, 14, 92**
See also CA 5-8R; 142; CANR 33; DAC;
DAM MST; DLB 68; EWL 3; MTCW 1,
2; RGEL 2; TWA

MacLeod, Alistair 1936- .... **CLC 56, 165**
See also CA 123; CCA 1; DAC; DAM
MST; DLB 60; MTCW 2; RGSF 2

Macleod, Fiona
See Sharp, William
See also RGEL 2; SUFW

MacNeice, (Frederick) Louis
1907-1963 .... **CLC 1, 4, 10, 53; PC 61**
See also BRW 7; CA 85-88; CANR 61;
DAB; DAM POET; DLB 10, 20; EWL 3;
MTCW 1, 2; RGEL 2

MacNeill, Dand
See Fraser, George MacDonald

Macpherson, James 1736-1796 .... **LC 29**
See Ossian
See also BRWS 8; DLB 109; RGEL 2

Macpherson, (Jean) Jay 1931- .... **CLC 14**
See also CA 5-8R; CANR 90; CP 7; CWP;
DLB 53

Macrobius fl. 430- .... **CMLC 48**

MacShane, Frank 1927-1999 .... **CLC 39**
See also CA 9-12R; 186; CANR 3, 33; DLB
111

Macumber, Mari
See Sandoz, Mari(e Susette)

Madach, Imre 1823-1864 .... **NCLC 19**

Madden, (Jerry) David 1933- .... **CLC 5, 15**
See also CA 1-4R; CAAS 3; CANR 4, 45;
CN 7; CSW; DLB 6; MTCW 1

Maddern, Al(an)
See Ellison, Harlan (Jay)

Madhubuti, Haki R. 1942- ... **BLC 2; CLC 6,**
73; PC 5
See Lee, Don L.
See also BW 2, 3; CA 73-76; CANR 24,
51, 73; CP 7; CSW; DAM MULT, POET;
DLB 5, 41; DLBD 8; EWL 3; MTCW 2;
RGAL 4

Madison, James 1751-1836 .... **NCLC 126**
See also DLB 37

Maepenn, Hugh
See Kuttner, Henry

Maepenn, K. H.
See Kuttner, Henry

Maeterlinck, Maurice 1862-1949 ..... **TCLC 3**
See also CA 104; 136; CANR 80; DAM
DRAM; DLB 192; EW 8; EWL 3; GFL
1789 to the Present; LMFS 2; RGWL 2,
3; SATA 66; TWA

Maginn, William 1794-1842 .... **NCLC 8**
See also DLB 110, 159

Mahapatra, Jayanta 1928- .... **CLC 33**
See also CA 73-76; CAAS 9; CANR 15,
33, 66, 87; CP 7; DAM MULT

Mahfouz, Naguib (Abdel Aziz Al-Sabilgi)
1911(?)- .... **CLC 153; SSC 66**
See Mahfuz, Najib (Abdel Aziz al-Sabilgi)
See also AAYA 49; BEST 89:2; CA 128;
CANR 55, 101; DA3; DAM NOV;
MTCW 1, 2; RGWL 2, 3; SSFS 9

Mahfuz, Najib (Abdel Aziz al-Sabilgi)
.... **CLC 52, 55**
See Mahfouz, Naguib (Abdel Aziz Al-
Sabilgi)
See also AFW; CWW 2; DLBY 1988; EWL
3; RGSF 2; WLIT 2

Mahon, Derek 1941- .... **CLC 27; PC 60**
See also BRWS 6; CA 113; 128; CANR 88;
CP 7; DLB 40; EWL 3

Maiakovskii, Vladimir
See Mayakovski, Vladimir (Vladimirovich)
See also IDTP; RGWL 2, 3

Mailer, Norman (Kingsley) 1923- . **CLC 1, 2,**
3, 4, 5, 8, 11, 14, 28, 39, 74, 111
See also AAYA 31; AITN 2; AMW; AMWC
2; AMWR 2; BPFB 2; CA 9-12R; CABS
1; CANR 28, 74, 77, 130; CDALB 1968-
1988; CN 7; CPW; DA; DA3; DAB;
DAC; DAM MST, NOV, POP; DLB 2,
16, 28, 185, 278; DLBD 3; DLBY 1980,
1983; EWL 3; MTCW 1, 2; NFS 10;
RGAL 4; TUS

Marivaux, Pierre Carlet de Chamblain de
1688-1763 .... **DC 7; LC 4**
See also GFL Beginnings to 1789; RGWL
2, 3; TWA
Markandaya, Kamala .... **CLC 8, 38**
See Taylor, Kamala (Purnaiya)
See also BYA 13; CN 7; EWL 3
Markfield, Wallace 1926-2002 .... **CLC 8**
See also CA 69-72; 208; CAAS 3; CN 7;
DLB 2, 28; DLBY 2002
Markham, Edwin 1852-1940 .... **TCLC 47**
See also CA 160; DLB 54, 186; RGAL 4
Markham, Robert
See Amis, Kingsley (William)
Markoosie .... **NNAL**
See Patsauq, Markoosie
See also CLR 23; DAM MULT
Marks, J.
See Highwater, Jamake (Mamake)
Marks, J
See Highwater, Jamake (Mamake)
Marks-Highwater, J
See Highwater, Jamake (Mamake)
Marks-Highwater, J.
See Highwater, Jamake (Mamake)
Markson, David M(errill) 1927- .... **CLC 67**
See also CA 49-52; CANR 1, 91; CN 7
Marlatt, Daphne (Buckle) 1942- .... **CLC 168**
See also CA 25-28R; CANR 17, 39; CN 7;
CP 7; CWP; DLB 60; FW
Marley, Bob .... **CLC 17**
See Marley, Robert Nesta
Marley, Robert Nesta 1945-1981
See Marley, Bob
See also CA 107; 103
Marlowe, Christopher 1564-1593 . **DC 1; LC 22, 47; PC 57; WLC**
See also BRW 1; BRWR 1; CDBLB Before
1660; DA; DA3; DAB; DAC; DAM
DRAM, MST; DFS 1, 5, 13; DLB 62;
EXPP; LMFS 1; RGEL 2; TEA; WLIT 3
Marlowe, Stephen 1928- .... **CLC 70**
See Queen, Ellery
See also CA 13-16R; CANR 6, 55; CMW
4; SFW 4
Marmion, Shakerley 1603-1639 .... **LC 89**
See also DLB 58; RGEL 2
Marmontel, Jean-Francois 1723-1799 .. **LC 2**
Maron, Monika 1941- .... **CLC 165**
See also CA 201
Marquand, John P(hillips)
1893-1960 .... **CLC 2, 10**
See also AMW; BPFB 2; CA 85-88; CANR
73; CMW 4; DLB 9, 102; EWL 3; MTCW
2; RGAL 4
Marques, Rene 1919-1979 .. **CLC 96; HLC 2**
See also CA 97-100; 85-88; CANR 78;
DAM MULT; DLB 305; EWL 3; HW 1,
2; LAW; RGSF 2
Marquez, Gabriel (Jose) Garcia
See Garcia Marquez, Gabriel (Jose)
Marquis, Don(ald Robert Perry)
1878-1937 .... **TCLC 7**
See also CA 104; 166; DLB 11, 25; RGAL 4
Marquis de Sade
See Sade, Donatien Alphonse Francois
Marric, J. J.
See Creasey, John
See also MSW
Marryat, Frederick 1792-1848 .... **NCLC 3**
See also DLB 21, 163; RGEL 2; WCH
Marsden, James
See Creasey, John
Marsh, Edward 1872-1953 .... **TCLC 99**
Marsh, (Edith) Ngaio 1895-1982 .. **CLC 7, 53**
See also CA 9-12R; CANR 6, 58; CMW 4;
CPW; DAM POP; DLB 77; MSW;
MTCW 1, 2; RGEL 2; TEA

Marshall, Garry 1934- .... **CLC 17**
See also AAYA 3; CA 111; SATA 60
Marshall, Paule 1929- .. **BLC 3; CLC 27, 72; SSC 3**
See also AFAW 1, 2; AMWS 11; BPFB 2;
BW 2, 3; CA 77-80; CANR 25, 73, 129;
CN 7; DA3; DAM MULT; DLB 33, 157,
227; EWL 3; LATS 1:2; MTCW 1, 2;
RGAL 4; SSFS 15
Marshallik
See Zangwill, Israel
Marsten, Richard
See Hunter, Evan
Marston, John 1576-1634 .... **LC 33**
See also BRW 2; DAM DRAM; DLB 58,
172; RGEL 2
Martel, Yann 1963- .... **CLC 192**
See also CA 146; CANR 114
Martha, Henry
See Harris, Mark
Marti, Jose
See Marti (y Perez), Jose (Julian)
See also DLB 290
Marti (y Perez), Jose (Julian)
1853-1895 .... **HLC 2; NCLC 63**
See Marti, Jose
See also DAM MULT; HW 2; LAW; RGWL
2, 3; WLIT 1
Martial c. 40-c. 104 .... **CMLC 35; PC 10**
See also AW 2; CDWLB 1; DLB 211;
RGWL 2, 3
Martin, Ken
See Hubbard, L(afayette) Ron(ald)
Martin, Richard
See Creasey, John
Martin, Steve 1945- .... **CLC 30**
See also AAYA 53; CA 97-100; CANR 30,
100; DFS 19; MTCW 1
Martin, Valerie 1948- .... **CLC 89**
See also BEST 90:2; CA 85-88; CANR 49,
89
Martin, Violet Florence 1862-1915 .. **SSC 56; TCLC 51**
Martin, Webber
See Silverberg, Robert
Martindale, Patrick Victor
See White, Patrick (Victor Martindale)
Martin du Gard, Roger
1881-1958 .... **TCLC 24**
See also CA 118; CANR 94; DLB 65; EWL
3; GFL 1789 to the Present; RGWL 2, 3
Martineau, Harriet 1802-1876 ...... **NCLC 26, 137**
See also DLB 21, 55, 159, 163, 166, 190;
FW; RGEL 2; YABC 2
Martines, Julia
See O'Faolain, Julia
Martinez, Enrique Gonzalez
See Gonzalez Martinez, Enrique
Martinez, Jacinto Benavente y
See Benavente (y Martinez), Jacinto
Martinez de la Rosa, Francisco de Paula
1787-1862 .... **NCLC 102**
See also TWA
Martinez Ruiz, Jose 1873-1967
See Azorin; Ruiz, Jose Martinez
See also CA 93-96; HW 1
Martinez Sierra, Gregorio
1881-1947 .... **TCLC 6**
See also CA 115; EWL 3
Martinez Sierra, Maria (de la O'LeJarraga)
1874-1974 .... **TCLC 6**
See also CA 115; EWL 3
Martinsen, Martin
See Follett, Ken(neth Martin)
Martinson, Harry (Edmund)
1904-1978 .... **CLC 14**
See also CA 77-80; CANR 34, 130; DLB
259; EWL 3

Martyn, Edward 1859-1923 .... **TCLC 131**
See also CA 179; DLB 10; RGEL 2
Marut, Ret
See Traven, B.
Marut, Robert
See Traven, B.
Marvell, Andrew 1621-1678 .... **LC 4, 43; PC 10; WLC**
See also BRW 2; BRWR 2; CDBLB 1660-
1789; DA; DAB; DAC; DAM MST,
POET; DLB 131; EXPP; PFS 5; RGEL 2;
TEA; WP
Marx, Karl (Heinrich)
1818-1883 .... **NCLC 17, 114**
See also DLB 129; LATS 1:1; TWA
Masaoka, Shiki -1902 .... **TCLC 18**
See Masaoka, Tsunenori
See also RGWL 3
Masaoka, Tsunenori 1867-1902
See Masaoka, Shiki
See also CA 117; 191; TWA
Masefield, John (Edward)
1878-1967 .... **CLC 11, 47**
See also CA 19-20; 25-28R; CANR 33;
CAP 2; CDBLB 1890-1914; DAM POET;
DLB 10, 19, 153, 160; EWL 3; EXPP;
FANT; MTCW 1, 2; PFS 5; RGEL 2;
SATA 19
Maso, Carole 19(?)- .... **CLC 44**
See also CA 170; GLL 2; RGAL 4
Mason, Bobbie Ann 1940- ... **CLC 28, 43, 82, 154; SSC 4**
See also AAYA 5, 42; AMWS 8; BPFB 2;
CA 53-56; CANR 11, 31, 58, 83, 125;
CDALBS; CN 7; CSW; DA3; DLB 173;
DLBY 1987; EWL 3; EXPS; INT CANR-
31; MTCW 1, 2; NFS 4; RGAL 4; RGSF
2; SSFS 3, 8, 20; YAW
Mason, Ernst
See Pohl, Frederik
Mason, Hunni B.
See Sternheim, (William Adolf) Carl
Mason, Lee W.
See Malzberg, Barry N(athaniel)
Mason, Nick 1945- .... **CLC 35**
Mason, Tally
See Derleth, August (William)
Mass, Anna .... **CLC 59**
Mass, William
See Gibson, William
Massinger, Philip 1583-1640 .... **LC 70**
See also DLB 58; RGEL 2
Master Lao
See Lao Tzu
Masters, Edgar Lee 1868-1950 ...... **PC 1, 36; TCLC 2, 25; WLCS**
See also AMWS 1; CA 104; 133; CDALB
1865-1917; DA; DAC; DAM MST,
POET; DLB 54; EWL 3; EXPP; MTCW
1, 2; RGAL 4; TUS; WP
Masters, Hilary 1928- .... **CLC 48**
See also CA 25-28R, 217; CAAE 217;
CANR 13, 47, 97; CN 7; DLB 244
Mastrosimone, William 19(?)- .... **CLC 36**
See also CA 186; CAD; CD 5
Mathe, Albert
See Camus, Albert
Mather, Cotton 1663-1728 .... **LC 38**
See also AMWS 2; CDALB 1640-1865;
DLB 24, 30, 140; RGAL 4; TUS
Mather, Increase 1639-1723 .... **LC 38**
See also DLB 24
Matheson, Richard (Burton) 1926- .. **CLC 37**
See also AAYA 31; CA 97-100; CANR 88,
99; DLB 8, 44; HGG; INT CA-97-100;
SCFW 2; SFW 4; SUFW 2
Mathews, Harry 1930- .... **CLC 6, 52**
See also CA 21-24R; CAAS 6; CANR 18,
40, 98; CN 7

Merleau-Ponty, Maurice
1908-1961 .... **TCLC 156**
See also CA 114; 89-92; DLB 296; GFL
1789 to the Present

Merlin, Arthur
See Blish, James (Benjamin)

Mernissi, Fatima 1940- .... **CLC 171**
See also CA 152; FW

Merrill, James (Ingram) 1926-1995 .. **CLC 2,
3, 6, 8, 13, 18, 34, 91; PC 28**
See also AMWS 3; CA 13-16R; 147; CANR
10, 49, 63, 108; DA3; DAM POET; DLB
5, 165; DLBY 1985; EWL 3; INT CANR-
10; MTCW 1, 2; PAB; RGAL 4

Merriman, Alex
See Silverberg, Robert

Merriman, Brian 1747-1805 .... **NCLC 70**

Merritt, E. B.
See Waddington, Miriam

Merton, Thomas (James)
1915-1968 . **CLC 1, 3, 11, 34, 83; PC 10**
See also AMWS 8; CA 5-8R; 25-28R;
CANR 22, 53, 111, 131; DA3; DLB 48;
DLBY 1981; MTCW 1, 2

Merwin, W(illiam) S(tanley) 1927- ... **CLC 1,
2, 3, 5, 8, 13, 18, 45, 88; PC 45**
See also AMWS 3; CA 13-16R; CANR 15,
51, 112; CP 7; DA3; DAM POET; DLB
5, 169; EWL 3; INT CANR-15; MTCW
1, 2; PAB; PFS 5, 15; RGAL 4

Metastasio, Pietro 1698-1782 .... **LC 115**
See also RGWL 2, 3

Metcalf, John 1938- .... **CLC 37; SSC 43**
See also CA 113; CN 7; DLB 60; RGSF 2;
TWA

Metcalf, Suzanne
See Baum, L(yman) Frank

Mew, Charlotte (Mary) 1870-1928 .. **TCLC 8**
See also CA 105; 189; DLB 19, 135; RGEL
2

Mewshaw, Michael 1943- .... **CLC 9**
See also CA 53-56; CANR 7, 47; DLBY
1980

Meyer, Conrad Ferdinand
1825-1898 .... **NCLC 81; SSC 30**
See also DLB 129; EW; RGWL 2, 3

Meyer, Gustav 1868-1932
See Meyrink, Gustav
See also CA 117; 190

Meyer, June
See Jordan, June (Meyer)

Meyer, Lynn
See Slavitt, David R(ytman)

Meyers, Jeffrey 1939- .... **CLC 39**
See also CA 73-76, 186; CAAE 186; CANR
54, 102; DLB 111

**Meynell, Alice (Christina Gertrude
Thompson)** 1847-1922 .... **TCLC 6**
See also CA 104; 177; DLB 19, 98; RGEL
2

Meyrink, Gustav .... **TCLC 21**
See Meyer, Gustav
See also DLB 81; EWL 3

Michaels, Leonard 1933-2003 ..... **CLC 6, 25;
SSC 16**
See also CA 61-64; 216; CANR 21, 62, 119;
CN 7; DLB 130; MTCW 1

Michaux, Henri 1899-1984 .... **CLC 8, 19**
See also CA 85-88; 114; DLB 258; EWL 3;
GFL 1789 to the Present; RGWL 2, 3

Micheaux, Oscar (Devereaux)
1884-1951 .... **TCLC 76**
See also BW 3; CA 174; DLB 50; TCWW
2

Michelangelo 1475-1564 .... **LC 12**
See also AAYA 43

Michelet, Jules 1798-1874 .... **NCLC 31**
See also EW 5; GFL 1789 to the Present

Michels, Robert 1876-1936 .... **TCLC 88**
See also CA 212

Michener, James A(lbert)
1907(?)-1997 .. **CLC 1, 5, 11, 29, 60, 109**
See also AAYA 27; AITN 1; BEST 90:1;
BPFB 2; CA 5-8R; 161; CANR 21, 45,
68; CN 7; CPW; DA3; DAM NOV, POP;
DLB 6; MTCW 1, 2; RHW

Mickiewicz, Adam 1798-1855 . **NCLC 3, 101;
PC 38**
See also EW 5; RGWL 2, 3

Middleton, (John) Christopher
1926- .... **CLC 13**
See also CA 13-16R; CANR 29, 54, 117;
CP 7; DLB 40

Middleton, Richard (Barham)
1882-1911 .... **TCLC 56**
See also CA 187; DLB 156; HGG

Middleton, Stanley 1919- .... **CLC 7, 38**
See also CA 25-28R; CAAS 23; CANR 21,
46, 81; CN 7; DLB 14

Middleton, Thomas 1580-1627 ...... **DC 5; LC
33**
See also BRW 2; DAM DRAM, MST; DFS
18; DLB 58; RGEL 2

Migueis, Jose Rodrigues 1901-1980 . **CLC 10**
See also DLB 287

Mikszath, Kalman 1847-1910 .... **TCLC 31**
See also CA 170

Miles, Jack .... **CLC 100**
See also CA 200

Miles, John Russiano
See Miles, Jack

Miles, Josephine (Louise)
1911-1985 .... **CLC 1, 2, 14, 34, 39**
See also CA 1-4R; 116; CANR 2, 55; DAM
POET; DLB 48

Militant
See Sandburg, Carl (August)

Mill, Harriet (Hardy) Taylor
1807-1858 .... **NCLC 102**
See also FW

Mill, John Stuart 1806-1873 .... **NCLC 11, 58**
See also CDBLB 1832-1890; DLB 55, 190,
262; FW 1; RGEL 2; TEA

Millar, Kenneth 1915-1983 .... **CLC 14**
See Macdonald, Ross
See also CA 9-12R; 110; CANR 16, 63,
107; CMW 4; CPW; DA3; DAM POP;
DLB 2, 226; DLBD 6; DLBY 1983;
MTCW 1, 2

Millay, E. Vincent
See Millay, Edna St. Vincent

Millay, Edna St. Vincent 1892-1950 ..... **PC 6,
61; TCLC 4, 49; WLCS**
See Boyd, Nancy
See also AMW; CA 104; 130; CDALB
1917-1929; DA; DA3; DAB; DAC; DAM
MST, POET; DLB 45, 249; EWL 3;
EXPP; MAWW; MTCW 1, 2; PAB; PFS
3, 17; RGAL 4; TUS; WP

Miller, Arthur 1915- ...... **CLC 1, 2, 6, 10, 15,
26, 47, 78, 179; DC 1; WLC**
See also AAYA 15; AITN 1; AMW; AMWC
1; CA 1-4R; CABS 3; CAD; CANR 2,
30, 54, 76, 132; CD 5; CDALB 1941-
1968; DA; DA3; DAB; DAC; DAM
DRAM, MST; DFS 1, 3, 8; DLB 7, 266;
EWL 3; LAIT 1, 4; LATS 1:2; MTCW 1,
2; RGAL 4; TUS; WYAS 1

Miller, Henry (Valentine)
1891-1980 .... **CLC 1, 2, 4, 9, 14, 43, 84;
WLC**
See also AMW; BPFB 2; CA 9-12R; 97-
100; CANR 33, 64; CDALB 1929-1941;
DA; DA3; DAB; DAC; DAM MST, NOV;
DLB 4, 9; DLBY 1980; EWL 3; MTCW
1, 2; RGAL 4; TUS

Miller, Hugh 1802-1856 .... **NCLC 143**
See also DLB 190

Miller, Jason 1939(?)-2001 .... **CLC 2**
See also AITN 1; CA 73-76; 197; CAD;
CANR 130; DFS 12; DLB 7

Miller, Sue 1943- .... **CLC 44**
See also AMWS 12; BEST 90:3; CA 139;
CANR 59, 91, 128; DA3; DAM POP;
DLB 143

Miller, Walter M(ichael, Jr.)
1923-1996 .... **CLC 4, 30**
See also BPFB 2; CA 85-88; CANR 108;
DLB 8; SCFW; SFW 4

Millett, Kate 1934- .... **CLC 67**
See also AITN 1; CA 73-76; CANR 32, 53,
76, 110; DA3; DLB 246; FW; GLL 1;
MTCW 1, 2

Millhauser, Steven (Lewis) 1943- .... **CLC 21,
54, 109; SSC 57**
See also CA 110; 111; CANR 63, 114, 133;
CN 7; DA3; DLB 2; FANT; INT CA-111;
MTCW 2

Millin, Sarah Gertrude 1889-1968 ... **CLC 49**
See also CA 102; 93-96; DLB 225; EWL 3

Milne, A(lan) A(lexander)
1882-1956 .... **TCLC 6, 88**
See also BRWS 5; CA 104; 133; CLR 1,
26; CMW 4; CWRI 5; DA3; DAB; DAC;
DAM MST; DLB 10, 77, 100, 160; FANT;
MAICYA 1, 2; MTCW 1, 2; RGEL 2;
SATA 100; WCH; YABC 1

Milner, Ron(ald) 1938-2004 ..... **BLC 3; CLC
56**
See also AITN 1; BW 1; CA 73-76; CAD;
CANR 24, 81; CD 5; DAM MULT; DLB
38; MTCW 1

Milnes, Richard Monckton
1809-1885 .... **NCLC 61**
See also DLB 32, 184

Milosz, Czeslaw 1911- ...... **CLC 5, 11, 22, 31,
56, 82; PC 8; WLCS**
See also CA 81-84; CANR 23, 51, 91, 126;
CDWLB 4; CWW 2; DA3; DAM MST,
POET; DLB 215; EW 13; EWL 3; MTCW
1, 2; PFS 16; RGWL 2, 3

Milton, John 1608-1674 ..... **LC 9, 43, 92; PC
19, 29; WLC**
See also BRW 2; BRWR 2; CDBLB 1660-
1789; DA; DA3; DAB; DAC; DAM MST,
POET; DLB 131, 151, 281; EFS 1; EXPP;
LAIT 1; PAB; PFS 3, 17; RGEL 2; TEA;
WLIT 3; WP

Min, Anchee 1957- .... **CLC 86**
See also CA 146; CANR 94

Minehaha, Cornelius
See Wedekind, (Benjamin) Frank(lin)

Miner, Valerie 1947- .... **CLC 40**
See also CA 97-100; CANR 59; FW; GLL
2

Minimo, Duca
See D'Annunzio, Gabriele

Minot, Susan 1956- .... **CLC 44, 159**
See also AMWS 6; CA 134; CANR 118;
CN 7

Minus, Ed 1938- .... **CLC 39**
See also CA 185

Mirabai 1498(?)-1550(?) .... **PC 48**

Miranda, Javier
See Bioy Casares, Adolfo
See also CWW 2

Mirbeau, Octave 1848-1917 .... **TCLC 55**
See also CA 216; DLB 123, 192; GFL 1789
to the Present

Mirikitani, Janice 1942- .... **AAL**
See also CA 211; RGAL 4

Mirk, John (?)-c. 1414 .... **LC 105**
See also DLB 146

Miro (Ferrer), Gabriel (Francisco Victor)
1879-1930 .... **TCLC 5**
See also CA 104; 185; EWL 3

Misharin, Alexandr .... **CLC 59**
Mishima, Yukio ... CLC 2, 4, 6, 9, 27; DC 1;
    SSC 4, TCLC 161
    See Hiraoka, Kimitake
    See also AAYA 50; BPFB 2; GLL 1; MJW;
    MTCW 2; RGSF 2; RGWL 2, 3; SSFS 5,
    12
Mistral, Frederic 1830-1914 .... **TCLC 51**
    See also CA 122; 213; GFL 1789 to the
    Present
Mistral, Gabriela
    See Godoy Alcayaga, Lucila
    See also DLB 283; DNFS 1; EWL 3; LAW;
    RGWL 2, 3; WP
Mistry, Rohinton 1952- ... CLC 71, 196; SSC
    73
    See also BRWS 10; CA 141; CANR 86,
    114; CCA 1; CN 7; DAC; SSFS 6
Mitchell, Clyde
    See Ellison, Harlan (Jay)
Mitchell, Emerson Blackhorse Barney
    1945- .... **NNAL**
    See also CA 45-48
Mitchell, James Leslie 1901-1935
    See Gibbon, Lewis Grassic
    See also CA 104; 188; DLB 15
Mitchell, Joni 1943- .... **CLC 12**
    See also CA 112; CCA 1
Mitchell, Joseph (Quincy)
    1908-1996 .... **CLC 98**
    See also CA 77-80; 152; CANR 69; CN 7;
    CSW; DLB 185; DLBY 1996
Mitchell, Margaret (Munnerlyn)
    1900-1949 .... **TCLC 11**
    See also AAYA 23; BPFB 2; BYA 1; CA
    109; 125; CANR 55, 94; CDALBS; DA3;
    DAM NOV, POP; DLB 9; LAIT 2;
    MTCW 1, 2; NFS 9; RGAL 4; RHW;
    TUS; WYAS 1; YAW
Mitchell, Peggy
    See Mitchell, Margaret (Munnerlyn)
Mitchell, S(ilas) Weir 1829-1914 .... **TCLC 36**
    See also CA 165; DLB 202; RGAL 4
Mitchell, W(illiam) O(rmond)
    1914-1998 .... **CLC 25**
    See also CA 77-80; 165; CANR 15, 43; CN
    7; DAC; DAM MST; DLB 88
Mitchell, William (Lendrum)
    1879-1936 .... **TCLC 81**
    See also CA 213
Mitford, Mary Russell 1787-1855 ... **NCLC 4**
    See also DLB 110, 116; RGEL 2
Mitford, Nancy 1904-1973 .... **CLC 44**
    See also BRWS 10; CA 9-12R; DLB 191;
    RGEL 2
Miyamoto, (Chujo) Yuriko
    1899-1951 .... **TCLC 37**
    See Miyamoto Yuriko
    See also CA 170, 174
Miyamoto Yuriko
    See Miyamoto, (Chujo) Yuriko
    See also DLB 180
Miyazawa, Kenji 1896-1933 .... **TCLC 76**
    See Miyazawa Kenji
    See also CA 157; RGWL 3
Miyazawa Kenji
    See Miyazawa, Kenji
    See also EWL 3
Mizoguchi, Kenji 1898-1956 .... **TCLC 72**
    See also CA 167
Mo, Timothy (Peter) 1950(?)- ... CLC 46, 134
    See also CA 117; CANR 128; CN 7; DLB
    194; MTCW 1; WLIT 4; WWE 1
Modarressi, Taghi (M.) 1931-1997 ... **CLC 44**
    See also CA 121; 134; INT CA-134
Modiano, Patrick (Jean) 1945- .... **CLC 18**
    See also CA 85-88; CANR 17, 40, 115;
    CWW 2; DLB 83, 299; EWL 3

Mofolo, Thomas (Mokopu)
    1875(?)-1948 .... **BLC 3; TCLC 22**
    See also AFW; CA 121; 153; CANR 83;
    DAM MULT; DLB 225; EWL 3; MTCW
    2; WLIT 2
Mohr, Nicholasa 1938- .... **CLC 12; HLC 2**
    See also AAYA 8, 46; CA 49-52; CANR 1,
    32, 64; CLR 22; DAM MULT; DLB 145;
    HW 1, 2; JRDA; LAIT 5; LLW 1; MAI-
    CYA 2; MAICYAS 1; RGAL 4; SAAS 8;
    SATA 8, 97; SATA-Essay 113; WYA;
    YAW
Moi, Toril 1953- .... **CLC 172**
    See also CA 154; CANR 102; FW
Mojtabai, A(nn) G(race) 1938- ..... CLC 5, 9,
    15, 29
    See also CA 85-88; CANR 88
Moliere 1622-1673 ..... DC 13; LC 10, 28, 64;
    WLC
    See also DA; DA3; DAB; DAC; DAM
    DRAM, MST; DFS 13, 18, 20; DLB 268;
    EW 3; GFL Beginnings to 1789; LATS
    1:1; RGWL 2, 3; TWA
Molin, Charles
    See Mayne, William (James Carter)
Molnar, Ferenc 1878-1952 .... **TCLC 20**
    See also CA 109; 153; CANR 83; CDWLB
    4; DAM DRAM; DLB 215; EWL 3;
    RGWL 2, 3
Momaday, N(avarre) Scott 1934- ...... CLC 2,
    19, 85, 95, 160; NNAL; PC 25; WLCS
    See also AAYA 11; AMWS 4; ANW; BPFB
    2; BYA 12; CA 25-28R; CANR 14, 34,
    68, 134; CDALBS; CN 7; CPW; DA;
    DA3; DAB; DAC; DAM MST, MULT,
    NOV, POP; DLB 143, 175, 256; EWL 3;
    EXPP; INT CANR-14; LAIT 4; LATS
    1:2; MTCW 1, 2; NFS 10; PFS 2, 11;
    RGAL 4; SATA 48; SATA-Brief 30; WP;
    YAW
Monette, Paul 1945-1995 .... **CLC 82**
    See also AMWS 10; CA 139; 147; CN 7;
    GLL 1
Monroe, Harriet 1860-1936 .... **TCLC 12**
    See also CA 109; 204; DLB 54, 91
Monroe, Lyle
    See Heinlein, Robert A(nson)
Montagu, Elizabeth 1720-1800 .... **NCLC 7,
    117**
    See also FW
Montagu, Mary (Pierrepont) Wortley
    1689-1762 .... LC 9, 57; PC 16
    See also DLB 95, 101; RGEL 2
Montagu, W. H.
    See Coleridge, Samuel Taylor
Montague, John (Patrick) 1929- ..... CLC 13,
    46
    See also CA 9-12R; CANR 9, 69, 121; CP
    7; DLB 40; EWL 3; MTCW 1; PFS 12;
    RGEL 2
Montaigne, Michel (Eyquem) de
    1533-1592 .... LC 8, 105; WLC
    See also DA; DAB; DAC; DAM MST; EW
    2; GFL Beginnings to 1789; LMFS 1;
    RGWL 2, 3; TWA
Montale, Eugenio 1896-1981 ... CLC 7, 9, 18;
    PC 13
    See also CA 17-20R; 104; CANR 30; DLB
    114; EW 11; EWL 3; MTCW 1; RGWL
    2, 3; TWA
Montesquieu, Charles-Louis de Secondat
    1689-1755 .... **LC 7, 69**
    See also EW 3; GFL Beginnings to 1789;
    TWA
Montessori, Maria 1870-1952 ...... **TCLC 103**
    See also CA 115; 147
Montgomery, (Robert) Bruce 1921(?)-1978
    See Crispin, Edmund
    See also CA 179; 104; CMW 4

Montgomery, L(ucy) M(aud)
    1874-1942 .... **TCLC 51, 140**
    See also AAYA 12; BYA 1; CA 108; 137;
    CLR 8, 91; DA3; DAC; DAM MST; DLB
    92; DLBD 14; JRDA; MAICYA 1, 2;
    MTCW 2; RGEL 2; SATA 100; TWA;
    WCH; WYA; YABC 1
Montgomery, Marion H., Jr. 1925- .... **CLC 7**
    See also AITN 1; CA 1-4R; CANR 3, 48;
    CSW; DLB 6
Montgomery, Max
    See Davenport, Guy (Mattison, Jr.)
Montherlant, Henry (Milon) de
    1896-1972 .... **CLC 8, 19**
    See also CA 85-88; 37-40R; DAM DRAM;
    DLB 72; EW 11; EWL 3; GFL 1789 to
    the Present; MTCW 1
Monty Python
    See Chapman, Graham; Cleese, John
    (Marwood); Gilliam, Terry (Vance); Idle,
    Eric; Jones, Terence Graham Parry; Palin,
    Michael (Edward)
    See also AAYA 7
Moodie, Susanna (Strickland)
    1803-1885 .... **NCLC 14, 113**
    See also DLB 99
Moody, Hiram (F. III) 1961-
    See Moody, Rick
    See also CA 138; CANR 64, 112
Moody, Minerva
    See Alcott, Louisa May
Moody, Rick .... **CLC 147**
    See Moody, Hiram (F. III)
Moody, William Vaughan
    1869-1910 .... **TCLC 105**
    See also CA 110; 178; DLB 7, 54; RGAL 4
Mooney, Edward 1951-
    See Mooney, Ted
    See also CA 130
Mooney, Ted .... **CLC 25**
    See Mooney, Edward
Moorcock, Michael (John) 1939- ...... CLC 5,
    27, 58
    See Bradbury, Edward P.
    See also AAYA 26; CA 45-48; CAAS 5;
    CANR 2, 17, 38, 64, 122; CN 7; DLB 14,
    231, 261; FANT; MTCW 1, 2; SATA 93;
    SCFW 2; SFW 4; SUFW 1, 2
Moore, Brian 1921-1999 ... CLC 1, 3, 5, 7, 8,
    19, 32, 90
    See Bryan, Michael
    See also BRWS 9; CA 1-4R; 174; CANR 1,
    25, 42, 63; CCA 1; CN 7; DAB; DAC;
    DAM MST; DLB 251; EWL 3; FANT;
    MTCW 1, 2; RGEL 2
Moore, Edward
    See Muir, Edwin
    See also RGEL 2
Moore, G. E. 1873-1958 .... **TCLC 89**
    See also DLB 262
Moore, George Augustus
    1852-1933 .... **SSC 19; TCLC 7**
    See also BRW 6; CA 104; 177; DLB 10,
    18, 57, 135; EWL 3; RGEL 2; RGSF 2
Moore, Lorrie .... CLC 39, 45, 68
    See Moore, Marie Lorena
    See also AMWS 10; DLB 234; SSFS 19
Moore, Marianne (Craig)
    1887-1972 ... CLC 1, 2, 4, 8, 10, 13, 19,
    47; PC 4, 49; WLCS
    See also AMW; CA 1-4R; 33-36R; CANR
    3, 61; CDALB 1929-1941; DA; DA3;
    DAB; DAC; DAM MST, POET; DLB 45;
    DLBD 7; EWL 3; EXPP; MAWW;
    MTCW 1, 2; PAB; PFS 14, 17; RGAL 4;
    SATA 20; TUS; WP
Moore, Marie Lorena 1957- .... **CLC 165**
    See Moore, Lorrie
    See also CA 116; CANR 39, 83; CN 7; DLB
    234

Oliphant, Margaret (Oliphant Wilson)
    1828-1897 .... **NCLC 11, 61; SSC 25**
    See Oliphant, Mrs.
    See also BRWS 10; DLB 18, 159, 190;
    HGG; RGEL 2; RGSF 2

Oliver, Mary 1935- .... **CLC 19, 34, 98**
    See also AMWS 7; CA 21-24R; CANR 9,
    43, 84, 92; CP 7; CWP; DLB 5, 193;
    EWL 3; PFS 15

Olivier, Laurence (Kerr) 1907-1989 . **CLC 20**
    See also CA 111; 150; 129

Olsen, Tillie 1912- ... **CLC 4, 13, 114; SSC 11**
    See also AAYA 51; AMWS 13; BYA 11;
    CA 1-4R; CANR 1, 43, 74, 132;
    CDALBS; CN 7; DA; DA3; DAB; DAC;
    DAM MST; DLB 28, 206; DLBY 1980;
    EWL 3; EXPS; FW; MTCW 1, 2; RGAL
    4; RGSF 2; SSFS 1; TUS

Olson, Charles (John) 1910-1970 .. **CLC 1, 2,
    5, 6, 9, 11, 29; PC 19**
    See also AMWS 2; CA 13-16; 25-28R;
    CABS 2; CANR 35, 61; CAP 1; DAM
    POET; DLB 5, 16, 193; EWL 3; MTCW
    1, 2; RGAL 4; WP

Olson, Toby 1937- .... **CLC 28**
    See also CA 65-68; CANR 9, 31, 84; CP 7

Olyesha, Yuri
    See Olesha, Yuri (Karlovich)

Olympiodorus of Thebes c. 375-c.
    430 .... **CMLC 59**

Omar Khayyam
    See Khayyam, Omar
    See also RGWL 2, 3

Ondaatje, (Philip) Michael 1943- .... **CLC 14,
    29, 51, 76, 180; PC 28**
    See also CA 77-80; CANR 42, 74, 109, 133;
    CN 7; CP 7; DA3; DAB; DAC; DAM
    MST; DLB 60; EWL 3; LATS 1:2; LMFS
    2; MTCW 2; PFS 8, 19; TWA; WWE 1

Oneal, Elizabeth 1934-
    See Oneal, Zibby
    See also CA 106; CANR 28, 84; MAICYA
    1, 2; SATA 30, 82; YAW

Oneal, Zibby .... **CLC 30**
    See Oneal, Elizabeth
    See also AAYA 5, 41; BYA 13; CLR 13;
    JRDA; WYA

O'Neill, Eugene (Gladstone)
    1888-1953 ... **DC 20; TCLC 1, 6, 27, 49;
    WLC**
    See also AAYA 54; AITN 1; AMW; AMWC
    1; CA 110; 132; CAD; CANR 131;
    CDALB 1929-1941; DA; DA3; DAB;
    DAC; DAM DRAM, MST; DFS 2, 4, 5,
    6, 9, 11, 12, 16, 20; DLB 7; EWL 3; LAIT
    3; LMFS 2; MTCW 1, 2; RGAL 4; TUS

Onetti, Juan Carlos 1909-1994 ... **CLC 7, 10;
    HLCS 2; SSC 23; TCLC 131**
    See also CA 85-88; 145; CANR 32, 63; CD-
    WLB 3; CWW 2; DAM MULT, NOV;
    DLB 113; EWL 3; HW 1, 2; LAW;
    MTCW 1, 2; RGSF 2

O Nuallain, Brian 1911-1966
    See O'Brien, Flann
    See also CA 21-22; 25-28R; CAP 2; DLB
    231; FANT; TEA

Ophuls, Max 1902-1957 .... **TCLC 79**
    See also CA 113

Opie, Amelia 1769-1853 .... **NCLC 65**
    See also DLB 116, 159; RGEL 2

Oppen, George 1908-1984 ..... **CLC 7, 13, 34;
    PC 35; TCLC 107**
    See also CA 13-16R; 113; CANR 8, 82;
    DLB 5, 165

Oppenheim, E(dward) Phillips
    1866-1946 .... **TCLC 45**
    See also CA 111; 202; CMW 4; DLB 70

Opuls, Max
    See Ophuls, Max

Orage, A(lfred) R(ichard)
    1873-1934 .... **TCLC 157**
    See also CA 122

Origen c. 185-c. 254 .... **CMLC 19**

Orlovitz, Gil 1918-1973 .... **CLC 22**
    See also CA 77-80; 45-48; DLB 2, 5

Orris
    See Ingelow, Jean

Ortega y Gasset, Jose 1883-1955 ...... **HLC 2;
    TCLC 9**
    See also CA 106; 130; DAM MULT; EW 9;
    EWL 3; HW 1, 2; MTCW 1, 2

Ortese, Anna Maria 1914-1998 .... **CLC 89**
    See also DLB 177; EWL 3

Ortiz, Simon J(oseph) 1941- .... **CLC 45;
    NNAL; PC 17**
    See also AMWS 4; CA 134; CANR 69, 118;
    CP 7; DAM MULT, POET; DLB 120,
    175, 256; EXPP; PFS 4, 16; RGAL 4

Orton, Joe ...... **CLC 4, 13, 43; DC 3; TCLC
    157**
    See Orton, John Kingsley
    See also BRWS 5; CBD; CDBLB 1960 to
    Present; DFS 3, 6; DLB 13; GLL 1;
    MTCW 2; RGEL 2; TEA; WLIT 4

Orton, John Kingsley 1933-1967
    See Orton, Joe
    See also CA 85-88; CANR 35, 66; DAM
    DRAM; MTCW 1, 2

Orwell, George ...... **SSC 68; TCLC 2, 6, 15,
    31, 51, 128, 129; WLC**
    See Blair, Eric (Arthur)
    See also BPFB 3; BRW 7; BYA 5; CDBLB
    1945-1960; CLR 68; DAB; DLB 15, 98,
    195, 255; EWL 3; EXPN; LAIT 4, 5;
    LATS 1:1; NFS 3, 7; RGEL 2; SCFW 2;
    SFW 4; SSFS 4; TEA; WLIT 4; YAW

Osborne, David
    See Silverberg, Robert

Osborne, George
    See Silverberg, Robert

Osborne, John (James) 1929-1994 .... **CLC 1,
    2, 5, 11, 45; TCLC 153; WLC**
    See also BRWS 1; CA 13-16R; 147; CANR
    21, 56; CDBLB 1945-1960; DA; DAB;
    DAC; DAM DRAM, MST; DFS 4, 19;
    DLB 13; EWL 3; MTCW 1, 2; RGEL 2

Osborne, Lawrence 1958- .... **CLC 50**
    See also CA 189

Osbourne, Lloyd 1868-1947 .... **TCLC 93**

Osgood, Frances Sargent
    1811-1850 .... **NCLC 141**
    See also DLB 250

Oshima, Nagisa 1932- .... **CLC 20**
    See also CA 116; 121; CANR 78

Oskison, John Milton
    1874-1947 .... **NNAL; TCLC 35**
    See also CA 144; CANR 84; DAM MULT;
    DLB 175

Ossian c. 3rd cent. - .... **CMLC 28**
    See Macpherson, James

Ossoli, Sarah Margaret (Fuller)
    1810-1850 .... **NCLC 5, 50**
    See Fuller, Margaret; Fuller, Sarah Margaret
    See also CDALB 1640-1865; FW; LMFS 1;
    SATA 25

Ostriker, Alicia (Suskin) 1937- .... **CLC 132**
    See also CA 25-28R; CAAS 24; CANR 10,
    30, 62, 99; CWP; DLB 120; EXPP; PFS
    19

Ostrovsky, Aleksandr Nikolaevich
    See Ostrovsky, Alexander
    See also DLB 277

Ostrovsky, Alexander 1823-1886 .. **NCLC 30,
    57**
    See Ostrovsky, Aleksandr Nikolaevich

Otero, Blas de 1916-1979 .... **CLC 11**
    See also CA 89-92; DLB 134; EWL 3

O'Trigger, Sir Lucius
    See Horne, Richard Henry Hengist

Otto, Rudolf 1869-1937 .... **TCLC 85**

Otto, Whitney 1955- .... **CLC 70**
    See also CA 140; CANR 120

Otway, Thomas 1652-1685 ... **DC 24; LC 106**
    See also DAM DRAM; DLB 80; RGEL 2

Ouida .... **TCLC 43**
    See De la Ramee, Marie Louise (Ouida)
    See also DLB 18, 156; RGEL 2

Ouologuem, Yambo 1940- .... **CLC 146**
    See also CA 111; 176

Ousmane, Sembene 1923- ... **BLC 3; CLC 66**
    See Sembene, Ousmane
    See also BW 1, 3; CA 117; 125; CANR 81;
    CWW 2; MTCW 1

Ovid 43B.C.-17 .... **CMLC 7; PC 2**
    See also AW 2; CDWLB 1; DA3; DAM
    POET; DLB 211; RGWL 2, 3; WP

Owen, Hugh
    See Faust, Frederick (Schiller)

Owen, Wilfred (Edward Salter)
    1893-1918 ... **PC 19; TCLC 5, 27; WLC**
    See also BRW 6; CA 104; 141; CDBLB
    1914-1945; DA; DAB; DAC; DAM MST,
    POET; DLB 20; EWL 3; EXPP; MTCW
    2; PFS 10; RGEL 2; WLIT 4

Owens, Louis (Dean) 1948-2002 .... **NNAL**
    See also CA 137; 179; 207; CAAE 179;
    CAAS 24; CANR 71

Owens, Rochelle 1936- .... **CLC 8**
    See also CA 17-20R; CAAS 2; CAD;
    CANR 39; CD 5; CP 7; CWD; CWP

Oz, Amos 1939- ...... **CLC 5, 8, 11, 27, 33, 54;
    SSC 66**
    See also CA 53-56; CANR 27, 47, 65, 113;
    CWW 2; DAM NOV; EWL 3; MTCW 1,
    2; RGSF 2; RGWL 3

Ozick, Cynthia 1928- .... **CLC 3, 7, 28, 62,
    155; SSC 15, 60**
    See also AMWS 5; BEST 90:1; CA 17-20R;
    CANR 23, 58, 116; CN 7; CPW; DA3;
    DAM NOV, POP; DLB 28, 152, 299;
    DLBY 1982; EWL 3; EXPS; INT CANR-
    23; MTCW 1, 2; RGAL 4; RGSF 2; SSFS
    3, 12

Ozu, Yasujiro 1903-1963 .... **CLC 16**
    See also CA 112

Pabst, G. W. 1885-1967 .... **TCLC 127**

Pacheco, C.
    See Pessoa, Fernando (Antonio Nogueira)

Pacheco, Jose Emilio 1939- .... **HLC 2**
    See also CA 111; 131; CANR 65; CWW 2;
    DAM MULT; DLB 290; EWL 3; HW 1,
    2; RGSF 2

Pa Chin .... **CLC 18**
    See Li Fei-kan
    See also EWL 3

Pack, Robert 1929- .... **CLC 13**
    See also CA 1-4R; CANR 3, 44, 82; CP 7;
    DLB 5; SATA 118

Padgett, Lewis
    See Kuttner, Henry

Padilla (Lorenzo), Heberto
    1932-2000 .... **CLC 38**
    See also AITN 1; CA 123; 131; 189; CWW
    2; EWL 3; HW 1

Page, James Patrick 1944-
    See Page, Jimmy
    See also CA 204

Page, Jimmy 1944- .... **CLC 12**
    See Page, James Patrick

Page, Louise 1955- .... **CLC 40**
    See also CA 140; CANR 76; CBD; CD 5;
    CWD; DLB 233

Patton, George S(mith), Jr.
1885-1945 .... **TCLC 79**
See also CA 189

Paulding, James Kirke 1778-1860 ... **NCLC 2**
See also DLB 3, 59, 74, 250; RGAL 4

Paulin, Thomas Neilson 1949-
See Paulin, Tom
See also CA 123; 128; CANR 98; CP 7

Paulin, Tom .... **CLC 37, 177**
See Paulin, Thomas Neilson
See also DLB 40

Pausanias c. 1st cent. - .... **CMLC 36**

Paustovsky, Konstantin (Georgievich)
1892-1968 .... **CLC 40**
See also CA 93-96; 25-28R; DLB 272;
EWL 3

Pavese, Cesare 1908-1950 .... **PC 13; SSC 19;**
TCLC 3
See also CA 104; 169; DLB 128, 177; EW
12; EWL 3; PFS 20; RGSF 2; RGWL 2,
3; TWA

Pavic, Milorad 1929- .... **CLC 60**
See also CA 136; CDWLB 4; CWW 2; DLB
181; EWL 3; RGWL 3

Pavlov, Ivan Petrovich 1849-1936 . **TCLC 91**
See also CA 118; 180

Pavlova, Karolina Karlovna
1807-1893 .... **NCLC 138**
See also DLB 205

Payne, Alan
See Jakes, John (William)

Paz, Gil
See Lugones, Leopoldo

Paz, Octavio 1914-1998 . **CLC 3, 4, 6, 10, 19,**
51, 65, 119; HLC 2; PC 1, 48; WLC
See also AAYA 50; CA 73-76; 165; CANR
32, 65, 104; CWW 2; DA; DA3; DAB;
DAC; DAM MST, MULT, POET; DLB
290; DLBY 1990, 1998; DNFS 1; EWL
3; HW 1, 2; LAW; LAWS 1; MTCW 1, 2;
PFS 18; RGWL 2, 3; SSFS 13; TWA;
WLIT 1

p'Bitek, Okot 1931-1982 .... **BLC 3; CLC 96;**
TCLC 149
See also AFW; BW 2, 3; CA 124; 107;
CANR 82; DAM MULT; DLB 125; EWL
3; MTCW 1, 2; RGEL 2; WLIT 2

Peacock, Molly 1947- .... **CLC 60**
See also CA 103; CAAS 21; CANR 52, 84;
CP 7; CWP; DLB 120, 282

Peacock, Thomas Love
1785-1866 .... **NCLC 22**
See also BRW 4; DLB 96, 116; RGEL 2;
RGSF 2

Peake, Mervyn 1911-1968 .... **CLC 7, 54**
See also CA 5-8R; 25-28R; CANR 3; DLB
15, 160, 255; FANT; MTCW 1; RGEL 2;
SATA 23; SFW 4

Pearce, Philippa
See Christie, Philippa
See also CA 5-8R; CANR 4, 109; CWRI 5;
FANT; MAICYA 2

Pearl, Eric
See Elman, Richard (Martin)

Pearson, T(homas) R(eid) 1956- .... **CLC 39**
See also CA 120; 130; CANR 97; CSW;
INT CA-130

Peck, Dale 1967- .... **CLC 81**
See also CA 146; CANR 72, 127; GLL 2

Peck, John (Frederick) 1941- .... **CLC 3**
See also CA 49-52; CANR 3, 100; CP 7

Peck, Richard (Wayne) 1934- .... **CLC 21**
See also AAYA 1, 24; BYA 1, 6, 8, 11; CA
85-88; CANR 19, 38, 129; CLR 15; INT
CANR-19; JRDA; MAICYA 1, 2; SAAS
2; SATA 18, 55, 97; SATA-Essay 110;
WYA; YAW

Peck, Robert Newton 1928- .... **CLC 17**
See also AAYA 3, 43; BYA 1, 6; CA 81-84,
182; CAAE 182; CANR 31, 63, 127; CLR
45; DA; DAC; DAM MST; JRDA; LAIT
3; MAICYA 1, 2; SAAS 1; SATA 21, 62,
111; SATA-Essay 108; WYA; YAW

Peckinpah, (David) Sam(uel)
1925-1984 .... **CLC 20**
See also CA 109; 114; CANR 82

Pedersen, Knut 1859-1952
See Hamsun, Knut
See also CA 104; 119; CANR 63; MTCW
1, 2

Peele, George .... **LC 115**
See also BW 1; DLB 62, 167; RGEL 2

Peeslake, Gaffer
See Durrell, Lawrence (George)

Peguy, Charles (Pierre)
1873-1914 .... **TCLC 10**
See also CA 107; 193; DLB 258; EWL 3;
GFL 1789 to the Present

Peirce, Charles Sanders
1839-1914 .... **TCLC 81**
See also CA 194; DLB 270

Pellicer, Carlos 1897(?)-1977 .... **HLCS 2**
See also CA 153; 69-72; DLB 290; EWL 3;
HW 1

Pena, Ramon del Valle y
See Valle-Inclan, Ramon (Maria) del

Pendennis, Arthur Esquir
See Thackeray, William Makepeace

Penn, Arthur
See Matthews, (James) Brander

Penn, William 1644-1718 .... **LC 25**
See also DLB 24

PEPECE
See Prado (Calvo), Pedro

Pepys, Samuel 1633-1703 ... **LC 11, 58; WLC**
See also BRW 2; CDBLB 1660-1789; DA;
DA3; DAB; DAC; DAM MST; DLB 101,
213; NCFS 4; RGEL 2; TEA; WLIT 3

Percy, Thomas 1729-1811 .... **NCLC 95**
See also DLB 104

Percy, Walker 1916-1990 .... **CLC 2, 3, 6, 8,**
14, 18, 47, 65
See also AMWS 3; BPFB 3; CA 1-4R; 131;
CANR 1, 23, 64; CPW; CSW; DA3;
DAM NOV, POP; DLB 2; DLBY 1980,
1990; EWL 3; MTCW 1, 2; RGAL 4;
TUS

Percy, William Alexander
1885-1942 .... **TCLC 84**
See also CA 163; MTCW 2

Perec, Georges 1936-1982 .... **CLC 56, 116**
See also CA 141; DLB 83, 299; EWL 3;
GFL 1789 to the Present; RGWL 3

Pereda (y Sanchez de Porrua), Jose Maria
de 1833-1906 .... **TCLC 16**
See also CA 117

Pereda y Porrua, Jose Maria de
See Pereda (y Sanchez de Porrua), Jose
Maria de

Peregoy, George Weems
See Mencken, H(enry) L(ouis)

Perelman, S(idney) J(oseph)
1904-1979 .. **CLC 3, 5, 9, 15, 23, 44, 49;**
SSC 32
See also AITN 1, 2; BPFB 3; CA 73-76;
89-92; CANR 18; DAM DRAM; DLB 11,
44; MTCW 1, 2; RGAL 4

Peret, Benjamin 1899-1959 .... **PC 33; TCLC**
20
See also CA 117; 186; GFL 1789 to the
Present

Peretz, Isaac Leib
See Peretz, Isaac Loeb
See also CA 201

Peretz, Isaac Loeb 1851(?)-1915 ...... **SSC 26;**
TCLC 16
See Peretz, Isaac Leib
See also CA 109

Peretz, Yitzkhok Leibush
See Peretz, Isaac Loeb

Perez Galdos, Benito 1843-1920 ..... **HLCS 2;**
TCLC 27
See Galdos, Benito Perez
See also CA 125; 153; EWL 3; HW 1;
RGWL 2, 3

Peri Rossi, Cristina 1941- .. **CLC 156; HLCS**
2
See also CA 131; CANR 59, 81; CWW 2;
DLB 145, 290; EWL 3; HW 1, 2

Perlata
See Peret, Benjamin

Perloff, Marjorie G(abrielle)
1931- .... **CLC 137**
See also CA 57-60; CANR 7, 22, 49, 104

Perrault, Charles 1628-1703 .... **LC 2, 56**
See also BYA 4; CLR 79; DLB 268; GFL
Beginnings to 1789; MAICYA 1, 2;
RGWL 2, 3; SATA 25; WCH

Perry, Anne 1938- .... **CLC 126**
See also CA 101; CANR 22, 50, 84; CMW
4; CN 7; CPW; DLB 276

Perry, Brighton
See Sherwood, Robert E(mmet)

Perse, St.-John
See Leger, (Marie-Rene Auguste) Alexis
Saint-Leger

Perse, Saint-John
See Leger, (Marie-Rene Auguste) Alexis
Saint-Leger
See also DLB 258; RGWL 3

Persius 34-62 .... **CMLC 74**
See also AW 2; DLB 211; RGWL 2, 3

Perutz, Leo(pold) 1882-1957 .... **TCLC 60**
See also CA 147; DLB 81

Peseenz, Tulio F.
See Lopez y Fuentes, Gregorio

Pesetsky, Bette 1932- .... **CLC 28**
See also CA 133; DLB 130

Peshkov, Alexei Maximovich 1868-1936
See Gorky, Maxim
See also CA 105; 141; CANR 83; DA;
DAC; DAM DRAM, MST, NOV; MTCW
2

Pessoa, Fernando (Antonio Nogueira)
1888-1935 ..... **HLC 2; PC 20; TCLC 27**
See also CA 125; 183; DAM MULT; DLB
287; EW 10; EWL 3; RGWL 2, 3; WP

Peterkin, Julia Mood 1880-1961 ...... **CLC 31**
See also CA 102; DLB 9

Peters, Joan K(aren) 1945- .... **CLC 39**
See also CA 158; CANR 109

Peters, Robert L(ouis) 1924- .... **CLC 7**
See also CA 13-16R; CAAS 8; CP 7; DLB
105

Petofi, Sandor 1823-1849 .... **NCLC 21**
See also RGWL 2, 3

Petrakis, Harry Mark 1923- .... **CLC 3**
See also CA 9-12R; CANR 4, 30, 85; CN 7

Petrarch 1304-1374 .... **CMLC 20; PC 8**
See also DA3; DAM POET; EW 2; LMFS
1; RGWL 2, 3

Petronius c. 20-66 .... **CMLC 34**
See also AW 2; CDWLB 1; DLB 211;
RGWL 2, 3

Petrov, Evgeny .... **TCLC 21**
See Kataev, Evgeny Petrovich

Petry, Ann (Lane) 1908-1997 .. **CLC 1, 7, 18;**
TCLC 112
See also AFAW 1, 2; BPFB 3; BW 1, 3;
BYA 2; CA 5-8R; 157; CAAS 6; CANR
4, 46; CLR 12; CN 7; DLB 76; EWL 3;
JRDA; LAIT 1; MAICYA 1, 2; MAIC-
YAS 1; MTCW 1; RGAL 4; SATA 5;
SATA-Obit 94; TUS

1, 3, 9; RGAL 4; RGSF 2; SATA 23; SCFW 2; SFW 4; SSFS 2, 4, 7, 8, 16; SUFW; TUS; WP; WYA

Poet of Titchfield Street, The
  See Pound, Ezra (Weston Loomis)

Pohl, Frederik 1919- .... **CLC 18; SSC 25**
  See also AAYA 24; CA 61-64, 188; CAAE 188; CAAS 1; CANR 11, 37, 81; CN 7; DLB 8; INT CANR-11; MTCW 1, 2; SATA 24; SCFW 2; SFW 4

Poirier, Louis 1910-
  See Gracq, Julien
  See also CA 122; 126

Poitier, Sidney 1927- .... **CLC 26**
  See also AAYA 60; BW 1; CA 117; CANR 94

Pokagon, Simon 1830-1899 .... **NNAL**
  See also DAM MULT

Polanski, Roman 1933- .... **CLC 16, 178**
  See also CA 77-80

Poliakoff, Stephen 1952- .... **CLC 38**
  See also CA 106; CANR 116; CBD; CD 5; DLB 13

Police, The
  See Copeland, Stewart (Armstrong); Summers, Andrew James

Polidori, John William 1795-1821 . **NCLC 51**
  See also DLB 116; HGG

Pollitt, Katha 1949- .... **CLC 28, 122**
  See also CA 120; 122; CANR 66, 108; MTCW 1, 2

Pollock, (Mary) Sharon 1936- .... **CLC 50**
  See also CA 141; CANR 132; CD 5; CWD; DAC; DAM DRAM, MST; DFS 3; DLB 60; FW

Pollock, Sharon 1936- .... **DC 20**

Polo, Marco 1254-1324 .... **CMLC 15**

Polonsky, Abraham (Lincoln)
  1910-1999 .... **CLC 92**
  See also CA 104; 187; DLB 26; INT CA-104

Polybius c. 200B.C.-c. 118B.C. ...... **CMLC 17**
  See also AW 1; DLB 176; RGWL 2, 3

Pomerance, Bernard 1940- .... **CLC 13**
  See also CA 101; CAD; CANR 49, 134; CD 5; DAM DRAM; DFS 9; LAIT 2

Ponge, Francis 1899-1988 .... **CLC 6, 18**
  See also CA 85-88; 126; CANR 40, 86; DAM POET; DLBY 2002; EWL 3; GFL 1789 to the Present; RGWL 2, 3

Poniatowska, Elena 1933- . **CLC 140; HLC 2**
  See also CA 101; CANR 32, 66, 107; CDWLB 3; CWW 2; DAM MULT; DLB 113; EWL 3; HW 1, 2; LAWS 1; WLIT 1

Pontoppidan, Henrik 1857-1943 .... **TCLC 29**
  See also CA 170; DLB 300

Ponty, Maurice Merleau
  See Merleau-Ponty, Maurice

Poole, Josephine .... **CLC 17**
  See Helyar, Jane Penelope Josephine
  See also SAAS 2; SATA 5

Popa, Vasko 1922-1991 .... **CLC 19**
  See also CA 112; 148; CDWLB 4; DLB 181; EWL 3; RGWL 2, 3

Pope, Alexander 1688-1744 ...... **LC 3, 58, 60, 64; PC 26; WLC**
  See also BRW 3; BRWC 1; BRWR 1; CD-BLB 1660-1789; DA; DA3; DAB; DAC; DAM MST, POET; DLB 95, 101, 213; EXPP; PAB; PFS 12; RGEL 2; WLIT 3; WP

Popov, Evgenii Anatol'evich
  See Popov, Yevgeny
  See also DLB 285

Popov, Yevgeny .... **CLC 59**
  See Popov, Evgenii Anatol'evich

Poquelin, Jean-Baptiste
  See Moliere

Porete, Marguerite c. 1250-1310 .. **CMLC 73**
  See also DLB 208

Porphyry c. 233-c. 305 .... **CMLC 71**

Porter, Connie (Rose) 1959(?)- .... **CLC 70**
  See also BW 2, 3; CA 142; CANR 90, 109; SATA 81, 129

Porter, Gene(va Grace) Stratton .. **TCLC 21**
  See Stratton-Porter, Gene(va Grace)
  See also BPFB 3; CA 112; CWRI 5; RHW

Porter, Katherine Anne 1890-1980 ... **CLC 1, 3, 7, 10, 13, 15, 27, 101; SSC 4, 31, 43**
  See also AAYA 42; AITN 2; AMW; BPFB 3; CA 1-4R; 101; CANR 1, 65; CDALBS; DA; DA3; DAB; DAC; DAM MST, NOV; DLB 4, 9, 102; DLBD 12; DLBY 1980; EWL 3; EXPS; LAIT 3; MAWW; MTCW 1, 2; NFS 14; RGAL 4; RGSF 2; SATA 39; SATA-Obit 23; SSFS 1, 8, 11, 16; TUS

Porter, Peter (Neville Frederick)
  1929- .... **CLC 5, 13, 33**
  See also CA 85-88; CP 7; DLB 40, 289; WWE 1

Porter, William Sydney 1862-1910 .
  See Henry, O.
  See also CA 104; 131; CDALB 1865-1917; DA; DA3; DAB; DAC; DAM MST; DLB 12, 78, 79; MTCW 1, 2; TUS; YABC 2

Portillo (y Pacheco), Jose Lopez
  See Lopez Portillo (y Pacheco), Jose

Portillo Trambley, Estela
  1927-1998 .... **HLC 2; TCLC 163**
  See Trambley, Estela Portillo
  See also CANR 32; DAM MULT; DLB 209; HW 1

Posey, Alexander (Lawrence)
  1873-1908 .... **NNAL**
  See also CA 144; CANR 80; DAM MULT; DLB 175

Posse, Abel .... **CLC 70**

Post, Melville Davisson
  1869-1930 .... **TCLC 39**
  See also CA 110; 202; CMW 4

Potok, Chaim 1929-2002 ... **CLC 2, 7, 14, 26, 112**
  See also AAYA 15, 50; AITN 1, 2; BPFB 3; BYA 1; CA 17-20R; 208; CANR 19, 35, 64, 98; CLR 92; CN 7; DA3; DAM NOV; DLB 28, 152; EXPN; INT CANR-19; LAIT 4; MTCW 1, 2; NFS 4; SATA 33, 106; SATA-Obit 134; TUS; YAW

Potok, Herbert Harold -2002
  See Potok, Chaim

Potok, Herman Harold
  See Potok, Chaim

Potter, Dennis (Christopher George)
  1935-1994 .... **CLC 58, 86, 123**
  See also BRWS 10; CA 107; 145; CANR 33, 61; CBD; DLB 233; MTCW 1

Pound, Ezra (Weston Loomis)
  1885-1972 ... **CLC 1, 2, 3, 4, 5, 7, 10, 13, 18, 34, 48, 50, 112; PC 4; WLC**
  See also AAYA 47; AMW; AMWR 1; CA 5-8R; 37-40R; CANR 40; CDALB 1917-1929; DA; DA3; DAB; DAC; DAM MST, POET; DLB 4, 45, 63; DLBD 15; EFS 2; EWL 3; EXPP; LMFS 2; MTCW 1, 2; PAB; PFS 2, 8, 16; RGAL 4; TUS; WP

Povod, Reinaldo 1959-1994 .... **CLC 44**
  See also CA 136; 146; CANR 83

Powell, Adam Clayton, Jr.
  1908-1972 .... **BLC 3; CLC 89**
  See also BW 1, 3; CA 102; 33-36R; CANR 86; DAM MULT

Powell, Anthony (Dymoke)
  1905-2000 .... **CLC 1, 3, 7, 9, 10, 31**
  See also BRW 7; CA 1-4R; 189; CANR 1, 32, 62, 107; CDBLB 1945-1960; CN 7; DLB 15; EWL 3; MTCW 1, 2; RGEL 2; TEA

Powell, Dawn 1896(?)-1965 .... **CLC 66**
  See also CA 5-8R; CANR 121; DLBY 1997

Powell, Padgett 1952- .... **CLC 34**
  See also CA 126; CANR 63, 101; CSW; DLB 234; DLBY 01

Powell, (Oval) Talmage 1920-2000
  See Queen, Ellery
  See also CA 5-8R; CANR 2, 80

Power, Susan 1961- .... **CLC 91**
  See also BYA 14; CA 160; CANR 135; NFS 11

Powers, J(ames) F(arl) 1917-1999 ..... **CLC 1, 4, 8, 57; SSC 4**
  See also CA 1-4R; 181; CANR 2, 61; CN 7; DLB 130; MTCW 1; RGAL 4; RGSF 2

Powers, John J(ames) 1945-
  See Powers, John R.
  See also CA 69-72

Powers, John R. .... **CLC 66**
  See Powers, John J(ames)

Powers, Richard (S.) 1957- .... **CLC 93**
  See also AMWS 9; BPFB 3; CA 148; CANR 80; CN 7

Pownall, David 1938- .... **CLC 10**
  See also CA 89-92; 180; CAAS 18; CANR 49, 101; CBD; CD 5; CN 7; DLB 14

Powys, John Cowper 1872-1963 ... **CLC 7, 9, 15, 46, 125**
  See also CA 85-88; CANR 106; DLB 15, 255; EWL 3; FANT; MTCW 1, 2; RGEL 2; SUFW

Powys, T(heodore) F(rancis)
  1875-1953 .... **TCLC 9**
  See also BRWS 8; CA 106; 189; DLB 36, 162; EWL 3; FANT; RGEL 2; SUFW

Prado (Calvo), Pedro 1886-1952 ... **TCLC 75**
  See also CA 131; DLB 283; HW 1; LAW

Prager, Emily 1952- .... **CLC 56**
  See also CA 204

Pratchett, Terry 1948- .... **CLC 197**
  See also AAYA 19, 54; BPFB 3; CA 143; CANR 87, 126; CLR 64; CN 7; CPW; CWRI 5; FANT; SATA 82, 139; SFW 4; SUFW 2

Pratolini, Vasco 1913-1991 .... **TCLC 124**
  See also CA 211; DLB 177; EWL 3; RGWL 2, 3

Pratt, E(dwin) J(ohn) 1883(?)-1964 . **CLC 19**
  See also CA 141; 93-96; CANR 77; DAC; DAM POET; DLB 92; EWL 3; RGEL 2; TWA

Premchand .... **TCLC 21**
  See Srivastava, Dhanpat Rai
  See also EWL 3

Preseren, France 1800-1849 .... **NCLC 127**
  See also CDWLB 4; DLB 147

Preussler, Otfried 1923- .... **CLC 17**
  See also CA 77-80; SATA 24

Prevert, Jacques (Henri Marie)
  1900-1977 .... **CLC 15**
  See also CA 77-80; 69-72; CANR 29, 61; DLB 258; EWL 3; GFL 1789 to the Present; IDFW 3, 4; MTCW 1; RGWL 2, 3; SATA-Obit 30

Prevost, (Antoine Francois)
  1697-1763 .... **LC 1**
  See also EW 4; GFL Beginnings to 1789; RGWL 2, 3

Price, (Edward) Reynolds 1933- ... **CLC 3, 6, 13, 43, 50, 63; SSC 22**
  See also AMWS 6; CA 1-4R; CANR 1, 37, 57, 87, 128; CN 7; CSW; DAM NOV; DLB 2, 218, 278; EWL 3; INT CANR-37; NFS 18

Price, Richard 1949- .... **CLC 6, 12**
  See also CA 49-52; CANR 3; DLBY 1981

Prichard, Katharine Susannah
1883-1969 .... **CLC 46**
See also CA 11-12; CANR 33; CAP 1; DLB
260; MTCW 1; RGEL 2; RGSF 2; SATA
66

Priestley, J(ohn) B(oynton)
1894-1984 .... **CLC 2, 5, 9, 34**
See also BRW 7; CA 9-12R; 113; CANR
33; CDBLB 1914-1945; DA3; DAM
DRAM, NOV; DLB 10, 34, 77, 100, 139;
DLBY 1984; EWL 3; MTCW 1, 2; RGEL
2; SFW 4

Prince 1958- .... **CLC 35**
See also CA 213

Prince, F(rank) T(empleton)
1912-2003 .... **CLC 22**
See also CA 101; 219; CANR 43, 79; CP 7;
DLB 20

Prince Kropotkin
See Kropotkin, Peter (Aleksieevich)

Prior, Matthew 1664-1721 .... **LC 4**
See also DLB 95; RGEL 2

Prishvin, Mikhail 1873-1954 .... **TCLC 75**
See Prishvin, Mikhail Mikhailovich

Prishvin, Mikhail Mikhailovich
See Prishvin, Mikhail
See also DLB 272; EWL 3

Pritchard, William H(arrison)
1932- .... **CLC 34**
See also CA 65-68; CANR 23, 95; DLB
111

Pritchett, V(ictor) S(awdon)
1900-1997 ... **CLC 5, 13, 15, 41; SSC 14**
See also BPFB 3; BRWS 3; CA 61-64; 157;
CANR 31, 63; CN 7; DA3; DAM NOV;
DLB 15, 139; EWL 3; MTCW 1, 2;
RGEL 2; RGSF 2; TEA

Private 19022
See Manning, Frederic

Probst, Mark 1925- .... **CLC 59**
See also CA 130

Prokosch, Frederic 1908-1989 ...... **CLC 4, 48**
See also CA 73-76; 128; CANR 82; DLB
48; MTCW 2

Propertius, Sextus c. 50B.C.-c.
16B.C. .... **CMLC 32**
See also AW 2; CDWLB 1; DLB 211;
RGWL 2, 3

Prophet, The
See Dreiser, Theodore (Herman Albert)

Prose, Francine 1947- .... **CLC 45**
See also CA 109; 112; CANR 46, 95, 132;
DLB 234; SATA 101, 149

Proudhon
See Cunha, Euclides (Rodrigues Pimenta)
da

Proulx, Annie
See Proulx, E(dna) Annie

Proulx, E(dna) Annie 1935- ...... **CLC 81, 158**
See also AMWS 7; BPFB 3; CA 145;
CANR 65, 110; CN 7; CPW 1; DA3;
DAM POP; MTCW 2; SSFS 18

Proust, (Valentin-Louis-George-Eugene)
Marcel 1871-1922 ..... **SSC 75; TCLC 7,
13, 33, 161; WLC**
See also AAYA 58; BPFB 3; CA 104; 120;
CANR 110; DA; DA3; DAB; DAC; DAM
MST, NOV; DLB 65; EW 8; EWL 3; GFL
1789 to the Present; MTCW 1, 2; RGWL
2, 3; TWA

Prowler, Harley
See Masters, Edgar Lee

Prus, Boleslaw 1845-1912 .... **TCLC 48**
See also RGWL 2, 3

Pryor, Richard (Franklin Lenox Thomas)
1940- .... **CLC 26**
See also CA 122; 152

Przybyszewski, Stanislaw
1868-1927 .... **TCLC 36**
See also CA 160; DLB 66; EWL 3

Pteleon
See Grieve, C(hristopher) M(urray)
See also DAM POET

Puckett, Lute
See Masters, Edgar Lee

Puig, Manuel 1932-1990 .... **CLC 3, 5, 10, 28,
65, 133; HLC 2**
See also BPFB 3; CA 45-48; CANR 2, 32,
63; CDWLB 3; DA3; DAM MULT; DLB
113; DNFS 1; EWL 3; GLL 1; HW 1, 2;
LAW; MTCW 1, 2; RGWL 2, 3; TWA;
WLIT 1

Pulitzer, Joseph 1847-1911 .... **TCLC 76**
See also CA 114; DLB 23

Purchas, Samuel 1577(?)-1626 .... **LC 70**
See also DLB 151

Purdy, A(lfred) W(ellington)
1918-2000 .... **CLC 3, 6, 14, 50**
See also CA 81-84; 189; CAAS 17; CANR
42, 66; CP 7; DAC; DAM MST, POET;
DLB 88; PFS 5; RGEL 2

Purdy, James (Amos) 1923- .... **CLC 2, 4, 10,
28, 52**
See also AMWS 7; CA 33-36R; CAAS 1;
CANR 19, 51, 132; CN 7; DLB 2, 218;
EWL 3; INT CANR-19; MTCW 1; RGAL
4

Pure, Simon
See Swinnerton, Frank Arthur

Pushkin, Aleksandr Sergeevich
See Pushkin, Alexander (Sergeyevich)
See also DLB 205

Pushkin, Alexander (Sergeyevich)
1799-1837 ...... **NCLC 3, 27, 83; PC 10;
SSC 27, 55; WLC**
See Pushkin, Aleksandr Sergeevich
See also DA; DA3; DAB; DAC; DAM
DRAM, MST, POET; EW 5; EXPS; RGSF
2; RGWL 2, 3; SATA 61; SSFS 9; TWA

P'u Sung-ling 1640-1715 .... **LC 49; SSC 31**

Putnam, Arthur Lee
See Alger, Horatio, Jr.

Puzo, Mario 1920-1999 .... **CLC 1, 2, 6, 36,
107**
See also BPFB 3; CA 65-68; 185; CANR 4,
42, 65, 99, 131; CN 7; CPW; DA3; DAM
NOV; POP; DLB 6; MTCW 1, 2; NFS 16;
RGAL 4

Pygge, Edward
See Barnes, Julian (Patrick)

Pyle, Ernest Taylor 1900-1945
See Pyle, Ernie
See also CA 115; 160

Pyle, Ernie .... **TCLC 75**
See Pyle, Ernest Taylor
See also DLB 29; MTCW 2

Pyle, Howard 1853-1911 .... **TCLC 81**
See also AAYA 57; BYA 2, 4; CA 109; 137;
CLR 22; DLB 42, 188; DLBD 13; LAIT
1; MAICYA 1, 2; SATA 16, 100; WCH;
YAW

Pym, Barbara (Mary Crampton)
1913-1980 .... **CLC 13, 19, 37, 111**
See also BPFB 3; BRWS 2; CA 13-14; 97-
100; CANR 13, 34; CAP 1; DLB 14, 207;
DLBY 1987; EWL 3; MTCW 1, 2; RGEL
2; TEA

Pynchon, Thomas (Ruggles, Jr.)
1937- ...... **CLC 2, 3, 6, 9, 11, 18, 33, 62,
72, 123, 192; SSC 14; WLC**
See also AMWS 2; BEST 90:2; BPFB 3;
CA 17-20R; CANR 22, 46, 73; CN 7;
CPW 1; DA; DA3; DAB; DAC; DAM
MST, NOV, POP; DLB 2, 173; EWL 3;
MTCW 1, 2; RGAL 4; SFW 4; TUS

Pythagoras c. 582B.C.-c. 507B.C. . **CMLC 22**
See also DLB 176

Rabelais, Francois 1494-1553 .... **LC 5, 60; WLC**
See also DA; DAB; DAC; DAM MST; EW 2; GFL Beginnings to 1789; LMFS 1; RGWL 2, 3; TWA

Rabinovitch, Sholem 1859-1916
See Aleichem, Sholom
See also CA 104

Rabinyan, Dorit 1972- .... **CLC 119**
See also CA 170

Rachilde
See Vallette, Marguerite Eymery; Vallette, Marguerite Eymery
See also EWL 3

Racine, Jean 1639-1699 .... **LC 28, 113**
See also DA3; DAB; DAM MST; DLB 268; EW 3; GFL Beginnings to 1789; LMFS 1; RGWL 2, 3; TWA

Radcliffe, Ann (Ward) 1764-1823 ... **NCLC 6, 55, 106**
See also DLB 39, 178; HGG; LMFS 1; RGEL 2; SUFW; WLIT 3

Radclyffe-Hall, Marguerite
See Hall, (Marguerite) Radclyffe

Radiguet, Raymond 1903-1923 ...... **TCLC 29**
See also CA 162; DLB 65; EWL 3; GFL 1789 to the Present; RGWL 2, 3

Radnoti, Miklos 1909-1944 .... **TCLC 16**
See also CA 118; 212; CDWLB 4; DLB 215; EWL 3; RGWL 2, 3

Rado, James 1939- .... **CLC 17**
See also CA 105

Radvanyi, Netty 1900-1983
See Seghers, Anna
See also CA 85-88; 110; CANR 82

Rae, Ben
See Griffiths, Trevor

Raeburn, John (Hay) 1941- .... **CLC 34**
See also CA 57-60

Ragni, Gerome 1942-1991 .... **CLC 17**
See also CA 105; 134

Rahv, Philip .... **CLC 24**
See Greenberg, Ivan
See also DLB 137

Raimund, Ferdinand Jakob 1790-1836 .... **NCLC 69**
See also DLB 90

Raine, Craig (Anthony) 1944- .. **CLC 32, 103**
See also CA 108; CANR 29, 51, 103; CP 7; DLB 40; PFS 7

Raine, Kathleen (Jessie) 1908-2003 .. **CLC 7, 45**
See also CA 85-88; 218; CANR 46, 109; CP 7; DLB 20; EWL 3; MTCW 1; RGEL 2

Rainis, Janis 1865-1929 .... **TCLC 29**
See also CA 170; CDWLB 4; DLB 220; EWL 3

Rakosi, Carl .... **CLC 47**
See Rawley, Callman
See also CA 228; CAAS 5; CP 7; DLB 193

Ralegh, Sir Walter
See Raleigh, Sir Walter
See also BRW 1; RGEL 2; WP

Raleigh, Richard
See Lovecraft, H(oward) P(hillips)

Raleigh, Sir Walter 1554(?)-1618 .... **LC 31, 39; PC 31**
See Ralegh, Sir Walter
See also CDBLB Before 1660; DLB 172; EXPP; PFS 14; TEA

Rallentando, H. P.
See Sayers, Dorothy L(eigh)

Ramal, Walter
See de la Mare, Walter (John)

Ramana Maharshi 1879-1950 .... **TCLC 84**

Ramoacn y Cajal, Santiago 1852-1934 .... **TCLC 93**

Ramon, Juan
See Jimenez (Mantecon), Juan Ramon

Ramos, Graciliano 1892-1953 .... **TCLC 32**
See also CA 167; DLB 307; EWL 3; HW 2; LAW; WLIT 1

Rampersad, Arnold 1941- .... **CLC 44**
See also BW 2, 3; CA 127; 133; CANR 81; DLB 111; INT CA-133

Rampling, Anne
See Rice, Anne
See also GLL 2

Ramsay, Allan 1686(?)-1758 .... **LC 29**
See also DLB 95; RGEL 2

Ramsay, Jay
See Campbell, (John) Ramsey

Ramuz, Charles-Ferdinand 1878-1947 .... **TCLC 33**
See also CA 165; EWL 3

Rand, Ayn 1905-1982 ...... **CLC 3, 30, 44, 79; WLC**
See also AAYA 10; AMWS 4; BPFB 3; BYA 12; CA 13-16R; 105; CANR 27, 73; CDALBS; CPW; DA; DA3; DAC; DAM MST, NOV, POP; DLB 227, 279; MTCW 1, 2; NFS 10, 16; RGAL 4; SFW 4; TUS; YAW

Randall, Dudley (Felker) 1914-2000 . **BLC 3; CLC 1, 135**
See also BW 1, 3; CA 25-28R; 189; CANR 23, 82; DAM MULT; DLB 41; PFS 5

Randall, Robert
See Silverberg, Robert

Ranger, Ken
See Creasey, John

Rank, Otto 1884-1939 .... **TCLC 115**

Ransom, John Crowe 1888-1974 .. **CLC 2, 4, 5, 11, 24; PC 61**
See also AMW; CA 5-8R; 49-52; CANR 6, 34; CDALBS; DA3; DAM POET; DLB 45, 63; EWL 3; EXPP; MTCW 1, 2; RGAL 4; TUS

Rao, Raja 1909- .... **CLC 25, 56**
See also CA 73-76; CANR 51; CN 7; DAM NOV; EWL 3; MTCW 1, 2; RGEL 2; RGSF 2

Raphael, Frederic (Michael) 1931- ... **CLC 2, 14**
See also CA 1-4R; CANR 1, 86; CN 7; DLB 14

Ratcliffe, James P.
See Mencken, H(enry) L(ouis)

Rathbone, Julian 1935- .... **CLC 41**
See also CA 101; CANR 34, 73

Rattigan, Terence (Mervyn) 1911-1977 .... **CLC 7; DC 18**
See also BRWS 7; CA 85-88; 73-76; CBD; CDBLB 1945-1960; DAM DRAM; DFS 8; DLB 13; IDFW 3, 4; MTCW 1, 2; RGEL 2

Ratushinskaya, Irina 1954- .... **CLC 54**
See also CA 129; CANR 68; CWW 2

Raven, Simon (Arthur Noel) 1927-2001 .... **CLC 14**
See also CA 81-84; 197; CANR 86; CN 7; DLB 271

Ravenna, Michael
See Welty, Eudora (Alice)

Rawley, Callman 1903-2004
See Rakosi, Carl
See also CA 21-24R; CANR 12, 32, 91

Rawlings, Marjorie Kinnan 1896-1953 .... **TCLC 4**
See also AAYA 20; AMWS 10; ANW; BPFB 3; BYA 3; CA 104; 137; CANR 74; CLR 63; DLB 9, 22, 102; DLBD 17; JRDA; MAICYA 1, 2; MTCW 2; RGAL 4; SATA 100; WCH; YABC 1; YAW

Ray, Satyajit 1921-1992 .... **CLC 16, 76**
See also CA 114; 137; DAM MULT

Read, Herbert Edward 1893-1968 ..... **CLC 4**
See also BRW 6; CA 85-88; 25-28R; DLB 20, 149; EWL 3; PAB; RGEL 2

Read, Piers Paul 1941- .... **CLC 4, 10, 25**
See also CA 21-24R; CANR 38, 86; CN 7; DLB 14; SATA 21

Reade, Charles 1814-1884 .... **NCLC 2, 74**
See also DLB 21; RGEL 2

Reade, Hamish
See Gray, Simon (James Holliday)

Reading, Peter 1946- .... **CLC 47**
See also BRWS 8; CA 103; CANR 46, 96; CP 7; DLB 40

Reaney, James 1926- .... **CLC 13**
See also CA 41-44R; CAAS 15; CANR 42; CD 5; CP 7; DAC; DAM MST; DLB 68; RGEL 2; SATA 43

Rebreanu, Liviu 1885-1944 .... **TCLC 28**
See also CA 165; DLB 220; EWL 3

Rechy, John (Francisco) 1934- ...... **CLC 1, 7, 14, 18, 107; HLC 2**
See also CA 5-8R; 195; CAAE 195; CAAS 4; CANR 6, 32, 64; CN 7; DAM MULT; DLB 122, 278; DLBY 1982; HW 1, 2; INT CANR-6; LLW 1; RGAL 4

Redcam, Tom 1870-1933 .... **TCLC 25**

Reddin, Keith .... **CLC 67**
See also CAD

Redgrove, Peter (William) 1932-2003 .... **CLC 6, 41**
See also BRWS 6; CA 1-4R; 217; CANR 3, 39, 77; CP 7; DLB 40

Redmon, Anne .... **CLC 22**
See Nightingale, Anne Redmon
See also DLBY 1986

Reed, Eliot
See Ambler, Eric

Reed, Ishmael 1938- ..... **BLC 3; CLC 2, 3, 5, 6, 13, 32, 60, 174**
See also AFAW 1, 2; AMWS 10; BPFB 3; BW 2, 3; CA 21-24R; CANR 25, 48, 74, 128; CN 7; CP 7; CSW; DA3; DAM MULT; DLB 2, 5, 33, 169, 227; DLBD 8; EWL 3; LMFS 2; MSW; MTCW 1, 2; PFS 6; RGAL 4; TCWW 2

Reed, John (Silas) 1887-1920 .... **TCLC 9**
See also CA 106; 195; TUS

Reed, Lou .... **CLC 21**
See Firbank, Louis

Reese, Lizette Woodworth 1856-1935 . **PC 29**
See also CA 180; DLB 54

Reeve, Clara 1729-1807 .... **NCLC 19**
See also DLB 39; RGEL 2

Reich, Wilhelm 1897-1957 .... **TCLC 57**
See also CA 199

Reid, Christopher (John) 1949- .... **CLC 33**
See also CA 140; CANR 89; CP 7; DLB 40; EWL 3

Reid, Desmond
See Moorcock, Michael (John)

Reid Banks, Lynne 1929-
See Banks, Lynne Reid
See also AAYA 49; CA 1-4R; CANR 6, 22, 38, 87; CLR 24; CN 7; JRDA; MAICYA 1, 2; SATA 22, 75, 111; YAW

Reilly, William K.
See Creasey, John

Reiner, Max
See Caldwell, (Janet Miriam) Taylor (Holland)

Reis, Ricardo
See Pessoa, Fernando (Antonio Nogueira)

Reizenstein, Elmer Leopold
See Rice, Elmer (Leopold)
See also EWL 3

Rosa, Joao Guimaraes 1908-1967 ... **CLC 23; HLCS 1**
See Guimaraes Rosa, Joao
See also CA 89-92; DLB 113, 307; EWL 3; WLIT 1

Rose, Wendy 1948- . **CLC 85; NNAL; PC 13**
See also CA 53-56; CANR 5, 51; CWP; DAM MULT; DLB 175; PFS 13; RGAL 4; SATA 12

Rosen, R. D.
See Rosen, Richard (Dean)

Rosen, Richard (Dean) 1949- .... **CLC 39**
See also CA 77-80; CANR 62, 120; CMW 4; INT CANR-30

Rosenberg, Isaac 1890-1918 .... **TCLC 12**
See also BRW 6; CA 107; 188; DLB 20, 216; EWL 3; PAB; RGEL 2

Rosenblatt, Joe .... **CLC 15**
See Rosenblatt, Joseph

Rosenblatt, Joseph 1933-
See Rosenblatt, Joe
See also CA 89-92; CP 7; INT CA-89-92

Rosenfeld, Samuel
See Tzara, Tristan

Rosenstock, Sami
See Tzara, Tristan

Rosenstock, Samuel
See Tzara, Tristan

Rosenthal, M(acha) L(ouis) 1917-1996 .... **CLC 28**
See also CA 1-4R; 152; CAAS 6; CANR 4, 51; CP 7; DLB 5; SATA 59

Ross, Barnaby
See Dannay, Frederic

Ross, Bernard L.
See Follett, Ken(neth Martin)

Ross, J. H.
See Lawrence, T(homas) E(dward)

Ross, John Hume
See Lawrence, T(homas) E(dward)

Ross, Martin 1862-1915
See Martin, Violet Florence
See also DLB 135; GLL 2; RGEL 2; RGSF 2

Ross, (James) Sinclair 1908-1996 ... **CLC 13; SSC 24**
See also CA 73-76; CANR 81; CN 7; DAC; DAM MST; DLB 88; RGEL 2; RGSF 2; TCWW 2

Rossetti, Christina (Georgina) 1830-1894 .... **NCLC 2, 50, 66; PC 7; WLC**
See also AAYA 51; BRW 5; BYA 4; DA; DA3; DAB; DAC; DAM MST, POET; DLB 35, 163, 240; EXPP; LATS 1:1; MAICYA 1, 2; PFS 10, 14; RGEL 2; SATA 20; TEA; WCH

Rossetti, Dante Gabriel 1828-1882 . **NCLC 4, 77; PC 44; WLC**
See also AAYA 51; BRW 5; CDBLB 1832-1890; DA; DAB; DAC; DAM MST, POET; DLB 35; EXPP; RGEL 2; TEA

Rossi, Cristina Peri
See Peri Rossi, Cristina

Rossi, Jean-Baptiste 1931-2003
See Japrisot, Sebastien
See also CA 201; 215

Rossner, Judith (Perelman) 1935- . **CLC 6, 9, 29**
See also AITN 2; BEST 90:3; BPFB 3; CA 17-20R; CANR 18, 51, 73; CN 7; DLB 6; INT CANR-18; MTCW 1, 2

Rostand, Edmond (Eugene Alexis) 1868-1918 .... **DC 10; TCLC 6, 37**
See also CA 104; 126; DA; DA3; DAB; DAC; DAM DRAM, MST; DFS 1; DLB 192; LAIT 1; MTCW 1; RGWL 2, 3; TWA

Roth, Henry 1906-1995 ..... **CLC 2, 6, 11, 104**
See also AMWS 9; CA 11-12; 149; CANR 38, 63; CAP 1; CN 7; DA3; DLB 28; EWL 3; MTCW 1, 2; RGAL 4

Roth, (Moses) Joseph 1894-1939 ... **TCLC 33**
See also CA 160; DLB 85; EWL 3; RGWL 2, 3

Roth, Philip (Milton) 1933- ... **CLC 1, 2, 3, 4, 6, 9, 15, 22, 31, 47, 66, 86, 119, 201; SSC 26; WLC**
See also AMWR 2; AMWS 3; BEST 90:3; BPFB 3; CA 1-4R; CANR 1, 22, 36, 55, 89, 132; CDALB 1968-1988; CN 7; CPW 1; DA; DA3; DAB; DAC; DAM MST, NOV, POP; DLB 2, 28, 173; DLBY 1982; EWL 3; MTCW 1, 2; RGAL 4; RGSF 2; SSFS 12, 18; TUS

Rothenberg, Jerome 1931- .... **CLC 6, 57**
See also CA 45-48; CANR 1, 106; CP 7; DLB 5, 193

Rotter, Pat ed. .... **CLC 65**

Roumain, Jacques (Jean Baptiste) 1907-1944 .... **BLC 3; TCLC 19**
See also BW 1; CA 117; 125; DAM MULT; EWL 3

Rourke, Constance Mayfield 1885-1941 .... **TCLC 12**
See also CA 107; 200; YABC 1

Rousseau, Jean-Baptiste 1671-1741 ...... **LC 9**

Rousseau, Jean-Jacques 1712-1778 .... **LC 14, 36; WLC**
See also DA; DA3; DAB; DAC; DAM MST; EW 4; GFL Beginnings to 1789; LMFS 1; RGWL 2, 3; TWA

Roussel, Raymond 1877-1933 .... **TCLC 20**
See also CA 117; 201; EWL 3; GFL 1789 to the Present

Rovit, Earl (Herbert) 1927- .... **CLC 7**
See also CA 5-8R; CANR 12

Rowe, Elizabeth Singer 1674-1737 ..... **LC 44**
See also DLB 39, 95

Rowe, Nicholas 1674-1718 .... **LC 8**
See also DLB 84; RGEL 2

Rowlandson, Mary 1637(?)-1678 .... **LC 66**
See also DLB 24, 200; RGAL 4

Rowley, Ames Dorrance
See Lovecraft, H(oward) P(hillips)

Rowley, William 1585(?)-1626 .... **LC 100**
See also DLB 58; RGEL 2

Rowling, J(oanne) K(athleen) 1966- .... **CLC 137**
See also AAYA 34; BYA 11, 13, 14; CA 173; CANR 128; CLR 66, 80; MAICYA 2; SATA 109; SUFW 2

Rowson, Susanna Haswell 1762(?)-1824 .... **NCLC 5, 69**
See also DLB 37, 200; RGAL 4

Roy, Arundhati 1960(?)- .... **CLC 109**
See also CA 163; CANR 90, 126; DLBY 1997; EWL 3; LATS 1:2; WWE 1

Roy, Gabrielle 1909-1983 .... **CLC 10, 14**
See also CA 53-56; 110; CANR 5, 61; CCA 1; DAB; DAC; DAM MST; DLB 68; EWL 3; MTCW 1; RGWL 2, 3; SATA 104

Royko, Mike 1932-1997 .... **CLC 109**
See also CA 89-92; 157; CANR 26, 111; CPW

Rozanov, Vasilii Vasil'evich
See Rozanov, Vassili
See also DLB 295

Rozanov, Vasily Vasilyevich
See Rozanov, Vassili
See also EWL 3

Rozanov, Vassili 1856-1919 .... **TCLC 104**
See Rozanov, Vasilii Vasil'evich; Rozanov, Vasily Vasilyevich

Rozewicz, Tadeusz 1921- ...... **CLC 9, 23, 139**
See also CA 108; CANR 36, 66; CWW 2; DA3; DAM POET; DLB 232; EWL 3; MTCW 1, 2; RGWL 3

Ruark, Gibbons 1941- .... **CLC 3**
See also CA 33-36R; CAAS 23; CANR 14, 31, 57; DLB 120

Rubens, Bernice (Ruth) 1923-2004 . **CLC 19, 31**
See also CA 25-28R; CANR 33, 65, 128; CN 7; DLB 14, 207; MTCW 1

Rubin, Harold
See Robbins, Harold

Rudkin, (James) David 1936- .... **CLC 14**
See also CA 89-92; CBD; CD 5; DLB 13

Rudnik, Raphael 1933- .... **CLC 7**
See also CA 29-32R

Ruffian, M.
See Hasek, Jaroslav (Matej Frantisek)

Ruiz, Jose Martinez .... **CLC 11**
See Martinez Ruiz, Jose

Ruiz, Juan c. 1283-c. 1350 .... **CMLC 66**

Rukeyser, Muriel 1913-1980 . **CLC 6, 10, 15, 27; PC 12**
See also AMWS 6; CA 5-8R; 93-96; CANR 26, 60; DA3; DAM POET; DLB 48; EWL 3; FW; GLL 2; MTCW 1, 2; PFS 10; RGAL 4; SATA-Obit 22

Rule, Jane (Vance) 1931- .... **CLC 27**
See also CA 25-28R; CAAS 18; CANR 12, 87; CN 7; DLB 60; FW

Rulfo, Juan 1918-1986 .. **CLC 8, 80; HLC 2; SSC 25**
See also CA 85-88; 118; CANR 26; CD-WLB 3; DAM MULT; DLB 113; EWL 3; HW 1, 2; LAW; MTCW 1, 2; RGSF 2; RGWL 2, 3; WLIT 1

Rumi, Jalal al-Din 1207-1273 ...... **CMLC 20; PC 45**
See also RGWL 2, 3; WP

Runeberg, Johan 1804-1877 .... **NCLC 41**

Runyon, (Alfred) Damon 1884(?)-1946 .... **TCLC 10**
See also CA 107; 165; DLB 11, 86, 171; MTCW 2; RGAL 4

Rush, Norman 1933- .... **CLC 44**
See also CA 121; 126; CANR 130; INT CA-126

Rushdie, (Ahmed) Salman 1947- .... **CLC 23, 31, 55, 100, 191; WLCS**
See also BEST 89:3; BPFB 3; BRWS 4; CA 108; 111; CANR 33, 56, 108, 133; CN 7; CPW 1; DA3; DAB; DAC; DAM MST, NOV, POP; DLB 194; EWL 3; FANT; INT CA-111; LATS 1:2; LMFS 2; MTCW 1, 2; RGEL 2; RGSF 2; TEA; WLIT 4; WWE 1

Rushforth, Peter (Scott) 1945- .... **CLC 19**
See also CA 101

Ruskin, John 1819-1900 .... **TCLC 63**
See also BRW 5; BYA 5; CA 114; 129; CD-BLB 1832-1890; DLB 55, 163, 190; RGEL 2; SATA 24; TEA; WCH

Russ, Joanna 1937- .... **CLC 15**
See also BPFB 3; CA 5-28R; CANR 11, 31, 65; CN 7; DLB 8; FW; GLL 1; MTCW 1; SCFW 2; SFW 4

Russ, Richard Patrick
See O'Brian, Patrick

Russell, George William 1867-1935
See A.E.; Baker, Jean H.
See also BRWS 8; CA 104; 153; CDBLB 1890-1914; DAM POET; EWL 3; RGEL 2

Russell, Jeffrey Burton 1934- .... **CLC 70**
See also CA 25-28R; CANR 11, 28, 52

Russell, (Henry) Ken(neth Alfred) 1927- .... **CLC 16**
See also CA 105

Russell, William Martin 1947-
    See Russell, Willy
    See also CA 164; CANR 107
Russell, Willy .... **CLC 60**
    See Russell, William Martin
    See also CBD; CD 5; DLB 233
Russo, Richard 1949- .... **CLC 181**
    See also AMWS 12; CA 127; 133; CANR
    87, 114
Rutherford, Mark .... **TCLC 25**
    See White, William Hale
    See also DLB 18; RGEL 2
Ruyslinck, Ward .... **CLC 14**
    See Belser, Reimond Karel Maria de
Ryan, Cornelius (John) 1920-1974 ..... **CLC 7**
    See also CA 69-72; 53-56; CANR 38
Ryan, Michael 1946- .... **CLC 65**
    See also CA 49-52; CANR 109; DLBY
    1982
Ryan, Tim
    See Dent, Lester
Rybakov, Anatoli (Naumovich)
    1911-1998 .... **CLC 23, 53**
    See Rybakov, Anatolii (Naumovich)
    See also CA 126; 135; 172; SATA 79;
    SATA-Obit 108
Rybakov, Anatolii (Naumovich)
    See Rybakov, Anatoli (Naumovich)
    See also DLB 302
Ryder, Jonathan
    See Ludlum, Robert
Ryga, George 1932-1987 .... **CLC 14**
    See also CA 101; 124; CANR 43, 90; CCA
    1; DAC; DAM MST; DLB 60
S. H.
    See Hartmann, Sadakichi
S. S.
    See Sassoon, Siegfried (Lorraine)
Sa'adawi, al- Nawal
    See El Saadawi, Nawal
    See also AFW; EWL 3
Saadawi, Nawal El
    See El Saadawi, Nawal
    See also WLIT 2
Saba, Umberto 1883-1957 .... **TCLC 33**
    See also CA 144; CANR 79; DLB 114;
    EWL 3; RGWL 2, 3
Sabatini, Rafael 1875-1950 .... **TCLC 47**
    See also BPFB 3; CA 162; RHW
Sabato, Ernesto (R.) 1911- .... **CLC 10, 23;**
    HLC 2
    See also CA 97-100; CANR 32, 65; CD-
    WLB 3; CWW 2; DAM MULT; DLB 145;
    EWL 3; HW 1, 2; LAW; MTCW 1, 2
Sa-Carneiro, Mario de 1890-1916 . **TCLC 83**
    See also DLB 287; EWL 3
Sacastru, Martin
    See Bioy Casares, Adolfo
    See also CWW 2
Sacher-Masoch, Leopold von
    1836(?)-1895 .... **NCLC 31**
Sachs, Hans 1494-1576 .... **LC 95**
    See also CDWLB 2; DLB 179; RGWL 2, 3
Sachs, Marilyn (Stickle) 1927- .... **CLC 35**
    See also AAYA 2; BYA 6; CA 17-20R;
    CANR 13, 47; CLR 2; JRDA; MAICYA
    1, 2; SAAS 2; SATA 3, 68; SATA-Essay
    110; WYA; YAW
Sachs, Nelly 1891-1970 .... **CLC 14, 98**
    See also CA 17-18; 25-28R; CANR 87;
    CAP 2; EWL 3; MTCW 2; PFS 20;
    RGWL 2, 3
Sackler, Howard (Oliver)
    1929-1982 .... **CLC 14**
    See also CA 61-64; 108; CAD; CANR 30;
    DFS 15; DLB 7
Sacks, Oliver (Wolf) 1933- .... **CLC 67, 202**
    See also CA 53-56; CANR 28, 50, 76;
    CPW; DA3; INT CANR-28; MTCW 1, 2

Sackville, Thomas 1536-1608 .... **LC 98**
    See also DAM DRAM; DLB 62, 132;
    RGEL 2
Sadakichi
    See Hartmann, Sadakichi
Sa'dawi, Nawal al-
    See El Saadawi, Nawal
    See also CWW 2
Sade, Donatien Alphonse Francois
    1740-1814 .... **NCLC 3, 47**
    See also EW 4; GFL Beginnings to 1789;
    RGWL 2, 3
Sade, Marquis de
    See Sade, Donatien Alphonse Francois
Sadoff, Ira 1945- .... **CLC 9**
    See also CA 53-56; CANR 5, 21, 109; DLB
    120
Saetone
    See Camus, Albert
Safire, William 1929- .... **CLC 10**
    See also CA 17-20R; CANR 31, 54, 91
Sagan, Carl (Edward) 1934-1996 .... **CLC 30,**
    112
    See also AAYA 2; CA 25-28R; 155; CANR
    11, 36, 74; CPW; DA3; MTCW 1, 2;
    SATA 58; SATA-Obit 94
Sagan, Francoise .... **CLC 3, 6, 9, 17, 36**
    See Quoirez, Francoise
    See also CWW 2; DLB 83; EWL 3; GFL
    1789 to the Present; MTCW 2
Sahgal, Nayantara (Pandit) 1927- .... **CLC 41**
    See also CA 9-12R; CANR 11, 88; CN 7
Said, Edward W. 1935-2003 .... **CLC 123**
    See also CA 21-24R; 220; CANR 45, 74,
    107, 131; DLB 67; MTCW 2
Saint, H(arry) F. 1941- .... **CLC 50**
    See also CA 127
St. Aubin de Teran, Lisa 1953-
    See Teran, Lisa St. Aubin de
    See also CA 118; 126; CN 7; INT CA-126
Saint Birgitta of Sweden c.
    1303-1373 .... **CMLC 24**
Sainte-Beuve, Charles Augustin
    1804-1869 .... **NCLC 5**
    See also DLB 217; EW 6; GFL 1789 to the
    Present
Saint-Exupery, Antoine (Jean Baptiste
    Marie Roger) de 1900-1944 .... **TCLC 2,**
    56; WLC
    See also BPFB 3; BYA 3; CA 108; 132;
    CLR 10; DA3; DAM NOV; DLB 72; EW
    12; EWL 3; GFL 1789 to the Present;
    LAIT 3; MAICYA 1, 2; MTCW 1, 2;
    RGWL 2, 3; SATA 20; TWA
St. John, David
    See Hunt, E(verette) Howard, (Jr.)
St. John, J. Hector
    See Crevecoeur, Michel Guillaume Jean de
Saint-John Perse
    See Leger, (Marie-Rene Auguste) Alexis
    Saint-Leger
    See also EW 10; EWL 3; GFL 1789 to the
    Present; RGWL 2
Saintsbury, George (Edward Bateman)
    1845-1933 .... **TCLC 31**
    See also CA 160; DLB 57, 149
Sait Faik .... **TCLC 23**
    See Abasiyanik, Sait Faik
Saki .... **SSC 12; TCLC 3**
    See Munro, H(ector) H(ugh)
    See also BRWS 6; BYA 11; LAIT 2; MTCW
    2; RGEL 2; SSFS 1; SUFW
Sala, George Augustus 1828-1895 . **NCLC 46**
Saladin 1138-1193 .... **CMLC 38**
Salama, Hannu 1936- .... **CLC 18**
    See also EWL 3
Salamanca, J(ack) R(ichard) 1922- .. **CLC 4,**
    15
    See also CA 25-28R, 193; CAAE 193

Salas, Floyd Francis 1931- .... **HLC 2**
    See also CA 119; CAAS 27; CANR 44, 75,
    93; DAM MULT; DLB 82; HW 1, 2;
    MTCW 2
Sale, J. Kirkpatrick
    See Sale, Kirkpatrick
Sale, Kirkpatrick 1937- .... **CLC 68**
    See also CA 13-16R; CANR 10
Salinas, Luis Omar 1937- ...... **CLC 90; HLC 2**
    See also AMWS 13; CA 131; CANR 81;
    DAM MULT; DLB 82; HW 1, 2
Salinas (y Serrano), Pedro
    1891(?)-1951 .... **TCLC 17**
    See also CA 117; DLB 134; EWL 3
Salinger, J(erome) D(avid) 1919- .. **CLC 1, 3,**
    8, 12, 55, 56, 138; SSC 2, 28, 65; WLC
    See also AAYA 2, 36; AMW; AMWC 1;
    BPFB 3; CA 5-8R; CANR 39, 129;
    CDALB 1941-1968; CLR 18; CN 7; CPW
    1; DA; DA3; DAB; DAC; DAM MST,
    NOV, POP; DLB 2, 102, 173; EWL 3;
    EXPN; LAIT 4; MAICYA 1, 2; MTCW
    1, 2; NFS 1; RGAL 4; RGSF 2; SATA 67;
    SSFS 17; TUS; WYA; YAW
Salisbury, John
    See Caute, (John) David
Sallust c. 86B.C.-35B.C. .... **CMLC 68**
    See also AW 2; CDWLB 1; DLB 211;
    RGWL 2, 3
Salter, James 1925- .. **CLC 7, 52, 59; SSC 58**
    See also AMWS 9; CA 73-76; CANR 107;
    DLB 130
Saltus, Edgar (Everton) 1855-1921 . **TCLC 8**
    See also CA 105; DLB 202; RGAL 4
Saltykov, Mikhail Evgrafovich
    1826-1889 .... **NCLC 16**
    See also DLB 238:
Saltykov-Shchedrin, N.
    See Saltykov, Mikhail Evgrafovich
Samarakis, Andonis
    See Samarakis, Antonis
    See also EWL 3
Samarakis, Antonis 1919-2003 .... **CLC 5**
    See Samarakis, Andonis
    See also CA 25-28R; 224; CAAS 16; CANR
    36
Sanchez, Florencio 1875-1910 .... **TCLC 37**
    See also CA 153; DLB 305; EWL 3; HW 1;
    LAW
Sanchez, Luis Rafael 1936- .... **CLC 23**
    See also CA 128; DLB 305; EWL 3; HW 1;
    WLIT 1
Sanchez, Sonia 1934- .... **BLC 3; CLC 5, 116;**
    PC 9
    See also BW 2, 3; CA 33-36R; CANR 24,
    49, 74, 115; CLR 18; CP 7; CSW; CWP;
    DA3; DAM MULT; DLB 41; DLBD 8;
    EWL 3; MAICYA 1, 2; MTCW 1, 2;
    SATA 22, 136; WP
Sancho, Ignatius 1729-1780 .... **LC 84**
Sand, George 1804-1876 ..... **NCLC 2, 42, 57;**
    WLC
    See also DA; DA3; DAB; DAC; DAM
    MST, NOV; DLB 119, 192; EW 6; FW;
    GFL 1789 to the Present; RGWL 2, 3;
    TWA
Sandburg, Carl (August) 1878-1967 . **CLC 1,**
    4, 10, 15, 35; PC 2, 41; WLC
    See also AAYA 24; AMW; BYA 1, 3; CA
    5-8R; 25-28R; CANR 35; CDALB 1865-
    1917; CLR 67; DA; DA3; DAB; DAC;
    DAM MST, POET; DLB 17, 54, 284;
    EWL 3; EXPP; LAIT 2; MAICYA 1, 2;
    MTCW 1, 2; PAB; PFS 3, 6, 12; RGAL
    4; SATA 8; TUS; WCH; WP; WYA
Sandburg, Charles
    See Sandburg, Carl (August)
Sandburg, Charles A.
    See Sandburg, Carl (August)

Sanders, (James) Ed(ward) 1939- .... **CLC 53**
See Sanders, Edward
See also BG 3; CA 13-16R; CAAS 21;
CANR 13, 44, 78; CP 7; DAM POET;
DLB 16, 244
Sanders, Edward
See Sanders, (James) Ed(ward)
See also DLB 244
Sanders, Lawrence 1920-1998 .... **CLC 41**
See also BEST 89:4; BPFB 3; CA 81-84;
165; CANR 33, 62; CMW 4; CPW; DA3;
DAM POP; MTCW 1
Sanders, Noah
See Blount, Roy (Alton), Jr.
Sanders, Winston P.
See Anderson, Poul (William)
Sandoz, Mari(e Susette) 1900-1966 .. **CLC 28**
See also CA 1-4R; 25-28R; CANR 17, 64;
DLB 9, 212; LAIT 2; MTCW 1, 2; SATA
5; TCWW 2
Sandys, George 1578-1644 .... **LC 80**
See also DLB 24, 121
Saner, Reg(inald Anthony) 1931- .... **CLC 9**
See also CA 65-68; CP 7
Sankara 788-820 .... **CMLC 32**
Sannazaro, Jacopo 1456(?)-1530 .... **LC 8**
See also RGWL 2, 3
Sansom, William 1912-1976 . **CLC 2, 6; SSC 21**
See also CA 5-8R; 65-68; CANR 42; DAM
NOV; DLB 139; EWL 3; MTCW 1;
RGEL 2; RGSF 2
Santayana, George 1863-1952 .... **TCLC 40**
See also AMW; CA 115; 194; DLB 54, 71,
246, 270; DLBD 13; EWL 3; RGAL 4;
TUS
Santiago, Danny .... **CLC 33**
See James, Daniel (Lewis)
See also DLB 122
**Santillana, Íñigo López de Mendoza,
Marqués de** 1398-1458 .... **LC 111**
See also DLB 286
Santmyer, Helen Hooven
1895-1986 .... **CLC 33; TCLC 133**
See also CA 1-4R; 118; CANR 15, 33;
DLBY 1984; MTCW 1; RHW
Santoka, Taneda 1882-1940 .... **TCLC 72**
Santos, Bienvenido N(uqui)
1911-1996 ... **AAL; CLC 22; TCLC 156**
See also CA 101; 151; CANR 19, 46; DAM
MULT; EWL; RGAL 4; SSFS 19
Sapir, Edward 1884-1939 .... **TCLC 108**
See also CA 211; DLB 92
Sapper .... **TCLC 44**
See McNeile, Herman Cyril
Sapphire
See Sapphire, Brenda
Sapphire, Brenda 1950- .... **CLC 99**
Sappho fl. 6th cent. B.C.- ... **CMLC 3, 67; PC 5**
See also CDWLB 1; DA3; DAM POET;
DLB 176; PFS 20; RGWL 2, 3; WP
Saramago, Jose 1922- ..... **CLC 119; HLCS 1**
See also CA 153; CANR 96; CWW 2; DLB
287; EWL 3; LATS 1:2
Sarduy, Severo 1937-1993 .... **CLC 6, 97; HLCS 2**
See also CA 89-92; 142; CANR 58, 81;
CWW 2; DLB 113; EWL 3; HW 1, 2;
LAW
Sargeson, Frank 1903-1982 .... **CLC 31**
See also CA 25-28R; 106; CANR 38, 79;
EWL 3; GLL 2; RGEL 2; RGSF 2; SSFS
20
Sarmiento, Domingo Faustino
1811-1888 .... **HLCS 2**
See also LAW; WLIT 1
Sarmiento, Felix Ruben Garcia
See Dario, Ruben

Saro-Wiwa, Ken(ule Beeson)
1941-1995 .... **CLC 114**
See also BW 2; CA 142; 150; CANR 60;
DLB 157
Saroyan, William 1908-1981 ... **CLC 1, 8, 10,
29, 34, 56; SSC 21; TCLC 137; WLC**
See also CA 5-8R; 103; CAD; CANR 30;
CDALBS; DA; DA3; DAB; DAC; DAM
DRAM, MST, NOV; DFS 17; DLB 7, 9,
86; DLBY 1981; EWL 3; LAIT 4; MTCW
1, 2; RGAL 4; RGSF 2; SATA 23; SATA-
Obit 24; SSFS 14; TUS
Sarraute, Nathalie 1900-1999 .... **CLC 1, 2, 4,
8, 10, 31, 80; TCLC 145**
See also BPFB 3; CA 9-12R; 187; CANR
23, 66, 134; CWW 2; DLB 83; EW 12;
EWL 3; GFL 1789 to the Present; MTCW
1, 2; RGWL 2, 3
Sarton, (Eleanor) May 1912-1995 ..... **CLC 4,
14, 49, 91; PC 39; TCLC 120**
See also AMWS 8; CA 1-4R; 149; CANR
1, 34, 55, 116; CN 7; CP 7; DAM POET;
DLB 48; DLBY 1981; EWL 3; FW; INT
CANR-34; MTCW 1, 2; RGAL 4; SATA
36; SATA-Obit 86; TUS
Sartre, Jean-Paul 1905-1980 . **CLC 1, 4, 7, 9,
13, 18, 24, 44, 50, 52; DC 3; SSC 32;
WLC**
See also CA 9-12R; 97-100; CANR 21; DA;
DA3; DAB; DAC; DAM DRAM, MST,
NOV; DFS 5; DLB 72, 296; EW 12; EWL
3; GFL 1789 to the Present; LMFS 2;
MTCW 1, 2; RGSF 2; RGWL 2, 3; SSFS
9; TWA
Sassoon, Siegfried (Lorraine)
1886-1967 .... **CLC 36, 130; PC 12**
See also BRW 6; CA 104; 25-28R; CANR
36; DAB; DAM MST, NOV, POET; DLB
20, 191; DLBD 18; EWL 3; MTCW 1, 2;
PAB; RGEL 2; TEA
Satterfield, Charles
See Pohl, Frederik
Satyremont
See Peret, Benjamin
Saul, John (W. III) 1942- .... **CLC 46**
See also AAYA 10; BEST 90:4; CA 81-84;
CANR 16, 40, 81; CPW; DAM NOV,
POP; HGG; SATA 98
Saunders, Caleb
See Heinlein, Robert A(nson)
Saura (Atares), Carlos 1932-1998 .... **CLC 20**
See also CA 114; 131; CANR 79; HW 1
Sauser, Frederic Louis
See Sauser-Hall, Frederic
Sauser-Hall, Frederic 1887-1961 ...... **CLC 18**
See Cendrars, Blaise
See also CA 102; 93-96; CANR 36, 62;
MTCW 1
Saussure, Ferdinand de
1857-1913 .... **TCLC 49**
See also DLB 242
Savage, Catharine
See Brosman, Catharine Savage
Savage, Richard 1697(?)-1743 .... **LC 96**
See also DLB 95; RGEL 2
Savage, Thomas 1915-2003 .... **CLC 40**
See also CA 126; 132; 218; CAAS 15; CN
7; INT CA-132; SATA-Obit 147; TCWW
2
Savan, Glenn 1953-2003 .... **CLC 50**
See also CA 225
Sax, Robert
See Johnson, Robert
Saxo Grammaticus c. 1150-c.
1222 .... **CMLC 58**
Saxton, Robert
See Johnson, Robert

Sayers, Dorothy L(eigh) 1893-1957 . **SSC 71;
TCLC 2, 15**
See also BPFB 3; BRWS 3; CA 104; 119;
CANR 60; CDBLB 1914-1945; CMW 4;
DAM POP; DLB 10, 36, 77, 100; MSW;
MTCW 1, 2; RGEL 2; SSFS 12; TEA
Sayers, Valerie 1952- .... **CLC 50, 122**
See also CA 134; CANR 61; CSW
Sayles, John (Thomas) 1950- .... **CLC 7, 10,
14, 198**
See also CA 57-60; CANR 41, 84; DLB 44
Scammell, Michael 1935- .... **CLC 34**
See also CA 156
Scannell, Vernon 1922- .... **CLC 49**
See also CA 5-8R; CANR 8, 24, 57; CP 7;
CWRI 5; DLB 27; SATA 59
Scarlett, Susan
See Streatfeild, (Mary) Noel
Scarron 1847-1910
See Mikszath, Kalman
Schaeffer, Susan Fromberg 1941- ..... **CLC 6,
11, 22**
See also CA 49-52; CANR 18, 65; CN 7;
DLB 28, 299; MTCW 1, 2; SATA 22
Schama, Simon (Michael) 1945- ..... **CLC 150**
See also BEST 89:4; CA 105; CANR 39,
91
Schary, Jill
See Robinson, Jill
Schell, Jonathan 1943- .... **CLC 35**
See also CA 73-76; CANR 12, 117
Schelling, Friedrich Wilhelm Joseph von
1775-1854 .... **NCLC 30**
See also DLB 90
Scherer, Jean-Marie Maurice 1920-
See Rohmer, Eric
See also CA 110
Schevill, James (Erwin) 1920- .... **CLC 7**
See also CA 5-8R; CAAS 12; CAD; CD 5
Schiller, Friedrich von 1759-1805 ...... **DC 12;
NCLC 39, 69**
See also CDWLB 2; DAM DRAM; DLB
94; EW 5; RGWL 2, 3; TWA
Schisgal, Murray (Joseph) 1926- .... **CLC 6**
See also CA 21-24R; CAD; CANR 48, 86;
CD 5
Schlee, Ann 1934- .... **CLC 35**
See also CA 101; CANR 29, 88; SATA 44;
SATA-Brief 36
Schlegel, August Wilhelm von
1767-1845 .... **NCLC 15, 142**
See also DLB 94; RGWL 2, 3
Schlegel, Friedrich 1772-1829 ...... **NCLC 45**
See also DLB 90; EW 5; RGWL 2, 3; TWA
Schlegel, Johann Elias (von)
1719(?)-1749 .... **LC 5**
Schleiermacher, Friedrich
1768-1834 .... **NCLC 107**
See also DLB 90
Schlesinger, Arthur M(eier), Jr.
1917- .... **CLC 84**
See also AITN 1; CA 1-4R; CANR 1, 28,
58, 105; DLB 17; INT CANR-28; MTCW
1, 2; SATA 61
Schlink, Bernhard 1944- .... **CLC 174**
See also CA 163; CANR 116
Schmidt, Arno (Otto) 1914-1979 ...... **CLC 56**
See also CA 128; 109; DLB 69; EWL 3
Schmitz, Aron Hector 1861-1928
See Svevo, Italo
See also CA 104; 122; MTCW 1
Schnackenberg, Gjertrud (Cecelia)
1953- .... **CLC 40; PC 45**
See also CA 116; CANR 100; CP 7; CWP;
DLB 120, 282; PFS 13
Schneider, Leonard Alfred 1925-1966
See Bruce, Lenny
See also CA 89-92

Schnitzler, Arthur 1862-1931 ..... **DC 17; SSC 15, 61; TCLC 4**
See also CA 104; CDWLB 2; DLB 81, 118; EW 8; EWL 3; RGSF 2; RGWL 2, 3

Schoenberg, Arnold Franz Walter
1874-1951 .... **TCLC 75**
See also CA 109; 188

Schonberg, Arnold
See Schoenberg, Arnold Franz Walter

Schopenhauer, Arthur 1788-1860 .. **NCLC 51**
See also DLB 90; EW 5

Schor, Sandra (M.) 1932(?)-1990 ..... **CLC 65**
See also CA 132

Schorer, Mark 1908-1977 .... **CLC 9**
See also CA 5-8R; 73-76; CANR 7; DLB 103

Schrader, Paul (Joseph) 1946- .... **CLC 26**
See also CA 37-40R; CANR 41; DLB 44

Schreber, Daniel 1842-1911 .... **TCLC 123**

Schreiner, Olive (Emilie Albertina)
1855-1920 .... **TCLC 9**
See also AFW; BRWS 2; CA 105; 154; DLB 18, 156, 190, 225; EWL 3; FW; RGEL 2; TWA; WLIT 2; WWE 1

Schulberg, Budd (Wilson) 1914- .. **CLC 7, 48**
See also BPFB 3; CA 25-28R; CANR 19, 87; CN 7; DLB 6, 26, 28; DLBY 1981, 2001

Schulman, Arnold
See Trumbo, Dalton

Schulz, Bruno 1892-1942 .. **SSC 13; TCLC 5, 51**
See also CA 115; 123; CANR 86; CDWLB 4; DLB 215; EWL 3; MTCW 2; RGSF 2; RGWL 2, 3

Schulz, Charles M(onroe)
1922-2000 .... **CLC 12**
See also AAYA 39; CA 9-12R; 187; CANR 6, 132; INT CANR-6; SATA 10; SATA-Obit 118

Schumacher, E(rnst) F(riedrich)
1911-1977 .... **CLC 80**
See also CA 81-84; 73-76; CANR 34, 85

Schumann, Robert 1810-1856 ...... **NCLC 143**

Schuyler, George Samuel 1895-1977 .... **HR 3**
See also BW 2; CA 81-84; 73-76; CANR 42; DLB 29, 51

Schuyler, James Marcus 1923-1991 .. **CLC 5, 23**
See also CA 101; 134; DAM POET; DLB 5, 169; EWL 3; INT CA-101; WP

Schwartz, Delmore (David)
1913-1966 ... **CLC 2, 4, 10, 45, 87; PC 8**
See also AMWS 2; CA 17-18; 25-28R; CANR 35; CAP 2; DLB 28, 48; EWL 3; MTCW 1, 2; PAB; RGAL 4; TUS

Schwartz, Ernst
See Ozu, Yasujiro

Schwartz, John Burnham 1965- .... **CLC 59**
See also CA 132; CANR 116

Schwartz, Lynne Sharon 1939- .... **CLC 31**
See also CA 103; CANR 44, 89; DLB 218; MTCW 2

Schwartz, Muriel A.
See Eliot, T(homas) S(tearns)

Schwarz-Bart, Andre 1928- .... **CLC 2, 4**
See also CA 89-92; CANR 109; DLB 299

Schwarz-Bart, Simone 1938- . **BLCS; CLC 7**
See also BW 2; CA 97-100; CANR 117; EWL 3

Schwerner, Armand 1927-1999 .... **PC 42**
See also CA 9-12R; 179; CANR 50, 85; CP 7; DLB 165

Schwitters, Kurt (Hermann Edward Karl Julius) 1887-1948 .... **TCLC 95**
See also CA 158

Schwob, Marcel (Mayer Andre)
1867-1905 .... **TCLC 20**
See also CA 117; 168; DLB 123; GFL 1789 to the Present

Sciascia, Leonardo 1921-1989 .. **CLC 8, 9, 41**
See also CA 85-88; 130; CANR 35; DLB 177; EWL 3; MTCW 1; RGWL 2, 3

Scoppettone, Sandra 1936- .... **CLC 26**
See Early, Jack
See also AAYA 11; BYA 8; CA 5-8R; CANR 41, 73; GLL 1; MAICYA 2; MAICYAS 1; SATA 9, 92; WYA; YAW

Scorsese, Martin 1942- .... **CLC 20, 89**
See also AAYA 38; CA 110; 114; CANR 46, 85

Scotland, Jay
See Jakes, John (William)

Scott, Duncan Campbell
1862-1947 .... **TCLC 6**
See also CA 104; 153; DAC; DLB 92; RGEL 2

Scott, Evelyn 1893-1963 .... **CLC 43**
See also CA 104; 112; CANR 64; DLB 9, 48; RHW

Scott, F(rancis) R(eginald)
1899-1985 .... **CLC 22**
See also CA 101; 114; CANR 87; DLB 88; INT CA-101; RGEL 2

Scott, Frank
See Scott, F(rancis) R(eginald)

Scott, Joan .... **CLC 65**

Scott, Joanna 1960- .... **CLC 50**
See also CA 126; CANR 53, 92

Scott, Paul (Mark) 1920-1978 ...... **CLC 9, 60**
See also BRWS 1; CA 81-84; 77-80; CANR 33; DLB 14, 207; EWL 3; MTCW 1; RGEL 2; RHW; WWE 1

Scott, Ridley 1937- .... **CLC 183**
See also AAYA 13, 43

Scott, Sarah 1723-1795 .... **LC 44**
See also DLB 39

Scott, Sir Walter 1771-1832 .... **NCLC 15, 69, 110; PC 13; SSC 32; WLC**
See also AAYA 22; BRW 4; BYA 2; CD-BLB 1789-1832; DA; DAB; DAC; DAM MST, NOV, POET; DLB 93, 107, 116, 144, 159; HGG; LAIT 1; RGEL 2; RGSF 2; SSFS 10; SUFW 1; TEA; WLIT 3; YABC 2

Scribe, (Augustin) Eugene 1791-1861 . **DC 5; NCLC 16**
See also DAM DRAM; DLB 192; GFL 1789 to the Present; RGWL 2, 3

Scrum, R.
See Crumb, R(obert)

Scudery, Georges de 1601-1667 .... **LC 75**
See also GFL Beginnings to 1789

Scudery, Madeleine de 1607-1701 .. **LC 2, 58**
See also DLB 268; GFL Beginnings to 1789

Scum
See Crumb, R(obert)

Scumbag, Little Bobby
See Crumb, R(obert)

Seabrook, John
See Hubbard, L(afayette) Ron(ald)

Seacole, Mary Jane Grant
1805-1881 .... **NCLC 147**
See also DLB 166

Sealy, I(rwin) Allan 1951- .... **CLC 55**
See also CA 136; CN 7

Search, Alexander
See Pessoa, Fernando (Antonio Nogueira)

Sebald, W(infried) G(eorg)
1944-2001 .... **CLC 194**
See also BRWS 8; CA 159; 202; CANR 98

Sebastian, Lee
See Silverberg, Robert

Sebastian Owl
See Thompson, Hunter S(tockton)

Sebestyen, Igen
See Sebestyen, Ouida

Sebestyen, Ouida 1924- .... **CLC 30**
See also AAYA 8; BYA 7; CA 107; CANR 40, 114; CLR 17; JRDA; MAICYA 1, 2; SAAS 10; SATA 39, 140; WYA; YAW

Sebold, Alice 1963(?)- .... **CLC 193**
See also AAYA 56; CA 203

Second Duke of Buckingham
See Villiers, George

Secundus, H. Scriblerus
See Fielding, Henry

Sedges, John
See Buck, Pearl S(ydenstricker)

Sedgwick, Catharine Maria
1789-1867 .... **NCLC 19, 98**
See also DLB 1, 74, 183, 239, 243, 254; RGAL 4

Seelye, John (Douglas) 1931- .... **CLC 7**
See also CA 97-100; CANR 70; INT CA-97-100; TCWW 2

Seferiades, Giorgos Stylianou 1900-1971
See Seferis, George
See also CA 5-8R; 33-36R; CANR 5, 36; MTCW 1

Seferis, George .... **CLC 5, 11**
See Seferiades, Giorgos Stylianou
See also EW 12; EWL 3; RGWL 2, 3

Segal, Erich (Wolf) 1937- .... **CLC 3, 10**
See also BEST 89:1; BPFB 3; CA 25-28R; CANR 20, 36, 65, 113; CPW; DAM POP; DLBY 1986; INT CANR-20; MTCW 1

Seger, Bob 1945- .... **CLC 35**

Seghers, Anna .... **CLC 7**
See Radvanyi, Netty
See also CDWLB 2; DLB 69; EWL 3

Seidel, Frederick (Lewis) 1936- .... **CLC 18**
See also CA 13-16R; CANR 8, 99; CP 7; DLBY 1984

Seifert, Jaroslav 1901-1986 . **CLC 34, 44, 93; PC 47**
See also CA 127; CDWLB 4; DLB 215; EWL 3; MTCW 1, 2

Sei Shonagon c. 966-1017(?) .... **CMLC 6**

Sejour, Victor 1817-1874 .... **DC 10**
See also DLB 50

Sejour Marcou et Ferrand, Juan Victor
See Sejour, Victor

Selby, Hubert, Jr. 1928-2004 ..... **CLC 1, 2, 4, 8; SSC 20**
See also CA 13-16R; 226; CANR 33, 85; CN 7; DLB 2, 227

Selzer, Richard 1928- .... **CLC 74**
See also CA 65-68; CANR 14, 106

Sembene, Ousmane
See Ousmane, Sembene
See also AFW; EWL 3; WLIT 2

Senancour, Etienne Pivert de
1770-1846 .... **NCLC 16**
See also DLB 119; GFL 1789 to the Present

Sender, Ramon (Jose) 1902-1982 ...... **CLC 8; HLC 2; TCLC 136**
See also CA 5-8R; 105; CANR 8; DAM MULT; EWL 3; HW 1; MTCW 1; RGWL 2, 3

Seneca, Lucius Annaeus c. 4B.C.-c. 65 .... **CMLC 6; DC 5**
See also AW 2; CDWLB 1; DAM DRAM; DLB 211; RGWL 2, 3; TWA

Senghor, Leopold Sedar 1906-2001 ... **BLC 3; CLC 54, 130; PC 25**
See also AFW; BW 2; CA 116; 125; 203; CANR 47, 74, 134; CWW 2; DAM MULT, POET; DNFS 2; EWL 3; GFL 1789 to the Present; MTCW 1, 2; TWA

Senior, Olive (Marjorie) 1941- .... **SSC 78**
See also BW 3; CA 154; CANR 86, 126; CN 7; CP 7; CWP; DLB 157; EWL 3; RGSF 2

Sherwin, Judith Johnson
See Johnson, Judith (Emlyn)
See also CANR 85; CP 7; CWP

Sherwood, Frances 1940- .... **CLC 81**
See also CA 146, 220; CAAE 220

Sherwood, Robert E(mmet)
1896-1955 .... **TCLC 3**
See also CA 104; 153; CANR 86; DAM
DRAM; DFS 11, 15, 17; DLB 7, 26, 249;
IDFW 3, 4; RGAL 4

Shestov, Lev 1866-1938 .... **TCLC 56**

Shevchenko, Taras 1814-1861 .... **NCLC 54**

Shiel, M(atthew) P(hipps)
1865-1947 .... **TCLC 8**
See Holmes, Gordon
See also CA 106; 160; DLB 153; HGG;
MTCW 2; SFW 4; SUFW

Shields, Carol (Ann) 1935-2003 ...... **CLC 91,
113, 193**
See also AMWS 7; CA 81-84; 218; CANR
51, 74, 98, 133; CCA 1; CN 7; CPW;
DA3; DAC; MTCW 2

Shields, David (Jonathan) 1956- ...... **CLC 97**
See also CA 124; CANR 48, 99, 112

Shiga, Naoya 1883-1971 ..... **CLC 33; SSC 23**
See Shiga Naoya
See also CA 101; 33-36R; MJW; RGWL 3

Shiga Naoya
See Shiga, Naoya
See also DLB 180; EWL 3; RGWL 3

Shilts, Randy 1951-1994 .... **CLC 85**
See also AAYA 19; CA 115; 127; 144;
CANR 45; DA3; GLL 1; INT CA-127;
MTCW 2

Shimazaki, Haruki 1872-1943
See Shimazaki Toson
See also CA 105; 134; CANR 84; RGWL 3

Shimazaki Toson .... **TCLC 5**
See Shimazaki, Haruki
See also DLB 180; EWL 3

Shirley, James 1596-1666 .... **DC 25; LC 96**
See also DLB 58; RGEL 2

Sholokhov, Mikhail (Aleksandrovich)
1905-1984 .... **CLC 7, 15**
See also CA 101; 112; DLB 272; EWL 3;
MTCW 1, 2; RGWL 2, 3; SATA-Obit 36

Shone, Patric
See Hanley, James

Showalter, Elaine 1941- .... **CLC 169**
See also CA 57-60; CANR 58, 106; DLB
67; FW; GLL 2

Shreve, Susan
See Shreve, Susan Richards

Shreve, Susan Richards 1939- .... **CLC 23**
See also CA 49-52; CAAS 5; CANR 5, 38,
69, 100; MAICYA 1, 2; SATA 46, 95, 152;
SATA-Brief 41

Shue, Larry 1946-1985 .... **CLC 52**
See also CA 145; 117; DAM DRAM; DFS
7

Shu-Jen, Chou 1881-1936
See Lu Hsun
See also CA 104

Shulman, Alix Kates 1932- .... **CLC 2, 10**
See also CA 29-32R; CANR 43; FW; SATA
7

Shuster, Joe 1914-1992 .... **CLC 21**
See also AAYA 50

Shute, Nevil .... **CLC 30**
See Norway, Nevil Shute
See also BPFB 3; DLB 255; NFS 9; RHW;
SFW 4

Shuttle, Penelope (Diane) 1947- .... **CLC 7**
See also CA 93-96; CANR 39, 84, 92, 108;
CP 7; CWP; DLB 14, 40

Shvarts, Elena 1948- .... **PC 50**
See also CA 147

Sidhwa, Bapsy (N.) 1938- .... **CLC 168**
See also CA 108; CANR 25, 57; CN 7; FW

Sidney, Mary 1561-1621 .... **LC 19, 39**
See Sidney Herbert, Mary

Sidney, Sir Philip 1554-1586 . **LC 19, 39; PC
32**
See also BRW 1; BRWR 2; CDBLB Before
1660; DA; DA3; DAB; DAC; DAM MST,
POET; DLB 167; EXPP; PAB; RGEL 2;
TEA; WP

Sidney Herbert, Mary
See Sidney, Mary
See also DLB 167

Siegel, Jerome 1914-1996 .... **CLC 21**
See Siegel, Jerry
See also CA 116; 169; 151

Siegel, Jerry
See Siegel, Jerome
See also AAYA 50

Sienkiewicz, Henryk (Adam Alexander Pius)
1846-1916 .... **TCLC 3**
See also CA 104; 134; CANR 84; EWL 3;
RGSF 2; RGWL 2, 3

Sierra, Gregorio Martinez
See Martinez Sierra, Gregorio

Sierra, Maria (de la O'LeJarraga) Martinez
See Martinez Sierra, Maria (de la
O'LeJarraga)

Sigal, Clancy 1926- .... **CLC 7**
See also CA 1-4R; CANR 85; CN 7

Siger of Brabant 1240(?)-1284(?) . **CMLC 69**
See also DLB 115

Sigourney, Lydia H.
See Sigourney, Lydia Howard (Huntley)
See also DLB 73, 183

Sigourney, Lydia Howard (Huntley)
1791-1865 .... **NCLC 21, 87**
See Sigourney, Lydia H.; Sigourney, Lydia
Huntley
See also DLB 1

Sigourney, Lydia Huntley
See Sigourney, Lydia Howard (Huntley)
See also DLB 42, 239, 243

Siguenza y Gongora, Carlos de
1645-1700 .... **HLCS 2; LC 8**
See also LAW

Sigurjonsson, Johann
See Sigurjonsson, Johann

Sigurjonsson, Johann 1880-1919 ... **TCLC 27**
See also CA 170; DLB 293; EWL 3

Sikelianos, Angelos 1884-1951 .... **PC 29;
TCLC 39**
See also EWL 3; RGWL 2, 3

Silkin, Jon 1930-1997 .... **CLC 2, 6, 43**
See also CA 5-8R; CAAS 5; CANR 89; CP
7; DLB 27

Silko, Leslie (Marmon) 1948- .... **CLC 23, 74,
114; SSC 37, 66; WLCS**
See also AAYA 14; AMWS 4; ANW; BYA
12; CA 115; 122; CANR 45, 65, 118; CN
7; CP 7; CPW 1; CWP; DA; DA3; DAC;
DAM MST, MULT, POP; DLB 143, 175,
256, 275; EWL 3; EXPP; EXPS; LAIT 4;
MTCW 2; NFS 4; PFS 9, 16; RGAL 4;
RGSF 2; SSFS 4, 8, 10, 11

Sillanpaa, Frans Eemil 1888-1964 ... **CLC 19**
See also CA 129; 93-96; EWL 3; MTCW 1

Sillitoe, Alan 1928- .. **CLC 1, 3, 6, 10, 19, 57,
148**
See also AITN 1; BRWS 5; CA 9-12R, 191;
CAAE 191; CAAS 2; CANR 8, 26, 55;
CDBLB 1960 to Present; CN 7; DLB 14,
139; EWL 3; MTCW 1, 2; RGEL 2;
RGSF 2; SATA 61

Silone, Ignazio 1900-1978 .... **CLC 4**
See also CA 25-28; 81-84; CANR 34; CAP
2; DLB 264; EW 12; EWL 3; MTCW 1;
RGSF 2; RGWL 2, 3

Silone, Ignazione
See Silone, Ignazio

Silver, Joan Micklin 1935- .... **CLC 20**
See also CA 114; 121; INT CA-121

Silver, Nicholas
See Faust, Frederick (Schiller)
See also TCWW 2

Silverberg, Robert 1935- .... **CLC 7, 140**
See also AAYA 24; BPFB 3; BYA 7, 9; CA
1-4R, 186; CAAE 186; CAAS 3; CANR
1, 20, 36, 85; CLR 59; CN 7; CPW; DAM
POP; DLB 8; INT CANR-20; MAICYA
1, 2; MTCW 1, 2; SATA 13, 91; SATA-
Essay 104; SCFW 2; SFW 4; SUFW 2

Silverstein, Alvin 1933- .... **CLC 17**
See also CA 49-52; CANR 2; CLR 25;
JRDA; MAICYA 1, 2; SATA 8, 69, 124

Silverstein, Shel(don Allan)
1932-1999 .... **PC 49**
See also AAYA 40; BW 3; CA 107; 179;
CANR 47, 74, 81; CLR 5, 96; CWRI 5;
JRDA; MAICYA 1, 2; MTCW 2; SATA
33, 92; SATA-Brief 27; SATA-Obit 116

Silverstein, Virginia B(arbara Opshelor)
1937- .... **CLC 17**
See also CA 49-52; CANR 2; CLR 25;
JRDA; MAICYA 1, 2; SATA 8, 69, 124

Sim, Georges
See Simenon, Georges (Jacques Christian)

Simak, Clifford D(onald) 1904-1988 . **CLC 1,
55**
See also CA 1-4R; 125; CANR 1, 35; DLB
8; MTCW 1; SATA-Obit 56; SFW 4

Simenon, Georges (Jacques Christian)
1903-1989 .... **CLC 1, 2, 3, 8, 18, 47**
See also BPFB 3; CA 85-88; 129; CANR
35; CMW 4; DA3; DAM POP; DLB 72;
DLBY 1989; EW 12; EWL 3; GFL 1789
to the Present; MSW; MTCW 1, 2; RGWL
2, 3

Simic, Charles 1938- .... **CLC 6, 9, 22, 49, 68,
130**
See also AMWS 8; CA 29-32R; CAAS 4;
CANR 12, 33, 52, 61, 96; CP 7; DA3;
DAM POET; DLB 105; MTCW 2; PFS 7;
RGAL 4; WP

Simmel, Georg 1858-1918 .... **TCLC 64**
See also CA 157; DLB 296

Simmons, Charles (Paul) 1924- .... **CLC 57**
See also CA 89-92; INT CA-89-92

Simmons, Dan 1948- .... **CLC 44**
See also AAYA 16, 54; CA 138; CANR 53,
81, 126; CPW; DAM POP; HGG; SUFW
2

Simmons, James (Stewart Alexander)
1933- .... **CLC 43**
See also CA 105; CAAS 21; CP 7; DLB 40

Simms, William Gilmore
1806-1870 .... **NCLC 3**
See also DLB 3, 30, 59, 73, 248, 254;
RGAL 4

Simon, Carly 1945- .... **CLC 26**
See also CA 105

Simon, Claude (Eugene Henri)
1913-1984 .... **CLC 4, 9, 15, 39**
See also CA 89-92; CANR 33, 117; CWW
2; DAM NOV; DLB 83; EW 13; EWL 3;
GFL 1789 to the Present; MTCW 1

Simon, Myles
See Follett, Ken(neth Martin)

Simon, (Marvin) Neil 1927- ... **CLC 6, 11, 31,
39, 70; DC 14**
See also AAYA 32; AITN 1; AMWS 4; CA
21-24R; CANR 26, 54, 87, 126; CD 5;
DA3; DAM DRAM; DFS 2, 6, 12, 18;
DLB 7, 266; LAIT 4; MTCW 1, 2; RGAL
4; TUS

Simon, Paul (Frederick) 1941(?)- ..... **CLC 17**
See also CA 116; 153

Smolenskin, Peretz 1842-1885 .... **NCLC 30**
Smollett, Tobias (George) 1721-1771 ... **LC 2, 46**
> See also BRW 3; CDBLB 1660-1789; DLB 39, 104; RGEL 2; TEA

Snodgrass, W(illiam) D(e Witt) 1926- .... **CLC 2, 6, 10, 18, 68**
> See also AMWS 6; CA 1-4R; CANR 6, 36, 65, 85; CP 7; DAM POET; DLB 5; MTCW 1, 2; RGAL 4

Snorri Sturluson 1179-1241 .... **CMLC 56**
> See also RGWL 2, 3

Snow, C(harles) P(ercy) 1905-1980 ... **CLC 1, 4, 6, 9, 13, 19**
> See also BRW 7; CA 5-8R; 101; CANR 28; CDBLB 1945-1960; DAM NOV; DLB 15, 77; DLBD 17; EWL 3; MTCW 1, 2; RGEL 2; TEA

Snow, Frances Compton
> See Adams, Henry (Brooks)

Snyder, Gary (Sherman) 1930- . **CLC 1, 2, 5, 9, 32, 120; PC 21**
> See also AMWS 8; ANW; BG 3; CA 17-20R; CANR 30, 60, 125; CP 7; DA3; DAM POET; DLB 5, 16, 165, 212, 237, 275; EWL 3; MTCW 2; PFS 9, 19; RGAL 4; WP

Snyder, Zilpha Keatley 1927- .... **CLC 17**
> See also AAYA 15; BYA 1; CA 9-12R; CANR 38; CLR 31; JRDA; MAICYA 1, 2; SAAS 2; SATA 1, 28, 75, 110; SATA-Essay 112; YAW

Soares, Bernardo
> See Pessoa, Fernando (Antonio Nogueira)

Sobh, A.
> See Shamlu, Ahmad

Sobh, Alef
> See Shamlu, Ahmad

Sobol, Joshua 1939- .... **CLC 60**
> See Sobol, Yehoshua
> See also CA 200

Sobol, Yehoshua 1939-
> See Sobol, Joshua
> See also CWW 2

Socrates 470B.C.-399B.C. .... **CMLC 27**
Soderberg, Hjalmar 1869-1941 ...... **TCLC 39**
> See also DLB 259; EWL 3; RGSF 2

Soderbergh, Steven 1963- .... **CLC 154**
> See also AAYA 43

Sodergran, Edith (Irene) 1892-1923
> See Soedergran, Edith (Irene)
> See also CA 202; DLB 259; EW 11; EWL 3; RGWL 2, 3

Soedergran, Edith (Irene) 1892-1923 .... **TCLC 31**
> See Sodergran, Edith (Irene)

Softly, Edgar
> See Lovecraft, H(oward) P(hillips)

Softly, Edward
> See Lovecraft, H(oward) P(hillips)

Sokolov, Alexander V(sevolodovich) 1943-
> See Sokolov, Sasha
> See also CA 73-76

Sokolov, Raymond 1941- .... **CLC 7**
> See also CA 85-88

Sokolov, Sasha .... **CLC 59**
> See Sokolov, Alexander V(sevolodovich)
> See also CWW 2; DLB 285; EWL 3; RGWL 2, 3

Solo, Jay
> See Ellison, Harlan (Jay)

Sologub, Fyodor .... **TCLC 9**
> See Teternikov, Fyodor Kuzmich
> See also EWL 3

Solomons, Ikey Esquir
> See Thackeray, William Makepeace

Solomos, Dionysios 1798-1857 .... **NCLC 15**

Solwoska, Mara
> See French, Marilyn

Solzhenitsyn, Aleksandr I(sayevich) 1918- .. **CLC 1, 2, 4, 7, 9, 10, 18, 26, 34, 78, 134; SSC 32; WLC**
> See Solzhenitsyn, Aleksandr Isaevich
> See also AAYA 49; AITN 1; BPFB 3; CA 69-72; CANR 40, 65, 116; DA; DA3; DAB; DAC; DAM MST, NOV; DLB 302; EW 13; EXPS; LAIT 4; MTCW 1, 2; NFS 6; RGSF 2; RGWL 2, 3; SSFS 9; TWA

Solzhenitsyn, Aleksandr Isaevich
> See Solzhenitsyn, Aleksandr I(sayevich)
> See also CWW 2; EWL 3

Somers, Jane
> See Lessing, Doris (May)

Somerville, Edith Oenone 1858-1949 .... **SSC 56; TCLC 51**
> See also CA 196; DLB 135; RGEL 2; RGSF 2

Somerville & Ross
> See Martin, Violet Florence; Somerville, Edith Oenone

Sommer, Scott 1951- .... **CLC 25**
> See also CA 106

Sommers, Christina Hoff 1950- ...... **CLC 197**
> See also CA 153; CANR 95

Sondheim, Stephen (Joshua) 1930- . **CLC 30, 39, 147; DC 22**
> See also AAYA 11; CA 103; CANR 47, 67, 125; DAM DRAM; LAIT 4

Sone, Monica 1919- .... **AAL**
Song, Cathy 1955- .... **AAL; PC 21**
> See also CA 154; CANR 118; CWP; DLB 169; EXPP; FW; PFS 5

Sontag, Susan 1933- .... **CLC 1, 2, 10, 13, 31, 105, 195**
> See also AMWS 3; CA 17-20R; CANR 25, 51, 74, 97; CN 7; CPW; DA3; DAM POP; DLB 2, 67; EWL 3; MAWW; MTCW 1, 2; RGAL 4; RHW; SSFS 10

Sophocles 496(?)B.C.-406(?)B.C. .... **CMLC 2, 47, 51; DC 1; WLCS**
> See also AW 1; CDWLB 1; DA; DA3; DAB; DAC; DAM DRAM, MST; DFS 1, 4, 8; DLB 176; LAIT 1; LATS 1:1; LMFS 1; RGWL 2, 3; TWA

Sordello 1189-1269 .... **CMLC 15**
Sorel, Georges 1847-1922 .... **TCLC 91**
> See also CA 118; 188

Sorel, Julia
> See Drexler, Rosalyn

Sorokin, Vladimir .... **CLC 59**
> See Sorokin, Vladimir Georgievich

Sorokin, Vladimir Georgievich
> See Sorokin, Vladimir
> See also DLB 285

Sorrentino, Gilbert 1929- .. **CLC 3, 7, 14, 22, 40**
> See also CA 77-80; CANR 14, 33, 115; CN 7; CP 7; DLB 5, 173; DLBY 1980; INT CANR-14

Soseki
> See Natsume, Soseki
> See also MJW

Soto, Gary 1952- ... **CLC 32, 80; HLC 2; PC 28**
> See also AAYA 10, 37; BYA 11; CA 119; 125; CANR 50, 74, 107; CLR 38; CP 7; DAM MULT; DLB 82; EWL 3; EXPP; HW 1, 2; INT CA-125; JRDA; LLW 1; MAICYA 2; MAICYAS 1; MTCW 2; PFS 7; RGAL 4; SATA 80, 120; WYA; YAW

Soupault, Philippe 1897-1990 .... **CLC 68**
> See also CA 116; 147; 131; EWL 3; GFL 1789 to the Present; LMFS 2

Souster, (Holmes) Raymond 1921- .... **CLC 5, 14**
> See also CA 13-16R; CAAS 14; CANR 13, 29, 53; CP 7; DA3; DAC; DAM POET; DLB 88; RGEL 2; SATA 63

Southern, Terry 1924(?)-1995 .... **CLC 7**
> See also AMWS 11; BPFB 3; CA 1-4R; 150; CANR 1, 55, 107; CN 7; DLB 2; IDFW 3, 4

Southerne, Thomas 1660-1746 .... **LC 99**
> See also DLB 80; RGEL 2

Southey, Robert 1774-1843 .... **NCLC 8, 97**
> See also BRW 4; DLB 93, 107, 142; RGEL 2; SATA 54

Southwell, Robert 1561(?)-1595 .... **LC 108**
> See also DLB 167; RGEL 2; TEA

Southworth, Emma Dorothy Eliza Nevitte 1819-1899 .... **NCLC 26**
> See also DLB 239

Souza, Ernest
> See Scott, Evelyn

Soyinka, Wole 1934- .. **BLC 3; CLC 3, 5, 14, 36, 44, 179; DC 2; WLC**
> See also AFW; BW 2, 3; CA 13-16R; CANR 27, 39, 82; CD 5; CDWLB 3; CN 7; CP 7; DA; DA3; DAB; DAC; DAM DRAM, MST, MULT; DFS 10; DLB 125; EWL 3; MTCW 1, 2; RGEL 2; TWA; WLIT 2; WWE 1

Spackman, W(illiam) M(ode) 1905-1990 .... **CLC 46**
> See also CA 81-84; 132

Spacks, Barry (Bernard) 1931- .... **CLC 14**
> See also CA 154; CANR 33, 109; CP 7; DLB 105

Spanidou, Irini 1946- .... **CLC 44**
> See also CA 185

Spark, Muriel (Sarah) 1918- ..... **CLC 2, 3, 5, 8, 13, 18, 40, 94; SSC 10**
> See also BRWS 1; CA 5-8R; CANR 12, 36, 76, 89, 131; CDBLB 1945-1960; CN 7; CP 7; DA3; DAB; DAC; DAM MST, NOV; DLB 15, 139; EWL 3; FW; INT CANR-12; LAIT 4; MTCW 1, 2; RGEL 2; TEA; WLIT 4; YAW

Spaulding, Douglas
> See Bradbury, Ray (Douglas)

Spaulding, Leonard
> See Bradbury, Ray (Douglas)

Speght, Rachel 1597-c. 1630 .... **LC 97**
> See also DLB 126

Spelman, Elizabeth .... **CLC 65**
Spence, J. A. D.
> See Eliot, T(homas) S(tearns)

Spencer, Anne 1882-1975 .... **HR 3**
> See also BW 2; CA 161; DLB 51, 54

Spencer, Elizabeth 1921- .... **CLC 22; SSC 57**
> See also CA 13-16R; CANR 32, 65, 87; CN 7; CSW; DLB 6, 218; EWL 3; MTCW 1; RGAL 4; SATA 14

Spencer, Leonard G.
> See Silverberg, Robert

Spencer, Scott 1945- .... **CLC 30**
> See also CA 113; CANR 51; DLBY 1986

Spender, Stephen (Harold) 1909-1995 .... **CLC 1, 2, 5, 10, 41, 91**
> See also BRWS 2; CA 9-12R; 149; CANR 31, 54; CDBLB 1945-1960; CP 7; DA3; DAM POET; DLB 20; EWL 3; MTCW 1, 2; PAB; RGEL 2; TEA

Spengler, Oswald (Arnold Gottfried) 1880-1936 .... **TCLC 25**
> See also CA 118; 189

Spenser, Edmund 1552(?)-1599 ..... **LC 5, 39; PC 8, 42; WLC**
> See also AAYA 60; BRW 1; CDBLB Before 1660; DA; DA3; DAB; DAC; DAM MST, POET; DLB 167; EFS 2; EXPP; PAB; RGEL 2; TEA; WLIT 3; WP

Spicer, Jack 1925-1965 .... **CLC 8, 18, 72**
> See also BG 3; CA 85-88; DAM POET; DLB 5, 16, 193; GLL 1; WP

Stevenson, Anne (Katharine) 1933- .. **CLC 7, 33**
See also BRWS 6; CA 17-20R; CAAS 9; CANR 9, 33, 123; CP 7; CWP; DLB 40; MTCW 1; RHW

Stevenson, Robert Louis (Balfour) 1850-1894 ...... **NCLC 5, 14, 63; SSC 11, 51; WLC**
See also AAYA 24; BPFB 3; BRW 5; BRWC 1; BRWR 1; BYA 1, 2, 4, 13; CD-BLB 1890-1914; CLR 10, 11; DA; DA3; DAB; DAC; DAM MST, NOV; DLB 18, 57, 141, 156, 174; DLBD 13; HGG; JRDA; LAIT 1, 3; MAICYA 1, 2; NFS 11, 20; RGEL 2; RGSF 2; SATA 100; SUFW; TEA; WCH; WLIT 4; WYA; YABC 2; YAW

Stewart, J(ohn) I(nnes) M(ackintosh) 1906-1994 .... **CLC 7, 14, 32**
See Innes, Michael
See also CA 85-88; 147; CAAS 3; CANR 47; CMW 4; MTCW 1, 2

Stewart, Mary (Florence Elinor) 1916- .... **CLC 7, 35, 117**
See also AAYA 29; BPFB 3; CA 1-4R; CANR 1, 59, 130; CMW 4; CPW; DAB; FANT; RHW; SATA 12; YAW

Stewart, Mary Rainbow
See Stewart, Mary (Florence Elinor)

Stifle, June
See Campbell, Maria

Stifter, Adalbert 1805-1868 .. **NCLC 41; SSC 28**
See also CDWLB 2; DLB 133; RGSF 2; RGWL 2, 3

Still, James 1906-2001 .... **CLC 49**
See also CA 65-68; 195; CAAS 17; CANR 10, 26; CSW; DLB 9; DLBY 01; SATA 29; SATA-Obit 127

Sting 1951-
See Sumner, Gordon Matthew
See also CA 167

Stirling, Arthur
See Sinclair, Upton (Beall)

Stitt, Milan 1941- .... **CLC 29**
See also CA 69-72

Stockton, Francis Richard 1834-1902
See Stockton, Frank R.
See also CA 108; 137; MAICYA 1, 2; SATA 44; SFW 4

Stockton, Frank R. .... **TCLC 47**
See Stockton, Francis Richard
See also BYA 4, 13; DLB 42, 74; DLBD 13; EXPS; SATA-Brief 32; SSFS 3; SUFW; WCH

Stoddard, Charles
See Kuttner, Henry

Stoker, Abraham 1847-1912
See Stoker, Bram
See also CA 105; 150; DA; DA3; DAC; DAM MST, NOV; HGG; SATA 29

Stoker, Bram . **SSC 62; TCLC 8, 144; WLC**
See Stoker, Abraham
See also AAYA 23; BPFB 3; BRWS 3; BYA 5; CDBLB 1890-1914; DAB; DLB 304; LATS 1:1; NFS 18; RGEL 2; SUFW; TEA; WLIT 4

Stolz, Mary (Slattery) 1920- .... **CLC 12**
See also AAYA 8; AITN 1; CA 5-8R; CANR 13, 41, 112; JRDA; MAICYA 1, 2; SAAS 3; SATA 10, 71, 133; YAW

Stone, Irving 1903-1989 .... **CLC 7**
See also AITN 1; BPFB 3; CA 1-4R; 129; CAAS 3; CANR 1, 23; CPW; DA3; DAM POP; INT CANR-23; MTCW 1, 2; RHW; SATA 3; SATA-Obit 64

Stone, Oliver (William) 1946- .... **CLC 73**
See also AAYA 15; CA 110; CANR 55, 125

Stone, Robert (Anthony) 1937- ... **CLC 5, 23, 42, 175**
See also AMWS 5; BPFB 3; CA 85-88; CANR 23, 66, 95; CN 7; DLB 152; EWL 3; INT CANR-23; MTCW 1

Stone, Ruth 1915- .... **PC 53**
See also CA 45-48; CANR 2, 91; CP 7; CSW; DLB 105; PFS 19

Stone, Zachary
See Follett, Ken(neth Martin)

Stoppard, Tom 1937- ... **CLC 1, 3, 4, 5, 8, 15, 29, 34, 63, 91; DC 6; WLC**
See also BRWC 1; BRWR 2; BRWS 1; CA 81-84; CANR 39, 67, 125; CBD; CD 5; CDBLB 1960 to Present; DA; DA3; DAB; DAC; DAM DRAM, MST; DFS 2, 5, 8, 11, 13, 16; DLB 13, 233; DLBY 1985; EWL 3; LATS 1:2; MTCW 1, 2; RGEL 2; TEA; WLIT 4

Storey, David (Malcolm) 1933- . **CLC 2, 4, 5, 8**
See also BRWS 1; CA 81-84; CANR 36; CBD; CD 5; CN 7; DAM DRAM; DLB 13, 14, 207, 245; EWL 3; MTCW 1; RGEL 2

Storm, Hyemeyohsts 1935- ... **CLC 3; NNAL**
See also CA 81-84; CANR 45; DAM MULT

Storm, (Hans) Theodor (Woldsen) 1817-1888 .... **NCLC 1; SSC 27**
See also CDWLB 2; DLB 129; EW; RGSF 2; RGWL 2, 3

Storni, Alfonsina 1892-1938 . **HLC 2; PC 33; TCLC 5**
See also CA 104; 131; DAM MULT; DLB 283; HW 1; LAW

Stoughton, William 1631-1701 .... **LC 38**
See also DLB 24

Stout, Rex (Todhunter) 1886-1975 ..... **CLC 3**
See also AITN 2; BPFB 3; CA 61-64; CANR 71; CMW 4; DLB 306; MSW; RGAL 4

Stow, (Julian) Randolph 1935- ... **CLC 23, 48**
See also CA 13-16R; CANR 33; CN 7; DLB 260; MTCW 1; RGEL 2

Stowe, Harriet (Elizabeth) Beecher 1811-1896 .... **NCLC 3, 50, 133; WLC**
See also AAYA 53; AMWS 1; CDALB 1865-1917; DA; DA3; DAB; DAC; DAM MST, NOV; DLB 1, 12, 42, 74, 189, 239, 243; EXPN; JRDA; LAIT 2; MAICYA 1, 2; NFS 6; RGAL 4; TUS; YABC 1

Strabo c. 64B.C.-c. 25 .... **CMLC 37**
See also DLB 176

Strachey, (Giles) Lytton 1880-1932 .... **TCLC 12**
See also BRWS 2; CA 110; 178; DLB 149; DLBD 10; EWL 3; MTCW 2; NCFS 4

Stramm, August 1874-1915 .... **PC 50**
See also CA 195; EWL 3

Strand, Mark 1934- .. **CLC 6, 18, 41, 71; PC 63**
See also AMWS 4; CA 21-24R; CANR 40, 65, 100; CP 7; DAM POET; DLB 5; EWL 3; PAB; PFS 9, 18; RGAL 4; SATA 41

Stratton-Porter, Gene(va Grace) 1863-1924
See Porter, Gene(va Grace) Stratton
See also ANW; CA 137; CLR 87; DLB 221; DLBD 14; MAICYA 1, 2; SATA 15

Straub, Peter (Francis) 1943- ... **CLC 28, 107**
See also BEST 89:1; BPFB 3; CA 85-88; CANR 28, 65, 109; CPW; DAM POP; DLBY 1984; HGG; MTCW 1, 2; SUFW 2

Strauss, Botho 1944- .... **CLC 22**
See also CA 157; CWW 2; DLB 124

Strauss, Leo 1899-1973 .... **TCLC 141**
See also CA 101; 45-48; CANR 122

Streatfeild, (Mary) Noel 1897(?)-1986 .... **CLC 21**
See also CA 81-84; 120; CANR 31; CLR 17, 83; CWRI 5; DLB 160; MAICYA 1, 2; SATA 20; SATA-Obit 48

Stribling, T(homas) S(igismund) 1881-1965 .... **CLC 23**
See also CA 189; 107; CMW 4; DLB 9; RGAL 4

Strindberg, (Johan) August 1849-1912 ... **DC 18; TCLC 1, 8, 21, 47; WLC**
See also CA 104; 135; DA; DA3; DAB; DAC; DAM DRAM, MST; DFS 4, 9; DLB 259; EW 7; EWL 3; IDTP; LMFS 2; MTCW 2; RGWL 2, 3; TWA

Stringer, Arthur 1874-1950 .... **TCLC 37**
See also CA 161; DLB 92

Stringer, David
See Roberts, Keith (John Kingston)

Stroheim, Erich von 1885-1957 ..... **TCLC 71**

Strugatskii, Arkadii (Natanovich) 1925-1991 .... **CLC 27**
See Strugatsky, Arkadii Natanovich
See also CA 106; 135; SFW 4

Strugatskii, Boris (Natanovich) 1933- .... **CLC 27**
See Strugatsky, Boris (Natanovich)
See also CA 106; SFW 4

Strugatsky, Arkadii Natanovich
See Strugatskii, Arkadii (Natanovich)
See also DLB 302

Strugatsky, Boris (Natanovich)
See Strugatskii, Boris (Natanovich)
See also DLB 302

Strummer, Joe 1953(?)- .... **CLC 30**

Strunk, William, Jr. 1869-1946 ...... **TCLC 92**
See also CA 118; 164; NCFS 5

Stryk, Lucien 1924- .... **PC 27**
See also CA 13-16R; CANR 10, 28, 55, 110; CP 7

Stuart, Don A.
See Campbell, John W(ood, Jr.)

Stuart, Ian
See MacLean, Alistair (Stuart)

Stuart, Jesse (Hilton) 1906-1984 ... **CLC 1, 8, 11, 14, 34; SSC 31**
See also CA 5-8R; 112; CANR 31; DLB 9, 48, 102; DLBY 1984; SATA 2; SATA-Obit 36

Stubblefield, Sally
See Trumbo, Dalton

Sturgeon, Theodore (Hamilton) 1918-1985 .... **CLC 22, 39**
See Queen, Ellery
See also AAYA 51; BPFB 3; BYA 9, 10; CA 81-84; 116; CANR 32, 103; DLB 8; DLBY 1985; HGG; MTCW 1, 2; SCFW; SFW 4; SUFW

Sturges, Preston 1898-1959 .... **TCLC 48**
See also CA 114; 149; DLB 26

Styron, William 1925- .... **CLC 1, 3, 5, 11, 15, 60; SSC 25**
See also AMW; AMWC 2; BEST 90:4; BPFB 3; CA 5-8R; CANR 6, 33, 74, 126; CDALB 1968-1988; CN 7; CPW; CSW; DA3; DAM NOV, POP; DLB 2, 143, 299; DLBY 1980; EWL 3; INT CANR-6; LAIT 2; MTCW 1, 2; NCFS 1; RGAL 4; RHW; TUS

Su, Chien 1884-1918
See Su Man-shu
See also CA 123

Suarez Lynch, B.
See Bioy Casares, Adolfo; Borges, Jorge Luis

Suassuna, Ariano Vilar 1927- .... **HLCS 1**
See also CA 178; DLB 307; HW 2; LAW

Suckert, Kurt Erich
See Malaparte, Curzio

Suckling, Sir John 1609-1642 . **LC 75; PC 30**
See also BRW 2; DAM POET; DLB 58, 126; EXPP; PAB; RGEL 2

Suckow, Ruth 1892-1960 .... **SSC 18**
See also CA 193; 113; DLB 9, 102; RGAL 4; TCWW 2

Sudermann, Hermann 1857-1928 .. **TCLC 15**
See also CA 107; 201; DLB 118

Sue, Eugene 1804-1857 .... **NCLC 1**
See also DLB 119

Sueskind, Patrick 1949- .... **CLC 44, 182**
See Suskind, Patrick

Suetonius c. 70-c. 130 .... **CMLC 60**
See also AW 2; DLB 211; RGWL 2, 3

Sukenick, Ronald 1932-2004 ..... **CLC 3, 4, 6, 48**
See also CA 25-28R, 209; 229; CAAE 209; CAAS 8; CANR 32, 89; CN 7; DLB 173; DLBY 1981

Suknaski, Andrew 1942- .... **CLC 19**
See also CA 101; CP 7; DLB 53

Sullivan, Vernon
See Vian, Boris

Sully Prudhomme, Rene-Francois-Armand
1839-1907 .... **TCLC 31**
See also GFL 1789 to the Present

Su Man-shu .... **TCLC 24**
See Su, Chien
See also EWL 3

Sumarokov, Aleksandr Petrovich
1717-1777 .... **LC 104**
See also DLB 150

Summerforest, Ivy B.
See Kirkup, James

Summers, Andrew James 1942- .... **CLC 26**

Summers, Andy
See Summers, Andrew James

Summers, Hollis (Spurgeon, Jr.)
1916- .... **CLC 10**
See also CA 5-8R; CANR 3; DLB 6

Summers, (Alphonsus Joseph-Mary Augustus) Montague
1880-1948 .... **TCLC 16**
See also CA 118; 163

Sumner, Gordon Matthew .... **CLC 26**
See Police, The; Sting

Sun Tzu c. 400B.C.-c. 320B.C. ..... **CMLC 56**

Surrey, Henry Howard 1517-1574 ...... **PC 59**
See also BRW 1; RGEL 2

Surtees, Robert Smith 1805-1864 .. **NCLC 14**
See also DLB 21; RGEL 2

Susann, Jacqueline 1921-1974 .... **CLC 3**
See also AITN 1; BPFB 3; CA 65-68; 53-56; MTCW 1, 2

Su Shi
See Su Shih
See also RGWL 2, 3

Su Shih 1036-1101 .... **CMLC 15**
See Su Shi

Suskind, Patrick .... **CLC 182**
See Sueskind, Patrick
See also BPFB 3; CA 145; CWW 2

Sutcliff, Rosemary 1920-1992 .... **CLC 26**
See also AAYA 10; BYA 1, 4; CA 5-8R; 139; CANR 37; CLR 1, 37; CPW; DAB; DAC; DAM MST, POP; JRDA; LATS 1:1; MAICYA 1, 2; MAICYAS 1; RHW; SATA 6, 44, 78; SATA-Obit 73; WYA; YAW

Sutro, Alfred 1863-1933 .... **TCLC 6**
See also CA 105; 185; DLB 10; RGEL 2

Sutton, Henry
See Slavitt, David R(ytman)

Suzuki, D. T.
See Suzuki, Daisetz Teitaro

Suzuki, Daisetz T.
See Suzuki, Daisetz Teitaro

Suzuki, Daisetz Teitaro
1870-1966 .... **TCLC 109**
See also CA 121; 111; MTCW 1, 2

Suzuki, Teitaro
See Suzuki, Daisetz Teitaro

Svevo, Italo .... **SSC 25; TCLC 2, 35**
See Schmitz, Aron Hector
See also DLB 264; EW 8; EWL 3; RGWL 2, 3

Swados, Elizabeth (A.) 1951- .... **CLC 12**
See also CA 97-100; CANR 49; INT CA-97-100

Swados, Harvey 1920-1972 .... **CLC 5**
See also CA 5-8R; 37-40R; CANR 6; DLB 2

Swan, Gladys 1934- .... **CLC 69**
See also CA 101; CANR 17, 39

Swanson, Logan
See Matheson, Richard (Burton)

Swarthout, Glendon (Fred)
1918-1992 .... **CLC 35**
See also AAYA 55; CA 1-4R; 139; CANR 1, 47; SATA 26; TCWW 2; YAW

Swedenborg, Emanuel 1688-1772 ..... **LC 105**

Sweet, Sarah C.
See Jewett, (Theodora) Sarah Orne

Swenson, May 1919-1989 ...... **CLC 4, 14, 61, 106; PC 14**
See also AMWS 4; CA 5-8R; 130; CANR 36, 61, 131; DA; DAB; DAC; DAM MST, POET; DLB 5; EXPP; GLL 2; MTCW 1, 2; PFS 16; SATA 15; WP

Swift, Augustus
See Lovecraft, H(oward) P(hillips)

Swift, Graham (Colin) 1949- ...... **CLC 41, 88**
See also BRWC 2; BRWS 5; CA 117; 122; CANR 46, 71, 128; CN 7; DLB 194; MTCW 2; NFS 18; RGSF 2

Swift, Jonathan 1667-1745 ..... **LC 1, 42, 101; PC 9; WLC**
See also AAYA 41; BRW 3; BRWC 1; BRWR 1; BYA 5, 14; CDBLB 1660-1789; CLR 53; DA; DA3; DAB; DAC; DAM MST, NOV, POET; DLB 39, 95, 101; EXPN; LAIT 1; NFS 6; RGEL 2; SATA 19; TEA; WCH; WLIT 3

Swinburne, Algernon Charles
1837-1909 .. **PC 24; TCLC 8, 36; WLC**
See also BRW 5; CA 105; 140; CDBLB 1832-1890; DA; DA3; DAB; DAC; DAM MST, POET; DLB 35, 57; PAB; RGEL 2; TEA

Swinfen, Ann .... **CLC 34**
See also CA 202

Swinnerton, Frank Arthur
1884-1982 .... **CLC 31**
See also CA 108; DLB 34

Swithen, John
See King, Stephen (Edwin)

Sylvia
See Ashton-Warner, Sylvia (Constance)

Symmes, Robert Edward
See Duncan, Robert (Edward)

Symonds, John Addington
1840-1893 .... **NCLC 34**
See also DLB 57, 144

Symons, Arthur 1865-1945 .... **TCLC 11**
See also CA 107; 189; DLB 19, 57, 149; RGEL 2

Symons, Julian (Gustave)
1912-1994 .... **CLC 2, 14, 32**
See also CA 49-52; 147; CAAS 3; CANR 3, 33, 59; CMW 4; DLB 87, 155; DLBY 1992; MSW; MTCW 1

Synge, (Edmund) J(ohn) M(illington)
1871-1909 .... **DC 2; TCLC 6, 37**
See also BRW 6; BRWR 1; CA 104; 141; CDBLB 1890-1914; DAM DRAM; DFS 18; DLB 10, 19; EWL 3; RGEL 2; TEA; WLIT 4

Syruc, J.
See Milosz, Czeslaw

Szirtes, George 1948- .... **CLC 46; PC 51**
See also CA 109; CANR 27, 61, 117; CP 7

Szymborska, Wislawa 1923- ... **CLC 99, 190; PC 44**
See also CA 154; CANR 91, 133; CDWLB 4; CWP; CWW 2; DA3; DLB 232; DLBY 1996; EWL 3; MTCW 2; PFS 15; RGWL 3

T. O., Nik
See Annensky, Innokenty (Fyodorovich)

Tabori, George 1914- .... **CLC 19**
See also CA 49-52; CANR 4, 69; CBD; CD 5; DLB 245

Tacitus c. 55-c. 117 .... **CMLC 56**
See also AW 2; CDWLB 1; DLB 211; RGWL 2, 3

Tagore, Rabindranath 1861-1941 .... **PC 8; SSC 48; TCLC 3, 53**
See also CA 104; 120; DA3; DAM DRAM, POET; EWL 3; MTCW 1, 2; PFS 18; RGEL 2; RGSF 2; RGWL 2, 3; TWA

Taine, Hippolyte Adolphe
1828-1893 .... **NCLC 15**
See also EW 7; GFL 1789 to the Present

Talayesva, Don C. 1890-(?) .... **NNAL**

Talese, Gay 1932- .... **CLC 37**
See also AITN 1; CA 1-4R; CANR 9, 58; DLB 185; INT CANR-9; MTCW 1, 2

Tallent, Elizabeth (Ann) 1954- .... **CLC 45**
See also CA 117; CANR 72; DLB 130

Tallmountain, Mary 1918-1997 .... **NNAL**
See also CA 146; 161; DLB 193

Tally, Ted 1952- .... **CLC 42**
See also CA 120; 124; CAD; CANR 125; CD 5; INT CA-124

Talvik, Heiti 1904-1947 .... **TCLC 87**
See also EWL 3

Tamayo y Baus, Manuel
1829-1898 .... **NCLC 1**

Tammsaare, A(nton) H(ansen)
1878-1940 .... **TCLC 27**
See also CA 164; CDWLB 4; DLB 220; EWL 3

Tam'si, Tchicaya U
See Tchicaya, Gerald Felix

Tan, Amy (Ruth) 1952- . **AAL; CLC 59, 120, 151**
See also AAYA 9, 48; AMWS 10; BEST 89:3; BPFB 3; CA 136; CANR 54, 105, 132; CDALBS; CN 7; CPW 1; DA3; DAM MULT, NOV, POP; DLB 173; EXPN; FW; LAIT 3, 5; MTCW 2; NFS 1, 13, 16; RGAL 4; SATA 75; SSFS 9; YAW

Tandem, Felix
See Spitteler, Carl (Friedrich Georg)

Tanizaki, Jun'ichiro 1886-1965 ... **CLC 8, 14, 28; SSC 21**
See Tanizaki Jun'ichiro
See also CA 93-96; 25-28R; MJW; MTCW 2; RGSF 2; RGWL 2

Tanizaki Jun'ichiro
See Tanizaki, Jun'ichiro
See also DLB 180; EWL 3

Tanner, William
See Amis, Kingsley (William)

Tao Lao
See Storni, Alfonsina

Tapahonso, Luci 1953- .... **NNAL**
See also CA 145; CANR 72, 127; DLB 175

Tarantino, Quentin (Jerome)
1963- .... **CLC 125**
See also AAYA 58; CA 171; CANR 125

Tarassoff, Lev
See Troyat, Henri

Tarbell, Ida M(inerva) 1857-1944 . **TCLC 40**
See also CA 122; 181; DLB 47

Tarkington, (Newton) Booth
1869-1946 .... **TCLC 9**
See also BPFB 3; BYA 3; CA 110; 143;
CWRI 5; DLB 9, 102; MTCW 2; RGAL
4; SATA 17

Tarkovskii, Andrei Arsen'evich
See Tarkovsky, Andrei (Arsenyevich)

Tarkovsky, Andrei (Arsenyevich)
1932-1986 .... **CLC 75**
See also CA 127

Tartt, Donna 1963- .... **CLC 76**
See also AAYA 56; CA 142

Tasso, Torquato 1544-1595 .... **LC 5, 94**
See also EFS 2; EW 2; RGWL 2, 3

Tate, (John Orley) Allen 1899-1979 .. **CLC 2,**
4, 6, 9, 11, 14, 24; PC 50
See also AMW; CA 5-8R; 85-88; CANR
32, 108; DLB 4, 45, 63; DLBD 17; EWL
3; MTCW 1, 2; RGAL 4; RHW

Tate, Ellalice
See Hibbert, Eleanor Alice Burford

Tate, James (Vincent) 1943- ..... **CLC 2, 6, 25**
See also CA 21-24R; CANR 29, 57, 114;
CP 7; DLB 5, 169; EWL 3; PFS 10, 15;
RGAL 4; WP

Tate, Nahum 1652(?)-1715 .... **LC 109**
See also DLB 80; RGEL 2

Tauler, Johannes c. 1300-1361 ...... **CMLC 37**
See also DLB 179; LMFS 1

Tavel, Ronald 1940- .... **CLC 6**
See also CA 21-24R; CAD; CANR 33; CD
5

Taviani, Paolo 1931- .... **CLC 70**
See also CA 153

Taylor, Bayard 1825-1878 .... **NCLC 89**
See also DLB 3, 189, 250, 254; RGAL 4

Taylor, C(ecil) P(hilip) 1929-1981 .... **CLC 27**
See also CA 25-28R; 105; CANR 47; CBD

Taylor, Edward 1642(?)-1729 . **LC 11; PC 63**
See also AMW; DA; DAB; DAC; DAM
MST, POET; DLB 24; EXPP; RGAL 4;
TUS

Taylor, Eleanor Ross 1920- .... **CLC 5**
See also CA 81-84; CANR 70

Taylor, Elizabeth 1932-1975 ..... **CLC 2, 4, 29**
See also CA 13-16R; CANR 9, 70; DLB
139; MTCW 1; RGEL 2; SATA 13

Taylor, Frederick Winslow
1856-1915 .... **TCLC 76**
See also CA 188

Taylor, Henry (Splawn) 1942- .... **CLC 44**
See also CA 33-36R; CAAS 7; CANR 31;
CP 7; DLB 5; PFS 10

Taylor, Kamala (Purnaiya) 1924-2004
See Markandaya, Kamala
See also CA 77-80; 227; NFS 13

Taylor, Mildred D(elois) 1943- .... **CLC 21**
See also AAYA 10, 47; BW 1; BYA 3, 8;
CA 85-88; CANR 25, 115; CLR 9, 59,
90; CSW; DLB 52; JRDA; LAIT 3; MAI-
CYA 1, 2; SAAS 5; SATA 135; WYA;
YAW

Taylor, Peter (Hillsman) 1917-1994 .. **CLC 1,**
4, 18, 37, 44, 50, 71; SSC 10
See also AMWS 5; BPFB 3; CA 13-16R;
147; CANR 9, 50; CSW; DLB 218, 278;
DLBY 1981, 1994; EWL 3; EXPS; INT
CANR-9; MTCW 1, 2; RGSF 2; SSFS 9;
TUS

Taylor, Robert Lewis 1912-1998 .... **CLC 14**
See also CA 1-4R; 170; CANR 3, 64; SATA
10

Tchekhov, Anton
See Chekhov, Anton (Pavlovich)

Tchicaya, Gerald Felix 1931-1988 .. **CLC 101**
See Tchicaya U Tam'si
See also CA 129; 125; CANR 81

Tchicaya U Tam'si
See Tchicaya, Gerald Felix
See also EWL 3

Teasdale, Sara 1884-1933 .... **PC 31; TCLC 4**
See also CA 104; 163; DLB 45; GLL 1;
PFS 14; RGAL 4; SATA 32; TUS

Tecumseh 1768-1813 .... **NNAL**
See also DAM MULT

Tegner, Esaias 1782-1846 .... **NCLC 2**

Fujiwara no Teika 1162-1241 .... **CMLC 73**
See also DLB 203

Teilhard de Chardin, (Marie Joseph) Pierre
1881-1955 .... **TCLC 9**
See also CA 105; 210; GFL 1789 to the
Present

Temple, Ann
See Mortimer, Penelope (Ruth)

Tennant, Emma (Christina) 1937- .. **CLC 13,**
52
See also BRWS 9; CA 65-68; CAAS 9;
CANR 10, 38, 59, 88; CN 7; DLB 14;
EWL 3; SFW 4

Tenneshaw, S. M.
See Silverberg, Robert

Tenney, Tabitha Gilman
1762-1837 .... **NCLC 122**
See also DLB 37, 200

Tennyson, Alfred 1809-1892 ... **NCLC 30, 65,**
115; PC 6; WLC
See also AAYA 50; BRW 4; CDBLB 1832-
1890; DA; DA3; DAB; DAC; DAM MST,
POET; DLB 32; EXPP; PAB; PFS 1, 2, 4,
11, 15, 19; RGEL 2; TEA; WLIT 4; WP

Teran, Lisa St. Aubin de .... **CLC 36**
See St. Aubin de Teran, Lisa

Terence c. 184B.C.-c. 159B.C. ...... **CMLC 14;**
DC 7
See also AW 1; CDWLB 1; DLB 211;
RGWL 2, 3; TWA

Teresa de Jesus, St. 1515-1582 .... **LC 18**

Terkel, Louis 1912-
See Terkel, Studs
See also CA 57-60; CANR 18, 45, 67, 132;
DA3; MTCW 1, 2

Terkel, Studs .... **CLC 38**
See Terkel, Louis
See also AAYA 32; AITN 1; MTCW 2; TUS

Terry, C. V.
See Slaughter, Frank G(ill)

Terry, Megan 1932- .... **CLC 19; DC 13**
See also CA 77-80; CABS 3; CAD; CANR
43; CD 5; CWD; DFS 18; DLB 7, 249;
GLL 2

Tertullian c. 155-c. 245 .... **CMLC 29**

Tertz, Abram
See Sinyavsky, Andrei (Donatevich)
See also RGSF 2

Tesich, Steve 1943(?)-1996 .... **CLC 40, 69**
See also CA 105; 152; CAD; DLBY 1983

Tesla, Nikola 1856-1943 .... **TCLC 88**

Teternikov, Fyodor Kuzmich 1863-1927
See Sologub, Fyodor
See also CA 104

Tevis, Walter 1928-1984 .... **CLC 42**
See also CA 113; SFW 4

Tey, Josephine .... **TCLC 14**
See Mackintosh, Elizabeth
See also DLB 77; MSW

Thackeray, William Makepeace
1811-1863 .... **NCLC 5, 14, 22, 43; WLC**
See also BRW 5; BRWC 2; CDBLB 1832-
1890; DA; DA3; DAB; DAC; DAM MST,
NOV; DLB 21, 55, 159, 163; NFS 13;
RGEL 2; SATA 23; TEA; WLIT 3

Thakura, Ravindranatha
See Tagore, Rabindranath

Thames, C. H.
See Marlowe, Stephen

Tharoor, Shashi 1956- .... **CLC 70**
See also CA 141; CANR 91; CN 7

Thelwell, Michael Miles 1939- .... **CLC 22**
See also BW 2; CA 101

Theobald, Lewis, Jr.
See Lovecraft, H(oward) P(hillips)

Theocritus c. 310B.C.- .... **CMLC 45**
See also AW 1; DLB 176; RGWL 2, 3

Theodorescu, Ion N. 1880-1967
See Arghezi, Tudor
See also CA 116

Theriault, Yves 1915-1983 .... **CLC 79**
See also CA 102; CCA 1; DAC; DAM
MST; DLB 88; EWL 3

Theroux, Alexander (Louis) 1939- .... **CLC 2,**
25
See also CA 85-88; CANR 20, 63; CN 7

Theroux, Paul (Edward) 1941- ..... **CLC 5, 8,**
11, 15, 28, 46
See also AAYA 28; AMWS 8; BEST 89:4;
BPFB 3; CA 33-36R; CANR 20, 45, 74,
133; CDALBS; CN 7; CPW 1; DA3;
DAM POP; DLB 2, 218; EWL 3; HGG;
MTCW 1, 2; RGAL 4; SATA 44, 109;
TUS

Thesen, Sharon 1946- .... **CLC 56**
See also CA 163; CANR 125; CP 7; CWP

Thespis fl. 6th cent. B.C.- .... **CMLC 51**
See also LMFS 1

Thevenin, Denis
See Duhamel, Georges

Thibault, Jacques Anatole Francois
1844-1924
See France, Anatole
See also CA 106; 127; DA3; DAM NOV;
MTCW 1, 2; TWA

Thiele, Colin (Milton) 1920- .... **CLC 17**
See also CA 29-32R; CANR 12, 28, 53,
105; CLR 27; DLB 289; MAICYA 1, 2;
SAAS 2; SATA 14, 72, 125; YAW

Thistlethwaite, Bel
See Wetherald, Agnes Ethelwyn

Thomas, Audrey (Callahan) 1935- .... **CLC 7,**
13, 37, 107; SSC 20
See also AITN 2; CA 21-24R; CAAS 19;
CANR 36, 58; CN 7; DLB 60; MTCW 1;
RGSF 2

Thomas, Augustus 1857-1934 .... **TCLC 97**

Thomas, D(onald) M(ichael) 1935- . **CLC 13,**
22, 31, 132
See also BPFB 3; BRWS 4; CA 61-64;
CAAS 11; CANR 17, 45, 75; CDBLB
1960 to Present; CN 7; CP 7; DA3; DLB
40, 207, 299; HGG; INT CANR-17;
MTCW 1, 2; SFW 4

Thomas, Dylan (Marlais) 1914-1953 .... **PC 2,**
52; SSC 3, 44; TCLC 1, 8, 45, 105;
WLC
See also AAYA 45; BRWS 1; CA 104; 120;
CANR 65; CDBLB 1945-1960; DA; DA3;
DAB; DAC; DAM DRAM, MST, POET;
DLB 13, 20, 139; EWL 3; EXPP; LAIT
3; MTCW 1, 2; PAB; PFS 1, 3, 8; RGEL
2; RGSF 2; SATA 60; TEA; WLIT 4; WP

Thomas, (Philip) Edward 1878-1917 . **PC 53;**
TCLC 10
See also BRW 6; BRWS 3; CA 106; 153;
DAM POET; DLB 19, 98, 156, 216; EWL
3; PAB; RGEL 2

Thomas, Joyce Carol 1938- .... **CLC 35**
See also AAYA 12, 54; BW 2, 3; CA 113;
116; CANR 48, 114, 135; CLR 19; DLB
33; INT CA-116; JRDA; MAICYA 1, 2;
MTCW 1, 2; SAAS 7; SATA 40, 78, 123,
137; SATA-Essay 137; WYA; YAW

Warburton, William 1698-1779 .... **LC 97**
See also DLB 104

Ward, Arthur Henry Sarsfield 1883-1959
See Rohmer, Sax
See also CA 108; 173; CMW 4; HGG

Ward, Douglas Turner 1930- .... **CLC 19**
See also BW 1; CA 81-84; CAD; CANR 27; CD 5; DLB 7, 38

Ward, E. D.
See Lucas, E(dward) V(errall)

Ward, Mrs. Humphry 1851-1920
See Ward, Mary Augusta
See also RGEL 2

Ward, Mary Augusta 1851-1920 ... **TCLC 55**
See Ward, Mrs. Humphry
See also DLB 18

Ward, Nathaniel 1578(?)-1652 .... **LC 114**
See also DLB 24

Ward, Peter
See Faust, Frederick (Schiller)

Warhol, Andy 1928(?)-1987 .... **CLC 20**
See also AAYA 12; BEST 89:4; CA 89-92; 121; CANR 34

Warner, Francis (Robert le Plastrier) 1937- .... **CLC 14**
See also CA 53-56; CANR 11

Warner, Marina 1946- .... **CLC 59**
See also CA 65-68; CANR 21, 55, 118; CN 7; DLB 194

Warner, Rex (Ernest) 1905-1986 ...... **CLC 45**
See also CA 89-92; 119; DLB 15; RGEL 2; RHW

Warner, Susan (Bogert) 1819-1885 .... **NCLC 31, 146**
See also DLB 3, 42, 239, 250, 254

Warner, Sylvia (Constance) Ashton
See Ashton-Warner, Sylvia (Constance)

Warner, Sylvia Townsend 1893-1978 .. **CLC 7, 19; SSC 23; TCLC 131**
See also BRWS 7; CA 61-64; 77-80; CANR 16, 60, 104; DLB 34, 139; EWL 3; FANT; FW; MTCW 1, 2; RGEL 2; RGSF 2; RHW

Warren, Mercy Otis 1728-1814 ..... **NCLC 13**
See also DLB 31, 200; RGAL 4; TUS

Warren, Robert Penn 1905-1989 .. **CLC 1, 4, 6, 8, 10, 13, 18, 39, 53, 59; PC 37; SSC 4, 58; WLC**
See also AITN 1; AMW; AMWC 2; BPFB 3; BYA 1; CA 13-16R; 129; CANR 10, 47; CDALB 1968-1988; DA; DA3; DAB; DAC; DAM MST, NOV, POET; DLB 2, 48, 152; DLBY 1980, 1989; EWL 3; INT CANR-10; MTCW 1, 2; NFS 13; RGAL 4; RGSF 2; RHW; SATA 46; SATA-Obit 63; SSFS 8; TUS

Warrigal, Jack
See Furphy, Joseph

Warshofsky, Isaac
See Singer, Isaac Bashevis

Warton, Joseph 1722-1800 .... **NCLC 118**
See also DLB 104, 109; RGEL 2

Warton, Thomas 1728-1790 .... **LC 15, 82**
See also DAM POET; DLB 104, 109; RGEL 2

Waruk, Kona
See Harris, (Theodore) Wilson

Warung, Price .... **TCLC 45**
See Astley, William
See also DLB 230; RGEL 2

Warwick, Jarvis
See Garner, Hugh
See also CCA 1

Washington, Alex
See Harris, Mark

Washington, Booker T(aliaferro) 1856-1915 .... **BLC 3; TCLC 10**
See also BW 1; CA 114; 125; DA3; DAM MULT; LAIT 2; RGAL 4; SATA 28

Washington, George 1732-1799 .... **LC 25**
See also DLB 31

Wassermann, (Karl) Jakob 1873-1934 .... **TCLC 6**
See also CA 104; 163; DLB 66; EWL 3

Wasserstein, Wendy 1950- ... **CLC 32, 59, 90, 183; DC 4**
See also CA 121; 129; CABS 3; CAD; CANR 53, 75, 128; CD 5; CWD; DA3; DAM DRAM; DFS 5, 17; DLB 228; EWL 3; FW; INT CA-129; MTCW 2; SATA 94

Waterhouse, Keith (Spencer) 1929- . **CLC 47**
See also CA 5-8R; CANR 38, 67, 109; CBD; CN 7; DLB 13, 15; MTCW 1, 2

Waters, Frank (Joseph) 1902-1995 .. **CLC 88**
See also CA 5-8R; 149; CAAS 13; CANR 3, 18, 63, 121; DLB 212; DLBY 1986; RGAL 4; TCWW 2

Waters, Mary C. .... **CLC 70**

Waters, Roger 1944- .... **CLC 35**

Watkins, Frances Ellen
See Harper, Frances Ellen Watkins

Watkins, Gerrold
See Malzberg, Barry N(athaniel)

Watkins, Gloria Jean 1952(?)- .... **CLC 94**
See also BW 2; CA 143; CANR 87, 126; DLB 246; MTCW 2; SATA 115

Watkins, Paul 1964- .... **CLC 55**
See also CA 132; CANR 62, 98

Watkins, Vernon Phillips 1906-1967 .... **CLC 43**
See also CA 9-10; 25-28R; CAP 1; DLB 20; EWL 3; RGEL 2

Watson, Irving S.
See Mencken, H(enry) L(ouis)

Watson, John H.
See Farmer, Philip Jose

Watson, Richard F.
See Silverberg, Robert

Watts, Ephraim
See Horne, Richard Henry Hengist

Watts, Isaac 1674-1748 .... **LC 98**
See also DLB 95; RGEL 2; SATA 52

Waugh, Auberon (Alexander) 1939-2001 .... **CLC 7**
See also CA 45-48; 192; CANR 6, 22, 92; DLB 14, 194

Waugh, Evelyn (Arthur St. John) 1903-1966 .. **CLC 1, 3, 8, 13, 19, 27, 44, 107; SSC 41; WLC**
See also BPFB 3; BRW 7; CA 85-88; 25-28R; CANR 22; CDBLB 1914-1945; DA; DA3; DAB; DAC; DAM MST, NOV, POP; DLB 15, 162, 195; EWL 3; MTCW 1, 2; NFS 13, 17; RGEL 2; RGSF 2; TEA; WLIT 4

Waugh, Harriet 1944- .... **CLC 6**
See also CA 85-88; CANR 22

Ways, C. R.
See Blount, Roy (Alton), Jr.

Waystaff, Simon
See Swift, Jonathan

Webb, Beatrice (Martha Potter) 1858-1943 .... **TCLC 22**
See also CA 117; 162; DLB 190; FW

Webb, Charles (Richard) 1939- .... **CLC 7**
See also CA 25-28R; CANR 114

Webb, Frank J. .... **NCLC 143**
See also DLB 50

Webb, James H(enry), Jr. 1946- ...... **CLC 22**
See also CA 81-84

Webb, Mary Gladys (Meredith) 1881-1927 .... **TCLC 24**
See also CA 182; 123; DLB 34; FW

Webb, Mrs. Sidney
See Webb, Beatrice (Martha Potter)

Webb, Phyllis 1927- .... **CLC 18**
See also CA 104; CANR 23; CCA 1; CP 7; CWP; DLB 53

Webb, Sidney (James) 1859-1947 .. **TCLC 22**
See also CA 117; 163; DLB 190

Webber, Andrew Lloyd .... **CLC 21**
See Lloyd Webber, Andrew
See also DFS 7

Weber, Lenora Mattingly 1895-1971 .... **CLC 12**
See also CA 19-20; 29-32R; CAP 1; SATA 2; SATA-Obit 26

Weber, Max 1864-1920 .... **TCLC 69**
See also CA 109; 189; DLB 296

Webster, John 1580(?)-1634(?) ...... **DC 2; LC 33, 84; WLC**
See also BRW 2; CDBLB Before 1660; DA; DAB; DAC; DAM DRAM; DFS 17, 19; DLB 58; IDTP; RGEL 2; WLIT 3

Webster, Noah 1758-1843 .... **NCLC 30**
See also DLB 1, 37, 42, 43, 73, 243

Wedekind, (Benjamin) Frank(lin) 1864-1918 .... **TCLC 7**
See also CA 104; 153; CANR 121, 122; CDWLB 2; DAM DRAM; DLB 118; EW 8; EWL 3; LMFS 2; RGWL 2, 3

Wehr, Demaris .... **CLC 65**

Weidman, Jerome 1913-1998 .... **CLC 7**
See also AITN 2; CA 1-4R; 171; CAD; CANR 1; DLB 28

Weil, Simone (Adolphine) 1909-1943 .... **TCLC 23**
See also CA 117; 159; EW 12; EWL 3; FW; GFL 1789 to the Present; MTCW 2

Weininger, Otto 1880-1903 .... **TCLC 84**

Weinstein, Nathan
See West, Nathanael

Weinstein, Nathan von Wallenstein
See West, Nathanael

Weir, Peter (Lindsay) 1944- .... **CLC 20**
See also CA 113; 123

Weiss, Peter (Ulrich) 1916-1982 .. **CLC 3, 15, 51; TCLC 152**
See also CA 45-48; 106; CANR 3; DAM DRAM; DFS 3; DLB 69, 124; EWL 3; RGWL 2, 3

Weiss, Theodore (Russell) 1916-2003 .... **CLC 3, 8, 14**
See also CA 9-12R; 189; 216; CAAE 189; CAAS 2; CANR 46, 94; CP 7; DLB 5

Welch, (Maurice) Denton 1915-1948 .... **TCLC 22**
See also BRWS 8, 9; CA 121; 148; RGEL 2

Welch, James (Phillip) 1940-2003 ..... **CLC 6, 14, 52; NNAL; PC 62**
See also CA 85-88; 219; CANR 42, 66, 107; CN 7; CP 7; CPW; DAM MULT, POP; DLB 175, 256; LATS 1:1; RGAL 4; TCWW 2

Weldon, Fay 1931- . **CLC 6, 9, 11, 19, 36, 59, 122**
See also BRWS 4; CA 21-24R; CANR 16, 46, 63, 97; CDBLB 1960 to Present; CN 7; CPW; DAM POP; DLB 14, 194; EWL 3; FW; HGG; INT CANR-16; MTCW 1, 2; RGEL 2; RGSF 2

Wellek, Rene 1903-1995 .... **CLC 28**
See also CA 5-8R; 150; CAAS 7; CANR 8; DLB 63; EWL 3; INT CANR-8

Weller, Michael 1942- .... **CLC 10, 53**
See also CA 85-88; CAD; CD 5

Weller, Paul 1958- .... **CLC 26**

Wellershoff, Dieter 1925- .... **CLC 46**
See also CA 89-92; CANR 16, 37

Author Index

Willingham, Calder (Baynard, Jr.)
1922-1995 .... **CLC 5, 51**
See also CA 5-8R; 147; CANR 3; CSW;
DLB 2, 44; IDFW 3, 4; MTCW 1

Willis, Charles
See Clarke, Arthur C(harles)

Willy
See Colette, (Sidonie-Gabrielle)

Willy, Colette
See Colette, (Sidonie-Gabrielle)
See also GLL 1

Wilmot, John 1647-1680 .... **LC 75**
See Rochester
See also BRW 2; DLB 131; PAB

Wilson, A(ndrew) N(orman) 1950- .. **CLC 33**
See also BRWS 6; CA 112; 122; CN 7;
DLB 14, 155, 194; MTCW 2

Wilson, Angus (Frank Johnstone)
1913-1991 . **CLC 2, 3, 5, 25, 34; SSC 21**
See also BRWS 1; CA 5-8R; 134; CANR
21; DLB 15, 139, 155; EWL 3; MTCW 1,
2; RGEL 2; RGSF 2

Wilson, August 1945- ... **BLC 3; CLC 39, 50,
63, 118; DC 2; WLCS**
See also AAYA 16; AFAW 2; AMWS 8; BW
2, 3; CA 115; 122; CAD; CANR 42, 54,
76, 128; CD 5; DA; DA3; DAB; DAC;
DAM DRAM, MST, MULT; DFS 3, 7,
15, 17; DLB 228; EWL 3; LAIT 4; LATS
1:2; MTCW 1, 2; RGAL 4

Wilson, Brian 1942- .... **CLC 12**

Wilson, Colin 1931- .... **CLC 3, 14**
See also CA 1-4R; CAAS 5; CANR 1, 22,
33, 77; CMW 4; CN 7; DLB 14, 194;
HGG; MTCW 1; SFW 4

Wilson, Dirk
See Pohl, Frederik

Wilson, Edmund 1895-1972 .. **CLC 1, 2, 3, 8,
24**
See also AMW; CA 1-4R; 37-40R; CANR
1, 46, 110; DLB 63; EWL 3; MTCW 1, 2;
RGAL 4; TUS

Wilson, Ethel Davis (Bryant)
1888(?)-1980 .... **CLC 13**
See also CA 102; DAC; DAM POET; DLB
68; MTCW 1; RGEL 2

Wilson, Harriet
See Wilson, Harriet E. Adams
See also DLB 239

Wilson, Harriet E.
See Wilson, Harriet E. Adams
See also DLB 243

Wilson, Harriet E. Adams
1827(?)-1863(?) .... **BLC 3; NCLC 78**
See Wilson, Harriet; Wilson, Harriet E.
See also DAM MULT; DLB 50

Wilson, John 1785-1854 .... **NCLC 5**

Wilson, John (Anthony) Burgess 1917-1993
See Burgess, Anthony
See also CA 1-4R; 143; CANR 2, 46; DA3;
DAC; DAM NOV; MTCW 1, 2; NFS 15;
TEA

Wilson, Lanford 1937- .. **CLC 7, 14, 36, 197;
DC 19**
See also CA 17-20R; CABS 3; CAD; CANR
45, 96; CD 5; DAM DRAM; DFS 4, 9,
12, 16, 20; DLB 7; EWL 3; TUS

Wilson, Robert M. 1941- .... **CLC 7, 9**
See also CA 49-52; CAD; CANR 2, 41; CD
5; MTCW 1

Wilson, Robert McLiam 1964- .... **CLC 59**
See also CA 132; DLB 267

Wilson, Sloan 1920-2003 .... **CLC 32**
See also CA 1-4R; 216; CANR 1, 44; CN 7

Wilson, Snoo 1948- .... **CLC 33**
See also CA 69-72; CBD; CD 5

Wilson, William S(mith) 1932- .... **CLC 49**
See also CA 81-84

Wilson, (Thomas) Woodrow
1856-1924 .... **TCLC 79**
See also CA 166; DLB 47

Wilson and Warnke eds. .... **CLC 65**

Winchilsea, Anne (Kingsmill) Finch
1661-1720
See Finch, Anne
See also RGEL 2

Windham, Basil
See Wodehouse, P(elham) G(renville)

Wingrove, David (John) 1954- .... **CLC 68**
See also CA 133; SFW 4

Winnemucca, Sarah 1844-1891 .... **NCLC 79;
NNAL**
See also DAM MULT; DLB 175; RGAL 4

Winstanley, Gerrard 1609-1676 .... **LC 52**

Wintergreen, Jane
See Duncan, Sara Jeannette

Winters, Janet Lewis .... **CLC 41**
See Lewis, Janet
See also DLBY 1987

Winters, (Arthur) Yvor 1900-1968 .... **CLC 4,
8, 32**
See also AMWS 2; CA 11-12; 25-28R; CAP
1; DLB 48; EWL 3; MTCW 1; RGAL 4

Winterson, Jeanette 1959- .... **CLC 64, 158**
See also BRWS 4; CA 136; CANR 58, 116;
CN 7; CPW; DA3; DAM POP; DLB 207,
261; FANT; FW; GLL 1; MTCW 2; RHW

Winthrop, John 1588-1649 .... **LC 31, 107**
See also DLB 24, 30

Wirth, Louis 1897-1952 .... **TCLC 92**
See also CA 210

Wiseman, Frederick 1930- .... **CLC 20**
See also CA 159

Wister, Owen 1860-1938 .... **TCLC 21**
See also BPFB 3; CA 108; 162; DLB 9, 78,
186; RGAL 4; SATA 62; TCWW 2

Wither, George 1588-1667 .... **LC 96**
See also DLB 121; RGEL 2

Witkacy
See Witkiewicz, Stanislaw Ignacy

Witkiewicz, Stanislaw Ignacy
1885-1939 .... **TCLC 8**
See also CA 105; 162; CDWLB 4; DLB
215; EW 10; EWL 3; RGWL 2, 3; SFW 4

Wittgenstein, Ludwig (Josef Johann)
1889-1951 .... **TCLC 59**
See also CA 113; 164; DLB 262; MTCW 2

Wittig, Monique 1935(?)-2003 .... **CLC 22**
See also CA 116; 135; 212; CWW 2; DLB
83; EWL 3; FW; GLL 1

Wittlin, Jozef 1896-1976 .... **CLC 25**
See also CA 49-52; 65-68; CANR 3; EWL
3

Wodehouse, P(elham) G(renville)
1881-1975 . **CLC 1, 2, 5, 10, 22; SSC 2;
TCLC 108**
See also AITN 2; BRWS 3; CA 45-48; 57-
60; CANR 3, 33; CDBLB 1914-1945;
CPW 1; DA3; DAB; DAC; DAM NOV;
DLB 34, 162; EWL 3; MTCW 1, 2;
RGEL 2; RGSF 2; SATA 22; SSFS 10

Woiwode, L.
See Woiwode, Larry (Alfred)

Woiwode, Larry (Alfred) 1941- ... **CLC 6, 10**
See also CA 73-76; CANR 16, 94; CN 7;
DLB 6; INT CANR-16

Wojciechowska, Maia (Teresa)
1927-2002 .... **CLC 26**
See also AAYA 8, 46; BYA 3; CA 9-12R,
183; 209; CAAE 183; CANR 4, 41; CLR
1; JRDA; MAICYA 1, 2; SAAS 1; SATA
1, 28, 83; SATA-Essay 104; SATA-Obit
134; YAW

Wojtyla, Karol
See John Paul II, Pope

Wolf, Christa 1929- .... **CLC 14, 29, 58, 150**
See also CA 85-88; CANR 45, 123; CD-
WLB 2; CWW 2; DLB 75; EWL 3; FW;
MTCW 1; RGWL 2, 3; SSFS 14

Wolf, Naomi 1962- .... **CLC 157**
See also CA 141; CANR 110; FW

Wolfe, Gene (Rodman) 1931- .... **CLC 25**
See also AAYA 35; CA 57-60; CAAS 9;
CANR 6, 32, 60; CPW; DAM POP; DLB
8; FANT; MTCW 2; SATA 118; SCFW 2;
SFW 4; SUFW 2

Wolfe, George C. 1954- .... **BLCS; CLC 49**
See also CA 149; CAD; CD 5

Wolfe, Thomas (Clayton)
1900-1938 ...... **SSC 33; TCLC 4, 13, 29,
61; WLC**
See also AMW; BPFB 3; CA 104; 132;
CANR 102; CDALB 1929-1941; DA;
DA3; DAB; DAC; DAM MST, NOV;
DLB 9, 102, 229; DLBD 2, 16; DLBY
1985, 1997; EWL 3; MTCW 1, 2; NFS
18; RGAL 4; TUS

Wolfe, Thomas Kennerly, Jr.
1931- .... **CLC 147**
See Wolfe, Tom
See also CA 13-16R; CANR 9, 33, 70, 104;
DA3; DAM POP; DLB 185; EWL 3; INT
CANR-9; MTCW 1, 2; SSFS; TUS

Wolfe, Tom .... **CLC 1, 2, 9, 15, 35, 51**
See Wolfe, Thomas Kennerly, Jr.
See also AAYA 8; AITN 2; AMWS 3; BEST
89:1; BPFB 3; CN 7; CPW; CSW; DLB
152; LAIT 5; RGAL 4

Wolff, Geoffrey (Ansell) 1937- .... **CLC 41**
See also CA 29-32R; CANR 29, 43, 78

Wolff, Sonia
See Levitin, Sonia (Wolff)

Wolff, Tobias (Jonathan Ansell)
1945- .... **CLC 39, 64, 172; SSC 63**
See also AAYA 16; AMWS 7; BEST 90:2;
BYA 12; CA 114; 117; CAAS 22; CANR
54, 76, 96; CN 7; CSW; DA3; DLB 130;
EWL 3; INT CA-117; MTCW 2; RGAL
4; RGSF 2; SSFS 4, 11

Wolfram von Eschenbach c. 1170-c.
1220 .... **CMLC 5**
See Eschenbach, Wolfram von
See also CDWLB 2; DLB 138; EW 1;
RGWL 2

Wolitzer, Hilma 1930- .... **CLC 17**
See also CA 65-68; CANR 18, 40; INT
CANR-18; SATA 31; YAW

Wollstonecraft, Mary 1759-1797 .... **LC 5, 50,
90**
See also BRWS 3; CDBLB 1789-1832;
DLB 39, 104, 158, 252; FW; LAIT 1;
RGEL 2; TEA; WLIT 3

Wonder, Stevie .... **CLC 12**
See Morris, Steveland Judkins

Wong, Jade Snow 1922- .... **CLC 17**
See also CA 109; CANR 91; SATA 112

Woodberry, George Edward
1855-1930 .... **TCLC 73**
See also CA 165; DLB 71, 103

Woodcott, Keith
See Brunner, John (Kilian Houston)

Woodruff, Robert W.
See Mencken, H(enry) L(ouis)

Woolf, (Adeline) Virginia 1882-1941 .. **SSC 7,
79; TCLC 1, 5, 20, 43, 56, 101, 123,
128; WLC**
See also AAYA 44; BPFB 3; BRW 7;
BRWC 2; BRWR 1; CA 104; 130; CANR
64, 132; CDBLB 1914-1945; DA; DA3;
DAB; DAC; DAM MST, NOV; DLB 36,
100, 162; DLBD 10; EWL 3; EXPS; FW;
LAIT 3; LATS 1:1; LMFS 2; MTCW 1,
2; NCFS 2; NFS 8, 12; RGEL 2; RGSF 2;
SSFS 4, 12; TEA; WLIT 4

Woollcott, Alexander (Humphreys)
1887-1943 .... **TCLC 5**
See also CA 105; 161; DLB 29
Woolrich, Cornell .... **CLC 77**
See Hopley-Woolrich, Cornell George
See also MSW
Woolson, Constance Fenimore
1840-1894 .... **NCLC 82**
See also DLB 12, 74, 189, 221; RGAL 4
Wordsworth, Dorothy 1771-1855 . **NCLC 25, 138**
See also DLB 107
Wordsworth, William 1770-1850 .. **NCLC 12, 38, 111; PC 4; WLC**
See also BRW 4; BRWC 1; CDBLB 1789-1832; DA; DA3; DAB; DAC; DAM MST, POET; DLB 93, 107; EXPP; LATS 1:1; LMFS 1; PAB; PFS 2; RGEL 2; TEA; WLIT 3; WP
Wotton, Sir Henry 1568-1639 .... **LC 68**
See also DLB 121; RGEL 2
Wouk, Herman 1915- .... **CLC 1, 9, 38**
See also BPFB 2, 3; CA 5-8R; CANR 6, 33, 67; CDALBS; CN 7; CPW; DA3; DAM NOV, POP; DLBY 1982; INT CANR-6; LAIT 4; MTCW 1, 2; NFS 7; TUS
Wright, Charles (Penzel, Jr.) 1935- .. **CLC 6, 13, 28, 119, 146**
See also AMWS 5; CA 29-32R; CAAS 7; CANR 23, 36, 62, 88, 135; CP 7; DLB 165; DLBY 1982; EWL 3; MTCW 1, 2; PFS 10
Wright, Charles Stevenson 1932- ..... **BLC 3; CLC 49**
See also BW 1; CA 9-12R; CANR 26; CN 7; DAM MULT, POET; DLB 33
Wright, Frances 1795-1852 .... **NCLC 74**
See also DLB 73
Wright, Frank Lloyd 1867-1959 .... **TCLC 95**
See also AAYA 33; CA 174
Wright, Jack R.
See Harris, Mark
Wright, James (Arlington)
1927-1980 .... **CLC 3, 5, 10, 28; PC 36**
See also AITN 2; AMWS 3; CA 49-52; 97-100; CANR 4, 34, 64; CDALBS; DAM POET; DLB 5, 169; EWL 3; EXPP; MTCW 1, 2; PFS 7, 8; RGAL 4; TUS; WP
Wright, Judith (Arundell)
1915-2000 .... **CLC 11, 53; PC 14**
See also CA 13-16R; 188; CANR 31, 76, 93; CP 7; CWP; DLB 260; EWL 3; MTCW 1, 2; PFS 8; RGEL 2; SATA 14; SATA-Obit 121
Wright, L(aurali) R. 1939- .... **CLC 44**
See also CA 138; CMW 4
Wright, Richard (Nathaniel)
1908-1960 ... **BLC 3; CLC 1, 3, 4, 9, 14, 21, 48, 74; SSC 2; TCLC 136; WLC**
See also AAYA 5, 42; AFAW 1; AMW; BPFB 3; BW 1; BYA 2; CA 108; CANR 64; CDALB 1929-1941; DA; DA3; DAB; DAC; DAM MST, MULT, NOV; DLB 76, 102; DLBD 2; EWL 3; EXPN; LAIT 3, 4; MTCW 1, 2; NCFS 1; NFS 1, 7; RGAL 4; RGSF 2; SSFS 3, 9, 15, 20; TUS; YAW
Wright, Richard B(ruce) 1937- .... **CLC 6**
See also CA 85-88; CANR 120; DLB 53
Wright, Rick 1945- .... **CLC 35**
Wright, Rowland
See Wells, Carolyn
Wright, Stephen 1946- .... **CLC 33**
Wright, Willard Huntington 1888-1939
See Van Dine, S. S.
See also CA 115; 189; CMW 4; DLBD 16
Wright, William 1930- .... **CLC 44**
See also CA 53-56; CANR 7, 23

Wroth, Lady Mary 1587-1653(?) .... **LC 30; PC 38**
See also DLB 121
Wu Ch'eng-en 1500(?)-1582(?) .... **LC 7**
Wu Ching-tzu 1701-1754 .... **LC 2**
Wulfstan c. 10th cent. -1023 .... **CMLC 59**
Wurlitzer, Rudolph 1938(?)- .... **CLC 2, 4, 15**
See also CA 85-88; CN 7; DLB 173
Wyatt, Sir Thomas c. 1503-1542 . **LC 70; PC 27**
See also BRW 1; DLB 132; EXPP; RGEL 2; TEA
Wycherley, William 1640-1716 .... **LC 8, 21, 102**
See also BRW 2; CDBLB 1660-1789; DAM DRAM; DLB 80; RGEL 2
Wyclif, John c. 1330-1384 .... **CMLC 70**
See also DLB 146
Wylie, Elinor (Morton Hoyt)
1885-1928 .... **PC 23; TCLC 8**
See also AMWS 1; CA 105; 162; DLB 9, 45; EXPP; RGAL 4
Wylie, Philip (Gordon) 1902-1971 ... **CLC 43**
See also CA 21-22; 33-36R; CAP 2; DLB 9; SFW 4
Wyndham, John .... **CLC 19**
See Harris, John (Wyndham Parkes Lucas) Beynon
See also DLB 255; SCFW 2
Wyss, Johann David Von
1743-1818 .... **NCLC 10**
See also CLR 92; JRDA; MAICYA 1, 2; SATA 29; SATA-Brief 27
Xenophon c. 430B.C.-c. 354B.C. ... **CMLC 17**
See also AW 1; DLB 176; RGWL 2, 3
Xingjian, Gao 1940-
See Gao Xingjian
See also CA 193; RGWL 3
Yakamochi 718-785 .... **CMLC 45; PC 48**
Yakumo Koizumi
See Hearn, (Patricio) Lafcadio (Tessima Carlos)
Yamada, Mitsuye (May) 1923- .... **PC 44**
See also CA 77-80
Yamamoto, Hisaye 1921- .... **AAL; SSC 34**
See also CA 214; DAM MULT; LAIT 4; SSFS 14
Yamauchi, Wakako 1924- .... **AAL**
See also CA 214
Yanez, Jose Donoso
See Donoso (Yanez), Jose
Yanovsky, Basile S.
See Yanovsky, V(assily) S(emenovich)
Yanovsky, V(assily) S(emenovich)
1906-1989 .... **CLC 2, 18**
See also CA 97-100; 129
Yates, Richard 1926-1992 .... **CLC 7, 8, 23**
See also AMWS 11; CA 5-8R; 139; CANR 10, 43; DLB 2, 234; DLBY 1981, 1992; INT CANR-10
Yau, John 1950- .... **PC 61**
See also CA 154; CANR 89; CP 7; DLB 234
Yeats, W. B.
See Yeats, William Butler
Yeats, William Butler 1865-1939 . **PC 20, 51; TCLC 1, 11, 18, 31, 93, 116; WLC**
See also AAYA 48; BRW 6; BRWR 1; CA 104; 127; CANR 45; CDBLB 1890-1914; DA; DA3; DAB; DAC; DAM DRAM, MST, POET; DLB 10, 19, 98, 156; EWL 3; EXPP; MTCW 1, 2; NCFS 3; PAB; PFS 1, 2, 5, 7, 13, 15; RGEL 2; TEA; WLIT 4; WP
Yehoshua, A(braham) B. 1936- .. **CLC 13, 31**
See also CA 33-36R; CANR 43, 90; CWW 2; EWL 3; RGSF 2; RGWL 3
Yellow Bird
See Ridge, John Rollin

Yep, Laurence Michael 1948- .... **CLC 35**
See also AAYA 5, 31; BYA 7; CA 49-52; CANR 1, 46, 92; CLR 3, 17, 54; DLB 52; FANT; JRDA; MAICYA 1, 2; MAICYAS 1; SATA 7, 69, 123; WYA; YAW
Yerby, Frank G(arvin) 1916-1991 ..... **BLC 3; CLC 1, 7, 22**
See also BPFB 3; BW 1, 3; CA 9-12R; 136; CANR 16, 52; DAM MULT; DLB 76; INT CANR-16; MTCW 1; RGAL 4; RHW
Yesenin, Sergei Alexandrovich
See Esenin, Sergei (Alexandrovich)
Yesenin, Sergey
See Esenin, Sergei (Alexandrovich)
See also EWL 3
Yevtushenko, Yevgeny (Alexandrovich)
1933- ...... **CLC 1, 3, 13, 26, 51, 126; PC 40**
See Evtushenko, Evgenii Aleksandrovich
See also CA 81-84; CANR 33, 54; DAM POET; EWL 3; MTCW 1
Yezierska, Anzia 1885(?)-1970 .... **CLC 46**
See also CA 126; 89-92; DLB 28, 221; FW; MTCW 1; RGAL 4; SSFS 15
Yglesias, Helen 1915- .... **CLC 7, 22**
See also CA 37-40R; CAAS 20; CANR 15, 65, 95; CN 7; INT CANR-15; MTCW 1
Yokomitsu, Riichi 1898-1947 .... **TCLC 47**
See also CA 170; EWL 3
Yonge, Charlotte (Mary)
1823-1901 .... **TCLC 48**
See also CA 109; 163; DLB 18, 163; RGEL 2; SATA 17; WCH
York, Jeremy
See Creasey, John
York, Simon
See Heinlein, Robert A(nson)
Yorke, Henry Vincent 1905-1974 ..... **CLC 13**
See Green, Henry
See also CA 85-88; 49-52
Yosano Akiko 1878-1942 .... **PC 11; TCLC 59**
See also CA 161; EWL 3; RGWL 3
Yoshimoto, Banana .... **CLC 84**
See Yoshimoto, Mahoko
See also AAYA 50; NFS 7
Yoshimoto, Mahoko 1964-
See Yoshimoto, Banana
See also CA 144; CANR 98; SSFS 16
Young, Al(bert James) 1939- ... **BLC 3; CLC 19**
See also BW 2, 3; CA 29-32R; CANR 26, 65, 109; CN 7; CP 7; DAM MULT; DLB 33
Young, Andrew (John) 1885-1971 ...... **CLC 5**
See also CA 5-8R; CANR 7, 29; RGEL 2
Young, Collier
See Bloch, Robert (Albert)
Young, Edward 1683-1765 .... **LC 3, 40**
See also DLB 95; RGEL 2
Young, Marguerite (Vivian)
1909-1995 .... **CLC 82**
See also CA 13-16; 150; CAP 1; CN 7
Young, Neil 1945- .... **CLC 17**
See also CA 110; CCA 1
Young Bear, Ray A. 1950- ... **CLC 94; NNAL**
See also CA 146; DAM MULT; DLB 175
Yourcenar, Marguerite 1903-1987 ... **CLC 19, 38, 50, 87**
See also BPFB 3; CA 69-72; CANR 23, 60, 93; DAM NOV; DLB 72; DLBY 1988; EW 12; EWL 3; GFL 1789 to the Present; GLL 1; MTCW 1, 2; RGWL 2, 3
Yuan, Chu 340(?)B.C.-278(?)B.C. . **CMLC 36**
Yurick, Sol 1925- .... **CLC 6**
See also CA 13-16R; CANR 25; CN 7
Zabolotsky, Nikolai Alekseevich
1903-1958 .... **TCLC 52**
See Zabolotsky, Nikolay Alekseevich
See also CA 116; 164

PC Cumulative Nationality Index

AMERICAN

Aiken, Conrad (Potter) **26**
Alexie, Sherman **53**
Ammons, A(rchie) R(andolph) **16**
Angelou, Maya **32**
Ashbery, John (Lawrence) **26**
Auden, W(ystan) H(ugh) **1**
Baca, Jimmy Santiago **41**
Baraka, Amiri **4**
Benét, Stephen Vincent **64**
Berry, Wendell (Erdman) **28**
Berryman, John **64**
Bishop, Elizabeth **3, 34**
Bly, Robert (Elwood) **39**
Bogan, Louise **12**
Bradstreet, Anne **10**
Braithwaite, William **52**
Brodsky, Joseph **9**
Brooks, Gwendolyn (Elizabeth) **7**
Brown, Sterling Allen **55**
Bryant, William Cullen **20**
Bukowski, Charles **18**
Cage, John **58**
Carruth, Hayden **10**
Carver, Raymond **54**
Cervantes, Lorna Dee **35**
Chin, Marilyn (Mei Ling) **40**
Cisneros, Sandra **52**
Clampitt, Amy **19**
Clifton, (Thelma) Lucille **17**
Corso, (Nunzio) Gregory **33**
Crane, (Harold) Hart **3**
Cullen, Countée **20**
Cummings, E(dward) E(stlin) **5**
Dickey, James (Lafayette) **40**
Dickinson, Emily (Elizabeth) **1**
Doolittle, Hilda **5**
Doty, Mark **53**
Dove, Rita (Frances) **6**
Dunbar, Paul Laurence **5**
Duncan, Robert (Edward) **2**
Dylan, Bob **37**
Eliot, T(homas) S(tearns) **5, 31**
Emerson, Ralph Waldo **18**
Erdrich, Louise **52**
Ferlinghetti, Lawrence (Monsanto) **1**
Forché, Carolyn (Louise) **10**
Francis, Robert (Churchill) **34**
Frost, Robert (Lee) **1, 39**
Gallagher, Tess **9**
Ginsberg, Allen **4, 47**
Giovanni, Nikki **19**
Glück, Louise (Elisabeth) **16**
Graham, Jorie **59**
Guest, Barbara **55**
Hacker, Marilyn **47**

Hammon, Jupiter **16**
Harjo, Joy **27**
Harper, Frances Ellen Watkins **21**
Hass, Robert **16**
Hayden, Robert E(arl) **6**
H. D. **5**
Hogan, Linda **35**
Hongo, Garrett Kaoru **23**
Howe, Susan **54**
Hughes, (James) Langston **1, 53**
Ignatow, David **34**
Jackson, Laura (Riding) **44**
Jacobsen, Josephine **62**
Jarrell, Randall **41**
Jeffers, (John) Robinson **17**
Johnson, James Weldon **24**
Jordan, June **38**
Justice, Donald **64**
Kenyon, Jane **57**
Kinnell, Galway **26**
Knight, Etheridge **14**
Komunyakaa, Yusef **51**
Kumin, Maxine (Winokur) **15**
Kunitz, Stanley (Jasspon) **19**
Lanier, Sidney **50**
Levertov, Denise **11**
Levine, Philip **22**
Lindsay, (Nicholas) Vachel **23**
Longfellow, Henry Wadsworth **30**
Lorde, Audre (Geraldine) **12**
Lowell, Amy **13**
Lowell, Robert (Traill Spence Jr.) **3**
Loy, Mina **16**
MacLeish, Archibald **47**
Mackey, Nathaniel **49**
Madhubuti, Haki R. **5**
Masters, Edgar Lee **1, 36**
McHugh, Heather **61**
Meredith, William (Morris) **28**
Merrill, James (Ingram) **28**
Merton, Thomas **10**
Merwin, W. S. **45**
Millay, Edna St. Vincent **6, 61**
Momaday, N(avarre) Scott **25**
Moore, Marianne (Craig) **4, 49**
Mueller, Lisel **33**
Nash, (Frediric) Ogden **21**
Nemerov, Howard (Stanley) **24**
Niedecker, Lorine **42**
O'Hara, Frank **45**
Olds, Sharon **22**
Olson, Charles (John) **19**
Oppen, George **35**
Ortiz, Simon J(oseph) **17**
Parker, Dorothy (Rothschild) **28**
Piercy, Marge **29**

Pinsky, Robert **27**
Plath, Sylvia **1, 37**
Poe, Edgar Allan **1, 54**
Pound, Ezra (Weston Loomis) **4**
Quintana, Leroy V. **36**
Ransom, John Crowe **61**
Reese, Lizette Woodworth **29**
Rexroth, Kenneth **20**
Rich, Adrienne (Cecile) **5**
Riley, James Whitcomb **48**
Ríos, Alberto **57**
Robinson, Edwin Arlington **1, 35**
Roethke, Theodore (Huebner) **15**
Rose, Wendy **13**
Rukeyser, Muriel **12**
Sanchez, Sonia **9**
Sandburg, Carl (August) **2, 41**
Sarton, (Eleanor) May **39**
Schwartz, Delmore (David) **8**
Schnackenberg, Gjertrud **45**
Schwerner, Armand **42**
Sexton, Anne (Harvey) **2**
Shapiro, Karl (Jay) **25**
Silverstein, Shel **49**
Snyder, Gary (Sherman) **21**
Song, Cathy **21**
Soto, Gary **28**
Stein, Gertrude **18**
Stevens, Wallace **6**
Stone, Ruth **53**
Strand, Mark **63**
Stryk, Lucien **27**
Swenson, May **14**
Tate, Allen **50**
Taylor, Edward **63**
Teasdale, Sara **31**
Thoreau, Henry David **30**
Toomer, Jean **7**
Urista, Alberto H. **34**
Viereck, Peter (Robert Edwin) **27**
Wagoner, David (Russell) **33**
Wakoski, Diane **15**
Walker, Alice (Malsenior) **30**
Walker, Margaret (Abigail) **20**
Warren, Robert Penn **37**
Welch, James **62**
Wheatley (Peters), Phillis **3**
Whitman, Walt(er) **3**
Wilbur, Richard **51**
Williams, William Carlos **7**
Wright, James (Arlington) **36**
Wylie, Elinor (Morton Hoyt) **23**
Yamada, Mitsuye **44**
Yau, John **61**
Zukofsky, Louis **11**

Nationality Index

PC-64 Title Index

Title Index

ISBN 0-7876-8698-0